BUILDING SHIPS ON THE NORTH EAST COAST

A Labour of Love, Risk and Pain.
Part 1 c 1640-1914

J F Clarke

Bewick Press
1997

First published 1997 by
The Bewick Press
132 Claremont Road
Whitley Bay
Tyne & Wear
NE26 3TX

©1997 J F Clarke

All rights reserved. No part of this book may be reprinted or reproduced or utilised in any form by any electronic, mechanical, or other means, now known or hereafter invented, including photocopying and recording, or in any information storage or retrieval system, without permission in writing from the publishers.

ISBN 1-898880-04-2

Printed and Bound in Great Britain by
Trade Union Printing Services Ltd
The Old Mill
30 Lime Street
Newcastle upon Tyne
NE1 2PQ

Table of Contents

Preface		iv
Chronology		vi
1	Introduction	1
2	Shipbuilding to about 1780.	5
3	The Changes in Shipbuilding Output - 1780- 1815.	25
4	Shipbuilding methods and the Changeover from Wood to Iron Hulls	43
5	The advance of the Northern Ports - c 1815- c1850	73
6	Shipbuilding on the Wear c1850-1880s	93
7	The advance of the Tyne [including Blyth] to c 1889	113
8	Shipbuilding on the Tees and at Hartlepool to c 1889	138
9	Radical Changes in the 1880s - iron to steel hull -oil tankers	155
10	Shipbuilding on the North East Coast c1889 - 1914	181
11	Warships Building and Supplying Overseas Markets to 1914	224
12	The workforce to c1870 & the formation of Employers' organisations	247
13	Labour relations in the later 19th century	293
Notes on chapters		359
Bibliography		363
Index		371

Ships named in text - Personal and company names - General

Diagrams

1.01 Coals from Tyne & Wear by sea 1660-1770	1
1.02 Coals from Newcastle 1702-4 by port	2
2.01 Apprentices Shiprwights' Company 1632-1773	5
2.02 Estimated workforce - apprentices over 35 years	6
2.03 Shipwrights' Company family yards 1719-1820	16
2.04 Size of ships from Hartley & Blyth 1770-1	18
2.05 Vessels built on Wear before 1771	21
3.01 Lloyd's Register 1776 tonnage by port	25
3.02 Admiralty Survey 1804 shipwrights by area / port	26
3.03 Tyne shipyards in Admiralty Survey 1804	27
3.04 Hurry / Mosley output 1761-1810	29
3.05 Number of Shipbuilders on Wear 1787-1815	33
3.06 Wear shipyards in Admiralty Survey 1804	34
3.07 Whitby output 1786-1813	38
3.08 Whitby & Scarborough in Admiralty Survey 1804	38
3.09 Paybill & workers employed Laing's yard 1800	41
3.10 Tonnage built Tyne, Wear & Whitby 1786-1813	42
3.11 North East Coast output 1786-1813	42
4.01 Wood ship *Hesperia* - work sequence by trade	44
4.02 Wear vessels length:breath ratio	57
4.03 Wood-Iron changeover in UK	61
4.04 Iron ship *Jessica* - work sequence by *black squad*	65
5.01 Tonnage Tyne- Wear & Rest 1815-1850	73
5.02 Output Northern Ports 1820-32	76
5.03 Annual Output all Gale yards 1813-57	77
5.04 T & W Smith output	78
5.05 Ships by Laing at South Shields 1807-31	79
5.06 Shipwrights in 1841 Census at Sunderland	83
5.07 Wear tons & ships launched by month 1839-46	84
5.08 Tees & Hartlepool output 1835-50	87
5.09 Steam vessels built on Tyne 1814-49	89
5.10 Wear top 20 yards 1820 & 1850	91
6.00 Sketch map of Wear with shipyards	92
6.01 Output Wear & the Rest 1849-1879	93
6.02 Wear no. of shipbuilders & ships/builder 1850-79	94
6.03 Wear ships by Lloyd's class 1847-69	94
6.04 Market for Wear ships 1853 by tonnage	95
6.05 Wm Pile jnr ships 1849-74	96
6.06 Wood ships built on Wear 1870-9	101
6.07 Changeover wood-iron on Wear	103
6.08 Laing wood to iron with composite tons	104
6.09 Doxford's changeover wood to iron	105
6.10 R Thompson jnr wood to iron with composite tons	106
6.11 Output of T R Oswald 1859-1875	109
6.12 Composite vessels 6 Wear yards	110
6.13 New ships steam & sail UK 1871-9	111
7.01 Value Mining & manufacturing 1863 Tyne Wear & Tees	113
7.00 Map of Tyne - shipyards	114
7.02 Tyne ports & Wear 1866-89 Output	115
7.03 Coal by Screw Collier to London 1852-62	120
7.04 Palmers output 1852-1889	122
7.05 Aggregate tonnage 4 Tyne yards 1852-1889	125
7.06 Tyne shipyards output 1889	137
8.01 Hartlepool Middlesbrough & Stockton 1866-89	138
8.02 Cumulative output at Hartlepool 1850-1889	146
8.03 Denton & Gray ships by tons	147
8.04 Denton & Gray £s / gtons 1864-1889	148
Sketch map Hartlepool	149
8.05 Hartlepool & Tees 1866-1889 output	154
Sketch map River Tees	154
9.01 Merchant & forg warships NE Coast - Rest 1880-9	155
9.02 Output four Tyne yards 1882-9	156
9.03 Output four Wear yards [medium 1882-9]	157
9.04 Output four Wear yards [large] 1882-9	157
9.05 Time rates & piecework Wear 1883-1905	162
9.06 Tonnage in Steel - Iron 1878-91 in UK	164
9.07 Tonnage in Steel - Iron 1878-91 on Tyne	169
9.08 Tonnage in Steel - Iron 1878-91 on Wear	170
9.09 Tonnage in Steel - Iron 1878-91 on Tees	171
9.10 Plates by material Laing 1882-93	171
9.11 Price mild steel & iron per Thompson 1884-91	172
10.01 Clyde & NE Coast 1889-1913	181
10.02 Output Tyne-Wear-Tees & H'pool 1889-1913	182
10.03 Cumulative tonnage 5 Tyne yards 1889-1913	183
10.04 Merc. & forg. warship Tees & H'pool 1889-1913	187
10.05 R Dixon - Richardson Duck - Ropner 1889-1913	188
10.06 Output at Hartlepool by yard 1889-1913	189
10.07 Cumulative tonnage by 6 Wear yards 1889-1913	192
10.08 Ships built by J L Thompson 1889-1913	194
10.09 Output at Blyth 1880-1913	195
10.10 Turnbull of Whitby 1843-1902	197
10.11 Doxford's output 1889-1913	200
10.12 Output North east Coast 1905-1913	200
10.13 Tankers built to 1906 on NE Coast	213
10.14 Tonnage of tankers built 1886-1914 on NE Coast	213
10.15 Shipyards aggregate 300,000t or more in 1901-13	223
11.01 Warship tonnage built on Tyne 1885-1913	228
11.02 Royal Navy tonnage 1885-1913	229
11.03 Royal Naval contracts 1895-1914 by type of ship	230
11.04 Armstrong warships by market to 1914	235
11.05 Foreign & Colonial Customers 1884-92	239
11.06 Overseas Owners 1888-1913 - Tees & H'pool	241
11.07 J Wigham Richardson foreign/home tonnage	242
11.08 Foreign owners - Tyne & Clyde 1888-1913	246
12.01 *ASE* membership 1851-1868 Leeds & NE Coast	262
12.02 Brown-Hopkins index 1821-1870	276
12.03 Average days per week Thompsons 1847-9	277
12.04 Wage rates some shipyard trades 1850-79	278
12.05 Palmers time & pw earnings Sept 1871	280
12.06 Deaths by age group Sunderland 1869	286
Ellison Street Hebburn 1871 census	facing 289
12.07 Population % in type of dwelling 1912	291
12.08 Rents 1905 & 1912	291

13.02 *ASE* membership 1872-1906	302
13.03 Wear Engine Works apprentices 1883	315
13.04 *ASE* membership Sunderland 1851-1911	317
13.05 Conciliation Boards NE Coast 1897-1906	322
13.06 Tyne shipbuilders men & apprentices 1909-14	344
13.07 Wear shipwrights & apprentices 1905	345
13.08 Unemployment Tyne & Wear 1894-1901	347
13.09 Unemployment UK & Wear 1902-1913	348
13.10 Workers employed 1902-10 on Wear by trade	348
13.11 Earnings 1886 & 1906 by trade	350
13.12 Earnings at Palmer's yard 1871-2, 1882 & 1886	351
13.13 Pieceworkers & timeworkers 1906	351
13.14 Shipwrights' weekly rate [& adjusted] 1881-1914	352
13.15 Comparison NE Coast Clyde 1906 earnings	353
13.16 Earnings by trade 1906 full-time hours	353
13.17 earnings distribution plater-riveter-shipwright	354
13.18 Earnings at Wallsend Slipway 1875-1914	355
13.19 Food Expenditure 1904	356
13.20 1911 % males in Shipbuilding North East & England &Wales	357

Illustrations and Insets

Sketch map of the North East	viii
Sailing collier	7
Emblem of Shipwrights	8
Shipwrights' Company account Widow Moore 1752-4	12
Masters & Mariners emblem	15
Chart - master shipwrights with 3 apprentices or more	16
River Tyne c 1750	22
Noah's Ark or the Shipwrights' Ancient Play, or Dirge	23
High Docks South Shields 1802	31
Sunderland - shipbuilders landings 1801 *Eye Map*	35
Map of Whitby showing shipyards & docks 1787	37
Shipwright's tools c 1700	45
Plan of Collier 1804	46
Illustrations on wood construction	47
Costs of *Mally & Jane* 1752	49
Timber sizes used on *Defence* 1836	53
Sketches of rig: ship & barque	57
Sketches of rig: brig - snow - brigantine - schooner	58
Sizes of wood ship & tonnage	59
Notes from Lloyds' Report on *QED*	63
Illustrations on iron construction	64
Composite ship half section	67
De Brus specification 1858	70
Trades in shipbuilding -employer's list 20th century	72
Baird & Barnsley letterhead	90
Wylam Dilly as a tug	91
Map of Wear - shipyards 1861	92
Launch of *La Hogue*	97
W. Pile's *Berean* 1869	107
Sketch map of the Tyne shipyards 1846	114
Smiths covered berths 1851	116
North Shields & *Alfonso XII* on stocks	117
Palmers' advertisement 1887	123
Palmer's yard s layout 1880s	124
George Hunter & Neptune Works - Swan Hunters	126
C J D Christie portrait	129
Readhead's West Docks 1890	132
Water ballast 3 early structures	135
Denton's self trimming collier	140
Sketch map of Tees with shipyards	142
Isabel Craggs	143
Sketch map Hartlepool - shipyards	149
Well deck steamer sketch	152
Layout of W Gray's shipyards	154
ss *Vaderland* tanker	175
ss *Gluckauf*	176
ss *Bakuin*	178
Fergusons converted to tanker	178
San Isodoro mid-ship section & pump rooms	180
Northumberland SB riverside view	185
ss *Queen Christina*	186
Half section turret ships 1892 1905	198
Bartram's *Castle Holm* 1875	203
Palmer's cable system	205
Bermuda floating dock lifting HMS battleship	210
Tanker *San Isidoro*	212
Merger Swan-Hunter & Wigham Richardson	213
rms *Carpathia*	214
tss *Mauretania*	215
Mauretania in shipbuilding shed	216
ss *Nullus Secundus*	223
HMS *Defence*	224
Elswick cruiser *Esmeralda*	227
HMS *Talisman*	232
Rivals - cartoon competition for naval contracts	233
Armstrong's Naval yard 1914	234
ss *Yat Sing* 1904	237
Train Ferry *Drottning Victoria* 1908	244
icebreaker *Ermack* in dry dock	244
ore carrier *Sir Ernst Cassel*	245
Emblem of the *ASE* [engineers' union]	272
King of the 9 Hours Movement John Burnett	274
Ellison Street Hebburn in 1871 facing	289
Robert Knight	296
William Mould typical foreman	304
Pages of demarcation allocations	319
Wallsend Shipwrights & Drillers Committee 1906	331
Michael Nairey's unique timeboard	336
ASE leaflet on overtime 1912	338

Preface & Acknowledgements

When my family and I came to the north east in the early 1960s shipyard cranes still dominated the landscape of the rivers and were ever visible on Tyneside as the coast line railway, or the buses travelled from Newcastle down to the seaside towns and back again. Similar sights and sounds were features of the region's other rivers. The scale of the activity was massively larger than any thing that I had experienced before. This work is a modest tribute to the many thousands of people who for more than two centuries built and powered ships for the world. I am indebted over my working lifetime to not only for the tolerance but the constant encouragement of my family in enabling me to carry out this research.

Over the years many people have helped my work and unfortunately they cannot all be named here. The staffs at the Tyne & Wear Archives Services, Cleveland Records Office and the Northumberland Records have invariably been most helpful. Likewise the staff of the region's libraries have always been most helpful. A special word of thanks from all those concerned with industry's history and mine in particular is due to Richard Potts for his most diligent efforts over a long period to recover and secure the deposit of so many shipbuilding records. Many people kindly read various parts of the text and made most helpful comments including Ray Chaloner, Ben Crowdy, Ken Douglas, Ron French, Peter Hepplewaite, Ann Garnham, Prof. Norman McCord, Brian Newman, Richard Potts, Archie Potts, Prof. Garrett Scaife, John Spence, Frank Storr and Brian Tebbutt. Material collected by David Rowe and John Oliver made parts of my work much easier and Ian Buxton has been helpful over many years. I am grateful to Peter Hogg who generously provided data he had collected, to A B Rodenby for allowing me to see an early wagebook of Robert Thompson and to Elizabeth Rowell for access to her grandfather's memoirs. The analysis of housing and occupations for Hebburn would not have been possible without the work of the late John Gascoigne. My thanks to Susan Fritz who designed the cover and provided advice on layout. My son Dominic has regularly had to sort out my computer difficulties and my daughter Leigh provided indispensable help with the index and other matters.

A very special thanks is due to my friend Joe Collerton, whose careful guidance has made this a much better book. My apologies to those whose advice I have not being able to follow. All errors and omissions are entirely my responsibility.

Acknowledgements
I am grateful to Richard Keys for permission to use his sketches of ship rigs. Full acknowledgement is made to the Records Offices of Tyne & Wear, Cleveland and Northumberland for permission to use material which they hold and to the various publications from illustrations have been used [*The Engineer, Engineering, Illustrated London News*, the transactions of the *NECIES, RINA, Institution of Marine Engineers* and *Institution of Mechanical Engineers*]

Joe Clarke

Statistical & other tables, together with lists of ships will be available on disk and CD-ROM format. Further information from

Clarke Ireland Associates
Churchill House, 12 Mosley St.
Newcastle upon Tyne NE1 1DE
tele no. [0191] 230000 fax [091] 261 0200
Email dominic@ciassoc.demon.co.uk.

Notes on conventions in the text.
The following conventions are flexibly followed through this book. Where words are quoted within the main text they are in *italics*, however where the quotation is set out separately then it is in one point smaller type. The names of ships appear in italics. The text is not referenced like a learned article or thesis and the foot-notes are used to provide information on possibly less familiar persons and at times for a particular direct reference. The notes related to each chapter provides a list of the some of the sources used for that chapter.

Where a ship's tonnage is given as 500t, the "t" is normally gross tonnage but prior to the use of steam engines this distinction is less significant. Where net tonnage [net] or deadweight [dwt] tonnage is used the abbreviation in brackets is used. Where ships or shipyards are named in some cases their tonnage, or relevant output, will appear in brackets for example *Mary* [200t] or Temple [33,000t]. In a similar way for the output of a yard or port the tonnage may be followed by the number of ships in brackets. Many shipowners well into the 19th century noted the size of their ships in *keels*, that is its capacity to carry that amount of coal: e.g the *Thomas* [12 keels]. With rare exceptions yard lists of vessels built do not exist for the early shipyards, that is why up to 1850 their will be frequent uses of the expression *at least* and then the number of vessels [or tonnage]. The number given represents vessels which have been identified from local Custom House Registers, Lloyd's Register, press reports or histories of individual ports. The *Statistical & other tables* [see p iv] will provide additional information for those requiring it.

The symbol k is used for knots: 9k = 9 knots, it was not unusual for trial and even log records to speed in knots to 3 decimal places such figures will sometimes occur in the text this is not because it is believed to be the correct figure but to show contemporary practice. This usually derived from prepared tables which translated a given number of knots in a certain time to a speed. A trial handbook changed a time of 64 minutes 10 seconds for the 9.6 knots from Newbiggin Church to Cullercoats Church into a speed of 8.976k.

The contemporary currency and weights are used:
"s" is used for shillings [$^1/_{20}$ of £] "d" for pre-decimal pence [12d = 1s]; where documents are quoted 5/- means 5 shillings and 5/6 five shillings and 6 pence [also 5s 6d.]. There are places where for ease of comparison shillings & pence are transformed into a decimal format - thus 4s 3d is 4.25s. "lb" or "lbs" is used for pounds weight [1 lb = 0.454 kilograms]. "cwt " is used for hundredweight - 20 cwt = 1 ton [= 1 cwt = 112 lbs = 50.8 kg] "qtr" was also used =28 lbs [12.7 kg] 1 ton = 2240 lbs [20 cwt] = 1016 kg. 11" is eleven inches - " is inch symbol [1" = 2.54 cm]; 11' is eleven feet [1' = 12" = 30.48 cm]. Contemporary practice for the thicknesses &c of plates regularly used vulgar fractions such as $^{18}/_{20}$" or $^{8}/_{16}$".

North East Coast Institution of Engineers & Shipbuilders - NECIES
Institute of Marine Engineers IMarE
Institution of Civil Engineers ICivE
Institute of Mechanical Engineers ImechE
[Royal] Institution of Naval Architects RINA
Iron & Steel Institute I&SInst
Institute of Marine Engineers IMarE
Institution of Engineers & Shipbuilders in Scotland IESSc
Mariner's Mirror MarMirr
North East Group for the Study of Labour History Bulletin [later North East Labour History] NELabB

A short chronology - North East Shipbuilding.
[for ships year of launch unless otherwise stated]

1294 Scarborough build a galley for the King
1294 galley built on Tyne - mouth of Lort Burn.
1346 shipbuilding by Thomas Menvill at Hendon on Wear.
1470 *ship* built for Bishop Booth at Stockton
1622 Company of Shipwrights of Newcastle upon Tyne.
1640s several ship carpenters at Whitby - sloops &c
1672 Goodchilds built vessels on Wear.
1679 Tindall's building at Scarborough
1685 Act to encourage shipbuilding

1720 Mary Wilkinson's yard at South Shields
1720s Headlams building at Stockton
1729 Robert Wallis yard at South Shields.
1750 Edmund Hannay building at Blyth
1750s Enoch White & G Boult built keels at Gateshead
1756 Wm Rowe started shipbuilding
1757 Thomas Fishburne building at Whitby
1758-9 Howdon Shipyard - Hurry, Mosley & Airey - dock
1760 Burns family building at Sunderland
1763 *Solebay* 6th rate frigate by Airey & Co
1767 A Topham building at Seaton Sluice

1770 Broderick building at South Shields
1770s John Summers - South Shore 1773 - *Mary* 329t
1773 Tonnage Act
1775 Shipwrights' Friendly Society at Scarborough
1778 Frigate by T & Mark Pye at Stockton
1778 *Union Ship Insurance Co* at North Shields
1780 Simon Temple's yard at South Shields.
1786 Custom House Registers
1789 The *Original* lifeboat by Greathead of South Shields
1793 Laing's yard began on Wear.
1795 *Shipwright's Association* started at South Shields
1798 New dry dock - Simon Temple
1798 *Lord Duncan*, 952t built on Wear.
1799 *Herculian* 3-decked Indiaman by Temple

1801 Shipwrights strike at South Shields
1802 *Admiral Attlin* for East India Co by Temple
1804 Temple shipyard at Jarrow
1804 William Rowe largest graving dock on Tyne.
1804-9 Warships built on Tyne and at Berwick
1805 John Laing & Co shipyard at South Shields.
1806 Thomas Foryth purchased Temple's yard.
1807 Crown's yard on Wear.
1808 *HMS Bucephalus* 970t.

1810 *Duke of Roxburgh* 417t bur
1810 Thomas Smith purchased Rowe's yard.
1811 Drydock at Blyth - Stoveld.
1812 High Dock South Shields - G & J Straker & T Wallis.
1814 *Tyne Steam Packet* [later - *Perseverrance*]
1818 Improved lifeboat - John Davison of Wear
1819 C Young & Son take over West Docks
1819 Tonnage Act provision for steam power space

1820 Hawthorns supply engine for *Indefatigable*.
1822 iron boat built at Hawks' Gateshead works
1824 17 weeks strike 7-year apprenticeship on Tyne
1824 *Albion* -Stockton built steam vessel.
1826 Austin's yard began on Wear.
1827 Gales shipyard on Wear
1828 Laings sell yard at South Shields.

1830 T D Marshall building ships
1832 *Columbus* - emigrant ship by Barrick of Whitby
1834 Reorganisation of Lloyds Register
1836 J P Denton shipbuilding at Hartlepool
1837 Lister & Bartram yard began on Wear.
1838 first dredger set to work on the Tyne
1839 *Star* iron paddle steamer by T D Marshall
1838-41 Doxford's first phase shipbuilding on Wear

1842 *Ellenborough* 926t by T & W Smith.
1842 *Bedlington* 214 t iron screw steamer.
1842 *Prince Albert* launched by Coutts at Walker
1844 *Q.E.D.* 271t. first screw propelled iron ship on Tyne
1845 Doxford with Crown joint shipbuilding venture
1845 *Experiment*, first steamer built on Wear.
1846 *Blenheim* 1600t by T & W Smith.
1846 Wear Shipwrights established trade union.
1846 J L Thompson's yard began on Wear. *Pearl*.
1847 Joseph Eltringham Boiler & Ship Builder
1847 *Conside* 259t iron screw collier by Marshall.
1847 Rennoldson marine engine building at South Shields.
1847 Gaddy & Lamb patent slipway at Tyne Main
1847 T Toward boilers & iron shipbuilder St.Peters.
1848 William Pile family yard at North Sands.
1848 George Clark's engine works started Sunderland.
1849 Parkinson & Coutts yard at Willington Quay.

1850 *Shipwrights of the Port of Tyne* revise their rules.
1850 Short's first yard on Wear.
1850 River Tyne Improvement Act
1851 Palmer Bros open yard at Jarrow.
1851 St Peters covered shipbuilding berths - T & W Smith
1851 Shipwrights' strike 7 year apprenticeship
1851 Hylton strike - 11 yards involved
1851 Doxfords and Crown ended partnership
1851 Amal Soc of Engineers - Newcastle branch
1851- Doxfords funding shipwrights Robt Reay & others.
1852 *Amity*, Laing's first iron ship.
1852 Dickinson's engine works opened.
1852 Charles Mitchell starts yard at Walker.
1852 Palmer's *John Bowes* - first successful steam collier.
1852 *Thomas Hamlin*, 1350t. -Parkinson & Coutts.
1852 *Loftus*, first iron vessel built on Wear.
1852 at North Shields Smiths launch *Termagant* 464t
1853 celebration first engine built at Palmers Nov. 25
1853 John Pile shipyard at Hartlepool.
1853 Leslie opens yard at Hebburn.
1853 *Wear Board of Conciliation* formed.
1853 *Wear Shipbuilders' Association* formed.
1853 Middlesbrough shipwrights strike for 5s
1853-4 Wear Conciliation Board - shipbuilding
1853 Pickersgill & Miller's yard began on Wear
1854 Robt Thompson jr opened yard at Southwick.

1854	ss *Brandon* first compound engine- Randolph & Elder
1854	*Zingari* first iron vessel at Smiths' Limekiln yard.
1854	Pearse & Lockwood yard opened Stockton
1854	Richardson-Duck yard opened south bank Stockton
1854	*Advance*, first iron ship built at Stockton.
1854	*Merchant Shipping Act*
1854	Wear -800 on strike - 6 yards continued to pay 6s/day
1855	Bartram's own yard begins
1855	*HMS Terror* by Palmer
1855	T Richardson concentrated on marine engines
1857	Palmer's Engine Works lighted by gas - Jun 26
1858	*De Brus*, first iron ship built at Middlesbrough -
1859	*Eglantine* first on South Shields Custom House register
1859	T R Oswald's iron yard on Wear
1860	Wigham Richardson opened his yard - 3 berths
1860s	Rogerson built sailing bulk oil carriers
1861	Daniel Adamson - patent triple expansion engine
1861	Tyne Improvement Act
1862	T Backhouse & Raylton Dixon yard at Middlesbro'
1863	Doxford's *Golden Sunset* no.1 iron ship
1863	W Gray partner Denton - Hartlepool shipyard
1863	Hodgson & Soulsby buy Drummond yard at Blyth
1864	Irvine launched his first ship at Hartlepool
1864	four ships launched on Tyne Aug 15
1864	Schlesinger & Davis shipyard at Wallsend
1864	Composite ship *Bertha Marion* - G S Moore on Wear
1865	North-Eastern Marine Works opened at Sunderland.
1865	Readhead & Softley take over shipyard
1865	First well-decker at Hartlepool
1865	Blair & Co marine engine works [formerly Hackworth]
1869	Withy Alexander at Hartlepool
1870	Robert Knight Secretary of the Boilermakers Society.
1871	Osbourne-Graham open iron yard at Hylton
1871	9-hours Strike on Wear and Tyne - Weekly pay on Tyne
1871	ss *Whitehall* first steamship launched at Whitby
1871	At St Peters ships built by Coulson, Cook [Mitchell]
1871	Wallsend Slipway Co. Ltd
1872	John Readhead & Co.
1873	R Dixon - Cleveland Dockyard [Backhouse retired]
1873-4	Yards of Oswald, Pile & Watson fail on the Wear
1874	W Gray sole control Hartlepool shipyard
1874	*Propontis* A.C.Kirk's triple expansion engine - Elder
1874	C S Swan & Co began
1874	Wallsend Slipway fitted a set of engines to *Castor*
1874	*Sexta* - A C Franklin's triple - Ouseburn Works
1875	*HMS Magician* composite gunboat by Doxford
1875	H S Edwards & Sons formed.
1876	Tyne Iron SB Co takes over yard of Cole Brothers
1878	Doxfords open an engine works.
1878	Wigham Richardson opens Neptune engine works.
1878	First steel boiler on Tyne by Wallsend Slipway - *Ethel*.
1879	*Britomart* - last wooden sailing ship built on Tyne
1879	electric light at Edwards' High Dock
1880	G.B. Hunter managing partner C.S.Swan & Hunter.
1880	Last wood ship on Wear - *Coppename* by Pickersgill
1880	iron ship begun at Blyth Hodgson & Soulsby -
1880	Boilermakers' headquarters moved to Newcastle.
1881	Scotia Engine Works opened.
1882	Triple expansion engine *Isle of Dursey* Alex Taylor
1882	Armstrong Mitchell's prospectus Nov. 22
1883	Priestman's yard opened on Wear.
1883	*HMS Wanderer* - composite by Raylton Dixon
1883	Blyth SB Co formed by W S Vaughan
1884	N E Coast Institution of Engineers & Shipbuilders
1884	Parsons' basic turbine & generator patents.
1884	Chilean cruiser *Esmeralda* launched at Walker
1884-5	warship *Panther* built at new Elswick shipyard
1884-8	deep depression in shipbuilding.
1885	first engine Gray's Central Marine Engine Works
1885	Wood & Skinner at Bill Quay.
1885	Swan Hunter first steel ship - *Burrumbeet*
1885	Wear Conciliation Board - shipbuilding
1885	Stephensons begin shipbuilding yard at Hebburn
1886	Armstrong's tanker *Gluckauf* design by Swan
1886	Gray's tanker *Bakuin*
1886	Amalgamation of Hawthorns & Leslie
1888	Neptune's *Alfonso XII* mail & passenger 5063t
1888-9	Labourers form lasting trade unions
1889	Tyne Dock Engineering Co Ltd
1889	Neptune first refrigerated ship *Hornby Grange*
1891	Furness-Withy formed
1892	*Turret* ships new design by Doxford
1894	Parsons Marine Turbine Co - first *Turbinia* trials.
1895	Swan-Hunter glass roofing 2 berth East yard
1895	MacColl & Pollocks engine works opened
1897	*Turbinia* at Spithead review.
1897	First working Diesel engine exhibited.
1897	first steel self-docking floating dock by Swan-Hunter.
1898	Laing a Limited Co. £300,000 capital
1898	*Ultonia* 8,056t first Swan-Hunter contract for Cunard.
1899	*HMS Viper* - turbine driven.
1899	Smiths' Dock Co Ltd formed
1900	Swan-Hunter 2 new larger building berths 750' covered
1901	T & W Greenwell started on the Wear
1903	*Swan, Hunter & Wigham Richardson Ltd.*- controlling interest in Wallsend Slipway. Tyne Pontoons & Dry Docks Co Ltd become Swan-Hunter's Dry Docks Dept.
1904	Stephenson's 700' graving dock opened at Hebburn
1906	Mauretania launched by Swan-Hunter
1907	Employers end of Wear Conciliation Board
1908	*HMS Ghurka* - oil fired destroyer - St Peters turbines.
1908	Laing goes into voluntary liquidation
1909	Smiths Dock shipbuilding on Tees.
1909	Craggs last launches
1910	Geared turbine fitted to *Vespasian*
1910	reorganised Laings starts with ship # 630 Feb
1910-	Brigham & Cowan using arc welding
1910	first Isherwood Tyne Iron SB ss *Leucadia* Jun 8
1910	Smith's first whale catcher
1910-1	Doxfords began work on diesel engine
1911	Smith's Engine Works first engine in *Lord Percy*
1912	Dreadnought cruiser *HMS Queen Mary* by Palmer
1912	Swan Hunter acquire Barclay Curle
1913	*Tynemount* elec propulsion.
1913	first Isherwood standard tanker by Laing - *San Joaquin*
1914	Armstrong's new Naval Yard at Walker

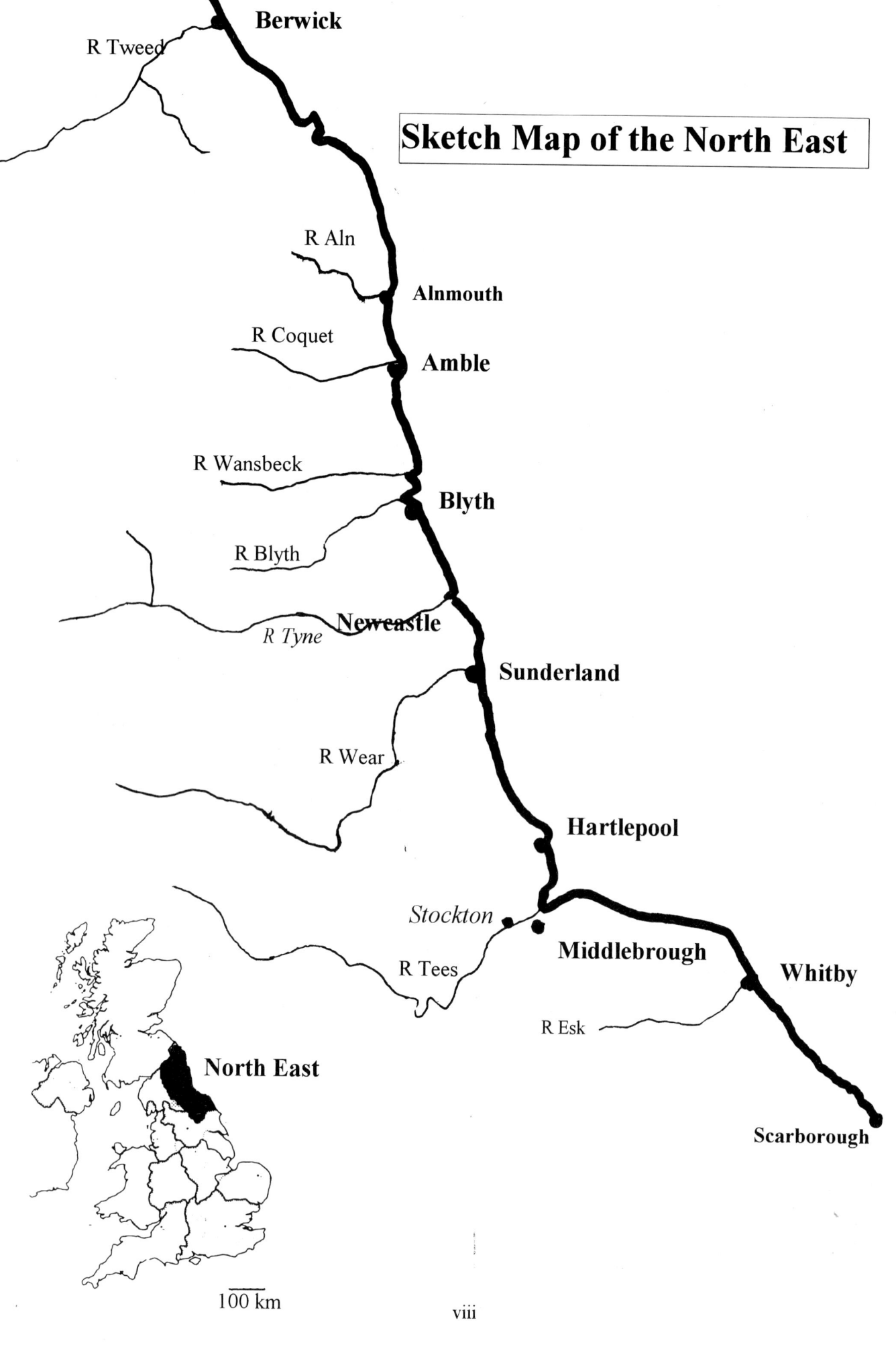

Chapter 1

Introduction

This is an account of shipbuilding on the north east coast, from Scarborough to Berwick[1], from the 17th century to recent times. It is a story which directly affected tens of thousands of families whose menfolk built the ships as well as the multitude of devices necessary for the vessels to sail successfully. Millions of people were affected, throughout the world, by the goods carried in these ships and many international conflicts were influenced by the warships built on the Tyne. Regional changes will, as far as space permits, be set in the background of national developments, with due consideration given to the many technical changes which so significantly affected the construction of ships and the industry. The growth of the workforce and its complex industrial relations are both central to this story of great achievement.

As soon as there was any significant amount of trade passing through a port it was necessary to have craftsmen, the shipwrights, on hand to facilitate repairs, over and beyond those which the ship's own carpenter could carry out; this man had also learned his skills as a shipwright. Many 19th century account books, in fact, list the shipwrights as *carpenters*. Once even a small group or family of shipwrights were at a port, especially if there was a local timber merchant, it was likely some shipbuilding would be carried out, at least sporadically.

New shipbuilding had few equals as an industry beset with cyclical fluctuations. This was hardly less true in the days of wooden ships than it was after the arrival of metal hulls, although from that time onwards, the larger yards frequently meant that the consequences of these fluctuations were more disastrous for both workers and their employers. Wars almost invariably inflated the industry and, usually temporarily, shipbuilding profits. Certainly, from the 17th century, in the immediate aftermath of a war a substantial depression of trade followed. Throughout the period of the 18th and early 19th centuries the number of *prizes*, ships captured, was of no small significance in terms of the English merchant marine. Such vessels were added to the trade fleet without the need of any new construction. Some 70 ports in England & Wales and a further 25 in Scotland were engaged in shipbuilding about 1800. As the years of the 19th century passed by, shipbuilding concentrated in particular ports, a trend which was strongly influenced by the construction of iron hulls. As will emerge, the metal hull required larger yards for economical working and this was a primary factor in this concentration.

The dominant economic factors in the development of the north east were the exploitation of coal, its shipment through the region's ports and the advantages which local coal supplies provided for industries such as engineering, iron & steel &c. As early as 1575 many ships from foreign ports were coming to Newcastle. Already by 1660 the coastwise movement of coal was very substantial; an annual average of 215,000 chaldrons or more than half a million tons [559,000] and in 1685, the unusually large amount of 297,000 chaldrons. With an average of 287,000 chaldrons from Newcastle alone for the four years 1729-32, it can safely be estimated that

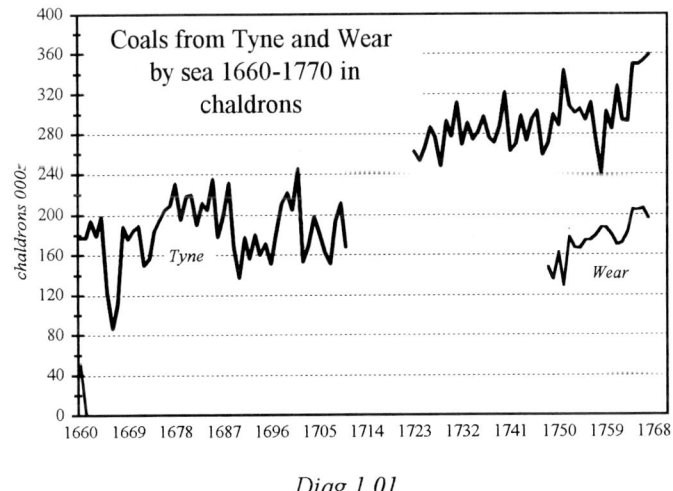

Diag 1.01

---

[1] *Engineering* in 1895 regarded Blyth and Whitby as *the extreme ports of what is regarded as North East Coast*; however Berwick is included here.

by then typically more than 300,000 chaldrons, or almost 800,000 tons, were shipped coastwise. *It is observable in this Place*, wrote Henry Bourne in his *History of Newcastle* of 1736, *when the Coal Trade is brisk, that all other Business is so too; and when it is otherwise ... there is a certain Deadness in all Traffick*. He cited a document from the Commonwealth period, dated Whitehall 17 April 1655, stating that 300 *Sail of Ships* were off Newcastle to take in coals, *which is so necessary a commodity for all Sorts of People*. On 20 April 1667, Captain John Earle wrote to the Navy Commission: *To-day we arrived with one hundred colliers at Tynemouth Bar*. If a single convoy contained 100 vessels, clearly many times this number were likely to arrive annually, creating the need for a very significant amount of repair work at least. A Trinity House[2] manuscript for the three years 1702-4 summarised information on 1,277 vessels *using the Coale Trade* at Newcastle; they came from 51 ports. These vessels carried 68,219 chaldrons, which amounts to about 13% of the estimated traffic in coal at that time. Bourne pointed in particular to the commercial importance to Newcastle's markets in providing the requirements of the ships which used the port, sometimes 300 or more vessels. On a single day, 8 March 1755, a total of 61 loaded colliers sailed from Shields.

This Trinity House manuscript provides the distribution of the vessels amongst the various ports; one sixth of the vessels, 211, were of Yarmouth and they carried almost one fifth of the coal shipped . From London just over 13% of the ships, 168, carried a sixth of the tonnage. There then followed Whitby, 98 vessels, and Ipswich 40. [see diag 1.02] These Ipswich vessels were significantly larger on average than those from any other port, carrying 144 chaldrons, compared with the overall average of 53.4 chaldrons. For nine months of 1634, the economic historian Nef calculated that the average cargo from the Tyne, coastwise was 58.4 chaldron [150t] and he gave the average cargo into London as 139t in 1638 increasing to 248t in 1701. After Whitby the numbers for Northern ports were Newcastle 71 vessels [8.2% of the coal], Scarborough 54 [3.8%], Sunderland 32 [2.7%], Stockton 27 [1.1%]. The combined north east vessels amount to just over a quarter of coal carried; vessels from 20 ports carried at least 1% of total in this document. The late Professor Edward Hughes pointed out that early in the eighteenth century *the coal owners neither owned nor had a controlling interest in the fleet of colliers plying between the Tyne and the Thames*.

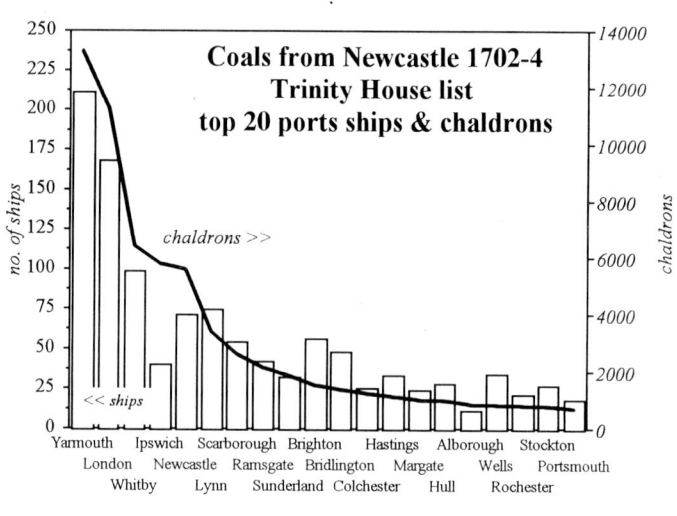

Diag 1.02

Forty-six vessels loaded at the Tyne staithes of the colliery owner Cotesworth [c1688-1725][3], from May to September 1710, a third 16 were Yarmouth owned, 12 from Scarborough, 4 from Sandwich and one from ten ports including Shields, Sunderland, Stockton and London. A mere two vessels were Newcastle owned. In the following six months period twelve of the 32 vessels came from Scarborough, nine from Yarmouth and two from London.

---

[2] Henry VIII set up a guild of seaman and mariners in 1517, which is the national usage of Trinity House. Trinity House was the name later given to the Society of Masters and Mariners of Newcastle [incorporated in 1492]: there was a Fraternity of the Blessed Trinity. Monarchs including Elizabeth I and James I granted charters to the Master, Pilots and Seamen of Trinity House Newcastle. They had the sole right to appoint pilots and were responsible for lighthouses. An Act of 1801 enlarged the powers and duties of Trinity House and jurisdiction extended from Whitby to Holy Island. The 1865 Pilotage Act changed the rules for pilots.

[3] See Joyce Ellis's work on Cotesworth e.g. *North History* pp 117-132 vol. XVII [1981]

Just under 54,000 chaldrons were sent coast wise from Sunderland in 1685, which was only a quarter of the coal sent from Newcastle. The next figure available for the Wear, in 1733, shows that the coal trade had almost doubled to 103,507 chaldrons, which was also a higher proportion [37%] of the Tyne trade of 275,243 chaldrons.[4] Certainly, between 400 and 600 vessels were engaged in transporting coal. Coasters averaged about 8 voyages a year and in 1777 made 4370 such round trips, which gives the likely number of ships involved as very similar to MacKenzie's estimated of 547 vessels in the 1820s. Writing in the early 1790s Hutchinson described *the great fleets* at Newcastle, sometimes 200 or 300 ships sailing in and out of that harbour on one tide. Following a statute of 1695, the *Seaman's Sixpence*[5] was collected monthly from all seamen. Data based on *sixpences* collected reflected activity in shipping. A comparison figures for the North East from 1735 with coal trade figures, where these are available, shows a not unexpected link. This link firmly emphasises the key role of the shipment of coal in the movement of shipping from the north east and the consequences of this for a substantial market for shipbuilding, which once well established could reach beyond this immediate stimulus. Despite the disputes about the precise rates of economic change during the eighteenth century there seems little reason to doubt that from about 1740 to the mid-1770s exports increased in value by about 50%. When the American colonists rebelled there was a sharp fall, but by 1790 the trend in growth had recovered. There was also a substantial growth in the population of England & Wales over the century, from about 5.83 millions in 1700 to 9.2 million a hundred years later. Over the years 1700-50, the combined total for Northumberland and Durham increased by about one sixth [16.44%] compared with a national growth of about 6%. However, during the second half of the century, the north east, at less than 22%, was well short a national growth rate of approximately 50%. It might perhaps be supposed that apart from the very significant growth in coal, the rest of the region's economy was not expanding particularly rapidly.

Not only the region's economic activity but that of the whole country and indeed world trade continuously affected the use of shipping and the demand for new vessels and the repair of the existing merchant marine. Wars and the threat of conflict always influenced the demand for ships and when the conflict ended there were usually set-backs in new building. All these wider political changes cannot be set out, but brief reference will be made as appropriate. It may of course be noted, that ideally such a history as this would start from the basis of many individual company histories; what is regional is that these many enterprises functioned within a given geographical area. That area no doubt gave it shared characteristics and resources but the regional industry was the aggregate of separate decisions. One of the regional characteristics was a strong and persistent family ownership of the shipyards. This was particularly so on the Wear and although on the Tyne some companies had a wider ownership, a family or personal ownership connection continued well into the 20th century. Even where there was wider share ownership, such as at Swan Hunter, the family influence remained strong; a Hunter was its chief executive when the firm was nationalised. There was a large number of yards of varying size, which continued despite the impact of the all too frequent fluctuations of demand. These yards prided themselves on the diversity of types of vessels, from small specialist craft to a few great passenger liners and large numbers of naval craft from the smallest to great battleships, they built. The sizes were even more diverse as will be illustrated from particular yards. Special efforts were required to establish and maintain standards of quality in ship construction. On the Tyne for a hundred years or so the Company of Shipwrights exercised this function, but the central role in this regard was under taken by the registration societies led by Lloyd's. There was a varied rate of response to the many technical changes within the industry. Although there was a long transition from wood to iron hulls, some yards never made the changeover and others began with the new material. For understandable reasons the changeover from iron to steel once underway was completed more

---

[4] see Nef app.D table facing p.380. Overseas trade was very much smaller - 1684-5 Tyne 21,014 chaldrons, Wear 8,434; in 1732-3 - Tyne 16,066 and a higher total on the Wear 19,535 chaldrons, 15% of total.

[5] The late Ralph Davis presented this data in 1956 Economica. A hospital for seamen, who were injured or lived to old age in the crown service, was established by charter of William & Mary in 1695. This was built at Greenwich. The sixpence was collected monthly for this and other naval charities.

quickly but again with variations. Metal hulls required larger yards and a new, more complex workforce initially recruited from an engineering background. Many of the shipwright's traditions persisted as the industry recruited new trades and the new craftsmen were offered the inducement of piecework, through which many secured high earnings. Unfortunately a great diversity of trade unions was the outcome of the slow evolution of workers' organisations. With the workers building metal hulled ships there were relationships between craftsmen and their helpers found in few other industries; until some years into the 20th century the squad leader paid his men The organisation of the employers for many years was on an almost ad hoc basis. Into the 20th century, within the region they were in separate associations. Conciliation was developed more successfully on the north east coast than elsewhere. The *custom of the port* or even a particular firm regularly influenced industrial relations but also other yard and workshop practices as well. Many support industries were needed for successful shipbuilding, sails and rope to mention two of the more obvious but there were many more vital components of *fitting-out*, the blocks, the masts and winches etc. These were established in years of the wood ships. After 1820, engineering through marine engines and other ship board equipment, played an increasingly important part in shipbuilding; this aspect is regarded here as an integral part of the industry. On the north east coast many shipbuilders also built engines and new specialist builders of auxiliary equipment expanded those trades which were also vital to wood sailing ships. Engineering added an additional dimension to the crewing of vessels. Skilled men were required in the engine room and these skills were first acquired in the marine engineering workshops, so that these became the schools for essential seagoing personnel. A local market for ships was always important but the main trading ports such as London and Liverpool were important for north east shipbuilders. Almost all yards had their regular customers who would given them the first opportunity for new work; there were no doubt reciprocal benefits. Although most of the larger yards periodically held a financial interest in ships they built, this practice was probably less developed than elsewhere. People are central to this story, even where blind impersonal economic forces were having their impact in the various yards employers, managers and men were trying to cope. Ships were built on speculation, work was taken on a prime cost basis of materials and labour, perhaps not even that to keep a yard operating. These themes briefly noted will hopefully emerge with this account of building ships on the north east coast.

Broadly the approach in this history will be in chronological order but certain aspects of the industry are given their own chapters, the workforce, marine engineering, shiprepair and major technical changes. Part 1 takes the story to 1914 but with certain topics, for example marine engineering from this period being covered in Part 2. Within the chapters covering the region overall [1, 2, 3, 5, 9 and 10] separate sections will deal with the main shipbuilding ports and selected individual yards will be used as examples of output at the level of the firm. Each river is dealt with separately in chapters 5,6 and 7 from about 1850 to 1889. Chapter 4 presents a short account of techniques of shipbuilding and the changeover from wood to metal hulls; changes at the main ports are considered in their own chapter. The 1880s are reviewed in chapter 9 both in regard to the prolonged depressions and the changeover to steel hulls and the introduction of the oil tanker. Two fields of particular interest on the north east coast warship building and sales overseas are considered in chapter 11. Labour issues and the organisation of the employers are reviewed in chapters 12 and 13. The very important matter of health & safety at work is covered in Part 2. In Part 2 the chronological account from 1914 to the 1980s is covered in chapters 20-26. Separate chapters are devoted to Marine Engineering [14], The Marine Steam Turbine [15],Technical changes in marine propulsion [16], Shiprepair [17], Profit & Loss in the Industry [18] and The Professional Society & Technical Education [19]. These chapters cover periods which begin before 1914.

Chapter 2

Shipbuilding to about 1780.

*[W]hen the Good-men of this Town began to trade and venture beyond the Seas,
they built many ships* - Gray in 1649.

By the 1660s Newcastle was the fourth most populous provincial town in England. Because of its coal *Newcastle, indeed, stood in relation to London not unlike that in which Egypt with her corn granaries stood to Imperial Rome.*[1] Coal played a central role in the development of shipbuilding. In addition to coal there were both glassworks and salt-pans, and before 1700 the beginnings of an iron industry. Vital to all of this economic activity were the wooden ships. A local timber supply was available. The wood on the Town Moor, Bourne stated, was *very famous for Oak Trees* and provided what was needed for hundreds of ships. Exactly where yards were is not recorded, however, about 1656 new slipways were added at St Lawrence to those at the Close-Gate.[2] Variations in demand for shipbuilding were already evident in the 17th century as reflected in the fluctuations of new apprentices enrolled in the Newcastle Shipwrights' Company [see diag 2.01]. In 1641, a total of 31 apprentices were enrolled and for some years there were probably about 100 apprentices on the Tyne. During the five years 1647 to 1651 only 57 apprentices were enrolled, compared with an annual average of 15 during the previous ten years. Over the years 1652-8, a total of 175 apprentice were registered, 35 in 1655 and 52 in 1656, probably linked with the new yards at St Lawrence. Less than 7 new lads on average enrolled during 1659-62. Not until 1668 did the numbers significantly move forward again. Many good years in the 1670s were followed by a very bad period. Only five apprentices were enrolled in 1680 and the numbers did not exceed ten until 1690. Some evidence suggests that foreign built vessels were moving coal. In 1685, Parliament passed an Act *For the encouragement of shipbuilding, greatly decayed in Newcastle, Hull, Yarmouth, Ipswich and other ports of England on the eastern coast, occasioned chiefly by so much employing of foreign built ships in the coal trade ... and other inland and coasting trades*. A duty of 5 shillings *per tun* was imposed upon the foreign vessels over and above existing duties. When four years later a petition was presented by *Mariners & Owners of Shipping, and others using Coal Trade*

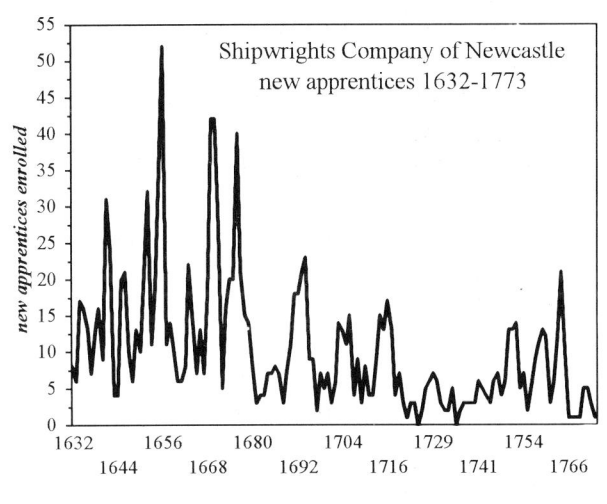

Diag 2.01

to have this changed, they stated that Charles II had allowed foreign-built shipping for the Coal Trade to replace the loss in a violent storm of more than 100 *considerable ships...about fourteen years since*.

Although there were upsurges, the 18th century did not start very well. For six years after 1717 only 21 lads were taken on and in 1724, for the first time, not a single apprentice was enrolled. This supports the evidence of the seven Tyne skippers, with more than 30 years experience, who stated in 1722 that shipbuilding had *formerly* flourished in Newcastle,

---

[1] Hearth Tax returns 1663-5 recorded 2,510 households in Newcastle, South Shields 567 households with about 5,000 on Tyneside as a whole see Fraser & Emsley. Lipson *The Economic History of England* [1956] p113.

[2] Shipwrights paid 2 shillings per tide to the Company when a ship of less than 100t burthen was brought on to these ways and 2s 6d for vessels over 100 t [order 29 Sept.1656].

but of late years few are built and many of the Ship Carpenters who commonly, when employed in their own business, earned above 4s/- a day and several of the Smiths are now obliged for want of Employ to get Bread for their familys to undertake the hard and dangerous work of Rowing in the Keels.

A very rough measure of the workforce may be estimated by the cumulative number of apprentices over a 35 year period; this is probably a minimum figure as it seems likely some lads were employed who were not enrolled with the Company [diag 2.02].[3] Some labourers were also probably employed in the shipyards and the assistance of the blacksmith was essential and the ship captains in 1722 who commented upon the decline linked them with shipwrights. There was a fluctuating but steady growth in shipwrights' work from the formation of the Company until about 1680. From the early 1680s there was a stepped but clear decline in the accumulated number of apprentices. Perhaps about 600 craftsmen were working as shipwrights from the mid-1670s to the mid-1680s and this had probably dropped below 500 by about 1700. By the early 1730s numbers were most likely below 250. Total membership of the Shipwrights' Company is unlikely to have exceeded 200 in 1717, when, in all, 192 members paid for the alterations to their meeting house. These members shared only 78 apprentices At this time, there were clearly substantial difficulties for shipbuilders. During the spring of 1729 many shipwrights were not being paid because the Master Builders were not paid by the owners of Keels and Masters of Ships for a *considerable time* after the work was finished. In future, it was resolved on 3rd May 1729, that every Master Builder should clear all wages due once in every three months, and *pay in the mean time* 15s for every 12 days worked. This is indicative of the operation of the fortnightly pay which was common on Tyneside up to the 1870s and in some trades even later. Penalties were to be enacted against ship owners, who failed to pay 6 months after the work was done. Shipwrights were also laid off unreasonably. In 1734 ten shillings was given to Robert Simpson and others *which they lost by being discharg'd from their work when they should not.*

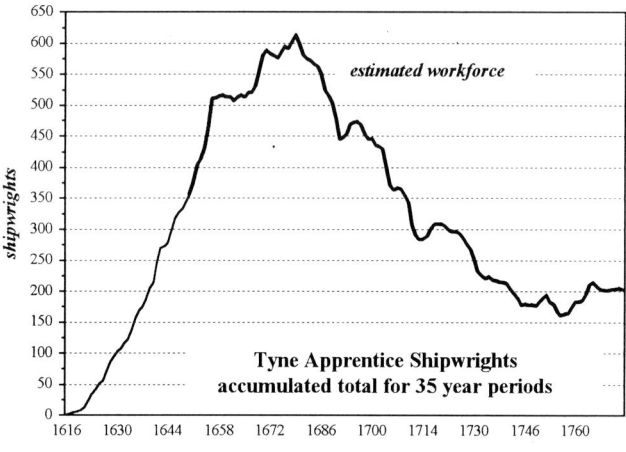

Diag 2.02

The Early Colliers.

Despite its frequent quotation, Daniel Defoe's comment, from the 1720s, may be recalled: at Newcastle *They build ships ... to perfection, I mean as to strength and firmness and to bear the sea; and as the coal trade occasions a demand for such strong ships, a great many are built here*. The collier was one of the principal vessels produced in the north east and for many yards continued to be an important part of their output as long as they survived. Unlike Defoe, one historian regarded the building of a new collier as *probably a rare occurrence* as such vessels *were known as the dregs of the fleet* and Ralph Davis stated the wooden ship *rotted through old age as colliers and hulks*. No doubt there were such vessels. Noting that *no eyebrows were raised at the Admiralty* when Cook selected Whitby vessels for his voyages of exploration, Parry wrote:

> Colliers had to be strong. They were solidly built of oak and their proportions were moderate; their tumble-home relatively slight; and they had robust transom sterns [and]... retained ... some of the virtues of the fluyt; their full section [i.e. a flat floor]; their capacious almost rectangular hold; their simplicity and economy of size. They had bluff bows and straight sterns, with no beakhead and only a modest cutwater, they were built for strength and carrying capacity, not for speed, certainly not for looks. Their qualities were widely appreciated.

In 1675, Coke wrote that the coal ships made *very good men-of-war, as the nation found in all the late*

---

[3] A crude measure, and should be treated as such. Thirty-five years might be a reasonable figure for a working lifetime [14 to 50]. No allowance is made for those leaving through other work or death, although this should not seriously affect the trend. The total seems to be of the right order of magnitude compared with 1804. See chap.3.

wars with the Dutch. There can be no doubt that new colliers were built in the 18th century, including some on the Thames; in 1789 the Blackwall yard constructed the *Crowley* [183t]. Design details were given for a collier brig in Steele's important work *Naval Architecture* [1804]. Lloyds' Register of 1776 described more than 100 vessels as *London Collier* and of these more than half were built after 1763.

Sailing collier

Keels were used to move the coal on the rivers Tyne and Wear. Clearly these craft were smaller [they carried about 21 tons of coal] than many seagoing vessels. They required, however, many of the constructional skills of the shipwright and as such were built and repaired by members of the Shipwrights Company.[4] Keel building was a source for skilled labour, of which an adequate supply was essential to enable industrial expansion to take place. Various estimates exist for the number of keels upon the Tyne; in the time of Charles I there were probably 200 and 320 in 1655. By 1725, Nef suggested as many as 400 based on the number of keelmen and more than 100 on the Wear. Such numbers represented a substantial amount of construction and repair work. These craft were estimated to be worth about £100 each. The Company of Shipwrights specified rates of pay for work on keels in 1679, 1729, and 1736. This work was not inconsiderable in value: Trewhitt in 1732 complained of a debt of £150 for work done on several keels. As early as 1421, by Statute, the Crown defined the size of these craft. This control was far from effective and in 1677, an Act was passed to set the size of keels[5] and a year later the manner of marking a vessel to indicate its capacity was laid down. Typical conditions for building wooden vessels were elementary, essentially a strip of river bank or beach on which the structure of the vessel could be erected and the hull satisfactorily launched on completion [see chap 4]. Fines imposed by the Shipwrights' Company provide a limited insight into the size of Tyne shipyards. Roger Durham jnr in 1717 worked with three men on Candlemas Day. The Brewhouses worked with between six and ten men in the 1750s and Richard Shaw employed up to nine men in 1753. Yards of this size are quite consistent with the survey of 1804 [chap 3]. The average tonnage for the British merchant vessels about 1800 was 108t: a 100t vessel was about 62' long; 20' wide. A typical ship was not very large.

The Company of Shipwrights of Newcastle Upon Tyne.[6]

A most distinguished naval architect, Sir Westmacott Abell [1857-1961] entitled his history of shipbuilding *The Shipwright's Trade*, thereby saluting a great and ancient craft. These very proud craftsmen dominated the wood yard. The journeymen and their apprentices usually provided about four out of five of those employed in a shipyard. Their work was described by that intrepid social investigator Henry Mayhew as *very hard, and demands not merely the customary skills and quickness of the handicraftsman, but great manual strength*. The ancient craft of the shipwright enjoyed the prestige of its own Guild or Company of Newcastle from late medieval times. Four shipwrights became Freemen of Newcastle upon Tyne in 1614, which suggests the Newcastle Company began just before this date. Ten more shipwrights were admitted to this distinction in 1624. The Shipwrights were better organised with an order book from 1622. Brand

---

[4] There were many references in overseer's reports showing Shipwrights doing this work, e.g 25 March 1721 *At a new Keel of Tho. Shafto ... At a new Keel of Tho. Wrangham.*

[5] *J.C.* in *The Complete Collier* of 1708 wrote: it is a great complaint that several Keels on that River *Wear* [if not on *Tyne*] which are not Admeasured according to that Act. [p51- 1979 reprint]

[6] This section could not have been prepared so readily without David Rowe's book *The Records of the Company of Shipwrights of Newcastle Upon Tyne 1622-1967* [Surtees Society 1971]. TWAS ref. GU/SH/1-4. See introduction on the early craft associations *struggling for power* for the government of Newcastle upon Tyne.

noted the following: *1613 Robbt Harrigad for carvell 1/- 1622 William Keisley for working on a ketch on a holiday 7d - of two for working on a flebote on a holiday 7d.* All this suggests some regulation before the formal rules of the Shipwrights' Company were certified by the judges of assize in August 1638. [Their play Noah's Ark is reproduced in the appendix] The Newcastle Company's powers did not extend beyond the River Tyne. Although it might be argued that the Company's regulations were a potential barrier to shipbuilding expansion on the Tyne, it was certainly not directly capable of deterring developments in other north east ports. On the contrary, perhaps any restrictions on the Tyne offered a stimulus to other ports. About 200 was the largest membership of the Company according to Rowe, who commented: *The Company was of no outstanding importance in the government or trade of the town, although the fact that a number of sons of masters and mariners (a very influential company) were apprenticed to members of the shipwrights' company suggests that the latter was considered a respectable occupation.* The place where the Company of Shipwrights met was described by Bourne as the *Carpenters Tower*.[7]

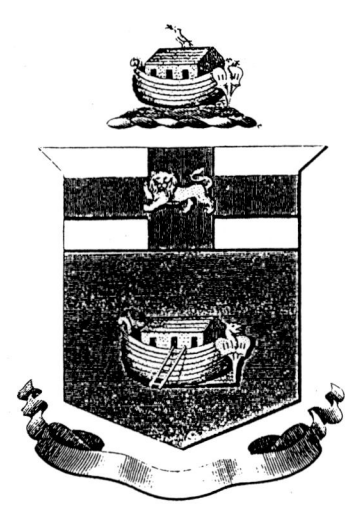

Emblem of the Shipwrights

On 30th May 1622 the shipwrights decided on orders *for the good government of the said fellowship*, which included members conduct at meetings and towards each other. These rules were intended to control the trade, firstly by attempting to limit the building of ships to Newcastle and that shipbuilding and repair work was done by craftsmen *free* of the Company. Apprenticeship was to be controlled by enrolment in the Company and some measure of quality control was exercised by inspection. As particular problems arose policy was defined by decision of the Company, for example on working with material supplied by the purchaser, changes to welfare benefits in difficult economic circumstances and on holy day working. It was laid down in 1622 :

> That noe brother of the said fellowship or any of his apprentices shall worke any day saleworke upon any holy day assigned by the church upon paine of 6d for every default, causes of extremities excepted.

There were 22 such holy days.[8] A *complaint* was upheld against Francis and Edward Greene on 10 February 1663 that they *had heretofore and ... doth now employ forreigners* [this included men from other British ports] *who never served to the trade to hew and square timber at or near their respective places ... which tends or may tend to much damage the Company.* It was ordered with the *consent* of Francis that no brother shall give shipwright's work to such persons under the penalty of 6s 8d for every offence.

Some thirty shipwright families enrolled ten or more apprentices before 1719 and a further 58 families between 4 and 9 apprentices. In all 188 shipwrights enrolled apprentices, although 58 of these had only one apprentice. Those original Freemen of 1614 were Rowland and Thomas Steel together with Robert, Anthony and Peter Wilkinson; a Thomas Steel was a steward of the Company in 1672-4 and enrolled his last apprentice William Hedley in 1674. Missing folios make the precise dates during the 1620s impossible to establish but it is likely that Thomas Steel enrolled the first apprentice that can be identified, Christopher Crosbie, in the early 1620s. A further 42 apprentices were enrolled by Steels and it is likely this yard operated for about 70 to 80 years. Peter Wilkinson took three apprentices during the 1620s and members of the family probably took almost 60 apprentices, and a Wilkinson was admitted by patrimony as late as

---

[7] Brand recorded that in 1716 the Company built *a very good and stately Square Tower, adorned at the Top Corners with 4 fair Turrets built in the form of a Lanthorn* as part of this building.

[8] St Paul, St Mark, St James, St Matthew, St Luke, St Andrew, St Peter, May Day, St Philip & James Day, Ascension Day, New Years Day, Candlemas Day, Whitsun Monday and Tuesday, St John , St Barnabas , St Bartholomew, St Mathias, All Saints Day, St Andrew, St Simon & Jude Day, and St Thomas Day.

1757. The Greene family also spanned the period from the 1620s to the 1690s. Edward Greene enrolled his first apprentice before 1630 and in all the family enrolled 49 apprentices, the last in 1687. A shipwright's memorial provides an indication of the output by a yard at this time. A marble plaque in All Saints' Church recorded:

> Under the adjacent Marble is inter'd the Body of Thomas Wrangham, the famous and beloved Shipbuilder of this Town, he married Jane daughter of Mr Robert Carr, by whom he left Issue two Sons and one Daughter... He built Five and Forty Sail of Ships.

Wrangham's output of just over two vessels a year was similar to wood yards of a century or more later. In the 1620s a John Wrangham was enrolled as an apprentice and in 1633 he took a Thomas as his apprentice. Presumably the Thomas who enrolled his first apprentice in 1641, and his son Thomas Wrangham jnr. took his first apprentice in 1669. In that year a shipwright, Thomas Wrangham, built the Glass House bridge[9] *on Account of Lands which the Town let him*, presumably when he started his own yard. Twenty years later, aged 42, he died of a fever. His two sons Thomas and William were also shipwrights; William took his first apprentices in 1702 and his seventh, the last, in 1717, the son of a Berkshire brickmaker. Many Wranghams were members of the Shipwrights' Company. John took apprentices during 1633-51, Avera from 1659-63, and Henry in 1690. In all, these Wranghams enrolled a total of 56 apprentices over the years 1633 - 1719, so, if the same yard, it lasted more than 90 years. All Saints' Church included a Seamen's porch and among annual legacies for the poor of the parish [prior to 1736] were the following from shipwrights: Thomas Smith £4 18s; John Collier £3; Edward Potts £20.[10] Many master shipwrights lived, and probably had their yards by the Glass House Bridge, including Thomas Wallis, Roger Durham, John Lattany and Cuthbert Preston. Maughlin[e] may serve as an example of a family moving into shipbuilding. George the son of a yeoman [William Maughlin] was apprenticed to Edward Preston in June 1693 and became a Freeman on 2 April 1701. He was joined by two brothers as a freeman; William in June 1704 and ten years later by Thomas, when he paid his *thirteen peny money* 4s 4d and 1s 6d for his fines.[11] Whether the George Maughlin [II], apprenticed in January 1706 to the above George Maughlin was related is not known: William the father of George [II] was a shipwright. Amram Maughlin, son of George, was admitted as a freeman in June 1733. George Maughlin was allowed to work at South Shields in April 1721. Before a year had passed however, he sought to recover his bond because he was not willing to continue at Shields. George Maughlin was an Overseer in 1726; a George Maughline one of the *Twelve* in 1764 and 1766; he was presumably the George *Maughling*, who took an apprentice on 26 April 1765.

There were numerous breaches of the restrictions on working on holy days and the number of men subject to fines gives some indication of the size of yard. Roger Durham jnr was fined 6d for each three offences in 1717; John & Stephen Brewhouse were regularly fined in 1754, 1755 and 1756. Both Brewhouse and Richard Shaw paid 17 fines in single years, showing a persistent breach of the rule. The numbers employed by Shaw varied, it was usually three men but on two occasions it was 5 and later up to 8 or 9 men. Robert Wallis over the years 1753-8 regularly employed seven men. Almost the same as some Wear wood yards in 1840s: Robert Thompson began his yard on the Wear in 1846 with his three sons and four men. Decisions on the limitation of apprentices were more restrictive than those later adopted by shipwrights'

---

[9] Bourne *The passage over it was very difficult and uneven 'till the Year 1729, when... it was made level and commodius both for Horse and Foot*. It may have been built by his father. Thomas jnr was described as *a Man of a most generous temper, of a plain and unaffected Conversation, and a sincere Lover of his Friend*

[10] The surname Colyer occurs in Shipwrights records from the early 1620s. In 1676 John Colier enrolled an apprentice, as did a John Collyer in 1689. Edward Potts took an apprentice in 1698, he was one of the Company's stewards in 1711-2 and also one of the Twelve.

[11] Money values across long time periods can be very misleading. *The Delaval Papers* for 1720-1 show:- masons 18d a day [16d in 1721], labourers 8d a day; joiners paid 16-18d a day. Men planting 8d and women at 4d for watering and weeding. Beef at $2\frac{1}{2}$d. per pound, eggs at 4 a penny. In October 1718, pay sheet for labouring men 2 at 10d/day, 14 at 8d, 1 at 7d, 1 at 6d & 1 at 5d. In Oct.1759 joiners 18d and 16d. [p 13-4 & p173]

unions. The Company resolved on 24 June 1696 *That noe brother ... shall be admitted to enter any apprentice in the Companyes book that is a Scotchman borne.*[12] If such an anti-Scottish attitude had persisted and had excluded the Scots, it is doubtful if iron shipbuilding would have flourished as it did on the Tyne in the 19th century. Not until 1709 does Scotland appear as a place of origin of the father of an apprentice; five other Scots were enrolled up to 1771, of whom one failed to complete his time.

The Shipwrights' Company successfully charged John Hubert of South Shields and fellow shipwright John Readhead and secured their imprisonment, because they worked at the trade when not freemen of Newcastle. They were not the only ones; John Hardcastle was fined in May 1648. This monopoly was severely criticised in Ralph Gardner's *England's Grievances Discovered in Relation to the Coal Trade* of 1651, where he accused the Company of preventing non-freemen shipwrights working at Shields. In reply, it was stated there were about 100 families in the company of free shipwrights and that *a competent number* of shipwrights always resided at Shields *to save ships in distress, and are ready upon all occasions to exercise their trade of shipwrights there or at any place within the river or port, either building or repairing of ships.* They went on to argue that *if any other strange ship carpenter, not free..., other than hyred ship carpenters coming in any vessel and working in the same,* work within the port, *they do as it were eat the bread out of the mouth of the free carpenters of Newcastle, their wives, children and families.* There must have been at least 100 Company shipwrights and perhaps 150 or more, counting the brothers and sons of the head of the family. The Commonwealth Committee of Trade decided such limitations were *very prejudicial to trade and navigation.* Nonetheless, the Company persisted in attempting to exercise control. An order made in February 1664 summarised this and other matters. They objected to the *reputed thirteenepenny men* who by refusing to become freemen or live in the town did not *pay Scott or Lott in the Towne.* Some 13d men lived at Gateshead and many shipwrights paid this money until they became freemen and some never became freemen. These shipwrights were *very much employed and abundantly worke* at South and North Shields [also *below or eastward of Walsend or Snowdon panns*] and as a result free brethren were *neglected and not employed.* In 1664 these 13d men were required to pay *five shillings lawfull english money over and besides the thirteene pence by them formerly yearly paid.*[13] On March 19th 1673, the Company decided that no freeman shall live at North Shields or South Shields to work as a shipwright *without license from the wardens and Society.* Richard Chambers, an apprentice, since 1669, of John Wilkinson of South Shields[14], saw his apprenticeship in jeopardy and sought the Company's help in finding a new master. The stewards and the *Twelve* [the Company's officers and managing committee] *fully argued and debated* the issue and unanimously agreed that Wilkinson for his contempt and offence, should immediately pay or give surety for £10 in lieu of the five years served by the apprentice. A new master in Newcastle was found for Chambers. Wilkinson immediately paid £5 and paid all the fine by the end of the year. Chambers became a 13d man and only became a freeman in December 1689. He certainly worked at Shields, in June 1705 he paid 10s for half a year working there and similar amounts were paid in 1712 and 1714. In the early 18th century the Company was at least tolerating work at South Shields; Thomas Browne, son of a deceased South Shields shipwright was enrolled as apprentice in 1698, likewise in 1713, the son of a North Shields shipwright was enrolled. An almost unanimous vote [62 to 2], in April 1721, allowed Richard Hudson to work at North Shields, *provided he enter the usual bond.*

Most of those who served apprenticeships under the Shipwrights' Company never enrolled any apprentices

---

[12] The rules of the Smiths of 1436 required that no Scotsman born *should be taken apprentice, or suffered to work , on pain of the forfeiture of 40s.* Half the fine *to the chamber of the town and half to the fellowship.*

[13] It is not clear how frequently the 13d was charged. A number of men when they became *free* paid amounts such as 2s 2d [i.e two 13d], 3s 3d or 4s 4d which suggests perhaps a monthly charge. In 1688 Thomas Chilton paid 13s in 13d money which is equivalent to a year if a monthly charge. The 13d may have stopped in late 1720s.

[14] John Wilkinson enrolled his first apprentice in 1655 and in all he took 13 apprentices, the last in 1695. Three Wilkinsons were amongst the earliest freemen.

of their own. More than 1,100 apprentices were enrolled during the years 1636-1750, excluding those by patrimony.[15] About 140 of these took more than two apprentices and there were another 46 or so who enrolled a single apprentice or two lads. Just over 100 of these apprentices never finished their time; 38 died and 67 more failed to finish. So perhaps about one fifth of these apprentices became master shipwrights, the total being probably slightly larger as not all members of a business owning family enrolled apprentices. Probably about three-quarters of the Company apprentices became working craftsmen.[16] It is almost certain that most of the master shipwrights not only worked in the yard but were actively engaged in actual construction. Brian Wall, the son of a mariner, became a freeman directly he finished his time in 1711. Five years later he took his first apprentice and he enrolled his second after another five years. When in 1723, the Company noted that Bryan Wall *hath given over keeping a yard and employing serrvants*, it was ordered that Wall was *at liberty to employ his servants with any other brother*. A year later, Wall and George Gordon were accused of *working forreigners stuff* [materials not supplied from Newcastle]. His third apprentice began in 1729, and then a very long gap followed before his final apprentice Thomas Curry, in 1748. Curry went on to be a major builder. Further evidence that Wall was then running a yard was an Overseers' report on poor workmanship *wrought at Mr Bryan Wall's* in 1749. His son entered by patrimony in 1741 and became a freeman in 1750. Various Company resolutions provide evidence that many members were employed just as craftsmen. It was decided in 1735 that if Richard Wilson persisted in not paying what was due to the Company it was resolved no brother *shall work with or employ him*; Wilson served as an officer of the Company. The Shipwrights' Company rules stated: *That noe Brother ... who is hired to worke stockeworke with any master workemen shall depart from the said worke until it be finished except it be for non payment of his wages* [penalty 3s 4d]. In 1712 fines were imposed on William Trumble and John Wilkinson for *leaving Captain Gile's shipp before it was finished*. Four members were fined in 1735 for leaving their work for John Thowburn *without any just cause* and were not permitted to work for anyone else until the work was completed for Thowburn. Action was also required against masters who had failed to pay their fellow Company members. These resolutions also give the payment for certain jobs. In May 1721, the *Twelve* ordered Robert Simpson for the work of doubling[17] done on Thomas Wallas's vessel to pay John Trumble, Henry Cay, Thomas Scott and Thomas Maughlin six pence per foot, less 3s 4d to be deducted *for the charge of the Companys meeting*. Two years later Thomas Wallas was required to pay Robert Simpson, Thomas Scott and John Carrier at the rate of *fourpence halfpenny p. foot for working the plank*. When the Overseers made their *Presentments* at the end of 1749 they reported: that Jacob Fisher and John Gibson were working *at Mr Trewhitts on board Capt. Garnett's ship* and John Wilson was employed at John Fawdon's. Jacob Fisher was certainly a master shipwright in 1757 and his son Ralph became a freeman. When in 1788, this *very respectable Brother* [Fisher then about 62 years old] was unable to work, he was paid 2s a week so that he might *live a little more comfortably than the hospital allowance can enable him to do*.

Many widows received benefits from the Company of Shipwrights, including those of master builders. Such benefits were very important to both the widows and children of the shipwrights. In 1686, 2s 6d was paid to each of 8 widows; others got 3s and 5s. Twenty four widows were named in an 1739 account; amongst those was Mary Wrangham. A number of widows continued to run their late husbands' businesses for some time. An early example was in South Shields: on 21 July 1720, permission was given to Thomas Forster to go to Shields *to serve widdow Wilkinson*[18] *as formerly he did performing all the laws and orders of the said company ... whilst his abode there*. Almost two years later he was told that he should not continue any

---

[15] See Rowe *Shipwrights Company ...* vol 1 p 10.

[16] Only one of 9 Trumbles were members of the Company took an apprentice and therefore presumably were usually working shipwrights. Four of them however held office.

[17] *doubling* was the term for covering with extra planking where the original timber hull was weak or worn; usually only used for planks thicker than 2".

[18] Disbursements in 1722 included 19s 4d for widow Wilkinson; there are many payments to widows named Wilkinson, in 1734 *Widd. Wilkinson of Shields 5/-... John Wilkinson's widd. 5/-*

longer at Shields, assisting Mary Wilkinson as her son was thought *sufficient to do it*. Mary Wilkinson paid her son's fines 11s in 1720. Widow Moore was paying fines throughout 1753 and into 1755 for two or three men working on holidays; thus although she was not a member of the Company, it required payment of these fines according to its rules. [see extract from Company of Shipwrights account book]. On 21 September 1750 the Company received from Mrs Moor[19] - 3s 4d *for a meeting of the 12*. At least two other widows paid holy day fines, Mrs Strother in 1712 and Widow Carrier during 1763-5. Another example of female employment[20] was that Robert Simpson's daughter undertook work for the Company ; she was paid in September 1715 *for two warnings of the Company & one of the Twelve 5s; to her more for keeping the cloaks 2s. 6d*. A *warning* here meant a notice, presumably of their meetings. Welfare payments sometimes covered funeral expenses. In 1686, fifteen shillings was paid for *widow Joblings buriall*, and £1 8s 10d was paid, in 1753, for Isabele Preston's funeral.

Shipwrights' Company account for Widow Moore

The details for Raiph Totherick's burial were *for a coffin 6s church dues 5s 10d gravemaker 1s waring company 2s expennses 5s 4d; in all £1 0s 2d-24 Dec 1674*. At the end of 1737 the Company paid *To Church dues for Tho. Ridleys funerall*- 9s 6d [Ridley, one of Wrangham's apprentices, became a freeman in 1718]. Two years later there began the first of a number of 5s payments to Ann Ridley, entered in 1758 as *Thos Ridley's Wid*. Finally on 29 September 1778, came *the charges of Ann Ridley's funeral* - £2. 4s 2d. When trade was depressed, benefits paid by the Company were suspended; thus, in 1767, having noted the *general stagnation* in trade and that many were unemployed, a range of exemptions and pay cuts for officers were agreed. Three years later *money given to Brethren whilst sick* were suspended for a year and the suspension continued through the following year, when shipwreck benefit was also suspended. Similar suspensions were made in 1781. With better times at the end of 1785 the sick money and shipwreck money was restored.

Other monopoly companies existed, particularly the Company of Hostmen which controlled the production and distribution of coal.[21] Queen Elizabeth I, desiring to raise revenue by imposing 1s per chaldron on coal, in 1600 granted the Hostmen a charter and confirmed their *alleged exclusive privileges* in exporting coals and grindstones. *This body exhibited all the characteristics of a highly developed monopoly,* wrote Lipson, *it approximated closely to a modern cartel*. The Hostmen, in 1663, sought a meeting with five or six of *the ablest* carpenters to confer about measuring keels; accurate measurement was important to market control. Regularly protests were made about the restrictive activities of the Shipwrights' Company but it also extended to other matters. The Hostmen complained, in 1655, that keels were damaged because ship

---

[19] A number of Moores or Moors were in the Company, it seems likely the deceased husband was Philip, son of a Newcastle plumber, apprenticed to William Trewitt in 1727. Phillip enrolled apprentices in 1744, 1747 and 1748.

[20] No doubt other women managed businesses. Welford listed *amongst the fellowship of brewers now living in now* [1637] *living in Newcastle* three women, out of the 35 with details of size of *mash tuns*. These were Mrs Mrgt Anderson [only six *tuns* were larger], Mary Andrew, widow, and Jane Hall. There were 20 other brewers [v.3.p349]

[21] see Dendy F W Extracts from the *Records of the Company of Hostmen of Newcastle upon Tyne* Surtees Society vol. CV [1901] also Lipson *The Economic History of England* v.II pp128-

carpenters left their timber below the high water mark and they wanted all timber or wood placed on the wharfs and staithes. In April 1705, they protested against the demand for *excessive wages*, stating that for working at keels per day, *their ancient dues were 1s. 6d.* and now 2s 6d and 2s 9d was asked for and paid. A year later, they contended that the ship carpenters' practices were *not onely prejudiciall* to the Hostmen but to the coal trade and to the *Nursery of Seamen and Navigation of England*, and had been *very destructive* to the *Trade and Welfare of this Port*. Complaints in regard to payments continued and in 1718 the Hostmen stated that the wages did *much exceed* those paid at any other port to shipwrights, which was *very extravagant*. In addition, there was *the exorbitant Demand they make of Bread and Drink, which they generally receive five Times a Day, amounts in all to about Five shillings p Day for each Man, which they take to be a very great Oppression and Hardshipp upon all Owners of Keels in this River*. This appears to be an exaggerated account of the well established customary *allowance* for shipwrights. Some Hostmen supplied timber for new construction or even repairs and were to say the least irritated when the Shipwrights tried to end this practice. On September 4th 1679 the Company of Shipwrights decided that no brother *shall presume to worke to or for such woodmonger or any other person that builds shipps or keeles who finde timber or other materials.*[22] The Hostmen declared a similar order, in 1718, *a great Prejudice... to this Company* and their Report on the matter denounced extravagant prices for plank, timber and other materials used in repairing Keels. They claimed these prices made it *insupportable* to the Keel Owners because the whole rents from the Keels did not exceeded by much what they have to pay for repairs. They pointed out that other craftsmen, such as house carpenters, millwrights, bricklayers and others *never refuse to work* timber or other materials provided. It was claimed these men were *much well satisfied* with the wages of *1s 8d p Day for each man, with twice a Day Bread and drink, which together never exceed 2s*, which was *so very much cheaper and easier* than the pay required by shipwrights. There is no evidence that the Hostmen's views directly influenced events.

The Overseers of the Company of Shipwrights were required to check standards of work and fine members who carried out *poor work*, for example in 1717 some of these fines were the following:
> *Thomas Wallas work at a butt wrought on a timber only a strake betwixt them on the starbard side forward at the old pink upon the dock insufficient.*
> *Wm Fletcher's work a plank wrought short at the hudden ends aft insufficient a butt wrought within seven inches of the skarf on the keel insuffiecient. His servant cawking of new work insufficient.* In 1749, amongst other matters, it was reported that at Wall's: *A gunwell that runs from abaft the main beam to fore the fore beam and natch'd out at the after end and the scarf at the fore end cut one inch short at one end and one inch and a quarter short at the other end* - an example of how very detailed the inspection was. Peter Forster was fined of 3s 4d *for cawking at Mr Beckwiths work insufficient.*

Standards of work were causing concern in 1757, when brethren were employing men that *have not been educated in* shipwright's work *which they are not capable of performing*. As a result customers were deceived and *manifestly injur'd*; and the Company's credit and character *greatly prejudiced*. A fine was to be imposed for employing and working with such persons. Conditions were changing with the expansion in the second half of the 18th century and in 1791 it was unanimously decided that the office of overseer was *of no use and... be abolished*; it had been by then a redundant function for many years.

Some information on pay is provided in the Shipwrights' Company's records. A complaint was made in 1674 *touching on* the wages and allowances of two men from Ipswich, and it was ordered that they shall be *constantly paid* 3s a day and 6d in lieu of their drink and 4d for whirrey [small sailing vessel] hire for work at Shields and other places on the Tyne. Clearly this cost for the *allowance* was much less than claimed by the Hostmen. The daily or tidal pay remained the manner of payment typical for shipwrights. Three shillings was similar to that earned in later years. In the summer of 1736 a day's pay was 2s 6d [or 2s a tide], which was also paid in 1778. A surviving bill for Hearn of North Shields for repair work in 1779

---

[22] Robert Beckwith was exempt - *he may freely proceed in the erecting and building of the shipp covenanted* because he had made the contract *sume long time* before the order. Robert became a freeman in 1676, in all the Beckwiths enrolled 31 apprentices, the family was probably engaged in shipbuilding or repair for about 80 years.

confirms this; he charged 3s a day which would represent the mark-up for a shipwright. During 1757 many more shipwrights than usual went to sea on warships or privateers as well as merchant ships. As a result there were not enough *Free* shipwrights at Newcastle to do the work required, in particular to do it as quickly as was necessary. Six shipbuilders[23] petitioned to hire the *not free*, they would agree to leave after eight days if required and the builder would pay the Company *for every shipwright one penny per day and also for every Hole Borer or Labourer that doth not handle edge tools one half penny per day*. These builders argued that otherwise this work would go to other ports, *greatly to the prejudice* of the Company and the trade.

A few words on the human weaknesses of the shipwrights, before considering the apprentices who are often seen as the more rumbustious members of a trade, There were many fines for members abusing each other. A brother was fined in 1673 for challenging another to fight *and giving him his glove*; presumably he had a duel in mind. There were no other examples of this; such episodes as Thomas Reed jun., a very senior figure, for *unbrotherly words* to James Lowson, and George Hindmarsh for saying to John Beckwith *Damn You,* were more common.[24] George Farmer was fined in 1717 for threatening to beat the overseers. Two examples of fines imposed for breaking the terms of apprenticeship: in 1711: Thomas Shafoe paid £2 for being married and *having a childe* before his apprenticeship was finished and in 1714 Thomas Baird paid £2 for marrying before he was out of his time. Occasionally a shipwright's defiance caused the Company's officers to appeal to the Common Council of Newcastle, and the case of Ambrose Preston[25] illustrates another aspect of the trade. A petition presented in January 1674 stated: *Ambrose Preston a burgesse and member of their society did worke in the trade of a shipwright to and with Thomas Burden a foreigner and particularly about masts and yards makeing for sale.* Traditionally shipwrights would work with the *carpenter* belonging to the ship under repair. [He was technically an outsider or *a foreigner*]. Preston defied the order against him and the Company raised its case again in March.

Apprentices were always a very important part of shipbuilding in wood, as this history will show. Periodically there were complaints of too many apprentices. In the spring of 1720, because apprentices were *very* numerous, *severall of the working brethren* could not get *any manner* of employment and *the rest of them do not get so much work as will sufficiently support themselves and their families so most of them are, in great want of the necessaries of life by not having employment*. The Company proposed that no master builder should take any apprentice, until the previous one had served three years and for working brothers this time delay should be five years. A £10 penalty for a breach of this decision was very substantial one. Twelve years later the problem was back and it was decided that £5 be paid when enrolling an apprentice and the lad should live with his master. Some relaxation came in 1748, when it was agreed that Master Builders could take two apprentices but not more, unless one of them had already served three years. In 1760 when Roger Almory already had six apprentices, the Company voted by 11 to 23 to prevent him taking another one. An outstanding exception to the practice of recruiting only one apprentice per year by a master was Headlam's yard. John Headlam, in 1743, acquired his freedom by patrimony as did T E Headlam in 1759. Joseph Nixon, son of a Gateshead dyer, became their apprentice in 1753, and in the next year the Headlams enrolled 7 apprentices. Only at the end of the year did Headlam pay £35 apprentice fees due on enrolment. The Headlams had 12 apprentices in 1759; the usual practice was then followed and 27 apprentices were enrolled over a 38 year period. About 15 shipwrights enrolled apprentices in the 1730s

---

[23] 27 Dec 1757 signed by Edward Trawhitt, Enoch White; Robert & John Gothard, Roger Almory and Jacob Fisher

[24] The rules of May 1622 included: [2] every brother... at every of ... their meetings shall decently and reverently use and behave themselves [3] noe brother... shall use any undecent or revileing words one to another or give the eye one to another or offer to strike [at meetings] [4] if any brother... shall in anger strike any other brother. . with his fist or any other weapon whatsoever in their. . .meeting house. The fines were 3s 4d for [2]&[3] and [4] 6s 8d.

[25] Ambrose Preston was an apprentice in 1646. If all the Prestons were related the family connection with shipbuilding continued until about 1750. An Edward was apprentice to John Colier in 1676 and his grandson was admitted by patrimony in 1743.

and the early 1740s, the number of shipwrights enrolling apprentices increased and during the 1750s about 25 shipwrights had apprentices. In 1764 a total of 21 apprentices were registered, followed by a reduction. It is likely that apprentice recruitment followed the movement of trade. The increase in work in 1757 was shown by the exemptions sought by five shipwrights noted above. By this time, it seems likely that boys were entering the trade without going through the Company. One of the master builders signing the exemption document, Jacob Fisher, never enrolled any apprentice with the Company and it is almost impossible to believe there were no lads working and learning in his yard. In 1765 there were about 70 young men, of whom 10 were in their final year, enrolled as Company apprentices serving 35 masters. At least 15 master shipwrights were operating on the Tyne, in or about Newcastle and Gateshead, over the fifty years 1726-76 and in some years as many as twenty-five. However, many of these men did not survive through the whole period; only Campion of the four who took an apprentice in 1726 survived until 1741.

Up to 1774, the Company register described more than 320 of the fathers of apprentices as yeoman, and there were 42 *gents*. Where trades were entered the sea and river dominated: 44 mariners, including masters, head the list, followed by 23 shipwrights and then 14 keelmen followed by 10 waterman. Many fathers were deceased, but remarkably only the names of two widows were entered. Almost all trades were represented - 8 weavers, 7 glassmakers, 4 butchers and 4 bakers but no candlestick maker. Another 49 occupations were recorded including surgeon, pitman and two Customs Officers. There was a single charity boy.

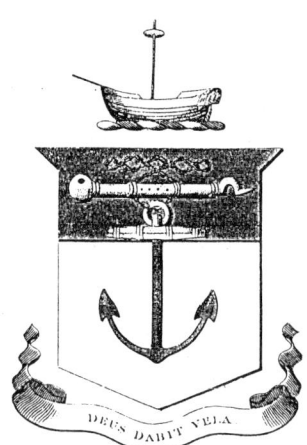

Emblem of Master Mariners

Joseph Campion's[26] last apprentice was John, son of Newcastle Keelman Stephen Goddard, enrolled in 1734. This name seems to have been variously rendered as Goddart or Gothart. In 1730 Robert Gothard, also a son of a keelman named Stephen, was apprenticed to William Henderson and in 1739 Stephen Gothart son of Stephen, Yeoman of Newcastle, was apprenticed to Robert Gothart [his first apprentice]. Four years later, in 1743, Thomas Goddart was apprenticed to John Goddart. The last apprentice by a Gothard [Robert] was in 1806, which if the family shipyard had worked continuously over those years would suggested a period of operation exceeding seventy years from 1739; very few of these early yards lasted so long. John took apprentices over the years 1763-5 and the last of these would have completed seven years year in 1772 but the next apprentice is to a Robert in 1788; there was no Gothard among the shipwrights in local Directory of 1778. So perhaps the yard was not operating between the early 1770s and 1788. It is likely the yard was worked continuously from 1788. In 1804 the yard employed 20 on the North Shore, of whom 16 were apprentices! Only six of these were indentured with the Company, which means presumably ten were normal trade apprentices. This shows the unknown factor in relation to the above discussion of apprentices. There is no means of knowing what other youths, outside those formally registered with the Company, were employed in the yards; such lads after about 1765 may have been quite numerous. During the 1790s Gothard built at least 2,436t, commencing with a vessel of 162t in 1790; no ships have been found for two of these years so the output may well have been higher. Assuming a shipyard was operating when the first apprentice was enrolled and continued until the last had completed his time, an estimated duration of working is presented in Diag 2.03 for those who enrolled three or more apprentices with the Shipwrights' Company. Despite the undoubted decline of the Company in the second half of the 18th century, membership was clearly valued, as was shown by the actions of James Storey. Early in July 1750, James Storey, son of a yeoman of North Shields, became an apprentice to John

---

[26] Thomas Campion took his first apprentice in 1691. A Mr Campion was one of the four shipwrights in March 1714, who helped manage the building of a meeting house. Joseph took his first apprentice John Fawdon in 1719.

Bruce [Brewhouse].[27] His master never registered his apprenticeship and was later in substantial financial debt to the Company. Many years after Bruce's death, James Storey sought in 1765 to have his apprenticeship entered so that he might become a freeman of the Company. Affidavits from shipwright Richard Shaw [North Shields] and yeoman William Farrow confirmed the apprenticeship and Storey was admitted. He paid his former master's fines and his own admission fee [52s 6d] in all £37-9s 6d, a very substantial sum in 1774. Storey enrolled his first apprentice in 1778. By 1788, when he enrolled his last apprentice, he was a substantial ship owner, with interests in eight ships [2,300t].

Shipwrights Company masters with 3 apprentices or more enrolled from entry of the first to the completion of 7 years by the last apprentice

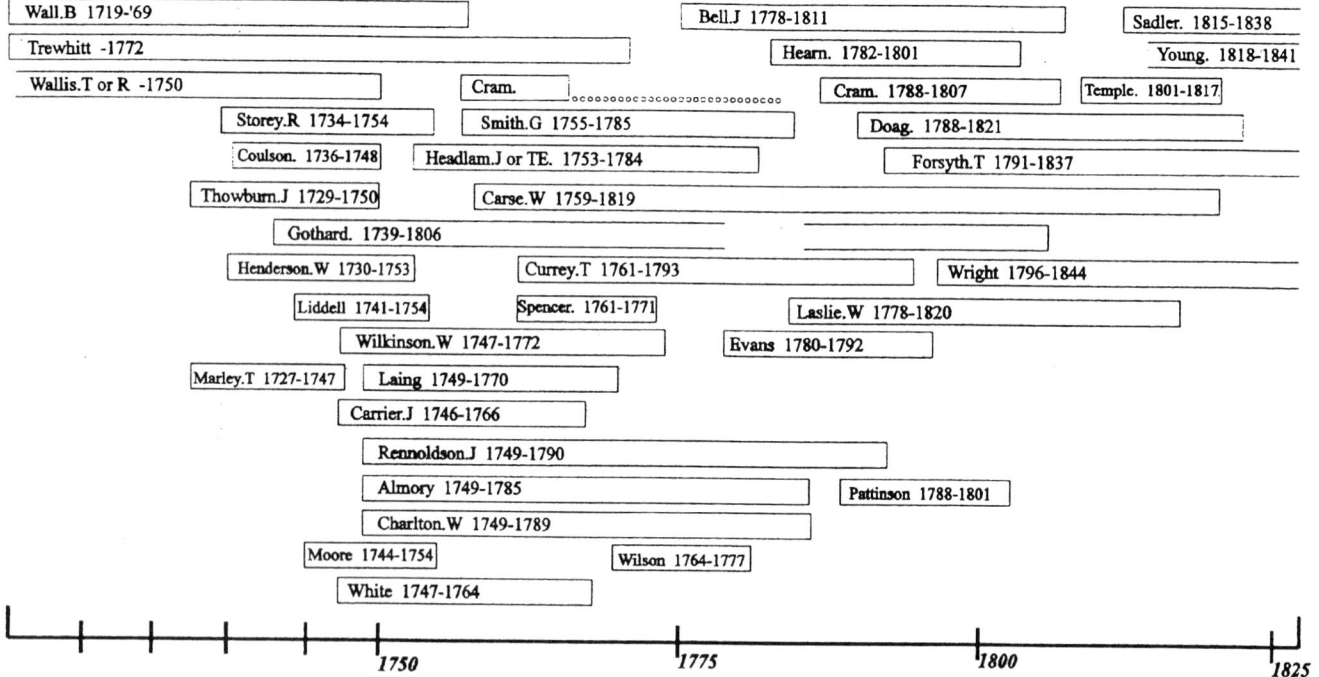

Other Individual Ports.

Gateshead.

Shipwright Thomas Reed offered keels for sale in 1705 and leased land with two smith's shops and a wet dock near Rock Staith on the South Shore. In 1655 a Thomas Reed was apprenticed as a shipwright and 14 years later Reed took his first apprentice and enrolled apprentices until 1717: Thomas Reed junior enrolled two apprentices in 1704 and two more a year later. Thomas jnr was a Steward to the Company in 1713-5, one of the *Twelve* in 1716, and one of two shipwright nominees to elect the Mayor of Newcastle in 1715. In the mid 18th century, Enoch White and George Boult were probably building keels, since they were offering them for sale. Although White was a member of the Shipwrights' Company, Boult does not appear to have been. White was one of those who sought permission in December 1757 to hire craftsmen outside the Company. The first record of the Whites was when James son of Enoch White, weaver of Bishop Auckland was enrolled as apprentice to Edward Blunt and duly became a Freeman in 1718. Enoch White took his first apprentice in 1747, others followed in 1752 and 1757. With his father one of the *Twelve* in

---

[27] see Rowe p.11, pp.63-4, 163-5, 168, 266-269; he gave the master's name as Brewhouse, a John Brewhouse was apprenticed to Roger Durham in 1727 and became a freeman in 1734, the apprentice taken in 1741 was to John Bruce [Brewhouse on p.257]. In 1774 the name is clearly Bruce.

1745, James jnr also became an officer of the Company and a James White took apprentices in 1753 and 1760. Such modest endeavours began more than 200 years of building vessels at Gateshead, albeit usually small. The Headlam family was the main shipbuilder at Gateshead during the second half of the 18th century and they continued building after 1800. The *Russell*, a fine vessel carrying upwards of 30 keels of coal, was launched in 1751 from South Shore yard, and a year later the *Experiment* for the West Indian trade. In 1767 a fine brig *Margaret & Winifred* was launched from Henry Forster's quay [off Hillgate] and in 1773 the *Mary* [329t] was launched by John Summer on South Shore, a large merchant vessel at that time. Later Summers apparently only built keels. Two block & mast makers in Hillgate supported shipbuilding and shipping.

South Shields.[28]

Shipyards nearer the mouth of the Tyne offered substantial advantages for repair work; a ship in distress would reach them more readily. Very often contemporary reports refer to *Shields,* without distinguishing between South and North Shields; the italicised word is used in these cases. This means returns for *Shields* may have included output from North Shields. Shipbuilding was carried out in the 1750s at North Shields, possibly earlier. The 335t *Northumberland* was launched there in 1758. Despite the hostility of the Shipwrights' Company it seems very probable that John and Anthony Wilkinson and George Selby were working at South Shields in 1674 and Anthony Nicholson and George Watt at North Shields. Mary Wilkinson was running a yard at Shields from 1720. This challenges the traditional view that Robert Wallis's arrival at South Shields in 1720 was the beginning of shipbuilding there. Members of the Wallis / Wallas family had early connections with the Company. In July 1648, a Thomas Wallis [son of George] became a Shipwrights' Company apprentice to T Colyer 1661. Robert Wallas, son of Thomas, was admitted a freeman by patrimony paid on 27 December 1726.[29] It is likely that Wallis purchased the land for his yard in 1729, which was when he registered his first two apprentices. The land was part of the estate of the deceased Martin Potter: *A Row or Onset of Houses at the East End of South Shields, with a yard and parcel of Waste Ground adjoining, and a Key or Wharf and the Coble Landing.* In 1738 the Shipwrights' Company resolved that: *to build any new vessel at Shields is against the interest of the Corporation.* Although 51 supported this decision, ten voted against the motion and eight shipwrights abstained, which suggests that a number of craftsmen probably saw a future there. Robert Wallis was called upon to stop building the ship which he had started, and when he refused, his licence was withdrawn. Wallis almost certainly completed this ship. He employed seven men over the years 1753-8. Legal opinion was taken by the Company as to how they could prosecute *persons not free* for working on the south side of the Tyne and stop them. The Company's control was slipping away despite many efforts to carry out the policy. Five shillings was paid on 16 January 1750 for horsehire and other expenses in going to Shields to serve writs and two weeks later another 2s and on 10 February a further 5s 6d. At this time 35s was paid to John Trewhitt and eight others for going to Shields *about foreigners working there* and for Thos. Robinson's *trouble* two days on the same matter.

Sailing ship captains very often held a financial interest in their vessels and at times were outright owners. Sometimes they extended their enterprise into shipbuilding. One such was Thomas Winship, who became the owner of the Low Dock at South Shields, after marrying *an agreeable widow*. By the end of 1766 he had 12 apprentices and so probably his yard exceeded twenty workers; he offered his *John & Thomas* for

---

[28] A most valuable collection of material is presented in *Notes on the History of Shipbuilding in South Shields 1746-1946* by Amy C Flagg published posthumously in 1979. Further references as Flagg.

[29] Shipwrights' apprentice register includes two other sons of a George Wallis - William enrolled in 1652 and George in 1655. Other Wallis names were in 1646 - Richard [no father's name], in 1661 - John [son of John] and in 1669 John [father George]. The following were admitted by patrimony: Henry [1698], Thomas [1699] James [1701]. Richard Wallas took 14 apprentices [1657-1713]; Thomas Wallas took 10 [1700-18]; Robert Wallas took 5 [1729-43]; Thomas Wallis - 2 [1727-31] and Thomas Wallis jnr 1 in 1731. A Robert Wallas son of Thomas was admitted a freeman by patrimony on 29 Sept 1716.

sale in 1764 and two years later a new ship [to carry 12 *keels* of coal]. Following Thomas's death in June 1768, his widow declared her intention *to repair such vessels as may be offered* until the Dock was sold. It is likely that the Brodericks took over the Dock [see chap 3]. George, son of South Shields Master Mariner Henry Smith, was apprenticed to Philip Moore in 1744. Smith enrolled an apprentice in 1755 and another in 1759, both from South Shields; 11 more were enrolled before 1780. He was a kind master. In 1777 because *of the hardship and ill treatment he suffered* from Smith, the Company ordered the transfer of a fourth year apprentice George Wray. Ships were sold by Smith from South Shields in 1760 and he was certainly practising his trade there in 1766. When a vessel was *suddenly upset* in Shields Harbour, in February 1769, Smith dealt with the problem. He may have played a part in building the Middle Dock; from 1768 there were references to Smith's Dock [a valuation of £36 in 1770].[30] George Smith's last apprentice, in 1778, was Simon Temple, who became a very ambitious entrepreneur and important shipbuilder. Temple completed his seven year period in 1785, and presumably Smith continued working as a shipwright until then. Fines were levied against Smith by the Shipwrights' Company from before 1753; he was regularly absent from meetings and appeared to work on every holy day. Smith was working with 8 men on St Marks Day 1753 and with 6 men on New Years Day 1756, although usually it was only with 3 or 4 men.

In 1762 the 242t *Isabella & Dorothy* was built at South Shields and no doubt there were others of which no record survives. Certainly by the 1770s, there was a well established ship building and repair capacity at South Shields. There were 35 Shields vessels in Lloyd's Register of 1776 and these were well above the average tonnage on that Register. The total of 9,825t, although only half that of Newcastle, was well above most British ports. Twelve *London colliers* built at *Shields* totalled 4,060t, slightly more than the 17 built at Sunderland. Six vessels exceeded 400t; both the *Expedition* [built 1760] and the *Westmoreland* [1765] were of 450t and the *Robert & Hannah* [1761] 460t. Not surprisingly therefore, 16 *Shields* vessels in the *ship* category [a *ship* had three or more masts, all square rigged] averaged 375t, which was greater than the average of the River Thames vessels! The first Newcastle Custom House Register [1786] included 1541t built at South Shields in 1778, with 278t at North Shields, 260t at Howdon and 469t at Newcastle.

Seaton Sluice.

Sir Ralph Delaval, a pioneer of the coal industry, developed the harbour works at Seaton Sluice for this trade and his other industrial interests. Increased trade from Hartley required better harbour facilities by the middle of the 18th century and Thomas Delaval [died in 1787, aged 56][31] organised this work. Two days after the harbour was finished on 20 March 1764, the *Warkworth* [13 keels] was the first vessel to sail from the new harbour. A summary of the ships which were used in shipping Hartley coal is given in diag 2.04. This shows that the vessels used were significantly larger than those from Blyth.

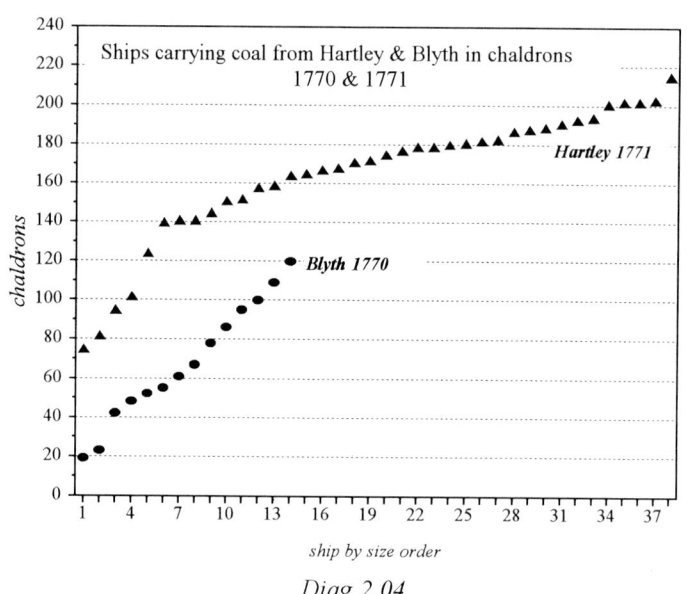

Diag 2.04

At a time when Blyth could only boast of one vessel belonging to the port, shipbuilding

---

[30] In July 1774 John Hall [probably the manager] showed potential buyers the *large & commodious Double Dock, a spacious Building Yard, Smith's Shop, Warehouses and all necessary Conveniences & Appurtenances*.

[31] Thomas 3rd son of Francis Blake Delaval [1692-1752] and brother of Sir John Hussey Delaval [1728-1808], owner of the Seaton Delaval estate. Thomas worked as a merchant in Hamburg. see W Percy Hedley *Northumberland Families* [vol.1 1968 pp 145-160 for an overview of the family]

was flourishing at Seaton Sluice. Robinson, the town's historian added that the volume of trade meant that ship carpenters were in *great demand for repairs*. In February 1767 Anthony Topsham, shipbuilder of Seaton Sluice, sold the Hull of the Ship *George and Thomas* to Mr William Dobson for £263 2s 6d. In 1777 the *Cumberland* [254t] was built. New building and certainly repair work continued; in September 1792, John Brown wrote, *I hope by this time the new ship will be launched, and the keel of another laid in down in lieu thereof. Mr Wright has quick sale for them.*

Whitby.

Except perhaps for those remembering the early circumnavigator James Cook, few recall just how significant Whitby was in British maritime affairs before 1800. The local historian Charlton wrote in 1779 that only fishing boats belonged to this port during the reign of Elizabeth, until after the erection of the alum-works at Gisbrough. As late as 1690, any Whitby ship wanting to *cross the sea for a foreign port*, required *a pilot, or master from London, Yarmouth, Hull, Newcastle, or some other noted sea-port town*. The creation of a harbour laid the essential basis for the development of Whitby. The alum trade for well over a century provided a regular need for vessels, particularly to carry coal. After gaining experience in supplying the alum-works with coal, as Charlton explained, their owners not wanting their ships to lie idle began to trade with other ports. They carried coal and other products and *thus by little and little was the navigation introduced and established at Whitby*. Shipwrights came to the town and so its own inhabitants could build new ships, with the *very plentiful and very cheap* oak timber in the neighbourhood. In Cromwell's times there were many ship-carpenters living in Whitby, a town of nearly 2,000, as well as those employed at sea; in addition to fishing boats they built sloops and brigantines for the coasting trade. By the time of the Restoration, the port had about 30 ships and this number doubled before the end of the century. Parliament decided to levy a farthing [$^1/_4$d] per chaldron of coal for repairing and rebuilding the piers of Whitby in 1702, an indication of the growing importance of this port. A petition to the Commons in 1745 stated that the farthing duty encouraged the building of larger ships. Three dry docks were made on the east side of the river Esk in 1734 capable of taking the port's largest ships. These docks encouraged ship owners to come for repairs both because the work was done *very compleatly*, and at a lower cost than elsewhere in Britain. Thomas Fishburne constructed a dock on the west side in 1757 and a second was added a few years later; these docks were seldom idle. The whale fisheries of Greenland opened a new opportunity for Whitby and two ships fitted out in 1753 were followed by many more. Nearly two hundred ships belonged to the port by 1755.[32]

James Cook's first voyage [1768-71], in the *Endeavour*, made this Whitby collier the port's most well known vessel, described by the Navy as a barque of 366t. A few years earlier one anonymous *Collier*[33] wrote of Whitby *filching* shipbuilding from the Tyne, in a pamphlet attacking the many Charters of Newcastle. Individual port output of *London colliers* in Lloyds' Register of 1776 was headed by Whitby - 14 vessels, a total of 4,300t. The oldest was the *William & Jane* of 300t built in 1718. The well established character of shipbuilding at Whitby was clearly demonstrated by the vessels on the 1776 Register. The Coates family, who built from about 1717 to 1756, are usually credited with being Whitby's first shipbuilders. After the elder Coates brother went bankrupt and his younger brother died, Thomas Fishburn took over the yard about 1745. He bought the yard in 1759 and shipbuilding on that site ended in 1830 [see Whitby in next chapter].

Scarborough.

A Patent Roll of 1252 noted the making of *a certain New Port with timber and stone towards the sea, whereby all ships... may enter, and sail without danger* at the town of Scarborough and authority was given

---

[32] Other trades related to shipping developed, such as sailmakers. By 1797 there were 4 canvas factories at Whitby employing 700 or 800 spinners and many weavers. Much of this work was for use by the Royal Navy and Charlton claimed it was made *to such perfection, and at so low a rate* that there was always a considerable market.

[33] Cited by Summers in his *History of Sunderland* vol I p420 from Colliers *Essay on Charters* [p 94].

to collect the following dues for five years: on every merchant ship arriving with merchandise 6d, every fisherman's ship with fish 4d, and every fisherman's boat 2d. In 1294 the king required the port of Scarborough to build a ship. Over subsequent years various actions were taken to maintain the port as a safe haven, for example a New Pier Act, in the reign of George II, which described this port as the only place between the Tyne and Humber able to offer refuge in bad weather. In 1805 more than twice as many Sunderland vessels put in for shelter as all other Coal Ports put together. The port had 20 or 22 ships of *large size* and many small *barques*[34] of between 20t and 60t burthen in 1638. Throughout the 18th century Scarborough was a port of no mean distinction; in 1730 the largest ship was 240t and the ships belonging to the town were estimated at almost 12,000t. By 1796 the port's 156 ships aggregated more than 25,000t.

Following the early 17th century builders Robert Hudson and Christopher Harrison, the Tindall family established a long running shipbuilding enterprise in Scarborough. From the first household assessments of 1679 up to 1720 they paid King's Rent for one building place, and for a second site before 1691. William Tindall was prominent in the town's government and his three daughters married shipbuilders Cockerill, More and Sollit. Shipyards extended some distance westward from the Old Piers. Like other shipbuilders Tindall owned vessels such as the *Free Briton*, which sailed between London and St Petersburg in 1762 and 1763. John Tindall in 1771 made the shipyard over to his 16 year old son. By the early part of the 19th century further purchases resulted in a compact shipyard. The Tindall's shipowning business helped their yard to survive for 150 years. Eight Scarborough built London colliers were listed in 1776. A Shipwrights' Friendly Society was instituted in 1775 and had 55 members in 1798, when two works made cordage and a third sailcloth. Shipbuilding, wrote Hinderwell in 1798, *forms an important object of employment ... is a great source of emolument; but it is precarious, and subject to sudden fluctuations*. Not much more than a generation remained for the port as a place for shipbuilding.

Stockton on Tees.
A letter from 1676 recounts the launch of *a pince betwixt 2: & 300 Tonnes Burthen*, the largest vessel to that date at Stockton, and another about the same size was ready. Headlams were working on the river Tees as shipwrights in the 1720s. In May 1726 John Headlam jnr, shipwright, took an apprentice and in about 1750 Michael Humphrey took over the Headlam yard. The *Elizabeth*, a Stockton built collier brig of 200t was still on Lloyds Register thirty years after her launch. With more than 11,000t on that Register of 1776, a significant amount of shipbuilding was carried out at Stockton. These vessels averaged 184t, twenty tons above the overall average, and although in the *ships* category they were not as large as those of other north east ports at an average of 314t. The 44 brigs [2 masts square rigged] averaged 146t.

The River Wear.
Although a ship was built on the Wear in 1346 little detailed information on shipbuilding before 1700 survives. At least one 17th century shipwright family can be identified; on 1st December 1666, Joseph, son of Sunderland shipwright John Letany, was enrolled as apprentice to John Lattany of the Newcastle Shipwrights' Company. He failed to complete his apprenticeship. Almost three years later Thomas Lattany, a son of a shipwright, was also apprenticed to the said John. Unfortunately he died before completing his time. Not until 1692 was another Sunderland boy, William Young, apprenticed with the Shipwrights Company. William Lidster of Coxgreen was apprenticed in 1707 to Paul Halliday, who also enrolled Sunderland lads in 1710 and in 1716. Meanwhile John, son of the Sunderland shipwright James Reed, was apprenticed to Thomas Reed jnr. Matthew Russell of a Cumberland family settled in Sunderland in 1717 and became a timber merchant and shipbuilder who *amassed a considerable fortune*.

Inadequate harbour facilities limited the size of vessels that could use the Wear in the 17th century, particularly in the winter months. The *ill Condition* of the Harbour, *J.C.* wrote in 1708, enabled Newcastle

---

[34] If the term was used accurately a bargue [*bark*] with the 3 masts like a *ship* but had a fore-and-aft rig on the aftermost or mizen mast.

to get the majority of the coal trade, because when storms raged there was *no safety offering* at Sunderland. There was no pier and *the Bar is so choked up, that there is great want of Water*. Ten chaldrons was the average coal cargo of in 1594 from Sunderland. This average increased to 18 chaldrons in 1634 and 23 in 1685, when the largest was 50 chaldrons. Wearsiders wanted improvements and an Act of Parliament in 1717 established the River Wear Commissioners. This Act described the town as *well Inhabited with rich and able Merchants and Tradesmen*, and that it would be of *great importance* for the publick benefit to have *a Port and Haven, capable of containing many Hundred Sail of Ships at a Time, and from whence may be loaded and sent great Numbers of Ships, with Coals, Salt, Glass, and other Merchandizes, to divers Places within this Realm, and also to Foreign parts*. The result would be *a constant Nursery and Supply of able Seamen, to Serve on Board the Royal Navy*, and also *great Numbers of poor People may be constantly Imployed*.

Apart from the handful of apprenticeships, a further indication of building or repair work was the vote by the Shipwrights' Company, in 1719, to allow their gaoled member William Fletcher *to send his servants to Sunderland or any where else to work* until his release. Boatwright Adam Nicholson worked in Sunderland in 1667 and his grandson Thomas, born in 1722, became a shipbuilder. A Nicholson built a 119t vessel on the Panns in 1768. Three Wear vessels on the 1776 Register, have no date of building and were probably constructed before the *Sarah & Jane* one of two built in 1743. The *James* 250t collier was entered as *old*. Amongst the largest vessels in this early period were: *Duke William* [500t] in 1748; *Providence* [420t] in 1762 and *George Elliott* [480t] in 1765. Like more than a few vessels at this time, the *Happy Jannet* was lengthened in 1772 and so had been originally smaller. The distribution of the size of the vessels [see diag.2.05] indicates a shipbuilding capacity comparable as regards size of vessel to any commercial port except London. At least five vessels were built in 1750 and their combined tonnage exceeded 900t. In 1754 almost 1,300t was certainly built on the Wear. During the 1760s output probably averaged about 1,500t or more a year judging by the tonnage of identified vessels. Cuthbert Vaux may serve as an early example of a local shipowner and business man who funded a shipwright team to build for him; he is entered as a builder in 1763 and for later work see the next chapter. From 1763 a few individual shipbuilders can be identified and a reasonably reliable list established from

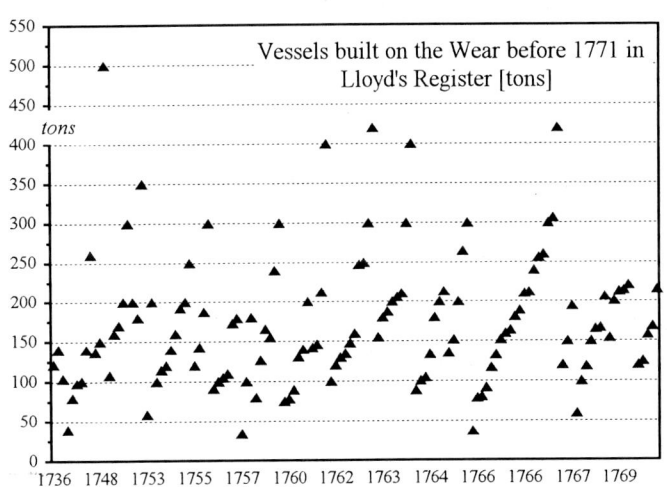

Diag 2.05

1783. Members of the Burn family were building for some 60 years from about 1760: a ship of 153t was built in 1763. Thomas Burn [1780-1862] was described by Brockie as *one of the prime masters of his craft and a man of great intelligence, and by no means contemptible scientific attainments*. His father died not long after Thomas's birth and his mother carried on the business. At the age of 17 years Thomas took over at Hylton, the yard moving later to the Old Jackdaw Dock at Bishopwearmouth. Burn's vessels had long lives, many exceeding 40 or 50 years and it was claimed that they were *as sound in the timbers* as at the time when they were built. Such success was due to always using *thoroughly good and well seasoned materials*. The banks of the Wear right back to Coxgreen, more than six miles from the mouth of the river, were almost literally studded with wood yards in the decades that followed. A firm base was laid for that advance by the late 1770s. Timber merchants and coal fitters often supplied financial support in a town where later people from almost all walks of life became, a least in a small part shipowners.

Some summary comments.

No accurate measure of output in this period is possible. More than 150 vessels can be identified as built on the Wear before 1776, and 85 at Newcastle and 94 at Whitby. These figures do not represent either total or relative output. The position in 1776 is reviewed in chapter 4. The average tonnage of the Wear vessels was 164t, the smallest was 32t and the largest 500t; both the Tyne and Whitby had higher averages 212t and 225t respectively. The 1786 Custom's Register includes a vessel of 340t from 1738 and one of 326t from 1749. Vessels built on the Tyne in 1762 totalled 1,883t in the first register, since those vessels would then have been almost twenty five years old in 1786, output may have exceeded 3,600t in 1762. The economic fluctuations so characteristic of shipbuilding were clearly present before 1776 and with it the need to provide assistance to workers and builders suffering distress. Shipbuilding at Newcastle increased during the 17th century with a total workforce reaching perhaps as many as 700 strong, including the blacksmiths and labourers, but there followed a decline and yards moved further down the river. At Sunderland the basis of its future expansion was already underway as the port improved and coal exports from the port sharply increased by about one-third between 1750 and 1765. This brief survey shows the extent of north east achievement in shipbuilding before the important impact of the American Revolution. Experienced shipwrights lived in all of the region's ports and the growth of coal production and trade generally provided the necessary base market for shipbuilders.

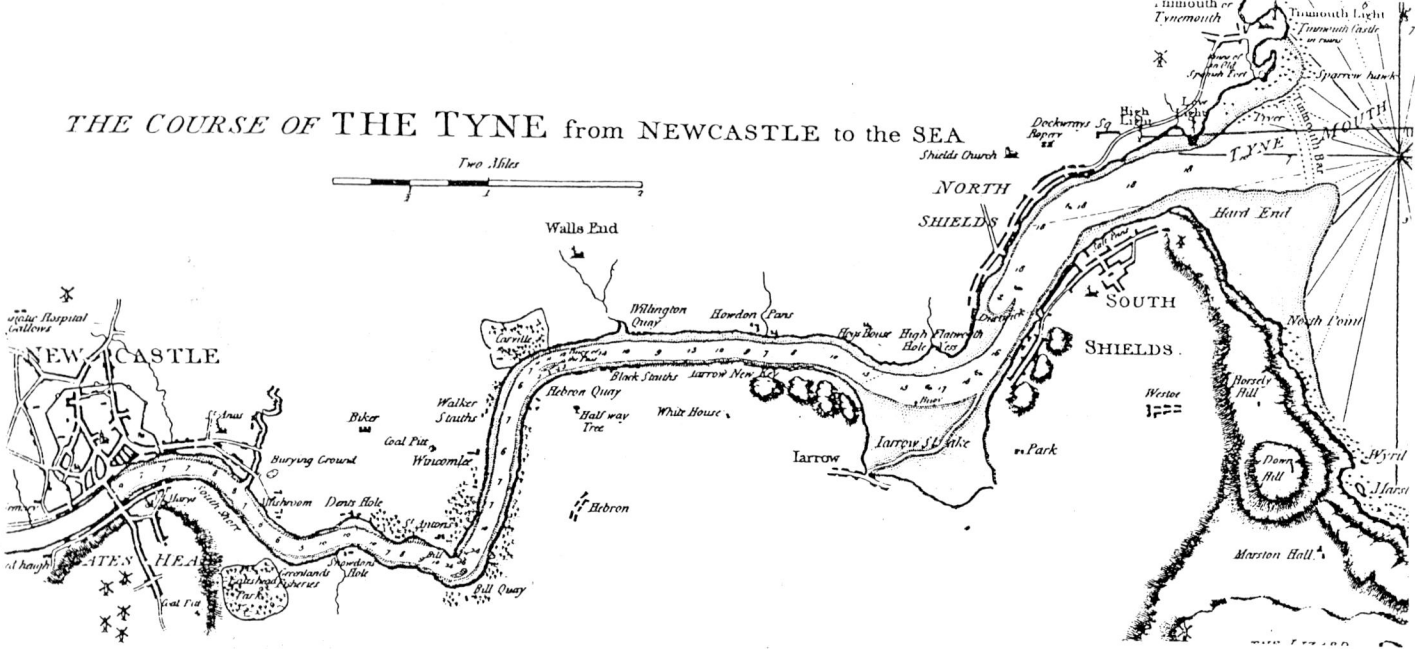

NOAH'S ARK or
THE SHIPWRIGHTS' ANCIENT PLAY

Deus incipitur.
Ere was this world that I have wrought
No marvel it is if I do show;
Their folk in earth I made of nought,
Now are they fully my foe.
Vengeance now will I do
Of them that have grieved me ill,
Great floods shall over them go,
And run over hoope and hill.
All mankind dead shall be,
Woth storms both stiff and steer;
All but Noah my darling free,
His children and their wives,
Ever more yet they trow'd in me,
Save therefore I will their lives.
Henceforth my angel free,
Into earth look what thou would
Greet well Noah in this degree,
Sleeping thou shalt him find:
Bid him go make a ship
Of stiff board and great,
Although he be not a wright
Therefore bid him not lett,
He shall have wit at will,
Be that he come thereto;
All things I him fulfill,
Pitch, tar, seam and rowe.
Bid him in any manner of thing,
To ship when he shall walk,
Of all kine kind of beast and fowl'
The male and female with him take,
Bid him go provey, say so,
In ship that they not die,
Take with him hay, corn and straw,
For his fowl and his fee.
Henceforth my angel free
Tell him this for certain:
My blessing with thee be,
While that thou come again.
Angelus dicat.
Waken Noah, to me take tent.
Noah bid, if thou hear this thing
Ever whilst thou live thou shall repent.
Noah respondit.
What art thou for Heaven's King
That wakens Noah off his sleeping
Away I would thou went.
Angelus dicat.
It is an angel to thee sent
Noah, to tell thee hard tidings;
For every ilk a wight for warks wild,
And many fowled in sins fair
And in felony fowly filled;
Therefore a ship thou dight to steer,
Of true timber highly railed,
With thirty cubits in defence,
Look that she draw when she is drest,
And in her side a door thou sheear,
With fenesters full fitly felt,
And make chambers both more and less,
For a flood that up shall burst;
Such a flood in earth shall be,
That every like life that hath lifeward,
Beast and body with bone and blood,
They shall be stormed through stress of storm;
Albeit thou Noah and thy brood,
And their three wives in your hand,
For you are full righteous and good,
You shall be saved by sea and land.
In the ship ere you enter out,
You take with you both ox and cow;
Of ilk a thing that life has lent,
The male and female you take with you,
You fetch in fother for your freight,
And make good purveiance for you prove,
That they perish not in your sight
Do Noah as I have bidden thee now.
Noah respondit.
Lord be then in this stead,
That me and mine will save and shield;
I am a man no worth at need,
For I am six hundred winters old,
Unlusty I am to such a deed,
Worklooms for to work and weild
For I was never since I was born,
Of kind of craft to burthen a boat;
For I neither ryss nor russ,
Spyer, sprund, spront, no sprot.
Christ be the shaper of this ship,
For a ship need make I must.
Even wo worth thou fouled sin,
For all too dear thou must be bought,
Good for thanks he made mankind,
Or with his hands that he then wrought;
Therefore or ever you blind,
You mind your wife and turn your thought,
For my work I will begin,
So well were me were all forth brought.
Deabolus intrat.
Put off Harro, and well away,
Thatever I uprose this day;
So may I smile and say,
I went, there has been none alive,
Man, beast, child nor wife,
But my servants were they;
All this I have heard say,
A ship that made should be,
For to save withowten nay,
Noah and his meenye;
Yet trow I mey shall lie,
Thereto I make a vow,

[24]

if they be never so slee,
To taynt them yet I trow
To Noah's wife will I wynd,
Gare her believe in me;
In faith she is my friend,
She is both whunt and slee,
Rest well, rest well, my own Dereday.
Uxor Noah dicat.
Welcome, Fewsthere, what is thy name,
Tyte that thou tell me.
Deabolus dicat.
To tell my name I were full loath,
I come to warn thee of thy skaith,
I tell thee secretly,
And thou do after thy husband read,
Thou and thy child will all be dead,
And that right hastily.
Uxor dicat.
Go devil, how say, for shame,
Deabolus dicat.
Yes, hold thee still le dame,
And I shall tell how;
I swear thee by my crooked snout,
All that thy husband goes about
Is little for profit;
Yet shall I tell thee how,
Thou shalt weet all his will;
Do as I shall bid thee now,
Thou shalt weet every deal.
Have here a drink full good,
That is made of a mightful main,
Be he hath drunken a drink of this,
No longer shall he learn :
Believe, believe, my own dear dame,
I may no longer bide,
To ship when thou shall fayre
I shall by by thy side.
Noah dicat.
This labour is full great
For like an old man as me,
Lo, lo, fast I sweat,
It trickles at our myn ee
Now home will I wende,
my weary bones for to rest,
For such good as God hath sent,
There I get of the best:
Rest well day, what chear with thee.
Uxor dicat.
Welcome Noah, as might I thee
Welcome to thine own wayns.
Sit down here beside me,
Thou hast full weary baynes:
Have eaten, Noah, as might I thee,
And soon a drink I shall give thee,
Such drink thou never none afore.

Noah dicat.
What the devil what drink is it
By my father's soul I have nere lost my wit.
Uxor dicat.
Noah, bode you tell me where about you wends
I give God a vow, we two shall nere be freinds.
Noah dicat.
O yes dame could thou layne
I would thee tell my wit.
How God of heaven an angel sent,
And bad me make a ship,
This world he will foredoe
With storms both stiff and steer fell,
All but thee and me, our children and wifes.
Uxor dicat.
Who devil made thee a wright,
God give him evil to fayre
Of hand to have such slight
To make ship less or more perfect,
Men should have heard wide where
When you began to smite.
Noah dicat.
Yes dame it is God's will,
Let be so thou not say,
Go make an end I will,
And come again full throng.
Uxor dicat.
By my faith I no rake
Whether thou be friend or foe,
The devil of hell thee speed,
To ship when thou shalt go.
Noah dicat.
God send me help in high,
To clink yon nail too'
God send me help in high,
Your hand to hold again,
That all may well be done,
My strokes be not in vain.
Angelus dicat.
God hath thee help hither send,
Thereof be thou right bold,
Thy strokes shall fair be kend,
For thou thy wife has cowld.
Noah dicat.
Now is this ship well made
Within and without thinks me,
Now home then will I wend
To fetch in my money,
Have good day both old and young ,
My blessing with you be.
Deabolus dicat.
All that is gathered in this stead,
That will not believe in me,
I pray to Dolphin prince of dead,
Scald you all in his lead
That never a one of you thrive nor thee.
Finis. Amen. [Brand v.II pp 373-9]

Chapter 3

The Changes in Shipbuilding Output - 1780-1815.

English shipwrights certainly had cause to rejoice when American independence put an end to competition from colonial builders. Joseph A Goldenberg[1]

This chapter will briefly review the position before all British ships were required by law in 1786 to register at a Customs port, the overall changes between 1786 and 1815, and then developments in various north east ports. War was a dominant factor in this period, with the American colonists to 1782 and the French and Napoleonic Wars 1793-1815 [with a short break]. Large numbers of ships were supplied to British owners from the north American colonies before their rebellion in 1776 began the creation of the United States of America. Just under half the vessels on the 1776 Lloyds Register[2] were British built. Almost one third of the vessels came from the British North American colonies and accounted for about 40% of tonnage in the British fleet. Foreign built vessels made up 18.5% of the Register's tonnage. British built vessels averaged just over 162t. In all the 3,464 British built vessels amounted to 561,563t and the American built added up to 361,435t [2,246 vessels]. Ten years later, more than 11% of the tonnage registered at Newcastle was built in north America [4,864t]. Perhaps not surprisingly only three of these ships were built after 1776. At Sunderland 4,110t of American vessels were registered. The north east was, of course, substantially below the proportion of American built ships in Britain as a whole.

Just over one third of the British tonnage on the 1776 Lloyds Register came from the *South-East*, with 19.3% built on the Thames and 9.8% in East Anglia. Goldenberg included Hull in his *North-east* so that his region accounted for just over 40%. The proportion falls to 28% when Hull is excluded. The leading position of Whitby [77,355t] is clearly shown in diag 3.01, the tonnage of the principal ports. This now attractive seaside resort was, in mid-18th century, only exceeded by the Thames as a provider of ships and is significantly greater than such ports as Hull [39,630t], Liverpool [36,465t] and Bristol [21,595t]. The River Tyne's 27,961t was about one-third of the tonnage of the London builders. Whitby was nearing the peak of its leading role and consistent with its leading position, almost 73% of Whitby's tonnage was in the category of *ship*. More than 90% of the London tonnage were *ships*, largely because of its long distance trade. Always regarded as vessels of good quality, these Whitby *ships* averaged 365t, only a mere two tons below the prestigious Thames's average. However, the Shields' average was higher still at 376t! Three of every five vessels built at Liverpool, Shields and Scarborough were in the class of *ship*. Only about two of every five vessels at Hull and Newcastle were *ships*; as a result the ratio for the Tyne as a whole was 46.5%.

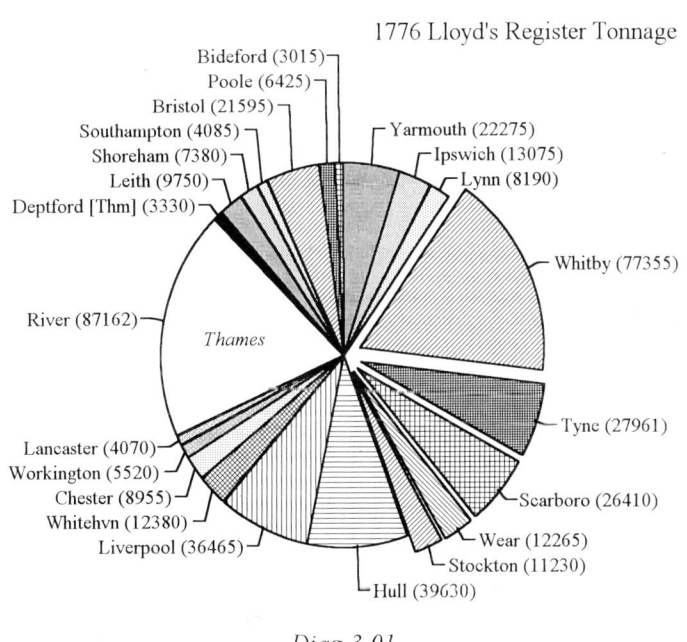

Diag 3.01

---

[1] see Goldenberg's *An Analysis of Shipbuilding Sites in Lloyd's Register of 1776* in *MarMir* v 59 [1973].

[2] This Register does not contain all vessels. A *ship* had at least three masts and square rigged on all masts - see also chap.4 for the use of terms such for other *rigs*.

Overall change 1786-1815.

Official figures show that over the years 1786-1813 north east yards provided just over 30% of the merchant tonnage launched in England and Wales, a total of 563,000t. The region moved quickly from about 20% in 1786-7 to 30% in 1790, and averaged more than 40% over the years 1793-5. Newcastle launched during 1786-1813 more than 200,000t, [Newcastle = all Tyne and included Blyth &c]. Not far behind was the river Wear with almost 9%, followed by Whitby at 7% and Scarborough was still able to deliver almost 2.5% of the total of England & Wales. Sunderland advanced most significantly at the outset. It built only about 3% [1786-7] but reached 12.5% in its highest year 1795; the Wear's aggregate output was about equal to that of Hull and more than double that of Liverpool.

A comprehensive survey of merchant shipyards was organised by the Admiralty in 1804, which showed that the north east accounted for about a quarter of the workforce in Britain.[see diag 3.02-the regional distribution] Shipwrights employed in the Tyne yards amounted to one in seven of all those in British merchant yards[3], exceeded only by the Thames. Just over 7% of the nation's shipwrights worked on the Wear. In England & Wales 63 ports built vessels in 1805 and 53 of these had built a vessel exceeding 100t, a figure just below 110t average of the UK register. Twenty-five ports in Scotland were building. More than 500 yards were listed in the 1804 survey. A revealing feature of the Survey was the proportion of apprentices. Almost 20% of the nation's journeymen worked in London, but only 6% of the apprentices, a craftsman to youth ratio of more than four to one, whereas on the Wear apprentices predominated. They were 59% of the shipwright workforce; with only just over 5% of the nation's men they had more than 10% of the lads. Almost half the workers on Tyneside were apprentices.

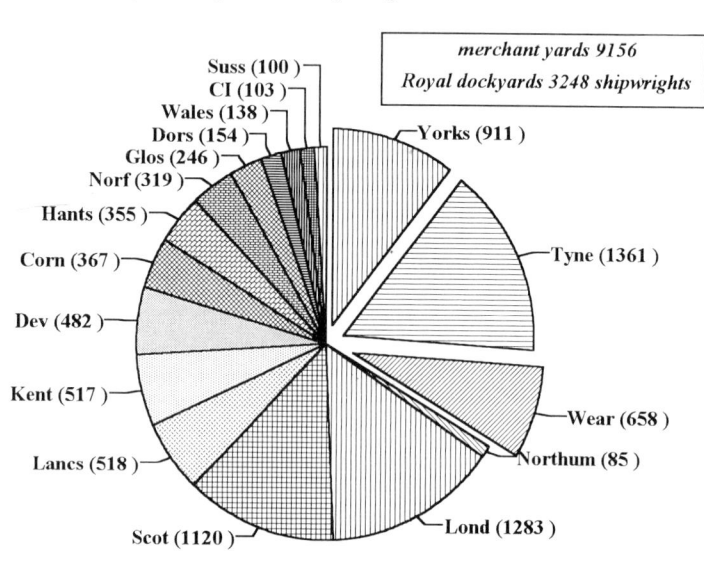

Diag 3.02

Individual North East Ports & shipbuilders.

North east output swept upwards from 13,000t in 1786 to 33,000t to 1800, and after four years on a high plateau there was a very sharp fall after 1803. More than 30,000t was the annual average for 1800-1804. Output fell to less than 12,300t in 1806 and averaged less than 14.000t over the four poor years 1806-1809.There were clearly significant changes in the distribution of shipbuilding within the region over the period 1786-1815. Increased output on the Wear has already been noted and the signals were there of the decline at Whitby, while South Shields advanced at the expense of Newcastle.

The Tyne [including Blyth].

A Newcastle Directory of 1778, listed nine shipwrights:
       at the *Mushroom* - George Cram, Thomas Curry and William Lashley

---

[3] No doubt some yards were missing, probably very few; there was no return for Stockton, where 1,470t were built in 1803 and 746t in 1804. An interesting note was added: *in Greenock, and its Neighbourhood, about 150 Shipwrights out of Employment, for want of Work.* The total at work was 309, including 118 apprentices.

on the *North Shore* - William Carse, Walter Middlemas and William Charlton,
on the *South Shore* - John Summers, Thomas Emmerson Headlam and John Rennison.

Of these men, only Middlemas and Summers do not appear in the records of the Company of Shipwrights, [assuming Rennoldson = Rennison]. Surprisingly, missing from the Directory was John Almory, who enrolled apprentices in 1760, 1765 and 1778. Carse built at least 13 ships [3,328t] over the years 1797-1815, he registered no ship locally during 1805-9, an example of the early vagaries in shipbuilding. Three ships built by Carse exceeded 300t. George Cram, who built 13 ships - 2,702t over the years 1787-1801, was also a sailmaker; in 1786 a Robert Cram, sailmaker, held shares in nine vessels with a total of 2,119t. It was not unusual for builders to hold shares in ships they built; Headlam, Laslie and Curry were shipowners. Curry's four vessels, together reached a total almost 1,300t in about 1785. The 1778 *Directory* also listed those engaged in the many trades related to shipbuilding: *Raff-yards, Rope-makers, Sawyers, Sailmakers, Anchor Smiths, Mast and Block Maker and Blacksmiths*.

No reliable overall output figures are available for the years 1777-1785. Tyne shipyards built at least 1,800t in 1777 and about 2,900t in the next two years. Just over 3,400t was the total of 10 vessels in 1781 and a slightly higher tonnage in the following year; the 21 vessels in 1783 almost reached 5300t. Apprentice enrolment and the Custom House Registers suggest that at least ten shipyards were active in 1778 and increased to fifteen by 1786. Thirty shipwrights registered nearly 200 apprentices over the years 1778-1815 with the Shipwrights' Company; eight of these masters only registered one each and nine men dominated, each registering ten or more. These were: Laslie 28; Doag 19; Carse and Gothard 16 each; Henry Wright 13; Simon Temple, Currey and the Forsyths [Tom - 10 and William - 2] 12 each and Hearn enrolled 10. These yards accounted for more than two-thirds of those enrolled [138 of 197]. Concern was expressed within the Company in April 1773 that *some Brethren have of late made a practice of taken apprentices to be free ... without having them bound by the Clerk*. Currey enrolled his last apprentice in 1786 and his last vessel [291t] found in the Register was launched in 1787. Over the period 1787-99 about 15 to 18 yards were building and 24 shipyards launched vessels in 1801, the highest number before 1815.

From 6,140t in 1786, *Newcastle* output [as official return = Tyne & Blyth] increased to 11,100t in 1800 and an average of more than 11,000t was built over the years 1800-1803. Output fell to 3,723t in 1808. At least three well established Tyne yards stopped building in that downward plunge, Walmsley, Broderick and Summers. More than 100 men registered vessels as shipbuilders on the Tyne between 1786 and 1815, 54 of these in two or more years. However, 35 yards accounted for 90% of the output and together Temple and Hurry constructed almost a third of the total tonnage. Twelve yards were on the North Bank and thirteen on the South Bank in 1804. There were 21 Block & Mastmakers & Boat-builders, employing 120 men and apprentices. Only 19 yards registered ships in 1804, the remainder were presumably working on repairs. The principal Tyne yards are shown by size in diag 3.03.

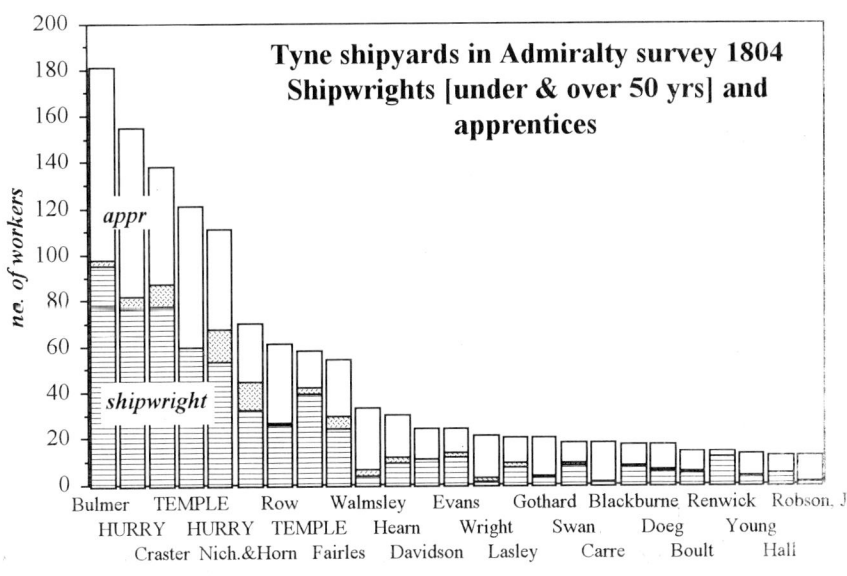

Diag 3.03

The Hearn family may serve to illustrate the progress of a Tyne wood shipyard. North Shields shipwright John Hearn carried out repairs in 1779 and may have already been building. His son Thomas was registered as an apprentice with William Carse on 30 December 1773 and duly paid his guinea on becoming a freeman in 1781. Three years later he enrolled his brother John as his first apprentice, and before the end of 1784 his second, the son of North Shields shipwright Eli Laverick. The *Happy Returns* [282t] was built in 1781, at the Low Lights, separating North Shields from Tynemouth. Hearn built at least 23 vessels, more than 6,000t, over the twenty years 1787-1806; the total output probably exceeded this. Almost half of these vessels were 300t or more. This yard headed the Tyne output of the vessels on Newcastle Register in 1787, with a total of 766t, the yard's largest tonnage in a single year. No ships by Hearn were registered locally in either 1789 or 1792. Probably however work was carried out in 1789 on one of the two brigs launched in 1790, with a combined tonnage of 601t. Usually one ship per year was built and the only other years exceeding an output of 500t were 1794 and 1795. The *Earl Percy* [269t] in 1806 was his last vessel. In 1804, Hearn employed 30 shipwrights, 18 of whom were apprentices, and two men were over 50 years of age. With this workforce, it is very probable that Hearn, like other shipbuilders, engaged in repair work and ship modifications of which no records survive.[4] Both Thomas and Joseph Hearn were shipowners. Six vessels in all more than 1,600t were owned in part or whole by the family in the mid 1780s. Shipbuilding was carried on to *a very great extent a few years ago* by the Low Lights, MacKenzie wrote in 1827.

The Hurrys at Howdon & Shields Dock.
Not far from Hearn's yard was probably the greatest of Tyne shipbuilding enterprises of the 18th century- Hurrys. Probably more than 150 vessels, about 40,000t,[5] were launched at the two famous Tyne yards of the Hurrys. This ship owning family, from Great Yarmouth, began shipbuilding at Howdon in 1758 and completed a large graving Dock there in January 1759. Francis Hurry was the resident managing partner of a business group of prominent Newcastle citizens, which certainly included Edward Mosley and Thomas Airey. Francis Hurry married Peggy, the third daughter of Thomas Airey, who was described by Richardson the historian of Wallsend as *a Newcastle shipbuilder*. His partners were engaged in the coal trade. The Fitter' Offices listed in the Newcastle Directory of 1778 included Mosley & Airey, near Love Lane, Quayside and a Henry Airey in Broad Chair. Almost certainly the shipbuilding venture was a joint enterprise of Airey, Mosley and Hurry. Their joint names appear together in the Port Registers from 1786, although not always in the same order. Indeed over the years 1787 to 1795, the name of Hurry does not appear as the builder in the Register but that of Edward Mosley, or Mosley & Co. and almost always jointly owned by various combinations including Aireys, Hurrys & Mosley. After the last appearance of Mosley's name[6] in 1796, Hurry was listed as the shipbuilder. Over the years 1787-1811, the total tonnage built credited to Mosley was 14,278t and 15,871t to Hurry. Airey, Mosley and Hurry were jointly owners of almost 7,500t of shipping on the 1786 Newcastle Register; that was almost one tenth of the Register's total. More significantly it was more than half of the locally built tonnage. Mosley & Airey were eighth in rank order in the Newcastle vend[7] in 1787, when as coal fitters they shipped 25,527 chaldrons. The downward trend of the shipyard's output seems to have begun with the ending of Mosley's active participation in the late 1790s. [see diag 3.04 below]

---

[4] His apprentices included two sons of Major Alexander Kyd of the Corps of Engineers, East India Company, James [Jan. 1793] and in November 1794 Robert, the last apprentice he enrolled with the Shipwrights Company.

[5] From the various registers 112 vessels can be identified but before this if the vessels given as built at Howdon and North Shields are added it reaches 140 - 38,475t. More than 28 vessels were likely to have been built over 1761-86.

[6] Edward son of a deceased York apothecary Rowland Mosley was apprenticed to Joseph Watson of the Hostmen's Company in 1734 and entered as a freeman in 1741. Mosley took an apprentice in 1751 and engaged his last in 1798. Mosley became Sheriff of Newcastle in 1758 and was mayor in 1767, 1774 and 1781. His wife Hannah, daughter of Henry Campleshon of York, died in 1784. The Aireys were also involved in the Hostmen's Company. Jonathan Airey became Master of Trinity House in 1765 and a Joseph Airey took the same office in 1786.

[7] The *vend* was a limitation of coal output agreed between colliery owners and traders.

Probably the first Tyne naval vessel built was the 6th rate frigate *Solebay*, in 1763, and the builder is given as Airey; it is most likely this was built under Hurry at Howdon.[8] Two Howdon war vessels were attributed to Baker[9], probably another financial backer of Hurry; these were: *Syren* [28 gun 514 *BM*] launched in 1779 and in 1781 *Argo* [5th rate frigate - 44 gun 892*BM*].[10] In merchant shipbuilding terms, the Howdon establishment was very substantial; there were four slipways as well as a double dry dock. The quay had a river frontage of 800'. A ropery and a sailmaking loft added an unusual combination to the yard. More shipwrights worked in Hurry's two shipyards in 1804, than any other merchant yard in Britain. At Howdon Dock 82 shipwrights and 73 apprentices worked and a short distance away at Shields Dock a further 68 craftsmen with 43 apprentices, in all 266. The largest yard on the Thames employed 173 [in 1804 survey]!

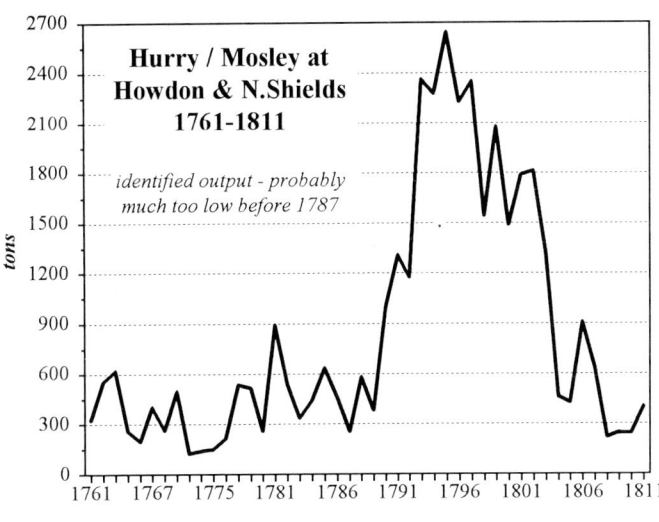

Diag 3.04

Over the five years, 1793-7, Hurry's output always exceeded 2,000t, about one third of the Tyne's output. These yards constructed a quarter of Tyne built and registered tonnage over the period 1787-1799. The partnership's second highest output was 2,538t in 1799 and in 1801-2 not far short of 2,000t was launched annually. A least a dozen merchant vessels exceeded 400t, including the *Albion* [448t] in 1791, the *Ocean* [481t] in 1794 and the *Brunswick* [486t] in 1795. If as seems likely Mosley & Airey's *Expedition* [326t], built in 1761 at North Shields was built by Hurry, it was the first of nearly 60 vessels exceeding 300t. After 1802 new output fell sharply, although what might have offered a ray of hope was the contract for the 18 gun *HMS Raleigh* launched in 1806. So large an enterprise as the Hurry business carried capital costs higher than was usual in wood shipbuilding, and so required not only a large output but also a steady flow of orders to cover its overheads. A commission of bankruptcy was issued against Francis and Thomas Hurry at the end of 1806. Two years later Francis Hurry died, on 8 October 1808, aged 79. Ships were built until 1811, but a total of 1,751t in the last five years was a mere two-thirds of 1795 alone. The *Tigris* [553t] in 1802 was the yard's largest merchant man and the last *Prince Regent* was 403t. The 285t *Triad*, built in 1803, was nearly rebuilt in 1834 and still appeared on the 1875 Register at 310t. Both the dry dock facilities and the tonnage of new ships built suggest that a great deal of repair work was carried out at Howdon. During 50 years this enterprise had substantial achievements but also raised the question whether, at that time, yards of this size were viable, given the fluctuating character of the demand for new ships and the ease with which a team of shipwrights could construct a ship on a stretch of open beach.

Row's shipyard at St Peter's.

William Row[e]'s yard at St Peters, probably started in 1756, was one of the most famous on the Tyne; 61 shipwrights, including 34 apprentices, worked there in 1804. By 1787 it was second only to Hearn in output with three vessels [625t] and during its years of operation built about 7% of the tonnage launched into the Tyne. In both 1794 and 1799 vessels in excess of 400t were built by Rowe, the *Crown* and the *Auspicious*. In March 1804 the largest graving dock on the Tyne was opened, capable of taking vessels of

---

[8] Archibald in *The Fighting Ship in the Royal Navy* briefly outlines the development of these frigates. The 6th rate was the smaller type, about 107' x 30' on the gun deck; the 5th rate was 124.3' x 34' on lower deck.

[9] John, a son of ffrancis Baker of Tanfield Lodge, was apprenticed to Thomas Airey in 1737; he was active in the Company of Hostmen, and became a City Alderman. It seems likely that he was the Baker given as shipbuilder.

[10] Richardson stated the *Madona* frigate, *above 30 guns*, was launched on 9 October 1782 [not listed elsewhere].

12 feet draught.[11] Almost 6,000t were built between 1786 and the end of the century and a further 5000t before the yard was sold in 1810 to the enterprising Smiths [see chap 5]. Rowe took William Smith as an apprentice in 1804, when perhaps the family had set its sights on the yard. A dozen vessels for the Admiralty were constructed at St Peter's during the Napoleonic wars [see below]. It is likely that the merchant William Row, who held shares in 11 vessels [2,500t] was also the shipbuilder.

Gateshead.
Although Gateshead never became a significant shipbuilding centre, at Friars Goose trawlers were built up to 1961 and there was also a tradition of boat building at Hillgate. One of the casualties of the dramatic slump about 1802-4 was a now forgotten yard of Summers, which between 1787 and 1803, built 19 ships, together more than 4,000t. In 1804 there were three yards on the South Shore: Boult and Renwick each employed 14 and boat builder Masterton six while at Felling 17 worked for Doeg. A workforce of 56 shipwrights at Gateshead was greater than the 36 at Swansea or the 46 working at the long established port of Appledore. Headlam launched a 288t vessel in 1779 and seven ships identified between 1787 and 1807 totalled 1,231t [this yard was not in 1804 Survey]. Hawkes & Co on the South Shore was listed in 1804 as employing three shipwrights and two apprentices. Four vessels were registered as built by Edward Hawke - in 1804 the *Hawk Packet* [171t], two years later the *Yariso* [209t] and *Northumbrian* [117t]. The famed iron master William Hawk's Gateshead works supplied anchors to the Admiralty from 1766.

South Shields.
South Shields was the rising shipbuilding centre on the Tyne between 1787 and 1815. The trend in output for South Shields & Jarrow over this period rose from less than 2,000t a year to more than 3,000t. On the local registers, the comparable output trend for the remainder of the Tyne began at 3,000t and increased to nearly 5,000t in 1799 but then merchant output fell back to almost 1,000t in 1808 and averaged about 2,500t in 1813-5., There were 10 shipyards and three repair docks at South Shields in 1781 when 11 ships were built and twenty years later facilities had expanded to 4 dry docks, 8 other repair docks and 12 yards, although seven of these were described as boat yards. Twenty-eight men and two women registered ships as builders between 1786-1815. The largest outputs were: Temple [33,000t], Bulmers [almost 14,000t] and both Nicholson & Horn and Broderick almost 6,000t each. There is no reason to suppose that Catherine Forster and Ann Broderick were merely nominal owners of their late husband's shipyards. Shipbuilder William Forster was at Shadwell Street in 1779 and seven years later, Catherine Forster informed *the Friends of her late Husband* and the public generally that: *she has employed proper Persons for carrying on the Business at South Shields; and a Continuance of Favours will be gratefully acknowledged.* Under Catherine's overall control a 256t ship was launched in 1787 and two years later one of 141t. No further new vessels have been found: a least one repair job on the *Harriot* was completed. No doubt the usual commercial hazards of the industry resulted in the bankruptcy of Catherine Forster in 1789, when the yard and its timber were offered for sale.

The Brodricks [Brodericks].
A Whitby family, the Brodericks[12] established a substantial business interests on the Tyne. Lockwood Broderick II was born in 1729 and a partnership between Brodrick & Hearn of North Shields was dissolved in May 1769, possibly the John Hearn discussed above. After starting his South Shields shipyard Broderick added a dock, probably on the same site; the assessment of Lockwood Brodrick for 1770 was £24. Building and repairs were carried out at the Low Dock, and in 1772 the *Content* was launched. When he remarried in January 1778, Broderick was described as *an eminent shipbuilder*. His new bride was the widow of a Newcastle iron merchant John Craister or Craster. When her husband died six years later, Ann Broderick

---

[11] *Smith's Dock Monthly*, in 1920, described the docking of the *Henry* and *Colpitts* as then *an event of great note ... than is the docking of a Dreadnought today*.

[12] A Brodrick was in partnership with Fishburn at Whitby from 1795 at least until 1815.

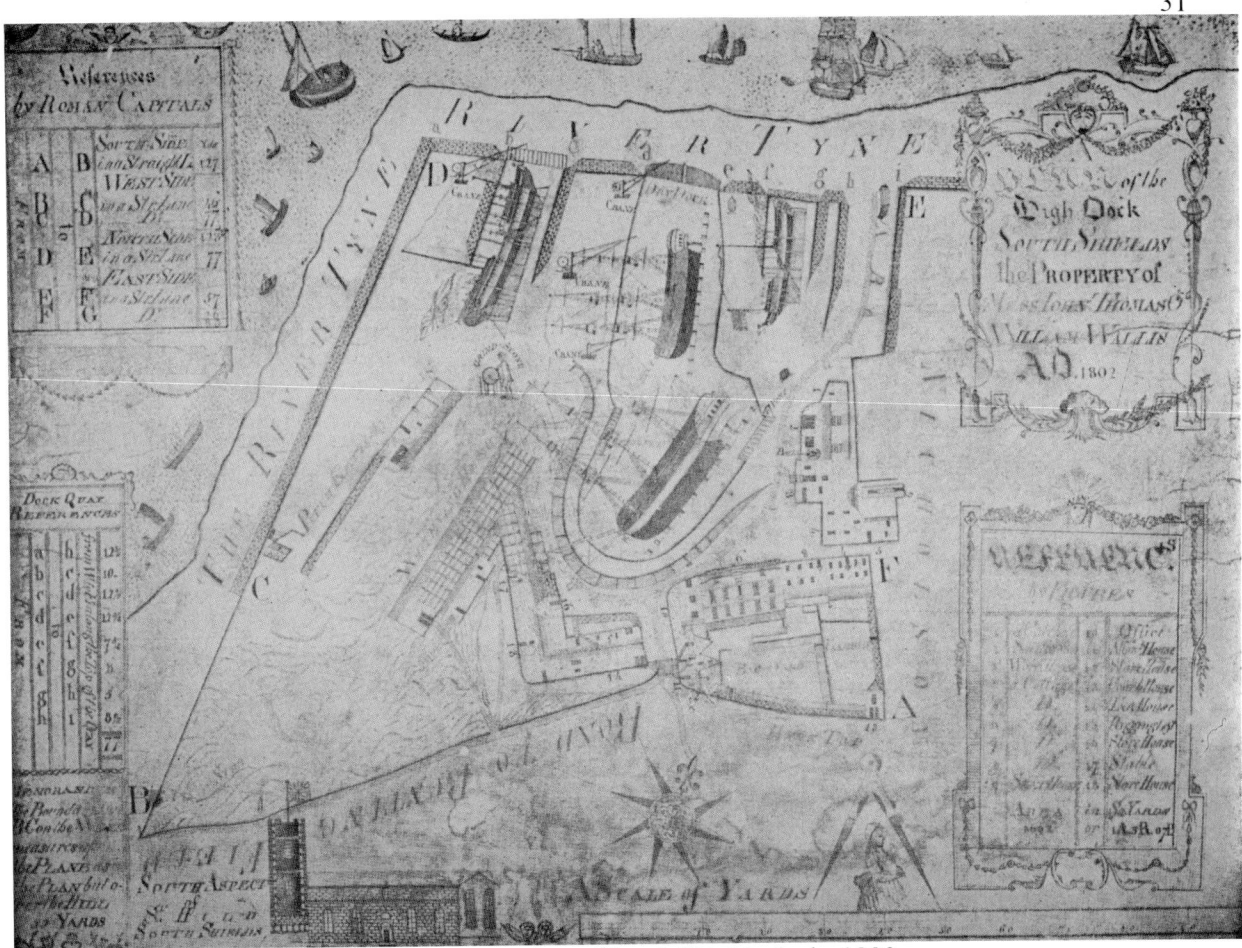

A contemporary plan of South Shields docks 1802

respectfully informed, through the local newspapers, *the Friends of her Husband* that shipbuilding and repair work at the Dock would continue. Fifteen vessels, more than 3,700t, were built by Ann Broderick over the years 1787-1799. A report of 31 absconding apprentices[13] suggests a yard of substantial size, probably not less than 60 workers. After some years at sea as Captain of the *Brodrick*, Mrs Broderick's son James took over the management of the yard with his step brother in 1787 when Lockwood Brodrick III came of age [Lockwood III died in 1802]. Five ships [1,465t] were launched in Lockwood Broderick III's name from 1800. James Craster acquired the business before April 1803, when it was referred to as *Mr Craister's Low Dock*. A ship was launched in both 1803 and 1804. This was the third largest yard on the Tyne in 1804, employing 138 shipwrights, including 50 apprentices. It seems clear that the bulk of the workforce was engaged in repairs. In March 1806, Craster offered for sale a 283t new ship, ready to launch presumably his final vessel. [It was not, however, registered locally in his name.] Not long afterwards the Dock was rented out: a Rate Book of 1807 recorded Wright & Co [late Brodrick] Dock £30. The 148t *Iris* was registered by the new occupiers in 1807. Henry Wright, with a partner Harle, worked the yard up to 1822. A Thomas Harle was an apprentice of Laslie in 1786 and Wright[14] was a friend of Roger Almory, of the established Newcastle shipbuilders. Henry Wright, son of a Newcastle master mariner, in 1804 on the North Shore employed 21 shipwrights, including 18 apprentices!

---

[13] Simon Temple jnr also suffered from the not unusual problem of absconding apprentices in 1794.

[14] The Wrights offer an intriguing problem. Henry an apprentice of Almory in 1778, became a Freeman in 1785 and a Wright was working at Seaton, 1787-1802, a Wright at Newcastle in 1799-1815; a Henry & William at Blyth 1802-7. By patrimony William Wright jnr entered the Shipwrights' Company in 1812 and became a freeman in December 1824. Henry enrolled his last apprentice in 1815; apprentices were taken in 1809 by brother William.

Richard Bulmer

In 1804 Richard Bulmer employed the largest workforce in a *single* shipyard on the north east coast - 181 shipwrights [Hurry had 155 at Howdon]. It is not certain if Bulmer was one of the Banks, Liddle & Co. *partnership* which launched a 380t ship in 1780 from the Middle Dock: a year later he undoubtedly was. Henzell[15] and Bulmer were both involved in 1784 by which time Banks had departed. Early in April 1785 the partnership between shipwright John Henzell and Richard Bulmer was dissolved. Bulmer must have prospered in the long run, probably through repair work. His business interests extended beyond Middle Dock. Bulmer's brother and partner Joseph began as an Insurance Broker in 1788 and in that year they offered Iceland cod for sale. A 300t ship was built in 1789 and at least five vessels were either repaired, rebuilt or lengthened by Bulmer in 1791. An advertisement of 1799 implied Bulmer owned more than one dock. Although he was mainly concerned with repairs and ship modification, Bulmer built almost 5,000t over the years 1787-1799 and in the first 14 years of the 19th century more than 8,100t. Even so substantial an entrepreneur as Bulmer faced problems of needing to build without firm orders, as press advertisements show:

    1786 February and September *Hull...at Middle Dock* for sale
    1789 March *a new Ship with a Poop Deck, now on Stocks - 300 Tons or upwards*
    1794 August *new Hull 340 Tons*
    1799 March a new ship *271 Tons, now building ... will be afloat 9 Ma*r.

Many fine large ships were built. Sixteen ships were over 300t and 9 of these exceeded 400t, including the *Lord Collingwood* [479t]. Serious financial problems beset the Bulmers in 1812 and a commission of bankruptcy was awarded against them.[16] Buyers were sought in October 1812 for the hull of a new ship as well as six colliers and early in the following year for the hulls of two vessels, of about 300t each, *copper fastened and one lately launched & the other nearly complete*. Ironically, Bulmer's total of 1,281t of new vessels in 1813 was only exceeded by Temple, who was then also in financial problems.

Simon Temple - father & son.

Simon Temple's father was born in 1728 and was the brother of a distinguished Master at Richmond School; their parents lived near Easingwold, Yorkshire. Simon sr was a master shipwright and married Ann Kell at St Hilda's Church, South Shields in April 1756.[17] Temple was selling ships from 1780 to 1783. When he went bankrupt in 1786, Simon Temple sr had 14 apprentices *most of them as good as men*, which suggests a workforce of perhaps 25 to 30. A new vessel was up for sale as well as the building yard and Temple paid his final bankruptcy dividend in 1788. In that year the *Eleanor* [158t] was built presumably by Simon Temple jnr [born 1759] and three vessels in 1789 [380t in all]. Temple worked at a number of sites at South Shields - *Temple's Low Building Yard* - *Temple's Dock* and *Mr Temple's High Building Yard*. More than 1,000t was launched by Temple for the first time in 1793, with four vessels [1,371t]. A year later he took over Evan's yard. A *terrible Fire broke out in Mr Temple's Dockyard* in September 1798, when work was under way on three West Indiamen. Some pitch kettles boiled over and the fire began during the workmen's dinner - *the Flames were making rapid Progress and had set a large Stack of Timber on Fire, when fortunately a Boy ran into the Market Place and gave the Alarm*. Although coming second to Hurry's yards until 1799, Temple thereafter built more than anyone else on the Tyne. On 7 September 1799 a copper fastened *very fine three-decked Indiaman* the *Herculean* [637t] was launched; she was *by far the largest Merchant Ship ever built* on the Tyne. Temple built 13 others exceeding 500t and more than 90 vessels were over 300t. The *Prince of Wales* [410t] was built in 1793. During 1802-3 the yard launched the *Lord Eldon* [571t], *Admiral Aspin* [594t] and *Indus* [601t]. In 1803 the *Intrepid*

---

[15] The Henzells were Newcastle glass makers; John's son Thomas was apprenticed to shipwright Trewhitt in 1746 and Moses son of Christopher Henzell in 1749. William Henzell was apprenticed in 1800 to Wm Laslie. Bulmer was probably the junior partner in 1784, the *bark Catherine* was for sale after repair in *Henzell & Cos Dock*.

[16] Nicholas Fairles was declared bankrupt in that month also. He built at least 13 vessels 2,305t during 1791-1813.

[17] see Flagg, she discussed the problem of *Who was Simon Temple ?* [p121 - 3]. He died in 1805 aged 77. This may have been his second marriage. It is not certain if Ann was related to the Kells, who were shipwrights.

[445t] was the first ship from Jarrow on the Register, the next was the *Admiral Gambier* in 1807.[18] Temple employed 121 shipwrights at South Shields in 1804, half of whom were apprentices, and another 58 shipwrights at Jarrow; together almost as many as Bulmer. Repairs were an important part of Temple's business but are impossible to quantify. Meanwhile his entrepreneurial ambitions expanded to acquiring land at Jarrow for mining coal, which later provided the site for a new shipyard, [at the West End of Jarrow Quay] at which the naval vessels were built. Three vessels were launched in 1808, totalling more than 1,600t. Apart from warships and the *Hound* of 1813, all new output was given as at Jarrow. The *Caledonia* [366t] of 1813 was the last Temple ship entered in the Register. In January 1806 Temple was *desirous to retire from Business* and sold the old yard, a double dry dock and building yard with the *Houses, Premises & Fixtures* at South Shields to a shipowner Forsyth.[19] Over stretched by his many business adventures, and not long after the launch of his last frigate Temple was in serious financial straits and bankruptcy followed. On 20 July 1811, the sale of his Stock in Trade, included:

> the Skelton of a new Ship, 100' Keel., framed 29' 4", another 88' 6" Keel, framed 28' 6", which may be built where they stand if the purchasers require it. Also the Hull of a new Ship, 261 t Reg., with a Mast, Rigging and One Suit of Sails, lying at Jarrow Wharf.

In May 1813 the shipyard was taken over by the Chief Assignees in the bankruptcy proceedings, Thomas & Robert Brown. Temple's personal final fate is unknown.

The Laings on the Tyne.

A Wearside family played an important role at South Shields. The Laing brothers Philip, John and James, began their business in 1806 and built almost 3,500t before 1816 to make them fifth highest builder in the town. A modest 145t vessel was the first but the second was the 326t *Plantagenet*. Repair work was an important part of the business and their dock was rated at £40: both the *Jonas* in 1810 and the *Bilboa* in 1811 were completely rebuilt and the brig *Hilton* lengthened. Three vessels were built in each year from 1813 to 1815. James married the daughter of master shipwright Cuthbert Heron in 1811, he was in charge of the Volunteers who fought the fire at Temple's yard.

Sunderland.

On the Wear five vessels totalling 1,352t were certainly built in 1779. For the early 1780s, data in Lloyd's Register and Customs Registers show the minimum output was as follows:

year	1780	1781	1782	1783	1784	1785
tons	793	2,623	1,749	4,045	2,911	2,798

With a single exception over the next seven years the Wear launched each year more than 2,000t and averaged above 2,300t. From 1793 the river's shipbuilders significantly increased their output and finally by launching 12,662t in 1800 exceeded the output of the Tyne. Over the four years 1800-1803, the Wear launched just under 40,000t and the Tyne 44,675t. After 1808-9 the Wear began to establish its leadership in the region. Over the years 1810-13 the Wear built more than 36,000t and the Newcastle ports less than 28,000t. A helpful factor was there young workforce, with 59% apprentices and only just over 6% of the shipwrights over 50 years of age compared with Whitby's more than 14% over 50 years and 52%

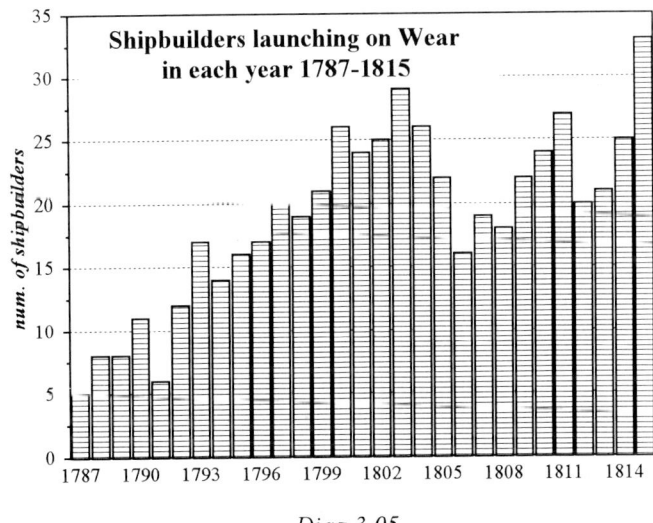

Diag 3.05

---

[18] Temple built the *Undaunted* at Sunderland in 1800 presumably he hired a team of shipwrights.

[19] Forsyth's new output was modest, 1,654t during 1805-10. Repair work was his main interest.

apprentices. There were many ambitious journeymen shipwrights. Surtees wrote in 1816: *In shipbuilding the Port of Sunderland stands at present the highest of any in the United Kingdom.* There were three relatively lean years 1806-8, with an average output of 3,625t; clearly very poor compared with 12,300t in 1811. Although 76 different builders were credited with at least one ship between 1787 and 1814, half of the output came from 11 yards. The many changing partnerships means that the total of 76 gives an impression of greater diversity than probably existed. Variations by year of the number of builders is shown in diag 3.05 and the yard sizes in 1804 for 24 builders in diag 3.06, which clearly shows the predominance of apprentice labour.

Laings.
Two shipyards, which began in 1793 headed the aggregate output over the period 1793-1816. The Laings and Benjamin Heward together built more than 14% of the total tonnage. The business started by the Scottish Laing family continued during almost the complete history of Sunderland shipbuilding. John Laing with his son David had a business on the North Sands and may have built before the mainstream yard began in 1792, when John was joined by his 22 year old brother Philip, a yeoman farmer from Fifeshire. The Laings built 71 vessels [14,000t] before 1816. Traditionally the *Horta* [162t] is regarded as their first vessel; however according to the Register the *Affiance* [108t] was completed three months earlier on 25 April 1794.[20] The Laings became substantial shipowners and regularly took a share in the ships they built, of which the *Sarah Scaling* [1798] was an early example. The *Fame* [375t] was launched in 1801 and 9 further vessels 300t or more were built over the following 14 years. The largest was the *Sappho* [419t] in 1809. Annual output exceeded 1,000t in 1811 and in 1814 six ships [1,615t] were launched. Few financial records survive, however in 1814 the *Polly* [283t] cost £5,426-14s, almost £20/ton. Laings employed an average of 72 workers, 58 shipwrights & apprentices in 1800. In 1804 Laing was the largest shipbuilding employer on the Wear with 53 shipwrights [30 apprentices and 5 men over 50 years of age].

Benjamin Heward and others.
Benjamin Heward started his yard when he was 42 years old and launched 11,400t to 1816. The shipyard was on the North Sands; it seems likely that at times he was in partnership with Booth and Blenkinsop. Both these men built on their own account and probably supplied the shipbuilding expertise. His first vessel in 1793, the *Astrae*, was a not untypical at 110t. However, three of his next four ships exceeded 200t. Before the yard was moved in 1803 to Southwick, two vessels exceeding 300t were built. Many of these

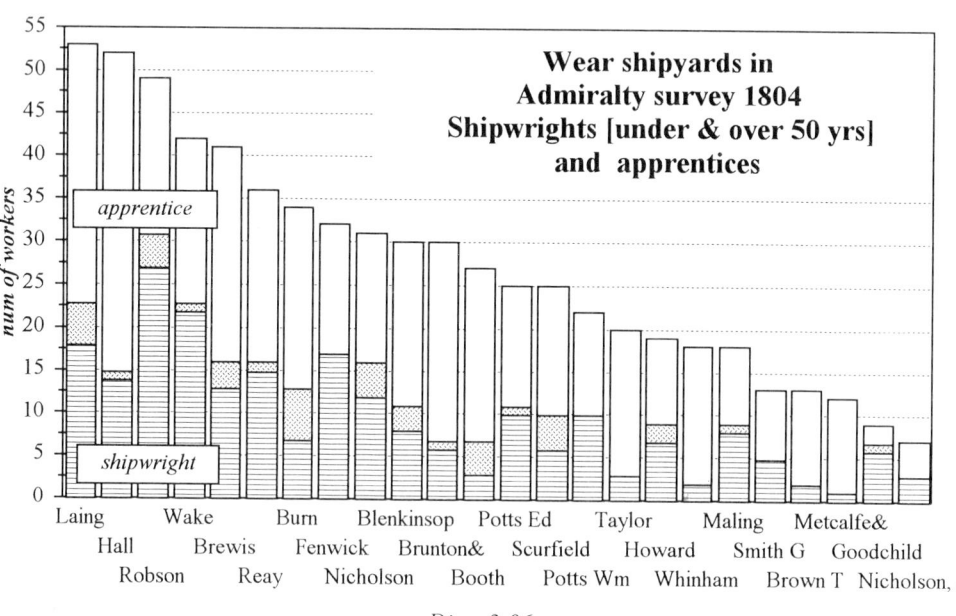

Diag 3.06

---

[20] The *Albion* [registration 14 Oct 1799] is the first vessel in a surviving Particulars Book and numbered 5 there is also a ringed *12* in pencil on the page. An explanation may be that Laing numbered differently. Both the *Affiance* and *Horta* were registered by John & David, the *Gemini* by John [17 May 1796] and the *Nerva* was the first by John & Philip [15 Dec 1797]. Thus *Albion* the 5th ship by J&P, was 12th in overall order on yard list.

vessels were built for himself and ten were 300t or more. The *Shannon* [419t] was launched in 1813 and was the yard's largest ship. The 1804 return listed a *Howard* [a typographical error?], who employed 9 shipwrights and 10 apprentices, a workforce quite capable of building the 284t of that year. Heward built at a number of sites on the Wear and his Deptford yard was taken over by the Laings. On 2 March 1798, a massive ship, the *Lord Duncan* of 925t, was launched at Southwick. This appears to be the last vessel by Thomas Havelock[21], a shipowner's son. Nine vessels by this builder have been identified, two in 1791, then the *Themis* [574t];a total of 3,363t over nine years. Wake and Reay between them accounted for almost 10% of output, while W. Potts, Burn and Nicholson[22] each had aggregates of about 4%. Only one vessel was built by 16 of these Wear yards, while another 12 only launched two. Such very short lived yards were uncommon on the Tyne. Jonathan Nicholson, employed three shipwrights and four apprentices in 1804 and built two vessels [217t]. Boat builder J Harrison employed four men & lads and built four vessels [299t] during 1805-9. A shipwright named Ralph Goodchild worked on the Wear in 1672 and this family name was linked with shipbuilding until 1821. They frequently built for their own use particularly for the trade associated with their many lime kilns. Typically their vessels were of 70t to 80t; their biggest vessel being a 97t schooner. A bank established by the Goodchilds failed in 1816 but their business activities continued. Between 1801 and 1821 fourteen vessels were built, a total of 1,006t. Goodchild employed nine shipwrights in 1804.

Part of an Eye Plan of Sunderland & Bishopwearmouth 1785-1790 by John Rain

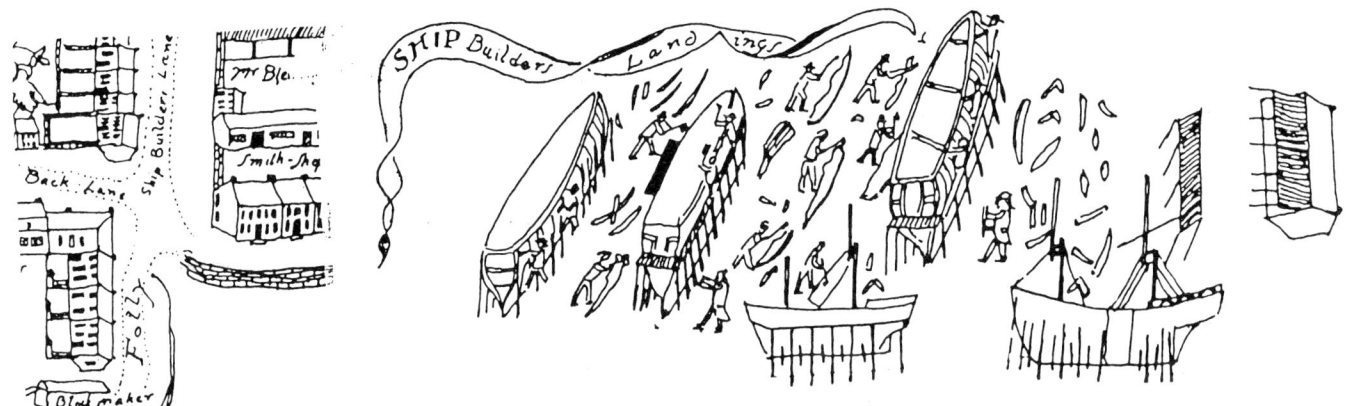

Ships under construction on the Wear in 1814.

Thirty-seven [8,410t] vessels were under construction on the Wear in December 1810: work in progress was on similar tonnages in the next two years [8,020t and 8,437t]. When work was continuous, it was unusual for the building of a new merchant hull to exceed six months.[23] The building capacity at Sunderland was at least double the tonnage on the slipways, in other words 16,000t or more. That level of ouput was almost reached in 1815, when more than 15,000t were launched. A summary of the work underway in March 1814 by Surtees listed 31 vessels [6,693t] on the slipways at 23 yards. Eight of these yards were each working on two vessels: Reay [660t], James Crowne [580t], Laing [414t], Radcliffe [395t], Hall [370t], both Adamson and Brown [350t] each and Hutchinson [320t]. The others only one vessel each, John Scott had nearly finished a 369t ship and Mrs Burn's 220t vessel being built *on spec* was a quarter finished and could be ready in July. James Crowne's *nearly finished* vessel *Agenoria* [182t] was launched in April. A half finished vessel, the *Stentor* [382t], which could have been finished in June was

---

[21] *Where Ships Are Born* described the yard, rather too grandly, as *perhaps the most important ... in the eighteenth century*.[p.19] An explosion at Port-au-Prince ended the career of the *Lord Duncan*, at a loss of £30000 to the builder. Havelock's son was the Sir Henry [1795-1857] of Indian Mutiny fame and other military campaigns.

[22] Thomas Nicholson died in 1781 aged 50; in 1798 both William Potts [aged 62] the Hylton Ferry shipbuilder and John Wright [aged 75] of Monkwearmouth Shore died.

[23] All four 200t vessels with only the *Keel laid* on 11 March 1814 could have been finished in July or August.

however not launched until August.[24] Of the 25 ships *on spec* in 1814, nine ships were nearly finished and the following sets out the stages of the other vessels:

two-thirds finished	2	half finished	6	quarter finished	1
Wales round	2	Floors across	1	keel laid	4

Eight of the 31 vessels, but only 14% of the tonnage, were iron fastened and the remainder had copper bolts. Three of the six vessels were on contract were for the builder himself - Reay [320t], James Thompson [1,123t] and Goodchild [80t]. Laing was building a vessel [154t] for the rope maker Grimshaw, Gales a vessel [180t] for the port of Greenock and Reay a 340t ship for Jno Hamilton.

Blyth.

Salt pans and a fishery existed at Blyth at the beginning of the 13th century and some trade in coal may have started later in that century. More than 3,000 chaldrons of coal moved coastwise before 1700 and this trade greatly expanded later. By 1800, the value of the port's shipping was estimated as £50,000, a year in which 43,440 chaldrons of coal left the port. Rope making was certainly carried out from 1762, with two rope-walks of 400 yards by six yards wide. These were still marked on maps a century later. As distinct from the occasional vessel continuous shipbuilding at Blyth was probably begun by Edmund Hannay[25] about 1750. At least 41 ships were built at Blyth between 1750 and 1799 and output averaged more than 400t over the years 1782-5. More than 900t were launched at Blyth in 1802. Although almost 1,100t were launched at Blyth in 1806, the average of the next three years was only 675t, but from 1810 until the defeat of Napoleon the average was 1,571t. Blyth advanced very significantly as a north east shipbuilding port after 1800, and its proportion of output on local registers increased substantially. From about 5% of the Newcastle register around 1790, output reached a sixth in 1806 and in 1810 Blyth built 20% or more of Tyne new tonnage. Edward Watts married Hannay's eldest daughter and he, too, began building ships. For a few years after Hannay's death in 1800, both yards were worked by Watts and then Wright took over Watt's yard. A second shipyard at Blyth was run by shipwright Watson in a partnership with Stoker. Shipowner George Davidson, with a partner Munroe, had certainly commenced shipbuilding by 1802. Wright built 500t in 1802. Others shipbuilders at that time were Manner & Bates, at the Low Quay, and Debord & Morrison at *upper end of the quay* and later at High Panns. Neither of these were in the 1804 Admiralty return. In 1804 Davidson & co. employed 36 shipwrights and there were 24 at H & W Wright's yard: 36 of these 60 were apprentices. Davidson built more than 8,500t over the years 1803 to 1819. Five shipbuilders launched more than 2,000t at Blyth in 1812 but usually only three registered new building. Charles Clark & Henry Taylor built from 1808 probably at Cowpen Quay and later Bowman & Drummond constructed a slipway. The first dry dock was built about 1811 by Stoveld.

Whitby.

Charlton's map of 1778 [below] illustrates the significance of shipbuilding at Whitby with its many dry docks and the little sketches of ships in frame showing the location of slipways. Having taken over the pioneering Coates yard, the Fishburns[26] confirmed their position as the leading Whitby shipyard and Thomas Brodrick [c1766-1829] became a partner in 1795. The *Esk* [629t] built by Fishburn in 1781 shows the scale of this yard and among other large vessels were *Coverdale* [579t] in 1795 and the *Cullandsgrove* [599t] in 1801. Thirty-five names appear as builders of ships on the Whitby Register between 1800 and 1815. Various combinations of partners accounted for this number of builders; for example amongst the family names in various partnerships were Barrick [4 names from 1790 - 1855]; Barry [3 names 1790-1830]; Chapman [4 names 1799-1817] ; Campion [5 names 1815-74; partner Chapman 1799]; Langburne

---

[24] Six builders launched vessels in January and February [Laing's two ships-548t]; 68 ships were launched in 1814, at 13603t double the tonnage under construction. The Gales launched in March, July, September and November.

[25] Hannay, the son of a parish clerk, was born in Bothal, near Ashington, and learned his shipwright's skills at the Scottish port of Leith. He became a shipowner as well as builder.

[26] Barry in 1833 spoke of a yard that built 150 vessels; probably Fishburn's; 114 vessels have been identified and the builders of a large number of Whitby vessels remain unknown. The *Esk* was 127' x 33' and mounted 44 guns.

Part of a map of Whitby 1778

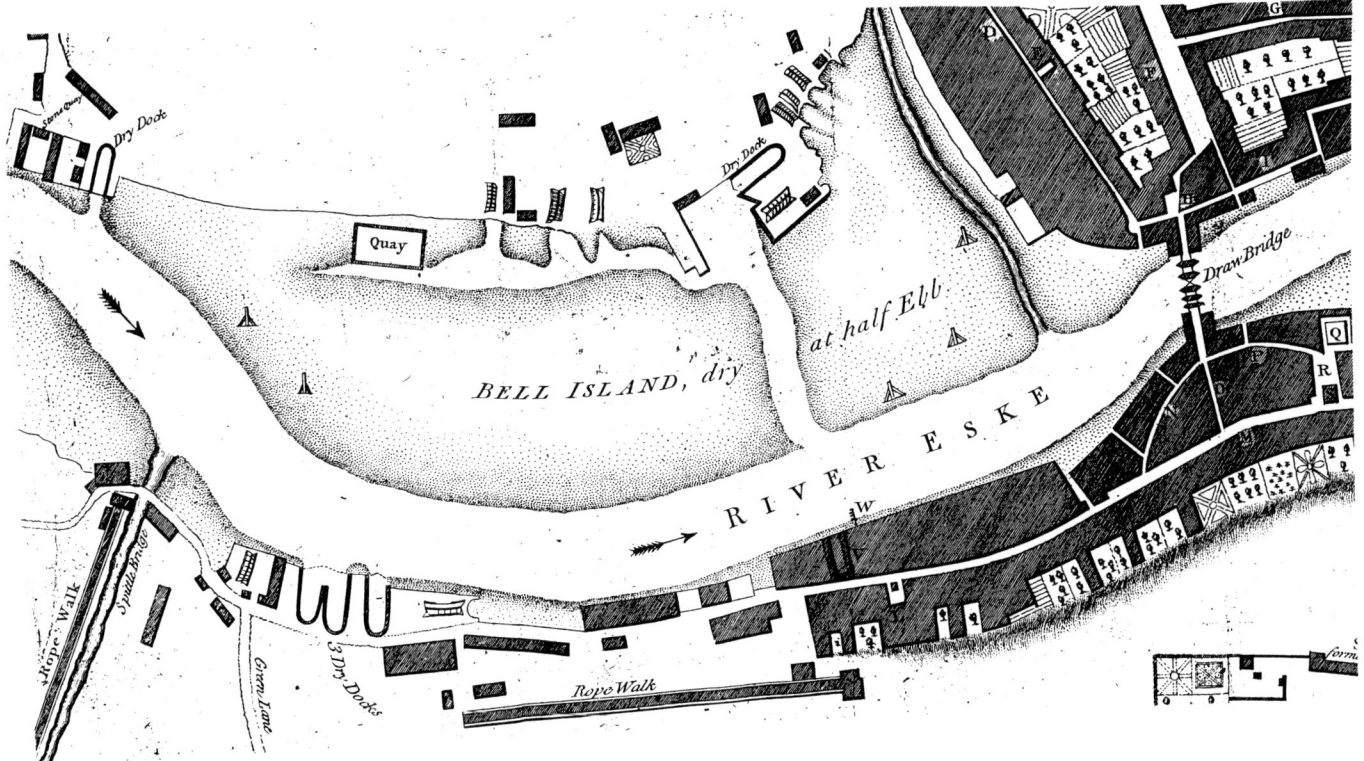

[3 names 1792-1835].[27] Peter Cato [c1775-1829], built on his own account and was in three different partnerships, with Eskdale, in addition to four years as partner to Smales. Charlton described the industry in 1797:

> Whitby has long been noted for building good ships for the merchants service and coal trade, but never was in so much fame on that account as at present. Our master-builders understand their business extremely well, and know the exact geometrical proportion all the parts of a ship ought to have in regard to each other. They are besides very assiduous and diligent in their vocation; and not only attend the shipyards themselves from five in the morning till seven in the evening, but also oblige everyone under them to do the same. And wages not being so high as in most other places, it follows of course that carpenters work is done both cheaper and better at Whitby than in any other port of England... many merchants who are desirous of having good ships, being convinced they no where else can be so well served, apply to our master-builders at Whitby, and frequently agree for turn on our stocks a year or two before their work can be done.

Owners booking work in advance was a remarkable tribute to the shipbuilding of Whitby, in contrast to the speculative building so frequently found at other northern ports. However, Charlton's claim that no port built annually the number of ships built at Whitby was being seriously challenged by the time his book appeared. Charlton's enthusiasm however is understandable, in the context of the port building 10% of the new tonnage of England & Wales over the years 1789-1794.

Generally, according to Charlton, 12 or 13 *large ships* were building about half of which were for Whitby, and the others for *London and other sea-ports*. His claim of 24-25 ships per annum was perhaps not too great an exaggeration, as between 1787-97, launchings exceeded 20 in each of seven years; with 26 in 1787. The value of new shipbuilding was estimated at almost £80,000 and repairs at £10,000 -£12,000. There were more than 300 shipwrights, *part of which always at sea*, and the remainder, with more than 100 apprentices *were building new ships*. A workforce of this size would certainly have been needed to produce new work and repairs of the amount given. In 1804, there were 265 shipwrights employed at eight

---

[27] On a site previously worked by Simpson and then Hustler, the Langborne brothers began their yard in 1760.

Whitby yards, 138 were apprentices [see diag 3.08]. Holt was the largest employer of shipwrights in 1804, a total of 79, thirteen more than Fishburns. His yard had just started although he had a short lived earlier partnership and in only two years between 1804 and 1813 did Holt's output exceed Fishburn and for the whole period the aggregate of 5,739t was less than the 7,292t by the older yard, despite no Fishburn vessels being launched in 1809. In 1804 the Langborne brothers employed 26 shipwrights, including only 9 apprentices, a smaller proportion than other yards, which may indicate a higher proportion of repair work. Many Berwick and Leith smacks were built by them. The overall output at Whitby for 1786-1813 is shown in diag 3.07.

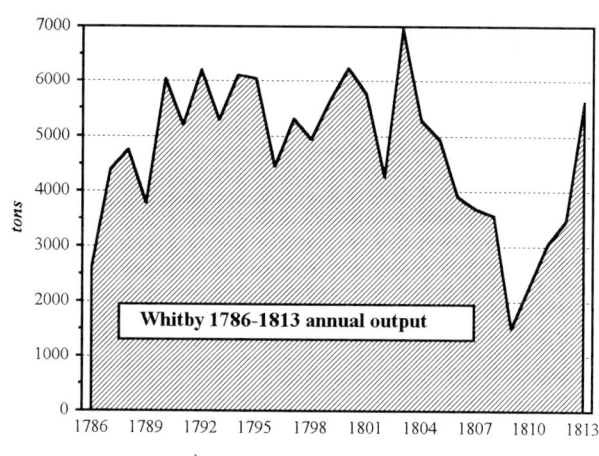

Diag 3.07

The leading position of Fishburn is unmistakable. Two-thirds of the tonnage between 1790 and 1813 can be identified with individual builders and of these vessels just over one-third of the tonnage was by Fishburns. Next in order of tonnage was Barry with 12%, Eskdale almost 11% and then Barrick with 9%. Those four yards together accounted for two-thirds of Whitby's output. Chapman, Holt and Langeborne each provided 7%-8%. Almost nine out every ten tons came from these seven yards. Block and masts were made at Whitby by the Smales from 1750 to 1871 and for a small number of years starting in 1807 the Smales were partners in small shipyards. Perhaps they were financing shipwrights such as Cato. With his son, Gideon Smales combined timber importing with a shipyard, which appears to have operated between 1807 and 1817. After building a vessel of only 98t in 1807, the next vessel [488t] launched was in 1809. Then two vessels [total 528t] in 1811. Like many other port business families the Smales were also shipowners. As will emerge later Whitby's former leading role was not revived after the war.

Scarborough.

There were 105 Scarborough built vessels in Lloyds 1776 register, with an average of 349t. An output of 2,000t a year was well within the capacity of this port and the 12 ships launched in 1799 reached 3,300t.

After 1803, two thousand tons were never again reached and the port averaged about 1,000t over the period 1805-13. A total of 146 shipwrights, including apprentices, in 1804 still placed the port 13th in rank order for Great Britain. There were seven yards at the port. Almost half these shipwrights, 70, were in John Tindall's yard, a quarter of the 48 journeymen were over 50 years of age. Over the twenty years to 1790, the yard turned out 35 brigs and 13 barques. During the following ten years, 35 vessels were built: 22 brigs, 10 barques and 3 snows. A quarter of the 1,800t built during 1801-3 was for the Tindalls and this proportion increased to a third during 1804-1812. Tindall's London based fleet was regularly supplied by his own yard and if the number employed in 1804 was about the norm, then it seems likely a substantial amount of repair work was also carried out. *The palmy days of Scarborough as a trading*

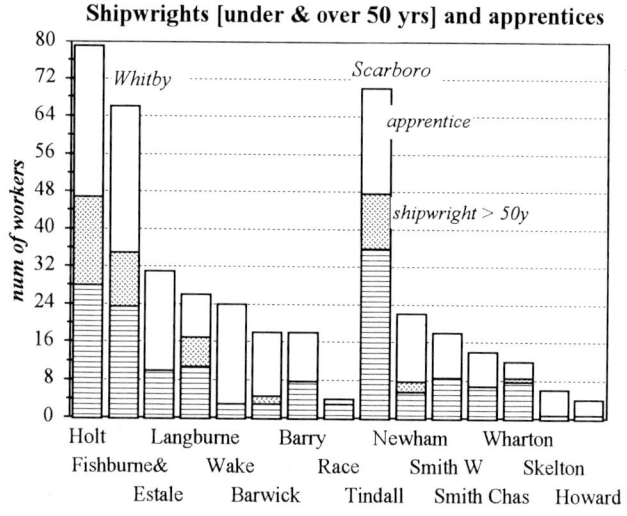

Diag 3.08

port, wrote Rowntree, *appear to have ceased in 1820 or thereabouts.* The end was summarised in a report by the Municipal Corporation Commissioners in 1835, *shipbuilding which was the principal business carried on here, has very much declined. It is not a place of much trade; it is resorted to as a watering place.*

The River Tees - Stockton.

Less than 300t were built in both 1786 and 1787 at Stockton. In the following year however output leaped to 1,137t, before falling to 707t and to less than 200t in 1790.[28] The years 1794-1804 were relatively good years. Unfortunately there was no return for shipwrights working on the Tees in the 1804 Admiralty Survey. A Mr Chapplelow, who was sent to buy timber for the government, according to the local historian Heaviside, was the *first that commenced a ship-building yard* on the Tees. Three shipyards were worked at Stockton in the 1780s, one of these by T. & Mark Pye from 1776 to 1790. A yard started at Portrack was soon abandoned. Thomas Haws built 24 vessels in the period 1782-1790, the largest being the *Aurora* [186t]. After his death in 1810, his son continued the yard and 40 vessels were built during 1790-1805, including the large *Highland Lass* [556t]. Other notable ships were the *Tottenham* [517t] launched in April 1802 for the East India trade, and the *Experiment* [750t]. Fine vessels were also built by William Mellanby who took over the Headlam yard and by Henry Markham who occupied the original Haw's yard up to 1815.

Speculative building.

Building a vessel *on spec* in the hope of finding a buyer was a regular feature of wood shipbuilding. Substantial evidence exists from the 18th century of this practice. In 1754 at South Shields, Robert Wallis offered *a New pink-sterned Vessel ... well built with Joiners' Work etc. completed.* John Wallis in November 1766 was selling a new ship *now on the Stocks* and in August 1767 he offered *a new Ship ready to launch.* From the Middle Dock ships *on the Stocks* were offered in both 1779 and 1780, the latter, *a good new Ship...380 Tons,* was a substantial vessel for the time. Others offering ships included James Evans - in October 1780 a Brig [14 keels] and a hull which was being built in 1786. Two hulls [220t & 130t] under construction were on offer in August 1801 and further vessels in 1803 and 1804. Broderick was trying to sell the *Mediator lately built* in 1784 and in 1787 Thomas Forsyth offered a new Ship *ready to launch.* Mrs Forster in October 1786 failed to sell a ship she was building and again advertised in December *a Vessel of about 18 Keels, which may be finished in six weeks if required.* In May 1806, Henry Taylor of North Shields wrote: *All the ships building on speculation are so done to employ the builders' apprentices, and to keep a few men in reserve for the purpose of repairing ships.*[29] He suggested that builders could lose 10% on speculative building. At South Shields Nicholas Fairles had three ships on his hands, for which as a builder his prime costs were £14,700 and although of *the first quality*, he could not sell them for 10% below his prime cost. In October 1811 Nicholson & Horn offered a new ship [163 tons burthen], which could be finished in a month. Leading shipbuilders such as Temple and Bulmer began work on vessels without a customer; in March 1812 Temple offered a *nearly ready* new ship for sale. As shown above 4 out of 5 vessels were being built on speculation in March 1814 on the Wear! Sunderland shipowner Henry Tanner explained in 1833 *they are mostly built ... upon speculation* and vessels were *lying six months after they are launched before they are sold* and *many ... are sold under very disadvantageous circumstances, from necessity.* Many of the smaller yards were worked on credit from timber merchants, who would also take over unsold vessels. Ships might be on the stocks for months, in various states of completion, while buyers were sought and then completion and outfitting would be related to the intended trade of the purchaser.

---

[28] Statistical comparisons pose problems for example, *Account... of Ships and Vessels* [1806] listed by tons only vessels built at Stockton 1790-1 and 1800-1: total tons [vessels]:*1790*- 516t [4];*1791* -661t [5];*1800*- 748t [5];*1801*- 250t [3]. The tonnages do not match those in *Cust 36/5*. Size of largest vessel by year -320t, 318t, 296t & 130t.

[29] Papers printed by *The Society of Ship-owners of Great Britain 1807* letter dated 2 May 1806: *There are employed four frigates or sloops, a gun brig, and two schooners for the government, on which are employed about 400 shipwrights, who, but for this employment would have been turned adrift.*

Naval Building on the Tyne and at Berwick.

In May 1806 government work was probably keeping about 400 shipwrights in work. During the Napoleonic war the following vessels were built for the Admiralty [with merchant ton equivalent]:

ROW at St Peters		guns	MerET	TEMPLE		guns	MerET
1804	*Acute*	12	340	1806	*Pandour*	22	920
1804	*Bouncer*	12	340	1806	*Crocodile*	22	920
1805	*Starling*	12	340	1807	*Banter*	22	920
1805	*Strenuous*	12	340	1807	*Rosamund*	24	920
1806	*Magpie*	2	160	1807	*Queen Mab*	26	920
1806	*Jackdaw*	2	160	1808	*Cornelia*	32	909
1806	*Skylark*	16	760	1809	*Nereus*	42	1900
1806	*Emulous*	18	760	1809	*Saldanha*	36	2400
1806	*Alacrity*	18	760	HURRY			
1808	*Shearwater*	10	470	1806	*Raleigh*	18	760
1808	*Woodlark*	10	470	TODD at Berwick			
1808	*Bucephalus*	32	976	1805	*Forward*	12	340
				1808	*Rover*	18	760

This was a tiny fraction, less than 3%, of Admiralty work done in merchant yards. Admiralty orders were concentrated in the south with more than half placed on the Thames. It seems rather surprising that Hurry, undoubtedly a more experienced shipbuilder than Temple, got only one of 23 ships listed, the *Raleigh* delivered in 1806. Clearly Temple and his foremen were not experienced enough to tackle the problems of naval vessels and meet the agreed delivery dates.[30] Three class 6th rate frigates, 540t, with 22 guns, were contracted to be completed in twelve months at just under £9,400 each, or £17 10s per ton.[31] What may have been the *finest* of Temple's frigates, the *Saldanha* of 36 guns, was launched on 8 Dec 1809. Two years later, she was tragically lost with almost all her crew. Although the *Crocodile* was launched a week ahead of contract, four of the other vessels were about a year beyond contract. Amongst the penalties for late delivery were: £200 on *Queen Mab*, £250 on *Nereus* and £300 on *Saldanha*. William Row had a rather better delivery record, although for being eleven months overdue on the *Bucephalus* he paid £150 and £100 each on *Shearwater* and *Woodlark*, each about 14 weeks late. However small a fraction of national output this naval work was it was a very important contribution to local employment over the years 1804-9.

Work & pay at Laings on the Wear in 1800-1.

A wage book for 1800-1 for Laings on the Wear has survived, which provides an insight into precise earnings and employment. Fluctuations within a single year were clearly shown in the wage bill and numbers employed throughout 1800 by the Laings [diag 3.09 below]. Over the year as a whole apprentices accounted for 56% of the days paid for, journeymen shipwrights for just under 26% and borers 7%, together almost 90% of the total days worked [contract work would reduce this percentage a little]. The total workforce varied between 56 and 87 and the apprentices were never fewer than 32, and increased to 41. On two particular weeks there were only 12 shipwrights in the yard and 38 apprentices; the greatest number of shipwrights working in a given week was 35 and average was just over 20. Shipwrights with their apprentices constituted at least 80% of the workers employed; three typical pay weeks were as follows:

payweek	apprent.	shipwright	borer	sawyer	hewer	blacksmith	total	
#10	36	19	4	2	2	4	69	*[1 joiner]*
#23	41	23	13	2	2	1	83	
#48	39	31	6	2	2	4	85	

---

[30] The *Crocodile* and *Pandoura* [renamed in 1807: *Cossack*] were both broken up at Portsmouth in 1816; also broken up were *Cornelia* [1814 at Sheerness] and *Nereus* [1817 at Deptford]; the *Banter* was lost in October 1808; two were sold by the Admiralty - *Rosamund* in December 1815 and *Queen Mab* [*Coquette*].

[31] When on 22 October 1805 two new contracts [for two sloops and two larger frigates] were signed with Temple none of the earlier warships were yet launched.

At this time Laings employed men in the separate trade of *borer*, who prepared the holes for treenails &c. Many years later when the Wear shipwrights had a well established trade union they attempted to secure this work for their members. During 1800 the shipwrights averaged $5\frac{1}{2}$ days a week although they did on occasion work overtime as did the apprentices. Less than a full week was usual [see chap 7] and of course that meant that average take-home pay was normally about 8% less than the full weekly wage. Other trades also worked less than full weeks, for example in the second pay week the hewers, sawyers and borers were each employed for five days and one borer for four. As always there were the blacksmiths and

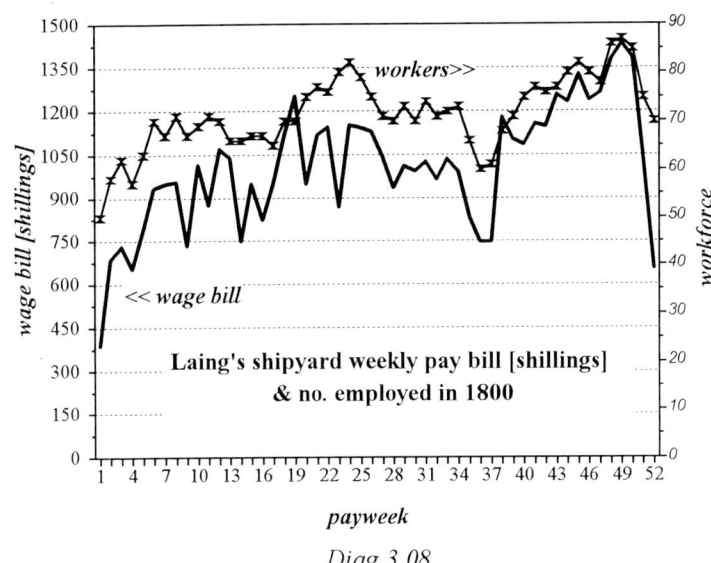

Diag 3.08

their strikers, usually three or four being employed. A joiner was not regularly employed, sometimes working in the yard for two or three days a week as required. This work was also done on contract. Another trade periodically needed was that of the rigger. The *Margaret* was launched on 31 March and probably for work on this vessel riggers were paid for 30 days work in April and May; three men in one pay period and four in the next.

The apprentices were listed first in Laing's wagebook with the amount of their *weekly pay*. Normally, the entry was not by days as it is for all the other workers; where however they have carried out extra work this is recorded in days. When an apprentice was absent from work, a deduction was entered. Under *extras* some of the older, and more able apprentices, were paid at higher rates. An example of this was the first pay week of the year, which included the Christmas and New Year, very few journeymen were at work [the total for all 9 men who worked was only $10^{3}/_{4}$ days]. This enhanced apprentice earnings and the following are examples of apprentice's *Extra* [the normal weekly pay is in brackets]. Sharp whose rate was 7s/week got 14s for 4 days:

Sharp 4 days @ 3s 6d. [7s /week]   *Adamsons* 4 days @ 3s 6d [8s /week]
Horsburgh 1 day @ 3s 6d. [7s /week]   *Christie* 1 day @ 3s 6d. [7s /week]
Lobin 1 day @ 3s 6d [7s 6d /week]   *Peter* 2 days @ 2s. [4s /week]
Carse 1 day @ 2s [6s 6d /week]   *Morris* 2 days @ 1s 6d. [6s 6d /week]

Shipwrights were paid 51d a day for the first two months of 1800 and from then until the end of January 1801. For a week there were no journeymen working and they then returned at 48d/day. The two rates for hewers show an interesting aspect of pay division. Michael and Gilbert Hodgson, as hewers, began the year on 45d a day and when later Gilbert was replaced by John Shaw, Michael's pay was increased to 54d and Shaw was only paid 36d. So the cost of hewing remained at 90d. Sawyers working in pairs were also not equally paid; at the outset it was 42d and 32d and the *top* man, literally in the act of sawing, was increased to 45d in February and in August to 46d. Blacksmith John Reed was a key figure, who started at 36d/day; his fellow *smiths* got 32d and 26d. Like other trades there was an increase in February, an extra 3d a day for Reed, later another 1d to 40d when his fellows got 34d and 32d. Both the number of borers and their daily pay fluctuated considerably. Those employed varied from three to as many as 13; in January some were paid 30d and one 26d. Eight weeks later the top rate was 36d with others on 34d /day. Thomas Sharer was employed throughout, though his job was not identified; he was paid 108d a week until the last pay of January, when he was paid an extra 36d a week for the previous five weeks and continued to work at the new rate of 144d for the rest of the year. There were also casual hirings as when labourers were paid 182d for *Digging a Dock to launch the Hope* at the end of July ; likewise the 84d to *lads* for bringing the *Leander* round from Shields. Labourers do not appear as part of the yard's normal workforce. A woman entered as *Nelly* was paid 30d in the first week of February *for Cleaning Oakum*. Further earnings were three weeks at 24d and one at 30d and finally a mere 6d. Six weeks later the entry was simply *Cleaning oakum* 48d but *Nelly* was back in November earning in one week 33d and two weeks later 24d. In a week in May, 90d was paid to *Women for Carrying water into New Ship*. Over the whole of 1800 those employed averaged less than 15s/week [30d/day], if however apprentices are excluded the shipwrights averaged about 22s 7d/week.

Some summary comments.

As noted at the start of this chapter, the absence of competition from North America provided an opportunity for the advance in shipbuilding, when it was an industry not making heavy demands on capital. When wartime demands diverted some output from the River Thames and other parts of the south, this for a short time at least helped the advance in new ports such as the Wear and Blyth. Over the years 1800-13, Sunderland merchant tonnage equalled that of the Tyne & Blyth. The movement between the three main centres on a 5-year moving average is shown in diag 3.10. Older centres were overtaken and they did not recover to the same extent from the depressed years 1804-8, almost an early foretaste of many subsequent depressions. Both ports and individual yards experienced substantial fluctuations.

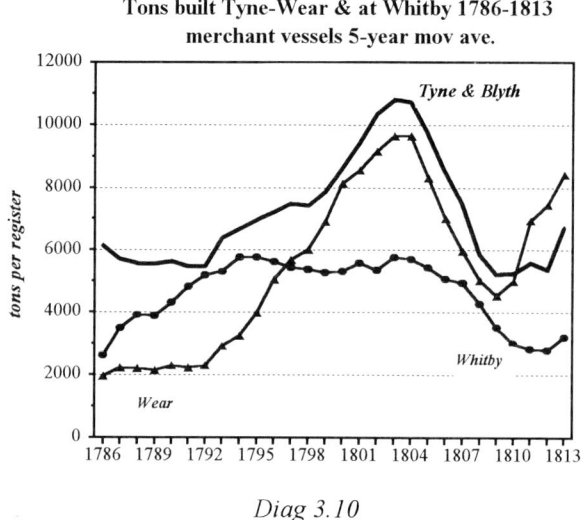

Diag 3.10

Shipyards lower down the Tyne took the lead away from those in Newcastle as was perhaps inevitable with many alternative competing demands on river frontage. A higher proportion of young workers was also an important factor at Sunderland, whereas the longer established centres naturally had more older men. The overall output over the period is shown below in diag 3.11. During the Napoleonic wars the region built about one-third of the merchant tonnage launched in England & Wales. By 1815 the basis was laid for a great advance in north east shipbuilding.

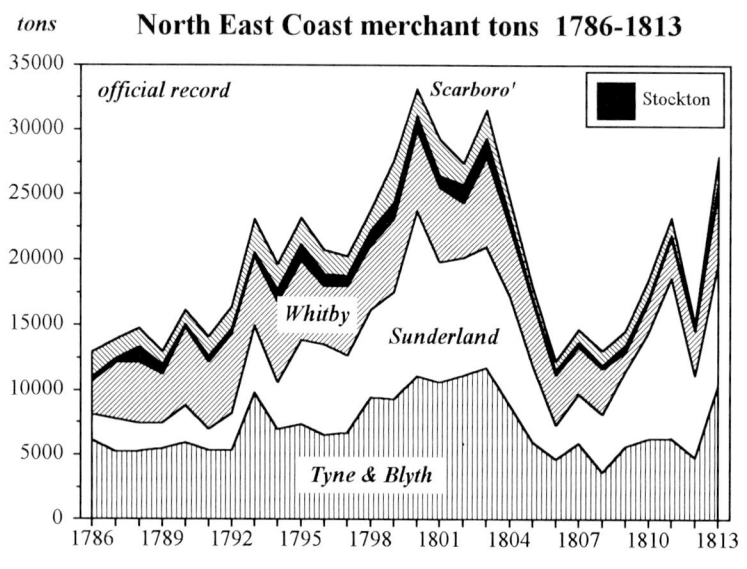

Diag 3.11

Chapter 4

Shipbuilding methods and the Changeover from Wood to Iron Hulls.

One of our ablest maritime historians, Farr, described the setting up of a wood shipyard: *it was a simple matter to set up launching ways and keel blocks, dig a saw pit, and build a lean-to for a small forge.* This was the usual very elementary procedure to begin merchant ship building. In addition a steaming oven was needed, and usually a crane or similar lifting device. On the banks of the Wear the increase from 36 to 76 yards in four boom years of the 1840s was confirmation of how little capital or equipment was needed. Yards could, of course, equally easily disappear. For centuries naval yards such as the Royal Dockyards were very substantial and more elaborate establishments, employing hundreds of men.[1] In the wood era this was of no matter on the north east coast. Advertisements for the sale of shipyards at South Shields provide summary views how the yard was presented to a potential buyer. Two examples from 1821, firstly Evan's yard possessed *Advantages for a Timber or Raff Yard superior to any other on the Banks of the Tyne ... extensive Sheds, a large Saw Pit and powerful Crane.* The Middle Docks consisted of *two Double Docks ... the Building Yards, Steamers, Cranes, Warehouses, Sheds, Lofts, Blacksmiths' Shop.* These Tyne facilities were more developed than the typical Wear yard. Capital equipment for building typical merchant ships was more akin to a jobbing builder than a cotton factory.

The work of the Shipwright - An Exacting Skill.

Noah's Ark,[2] the subject of the Shipwrights' Guild miracle play performed at Newcastle, may serve as a symbol of the ancient craft of the shipwright whose task it was to shape the multiplicity of timbers in a ship, erect these individual members successfully and then render them watertight. There was a multitude of complex shapes [see examples in diagrams]. A writer on the East India trade in 1701 stated:

> of all things to be performed by the labour of Man, perhaps there is not a more variety in anything than in a Ship: The manufacture of the Keel, the Ribbs, the Planks, the Beams, the Shrouds, the Masts, the Sails, almost thousands of other Parts, together with the composition of the several Parts, require as much variety of skill.

He proposed the organisation of mass production - an *Artist whose whole and constant employment shall be the manufacture of that single part.* The demand for wood ships was never so great or consistent as to allow such specialisation to occur.[3] Each shipwright was required to have the skill of shaping and erecting all those different parts and, in the typical merchant yard, without what would later be an engineering drawing. A distinguished London shipbuilder, Ditchburn, stated the frames alone of 1,000t wood ships required 1,600 pieces of timber and obviously as many joints, and the ship as a whole many more pieces.

A recognition of the very physically demanding nature of the shipwright's work was reflected in the 1804 Admiralty inquiry, which asked for a count of the men over 50 years. The shipwright's work according to the Victorian social investigator Henry Mayhew was *very hard, and demands not merely the customary skills and quickness of the handicraftsman, but great manual strength; they must either carry heavy*

---

[1] In March 1814 the numbers in the various Royal Dockyards were, [in brackets = *shipwrights & caulkers*] : Portsmouth 4,257 [1,562], Plymouth 3,869 [1,432], Chatham 2,672 [850], Woolwich 2,026 [627]; Deptford 1,886 [582] and Sheerness 888 [316]. In 1830 the figures were Portsmouth 2,079 [917], Plymouth 2,123, Chatham 1,382 [602], Woolwich 742; Pembroke 454 and Sheerness 470. Highly sophisticated techniques of shipbuilding existed in 15th century Venice and 18th century Holland.

[2] In 1921, a shipwright at Smith's Dock claiming the *most interesting job* in the yard wrote: *It is an undoubted fact that my trade is the Aristocrat of trades in general, having as its Patron, one Noah, of Biblical fame, whose masterpiece, the Ark was a triumph of the Shipwright's art, and independent of the aid of all the other trades.*

[3] Two centuries later in the 1914-8 War, a programme of wood shipbuilding was successfully carried out, with elements of mass production, in the USA. *Considerations of the East India Trade* [1701] in McCulloch edit *Early English Tracts of Commerce* pp 592- . [1856 - repr 1952]

beams or woodwork from the workshops to the ships...and with these must ascend and descend ladders. [It was more usually to have a ramp]. The arduous character, and indeed hazardous nature, of shaping timber with adze should not be overlooked. Mayhew described the caulker's work is *especially hard* and working *in all positions of the body - recumbent or half recumbent* added to his fatigue. When working on the bottom of the ship they had hardly room to stand. *Accidents were not infrequent* even at the prestigious naval yards[4]. Lloyd's Chief Surveyor Creuze stated in 1845 that shipwrights in the Royal Dockyards were *frequently pensioned from hurt before they are invalided from age*. A London shipbuilder, G F Young in 1848 spoke of *the great liability to frightful Casualties*, which a working Shipwright faced. The death rate for shipwrights, aged 20-25 years, in 1860-1, was very much higher than for males generally, nearly 12% of the deaths among shipwrights in seven northern towns were in this age group, compared with 7.2% of all males in the Northern Counties. Shipwrights on the Wear wanted their infirm brethren to act as labourers, when their strength no longer enabled them to justify a craftsman's wage. The shipwright's skill continued to be acknowledged. William White, the distinguished Director of Naval Construction and one time manager of Armstrong's Elswick naval shipyard, wrote in 1877: *Manual work is ... almost a necessity in the greater part of building a wood ship*. In contrast iron was obtainable in almost all of the sizes and form required and so *less* [was] *required in fashioning and combining the pieces than in the case with wood. Anyone who has witnessed the rapid progress of framing an ordinary iron ship compared with the erection of the ribs of a wood ships, cannot fail to have noticed the much greater simplicity of operation required in the iron ships*. A Sunderland shipwright stressed this point in 1855, arguing that iron shipbuilding was *the introduction of machinery into the art of shipbuilding as well as an entirely new class of skilled and unskilled workmen... It is unskilled labour's opportunity in shipbuilding*. Their skill in erecting and aligning the frames and other such tasks extended over into working iron. Adaptability in the shipwright was particularly important in repair work and many of these men would be switched between *new* and *old* work. The shipwright was the central dominant figure in the wood yard as shown in the wages paid to the various workers building the wood ship *Hesperia* at Doxfords in 1863 [diag 4.01]. By this time iron beams were generally used on wood hulls. Earlier the workforce at Laings in 1800 illustrated the total dependance on the shipwright, at that time boring, drilling holes, was done by a separate group of workers, this work was later recovered by the shipwrights on the Wear.

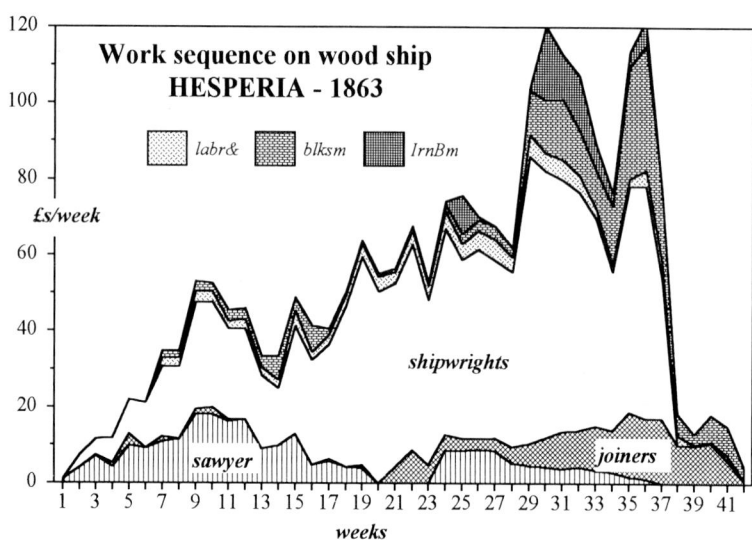

Diag 4.01

The shipwright's tools.

Shipwrights owned their own personal tools and the more prudent saved regularly to enable them to keep them in good condition and renewed as required. John Horsley's excellent account *Tools of the Maritime Trades* should be consulted for a detailed account of these tools. A Swedish book of 1691, contained an illustration numbering 46 shipwright's tools. Work in the mould loft required a scrieve hook [which might be made from an old file], a scribing knife, sweeps [rather large compasses, arms up to about 54"] and for a similar purpose a pair of trammel heads. Bevel gauges and rulers were also required. Straight lines were

---

[4] Approximately one worker in every six lost time at the Portsmouth Dockyard during 1830-2 due to *hurt*, a total of 4,771 days in an average year, injuries to shipwrights were much more common. Over those three years 72 of every 100 shipwrights suffered a *hurt*, this trade accounted for 60% of the time lost but only 40% of the workers!

made by a well chalked string stretched between two nails and they *pinged* to mark the line. The peg-poll adze was the great symbol of the shipwright's craft and he also used a variant, the scarphing or strap adze; at least three types of dupping adzes were sometimes used. A wide range of axes were used. Horsley described the shipwright's axe as a large bladed version of the Kent felling axe and there was a Newcastle ship axe. Hammers were needed for many purposes, as were a variety of chisels and gouges. Fifteen types of caulking irons were available in addition to the *long-arm* horsing type. A crucial part of the caulking was the caulking mallet, Horsley wrote *the caulking mallet sings while it works, the note it makes when it strikes the iron being quite musical*. The head was of lignum vitae, beech or American *live* oak. For heavier

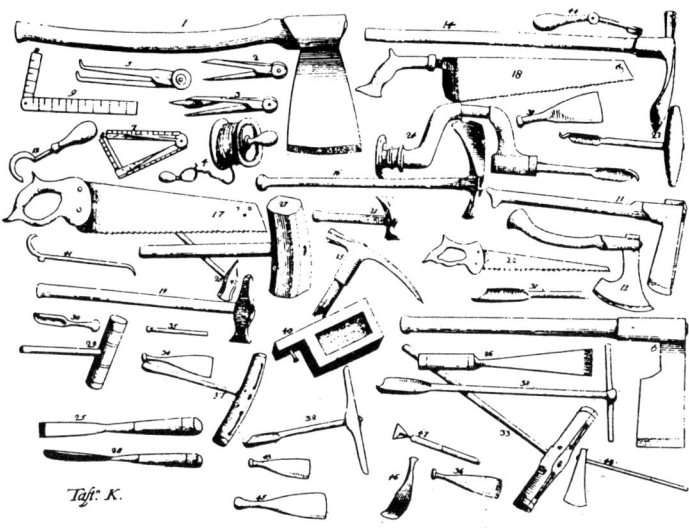

The shipwright's tools from 17 century book.

work the *bettle, bittle* or caulking hammer was used, the ends iron bound to prevent splitting. Tapering iron rings were used on the mallet. Long spouts, to reduce spillage, were provided on the pitch ladles used on the decks and a stiff bristled brush called a mop was used for applying the pitch on the sides of the vessel. A wooden oil box, with linseed oil, was used to lubricate the *irons* to stop them sticking. There was also a rake or hoe for removing old oakum. For boring holes there was a range of augers and bits, gimlets and braces. Many other tools were used such as planes, clamps and scrapers.

Building a wooden ship.

An important economic factor for the shipbuilder was the availability of adequate space so that the timber could be spread out in order to enable the shipwright to select the most suitable piece for each part of the vessel under construction, thereby reducing waste. Liverpool shipbuilders stated in 1850 that a lack of such space was one of the explanations for their lack of prosperity.[5] Their yards were *too narrow for canting the timber* and it was claimed that as much space could be secured at Sunderland for £50 as at Liverpool for £500, almost certainly an exaggerated comparison. Bartram on the Wear in the mid-1850s paid £20 a year rent for his modest yard and a further £10 for the Quay he used. Laings paid a rent of £300 in the 1840s. It was also of course true that land was likely to be much cheaper on the banks of the Wear than on the Tyne. The annual rental, for local taxation purposes, offers some evidence of property values. In 1812, South Shields docks were rated as follows: Richard Bulmer and Nicholson each at £100, Wright at £75, Metcalfe at £66, Laing and Forsyth at £60 and Blackburn at £40. Very much lower was £7 for Attley, Swan & Co's shipbuilding yard in 1807, and that of James Evans at £4 in both 1807 and 1812. At Sunderland in 1803, Robson's dock and shipyard was rated at £67 10s and the great rope works of Grimshaw at £90. Philip Laing's dock was rated at £75 in 1827 and during the late 1820s building yards were rated from £12 to £40, mostly less than £20.

Sawing.

Many builders purchased timber in logs rather than in the form of planks and although some had their own sawyers they also contracted for sawing. In 1800 Laing paid 3s per 100' for sawing 511'. In June and December 1858 John Brown carried out sawing for Bartram. The total of 9360' of Yellow Pine was sawn

---

[5] see *Shipbuilding in Liverpool* - evidence before a committee of the Town Council [1850] - Peter Chaloner, shipbuilder since 1805; Clover and Royden *size not enough ... crammed space ... moving timber.*

at 24d per 100' but the 2028' of American Elm at the much higher charge of 42d per 100'. These prices were lower than those agreed between the Master Shipbuilders and Sawyers on 4 June 1857, which were *per 100 feet: 78d* -Iron wood; *60d* -African Oak, Australian Oak and Greenheart; *48d* -Elm, Teak, Beech & Birch; *45d* -English and other Oaks, Mahogany and Pitch Pine; *36d* - Red Pine, White Wood, Dantzic, and Memel; *30d* -Yellow Pine. The basic rates were subject to qualifications, such as 24" deep or more an extra 2%; a measure and a half for circular, feather-edge, bevelled work and old wood. Non-plank work, such as knees and stanchions, were 20' each, minimum, and *Keel-scarf 15 feet, Keelson do. 20 feet, Stem and stern-post do. 10 feet each.*

Ships plans.

With the exception of naval vessels or those for such vast companies as the East India Co, detailed drawings were not prepared. No doubt some sketches were made by the master shipwright or his foreman but the starting point for shape and form was usually a half model to a suitable scale from which the shapes of the various parts of the ship could be taken. Later the ship's lines were laid out full size in the mould loft from scaled drawings. Many vessels were however probably built without even such facilities. Robert Thompson when he was building in the late 1840s used *an inn tap room near the yard served as a designing office.*[6] Only after the building of iron ships began were drawing offices usually found in north east shipyards, unless the occupants were hidden from the census of occupations. Before 1800 the conventional sheer draught plan had emerged.[7] A plan of a collier brig published in 1804 illustrates such a drawing [see below]. The grid of lines enabled all the various shapes to be formed. The profile was the engineer's drawing front elevation [marked F] and directly beneath a half breadth plan [P]. In the side elevation [S] on the left, either side of the centre line is presented the cross-section at various points along the length of the vessel. Economy of line was achieved by the after-body being drawn on the left-hand side of the centre line and the fore-body on the right-hand side.

Plan of a collier brig published in 1804

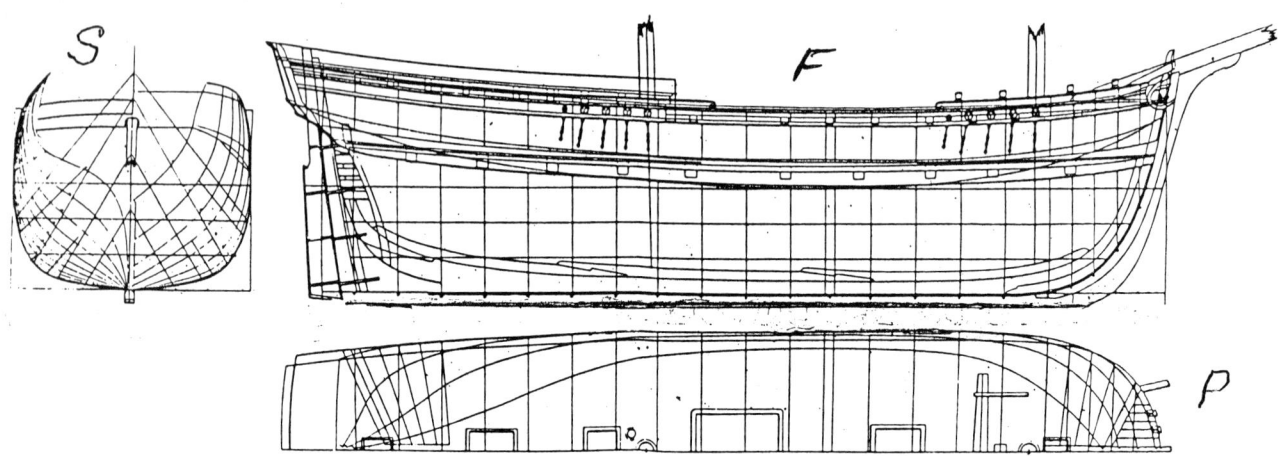

T.R. Blankley in his *Naval Expositor* of 1750 set out the names of each specific part of a ship. In the order of building on the stocks, he numbered 81 components. The following is a brief outline of the main stages of building a wooden vessel [see also sketches]. The keel blocks were set up on ground which was capable of taking the weight of the ship and with a slope to assist the launching. To secure adequate strength where more than one piece of wood was used for a part of the ship's structure, the two pieces of timber were

---

[6] In the 1860s the top floor room of the East House Inn was used for *laying off* - the rear of the Inn faced shipyard.

[7] A conventional system of presenting ships lines developed from the mid-17th century. Illustrations from about 1586 show a shipwright's drawing office and sheer plans, where complete cross-sections appear on the elevation. In 1670 Deane's drawings have the fore and aft sections drawn as half views either side of the centre line, which as became the usual practice. [as the collier plan of 1804]

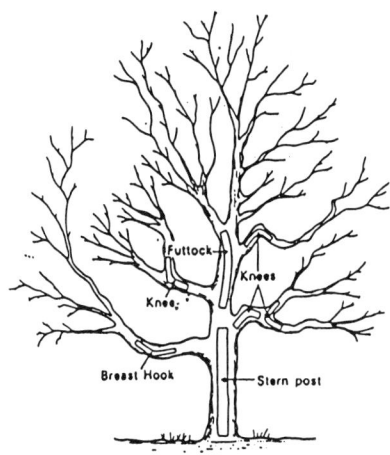

This sketch shows how different timbers were selected from particular parts of a tree

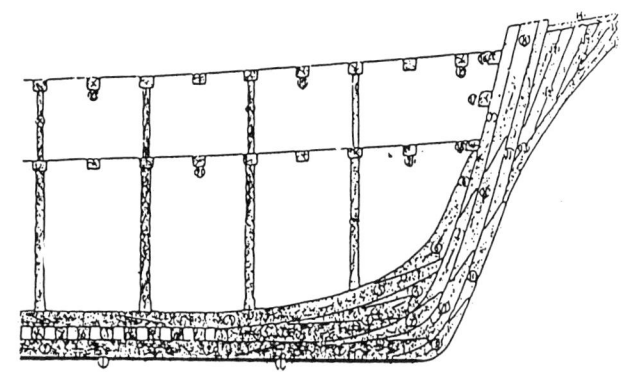

Part of drawing showing the variety of timber shapes in the forward end of a ship [from Paache]

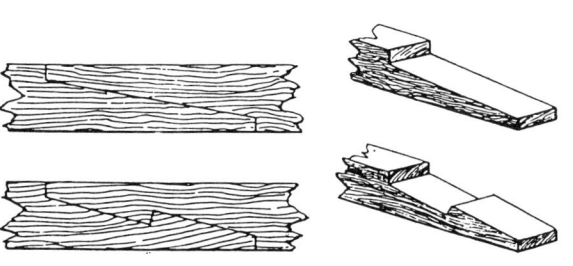

Examples of scarph joints

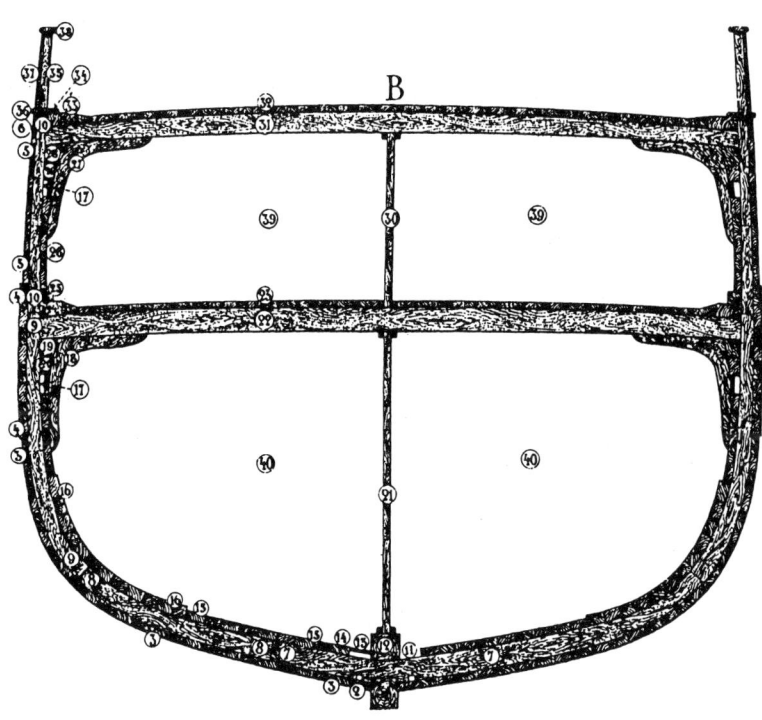

Structure of wood ship mid-section this shows wood knees [Paache]

Part of Carmichael Drawing showing early stage of construction & nearly completed ship

On iron ship on the left and a wood ship [fast clipper given length breath ratio] on Wm Pile's letter head

scarphed together. To form the keel timbers were joined in this way [on a small vessel if possible a single piece of the required length was used]. Some shipowners specified the number of pieces to be used, often three. The prepared keel was laid on the blocks, then followed the scarphing of the stem and sternpost to the keel. Transom and fashion pieces were then assembled to provide the main shape for the stern, and shored to keep in correct position. Floors, which were the lowest and only timbers of the frame to cross the keel, were set up and temporarily bolted to the keel. Suitable flexible lengths of fir were temporarily attached to the outer ends as a ribband to hold position. This provided an indication of the shape before the floors were firmly fastened and then the keelson was placed over floors and permanently bolted right through the keel. In order to work up to the level of the deck, elementary staging and gangways were prepared, resembling scaffolding on early building sites. Poles were driven into the ground and planks were laid on cross timbers fixed to each pole. Access to this staging was by ladder and / or gangways. This staging was dismantled and re-erected for the next vessel built.

Suitably shaped timbers were prepared as futtocks [1st-2nd-3rd]. On any vessel these futtocks were required in many shapes and sizes because the hull changes its form, from amidship to stem and stern. When the futtocks were assembled together the frames were formed and the structure then resembled the bones of a fish curved upwards. Another ribband was added when frames reached the breadth of hull. The first futtock overlapped the floor head and the heel of the second futtock and so on. Planks were fitted across the frames to keep them in place until the deck beams were fitted. The outer face frames were bevelled to allow a good fit for hull planking and the planking usually went from the main wales downwards and from the keel upwards. As this was completed the ribbands were removed. A steam oven was used to enable planks to be bent more easily to the form of the hull. *Strake* was the term used for a line of planking extending the length of the vessel; it was also used for iron plates. *Wales* was the strake of thick plank at about the load-water line. As with other sections which could not be obtained in one piece, the beams were scarphed and held in position by lodging or hanging beams. Sections such as knees could only come from particular parts of a tree, the scarcity of which helped to inspire the early adoption of iron knees in Britain. Iron knees were cheaper. An American naval architect J V Griffith disapproved in 1856:
> Iron has often been used for knees, and continues [to be] in England and her provinces. The scarcity of forest grown knees has compelled this course; but we have never seen the hanging or dagger knee of iron that bore a proper comparison in strength with the well-grown white oak knee; and the only thing ... in their favour [they] occupy less room.

Once the beams were firmly secured, the decks were laid. All the various components of the vessel were held together either with iron or copper bolts and extensively with *treenails* [also called *trunnels*][8], which were round pieces of timbers usually from 12" to 30" long. Some *treenails* 36" and 48" long, made of fir, were used in the north east; oak was also used for *treenails*. Caulking to make the vessel water-tight also forced the whole structure under tension, which increased the rigidity of the structure [this term was carried over into iron building but the operation was different- see below]. Although in the Government's naval yards and a small number of merchant yards this caulking was given to a separate group of workers, on the north east coast it was shipwright's work. Oakum or unpicked rope junk was driven with a caulking iron into the space between the outer ships planks of the hull and deck and then hot pitch or similar resinous material was poured on to form protection against water. White oakum was prepared with untarred rope. Many high class ships had copper bottoms, in fact the *copper bottom* was usually a yellow alloy metal. This material was used to kill the animal and vegetable products that fixed themselves to ship's bottoms, particularly in tropical waters or if they were stationary for long periods.

A brief comment on costs. Although Bartram, at Sunderland, bought crooks [used for knees] from Stettin, he relied mainly on iron knees, which cost 17s 6 to 18s a cwt. On Wearside Mary Lightfoot was one of the

---

[8] An additional year was allowed ... if fastened externally with treenails, and with copper or yellow metal bolts, to the exclusion of iron, in the outside planking, keel, keelson, deadwood, stem and sternpost, ... the hanging knees and riders, hooks and crutches [bolts ... must pass through the outside planking].

main suppliers of oakum, which cost Bartram 23s -24s a cwt and pitch cost him about 9s-6d a cwt: he spent about £30 a year on oakum and pitch. Doxfords purchased oakum on a regular basis from Durham gaol. A copper bottom was a very expensive addition to a ship's first cost; in 1848 Money Wigram stated that a 12 year ship, copper bottomed ready for sea would have a mean price of £24. Bartram paid £241 for yellow metal sheathing for the *Sarah Jane* [366t] in 1866. There would in addition be a cost for fitting the sheathing as well as the underlying felt or paper. One owner estimated an extra cost of 20s -25s a ton to sheath a bottom; Bartram's metal alone was 13.17s/ton.[9]

Fitting Out.

After the hull was launched much more work remained to be done in fitting out. This fitting out work and generally preparing a ship for sea was always a most important matter but tends to be neglected, as though the vessel was finished when the craft entered the water. Many other trades in addition to the shipwright were involved in finishing the vessel after its launch. The Letterbook of Ralph Carr shows that it cost £1537 14s 4d to complete the *Mally & Jenny* ready to go to sea in 1752. This total included the provisioning of the ship [£100] and £55.81 spent by the owner in building. The construction costs are set out opposite. The bill for shipwright Charlton[10] and the iron work required for the hull was just under 60% of the total. The ropes cost about 40% of the shipwright's bill and the sails nearly 20%. The *Shipbuilding Outfit* included - the masts, the yards, the sails, anchors, chains, ship chandlery, and a variety of cooking utensils, colours, spy glass *&c., &c., and a Variety of little Things*. The type of vessel and its trading purpose determined its outfit and this could dramatically effect the final cost of the ship and the work required. Scarborough shipbuilder and shipowner, Tindall stated in May 1848: *The Expense of building Ships is in the Outfit. At Scarborough for an Eight Years Ship it would be 8l. a Ton, and Four Guineas for the Outfit.* Ships of a higher class would have more costly outfits. The sums entered for rigging in some Wear builder's account books do not make it clear whether this is for contract work or supplies, it was not unusual for yard to recruit workers to carry out such work although probably regularly using contractors with the same employees. The hull for Edward's *Elizabeth* in 1831 cost £1,697 and the *outfit* £706; that was a typical ratio for wood ships. Bartram's *Olive Branch* [200t] cost for rope was £118.5, anchors & chains £142 and £137 for sail. The making of masts, blocks and rigging &c was usually carried out by specialist works; special timber supplies were required for masts.[11]

A summary of cost of ship 1752 MALLY & JENNY

		£ s d
Wm Charlton for	*Hull*	700-
Wm Cramlington	*Ropes*	283- 7- 6
Adam Bird	*Ironwork*	158-19- 0
Thoms Durham	*Sailcloth*	76-14- 5
Isaac Kirton	*Sailmaker*	59-18- 5
Natl Taverner	*Blocks*	22
Masts Yards & Booms unmade		43-16-10
Robt Porter	*Boats*	16- 8
Geo Lowes	*Joiner Work*	23- 2-11½
Wm Spoor	*Glazing & painting*	7-10- 0
John Harrison	*Rozen Oil &c*	2-10- 4
Lowes	*Pewter*	10- 4
H Metcalfe	*Cooper*	7-10- 8
Isaac Wilson	*Plumber*	3-19- 3½
Geo Carr	*White Oakum*	1- 7- 7½
John Lothing	*Spikes & Nails*	3-19- 4
Deals for Ship		19-14- 7
J Smith	*Brazier*	7-12- 0
Jhno Cap	*Mast-maker*	13-18- 8
T Matthews	*Butcher*	14- 3- 4
Mrs Gray	*Baker*	3
The Brewers Bill		2- 9s
Isaac Kirton	*Ship Chandler*	5-19- 8
Brown & Shaw	*Checks to Mast*	3-16s
Charge disbursed by self in Building		55-16- 3

Some other craftsmen.

Amongst the other craftsmen regularly involved in shipbuilding were wood carvers, boat builders, blockmakers, blacksmiths, painters and joiners. Many wood ships needed the blessing of a figure head.

---

[9] *Sel Ctte on the Navigation Laws* 1848. Tindall said a 12yr ship could be built for £12-10s + outfit £5 and another £1-5s for *coppering* in all £18-15s, significantly less than Money Wigram's figure. yellow metal - 70% copper & 30% tin. Barry's evidence in *Sel Ctte on Manufactures...* 1833 is printed as *30l.* per ton, [a misprint for 30s!]

[10] Charlton enrolled his first apprentice in 1749 and by 1769 had registered seven.

[11] As with knees, iron masts were built for some wooden hulls.

Such symbols were carved with skill, and often the craftsman's love, and were probably always specialist work. The Lindsay family regularly carved for Laing and later enjoyed the patronage of Queen Victoria. Lindsay carried out the work on the *Anne* in 1819 for £5 5s and in the following year on the *Thisbe* for £8 11s; his work on vessels in the 1860s were between £34 and £63 but may well have included more than the figure head. Others who worked for Laings were Wilson and Tate. R S Branfoot carried out this work for Bartram, costs varied from £5-15s to £6-15s. Any boats required for a ship were usually purchased from specialist builders; for example in 1866 Bartram was supplied with two for the *Sarah Jane* for £26.50 by James Aitken and three for *Waterlily* by Potts & Burn [£36]. On occasion the shipbuilder's own men might do such work. The blacksmith was universally required in this as other industries. Painting, which became much more significant on iron vessels, was frequently subcontracted to painters. Bartram's 1855 accounts show painting costs as £143-15s, and although such work does not appear in 1856, in 1857 this item at £53-10s was about equivalent to the wages of a labourer a year. In the 1860s Elliott who painted ships for Bartram's ships also worked on two houses he had purchased. The term *carpenter* is frequently used instead of *shipwright* and is the one usually found in account books. However, the work normally associated with a *house carpenter* was in a shipyard performed by *joiners*, as both these trades were wood workers demarcation disputes poisoned relations on all too many occasions [see chap 13].

Timber.

Timbers used in wood construction were often 12" square or even larger. A great diversity of types of wood was used in building a ship and the type of timber played a significant part in the classification which Lloyd's gave the vessel. Lloyd's Rules in 1870 listed twenty different categories of timber.[12] After many years of using British supplies of timber for ship construction, by the beginning of the 19th century the north east shipbuilders were using very large supplies of imported timber from both the Baltic countries, Prussia, Russia and North America. Imports were not unimportant earlier: for example in 1776, timber was brought into Newcastle from Denmark, Norway, Germany and Poland. While all of this was not for shipbuilding, the 115 *middle masts* and 281 *small masts* together with the 26 *Great Masts* were for this purpose. Masts offered particular problems, which Rees pointed out in 1814:

> Masts are long fir trees, or several fir trees coaked or douelled and bolted together...All large masts, previous to the American war, were made in New England, white pine, having been found the highest, and all respects the best suited to the purpose; but since then masts from Riga have been procured. As the largest trees from that country seldom exceed 24" in diameter, and more frequently from 19 to 21.[13]

The oak-knees from Denmark, Norway, Prussia and Germany, in 1776, were for shipbuilding, and probably the oak timber and planks. Poland supplied 4,530 treenails. Oak Timber and knees were imported from Holland and Germany in 1819 into Sunderland as well as the following from Russia and Canada

Russia		*British Northern Colonies*	
Fir Timber	54 loads 36 feet	Birch Timber	86 loads 45 ft
Masts	46 loads 14 feet	Fir Timber	1,601 loads
Masts by tale	70 [number]	Oak Timber	102 loads 34 ft
Spars	c 1,224	Elm Timber	15 loads 29 ft
Fir timber	1,063 loads	Masts	62 loads 47 ft
Oak timber	82 loads 29 feet	Masts by tale	67
Masts	129 loads 27 ft	[a load = 50 cubic feet; roughly 13.5"dia x50']	
Masts by tale	10		

---

[12] East-India Teak; 2. English, African & Live Oak...; Greenheart; 3. Cuba Sabrien, Pencil Cedar...; 4. Danish Oak, other Continental White Oak...; 5. N. Amer. White Oak; 6. Stringy Bark, and Red Cedar; 7. Pitch Pine, Larch, Hackmatack...; 8. Second-hand English Oak &c from group 1 9. Cowdie, Huon Pine; 10. Red Pine; Danzig, Memel, Riga and Amer.; 11. English Ash; 12. Foreign Ash and Rock Maple; 13. American Rock Elm and Hickory; 14. Grey Elm: European and Amer; 15. Black Birch and Black Walnut; 16. Spruce Fir, Scot. Fir & Scandinavian Red Pine; 17. White Cedar; 18. Beech; 19. Yellow Pine; 20. Hemlock

[13] Laing in the 1830s and 1840s used yellow pine and red pine for masts, and some of these came from Quebec, he purchased at least some masts already made, perhaps all of them.

American elm was first brought into Sunderland by shipbuilder Tiffin in 1818. This material became the *material most commonly used* for *Deadwood*[14] in the north east. Surveyor Bayley in 1844 described this as an erroneous practice - *because it is a part of the ship particularly liable to decay if she should be perfectly watertight and ought therefore to be of the most durable material, at least of the same quality as required to be used for the Floors & First Futtocks, the same remarks apply to the Fore Deadwood.* He stated as an example that the elm in the *Sarah* of Grimsby was found to be *perfectly rotten*. Smaller knees were imported at a low rate of duty, however, lower masts, top masts and spars from Riga, Memel, Dantzic or Norway were subject to *nearly to a prohibition* because of duties imposed. The arrival of Sierra Leone oak at Sunderland improved the quality of Wear ships according to the Newcastle shipowner, Thomas Hedley. This timber from Africa was also used at Sunderland for repairs. In 1833, Hedley had 13 ships bound from Sierra Leone to Sunderland *with large cargoes, all laden with oak ... 400 loads of timber in some of them*. Imports had only begun *a few years ago* and the timber was cut into plank at Sunderland, replacing Dantzic plank and Memel oak. It offered *a very great advantage* to the shipbuilder because although English oak was obtainable for *timbers, &c., you cannot get it for planking of lengths equal to Sierra Leone*. One piece was 166' and another piece in West India Dock was 6 loads [i.e. 300 cubic feet - roughly 2' dia 100']. Many Prussian ships brought in timber to Sunderland and took away coal. American fir and ash was generally used. During 1844 a total of 3,395 loads of timber was imported coastwise into Newcastle. The North American Colonies supplied the greatest amount from overseas, including 13,621 loads of *Fir and Hardwood*. There were 4,242 loads of the same timber from Prussia with smaller amounts from Norway & Sweden. Germany with Prussia supplied the bulk of the oak brought in, 1,538 of 1,631 loads. The French supplied nearly two-thirds of the 62,000 treenails imported; the large masts were shared between North America [10] and Russia [6]. From Africa 380 loads of teak were almost certainly intended for the shipyards.

Two Sunderland builders, each with 5 vessels to their credit in 1834, used oak from various sources - English, African, Hambro and other places as the principal timber for the frames and beams. Timber for the outside planking was more varied: a similar range of oaks but also American elm, beech, pitch pine or red pine and in addition to these inside planking included blue gum. Red and yellow pine was used for the decks. It seems likely that the particular timber used may well have as much anything as to what was immediately available. Built in 1836, the *Defence*, a typical vessel, contained seven different types of wood. The oak used came from England, Africa and America, and the planking from the first futtock to the light water mark was *foreign white oak*. Elm from England and America was used for the keel, with the main keelson of African oak and the false keelson of American oak. American elm was used for the outside planking from the keel to the first futtocks; then came the foreign white oak to the light water line; above this it was a combination of English and African oak.[15] Wallis at South Shields in 1844 built a 400t ship with the following mix of timbers:

> Stern Post Africa no.2, a wood of hard grain and pale colour. Upper transon Africa Silver Oak remaining transon English Oak - Inner Post English Oak - deadwood on keel American Elm - next above oak - fore deadwood Africa Silver Oak -lower piece of stern African Mahogany - Upper Piece Africa Apron Silver Oak.

The *Heversham* built at South Shields 20 years later also had bottom planking of American Rock elm. Three inch yellow pine planks were used for the upper deck. This wood was also used for the bowsprit and lower masts while the remainder of the masts, yards &c were of red pine.

---

[14] *Deadwood* was the term for the large pieces of timber fitted on the keel at the stem and stern-post, for the purpose of raising the floor-timbers and bolting the heels of the cant-timbers - these were sloping pieces.

[15] A summary of survey: *Oak English*: bilge planks; ceiling remainder; clamps; light water m.-wales; sheer strakes; wales & black strakes; beams deck & hold; floors; first futtock; futtock other; stem, stern post, transoms &c; top timbers. *Oak African*: clamps; stringers; gunwales; light water m.-wales; sheer strakes; wales & black strakes; waterway; beams deck & hold; keelson main; stem, stern post, transons &c *Oak foreign white*: first futtock-light water mark *Pine yellow*: upper deck; bowsprit; mast lower *Pine red*: mast remainder &c *Elm American*: keel-first futtock heads

Bartram's shipyard spent a total of £10,680 on timber over the years 1855-9. The amount for each year varied and it was £3,250 in 1857. In that year, the yard used oak from Africa, from America deal, elm, red pine, from Quebec yellow pine and elm, spars from Norway and fir from Sweden; also from the Baltic fir and oak, which came from Dantzic and Stettin, together with East India teak and greenheart. More than three quarters of this money was spent on oak, of which 39% in cost terms was English oak. In 1858 more than 84% of the cash spent on timber was for oak. However in 1858 oak only accounted for 53% of expenditure, while East India teak reached almost 27%; this timber was purchased in September 1858 and cost £11-10s [230s] a load. Greenheart was only purchased in 1855-6 [1.35% & 0.67% of timber costs respectively] at 220s / load compared with African oak at 240s a load in 1855. In 1857 English oak plank was at 220s. From the Baltic oak planks were purchased at 142s 6d in 1857 but for only 120s two years later. From Stettin oak logs averaged approximately 100s a load. English oak as timber averaged about 65s a load. The combined purchases of pine, including red and yellow was just over 9%, overwhelmingly yellow pine. Although some yellow pine was bought in 1859 for 65s the average price was 76s. Red pine cost 105s in 1857 but was later available at 90s. The price of the elm was usually about 105s but there was an exceptional purchase in 1856 entered at 47s -6d. Purchases were usually by the load [50 cubic feet], but some pieces such as the keel timber were priced by the foot. Elm was usually used for the keel as in the *Defence* above. Prices per foot for English elm were from 2s 3 to 2s 9d but there were purchases at 1s 3d, presumably for much smaller vessels. More than 20 merchants supplied timber to Bartram during 1855-9 but the bulk of the timber, came from four firms. Overall W W Robson was the dominant timber supplier, accounting for almost 41% in cost terms.

Lloyd's Register and their Surveyors.

A modest Wear shipbuilder Bartram paid about £100 on survey costs during 1855-9, which was then charged at 1s per ton by Lloyd's. There can be no doubt the shipbuilders got good value for money, given the then *primitive* state of what would now be technical support staff. A new era began for Lloyd's register when the two conflicting or competing shipping registers[16] were reconciled in 1834. The Lloyd's surveyor and his managing committee became both the guardians of sound standards of good construction and also the stimulators and teachers of those who wanted to build better vessels. A theme running throughout the history of shipbuilding was the role of Lloyd's' Surveyors in improving the standard of shipbuilding. Bayley wrote in July 1844 they were *most assiduous* in encouraging the Builders *to improve the method of Building*. Those appointed as surveyors were men with direct shipbuilding experience. The first two appointed at Sunderland were John Brunton then aged 32 and John Punshon Denton a year older. Part of the Brunton story has already been related and Denton became a shipbuilder at Hartlepool. Brunton wrote in the *General remarks* on the *Defence*, built in 1836:

> Frame of the ship throughout is all sound and healthy, well wrought and shifted, and regularly spaced; knees and hook, all English oak, good arms and well squared. Quality of planking all good throughout, very well wrought and shifted, and clear of sap or defect; treenails of English oak and blue gum wood, turned, appears all good and sufficient; upper and lower beam fastenings, hooks, &c. all very well fitted and securely bolted and clenched, all copper fastened. Her general appearance is firm and substantial throughout.

A vessel surveyed by Lloyd's in the wood era was allocated a class of a number of *years* [6-7-8…12] accompanied by a letter.[17] To secure a particular classification stated minimum dimensions were required for the various parts of vessels of different tonnages as well as a particular type of timber. Each category of timber was allocated a *year* classification. To achieve the highest A class for 12 years in 1834, the

---

[16] The Register issued by the underwriters [Lloyd's] was known as the *Green Book*. The register issued by the *Society of Merchants, Shipowners and Underwriters* in 1799 was known as the *Red Book*, which was strongly influence by the ship owners.

[17] There is not space here to expand on the classification system - see references in notes. For many years *country-built*, that is not built on the Thames, were automatically given a lower classification. Class A and AE were first class. The *years* related to the period after which a survey was required to retain classification.

whole of the timbering was required to be of English, African or Live Oak or else Teak. [the inset shows the application of these dimensions to the snow *Defence*]. These figures show the substantial size of the timber used. Lloyd's tabulated dimensions up to 2,000t for wooden hulls. In 1870, teak carried a 14 year class, the oaks, in group 2, were allocated 12 years, however the North American White Oak only 8 years, the same as red cedar and pitch pine. These timbers could be used for the lower outside planking [top of Keel to $^2/_5$ of the depth of hold, for 12 year class]. A similar planking class was available for groups 13 & 14 [various elms], although for floors they only rated 7 and 5 years respectively. Group 16, spruce fir, Scandinavian red pine and Scotch fir was only given a 6 year class. A year could be added to all timbers, except teak, *if salted while building* provided according to Rule and *the satisfaction of the Surveyors.*[18]

Wearside builders were quite prepare to challenge Lloyd's Rules and in October 1834 William Gales wrote on behalf of himself and other builders in regard

Timber sizes on the snow Defence of 1836

Length 90' ext breadth 26'6" hold 16'8"
Scantlings of Timber [moulded]

	inches	inches middle	inches ends
Timber	12		
Floors sided	12	$12^1/_2$	$10^1/_2$
1st futtocks	9, 10	$9^1/_2$	
2nd futtocks	10	$8^1/_2$	
3rd futtocks	8, 9	$6^3/_4$	
Top timbers	7, $7^1/_2$	5	
Deck beams [21]	9	9	$5^1/_2$
Hold beams [12]	11	11	8
Keel in three lengths	$10^1/_2$	$9^1/_2$	
Keelson	$10^1/_2$	$14^1/_2$	

Thickness of Planks

Outside	inches	Inside	inches
Keel to bilge	3	Foot waling	3
Bilge planks	$4^1/_2$	Bilge planks	4
Bilge to wales	3	Ceiling in flates	$2^1/_2$
Wales	$4^3/_4$	Ceiling bilge to clamp	4
Topsides	$2^3/_4$	Hold beam clamps	$2^1/_2$
Sheer strakes	$3^1/_4$	Deck beam clamps	$2^1/_2$
Plank sheers	3	Ceiling 'twixt decks	$4^1/_2$
Water-ways	4, 3	Hold beam shelfs [10]	5
Upper Deck	3	Deck beam shelfs	5

to classification related to planking. They contended that good quality elm was a better material to use up to the light water line than either Quebec or Memel oak. This contention was most carefully considered and it was concluded that for that position Quebec oak was not considered equal to foreign white oak but *it did not deem it expedient to recommend any alterations in the Rule*. Attempts by both Gales and Philip Laing to have the years assigned to vessels upgraded were unsuccessful. Too speedy a construction might contributed to the reduction of a ship's class; a Wear hull completed in nine weeks resulted in a reduction. The Surveyors stated *We have reduced this vessel from 10 to 9 years although built of English and African oak, timber and planks thoroughly copper-fastened, on account of being rapidly built and the sternframe imperfect.*

When the first rules were issued for iron ships in 1855, similar tables of dimensions were produced. An important difference was that the dimensions used resulted in the allocation of only three classes - 6, 9 or 12 years. To qualify for 12 years frames were required to be not more that 16" apart, while for a lower class [6 -9 years] it was 18". For a 200t vessel ½" garboard strakes qualified for 12 years, $^7/_{16}$" for 9 years and $^3/_8$" for 6 years. *Frames or Ribs* were give as $^5/_{16}$"x 3"x 2" for 200t and $^5/_8$"x 6"x 4"for 2,000t. Such structural components were the same size for all years; the keel was 6"x 2" for 200t and 12"x 3"for 2,000t. Rivet diameters were also specified, by thickness of plate: $^3/_8$" up to $^3/_8$" thick, then $^3/_4$" up to $^5/_8$"thick and for $^7/_8$"to 1" rivets were 1"diameter. These rules were revised in 1863 and the years replaced with classes *a, b* and *c*. The very able Bernard Waymouth[19], then London surveyor was soon arguing for a more

---

[18] Salting - *Lloyd's Rules* required that during construction - the openings between the timbers of the frame, at the extremities of the vessel, from the deadwood to the height of the air courses formed midway between the keelson and the hold beam clamps, and also the buttocks, be filled with salt, and the spaces of the upper air course and the gunwale be filled before the planksheer is fitted; and within six months of the date of launching, the salting be completed so as to fill the spaces between the transoms and between the timbers of the frames at each end of the vessel for one-fifth her length, from the deadwood to the gunwale, and amidships from the upper part of the bilges to the gunwale... Suitable stops were required to retain the salt... details for other parts were included in rule.

[19] Bernard Waymouth [1824-1890] was at Newcastle in 1857. He became a Principal Surveyor in 1871 and was secretary to the Society from 1872 to 1890. Martell became Chief Surveyor in 1872.

substantive revision of the iron rules and with the assistance of Benjamin Martell overcame the resistance of the senior surveyors Martin and Ritchie. By 1871 there were new symbols *100A1, 90A1,* etc and in 1871 there were issued more elaborate and comprehensive tables setting out the dimensions for the various components of the iron ships. A shipowner by contract could and often did lay down his own requirements and some builders would build above the minimum standard. These tables greatly reduced the work required of design staff.[20]

Some comments by Lloyd's Visiting Committee.
Problems with the use of elm noted above continued. In August 1849 Lloyd's Visiting Committee found three Sunderland shipyards working elm *too high* and a year later a number yards on the Tyne were similarly criticised. The elm was objected to at Ilwaines and was immediately removed. Aware of commercial problems, Chief Surveyor Creuze,[21] endeavoured to widen the areas of approval for various timbers and wrote to his Managing Committee in December 1845 pointing out that it would be *a great boom* to the shipbuilders if Danzic Oak was admitted for the second futtocks on *8 year* class ships. Shipbuilders had *great difficulties* in getting crooks [curved pieces] of English Oak, because an *8 year* ship *cannot command a price sufficiently high to enable the Builders to have good crooks* and as a result 2nd futtock were *of necessity therefore sappy, rainy and very often not well grown*. He contended that Danzic Oak would not have these defects. More than a year later, having failed to secure sanction for his proposal, he pointed out that such a change would mean *a great saving in valuable English oak timber.* As these *8 year* vessels were usually colliers, *the compass 2nd futtocks in the midship body* [were] *well down.* Bayley did not find *so marked an improvement* on the Tyne as on the Wear, where there were some men who appeared *determined to produce good ships & I hope that this spirit will in the course of time lead to a general improvement in all respects.* Clearly there had been significant improvement in the timber used on the Wear, Bayley had *never seen so much Timber of really good quality* at Sunderland; the English Oak <u>remarkably sound</u> *and well grown*. The African Timber was of good quality, however there was *little of no. 2* [African] *to be seen either in the building yards or in the Timber Wharfes.* Workmanship was also an issue. It was rightly stressed that far from a lower class allowing an inferior standard of workmanship, if anything the opposite should be true that the less good materials required better workmanship. Lloyd's Rule was clear: *The workmanship in vessels is to be well executed, and equally so for all grades.* In 1844 a Visiting Surveyor wrote: *n.b. The shifting of the Plank regularly 3 between is now becoming very general on the River Wear so much so that I have omitted to particularize it in the description of each vessel in class 10 years & upwards.* In 1850 visiting the Wear the Surveyor noted that Greenheart, Teak and Morra, had *almost wholly superseded* English Oak and therefore the Rules should be modified. Local oak rarely exceeded 9" in width whereas these new timbers did, and so the number of fixings needed to be increased for the wider planks.

Many problems in regard to securing the use of good materials continued to emerge and even normal good yards could and did lapse, while others were considered evasive. Two vessels at Hutchinsons were criticised in 1844. A number of the deck beams on a 260t vessel [intended as *8A*] were *all extremely sappy and rainy*. These with several planks *all more or less broken* were removed. On a second ship Brunton had *marked 89 timbers to come out, not one of which is fit to remain.* Five years later on a 350t barque *a great deal of South American hard wood apparently of a very variable quality* was used and it was vigorously pointed out that *none of the inferior description* [was] *admissible.* Hutchinson was described as having *the character of Building rather to the letter than the spirit of the* rules. Matters were bad at

---

[20] Pollock: the existence and influence of the Registration Societies are such that the codes of scantlings and the structural supervision instituted by then together constitute the only guarantee of structural strength generally, [their work] obviate[s] the need for strength investigations generally or at least ... discourage[s] shipbuilders from independently instituting them. Small drawing offices placed considerable reliance on very competent foremen.

[21] Augustin Creuze [died in 1852] succeeded George Bayley in 1844 as Principal Shipwright Surveyor. He attended the first Royal School of Naval Architecture and wrote on Naval Architecture in *Encyclopaedia Britannia* [7th ed].

Bartram & Lister, where the English Oak frame was *extremely rainy & sappy* on a 100t vessel. On a 270t [*8A*] vessel the stern and stern frame was *so indifferent* as not to be *eligible* and *The Timber provided is small, sappy and of moderate quality - but little of it applicable for building a vessel of her intended size and class*. Failures by Crown were sharply criticised in January 1849, when a 500t bargue under construction intended as *12A* was

> by no means worthy of that grade, her frame must be seen again & the specimen of the treenails I saw backed out, being very contrary to rule ... when the vessel was completed, the treenails would again be severely tested before any class could be assigned. He promised everything, but ... he endeavours every evasion.

Having regarded Crown as *a very slack builder*, in August he was *happy to say that this frame is an improvement, and shows some anxiety to abide by the rules. They are ... working the Elm too high*. A year later, however Crown was told that the frame for a 700t ship *as prepared & the timber lying about was not fit for this class* [13 year] *... much was not fit for any class*. The worst vessel on the Wear was at Petries, who had continuously neglected the advice of the local Surveyor Brunton, *several timbers...very inferior... top timber generally being poor* and the elm was *5 strakes too high aft & 2 strakes too high forward*. There was praise at other yards. At R Wilkinson's yard the frame was found to *very sound* in 1844 and five years later Wilkinson was advised to prepare for 12A the 350t vessel intended to be 10A, because *so few timbers objectionable and so much very superior*.

Even Laings was not free from critical comment. On a vessel in 1844, about half in frame of English Oak, *objectionable timbers* were to be removed. Similarly, although the floors were large they were found to be *badly squared. Timbers of the Frame stout, rough and badly squared at present. Several of the Timbers shaky & the chock grains cut and defective in many instances. This frame required to be well dubbed out, ... and all the grain cut and defective chocks in order to make it eligible for 11A*. Such cases were exceptional at that yard. Other comments were: in 1852 the 1,160t vessel *finishing in a manner very creditable to the Builder*. When in 1855 the *La Hogue* was inspected the Visiting Committee noted that *in common with all the Surveyors and other persons who have seen this ship* they admired the *excellence of the materials and workmanship* and expressed their *admiration of this beautiful model of British Naval Architecture*. Laing was for many years a major trader in timber and purchased prepared timber at its point of origin, as was reflected in the report on a 700t vessel, which had a frame of *good quality and well squared British Oak. The whole scantling converted in Herefordshire where the timber was grown a saving in freight ...*

During Lloyd's visit to Hartlepool some timbers unfit for grade were found at the Pile yard but particular concern was expressed on an 8' plank, which had been steamed and was about to be wrought when a fault about $^3/_4$" thick for nearly its whole length was observed. When it was removed, the plank itself was found to be *very sappy, and utterly unfit* to be used. They commented that *the case exhibited in a very strong light, the difficulty, not to say impossibility, which exists for a Surveyor to detect such work if the workmen are desirous of deceiving them*. Pile expressed *extreme regret that the foreman should have contemplated using so defective a plank*, he would not allow it. The fundamental point of the limits on supervision was well made. Such vessels depended upon skilled, diligent and honest craftsmen. Newly introduced timbers presented other problems. In the case of Greenheart the sap *nearly... resembles the heart of this wood*, which made the detection of sappy wood more difficult. The *Calabar*, built in 1853 to the *13A* class, was examined five years later in Dock and it was discovered that the Australasia Hardwood used for the ceiling had suffered premature decay [it was supposed to be Teak and Ironwood[22]]. A sample was sent to the General Committee of Lloyd's and a list prepared of all Sunderland ships in which this timber was used. The earliest one was the *Cuba* of 1844 and six further ships had this wood up to 1850. followed by three each in 1851 and 1852. The material was extensively used over the four years 1853-7 on 98 vessels, which made a total of 111 with the defective wood; many of these vessels were by

---

[22] *Ironwood* - was a name given to extremely hard woods chiefly of tropical origin

Laing. Surviving evidence has not revealed the follow-up to this. As always new materials must be proved sound or otherwise in *long run* use.

Lloyd's Staff realised they could not relax their vigilance; when Bayley proposed another Surveyor for Newcastle he wanted a *real good one* who both knew his business and would not be *afraid of the great men of the Tyne*! Even such a great yard as that of T & W Smith was on occasion found wanting: in 1844, on a *12A* vessel some of the Timbers were found to be *rather sappy*. Eleven years later a 1000t wood ship built under cover was *generally square & good* with a *good frame, well squared & wrought*. At Edwards the floors were mostly English Oak of *fair size & quality* but several timbers were *druxy*[23] *and defective*. Work was found to be *well done* at Metcalfes, *evidently an effort to do better than has been their usual practice*.[24] The *extremely improper* caulking of the bottom *before Beams fastenings is put* at Hutchinsons indicated the continuing difficulties in securing the best standards. Vessels intended to be one class might end up a lower one as in the case of a bark started as 12A year vessel and *being finish for 10A*. Iron knees also received attention and in 1850 Candlish was reported as having *bad fitting of iron work: The Deck knees not worked correctly*. It was noted, in 1855, that the Piles were using *substantial iron work in knees and Riders*.

The quality of Sunderland vessels.

Eleven Sunderland shipbuilders were listed as subscribers to Peter Hedderwick's *A Treatise on Marine Architecture* [1830], evidence of a desire to acquire some additional grasp of the *Theory and Practice of Shipbuilding*. There were eight subscribers from the Tyne.[25] Steadily standards were raised as Lloyd's surveyors influenced the practices in the yards and insisted that requirements were met and not fudged. No doubt some poor work got through but even a cursory consideration of the construction of a wood vessel will make clear how very difficult it was to ensure that every piece of timber was what it should be and properly shaped. In 1836, Shipwright Surveyor George Bayley felt able to tell the *Select Committee on Shipwrecks* in regard to Sunderland:

> The improvement is most decided, and quite astonished me in going through that port, and several of the builders there applied to me for information where they could get instruction in the higher branches of the art, for now they thought it was worth their while to do it according to science or in a scientific manner: they told me that they would like to work according to the rules of the art.

Bayley's assessment certainly did not mean that vigilance had ceased to be necessary. However, the view of the South Shields Seamen's leader Woodroffe in the 1830s that Sunderland ships were *the worst built in the world* is not sustainable. No one could assert that no bad ships were built on the Wear. Many vessels were in the lower Lloyd's classes, but that is a different matter. In 1833 a Liverpool shipbuilder James Aitken linked the Tyne and Wear in his condemnation: on Newcastle *instances of very cheap ships... inferior ships; they have proved to be badly constructed, often with a great deal of sappy*[26] *timber, which is rotten in a few years; they are in bad repute with us: with the exception of...one or two builders*. When challenged in later questions about the vessels of the Liverpool shipowners built at Sunderland, he conceded that the one he had seen was *a very fine vessel*. He commented it was *bought uncommonly low from a builder that had since failed* and he continued *There are some names in Newcastle as good as any in the kingdom*. Finally he stated *They build very good ships at Whitby; Newcastle and Sunderland stand*

---

[23] *Druxy*: Of timber: having decayed spots concealed by healthy wood [1589 - earlier dricksie]

[24] The timber used was noted as: *frame* Eng Oak except 10 or 12 *timbers one side* #2 Silv Oak *lower deck shelf* #2 Silv Oak *Outside plank* mixed Eng Oak, E. India Teek Afr Tim #1 & #2.

[25] Peter Hedderwick *A Treatise on Marine Architecture* ... [Edinburgh 1830]. The shipbuilders were: at *Sunderland* - Adamson W, Alison James, Gales John M, Gales Thomas, Hall George & W, Laing Phillip, Liddell George & Robert, Mackie Joseph, Mills George, Potts William, Reay Robert, Scurfield Robert, Storey John and from the *Tyne* - Brown Thomas [Jarrow], Doeg Alexander, Hopper Ambrose & R, Laing James [South Shields], Scott William [Walker], Smith William, Wetherley John [Howden Pans], Winlow John [St Peters].

[26] *Sappy* -Full of moisture; wet; sodden.

the worst with us. Almost all these generalised views have no evident statistical basis and against these critics may be set the statement of a London dockmaster that Sunderland ships navigating the north east coast were *Decidedly a better class than those of London...they can sail without ballast.* Although it has been suggested that Sunderland built ships were dumpy, in fact the length to breadth ratio of Wear vessels was similar to the ratios in contemporary textbooks and well within an expected spread of individual values. The length was typically about 3.4 times the breadth around 1800 [see diag 4.02].

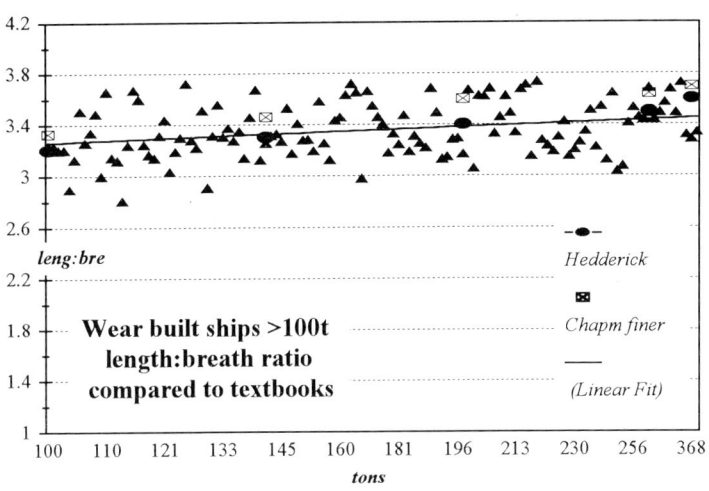

Diag 4.02

There was a dramatic increase in that ratio once metal hulls were introduced when the ratio became typically 7:1. Over the years 1855-65, wood vessels by Robt Thompson jnr had a ratio of about $4\frac{1}{2}$ to 1. The length to breadth ratio to tonnage for Thompson's iron/steel steamers over 40 years period fluctuated from below 7 to above 8 and three ships reached a 9:1 ratio. As with so much else the requirements of the shipowner was the dominant factor in such design decisions.

Ship types.

In the early nineteenth century Lloyd's Register described 18 types of vessels by suitable abbreviations. These were: Bargue [Bk], Brig [Bg], Brigantine [Bn], Cutter [Cr], Dogger [Dr], Galliott [G], Hoy [H], Ketch [K], Lugger [Lr], Polacre [Pol], Ship [S], Smack [Sk], Sloop [Sp], Schooner [Sr], Schoot [St], Steamer [Stm], Snow [Sw] and Yacht [Yt]. Not all of these will be described here. Some were very similar and with regional associations; for example the dogger was similar to the ketch and the polacre was a brig associated with the Mediterranean. The number of masts and their rig were distinguishing characteristics, Keys[27] has shown that ten different types operated on the Northumbrian rivers of the Aln and Coquet. A *ship* had three or more masts, all square rigged, while the *bargue* [*bark*]with the same number of masts had a fore-and-aft rig on the aftermost or mizen mast. The *brig, snow* and *brigantine* each had two masts; the *brig* and the *snow* were both square rigged, *snows* however had a try-sail mast abaft [towards the stern]. On *brigantines* only the fore mast was square rigged and there was a fore-and-aft rig on the main mast. *Schooners* might have two or three masts; two masted vessels were usually either fore-and-aft rig only or with square top sails on fore mast. Three masted *schooners* usually had fore-and-aft rig, with square top sails on fore mast. A single mast was the feature of the *sloop,*[28] normally worked with fore-and-aft rig. Combinations of these

Ship

Barque

---

[27] Richard Keys's study provides an excellent insight into local ship ownership and their sailing ships.

[28] *Sloop* was used for naval vessels - in the wood era usually auxiliaries and in World War II escort vessels.

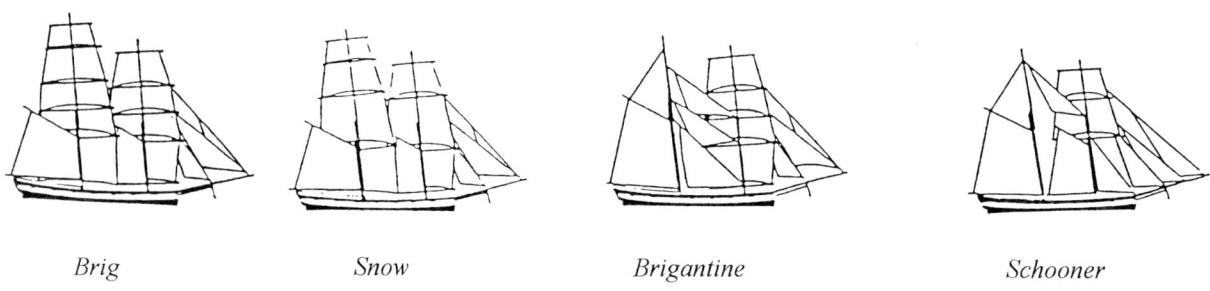

Brig *Snow* *Brigantine* *Schooner*

types were referred to as hermaphrodites, for example the *schooner-brig* and the *snow-brig*. Of special importance for the north east was the collier brig. Of the 93 *London Colliers* in Lloyd's of 1776, with an identified rig - 51 were *brigs*, 47 *ships* and a *snow*. A type not in the Lloyd's list was the wherry, a decked single masted vessel with a shallow draught, which were built on the Tyne.

On Lloyd's Register of 1776 *brigs* accounted for 25% of the Whitby tonnage [*ships* 72%]. Just over half the Tyne tonnage comprised of *brigs*. Almost two-thirds of the Wear tonnage was made up of *brigs* and almost all the remainder 35.8% of *ships*; less than 1% was for *sloops*. There were 44 *snows* among 97 ships with identified rigs built on the Wear in 1834. The others were 28 *bargues*, 8 *brigs*, 8 *schooners*, 6 *ships* and 3 *sloops*. Of the more than 700 Wear built sailing vessels on the Sunderland Register in 1856, nearly half [47.6%] the tonnage was of *snows*, slightly more than a third *barks*, nearly 12% *ships* and only 1.64% *brigs*.[29] A *bark* rig was most frequently used for wood ships built on Tyne in the 1850s, a total of 11,203t. There was one 3-masted schooner of 350t. There were 20 *snows* and 17 *brigs*, [average 232t]; the 39 *sloops* and 11 *wherries* were smaller craft about 25'-30'; 15 other schooners averaged just over 80t.

The measurement of tonnage.

Tonnage is a term which was used in various ways and the definitions for business and official purposes have changed many times since the 17th century. It is the most usually used indicator in assessing changes in the amount of shipbuilding and it needs therefore to be interpreted with more caution than is usually applied.[30] Changes in the forms of ships, the different types and their construction material all complicate the use of this measure, for example in the overlap of wood and iron-hulled ships. It should immediately be noted, that the capacity of a ship to carry a given weight of cargo tonnage is also limited by the bulk characteristics of the cargo and arguments related to increased deadweight capacity will be irrelevant to a ship owner whose trade is not able to utilise that apparent gain. These notes are intended to offer a working guide to the reader, with specific examples, and further references are listed in the bibliography. The terms involved include: *measured* tonnage [*Builders measure*], *gross* tonnage, *net* tonnage *registered* tonnage *deadweight* tonnage and tonnage *below deck* and particularly for naval vessels *displacement* tonnage since such craft are not normally carrying cargo. Of particular importance to the north east is the *keel*.[31] Legislation regulating the size of craft carrying coal was passed long before rules for general cargo [see chap 2]. The buyer of a ship by contract wanted to set down his requirements and at the end of the eighteen century this would refer to its *burthen* and *register* tonnage. The use of *keels* was very extensive and this was often noted in addition to BM [Builder's Measure], shipowners and their insurance clubs recorded a ship's size in *keels*. After examining the Wear vessels of 1834, Nell concluded that the

---

[29] An analysis of the 1851 Register by Patterson showed 59% snows, 13% schooners [almost all under 150t], 12% barques, less than 4% brigs and just under 1% [9 vessels] were ships. Only 3 of the 48 sloops exceeded 50t.

[30] Farr wrote *It must be admitted that tonnages are a nightmare to the serious student of maritime history* [p 5]

[31] The term keel probably came from Anglo-Saxon times, however, the Crown set a measure for keels to enable an effective collection of taxes by statute 1422. A keel should have the *portage* of 20 *chaldrons* equal to 8 waggons with a capacity of 126 cubic feet. All vessels were to be suitably marked for the correct load.

registered tonnage was *no indication of their carrying capacity*. He estimated that 14.6t [of vessel tonnage] was required for a *keel* of coal in a 175t collier and this was down to 11t in a 330t vessel; a 175t collier carried 12 keels and a 330t vessel 20 keels. Sunderland shipowner, J White, was then allowing about 16t / *keel*.

A distinguished Admiral, Sir William Monson [1568-1643] included the formula *L x B x D / 100* for calculating tonnage in one of his naval tracts. Edmund Bushnell in his *The Complete Shipwright* [1678] gave the rule used by Thames shipwrights as the length of the keel x the maximum outward depth x half breadth divided by 94 [or 100]. This assumes that depth was half the breath with a small allowance for shape instead of full rectangular block volume. He was aware that this did not measure carrying capacity and proposed more sophisticated calculations to allow a suitable deduction for the rounding of the vessel. Legislation gave a new definition in 1694, that

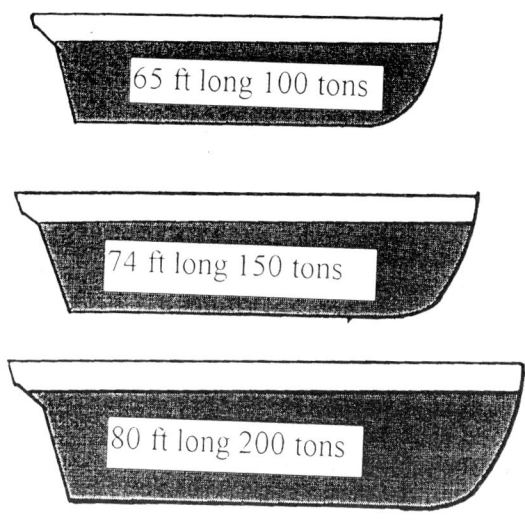

Size of wood ships & tonnage

65 ft long 100 tons

74 ft long 150 tons

80 ft long 200 tons

tonnage equalled *L x B x Depth of Hold / 94* and in the case of two deck vessels, if the 'tween deck space was used for cargo then the depth was measured from the underside of the upper deck. Although William Sutherland in his *The Shipbuilders Assistant* [1711] was critical of this method of tonnage measurement it continued in use, and the divisor 94 was confirmed in the Act of 1720.[32] From 1773 tonnage measurement was compulsory, with a slightly modified formula *[L-0.6B]xB x0.5B/ 94*. This is generally known as the *Builders' Old Measurement Rule* [BM]. Laing's Particulars Book shows that he used this formula about 1800. North east builders continued to use and record the Builders' Measure for their own purposes into the 1880s: it was legally abandoned in 1835. Laing's book had another formula:

> To find the number of Keels a ship will carry Keel x Ex breath x Depth x 56 and prick off the first five figures from y Right the Other will be y Keels or keel + $^2/_3$ of rake x frame breadth x depth divided by 96 divided by $21^1/_5$ gives the keels.

The word *keel* as used in this formula could be confusing as in the singular it means the part of the ship and in the plural the measure for coal. There is no reason to suppose that these two formulae directly influenced the size of rake [the overhang of stem and stern over *neat* keel] nor the difference between the breadth of the frames and the extreme breadth, however it is very likely that either would have given the same result if rounded to a whole number or even a half.

Clearly the arrival of steam raised the need to allow for engine room space and an 1819 Act made an allowance for this by diminishing the length of the keel for calculation purposes by the length of machinery space. There was a government Commission of Inquiry in 1821 and twelve years later one by the Admiralty.[33] A new Act was passed in 1835 and the expression *New Measure* was used for many years.

---

[32] *Take the length of the keel within board, so much as she treads on the ground, and the breadth within board by the midships beam, from plank to plank, and half the breadth for depth...* [quoted from Salisbury 340]

[33] A method to calculate internal capacity was set out. The length of upper deck between the insides of the stem and the sternpost was divided into six equal parts - depth of hold measured A C E, each divided into 5 parts; sum of breadths measured a1, a4, c2, c4, e1, e4. a1+a4+c4+e1+[3 x c2]+[2 x e4]- sum of depths A+C+E. Internal length measured at half height of depth of hold amidships the len x sum of breadths x sum of depths / 3500 [35 cub ft seawater = ton].

This new formula took the length at half the midship depth and the breadth and depth was taken at a number of points along the hull, the result being divided by 3500. Laing's first iron ship the *Amity*, in 1853, was entered in Particulars Book as *Admeasures 479 $^{3409}/_{3500}$ tons*! There was no consistent relationship between the old method of calculation and the new. For some vessels the difference was small and in other cases much larger but might be an increase or decrease. Following an Admiralty Commission in 1849 a new bill was introduced and rejected. However, the secretary to the commission, the naval architect George Moorsom, devised the system which became law in the Merchant Shipping Act of 1854, and has essentially remained the basis of tonnage calculation since that time. This was a technique for accurately measuring the internal volume of the vessel and dividing by 100 to give the *gross tonnage* figure. Clearly once there was machinery this occupied space not available for cargo. Space was required for fuel in addition to crew accommodation and ship's stores. The various complications of the calculation of such spaces cannot be examined here, but when this space was deducted the result was *net tonnage*. Both of these values appear in various registers and as such are equally entitled to the term *registered*. It was usually on the basis of net tonnage that such ship charges as port & harbour dues &c were calculated. North east coast builders, such as Doxfords, in the late 19th century produced designs which reduced these charges [see chap 10]. Particularly important for shipowners was *deadweight tonnage*, the actual weight of cargo a vessel could carry at her water-line. For many trades with bulky cargoes this figure was less important and for such dense cargoes as iron ore the holds were not fully occupied. This value relates to the *displacement tonnage* which is the actual weight of the ship, measured by the volume of water it displaces. Naval vessels are usually given in *displacement* tons. These qualifications should be borne in mind when considering figures given; usually shipbuilders reported their output in terms of *gross* tonnage and as already indicated this is what is intended when a figure is followed by *t*. In the twentieth century particularly with oil tankers deadweight is the figure most usually quoted and the Diesel engine technical press from 1920 usually gave such vessels in deadweight, which was about 50% higher than gross tons. The illustrations show the dimensions of vessels related to their tonnage.

Building iron ships - Wood to iron hulls - the long transition.

It may be argued that the greatest of all shipbuilding *changes* was that from wooden hulls to iron hulls. Already some of the advantages that iron offered the shipbuilder have been indicated, in particular the ability to shape the material without a loss of strength or the need to find a suitably formed part of a tree.[34] With wrought iron of a suitable quality, strength was combined with lightness of structure, it was estimated that 1,000t hull weighed 35% less than a comparable wooden one, thus allowing more cargo. The thinness of the metal hull, fractions of an inch, compared with the solidity of the wooden walls, many inches, was a more likely cause of concern than the issue of buoyancy. For countries with an iron industry and declining forests it offered reduced dependence on timber imports.[35] Charles Palmer said the *only serious drawback to the use of iron hulls is their liability to fouling*.[36] When in 1861, the Tynemouth MP, W S Lindsay fiercely attacked the provision of £949,371 for timber, the Prime Minister retorted that the House

---

[34] A pioneer of the iron , Grantham wrote: *the shipbuilder [racked] his brains and [tried] his patience, in seeking for crooked timber necessary to frame a sharp floor ... How often is he obliged, though he knows it to be injurious to scarf the frames, for which no timber can be found sufficiently large to enable him to avoid such defects...*

[35] White, in his *A Manual of Naval Architecture* [1877], wrote: *Iron shipbuilding originated in this country ... has been the source of great advantage. It has rendered us practically independent of foreign supplies of shipbuilding materials ... The United States, Canada, France and Italy, all furnished with ample supplies of suitable timbers...*

[36] Fincham wrote in 1851: *The formidable character of this species of mischief threatened to fix a disadvantageous limit to the employment of iron ships and vessels both for commercial and naval purposes.* Grantham, who was not likely to exaggerate, said in 1870: *A ship at the end of four months...anchored in harbour, it was found she could hardly move, the amount of coral and shells had accumulated to such an enormous extent on the bottom ... portions of the coral...was 4 inches thick in many places and had a very rough surface. I have supposed this to occur upon some of our fast iron-clads - the Warrior ... at least half their power would be wasted...by the decrease of the speed.*

must not suppose that iron ships will wholly supersede wood ... You cannot send iron ships to keep the sea for any length of time where they cannot clean their bottoms. Nine years earlier, in 1852, the Lloyds Visitation Committee felt

> it their duty again to advert to the great extent to which Iron Shipbuilding is now carrying on, which they have reason to believe will still be increased at Hull, on the Tyne and at Greenock, Dumbarton and Glasgow, and the very great importance of introducing, if possible, some rules, by which at least the Surveyor & the Committee might well be able to judge of the fitness of Iron, from its size and quality for the Ribs, Plates, Beams etc of Iron Ships.

The notable absentee from this list is Sunderland, then the leading building port in the country and still very firmly wedded to wood!

Almost a generation passed from the first builders of iron ship in the 1830s to the 1860s when 50% of Britain's new tonnage was of iron. There were marked time differences in reaching the point at which half the new tonnage was of iron. In Britain this occurred in 1862 but in the USA it was not until 1900![37] More than half the Tyne tonnage was of iron hulls by 1854 and on the Wear this position came 14 years later. It was the end of February 1852 before the first iron hull was completed on the Wear. The national changeover to iron is shown in diag 4.03. At the end of the Crimea War, iron ship building declined more than wood: from 108,200t of iron in 1855 it fell to 67,400t in 1856, a reduction of 37% whereas the tonnage in wood was reduced by about 17%. Not until 1862 did the iron tonnage exceed that of 1855. The story began in 1787.

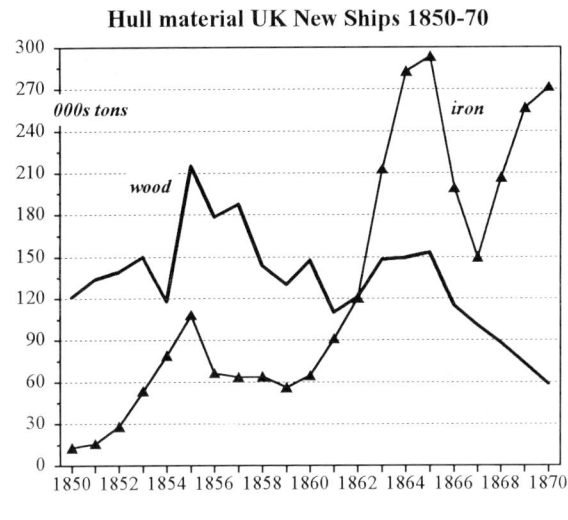

Diag 4.03

John Wilkinson [1728-1808], the great ironmaster, constructed a 70' iron barge, the *Trial*, in 1787; although some wood was used in the construction, the hull was made from $^5/_{16}$" plates. Wilkinson described it as answering *all my expectations* and thought it had *convinced the unbelievers*. River vessels were to become one of the early fields of application for iron, including in British African colonies and in India, but such vessels came many years after Wilkinson's experiment. Not until 1819 do we find another clearly documented example, when the *Vulcan*, a barge with a 56' keel was built to work on the Forth & Clyde Canal. In 1821, there was the first of many prefabricated vessels; the parts for the *Aaron Manby* were made at the Horseley Iron works, in Staffordshire, and then assembled and finish rivetted in the Thames. This vessel later sailed to France.[38] Lairds began the continuous building of iron ships in the 1830's on Merseyside including the *Garry Owen* in 1834. John Fincham, Master-shipwright of Her Majesty's Dockyard, Portsmouth, wrote in 1851: *The suitableness of iron as a material for shipbuilding, and the rapid increase, recently, of its application ... merit some notice.* He pointed out that Laird *proceeding upon a large scale prosecuted this branch of art with uninterrupted success*. There were 37 iron vessels in all 9,500t on Lloyds Register of 1845; of which London accounted for 3,357t, Scotland 1,954t, Liverpool 1,496t and Hull exceeded the Tyne's modest 498t. It is possible that a few vessels were not on the Register.

---

[37] An American naval architect and author, John W. Griffith, wrote in his *The Shipbuilder's Manual* of 1858: *It is ... quite certain that, in a wood country like this, years must elapse, and even generations pass away, before wood, as a material for constructing vessels will be abandoned.* This man was not a conservative.

[38] This vessel was working 24 years later. In 1823, a small iron steamer, built by Grantham worked on the River Shannon in Ireland; this great pioneer of the iron ship published his *Iron As A Material for Shipbuilding* in 1842. A Pennsylvania boiler-maker, John Elgar, in 1825, built the first iron boat 60' long, in the USA

On 15 June 1822, the foreman blacksmith of Hawks launched an *iron boat* into the Tyne at Gateshead. Local historian MacKenzie wrote a year later: *This circumstance may form the commencement of a new era in naval architecture upon the Tyne.* This boat was 31'7"x 4'6" wide and weighed about 340lbs; arrangements were made for 6 oars and it was said only to draw a half inch of water. Almost twenty years passed before a pioneering endeavour began the realisation of MacKenzie's prediction with *a notable experiment in naval architecture,* in the words of Martin & McCord.[39] The Bedlington Coal Co, to gain better access to new seasale markets, decided to use an iron steamer and in March 1841, the little known twin screwed ss *Bedlington*[40] [400t *BM*] was launched, with the unusual feature of tanks for water ballast. T D Marshall built both the ship and its 43 *nhp* side lever engines. Her deck had a great open hatchway, and three lines of rails enabled the normal load of 40 coal waggons to move within the hold. Abbot of Gateshead provided the derrick used to load and unload the wagons. Great difficulties were experienced in keeping the *Bedlington* operational and in 1845, its last full year of working, accounts revealed more than 120 days of work on the vessel. This work included repairs on gearing- *spurs wheels &* for which 76 cogs were required at 5d each; steam pipes, work on *fraiming* and the side of the boat and in June *repairing the boat bottom whare she was leakey*. New plates for the boat side were almost regularly required as well as iron for bolts and rivets. Craftsmen from the collieries carried out most of this work. During 1845 the millwrights and smiths working on the ship were paid almost £100 [equivalent to at least 2 man-years work]; colliery stores cost £16 -8-4 and there was also the following outside payments:

      Thomas Toward *bulwarks* £5-0s-11d   T D Marshall *machinery* £96 -13s -2$\frac{1}{2}$d"
      T Wallis *repairs & timber* £10 -2s -3d   A Woodhouse *machinery* £10 - 6s
      Luke Turnbull *boiler* £26 -14s -10d   Abbot *casting* £3 - 9s   W Milburn £2 -2s

Without wishing to deny that some of these problems might not have been avoided, radical technical changes give rise to the unexpected. It is essential to realise that particularly in the absence of experienced skilled people, inevitably this venture was likely to have more than its fair share of difficulties. This maintenance work is cited to illustrate the point. Nor it may be added are technical innovators necessarily commercially successful. Gibson of Newcastle bought the Aberdeen built iron *Vulcan* for use in the coal trade but she was sold when found not *to answer as a collier, on account of her straining.*

Marshall started with a smith's business and went on to build engines for tug boats. He later took over the shipyard of Andrew Woodhouse. The business records of ss *Bedlington* suggest a continuing link between Woodhouse and the yard. After building some wood vessels, Marshall in 1839 built his first iron vessel the *Star* and so began iron ship construction on the Tyne [he went on to build 99 iron vessels]. Nonetheless it might be argued that the pioneer was John Coutts [*Coattes* in Lloyds report]. He began in 1842 with the *Prince Albert*[41] and built the *Flash* [216t] in 1843. As early as July 1844 the men from Lloyds reviewed with great interest the 271t the iron barque *Q.E.D.* just launched by Coutts. Extracts from their report is given below. There is clearly evidence here of a *double bottom* but no comment on water ballast as such. By 1850 there was a basis for iron shipbuilding on the Tyne.

Iron shipbuilding was a new development on the Tyne, rather than mainly a changeover amongst wood shipbuilders as it was on the Wear. Although James Laing was the pioneer and built his first iron vessel, the *Amity*, in 1853, iron was not a significant part of his output until 1858. His final wood ships were built in 1866. Unlike the Tyne, where men with a metal working or engineering background such as Marshall started iron shipbuilding there were few comparable men on the Wear. Workers in the boilermaking trades were more numerous on the Tyne than the Wear. The changeover in individual Wear yards is discussed in chap 5. At Hartlepool although John Pile's yard did build some wood hulls it was essentially an iron yard and its third ship was of iron. Two iron steamers were built in 1856. Strangely in 1861, two vessels of

---

[39] This section is based on *The Steamship Bedlington, 1841-54* Martin & McCord *Maritime History* no.1 pp 46-63.

[40] The total cost was £4924 or £23/regt. Coal wagons were loaded directly into the hold of the vessel by means of a steam derrick operated from the ship's engine, which was disconnected from the screw for this purpose.

[41] 155ft x 19.5ft and depth of hold 9.5ft, plate thicknesses $\frac{3}{8}$, $\frac{5}{16}$ and $\frac{1}{4}$ inches

> *Notes from Lloyds' Report on Q E D*
>
> Q ED was to be propelled with a screw when necessary, particularly in ascending the Seine to Rouen. Ribs 18 inches apart of double and single angle iron alternatively 3 ½ in x 2 in - rivetted through the plates with $^5/_8$ and $^3/_4$ rivets about six inches apart. The outside plating is lapped at the edges to the turn of the bilge with 6 rivets in each foot, thence up flush at the edges with 12 rivets in each foot - Flush Butts throughout.
> Floors $^3/_8$ in Plate and 2 in angle Iron at top - 10 inches deep. Ceiling is Flat and up above turn of the Bilge $^1/_8$ in Plate close rivetted at butts and edges, and to the alternate frames or ribs - being a complete internal Skin, quite watertight. The rivetting of this ceiling is about 8 rivets per foot in length.
> She has two watertight Bulkheads formed with $^1/_8$ in Plate and diagonal Ribs 3 feet apart on each side of the Bulkhead. Bottom Plates Bilge upwards $^3/_8$ thick from Bilge downwards was unable to ascertain (excepting by report) the thickness of the plates - they are stated to be $^1/_2$ inch next the Keel and then $^7/_{16}$ to Bilge - Wales $^5/_{16}$ - The Keelson is of plate Iron 12 inches broad and $^3/_8$ thick - the keel is an curved plate thus [sketch] forming a watercourse and the Keelson is worked downwards from the Ceiling between the Floors.
> The Stem and Stern Post are formed with a solid Iron Core and securely rivetted. The opening for the propeller is about 6 feet by 2 ft 3 in worked with a double post and a broad knee foot apron{?}
> The Deck Beams are formed in the usual mode with plate iron, and double angle iron on the top - the decks are secured to the Beams by Coach screws from below and some screw bolts from above through the deck and secured with a nut under the angle iron.
> She has a Bilge piece on each side for the purpose of keeping her upright when laying aground, and to enable her to hold a good wind. formed like the small sketch in the margin projecting from the bottom about 12 ins & forming nearly an equilateral triangle and secured at the angles by single iron

almost the same dimensions for a London owner were built in the different materials: *King Arthur* [1,211t] of iron and the *King of Italy* [1,230t] of wood! When William Gray became Denton's partner iron replaced wood and the yard laid its first iron keel of the sailing ship, the *Dalhousie*[42], on 4 July 1863 and she was launched on 23 January 1864. [see chap 7] Ten years earlier the first iron ship was built on the Tees, ss *Advance* [336t] and ss *De Brus* was built in 1858 at Middlesbrough [the specification in appendix].

The workers required to build iron ships.

Few wood shipwrights took up the new skills required in iron construction and indeed why should they have done? Firstly there was a long period of transition in many yards and there remained the continuing repair work on the wooden ships afloat for decades to come. More importantly, a great deal of work remained for the shipwright on the iron ship. Wood shipwrights for many years held the workers in iron shipbuilding withe contempt as at best semi-skilled. Mayhew recorded that the regular London shipwrights called the iron workers *boilermakers* and described *them as an inferior class to themselves, made up from all descriptions of workers in iron, including many boys and unskilled labourers.* The group of skilled trades which was central to the construction of iron ships became known as *the black squad*[43], and they were first recruited from trained boiler-makers. These men had the skills to shape accurately the iron plates, which, after being riveted together were rendered steam tight by caulking the joints to provide the boilers for stationary steam engines and locomotives. In the boiler-shop, a craftsman would carry out all aspects of his trade, just as the wood shipwright had done. The first craftsmen who entered the iron

---

[42] It was not built under survey Lloyds Reg -177.3' x 29.4' x 18.5', - 696 t; Spaldin 715t and 1050 dwt.

[43] This group included: angle-iron smiths, platers, riveters, caulkers, holder-upers, drillers and their helpers.

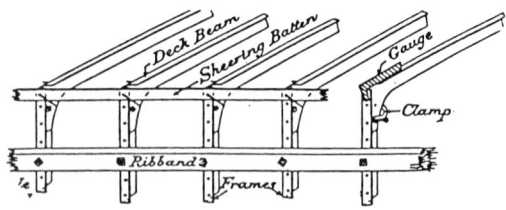

Picture of staging for HMS Nelson 1905 at Palmers

Textbook [Holms] illustration of staging &c

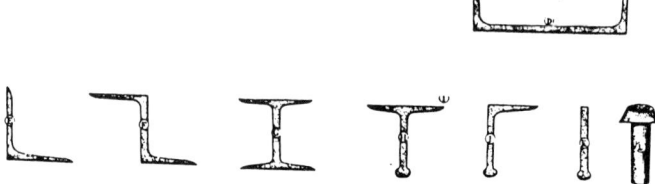

Rolled sections used on ship construction

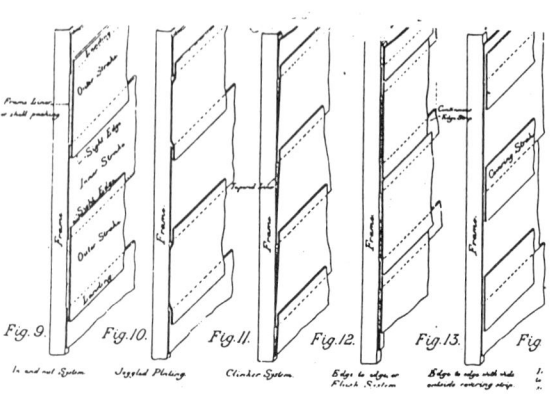

Various plating arrangements

Diagram of bending slabs

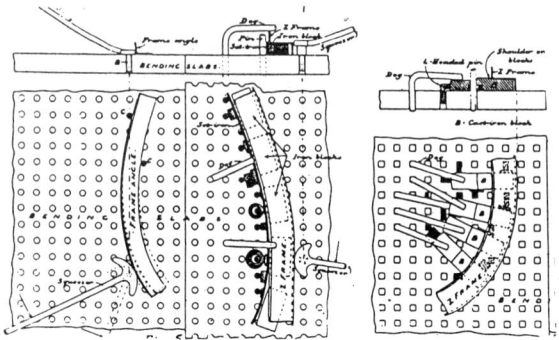

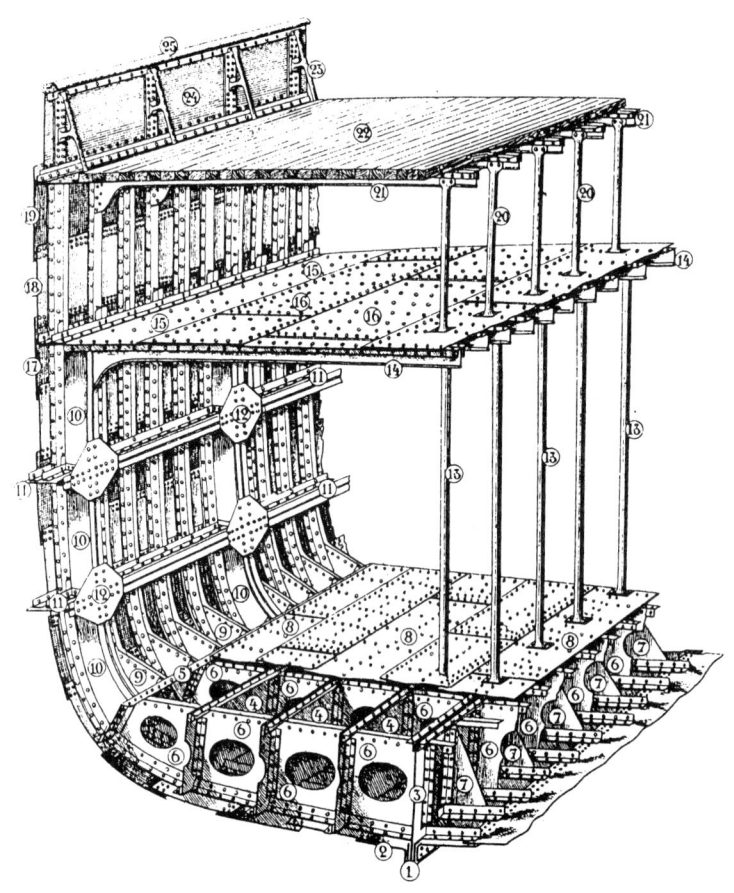

Paache illustration of iron ship

shipbuilding had that combination of skills, but this situation was quickly changed in the shipyards. Although most of the basic procedures in building an iron hull followed that of the wooden walls, the blocks were laid followed by the keel. The illustrations [opposite] show the staging [and the ribbands], which have a clinical abstraction but the photographs reveal the more primitive reality. The preparation of the iron frames brought a sharp change; the mould loft was now essential. This was work which continued to be done by shipwrights.[44] A single piece of metal would take the shape of the frame in place of a number of separate shaped timbers scarphed together, although in the early days scarphing was often required because iron pieces were not available in the length required.[45] Firstly, an *angle-iron smith* prepared the iron angles in a special furnace and then shaped them to the required dimensions of each frame. The heated angle irons were hauled on to a floor of cast iron blocks with holes into which were fitted the pegs positioned from templates prepared from mould loft layouts. The separate trade of *plater* was created, a craftsman who specialised in shaping and fitting plates, who was usually assisted by four *labourers, helpers* who carried and manipulated the plate at the various work locations. Those plates were not only taken to ship's side for marking and later erection but the rivet holes had to be punched. Likewise these plates required suitable bending which was carried out on special rolls. This shipyard equipment developed through the 19th century and generally such machines were bought outside the region. A pair of *riveters* worked with a *holder-up-er* [holder-on], who firmly supported the rivet in place with a heavy *hammer*, while the rivet was closed. It should be noted one of the pair of riveters was required to become *left-handed*. Rivets were heated in a moveable fire, with a foot operated bellows by a *rivet heater*. This was no routine task. Unless the temperature of the rivet was correct, bad work resulted. The heater tossed the red hot rivet with his tongs to a *catcher*, who passed it to the riveter. The critical matter of providing the essential water tight seal was carried out by the *caulker*; the term used for sealing timber joints on the wood vessels. There were also *hole-cutters* or *drillers*. Ultimately a much wider range of trades emerged which by the late 19th century exceeded thirty.[46] A most significant change was the introduction of piecework payments, a method of payment traditionally rejected by craftsmen. Iron shipbuilders, added to this new feature, paying the leading craftsman for the work done and so it was the plater who paid his *helpers*. There developed a very different social structure in the iron shipyard from the wood yard. Many Scots skilled in iron shipbuilding came to the north east.

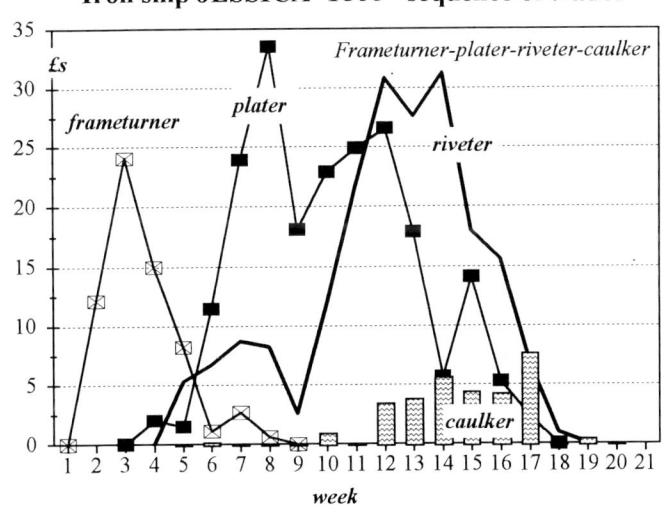

Diag 4.04

The need for multiple berth yards.
A consequence of this sub-division of trades was the building simultaneously of a number of ships, because otherwise each trade would be laid off as its work was completed until it was needed again. This sequence in terms of wages paid can be seen for an early iron ship at Doxfords [diag 4.04 above]. In building ss

---

[44] An 1870s union document listed almost 100 separate task carried out by shipwrights in the iron yard. Beginning with: 1. Lay keel blocks; 2. Make and put up Standards, Stages and Gangways; 3. Put up Frames, Beams and Carlings; 4. Make, run and take off Ribands; 5. Do all Shoring and Fairing and Lining and Shearing; 6. Make all moulds, whether upon the Boards, aboard of ships or in the Loft; 7. Build all Bilge Blocks.

[45] Some of the specifications given by Grantham in 1858 included the words *in as long lengths as possible*.

[46] Shipbuilding Employers' records listed more than 90 categories in 1940s see appendix.

Jessica, the frame turners have more or less completed their work in six weeks, when the platers were getting underway. Although some riveters follow the platers almost directly the bulk of their work peaks later and of course the caulkers can only follow on after the riveters. There are similar complications with the other trades, for example the shipwrights had many tasks in the early stages, including aligning the frames and if there were wooden decks, then the caulking of those would come at the end. In addition to the painting required on iron vessels, the inside bottom was cemented to protect the iron from water. Both of these activities were carried out by contractors for many years. Outfitting trades, such as joiners, fitters and plumbers, were normally required much later in the process of construction, much of it after the launch. For steamers the marine engine was built while the hull was under construction. Usually after the launch the hull was towed to the engine works for the installation of the engine, the boiler, and many associated devices not least the pipework. Sufficient parts of the deck had to remain open so that the machinery could be fitted, an operation largely overlooked in accounts of the industry. The iron shipbuilder with four berths would have liked a keel laid on berth #1, the frames up on berth #2, the plating well underway on berth #3 and the hull on berth #4 nearly ready to launch - few order books allowed this ideal situation.

The Composite Ship.

In composite ships an iron frame provided the main structural strength, and a hull of wood planking offered an acceptable solution to the problem of fouling.[47] A wooden hull could be sheathed with copper without the damaging electrolytic action of combining iron and copper of the metal hull.[48] Despite the claim, in the *Annals of Lloyd's Register* that *The transition from wood to iron as a material of construction...was not effected without the introduction of an intermediate stage*, i.e. the composite ship. This was not so, with a few exceptions such as Robert Thompson [see chap 5]. Composite ships were not built in any quantity until after more than half of Britain's new tonnage was of iron and at no time was a significant number of the British builders constructing composites. At least two authors, albeit in brief comment, also imply a phase of this kind of construction and both date it earlier than it took place in construction terms. Unger wrote of *the composite hull of the early nineteenth century* and Slaven stated *Linking their new designs ... for a time to the composite form, British builders tipped the scale back in their favour ... from the mid 1830's.*[49]

As early as 1839, Watson of Dublin took out a patent for a composite construction and probably built a vessel, and in that year also Capt. Andrew Henderson built a composite steamer, the *Assam*, in India. The key starting point was an 1849 patent [#12824] taken out by John Jordan of Liverpool. At this port a year later, the 50' long *Excelsior* was launched and early in 1851 the *Marion Macintyre* [283t]. The *Tubal Cain* was registered by Lloyd's on 5 August 1851. Rankine distinguished four main types.[50] However only the Jordan type was used extensively; other types were likely to have been much more expensive in construction. The great advocate of iron vessels, William Fairbairn expressed his rejection of composites in 1865. After noting that the system was *for some time highly appreciated*, he commented that a

---

[47] *The Annals of Lloyd's Register* [1934] Up to 1884... Experience showed that the bottoms of iron ships were more or less subject to fouling and corrosion... the speed became greatly reduced after the vessels had been some few months at sea ... although some of the compositions ... effect the result to a considerable degree, yet it must be admitted that to a large extent the same difficulty exists now as at the beginning. p.83.

[48] MacGregor wrote: Composite ships hold several advantages over both wood and iron craft, compared with wood-built ships, they could stow a relatively larger cargo... they did not become strained or water-soaked, but possessed the strength of iron hulls which enabled hard driving, without suffering too much stiffness which prevented speed in strong winds. In light breezes they were as fast as wooden ships and delivered their cargo in excellent condition.

[49] *The Annals* [1934] p.87; Unger pp 42-3; Slaven p110 in *Dynamics of Victorian Britain* ed Roy Church.

[50] Apart from the Jordan there were: inner skin, outer skin wood; Hein's system complete skin of iron-Z beams filled between with timber; iron frames embedded between two wooden skins and wooden bottom iron topside.

consideration of the properties of the materials showed that the system was *not an eligible one, and for seagoing ships was utterly at variance with sound principles of construction.* In regards to strength the composites were *exceedingly defective compared* with iron vessels.[51] In 1857, Bilbe & Perry of London built the composite colonial clipper *Red Riding Hood*. Only two tea-clipper [built in 1857-8] were listed by MacGregor as built before 1863, he suggested that for some years, *owners and builders were presumably watching the performance of the few composite ships afloat. Then, in 1862 and 1863, there was a rush to build such ships.* There were 29 composites among the 36 tea-clippers listed by MacGregor as launched during the seven years 1863-9. Published national records only separated composite ships between the years 1866 and 1882 and it is not until 1867 that Lloyd's published their rules for composite ships, with splendid drawings. Nationally the largest

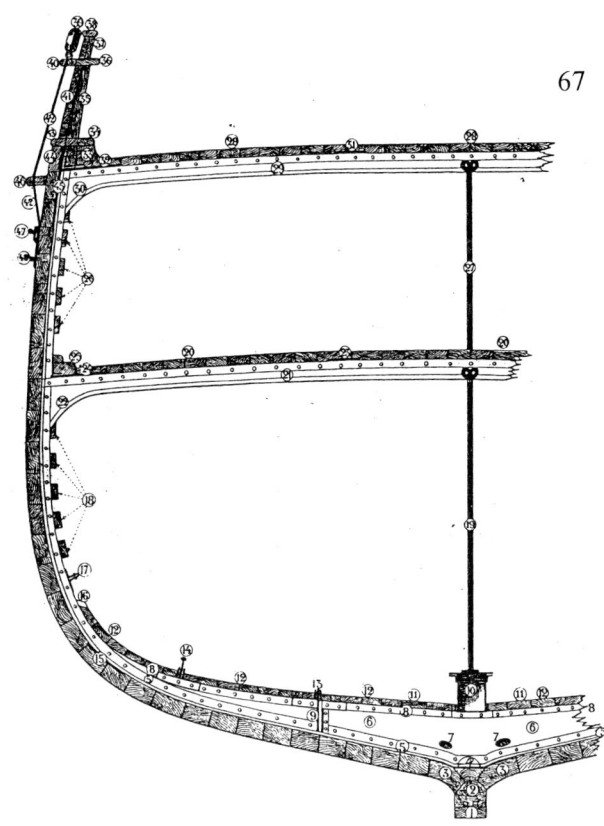

Half section of a composite ship

tonnage of composite ships was in 1866, when it was one eighth of the sailing tonnage but less than 8% of the total tonnage. After three years at about 7%, it dropped to 3.6% in 1870 and was only 0.6% a year later. The opening of the Suez Canal, at the end of 1869, enabled the iron steamer to compete with the composite clipper on voyages to China.

Of the vast array of shipbuilders on the Wear only 12 ever built even a single composite vessel, and three of these launched only one. Seven Wear builders in 1867 shared ten composite ships between them. This compared with 23 iron and 100 wood vessels launched. There was little composite building elsewhere in the north east. When in an 1870 paper, Palmer failed to mention composite ships, Teesside shipbuilder, Raylton Dixon, commented *for the trade of the eastern seas, the custom has been to employ ships having an internal framework or iron but sheathed with wood.* Palmer responded by supporting Fairbairn's view - *I look upon a composite ship as an unsatisfactory compromise between wood and iron, and I think it is such a compromise as must day by day go out of fashion. Combining wood with iron must always render a vessel weaker than constructing of iron alone.* When further pressed on fouling, Palmer contended that the cost of docking, scraping and repainting was more than compensated for by the advantages of iron. Very few composites were built on the Tyne, in 1867 the *Brisbane* [451t] by T & W Smith, and at South Shields the *Tynemouth* [386t]. Established iron builders were unlikely to show a keen interest in this form of design. One north east shipbuilder, Harkess at Middlesbrough appears to have started with composite ships, the first four ships identified as by this yard were all composites; from 1871 he built in iron.[52] Only one composite was built at Hartlepool, the *Taunton* [688t] by Denton Gray for Watts Milburn of Newcastle in 1867.

---

[51] Bennett Woodcraft - List of Patents; Rankine p.191; Fairbairn *Treatise on Shipbuilding* p71. Jordan read a paper to the *Institution of Scottish Engineers and Shipbuilders* in 1863 [pp25-], and there were papers at the INA in 1864 & 1865 and one contributor supported a complete iron ship with a sheathing of wood outside. INA - v.5 Grantham, C. Lamport, G L Abegg; v.6 A McLaine and in v.8 [1867] a second memoir from Scott pp168-.

[52] These ships were for Jones Bros of Newport, Wales and included in 1870 the *W H Harkess* [499t]. The only vessels in the name of Riddle were composites built in 1865, the *Challenge* and *Conqueror* [599t].

Support Industries.

Support industries were needed to provide sails and the related pulley blocks, anchors, chains and ropes. In 1776, sail cloth was imported from French Flanders [75 *ells*], Germany [32 *ells*] and Holland [58 *ells*]. Sailmakers, like the many other support industries were vital to the success of shipbuilding. Unfortunately a detailed study cannot be pursued here. A small number of the shipbuilders in the late 18th century made their own sails but normally these were purchased. Twenty sailmakers were listed in a Sunderland Directory of 1827 and this number increased to 29 by mid-century. Throughout the 19th century and for some time beyond steamers carried sail, for example a 3-masted steamer built by Richardson Duck in 1855, carried two each of fore sails, fore top sails, for topmast stay sails, main sails, main top sails and *the rest as usual*. When the propeller of Laing's *United Services* was washed away off the coast of Canada, she arrived 11 days later under canvas off the south coast. On the earliest surviving maps the rope walks are to be found and on Wearside covered-in walks continued into the 20th century. Rope, wire and cable was also essential not only for new vessels but for the maintenance of those already afloat and on the north east coast firms in this field were also suppliers to the coal industry. Hood Haggie & Co began making rope as early as 1789 and moved in time from hemp ropes to iron cable. Starting at Gateshead works were established on the north bank of the Tyne. A member of this family established a works at Monkwearmouth. Twenty ropemakers were operating on the Wear in 1820, including Webster & Grimshaw, who began in 1780 and in 1797 opened probably the world's earliest factory for machine-made rope.[53] Wire ropes were made from 1840. Both were major employers and employed many women.[54] Chain making was a well established industry at Gateshead and amongst the leading companies were Hawks and Abbotts. Hawks, a foreman blacksmith from the Crowley Irons Works in the mid eighteenth century established his own business working old ballast iron [kentledge]. Gateshead historian Frank Manders has summarised the firm's progress and the changing partnerships. The firm was innovative and early users of steam; a patent for chain making was taken out in 1804 and for a testing machine in 1812. This was an essential instrument for quality work. The enterprise of Hawks Crawshay embraced many aspects of engineering as it developed including some marine engines. A reliable anchor was an essential part of a ships equipment.[55] Francis Martin , in the mid-1860s, achieved a practical anchor capable of holding by both flukes and Hawks of Gateshead offered the practical assistance that was required. They later supplied a 6.5 ton *Martin* anchor for the *Victoria* and two of a similar size for *Sanspareil*. About 100 tons of anchors were supplied to the Admiralty up to 1888. When a year later Hawks Crawshay closed, a former fitter Henry Charlton [born 1833], the firm's manager, took over a part of the works and continued to produce this patent anchor and later built the improved *Martin-Adelphi* of 1894. From the 1770s, Joseph Abbott worked as a master brazier, brass founder & copper smith and his sons carried on the business. By 1827 they were manufacturing chain cables. By 1831 the number employed had reached 190; ten years later the number had reached 640 men and boys and in 1834 William Brown, one of the employees became a partner. Following the death of John Abbot in 1863, both his son and partner William Brown, having no sons, decided to established a Limited Liability company.[56] This company was a major supplier to local

---

[53] The *Patent Ropery* was in a four story building [100' long x 30']with a 16 hp steam engine. *The use of the long rope-walk is totally excluded and the whole is performed by the machinery.* Working only by day output was 500 tons of cordage a year, in 1804 partly to meet government orders 800 tons was produced. [Garbutt p409-410]

[54] A riveter [b 1903] recalled hearing the Haggies Angels: the girls who worked at Haggies Ropery ... Perhaps the first girls to do factory work. As early as five o'clock in the morning you could hear the patter of their clogs ... The shipyard workers used to time themselves to get up for work by the sound of the Haggies Angels

[55] A Roman alter piece found in the bed of the Tyne bears a form of anchor which continued into the 19th century. In 1819 a clerk Richard Perring of the Plymouth Yard drew attention to anchor failures and his proposed modified form curved arms became known as the *Common* or *Admiralty* anchor and was still widely in used after 1900.

[56] The business was set out as *chain, cable, and anchor manufactures; engine and boiler builders; iron founders, brass founders, and finishers; copper-smiths, iron-merchants, and manufacturers of forged iron work; copper and tin merchants, and general ironmongers.* Thomas Hood Henderson was the first chairman, when John George Abbot died in 1867, his brother in law L W Adamson joined the Board and succeeded Henderson as Chairman.

shipbuilders. *Abbot's anchors and cables were as well known as the proverbial Gateshead grindstone* according *The Shipping World*: contracts were held with the Admiralty, the East India Company and their products supplied to many European countries. Abbots manufactured the improved *Rogers* anchor introduced in 1833 as well both the *Trotman* and *Tyzack* designs and marketed their *Lion* anchor, which was widely used on cargo ships. Anchors from 1 to 70 hundredweights [50 kg to 350 kg] were produced, in addition to the common type. The works covered 14.5 acres with an extensive river frontage and about 2,000 were employed in 1888. The heat from 32 puddling furnaces was used to raise steam in eight Raistrick boilers, an early example of fuel economy. Average output was about 100 tons of chains and anchors a week. Abbots had their own test house for chains and supplied the machinery to Lloyds for the Proving Houses at Low Walker and Sunderland. In 1871, Wasteney Smith of Newcastle took out a patent for the first *satisfactory type* of stockless anchor, which he manufactured on Tyneside. The great advantage of drawing up the shank into the hawse pipe resulted in the almost universally adoption of the stockless anchors. Four anchor iron smiths had small businesses at Sunderland in 1820, two of these William Nicholson and the Lumsdens expanded their activities and were regular suppliers to Wear shipbuilders. W L Byers produced the *Reliance* a *very strong and efficient type* of anchor. Ship's block were needed in large numbers and the Admiralty's requirements during the Napoleonic wars led to the first comprehensive British example of mass production with specially designed machines.[57] Although it was suggested in Liverpool that someone in the north east had applied these techniques no evidence has been found of this. Small businesses supplied each shipbuilder's needs of blocks. There were ten blockmakers on the Wear in 1820. Amongst specialities required were accommodation ladders which were supplied by Linklaters Patent Ship Fitting Co of North Shields.

The importance of outside expertise.

However much at times the officers of classification societies might be a thorn of the shipbuilder in a hurry or under cost cutting pressures, overwhelmingly they were a regular and important source of advice and help to the shipbuilders. Similar remarks would apply to those appointed by owners to supervise construction and in the particular role of the Admiralty officials. A very important group were the consulting partners of naval architects and marine engineers; these were frequently employed by shipowners to produce design plans & specifications and also to supervise construction. There were also special cases such as the civil engineers who produced designs for floating docks. These specialists were always men with substantial experience in design, construction and management work in commercial and or naval yards. This reservoir of skilled knowledge reduced the need, however undesirably perhaps, of individual yards maintaining on their staffs an adequate supply of designers.

At the time when the changeover in iron construction for new ships had just passed the half-way mark there was still a substantial shipbuilding industry in the South of England. Early in 1863 it was estimated that there was about 87,000t of iron shipbuilding under construction on the banks of the Thames and nearly 10,000 workers employed. Almost a million pounds [£976,531] was Palmer's estimate of the value of iron shipbuilding produced on the Tyne, Wear & Tees in 1862. This was based upon more than 57,000t built, which he distributed approximately as 56% on the Tyne, 27% on the Wear and 17% on the Tees. A year later the tonnage had increased to more than 90,000t and this he calculated at £18/ton [a £1 more than 1862] and so it was worth £1,643,328. About two-thirds of a ton of iron was used for each ton of shipping.[58] He gave the number of workers as 4,060 on the Tyne, 2,500 on the Wear and 1,550 on the Tees in 1862; those figures suggested an output of just under 8t/man-year on the Tyne and only 6.24t on the other two rivers; such a difference was very unlikely. He argued that these figures showed that *with the single exception of the coal trade, iron shipbuilding is the most important branch of industry in this great commercial and manufacturing district* of the Tyne, Wear and Tees.

---

[57] A most useful description is available in K C Gilbert's *The Portsmouth Block Making Machinery* [1965]

[58] It is not clear what tonnage Palmer used - possibly OM; the almost exact coincidence of the division between the three rivers is also surprising. Unless he excluded Hartlepool from the *Tees* figure was an under estimate.

De Brus 1858 *Specification*

285 tons OM   171 net tons   length 146 ft   breadth 20 ft - depth of hold amidships 11.5 ft load draught 9.5-10 ft
Engine 40 nhp   26" diam   24" stroke 15 psi - R & W Hawthorn

Keel & Stem	bar iron 6" x 2" welded into one piece
Screw Frame	forged iron properly proportioned throughout & in accordance with Lloyds rule general section 6"x 4" to be welded to keel
Frames	angle iron 3" x 2" x spaced 18" apart reverse angle iron 2" x 2" x $1/4$" running along tops of the floors well round the bilge and up to the gunwale stringer alternately.
Floors	plate iron 11.5" deep $5/16$" thick on every frame extending from bilge to bilge deeper at extreme ends of vessel.
Main Keelson	plate iron 9" deep x $5/16$" angle iron on each side top & bottom 3" x $2^1/_2$" x $5/16$" rivetted to reverse angle irons on tops of floors and run as far fore and aft as practicable and continuously through all bulkheads.
Bilge Keelson	one on each bilge formed of angle iron 3" x 2" x $1/4$" rivetted back to back with a plate 4" x $1/4$" between forming breast hooks and crutches at ends. To be rivetted to reverse bars on frames and run continuously through all bulkheads.
Engine & Boiler Seats	of form and strength to drawings supplied by the engine builders
Bulkheads	Four watertight bulkheads of $1/4$" plate; plate properly stiffened by vertical angle iron bars 2" x 2" x $1/4$" spaced 2' 6" apart. In addition to being rivetted to the framing attached to outside plating by knee plates $1/4$" thick fore and aft side alternately
Deck Beams	On every alternate frame of angle iron $4^1/_4$" x 3" x $5/16$" back to back & attached to frames by knee plates $5/16$" thick having at least $12^1/_4$" arms.
Hold Beams	as Deck Beams attached only to every eighth frame.
Gunwale Stringer	To run all round vessel plate iron 14" x $1/4$" rivetted on top of beams and secured to outside plating by angle iron 3" x $2^1/_4$" x $5/16$"
Hold Beam Stringer	To run all round vessel on tops of hold beams and rivetted thereto. plate iron 11" x $5/16$" secured to reverse bar on every frame by bracket or knee on every alternate frame.
Ceiling Plate	To run all round vessel plate iron 11" x $5/16$" rivetted to a reverse angle iron on every frame about two feet below deck beams.
Beam Clamp	of plate iron as Lloyds rules about 10" x $5/16$" running on tops of Deck and Hold Beams on each side of hatches where practicable running fore and aft and attached to stringer plates at the ends.
Hold Stanchions	To be on every alternate deck beam where practicable and convenient and formed of the best round bar iron $1^3/_4$" diameter opened out at the bottom to rest on the keelson and bolted or rivetted thereto and to deck beam.
Funnel	To have a close funnel of wood or iron and according to drawing supplied by the Engineers
Coal Bunkers	plate iron $3/16$" thick stiffened by vertical angle iron every four feet. In form as required by Engineers. capacity to hold at least 35 tons of coals or say for about 120 hours full steaming. To be fitted with necessary ports on deck and below.
Rudder Stock	of Best bar iron 3" diameter at head and 2" at keel. Frame properly proportioned and plated with $1/4$" iron
Plating	Garboard Strake $7/16$"; Thence to upper part of bilge $6/16$"; Thence to shear strake $5/16$"; Shear strake $6/16$". All plating to be double rivetted to Keel, Stem and Stern Post. The plating next on each side of the Garboard strake to be double rivetted thereto. All butts are to be properly strapped and doubled rivetted. Longitudinal joints lapped and single rivetted except where otherwise specified. To have proper filling-in pieces where necessary between frames and plates, the plating being wrought in inside and outside sheets.
Rivetting	All rivets to be of best quality and of size and distance apart in accordance with Lloyds Rules, to be countersunk and flush on outside plating
Stern	To have an elliptical or round stern with a half poop raised, the frames being prolonged to form the sides and plated above the shear strake $5/16$"
Decks	well seasoned yellow pine $5^1/_2$" x $2^1/_4$" properly seasoned, laid dressed and caulked. To have one good coat of pine oil.
Bulwarks	To be 2 ft 9 in high to top of rail above top of the waterway. Stanchions of English oak not less than 4" x 3" spaced 4 ft 6 in apart properly secured to ships sides. Rails of red pine or American elm 8" x 3" properly tenoned to stanchions with neat bead outside.

Planking	of Baltic Fir or Pine about $1\frac{1}{4}$" thick.
Waterway	red pine about 12" x 6" Stettin oak round bows if desirable
Hatches	Combings of hard wood about 8" x 4" or red pine of similar size protected by iron plates on three sides $\frac{1}{8}$" thick. Carlings of ash or elm, suitably arranged coverings of Baltic fir or pine with rings or other arrangements for lifting, To be complete with tarpaulins, bars, locks.
Hold Platform & Ceiling	Memel or Baltic fir or pine $1\frac{3}{4}$" thick to turn of bilge. Above turn of bilge to be ceiled at intervals $1\frac{1}{4}$" thick as required for carrying a general cargo.
Lumber Strake	red pine with rings for lifting
Cabin Floor	yellow pine $2\frac{1}{4}$" properly secured &c
Cabin	The half poop to form a neat cabin for Captain and Steward. Horsehair seats, neat mahogany table with iron stanchions fixed to the floor, plain swing candle lamp for each berth or state room and oil lamp for saloon, neat oil cloth, side and deck lights as necessary. Stewards pantry fitted up complete as usual. Captain's state room neatly fitted up with table, desk, drawers& lockers. No passenger accommodation but this can be added at the owners wish and expense if desired. To have companion staircase &c as necessary and usual.
Deck House	suitable deck house fitted up with accommodation for mate and engineers also small neat galley with cooking stove complete. To be connected by bridge with neat rail, steps &c
Forecastle	plainly fitted up for crew with all the usual necessaries, plain stove and swing lamp. Deck lights &c, as necessary.
Skylights	neat Cabin Skylight protected by wire guard and arranged for ventilation. Engine skylight glazed with rough plate glass $\frac{5}{16}$" thick protected by strong wire guards, to be arranged for ventilation
Windlass	a strong windlass fitted at the heel of the bowsprit, and also a strong winch.
Steering Gear	neat steering wheel, tiller ropes or chains, blocks, standards &c complete arranged at the stern of the vessel
Boats	In accordance with Merchant Shipping Act 1854 with all the usual and necessary davits, blocks, falls, slings and chocks complete.
Painting	The whole of the ironwork inside and out where exposed to have two coats of paint of a suitable colour. The bottom outside below the water line to have a third coat good red lead and black above. Bulwarks to have three coats of paint to be black outside, inside and stanchions to be painted stone colour or grained in oak and varnished, deck beams covered with wood and painted white. Deck House grained in oak inside and out or neatly in stone colour, but to correspond with bulwarks. Forecastle neatly painted in stone colour.
Anchors, Chains &c	Two bower anchors of 10 cwt each with iron stock complete, 150 fathoms 1" stud chain cable, one stern anchor 4 cwts, one kedge 2 cwts, 75 fathoms 6" stern hawser or iron in proportion strength, 75 fathoms 4" hawser, two mooring lines 3" hemps 25 fathoms each.
Rigging	as a two masted topsail schooner, with all necessary masts, spars, booms, sails &c complete, also a derrick boom. Standing rigging of wire rope, running gear of best hemp and chain where necessary, complete in every respect and of the best materials and workmanship.
Miscellanea	2 Hawse pipes and chain stoppers, 2 Catheads and gear complete, 6 mooring bits, One Octagon binnacle with two lamps, also for bridge with one lamp, best dipping needles to each and two spare flies complete and adjusted. One Life buoy and line, 1 kedge buoy and line, 2 draw buckets and ropes, 4 pails or fire buckets, 2 brooms, 2 mops, 2 crowbars, 4 cork fenders, 6 scuppers, 1 beer cask, 1 ale cask, 1 water cask 120 gallons, 2 mess kits, 2 harness casks, 2 flour casks, signals lanthorns and gear complete as usual, 1 brass bell ship's name engraved thereon, One Bourgee and three other colours, 1 best day and night telescope, necessary leads and lines, One half hour glass, One log reel and line complete, 1 windsail for engine room.
Carved work	plain neat carved work at bow and stern

Delivery in the Tees complete as above specification exclusive of plate, linen, general cabin, cooks and stewards stores, manning and provisioning. It is specially understood that as this vessel is to be built under special survey to the present 9 years A1 Class at Lloyds any alterations required by the surveyors and made by the builders shall in no ways vitiate this contract anything therein contained to the contrary notwithstanding.

[*The Cleveland Industrial Archaeologist* no 15 from Letter Books of the Owners of the Middlesbrough Estate]
Pease option to buy from Rake & Kimber for £5,350 at 285t OM this was £18.78/OMt and £30.25/t.

Trades by the shipbuilding employers in 20th century. [piece/time workers & apprentices separate]

1	Angle Back Handers	40	General or Yard Labourers	83	Pumpmen
2	Angle Iron Smiths	41	Holders On	84	Red Leaders & Cementers
3	Angle Iron Smiths Apprentice	42	Iron Saw men	85	Red Leaders & Cementers App
4	Angle Iron Smiths Strikers	43	Iron Shifters & I. Stocktakers	86	Riggers
5	Beltmen	44	Iron Stocktakers	87	Riggers App
6	Blacksmiths	45	Joiners	88	Riggers' Labourers
7	Blacksmiths Apprentice	46	Joiners App	89	Rivet Catchers
8	Blacksmiths Strikers	47	Joiners Machinists	90	Rivet Heaters
9	Boat Builder Block & Spar Makers	48	Joiners Machinists App	91	Rivet Testers
		49	Joiners' Labourers	92	Riveters
10	Boat Bld Block & Spar Mkrs App	50	Liners Off	93	Riveters App
		51	Locomotive Drivers & Firemen	94	Sailormen
11	Boilermen & Firemen	52	Locomotive Firemen	95	Sawyers [Wood]
12	Brass Finishers	53	Loftsmen	96	Sawyers [Wood] App
13	Brass Finishers App	54	Machinery Attendants	97	Scarphers
14	Bumpers Up	55	Machinists	98	Sheet Iron Workers
15	Burners	56	Masons & Bricklayers	99	Sheet Iron Workers App
16	Caulkers	57	Masons' Labourers	100	Sheet Iron Workers' Labourers
17	Caulkers App	58	Millwrights	101	Shipwrights Iron Work
18	Coppersmiths	59	Millwrights App	102	Shipwrights Iron Work App
19	Coppersmiths App	60	Miscelaneous Female	103	Shipwrights Labourers
20	Coppersmiths Helpers	61	Miscelaneous Male	104	Shipwrights Woodwork
21	Countersinkers	62	Miscelaneous Male youth	105	Shipwrights Woodwork App
22	Cranemen [Electric]	63	Model Makers	106	Slingers
23	Cranemen [Steam & Electric]	64	Model Makers App	107	Slippers & Packers
24	Drillers	65	Motor Lorry Drivers	108	Smiths Finishers
25	Drillers App	66	Packers	109	Smiths Finishers' Helpers
26	Electricians Temp Plant & App	67	Painters	110	Stagers
		68	Painters App	111	Steam Hammer Boys
27	Electricians Temp Plant & Electric Light	69	Painters' Labourers	112	Steam or Motor Launchmen
		70	Patternmakers	113	Storemen
28	Electricians Wiremen	71	Patternmakers App	114	Toolsmiths & Fettlers
29	Electricians Wiremen App	72	Planer	115	Turner
30	Electricians' Labourers	73	Plater	116	Turner App
31	Enginemen	74	Plater App	117	Watchmen
32	Fitters	75	Plater Helper Blocks & Boards	118	Welders Assistants
33	Fitters App	76	Plater Helper Boards	119	Welders [Acetyl & Elect] App
34	Fitters' Labourers	77	Plater Helper P&T	120	Welders [Acetylene & Electric]
35	French Polishers	78	Plater Helper T workers	121	Wood Machinists
36	French Polishers App	79	Plater Marker	122	Wood Machinists App
37	French Polishers female	80	Plumbers	123	Wood Stocktakers & Labourers
38	Furnace Men	81	Plumbers App		
39	Gatemen	82	Plumbers' Labourers		

Chapter 5

The Advance of the Northern Ports c1815-c1850

From the end of the Napoleonic wars to the beginning of the Crimean war there were significant changes in shipbuilding, a substantial expansion in output, as well as the emergence of steam propulsion and the introduction of the iron hull. The British registered merchant fleet increased from two and half to four million tons. Over the country as a whole however, the upward movement did not begin until mid-1830s, when the total was still at about the level of 1815.[1] A 66% increase took place in the tonnage of British merchant vessels over the fifteen years 1838-1853. Such an advance in shipping clearly required an expansion of shipbuilding. During this period, the cyclical characteristics of shipbuilding were displayed to the full both nationally and at individual ports; with peaks in 1819, 1825, 1835, 1840 and 1847 [see diag 5.01]. The cyclical variations were not peculiar to shipbuilding alone, but part of the capitalist system of production, always seriously affecting the capital goods industries, although the builders of ships were most grievously damaged. Financial institutions were essential to industrial and commercial expansion. Local banks existed from mid-18th century.[2] A most important stabilising influence was the opening of a branch of the Bank of England in Newcastle in 1828; nonetheless many of the early banks led McCord to describe the years 1826-57 as a *major period of banking instability*. During the financial crisis of 1847 the Bank of England ensured the survival of the District Bank [founded in 1836], which finally collapsed in 1857 and this marked *the end of a period of instability in local banking*. Helpful banks played vital roles in the survival of many companies when they faced critical financial situations The use of steam and iron both offered some advantage to those ports with an established basis in mechanical engineering and iron working trades. Initially steam was overwhelmingly employed on river boats and tugs, and a lead was established in both these areas on the Clyde by 1850. However change to iron came much more hesitantly on the Wear. Sunderland continued to grow from the base already established by 1815 and in wood shipbuilding increased its output to become the premier building port for commercial vessels. The fluctuations in output did not deflect the great advance of the northern ports. However, Sunderland with its profound dependence on building ships suffered dramatically in the severe slump of the mid-1840s.

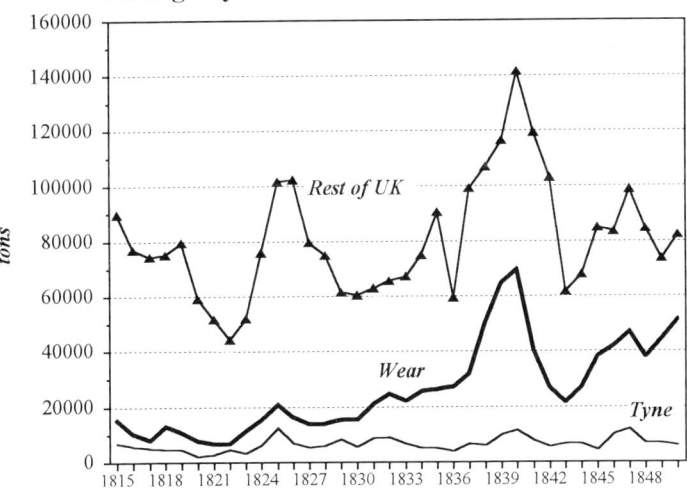

Diag 5.01

Changes in the post-war years 1815-1820.

Nationally tonnage launched fell sharply from 102,900t in the last year of war to 84,700t in 1816. This fall continued into 1817 at 81,300t and was followed by an increase through 1818 to 89,100t in 1819, then collapsed again to a mere 66,700t or only two-thirds of 1815. Even more severe falls in output were

---

[1] Care must be exercised in regard to these early figures. The sharp fall of almost 10%, between 1826 and 1827, of the merchant tonnage was due to the removal of ships which were lost but had remained on the register.

[2] Professor Norman McCord identified the Newcastle firm of Bell, Cookson, Carr & Airey, as *The first local firm recognisable as a bank* set up in 1755 and many others followed in the other major towns in addition to those on Tyneside. McCord [1979] is an invaluable brief survey pp59-65 & 147-8; also M Phillips [1894]

experienced on the north east; on the Tyne, less than 1,400t was launched in 1820 compared with more than 7,000t in 1815. Output on the Wear almost halved between 1815 [15,000t] and 1817 [under 8,000t] and then leaped back to more than 13,000t in the following year. After almost 11,000t in 1819 it only just exceeded 7,000t in 1820. Great distress was felt in ports such as South Shields, *a large number of shipwrights and other shore workers being thrown idle in addition to the seamen*. The post-war depression of shipping in 1816, according to Henry Nelson, was *on account of the great quantity of tonnage that was thrown out of employment by the Government in the transport services*. Many ships were advertised for sale at South Shields and their low prices reflected the surplus supply, for example in April 1817, £650 for the good brig *Two Friends* [153t - only just above £4 / t], repaired in the previous year. The *Amphitrite* [241t], built at Sunderland in 1747, was offered for sale in April 1816; this shows just how long ships were worked.

On the Tyne.
Just over 20 builders launched new vessels on the Tyne in 1816 and four years later only 14 did so. A shipyard was commenced by Richard Farrington at St Anthony's and the pattern of output was similar to yards on the Wear rather than the Tyne. His first vessel in 1817 was the *Hew Singers* [158t], in the next year the *Cicero* [185t], then for two years no new vessel was built. Alexander Doeg's well established yard failed in 1816; he had enrolled his first apprentice 29 years earlier in 1788. He built at least 24 vessels during the years 1791-1816, in all more than 4,200t. Laslies worked as master shipwrights from the end of the 1770s and they followed Doeg into failure; nothing was launched in 1816 and their last vessel was completed in 1817. At South Shields James Evans jnr, whose father took his first apprentice in 1780, after launching almost 3,000t in the war years, then experienced two barren years and the last ship was launched in 1818; almost certainly repair work continued at least until 1826. Another older yard that failed was that of William Carse, with his last vessel in 1815, and Kell failed to register a single ship from 1816 until 1824. Even the low new tonnage built in the post-war depressed years was largely due to speculative building at South Shields. Nicholson offered two ships for sale in both 1818 and 1819 and Bulmer in February 1819. Advertisements for a Forsyth vessel appeared weekly from 10th October 1818 until the end of the year, offering the *Hull of a new Ship ... Burthen per Register, 384 Tons; copper fastened, built...of the best Materials and particularly adapted for the East & West Indies Trade*. Another casualty was the Bulmers' very substantial enterprise, whose difficulties in 1813 were noted above. Not only did they build at least 1,881 tons over the years 1815-9 but in both 1816 and 1817 they launched the largest vessels on the Tyne - *Lord Sidmouth* [406t] and *Asia* [410t]. However, in June 1819 a commission of bankruptcy was issued against the shipbuilders Joseph Bulmer the Elder and the Younger and also against Timothy & Richard Bulmer, rope manufacturers. The final act for a distinguished South Shields yard was the offer for sale of the brig *Juno* [219t] in January 1820.

Declining business obliged Nicholson, Horn & Co to offer their premises for sale in May 1817, which suggests that shiprepair was not then offering adequate profitable opportunities. New building by this yard was well below capacity; with two slipways four vessels a year would have certainly been possible. No buyers came forward and the partnership was dissolved in December and the yard briefly continued as Nicholson & Co under the management of Cuthbert Young. A single vessel of 231t was launched in 1818, as was the case in 1815 and 1816. Young with his son took over the yard, although it is likely Nicholson continued to hold some financial interest in the business. Vessels were attributed to C Young[3] in both 1816 and 1817 although it was not until November 1818 that he used the local press to inform the Public that he was running the West Docks, *lately carried on by Nicholson & Co*. Thirty ships [7,511t] were built by this yard before failing in the depression of the 1840s. Many builders failed to register any new tonnage in single years and sometimes for many years. For example, after the *Heworth* [291t] in 1816, Huntley does

---

[3] Flagg described Young as *a Shieldsman by birth*, who after a time at sea owned his own vessels. During 1817 he managed the High Dock for Wallis. The *Acorn* [119t] in 1807 and *Iris* [342t] in 1811 were registered with C Young as the builder, perhaps these were built by shipwrights on his behalf, rather than that he then owned a yard.

not appear again as a builder until 1823. The name appears only in seven years during the period 1816-29. Stephenson[4] appears even less frequently, only in six years between 1815 and 1839. The 327t *Ellens* was the largest vessel built in 1818, Joshua Donkin was registered as the builder. No other vessel appeared in this man's name so almost certainly someone else built it on his behalf. George Straker ended his seagoing days about 1812 and joined a group with his brother Joseph, including William Wallis and J Hunter, to continue the Wallis shipbuilding business. They too were in serious difficulties; no ships appear to have been launched in the years 1815-17, and when in 1818 the partnership was dissolved, the dry dock and *good slipway* were offered for sale. On 26 October George Straker, in partnership with George Barrass, announced the resumption of business and launched a 227t vessel in 1818 but then three years elapsed before the next ship was completed. Only two Tyne yards launched vessels in each of the five years 1816-20, the Laings [exceeded 2,500t] and T & W Smith [almost 2,000t].[5]

On the Wear.

The dominance of the Wear over the Tyne was shown in diag 4.01above. Despite the large fall in output from 1815 to 1816 at Sunderland 25 of the 31 builders continued. Other yards failed in the following year, when 21 shipbuilders registered new vessels. The numbers increased to 29 in 1818 and in all some 50 names appear on the Custom House Register as builders during the period 1816-20. Some of these new yards managed to survive over many years, although not always continuously. William Gales, a foreman in Potts yard before starting his own business in 1813, headed the Wear's output for 1815-20 with more than 5,800t. Second place was occupied by Laings [3,926t] followed by Oswald Partis with 3,431t; no other builder exceeded 2,500t. Among the long established yards that closed in this period was John Booth, who began with the *Mary* in 1786.[6] Despite some years with no new work Booth built at least 40 vessels, almost 7,000t, an average size 168t. This output included the 301t *Henry* [1799], and 297t *Oscar* [1814].

Newcastle Shipwrights' Company revisited.

Despite its greatly reduced importance the Shipwrights' Company continued for many years to recruit apprentices. Fifty were enrolled over the five years 1810-4, only four in 1815 and two in 1816. The next enrolled was by Thomas Young in April 1818 and then a three year gap until Farrington enrolled his first apprentice. During 1824-28 no less than 39 young men were enrolled and over the years 1830-4, a further 36. Apparently in the good years apprentices did continue to enter the Shipwrights Company. No less than 31 apprentices were enrolled with William Smith as their master; the first three in 1823 followed by five in 1824. As business collapsed after the 1825 boom some Company apprentices changed masters. Joseph Man, enrolled with Farringdon in October 1825, transferred to Ambrose Hopper before the end of the year. When in turn Hopper's business also declined Man then chose William Smith as his new master. Two other apprentices Robert Fairs [he later had his own yard] and Thomas Willis also went to Smith.[7] In 1827, the Company attempted to exercise its authority over James Evans of South Shields, who was presumably normally only doing repair work since his only new ship after 1815 was the *Traveller* [241t] in 1818. He enrolled two apprentices in April 1826 and a year later, the Shipwrights' Company secretary, Bainbridge, wrote to Evans:

> as your two apprentices...are not employed by you or a free brother shipwright, they will not be admitted to the freedom of the company...the young men are to attend at the next quarterly meeting ... in order to procure if possible a master with a free brother or brothers who are actually carrying on the business of a shipwright.

---

[4] Farringdon enrolled Christopher and Wm. Soulsby Stephenson, sons of shipwright James in 1821 2; both were later transferred to Wm. Wright jnr, so the building may be by the father and later the sons.

[5] Almost certainly all T & W Smith vessels have not been located, which might modify this position.

[6] Booth with Blenkinsop were at times partners with Heward. There are no vessels identified for Booth in 1787, 1789 or 1791, but Blenkinsop built in those years. Booth launched ships in every year to 1805 but none in 1806.

[7] The unfortunate John Bowlt, late apprentice of Sharpe, tried to find a new master in December 1831, but *no one would take him in consequence of disease.* [cholera?] Bowlts built small vessels at Bill Quay from 1820.

Evans did not attend the June meeting and as the lads worked for a non-freeman, it was resolved:
> no apprentice be entitled to the freedom of this company unless he serve the full term of seven years with a free brother or brothers of this company actually carrying on the trade or business of a shipwright.

Although the Company continued, it was no longer an important or even relevant factor in shipbuilding, except for such honorary status[8] it could give and later scholarships and prizes. Working craftsmen formed trade unions and the employers, at that time, wanted no part of any restricting collective of their own.

The Northern Ports 1820-1832.

Official figures for the period 1820-32 show just how far Sunderland stood above the other Northern ports [see diag.5.02] and the Tyne moved decisively ahead of both Liverpool and Hull. In 1820 both Hull and Liverpool launched a higher tonnage than Newcastle but by 1824 the Tyne had passed Hull and a year later Liverpool. This position was never subsequently lost. Nationally output fell from 66,700t in 1820 to 50,900t three years later and then climbed to a peak of 122,500t in 1825. Once again after a good year there was a slide down to 75,500t in 1830 before increasing to 90200 two years later. Ouput at Whitehaven, Whitby, and Stockton in 1832 remained largely the same as in 1820, however at Scarborough output was undoubtedly pointing to the decline of shipbuilding there, the tonnage in 1832 was less than 10% of 1825.

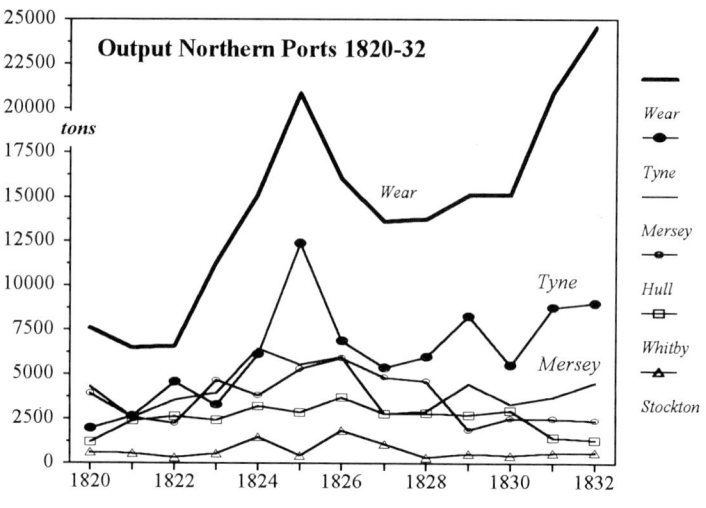

Diag 5.02

On the Wear.

A threefold increase in output was achieved on the Wear between 1822 and 1825, when output for the first time exceeded 20,000t compared with an average of just under 7,000t over the years 1820-2. Between 1823 and 1825 the number of shipbuilders doubled. When tonnage on the Wear fell by 23% from 1825 to 1826, the number building fell to 28; many of those were single vessel builders and some were new starters. Between 1830 and 1832, output on the Wear increased by more than 60% to reach 24,519t and there was the usual increase in the number of builders, this time from 33 to 42. Shipping belonging to Sunderland, increased from 80,000t to 129,000t between 1822 and 1832, a gain of 60%. From a fleet of about 600 vessels in 1815, Sunderland advanced to 1,000 ships in 1850, and the average tonnage increased from about 150t to 200t. The local expansion of shipping was the base for the advance of the Wear to the leading port for building wood ships. From 11% of UK new tonnage in 1820, the Wear reached 27% by 1832. Individual yards did not always follow precisely the overall trends and a small selection of the Wearside yards will show such variations. Continuing success was achieved by the Gales, with an annual average of 1,113t compared with Laing's Wear output of 808t in the six years to the boom year of 1825. William Gale turned out 1,680t in 1826 and only in 1829 was his output below 1,000t. John Mowbray Gale began building in his own yard in 1827 and by 1831, with 1443t he almost equalled brother William's tonnage; John averaged more than 1,000t a year during his first nine years in business. Over the years 1816-1849, the Gale family launched at least 60,000t and 242 ships, compared with Laing's 35,000t and 107 vessels. Another builder in this 1,000t a year class was John Storey, who had *perhaps the largest yard on the North Sands*. Storey came to Monkwearmouth to start a rope works and moved to sail making before

---

[8] William Wright enrolled as an apprentice Robert, son of Newcastle shipowner Nicholas Armstrong, in 1834. This and later enrolments must surely have been for the privileges of the Shipwrights' Company.

turning to shipbuilding in 1821, when he launched 332t and two years later it was over 900t; almost 10,600t were launched over the eleven years 1825-35. Robert Thompson ran the yard for Storey and his son Joseph Lowes served his apprenticeship there. He managed a yard for Elliot from 1837 to 1840. This very able shipwright with his sons established the world famous yard of J L Thompson as will be related below. Luke Crown started his yard in 1818 and with 1,215t headed the river in 1824. A James Crown built no new vessels during 1819-21 and then launched again in 1822, only to fail in 1826 with the onset of the next decline, Luke launched nothing in that year either. Almost 24,000t [97 ships] were built by Crowns during 1816-1849. Typical

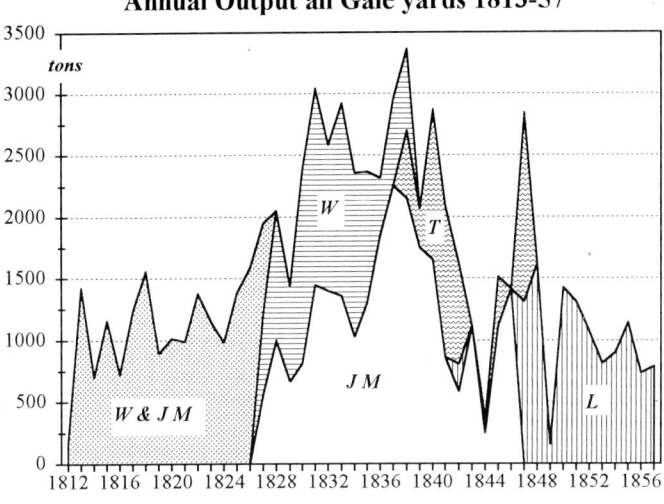

Diag 5.03

of the modest yards was that of Thomas Rowntree at Ayres Quay, the *Agenoria* [119t] being his first vessel in January 1820. After his second launched six months later there was a gap until the *Pleiades* in March 1825, after which vessels were built in every year until 1842., Almost all his 54 vessels were in the 200-260t range. Wilkinson began his shipyard, in 1825 and in three years exceeded 1,000t; he built more than 70 vessels with an average of 262t, amongst the highest yard averages on the Wear.

On the Tyne.

Almost 81,000t were built on Tyneside over the period 1820-32. This was just over 43% of the Wear's tonnage. An output of 12,390t [57 ships] in the highest year 1825 was almost double the annual average of 6,230t. Over these years more than a hundred large ships and many excellent vessels were built at South Shields, described as *the most important centre of wood shipbuilding on the Tyne* by the town's historian, Hodgson. The massive fall back in tonnage in 1826, to 6,892t caused great distress and when 400 of 630 shipwrights were unemployed their Union spent £800 on a new ship to provide work. A similar fall in output on the Wear was very serious, from 20,818t to 16,055t but proportionately less only about 25% compared with 44% on the Tyne! As output continued to fall, MacKenzie commented in 1827, *shipbuilding at present is in a languishing state*. A shipping family, the Metcalfes, had a dock at South Shields from 1813 and over the ten years 1823-32 built at least 21 ships, almost 5,500t, the largest total on the Tyne for those years. Joseph Farringdon was admitted to the Shipwrights' Company in 1821 and built five vessels during 1821-5: then the yard failed and his apprentices were allocated to new masters. He began shipbuilding again in 1829, with two vessels, and the final craft the *Porcia* [149t] in 1830, a total of 1,793t. Straker built almost 4,500t during 1820s, to which Edwards added a further 1,651t in 1830-32, together making this yard the highest builder on the river. *A very beautiful new ship*, the *Isabella* was launched in September 1829 by Straker. His newly patented windlass[9] was praised by Sykes, who described it as *one of the greatest improvements in that important part of naval architecture*, probably an exaggerated claim. He more accurately pointed out another hazard for shipbuilders. On 2 February 1825 a tremendous hurricane struck and *the greatest sufferer* was the shipbuilder Wall, at the Low Lights. The sea smashed the quay in front of the yard and swept away the two vessels on the stocks. The timbered and partly planked brig [120t] was completely wrecked and even though the nearly finished sloop was saved, the estimated loss was nearly £700.

---

[9] The claim was that a 13 cwt anchor required 6 men by an ordinary windlass compared with a man & boy on the patent windlass and a load of about 26 cwt managed by two men compared with 8 men and boys.

T & W Smiths

T & W Smith were probably the most important builders on the Tyne, although it seems likely that many of the ships built for London did not appear on the local register. Their 13 ships 1821-32 equalled 4,427t.[10] When the successful merchant Thomas Smith of Heaton Hall placed his son William as apprentice in the shipyard of William Rowe, he was, however unconsciously, beginning a shipbuilding *dynasty* that would last for more than 170 years. In 1920, *Smith's Dock Monthly* described the Company as *The Oldest Tyne Shipbuilders*. Smith sr[11] was a Free Burgess of the City of Newcastle and had a substantial rope works and the family's trading interests provided many orders for ships over the years that followed. By the time the young William had completed his apprenticeship, his father had purchased the Rowe yard at St Peter's. Although Rowe was not a member of the Company of Shipwrights, William, son of Thomas Smith *Ropemaker & Free Burgess* was admitted as a Freeman on 27 December 1822 by *Presentation*. Smith's output is shown in diag 5.04 based upon figures given by Messent, the Tyne Commissioners' Engineer[12], until this family ceased to use the yard at St Peter's. The beginning was modest with an annual average over the first 24 years of only 380t, in all 29 ships. There were four vessels of 400t or more before 1832, including the *Duke of Roxburgh* [417t] in 1828. On Boxing Day 1829, the Newcastle people cheered the launch of the *George Green*.[13] She was described as *the finest merchantman ever constructed in the port* and *considered by scientific men to equal any London-built vessel*. This ship, like the *Duke* was built for the Thames shipowners and shipbuilders Green &

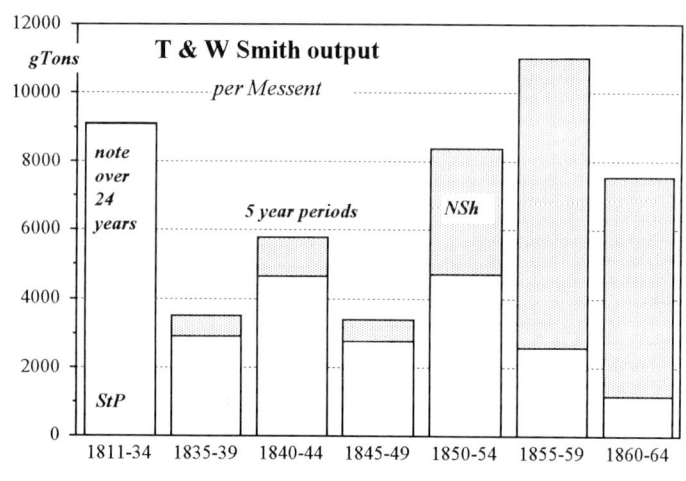

Diag 5.04

Wigram, clearly showing that the St Peters yard was capable of challenging the famous London yards for the quality of vessel built. Tragically this fine ship, intended for the East India trade and *principally for passengers*, was lost on her journey to London on 30 January 1830. Her replacement, the *Duke of Northumberland*, was launched early in 1831. The Smith family became major ship owners and developed their own passenger clipper line, London - The Cape, Madras & Calcutta, built and sailed a fleet of colliers Tyne-London, while maintaining coal hulks at Greenwich & warehouses in East India Docks.

The Laings at South Shields.

Usually the Laings are only considered as Wear shipbuilders, however, their Tyne activity was for some years very important. Indeed they were ranked fifth in aggregate Tyne output over the years 1816-49, despite the yard closing in 1831. At least fifty vessels were built, in all 10,900t [average 218t], and many

---

[10] From local registers &c 392 ships, with 62,285t, have been positively identified; this tonnage is only 77% of the official Newcastle total for the years 1820-32.

[11] Thomas sr [died 1836] was apprenticed to a ropemaker, whose daughter Mary Pearson he married. His son Thomas [born 23 Nov.1773] went into ropemaking and William [born 15 Jul 1787] became the shipbuilder.

[12] His total for the period to 1850 corresponds with those in list 22544t- 50 ships [Messent 21808 tons].

[13] Sykes *Local Records*: An excellently finished and beautiful vessel ... her interior being fitted up with unusual neatness and elegance ...frigate style ... the ports...on each side, had each a patent light in the centre, which hauled up for the admission of air into the cabins and lower deck; she was also fitted with a double tier of windows in the stern and quarter galleries ... Some beautiful carved work on the stern represented the armorial bearings of the gentleman whose name she bore; her cutwater surmounted by a bust of the same individual.

of these were built on speculation. The *Palambam* of 398t was the largest vessel built and four others were 300t or more. [see diag 5.05] A single steam boat was built, the *Britannia*, in 1823, powered by two 25 hp engines supplied by Hawkes.[14] A substantial amount of repair work and rebuilding was carried out, and in 1824 the rebuilding of the *Commerce* cost £2,150. Later work included the *British Queen*, which was *fresh sheathed* in 1828 and one of the last repairs was to the *Fort Augustus* in 1830. In March 1822 the local press announced the breakup of the original partnership but James and John continued certainly for some time. Many later references were to John Laing & Sons. The business was offered for sale or to let in March 1828. Philip Laing jnr managed his own slipway for a time. Those interested in buying the business in April 1829 were to apply to *Philip Laing*. They were offered -

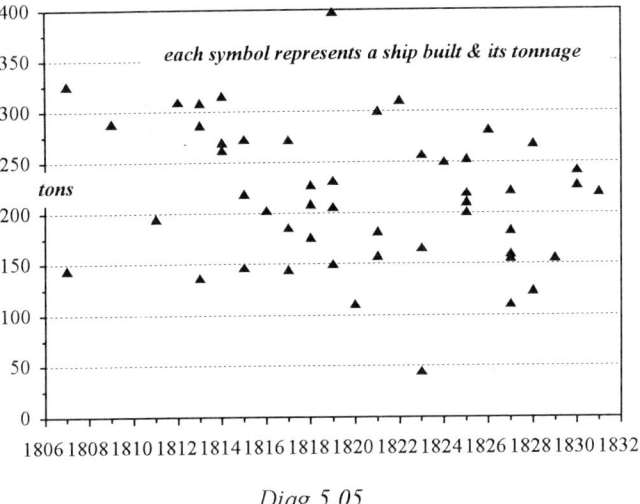

Diag 5.05

extensive Shipbuilding & Timber Yards - a Patent Slipway will be completed - large Warehouses, a Moulding Loft, and Blacksmiths' Shops on the Premises, and the Tenant or Purchaser may be accommodated with the Whole of the Builders' Tools and Carpenters' Utensils and a very large sawpit.

The lower Yard was suitable for a *Chain Cable & Anchor Business* or any other manufactory; *an extensive & convenient Yard* was available for the *Deposit of Cargoes of Timber*, which could be charged at *Twopence per Load per Month*. The *Vistula* launched in 1831 was the last ship built by Laing at South Shields. A number of Laing's apprentices joined Edward's yard when the Wear builders left Shields.

Around Gateshead a number of small yards were active in the 1820s. There were boat builders at Hillgate and ships were built at Friar's Goose. These yards included Boutland who built 15 vessels [1,662t] and George Huntley 8 vessels [1,082t]. Grays were very active on the South Shore. Various partnerships were linked with the Grays, including Robson & Roberts. The block & mast maker Andrew McLeod stated that the one shipbuilder at Gateshead in 1830 employed about 25 men and the two boat builders about 20; he had 11 *hands* and three blacksmiths.

Shipbuilding in the 1830s.

The tonnage of ships built and registered in the UK increased from 74,000t in 1830 to more than 105,000t in 1835. A bad year followed with less than 78,000t of sailing ships and then output increased sharply, exceeding 201,000t [1,296 vessels] in 1840. Evidence from north east shipbuilders and others to a Parliamentary Committee provided a contemporary picture of the industry in 1833. Shipbuilding and repair had *diminished very much ... for the last five years* according to Tyne shipbuilder Thomas Young. However, the tonnage launched on the Tyne hardly supported such a claim.[15] Others also saw it that way, Wear shipowner Henry Tanner said that shipbuilding *has very much declined at Shields; it is almost annihilated*. Vessels were smaller, at an average of 166t. Undoubtedly new work was less than the boom year of 1825; the yearly average was 7,518t over the period 1828-32. Young's own output may not have done so well[16]; he said *We have sometimes lain idle for three or four months together*. Ships not infrequently remained a long time on the stocks and then the shipwrights were often switched to repair

---

[14] There is some confusion on p50 of Flagg, where it is stated the *Carnation* was steam propelled.

[15] Hull could justify such an assessment. Edward Gibson, owner of two shipyards there, said *very few [ships built] now at Hull*, the average of the four years 1829-32 was a mere 2,325t and an average of only 84t per vessel.

[16] Young:1825: *645t*[2];1826: *60t*[1];1827: 0;1828: *401t*[1];1829: *508t*[2]; 1830: 0; 831 *492t*[2]; 1832: *242t* [1]

work. After Young failed to sell two recently built ships *for what they cost us* he was *induced to navigate them, hoping ... better price*.[17] The yard's most recent ship [*Nautilus* -400t], was sent to sea at £13/t *about price cost of her as a plain ship*, that is a vessel with no special outfit for a particular trade. Repair work was probably diminishing on the Tyne; many docks could not be let and half were unoccupied. At South Shields ten firms held 13 graving docks; the seven unoccupied could repair 11 ships, while the remaining six could only take 8 ships. It was claimed that nearly all the South Shields docks were employed in 1823. However, there was a very changed situation in 1832. Amongst those untenanted *were: Laing's* double dock since August 1828, *Craister's High Dock* since November 1828, both of *the Fairless Docks* since August 1831 and the *Forsyth's* double dock had been vacant since August 1832. Only one of the two *Middle* double docks was in use by W Stoveld. C Young & Son occupied the three single *West* Docks, and James Edwards the double *High Dock* and lastly T Metcalfe worked a single dock. *Craister's Docks* were let for £500 up to 1821 but was then empty until 1823 when the rental was halved; for occasional use rental/ton earned an average about £120/yr. A remarkable and surely unexpected example of pressure to employ men was given by Young. After they had laid men off, when work was coming in *the shipowners have resorted to employing the men themselves, and on that account we have set them on again.*

Tyneside shipowner, Thomas Brown, who was also a manufacturer of canvas and a partner in both a colliery and shipbuilding & repair company[18], acknowledged that shiprepairing *has been a steadily profitable business, but shipbuilding has not been good on the Tyne*. Ships were generally bought at Sunderland, where recently Brown bought a new ship, fitted out, for £8 10s a ton. Shipowner Hedley confirmed this and stated *we are obliged to go to Sunderland for A.1. ships for the corn trade ... we have so few of that class and suitable size at Newcastle*. Prices on the Wear were *in many instances* 25s to 30s a ton cheaper in the first cost of a ship. Young stated that building costs were *considerably less than at Shields*. Sunderland shipowner Henry Tanner said he could get a ship complete for coasting trade for about £9/ton. A collier in coasting trade cost £8 -10s /reg. ton according to Wearside shipowner and importer of timber, John Spence[19] and for East Indies trade, copper fastened - £11- £12/ton *fitted completely for sea, except coppering* of the bottom. The average price of vessels at Whitby increased from £12 in 1822 to £18 four years later, dropped to under £13 in 1828 and then to £12.25/ton. Prices rose in 1830 to £13.5, before falling to £11, which remained approximately the price per ton until 1837. A factor in the average prices were a mixture long distant traders which were more costly than those to the Baltic, which in turn cost more than coastal vessels such as colliers. The collapse in second-hand ship prices was illustrated by £1,800 being the *utmost bid*, in 1833, for a vessel completed at a cost of £4,295 in 1826. Many shipbuilding materials were cheaper in 1833 than 5 years earlier.[20] Barry of Whitby estimated a 15% fall in the cost of shipbuilding since 1825 and at that port hulls cost £8 /ton. He cited the following prices, presumably for completed vessels: £12.84 for Baltic trade in 1828 and two years later Barry built for himself a 159t, copper fastened, with a *first cost* of £12.64/ton. However, for a time the very important part of completing a vessel, fitting out, was carried out on the Tyne for some Sunderland built vessels.

Despite Young's pessimism, over the years 1833-40, he built 13 vessels, more than 3,600t, and also enlarged at least three vessels. He was fourth in rank order of output on the Tyne behind T & W Smith, Reay and Metcalfe, followed by Straker who built nine ships [2,671t]. One of those who stopped new

---

[17] The Youngs with 24 vessels, nearly 6,000t, were substantial shipowners; Brown said Thomas Young *has made a considerable fortune as a shipbuilder and dock owner*; When asked by an MP - *have not they [his docks &c] paid you over and over again?* Young replied *I decline answering that question*. [Q7809]

[18] Brown T & R jnr built five vessels 2,162t over the years 1831-3. As shipowners, they held interests in 24 ships.

[19] He owned *directly and indirectly* less than 700 tons. Spence was involved in shipbuilding in 1811, 1814 and occasionally between 1830 and 1860, at least three different partners, probably the shipwrights who built the ships.

[20] Young gave these price changes for 1818,1825 and 1833 :*cordage* /cwt -55s; 54s and 34-36s. *sails* /yard -2s 3d [1818]; 1s 9d.[1833] *iron anchors* /cwt - 33s; 30s and 25-26s. *cables* - 42s; 30s and 18s.

building in 1834 was George Kell, who began with the *Don* [336t] in 1814 and over the next two years he built 3 ships [830t] probably at Jarrow. A gap followed until the mid-1820s boom. Between 1824-34 he built 14 ships, about 3,600t, ending with the *Crusader*, 280t. Much of his work was in repairs and he occupied the Low Dock at South Shields and later Craster's dock.[21] Ambrose Hopper started his yard on the North Shore in 1825, with two vessels of 85t and 152t; the next new vessel was in 1828. His total tonnage to 1840 was 3,122t, effectively the end of new building with only the 53t *Sunniside* seven years later. This small yard enjoyed a moment of glory on 4 February 1837. More than half a page in Richardson's *Local Historian's Table Book* recounted the launch of ss *Vesta amid an immense multitude of spectators*. The vessel *presented a beautiful spectacle* [and] *went into the river with such ease, so slowly and majestically, that the people on board were scarcely conscious of her motion*. Owned by the Newcastle Steam Navigation Co, she could accommodate 50 persons, for whom the 80' of deck between the first and second cabins presented *an inviting promenade*. The *best cabin, or saloon* was *a lofty and very elegant apartment, twenty-two feet long ...splendidly lighted with plate glass, there being four stern windows, besides others, and...in the panel work several large mirrors*. The *Vesta* was 150' overall, 300t [OM] and the height between decks was 6' 7", powered by two 70 nhp engines. The crew's accommodation, 12 berths for seamen, deck houses for the master, mate and stewards, was said *to afford every comfort and convenience*. William Reay, owner of a timber yard at Walker started a shipyard in 1831. Three years later he launched *a splendid large, fully rigged ship*, which required 100 tons of ballast. Reay advanced his yard from single vessels in both 1831 and 1832 to the capacity of launching eight ships in 1840, a total of almost 1,600t, matching any yard on the river. Over a 12 year period he built more than 5,600t. An ambitious Scot, John Coutts, took over the yard in 1842. With its three berths and a river frontage of 107' this site became home to many famous shipbuilding endeavours.

Straker & Edwards
Surviving records do not enable a clear understanding of the Straker/Edwards management arrangements. James Edwards, an Irish land agent, from Dublin, married George Straker's daughter Elizabeth in 1821 and it seems likely that the son-in-law was involved in the management of the shipbuilding and repair activities from then onwards. Names of apprentices *bound & engaged* to James Edwards survive from 1826, and the yard may have had as many as 40 apprentices in the mid-1830s [records do not show how long they stayed]. There was a valuation of the yard's stock in March 1830, at the time when Edwards took full charge of the High Dock; the total valuation being £1,816 -3s-8d. Details of Edwards first 31 vessels provides a useful picture of how work proceeded on the blocks and labour costs. Although the average size was 302t, vessels varied from the *Flora* of 95t to the 670t *Viscount Melbourne*. Remarkably the days between *laid down* and launch were even more variable. The overall average was 285 days. Two hulls only took 92 days to build, the *William Wallis* [303t] and the *John* [186t].The *Flora* was laid down in September 1833 eight days before the larger *Bacchus* 145t and both were launched on 10 June 1834 - 277 days! The *Adam Lodge* [566t] was 248 days from laying keel to launch and the *Viscount Melbourne* more than twice as long 561 days. Any of these vessels, with continuous work and an adequate number of shipwrights, could have been completed in under 180 days and most in under 100 days. Such irregular periods of construction were not peculiar to Edwards; some vessels at South Shields yards were on the stocks for two years or more. Either vessels were being built on speculation and/or the work on them was undertaken when there was no repair work or an owner delayed completion. These 31 vessels aggregated almost 9,400t in the period 1830-1844. [at 600t/year output could have reached 9,000t per berth] The number of vessels on the stocks varied from one to three. Edwards' son Harry Smith took over the business at the death of his father in 1856. [see chap 7]

On the Wear.
More than 145 names appear on the Customs Register as builders on the Wear over this period, of whom more than half launched vessels in two years or more. Shipowners and timber merchants continued to

---

[21] £400 spent on new sheathing & repairs on *Juno* in 1825 and £500 on *Young Regulus* in Kell's dock.

commission and fund a shipwright to build, often only a single vessel. About 100 vessels were built annually on the Wear during 1831-4. An upward movement began which dramatically increased to almost 70,000t in 1840. The inevitable disastrous collapse followed, which affected thousands of people. Some of the new builders, who started in the early 1830s,[22] survived into the troubled 1840s and some beyond that. Undoubtedly the most important new entrant was Peter Austin, whose yard continued until the very end of shipbuilding on the Wear. At various times Austin was in partnership with Mills. Many yard owners had the surname Mills, for example John Mills [1836-9], George & J Mills [a single vessel in 1835] and James & R Mills [one vessel in 1842] and Sampson & Peter Mills. This last yard built 15,000t over the years 1832-43. Some 12,000t [45 ships] can be attributed to Austin, over the period 1831-49 and almost another 12,000t [36 ships] to the Austin & Mills partnership. William Byers started in 1832 and built almost 19,000t over 25 years. Others were Edward Brown, who built more than 8,600t, Dobbinson [8,450t] and George Frater [7,300t]. Sometimes a new builder turned out an unexpectedly high tonnage in a short period; for example W Cornforth launched the *Barbara* in April 1832 and his last the *Incertus* in October 1834, a total of 2,400t. Other such cases were more frequent in the 1839-40 boom phase. With 50 vessels over the eight years 1833-40, J M Gale continued to lead the output on the Wear and when to this was added the output of the other yards of the Gale family averaged more than 2,500t over a number of years. Sampson & Peter Mills enjoyed for those years second place on the River, with a total of 46 ships, followed by Watson with 41 and Leithhead with 36; temporarily the Laings occupied a lower position in the Wear output league table.

The famous Doxford family began its faltering early years in shipbuilding. From the early 19th century they were in the timber trade. A surviving account book, unfortunately with gaps, shows joint family business activity from 1833.[23] John [b.1786] and Joseph [1790-1851] were timber merchants. There was a brief partnership between George & Joseph and more extended joint business activity between Joseph & William. Houses were purchased and the rents provided a regular income.[24] Shipbuilding was started by William [1812-1882], son of Joseph and Elizabeth [nee Chapman]. William married Hannah [1814-95], daughter of the glass manufacturer Robert Pyle. Although the Doxford tradition suggested that the yard began in 1840, the *William & Catherine* was built in 1838 by William, followed by the *Betsey & Jane* in 1839; four vessels were built in 1840 and two in 1841. William Doxford's bankruptcy [he was also a dealer & chapman] in 1841, ended his shipbuilding for four years. After a single vessel, the *Amelia Mary*, Joseph Doxford's career as a shipbuilder ended in on 27 August 1841, when his premises at Monkwearmouth Dock, shipbuilding stock & materials were offered for sale. For six years, 1845-1851, Doxford and William Crown[25] jointly built vessels at Low Southwick. The Doxfords later funded shipwrights to build on their behalf [see chap 6].

The boom of 1839-40.

Ten Wear builders launched 10 ships or more in the two boom years 1839-40, on the Tyne only Reay matched this performance. Watson with more than 4,200t [17 ships] headed the 19 Wear builders who launched 2,000t or more. J M Gale followed with 3,400 [13 ships], H & W Carr 3,325t [14 ships] and S & P Mills with 3,309t [12]. The *Agricola* [564t] the largest ship in 1839 was built by Adamson and a year later Laing built *the John Line* [695t]. More than 80 builders were active in both 1839 and 1840, however

---

[22] The brig *Lord Seaham* began the shipments from the new coal port Seaham on 25 July 1831. A repair facility and shipyard was started by William Henzell and later by Potts, probably an off shoot of his Sunderland business. Henzell built 16 vessels between 1836 and 1851, including the 308t *Mary Sophia*, a total of 3,100t

[23] Corder found a William Doxford born in 1750 at Embleton; William [1750-91] married an Elizabeth White of Bishopwearmouth in 1779; four surviving sons and two daughters. Accounts in the surviving ledger related to Joseph, William [1782-] and George [1784-1861]. George's son Joseph became a wine merchant.

[24] These included 1 Bedford St, 2 Low Southwick and a house in Brougham St.

[25] There is uncertainty over which Crown this was - Clement William or were both names used for the same man?

about 30 of these men only each built a single vessel. Some builders launched two vessels in the same month. During six months of 1839, twenty or more builders launched a vessel a month and 30 yards launched ships in May 1840. During April and May alone more than 17,000t [57 ships] were launched. No one had ever previously known such prosperity. No records survive as to the profits made but clearly few shipbuilders secured enough reserves to survive in the subsequent slump. Boys were flocking into the shipyards: the number of shipwrights at 1841 census are shown in diag 5.06 below. One lad [under 20 years] in three at work was described as a shipwright in both Bishopwearmouth and Monkwearmouth; in Sunderland it was one in eight! In Wearside as a whole one lad in five was entered as a shipwright. In Jarrow, which included South Shields the comparable figure was one in 10 and at Tynemouth one in 30; in Great Britain as a whole slightly more than one in every 200. For these lads and their families harsh times soon arrived.

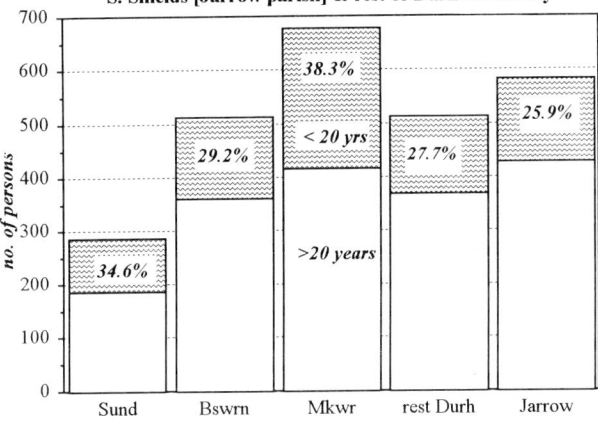

Diag 5.06

1840s - some years of severe depression.

Nationally the tonnage of sailing ships launched slumped from more than 200,000t in 1840 to less than 77,000t in 1843, in other words to less than 38% of the peak. At the end of 1844, Lloyd's surveyors reported 290 vessels under construction at 61 ports; 45 yards were building on the Wear, 25 on the Tyne and two more at Blyth, 8 at Stockton & Hartlepool and three at Whitby, a total of 83 yards on north east coast. Almost 30,000t was building in the region, nearly 43% of the total reported 69,364t. At Sunderland 100 ships, just over 27,000t, were launched in 1844, and improved output continued until 1847, when almost 47,000t were built; this was an increase of 74% compared with a national increase of about 46% [UK from 88,900t to 129,700t]. A financial crisis, not unrelated to the consequences of the Irish famine and the vast expansion of railway investments, caused substantial problems in 1847. A downturn occurred nationally falling back by 20% between 1847 and 1848 and the fall continued into 1849 [129,700-107,200-105,500t]. On the Wear there was a similar decline from 1847 to 1848 but then the trend moved upwards.

Launches declined sharply on the Wear from the beginning of 1841 [see diag 5.08]. There was then a sustained trough from May 1842 to the start of 1845. The bankruptcies of the shipbuilders began as early as August 1840 with James Carr of Southwick; a timber merchant Mitclam held security on Carr's ships and yard.[26] At least forty builders failed, including many long and well established yards, in this the first of all too many sustained depressions. The stark distress was summarised by the *Sunderland Herald*: There were 31 empty shops on the High Street in February 1843 and during June 500 workmen were on relief. A thousand empty houses and 133 empty shops showed the plight of the town. Shipbuilding offered work for a thousand where more than three times that number had been employed, the craftsman's weekly pay had fallen from 31s 6d in 1841 to 19s 6d a year later. The Sunderland historian Potts wrote:

> It was a sad sight, when going down the river, to see so many yards idle: the tall cranes standing for which no purchaser could be found,[27] whilst others had been taken down and removed to the merchants premises to save the rent of the yard; saw pits were pulled up, and desolation reigned supreme where a busy hive had been.

Many other places also suffered severe distress. On the Tyne the men stated they were paid 4s/day

---

[26] The timber merchants Grenwell & Sacker had almost 20 hulls in the North Dock from failed yards in 1841-2.
[27] Potts purchased one for £25 in August 1844.

[24s/week] in 1840. A *long and bitter strike* in 1841 followed the reduction of work to the point where even for the best employed shipwrights earned an average of only 14s 7d/week and the worst a mere 6s 4d. Robert Anderson as spokesman for the port of South Shields told a Parliamentary Committee that the *ordinary problems of relief* were *complicated in periods of extraordinary depression.* There was a public meeting in July 1843 which sent a deputation to demand work or relief; the unemployed were *chiefly* shipwrights and factory labourers [the chemical works had closed because of smoke nuisance].

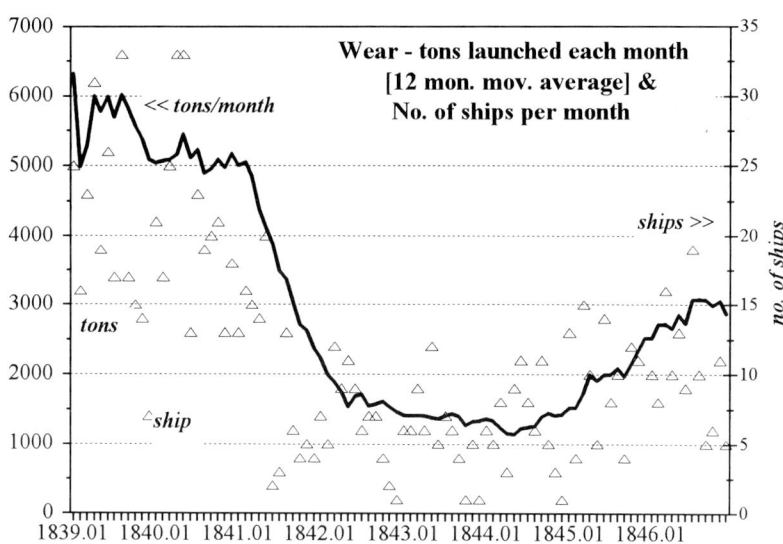

Diag 5.07

Despite launching 1,229t in 1841, Tom Gales's Hylton yard failed, *much to the surprise of almost everyone.* Vessels were built in 1842 and he managed a few more ships but none after 1847, when his liabilities were £9,000. A year earlier J M Gales launched the last of their 96 ships, built over 20 years and almost reaching a total of 25,000t. The family began building ships in 1812[28] and L Gales followed Thomas and continued until 1857. Frater, after eleven years, launched no more after 1841. Ten others, who had built at least three ships, also finished then but they had all started after 1837. A further seven builders, all of whom had built more than 1,500t, ended in 1842, including T S Dixon [started 1828]. By 1843 what seemed firmly established yards closed: J Bell had started in 1818, Rowntree in 1820, J Storey 1821, Kirkbride & partners 1824. Although S & P Mills had only begun in 1832, they had built at least 54 ships, almost 15,000t by the closure in 1843. Thirty-six builders of more than two vessels ceased new work; others, such as Naisby, Chilton, Lumsden and Doxford, were bankrupt but did return to the industry. Bankruptcy was rather more than an occasional occupational risk.[29] Seventeen yards did manage to launch at least one ship in each year 1842, 1843 and 1844, Laings built nearly 3,000t [7 ships], Ralph Hutchinson 2,614t [10 ships]and Crown just over 2,000t, although he was also bankrupt. Among those with a long term future who also achieved this distinction were Lister & Bartram [5 ships- 1,414t], Austin [3ships - 1,167t] and Austin & Mills [5ships - 1,044t]. There were other failures later in the 1840s, including some well established yards, Dobbinson in 1846, after 40 ships and 16 years, James Leithhead in the following year [another Leithhead returned in 1849] and in 1849 Joseph Helmsley, after building for 17 years. Despite all this 340,000t were built on the Wear in 1840s.

Reasons for low costs on the River Wear.
Tyneside shipowner Brown stated that part of the explanation of lower costs at Sunderland was that many builders were *barely above the position of artisans*; in using such men he had supplied *to a certain extent, the material and capital.* The Wear *carpenters* were of *a better class* and on the Tyne there were *a great many old carpenters, and a great many apprentices; in fact Shields is the nursery for carpenters for Sunderland and as a new port very few carpenters exceed the age of 45 or 50.* A third of the shipwrights

---

[28] As noticed earlier, a Lawson Gales of Hylton was building in 1770s.

[29] Other bankruptcies on Wear included: H. Carr; Henderson & Co; Lancester; Leithhead; Noble; C. Potts; W. Thompson; Andrews, Atkinson & Pyle; Briggs; Brown, Bamfield & Co; Brown & Co; Corn; Cairncross; Davy & Co; R. Dixon J; Dixon H; Dobinson; Feater & Co; Hull & Co; Jolly [Jolie] & Co; Kearsley & Turnbull; Kewin & Co; Laws & Co; T. Lightfoot; Mackie & Co; Moore & Co; Robt Reay; W. Sutherland; Spowers & Co; Taylor; W. Thompson; Todd & Wilson; J. Watson.

on the Wear were under 20 years of age in 1841. The census of 1851 showed that 58% of the Durham shipwrights were under 30, compared with 51% in Northumberland and only 38% in London. Wear shipbuilders recruited lads on the Tyne. In April 1824 John Robson, of Monkwearmouth, advertised in the *Newcastle Courant* for *A number of young men...to serve an Apprenticeship as Shipwrights*, they were to be 16 to 20 years and of good background. Some years later Joshua Wilson explained in 1848, how *the Sunderland People* were able to build so much more cheaply than the rest of the World:

> there is a large Export of Coals ... Freight both Ways...That gives us a very great Advantage in the Baltic and Hamburg and other Countries to which we carry Coals every Day. It also gives us an Advantage in getting timber from the South of England and London ... out of Yorkshire, English Timber.. we have a great Assortment of Timber... American Elm...Danzic Oak Plank ... our builders place each Description of Timber in that position of the vessels to which it is best adapted. Now in the Ships of the Size built at Sunderland the Timber is small [on the Tops], and the English Timber actually costs less than they could import Foreign for that Purpose ... I consider that one great Saving is in the Workmen; the Workmen of Sunderland can do at least twice as much Work as those on the Continent, if not more. I believe they can get through a great deal more Work than any other Workmen in the Kingdom; the Tyne Shipwrights cannot compete with ours. ... another great Advantage that the British Shipowner has is in the Outfit of the Vessels; the Ironwork, which is a very great thing, for Anchors, and Chains, and Fastenings, is very cheap in England. We have large Works for finishing Iron in Sunderland and the Iron Mine is in the same County. We have Coals for very little indeed, because the Refuse Small does for working it ... instead of using Copper, we generally use ... Muntz's Metal[30] or Yellow Metal; it is ... considered better for fastening Vessels, as being harder than Copper ... the Men in fitting out Ships have great Skill and Activity. I have heard Workmen say that a Sunderland Blockmaker would do Three Times as much Work as a Shields one; a good deal of that may be Brag; still everything is adapted for it, like as everything is adapted in Manchester for carrying on the Cotton Trade, and I consider that one great Reason why we excel in Cheapness of Shipbuilding ...Another thing ... all the refuse Timber that will not go into a Twelve Years Ship is put into this lower Class Vessel; for the Coal Trade there is a very large Demand for those cheap Vessels. In London ... a good deal of this refuse Timber is wasted.

He endorsed Brown's view that a *large proportion* of the shipbuilders were *little better* than labouring men and if they made their wages, and *perhaps £100 or £200 a year, they were very well off*. A builder told him he *could make £100 by converting the Timber when another would make nothing because one Man will cut his timber to waste and another will fit it with much less waste*.[31]

The Tyne.
As on the Wear, 1839-40 were good years on the Tyne and at least 21,000t were built; launches dropped to about 8,000t in 1841. However the annual average during 1842-5 was not much above 6,000t. More than 10,000t were built on the Tyne in 1847 and the Lloyd's agent at North Shields provided a snapshot of the activities in April of that year. Six yards had no ships under construction: at South Shields-Blumer[32] and Barker; Boutland at Bill Point as well as Hopper, Straker & Love and Winlow. Blumer lost between 40s and 50s a ton when he sold his new vessel of 332t for £2,700. Other builders had ships on their slipways for a long time -Thomas Young 370t *a full year on*, James Young 280t *standing two years*; Forsyth 250t *two years building*; T. Metcalfe & Son 380t *stand still ... also Two Years on*. Work was proceeding on two of three vessels at Edwards, including a 12 year ship, while T & W Smith were building 1,400t all high class ships. Other work included -Trotter & Young 380t, C Smith 300t, Cunningham 270t, Wallis 170t, Gaddy & Lamb 130t and Arvin 70t. Poppelwell, of Lloyds, wrote in April 1847 *during my life* [on the Tyne] *never so few building*. There were then 15 vessels were on the stocks, 5,500t wood and

---

[30] G F Muntz patented his metal in 1832; it was about 3 parts copper to two parts zinc.

[31] Wilson pointed out that it was not *the practice of the Port* at Sunderland to include a chronometer in the outfit. This saving was not very great and presumably was discounted by the fore knowledge of the buyer. Cheap material MacGregor claimed was the major factor in Sunderland's success. His view that *no owner of repute would purchase a ship built there unless he had supervised her construction* must be doubted. pp86-7 *Tea Clippers*.

[32] Blumer had rented Laing's slipway at South Shields from 1839 to 1845 at £200/year, Bushell paid rent in 1846-7.

800t iron [Coutts 400t and Clay 400t]. Matters were little better a year later, when he commented that new ships were unsaleable on the Tyne: *We have not One Order for a Shipowner or Merchant for building a Ship. Master Shipwrights*, with their apprentices ,only work on new vessels when no dock repairs were required. When Edwards saw *Ruin stared him in the Face*, when he sold a 692t vessel at £12 a ton, which was £4/t below prime cost. Output was about 7,000t in 1848 and 1849. At this time amendments to the Navigation Laws were vigorously debated and many petitions were sent to Parliament.[33]

Whitby.

As elsewhere, after the end of the war in 1815, shipbuilders at Whitby left the industry. After constructing nine vessels [2,844t] over four years, *Whitby Builders* appeared well established but they do not appear on the register after 1815. Smales and Chapman struggled through to 1817 and Holt until 1819. New yards by Falkingbridge and Spencelayh began in 1819; output from both yards was modest. Falkingbridge built 16 vessels over the 27 years to 1846 [average 56t]; clearly this business dealt in small craft. Spencelayh's vessels were larger at 127t average but he only built 11 vessels over a 17 year period until the yard ended in 1835. The name of Fishburn ceased to appear in 1822. Although Thomas Broderick continued, the output was very small only nine sailing ships, in all 2,018t spread over the period 1823-75. The rising trend in 1824 may have prompted William Hobkirk to begin shipbuilding and over the next 26 years he launched 33 vessels, just over 6,000t; Thomas Hobkirk took over in 1850. Sunderland shipowner John Spence in 1833 regarded Whitby as *hardly a building port at all*. This was too harsh a judgment but Thomas Turnbull as a Whitby shipowner stated that *the town was in a very depressed state at present* [July 1833], only 4 of 14 slipways were occupied. He explained that Whitby could not compete with the low rate of other ports, Sunderland and Shields ships were 15% - 20% cheaper, he added these ships *will answer every purpose during the 10 years that stands upon the first letter* [Lloyd's classification]. Turnbull began shipbuilding in 1840 and the yard continued until 1901. Before 1830 there were eight yards at the port but it had by then declined to four. A contributory factor to the immediate decline was the decision of Robert Barry in 1830 to leave shipbuilding, because he *could not make it pay*. The Barrys had built on the same site for more than 70 years. The Barry family made their money as shipowners. Robert was unequivocal on the financial gains from building new ships: if *a shipbuilder had invested his whole capital in the funds eight or ten years ago, and had retired ... he would generally be richer* than having continued to work his yard. *If all the shipbuilding establishments in the kingdom were thoroughly examined, they would all be found to exhibit a loss at present*. He offered his reasons why firms continued: *people that have establishments cannot lay them down immediately,*[34] *and they must go on doing something...They cling to it with the hope that it will ultimately become more profitable...Like a drowning sailor, they cling to it till the property is gone*. Only three vessels were building at Whitby in December 1844. Two of these were on contract and Barrick was building for sale the largest vessel, a 290t 12 year ship. Lloyds had their difficulties with the Barrick yard, in 1850 chief surveyor Creuze described Barrick as *one of the most blasphemous, foul mouthed and malignant men I have ever met ... complaints* [from whom] *entitled to little credit or consideration.*

The Tees & Hartlepool.

The Tees, like the Tyne, gained its significance as a shipbuilding centre with the arrival of the iron hull. Nonetheless there was some progress through the 1830s and 1840s, with high levels of output in the boom years 1838-40. There was a ship carpenters' community at Stockton, which turned out with two banners

---

[33] *Navigation Acts*. Petitions against any Alterations came from South Shields and Middlesborough signed by Shipowners, Shipbuilders, Merchants, Shipwrights, Mast & Blockmakers, Ropemakers &c, Master Mariners and Seamen. Petitions for a Select Committee before any Alteration from Sunderland, South Shields Hartlepool and Scarborough. Various Navigation Laws had regulated overseas trade for centuries, including rebates and duties and the ownership and manning of ships. The particular concern related to timber, particularly that coming from North America.

[34] Like Tynesider Thomas Young in 1833 *we have a large establishment, which we are obliged to continue.*

in 1832 to celebrate with other workers the Reform Bill. A sale of the three ships of the Stockton Marine Co. in 1830 indicates the prices of secondhand vessels: 226t - £4/t; 177t £5.14/t and 108t £5/t. Coal and other trades were advancing. In 1834 the first coals were shipped from Haverton Hill staithes and a year later the Hartlepool Docks & Harbour opened for trade and the first shipping company was established there. Thirty eight different names[35] appear as shipbuilders in registers for the period 1835-50; most of these were for a single vessel or two. On 5 March 1833 the *Middlesbrough* [300t] was launched by Laing at Middlesbrough shipyards. A year later Holmes, J G [& Harding] began a yard which survived until 1853 at least, in 1835 they launched *Otnaburgh* and apart from the depressed years 1843-4 completed at least a vessel in each year. Between 1835-50 Middlesbrough shipyards turned out about 4,500-5,000t, and Holmes built about 3,500t and launched four vessels in 1839 including *Wellington* [308t]. In the 1842 Directory he was the only shipbuilder listed at Middlesbrough. Three vessels were built by Cudworth in the boom 1838-40. The first steamer at this port was the *Fortitude* of 21t, built by Nicholas Arkley followed by tug *Sunbeam*, both in 1840. John Langdale had a timber yard and built ships during 1844-7; this yard was later used by Rake & Kimber.

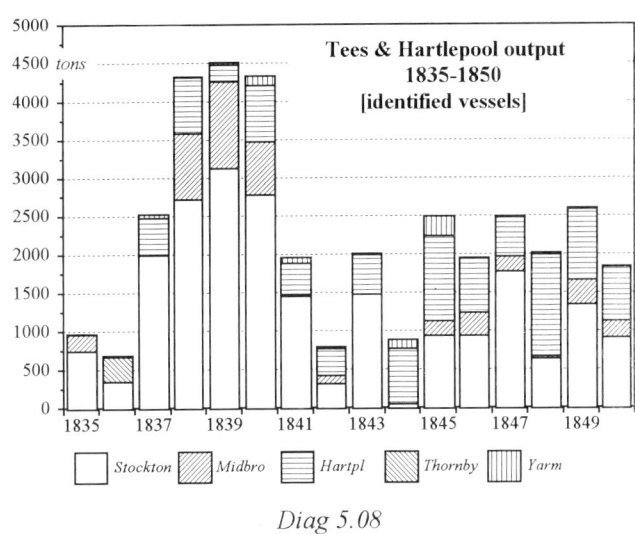

Diag 5.08

Overall output is summarised in diag 5.08. A new shipyard was opened in 1836 at South Stockton [Thornaby] by Spence; his first vessel was the *Coundon* [340t], and he built almost 2,500t before the yard closed in 1843. In that year T.Lane built the first steamboat at Stockton - *English Rose* which appears to be his only venture into shipbuilding. At Portrack William Mellanby had a yard from 1826; new output seems to have been erratic. The activities of the Turnbulls, shipowners and builders, are considered in chap 8. More than 22,000t were constructed at Stockton in the period 1835-50; almost half of that was in the years 1837-41. As much as 10,000t was probably built at Hartlepool.

Denton's yard dominated wood shipbuilding at Hartlepool, not far short of three-quarters of the port's output being by his yard. However, the industry began with a joint venture between the blacksmith Thomas Richardson, of Castle Eden, and the Sunderland man Joseph Parkin with interests in shipping. Their first site was hardly suitable but they launched the very respectably sized *Castle Eden* [258t]. Parkin & Richardson[36] built only six vessels, a total of 1,204 tons, and Richardson moved back to engineering and a distinguished future [see chap 15]: he briefly returned to wood shipbuilding, with one ship in both 1845 and 1846. When Parkin & Richardson moved, John Punshon Denton [1800-1871] took over their old yard at Middleton. The son of a Sunderland shipowner, Denton was for a time Lloyds surveyor on the Wear before moving to Hartlepool in 1836 and undertaking some repair work. At 94t the *Petrel*, Denton's first vessel, was a modest start in 1839. Half of the first ten vessels were registered for Denton, one in partnership with his in-laws the Sunderland Ords. The Ords continued to buy ships, four more before 1852, just as Denton himself continued to share ownership of the vessels he built. His largest wood ship was 582t, launched, in 1854, as the *Ocean Flower* [renamed *John Masterman*] for the London shipowners Lidgett & Co. The longest vessel was the *Armais* [501t], at 144' 6" built for Ord in 1851, and almost as long was

---

[35] These include a W Pile in 1838 and a J.Pile in 1842.

[36] Wood in his *History of Hartlepool*, described the personal links and continuity in a family of shipwrights. In 1837 Thomas Sanderson went from Wearside to work for Parkin & Richardson on the *Richmond Lass* and went on to work on the first ship built at Middleton the *Thomas Wood*. Anthony Turnbull, as a boy, worked with him and later became foreman shipwright at Denton Gray and his great grandson held the same job at Gray's Dockyard.

the *Alliance* [507t] for Henderson of Liverpool in 1848. Denton's business through its later partnership with Gray was the single shipbuilding continuity from before 1850 into the twentieth century. Whitby born, John Winspear [1816-74][37] began with a schooner [74t] built on speculation in 1841 probably at Middleton. In all he launched seven vessels scattered over the years from 1841 to 1858 but mainly carried out shiprepair work. Ship surveyor Luke Blumer with his son George began a yard in 1849 [see chap 8]. When Hartlepool received a new charter in 1850, Blumer became a councillor and Denton an alderman.

Early steam power and the tug boat.

Once steam was successfully applied to land engines a small number of men hoped to apply it to ship propulsion. The first practical regular application of steam power was to river boats and particularly tug boats. From the 1770s a number of French engineers experimented with steam propelled vessels. In the newly formed United States of America, John Fitch [1743-98] and James Rumsey [1743-92] were also trying to overcome the many problems of successfully installing an engine on a ship. Another American Robert Fulton [1765-1815], travelled to England to study engineering and in 1793 sent the plan of a steam engine to Lord Stanhope. He continued his studies in France with a famous mechanic Etienne Calla [1760-1835]. After many unsuccessful attempts Fulton built his submarine *Nautilus* in 1801. He also built a steam boat, which towed two vessels in a trial on the Seine in 1803. Fulton returned to the U S A and in 1807 his *Clermont* made its trial run, arguably the first commercial steamboat. An Englishman named Dyer travelled on the *Clermont* In 1811, he tried to introduce steam navigation in Britain, but found *a strong conviction that it would not answer in this country*, because of the smaller rivers. Fortunately more adventurous men had already, indeed for many years before 1811, been carrying out experiments north of the border. Scotsmen were signalling their future leading role. William Symington supplied Thomas Miller with an atmospheric engine in 1788 which propelled a boat, with the poet Robert Burns on board. Symington also supplied the engine for the pioneering and better known tug boat *Charlotte Dundas*, whose successful trials were carried out in 1802.

About half a dozen river steamers were working on the Clyde before the *Perseverance* made her first run on the Tyne on 3rd June 1814. Beginning in the local Race Week 1814, the Shields-Newcastle service has been claimed as the *first English River...regular passenger traffic by steamboat*. When this proved unprofitable John Price, of Gateshead, decided to use two paddle steamers for towing sailing ships.[38] His first endeavour was to tow the *Friends' Adventure* two miles across the Shields Bar in July 1818. An article in *Smith's Dock Journal* in 1929 suggested that this was the *first tug-boat*; this claim is not sustainable.[39] In August 1816 the *Majestic* towed the *Hope* from Deptford to Greenwich, on the Thames, and in October 1816 the *Charlotte* towed a vessel out of the Mersey. Interestingly, the Oxford dictionary dates the word *tug* from 1817, when a steam boat of this name was specially built at Dumbarton. These humble craft enabled sailing ships to avoid being harbour bound due to adverse winds and went on and continue to form a vital role in the maritime field.

An engine from the Birmingham firm of James Watt powered the *Eagle*, used on the Tyne from 1816. The engine builder for the second Tyne steam vessel, the *Swift,* in 1815 is however unknown. Building engines for those early river steamboats and tugs laid the basis for the marine engineering on the Tyne. Fifteen vessels were used for towing purposes on the Tyne by 1822; Jonathan Robson of Gateshead engined six of these and Hawthorns of Forth Banks four. Hawks of Gateshead added to its many achievements the 14hp

---

[37] see *John Winspear A Hartlepool Shipbuilder* D McLaren Kerr [Hartlepool 1982]

[38] A very importance source for this section is P.N. Thomas *British Steam Tugs*. The classes of tug include: harbour or dock tugs; river tugs; ocean-going tugs; Thames craft tugs and tenders and naval tugs. J H Proud's *150 years of the Maltese Cross,* a study of the Tyne, Blyth and Wear Tug Companies provides invaluable information on tugs up to 1992. See also his *Seahorses of the Tees* [1985].

[39] See R. N. Appleby Miller *The First Tug-boat*. Appleby was aware of the *Charlotte Dundas* but commented *she was scrapped. Smith's Dock Journal* pp249- Sept. 1929.

engine for the *Safety* in 1821 and three years later this works built the 30hp *grasshopper*[40] engine for the *Newcastle*. Robson's works continued to be a well respected boiler works and the young Wigham Richardson served his time there. Just over 10% of the tugs operating throughout the UK were on the Tyne. By 1827 some 38 such vessels were plying the river. Their largest task was towing of vessels. As the contemporary MacKenzie wrote

> This has become a matter of great importance to those concerned in the shipping of coals and goods ... large fleets never remain wind-bound in harbour, when there exists the least chance of making progress at sea.

In the 1860s there were upwards of 250 *native steam tugs* on the Tyne and almost 100 more on the Wear and Tees, all with engines *almost identical* in type to those fitted in 1820. These early engines devoured coal which restricted the application to either towing or river traffic so that fuel could be readily taken on board when required. *A notorious coal eater*, the tug *Monarch*, occasionally borrowed coal from her tow. The Tyne was described as *the home of tug building from the very early days of tugs and towing*. Tyneside's strong engineering base was no doubt a major factor in this achievement, relatively few tugs were built on the Tees or the Wear. A remarkable example of Geordie ingenuity, the combination of locomotive and boat, provided a primitive tug in 1822. This strange craft was created to overcome the consequence of a strike of the keelmen, which prevented the movement of coal down river to be loaded for shipment by sea. A keel was adapted to take the famed early locomotive *Wylam Dilly* minus its wheels, with its power geared through paddles to pull a number of keels loaded with coal.

At least 360 steam vessels were built on the Tyne before 1850 [see diag 5.09] and perhaps a dozen were built on the Wear. Thomas Richardson of Hartlepool supplied the engines for the *Flying Dutchman* built at Sunderland in 1851. Almost all these early steam vessels were paddle driven and although there were many early experiments with screw propulsion this did not seriously emerge until after 1854. North Shields [with 149 vessels], South Shields [78] and Gateshead [63] were the principal centres for tug boat building. Eleven Tyne yards each built nine steamers or more before 1850, and a further eleven constructed four or more. In all sixty builders built at least one of these early steamers. About half of these were built by six yards: the largest number by Dowey of North Shields with at least 48. His first steamer, the *Jane*, was registered in 1826. Woodhouse, of South Shields,

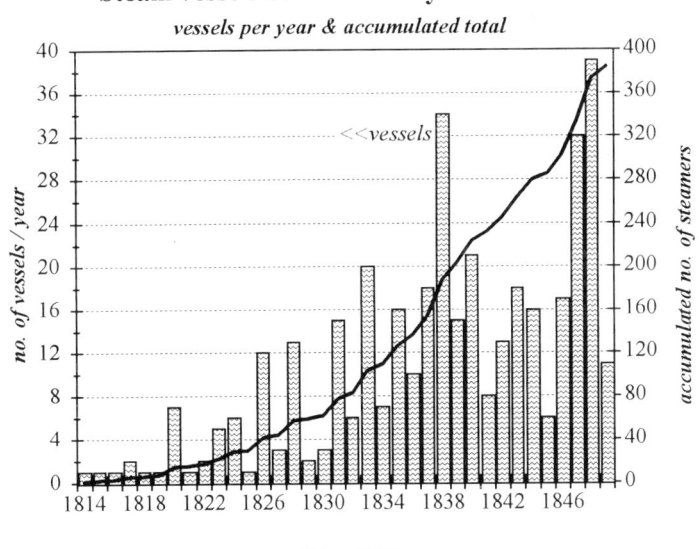

Diag 5.09

built two steam vessels in 1835 and completed 34 by 1849. At Jarrow, Daniel Bider began in 1838 and built more than 30 steam vessels by 1848. He later moved to North Shields. Cooper & Gardner at North Shields, launched two steamers in 1840, and more than 20 vessels were built before 1850, including the *Water Witch* [30 hp] in 1843 and a year later the *Chieftain* [45 nhp]. Nearby Bell also built tugs, and was in a sometime partnership with a Cooper. The number launched in a particular year varied considerably, as diag 5.09 shows. This was also true for individual yards. Stephen Wood at Gateshead built an average of one steamer a year during 1828-1846 but six were registered in 1833 and three in both 1831 and 1838. Bowlt also averaged one a year from 1820 until 1836; his first, the *Tyne*, was engined by Robson. Tyne tugs, in 1830s, were *generally small* [50' -70' long] compared with other shipyards elsewhere in Britain,

---

[40] Engine and boiler design is reviewed in chap 14.

according to Thomas. From 1840s an increased number of tugs were built on other rivers. Tyne built tugs for local owners were later sold to other ports. An 1852 Admiralty survey of the tugs in use in London, Bristol and Liverpool, showed that 40 were built on the Tyne, 11 on the Thames, 10 at Liverpool, three at Southampton and Bristol and two each on the Wear and Tees.

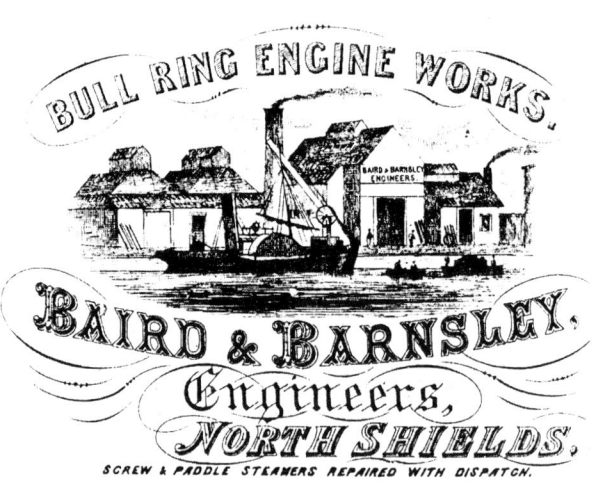

Wood remained the principal material for tug hull construction[41] for many years after iron became the main ship construction material on the Tyne. In 1868 on that river, only 12 of the 236 tugs and ferries were of iron; on the Wear in 1860 only one of 48 tugs was of iron and only two iron hulls of 22 on the Tees. Very probably the bumping and other stresses to which tugs were subject made timber a more suitable material and the cargo space gains of the metal hull were not relevant. Almost 400 wooden hulled vessels, under 150t, were built on the Tyne between 1856 and 1872 and another 100 over the next twelve years. At least a further 36 were added before the end of the century. One of the Tyne built tugs the *Monarch* has a fame hardly realised, being portrayed in Turner's famous painting *The Fighting Temeraire*. She was built at North Shields in 1836-7 for John Watkins of London [64'10" x 13'11" draught 4' 6"].[42] Many examples might be given of the long life of these Tyne tugs. The *Prince of Wales* was built at Low Walker in 1861 and was not broken up until 1915. Others exceeded this period of 54 years. The *Favourite* built in 1828 at North Shields was on the Register until 1891; Thomas pointed out that in 1845, the dimensions were given as *52'2 x 11 x 3' dr -10t with an* 8 nhp engine and in 1878 as *54'3 x 12 x 6'1- 24t 9 nhp*! The tonnage of these early steam vessels if simply added to that of wood sailing vessels gives a misleading impression of the amount of work they required; a tug could cost three to four times per ton more than a cargo vessel. The tonnage deducted for the engine room, certainly on vessels up to 50t invariably exceeded the registered tonnage and not infrequently was twice as much, for example Bider's *Emperor* in 1847 had a gross tonnage of 73t but the engine room at 52t made the net tonnage 21t. All these the engine rooms, especially on small craft, occupied a substantial part of the vessel's length. The average of 300 Tyne built tugs from 1851-1913 was 117t.[43] While few of the early pioneers of tug boat building survived beyond the 1880s, their tradition was carried forward by Eltringham, Rennoldson, Hepple and Readhead. A tug, *Old Trafford*, built in 1907 by Eltringham, is on display as *Reliant* in the National Maritime Museum. Wood tugs were built on the Tyne up into the 1890s.

Some summary comments.
In Lloyds Register of 1844 there were 37 iron vessels [almost 9,500t], of which nearly 28% was from Scotland; London with 3,357t exceeded the Scots. Both Liverpool with 1,496t and Hull exceeded the Tyne's modest 498t; possibly a few vessels were not on the Register. These figures show the ground to be made up in iron construction on the north east coast. The redistribution of shipbuilding output between the north

---

[41] Although the work was similar to other craft, they had their own peculiarities. Firstly a clincher [planks overlapped at edges] technique was used this gave a stronger structure. A description given in 1933 claimed it was a craft which *needed a high degree of skill, an eye for symmetry, and a thorough knowledge of how the details of the under water form affected the performance of the finished tug* and that the two shipwrights working on each side would *usually* race each other to finish first. Smith's Dk Jrl May 1933

[42] Watkins arranged the design with H S Wait and the Waits made the engines. Richard Arkley was the builder.

[43] Tugs were frequently below 100t, and so will be excluded from many aggregate tables of tonnage.

east ports, which began before 1815 was carried forward in the years to 1850. Although the Tees had yet to fully emerge, both Whitby and Scarborough had greatly declined and Sunderland moved forward. With the exception of Smith/Edwards not one of the 30 men on the Tyne who registered vessels in 1849 would be a major shipbuilder in later years. In contrast most of the future leaders on the Wear had already established their yards and diag 5.10 below summarises the great advance of output on that river between 1820 and 1850. These top 20 yards had a combined output five times greater in 1850 compared with thirty years earlier, the average tonnage was more than doubled and from just over two ships/year there was nearly five per yard. The largest ships built on the Wear moved steadily upwards from less than 500t in the 1830s to more than a 1,000t in 1849.

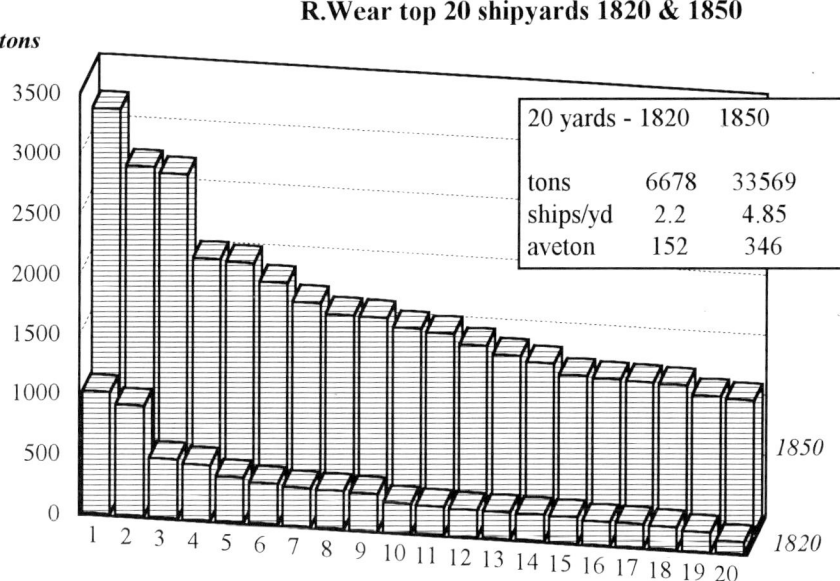

Diag 5.10

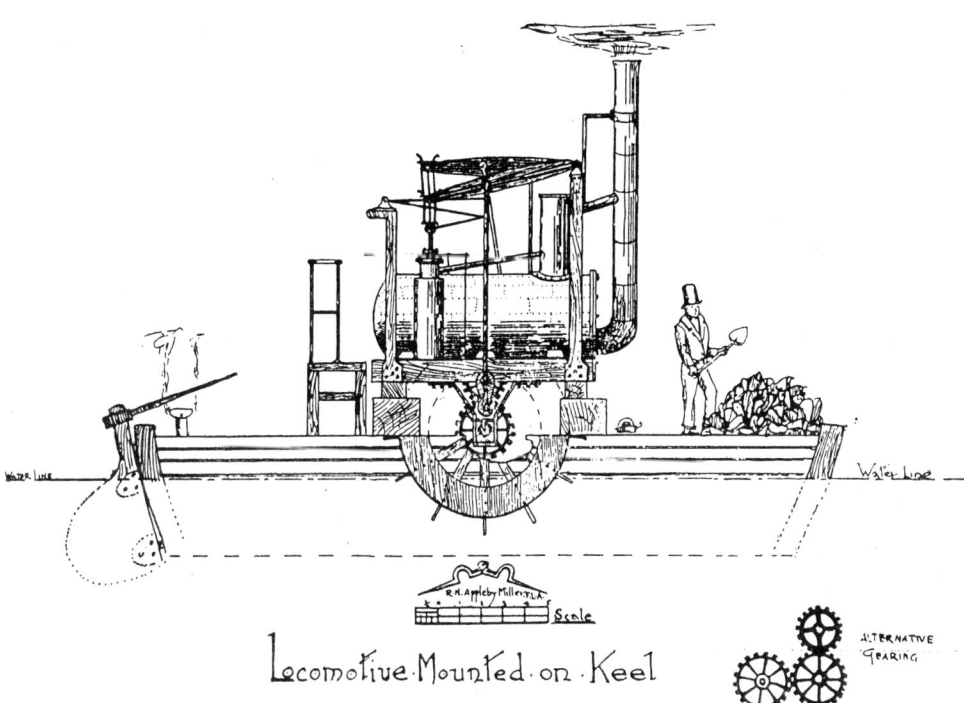

River Wear Shipyards 1861

G W & W J Hall - graving dock

North Sands 5 yards
Wm Barkley
J Blumer
B & J Gardner
R Thompson & Sons
Wm Pile jnr

A Simey - Strand Slipway

Wreath Quay 2 yards
G Peverall
J Barkes

Laing's Cornhill graving dock

Southwick 9 yards
D A Douglas
Pickersgill & Miller
Rawson & Smith
J & G Mills
R Thompson jnr
James Hardie
W Petrie
W Chilton
J & J Brown

North Hylton 10 yards
R Bartram
Gibbon & Nichol
B Hodgson
J Errington
Todd & Brown
Gray & Young
L Wheatley
Sutcliffe
Sykes Talbot
John Pile

One mile

South Dock 3 yards
Taylor & Scouler
J Haswell
J M Reed

Low Street 2 yards
R H Potts & Bros
J T Alcock

Bishopwearmouth 2 yards
S P Austin
J Hutchinson

Ravenswheel 2 yards
J Davidson
T Stonehouse

Ayre's Quay
Metcalfe & co

Deptford 3 yards
Richard Thompson
J & J Robinson
James Laing

Pallion 10 yards
W Doxford
T R Oswald
G Short
Wm Briggs
G Watson
J Watson
W Ratcliffe
W Adamson
James Robinson
T Robson

South Hylton 3 yards
J Lister
Wm Naisby
Edw Potts

Chapter 6

Shipbuilding on the Wear c1850-1880s

Sunderland - the greatest shipbuilding port in the world was the proud claim made by the *Sunderland Herald* in 1850. This chapter reviews the changes on the River Wear from about 1850 to 1880, during which many wood yards somewhat belatedly made the changeover from hulls of wood to iron and Sunderland's leading position was challenged. The distinction of being the greatest centre in wood shipbuilding, in part at least, helps explain the seven year delay in the adoption of iron compared with the rest of the country.

Overseas trade to and from the United Kingdom doubled in money terms between 1854 and 1870. Between 1850 and 1866, the UK Register increased by 3,000 ships to 28,971. It then fell back to 25,892 in 1871. However, the tonnage had grown by 60%, with the average size of ships increasing from 137t to 220t. Shipping was strongly influenced by both the Crimea War [1854-6] and the American Civil War [1861-5], and the additional factors of the discovery of gold in both Australia and California, and emigration from Europe. Although the imports of coal by sea to London fell by rather more than 10%, coal exports overseas increased almost fourfold from 3.2 million tons in 1850 to 12.2 million tons in 1870. Coal moved by sea increased from just over 6,000,000 just over 15,000,000 tons. In Northumberland and Durham coal output almost doubled, increasing from 15.4 million tons [1854] to 29.2 million tons in 1871. At mid-century the Cleveland iron ore field had barely begun and output increased from 865,000 tons in 1854 to more than 4 million tons in 1870. There was a tenfold increase in the output of pig iron in North Yorkshire from 101,000 tons [1854] to more than a million in 1871. This expansion made the increase in output in Northumberland and Durham from 174,000 tons to 793,000 tons seem modest. Between 1851 and 1871, Northumberland and Durham increased in population by 54.1%, double that in the rest of England & Wales. Vigorous expansion characterised industry in the north east. The 6,000 miles of railways in Great Britain in 1850 more than doubled before the end of the 1860s.

Broad trends in shipbuilding output.

Shipbuilding output shown as a 9-year moving average provides a most useful summary picture, evening out the fluctuations due to the trade cycles [see diag 6.01 note the two scales]. From the early 1850s to the start of the 1870s the rest of the country shows a steadily upward movement. At the outset of this period the Wear was at a high point, aggregated output over the years 1846-54 being about one-third of total national output [the Tyne was probably about 8%]. After the end of the Crimean war, the trend shows the decline at Sunderland, whereas elsewhere the upward movement continued strongly, so that the lead held by the Wear was lost. The two lines move together from 1864 to 1871. Over the period 1855-70, the Wear's proportion of national output, in simple tonnage terms, was just over one-fifth compared with an earlier level of about one-third. The failure to change from wood to iron quickly enough was undoubtedly a factor in this relative decline. However legitimately a moving

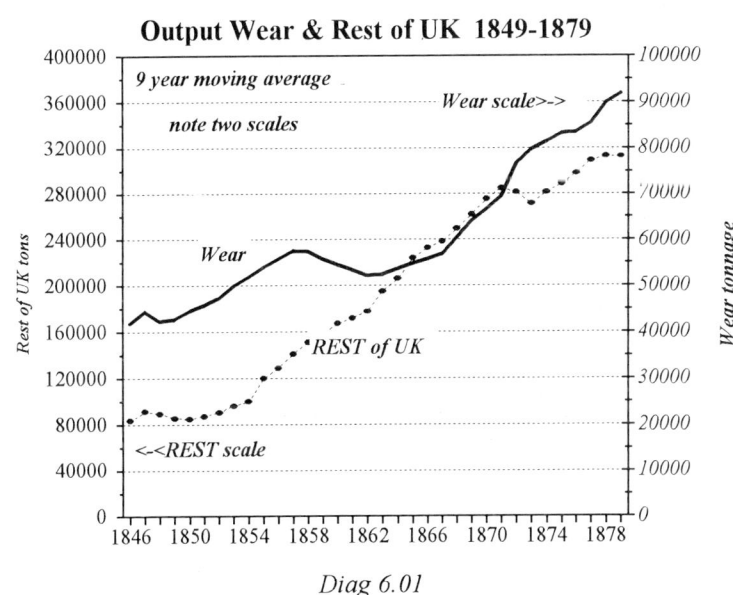

Diag 6.01

average may help our understanding, it masks the difficulties of the individual shipbuilder who was trying to sell a ship or secure orders during those 9 years [which were averaged].

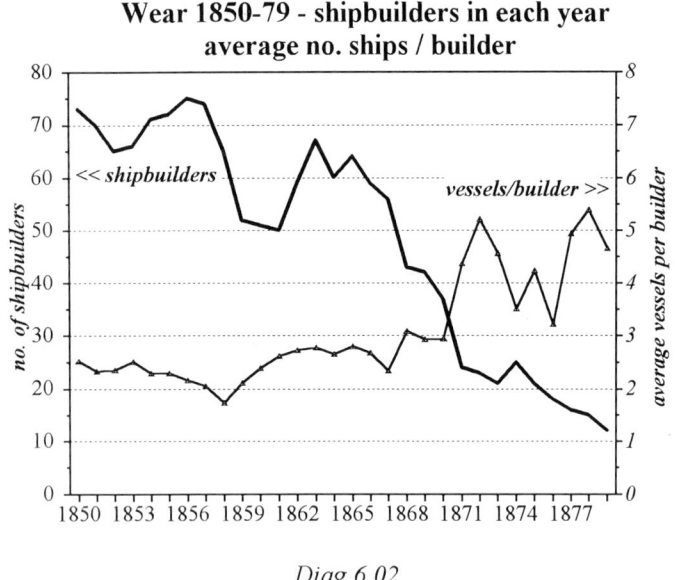

Diag 6.02

After 1857 there was a clear downward trend in the number of shipbuilders on the Wear, with fluctuations [see diag 6.02]. Over the years 1850-7, an average of about 70 yards launched about two vessels each annually. Not until 1868 did the number of yards fall below 50 and as iron construction advanced the numbers reduced to the 13-14 yards which continued until the 1920s. There were 100 vessels on the stocks on the Wear in January 1850 and at the end of the year 74, of which a mere 17 were sold. Speculative building continued to dominate Sunderland's output; as 1863 began, only 58 of 99 vessels launched were sold when launched. Various mutual insurance associations were established by north east ship owners to cover the substantial losses of shipping which occurred throughout much of the 19th century. The insurance clubs at Sunderland did not rely on the *Liverpool book*;[1] indeed it was proposed in the Notice for the annual meeting of the Wear Assurance Association that *the Liverpool class* be expunged. These clubs continued to record a ship's carrying capacity in *keels*, reflecting the persistence of the central role of carrying coal. The following requirements were proposed for insurance:

> Ships not permitted above 17 tons to a keel, if loaded wholly or in part with Railroad Iron; nor above 5 tons per keel of Pig Iron or Iron Ore ... or Pig Lead, Copper Ore, Marble, Metallic Sand, Spelter or Zinc.

The market for Sunderland ships.

Ships of a lower year classification dominated for many years, with roughly 80% of Wear built wood ships classed *10* years or below until the end of the 1860s. Although in the early 1850s about half were *8* years or less, there was a clear downward trend in the number ships in this class [diag 6.03]. These vessels should not be considered as evidence of inferior work at Sunderland but rather that the owners wanted vessels at a price that matched this class.[2] There clearly was a substantial market for these ships. Many fine vessels in higher classes were built. London was a major market for Wear ships and in 1853 purchased some 35% of the tonnage [27% of ships, larger

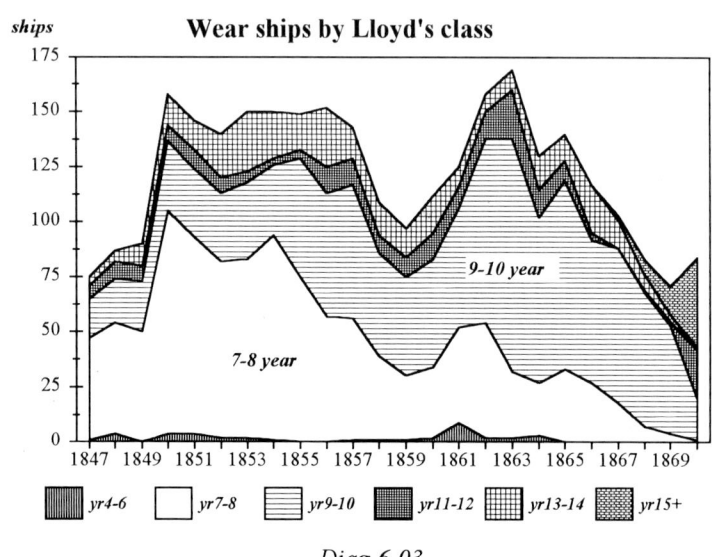

Diag 6.03

---

[1] As noted above shipowners in so called the *Outports* were anxious to be adequately represented in the management of Lloyds, and in 1835 there was created the *Liverpool Register of Shipping* as an alternative Society.

[2] In 1849 a Newcastle owner required a ship by Wm Wilkinson to be completed as 10A, frame surveyed 12A!

than average]. Tyne and Wear owners accounted for 41% of the output, as would be expected, while nearly 5% went to Liverpool and 3% to Scotland [diag 6.04 below]. Eight years later, in 1861, London sales fell to just over 28%, and purchases by Sunderland owners increased from a quarter to a third; the proportion sold to Liverpool also increased to 7.5%! Twenty ships were built by the Piles for the North Shields shipowner Kelso, for Pile's partners the Hay family 18 and they also supplied the principal London owners: Green, Willis, Walker, Nourse, Devitt & Moore, Ellis Tyser &c. A small indication of the future overseas market was emerging with the sale of ships to Germany.

Output in the 1850s

Shipbuilders on the Wear began the 1850s very well, more than 51,000t being launched in 1850, increasing to not far short of 70,000t by 1853. An average exceeding 66,000t was completed for the next three years. The demands for ships during the Crimea war resulted in many orders. Wear shipbuilders claimed in 1852 that *the large capital* they employed *far exceeded that of any other port in the United Kingdom*. Lloyd's Visitors noted in the summer of 1853 the marked contrast between complaints elsewhere of a scarcity of workers, whereas it was quite evident, and was indeed acknowledged, that at Sunderland where much activity prevailed there was no lack of shipwrights or others for shipbuilding purposes. Wearside youngsters were ever willing to build ships.

Laing's yard headed the output over the 1850s with almost 27,000t; however, the combined output of the three/four Pile family yards reached some 37,000t and 84 vessels compared with Laings 49 ships. The third largest output was by the Watsons [taking all with that family name] and the fourth place belongs to the joint output of the two yards in which Austin had an interest. These businesses were followed by the Robert Thompson snr yard with 44 vessels and nearly 21,000t. Each year saw at least one vessel of a 1,000t or more launched into the Wear; 19 were built during the 1850s and a further 13 during 1860-6. Laings [8], Pile [9] and Watson [5] were the main builders of these large fine wood ships.

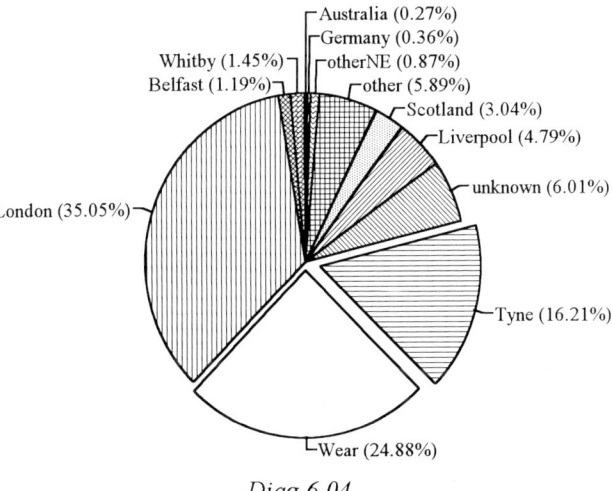

Diag 6.04

The Pile family.

A distinguished contribution was made by the Piles to north east shipbuilding. The family came from farming, probably in the vicinity of Rothbury. The shipbuilding role began with William [c 1795-1858][3], and was continued by his three sons John [1820-1903], William [1823-1873] and James [c 1827-1901]. Shipwright William Pile certainly built five vessels over the years 1818-20, all about the same size, averaging 188t, and a further vessel the *Arno* of 184t in 1823. It is possible that he built others but more likely he worked as a journeyman craftsman or foreman. Young William III learned his trade at the Lightfoot's Hylton Dene shipyard, after first working at John Hay's Ropery, little then realising the importance of future links with the Hays. Like many able journeymen he became a yard foreman but soon joined his father in a small yard at Fatfield, possibly in partnership with W T Wang, timber merchant & shipbuilder. The first clipper bow on Wear was built in 1845 at Pile's Southwick yard. By 1848 the Piles, William and son John, had a yard on the North Shore. Brother John went south to Hartlepool where he played a key part in the introduction of iron shipbuilding [see chap 8]. William's younger brother James

---

[3] This William was the son of William I [1766-1841 -married 1792 Ann Walker]; William II married Mary Hunter [1803-1864] in 1823 but the first child John was born in Feb. 1820. William III married Isabella Rickaby [1822-1908] daughter of a miller, four of their children attended their father's funeral.

married Ann [1829-1892] the daughter of a local grocer named Smart. James Pile and Smart in partnership built vessels from 1852 to 1858, one of these being attributed to James alone. Many were registered with John as the builder, including *The Spirit of the North* and *Flying Dragon* both about 670t for London in 1853, and a year later *The Spirit of The Age* [878t]. In 1852 William's yard launched *King Richard* [1300t] and the *Roxburgh Castle*, his first ship for the distinguished London shipowner Richard Green [1803-63]. The diary of Alexander Whitehead *China and Back 1857* described the maiden voyage of the *Vanguard*,[4] which Pile built in 1857. Rigged as a ship, the *Vanguard* traded on the China route during the period 1857-65, and later,

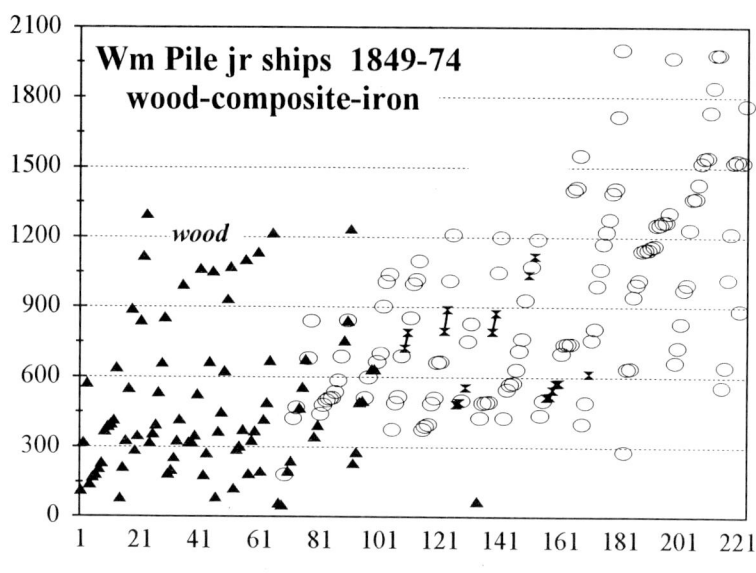

Diag 6.05

with a barque rig, sailed to China in 1869. After she was sold to John Baker of London in 1870, she was extensively altered, with 7' added to her original 154' and in 1873 sailed to Japan. In 1874 damage repair was carried out and four years later she left the register. Certainly no later than 1855, William Pile III was in charge of the Wear shipyard and more than 220 vessels can be identified with this man's design and constructive genius [see diag 6.05]. In all the family built in excess of 175,000t on the Wear, more than 5,500t in 1853 alone. Like other yards they experienced a sharp fall after the Crimea war ended. Output in wood stayed above 2,000t per year and the take-off in output came with the introduction of iron.

Blackwall Frigates, Clippers and the Wear.

Much admiration has always been bestowed on fast sailing vessels and the Scots are rightly famed for building many of these. The achievements of the Wear were however not inconsiderable. *Clipper* is used as a generic term applied to very fast sailing ships; these usually had a fine form, which was expressed as a co-efficient of fineness. In 1853, Pile launched the *Crest of the Wave*, which was described by MacGregor as *an extreme clipper* [an estimated fineness of 0.56]. The *Spray of the Ocean* [1854] was equally fine. On her maiden voyage, the *Crest* reached Melbourne in 73 days; as a tea clipper she could carry 920,000 lbs of tea, and she sailed for almost forty years. Pile's brother John built the *Spirit of the North*; although an *10A1* she was *a quite fast vessel* and sailed for thirty years. Despite its 700t the *Spirit of the Age* was rigged as barque from her launch. Although MacGregor suggested she was *probably built on more extreme lines* than *Spirit* of 1853, the ratio length to breadth hardly supports this [5.63 to 5.4]. Accident seemed to dog the *Spirit of the Age*: in 1857, her anchor fouled a submarine cable and in 1859 she was struck by the Admiralty steam tug *African*. Although repaired, on her next voyage to Shanghai she began to leak badly and was condemned. Pile was always a daring designer. The Blackwall Frigates were mainly built for the Indian trade and many were built on the Wear. Laing built many fine ships for Duncan Dunbar. The praise of Lloyd's Visiting Committee for the *La Hogue* [see chap 3] was justified by her performance. In his *The Blackwall Frigates*[5], Lubbock wrote:

---

[4] R C Bell *Diaries from the Days of Sail* [1974] - Whitehead recorded the work often necessary after a long voyage - at Hong Kong - 21 Oct. *eight carpenters caulking* and how a seaman might see another vessel: 27 Jan. *I had to go up to the Tynemouth with two barrels of pork. She is an ugly beast.*

[5] An historian of the Thames shipyards, Banbury, wrote *Strangely enough these ships, so closely linked with the Thames... were more often built away from the Thames than on it... seventy-eight were built on the Tyne* p.181

The launch of *La Hogue* from Laing's yard

La Hogue ... specially built for the Australian passenger trade [was] for many years a favourite ship to Sydney. She had splendid accommodation ... a poop 96 feet long, a big midship house and long top gallant foc's'cle might almost be said to be an extra deck. Her passages to Sydney were extraordinarily regular, averaging about 90 days outward and a few more days coming home...was also celebrated for her immense figurehead.

Although the first seven of these ships were built at the Blackwall yard, Thames builders only provided 36% of the total tonnage built whereas the Wear's constructed 40% in all 48,721t [see diag 5.06]. Remarkably Banbury [see fn 5] attributed this output and Laing's *Duncan Dunbar* to the Tyne. Laing, with 28,624t was the largest supplier after the Blackwall yard; indeed after 1842 Laing provided 7 tons for 8 eight by the famous Thames yard. Ten of these ships [10,616t] were built on the Tyne by T & W Smith. Other Wear builders were Pile with almost 9,974t, which almost equalled Smiths; their first vessel was in 1840 and Piles twelve years later. Six ships, more than 7,000t, attributed to Marshall were probably built by Watson [see below], Doxford, Reed and Haswell each built a single Blackwall Frigate. [For further information on fast sailing ships the reader see consult MacGregor & Lubbock.] Wear builders[6] made an important contribution in this field but it was not their main area of work as it was for some Scottish yards.

William Briggs

Many fine large vessels were built at the shipyards of a neglected figure in the history of shipbuilding on the Wear, William Briggs. As a successful timber merchant and shipowner Briggs almost certainly directly or indirectly financed many yards. He was a shipbuilder for more than twenty years. William was born on 18 May 1803 and twenty-two years later married Margaret, daughter of the shipwright Joseph Hedley. On his death in July 1871, his gross estate was £240,000. There were certainly trading relations between the Doxford family and the Briggs from 1833 and Corder suggested that Briggs' name was on occasion attached to the gates of Doxfords as evidence that they were financially secure. Evidence survives of Briggs' financial support for Doxford's yard developments of the late 1860s and early 1870s; this relationship continued after the death of William sr.[7] Apart from listing the Briggs family yard, Lloyd's surveyors in 1861 linked two other yards to *Briggs & Sons* - Mills and a Thompson [probably Richard]. This is evidence that Briggs was financing these two and probably other yards, such as John Reed, on various occasions for which no direct evidence survives.

---

[6] Lubbock *The Last of the Windjammers*; MacGregor - his many works listed in bibliography ; Fletcher *In the Days of Tall Ships* Fox Smith *Famous Ships*; Capt. Sherwin *Great Days of Sail*

[7] Sir William Doxford's was still concerned about Briggs's attitudes in the early 20th century.

From 1849 William Briggs owned a yard at Pallion and it seems most likely that the management skills were provided by Michael Clarke.[8] The local papers recorded vessels as built by Clarke, but often the Customs Register gave Briggs as the builder, for example of the *Miaza* in 1850. The yard began with the typical modest output, a 157t vessel in the first year and one of almost identical size in 1850; however in that year the *Gem* [353t] was attributed to Clarke. Few vessels of under *10 year class* were built after the *John Myers* [322t] built in 1851. Two much larger ships the 720t *Alma* [*11yr*] and *Empress Eugenie*, 653t [*12 yr*] were launched in 1854, both by Briggs/Clarke. Thereafter *13 year* ships became typical of the yard's output, with many vessels going to London and Liverpool. No output was attributed to W Briggs in 1857 and 1858, and for Clarke only the *Cornelia* [374t] for London. However, John Reed built a considerable number of vessels, including the *Phantom* [508t- *13yr*] in 1857. The *Sunderland Herald* listed Reed as the builder and Lloyd's Register gives Briggs as the builder of the *Latona* [693t] in the same year. The *Holmsdale* [1,257t] by Reed was by a large margin the biggest vessel built on the Wear in 1858. Financial support may have been the only connection between Briggs and Reed or perhaps Clarke had gone and left him without a manager to his liking. Presumably Briggs' success with London shipowners, apart from business acumen, helped him to secure Admiralty orders for six gunboats of the *Britomart* class and two further vessels in 1860. No other Wear yard secured similar orders. As many as 300 men may have worked at his yard building these gunboats, with the shipwrights paid 8s a day. Briggs never built an iron hull. The historian of sailing ships Lubbock stated that the *best remembered* ships in the Mauritius coolie trade were those of John Allan of London and continued *most of his fleet were sturdy, wooden ships of between 600 and 1000 tons, built by Briggs ... handy, seaworthy vessels, but without any pretensions to speed*. Other Allan vessels were the *Mars* [by J & R Mills, a link with Briggs] and the *John Allan* 734t [1864][9], three others were *Latona, Medusa* [848t in 1862] and the *composite Bride* [830t in 1870]. This was his longest ship - 189.4'. The yard did not carry on after the death of William Briggs sr, total output having been about 26,000t and 60 vessels.

Another Briggs [James][10] was also building on the Wear; he was not related to William. James Briggs launched his first ship the *Launceton* [640t] in 1853, and in 1855 the *Queen of The North* of 908t. Such large ships continued, with the *Warrior Queen* of 988t [*13 year*] and in 1858 the *Mary Shepherd* [905t] for the owner of the *James Shepherd*, built by William Briggs. Both Briggs were supplying a very similar market. When in 1854 James Briggs was taking on apprentices from other yards, the Employers' association sent Alcock and Austin to see his partners, the timber merchants Bradley & Potts, at North Quay. Presumably they were financing this yard. After 1860 there was a gap in output until he began building at Hylton in 1865, then vessels of a lower class - two *7-8 year* [183t & 280t] vessels for the Wear. A year later the *Holly Bough* [324t - *9yr*] for Whitby was the last output by James Briggs. Almost 13,000t were built during 1853-60; the average of 536t was substantially above that of the Wear overall, which was less than 400t.

John Smith.

A name no longer recalled from this period is John Smith, who began in shipbuilding in 1849, when his 550t vessel was noted by Lloyd's as a vessel for *a high class*. A year later he launched a 655t vessel classed 12A. Lloyds Surveyor, Waymouth, noted that Smith, like many other gentlemen in Sunderland who build ships, *has several sources of living*, he believed he was an ironsmith. His foreman was responsible for building the vessels which were *satisfactory*. In this as in other cases the foreman's name was not recorded. Smith's work over the following five years was very successful, exceeding 14,500t, an annual average of

---

[8] The Wear shipwright Gamsby [see chap 12] told the Employers Assoc. in Apl 1853 - Wm Briggs had Clarke and Reed building for him at 5s/day and in Dec. 1854 Briggs was giving *6s at Michael Clarke's yard.*

[9] *John Allan*, licence for 267 adults, 6'6" head room under beams & special ventilating air shafts in addition to her hatches - about 26 days India to Mauritius - *strained in bad weather and began to leak badly* in autumn 1878

[10] A J. Briggs built single vessels in 1838 [275t], 1839 [236t] and one of 75t in 1844 and a year later a 280t.

2,500t better than most Wear builders; the yard was second to Pile in 1852 and headed the river's output in 1853. Smith's death ended this enterprise and the last three ships were completed by his executors.

Years of decline 1855-1859
Years of decline followed the end of the Crimea war; less than 55,000t were launched in 1857 and in 1858 output was only two-thirds that of 1856. In January 1859, *The Sunderland Herald* described shipbuilding on the Wear as in *a state of things ... so very bad that none of their previous annual reviews statements have evidenced such a crippling of the trade, if we except the disastrous year of 1848*. It continued to declare that *overbuilding* had taken place and to this *much of the present depression in the ocean carrying trade* was *attributable*. As this was *already correcting itself at the headquarters of British shipbuilding* [Sunderland], with similar reductions at other ports, *the balance between supply and demand will soon be regulated*. However, the opinion of those *who have long watched the operation of great fluctuations in the shipbuilding trade that no change for the better may be looked for in the present year*. A year later the editor was still claiming that the the law of supply and demand would *ere long equitably adjust the shipping interest* and so *assist in creating a state of prosperity*. He went on to argue that it would be *more healthful if gold fevers and war excitements (which are always profitless in the long run) had nothing to do with it*. In the USA, the *Boston Post* blamed their depression on Britain: *Empty yards, idle workmen, ships waiting for freight, and a loud cry that American shipping is ruined by British competition.*

Shipbuilders on the Wear leave the industry.
Many long established shipbuilding families left the industry in the late 1850s. With the *Lizzie Scott* in July 1857, Lawson Gales ended more than 45 years of building by the family at Hylton, although like many others they had their empty years during the bankruptcies of the 1840s. Also in that year the Tiffins, who went back certainly to 1790, completed their last ship the *Vigilant*. Not long after completing his last ship the *Lucknow* [671t] in 1858, George Booth left for New Zealand having begun shipbuilding about 1790. His output for the nine years, 1850-8, reached almost 16,000t [39 vessels]. An able builder, Lightfoot, who built his largest ship the 593t *Colonist* in 1851, ended 33 years of business with a small 110t vessel in 1859. Byers began building in 1832 at the Strand and later added a patent slipway and gridiron, which probably means that repair work replaced new shipbuilding in years such as 1850 and 1852. A sequence of large fine ships: *Her Majesty* [848t], *Royal Family* [916t], *Constantia* [626t] and *Northumbrian* [639t] were launched in 1854-5 before Byers became a bankrupt in the summer of 1857. There were other failures, although in at least one case stopping building was due to a reluctance to change from wood to iron. Thackray noted that his uncle William Abbay, who was at Ayres Quay 1845-58, never changed to iron and then wrote:

> It was owing to this change that my father[11] gradually gave up shipbuilding, but he kept on the timber yard till about 1867, although in 1857 he had entered the iron trade with Samuel Tyzack and John E Bell.

From the yard at Ayres Quay, his father, in partnership with Pearce, launched the 112t *Snowdrop* in 1851; it was registered as built by Abbay. A year later the 665t *Priam* [12A], was built by Pearce & Thackray for the port of Goole, it seems likely that Abbay had a hand in this vessel also. Abbay built two ships for Goole in 1853 and six months after he had launched his last vessel the *Honour* in May 1858, Thackray launched a new barque, the first in his own name and his largest vessel, 466t. Three ships were supplied to Goole in 1859, the fourth was a small 47t craft for Cape Town and only the *Ann Brass* [92t] was built in 1860. There was no new building in 1861 and the final ship was the *Barbara* for Scotland in 1862. Presumably a wish to continue the Abbay business and provide an outlet for his own timber yard accounted for Thackray starting wood shipbuilding so late, when the future of iron hulls was so clearly to be seen. Yet others were doing the same.

---

[11] Thackray was never a large builder. Abbay was also a shipowner- his first output was for himself.

The late starters in wood construction.

New wood shipyards were started on the Wear throughout the 1850s and the profitable times of the American Civil war encouraged others to do so. A market for new wooden ships continued; early in 1863 quotations were *fully 10 per cent higher* than a year earlier and by the end of the year, *9* year wood ships were at £11-10s to £12 a ton. In January 1862, the *Sunderland Herald* wrote:

> The American difficulty will no doubt have a most favourable effect on British shipping, and there is every reason to believe that the builders on the Wear will be amongst the first to experience the benefits which will accrue to the commerce of this country by the unhappy quarrel...between States which have long threatened to become our most formidable rivals in the carrying trade of the ocean.

At that time only 37 of the 88 vessels on the stocks were sold and it was reported that *needy builders* were *occasionally selling at less than cost price*.[12] Many new wood yards achieved a substantial output and lasted for many years, for example:

	tons	years		tons	years
Gardners-G- B & J -J	16,928	1855-76	Gill	9,566	1857-74
Gibbon & partners	16,000	1863-76	Richardson W	7,697	1857-76
Thompson Rich	10,283	1859-76	Metcalfe	6,172	1859-70
Adamson W	10,458	1858-70	Dennison & Pearson	5,143	1858-72

These tonnages combine family surnames in the case of the top two and so may not represent exactly the same enterprise or partnership. A continuity of building suggested a connection, as it did in the case of Dennison & Pearson. Richard Thompson continued vigorously into the 1870s; indeed more than 60% of his output was in the 1870s. Gill built a vessel in 1857, followed by a gap until continuous output began in 1862 and continued until 1874. No vessels were however launched in either 1869 or 1873. The *Humbleton* was on the stocks more than a year before being launched in January 1870. Similarly, Richardson built a vessel in 1857 and then for the next four years was in partnership with Green[13]; from 1863 Richardson was on his own. Adamsons were both shipbuilders and owners in an earlier period, however after their departure in the early 1840s almost twenty years passed before William Adamson began this new yard, which over a thirteen year period built 29 ships. Adamson was part owner of seven ships in 1856 and he was the sole owner of eight ships in 1874. At least 30 yards built wooden ships in the 1870s. Some other yards such as Simey & Co, which began in 1861 and constructed 33 ships [in all 15,142t] but who finally built in iron until 1879. Although only lasting five years, 1862-6, G S Moore & Co began *composite* [wood hull on iron frames- chap 4] shipbuilding on the Wear; the yard had began with three small wood ships and an iron vessel. Shipowners J & E Lumsden, who as anchor manufacturers had a continuous direct link with shipbuilding, operated a yard from 1865 to 1869; ten wooden vessels [3,071t] were built. Robinsons built ships over many years and while there are many difficulties in sorting out family links, John Robinson had almost 19,000t to his credit over the years 1846-69. A second yard at Deptford was run by James Robinson and built at least 25,000t during the years 1839-67. Starting in 1846, James Hardy launched more than 24,000t at his Southwick yard, his last ship was in 1869. His partner in 1853 was Clarke, who had so many links with various builders! A partnership, Naisby & Reay built 5,280t over the period 1863-71 and in addition almost another 14,000t was registered by Naisby alone.

The Last Years of Wood on the Wear.

As late as 1868 there were 40 wood yards on the Wear and two years later 28. These yards launched 44 wood ships totalling 15,600t in 1870 [more than in 1830]. A *carpenters* yard, Wilson Brothers, was added to the 13 surviving wood yards in 1871. This *new* yard may be related to Chilton, Wilson & Co, which *Turnbull's Maritime Guide* for 1871 listed amongst 64 *Principal Shipbuilders on the Wear*; Chilton began in 1829. Only the 122t *Priscilla* for Chester was built by the Wilson Brothers. The final wood ship phase

---

[12] *[T]he fair market value* for an 8 yr ship 200-400t BM was £9-£10; and £1 added for higher years, e.g. 13 yr - £14-£15, [for a Baltic outfit but no metal sheathing]. Ships of 700t or more for 10yr £14-£15 and 13yr £17-£18.

[13] Green built in partnership with Robinson during 1856-7.

of 163 ships and 61,662t during the 1870s is shown in diag 6.06. After the *Claudia* [373t] in 1871, Douglas reappeared in 1875 to launch his last vessel, the *Sarah & Mary* [133t]. Both Richard Thompson and William Richardson finished in 1875. Two years later Crown built his last wood ship, the *South Milton* [607t] and the Gardners finished with the *Halia* [549t]. One of the Gibbons continued into 1878 with the *Cricket* [333t]. Pickersgill continued to bear the palm of the last wood builder in 1880. Scotland was the market for 7 of the last 8 wood vessels, the other one went to Wales.

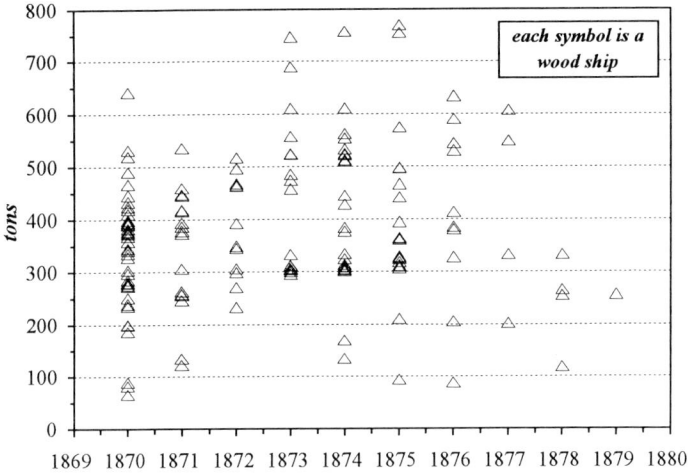

Diag 6.06

Lloyds and Wear Shipbuilders.

The Lloyds Visitation Committee, usually headed by the chairman of Lloyds, regularly went to review shipbuilding at the *outports*,[14] although not all were visited annually. Sunderland and Newcastle were visited in September 1851. As was noted in chapter 3 even in the most reliable of yards occasionally defective timbers were found. Samuel Austin was highly regarded, surveyor Bayley: wrote *the work throughout is well done*. At Abbay's yard in 1849 a *very creditable vessel* [270t] was seen. In August 1852, it was noted as *worthy of remark* that twenty *13* year and three *12* year ships were building on the Wear and three years later Lloyd's, *with pleasure*, attributed *the vast improvement exhibited in this Port* to the efforts of their Surveyors. Very high quality was achieved: A F B Creuze FRS wrote, as part of his internal Report in April 1851, *the high classed ships building at Sunderland will bear comparison with the high class ships of any other port*. In 1855 at Thompsons *materials, workmanship & form* [were] *unexceptionable* and at Piles a 1,100t vessel was of *good material & workmanship*. Lloyd's committee in July 1858 noted *with much satisfaction* that the number of ships under Special Survey[15] had increased over the previous two years especially for the lower grades. This of itself did not mean that all was well. When Metcalfe, Welsh & Co began in 1861, it was complained that: *The persons engaged in building were without Capital and generally both materials and workmanship were of an inferior description*. Surveyor Lawrence reported in July 1862 that in some cases, even Special Survey, he had *great trouble* in getting the builders to carry out his instructions to bring the ships within the Rules. Authority was asked by the surveyors to refuse to survey until it was clear that the vessel was likely to secure a grade, and to be able to give up a survey and give no class. After four years as a shipbuilder, Liddell in 1863 was described *as being professionally quite unequal to the construction of a ship* and as a result Lawrence claimed that he [the surveyor] had *to build* the ship, undoubtedly an extreme case. This yard continued until 1870 and the 21 vessels built averaged just over 200t. It was apparent that some builders believed that the quality of workmanship *may degenerate* with a lower classification, this was against the Lloyds Rules, which designated the *year* in regard to the materials used and did not accept shoddy workmanship for any class.

Shipbuilders were always very concerned about how Lloyds and its local surveyors functioned. Following letters in July and August 1852, both Laing and John Pile protested to the Visiting Committee in regard to the operation of new rules. They claimed it cost them *some hundreds of Pounds more than they*

---

[14] The following section is based upon Lloyds' reports, particularly of the Visitation Committee 1851-1879.

[15] Special Survey was used to describe a vessel which was surveyed from the laying of the keel until completion.

calculated at the time of contracting, and secured a six months adjustment period. Both men expressed *their entire approval* of the increased Topside Planking. Throughout all these visits it is very clear that the men from Lloyds were constantly seeking the views of builders and seeking assurances for any Rule changes they made. When in 1856 the Visiting Committee wanted to transfer Lawrence to Newcastle *two very respectable Shipbuilders*, Austin and Pearson, convinced them that he should stay on the Wear. At this time the assistant to Lawrence was the young Benjamin Martell, *whose diligence & ability* was praised, a young man bound for a very successful career. Lloyd's Rules and the Special Survey were the subject of *a lengthened discussion* at a meeting of the Wear Shipbuilders' Association in May 1857 and a committee [Laing, Spence, Pile, Alcock, Watson & Miles] was to consider the matter. In June 1858 Laing read the new Rules to their meeting and after the visit of July he asked for support in August to secure a modification of the Rules. Austin's son in 1863, expressing a strongly held local opinion, asked unsuccessfully for the removal of Surveyor Mumford. A note from Laing *expressing in forcible terms his objection to Mr Mumford* was read at the Wear Shipbuilders Association a year later and a resolution was passed objecting to the Surveyor.

These surveyors faced many problems in carrying out their work. At times as many as a hundred vessels were on the stocks from the mouth of the river to Hylton. In 1861 Simey had 25 yards [37 ships] in the *High District*,[16] Darling in *Middle District*- 16 yards, 2 dry docks & a slipway [28 ships] and Lawrence in *Lower District* 14 yards [20 ships], 6 dry docks & 5 slipways; a total of 85 vessels were under construction in November. There were not always three surveyors on the spot. A critical problem was how they were to move about. When this was considered in the 1840s, a fixed allowance was made for land transport; boat hire was described as expensive. Creuze pointed out in 1847 that land conveyance was *indispensable for efficient superintendence ... in the upper portion of the River* and would save time elsewhere. Both horses and the *common Cabs or Flys [lately established]* were used; such cabs were understandably more readily available in the *Lower District*, the urban area. The Chief Surveyor was adamant that proper control could only be exercised by *constant superintendence* which required *a liberal expenditure in conveyances*. When the wood yard of Alfred Simey & co began in 1861 Lloyds faced a problem. Alfred was the son of Lloyd's Wear Surveyor Simey and when questioned by the Visiting Committee on his connection with the new yard, Simey snr stated he had *no interest whatever*. He was not a shipowner and had *no interest in Shipping, except in regard to interest in Money lent and secured in such property*. The committee was almost certainly aware that T B Simey had run his own yard on the Wear before becoming a surveyor.[17] After the General Committee had considered the matter, a year later Simey's services were *discontinued*, his plea to remain for 12 months was rejected and he was required to leave by the end of the year, with an annuity of £200 a year. The influence of these generally very talented and helpful surveyors must have helped to extend the market for Wear ships.

There were still a vast number of wooden vessels sailing the seas of the world and in need of ongoing repair, so providing work for those with skills in repairing wood ships for many years. It is surely a significant indicator of the continuing importance of wood ships that Lloyd's continued to up-date their regulation of wood ship building. Rule changes were made in 1870, when the *years* allowed for some timbers were reduced and others such as East India teak extended. As late as 1878 revisions resulted in some timbers being removed from tables while the grade was raised for certain other timbers when salted e.g. American Oak and Fir timber. Perhaps not surprisingly, but none the less worthy of note, the comment *there can be little doubt that wood vessels were never better than when they were being superseded by iron vessels*. So it may be fairly concluded that those Wear built vessels of the late 1860s and early 1870s were amongst the best.

---

[16] High District was from Hylton to Pallion Quay; Middle to Robinson's yard from Metcalfe's Hylton works to R Thompson at Low Sands, Lower Laings to South Dock, Stonehouse Ravenswheel to North Dock and the sea.

[17] This was not unusual, many Lloyds surveyors had for a time built ships e.g. Brunton and Wang; usually they found a Surveyor's salary a more reliable means of livelihood. Others like Denton became shipbuilders.

The adoption of iron hulls - the long transition from wood.

In the autumn of 1850 the *Sunderland Herald* had taunted *Ere long our shipwright yards will be mere places for repairs*. That certainly did not prove to be the case, and as already made clear a substantial demand for wood vessels continued for the best part of a generation. At the end of February 1852, the first iron hull, the 77t *Loftus,* was completed by the engineer George Clark with John Barkes. Although James Laing built his first iron vessel the *Amity* [479t], in 1853, iron was not a significant part of his output until 1858, when his three iron vessels totalled 3,083t. He continued to build in wood until 1866.

The increased demand for shipping stimulated by the American Civil War [1861-5] was one factor in postponing the changeover from wood to iron on the Wear. Less than 47,000t was launched in 1861. This was followed by an increase of 10,000t in 1862 and output averaged more than 71,000t over the years 1863-5. Three yards were building in iron when the war began and only 30% of the increase in 1862 was of iron. However, in the following year the proportion of the increase in iron was even less - 16%. The iron tonnage increased in 1864-5, while wood output fell. For two years after 1865 the output in iron fell more sharply than the post-war fall in wood ships; this can be vividly seen in the case of Laings [see diag 6.08 below]. A very sharp upward movement in the iron tonnage from 1867, signalled the final phase of wood shipbuilding on the Wear [diag 6.07]. Almost 130 iron ships were launched before 1865 [10,600t], overwhelmingly due to Laing, Pile, Oswald. Doxford launched their first iron vessel in November 1863. In the war years, both London and Liverpool merchants increased their purchase of Sunderland ships and *composite* vessels mainly went to London. In 1867 the *Sunderland Herald* quoted *from a trustworthy source* the following prices at the port.

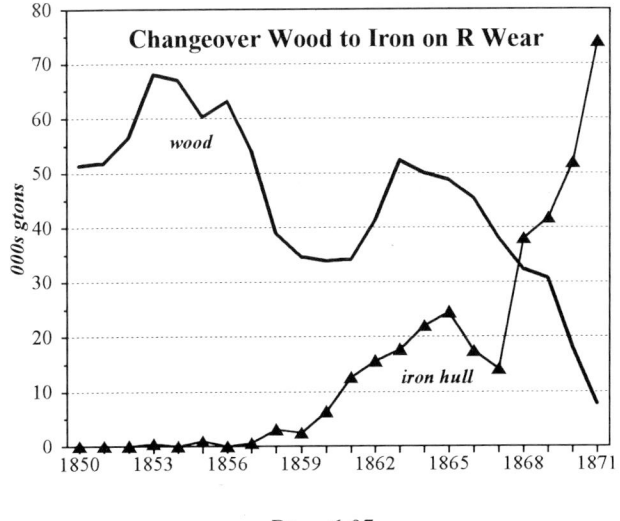

Diag 6.07

Wood Baltic outfit	8 year £10 /ton OM
	9 year £10-10s to £11 /ton OM
	10 year £12 to £12-10s /ton OM
Wood India outfit	13 year £15-15s /ton OM
Composite / to outfit	14 year £15-10s to £16-10s
Iron according to outfit	12 year £14-15s to £15-15s

Given the increased carrying capacity and class of iron vessels, there was little difference even in first cost between iron and wood, when Sunderland was about to build half its output of iron. *The Sunderland Herald* gladly noted that in *the severe commercial crisis through which we have passed, the shipbuilding interest in this port has not suffered,* to the same extent as other ports, this was indeed true. On the Wear output overall fell by about 12% and wood tonnage by only about 6%, while nationally tonnage fell by about 28%! Possibly the wood builders, with a longer experience of their craft, could respond more quickly to price changes, whereas the Wear iron constructors still had a limited experience to draw on.

Unlike the Tyne, where men with a metal working or engineering background such as Marshall started iron shipbuilding and a number of similarly skilled Scots soon joined them there were fewer comparable engineers on the Wear. The suitably skilled metal workers to get iron shipbuilding underway were more numerous on the Tyne than the Wear. Ambitions as great as Palmer's may have inspired Oswald, the second man to built iron ships on the Wear, he did not have Palmer's financial reserves nor his commercial experience. From the outset this young man only intended to build in iron, his volatile colourful career only lasted 16 years at Sunderland. Iliff & Mounsey was the only other yard to start with iron vessels, their first launch being in 1866, seven years after Oswald. All the remainder were the result of changeovers in wood yards up to the 1880s. There was certainly no compelling force of the size of vessels to require the adoption of an iron structure, however much iron might be used as reinforcement in wood vessels. Up to 1863, only the *Hector* [1,614t] of the iron vessels exceeded Laing's last wood vessel the *Parramatta* of 1,521t.

Examples of the Changeover to Iron in some Wear Yards.

Laing.

The changeover to iron hulls in a number of yards is explored, with selected aspects of the yard's history where appropriate. Although James Laing, the leader of the Wear shipping and shipbuilding community, took thirteen years to pass completely from building in wood to iron hulls [1853-1866], from 1858 onwards the iron tonnage exceeded that of wood [see diag 6.09]. After two iron ships in 1855, Laing launched no iron ship in 1856 and only ss *Hercules* [850t] in 1857. Iron tonnage was then steady for three years at just over 2,000t / year, including in 1858 ss *Asia* [923t] and ss *Admiral Kanaris* [928t]; there can be no doubt that by then iron shipbuilding was very firmly established at the Deptford shipyard. As with other yards, during the changeover to iron there was a significant increase in output albeit with the usual cyclical fall backs. A new standard was set for the river with ss *Hector* launched in March 1863; she was more than 284' long, just under 2,000t, and was powered by George Clark engines. Laing launched his final wooden vessel, albeit with iron beams, in May 1866. The noble *Parramatta* [1,521t] was a three mast sailing ship for the London owners Devitt & Moore, 231' long with length to beam ratio of 6:1, a very fitting conclusion to more than 60 years of wooden walls, and the composite *Torrens* was still to come.

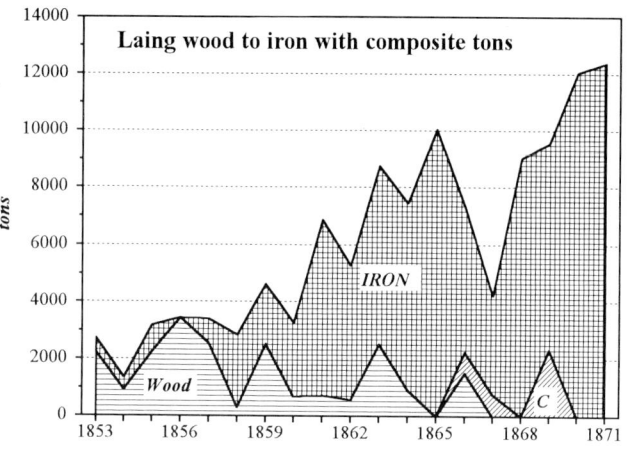

Diag 6.08

Pile.

A great leap was taken by Pile late in 1861 into iron hull construction. Not far short of 2,600t [5 ships] were launched in iron in his first year of iron compared with 2,200t in wood, thus directly the new material was taken up it exceeded the tonnage in wood. At Pile's yard a phase of *composite* construction certainly continued to provide work on hulls for his wood shipwrights until 1869, apart from their essential work on iron vessels. Iron ship no.1 was the sailing ship *Ganges*[18] [839t], launched in July 1861 for Scottish owners, but later owned in London; however, ss *Wisbech* [#2] was launched a month earlier. Three wood vessels were built for London in that year, the largest being the *Glenaros* [675t], and for the North Shields owner J R Kelso, the *Kelso* [556t]. This owner continued to buy wooden walls from Pile for a further two years; Kelso then purchased composite vessels until the iron *Blyth* and *Marmion* in 1870. Two of the four wood ships in 1862, the *Lord Warden* [1,237t] and the *Queen of the Age* [757t] were supplied to London. A year later two of the yard's final three wooden vessels were also for London: the *Arab Steed* [635t] for a regular customer, Walker, for the New Zealand trade and the last wood ship the *Colorado* [499t] launched in September 1863. As he began the changeover to iron, Pile was about £15,000 in debt to the timber merchant William Hay. The debt was discharged on the basis that his nephew Richard Henry, son of the ropemaker John Hay, became a partner. This financial link lasted until 1866; when perhaps a collapse in output encouraged the Hays to pull out. Like Oswald he went on towards the end of the 1860s

---

[18] Lubbock wrote: *The Ganges has always been considered the clipper of Nourse's fleet. Unfortunately her speed was entirely spoiled when* following *the evil example* of British shipowners she was lengthened by 35' in 1881. Other Pile vessels for Nourse were *Jumna* built in 1867 and still with Nourse in 1895 and *Syria* 1,010t [1868].

to build some of his own engines. Only a few of these engines have been found in the records and he continued to be supplied by specialist marine engine builders. Two 1,000 tonners, the *Trevelyan* and the *Himalaya*, launched in May and November 1863 joined the Shaw Saville Line and a year later the *St Leonards* [999t] followed. Two other iron vessels were supplied to London. A notable launch in 1869, was ss *Ariadne* [1,412t][19] for the Belgian Royal Mail Co. She was Pile's largest vessel to that time, being 254' long [length: beam - 7.89]. This ship was one of the few at the time with part double bottom and had a spar deck and two masts. A larger ship, ss *Galatea* [2,001t], was supplied a year later; she was almost 290' long [length: beam 8.18] with three decks and five bulkheads. Both of these ships had Hawthorn engines. These are but a few examples of Pile vessels. More than two-thirds of the total output of William Pile was in iron.

Doxfords

The next wood builder to make the transition to iron was Doxford, who have a much more complicated story than is usually realised. A joint partnership for shipbuilding with William Crown[20] existed from 1845 and continued at Low Southwick until 1851. Almost 5,200t [17 vessels] were built with Crown, of which the largest was the *Duke of Northumberland* [571t] in 1851. A gap follows, 1852-7, when no vessels were built by Doxfords. Despite his long sustained efforts Corder could not *trace* where Doxford was between 1852 and 1857 or any launches, almost certainly because there were none directly attributable to a Doxford. However as timber merchants, they were funding shipwrights to build. A shipyard at Coxgreen was probably used by these men and their workers. Surviving accounts show that there were financial arrangements with three shipwrights: Reay, Johnson, and Jobling.[21] All three men have ships attributed to them that appear in the Doxford profit & loss account. For Reay in 1854 the *Maize* [#2], *Britannia, Faith* and the *Vibilia* in the following year; for Johnson *Reward* [1853], *Britannia* [1854 #1], *Cadiz* [#3] and *Chase* [378t - #2] in 1855. Both Reay and Johnson built Britannias. These were usually *8* year vessels. Doxford's Profit & Loss account also recorded in regard to Coxgreen: in 1856 *Celandie* [#14] and *Alacrity* [#15] and in 1857 *Maynards* [#17] and *Dependent* [#18]. Money was paid regularly to these three shipwrights. There were continuous cash payments to Reay from October 1851 to March 1852, followed by further payments in May and December 1852, and in May 1853. Amongst other payments the monthly sums from January 1855 to July were for *shipbuilding by Reay*. More than £16,965 was paid to Reay, in a sequence which continued until October 1856. Cash payments to Johnson were smaller, a total of £2,305; they were made from January to October 1854 and began again in July 1855 and continued until August 1857. Interestingly the chief shipwright foreman at Pallion was William Johnson and under him a Jonathan and Ralph Johnson, each separate from the general craftsmen in the wage book ,although Ralph was on their pay rate, probably from the same family. Jobling received monthly payments from January 1856 to May 1857, in all £2,531. Entries in the manner usually interpreted as wages were paid to Reay also. These accounts seem to be a clear example of the acknowledged practice of

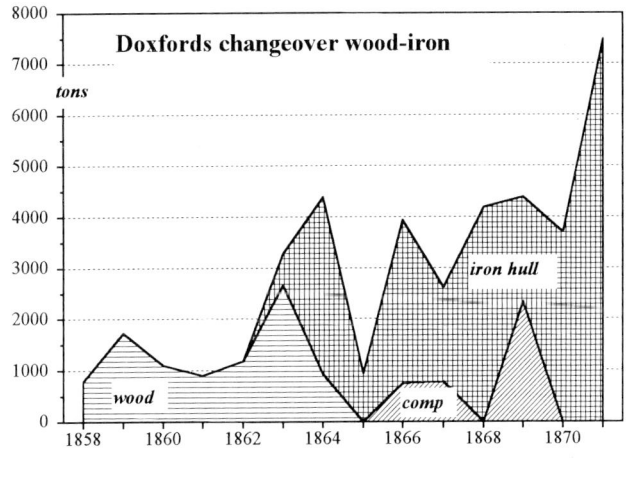

Diag 6.09

---

[19] another *Ariadne* was built by Pile in 1870; 1,003t engines by NEM

[20] As already indicated the Crowns had to say the least a complex family pattern in terms of shipbuilding and there is some confusion whether this is Clement William or whether these names were used for the same man.

[21] All these men are later found in other partnerships.

a timber merchant funding a master shipwright to build for him.[22]

Output by Doxfords was modest over the years 1858-1862 [diag 6.10]; however, the two largest wood hulls were each almost 900t the *Belgravia* and the *Alexandra*. The change to iron came in 1863, when in addition to four wood ships, Doxfords built their the first iron vessel, the *Golden Sunset* [626t] launched on 10 November. Wages for iron building were first paid on 25 April and eight months later the ship was completed. From September 1862 to August 1864 wages were paid at the Low Yard, Pallion, for wood shipbuilding; the *Chaudiere* [520t] and the *Hesperia* [513t] were built and then wood shipbuilding ended. A few *composite* ships were built starting with the *Zoe* in 1865, two years later the *Jung Frau* [584t] and in 1869 - *Invarine* [685t] and *Temesa* [734t] and then the full transition to iron was completed. In March 1869, Doxfords purchased Pallion Quay Quarry in order to extend the yard for the building of iron & *composite* ships and by July that the shipyard was ready. It was not very long before the ambitions of the young William Theodore Doxford and his brother added an engine works to create a comprehensive enterprise with a future few companies matched.

Thompsons.

The Thompson family were a special case. Robert Thompson jnr was more inclined to innovate than his father and for about ten years, 1865-74, his output moved ahead of his father's yard. In the 25 years to 1879 the aggregate tonnage of Robert jnr 's yard was 84,596t, almost 4,000t more than his father's yard.[23] Robert jnr made the transition from wood to iron through an intermediate phase of *composite* ships, which was exceptional [diag 6.10]. He built his first composite, the *Southwick* [337t] in 1865, and thereafter no wood vessel was built. Yard numbers 24-36 & 38-42 were all *composite* ships; *Per Ardua* [787t], a sailing ship for Liverpool, was launched in February 1871. Five years later the final *composite*, *Helena Mona* [670t], was built for London. Robert jnr launched his first iron vessel in October 1868 the *Ireshope* [1,113t][24] for the Tyne based Middle Dock Co. and 8 months later the second iron ship *Ocean Mail* [1,039t]. The yard's first steamer was ss *Canadian* in 1870. Two ships ss *Min* and ss *Sumida* [1,243t] supplied to Japan in 1874 were indicative of the yard's prestige. Robert's yard offered the ideal training ground for his nephews in iron construction.

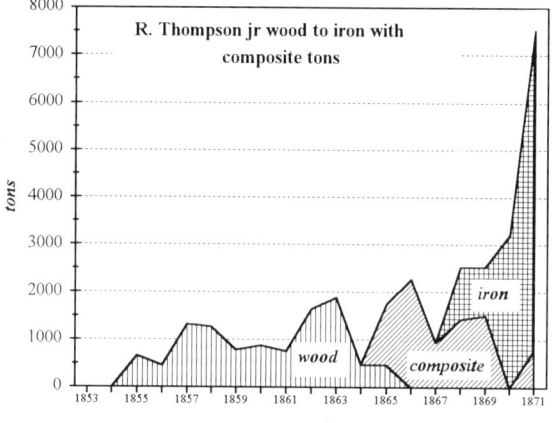

Diag 6.10

An unmistakable downward trend at the senior Thompson yard was probably linked to continuing to work in timber alone. Output in 1851 was 3,440t and 1,366t in 1857; four vessels in 1859, a total of 1,664t placed the yard fourth on the river with about 4.5% of the output. It never matched that total again until after iron was introduced. Other factors may have affected the output. Robert Thompson snr retired in April 1860 and died before the end of the year. His son Robert purchased Candlish's patent slipway & yard. His brother John started his own yard in North Dock. When Blumer moved to the North Dock, their landlord Hedworth Williamson obliged the Thompsons to move on to Blumer's yard while Pile occupied

---

[22] December 1853 accounts for Reay gave costs for *Faith*, hull £2,250 and the outfit £797. Monthly wages were entered regularly for Coxgreen yard from January 1854 to May 1855. The earliest entry for Coxgreen was £11-12s in Sept 1853.- Wage payments began at Pallion in June 1857, £11-12s.

[23] Robert jnr started eight years after his father yet exceeded, in aggregate, the senior yard by 1869 and up to 1873 [i.e. 1855-73] was 13,000t ahead.

[24] This ship's dimensions may be compared with the 945t wood ship *Solway* [*13yr*], built in 1857- 176 ' x 33' [len: bre *5.33*] 22' depth, the same depth as the iron ship, which was 207' x 35' [len:bre*5.91*].

theirs. Their rent was doubled from £35 to £70 a year. The two vessels built in 1869 together were only 821t, which was not much more than 1% of the Wear's output; there was an even lower tonnage 783t in 1870. Small vessels were being built compared with the 900t to a 1,000t ships built in 1853-5. Robert [1850-1908] and Joseph Lowes jnr [1853-1903], grandsons of the founder, were sent to uncle Robert's yard to learn iron construction. On their return iron shipbuilding began at the North Sands Yard with a dramatic change of fortune, three iron vessels being built in 1871. They totalled 3,210t, which was not far short of 4% of the total Wear tonnage of that year. A year later five vessels, 5,358t, maintained the 4% proportion.[25] There certainly must have been a renewed vigour, perhaps in no small part due to the young Robert, who would have been retained by his

THE BARQUE BEREAN BUILT BY WILLIAM PILE IN 1869 WAS ONE OF THE FASTEST SHIPS ON THE LONDON-TASMANIA RUN

uncle if he had been willing to stay with him. The old firm took a new name, J.L.Thompson. At North Sands there was a sharp transition, one year wood and the next iron; on 3 August 1870 the last wood ship was launched, the *Peace* [383t].[26] Eleven months later on 3 July 1871, the first iron ship ss *Black Sea*[27][1,902t , yard #105] was launched and ss *Celsus* [yard #104] went down the slipway on 30 September. *Celsus* was laid down first *on spec*, and so once there was a contract for #105, she was completed first. Finally, two weeks before Christmas, the *White Sea* was launched, a four fold increase in tonnage launched vividly illustrating the rapid advance once iron was adopted. Like other yards, North Sands fell back in 1875; nonetheless the yard just about exceeded the new tonnage by Robert jnr. After that the senior yard stayed ahead in each year, launching in aggregate more than 100,000t over the years 1876-82, compared with just under 70,000t from Robert's yard. J L Thompson headed the annual output, on the Wear, almost continuously from 1885 to 1900.

Shorts - Bartram - Austin.

Short Brothers also changed from wood to iron between 1870 and 1871. Although not declining quite as badly as the senior Thompson yard, output in 1870 at only 734t, even lower than Thompson. *Nanuphar*, the last wood ship[28], was launched in November 1870 and five months later Shorts launched their first iron vessel, ss *Hugh Streatfield*. Five iron ships were launched in 1871. Two of these were engined by Richardsons of Hartlepool, two by the Ouseburn Works and the fifth by Oswald. Two years later two iron ships were sold to Germany and another to Spain. A single wood vessel [399t] was built by Bartram in 1870 and in March 1871, he launched his last wooden hull, the *Myrtle* [417t]. Haswell joined Bartram and presumably provided the capital, which enabled iron construction to begin towards the end of 1871. Their first iron vessel, ss *Ardmore*, was launched in June 1872. At 927t she was twice the tonnage of any wood vessel built by Bartram; ss *Zeus* [1,016t] followed in September, powered by the locally built Dickinson engines. A four year gap marked the changeover at the second oldest shipyard on the river, Austins, who

---

[25] Robert jnr was still ahead - 7,518t [1871]; 8,186t [1872] but by 1874 the gap was almost closed 6,779t & 6,428t

[26] A Frenchman offered £4,000 for *Peace* but Thompson wanted £4,500. She was on the stocks for 12 months. She made £500 on a chartered voyage and while she was at Alexandria, *Peace* was sold to Hedley of Blyth for £4,000.

[27] It was *laid off* in the attic of 79 Dock St [later New Dame Dorothy St]. Geo Clark twin compound engines, 120 nhp, with two masts and two decks 226.2' x 30.7' x 16.8'.

[28] In the depressed year of 1876 Shorts built a 88t wood hull *Champion of the Seas* for Thurso owner.

continued to build in wood until July 1869, when the *Choles* [409t] was launched for a Scarborough owner. Only six vessels were built over the five years 1865-9, in all about 2,300t. There is no record of new ships during 1870-73, when no doubt repair work continued. One of the greatest figures in shipbuilding, George Hunter, then arrived as a junior partner; having lost his job as manager with the closure of Pile's yard. Iron construction began and in 1874 the *Knight Templar* [1,546t] and the *Barambio* [754t] were launched, for North Shields and Bilbao. In 1876 ss *Fenton* was built with a cellular bottom construction, which was Hunter's contribution to satisfactory water ballasting. During the six years of the partnership, approximately 20,000t [21 ships] were launched, which was more than the total built in wood over the sixteen years 1854-69 [52 ships]. The Tyne offered new opportunities and Hunter joined up with the Swans and began his rise to fame as related below.

Crown - Pickersgill and other yards.
Over the years 1870-7, Crown built 21 wood vessels, in all 9,000t. Crown [as Strand Slipway] in 1879 built the yard's first iron ship, the *Ferdinand Corvilain* for Belgian owners. The last wood merchant ship on the Wear, the *Coppename* [336t] was built by Pickersgills in 1880.[29] This apparently innovation resistant yard survived until the end of shipbuilding on the Wear. Fleetwood owners were supplied with 12 wood vessels during 1870-4, including the *William C Seed* [757t]. London and Spain took the remaining two vessels in 1870-1. William Pickersgill learned his trade at Laings and began shipbuilding in partnership with Miller, and their first vessel was launched in 1854. About 30 vessels were completed before the partnership ended in the spring of 1863. Many vessels were built *on spec*, and when the partnership ended an unsold planked barque [470t] was on the stocks and later sold as the *Beaufort*. William jnr [1847-1936] was apprenticed to the timber trade and joined his father's yard as a craftsman, later becoming foreman and taking over the management in 1880. Not long after they had acquired extra land to begin iron building William sr was killed in an accident at the yard. ss *Carmargo* [948t] and the *Stuart* [1,380t] were the first two iron ships. Pickersgill [with partners] built more than 20,000t of wooden hulls

Four iron ships were built by John Haswell during 1864-6 at his South Dock yard, after building in wood from 1837.[30] He launched the *Magnet* [484t] in February 1866 and from this yard Iliff & Mounsey followed with the ss *Lasborough* [965t] in June. This new yard's output remained modest; in 1867 four of the five vessels were each about 390t and the fifth 194t. Work was under way on the first of their two largest vessels, near sister ships for London, ss *Nile* [1354t] launched in January 1868 and six months later ss *Niger* [1442t]. A number of very similar sized ships were built by this yard, seven about 390t[31] and five about 530t, out of 28 identified vessels. Late in 1870, the partnerships dissolved, Iliff continued on his own for a time and Mounsey was joined by Foster over the years 1873-9. Following two vessels by Foster on his own in 1880, the business became the Sunderland Shipbuilding Co, known locally at *The Limited*.

Oswald & Castletown
Thomas Ridley Oswald was born in 1836. He entered the yard of his uncle James Laing[32] when he was 16 and later worked in the famous Millwall Yard on the Thames. On his return to Wearside, aged 23 years, he devoted all his energies to the new iron hull and began with the *Carn Tual* for a Belfast owner in 1859. Seven iron vessels were launched in 1860, in all almost 3,800t, the smallest being 193t. His largest *Baronsmore*, [859t] was also for Belfast; other ships went to Liverpool, Hull and London. Oswald's output

---

[29] Probably of Scottish origins, William sr was born at Chester-le-Street. No evidence has been found to support claims that he began a yard at North Dock, he would then have been 15 years old! [see S P Russell in DBB.]

[30] Haswell began building ships at North Hylton in 1837, later moved to Ayres Quay and then to the South Dock. Like many others he launched no ships during 1844-8, nor in 1858. A Haswell was partner to Bartram from 1872.

[31] R H Penney of Shoreham bought five ships.

[32] Elizabeth [died 1889] daughter of Philip Laing married William Oswald [1795-1896] in 1828, and their son Thomas Ridley married Isabella Lambert; there is some confusion with Corder who gives marriage to Francis Alice [Webster], however pedigree shows Frances marrying Thomas Rudd.

made steady progress and he became the biggest iron builder on the Wear and went on to head the river's output in the four years 1868, 1869, 1870 and 1871 [there was little difference between Oswald, Laing and Pile in 1870 and 1871]. Oswald's exuberance brought his first financial failure in 1861. The local paper wrote of *the grossest of reckless trading* and commented *Where iron shipbuilding was undertaken by prudent capitalists conversant with the details of the business, it has never failed, so far as we are aware, to flourish*. That opinion was far from true. Undeterred, Oswald continued and displayed the scale of his ambitions at Castletown, by creating both an iron works to provide his own supplies of materials, and his own engine works. He was investing regularly. The auction list after bankruptcy claimed that the *majority of the tools* were purchased after 1870.[33] Oswald ships were of a wide variety of sizes [diag 6.11]. The *Pera* at 1,231t was the first of many vessels over 1,000t and in 1871 five ships were built exceeding 2,000t. As 1869 began, there were on his slipways:-three iron vessels being plated, a fourth rivetted, a fifth framed and work had begun on a sixth ship and also on a *composite* ship. Six years later, in January 1875, matters were not so happy; only one ship was fitting out, and one each framing and plating but the yard was only preparing the materials for the remaining five vessels. However, eight vessels were completed before the end of the year, seven for Liverpool and one for London.

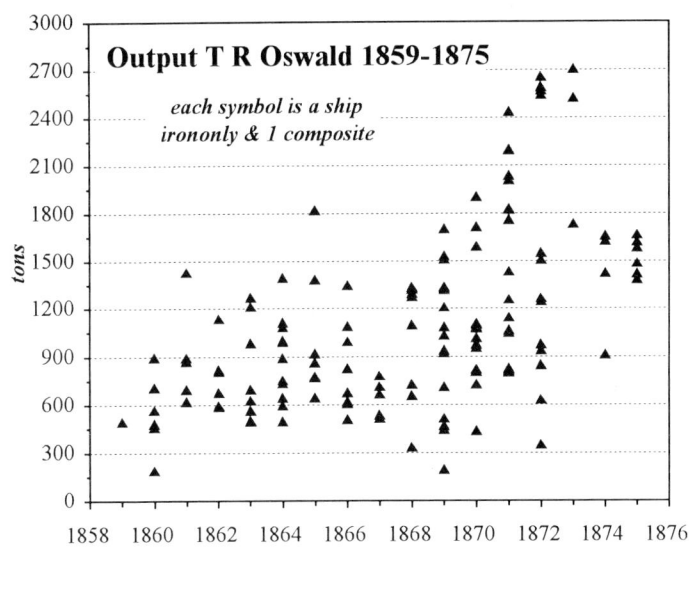

Diag 6.11

A very forceful personality, Oswald had many tussles with Lloyds. Their visiting committee in 1870 found a general approval for the basis of their new iron rules but he *appeared annoyed because the Committee had not sanctioned* [his] *proposal to use thiner plating*. Also, he expressed with *much frankness* the desirability of competition between Lloyd's and the Liverpool Registry. True to this attitude, he registered many of his ships at Liverpool, ten in 1868, a year in which Iliff & Mounsey registered eight, Doxford and Laing three each and Pile one. Oswald claimed Lloyds took as many weeks to make a decision as Liverpool took hours; he complained of three weeks over one ship, which he considered needed *the immediate and careful* attention of the committee. Nine vessels were under construction during a visit from a Lloyds party, who in their *hurried look ... did not observe anything objectionable*. Four years later in 1870, they were critical; although the rivets tried were sound, the work and finish *throughout were rough*. More specific comments followed; a large cargo port was badly located relative to the butts, angle iron fitted in *a most objectionable manner*, a flange not broad enough. Spaces were *made good by fitting pieces in some cases in two thicknesses, throughout a great portion of the vessel and many scantlings below required dimension*. Perhaps all these were signs that the financial pressures were affecting the quality of work. After surviving his various financial set backs, when bankrupt for the third time in 1875, Oswald left the Wear, taking with him the frames of the ship on his slipway. With these frames and a partner John Mordaunt, he began again in shipbuilding at Southampton.[34] The history of Oswald's yard was an example of the commercial hazards of innovation, especially if undertaken on a large scale. Unquestionably, however, this enterprise was an important factor in establishing iron shipbuilding on the Wear, where a

---

[33] *The Engineer* wrote since the bankruptcy *the machines have never worked, but have simply been kept cleaned*.

[34] The Southampton firm went into liquidation after the 1889 boom of 1889 and the ever persistent Oswald began again in Wales. Corder MSS, Rance *Victorian Shipbuilding At Southampton*; W H Mitchell *The Woolston Ships* [Oswald Era] ; various newspaper clippings Southampton City Library.

110

substantial number of men learned and practised shipbuilding skills. During 1859-75, his total tonnage exceeded 160,000t [almost 150 ships], which was more than any other builder. Laing's total was about 145,000t and Pile's, who ended two years earlier, 137,000t. Oswald's annual output regularly exceeded 10,000t.

Building Composite Ships.

G S Moore pioneered the *composite* ship on the Wear, with the launch of the *Bertha Marion* [544t] in January 1864; six *composites* were built by this yard. During 1864-71 on Wearside, the output of 67 *composite* ships totalled 42,648t and a few more were built later. About 30% of the national tonnage of composites were Sunderland built in both 1865 and 1866 and almost 39% in 1869; this amounted to about 13% of the output on the Wear over those years. London took more than half this tonnage, the Tyne about 7,000t and the Wear less than 6,000t. Both, Pile and Robert Thompson jnr, each built 17 composite ships; Thompson's vessels were smaller, in all 8,200t. Nearly two-thirds of Pile's 12,000t was for London and none for Sunderland. These North Sands vessels were of the splendid standard typical of the Pile yard. The *City of Adelaide* [791t[35]], built in 1864 for Devitt & Moore, was a very fast ship, with a 65 day run from London to Adelaide. A year later, the same shipping line purchased the *St Vincent*, regarded by the company as the fastest they ever owned; she was still afloat in 1905. Laing's first *composite* was the *Sumatra* [733t] launched in 1866 for Palermo and five more followed, including the *Beltane*, on which Lubbock lavished praise. A favourite among north east admirers is the *Torrens*, on which the author Joseph Conrad once served as a mate. This was a beautiful ship with remarkable achievements to her credit, including a voyage from Plymouth to Adelaide in 67 days. This 221' long passenger clipper of 1,276 t was built in 1876 and had a working life of 34 years. Conrad wrote of her: *The way that ship had of letting big seas slip under her did one's heart good to watch. It resembled so much an exhibition of intelligent grace and unerring skill that it could fascinate even the least seamanlike of our passengers.*

Fourth in output terms of *composites* on the Wear was Peverall's yard at Wreath Quay with 9 vessels, 5,707t. George Peverall had with various partners built wooden ships for 12 years before being declared bankrupt in January 1862.[36] Within a year he was back in business and built two large wood ships for London and a third for Sunderland and changed to *composite* ships. Peverall headed the Wear's output for this class of vessel in 1864, with three *composites*: the *Oriental Queen* and the *Fi-wan* were almost 900t. In 1865 he again headed the River for *composites* but again he was in financial straits. After launching 2,151t in nine months, his failure was reported on 5 October 1866, another example of the chequered history of so many Wear yards. It can only be wondered if the largest composite on the Wear, the *Forfarshire*, launched in March 1867 and attributed to John Morrison, his *only* vessel, may have been the last on the stocks at Peverall's yard. As stated elsewhere owners would become *builder* to avoid bankruptcy seizure. Blumer like Moore built six *composites* and almost an equal tonnage,

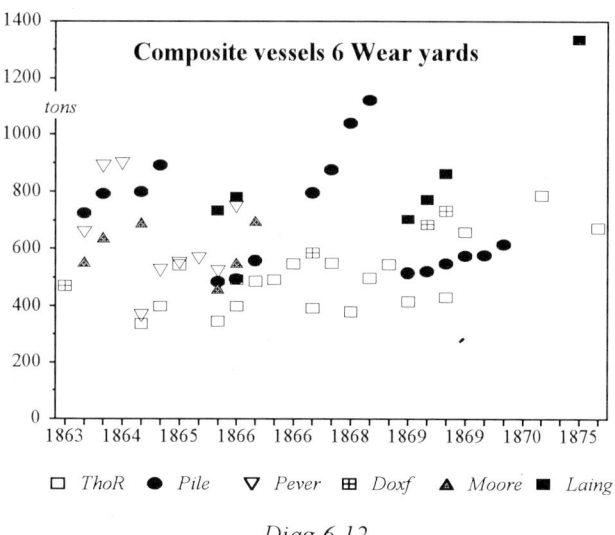

Diag 6.12

---

[35] *Sobraon* [1866] by Hall of Aberdeen, was probably the largest composite - 317' overall, 2,131regt; in 1911 became a training ship with the Australian Federal Government. This lifespan showed the durability of these ships.

[36] Peverall's various partners were Wallace, Charlton and Davison. He started with the *Lady Zealand* [68t] in 1851 and launched the 375t *Rebecca Stout* in 1852. Continuous shipbuilding did not begin until 1857 and he built 17 wood ships. Three large ships built for London owners included the *Gresham* [965t]. He was bankrupt in Jan 1862.

about 3,600t. Doxford constructed four *composites* and Briggs, Nicholson and Gardner one each. Composite output by six yards on the Wear is shown in diag. 6.12.

The 1870s and the failures of Oswald, Pile and Watson.

Tonnage launched increased from 70,000t in 1870 to 134,000t two years later. The Wear recovered part of its lost position with the extension of iron building and from just over 20% of the national output this figure leaped in 1872 to more than a third, when 122 ships were launched. Three of the yards, Oswald, Pile and Watson, who played a central role in this achievement were all closed within less than four years. Although 1873 saw a dramatic fall back to 99,000t, this was much larger than the average of the 1860s. The fall continued through 88,000t [1874], then just under 80,000t before the low point of the cycle of 54,000t in 1876. The output increase in the rest of the country came later than on the Wear, between 1873 and 1874, and was associated with a remarkable upsurge in new sailing vessels and for a few years a sharp decline in steam ships [diag 6.13].[37] These sailing ships were built of iron, the tonnage of wood sailers hardly changed.[38] Although many fine sailing ships were built on the north east coast, Scottish shipyards were the major contributors to this increase. Nationally sailing ships as a percentage of tonnage increased from 24% in 1873 to not far short of 66% in 1876, before falling back to 49%. In 1878 sail was one third of total net tonnage; in 1879 it was down to 16.6% and in absolute terms just above tonnage of 1871. About 47% of net tonnage was sail over the period 1874-8.

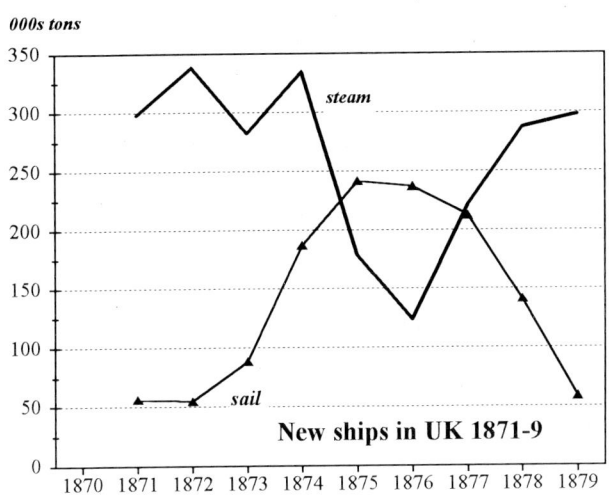

Diag 6.13

Osbourne, Graham & Co started a new iron yard at Hylton in 1871. This was an example of the Scots still making their invaluable contribution to new yards. Edwin Graham[39] [1837-1897], served his time at Dennys of Dumbarton and after a time with a naval architect in London he joined Oswald as chief draughtsman. Two years later he returned to Scotland to take over the management of John Key's yard at Kinghorn, Fifeshire. Presumably the attraction of the expanding yard of Oswald's brought him back to the Wear as shipyard manager from where he went to join Osbourne. In October 1871 the launch of the *Flor De Maria* [771t] for Bilbao was the first vessel beginning 55 years of shipbuilding. A year later 4,627t [4 ships] were launched followed by 5,605t [7 ships]. A 1,370t vessel *Wye* was ordered by the Admiralty in 1873. Unusually there was a very short-lived iron yard. John G Gulston launched the *Nautilus* [718t] for London in November 1874 and three vessels in 1875. One of these *Lady Eleanor*, stuck in river's mud at the launch, a not unusual hazard if due care was not taken. Local railway navvies freed the ship. After constructing the first sheer legs on the river and the first steam ferry built there Gulston failed to continue beyond 1876.

In 1871, Oswald launched more than 28,000t, Pile more than 18,000 and Watson 7,400, those yards together more than 54,000t, to which Laings added more than 12,000t. A year later the leading position was reversed, with Pile at nearly 22,000t, Oswald nearly 20,000 and Watson 6,500, together more than

---

[37] see G S Graham *The Ascendency of the sailing ships, 1850-85 EconHistRev* 2nd series v.11 [1956]

[38] In 1872 there was 39,200t of wood sailing ships and 15,100t in iron and in 1875 wood was totalled 41,600t and iron 198,800t. The figures for 1877 were 42,500t wood and 169,700t iron.

[39] A founder member of the NECIES, also a member of INA & Inst of Scot; he died on 22 Feb 1897

48,000t, and three other yards exceeded 10,000t: Laing 15,300t, Iliff 12,000t and Doxford nearly 11,000t. Twenty-three yards launched ships in that year. The biggest falls in output between 1872 and 1873 were at Oswald and Pile whose combined output of 13,400t was less than 29% of their best year; Watson increased his output to more than 10,000t. From Oswald's Pallion yard in 1872 two ships went to Germany each exceeded 2,500t - *Thorwald* and *Washington* and in January 1873 ss *Wallace* of 2,708t! Even with such fine ships and the high output of 1872, Oswald went bankrupt with liabilities of £300,000 and the Pallion yard was offered on a 21 year lease. By some means he resumed, but when three years later he failed again the works was dismantled.[40] It is not clear where Oswald was building after the 1872 bankruptcy. *The Engineer* wrote this failure *caused a considerable sensation in the engineering world*. Vessels launched in 1873 had Oswald engines, which would certainly imply that work continued at Castletown and that the ships launched were large. A multiple berth yard was needed for the 1875 launches in February, March, May, July, August, September and finally the *Champion* [1,487t], in October to take place. So ended an ambitious man's enterprise and only the tall chimney's of his iron works continued to remind Wearsiders of a once great works. Pile died in 1873 with liabilities in excess of £170,000 and his remaining ahips were completed by others. His many ships, certainly more than 200, were very worthy achievements in naval architecture. Watson[41] also failed in 1874 with debts of about £77,000. Like Pile he was a very able designer and builder of ships, but his frequent financial problems meant that the owners of his vessels, such as Marshall[42] were registered as the builders to avoid the very real risk of confiscation for payment of debts. Although his last vessel was numbered 429, it seems unlikely he built that many.[43] Watson built in wood until January 1869, when he launched the *Miss Preston* [449t] and later that year his first iron ship the *Glance* [912t], which like many others was for London owners. With his departure three great figures, who had played significant roles in Sunderland shipbuilding, had gone. Each was unable to master the financial hazards of this ever fluctuating industry.

Iron construction brought a new pattern to Wear shipbuilding and about a dozen very much larger yards replaced the scores of yards of the wood era. In 1882 articles by W Clark Russell[44] appeared in the *Daily Telegraph* on the ports of the north east and the Bristol Channel. At Sunderland he saw a letter of congratulations from the Captain of a 40 year old Laing ship, which had just arrived in Australia from London with her cargo in perfect condition. His guide rejected out of hand the suggestion that since Bristol had been almost killed as a port by the narrowness of the Avon, Sunderland might suffer the same fate. He was told *that before long Sunderland will have the distinction of being the first port in the world as regards both number and size*. Russell wrote of a *wonderful picture* of the five miles of thriving industry on the banks of the Wear -

> You see the yards, the factories, the works; you hear the harsh roar of the giant Labour; you behold every yard crowned with fabrics in course of construction, while the river teems with newly-launched ships; every acre of land is the basis of some great commercial undertaking... Moribund! Not yet... There is many a heavy kick in this old horse yet; nor can I turn my back on the famous port without saluting the magnificent evidence of human skill, courage, and perseverance which I find in her, and which will take a place among my most inspiring memories.

---

[40] The sale of the machinery, in May 1877, was extensively covered by *The Engineer* [pp 346,363-4, 380-1]- given that much of this machinery was installed in the 1870s those at the sale got many bargains.

[41] Shipbroker Geo Swainston held £42,000 of the debt; Watson left Sunderland for Canada in 1877. A short lived attempt was made to revive the yard as Hardcastle & Watson 1877-9, four ships were built.

[42] Three examples of this were *Kent*[445t], *Winchester* [1,157t] and the *Essex* [1,255t] in 1862-3.

[43] A total of all the ships identified as built by a Watson fall far short of 429. A number of shipbuilders changed their numbering systems e.g. Laing moved from #339 to #500 in 1890 and others started at 100.

[44] The writings of Russell [1844-1911] helped improved conditions in the merchant service, in which he served [1858-66].

Chapter 7

The advance of the Tyne [including Blyth] to c 1889.

The [British Association] visitors proceed ... by steamboat, and so had an admirable opportunity afforded them of peering beneath the banks of smoke which almost hide this river and the tremendous ranges of factories and works which line its steep banks on either side. Though the picture is a very dark one, still, in its way, there is no river in the world which presents such a wonderful picture of manufacturing industry as the Tyne. Everything around - houses, workshops, the wharves and the river itself - is blackened to a blackness that would be scarcely believed possible even in the grimy districts of the Black Country itself, while the countless chimney stacks rise into the air in all directions, pouring forth dense volumes of white smoke from the chemical alkali works, or black smoke from the foundries, which as they mix make regular stratifications in the air, almost thick enough to keep out the sunlight. No matter where the eye turns, the view is all the same - it is steam, fire and smoke in every direction for miles, with occasionally a background still more hideous over all. Never did industrial labour assume a more unattractive aspect than it does on the Tyne, where peaceful employment looks more tremendous and dangerous to the eye than almost any horror of war. The great yards of Messrs. Palmers at Jarrow are some miles down the river ... tolerably isolated, so that from the water they are pretty equally divided between flame, steam and Smoke.

That was a vision of the Tyne as described by *The Engineer* in 1863. Jurisdiction over the river was the subject of many long and often bitter disputes; the secretary of the Tyne Commissioners, James Guthrie, wrote in 1880- *Perhaps in no Port in the Kingdom have there been ...more contests.*[1] This will not be pursued here beyond noting that about 1850, and indeed for a further ten years, the whole future of the port was in potential jeopardy due to the lack of care of the river. Shipbuilding's future was linked to the success of the port. In 1849 an Admiralty inquiry pointed out that water at the bar was still only 6' as it had been in 1813; in contrast Sunderland had gained 4'-6'. As that Inquiry proceeded, the *Norval*, drawing less than 12' was grounded in Hebburn Sand at high water. Three large American vessels were grounded together on the bar in May 1861; vessels over 12' could only get up to Newcastle at high Spring tides.[2] Such was the situation even after the actions following the Tyne Improvement Act of 1850, when control passed from the Newcastle Corporation to the Tyne Commissioners. Dredging began in a modest way from 1838 and was stepped up from the mid-1850s, but was still under half a million tons per year when in 1859, J F Ure from the Clyde became the engineer. Ure developed a new plan and by 1863 almost two and a half million tons were dredged from the Tyne. During the following ten years the annual average removed was about four million tons, a measure of the seriousness of the problem.

More than 720,000t of shipping was owned on the north east coast, compared with 1,407,000t on the Mersey and 1,059,000t on the Thames. The shipping owned on the Tyne in 1863 was divided as follows:

	num.	tonnage	£s
sailing vessels	1,406	371,480	223,000
merchant steamers	26	9,817	245,000
tugs & river craft	241	3,971	125,000
total	1,673	385,268	2,700,000

A thriving industrial situation, increased coal, iron

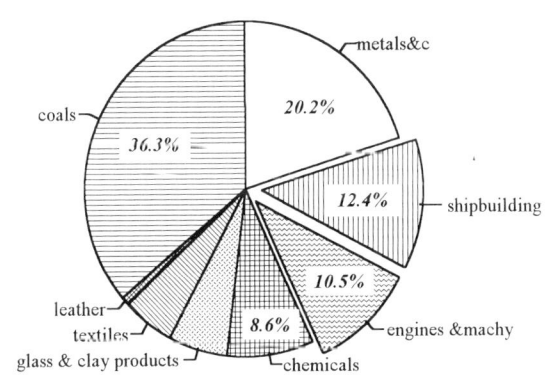

Diag 7.01

---

[1] The opening page of his book *The River Tyne* ; see also *The Making of the Tyne* R W Johnson [1895]

[2] Opposite Richardson's Neptune yard in 1860 there was only about 6 feet of water at low Spring tide.

28 Tyne Shipyards in 1846

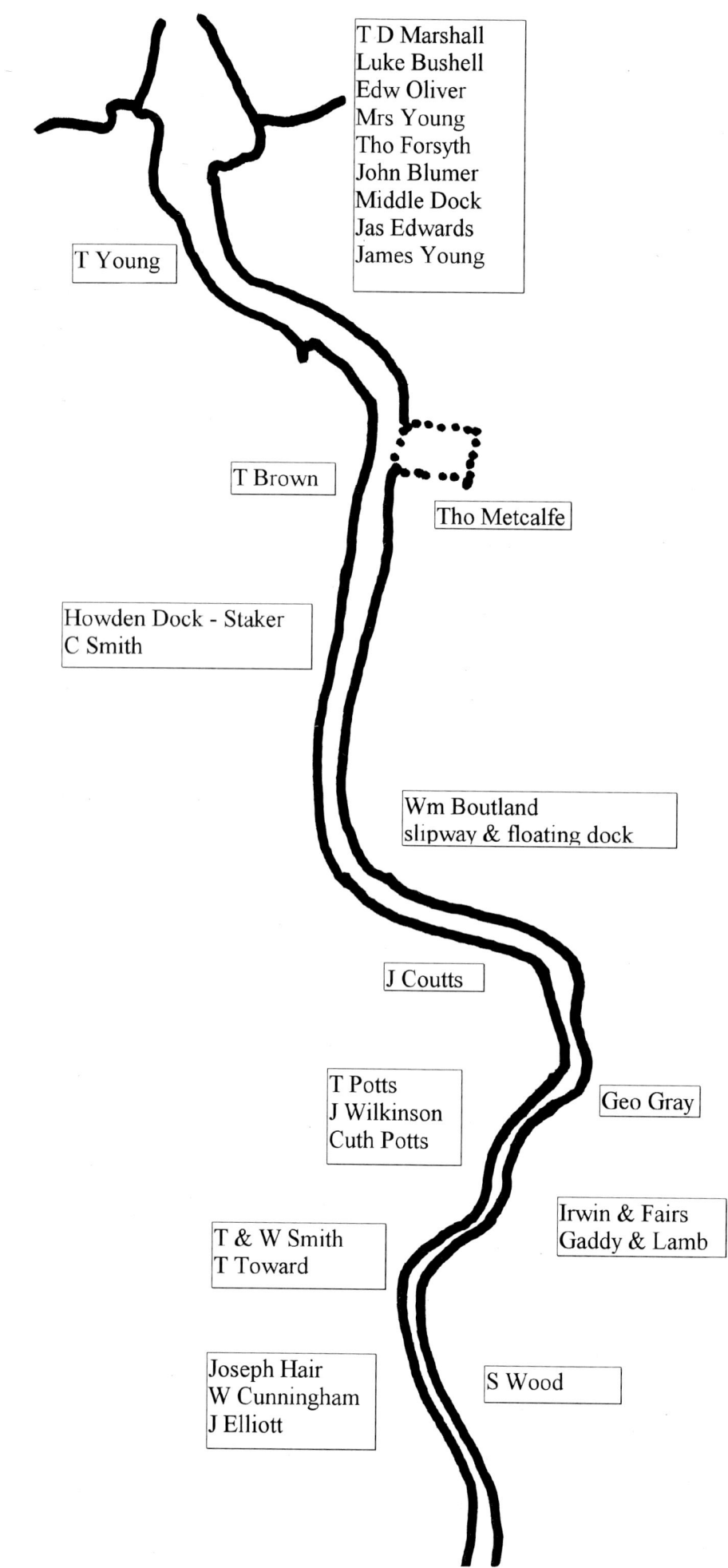

ore and iron production, was providing a basis for the advance of shipping. The British merchant marine increased from four million tons in 1853 to seven millions in 1882. Carrying capacity increased even more substantially, because iron hulls carried more cargo and steam power enabled more miles to be travelled in a given time [in 1883 steam tonnage first exceeded sail]. The leading role of coal in Mining & Manufacturing Products for 1863 is shown in diag 7.01. Shipbuilding was 12.5% and engineering 10.5% of the total and of course used a high proportion of the metals produced. The advance of shipbuilding on the Tyne [including Blyth] from about 1850 to the 1880s will be examined in this chapter, including the last years of wooden hulls - the new iron yards - the screw collier -the managers who become shipbuilders - water ballast and Lloyds. On the Tyne from an annual average of about 7,000t in the early 1850s output by the 1880s reached on average almost 170,000t, a 24-fold increase. Nationally, over that period, the increase was less than four-fold. For the 1850s and 1860s, uncertainty remains on individual yard output, Custom House registers did not regularly identify the builder, nor did Lloyds; in contrast, given the greater significance of shipbuilding on the Wear, the local press published launchings annually.

In about 1850, on the north bank of the Tyne there were 12 shipbuilding or repair yards and 18 more on the south bank. They were almost all building in wood and some continued to do so into the 1870s. Iron shipbuilding exceeded wood on the Tyne in 1854. As elsewhere after the Crimea war there was the usual post-war collapse; from 1859 there was an upward sweep and output reached 50,000t in 1864. Two factors stimulated a sharp advance from about 1860, the established iron yards expanded their output and Wigham Richardson opened his yard, to which was added the impact of the American Civil War. By the end of 1865, ten of the 20 yards building on the Tyne were working in iron and this iron tonnage was almost ten times the wood ships under construction. Only T & W Smith were using both materials in 1865; they built four iron vessels totalling 3,310t and a wood ship of 400t. Two wood yards were each building two vessels and the other wood yards only a single vessel. The official figures from 1866 for the Tyne and Wear are summarised in diag 7.02. Again they show another post-war fall, much sharper on the Tyne than the Wear. This was probably partially due to the reduction in iron hulls being greater than wooden hulls.[3] Both rivers have a similar general pattern although the exact times of change vary. A second severe slump occurred in the mid-1870s, when from more than 91,000t in 1874, Tyne output fell to less than 32,000t in 1876, in other words for every three tons built in 1874, little more than one ton was built two years later; the output of 1874 was not reached until 1880. A prolonged depression devastated the 1880s a fall more severe than that of the 1870s. [see chap 9] Nonetheless, an unmistakable upward linear trend is clear, much greater on the Tyne than on the Wear; on the Tyne this linear trend was from 30,000t to 120,000t while on the Wear from 60,000t to 90,000t. A slower adoption of iron and steam were influenced in this difference, as well the absence of warship output.

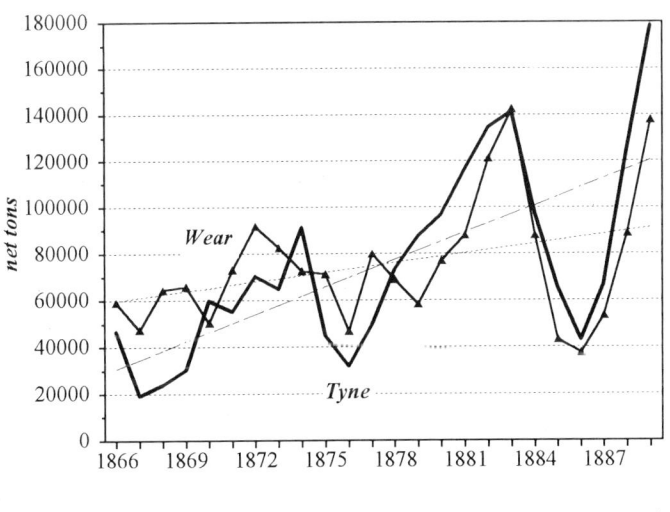

Diag 7.02

The final stage of wood and T & W Smith.
Almost 100 wood ships of 400t or more were launched on the Tyne after 1850. In 1873 the *Merlin* [248t], was probably the last Tyne wooden hull, launched by Banks at Howdon. The yards of T & W Smith, *the oldest Tyne shipbuilders*, no doubt had the highest aggregate output in wood on the river, but no precise

---
[3] Nationally the iron tonnage fell by 43% between 1865 and 1867, whereas wooden ships fell by 35%.

Smith's covered berths of 1851 as presented by the Tyne Iron Shipbuilding Co Ltd.

figure can be put on this. During the five years up to 1850, Smiths operated at both St Peters and North Shields; in that period, according to Messent two ships [2,779t] were built at St Peters and four at North Shields together only 620t. A very important development was undertaken by Smiths in 1851, the building of the first covered berths on the Tyne.[4] The scale of Smith's yard and this innovation can be seen in the illustrations. The *Practical Mechanic's Journal* described the construction and commented: *So far a roofed slip is almost unknown amongst them* [private commercial shipbuilders], *but they are gradually awakening to a sense of its value, and the system promises soon to become general.* This prediction was completely wrong; no one on the north east coast followed Smiths's lead. Both the design and supervision of the construction was by the Glasgow firm of Bell & Miller: a double roof covered two slipways and had the very important new feature of overhead travelling cranes. These cranes with a both a longitudinal and transverse movement could *take up loads to any corner of the building, and thus materially diminish the expenditure of manual labour*. The glass roof was 247' long and the berths were certainly more than capable of taking any vessel of that time but strangely the two spans were unequal; between the centre lines of supports one was 61.5' and the other 55.5'. Despite the undoubted substantial potential gains from the use of such cranage there was no sustained attempt again for almost 50 years. However, about 20 years later when Palmers were building two armoured cruisers gantry cranes supported on a wooden structure were in use at two building berths. Few shipbuilders believed they could secure sufficient regular orders to make such a large capital asset commercially sustainable. Although some builders in wood questioned the merits of the technique of a covered yard, this was unlikely to have been a deciding factor.

Under this roof Smiths built the largest Tyne wood vessel, the screw frigate *Carlo Alberta* for the Sardinian government. Launched on 23 May 1853, she ended on a sand bank on the south shore when a warp broke but fortunately got off unharmed. This three decker, pierced for 50 guns, was 245' extreme length, 50' breadth and 32' deep, by builders measure 2,500t. It was necessary to dredge 200,000 tons out of the Tyne to create a special channel to enable the frigate to reach Shields Harbour [dredging cost £1,600]. She was docked for coppering at Shields on 23 June. Four weeks later she was taken to Peggy's Hole where she waited for six months for her engines, 400 nhp supplied by Stephensons. The *Carlo Alberta* sailed on 20 February 1854 for Woolwich to be armed there. Before work began on the covered yard, Smiths were extending their facilities at the Limekiln Shore at North Shields both at the yard and a graving dock. On 21 February they launched their first vessel *Termagant* [464t] from the new yard and less than four months

---

[4] For many Swan Hunter have been considered the first to provide a covered shipyard on the Tyne.

A picture of North Shields of the 1860s.

As recalled in 1919 by foreman shipwright, William G Henry:

between the Low Lights and the Wooden Bridge Bank ... a hive of industry ... thirty-five public houses. Starting at the Low Lights - the tanning industry of J R Proctor - Tyzack's forge - anchors, chains & patent windlasses - Carr's pottery & brewery - Tynemouth Gas Works- Robt Stewart, shipwright - repairing yard - behind and next to lighthouse Dowey's boat building shops, where many of the Tyne tugs were built... school children usually took a half holiday whenever a launch had to take place. On the opposite side Mr Almond's engineering shop... famous for the building of new and repairing old tugs' engines. Edward Hadaway... a shiprepairer... the ships' bottoms were first fired with whin bushes and then scrubbed with wire brushes before being given a coat of hot tar mixed with arsenic [and] his floating workshop, commonly known as *the Barge*... John Black's blacksmith's shop, Mr Elsdon Storey's ship repairing works with gridirons for overhauling ships., Mr Avery's sail loft, above Mr Cleugh's bakery, Mr Michael Morton's block and mast making shop, Wardle & White's bakery, and Mr Marshall Gray's block and mast making shop. At Dowson's Quay - Mr W. Charlton's block and mast making shop, - close by Joseph Ellis's blacksmith's shop, also Tyzack's other blacksmith's shop- a little further along - Pickering & Anderson shiprepairers with two gridirons noted for salving of vessels on the Black Middens and Herd Sands - Mr Duncan McGregor's marine store -Wm Johnson's block and mast making shop. At Maitland's Quay Mr John Kelso had his sail making business - Pow & Fawcus blacksmith's shop were well known for their patent windlasses and chains...the harbour Master's Office... Wascoe's brewery close to the Custom House Quay better known as Wooden Dolly Quay - Harcuss and Stroud, block and mast makers, Wm. Gibson sail maker, Mr Matthew's plumbing shop. Close by the river police station - Robt. Pow's blacksmith's shop- dock and shiprepairing yard [of] Mr Emmanuel Young - Spencer's tobacco works.

Henry began work at the age of $10^1/_2$ years at Charlton's block makers and at 14 was apprenticed to Emmanuel Young.
From Smith's Dock Monthly October 1919 pp 166-7.

ALFONSO XII *on the stocks showing the yard, stocks and workmen. She was launched in 1888.*

later ss *Tyne*[5] for mail and passenger service in the West Indies. ss *Zingari* [342t][6] was the first iron vessel from Limekiln yard in 1854. An iron screw collier, ss *Chasseur*, was taken over by the Admiralty while under construction and converted into a floating workshop. She sailed for the Crimea in August 1855. Six gunboats of the best English oak were also built for the Crimean war, powered by 60 hp engines. During 1850-4, the four ships were built at St Peters averaged 1,184t, while the 18 built at North Shields averaged 2,02t, a combined total of 8,375t. Smiths built 78 ships [37,000t], over the years 1850-1869. Wood construction continued, and in July 1862 there was only a modest 300t wood vessel on the stocks. The last in wood the *Sally* [307t] was launched in May 1869. Earlier wood vessels included the *Hotspur* [1,142t], in 1851, *Gosforth* [800t] and in 1861 the *Saint Lawrence* [1,094t]. After 50 years shipbuilding by Smiths ended at St Peters in 1861; over the five years 1855-9, more than 8,300t were built at North Shields compared with 2,622t at the older yard. It would appear that Smiths were showing less interest in new shipbuilding; over the years 1860-5, output was less than one-tenth of Palmer's and not as much as the newly started Wigham Richardson. From 1850 to the end of June 1887, T & W Smith built 118 ships, almost 95,000t; more than 90% of this was built at North Shields. Short of turning down orders it was difficult not to have increased output in the early 1880s, but Smiths launched less than 26,000t in the five years 1880-4. Edwards began at Howdon in 1883 and built more than 14,157t [18 vessels] before the end of 1884. He was one of the men, with family links, who continued the Smith's yard tradition.. No ships seem to appear in the name of T & W Smith after 1890. [North Shields in 1860s see inset opposite]

Others on the Tyne.
Many fine vessels came from South Shields. William Marshall launched the *George Marshall* [1,361t] in 1854. His brother George, was a substantial businessman, owner of a timber yard and shipowner, and a member of the Lloyds General Committee. Lloyd's visitors in August 1855 praised the *Gertrude* [949t], which was also built for George. Three years later the *Surrey* [1,089t][7] was Marshall's last ship in wood. Andrew McLeod, with his partners, were owners of wooden vessels and shipbuilders. They built amongst others the 1,055t *Octavia* in 1851 and the 954t *Asiatic* [1852] and owned the *Heversham* [490t][8] one of the few vessels identified as built by W P Greenwell in 1856. Other examples from South Shields were 500t *Britomart* by Wilson[9] in 1869, the *Hawkhope* [337t] in 1870 from Middle Dock, James Young's 268t *Renovation* in 1872 and finally the *Zulu* by Winlo in March 1872. At Gateshead one wood ship a year of about 200t was regularly built, the last being the 380t *Lewis M Lamb* in 1871. On the North Bank, William Cunningham who had first built at the Mushroom/ St Lawrence in 1839 built the 710t *Merrington* in 1854 and probably the 447t *Hotspur* a year later: in 1860 the *Danube* [201t] was also built at St Lawrence. The first identified ship by Banks at Howdon was the *Babthorp* [192t] in 1861 and he usually launched a ship per year until the *Merlin* [248t] in November 1873. Laing Brothers as typified many mainly repair yards were in August 1856 making the frame for a vessel *already...2 years in course of building*, and Lloyd's commented *The frame, generally and the Workmanship, so far as it has progressed superior for the grade* [8 yr] *contemplated*. At Rennoldson's yard in 1873, the Surveyor pointed out the *superior workmanship and finish* on a 216t vessel. However, when the air ports at the extremities of this ship were removed *several of the Frame openings were found not to be filled with salt*. After a claim that the salt had settled down, the spaces were refilled.

---

[5] 120 nhp engines by Hawthorns. Reg.tons 165 however 300t burden - dimensions 157' x 22.5' x 10'.

[6] This ship was for Ralph Ward Jackson to trade from Hartlepool to Hamburg ; 157.8' x 25.1' x 12.3' is given in Lloyds as 217/ 342t, Newcastle register 327/ 423t - engines 75 nhp by Stephenson - 2 cyl 34.5"dia x 34.5" stroke.

[7] Her bottom was still in excellent condition when she docked at South Shields 22 years later. The *Shields Gazette* commented: "A noble vessel in appearance ... While... in the Tyne she was the object of admiration to the old salts of the past generation as she was a splendid specimen of the fast disappearing *wooden Walls of old England*."

[8] described by MacGregor in *Chinabird* [p285]

[9] Flagg misdated this to 1879 and then described it as *the last wooden ship built at South Shields*.

Iron Shipbuilding.

Three Scotsmen, Coutts, Leslie and Mitchell, should be remembered as important pioneers of iron building on the Tyne. Although the output of Coutt's yard did not compare with the other two, it can be argued that Mitchell came to the Tyne because of Coutts. J H S Coutts [1810-1862],[10] the son of an Aberdeenshire farmer, worked as an architectural draughtsman with shipbuilders Simpsons in Aberdeen, where he met Mitchell. In about 1840 he came to the Tyne and acquired the Low Walker site [3 building berths and a river frontage of 107'] previously used as a wood shipyard by William Reay, who registered his last vessel in 1842. Coutt's first launch was the paddle steamer *Prince Albert* on 24 September 1842. The day after this launch, Charles Mitchell joined him as a draughtsman. Another great north east shipbuilder Raylton Dixon was an apprentice at this yard. Coutts probably built in all about 20 vessels, including the pioneering *Q.E.D.* [see chap 4]. John Parkinson ,a joint owner of the *G.F.D.* [built in 1847], became Coutt's partner, when the Low Walker yard was sold to Miller, Ravenhill Ltd in 1848. In February 1849 Coutts secured the lease of some ground at Willington Groins on a 75 year lease at £60 a year with the liberty to lay down a patent slipway and erect the necessary buildings. There followed a four year partnership with John Parkinson, after which Coutts continued alone. ss *W S Lindsay*, their largest vessel at 1,300t was the subject of controversy and correspondence in *The Times*. This ship was launched with great ceremony at the end of September 1852. When, however, she set sail for Australia with 300 passengers of board she was soon obliged to return to London. When blame was being laid at their door the builders responded by pointing out that the vessel was not built for trade to Australia. They had been asked for a fast sailing clipper and both the drawings and models had been approved. During construction, with the vessel *far advanced* Lindsay decided he wanted *a third or spar* deck, which added 7' to the depth [the original 18' became 25.5']. Lindsay[11] rejected the advice against this change and had 150 tons of pig iron fitted in the bottom of the ship to change the centre of gravity, but the ship rolled badly. Faced with his later criticism, Coutts & Parkinson pointed out that Lindsay had placed an order for a second vessel after paying tributes to their efforts.

Miller, Ravenhill & Co [1849-1855].

Joseph Miller [1797-1860], with a fellow Boulton & Watt trained engineer Barnes, established an engine works in London. After Barnes moved to France, Miller began shipbuilding in partnership with Ravenhill at Blackwall. Miller, Ravenhill began building early in 1851 at Walker. The *Chusan* [699t]was launched in 1852 for the P & O Line, and was the Line's first steamer to voyage to Australia: the oscillating engines were built at their London engine works. Two large vessels were built in 1853 - *Fiume* [*Iquique*] of 573t and *Memora*. This was an isolated example of a southern shipbuilder moving to the north east coast. Fast steam boats for the Rhine were also built at the yard, and the paddle steamer *Newcastle*, launched in June 1854 for the Government. Two months later they launched their largest Walker built ship the *Tyne*, an iron paddle steamer for the Royal West Indian Mail Steam Packet Co [400hp oscillating engines by London works]. She was nearly 300' long, Lloyd's has 1,603t but higher figures appear elsewhere - 1850t according to *Newcastle Journal* at the launch. Soon after this the firm left the Tyne.[12] James Skinner [see below] served his time at this yard. A potential apprentice John Wigham Richardson gave a colourful account [in 1905] of a visit with his father to the yard:

---

[10] I am indebted to Ron French for information on Coutts. John Henry Sangster Coutts was the son of farmer and he married Margaret Milne. They had 5 sons and 2 daughters. Coutts died at Tynemouth 18 August 1862.

[11] William Schaw Lindsay [1816-77] went to sea at 15, became a captain and later established one of Britain's largest shipowning companies. In 1851 he said that in 20 years *there will hardly be a sailing vessel employed between the ports of our seaboard*. Liberal MP for Tynemouth & North Shields 1854-9 and for Sunderland 1859-65. He wrote the *History of Merchant Shipping ...* [4 vols. 1874-6]

[12] The machinery was auctioned in 1855, starting on 16 April. In August the lease of *spacious premises* 340' river frontage was offered for sale. Miller retired to South Carolina in 1852, where he died in 1860. Ravenhill took a new partner Salkeld. I am grateful to Ron French for information on this yard.

the office entrance door suddenly flew open, and a man in his shirt sleeves - the head cashier - literally kicked out another man ... manager of the yard [John Vernon]. The latter stood swearing at large, and finally took refuge in a public house, which is now the time office of the Neptune Works. My dear father was inexpressably shocked, and expressed the hope that I would never come near the place again...I was destined to spend many of my days in that very office.

Vernon ran the yard between 1855-8; only a single small vessel has been firmly identified with his business.

Palmer's enterprise at Jarrow.

The dominant figure of Charles Mark Palmer will ever be associated with the town of Jarrow. As David Rowe wrote *His association with Jarrow was absolute,* and the growth of Jarrow from a small colliery village to a world renowned industrial centre has been described as a nineteenth century romance. Many thought of Jarrow as *Palmers Town*. When Palmer began his shipyard at Jarrow[13] in 1851 he was already a well established businessman. He was born in South Shields in 1822, the son of a timber merchant and shipowner. He moved from the local school to then famous school of Dr J C Bruce in Newcastle. After initial training in a Newcastle shipbroker's office, he spent some time in Marseilles and then joined his father's firm, Palmer, Beckwith & Co. He had personal ambitions; as Rowe wrote, he was a *larger-than-life* entrepreneur, who was *a great showman and advertiser, regarded by his contemporaries as a remarkable man with boundless energy, always anxious to expand his empire and reduce his dependence on others*. Charles established links with the local coal owner John Bowes [1811-85][14] and he became a partner in the Bowes Marley Hill Coking Co: before long Palmer was the managing partner and a successful business was developed.

Precisely why Charles, in partnership with his brother George, started shipbuilding we may never know. The conventional view is that it was to solve problems of transporting coal; however it may be noted that the first vessel completed was an iron steam tug the *Northumberland*. Nonetheless undoubtedly their second vessel ss *John Bowes* was a dramatic start to starting the regular movement of coal by steam propelled colliers and helped to inspire the adoption of water ballast. The *John Bowes*[15] was launched on 30 June 1852 and a month later picked up her first cargo of coal at Sunderland. She sailed the seas for just as long as Palmer's company lasted and sank of the coast of Spain [after many name changes[16]] in 1933, the year the gates shut on the Jarrow shipyard. Palmer set up the General Iron Screw Collier

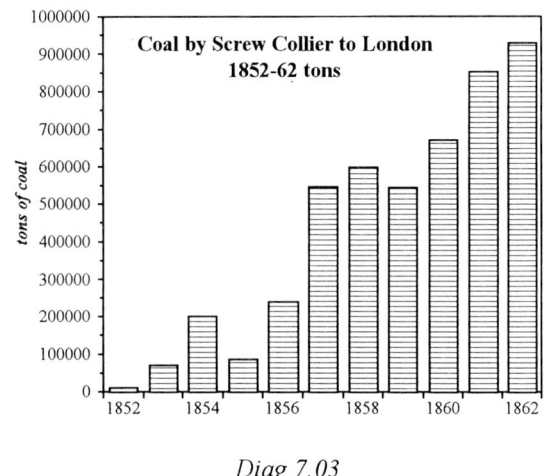

Diag 7.03

Co. [capital £2,500,00] to stimulate the successful application of this type of vessel for shipping coal[17];

---

[13] Thomas Metcalfe, who also had worked at South Shields, had a wood shipyard on this site from the late 1830s.

[14] John Bowes was the only and illegitimate son of the Tenth Earl of Strathmore. He was denied his father's title and Scottish inheritance but was allowed the estates in the north east of England [42300 acres in 1879]. He inherited mining investments and a share of the Lord Ravensworth & Partners interests. The Marley Coal Co. was formed in 1841, Bowes did not manage it very well and it got into debt. His gross personal estate was £145875 [compare with Palmer's £15226], he had no heirs and the estate went mainly to maintain the Bowes Museum.

[15] A modest sized vessel 437t, net 270t [149' x 25.7' x 15.6'].

[16] Name changes were 1889 *Spec* [Norwegian owners], 1900 *Transit* [Swedish owners], 1908 *Carolina* [owned at Bilbao], 1920 *Valentine Fierro* [new owners Gijon] and finally *Villa Selgas*.

[17] A quarter of a million tons of coal was carried to London by rail in 1851 compared with 3.25 million by sea, ten years later that carried by sea had only increased by $1/3$ million tons, however the railways carried 1.64 million tons almost equal to half that shipped. By 1867 the coal to London carried by rail exceeded that carried by sea.

in addition he organised the development of the machinery to unload the coal more quickly on the Thames. There was an immediate rapid expansion of the shipyard's output from 920t in 1872, to 3,539t in the next year and then 7469t. Approaching a million tons of coal were transported by screw collier within eleven years of the first trip by the *John Bowes* as diag 7.03 below shows. The average size of cargoes did not increase dramatically, rising from 579t in 1852 to 656t in 1861. Before very long the building of colliers, although continued, passed largely to other yards. Almost every type of vessel was built at Jarrow and their naval work began during the Crimean War.

Like all successful managers, Palmer knew that the key to success was in the selection of the right people for the job and he found his shipbuilding manager in Scotland - John McIntyre, then at Govan. The essential points of the agreement between Palmer Brothers & Co and McIntyre in 1852 were that

> *McIntyre Ship Builder* was engaged *as Shipbuilder and manager in their trade of Shipbuilding at Jarrow for five years from 10th May next yearly salary of £150 for first year and £200 for each of remaining four years.* The Company *will furnish* [him] *John McIntyre with the house and pertinents at Jarrow... at present occupied by Mr Robertson* [present manager], *or other suitable house, rent free during the subsistence of the said engagement and defray removal expenses.* McIntyre *shall give and devote his whole time and attention to the business he will not divulge any of the affairs or secrets of his employers.*

The shipbuilding foreman, Clydesider William Cleland, was one of those who witnessed McIntyre's signature. Both later started their own yards. When a ten years agreement was negotiated in January 1860, McIntyre was to receive £7 per cent of the net profits in first year and thereafter £10 per cent. However the Company guaranteed a minimum of £1,100 per annum; both sides entered under a bond of £5,000. Very soon the directors bought off the percentage of profit arrangement and from 30 June 1862 under a new agreement McIntyre was paid £1,500 a year and no percentage of profits. McIntyre also wanted the best men; in particular he wanted to bring a particular draughtsman to Jarrow. He had been empowered to offer £100 per year. The draughtsman was already earning that on the Clyde and asked for a further £20 to move. Feeling he could only offer an extra £10 without authority from Jarrow. McIntyre wrote for approval of this to George Palmer: *during the long experience I have had in working to his drawings you will in a very short time I am positive not think he sought over much.* Unfortunately it is not known if he came. Once it was known at Govan that McIntyre was leaving, a number of workmen offered their services. Palmer had mentioned wages of 26s per week, McIntyre wrote:

> I shall have two or three good hands for 25/ per week I have 2 first rate workmen which I offered 27/ per week and enshure [sic] them of five years work, I propose them getting houses and taking too or three of the young men as lodgers you will write me if that could be easily attained to, & father they have asked me the fare to Newcastle by the steamer you will let me know that for without a few good men we can not make good work... you wrote me how your rivetters are paid our best hands here have 19/ per week I should like to have two or three good rivetters bespoke a good deal depends on good rivetting for good looking work, I hope to have word from you by the end of the week.
>
> P S I almost forgot, I should feel very happy if you thought proper to drop the draftsman a note...

For more than 20 years McIntyre was a central figure in the development of the shipyard. Although he made major contributions to developing the application of water ballast he was not at Jarrow in time to have been responsible for the design in the first collier. Water ballast designs and their application were major contributions to shipping and these advances benefited greatly from the lead given by Palmer and his Jarrow yard. John Price, of whom more later, became general manager in 1876; he resigned in 1894.

Stephensons engined the ss *John Bowes* with a two cylinder engine placed aft [34"dia x 26"stroke].[18] Robert Stephenson believed that *he was, in some measure, instrumental, in conjunction with Mr Palmer, in first bring into notice the system of screw colliers.* Palmer's own engine works was soon started, although for some years it did not provide all the engines required; the first, for ss *Jarrow* [yd.# 8] was completed in November 1853. Four years later about 300 were employed in the engine works. F C Marshall managed the engine shops, which expanded throughout the 1860s.

---

[18] Thompson & Boyd fitted a new engine in 1864. A compound engine was fitted at Dumbarton in 1883.

Charles Palmer extended his business interests to support his yard by playing a part in a number of shipping companies, and brought together a number of Tyneside firms to form the Tyne Steam Shipping Co. Ltd, of which he was chairman. He was also involved in the National Steam Navigation Co [later the Liverpool & Great Western Stm Co] and his yard built their first six steamers. He became the first north east shipbuilder to form a limited liability company to own and manage the Jarrow enterprise: Palmer's Shipbuilding and Iron Co. Ltd. was registered on 21 July 1865, with a nominal capital of two million pounds, divided into 40,000 shares at £50 each. A group headed by the Manchester chemist H D Pochin promoted the new company, whose stock[19] was readily taken up. Palmer was to receive £505,000 for real & personal estate, £200,000 for goodwill & contracts together with a further sum for stocks &c. and he continued as chief executive on £3,000 / year plus an additional £300 for every £10,000 profit above £100,000.

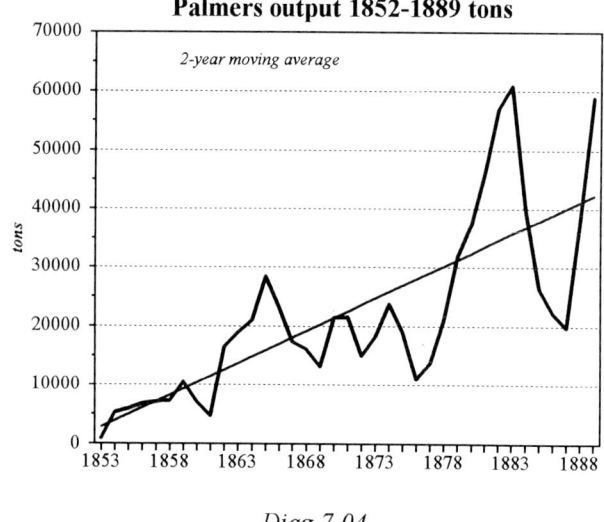

Diag 7.04

Output at Palmers is shown in diag 7.04 and although over the period 1853-89 there is an upward linear trend the violent fluctuations are only too evident. After the initial rise there was a fall back in 1860-1 to less than 5,000t, before the rapid increase to 31,000t in 1865. Almost 20,000t was built annually on average of over the years 1866-78. From the very depressed year of 1876 [8,635t[20]] there was a sevenfold increase in tonnage to 1883 [61,113t]. For the years 1881-3 the average was 57,200t, a level equal to the output for the whole of the Tyne 20 years earlier. The peak of 64,669t in 1889 was not equalled before the Great War [warship work complicates this simple comparison]. By 1857 Palmer had decided to make his own iron, and purchased ironstone mines[21]. Four blast furnaces were erected at Jarrow, and in 1862 he set up the Bede Metal Co. to supply the required copper products. As a result of these actions, when the ss *Erin* was launched in June 1864 the *Newcastle Courant* wrote *we believe every part of it, including engines, boilers and other machinery, has been built by Messers Palmers.*[22] From 1861 to 1869 Palmers also built on the north bank at Howdon, as they did again to achieve that remarkable output of 1881-3, when 32 of the 90 vessels were constructed there. Lloyds' Visiting Committee described the location as Willington Quay as *extensive building premises.*

HMS Terror, the first iron warship on the Tyne, was built in three and a half months at Jarrow in 1856,[23] she had a displacement of almost 2,000t [see chap 13 for review of naval work]. ss *Hudson* launched in June 1858, at 3,000t, was the first of the passenger and other large vessels built, more than 120 ships

---

[19] Wilkinson's analysis was as follows: 73 people between them subscribed £1,613,650 - 11 bankers and financiers subscribed £266,250, eight engineers between them £55,000. Twenty three Londoners took shares of £374,000 and a similar number in the Manchester or its vicinity subscribed £296,000, the nine from Newcastle about £90000.

[20] The value of that output and in 1877 would have been greater than the tonnage suggests because of naval work.

[21] At Port Mulgrave near Whitby, 1,000 tons /day were raised in 1883, the blast furnaces were 85ft tall by 24ft diam. The forges produced 1,000t of puddled bars /week- rolled into plates and angles of the largest sizes used.

[22] *The only works in England where every branch of manufacturing is done on the premises- from the delivery of the ore at one end of the yard till it leaves the docks at the other in the form of a finished Ship. The Engineer* 1863

[23] Delivery was under a substantial financial penalty in the event of delay. Palmer said *she would have been completed in three months, had not the declaration of peace slackened the energies of our men, which up to that time, had been maintained so nobly by their patriotic feelings.*

exceeding 2,000t were launched before 1890, excluding warships. Two large mail paddle steamers the *Connaught* and *Hibernia* [*Leinster* chk!] 3,183t[24] were launched in 1860, unusually with their engines and boilers on board. Eighteen ships were built of the order 4,000t or more, including in 1862 the ss *Greece* 4,310t and ss *Holland* 3,847t. During 1863 two sister ships the *Virginia* [2,888t] and *Georgia* were launched for the cotton trade. The *Nevada*, the sixth for the Liverpool & Great Western Stm Co [chk], was launched in October 1868. She carried 70 first class passengers and 1,200 emigrants. Many famous shipping lines were purchasing ships from Jarrow by the 1860s. Showmanship was exhibited to the full on Saturday 15 August 1863, when Palmer arranged for the simultaneous launch of two vessels from Howdon and two from Jarrow, from the north bank the ss *John McIntyre* [985t] and ss *No.1 for the Japanese Government* [730t] and from the south bank ss *Europa* [1,284t] and ss *Latona* [699t]. Modest sized craft such as tugs continued to be built. There were three dredgers and in bad years even barges, with a dozen barges built in 1884. A number of ferries were built and a landing stage for India in 1860. Although many large vessels were built, most ships until the 1870s were 1,000t or less; thereafter they move up towards 2,000t. Almost 400 vessels were built before 1881 totalling more than 440,000t. The cumulative output of the four leading yards is shown in diag 7.05 below.

PALMERS SHIPBUILDING & IRON COMPANY LIMITED,
JARROW-ON-TYNE.
(THE MOST EXTENSIVE SHIPBUILDERS IN THE WORLD.)

Manufacturers of every Requisite in connection with the Construction of Steam Ships.

IRONMASTERS. { MINE OWNERS AND IRON ORE IMPORTERS.

MANUFACTURERS OF PIG IRON.
Cleveland Pigs—Brand "Jarrow."
Hematite Pigs—Brand "Tyneside."
Kentledge, Castings, &c.

MANUFACTURERS OF IRON & STEEL.
Steel Ingots and Blooms.
Plates and Angles.
Tees, Sheets, &c., &c.

MAKERS OF MARINE ENGINES & BOILERS.
Stationary Engines.
Forgings, Castings, &c.

SHIPBUILDERS IN IRON & STEEL.
War Ships of every Class.
Armoured Vessels and Cruisers.
Torpedo and Despatch Boats.
Mail and Cargo Steamers.

SHIP REPAIRERS.
GRAVING DOCK—
Length - - - - - - - 440 Ft.
Width of Entrance - - - - 70 ,,
Depth of Water on Sill and Blocks
Ordinary Spring Tides - - - 18 ,,
Neap Tides - - - - 15 ,,
PATENT SLIPWAY—Length - - - - 600 ,,

This Company stands on the Lists of the British Admiralty, the Indian Government and the Crown Colonies as Manufacturers of Steel and Builders of Ships and Engines of all kinds.

Advertisement for 1887 Newcastle Exhibition

John Price [1833-1903] became general manager at Jarrow in March 1876. He completed an interrupted apprenticeship [the firm failed] at George Clarks. For three years he joined the glass bottle making works with which his father was associated. He served for about a year on the HM floating factory *Chasseur* in the Crimea. In 1858 he joined Pile, Spence as an engineer and later became the superintending engineer with the West Hartlepool Stm. Nav. Co. Soon after the establishment of the Registry at Liverpool, Price joined them as surveyor in March 1863 and later became chief surveyor. For the *Shipping World*, Price was the *guiding spirit* of the Underwriters' Register and he moved from Liverpool to Jarrow. Price stayed for almost twenty years: he retired in 1894. The *Shipping World* wrote in 1883 *it is only since he took the reins that the present prosperous state of affairs has existed at Jarrow*. Palmers also made its contribution to the late expansion of sailing vessels. Two were launched in 1884, the *Scotsman* [937t] and *Otterspool* [1,875t], a year later *Four Winds* [1875t] and *Dovenby Hall* [3,068t] and finally in 1893 *Lydgate* [2,534t]. He was active in many professional Institutions and ended his career on the Board of C S Swan & Hunter Ltd. He was twice mayor of Jarrow and later a magistrate at Wallsend. During his years of management

---

[24] *Shipping World* commented in Oct.1883 : *The original firm got into some discredit by the Galway mail steamers, but has since abundantly redeemed its reputation.*

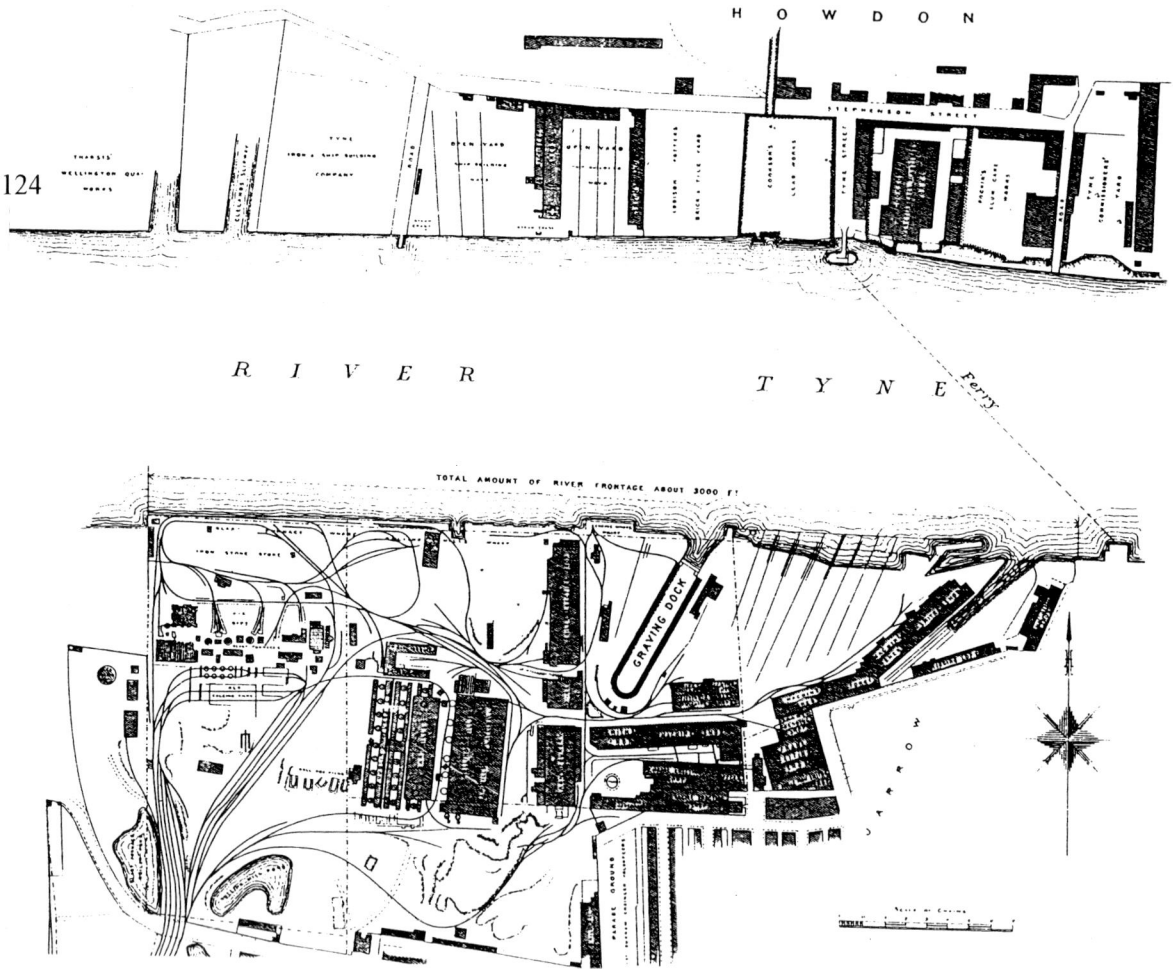

Plan of Palmer's shipyards 1880s

more than 460,000t[25] of shipping was launched, in addition to the creation of Siemens Martin steel making equipment. Price established a firm basis for naval work; many cruisers were built and in his last years at Jarrow the battleships *Resolution* and *Revenge*.

Charles Mitchell and the crucial amalgamation with Armstrong.

Charles Mitchell [1820-1895][26] was important not only as a major pioneer of iron shipbuilding on the Tyne in his own right but also as a contributor to the formation of Swan Hunter and as providing the base for Armstrong's shipbuilding work. He was also a key figure in the formation of the Wallsend Slipway Co [see chap 14]. Mitchell was born on 22 May 1820; his elementary education was at Ledingham's Academy followed by attending grammar school in his home town of Aberdeen. In 1840 he took first prize in chemistry while studying at Marischal College, Charles served his time as an engineer at W Simpson & Co. When he joined Coutts as a draughtsman he was paid 10s a week. In order to gain wider experience in October 1844, Mitchell moved to Maudslay & Field the famous London engineering works and a major supplier of marine engines to the Admiralty. The young Charles lived with a French family in order to learn French. After eight years away from Tyneside, Mitchell returned in 1852 to establish his own yard at Walker, adjacent to Coutts's former yard. A partnership with Matthew R Bigge, of Fenham Hall, provided. financial support The first vessel, ss *Havilah*, was launched on 17 February 1853; this ship was still trading ten years after Mitchell's death. Just before his 34th birthday in May 1854 Charles married Anne, the eldest daughter of William Swan of Walker. Two of her brothers, Henry Frederick and Charles Sheriton became his business partners.

---

[25] His obituary in NECIES claimed 650,000t, this figure seem to be the total by the yard to his retirement.

[26] After the sale of the shipyard, Mitchell purchased Jesmond Towers, former home of Burden Sanderson, and provided the funds for the erection of St George's Church, Jesmond [1888], probably providing as much as £30,000. He also made generous donations to Marischal College Aberdeen. He died 22 August 1895. His son, an accomplished artist, designed the mosaic figures above the altar of St George's, and died aged 48 on 28 Feb 1903.

Output of the yard expanded rapidly, from the first year's 1,500t to almost 6,000t in 1857; like other yards it suffered from ups and downs; however more than 10,000t was launched in 1864. In December 1854 the *Hesperus*, built for Hamburg, was purchased by the Admiralty to carry iron rails from the nearby Walker Iron Works to the Crimea. A large number of barges were built, particularly for India, and some of these were built in 1857-8 on the old Coutts's site. Mitchell became one of the first shipbuilders to use steel in ship construction; he supplied a flotilla of river vessels to India in 1859-60. The understanding reached with Armstrongs,[27] in the 1860s, that Mitchell would build the ships which the Elswick works armed, was an undoubted boost to the Walker yard. More than 15,000t of war vessels were built over the years 1864-8. Inevitably there was the occasional lack of success. For example, in May 1864, ps *Waverley* [later *St Magnus*] was launched for the North British Steam Packet Co but according to the historians of railway steamers she seemed *not to have come up to the requirements of the N.B.S.P.Co.*[28] Although they described this steamer *as the fore-runner of a great many others*. Over the 1870s Mitchell's output exceeded that of Palmers; the Low Walker yard turned out 229,000t compared with 199,000t by Jarrow; these included a substantial number of orders from the north east shipowner Milburn. A new specialism was brought to the Tyne in 1873, when ss *Hooper* [4,935t], the first of three specialist telegraph cable laying ships, was built. This ship was launched within 100 working days of laying the keel. The equally large twin screwed *Faraday*[29] was launched in 1874 and five years later ss *Pouyer Quertier*. Fourteen passenger vessels were built between 1872 and 1877, starting with ss *Japan* [2,440t] and including ss *St Osyth* [3,541t]. At least three of these later sailed under the Japanese flag. In 1878, ss *Ethel*, for Tyne shipowner Rogerson, was one the first vessels to have both a steel hull and boiler [see chap 15]. Palmers restored their dominance on the Tyne by launching more than twice Mitchell's tonnage over the years 1880-4. Mitchell's yard achieved its highest output, 29,000t, in 1870. A wide variety of vessels were built, 79 paddle driven and more than 50 vessels were over 2,000t. The future picture of Tyneside shipbuilding was further sketched in when on 16 November 1882 Mitchell's firm was amalgamated with Armstrong's vast armaments works. Mitchell's yard was valued at £250,000 and he became a director of the new enlarged company. During the Exhibition of 1882, Armstrong spoke of his firm *gradually sliding into* shipbuilding. Henry F Swan became a managing director in 1882 at the Walker yard. Very soon Swan was involved in inventing and designing the tanker, the type of ship which ultimately so dominated shipbuilding. His first, the *Gluckauf*, was built in 1886 [see chap 9].

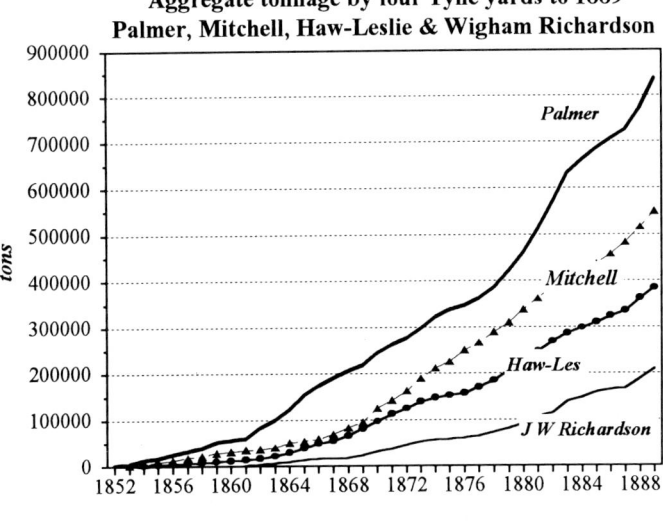

Diag 7.05

---

[27] William George Armstrong [1810-1900], the only son of a corn merchant, trained as a solicitor but carried an early interest in mechanics into a range of experiments which secured his election as an FRS in 1846. In that year with a number of partners he set up the Newcastle Cranage Co to supply hydraulic cranes and a year later Armstrong & Co, an engineering works, was started at Elswick. During the Crimea war Armstrong worked on improving military equipment and produced by 1857 an 18 pounder gun with a rifled bore. Two years later he was appointed the Government's Engineer of Rifled Ordnance and Superintendent of the Royal Gun Factory at Woolwich, as well as being knighted. His partners established the Elswick Ordnance Factory adjacent to the engineering works. In 1863, after resigning his government posts Armstrong reorganised the two works at Elswick which were amalgamated and substantial overseas arms contracts were secured.

[28] See Duckworth & Langmuir pp118-9

[29] See INA v.17 pp 200-210; v 24 p88

George Burton Hunter [1845-1937]

George Burton Hunter was born in Sunderland on 19 December 1845. When his father Thomas [1805-1887], was unable to find work as a potter, he became a shipwright's apprentice at Hall's of Monkwearmouth. He went to sea as a ship's carpenter. After he became a ship's Captain to become a shipowner he built his own vessel. George's mother, Elizabeth, was the eldest daughter of a Sunderland master mariner, William Rowntree. Although for a time an active Baptist, she practised her faith as a staunch Anglican, and this religious background influenced her son. George had little formal schooling and in 1853, his father took the boy round the world in his three-master barque, the *William & Jane*. Despite not learning to read until he was ten, the boy diligently used *Cassel's Popular Educator*. His working life began at 13 years of age with two years with Thomas Meek, the Wear Commissioner's Engineer and then a shipwright's apprenticeship to his cousin William Pile. At twenty he was in charge of the drawing office and outside work; he widened his experience in Robert Napier's Govan yard. Hunter returned as Manager of Pile's yard in 1871 and when this yard closed in 1873, he became the junior partner in the shipyard of S P Austin. An insatiable capacity for work was his hallmark and he described his recreation as a *change of employment*. A forceful and controversial speaker, he frequently wrote to the newspapers to defend his views. In 1900, he made his only attempt to enter Parliament as joint Liberal candidate with the leader of the Shipwrights' union, Alex Wilkie. From his arrival in Wallsend he was actively involved in the affairs of the area and lived in Wallsend for ten years before moving to Jesmond. He served on both the School Board and the Local Board of Health and was the second Mayor of the Borough. Local hospitals and St Luke's Church benefitted from his financial support and he donated park land to the borough. Although never very keen to write technical papers, his contributions to discussions were invariably valuable and to the end of his days he delighted in the *know-how* of his long learned empirical knowledge. He was created a KBE in 1918. George married Annie, the daughter of Charles Hudson of Whitby and niece of the *Railway King* George Hudson, in 1873. A year after Annie died in 1927, aged 82, Hunter retired as Chairman of the Company. They had two sons and three daughters. He refused alcoholic drink and supported a petition to parliament for prohibition; he also actively supported the Society of Non-smokers. *Esperanto* [an artificial language intended for universal use] had a special place in his heart and he advocated spelling reform. He died in his 92nd year on 21 January 1937, leaving an estate of £152,363.

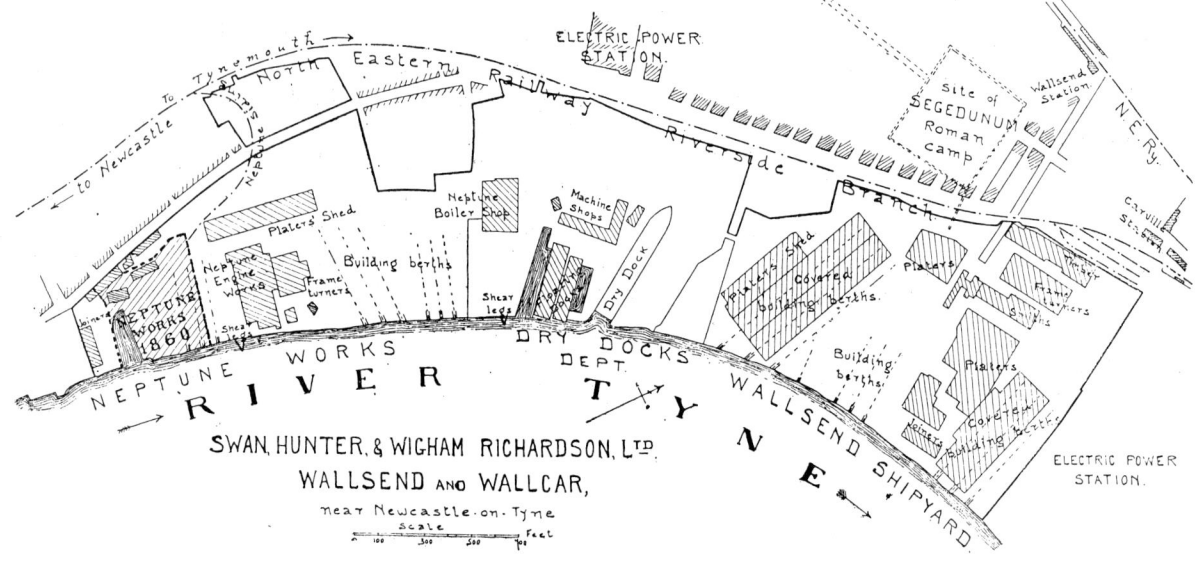

The beginning of Swans.

Coulson, Cook & Co [1871-4] C S Swan & Co [1874-1880]

Many overseas orders were secured by Mitchell including from Russia, China and Germany. He not only built warships for the Russians, but was invited to St Petersburg to organise plans to change their naval yards from wood to iron construction; he was awarded the Order of St Stanislav. A diamond encrusted gold snuff box, valued at 3,000 guineas, was presented by the High Admiral, the Grand Duke Constantine to both Mitchell and his brother-in-law H F Swan.[30] The young Swan showed himself so competent that Mitchell left him in charge in Russia and he lived there for a number of years supervising the work of these yards. With his increased orders Mitchell arranged for two of his senior managers to open a shipyard at St Peters - Coulson, Cooke & Co in 1871. This yard's output was very modest and was later included as the starting sequence for Swan's ship numbers; however it moved in October 1873 to a site exceeding six acres at Wallsend, adjacent to Schlesinger & Davis. A year later, Mitchell resumed full control and placed the yard in the hands of Swan, with the formation of C.S. Swan & Co. Swan left the post of managing director of Wallsend Slipway to take up his new role. Thirteen ships, a total of 5,265t, were built by Coulson, Cook & Co, the largest only 533t and the average about 405t. It is difficult to understand what caused Mitchell to set up a yard with such a small output. Charles Swan arrived as managing director in the summer of 1874. Output in 1875 included ss Whitley [#14] of 1,139t, ss *Stelvio* [1,753t], ss *Monte Moro* [1,777t] and four tugs [three for Russia]. The yard was now in the normal field of cargo steamers. During his first five years more than 37,000t [30 vessels] were built. Tragically in 1879 Charles Swan was drowned; he fell overboard on to the ship's paddles while returning from Russia. The second half of the great Company's name was added when George Hunter joined the Tyneside yard and from 1 January 1880 became managing partner.

Swan-Hunter.

The advance continued when George Hunter took over, and over the period 1880-5, forty-five ships were launched, more than 62,000t. When George Hunter died in January 1937, the *Newcastle Journal* wrote: *No man did more to give the Tyne and the North East, the high place they hold for shipbuilding*. The life of a man who merited such a judgment deserves more than a few lines of biography [see inset opposite]. In 1880, when Hunter joined the Wallsend shipyard, a new partnership was formed, C S Swan & Hunter, and he himself had *only £5,000 capital in it*. About 700 were then employed, and numbers increased as output rose to 20,000t in the boom year of 1883 and in the next peak year, 1889, to more than 28,000t. The annual average for 1885-9 was 15,400t. The increasing size of vessels may be seen from ss *Lamport*, 2247t and 318' long, built in 1882. A year later ss *Monkseaton* [2,900t] became the largest vessel, until the ss *Fifeshire* [3,720t] launched in 1888; she later sailed as *Itsukushina Maru*. Vessel types began to go beyond the cargo type and in 1886, two sister ships were built for the M S & L Railway Co ss *Warrington* and *Northenden*, the first engined by Westgarth and the second by Wallsend Slipway. Eight engine builders supplied the machinery for a sequence of ten ships built in 1885-6. James Huddart, the Australian shipowner, took delivery of a number of vessels including ss *Courier*, which achieved 18k. Forty-one vessels of 2,000t or more were launched in the 1880s and total output was 146,500t. Land was purchased, in 1883, from the adjacent Alkali Works and on these 16 acres, what became the East yard was created. By then Swan Hunter were building more than 10% of the Tyne's output and had moved into third place behind Palmers and Armstrong-Mitchell. Soon afterwards the yard's first two steel ships were built and in 1889 their first oil tanker ss *Circassian Prince*, built to carry 3,427 tons of oil.

A surviving letter by Hunter, dated 8 March 1889, apparently to a new working partner / potential investor provides an insight into how he then viewed things. Hunter distinguished the value of the business between the value of buildings, plans &c and the amount of Partner's Capital on which dividends had to be paid

---

[30] There is some confusion of which of two brothers was given this snuff box. *The Mid-Tyne Link* [1905 - p82] stated Henry Frederick; however in *Launching Ways* [1953 - p. 23] Charles Sheriton is identified for the honour.

which was *£52,000 or a little over* [capital included goodwill valued at two years average profits].

The yard was rather small when business was good in 1881-2-3 & too large [in] bad years 1885-6-7...we lost considerably in 1886 & 1887 while in another year a customer failed by whom we lost over £4,000. The nett profit ... over the nine years 1880-1888 has averaged £7,301 - my salary of course is additional. I do not consider £7,000 per annum is a measure of what the business will make. Alone I have found the work too much for me and have not been able to keep the yard fully employed from 1884 to 1888[31] and could have done much better with a smaller yard that is the reason I want assistance.

I shall be disappointed if we do not make £20,000 profit this year and an average profit of £12,000 to £15,000 over many years to come that however I cannot guarantee. I feel satisfied with our prospects now in any case and especially if you join me in which case we shall do more work and improve our economy. I agree to £1000 salary but prefer the one sixth share of profits for reasons which I can explain. I should prefer your having jointly with myself an additional percentage of the profits over 5%; added to the salary and one sixth share of the business. [He was hoping for an early reply. Unfortunately the enclosures have not survived]

Some Other Tyne Yards

Andrew Leslie - shipbuilder and Hebburn [32]

An ambitious Scot named Andrew Leslie [1818-1894], with £200 in his pocket, decided in 1853 to start an iron shipyard and boiler works at Hebburn. The site was a small piece of open country east of Hebburn Quay. After a brief partnership with Coutts, Leslie was sole owner of the business. While he recruited the bulk of his skilled craftsmen from Scotland, there were also many Irish workers amongst the 200 he was soon employing. There were few if any facilities for his workers, and many disputes with the local pitmen when the blacksmith's shop was erected across a path they used. Houses were built for the foremen and for a time Leslie's own home was beside the yard. James Skinner [1836-1920], who thirty years later opened his own yard [Wood & Skinner], was the only draughtsman for many years, and he with Leslie prepared the estimates for ships. Although in the early years there was a very high turnover of workers[33], many stayed with him all their working lives, such as head foreman John Matheson. In the early 1860s Leslie was rescued from financial difficulties by Thomas Coote, a south of England businessman who put at least £13,500 into the business. This investment secured for his son Arthur [1841-1906] a one-third partnership share. This young man had served his apprenticeship at Denny's Dumbarton yard and he later married Leslie's adopted daughter.

Leslie's first vessel, the *Clarendon*, was a very impressive 1,000t; the Tynemouth MP W S Lindsay was the principal shareholder in this vessel. Many ships were build *on spec*, in the hope of finding an owner. When no buyer was found Leslie traded with the ship until he could sell it. The influx of capital from Coote resulted in an upward trend in output; wages paid in 1873 were £130,000. Leslie was a good salesman and established contacts with Russia where 12 of his 20 twenty vessels were sold. He forged a close connection with the Liverpool firm of Holts, building the *Copernicus* in 1861 and after that a Holt ship was usually to be found on the stocks. In some years this firm accounted for more than 40% of the yard's output and Holt's *Smyrna* was the first Tyne built ship with twin compound engines. Notable paddle steamers were also built by Leslie: in 1868 the *Duke of Sutherland*, which reached 15k and the remarkable cross-channel

---

[31] That was no failure. No shipbuilders however well established were able to do that.

[32] see *Power on Land and Sea*. Leslie was the only son of a displaced crofter of the Shetland Islands. At 13 Andrew went to Aberdeen to work, became an apprentice boilermaker and later a foreman; he studied in evenings and learned engineering drawing from Mitchell. In the 1840s he set up his own business as a boilermaker & general blacksmith and built two small iron vessels at Aberdeen. A life-long Presbyterian, he gave £9,000 for the building of St Andrew's Church at Hebburn. His home was at Wallsend, where he was very active in the local community. He was a River Tyne Commissioner and a J.P. for both Northumberland and Durham, a Unionist in politics. His wife Margaret Jordan was the daughter of a Leith merchant. Leslie died on 27 Jan 1894, leaving £161,275 (gross).

[33] Over the period May 1855 to August 1856 more than 650 names appeared in the pay book and in any one week rarely were more than 200 employed. Labourers in particular did not stay long, some only one or two days.

steamer the *Calais-Douvres*, which was twin hulled, with paddles between the hulls. In the years leading up to his retirement in 1885, he saw output fall off dramatically in the depression of the 1880s. While he owned the Hebburn yard 255 ships were built, totalling more than 300,000t. One of the last young men to learn his trade in Leslie's yard, J T Batey [1862-1951], became managing director of the yard and a national leader of the industry.

The Neptune Yard - J Wigham Richardson.

A young Quaker, John Wigham Richardson [1837-1908] at 15 years went to work with a distant relative, Senhouse Martindale at Liverpool. On his return Robert Hawthorn suggested to his father that he should serve an engineering apprenticeship with the steam boat builder Jonathan Robson at Gateshead. Daily he set off to start at 6.00 am with his can of *cafe-au-lait* and in the evenings was coached in mathematics and French. He finished there in the summer of 1856 and went to London to study. His University studies ended when the collapse of the Northumberland & District Bank placed the family finances in some disarray. After his return the young John joined the drawing office of Hawthorns. He became another early starter in iron shipbuilding on the Tyne, when his father in 1860 provided the finance to start his own shipyard. His manager was a very able and experienced Scotsman, C J Denham Christie [1830-1905],[34] who became a partner in 1862. This was a most useful combination, and

Charles J D Christie

Christie developed into a great naval architect. Richardson suggested that his technical ambition for perfection could impair practical commercial considerations. However John Wigham was a countervailing influence with an indomitable drive and the energy to advance his company. Richardson benefited from his Quaker education and retained wide interests throughout his life and showed an understanding of workers which few matched. This did not deter him from strongly standing up for his view of employers' rights. Another Scot, John McLeod Campbell, [1841-1903] became shipyard manager in 1877 [he started his own yard in 1881].[35] Two years later Richardson recruited a very able marine engine designer John Tweedy [1850-1916] from George Clark, for his recently started engine works. The Neptune yard built a variety of vessels and was particularly successful in securing overseas orders [see chap 12].

Output in the yard began modestly, with about 200 employees, a number similar to Leslie when he began. An annual average of just over 2,000t was built during the first five years and 2,500t in the next five. In the disastrous year of 1867, Richardson was asked if he wanted the hay mowed on his slipway. The 124t ss *Dhu Hearth*, the even smaller *Achillens*, a caisson for the Middle Dock Co and six buoys for Trinity House made up the output for the whole year. An important contract for a train ferry for the Prussian government came in 1865, the ps *Ruhr*, the first of many such ferries built by the Neptune yard. Apcar & Co were supplied with ps *Electric* [395t] in 1864 and a year later with two sister ships, the first vessels over 1,000t. This company also bought the first ship over 1,500t, ss *Hindostan* in 1869. During the 1870s output averaged about 6,000t. Laverello in 1870 received the first of 9 ships delivered to him before 1899,

---

[34] Christie was an apprentice at Dumbarton, went to sea on the *Waterloo* [Sunderland built in 1848] and then became foreman at Clayton's of Liverpool, where a water ballasted screw collier was built in 1855. He worked as manager at Alexander Denny's yard [who had left the family business] until he failed in 1857, directly after his marriage to a Miss Pond. Christie then worked for some time for Brunel on the *Great Eastern*, which he said would never pay. He then worked at the Willington Quay slipway of Adamson & Ronaldson, Spencer suggested Christie as a possible partner.

[35] Campbell was born in Invernesshire and served his time at Cairds of Greenock as a shipwright; after a period in a Dublin shipyard drawing office, he went to sea as a ship's carpenter; in 1866 returned to Cairds, served as a draughtsman with the Humber Ironshipbuilding Co, [Greenock] and after some years as assistant foreman carpenter he became a manager. His joint venture in 1881 was with Mackintosh and Bowstead.

in all almost 19,000t, becoming the yard's largest single customer up to that time. His ss *Espresso* [1,935t] was almost 300' long. Three, near sister ships, were supplied to Laverello in 1872-3, *Nord America* [2,175t], *Sud America* [2,246t] and *Europa* [2,237t]. These were each about 314' x 35.5' x 27.5'. Ten years passed before any other Neptune vessel exceeded this length. In 1883 ss *Milburn Tower* [2,872t] exceeded 330' and two years later ss *Restitution* [3,363t] at 340' was the first over 3,000t. In all 31ships greater than 2,000t were built in the ten years after 1878. A great leap forward was made with the steel hulled ss *Alfonso XII* [5,036t][36] launched on 29 March 1888, Christie's *masterpiece of design*. She was for the Spanish mail service and the Neptune engine works constructed the 4,500 hp engines [34", 55", 90"/ 60"]. This was the largest non-warship built on the Tyne up to that time. Described as *fitted up luxuriously for 240 passengers and 800 emigrants* [at the time *emigrants* were not thought of as *passengers*]. The account in the *Shipping World* continued:

> The decks are arranged to mount guns in the case of need. All the loading and unloading, as well as the steering will be effected noiselessly by hydraulic gear. The lighting throughout will be by electricity. There are large cooling rooms for keeping fresh milk and vegetables for the whole voyage. In the music room there will be a magnificent piano [on wheels for moving to other places]. The cabins will be fitted up'... with vari-coloured windows and every fitting will be silver plated. The grand entrance will be in coloured marbles, and in imitation of the grand staircase at the Opera House in Paris.

An average of 13,500t was launched over the years 1880-4, but in 1881 it reached almost 16,000t and nearly 25,000t in 1883. Neptune suffered less than most other yards in the mid-1880s slump; output in 1886 was 5,566t, and in the worst year 1887, only the *Port Fairy* [2,539t] and *Hindoo* [420t] were launched. Not until 1896 was the total of 1883 exceeded. By the end of 1889 Wigham Richardson had launched more than 200,000t in aggregate, and the yard was poised for further advance and almost doubled the aggregate over the next ten years. The 178 ships built went to more than 60 different customers.

A new yard at Wallsend - Schlesinger Davis.

A new yard was started at the west side of Wallsend parish in 1863 by a former Stephenson apprentice C A Schlesinger[37] in partnership with F B Davis, who not only trained at Mitchell's but also worked for that yard for four years in India. Their manager Henry Raincock also came from Mitchells. M C James was the chief draughtsman, and later was a key figure in Tyne shiprepairing. Two sailing ships were launched before their first steamer, ss *Llandaff* [441t], in 1865. The yard lasted almost thirty years and although ship numbers reached 167, only 134 have been firmly identified, about half these under 1,000t. A dozen or more exceeded 2,000t. In 1868 ss *Kielder Castle* was their first of more than 1,000t. Three years later ss *Urbino* [1,535t] for Wilsons of Hull was engined by Holmes of that port as was ss *John Dixon* [1,522t] a year later. Four vessels exceeding 2,200t were launched in 1881 and by then Davis had bought out his partner. In 1883 his cashier Wood left [see Wood & Skinner below]. The largest ships were launched at the 1889-90 peak: ss *Sullamut* at almost 3,700t and over 370' long; her 2,500 ihp triple expansion engines were made by the Wallsend Slipway Co. About 12,000t were launched in the first five years, and this was almost trebled in the next five [33,600t] and almost 48,000t were built during 1875-9, not the best of years. In the first half of the 1880s output averaged more than 11,000t per year. This Company failed as output fell in the 1890s and closed in 1893. Four years later the site was taken over by Swan-Hunter.

Tyne Iron Shipbuilding Co Ltd & local shipowners.

Marshall's old yard at Willington Quay was taken over by the Cole Bros and they began with two vessels of almost 1,000t in 1871. When W J Bone was appointed manager, Lloyd's were impressed with the work of their former surveyor colleague; in 1874 they reported *workmanship* [now] *excelled any they had previously examined*. Their largest vessel was the 267' long sailing ship *Cambridgeshire*, [1,766t], built for London owners. The North Shields Stag Line ordered three ships, the first, ss *Amaryllis* [1,714t] was

---

[36] She was 426' overall x 47.8' x 36', the comparable dimensions of the cable ships by Mitchell in 1873-4 : *Faraday* [4,908t] 360.4' x 52.3' x 34.7' and the *Hooper* [4,935t] 338.2' x 55' x 34.6'.

[37] Schlesinger was active in local government was sixth in the first election to Wallsend Board of Health.

launched in October 1874 and the third in April 1876; they each cost about £28,000. In all at least 25 vessels were built, totalling more than 25,000t, by the Cole Bros. The yard failed in the depression of 1876 and their last vessel was completed by Bartram & Haswell on the Wear. In September 1876, Bone joined a group to form the Tyne Iron Shipbuilding Co Ltd, on this site: it was overall a very successful commercial venture. Incorporated on 9 October 1876, this new company had a nominal capital of £30,000 [£10 shares]. The shareholders were Bone [100], shipbroker H A B Cole 50 [one of Cole brothers], and shipowners - J. Robinson jnr [100], J F Common [100], G Cleugh [50], Charles Tully [50] and Robert Firth, a chemist [25]. In 1877 £15,405 of the capital was called up and increased a year later to £18,000. Not until 1899 was the whole of the £30,000 called up.[38] Two vessels were built in 1877, almost 3,500t. Over the next seven years the 52 ships completed amounted to an average of about 12,500t a year. Nine vessels [13470t] were launched in 1879. Only the ss *Springhall* [587t] was launched in 1886. In 1883, the largest vessel for this period ss *Energia* [3,177t] was built, together with two other vessels over 2,500t. Almost £35,000 was paid in dividends over the first ten years, despite no payment being made in the depressed years 1886-7-8. The Robinson family increased their share holding to 2,950 shares. Their *Stag Line*[39] was a most important customer, ordering 10 of the first 33 ships built [1876-1881]. All the *Stag* ships from #26 [1877] to #45 [1904] were all built by Tyne Iron SB. The first ss *Laurestina* [1,919t] was launched in September 1877. There followed three ships at about 1,360t, 6 ships about 1,950t and two at 2,050t.

Stephenson's yard.
Inspired perhaps by the rising output of the early 1880s, Stephensons moved into shipbuilding, although by the time they acted a slump was worsening. In November 1885, the *Shipping World* reported that *the old and historic firm of ... Robert Stephenson ... and the young shipbuilding establishment of ... McIntire & Co Limited,*[40] *of Hebburn united for carrying on shipbuilding, engineering and dock construction.* The failure of his attempt to establish his own yard resulted in John McLeod Campbell becoming the new yard's manager and he remained until shortly before his death in 1903. The yard, between Leslie's yard and the Nicholson Boiler Works, had a river frontage of 800' and five berths [17 acres]. Months passed before the first keel was laid. In February 1888 it was reported that
> to avoid the cost of transporting heavy boilers from Forth Banks to the Tyne, they are erecting a boiler shop within the shipyard ... A splendid 100 ton shear-legs for hoisting machinery ... has been erected, and branch rails lead from the North-Eastern Railway system and from the contemplated boiler-shop direct to the shears... it is intended to make a graving dock [400' x 73' and 20' deep] in a few months we hope to see the joiners' shop, the moulding loft, the saw-mill, the scrive-boards, and the plates and angle furnaces busy as beehives.

The good years, 1888-1890, gave the new enterprise a sound start for but it never lived up to its high hopes.

Readheads.
Two former key workers at Marshall's Willington Quay yard, Softley [general manager] and Readhead [chief engineer], in partnership, establish a shipyard at Pilot St. South Shields in 1865. A Readhead yard continued almost to the end of Tyne shipbuilding. The partners had £2,800 of their own capital, and more than 80

---

[38] A further 100 shares were issued in 1918 and a reconstruction of the capital in 1919 with the issue of 124,000 new £10 shares. Seven years later following a voluntary winding up, the freehold & leasehold property, &c. was sold to Armstrong-Whitworth for £31,000. Total return to shareholders per £10 share - £13- 3s - 2d.

[39] See *Stag Line* and *Joseph Robinson and Sons* - N J Robinson. James Robinson was born in Whitby in 1768 and went to sea, later settled at North Shields. In 1817 he bought the 218t *Blessing* Wear builtin 1805. After his death in 1833 his wife Grace took over the management. Her sons were the brig's master at various times and after his mother's death in 1844 Capt. Joseph took over as sole owner. When the *Blessing* was lost in 1846, the insurance money was used to order the *Stag* from South Shields. By 1871 Joseph had a fleet of one brig and eight barque in all 3,282t, eight years later he had 11 steamers [16113t]. Nicholas J Robinson played an active part in the NECIES.

[40] This yard only built 4 ships, 6410t, it began in 1883 and closed in October 1884.

Readheads - West Docks 1890.

vessels were built over the following nine years.[41] A small iron sailing collier brig ss *Unus* [183t] completed in October 1865 was the first vessel from the partner's yard. More than a dozen tugs were built, including ps *Washington* built in 1870 which worked for 82 years; the *President* built in 1876 lasted a year longer. Constantinople was the home port of the tug *Unione* launched in July 1866 and her engines were also built by the partners. Lloyds first used their classification symbol, 100A1, on the yard's sailing barque *Lizzie Leslie* [later *Familia*] launched in October 1866. The first 50 vessels averaged less than 200t and over the years 1870-4, the next 54 averaged 574t and it all amounted to 31,000t. A number of 1,000t ships were built, including the sailer *Border Chief* in 1870. There were separate businesses in 1874.

John Readhead [1818-1894][42] worked as a millwright at Earsdon Colliery. At the age of 32, perhaps with a view to new opportunities, he started work at T D Marshall's shipyard at South Shields. Given that his background was in engineering he must have applied his abilities while working there with Softley to gain the knowledge, which later secured him such respect as a shipbuilder. His engineering experience explained the fact that from the outset the Company built its own engines and boilers. Over the period 1875-9 Readhead launched 47 ships [average 855t], a total of more than 40,000t; this included ss *Sagunto* [950t] built in 1875, and still trading ninety years later, under the name *Enrique Maynes*. Readhead's ships, in time, established the firm's reputation for building long lasting vessels. Narrowing the gap of average tonnage Readhead averaged 1,407t over in the early 1880s, which was higher than Smiths or Mitchell; his output averaged more than 15,000t during 1880-4. His early years were not helped by an explosion in the boilershop in 1875. During the depression of 1879, Readhead delivered ss *Trewidden* to Edward Hain[43], the first of a continuing line of vessels built for this Cornish shipping Line. The relationship between these two companies was described as *unique in the annals of the merchant marine*; with 87 ships supplied up to 1965, an average of one a year! The first Hain vessel was 1,730t [115 nhp engine] and cost £18,000. Thirteen further ships were built for the firm between 1881 and 1888. Edward Hain recalled in 1913:

> my father and myself ... first came into the yard - the old yard- as entire strangers; ...a young man... asked us our business and, I suppose, observing our intentions to be quite honest, took us under his wing and showed us everything there was to see. He took us on board a steamer fitting out at the jetty, which was something like the ship we required, and before very long I signed our first contract with John Readhead...

---

[41] After 1874 Softley continued for a time of his own. His sons went into voluntary liquidation in 1880.

[42] John Readhead began a family tradition of dedication to the Conservative Party, and was President of the South Shields Association. He was very active in local government, served as Mayor, in 1878-9, and represented the town on the Tyne Commission, from 1883 until his death. He had two daughters and five sons and took a very keen interest in bowls. An active Churchman, the Chief Constable led his funeral cortege and his pall bearers were chosen from his oldest foremen.

[43] Edward Hain [1851-1917] persuaded his father they needed to replace the wood sailing ships with iron steamers, MP for St Ives 1900-6 and knighted in 1910. Left an estate £628,677 gross, his line was then purchased by the P & O Line, who wisely decided to continue the existence of the Hain line.

This young man was Readhead's son, James [1852-1930] who remarked: *fortunately I asked their business in a pleasant manner*. Such contacts symbolised the personal level of contacts, as well as the family nature of the shipyard, which characterised much, probably most, of the shipbuilding industry on the north east coast throughout almost all its history, certainly until the 1960s. Readhead's older sons served their apprenticeship at Marshalls but James at 15 started in the Readhead & Softley yard and devoted his attention to shipbuilding. At the Union British School, a young James met Walter Runciman[44] and a firm personal friendship was established. In later years the yard built many ships for Runciman. The growth of the business compelled John Readhead to purchase a new site, the West Dock early in 1880, and in the following year the first ship, ss *Jane Kelsall*, was launched from there. Readhead continued to own and work at the Pilot St Engine Works until 1896. There were four vessels under construction in the Lawe Yard in 1881 and vessels of 2,000t were being built. When son William came of age in 1888, the firm became *John Readhead & Sons*.

Some other managers who established their own yards.
William Cleland [died 1876] left Palmers in 1866 and took over the Willington Patent Slipway. He invited repair work for wood or iron vessels and like his former employer formed a limited liability company, W. Cleland & Co Ltd, a much more modest one. Although a few vessels were built in this period, the work at the Willington Slipway was overwhelmingly ship repairs. The 1880s was the last phase, in which men who had risen through the ranks from craft apprentice opened their own shipyards. In 1883 James Skinner [1836- 1920], Leslie's manager, joined with William Wood [died 1914, cashier at Schlesinger & Davis] to open a yard at Bill Quay. Time was required to secure sanction from the River Tyne Commission and the first ship was not launched until 1885. By then the depression was under way, Wood & Skinner built only 1,600t in the first two years including the Tyne Port Authority's Floating Hospital in 1886 [yard #3, it was used until the late 1920s]. Output reached almost 9,000t in 1889 and a total of 17,500t was launched in their first five years. Also in 1883, the Scot William Dobson [1833-1907], Mitchell's manager, started his own yard at Low Walker. He launched 2,500t in 1883 and apart from the disastrous 1885 [only 975t] no year was lower. In 1888 he exceeded 9,000t and reached 12,500t in 1889; over his first seven years 36,000t were built. Campbell, Mackintosh & Bowstead launched their first ships in 1882 and their last small craft in 1886. In all they built 17 ships, a total of more than 30,000t.

Some of the small shipyards.
Side by side with these medium and large shipyards were the small companies which together played a useful part in complementing the work of the larger establishments. Following the death of his father, James Purdy Rennoldson, extended their engineering business to include shipbuilding and repair. In 1863 he acquired a shipyard with a patent slipway at South Shields [once part of Wallis' yard]. They built and repaired wood vessels and extended the yard in 1872. After his death, his two sons carried on and one of these, Charles, later set up his own business; at least 35 vessels [3,358t] were built over the years 1850-87. Joseph Toward Eltringham [born 1848] took charge of his father's yard and built small iron vessels. A typical size was ss *Fiery Cross* of 139t in 1870. Amongst the larger vessels were *Biscayan* 494t in 1873. Hepple was regularly building wooden hulled paddle vessels from 1863 and some with iron hulls from 1870 and by the end of the 1880s almost all were of iron. Each of these yards continued into the 1920s. Both Eltringham and Hepple each built about 21,000t over the period 1850-87, Hepple built many more vessels 283 compared with Eltringham's 133 and so on average Eltringham's craft were about twice as large.

---

[44] Walter Runciman [1847-1937] was born in Dunbar, Scotland, ran away to sea and became a master. In 1885 he bought his first ship and in 1889 began the South Shields SS Co renamed the Moor Line. Later he controlled Anchor Line and became the second largest shipowner in the north east. Liberal MP for Hartlepool 1914-8, a baronet in 1906 and a baron in 1933.

Blyth.

The earlier potential for the advance of shipbuilding at Blyth was not realised for some time. A mere four vessels were built in each of 1850 [769t] and 1851 [1,085t]. Output increased in the next two years to reach 1,980t [five ships] in 1853. Bowman & Drummond continued their yard until it was bought by Hodgson & Soulsby in 1863. This partnership also took over Robinson's shipyard in 1879. The wood shipwrights' union established a yard in 1868 - the Blyth Union Cooperative Shipyard; the founding members were Richard Lough and a Mr Heron. Runciman recalled the position in 1863:

> There was only one slipway and a dry-dock ... which belonged to Mr Robinson, and a wooden floating dock owned by the Soulsby Brothers ... and many of the colliers were laid on the land at Hodgson's Mill, and the caulking and coating of their bottoms was done by listing them over.

These sailing ships turned in some good performances, for example Soulsby's brigantine *Smiling Morn* built in 1870 made 12k fully laden. At the height of the boom of 1883, the basis of the future was laid: Birkenhead born W S Vaughan founded the Blyth SB Co and remained head of the Company for forty years until 1923. Vaughan served his time in engineering at the Glasgow firm of Napiers and held various posts on the Tyne before starting his own yard. Five iron ships were launched in 1884 - 5,067t, which fell back to 1,154t in 1885 and no new ships in 1886. Then growth began again from 2,160t to 6,851t in 1888 and the 8 ships in 1889 totalled almost 11,000t, which compared with many Tyne yards.

Water ballast.

Some method of ballasting a ship without cargo was necessary to keep the vessel seaworthy. In 1855, E E Allan outlined five methods of ballasting colliers at the Institution of Civil Engineers. These were: sand ballast; bag water ballast; three variants of bottom water ballast [water contained between the floors or in a double bottom formed for the purpose, or water in iron tanks fixed on floor or ceiling], and gave his estimates of the costs and benefits of each type of ballast. *The general adoption of water ballast in merchant steamers*[45] *owes its existence entirely to our steam colliers*, according to Benjamin Martell, Chief Surveyor of Lloyds, in 1877. This feature of ship design with the associated double bottoms was linked to the north east shipbuilding. Martell reminded the INA of the considerable inconvenience of earlier forms of ballast and the *unsightly mounds or ballast heaps* [which] *rendered valuable land unsuitable for industrial purposes*. All those transporting coal did not instantly adopt the steam collier; however, the arrival of steam power and the reduced voyage time increased the need to reduce the time in port dealing with solid ballast. According to one defender of the sailing collier, Hugh Taylor MP, coal and shipowner, the great problem for the shipowner was *detention in harbours* and he contended that with greater facilities in loading and unloading, the screw colliers could not compete with sailers. He had tried for a year the bagged water ballast patented by Dr White[46] of Newcastle and stated that on the *Devonshire* he had saved £120 compared with the ordinary ballasting, in addition to a *great saving of time*. As soon as the cargo was cleared, the ship could start, *instead of waiting all night, and frequently two days, for ballast*. [see fn 43] This scheme *found little favour*, the rolling of the vessel chaffed the bags and sometimes they tended to burst which could endanger the ship.

Palmer frankly explained the efforts to achieve a satisfactory system of water-ballast in the *John Bowes*:
> the ceiling... of iron, [was] found... unserviceable, as it could not be kept tight: he replaced the iron ceiling with one of timber, but with the same result. He then tried large tanks in the sides, containing 70 or 80

---

[45] He pointed out that in the merchant ships double bottoms were usually associated with water ballast. In naval vessels double bottoms were fitted *chiefly as a source of additional strength and security in the event of accident occurring to the outer bottom* [as in the *Great Eastern*].

[46] Dr David Blair White claimed the first *practical experiment in ballasting with water* and cited the log of the *Benton*. Her coal was discharged by 4.30 p.m. on 13 June, weighed anchor at 5 p.m. and began to fill the rubber and canvas bags with water off Woolwich. By 8 p.m. the ship was all ballasted. She arrived off Tynemouth Castle on 19 June *during all the time the bags were found perfect*. There was a special ballast pump. In the 18th century, Berwick traders carried live trout to London in wells or tanks in their ships, not strictly ballast, of course.

tons of water, but was compelled to remove them, least they should strain the ship...then had recourse to bag-ballast, which he was eventually obliged to reject. For the steamers...since built, he had adopted the plan of large flat iron tanks, running from one end of the hold to the other, with spaces underneath, so as to admit of painting and repairing, with other tanks fore and aft; so far as his experience had gone, he had found it very efficient.

It is certainly not surprising that there were difficulties in mastering this new technique but they pressed on in a determined way at Jarrow. Launched in 1854 ss *Samuel Laing*, fitted with iron tanks in the bottom of the ship was successful and more than twenty years later a Lloyds surveyor reported *the tanks originally fitted remained serviceable*. In ss *Rouen* of 1857, the fitted inner bottom entered *into the structural arrangement of the vessel similar in principle to the double bottom*. In *all probability,* Martell said, the coastal coal trade *would in have been lost to ship owners had water-ballast steamers not been introduced and developed*. Supporting this view Samuel Austin said the double bottom principle was *an absolute necessity* in the coasting trade, without which coasters *could not possibly be employed profitably*.

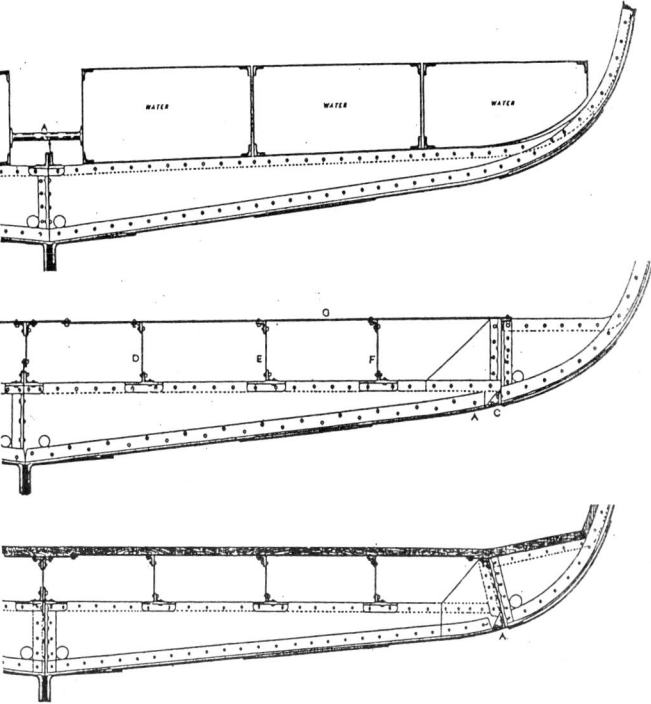

Examples of Water Ballast in Double Bottoms

Martell argued against those who opposed the use of water ballast for the foreign trades, claiming it offered no advantages. He pointed out that on a £20,000 steamer in the Mediterranean trade, solid ballast could cost £1,000 a year [equivalent to 5% on the first cost of the ship]. It might be higher on the Baltic routes because of more journeys. Many underwriters and others had held a *great prejudice* against vessels fitted with double bottoms and such ideas persisted for some time. The overloading of inadequately designed vessels with the attendant losses had contributed to such ideas. At Jarrow the improved design of the MacIntyre arrangement followed. Later many other north east firms offered new designs, for example Withy and Laing. George Hunter made an important contribution on the Wear; Austin said that by their *rather novel mode* every part of water ballast could be kept *absolutely free from corrosion* by *having facility for the due painting of the iron*. Bone developed a design for use with sailing vessels taking coal to Almeria or Valencia and returning with ore: 150 tons of water ballast was pumped out by the crew while the cargo was unloaded. The improved turn-round time and no cost for dry ballast saved £40 each voyage. A leading role was played by the north east in developing designs for water ballast and its application to the great benefit of shipping.

Comments by Lloyd's on Tyne yards in the 1870s.[47]

The desire of many shipbuilders to secure minimum scantlings &c for iron vessels resulted in the formation of a Registry at Liverpool separate from that at Lloyd's. Until about 1870 many north east built ships were on this Liverpool Register [some were on both]. Lloyd's Surveyor Reed reported in the summer of 1870:
> previous to the issue of the issue of the new Rules [which adjusted previous requirements] we had not a ship building in Messers Palmers, all being built for the Liverpool Book, but in the short period which has elapsed since the promulgation of the new Rules, we have 8 to survey, Liverpool 1.

---

[47] The Chain Cable & Anchor Act was passed in 1864 and Lloyd's gave close attention to the Testing Establishments at both Newcastle and Sunderland. The Proving House at Walker had cost about £10,000 and employed about 15 men. Their work to June 1865 showed a 14.8% breakage and that the weld rather than the iron seemed to be the problem.

At the end of 1869 the bulk of Mitchell's work was also under the Liverpool Survey but this position had changed by the early autumn of 1870, when manager Dobson showed Waymouth round the yard and only one of seven vessels building was under the Liverpool Survey; Dobson expressed his approval of the *New Rules*. At Palmers, Lloyd's described the work on the four vessels under construction as *very satisfactory generally* and the vessel fitting out was *flush plated and appeared a very satisfactory structure*. Waymouth was not so happy at Hebburn, where the work *did not give as good an impression as that in Palmer's yard*. Two years later, all eight vessels building at Smiths were subject to Lloyd's as were the eight vessels under construction at Palmer's yard. There were no complaints on workmanship at Hebburn, where both Leslie and Coote escorted the party; in 1877 the work was *highly satisfactory*, indeed two members of the party who missed the main visit came on the next day to see the work in progress.

Carelessness could cause some *unpleasant feeling,* as at Mitchell's when an anchor chain test certificate was *said to be lost*. During September 1873, when the cable laying ship the *Faraday* was framing at Mitchell's yard and four other vessels were under construction, Lloyd's complained in regard to the half plated #292 that the Fore-Foot plate *being badly fitted, and the holes not conforming well with each other, was to be renewed*. Another example of a generally very good yard lapsing was at Softley's where the workmanship was *sound, but rather rough in finish*. In concluding his 1873 report Martell pointed out that *great differences exist in the soundness of work, and the carefulness with which it is arranged and finished, in shipyards contiguous to each other*. When in 1874 as usual the *arrangements and work* at Palmers were *highly satisfactory*. It was discovered however, that the bilge plates required firing before passing the Rolls, which indicated that the iron was not as malleable as it should have been for those parts. The *objectionable plates* were removed. Martell regretted that the quality of iron used for shipbuilding had been deteriorating, however, there was *an improvement observable*. He saw the need for *increased vigilance of staff* and stated that the Surveyors should arrange their duties to meet *the growing desire amongst Shipbuilders to obtain a reputation for good workmanship as well as increased knowledge of iron*. Difficulties emerged at Neptune in 1875, Lloyd's Visiting Committee described #93 as showing *A want of care in the arrangement and practical details - many of the rivet holes not conforming well, & many rivet holes carelessly spaced*, and made a similar comment on # 94. Cooke, the local Surveyor, defended the yard explaining it had only recently built under Lloyds and there were *a few such holes in almost all vessels*. Although two years later work was still *not so satisfactory as could be desired*, the Visitors were satisfied that the local Surveyor Reed was taking actions *to effect an improvement*.

In August 1879 Lloyd's party found workmanship on Tyneside *generally very satisfactory... but at Readheads it was not so*. Bracket knees were described as *small and not well secured* and in the case of #153 the rudder truck *very badly fitted and could not be made water tight without cement packing...some frame angles reedy and cracked in the throat*. John Readhead was very angry and set out to refute the adverse comments over four foolscap pages. Waymouth's remarks were regarded as *very harmful and damaging to our reputation*. On 4 September the Company wrote:
> Our Principal regrets that he [was not] on the premises ... the more so as we learn ... Mr Waymouth took occasion to express himself to our Mr James Readhead in a manner not by any means complimentary to the character of our workmanship; and further stated in the presence of the Committee ... we were doing Slop work ... after 15 minutes in the yard and looking at two vessels Mr Waymouth must justify his remarks...

Readheads *confidently* invited consultations with the local surveyors, past and present, and stated their willingness to carry out Lloyd's suggestions. A list of customers, who had *10 years practical experience of their work*, was supplied so that they could give their views. Detailed comments were made on all the points except that of the rudder trunk. The three local surveyors prepared a detailed report and saw together John Readhead and his son James; they noted *The candid way in which Mr James Readhead, on the part of the firm, admitted the justice of our criticism* and expressed readiness to remedy and *the points will be observed in the future*. It was agreed that in future all rudder trunks would be caulked iron to iron and made water tight without the use of cement and felt. These surveyors concluded *on the work at present*

being turned out:
> there is great deal of it which is very satisfactorily performed, such as the fairness with which the vessels are laid off and framed and the consequent fairness of the shell plating without packing the frames, and the generally close fitting butts; [but] bound to say...that certain other important parts of the workmanship now being turned out are not satisfactory...can only be obviated in the future by the builders themselves ... exercising more thoughtful care in the arrangement of the details than has hitherto been displayed, previous to laying their vessels down, and by their cordially co-operating with the local Surveyor on workmanship.

Lloyd's surveyors continued to play their vital role in the advance of iron shipbuilding and in maintaining standards throughout the industry. Mistakes and carelessness are a continuous part of human activity; both managers and inspectors need eternal vigilance.

Some summary comments.
Probably as much as three millions tons of shipping were built on the Tyne over the forty years 1850-89, although nearly half of this was built in the 1880s, so great were the booms of 1883 and 1889. Almost 282,000t were launched in 1889, in all 152 ships. By then the future structure of the industry on the Tyne was in place. The number of yards had been halved compared with 1850. Output by each of the Tyne yards for 1889 is presented in diag 7.06. Palmers headed the world's output in 1882-3 and again in 1888; Jarrow was second to Grays of Hartlepool in 1887. Scottish yards were regularly pressing for the first position and frequently achieved it. Certainly by the late 1870s the Tyne had more than restored the position in shipbuilding she had previously lost to the Wear.

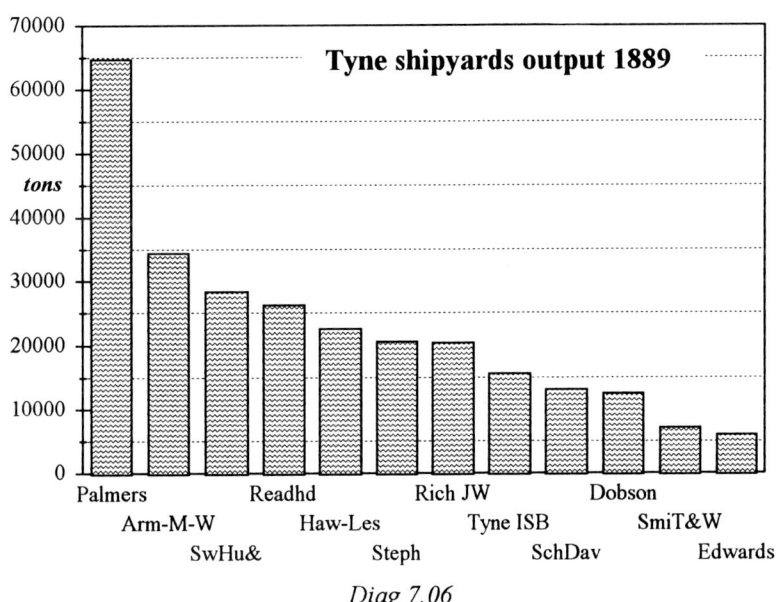

Diag 7.06

Chapter 8

Shipbuilding on Teesside & at Hartlepool c.1850-1889.

On the banks of the Tees what thistles once did grow,
Where our iron ships are built - which now are all the go:
They are rivetted so well, and their models are so fine,
That the Tees takes the shine from the Clyde and the Tyne.
[H Heaviside 1865]

The expansion of the Cleveland iron industry in the 1850s offered a great opportunity of a supply of low cost iron[1] together with the stimulation of increased trade associated with industrial and population growth. Shipping clearing the Tees increased sixfold between 1853 and 1887. Wood construction had not been established as extensively on either the Tees or at Hartlepool as it was on the Wear, and local timber merchants were not playing the same role of funding enterprising young shipwrights through credit and cash. These circumstances probably made the adoption of iron construction easier, and it is in building metal hulls that the area acquired its shipbuilding distinction. Only one 20th century yard, at Hartlepool, had a history going back to before 1850, if William Gray's enterprise is considered a direct continuation of Dentons. After 1869 there were three shipbuilders at Hartlepool and the dominant role of Grays will emerge below. There were six major builders on the Tees, and of these Richardson Duck was the only one with a continuous history from the early 1850s. Pearse's yard at Stockton began in 1854 and was taken over by Ropner in the 1880s and continued into the 1920s. From 1850 to 1889 there was a greater rate of growth in shipbuilding on the Tees and at Hartlepool[2] than on either the Wear or the Tyne. It is unlikely that the average of 1850-2 at either location was much more than 1,000t; however just over 2,500t were built at Hartlepool in 1854, and about the same amount over 1854-5 on the Tees. In 1883 more than 92,000t were built on the Tees and a year earlier 73,210t at Hartlepool; this was almost a 30-fold increase.[3] More than half a million tons were built by three yards at Stockton before 1890. The output in net tons is shown in diag 8.01.

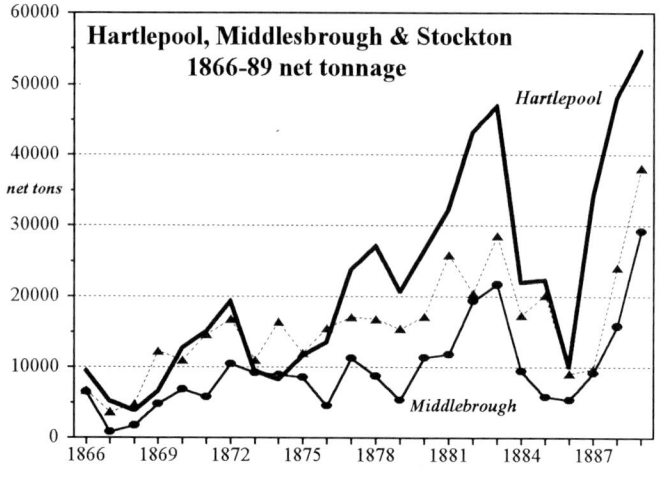

Diag 8.01

On Teesside.

At least 16 men built wood ships on the Tees before 1850, excluding tug builders; probably only three built in wood thereafter.[4] William Turnbull & Co was building until 1860, when two ships [177t & 334t] were launched. When Lloyd's Visiting Committee came to Stockton in 1850 the only work they commented upon was a 360t vessel in Turnbull's yard, and they described him as *highly respectable.* Output at this yard exceeded 1,000t in both 1852 and 1853; the *Westminster* [731t], built in 1855, was probably the largest

---

[1] A more important specific development for shipbuilding was the opening of a large plate mill [80 hp engine] to manufacture ship plates at Hartlepool, on 11 Apl 1865, by Head, Ashby & co - Hartlepool Rolling Mills.

[2] Bert Spaldin's valuable *Shipbuilding of the Hartlepools* was a most helpful starting point for that port.

[3] A linear trend of the official output 1866-1889, shows increases 5.3 Tees & Hartlepool; 4 for Tyne and 1.5 Wear.

[4] In 1849, W Scrafton & J Smith leased Langdale's site. Only the *Concord* [208t] in 1851 has been identified

wood ship constructed on the Tees. After Turnbull's death his wife Ann continued the business. There may have been some links with Robert Craggs, who started shiprepairing in 1835. Craggs occasionally built new ships, including the *Remembrance* [220t] in 1862. At the end of 1866 he took over the Leach & Coates yard at Middlesbrough, and built some wood vessels up to 1870. James Jackson and J H Leach appear to have been largely tug boat builders. Jackson is said to have built 20 tugs for Leach, and Leach to have built 60 but it seems more likely that the 20 were included in the 60. At least one of these tugs, *Victor*, was engined by Rennoldson of South Shields; the last identified was the *Emperor* of 1865, at which time the yard was up for sale. The first iron ship built on the Tees, ss *Advance* [336t], was launched on 26 January 1854, by the Stockton Iron Shipbuilding Co and engined by Hackworth & Fossick. Soon after the launch of the *Advance*, Richardson & Duck took over the yard. Four years later, Rake, Kimber & Co completed the first iron vessel at Middlesbrough, ss *De Brus* [177t - see specification in appendix]. Only one other vessel appears to have been built by Rake & Kimber, ss *Essequivo*; both ships had engines by Hawthorns.

Pearse & Lockwood.

Pearse & Lockwood began in February 1854 and six months later launched the *Iron Age*. This yard was on the Durham side of the river, close to the Clarence Staithes. Soon after the first launch it acquired the site of the earlier wood yard of Markham. In August 1855 Pearse was altering and strengthening a collier *for foreign service* and he launched the ss *Osprey* [386t] in that year and at least three iron ships were built in 1856. The yard was *honourably mentioned* at the International Exhibition of 1862 and built many large and interesting ships by the standard of the times. Before it closed in the mid-1880s slump Pearse launched 229 vessels. In its first ten years a total of 42,588t was built, including 34 steamers [3,680 hp], 20 sailing ships and ten barges.[5] Although from the outset ships were engined by Hackworth & Fossick, some Tyne made engines were used; Hawthorns supplied those used on two steam powered barges for the river Danube in 1858. Hackworth's works under Blair engined almost all the Pearse ships after the mid-1860s, though six were supplied by NEM. Pearse launched their first 1,000t vessel in 1859, ss *Euphrosyne* and a year later ss *Zaire* [1,470t], accommodated 40 first class passengers, 36 second and 60 third class. Rivers in India required vessels of shallow draft and Pearse supplied at least two of these vessels and one of these had steel plates. In 1861 he built a most remarkable vessel the *Talpore* [*Indus*]; Heaviside called it *The Great Eastern of the North* and the local press rated her at 3,900t. She was a shallow draft vessel to be able to carry 3,000 troops for the Lower Indus River, with sleeping arrangements for 800 troops, together with 300 tons of stores and wood fuel for 18 hours steaming. The *Talpore* was 375' long and 46' moulded beam but 72' across the paddles, with a depth of 5' and a draught of only 2'; thin steel plates were used to meet these stringent requirements. After completion at Stockton, this vessel was taken apart and shipped to the Thames, where she was reassembled and tested and then once again taken apart before despatch to India. The ship was finally constructed in India. A year latter a paddle steamer was also supplied to the India government. Blockade runners in support of the Confederates in the American Civil War provided orders for many British yards; three Pearse ships were involved in this blockade running: ss *Gladiator* [592t], ss *Bermuda* [898t] and ss *Bahama* [888t], built respectively in 1860, 1861 and 1862.[6] There was also a complex story related to ss *Southern* [2,245t]. *The Engineer* reported that she was for the Confederates and some diplomatic activity followed. Federal officials investigated the reports and they suggested she made 18k on her trials. Allegations of a strengthened deck and gun ports were unfounded. Heaviside suggested that a former editor of the *Newcastle Daily Chronicle* travelled on a trip to Scarborough *as a spy ... to ascertain whether she had been built run the blockade*. She was *fitted up in the best style* for 68 passengers and intended for trade in the Mediterranean.[7] A longer and angled slipway

---

[5] One of the barges built in 1861 carried 24 wagons, each of 13.25 tons.

[6] This account is based on Peter Barton's highly informative article *The First Blockade Runner...* in *MarMir* Feb 1995 pp 45-64, which provides much more on this whole phase in the history of north east ships.

[7] A dissatisfied owner soon sold her *as there is no prospect of her soon being able to go into that for which she was built*. Barton commented: *he leaves to our imagination the exact purpose for which she had been built*.

was need to build larger vessels and houses were knocked down to provide the space required. Two ships of about 3,000t were built for the British & South American Steam Navigation Co in 1865-6 - ss *Chilean* [2,845t] and ss *Germany* [3,117t]. Pearse built the 3,724t ss *Denmark* [342.9' long] in 1866; this size was not exceeded for 20 years. Only Raylton Dixon exceeded this size on the Tees in 1886 and up to 1889, no vessel at Hartlepool was so large. Rarely, if ever did a yard build so many of its larger vessels so early in its history and in 1863 they stated *We have as much work as ever we can do.* After that spell in the middle 1860s it was not until 1874, that Pearse again build a vessel over 2,000t, ss *Blenheim*. A number of fine sailing ships were also built; these were generally smaller, however the *Royal Victoria* was 1,298 OM. The *Hudson* [833t] built in 1869 belonged to the Shaw Saville Line; she was probably the last sailer.

The Engineer published a brief report on the Pearse yard in 1863. About 400 men were employed on wages that averaged about 25s/week: only 15-20 of those were wood shipwrights. Their reporter wrote that
> iron shipbuilding has been mainly executed by unskilled labour - a great number of Irish labourers taking it up in the last few months, and receiving higher wages than were ever earned by wood shipwrights.

What was and did remain true was that piecework craftsmen did earn more than the shipwrights, but to suggest these were labourers who had in months acquired those skills is misleading. At that time Pearse had on the stocks three ships of about 500t and one of 2,000t. It may reasonably be assumed that at this time this yard could readily average 4,000t / year, which was about 10t / man, and this is also about the ratio for the larger Richardson Duck yard. The ships built by Pearse, Heaviside wrote in 1865, *have been much admired, and they have greatly contributed to give a high character to iron vessels built at Stockton.* Ten years later the yard supplied *ss Hokkaido Maru* [643t] to Japan. In 1882, Pearse launched almost 17,700t and in 1883 more than 22,700t. The yard built more than 180,000t over its 43 year history!

Richardson, Duck & Co.

Roughly opposite Pearse on the south bank was the yard of Richardson, Duck & Co, which started in the early 1850s. During its first ten years Richardson, Duck built more than 55,000t, made up of 50 screw steamers, a single paddle vessel, 10 sail and 29 barges. These barges, usually for the iron companies, were a significant part of the output, comprising more than half the total tonnage in 1860. After the partnership expanded their capacity by taking over the Rake Kimber yard at Middlesbrough in 1859, a young Raylton Dixon was put in as manager; however unintended this was the first step to a new shipyard. [see below] In 1865 about 600 were employed, with wages were at about 24s/week. There were on stocks at that time three steamers, total 1860t and 15 barges [3,600t] and three steamers were fitting out. In September 1865, the prospectus for a limited company [discussed below] described Richardson, Duck & Co thus:
> Draughting Loft...extensive Joiners' Shops, with Planing & Mortising Machinery...Saw Mills with Stores for drying and seasoning Timber. Large Sailmaking and Rigging Lofts Smiths Shops, Furnaces and Powerful Machinery for Punching, Drilling, Shearing and Bending Plates and all requisite Machinery for the construction of Ships of the largest size. 6 acres freehold 874 ft river frontage now capable of Building 10,000 tons of Shipping Annually which can be increased.

The value of the previous year's output was stated as exceeding £140,000. Over the years 1870-2 average output was just over 10,000t; a similar level of output was achieved over the period 1877-81.

Many good sailing vessels were built at this yard, such as the *City of Sidney* [1,130t] in 1863, up to then the largest sailer built on the Tees; it was a Black Ball Line Australian packet. A year later two of the three sailers were over 1,320t. The first vessel over 1,000t was the ss *Palikari*, in 1860 and three years later ss *Bolivar* exceeded 2000t. Like Pearse, Richardson built an early steel vessel [Mersey puddled steel], the 70' long *Little Lucy* in 1859. Four vessels were linked to

Denton's self trimming collier

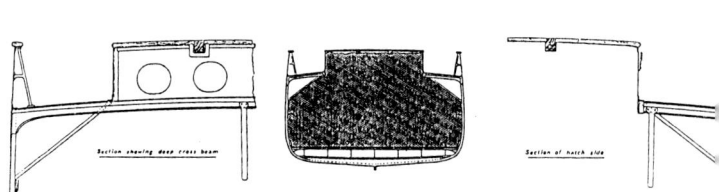

the blockade running: *Modern Greece* [754t], *Patras* [264t] *Harriet Pinkney* [715t] and *Justitia* [783t]. The first two were built in 1859 and the other two in 1862. Although the principal suppliers of engines were Blair and Thomas Richardson, Holmes of Hull engined at least 18 vessels and Thompson & Boyd at least five. Richardson Duck were one of the north east yards that responded vigorously to the upsurge in orders for sailing ships in the 1880s; of 24 iron sailing ships built in the 1880s; twelve were about 1,750t, and two in 1889 were 2,400t.[8] These vessels were praised by Lubbock in *The Last of the Windjammers*: with the words *Most of Richardson, Duck & Co's ships could sail*. He discussed the four iron masted *Afghanistan* of 1888 [2,286t], which was sunk in a collision in June 1905. The *Ulidia* [2,405t] was *one of those splendid ships* which due to a short life was forgotten; this full rigged ship made the Sydney - Maryport run in 88½ days, loaded with 3,650 tons rail iron [11,993 rails] and cost £23,000. *Two the fastest ships in the last days of sail*, was the description of *that wonderful pair, Oweenee* [2,432t] and *Muskoka* [2,357t] of 1891.[9] *The Highlands* of 1892 was a *fine Stockton-built four mast barque* and became the last sailing ship owned by C W Kellock of Liverpool. This owner had the highest reputation; Lubbock wrote *no ship sailing under their flag was anything but first-class in everyway* and this included the Richard Duck ships.[10] More than 21,000t were built by Richardson in 1882 and 1883; by the end of the 1880s the yard had completed more than 350 ships and 270,000t.

Craig-Taylor, a family yard.

A family yard, Craig-Taylor, began at Stockton in 1884. G B Craig had come from the Tyne and his partner was Herbert Taylor. A modest output of 1,602t in 1885 included ss *Expedit* [552t]. Having survived relatively better than many during 1887, building the steel hulled ss *Benholm* [1,438t], they advanced over the next three years from an annual output of 4,507t to 6,519t and finally to 10,450t in 1889. Output in 1888 included two vessels of about 2,300t. One of these ss *Persian Prince* was for James Knott and a year later ss *Petrolea* [2,330t] was supplied to Stuart of London. These ships clearly confirmed the yard's ability to meet the usual market requirements; later they supplied many vessels to overseas customers and regularly built tankers [9 up to 1906].

Shipyards at Middlesbrough.

In the 1870s three shipyards Dixon, Craggs and Harkess, were situated on the south bank of the Tees between the vast works of Bolchow-Vaughan and the coal drops by the entrance to the Middlesbrough dock. The Tees Conservancy graving dock was further down stream. William Harkess [died 1886] came to Middlesbrough in 1853 and began his family yard in 1856. No specific vessels have been positively identified before two composites in 1866 and one in each of the following years; the *Elizabeth Graham* [598t] was the largest of these. An iron steamer was launched in December 1871, ss *Jones Brothers* [695t], for Welsh owners. For the same owners a larger steamer [762t] followed nine months later. Both were engined by Pollitt & Wigzell of Middlesbrough. The yard's largest ship *Carrie* [1,440t] was built in 1883. Harkess' son took over the yard in 1886. Apparently no new ships were built during 1885-8 and then 2,700t were launched in 1889. On the basis of yard numbers 120 vessels were built up to 1889. A yard run by Candlish-Fox only lasted about three years 1864-6 and built more than 3,000t in the first year. Heaviside, in 1865, wrote of two iron yards at Middlesbrough, together with one for composite ships and Leach's wood yard. Backhouse-Dixon and Candlish-Fox & Co, were no doubt the iron yards, but it is not clear which was the composite yard. Two composites were registered as built by one Riddle in 1865, there do not appear to be any other vessels registered by Riddle. Perhaps they were built by Harkess.

---

[8] This increased demand for sailing ships in July 1883, at Stockton pushed *a lot of inside platers and riveters in the streets*. This switch to sail also repercussions on engine work.

[9] *Muskoka* loaded: 3,709 tons of nitrate, 3,721 tons wheat, 3,713 tons coal, 94,578 cases of oil, 17,062 bales of hemp and 2,111,000 feet of timber. Sail times included: *1891-2*- Tees-Port Pirie 71 days; *1899* New York- Sidney 85 days; *1900*- New York-Shanghai 124 days. 1917 converted to oil tanker as *Ortinashell*- 1920 fire & beached.

[10] *Arracan* [1892- 2282t] *distinguished herself* ...Calcutta- Falmouth 97 days in 1894, London- Mauritius 63 days 1902. In 1908 coal caught fire and sold to Germans renamed *Carla-Fehmarn* - to breakers 1924.

Shipyards on the Tees

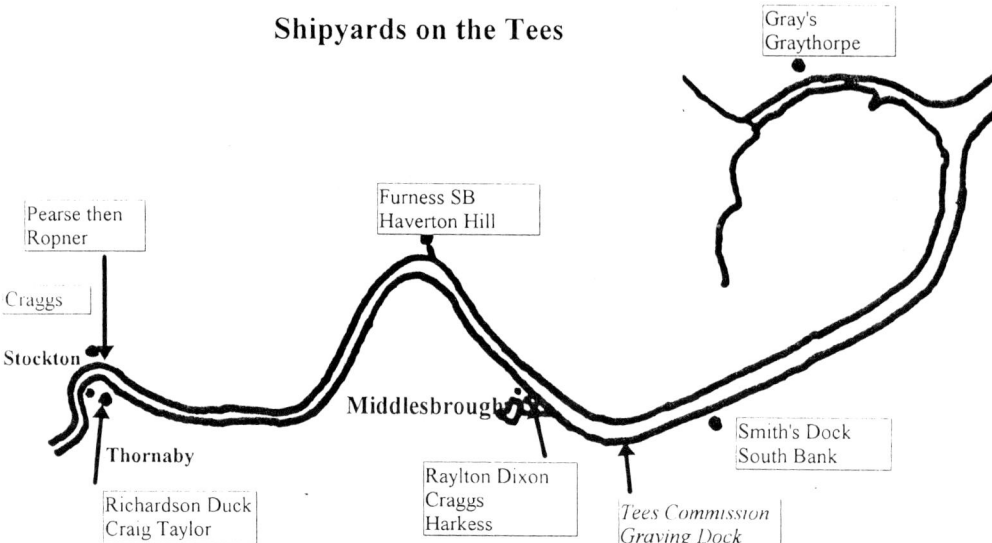

Raylton Dixon - a great shipyard.

Raylton Dixon [1838-1901][11] with Thomas Backhouse, established their own shipyard in the old Kimber Rake yard in 1862, which Dixon was managing on behalf of Richardson-Duck. To this they added later the Candlish Fox yard. Their establishment became the Cleveland Dockyard and went on to become the leading builders on the Tees and a well respected yard world wide. More than 80 vessels had been built when Backhouse retired in 1873 and Dixon took over with his brother Wayman, who was already working at the yard. A sailing ship *Cherwell* [1,170t] was launched in 1864 and two years later ss *Sunda* of 1,886t was launched and in 1873 ss *Kong Sverre* [2386t]. Both steamers were engined by Richardson of Hartlepool, who remained the principal supplier of machinery until after 1890. In October 1875, Dixon launched a rarity on the Tees, a naval vessel, *HMS Tourmaline*, an armoured composite corvette, and later built other composites for the Royal Navy.[12] From 1878 most ships were over 2,000t and 17 ships in the 1880s exceeded 2,500t. At, 4,340t ss *Santiago* in 1886, powered by 600 nhp engines by Richardson was the largest on either the Tees or at Hartlepool; it was built for the North Atlantic route of the Wilson Line. At least 110,000t were built before 1880. The 90 vessels built during the nine years 1882-9 added up to 162,500t, which was an average of 18,000t a year; more than 27,000t were built in 1882, and more than 30,000t in the following year. About 2,300 were employed at Dixons in 1883, when they built 16 steamers, a sailing barge [440t] and the composite *HMS Wanderer*. In 1887 Dixon took over a shipyard set up on the site of the old Teesside Iron & Engine Works in 1879, but never used. With the increased capacity 40,689t was built in 1889: the 18 vessels averaged 2,260t. Dixon launched 38% of the output on the Tees during 1882-9 and almost 48% in 1889.

Craggs

After more than 20 years mainly in shiprepair at Stockton, in November 1866 R Craggs took out a 5-year lease on the Leach & Coates yard. Only a small number of vessels have been identified before 1880. The yard averaged more than 4,000t annually over 1882-4, before three barren years. A series of six similar vessels 1,235t, all engined by Westgarth were built in 1883-4. Craggs converted the *Fergusson* to carry oil for J M Lennard of Middlesbrough, in 1885 and this shipowner was supplied with the tanker ss *Attila* [2,141t] in 1889. The remaining four ships built in 1889 averaged 855t. H G Craggs was regularly involved in innovative work, as will emerge in later chapters. He patented a design of vessel for carrying timber and cotton as shown in *Isabel Craggs* [see illustration].

---

[11] Dixon was born in Newcastle, the second son of Jeremiah Dixon, who held a *responsible position* in a banking firm. He was educated at private schools and an apprentice at Coutts and later worked at Mitchells. He joined INA in 1868. Deeply involved in local politics, he served on the town council and was mayor in 1888; unsuccessful Conservative candidate in the 1885 general election and knighted in 1890. He had many commercial interests including a chemical manufacturing company. In 1863 he married Elizabeth Walker of Glasgow; they had two sons and six daughters. He left £124,080.

[12] Dixon built *HMS Dolphin* [925 dpt] in 1882. The *Dolphin* became a hulk in 1907, a submarine depot ship 1912, foundered in 1925, then raised and used as an accommodation ship.

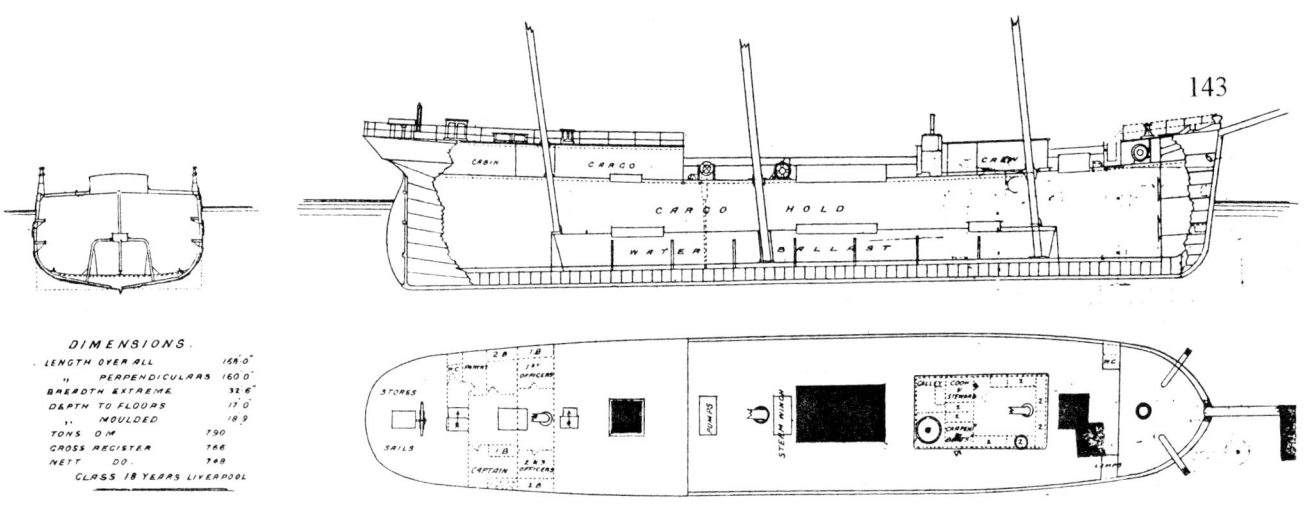

Isabel Craggs

The failed merger.

Through legislation passed in 1855, 1857 and 1862 general limited liability became available to industrial enterprises. An attempt to establish a large limited liability company, bringing together the then leading Tees shipbuilder and a Hartlepool shipyard and an engine works failed. A prospectus was issued on 6 September 1865 to raise a capital of £500,000 for Richardson, Denton, Duck & Co Ltd. The three firms were described as having *old and well established business connections, and are now in full and profitable operation, which will secure...an immediate return upon the investment*. It was argued:

> The experience demonstrates that the combination of Marine Engineering and Shipbuilding under one practical supervision, greatly enhances the success of both Departments tending not only to cheapen production but also to secure greater excellence of workmanship. This combination will also offer facilities for repairing both Ships and Machinery with more expedition and at diminished cost.

The valuation of output of the three companies in the previous year were given:

Engine Works & Iron Manufactory of Thomas Richardson & Sons. £256,000
Richardson, Duck & Co £140,000
Patent Slipway and Shipbuilding Yard of Denton Gray. exceeds £100,000.

It was claimed that in all the establishments the machinery was *of the most modern construction and includes all recent improvements for economising labour*. Shares were £50 but it was anticipated that not more than £25 per Share would be required; £2 on application, £3 on allotment and £5 on 1 January 1866. The combined enterprise quickly failed. On 18 September 1866 it was resolved that the original vendors would *take back their respective their respective businesses*. Shareholders would get their money *back at par, with interest, in instalments of 3, 7 and 10 years*. Clearly if this merger had succeeded it would have been a truly massive company in shipbuilding terms, the combined tonnage of Gray and Richardson Duck was 80,000t in 1889, when Palmers turned out 64,669t and Russell on the Clyde 46,500t. Earlier in 1865 Pile, Spence had formed an equally large financially company as will be explored below. With a few exceptions it was more than another 20 years before the limited liability company became the usual form of industrial organization for shipbuilding and marine engineering.

Shipyards at Hartlepool.

When men from Lloyds visited Hartlepool in 1855, they expressed *their gratification at the great improvement already affected in this Port, which bids fair to rival any other on the East Coast*. Three builders continued to build in wood at Hartlepool until 1866. Winspear and Blumer only worked in wood and were primarily engaged in repair work. John Winspear employed 20 workers in 1851 and over the years 1854-5 showed he could match a typical wood yard; his three vessels were 229t, 249t and 328t. *Practical Shipbuilder* was the description emphasised by Blumers when Luke and Son[13] started in 1848. They launched their first vessel, a snow [278t] in 1849, they were its first owners. Only eight other vessels appear to have been completed up to 1866. Their tenth vessel *John and Mary* [219t] was completed by

---

[13] Later it was George Blumer and finally George and Son [a Lloyd's report rendered the name as *Bloomers*].

Denton and seems to have been the last wood vessel.[14] J P Denton continued to build wood ships until Gray joined him in 1863 [see below] and the yard changed to iron.

Richardson Brothers.
The first iron vessel at Hartlepool ss *Sir Colin Campbell* [536t] was built by the short lived Richardson Brother's iron yard [1855-7]. A year later the Richardsons built their largest ship ss *Ireland* for the almost ever present W S Lindsay. She was 233' long, with accommodation for 80 first class passengers in addition to 1,200 tons of cargo. Another large ship [1,000 tons burthen] was built for the Indian Company Apcar in 1857, and in the same year two vessels were sold to Sweden and a fourth to the iron manufacturers Bolchow & Vaughan. Despite such output the Richardsons, like many others, were in financial difficulties, with liabilities of about £30,000 by the end of 1857 and the final vessel on the stocks was completed and launched by John Pile. From then on the Richardsons concentrated on marine engine building and gained world recognition [see chap 14]. The yard remained empty until the Piles took it over in 1863 and Thomas Pile briefly maintained shipbuilding there until another recession saw them also fail.

John Pile and Joseph Spence.
As already stated the Piles were very adventurous in shipbuilding and 33 year old John, encouraged by Ralph Ward Jackson,[15] set up a two berth yard with dry dock at Hartlepool in 1853-4. His last vessel at Sunderland was called *Port Jackson* and years later the *Shipping World* described John Pile as *a clever and successful builder of wooden clippers on the Wear.* This background was probably reflected in a mixed output of wood and iron hulls until 1861. Pile played a key part in introducing iron shipbuilding at Hartlepool; and his yard was considered as *rivalling the best firms in the kingdom in the new industry.*[16] He began with the wood *ship Mirage* [833 rt] launched on 20 December 1854 for a Liverpool owner. Mrs Jackson christened yard #4, the 1,350t wood steamer *Istanboul* [later *Turkish Empire*][17] built for Wood & Co timber merchants of Sunderland. On 2 February 1856, Pile launched his first iron ship, ss *Demetrius* [yard #3]. She was for London owners and carried 20 first class passengers and 800t of cargo. When in 1856 the Swainson Dock was opened, a new shipyard and graving dock there was leased by Wood, Spence & Co. to be managed by Pile; thus did the links between timber merchant, shipowner and shipbuilder continue. Not until February 1858 was *Early Morn* launched from the new yard [South Yard]. Seven of the first 12 vessels were of wood, but after 1858 only a single wood vessel was built, the sailing ship *King of Italy* [1,230t] in 1861, the largest tonnage built until then. Strangely she was supplied to Higgins of London, who also had an iron sailer, *King Arthur*, in the same year; she was marginally longer but with a slightly smaller tonnage 1,211t. Two very fine iron 1,000t sailing ships were supplied to Liverpool in 1861, *Sam Mendel* which survived until 1909 and *City of Agra* until 1907. George Pyman,[18] who became a major figure in local shipowning, ordered his first screw collier *George Pyman* [691t] in 1865. One vessel

---

[14] Whitby born Mark Dring and his partner John Pattison occupied Blumer yard from 1869 to 1873 as ship repairers and then moved to Winspear's yard.

[15] Jackson [1806-1880] played an important part in the development of West Hartlepool. He practised as a solicitor in Stockton, in 1829 married Susanna [1806-65] daughter of Charles Swainston. Jackson suggested building a dock and harbour at West Hartlepool, when the Stockton & Hartlepool Railway was formed. In June 1847 the harbour was opened and further railway development followed and a second dock in 1853. A Town Improvement Act was secured in 1854.

[16] In 1889, when he was presented with a marble bust, Alderman Thomas Furness said the town was *very much indebted to him* and that the town was *reaping the benefits* of his *great energy* in earlier times.

[17] The bunkers were for a passage to India without fresh coal but the vessel was later changed to a sailing ship.

[18] Pyman [1822-1900] started work as a fisherman at 10 years of age. He was later a bound apprentice and became a captain, with his own vessel. In 1850 he became a ship chandler and four years later was in partnership with a shipbroker T. Scurr. By the 1860s he was a coal exporter and part owner of 5 vessels; later companies included Pyman Bell at Newcastle, Watson & Co at Cardiff and Pyman Bros of London. He was active in both the town council and harbour authorities.

worked for more than 70 years, the tug *Conqueror*, which was delivered in 1861, operated in the local docks until 1902, then went to Sunderland and was only broken up in 1934. Joseph Spence[19] boasted that *the largest cargo* run into Charleston during the Civil War was by their *Lloyds*; she was renamed *Sea Queen*. This vessel sailed for Matamoros, just over the border in Mexico from which cotton was regularly traded. A luxuriously fitted paddle steamer *Whisper, a capital sea boat* in the words of the captain who took her on a blockade run, was launched in 1860; an illustration survives of her flying the Confederate flag. In a different but related direction, when the Federal government took some Confederate agents off the British ship *Trent*, diplomatic problems followed and the British government chartered the Pile built *Spartan* to help carry more troops to Canada.

A substantial amount of repair work was carried out, more than 100 vessels being repaired in 1863 and a number of vessels were lengthened. The Jackson dry dock was extended to 386' in 1860, with a pumping engine supplied by Richardson which could empty the dock in seven hours. Thirty feet was added to the *Sheldrake* in 1861. Other ships lengthened included ss *Venezuelan* and ss *Christobal Colon*. Conversions were also carried out: the paddle steamer *Leipzig* was changed to screw propulsion. A steam barge, the *Avon*, the very last vessel in 1867, was both lengthened and made suitable for sea-going before her launch. A second 80 ton sheer legs were added to the Company's facilities in 1863, when the shipyards covered more than 8 acres, with a river frontage exceeding 500'. As many as 2,000 or more were employed by 1863; the yard being one of the largest employers on the north east coast.

Before the end of 1859 Pile was in partnership with Spence and from yard #24 the shipyard was Pile, Spence & Co. At the Middleton yard four vessels in 1864-5 were built under title T H Pile & Co by another brother Thomas Hunter. After it was decided that the West Hartlepool Harbour & Railway Co could not legally finance shipping operations, Pile & Spence took the company over. This made them the owners of nine ships. A euphoria of expectations resulted in Pile, Spence forming a limited liability company, with a capital of £500,000 in £20 shares[20], early in 1865. This company included not only the shipyards and dry docks but also the West Hartlepool Steam Navigation Co, the West Hartlepool rolling mills and blast furnaces, the Stockton rope works, London premises and other business interests. The *wholly subscribed shares* were allocated in February but the new company was to be very short lived. The extensive London financial house of Overend & Gurney stopped payment in financial crisis of *Black Friday* 11 May. This caused commercial panic well beyond the City of London and reached Hartlepool. Pile & Spence ceased trading on 25 July. The liquidator took over the completion of four ships and a barge.

Over the three years 1863-5, Pile & Spence built an average of 10,800t and the combined output of the three Pile yards at Hartlepool exceeded 74,000t over the years 1855-67. The Pile yards supplied vessels to 49 shipowners. Seven iron steamers went to the Greek & O S N Co, one of which sank on her maiden voyage.[21] Stephan Xenos placed many orders in the north east. Repeat orders from a range of owners reflected the quality of Pile's ships, for example - McKinnon of Liverpool [9] and West India & Pac SS Co [6]. The West India & Pacific SS ordered the greatest tonnage, more than 11,000t; this included ss *Columbian* [2,158t] in 1866 and ss *Australian* [324'] a year later. Fifteen years passed before another vessel as large as ss *Australian* [2,477t] was built at Hartlepool. These two ships and ss *Himalaya* for the British India Co [ss *Persia* was delivered in 1863] were completed by the liquidator. A wide variety of high quality vessels were built, in wood and iron, sailing ships and both screw and paddle propelled. Very few,

---

[19] Spence had retained a financial interest in ss *Lloyds*. Barton pointed out the likely confusion amongst US government officials between *James* Spence, of Liverpool, who was the financial agent for the Confederacy and a propagandist for their cause and the Hartlepool Joseph Spence. His Wear built *Peterhoff* was seized and his *Gipsey Queen* brought cotton from Matamoros in 1962. -again reference should be made to Barton's articles.

[20] About 260 shareholders had subscribed to the Limited Company. John Pile [3,900 shares] and Joseph Spence [4,850 shares] together were allocated just over a third of the shares.

[21] One was ss *Wave Queen*, an unfinished Richardson vessel which Pile completed [renamed *Admiral Miaulis*].

in shipbuilding, could sustain the scale of financial enterprise that was finally attempted. Denton-Gray did not surpass the aggregate of the Pile yards until 1872 [diag 8.02].

Denton & Gray.

John Denton built 25 wood vessels [average 372t] before William Gray[22] joined him as a partner in 1863. The largest wood ship was 582t and sold to a London owner. Four ships went to Nichol at Liverpool, his largest single customer; three of the last five were for Gray and a fourth for Denton & Gray. At first, although the capital was equally divided, the profits were to be 55% for Denton and 45% for Gray; perhaps the amount of time Gray gave to

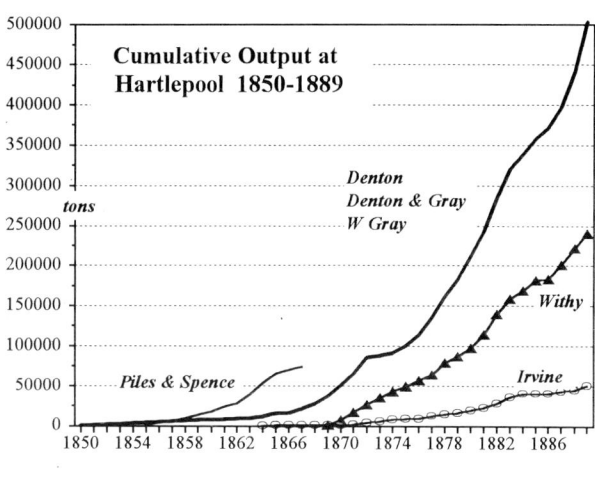

Diag 8.02

the company was a factor but also perhaps again he was considered not to have shipbuilding know-how. Gray was one of the very few on the north east coast who headed a shipbuilding company but was not trained to that trade. On 4 July 1863 the first keel of the new partnership was laid for the iron barque *Dalhousie* [715t], sold before completion and renamed *Sepia*. The engine builders Richardson partially financed the construction of the first iron steamer[23] launched later in 1864. With two exceptions, Denton & Gray constructed only in iron: the yard completed Blumer's wood vessel, *John and Mary* [219t], and their only composite vessel the *Taunton* [688t] in 1868. Two of the first six vessels built were for the Gray family; the *Golden Horn* [1,187t] which was started *on spec* became the first steamer in Gray's own fleet. In 1867 they built ss *Borneo*, a three-decker of 1,770t with accommodation for 64 first class passengers, which two years later she was used as a troopship by the government. In 1867 they built ss *Borneo* a three-decker of 1,770t with accommodation for 64 first class passengers, two years later she was used as a troopship by the government. Ropner's first venture into shipowning was ss *Amy* [583t] launched in July 1868; he and his partner Appleby each held $24/64$ and Denton and Gray $8/64$ each.[24] The range of ship sizes built over the period 1850-89 is shown in diag 8.04. Nearly 79,000t and 87 ships were built during the ten years of partnership. Output over two years 1863-4 averaged 3,100t. After a very poor 1866 output leaped to almost 5,600t in 1867 and surpassed 20,000t in 1872. In 1869 Denton-Gray launched their last vessel, ss *Woodham* [1,340t], from the Middleton yard [see Withy below]. In August 1868 they had leased the old Pile Spence yard for 14 years and almost immediately took a ship into the dry dock for repairs. The first

---

[22] William Gray [1823-98] was born in Earsdon, the younger son of a successful Blyth draper. After attending the John Bruce Academy in Newcastle he joined his father's business. He started his own drapery business and began investing in wood ships. He became a major shipowner and by 1887 he was manager of at least 12 steamers and had substantial finance interests in 70 more. He was President of the UK Chamber of Shipping in 1891. In 1868 with Pyman formed the East Coast Iron Ship Insurance Co and thereafter he was a director of various marine insurance clubs. Gray unsuccessfully stood as Liberal-Unionist candidate against Christopher Furness in 1891. He was knighted in 1890. He married Dorothy Hall, daughter of a sea captain, in 1849. He left £1,534,704.

[23] ss *Dolmenbaktchi* was for the Egyptian government -renamed *Dessouk* - 1,389t 240' long 200 nhp

[24] Emil Hugo Oscar Robert Ropner [1838-1924] was born in Magdeburg [Prussia] son of an army officer; his parents died of cholera in 1848. Robert emigrated to England in 1857, he worked in a bakery at Hartlepool, and a year later married Mary Ann Craik daughter of another baker. After a short time in a coal exporter's office as a clerk moved in 1860 to an other coal exporter, Thomas Appleby, and became a partner early in 1866. By 1874 Ropner had his own business concentrating on coal exporting. In 1884 he was part-owner and manager of 18 ships [29,000t]. Naturalised in 1861, he was active in politics at both Hartlepool and on the Tees; a Unionist and tariff reformer, he twice failed to win the Stockton seat before being elected in 1900, he left the Commons in 1910. He was knighted in 1902 and made a baronet in 1904. He formed the Pool Shipping Co Ltd in 1903, all directorships held by the family. He left £3,615,828. *SS Amy* was wrecked in September 1868.

vessel launched from the former Pile yard was ss *Ouse* [705t]. The partners and the engine builder Richardson jointly owned ss *Euxine* [1,346t] which was launched in February 1870. She was chartered to the Great Northern Telegraph Co for cable laying in the Far East and was suitably renamed *Great Northern*. Many vessels were built for Germany, including the last ship by the partnership, the ss *Luxor*, launched in March 1873. About 1,150 were employed in 1871, when 14,000t were launched.

When Denton died in December 1871 the lack of a formal partnership between Gray and Denton complicated arrangements. Richard C Denton, the eldest son, was employed from 1863 and was outdoor manager in 1869, with a salary of £300 plus 5% of the profits over £4,000. His brother joined the firm in 1869. Gray was not willing to accept Denton's proposal that both sons became partners in the firm, though he would take Richard firstly with a one-third share, increasing to half after five years. Having completed his education in Germany, Gray's son Matthew joined the firm as a clerk in March 1873. When court hearings failed to offer an acceptable solution, the partnership dissolved. Gray proposed a company based on his contribution of £40,000 of capital and Richard Denton £20,000; this was not accepted. A price was paid for the uncertainties of 1873-4; over the two years only 6,274t were launched compared with 16,722t by Withy at the Middleton yard.

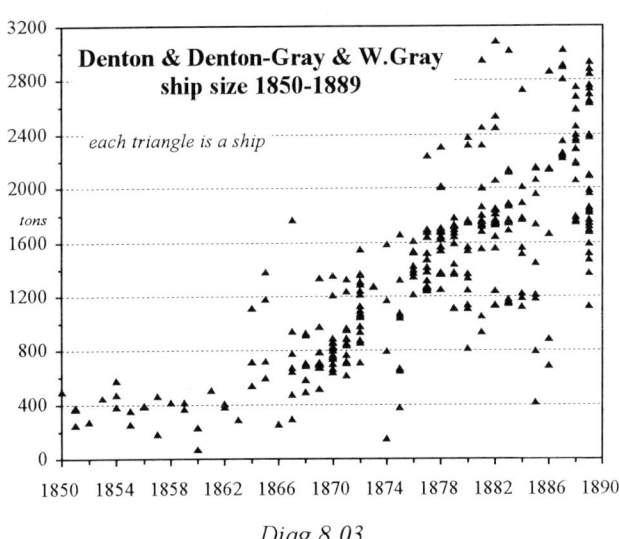

Diag 8.03

William Gray & Co.

In 1874 when William Gray had sole control, a most notable vessel was launched, ss *Sexta* with a triple expansion engine [see chap 15]. As the name suggests this was the sixth for the Flensburg Nav Co. Gray was the only builder at Hartlepool constructing sailing vessels in the 1870s and just over 13% of the yard's tonnage for 1874-8, significantly less than the national average. However in 1875 sail was almost 28% of Gray's output and reached 33% in 1876; their customers for these sailing ships were for London [almost 4,300t], the Tyne based Middle Dock Co. [3,070t] and Swansea [2,363t]. Four iron sailing ships were built in 1884-5 and the *Midnatsol* [1216t] for Norway in 1885 was built with a steel hull. In 1877 ss *Zanzibar* [2,245t] was the first ship over 300' long and five years later *Durham City* for Furness was the first to exceed 3,000t. The only other vessel of this size was ss *Gulf of Venice* in 1883. Even allowing for the very low start in 1874, the average for 1874-9 was 17,345t compared with 7,852t during the partnership. This period included 1878, when it is claimed that for the first time Gray exceeded the output of any shipyard in the country, with 26,260t. An almost unbelievable 321,000t were built in the 1880s, with 41,927t launched in 1882 placing Gray immediately behind Palmer's 60,379t. Five year's later in 1887, Gray was second to Harland & Wolff, but there is no doubt that the Hartlepool yard was in first place in 1888, with 50,307t, 3,000t more than Palmer.[25] This firm over the years 1870-72 supplied about 3% of the UK output and after the setback in the transition to Gray as sole manager this level, or rather better, was reestablished, with 3.7% over the years 1878-80. In the last years of the 1880s the percentage reached about 5%. A total of 425,000t and 238 ships were built before 1890.

---

[25] There are problems of interpretation, e.g. tonnage launched or completed. The figures used are those in *Shipping World*. See also table by Hunter & de Russett - they placed Mitchell first [24,722t] and Palmer second; there is no doubt Gray was above this either by Craig's 26,556t or the slightly lower total from Spaldin list. In 1882, they wrongly placed Elder second with 31,686t [Craig 37,298t for Gray] - first. NECIES v XXVI p114.

Gray supplied more than 70 customers over the years 1874-89. Ropner, with an average of a vessel a year, was the best customer, purchasing 33,627t, followed by Furness[26] and the London owners Watts Ward each exceeded 21,000t. Together three Pyman companies took almost 20,000t and Gray himself almost 15,000t. Appleby bought eight ships, in all 13,600t, and the West Hartlepool Steam Navigation Co almost as much. Three ships or more were purchased by each of 35 customers. Even in the very bad year of 1886, Gray delivered nine ships, more than 14,000t, including three up-river colliers, usually known as *flat-irons*.

The first steel vessel was ss *Shagbrook* launched in 1884. Nine of the next 14 vessels were however of iron, the last being a pioneer tanker *Bakuin* [a near miss as the *first* tanker - see chap 10]. An unmistakable downward movement in ship prices is shown in diag 8.04, based on Craig's figures. As always there were sharp increases in booms and declines in depressions, but the trend shows approximately a halving of the price between 1864 and 1889. As demand rose out of the depression Gray leased a site for a new shipyard, which had the advantage of being beside the Dock Authority's Central Dry Dock. It was laid out for 3 berths up to 450' in length [see illustration]. The ss *Missouri* [2,845t] was the first vessel launched from this new yard in December 1888.

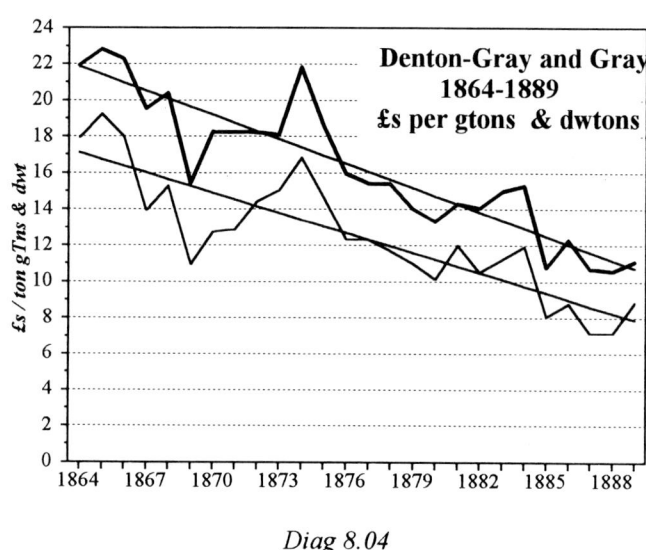

Diag 8.04

Gray's shipbuilding created a substantial demand for marine engines. A total of 28,364 nhp was fitted in Gray ships over the years 1864-83, at a cost of at least £1.25 million [at £45/hp]. A sequence of purchases from Black Hawthorn, of Gateshead, in the years immediately before the boom of 1883 [1816 nhp], might suggest that there were difficulties with local supply. Blair and Richardson were the main suppliers. Up to 1879 Richardson supplied 5,187 nhp compared to Blair's 2,079 nhp. This relationship changed dramatically in the five years 1880-1884 when Blair became the principal supplier, with 8,494 nhp, more than double Richardson's 4,052 nhp. Other suppliers were NEM 460 nhp, George Clark 219 nhp, Wallsend Slipway 200 nhp and Oswald 35 nhp. The first engine from Gray's new engine works Central Marine Engine Works [CMEW] was installed in ss *Enfield* in 1885. A decision to build an engine works had been made in 1881 or 1882 according to Craig, who wrote: *In view of the outstanding achievements of the established north-east coast marine engine builders, it required considerable courage ... to embark on the considerable capital expenditure*. Data does not survive to enable an assessment of its financial success, but if it followed the pattern of other marine engine works, the investment would have been justified. An able management team was recruited and the CMEW had a distinguished history for many years [see chap 14].

Withy Alexander & Co [1869-1874] and E Withy & Co.
Financial support by Denton-Gray for their head cashier, Edward Alexander Withy, and Edward Withy

---

[26] Christopher Furness [1852-1912] was a central figure in the industrial and commercial activities of the north east, including shipbuilding. He was born at West Hartlepool, the seventh son of Thomas Furness who after a time as a coal trimmer started a grocery business, which the brothers expanded under the leadership of the eldest, Thomas [b.1836]. Thomas Furness & Co were importers and exporters, ship chandlers and coal factors. They acquired ships and Christopher decided to develop this business. In 1882 Christopher established the Furness Line [capital £100,000].

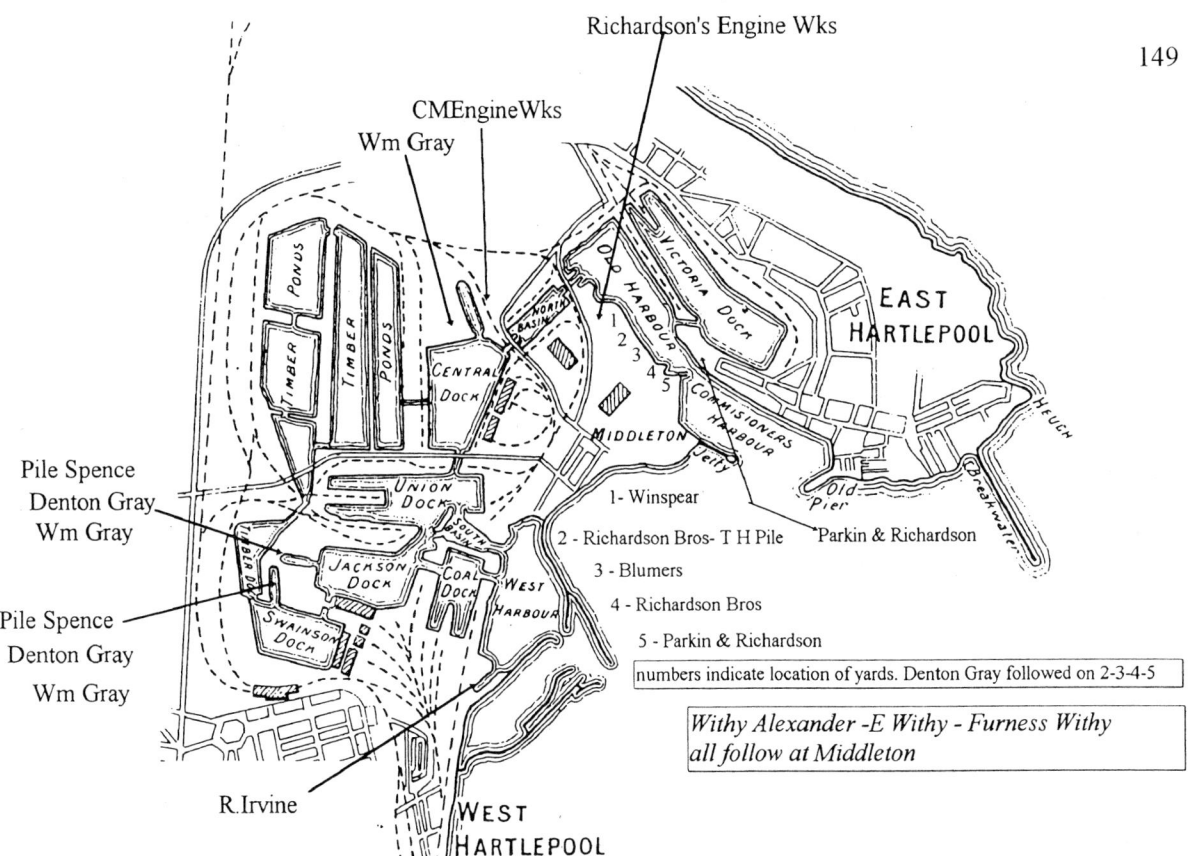

Approximate location of Shipyards & Engine works at Hartlepool

enabled the immediate continuation of building at the Middleton shipyard after their departure in 1869. It was agreed that for five years Denton-Gray were to receive one-third of the profits. Edward Withy, had worked for Richardson, Duck and been a marine inspector for the P & O, was the managing partner. From the outset the yard built in iron but its advertisement is informative in two respects, it read :

> execute REPAIRS for WOOD or IRON VESSELS at Moderate Charges for Material. Shipwrights Wages are now only charged 5s 6d per day, and they work full time without beer or allowance.

This is clear evidence of the persisting need for repairs for the vast number of wooden ships still in service and that the shipwrights' tradition of allowances was still an issue for comment. Withy was fortunate in starting on a rising curve for shipbuilding and output exceeded 10,000t in their third year. Construction began early in 1869 in advance of the formal handover and the first vessel was a modest 158t sailing ship for Spanish owners. Three other vessels were launched in the first year, another for Spain and two for Cory Lohden. Three hopper barges followed in 1870 for the Hartlepool Harbour authorities and the first two of 11 vessels for Ropner, the yard's second largest customer. Three ships in 1871 exceeded 1,000t, including one for Pyman, who purchased two other vessels. Although there was then a decline, the yard was at least as successful in securing, or maintaining new work, as most other north east yards during 1872-7. This success was in part due to supplying 4 ships to Germany, a total of 5,893t in 1872-3, a third of the total output; Kosmos SN was the best customer up to Alexander's retirement in 1874.

The Middleton yard was enlarged in 1873, by the addition of the adjoining slipway of Dring & Pattinson; the slipway was replaced with a building berth allowing the building of five ships at once. At the end of that year Alexander retired and soon afterwards the five-year arrangement with Gray ended. Withy Alexander & Co became simply E Withy & Co. In 1883 Furness acquired an interest in the company and later became the largest shareholder when Edward emigrated to New Zealand in 1884. Younger brother Henry [1852-1922] became managing director. In 1891 it became Furness Withy & Co Ltd [see chap 11]. Thomas Richardson and Edward Withy entered an agreement on 7 August 1874 similar to a number made between engine builders and shipbuilders to provide work in slack times.

> [They] mutually agreed to build yard #52 on joint account *a duplicate of No. 50* [but] *with only two masts ... a close iron bulwark and monkey forecastle instead of a partially open bulwark.* Richardson was to provide a *pair of compound engines* 130 nhp *with governors and spare propeller...according to their usual specification.* Price for the hull was £18,960 and for the engine £7,570 *on basis of half cash, half six months on completion.* Either party could sell the vessel for £26,530 or more, if they mutually agree to sell for less or obtain more the nett loss or gain divide *in proportion to the respective prices of hull and engines...each take proportionate share of whatever paper* [bills of exchange] *may have been taken.*

This ship was launched as *Bertha* and completed as *Kate Fawcett* in 1876.[27] Four vessels were supplied in 1873-6 to G Steel of Hartlepool followed by 21 to Steel Young of London and one to G Steel of London; together these ships made up a sixth of the total tonnage built by Withy up to 1889. Steel's 40,233t were substantially more than the 16,926t for Ropner/Appleby, the second largest customer. In 1877, a vessel with steam powered cranes, winches and windlass was launched as the *Scotsman* [1,827t]. Before she was completed however, Steel, Young bought her and she was renamed ss *Marlborough*. Local shipowner G Horsley was supplied with 7 ships between 1879 and 1889, to make them the third largest customer with 13,846t. Five vessels were built for the coalowner Marquis of Londonderry, including the *flat-iron Van Tempest* in 1884, which carried 900 tons of coal at 9 k. The *Manchester, Sheffield & Lincolnshire Railway Co* used the ss *Ashton* built Withy in 1884 until 1916, when she was sold.

A mild steel hull was first used at Hartlepool by Withy for Steel, Young in 1880. On 21 August ss *Cyanus* [1,635t] was launched, built of Siemens Martin steel[28] and also constructed on the longitudinal bracket system invented by Withy & Sivewright.[29] Withy extolled the superior mechanical qualities of steel. He acknowledged that this vessel cost £1,779 more but the steel vessel weighted 94 tons less, thus allowing 4% more dead weight.[30] This design resulted in a large portion of light scantling which meant the full weight reductions were not gained. It was Withy's first experience of handling steel;

> it had not been worked in any special way, but none had been broken or condemned ... an item of economy ... in favour ... of steel. A few steel plates and angle-bars had been left over from that vessel; and wherever there was difficulty in flanging to be done on an iron vessel, for instance in the angle-iron collar round the lower end of the rudder trunk, he had frequently found that the men had taken up a piece of steel for making it.

Nonetheless, despite Withy great enthusiasm, it would seem that neither the purchaser, nor other shipowners, were immediately convinced of the merits of steel, and the next 9 ships ordered by Steel were all of iron. Three steel vessels were built in 1885, including ss *Washington City* [2,296t] for Furness. The only vessel launched in 1886 was of iron and there was only one more iron ship ss *Lydie* in 1887 at Withy's yard. Steel's as owners shared another first with the yard, their *Para*[31] in 1884 was the first Withy vessel with a triple expansion engine. The ss *Wastwater* [2,874t] for the Australian owner J Huddart was the

---

[27] She was a three deck cargo boat - 245' x 36.6' x 23'- with water ballast in two holds, steam winches Class 90A1.

[28] The use of steel had already been discussed on Teesside. The President of the Cleveland Institution of Engineers, Thomas Whitwell, in Nov 1877 noted the order on the Tyne for a *mild steel* vessel and said it was *another influence which may at some future time affect our local trade*, but he thought the price of steel might not cover the gain in lightness [20% in the hull] and *The question of the corrosive action of sea water on steel plates has yet to be determined.* A year later Gjers, the new President, commented it may said that steel *is threatening to surpass iron in shipbuilding*' but there were *good reasons for believing,* [that] *unless steel plates come down very much in price,* [they] *would be used only under exceptional circumstances.*

[29] G W Sivewright became manager of the yard and dry dock at the Withy yard.

[30] *Cyanus*. Particulars: 273.7' x 34.2' x 19.6$\frac{1}{2}$'. 1,635t 1,060.6 net -total equipped weight 1,133t total dwt on 18.4' mean draught 2,434 t.-water double bottom 431t - cubic capacity 103,410 ft^3 - mean draught in ballast 9.3'. *total weight:* steel net 688t. cost £6,966.   cost iron £5,187 weight 782t

[31] The efficiency of the triple expansion engine on ss *Para* was shown in comparison with ss *Ingram* and ss *Wandle*, both with compound engines. All three ships had a similar tonnage [1748t-1790t]. The compounds had a boiler pressure of 75 psi sailed at 8.5k with 570 ihp and 580 ihp, while ss *Para* made 9k, 620 ihp working at 150 psi. Coal consumption per day was - 13.75t, 14t for compounds and 10.25t [ss *Para*].

largest ship built at the Middleton yard before 1890 and was constructed on the web frame principle. This design facilitated carrying bulky items by eliminating hold beams. It was then *universal practice* at Withys to design with web frame and cellular bottom, a decision made after calculations of hogging, sagging and racking strains *likely to occur in cargo vessels under all conditions at sea*. Naval architect Sivewright claimed that the actual results had verified their approach. Edward Withy was both an energetic and innovative shipbuilder. He read papers to the technical institutions and regularly contributed in discussions. His emigration no doubt influenced the later history of this yard but many fine vessels were still added to the 166 ships of 240,538t built before 1890.

Irvines.

Ward Jackson appointed the Glaswegian Robert Irvine as marine superintendent for the West Hartlepool Shipping Co and Irvine combined this job with some ship repair work from 1860. In partnership with Alexander Currie, previously head foreman shipwright at the Pile Spence yard, Irvine leased a site for a shipyard in 1863 [Currie left the partnership in 1866]. Their first vessel was ss *Island Queen* [319t] for John Pile. Three modest iron sailing ships were built in 1865. Shipbuilding was stopped while a dry dock was built, and a single small steamer was built in 1866. Repair work appears to have largely occupied the next four years, with only a 101t steamer in 1870. Two vessels were built in 1871 each of about 960t, one for Irvine himself and the other for Cory. Up to 1884 a number of vessels of similar size were built, seven about 1,100t, six about 1,350t, four for himself about 1,600t and four about 950t. Regular new shipbuilding began in 1877,[32] and three of the five vessels during 1877-9 were for Irvine. A total of 15,610t were built during 1880-4, the highest annual total being 8,138t in 1883. There were no new ships in 1885-6 [yard #53-#59 were not used] and 10,000t in the last three years of the 1880s. Irvine was his own best customer, eight of the 47 ships built before 1890 were for himself, in all 22% of the tonnage. Robert Irvine retired in 1887 and his sons took over the management of the business.

Comments by Lloyd's Visiting Committee on Tees & Hartlepool.

When Lloyd's visited both Richardson-Duck and Lockwood-Pearse in August 1855, the former stated they wished to carry out Lloyd's *Rules*. At John Pile's yard at Hartlepool in 1855 Lloyd's commented that an iron steamer which was so *badly wrought* as to be *unfit for class intended*. A Foreman conducted the Lloyd's visitors round the Richardson Brother's iron yard and they commented: *The workmanship not of the best quality. Spacing of Frames very irregular varying from 15 inches amidship to 20 inch at the ends of the Ships*. This is perhaps an example of the problems of introducing the new technique of iron shipbuilding by metal workers who were not as familiar as the shipwrights with a balanced layout of the ship's structure. At Pearse's yard in 1856 Lloyd's noted that the edges of the plates were double rivetted up to the edge of the bilge, but in the case of another ship it was pointed out that *many rivet holes* [were] *punched much too close to the edge*. They were assured this would be avoided in future. Apparently unknowingly, a party from Lloyd's came to Stockton in Race Week 1868, and consequently they found no work in progress. Complaints of Lloyd's survey being *too strict* were made by Richardson and his manager in the autumn of 1870; they were at the time building two vessels [1,386t & 1,539t] for the rival Liverpool register. Lloyd's visitors noted that from the *limited opportunity for observation* the work appeared satisfactory. Lloyds insisted that the plates delivered *slightly below required thickness* must be rejected, this was either neglect or oversight and the departure from the Rules, even if a hardship must be rectified as it was the yard's error. Remarkably the men from Lloyds returned to the Tees again during Race Weeks and in 1876 found Raylton Dixon's yard closed; usually they toured the yards even if no workers were present. On this occasion although generally the work at Pearse's was very satisfactory on one vessel the rivetting was not as good *as might be desired*. The masts from Head Wrightson, were of *a very massive character*, however, the *yards* supplied by this famous engineering works were not considered *suitable*. At Withy's yard in 1876 Lloyd's visiting committee saw three long raised quarter decks vessels under

---

[32] Yard numbers 5, 7 and 11 were used for repairs. #19, #20 [1876] were not built and #25-#29 [1879] were not used.

construction and commented that *continuous strength is well maintained by the introduction of iron decks, the efficient shifting of the stringers and the doubling of the main strake at the break.* This was a development of the well-deck design.

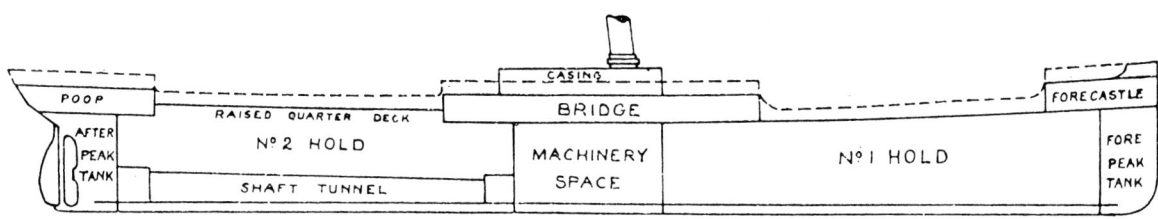

VESSEL WITH A POOP, A RAISED QUARTER DECK, A BRIDGE, AND A FORECASTLE. WELL DECK.

The Well-deck Steamer.

The welldeck steamer, a form of vessel originally very much a product of Hartlepool was widely built throughout the north east. Unjustified criticism over many years was bitterly resented by the builders of these ships. There were some early problems with the use of plating which was too thin on the bridge. Precisely which ship was the first welldeck type is disputed, Spaldin suggested the *Lizzie English* built by Denton-Gray in 1867. Naval architect Sivewright, speaking to NECIES in 1889, stated that all vessels before 1865 for shipowners on the north east coast were *flush deck* and as long as dead-weight cargo was carried there was no inconvenience with regard to trim. There were trim problems with homogeneous cargoes, which completely filled the hold, and to overcome these difficulties a *large portion of the forehold* was enclosed which resulted in a loss of earning capacity. After trying double-deck vessels, the raised quarter deck was adopted. Gray became an extensive builder of these vessels He told the *Royal Commission on Loss of Life at Sea*, that since 1874 he had built 115 such ships and none had foundered or gone missing but four of the 29 flush deck vessels were missing and one had capsized. These figures suggest that three-quarters of Gray's ships were well-deckers. Sivewright said all the vessels for Hartlepool owners built in the previous four years were of the *well-deck* type, *upwards of 350* built, exceeding half a million tons. Local shipowners were *satisfied* with *the results of the all round trading of these vessels* There was *a very critical time* in 1880, when the Board of Trade *detained these vessels for alleged overloading.*

Disputes arising from the practice of loading to a freeboard of about one-tenth the moulded depth resulted in the Parliamentary Load Line Committee [1883-5] and in evidence shipowners argued that the *well-deck* type was *one of the safest class of cargo boats in use.* This detailed argument cannot be pursued here but it may be noted that Sivewright contended that the *design of the raised quarter deck type of vessel has been so carefully studied and improved in the last ten years*[33] *that, from actual sea experience, this type had proved to be one of the strongest class of cargo boats that is now being built.* Many of the leading shipbuilders discussed Sivewright's paper, which Wigham Richardson described as *one of the most sensible papers ever read.* He had first heard of the design from John Pile, who saw the quarter deck as compensation for the space occupied by the tunnel. Richardson was critical of the *break* amidship especially in larger vessels. Henry Withy objected to the raised quarter deck being described as a *break.* At Laing's yard they had developed a design extending the raised quarter deck through to the stem, and called the type a semi-spar decked ship. Shipowner F Yeoman [Hartlepool] reported that almost at the end of its sixth year the Well-Deck Steamship Insurance Association had not paid for a single *missing* steamer,

---

[33] Henry Withy said that the first bridges were *very poor structures ... the side plating was very light.* Most of the objections were because the bridges of one or two of them *stove in ... a local weakness ... properly overcome by carrying the frames to the top of the bridge and by making the side plating and end bridge much stronger.*

with an annual average of about 350 vessels insured. Edward Withy contributed to the debate on well-deck ships at the INA.[34] In 1882 he pointed out that in London *particularly there is a great prejudice against these wells* and explained that of 101 ships built in last 13 years, 75 were well-deckers, some had long poops, some quarter decks but all had *wells*. Lloyd's surveyor Martell *perfectly* endorsed Withy's statements and continued: *There can be no comparison between the ships that were commonly called well-deck ships now as compared with what they were some years ago; the safety of them has been immensely increased*. In July 1891, Martell in a paper on ships types, loading and safety at sea, said unequivocally the *well-deck* type *has proved itself, by reliable statistics, to have exceptional immunity from loss, as compared with other types of vessel*. The advance of this design and the steady improvement in the construction techniques involved provided north east shipowners with a ship many wanted.

Marine Engineering.

This topic is mainly covered in chapter 15. In line with the general character of British engineering, on the Tees as elsewhere for many years almost all competent engineering works were prepared to build marine engines. The iron masters Bolchow & Vaughan built the engine for *The English Rose* in 1843. Gilkes & Wilson [Teesside Engine Works] also built marine engines. However, two works began to specialise in marine engines - Thomas Richardson and Hackworth & Fossick [later Blairs]. Richardson's works began at Castle Eden, in 1838, Hartlepool. From the famed Hackworth family Thomas Hackworth with George Fossick, in 1840, opened a works at Stockton to build locomotives and later turned to marine engines. This company after the deaths of the original partners became the justly well respected Blairs when their manager took over the works. Thirty companies supplied engines for 550 ships built between 1850 and 1889 at Hartlepool, 13 of these however supplied only a single set of machinery. Thomas Richardson built almost half of these engines, 271, followed by Blair with 149 [plus five by Fossick & Hackworth]. CMEW in its first five years supplied 58 sets and from Teesside a single engine each by Joy and Westgarth. Eight Tyneside works supplied 38 engines, headed by Black, Hawthorn with 15, R & W Hawthorn 7 and Thompson & Boyd 6. Ten engines came from George Clark at Sunderland and seven from NEM. Six Scottish firms provided 10 engines and Brassey and Jack provided a few engines from Liverpool. A ten year gap between the triple expansion engine in ss *Sexta* in 1874 and the next Teesside or Hartlepool vessel with a triple masked the efforts of Robert Wyllie [1850-1886], in particular, to secure the adoption of the new design. However from 1884 the situation changed: Richardsons, Blair and CMEW were all very active in constructing the new engine, over the years 1884-6, they built respectively, 24, 16, 4 engines to which Westgarth added one. Some owners preferred to continue with compound engines.

Some summary comments.

The very marked upward trend in the combined output of the Tees & Hartlepool is shown in diag 8.09 [below]. Much capital was invested in both shipbuilding and marine engineering on the Tees and at Hartlepool by 1889. There was a substantial skilled and experienced workforce of which many semi-skilled men and labourers were a vital part, described by a local historian as *steady, sober and reliable*.[35] Their frequent industrial disputes are examined in later chapters. Organised by skilled management the Tees and Hartlepool were major centres for British, nay world shipbuilding. Firms such as Grays were capable of equalling any in the world and many others were not far behind. A brief reminder of what had been achieved by British shipbuilders at that time, Jeremiah Head stated that two Hartlepool steamers ss *Oscar II* [4,600dwt] and ss *Aldworth* could carry a ton of cargo 1 knot on $^1/_2$ ounce of coal at a speed of 9 knots!

---

[34] Withy argued that in *considering the safety of ships, we...should have a fair margin to meet any contingency*, but that was not *part of the creed of every shipowner*. He suggested the doubters took a trip *under the ordinary conditions of lading which they not only sanction, but enforce*. The issue was *not ordinary commercial ones, but human lives*.

[35] Labour issues are explored in chapters 12 & 13. Both Teesside and Hartlepool had a major industrial dispute in the 1860s. Various press figures for pay suggest that the average per employee of about 25s-26s a week. That figure masks the high earnings of the piecework craftsmen and the much lower earnings of labourers and apprentices.

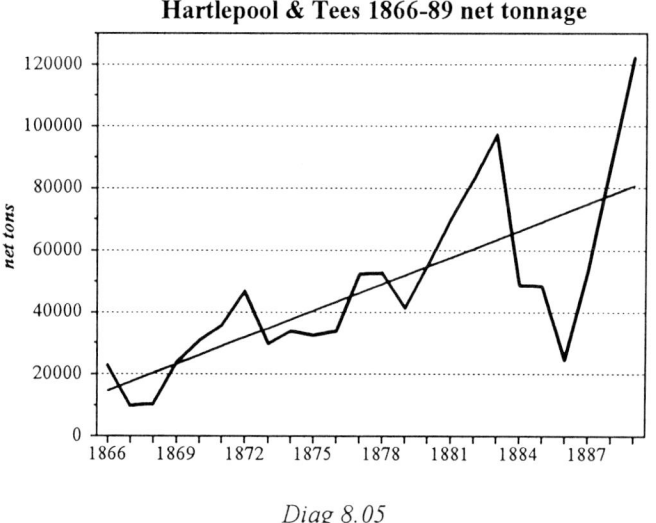

Diag 8.05

Plans of W Gray's shipyards at Hartlepool in 1880s.

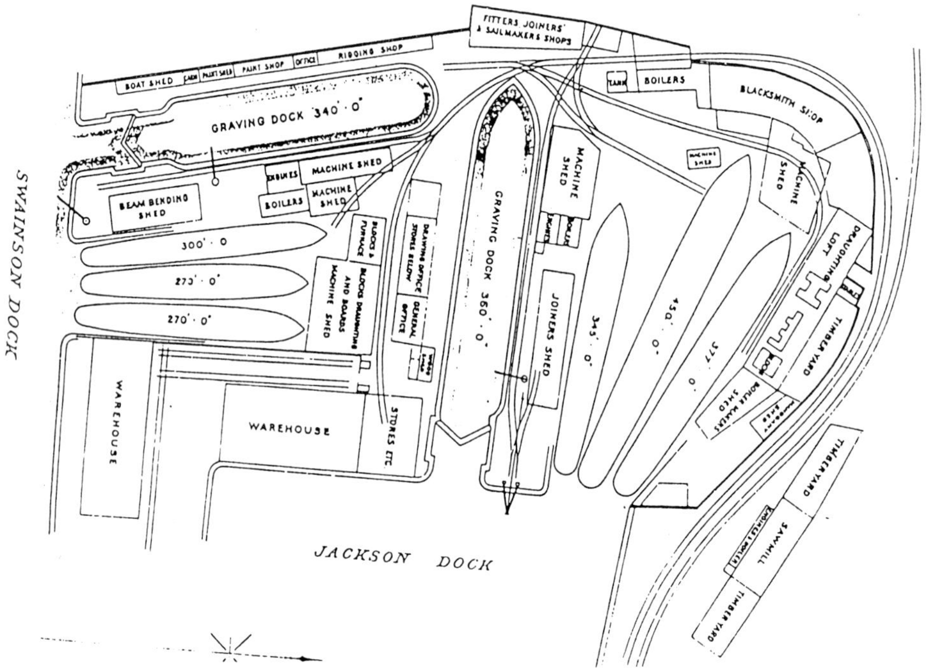

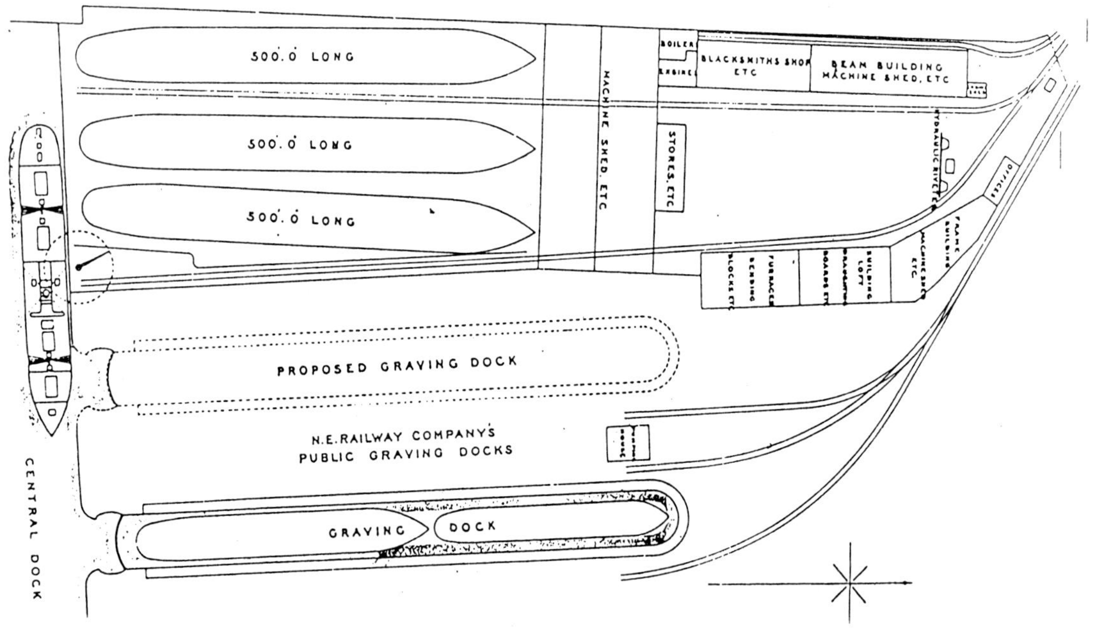

Chapter 9

Radical Changes in the 1880s - iron to steel hull - oil tankers.

In almost every way the 1880s was a period of dramatic change, with a national economic depression so severe that a Royal Commission was set up to examine the causes of it and for shipbuilders two booms and a depression such as they had never previously experienced. The most enduring features in shipbuilding were three very significant technical changes, the use of steel, a new form of steam reciprocating engine, and the oil tanker. From the low point of 1879 tonnage launched dramatically advanced to a peak in 1883, only to be followed by a prolonged depression spanning the years 1884-8. Steel hulls replaced those of iron in the 1880s and the triple expansion engine was adopted and established its position as *the* means of propelling commercial ships. A new specialised form of vessel, the oil tanker, emerged from north east shipyards and from 1889, frozen meat vessels also were regularly built. This was also the time when Charles Parsons provided one of the north east's greatest contributions to society and technical progress, the steam turbine, the fundamental prime mover for the generation of electricity and later a major source of marine propulsion [see chap 15]. By the end of the decade the labourers and non-craft workers had formed enduring trade unions and an effective Conciliation Board was established in the Wear shipyards. This chapter reviews the overall economic changes, the impact of the depression on labour, and the introduction of the steel hull and the oil tanker.

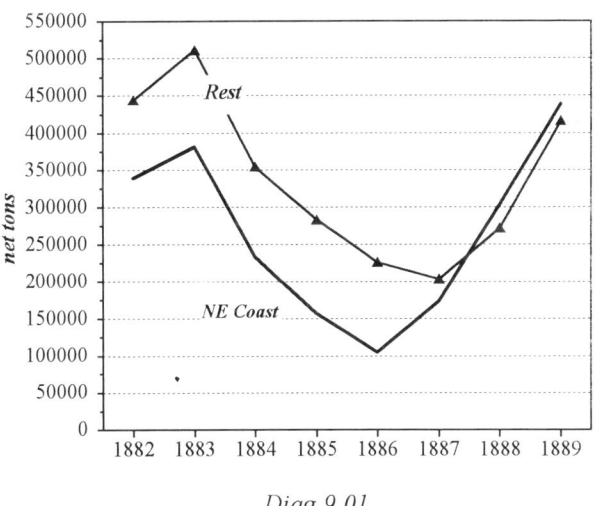

Diag 9.01

The tonnage launched in the 1880s on the north east coast and in the rest of the UK is shown in diag 9.01; the pattern of decline is similar except that the north east reached its nadir a year before the rest of the UK but although it started this cycle at a lower point it ended above the remainder of the industry. A similar pattern of change occurred in each of the north east areas. A comparison of the worst three consecutive years with the best three shows the Wear at 48.1%, the Tees & Hartlepool at 48.5% and the Tyne at 52.6%.[1] There was substantial variation between the individual shipyards as shown by comparisons of the average annual output of 1884-6 with the output in 1883. On the Wear Doxford and Laing maintained 71% and 68% of their 1883 output and Crown, Austin and J L Thompson 42% and 45%. The greatest falls were Blumer [5%] and Bartram [12%]. On the Tyne, Hawthorn-Leslie [70%] and Armstrongs [65%] had figures similar to the best on the Wear, and Wigham Richardson and Readhead were at about 55%. Palmers and Swan Hunter were at about 40%; Schlesinger Davis reached only 13% and T & W Smith a mere 7.5%. In the south of the region Richardson Duck averaged half of the 1883 output, Gray 45% and Withy 40%, while Raylton Dixon was a mere 24% and Irvine not quite 13%.

The rising curve of output to 1883 inspired the opening of a number of new yards. These included probably the last examples of shipyard managers successfully finding financial support to begin their own yards. On the Tyne, Skinner from Andrew Leslie's joined with Wood to begin a yard at Bill Quay and survived,

---

[1] The comparison over four years [1884-7 & 1880-3] was Wear 52%, Tees & Hartlepool 59.1% and the Tyne 55.9%. There was a variation within Teesside: Middlesbrough 46.4% [39%], Stockton 61.3% [62.4%] and Hartlepool 59.1% [44.1%]. Bracketed figure is for three year comparison.

whereas McIntyre's venture very soon merged with Stephensons. Mackintosh & Bowstead came and went with hardly a whiff of recollection surviving.[2] Having proclaimed Palmers as the largest shipbuilding firm in the world at the end of 1882 the *Newcastle Daily Chronicle* commented: *So far the cry ... heard constantly for three years past that steam tonnage is being over-built, and that collapse might be expected before long, does not seem to have had any substantial foundation.* A year later that collapse began in earnest and in few places was it deeper than at Jarrow. After two years of launching 60,000t output fell below 30,000t in 1884. Even lower output followed during the next three years [see diag 9.02: note Palmers on *right hand scale* is double scale for other yards]. In 1884 Palmers closed their yard at Howdon. The combined output of the three years 1885-7 only just exceeded that of 1889 alone! In 1884 Toward's yard and the small yard of G K Smith were closed. After launching 6,408 tons McIntyre's new yard at Hebburn stopped work in September 1884. At T & W Smith the workers employed were reduced from several hundreds to 50 or 60. In contrast to the closures, Armstrong-Mitchell's new Elswick shipyard, adjacent to the armament works, was opened and during 1884 was constructing two steel cruisers for the Austrian Government. Work on foreign warships enabled Armstrong-Mitchell alone to increase output from 1884, while the others either continued to decline or remained in a very depressed state. An average of 7,590t over the years 1884-6 by Swan Hunter compared with 20,000t in 1883 and 28,300t in 1889.

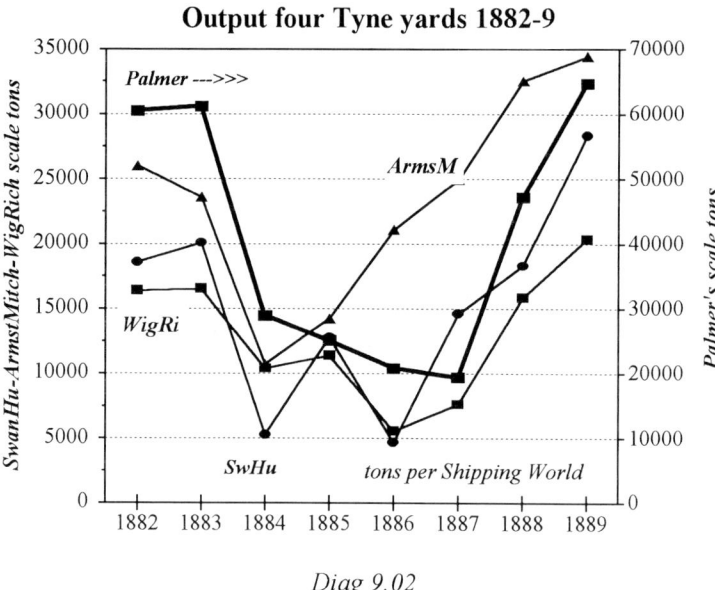

Diag 9.02

There were new yards and changes in the management in others on the Wear. The site used by Iliff, Mounsey and Foster[3] at the South Dock was taken over by the Sunderland SB Co in 1880 and in 1882 launched more than 17,000t. In the next year, however, output fell to 12,482t. At North Sands Baxter & Co launched their first two vessels in 1881: they only lasted four years, building a total of 8,737t. John Priestman [1855-1941][4], a baker's son who became chief draughtsman at Pickersgill, started a yard a Southwick in 1882 and was successful enough to launch 7,500t in 1883 and the yard continued for fifty years in his sole ownership. Shipowners Thomas and William Kish briefly joined with J H Boolds and built on part of Oswald's old Pallion yard; during 1882-4 they launched 14 ships [15,813t]. When the Kish Brothers left, Boolds joined an engineer, Edmund Sharer[5] and during 1885-7 they built new ships [10,010t]

---

[2] The Tyne General Ferry Co, owned by the shipowner Rogerson built between 1881 and 1889.

[3] In 1873 Illiff ended his partnership with Mounsey, who then was joined by Robert Foster, and when Mounsey retired in 1879 Foster briefly continued on his own . Foster launched two ships each 1438t in 1880 and the first by Sunderland SB ss *Blodwen* was launched in Nov 1880.

[4] Priestman was born at Bishop Auckland and entered Blumer's yard as a boy and must have shown the talent which enabled him to get drawing office experience. He produced various designs of tramp steamers and through skilled investment, including South African gold mines, amassed a substantial fortune; he left £1,504,774 and his substantial donations to charities included £20,000 in 1939 for the Sunderland Technical College library. He was a Conservative who served for more than 20 years on various local councils. An active Anglican and keen organist. He married twice and had only one child Barbara Marie. He was knighted in 1923 and made a baronet in 1934.

[5] Edmund Sharer was the son and grandson of shipyard managers at Laings. He moved to Beardmore's on the Clyde, where he went on to become general manager of the shipyard. He retired in 1912.

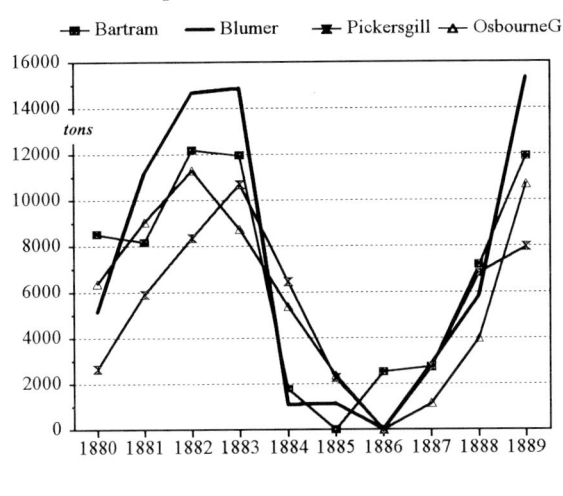

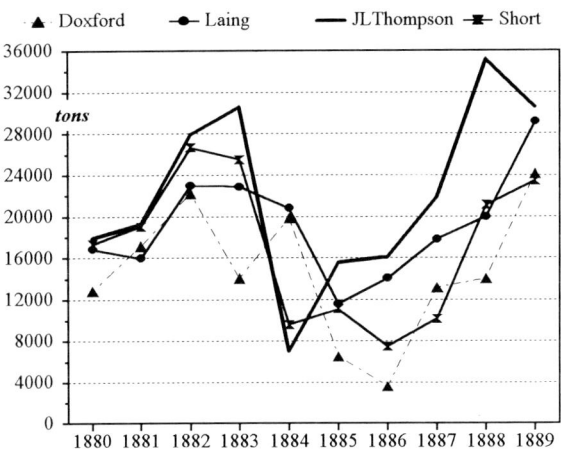

Diag 9.03 *Diag 9.04*

and the yard closed. The North of England SB began in 1882, with *Mozart* [2,390t] and completed 12 ships at an average of almost 2,000t before closing in 1886. Two diagrams show just how deep this slump was for four well established yards [diag 9.03] and how the four largest yards performed [diag 9.04]. A notable feature here is the rise by J L Thompson from 1884 and this signalled the fact that the North Sands yard was about to head the Wear's output throughout the 1890s [with a single exception]. In all three north east centres there was a marked change in the size of ships built between 1881-3 and 1888-9. On the Tees the average size increased from 1,736t to 2,145t, a rise of 24%. On the Wear the change was from 1,672t to 2,022t an increase of 20% and on the Tyne the gain was 17% from 1,586t to 1,872t.

The first Great Depression - the mid-1880s and the working people.

The depression of 1884-7 was a devastating new experience for many thousands of working men and their families, especially on Wearside. Ultimately, conditions at Sunderland were so bad that food was taken from pig-troughs. The Medical Officer of Health reported: *Their homes are bare of furniture, their clothes are scanty, the season promises cold, and fires are luxuries they cannot afford.* The *Shipping World* wrote: *The present suffering is among a class of highly respectable artisans, self-reliant, proud workmen, who will endure long, rather than disclose their poverty and want*; the trade was never before *in such wretched state*. Payment of donation to their unemployed by the South Shields *ASE* vividly showed the onset of this collapse in work available; from an average of about £20 a fortnight during 1882-3 it rocketed to £500 in December 1884. As early as October 1883, *The Shipping World* reported that 1,000 men might be laid off at Raylton Dixon's shipyard; then employing 2,300. The trade union evidence to the Royal Commission on Depression in Trade and Industry was unanimous that the like had not been experienced ever before:

> Hartlepool Boilermakers: *none witness anything like the present depression ... So much so that we are on the verge of starvation* - more than half their members were unemployed.
> Hartlepool *ASE*: *1884 and the first three months of 1885 the depression was severely felt, more severely than was ever known in this district.*
> South Shields Ironfounders: *More depressed than any former period: 60% of the skilled men were unemployed, 47% of the unskilled but only 10% of the apprentices.*[6]

At Stockton, *fully half* of the Boilermakers were unemployed and the carpenters estimated that on the Wear more than 40% of their members were out of work. Generally, engineering workers were not quite so severely hit as the shipyard workers. The labour force at the Wallsend Slipway Co dropped from 1,245 to

---

[6] Little wonder, perhaps that the Newcastle secretary added the comment: *I think I may safely say no boys (are) out of employment, as they are a source of great profit to the masters.*

812 in a year and, for two more years, remained below 850, while average earnings fell from £89 per man to about £70. If this marine engine works was typical then about 30% of engineering workers were idle for three years, and this firm may well have been better than average because of the work they did for Armstrong.

In the boom the iron hands in the shipyards *averaged from 17s to £1 per day of 9 hours, and expert hands at piecework enjoyed even much higher earnings,* according to the *Shipping World.*[7] This journal reported that the notices of wage reductions of 10% to 20% were posted in the shipyards from the Tees to Blyth in January 1884 *excited no surprise among the workmen* and there was *every probability of an amicable settlement.* Wisely the employers gave three months notice[8], which allowed time for negotiations. These proposals would have reduced the rates to those of 1879 and the Boilermakers were both unhappy and *astonished at such an unreasonable demand.* A very concerned Knight, leader of the Boilermakers' Union, hoped *our members will take matters calmly and quietly, and be willing to be guided by those in authority.* He found it difficult to believe that the Tyne & Wear employers had *any intentions of enforcing the reductions proposed,* if they did, then *a rupture* must follow. He was *very sorry* about this prospect *after working amicably with them for so many years.* Knight personally led a deputation to the Wear employers on 4 February and despite *a very agreeable and courteous reception* his offer of a 5% reduction was rejected. Ultimately, the agreement reached avoided a stoppage on Tyne and Wear. From March, the platers' rates were reduced by 10% and the riveters and holders-up by $7\frac{1}{2}$%. By April 1884 the streets of Sunderland were *full of idle men* and *scarcely a quarter of* the Wear Boilermakers were *in employment.* The *Shipping World* stated 7,000 workmen were *lying idle;* in some yards only the apprentices were working. Little wonder that when the helpers resisted the reductions by strike action they failed, as did a strike by the Teesside Boilermakers against the proposed 10% reduction.

During the summer of 1884, new reductions threatened as the slump failed to ease off, and in June, the *Shipping World* wrote that shipbuilding was *about as bad as it can be.* There were new reductions of 5% and $7\frac{1}{4}$% for boilermakers and a 1s cut for the shipwrights. The Boilermakers Society circulated a hundred French shipyards in an attempt to find work for members and James O'Neill with another official visited such ports as showed any interest, but this brought little return. The autumn and winter were bleak. On Tyneside, many yards were only able *to keep apprentices and a few workmen going;* often it was repair work alone which kept yards from closing. Trade unionists continued steadily organising work and the Boilermakers found some slight consolation in securing *for our members* the shipyard of Harkess, which was previously worked by *carpenters.* Further reductions were expected, and in January 1885 the relentless wage cuts came on all three rivers but, as before, it was only on the Tees that they were resisted by strike action. The men were out for 17 days before accepting a 7% cut in piecework rates. Some hopes were raised in the early months of 1885, when the *Shipping World* estimated an increase from 3,000 to 4,000 in those working in the shipyards.

The Wear Board of Conciliation.

Wearside was still rising from the position of being *the cockpit of the North of England,* in the words of James Laing, *continually fighting and struggling.* In Sunderland there was *sure to be a dispute of some kind on every vessel* before work began, according to a Boilermakers' Report and *half a dozen before she is finished.* Yet it was on the Wear that the first successful conciliation board was formed. This Board unlike its predecessor of the 1850s, which was based on the principal shipyard trade of the shipwrights,

---

[7] Herbert Rowell cites two examples in his *Memoir*: frame bender James Gainer *when he found he couldn't average £8 week ... he would leave* and Mick Mulherion he *certainly earned more than 1 a day.* These were exceptional. Very few men earned such amounts.

[8] The notice for the Tees was due to expire on 18 February and for the Tyne & Wear on 4 March. Already on the Tees there were attempts to reduce rates, according to the Boilermakers, and these reductions did not become evident until pay day; as a result small disputes were *more numerous than ever.*

did not include *the black squad*, the key workers in the 1880s. Many disputes involved shipbuilding trades other than the Boilermakers and their helpers. When the Wear and Tyne shipbuilders discussed a Board of Arbitration in June 1884, Laing saw great difficulties in the suggestion. In the midst of the many disputes, in March 1885, John Price advocated a Conciliation Board, but some weeks later Laing still *thought it difficult to hit upon a satisfactory basis.*[9] Haswell later related that after several strikes, lasting two or three days, involving blacksmiths, joiners and carpenters in the shipyards, it was considered *the time had come when a conciliation board should be formed* to which all such disputes could be referred. On the invitation of the Wear Shipbuilders' Association, sixteen trade unionists met six shipbuilders to discuss the formation of a conciliation board on 24 June 1885. Most of those six shipbuilders, James Laing, S.P.Austin, R.Thompson, Bartram, Doxford and Graham, had recollections and or some direct experience of the earlier 1850s Board. The principle was readily agreed and a trade unionist seconded Doxford's motion to establish a committee to draw up a code of rules. Within weeks the drafting committee began work, under the chairmanship of Doxford, and the rules were finally signed in November[10]. As a result of this Board activity, Laing told the *Royal Commission for Labour* in 1892, since then *we have had no strike on the Wear*. Wide agreement on the need to avoid stoppages was an essential feature for the success of such a Board as well the considerable understanding of the concept of conciliation. In addition, the vital point for the employers, was that *pending the settlement of any questions ... there shall be no stoppage of work, and the wages ... or other working conditions shall, until settlement, be those current at the time of the notice.*

Both Laing and Doxford emphasised the conciliation aspect to the Royal Commission on Labour [1894]. Laing said: *you will notice the title of the thing is Conciliation. It is with a view to bring the parties together - not so much for the purpose of arbitration, because we have no power really to enforce any award, the main purpose of it is conciliation.* Doxford explained that the Chairman had no casting vote adding [there is] *not any means of enforcing decisions, but personally I think that position is better than it would be if we had ... power to compel compliance ... I think myself that the working men are being gradually educated up to the point of seeing the advisability of abiding by any decision.* Robert Thompson, as President, told the NECIES:

> Such stoppages [demarcation disputes on the Tyne] point to the necessity of forming boards of conciliation, such as exists on the Wear, and which has worked very successfully, so that every effort may be made to come to an amicable agreement without the necessity of reverting to a strike. The men could remain at work during the discussion of the question raised, and so avert that which causes so much misery and commercial loss ... It is essential that capital and labour should recognise that their interests are identical.

Both sides agreed that by reasoned discussion acceptable solutions to problems could be reached. It should not be assumed that the continuation of work only benefited the employers. This permanent organisation and its procedure offered the men the belief that they would get a fair deal and so would not suffer as a result of continuing to work when a difficulty arose, as well as the loss of income during a strike. Rule 7 stated

> Questions between the parties shall in the first instance be referred to the Departmental Boards and failing a settlement by such Departmental Boards shall then be referred to the General Board, or if the parties concerned agree to the Board of Referees. [in practice failure to agree went straight to the Referees][11]

Departmental Boards for each trade provided an organisational form in which the men developed some faith and trust. The Conciliation Board included the shipwrights, joiners, blacksmiths, drillers and painters but not the Boilermakers; who contended that they were perfectly satisfied with their existing arrangements with

---

[9] At the Wear Shipbuilders Association when Foreman, of the Trades Council, wrote about Conciliation Boards.

[10] As with the earlier Board some printed accounts are misleading. Lord Amurlee quite wrongly wrote that *decisions of the new board were followed through the north east coast.*

[11] Six representatives of the employers and the same number from *each branch of the workmen*. Two referees were nominated [one by each side] from a list of 14 named *disinterested gentlemen* and the two referees elected a chairman from - Lord Ravensworth. Mr Cowen, Mr Burt M.P. and the Registrar of the Sunderland Court.

the employers. Laing said that relations with the Boilermakers were satisfactory; although they were not members of the Board, they were consulted beforehand. Like Benjamin Browne, Doxford, based on his experience, said: *my personal views are very strongly in favour of strong unions, both on the part of the men and the employers. I believe the stronger the unions are, the less likely there will be strikes.* He preferred to deal with the Boilermakers than the smaller societies - *they take broader views of the subject under discussion.*

During the period March to May 1886, the Wear Conciliation Board arranged reductions in wages for the shipwrights [1s 6d], the joiners [1s 6d], only the time wages of the blacksmiths were reduced by 2s and piecework rates were cut for the drillers by $2\frac{1}{2}\%$. Advances were arranged as trade improved - in August 1888, in February and July 1889 and in 1890. All of these wage changes were settled by the Departmental Boards except the shipwrights' reduction. At the time, the proposed Tyne reduction for shipwrights was only 1s, compared with the 1s 6d on the Wear, but the Wearsiders worked an hour per week less than the Tynesiders. Mr Ellis, Registrar of the Sunderland Court, was Chairman of the referees and their decision on the reduction was accepted without stoppage. An issue not resolved at the Departmental Board was concerned with *docking of vessels* and again difficulty was related to reaching parity with the Tyne in regard to the number of men employed. When men were not willing to accept the decision given in February 1889, the employers not wishing to risk any breakdown, given the overall value of the Board, for three years did not attempt to enforce the award. Whereas the Tyneside shipbuilders offered many objections to the shipwrights' restrictions on overtime working this was regulated to the satisfaction of the Wear employers by the Board, in 1888. This was a further indication of the success of this Wear Conciliation Board.

Trade Union responses to the Depression.

New expedients were forced on the Boilermakers' Society by this prolonged depression. A ballot vote, reported in October 1885, decided, by 3,336 votes to 2,801, that *pieceworkers shall in future be restricted to earning not more than time and a half* and, by a majority of 1,500, that *no piecework shall be allowed on repair work*. The loss of earnings implied in these decisions showed how gravely members viewed the situation. The *Shipping World* wrote *platers, framebenders and angle iron smiths have been in the habit of making three or four times their day wages, and rivetters and caulkers at least double.* Whereas before a team of platers *in a properly appointed yard* put up 18 plates a day, this would now be reduced to 9. The journal continued: *The shipbuilders who are lucky enough to have work ... cannot tolerate interference of this kind with their methods and arrangements, especially at a time when the circumstances of trade place them in a position to resist dictation and, if necessary, to carry out their work independently of the unionists.* It seems, however, that these decisions caused little real difficulty. The *Shipping World* failed to report any actual problems. Nor was Knight asked about this issue at the *1886 Royal Commission*, which included Palmer and a shipbuilder named Pearce, neither in any way sympathetic to trade unions. Some employers had reverted to timework. Austin told his fellow employers in October 1885, that *since timework had been tried a great change for the better in general discipline and attendance* and savings of £340 in one case 8s/ton of iron worked. Blumer, in December 1886, was in favour of the general establishment of timework; others agreed that it *might well work in dull times* but it was *a hindrance ... in brisk times.*

Agreement on the fourth wage reduction in two years occupied the employers over two meetings. Notices of reductions were posted in December 1885, due to expire on 6 January 1886 on the Tyne and Wear, and ten days later on the Tees. All efforts to find a settlement failed and on 7 January, the Boilermakers resolved on strike action. O'Neill's proposal, to resume on the old terms while lists of high earning jobs were submitted and examined, was endorsed by the Wear Boilermakers on 19 January, and later agreed on the Tyne. With little hesitation, the employers rejected the proposal and continued to demand a $12\frac{1}{2}\%$ cut in piecework prices and 10% in time rates. Some Wear shipbuilders wanted to finish their work, if need be at the old rates; however, outward division was avoided and the employers on the Tyne and Wear continued to act together. Interestingly, the *Shipping World* hoped *that the Sunderland masters will see their way clear to transact their business as formerly, and treat with the men of the Wear direct, so that all complications arising out of the combination with the Tyne may be avoided.* Rumours that some employers would break ranks were unfounded. During discussions with the Boilermakers on 5 February, the employers eased their position: they were *prepared to take into favourable consideration any modifications the men may propose to the reduction already notified, the amount ... not being a hard and fast line.* The Tynesiders were almost totally opposed to any reduction [only 60 voted to accept a reduction] and the men refused to give their representatives powers to accept one. In contrast on the Wear, there appeared to be some willingness to settle, which probably accounted for the attitude of the *Shipping World*.

Strike benefit was paid on 6 February, 8s weekly per man. Four days later the employers offered to accept a 10% cut on piece rates and 2s on time rates. The negotiators rejected this proposal; indeed, they had no powers to accept it. Considerable efforts were made amongst the Boilermakers' membership to secure a delegation with full powers and an offer of a reduction. Finally, on 18 February, delegates from all the Tyne and Wear Lodges meeting at Sunderland, decided to empower their representatives to offer:

> [1] that the alleged high paid jobs in each yard be pointed out by the employers or their managers to their workmen and the district delegates, and to be reduced by 5% in all branches of the trade.
> [2] that all middle or average paid jobs be reduced $2^1/_2$% on piecework.
> [3] that the workmen in each yard have the option of pointing out any lowly paid jobs which shall not be reduced in any of the different branches of the trade.
> Time wages to remain as at present viz. Angle Iron Smiths and Platers 33s, Riveters & Caulkers 31s, Holders-up 25s weekly. Repair work to remain in each yard in its present condition at the price on both rivers. Government work to be arranged for the future as has been the custom in the past. This to apply to all advances or reductions in future.

Later that day, after four hours of discussion, the employers rejected these proposals as impracticable and then offered a 10% reduction for the platers and angle iron smiths, and $7^1/_2$% for the riveters and caulkers, and 2s off time rates. Greatly surprised at the rejection of their offer, the trade union negotiators rejected the revised reductions. Six days later, a meeting of delegates from 27 Lodges worked on a proposal that attempted to discriminate between the various jobs done by each trade. The platers would accept a $7^1/_2$% reduction on frames, beams, shells, keels and stringing but only 5% on decks, tank tops and tank sides, bulk heads and keelsons, whilst other work was to remain at existing prices unless proved highly paid. The Angle Iron Smiths offered a $7^1/_2$% reduction on all iron work except bulkhead collars but they wanted no reduction on steel work, an expression of some difficulties in working the new material. There were similar detailed proposals for the other trades, however as before, time rates to remain unchanged. Negotiations began at 2.40 p.m. and after three separate consultations by both sides, this dispute was settled at 7 p.m on 24 February. The employers secured a simple settlement and agreed to the reductions finally proposed by the delegates - $7^1/_2$% from the Angle Iron Smiths and Platers and 5% from the riveters and caulkers; and a reductions of 1s per week on time wages; this reduction to be made off the present lists and rates, as usual in each yard, and to apply also to repair work. So ended a seven-week strike of between six and seven thousand men, who returned to their yards the next day. This, the largest strike in the north east of the *black squad*, reflected the deep despair of these men in the face of cut after cut in wages with increasing unemployment and no sign of relief. When two local yards had just gained two Government contracts, these craftsmen could not see why more cuts were needed then. This dispute reinforced Robert Knight's[12] opposition to strikes. Fluctuating employment conditions, even after a brief improvement in 1887, lead the *Shipping World* to comment that the men in the shipyards of the north east were *somewhat demoralised*.

---

[12] Cummings wrote: Large sums spent on disputes, mostly justified by the action of employers. *Robert Knight, who, looking back upon his 15 years of continual strife, determined, despite the fact that the employers had insisted upon large and unreasonable reductions, to preach forbearance, educate the members in a belief in conciliation and prove to the employers that conciliation and reason was best for all concerned...To a large extent, success was attained.*

The very sharp reductions which the black squad suffered in the depression are shown in diag 10.05 [below]; plater's piecework prices fell to less than 70% of the 1883 level; it fell almost as much for the caulkers. Neither trade recovered to earlier price levels; the scale of changes for time rates was less, but still more than 10%. Unemployment cost the Boilermakers' Society dearly during the four years 1884-7; almost £160,000 was paid out in home donation, more than £57,000 in 1884 alone. In comparison dispute costs were less than £12,000 [7.5% of home donations]. Funds fell from £108,545 in January 1884 to less than £22,000 three years later. Sunderland members were paid £7,700 in home donation in 1884. During these years, there was a regular flow of funds from the non shipbuilding areas to the badly affected ports.[13]

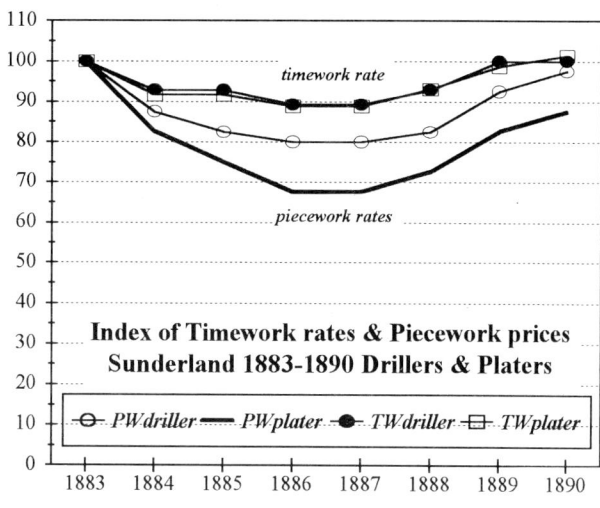

Diag 9.05

Austins, in 1888, returned to piecework *so that a large number of men can be kept in employment*; the famine of orders ended and the road to another feast of work had begun. On Teesside the *black squad* speedily wanted to recover lost earnings. The Boilermakers sought an increase of 12½% in June 1888 and men stopped work at nine firms on Teesside.[14] A wage advance was settled by normal negotiations on the Tyne and Wear with a general advance of 5% in August. A strike on Teesside was against the Union's advice and without the sanction of the Executive Council. About 2000 men were on strike for two weeks, which made about an equal number of other workers idle. At one Middlesbrough shipyard 400 men struck and 500 others were made idle. At Stockton, comparable figures were 541 and 380, while, at a Hartlepool yard, 350 unskilled were reported as striking with the 500 skilled men and a further 400 were idle as well. When employers' offered increases of 5% on piecework and 1s on time rates, the men returned to work. Understanding and trust continued to be lacking on the Tees; the employers stated: *we find the workmen don't believe the statements of the employers and are generally afraid to trust their own delegates who meet the employers*. Four years later, William Gray reiterated this point in written evidence to the *Royal Commission on Labour*, giving as the cause of disputes - *the refusal of the men to abide by the decision of the executive* [of the union].[15] Teesside remained the area most ready to strike.

Early in 1889, Boilermakers negotiated a further wage increase of 5% for the Tyne and Wear without a general stoppage. However, at South Shields, 25 smiths defied their union and were out for a week to gain a 3s increase. On the Tees, again, matters did not go smoothly. Two thousand boilermakers, *kicking over the traces*, in the words of their delegate Rothwell, refused to accept the employers' offer [the same as Tyne & Wear] and struck, on 15 January. In just over three weeks the strike did gain them a greater advance,

---

[13] An analysis over a 12 year period, showed the net weekly balance for 20 boilershop branches to be 4d but a similar number of shipyard branches averaged only a 1d per week. The balance was negative in the branches at Howdon -1½d and Wallsend -½d, other north east examples were Jarrow +½d, Sunderland #1 +2d and Sunderland #2 +1¼d.

[14] The Board of Trade reported it as a general strike of platers &c on the Tyne, Wear and Tees, their own detailed reports only linked one Tyneside firm, at Low Walker - strike #114.

[15] Furness Withy and the Teesside & Hartlepool Shipbuilders' Association both gave as the means of avoiding disputes: *The endeavouring to obtain a just conception of the various cases. . .the arrangement of same by conference and conciliation. Very important that workmen should loyally accept decisions mutually arrived at in this way.*

$7\frac{1}{2}$%, but with other consequences. The Teesside employers joined with the employers of Tyne and Wear for all negotiations with the Boilermakers and thus the Teesside men lost their local power to settle wages. At Middlesbrough, the men would have been back earlier but the helpers refused to return until they had received a similar advance and despite a five day strike at Stockton, the helpers were obliged to accept 6%. A further wage increase was negotiated, in July, on the Tyne and Wear, and another 5%, on the Tees. The men asked for 10% but parity was now restored when they were obliged to accept $2\frac{1}{2}$%. A strike was avoided, although the settlement was made four months later than on the other two rivers. The helpers objected to $2\frac{1}{2}$% increase and some 820 men stopped work in Stockton and Hartlepool, for two weeks. The employers intervened and the helpers gained 4% on piecework and 1s on time work, a weekly rate of 27s 9d, which was 9d above rate before the reductions of 1884. [see chap 13 for helpers' trade unions].

Mild Steel & Shipbuilding - the Failure of Bessemer Steel.[16]

Wrought iron was replaced for engineering constructional purposes by *mild steel* in the third quarter of the 19th century. 1856[17], the year of Henry Bessemer's great invention, is far too widely is seen as the occasion of the arrival of *mild steel*, while the critical role of the open-hearth process in the extension of the successful use of *mild* steel plate goes largely unacknowledged. *Steel* made by the Bessemer process was very successful for railway track but as late as 1881 in the UK 2,681,000 tons of wrought iron were made compared with 1,778,000 tons of steel. Bessemer himself acknowledged in 1879 that *the first announcement of his invention...was succeeded by disastrous results*. There was more than a little confusion as to what should be called *steel* in the 19th century. Ferrous materials in commercial use contained other elements; steel was the term usually understood to mean a material with sufficient carbon to enable it to be hardened by heat treatment so that it could be used for example as a cutting tool. Cast iron with a significantly higher proportion of carbon, while strong in compression and weak in tension could be brittle. As new materials were developed in the nineteenth century a debate arose on the use of various terms. The engineer William Pole in 1872, commented:

> if the Bessemer process could be successfully adapted to the production of the best kind of wrought iron, and were so used honestly and avowedly, it would be a much greater benefit to engineering manufacture than flooding the market with a mass of the more pretentious material, too often of a very doubtful character.

Steel is popularly described as holding a mid-position between cast and wrought iron with respect of the amount of carbon it contains, wrote boiler inspector, Robert Wilson, in 1879. For him steel fell in the range 0.33% to 2% of carbon. When the amount of carbon in Bessemer steel reached about 1.25%, this steel had its *greatest strength* about 70 tons/sqin, which was clearly not a *mild steel*. Plates for a Liverpool ship in 1864, had 0.5% carbon and a tensile strength of 44 t/sq.in. In 1871 steel maker Howell considered 0.2% C the maximum for steel for shipbuilding. The Scots marine engine designer, A. C. Kirk , agreed about this confused position stating *that which sells commercially under the name of steel is not steel at all - it is simply a high class of iron*. Problems of definition continued into the 20th century.[18]

It was implied by Pollard & Robertson that steel was well-established in shipbuilding before 1880; that

---

[16] This topic was examined in *The Introduction of the Use of Mild Steel Into the Shipbuilding and Marine Engine Industries* - J.F. Clarke & F.Storr [Newcastle Polytechnic 1983]. Detailed information will be found there and in Frank Storr's PhD thesis *The Development of the Marine Compound Steam Engine* [1982].

[17] Bessemer's famous 1856 paper clearly implied an established industrial process. His American advocate, James Dredge was more modest, adding that the invention *was of course in an experimental stage*. Beesemer [1813-1898] made many inventions and a visit to Napoleon III helped stimulate his work on producing a strong iron.

[18] An American metallurgist A Sauver [1863-1935] wrote: Our difficulty lies in the lower limit, namely some 0.20 to 0.25% carbon ... the custom [was] to give the name steel to the product of the refining of iron or from remelting scrap, quite regardless of the carbon it may contain, provided it has been obtained in a liquid form and is malleable.

was not so as diag 9.06 shows.[19] Before shipbuilders could adopt any new material on offer they needed to be assured of its qualities and its suitability for working economically with the available shipyard machinery. A commercially acceptable price was also required and the views of both the Admiralty and the registration societies such as Lloyds would also strongly influence the use of any new materials. By no means the least significant factor was the attitude of shipowners. *Mild* steel, a low-carbon steel with a tensile stress of 26-32t/sqin, was adopted for boiler construction some years earlier than its general use for ship construction. Far from neglecting the new material, the Admiralty carried out tests on steel in 1857. The results were *not satisfactory* but Jeans argued that cost was the principal deterrent to use. They tested Howell's *homogeneous metal* and the engineers wrote of the *superior strength of this iron* and according to Jeans it was long considered the softest and most tenacious kind of cast steel produced, being

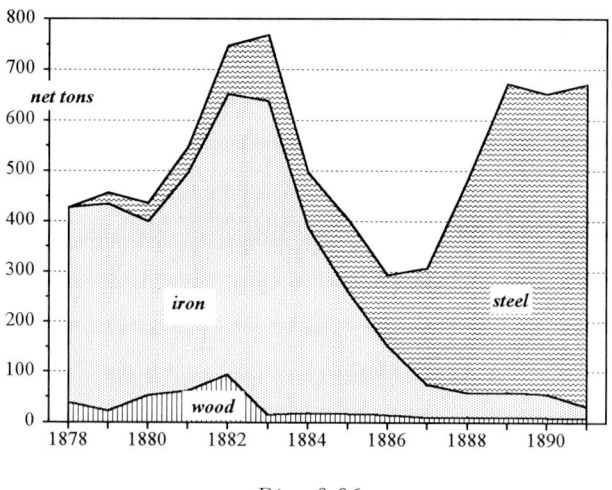

Diag 9.06

the poorest in carbon. Pioneers of land steel boilers, such as Daniel Adamson, purchased plates with a extra one inch all round to be sheared off and tested before the plate was used and rivet holes were drilled. Those were costs no merchant shipbuilder could seriously contemplate, any more than that of reaming out holes after punched plates were annealed, which Bessemer said gave satisfactory results. He preferred to use *the weakest material we make* for boiler plate, by which he meant a tensile strength of *only 32 or 33* and claimed that then they *never get a fracture*. Almost twenty-five years later, Gross of Sheffield, stated that specifications required limits of 26 to 30 tons because *no man living could make a large plate without the latitude of 2 tons per sq in of tensile strain*. He made clear that while chemically there was no difference: the critical factor was in the rolling - *a very great question in the manufacture of steel*. It would seem that Bessemer did not grasp this fundamental point, as he wrote: *it is physically impossible for the Bessemer process to produce a single isolated plate of such bad quality, for the simple reason that Bessemer steel is never made in less than 5-ton batches, every part of each blow being equally good or bad.* He did not acknowledge that there were many problems in working his material in large size plate work.[20] The presence of impurities caused undesirable characteristics, and this was soon recognised for the elements sulphur and phosphorus, and from 1872 until after 1900 there were disputes about the effects of nitrogen. A Swedish metallurgist, Tholander, pointed out in 1889 that there was a very much higher percentage of nitrogen in Bessemer steel than in samples from the open-hearth process and he was convinced this contributed to defects in Bessemer steel. Harbord & Twynam in 1896 disputed that the proportion found in commercial steel had any *detrimental effect*. By 1914 Stromeyer was not in any doubt: Nitrogen *... shares with phosphorus the inevitable distinction of making steel unreliable*. Bessemer steel

---

[19] They wrote reads *With the exception of the turbine engine, most of the important innovations covered in this chapter were well-established by 1880 ... steel allowed increasing size and speed...* [p.23], however, they were aware that not until 1890 were *virtually all* Clyde ships of steel.

[20] Many engineers recognised the dangers of working in the *blue heat* range; this term was used to cover the range from light straw to blue. Faupel wrote, in 1964, *generally... low carbon steel goes through apparent strengthening around 200 to 300^0C* [blue brittle range] *which should ordinarily be avoided in design.*

was not suitable for ship construction *under normal yard and commercial conditions*[21]; at least one naval architect wanted to blame the shipbuilders [see below]. There was, also, a problem of corrosion, which affected all mild steels.

Apparently contradictory experimental evidence was produced on the hotly debated issue of the relative corrosion resistance of the two metals.[22] The proponents of steel argued for the superiority of their material over wrought iron. When tests by the Admiralty and an independent researcher indicated the superior resistance of wrought iron over mild steel, these results were challenged, particularly in regard to use in boilers. Siemens had found that in the open air wrought iron did corrode less than mild steel but he had not found that so in boilers, nor had Lloyd's surveyor Parker. Interestingly, with all his experience and advocacy Adamson was prepared to say in 1878:
> Should it ultimately be proved that sea water will destroy steel quicker than wrought iron, we might continue the application of wrought iron for the skin of the ship but ... nothing should ... prevent the whole framework of every ... vessel being constructed of Bessemer or Siemens-Martin steel.

This almost sounded like an echo of the composite ship. Admitting some uncertainty Jeans argued *the probability* was that corrosion with mild steel *would set in less readily than with ordinary qualities of shipbuilding iron*. Experience did not confirm such optimism. *The Shipping World* wrote in 1895:
> Shipowners are beginning to have some misgivings about the durability of steel steamers ... experience is proving that steel is a much more perishable material than iron, especially where it cannot be frequently painted; and some owners find that steel vessels five years old are not in such good condition as iron ships three times that age.

A few years later the Hartlepool shipowner, Otto Trenchmann, wanted to know *how he got at the inside tanks to paint them, to prevent corrosion, for that, in steel ships, was one of the great factors they had to deal with after the vessel was seven or eight years old?* Steel hulls raised the issue of a suitable protective coating even more sharply than the wrought iron hull.

Steel for Ships.
A distinguished economic historian Clapham wrote: *No doubt, as Bessemer always and inevitably believed, sheer conservatism in the shipyards explained much*[23] and few historians appear to have differed from that view. This is not a valid line of argument. Any argument that there was an unjustifiable delay must hinge on whether or not Bessemer's material was suitability for shipbuilding. Early in the 20th century Lloyd's Rules prescribed that *Steel for Shipbuilding shall be made by the Open Hearth Process, acid or basic,* which was a ban on Bessemer steel after almost fifty years of development [previously the rule required the material *to withstand* prescribed tests]. Palmer, unquestionably a pioneer of iron shipbuilding, pointed out in 1870 that in addition to a much higher price builders stayed with ordinary iron rather than steel because *the uncertainty of manufacture has...been so great, that few have ventured to run the risk of the reduction of scantling necessary with a more costly* material. Puddled steel rather than mild steel was frequently used for the first vessels with steel hulls. There are references to steel punts on the Rhine in the early 1850s and the first British endeavours were in 1858. Lairds of Birkenhead built the

---

[21] Berrier-Fountaine of the French naval yard stated that *steel* required *to be treated with more care and precaution than iron. It will not bear, without suffering more or less, violent blows from iron hammers, or irregular tears produced by using hand chisels*; wooden beetles and mallets were substituted and they introduced hydraulic equipment. Gas heated furnaces replaced the common furnaces and many other changes were made. Jeans supported Barnaby's view that a material which needed *such care in its treatment* stood *a very poor chance in an ordinary shipyard.*

[22] Thomas Turner, Professor of Metallurgy at the University of Birmingham, wrote: Great differences of opinion have been expressed on ... the relative corrosion of iron and steel, and various experimenters have obtained results which are apparently most contradictory...Perhaps no other property [resistance to corrosion] of wrought iron has had a greater influence in causing the puddling process to survive.

[23] Clapham also wrote: Siemens set himself to meet the Admiralty challenge, and satisfied their most exacting requirements with a uniform mild steel.

Ma Roberts [23t] for the explorer Dr Livingstone, and Cairds on the Clyde built the *Windsor Castle* [93t]. Pearse at Stockton built a shallow draught troopship for use on the River Indus in 1859 and Richardson further down the Tees built the *Little Lucy* with Mersey puddled steel. On the Tyne, Mitchell built a flotilla of flat bottomed river boats for India. The most extensive builder in steel was Samuda on the Thames. Up to 1870 he had built 20 vessels[24] *wholly of steel* and eight *partly* of steel. Bessemer in his *Autobiography* named 18 vessels as *Bessemer steel ships*. Five were built in 1863, seven in 1864 and five more in 1865; the claim that these ships were built of *Bessemer* steel must be doubted. Jones, Quiggin of Liverpool built six ships usually cited. Surviving specifications for the Jones-Quiggin ships provide a more complicated picture. The first page of each specification is marked *Steel*. The following are examples of the material used. In all five vessels where details survive, the Keel, Stem and Stern Post were of *iron*. The term used in the case of the *Banshee* and *Domitilla* is simply *steel*. In the other cases, the material was specified as: *All Steel to be understood as puddled unless otherwise stated*; therefore not Bessemer steel. The bulkheads on the *Clytemnestra* were *iron* and, as on the *Hope*, the hold stanchions and floors were of *iron*. Steel was used for the frames on the *Banshee*, *Clytemnestra*, and *Formby*. Only on the *Hope* was Bessemer steel specifically mentioned: *In Engine Space to stay the sides there are two 15" x 20" & angles 3 x 3 x$^3/_8$" box beam Bessemer steel plates $^3/_8$" & $^5/_{16}$"*. There is little doubt that steel was employed for items on board some ships, but that is far from it being the main construction material used.

A number of advocates for steel spoke at meetings of the INA. Rochussen, speaking in 1866 argued that ships were *likely to be of steel* in the future and contrasted the 22 ton tensile strength of iron, which *will set under a strain of 11-13 tons* whereas *mild steel of 32 tons will recover itself under a strain of 22-24 tons* [this was an exaggerated claim- see chap 15]. Plates 30' long by 6' wide were projected,[25] and for Rochussen the failures *more often originated with the ship constructor, who, careless or ignorant of the nature of steel, uses hard metal, where only mild could be tolerated*. Grantham declared for *puddled steel* and when he *most carefully watched* over the construction of three steel ships, and the plates were *carefully selected*, in his recollection not *a single rivet hole* cracked, nor was there *a single fracture* in bending angle bars. He was *quite satisfied that with proper care - and it all depends upon care - steel will supersede iron*. The critics were not denying the future success of steel. An undoubted friend of steel, Scott Russell, noted *we all need educating in the use of steel* nonetheless added *it is very difficult to get steel of sufficiently good quality for practical purposes*. The Chief Constructor of the Navy, E J Reed[26] expressed the widely held *view: over and over again, the steel breaks through its rivet holes ... we have not yet obtained results which at all justify us in using steel wholesale in the construction of ships*. Belfast shipbuilder Eric Harland, supported Reed and commented *My idea of a ship is that you should be able to kick her about like an old shoe without knocking a hole in her*. Wilson, from the Sheffield firm of Cammell, producers of Bessemer rail steel since 1861, acknowledged as late as 1875: *in respect to Bessemer steel, there is this difficulty - the want of absolute uniformity...we cannot yet say that Bessemer plates can be treated without extreme care in working them into structures*. After seeing *a great deal* of the use of steel in shipyards, and in its manufacture, Lloyd's Chief Surveyor Martell found *it not so reliable*

---

[24] The two largest [*Scud* and *Foam*] *wholly* of steel were 757t in 1861, a Prussian frigate [3404 t OM] in 1866 was the largest of those partly of steel - deck plating, stringers and yards. In 1878 twenty cargo boats [16t] for Madras were of Siemens steel.

[25] Pollock wrote in 1905 that iron plates were 10' -12' x 3'6" and later reached 12'-16' x 3'6"-4' and that steel plates *now commonly used* 24'-32' x 5' and *leading yards* have reached 34'. After 1893, Consett Iron Works provided Furness-Withy with plates 64' x 4' and for frozen meat trade mid-ship body 67' x 5'6". In 1901 for the Colville steel works plates of 50' x 11'6" were normal.

[26] Edward James Reed [1830-1906] was a shipwright apprentice at Sheerness, who attended the School of Naval Architecture. He was for a time editor of the *Mechanics Magazine* and appointed Chief Constructor of the Navy in 1863. In a career dogged by controversy a notable achievement was his success in securing Admiralty support for the first ship model tank at Torquay. From the Admiralty in 1870 he went to Whitworth's in Manchester and designed ships for foreign navies. Reed was a Liberal MP from 1874-1905, Knighted in 1880 and an FRS.

in character that we like and can depend upon.

Lloyd's and the use of steel.

Lloyd's were certainly willing to provide a special survey for steel vessels. Instead of the one-third reduction in scantling cross-sectional area requested, because of higher strength, in 1866 for a vessel of Barrow haematite steel, Lloyd's only allowed a one quarter reduction in the sizes. This was decided after consultation with the Liverpool Registry and the classification was *Experimental*. After four experienced surveyors visited the steel plant and conducted experiments with steel, of not less than 30t/sqin, it was agreed to allow frames a quarter reduction on iron ship sizes. Many ship designers hoped for greater reductions in scantling dimensions when using steel than Lloyd's were willing to allow, e.g Reed in 1878 said that in practice *our steel scantlings...[can only come down] to 13 or 14%* and Denny in 1880 suggested that *by no means the least obstacle to an enlarged use of steel* was the practice of testing adopted by Lloyd's. Such testing it could be argued was necessary to establish confidence in the new material. West, of the Liverpool Registry, pointed out in 1882 that low-priced contracts resulted in poor quality materials and that *the elaborate and stringent tests* for steel were *beneficial* for high standards. Shipbuilder Samuda supported that attitude, saying that *everyone must be satisfied* that Lloyd's approach was a *very satisfactory course ... a most careful supervision* at steel works and local inspectors testing every plate. Two years later shipyard manager and naval architect John stated *the Committee at Lloyd's Register, influenced by their principal officers, were among the first to throw themselves heartily into the matter, and to propagate the new movement.*

The solution - Siemens Martin steel and the contribution of James Riley.

A Report from Lloyd's appeared in the INA Transactions of 1877. A year later when Martell spoke on *Steel for Shipbuilding*, he recalled the doubt existing until recent developments *had induced shipowners ... to look forward with the greatest interest to the possibilities of [mild steel] becoming the material for shipbuilding in the immediate future*. Although he said that both types of material, Bessemer and Siemens, had *abundantly proved that mild steel*, with the approved properties could be produced. Some years later he was rather more specific: *When it was shown to the public in 1876 that mild steel, produced by Siemens-Martin, or acid process, could be made of a ductile, reliable quality, suitable in all respects for shipbuilding purposes, of a much superior character to that of ordinary ship iron.* It clearly should be the duty of any inspecting authority to be convinced of the soundness of any changes, particularly structural ones which affect the safety of human life and this the Society of Lloyd's Registry attempted to do, without unduly delaying technical change. Martell in an 1883 Memorandum reviewing experience argued for a 20% reduction in scantlings. He was responsible for drawing up Lloyd's Rules for Steel ships issued in 1885. If this may seem a delay, it must be noted that special survey had been used for such vessels for a long time and adequate sea going experience was required before formulating satisfactory Rules, which once in existence are difficult to change quickly. The rules were broadly in line with what was agreed with Elders for their vessels in 1877. A neglected figure in the history of technology is Siemens works manager James Riley [1840-1911][27], who carried out experiments extending over many months, and carried out various tests, to achieve *the desire of Dr Siemens that ... the Company should turn attention to the production of steel of the finer qualities* suitable for shipbuilding and boiler-making. It was Riley's great achievement to produce an open-hearth steel, which greatly reduce the demanding workshop practices which were first required in working steel plates. His INA obituary concluded: *It is not too much to say that* his 1876 *paper led the way to the now universal use of this material for shipbuilding* and the journal *Engineering* agreed, *Mild steel ... owes its introduction largely to him.* Another vital advance in production technique came from the Landore Works, the manufacture of seamless steel tubes. Two German brothers named Mannesmann in 1885 patented a process developed from an idea first conceived by Reinhard twenty years

---

[27] Riley was born in Halifax and appears to have learned the trade of millwright. He moved to Middlesbrough and rose to be foreman at the iron works of Cochrane, before moving at the age of 29 to Barrow, from where Siemens recruited him for his Landore, near Swansea.

earlier.[28] Siemens Landore workers began to operate the process from 1887 and remained the principal supplier of these tubes for 20 years or more. Such apparently simple matters as a reliable tube are critical factors in many technologies.

The Attitude of the Admiralty.
A President of the Mechanical Engineers, E A Cooper, was in no doubt in 1880: *I do think that great praise and the thanks of the country are due to the Admiralty for the way they took up steel, as soon as they were assured that good mild steel of regular quality could be made.* This sharply contrasts with the anger Bessemer vented against *our quietly-sleeping Admiralty officials* and *their ten years' indifference and apathy.*[29] Officials of the Admiralty carefully examined the possibilities of steel from the outset. Barnaby, Chief of Naval Construction,[30] felt obliged to make his views clear in 1875: *The uncertainties and treacheries of Bessemer steel, in the form of ship and boiler plates, are such that it requires all the care which it has bestowed upon it at L'Orient to avoid failure. The question we have to put to the steel makers is , What are our prospects of obtaining a material which we can use without such delicate manipulation, and with so much fear and trembling ?* As this comment made clear the problems were primarily with plates, a point Bessemer never seemed to grasp. French naval yards which had taken the lead were using open-hearth not Bessemer steel! It was a French pioneer in the use of steel who rebutted the unjustifiable accusation of overt conservatism made against the Admiralty. Addressing the INA, Marc Berrier-Fontaine began by doubting whether he would be able to add *any important matter of experience* to the papers of Barnaby, Riley, Denny, Martell and West and continued that if the French were first it was *necessary to admit that the British Admiralty very quickly followed in this line.* Brown, the historian of the Royal Corps of Naval Constructors, wrote: *William White visited Le Creusot, studied the methods used, and then persuaded the Landore works...to produce a steel of comparable quality.* In 1877-8 two despatch vessels *Iris* and *Mercury* were constructed of open-hearth steel. Siemens paid tribute to the *very positive role* of William White, who in addition to being responsible for the British Navy's first steel warships also designed a steel warship for the Argentine Government - *Almirante Brown* [4,200dspt].[31] Over the years 1864 to 1875, the Royal Navy continuously used steel for certain parts of the internal framing of iron ships, but always under *special precautions. The Shipping World*, in June 1883, clearly acknowledged the Admiralty's *role*:

> It is satisfactory ... to remark that the Government ... had the temerity to employ it [steel] to some extent in ... our vessels of war; and it is fair to suppose that this fact alone had considerable effect in bring the question of its use into prominence, and in shortening the time when confidence in it should be established.

The Changeover to Steel Hulls Gets Under Way.
Once again the Scots led the way with this major innovation in merchant shipbuilding. Elders in 1877 made the first proposal to Lloyd's to use Siemens-Martin steel; two paddle steamers were built for the London,

---

[28] See *History of Technology* vol 5 pp 63-4 & 629. A hot billet was drawn forward by two rollers and a suitable mandrel formed the inner diameter in the cavity generated by the rotation of the two rollers, the tube was fed to Pilger mills [British patent 1891]. The Swansea plant had six machines capable of working rods up to 10" diam.

[29] Although Bessemer contended that the Admiralty were lagging behind the USA - *the great metallurgical revolution ... had already extended in full force to the energetic people of the United States*: a US government report of 1885, stated -*The use of steel ship-building was by no means so advanced as in other leading branches of iron construction. Only one establishment appears to have given the subject practical attention*!

[30] Barnaby [1829-1915] assisted Watts in designing HMS *Warrior*, Britain's first iron hulled armoured ship. He was DNC 1875-1885,

[31] Its builder Samuda said it was *the first vessel afloat ... constructed entirely of steel and coated with steel faced armour. The Siemens-Martin steel used here, in all respects a superior material to iron...much more ductile both hot and cold ...where properly prepared and annealed where necessary, and properly coated with paint, has in no instance given any symptoms of unreliability or of premature decay.*

Brighton & South Coast Railway Co., with a 20% reduction allowed in the thickness of plates and angles on that used for iron. Denny, the Dumbarton shipbuilders, offered steel vessels to their customers beginning with Irrawaddy Flotilla Co in 1876, with a steel vessel at a mere £200 above the *iron* equivalent. Bessemer steel was used on the *Taeping*; however, it seems that the transverse frames were of iron. At a price of £12,400 this vessel cost £35.7/ ton. This yard was one of the great pioneers in the use of steel[32], as it was later of Parsons steam turbine, and as early as 1884 all output was of steel. In 1879 William Denny III encouraged both the Union SS Co of New Zealand and the Allan Line to use steel. When on New Year's Day 1880, the ss *Rotomahana*, was badly damaged by striking a rock, the Union SS Co was impressed with the performance of the steel used.[33] Denny reported the outcome to the INA and Withy to the Mechanicals in 1881. Other builders also quoted the examples of the durability of suitable steel and such comments helped create an awareness of the success of mild steel. The first steel transatlantic steamer was ss *Buenos Ayrean* of the Allan Line in 1879; Doxfords were then building the first of three Allan Line iron ships, the last of this Line. Widespread adoption by the major shipping Lines, did not follow although many had at least one steel vessel before 1885. By 1883, when the continuous use of steel was just beginning on the north east coast one third of the Scottish tonnage was of steel, a year later all the Denny and Caird output was steel.

Once Siemens-Martin steel was available to the builders, product champions such as Dennys could convince shipowners to buy steel vessels, although not all owners were instant converts, nor were all builders; in August 1881, John Price, the general manager of the Jarrow Shipyard told the Mechanicals that at present cost that there was *only one condition* justifying the use of steel - where *the dimensions of the ship are absolutely limited by the conditions of her trade*. He added that such a condition existed *hardly anywhere in the ordinary carrying trade*. More than 10% of Palmers shipbuilding output in 1884 was with steel hulls. This proportion doubled the following year and then went to almost 70% a year later, and by 1888 all output was in steel. In that year at the INA, Price suffered embarrassing attacks not only from Denny but also Withy, and Tyne shipowner Rogerson, all of whom claimed he had exaggerated cost differences. Anxious *to clear himself from suspicion that he had any antagonism to steel,* Price protested, *he believed steel was a better* material. The question was to find out which was the *better investment*. Perhaps *The Engineer* had found part of the reason for reluctance to change at Jarrow. In January 1886 it commented *the fact that the Palmer Shipbuilding Company has begun the production of steel plates must be looked upon as significant. There were reasons why that company should adhere as long as possible to iron ... it had its works ... fitted up for the production, cheaply and efficiently of iron plate.* This journal was not yet completely

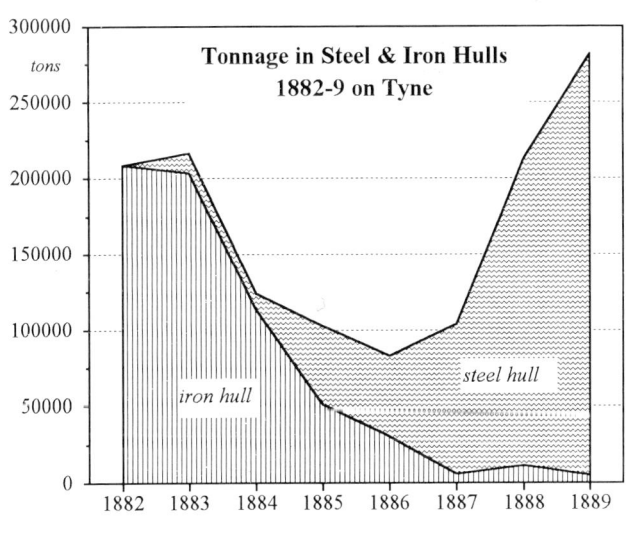

Diag 9.07

---

[32] In 1879-80 Denny built the P & O's first steel ship ss *Ravenna*. Cable Boyd, P & O's historian, suggested the next four ships were of iron because of a lack of supplies of shipbuilding steel. He wrote that the *Ravenna was such a success that iron was abandoned as soon as possible,* although *her cost was great, several thousand pounds more than that of her bigger sisters.* Dennys made just over £1,000, a mere 1.3%, on a final price of £8,2521.

[33] A letter from the company commented: *This experience has shown clearly the immense superiority of steel over iron. There is little doubt that had the Rotomahana been of iron, such a rent would have been made in her that she would have filled in a few minutes. A number of frames were set back by the force of the blow, the bulkhead was bulged and the plate was corrugated and yet there did not appear one crack anywhere.*

convinced: *Whether or not the steel vessel may prove to be the best under all circumstances cannot be definitely said, but the tendency towards its use ... has been very decided.* The changeover on the Tyne is shown in diag 9.07.

Following Mitchell's work on the *Ethel*, five steel gunboats of about 370t were built at the Walker yard in 1879 and three more of 412t in 1881; these were all for China. Nearby Wigham Richardson built ss *Madrid* of nearly 2,000t in 1879. Seven steel paddle steamer were built by the Tyne General Ferry Co between 1881 and 1889. Given the experience at the Mitchell yard it was not surprising that Armstrong's moved fairly quickly into steel hulls, with the *Czar*, for Russia in 1883 as well as the cruiser *Esmeralda* for Chile. More than half the tonnage in that year was of steel. It fell back to just over 6% in the following year; however, in 1885 all the vessels launched were steel. Although in 1888, almost 20% of the tonnage was iron, Armstrong ships were from then on made of steel. Eight Tyne yards built in steel in 1884, including Palmers [10.7%], Leslie [15.3%], Dobson [12.9%] and Wigham Richardson [4.9%], overall 8.5% of total tonnage. More than a quarter of the output of Edward's yard was in steel and the small yard of Hepple built a steel vessel also. Excluding the smallest vessel, the average size of the 16 steel vessels was 651t, compared with the overall average for the river of 1,044t. In the very depressed year 1885, steel output just exceeded half the total. About half the tonnage at Richardson, Edwards, Tyne Iron SB [a ship] and Wood & Skinner [a ship] was in steel. Richardson's ss *Alfonso XII*, at 5,063t was the largest steel vessel built on the Tyne. Swan Hunter began steel construction with ss *Burrumbeet* [2,600t] in 1885 a year in which more than two-thirds of their output was steel, it dropped to 61% in 1886. Thereafter vessels from the Wallsend yard were normally of steel. Not until 1886 did Redhead and Schlesinger-Davis build in steel. Almost 95% of the Tyne's output was steel construction in 1888, when a third of Dobson's tonnage and 40% of Wood Skinners was still iron.

Doxford's led the way on the Wear; three steel ships were built in 1883, a third of yard's output. A year later no steel vessels were launched on the Wear, but in 1885, eight of the 16 Wear yards built at least one vessel in steel. Six of the these vessels were under 1,000t. J L Thompson turned out four steel ships [8,392t], 54% of their output and a year later three-quarters of the tonnage was steel. After that the North Sands yard built in steel. More than 81% of the Wear's output was in steel, in 1887, and, a year later 98.6%. [see diag 10.08] Bartram's only vessel in 1886 was of steel and the yard continued to use this material, Short Bros began in 1887, with four of six vessels of steel. Pickersgill could have moved straight into the steel era since their first iron ship was launched in 1880 and a mere eight years later all the output was steel. In 1885, only 9% of Robert Thompson's output was steel and 12.4% of Laings, who moved to steel in 1887, the depression delayed Robert Thompson's changeover until 1888. Blumer first used steel in 1887 [52% of tonnage] and steel only in 1888, but almost 20% was iron in 1889.

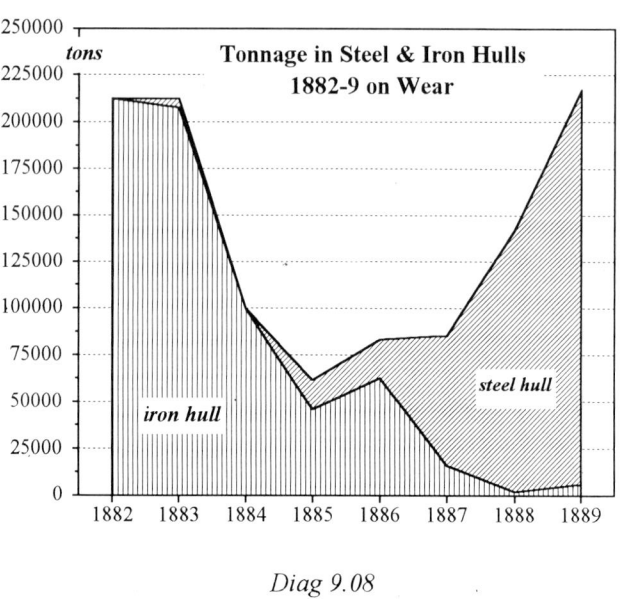

Diag 9.08

On Teesside, Raylton Dixon was enthusiastic for steel. He reported how the first plate in the yard was transformed into *a well made round hat*, which proved there was *not much difficulty* in working it. His men liked Siemens steel and they had not had a single piece condemned; it was worked at the same price

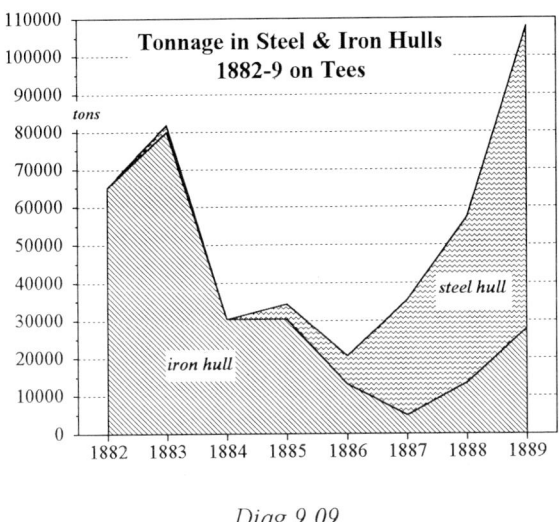

Diag 9.09

as iron. In 1883, Dixon built a 1,833t steel ship and apart from the requirement of his customers such as trawler owners who wanted iron, steel was the normal material from 1886. He built one of the largest steel vessels in the region in the 1880s, ss *Santiago* of 4,340t. Richardson Duck was rather slower in adopting the new material, with its first steel vessel in 1887 and over the three years 1887-9, iron output was 40% of the total. The long established Pearse yard built steel hulled ss *Mount Kembla* [716t] in 1885, his output in 1886 was in iron but in his last year it was all steel. When Ropners took over the yard they were steel builders from the outset. At Hartlepool, in 1885 more than half the tonnage Edward Withy's yard was of steel and 58% of Gray's output. By 1887, just over 93% of the district's output was in steel, although this proportion dropped in succeeding years. A substantial tonnage of iron hulls were built in 1889 as diag 9.09 shows.

Continued use of iron on parts of steel hulled ships.

Some parts of the many early vessels continued to be of iron. Swan Hunter used steel for half the plating amidship on ss *Antwerpen* in 1887 and later the inner bottoms of the *Avalon* and *Knutsford* were also of iron. Floors of iron were used by Richardson Duck in 1888. Although many decks continued to be made of wood, iron decks were regularly used and as on Swan's *Kara* this continued to be the material used with only part of the deck of mild steel. In ss *Port Denison*, built at Hebburn, 251t of iron plates were used and 756t of steel; thus about 25% of the plates, by weight, were iron. In 1889 at that yard, 14% of the plates for the *Nairnshire* were of iron and 27% of those on ss *St Clears*. The relative amount of steel and iron in plates used by Laing is shown in diag 9.10. On some ships half the tonnage of plates was iron and only in a few cases was the amount of iron less than 15%. A higher proportion of steel was used for angles &c than plate.

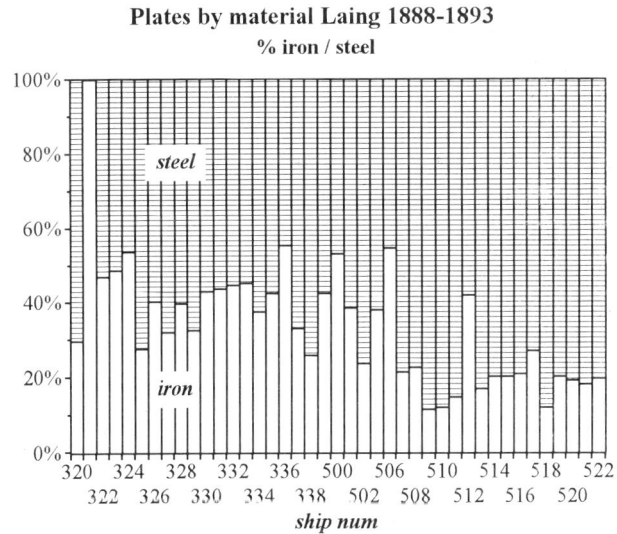

Diag 9.10

Cost of iron and steel.

Unless material costs were low enough shipowners were unlikely to commit themselves. Iron or steel used on a vessel constituted a very important part of final cost. Clearly the weight reduction due to steel contributed in two ways; firstly if 14% less steel is used than iron a price differential of 14% will leave that particular raw material cost remaining the same and secondly for deadweight cargoes there would be the possibility of carrying extra *deadweight* cargo to the extent of the weight of metal saved. Of course, not all cargoes were *deadweight* and so this operating gain was not then available. Although Lloyds allowed a 20% reduction on scantlings and Martell believed this allowed saving on the weight of metal of 18% on a steamer and more on a sailing ship. Commercially available sizes of materials[34] and design did not allow the full theoretical saving. Denny's experience, to 1881, was that the ratio was between 13% and a little over 14% and this seemed to be the consensus amongst fellow shipbuilders. By 1884 John was claiming that a steel ship was as cheap as iron in first cost per deadweight ton carried. A year later J H Biles found it *difficult to see* why any further iron cargo ships should be built on the Clyde; his figures for materials saved was from 13.9% on a 1,500 ton ship to 13.3% for a 4,500 ton ship. In 1878 the view was that a steel ship was about 25% dearer than an iron. Tables of costs were presented and argued about. All prices in the 19th century were strongly influenced by the business cycle, which was further complicated by the slump in shipping over the years 1884-8. In addition the precise price at which any yard purchased is not generally known and published prices are not necessarily the most reliable guide. Nonetheless, there is no reason to question the downward trend in prices presented by Riley in 1885. A very sharp fall in the late 1870s resulted in the steel plates selling for about £10/ton at the bottom of the slump from twice that figure in 1876. In the jump that followed as industry moved out of deep depression, the price increased to £13 followed by a steady downward trend to about £7/ton in 1885 according to Riley. One historian, McCloskey, calculated the ratio of ship plate steel to iron prices in Scotland as falling from 1.43 in 1880 to 1.06 in 1888 and in North Yorkshire from 1.48 to 1.12 in 1888. His figure for Scotland in 1885 was 1.21. Contemporary naval architect Biles gave a somewhat higher ratio of 1.30. North east iron master, Lowthian Bell, gave a ratio 1.88 for 1880 [plates iron £6.25 and steel £11.73] and in 1886 a ratio of 1.32, which was lower than McCloskey's 1.41. Such variations are not surprising but they do suggest guarding against apparent precision of clear lines of movement beyond broad trends. Prices paid by Hawthorn Leslie for plates between 1886 and 1893, do show finally the closing of the gap but generally steel was about 20% dearer per ton. For ships #267-272 in 1889, Laing paid £5.85 for steel plates and usually £4.66 for iron [2 ships were at £4.82], which meant steel was 25% higher per ton. Robert Thompson, as President of the NECIES in October 1892, reviewed both freight rates and prices of iron and steel from the summer of 1884 to the end of 1891. His figures show significant variations within single years[35] and diag 9.11 shows the lowest yearly figure for plates and angles in steel and iron; there was at least a difference of £1/ton for plates until 1890, the mean figure being £1.17, and as a percentage of the iron price, steel was 24% higher. Clearly once steel could be bought for not much more than 20% above iron, it was in cost terms alone competitively effective. Two further factors were involved in the cost equation: firstly the money recovered by the use of scrap wrought iron and secondly, for a time, the cost of testing plates. As much as 10% of iron might become scrap, and iron shearings were *easily repiled and rolled into plates, at the same time improving plate.* In

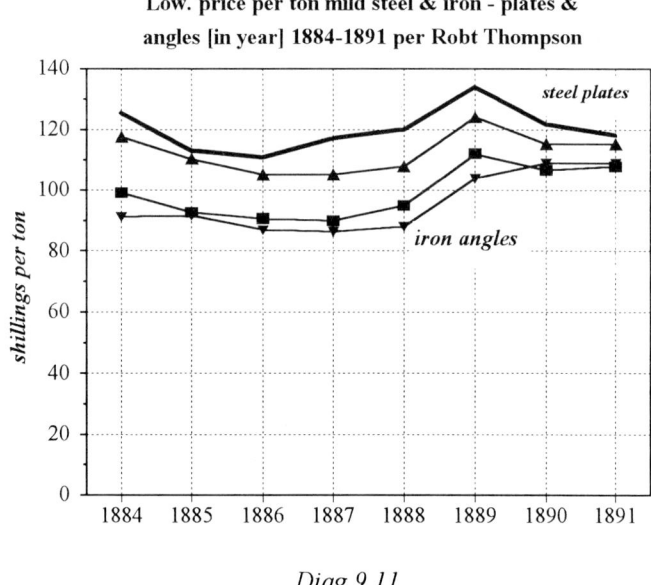

Diag 9.11

---

[34] Although there is a multitude of sizes [probably too many] available to shipbuilders they were not infinitely variable, even plates varying in .05" will not allow the full exploitation of a 20% [or any fraction] of reduction.

[35] Prices for plates fell steadily from 142.6s in Mar.1885 to 110.6 in Sept 1886; angles however, fell from Mar 1885 [125s] to Sept 1885 [110.6s] and then rose to 125s in Dec 1885, before falling again to 105s in Sept 1886. Steel plates increased from 135s in Jan.1888 to 137.6s in Mar. before plummeting to 120s in May, after 10 weeks at that low level, it climbed back to 137.6s in October but after a month fell again to reach 133.9s in Mar 1889. What might seem almost a bizarre phenomena occurred in the boom of 1889; wrought iron plates increased from about 120s a ton to more than 160 at the end of the year but by May 1890 down to 107s and then moved back to 118s.

contrast steel shear scrap reduced almost to the value of pig iron. It was estimated that the cost of testing a large plate was £1 per ton of steel in a Scotch yard in 1888.[36]

Basic Steel.
Steel from the Cleveland ore fields was described as basic steel, and the suitability of this material for ship construction was very important for the north east. When INA meet in Newcastle in July 1888, two papers were devoted to basic steel. Percy Gilchrist, a key figure in developing the successful process of making basic steel, opened the discussion in which four shipbuilders related their experience. Price of Jarrow, while clearly wanting satisfactory basic steel for shipbuilding, could only tell a tale of woe, 20 broken frames in one ship, beams 40' long and 10" deep, which *would not bear throwing down off the men's shoulders on to the ground* and when the men *applied a little pressure, off they went like a pistol shot, breaking through their entire section.* Clydesider F.J.Trewent, who worked at Swans and Hawthorn-Leslie, felt obliged to *corroborate what Mr Price has so ably stated ... We found that shell plates, after being punched, simply by being put through the plate rolls, broke through a row of rivet holes. This occurred frequently, even when dealt with very tenderly.* On a ship nearly ready for launching, a corner rivet had broken off and when the riveter tapped *the plate very smartly with a quarter hammer* flaws and cracks appeared; when other plates were also tapped, they were *cracking in all directions*. These were Bessemer steel. W. John had already explained that often it was not known what makes the plates were. In his own yard where 500 tons of supposed basic steel were condemned, it turned out *that a large proportion ... was Bessemer steel made by the acid process*. Although at that time Sunderland shipbuilder Laing did not have *that confidence in it which I desire*, he was confident that *by the application of chemical science to metallurgy...in the course of time, we shall be able to produce, by the basic process, steel, which, in all respects, will come up to the requirements of shipbuilders*. So indeed it was as the open-hearth manufacturers developed their techniques to the production of uniform reliable material for shipbuilding.

Attitude of the Workers.
There is no evidence of reluctance by workers to use the new material. Angle-iron smiths wanted changes in their piecework rates and the larger plates created difficulties for the platers' helpers due the inadequate lifting and transporting equipment in shipyards [see chap 13]. As might be expected, younger, less experienced men took more quickly to the new material. This was documented for the French experience and no doubt was equally true in Britain. In his *The Practical Boilermaker Iron-shipbuilders and Mast Maker* [1880], Robert Knight, of the Boilermakers' Union, showed his awareness of the qualities of steel. He wrote:
> If ... steel rivets were substituted for iron, the size might be reduced in proportion to their extra strength ... and this [with equal spacing] would leave a stronger joint. But it will naturally occur to anyone who gives the subject serious consideration ... there must be further advantage in using steel plates, in as much as these are nearly 50% stronger than iron.

He cited *lighter construction* when used for mast making. Like others who were well informed he pointed out that *much uncertainty* existed as to the quality of Bessemer plates, *until recently* and noted the considerable extra cost compared with iron. Although the adoption of *mild steel* largely advanced during a depression, which would have rendered trade union resistance more difficult, in Scotland the changeover largely preceded the depression. In any event there are no indications that the Boilermakers' Society wished to resist the new material; their main concern, certainly on the north-east coast, was the unemployment and sequence of four wage reductions caused by the depression. The working craftsmen were not an obstacle to this change. A factor in using iron was that the general familiarity with the material meant that foremen, workers and managers could more readily detect the faulty iron material even without specific testing, which they could not do with the unfamiliar *mild* steel.

---

[36] As early as 1877, boilermakers complained of the cost of testing of plates; a strip was cut off from two edges of the plate and tested. A few firms had their own testing machines and boiler inspector Fletcher urged others to follow their example. Managers objected to the cost of *an idle unproductive machine*.

Any suggestion of British backwardness in introducing steel is not sustainable, though it is possible that metallurgical staffs and representatives capable of resolving customers' problems might have increased the speed of adoption. The absence of uniformity in test procedures, even for tensile strength, did not facilitate comparisons. Into the 1880s materials were being supplied without a clear, let alone precise knowledge of consumers' specific requirements.[37] Neither the Admiralty nor the shipping registries such as Lloyds appear as restricting factors; if anything the contrary view emerges. Leading officials in these organizations most carefully examined and tested the new material and urged it forward once a steel emerged suitable for its intended use. With the sole instance of the French naval yard, nowhere else did shipbuilders act before the British industry. Shipbuilders were not selling to a wide consumer market but to a limited number of owners, and their views or those of their marine superintendents, were always a critical factor in regard to any innovation. Papers read to the professional Institutions were important in establishing the technical acceptability *of mild steel*. Unlike the scientist who basically convinces his peers, the technologist after convincing his peers must sell to a buyer, so the price must be right.

Oil Tankers.

TANKERS - Such is the concise nomenclature applied to oil-in-bulk carrying vessels... It is ingenious if not Elegant. The Shipping World 1 Oct 1890.

Another great innovation, with many hazards, of this decade was the tanker, which advanced rather more slowly than *mild* steel hulls. In 1861 the brig *Elizabeth Watts* [224t] loaded with the first full cargo of oil in barrels sailed from the USA for London. Barrels were extremely wasteful of cargo space and added significantly to weight; a barrel weighed about one fifth of the weight of oil in it and a vessel capable of carrying 2,000 tons would only carry a little over half this amount, 1,030 tons. Selling the barrels in London could result in a loss of £350 a voyage, in addition to the unloading costs. So there was a substantial incentive to finding a better way to carry this new valuable cargo. Many of the essential features of the tanker were laid down in the 1880s and north east shipbuilders played the leading part in creating this new vessel, both in terms of design and production. Liquid cargoes was carried from the earliest times but usually in containers. Many centuries ago the Chinese developed the use of bulkheads; and they carried oil next to the skin of vessels with bulkheads dividing the hull into eight tanks; the junks used for this trade were small. However, the tanker did not evolve from these early endeavours. The tanker dominated shipbuilding after 1945 in a way that no other type of vessel did. A seemingly insatiable demand for petrol and oil products, within a relatively short period of years, resulted in these ships reaching a size that few, if any, naval architects would have thought possible in 1945.

Oil was widely used in Russia and many vessels were developed there for its transportation along rivers and across the Caspian Sea; 286 oil carrying vessels operated on that inland sea in 1907. Almost half, 137, were steam propelled. Ludwig Nobel after migrating from Sweden to Baku, is said to have conceived of carrying petroleum in bulk right up to the plating of the ship and indeed in 1878 the *Zoroaster* was the *first true steam tanker to see service in her intended trade*. Events on Tyneside began with the Newcastle entrepreneur John Rogerson, who used his *Mary Rogerson* to carry oil in barrels before purchasing in 1863 the *Atlantic,* a sailing vessel built at St Peters. This ship was intended to carry oil in bulk; iron sheets partitioned the hull and hollow masts provided a kind of expansion chamber. She may have only carried one cargo of oil. American maritime historian Frear regarded the *Ramsey*, launched in 1863 on the Isle of Man, as the *first step in the evolution* of the tanker; she could carry 1,400 tons in iron tanks. From 1869 to 1872 the *Charles*, a sailing vessel of 794t, regularly carried oil in 59 tanks, placed in rows in the hold

---

[37] Parker said the makers of the steel *had never seen a marine boiler [and] had no idea that these plates had to be heated, worked and tortured in this manner.*

and between decks. Three vessels were built at Palmers specifically designed to carry oil. The *Vaderland* [2,748t] was launched in August 1872, followed by the *Nederland* [2,839t][38] and the *Switzerland* over the next two years. An important design feature was a short expansion trunk and there was a complete inner skin 26" from the outer plating [this gap reduced to 20"]. However, this inner skin was ultimately regarded as more of a hazard than a benefit.[39] These were owned by a Philadelphia based company but belonged to the port of Antwerp. None, however, actually carried oil. When the *Vaderland* arrived at Philadelphia with emigrants, remarkably the normally intended return *cargo*, the American authorities objected to this plan. They would not, very understandably, permit an oil vessel to alternate as passenger ship and the Antwerp authorities were unwilling to permit the construction of oil storage tanks. So these potentially pioneering vessels reverted to normal cargo trade, which may have included cased oil. As late as 1908 many tankers carried general cargo on return journeys. A member of a family with a long connection with Palmers, McAllister, pointed out that the *Vaderland* [see illustration] had five key features of a tanker:

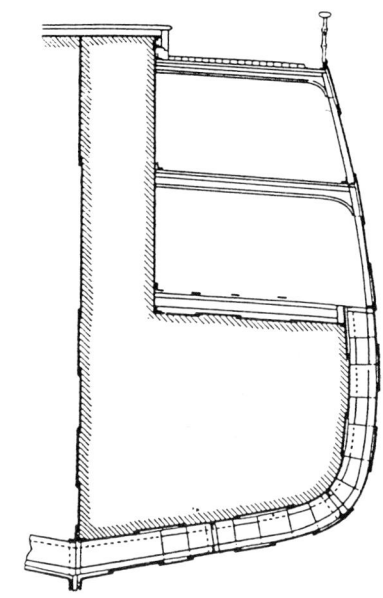

Section of ss *Vaderland* shows double skin

1. All five tanks were equal and of moderate length;
2. Centre-line bulkheads divided the tanks into pairs;
3. the internal structure of tanks formed natural cofferdams;
4. separate expansion trunks for each tank;
5. machinery was aft.

Mitchell's Walker yard supplied a number of vessels to the Nobels starting with the *Massis* in 1881; this 411t steamer had a deep tank amidship to carry 80 tons of petroleum. She was designed to pass through the lock systems between the Baltic and the Caspian Sea and depended upon shore facilities to load and discharge her cargo of oil. Two years later the Nobels were supplied with the *Poseidon* and the *Armeniak* [149'], which carried 492 tons of oil and was described by naval architect Watson as *a true tanker*. Oil cargo tanks extended to the hull shell for more than 40% of the ship's length, with a centre line bulkhead; the cargo hatches allowed for any expansion of the oil. There was a large water ballast tank at the end of each cargo tank. In order to pass the locks the *Poseidon* was built in two sections, together 210' long, and had a bulk oil capacity of 287 tons, carried in the double bottom MacIntyre tanks and a deep tank; it had a steam driven cargo pump.[40]

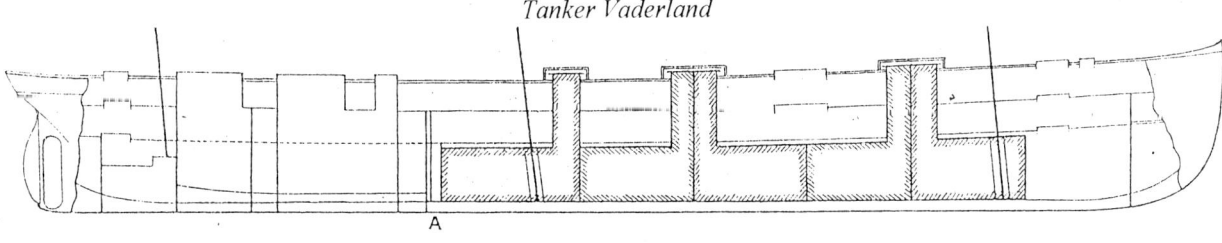

Tanker Vaderland

---

[38] *Vaderland*- 320.5' x 38.5' x 23.8' with 3 bulkheads. *Nederland*- 329.2' x 38.6' x 30.5'; 290 nhp engines.

[39] Swan wrote in April 1885 of the *great disadvantage* of the ordinary double bottom for the petroleum vessels - *if crude oil be carried in it, or if by any chance the space becomes filled with gas, it cannot be entered until the gas is entirely expelled, which would be extremely difficult to do.*

[40] Another Mitchell ship the *Hooper* [5,046t] finally became a tanker. No doubt Swan had supervised the construction of this cable ship delivered in 1873. As the *Silvertown* she was acquired by the Anglo-American Oil Co in 1916 and fitted with cylindrical tanks for carrying oil. In 1920 she became a bunkering vessel at Southampton. Under the name, *Francunion II*, in 1924, she became a fuel supply ship at Algiers and was finally sold to the ship breakers in 1935. One of many examples of the durability and adaptability of north east ships.

Henry Swan and the Gluckauf.

Swan's *Gluckauf* usually carries the accolade of being the first tanker. Henry William Swan, the son of a farmer at Walker, served his apprenticeship at Charles Mitchell's yard. Swan's sister Anne married Mitchell in 1854. When only 20 years of age, in 1862, Swan was sent to supervise the building of warships at Kronstadt and three years later took over charge of the Walker yard. During 1885 Swan was transforming the ideas of his patent[41] into the design of full scale oil tankers. Some naval men who had seen the design told him that such a ship could not stand the rough passage of the Atlantic. On 25 November 1885 the keel was laid for the first Swan tanker on the yard's own account. At this time, Heinrich Riedemann, a shipper of oil from Bremen, was arranging for 72 tanks to be fitted into the composite vessel *Andromeda*. *In all Germany* he could not find a shipbuilder who would risk building a tanker with the oil going to the plating. On a visit to Tyneside at the end of that year Riedemann was shown the vessel by a young Saxton White while the frames were being erected; he agreed to buy the ship, which he called *Good Luck* - the *Gluckauf*. The building work of the *Gluckauf, one of the largest experiments* in oil transport, was *rapidly pushed forward*; she was completed in under seven months.

Swan's tanker Gluckauf.

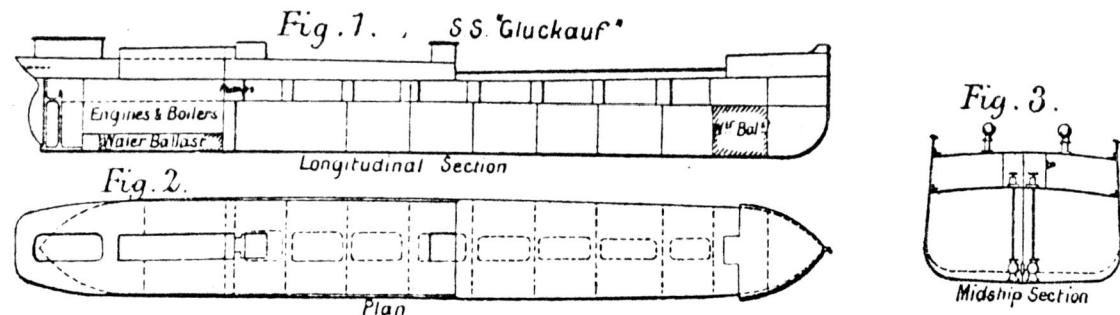

McAllister's five features of the *Vaderland* are usually regarded as advances in design made in the *Gluckauf*. However, in addition ss *Gluckauf* had oil main expansion joints, vapour pipes on top of each expansion trunk, strengthening grid irons on tanks, pump room below deck and a short bridge amidship. He also used countersunk rivets in all oil tank work and stressed the elimination of the normal double bottom.[42] These were decisive contributions to the design and building of oil tankers. When in April 1886 *The Shipping World* discussed Swan's invention, it noted the success by Nobel in bulk carriage on the Caspian Sea and that there were many rival schemes. The fundamental principles identified were:

> the subdivision of the hold spaces into numerous oil-tight compartments;
> the installation of powerful pumping appliances for clearing the holds of cargo;
> the device of arrangements for burning liquid fuel in the boilers;[43]
> plans for isolating the cargo holds from the boiler-rooms;
> special provisions for ventilation and changes in bulk due to temperature change

and the journal finally pointed out that because a liquid cargo was a shifting cargo steps were taken to ensure that the compartments were *kept practically full*. In April 1886, Swan stated that his vessel was *deliberately intended to make her return voyages without cargo*, and so must be *sufficiently immersed when in ballast trim* for long voyages, including crossing the Atlantic in all weathers. Whereas *rarely* was

---

[41] Four patents stand in Swan's name in 1885 [#15711], two with a J Casey were concerned with sewage carrying.

[42] The *Gluckauf* did not have a double bottom under the oil compartments. Swan argued that the conical form of his patent placed the centre of gravity, both in ballast and with a cargo, in a position to give the vessel excellent sea-going qualities. The conical form allowed any gas by chance in the ballast space to be entirely expelled and gave greater facility for examination, painting or repair. In fact the conical form was not used. He stated the double bottom would function on the *petroleum ship* as on a screw collier and was not available for crude petroleum.

[43] The proposal of oil burning boilers was not followed outside of Russia for a long time; there were hazards in handling bunker coal on oil vessels. Many vessels supplied by Mitchell for the Caspian Sea, e.g ss *Yang* in 1888, were fitted with boilers to burn petroleum waste.

an ordinary vessel ballasted to more than 15% of her maximum dwt capacity in Swan's system over 50% could be carried. No oil compartments were used for ballast purposes. His ship could carry either a full cargo of refined petroleum, or one half refined and one half crude oil.

Just a fortnight after the completion of the *Gluckauf*, Lloyds surveyor Martell delivered his pioneering INA paper on *The carriage of petroleum in bulk on over-sea voyage*. Opportunities were being lost by British shipowners, according to Martell,, as their efforts *have been little exercised in competing with foreign shipowners for the oversea carrying trade in petroleum*. With more than one and half million tons exported from the USA alone in 1885, there was an opportunity lost in a freight market worth £1,500,000; almost all of this in 1885 was carried in barrels. As *The Shipping World* pointed out, the *crowded state of the chamber showed the subject was one of absorbing interest*. However, a rather annoyed Swan commented *It is, perhaps, rather strange that the only steamer that has yet been specially built to cross the Atlantic is not represented in* [the] *diagrams*[44]. In discussion Swan said he had *given very great attention* and *done a little toward advancing knowledge* on the question of carrying oil in bulk. Most proposals had *unnecessary complications* and he identified the *great difficulties* as *the questions of the leakage and the change of bulk of the liquid cargo ... and last but not least, the danger ... by reason of the gases ... evolved from the cargo*. He then showed diagrams of the *Gluckauf* and his patent. Swan argued against the inner tanks on the grounds of being *quite inaccessible* for repair and that if struck by another vessel the inner tank would be penetrated anyway. In the case of the *Gluckauf*, he contended

> it would be possible to imagine the ship's bottom entirely knocked out, and yet she would float and come to her port of destination without any serious casualty. The lightness of the oil itself is such that it will remain in the upper half even though damage occurs here [to which he pointed - not shown in INA text].

Kirk's view that there was *not the slightest difficulty in making oil compartments perfectly tight* was *entirely* endorsed by Swan. During construction the *Gluckauf* was treated as a boiler and *every compartment as a boiler compartment* and they were tested up to double pressure. On trial with tanks filled to the upper deck *only one rivet ... showed a tear*. When the *Gluckauf* sailed from the Tyne on 10 July 1886 she was the first ocean going tanker with oil to her skin. She carried just over 3,000 dwt [equivalent to about 18,000 barrels - about three-quarters of her dead weight]; her dimensions were just over 300' long, 37.2' wide and 24' moulded. She reached 10.5k on her trial and had a sea speed of 9k. The reception at New York was not friendly. The coal merchants refused to refuel the vessel and she bunkered at St Johns. Her name failed to bring good luck as she was wrecked on Long Island on 24 March 1893. For months she was *an object of interest ... with her stern under water and her fore-body reaching high up in the air*, an indication of the soundness of her structure. John McGovern in 1930 held the view that the *Gluckauf may be regarded as the basis of the modern tanker with which we are familiar to-day*. Four more vessels were ordered by Riedemann and many tankers were built by Armstrongs for other owners, more than 50 in the ten years after the *Gluckauf*. In 1888, the Kerosene Co of London was supplied with ss *Elbruz*, able to carry 4,000 tons on a light draught of water. A year later, the oil fired *Phosphorus* of 1889 carried 740,000 gallons of oil, with 300 gallons in the bunkers, and ss *Lumen* [3,500 tons of oil and coal carried]; both were classified by the Paris based Bureau Veritas. Early in 1887, Palmers launched ss *Era* [1,850t], which carried about 2,000t of oil and a year later the much larger ss *Oka* [3,095t]. Both were designed by Sir E J Reed [1830-1906] and followed a Flannery type design. These vessels were described in 1940 by Frear as bringing *to an end a chapter in the evolution of the marine transport of oil and established a precedent in design which has undergone no fundamental change except in equipment and details of construction up to the present time*.

Remarkably Gray's first tanker, the British owned *Bakuin*, was launched at Hartlepool on 17 June 1886, the day before the *Gluckauf*. However, the Armstrong-Mitchell ship was completed on 13 July and Gray's tanker on 7 August. The *Bakuin*'s engines were aft with a double bulkhead before the boiler space and also

---

[44] Swan said that when approached *some weeks ago* by Martell he was under express orders of owners not to supply information and later Martell said he had sufficient information.

at the fore-end; she had electric light installed and could discharge a full cargo of 1950 tons in 12 hours. Some contemporaries, such as Martell, considered the *Bakuin* the better of the two ships. Nonetheless, Lloyds would not classify this new vessel unless alterations were carried out. North east builders already regularly used the Bureau Veritas.[45] After limited scantling alterations Bureau Veritas approved the design. Probably because of his ability to extend remarkable credit to Marcus Samuel [1853-1927], the founder of Shell Oil Company, William Gray secured an order for six tankers. The first, ss *Murex*, was launched on 27 May 1892. Samuel had overcome the resistance of the owners of the Suez Canal to tankers passing along this vital waterway to the Far East and the *Murex* was the first oil tanker to make this passage. A firm of consulting naval architects & engineers Flannery, Baggallay & Johnson drew up the plans and specifications[46] of these tankers; the oil tanks when required were used for water ballast. The *Murex* [4,900dwt] measured 349' x 43' x 28'. She was schooner rigged and two of her three masts were of iron and the third of wood; the poop deck was 230' long and there was also a top-gallant forecastle. Two powerful pumps, supplied from London, were capable of pumping out 4,200 tons of oil in 12 hours and the electric light installation was installed by Clarke, Chapman & Co who also supplied the winches.

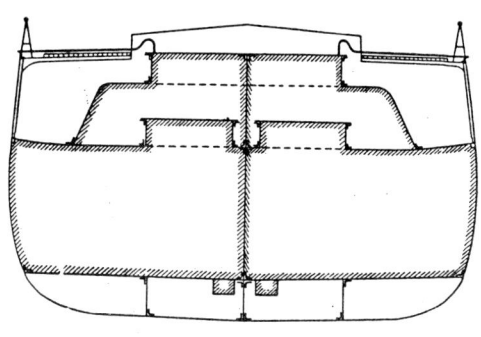

Section ss Bakuin

On Teesside in 1885, after discussions with local shipowner J M Lennard and a representative of Nobel Bros, Craggs was given an order to convert the *Fergusons* [1,551t] to carry oil in independent tanks fitted exactly into the cargo spaces. [see illustration] Probably this ship made the first trip from Britain to Batoum for oil. Other north east builders entered this field early. Three conversions were carried out by Hawthorn Leslie, one of which suffered a tragic explosion. The *Marquis Scicluna* [1,665t][47] sailed between Batoum and Fiume in the autumn of 1886 and the other two, ss *Chigwell* and ss *Petriana*, like the *Bakuin*, were for Alfred Stuart of London. The machinery of ss *Chigwell* was amidships and the tanks extended from side to side and from the double bottom upwards. Hawthorns built their first tanker, the *Looch*, in 1886 and the *Hafis* a year later. A combined loss on these two hulls of £9,045, on a price of £31,542, demonstrated the risks in estimating costs on new designs. Renamed the *Chaumin*, ss *Looch* continued in service for more than 60 years! In 1889, Swans built the *Circassian Prince* their first tanker for local shipowner James Knott. In the same year Robert Thompson launched ss *Wild Flower* [2,656t] for Wear ship owner J S Barwick. She carried 3,000 tons of oil. Tankers did not become a regular part of the output of Thompson but they did for Laings, who built for Samuel in the 1890s. [see chap 11]. A yard apprentice,

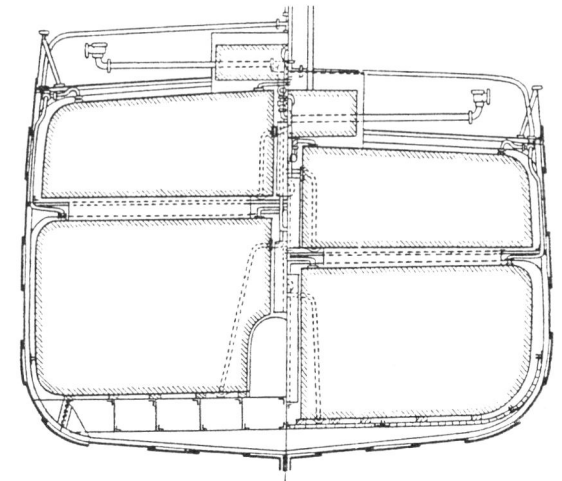

Section of Fergusons

---

[45] Their Newcastle Surveyor John Gravell was born in Italy and trained there; he regularly contributed to NECIES.

[46] Flannery's design carried the oil to the ship's bottom, with cofferdams at the end of each tank space and engines aft.

[47] This was claimed to be the first steamer with oil in bulk against the skin of the ship. A longitudinal bulkhead divided the vessel for and aft. Four transverse bulkheads were added in addition to existing engine room bulkheads and an oil tight platform was fitted on top of the tanks. Coote's estimates for the cost of these conversions was too low and he surrendered shares to the value of £16,500 to cover the losses to the newly formed Hawthorn-Leslie.

J W Stewart, in 1939 recalled ss *Wild Flower* as

> a fully developed tanker ... engines aft and ... oil carried below the second deck ... Later they added an expansion trunk up to the upper deck ... while lying in the river Wear, pumping the residue out of the tanks, the refuse oil floated on the surface. This took fire due to a rivet heater boy's throwing red-hot ashes over the side of a nearby vessel being repaired. The whole river was on fire for hundreds of yards.

A description of vessels provided for the Caspian Sea in the 1890s was given by shipbuilder Dobson. These craft went from St Petersburg up the River Neva, passed through the Marinsky Canal to the River Volga and then travelled the hundreds of miles to Astrakan on the Caspian Sea.

> The ships were all built the full size of the locks in the Canal, except those which were nearly twice as big. The latter were joined almost amidships, the two parts only being bolted together to steam across the North Sea. On arrival at the locks, the two parts were separated and they continued their independent journeys ... to Astrakan, where they were rejoined with doubling plates riveted across the joints. Before being separated ... all possible internal weight were suitably moved in order to trim the two separated pieces to an even draft restricted to 6 feet 9 ... This restricted draft made trimming by water ballast impossible and it even necessitated fitting large lightly built steel pontoons or camels specially shaped to fit on each side below the after end of the ships where the twin-screw machinery was fitted. These pontoons were carried across on the ship's deck, were bracketed below the stern and they remained there all the way down the Volga to Astrakan, where they were scrapped. These ships had necessarily to be of very light construction on account of the shallow draught, ... the design and workmanship had to be especially good to make and keep them, oiltight. They had the usual longitudinal and transverse bulkheads, expansion trunks and coffer dams, elaborate pumping system, electric light, etc... they were amongst the earliest steamers to burn oil fuel. Some... steamed at 12 knots.

The Risks of Explosion and Fire.
Rather hopefully Swan argued that his oil vessels

> should be insured at a very moderate rate, as not only are they structurally much stronger than ordinary merchant ships of the highest class, but their sub division into such a number of absolutely tight compartments renders them practically unsinkable and the risk of fire is reduced to a minimum.

The risks on all tankers were greater than other vessels. A serious explosion on the *Petriana* at Liverpool killed ten men, including an extremely able 26 year old engineer Ivan Mavor. This young Scotsman was trained in John Elder's works and had come to Tyneside as a draughtsman at Armstrongs, rising to be assistant manager at the Low Walker yard. He became manager of the Hebburn shipyard in the year of his death and was married only three weeks before his death. *It would be a great misfortune*, argued *The Shipping World* in February 1887, if this fatal disaster hindered the development of the *sea carriage of petroleum in bulk*, and noted with satisfaction that the jury had found that the accident was not due to the system of bulk carriage. Naked flames must be avoided particularly when loading or discharging and the journal contended that electric light was *particularly suitable for petroleum ships*. In November 1891, the Armstrong built *Lux* was lost and only six of the 26 on board were saved. An explosion on the Swedish built *Petrolea* on 14 June 1892 killed both the ship's crew and men on coal laden lighters nearby The Board of Trade Inquiry concluded *the tanks were filled objectionably, if not perilously, full*. The expansion trunks allowed for about 1.25% with a full cargo. She left Batoum with 2,229 tons [the design load was 2,200 tons] and suffered strong gales in the Black Sea. Some days later the third engineer reported that the bilges were on fire and explosions followed. The primary cause of the accident was held to be the *absence of any adequate separation between the side bunkers and the non-cargo spaces aft* and in this respect the design of the vessel was *radically defective.* F Wailes[48], the surveyor for the underwriters of the *Petreolea* and supervisor of *extensive repairs to numerous oil vessels*, pointed out that in regard to safety *both constructors and shipowners require to treat tankers in every respect upon totally different lines to*

---

[48] Wailes served his time at Wigham Richardson and rose to be chief draughtsman. His later posts were: on the Wear as assistant shipyard manager at Davison & Stokoe, manager of the ships department at Wallsend Slipway and marine superintendent to Henry Bucknall & Sons. In 1887 he started his own consultancy practice- Wailes, Dove & Co. A Founder member of NECIES and author of three papers. He died 17 December 1895, aged 45 years.

ordinary cargo steamers. He advocated the Board of Trade issuing a special certificate to seamen and fireman who were proved *capable and reliable in this trade* and suggested there were serious problems in getting reliable crews. The *Bakuin* was destroyed by fire in Callou Bay in Peru in September 1902. The safety with which oil was carried in bulk on the Caspian and elsewhere was due to the *very great care* taken by those in charge. None the less, there were many serious accidents and not only in the early years. The Boilermakers negotiated an agreement in 1894 to reduce the hazards of repairing oil vessels [at higher rates], it required *that an expert's certificate shall be obtained daily to the effect that the tanks are absolutely safe.* [Ordinary rates applied to *cleansed* oil vessels, which had carried perishable goods as the last cargo.]

Many highly significant changes were carried through in the 1880s on the north east coast, the steel hull, the triple expansion engine and the oil tanker, by able managers and a very skilled workforce, who readily accepted the technical changes. Both workers and their employers suffered a prolonged depression, which resulted in both sides revising at least briefly the practice of piecework to cope with the lack of work. A model, not copied, of conciliation was established on the Wear and many *unskilled and semi-skilled* workers were organised in trade unions. Truly a dramatic ten years.

Two sections of tanker *San Isidoro* as reproduced in *Engineering* in August 1914.

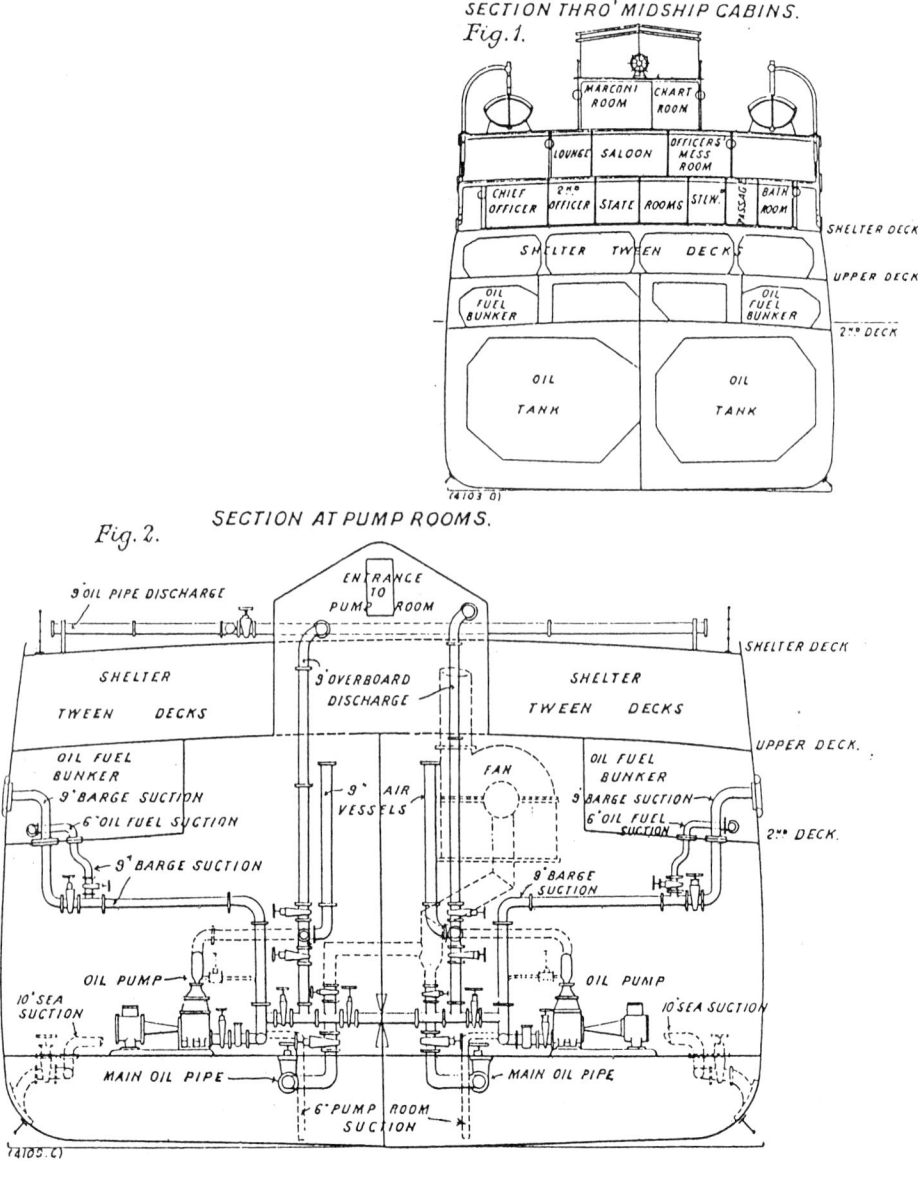

Chapter 10

Shipbuilding on the North East Coast c1889-1914.

By the late 1880s some Tyne shipbuilders were challenging the prestigious standing of the Clyde. In May 1888 *The Shipping World,* wrote of the *extraordinary advances* in the *class of ship* built, which established *the fact that henceforth the North East Coast will divide with the Clyde the work of building the largest class of passenger ship.* The journal cited ss *Mei Shih, Alfonso XII* and *HMS Victoria*. This prediction was never quite realised; the skill, however, was available and in time so was the capacity. North east yards were not then building ships as large as the biggest on the Clyde; in 1890 the Tyne's largest was Palmer's ss *Europe* [5,300t] but the Clyde's ss *Normania* [8,249t] was almost 3,000t bigger. Although *Engineering* in 1891 described the north east as *undoubtedly the most important shipbuilding centre in England,* it pointed out that tonnage did not coincide with value. *Without entering into the question as to whether or not the value of the work done on the Tyne corresponds proportionately with that completed on some other English rivers, we give the former precedence by virtue of the greatly increased tonnage of vessels added there to the shipping of the country.* Three years later, *Engineering* acknowledged the improved quality and that the *status* of north east yards *for workmanship has improved in the esteem of shipowners,* and more firms *stand on equality with the best on the Clyde than formerly.* In 1894, the Clyde only sent a single vessel, 2,100t, to a north east owner but 46,558t was sent to Scotland from the north east!

This chapter begins with an overview of the period 1889-1913, followed by a review of the Tyne, Tees & Hartlepool, Wear, Blyth and Whitby. Particular topics are examined: Doxfords & the Turret Ship, the depression of 1908-10, Laings in voluntary liquidation, and improvements in the shipyards, including the use of electricity. Some changes in ship structures are briefly described together with some comments on sailing ships, colliers, trawlers, tugs and the advance of the tanker. The final section is on Swan Hunter and J Wigham Richardson, probably the greatest shipbuilding company in the world in the years immediately before 1914.

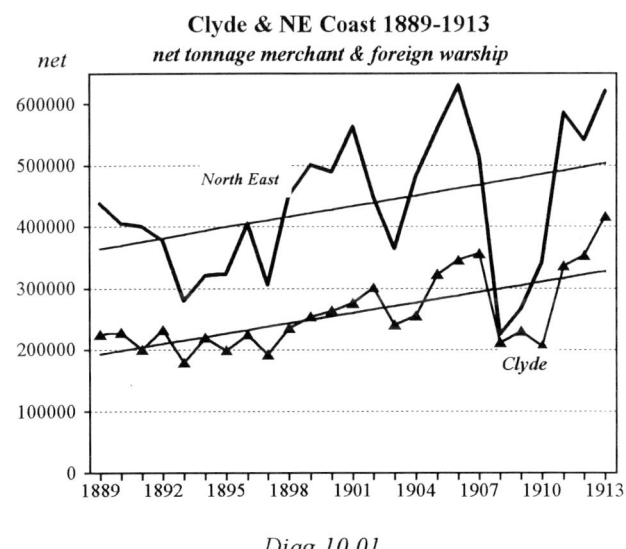

Diag 10.01

Overview 1889-1913.

When shipbuilding emerged from the depression of the mid-1880s, the aggregate total of the north east in 1889 was almost 720,000t, which was more than double the output of the Clyde in 1890. The Clyde, like the Hartlepools and the Tees, reached a peak in 1890. Over the 25 years to the Great War, with the usual fluctuations in the demand for merchant shipping, output increased by about half, and overall probably the Clyde increased slightly more than the north east.[see diag 10.01] A vast increase in naval expenditure strongly affected output on both the Tyne and the Clyde. The north east with the Clyde accounted for 80% of the output of the UK. By July 1889, the Boilermakers' leader, Robert Knight sensed trouble ahead:

> Don't forget the terrible experiences of the late four years of bad trade, and think the present rush in shipbuilding is going to last forever, as it won't; and we are much afraid that at the present rate of shipbuilding a similar collapse to that which took place at the latter part of 1883 will soon overtake us. We surely have a sufficient feeling of self preservation, and of parental love for our families, to prevent a repetition, if possible, of the experiences of 1884-5-6 and 1887; if we have not, our manhood is not

worth much.[1]

The Shipping World pointed out, in August, that the addition of 109,910t to the Register when only 35,715t were removed, might mean *The worthy Secretary will have still greater justification for lifting up his parable*. Boom conditions continued on Teesside, certainly until the end of the year and output was still high in 1891.[2] Nationally the merchant work in hand in January 1890 stood at 873,000t but by October it was only 652,000t. There was a sharp downward trend in the north east until 1893. So pessimistic was the outlook for Tom Richardson in October 1894, that he said: *With the late disastrous record of shipbuilding and engineering industries ... it is highly improbable that any capitalist will start a new ship yard or engine works amongst us*. A hesitant upward movement had then begun in shipbuilding. Early in 1894, *Engineering* wrote of *indifferent promises of activity* and the *great courage* of the shipowner who placed orders when freight rates were so low. It was suggested that old ships were being replaced to gain the economy of new vessels: *the hope of economy lies in the adoption of the most modern machinery in vessels of general cargo capacity... a 9-knot speed at minimum coal consumption was required for the majority of steamers*.[3] The Clyde managed to secure a much steadier level of output over the years 1889-93. Following a peak in 1896, both regions fell back in 1897 when a major engineering dispute affected output. A massive increase in tonnage launched took place on the north east coast between 1897 and 1898, a rise of 52% to 846,027t. Four to five good years were experienced during 1898-1902. Although the movements on the three rivers were similar there were year on year individual variations as shown in diag 10.02. During the four years 1898-1901, almost 3,500,000t of merchant shipping were built on the north east coast.

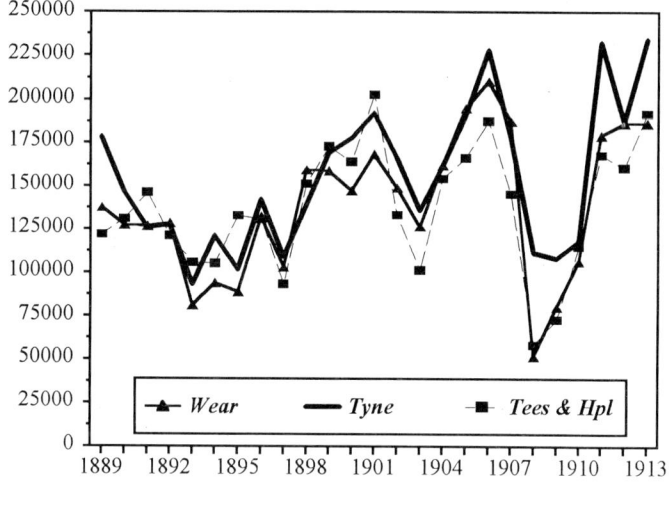

Diag 10.02

The Glasgow Herald wrote in January 1902:
> Shipbuilding is becoming more and more an international industry. America and Germany[4] have advanced immensely ... the well-nigh boundless wealth of the one and the feverish anxiety to get on of the other promise still greater developments ... America is forming shipbuilding companies with immense resources, and Germany is turning out liner after liner of the first class, capable of beating anything yet built by British firms.

The American threat did not materialise and a successful response was made to the German liners. From 900,000t in 1901, north east output fell to less than 650,000t two years later.[5] *The Glasgow Herald* regarded the *general state of trade* as *bad* and pointed out that after the end of the South African War [31 May 1902] a large number of vessels were *suddenly* thrown on the freight market. From the low point of 1903, output rose very sharply to more than a million tons in 1906 and although there was a fall in 1907,

---

[1] In the four years of bad trade *7,000 members in want of work for the whole of that time* [an average of 25%]. It cost the Society £400,000 to keep them and their families *from the relieving officers or the workhouse*.

[2] *The Shipping World* reported continuing speculation; one owner sold a vessel on contract for £14,000 clear profit.

[3] The journal was concerned that engines had *too little power to hold the fully laden ship up to gale. Many steamers might be named... on which the designer would not hazard a voyage across the Bay of Biscay in a gale*.

[4] *The Marine Engineer* wrote in Jan 1896: *There cannot be the slightest doubt that the German builders are putting forth strenuous efforts to get on terms of equality with the builders of the U K*

[5] In official net output terms the fall was from 563,035t to 364,501t, which was a fall of 35%.

the tonnage launched was at the level of the 1901 peak. Eleven of the top 16 places in the table of national output were held by north east yards; they were first, second and fourth, with Harland & Wolff in third place. Twenty-five ships were launched by both Swan Hunter, 118,039t, and Doxford 106,058t. William Gray built 85,111t. A massive depression followed across the years 1908-10, which is examined below. With a fall of 50% the Tyne did rather better than the Wear or Tees, if such can be described as better; in the north east as a whole output was not even 40% of the 1906 peak. From the nadir of 1908 output increased up to the outbreak of war. The regional failure to increase in 1912 was due mainly to a fall on the Tyne. A capacity to build at least a million tons a year existed on the north east coast and the average of 1911-3 was almost at that level.

The Tyne 1889-1913.
After the few unsuccessful new yards in the 1880s, with minor exceptions the pattern of shipbuilding on the Tyne was set in the early 1890s. T & W Smith made their last return of new ships in 1890 and during 1891 they constructed the first part of a pontoon dock for their own use, extending their activities in ship repair. Edwards continued the family heritage in new building and finally Smiths Dock emerged as a limited company in 1899 and moved its shipbuilding work to Teesside in 1909. Early in 1893 Schlesinger Davis closed their yard *pending an improvement in business*. This never came and the site later became part of Swan Hunters. A new enterprise, Northumberland SB, began in 1899 on the site of Edward's Howden yard. Stephensons stopped new building in 1909. A late newcomer was Charles Rennoldson, who opened a new yard at South Shields in 1914. By the turn of the century Palmers' Jarrow yard was losing its dominant position and fell to third place behind the new Swan Hunter enterprise and Armstrongs. Over the period 1889-1913, the combined output of Swan Hunter and Wigham Richardson totalled 1,833,000t, Armstrong 1,100,000t and Palmers 856,000t [see diag 10.03]. Up to 1902 the separate figures for Swans and Richardsons were 53,6714t and 311,625t. With almost 65,000t in 1889, Palmers launched more tonnage than Armstrong and Swan Hunter combined, and they continued to head output on the Tyne until 1893, when Swan Hunter first achieved the highest tonnage on the Tyne. Palmers regained the lead in 1894, but then only headed the river once more, in 1901. Armstrong held first place in four years [1895-1896-1899-1900], while in 1897 and 1898 Swan Hunter had the highest tonnage. From 1902 to 1913, the Swan Hunter yards had the highest output not only on the Tyne but in the UK as a whole.

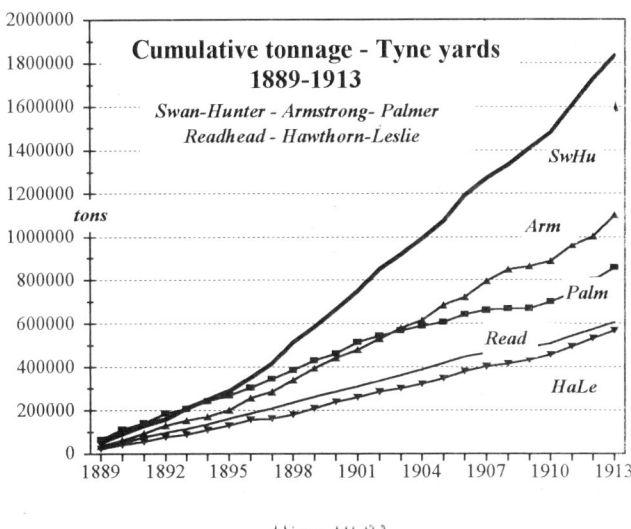

Diag 10.03

There was a downward trend on the Tyne from 1889 to 1893, with 1891 a third lower than the 1889 peak. This may give a misleading impression since two battleships were under construction at Jarrow and such vessels took more than a year to construct, so the tonnage increased between 1891 and 1892 unlike the other three ports. Palmers output increased by 50% and Armstrongs by 20%. In the depressed year of 1893, Swan Hunter, with their highest total to that time [31,088t] and Wigham Richardson were the only Tyne yards to improve on the previous year. *Engineering* suggested that the reason the Tyne was able to sell 11,412t to Glasgow was *that the price was very low*. Those ships were by Hawthorn Leslie, ss *Perthshire* [5,550t] and ss *Buteshire* [5,574t] both engined by St Peters; the loss on the engines was £2,527 and on the hulls £2,758, which was a loss of about 10s / ton. No ships were launched at Stephenson's

Hebburn yard. They did, however, construct 6 iron lock gates, an iron pontoon and a floating dock. Edwards Brothers began building at North Shields in 1893 and launched three iron screw trawlers. From 1894 there was an upward trend to 1898 on the Tyne, and then a remarkably steady period up to 1902, five consecutive years with an output of 300,000t or more. Wigham Richardson's output of 8,273t in 1894 was less than half the tonnage of the previous year; however over the five years 1898-1902 the total launched was 165,111t, an annual average of 33,000t! There was also a sharp fall at Armstrongs, more than a third from 1893 to 1894. They went on to build almost 250,000t in those happy five years 1898-1902, during which Palmers launched just over 200,000t. A brief return to building was made at the Scotswood SB yard during 1894, with a single vessel of 1914t, a paddle steamer for Monte Video, and the small yard of Anderson & Laverick built four small craft, one of timber before closing. Wood & Skinner seemed to be struggling with less than 2,900t in 1893. They more than doubled this a year later, but they did not quite reach 3,000t in 1895, from which they climbed steadily to reach 11,300t in 1899.[6] In 1902 output was only 6,500t and over the five good years the average was less than 9,300t compared with more than 10,000t in 1890. Not unreasonably, *Engineering* described the 21,105t launched on the Tyne in 1897 as *over the average* despite the engineering dispute. Three merchant vessels in excess of 7,000t were built on the Tyne for Liverpool owners: ss *Monarch* [7296t] by Swan Hunter and two by Palmers. Twelve vessels exceeding 6,000t built in 1898 and in all 51 above 3,000t showed the increasing size of vessels. None of the merchant ships built by Hawthorn Leslie during 1899-1901 was under 5,000t; in 1900 ss *Canadian* was 9,301t. At South Shields, Readhead's 8 vessels averaged 3,400t. With the massive warship output Armstrongs headed the Tyne's output in 1899 with 57,543t, double that of 1897. Christopher Furness[7] was among those promoting Stephensons as a limited company and he ordered some of his new ships from the yard. During 1900 Stephensons were busier than ever before. In addition to three cargo ships [each 3,871t], they also constructed 6 pontoons with a combined displacement of 20,100t. Four dredgers, designed by Lindon W Bates, were built by Armstrongs, with the machinery and dredging equipment provided by Wallsend Slipway. These vessels sailed to Queensland under their own steam. Icebreakers were built by Armstrong, usually for Russia, in 1895 ss *Saratovskaia Ledokol* and ss *Saratovskaia Pereprava*. The latter was a train ferry with a hydraulic elevator to raise railway carriages to suit the varying water levels on the Volga. Both were built in sections to enable them to pass the locks [see 11 for *Ermack* and *Sampo*]. Armstrong built ss *Scotia* in 1901, combining ice breaking with transporting railway trains across the Straits of Canso for the Canadian Government; 9 Pullman cars and an express locomotive with tender, were carried on specially strengthened ends. Although only 1,461t, ss *Scotia* was powered by 2,000ihp engines equal to 1.37hp/ton. Eight ships [51,291t] were launched from Jarrow in 1901, ranging from the battleship *HMS Russell* [14,000t] to the smallest of 3,872t.

Output from 1902 to 1903 fell much less on the Tyne than elsewhere in the north east. However, in the third quarter of 1902, work in hand stood at 156,000t and by the end of the year several yards were on three-quarter time and at others many workers were laid off. The fact that the tonnage launched by Swan Hunter's combined Wallsend and Neptune yards was only slightly above Wallsend alone a year earlier shows how serious the fall was for that Company. The combined output of these two yards in 1902, or 1898, was not exceeded until 1906. Steamers were built *on spec* in 1903 and one [#727] at least remained unsold a year later and rather surprisingly, *several stock ships* were *on hand* in May 1906. Readheads alone increased output. This South Shields yard probably does not get as much recognition as it should; in simple trade return tonnage its output, although not so varied, was greater than Hawthorn Leslie. A new *Turbinia*, a very different vessel from its famous namesake, was launched by the Hebburn yard in 1904; she was the first turbine propelled vessel in American waters and designed for passenger service on the Canadian Lakes. Each of the three propellers was powered by a Parsons Marine turbine and a speed above

---

[6] The eight vessels included: ss *Crewe* of 3,139t, two fishing craft for Grimsby and the remaining five for Norway.

[7] As *Engineering* reported in July 1899 *a very strong board*: Joseph Pease, Raylton Dixon, Furness J A Pease, Philip Watts and Henry Withy. See M W Kirby *Men of Business and Politics* he wrote: *There can be no doubt that Robert Stephenson & Co and Henry Pease & Co were sustained in part for non entrepreneurial reasons.*

22k was achieved on the trials. Northumberland SB exceeded 40,000t in 1904, which placed the yard second in output terms behind Swan Hunter. According to the *Glasgow Herald* in January 1904, at Palmers, although the outlook towards the end of the year showed *a noticeable* improvement, trade was *quiet, and the work in hand compares very indifferently with that of past years, and with the large productive capacity of Palmers establishment.* Just under 22,000t was launched at Jarrow in 1904 and even less, 16,000t, a year later.

Almost 1,100,000t were launched into the Tyne during the three years 1905-7,[8] including the tss *Mauretania*. Swan Hunter built 280,000t, Armstrongs 178000t, Northumberland SB 140,000t and remarkably Stephensons 102,000t.[9] There followed Hawthorn Leslie 82,000t, Readhead 79,000t, Palmers 72,000t, Dobson 51,000t, Tyne Iron SB 46,000t and Wood Skinner 38,000t. The sharp relative decline of Palmers is clear, seventh place in aggregate output over three *boom* years; the Jarrow yard was on a downward trend from 1899 to 1909. During 1905 a large amount of work was done on the hull of *HMS Lord Nelson*, launched in May 1904, as usual there was more work on warships after the launch than on merchant ships. This meant that the level of activity in the shipyard was not adequately shown by the tonnage launched. Other than the *Mauretania*, only two ships over 9,000t were built during 1905-7: ss *Teucer* [9,390t] by Hawthorn-Leslie in 1905 and ss *Arawa* by Swan Hunter in 1906. The Hebburn built ship had the unusual feature of having no masts. Two large pillars were built, both forward and aft, for the derricks, capable of lifting weights up to 36 tons; the forward pillars were joined by a bridge 80' above the water line. The turbine driven ss *Viking* for the Isle of Man, built by Armstrongs in 1905, was the first vessel of its kind built on the Tyne. She could carry up to 2000 passengers and special attention was given to ventilation; her guaranteed speed was 22k. Seven of Armstrong's 16 vessels were under 400t in 1905, a year that included *HMS Achilles* [13,660dt] and a Japanese battleship *Kashima* [16,383dpt]. Ships launched by Readhead and Tyne Iron SB averaged almost exactly 4,000t in 1905, Dobsons 3,100t and Wood Skinner 2,000t [excluding small craft].

General View of Northumberland SB from the river.

Northumberland SB.

Rowland Hodge purchased Edwards's yard at Howden in 1898; it had been closed for three years. Not long afterwards the Northumberland Shipbuilding Co, a private limited company, began building. Seven ships [20,330t] were launched in 1899. The first, ss *Ravenshoe* [3,592t], was built for the Cardiff coal magnate John Cory a director. Sir Christopher Furness together with the Sunderland shipowner J S Barwick

---

[8] *The Glasgow Herald* reported that in October 1905 many north east yards had 12-18 months work in hand and one firm 25 ships on the books. Orders fell off in November. A cargo steamer changed hands twice during building with a profit of £1,800 each time. Quotes in summer 1904 previous £5.63/dwt and £6.5 - £6.63 in January 1906.

[9] Annual tonnages launched from 1904 were: 8,432t, 32,750t, 39,131t, 30,144t. In 1908 less than 6,000t were launched and in 1909 the final year only 4,386t- ss *Navarra*. Stephenson's ships were usually just under 4,000t, the largest of 4,800t, *Montauk Point* and *West Point* were built in 1899. Blair supplied many engines.

acquired financial control in 1901, Furness became chairman and Hodge was Managing Director. These three in 1904 were described as *practically the sole proprietors*. The original site was not adequate for the ambitions of this new part of the Furness commercial complex and three acres were purchased to extend the site to about 11 acres with a river frontage of 800'. An additional berth for vessels up to 10-12000dwt was added and by 1904 the yard had five berths capable of constructing ships up to 650' long. New shipyard machine tools from Glasgow replaced obsolete tools and hydraulic machinery was purchased from Fielding & Platt. Virtually a completely new shipyard was created with *a complete Installation* of electrical lighting and power plant. Construction was described as by *the most progressive methods*, including the use of joggled plates [see below]. If as was claimed that *all work where possible is hydraulically rivetted on the ground before being fitted in place*, it was an early example of prefabrication. The pole derrick cranes [see illustration], however, suggest that not very large sections could have been involved. Eleven winches could lift loads of three tons at 50' per minute. The yard claimed to be the only shipbuilding company in the Kingdom *entirely supplied with energy and light from a public electrical supply company*.[10] The new Company was very proud of the electrical set-up. Apart from the hundreds of incandescent lamps there were 50 arc lamps. *One of the finest and largest of its kind in the North of England*, was the Company's description of the Steel & Iron Machine Shop in the East Yard: it was 300' x 64'. Both the Mould Loft and Joiners' Shop were located above the ground floor which housed the heavy shipyard tools, the Fitters' & Plumbers' Shops as well as a general store. An even larger Machine Shed, 320' x 80', with the frame furnace, was newly constructed in the West yard, with a Mould Loft above it. In 1901, *The Marine Engineer* commented that Northumberland SB was *likely to be amongst the first half dozen firms* [world wide] *certainly remarkable for a firm that has been but a little over two years in existence, and it seems to point to the occurrence of great things in the future*. A year later many of the yard's vessels sailed for South Africa under Government charter.

A move towards a standard ship was the very important initiative undertaken by Hodge, and a design was prepared of *a size to suit the requirements of the majority of Shipowners*. It was a spar deck steamer to carry 7,000 dwt on a moderate draft capable of 10k at sea, with the dimensions - 360' bp x 48' x 30.8' depth moulded.[11] Many such vessels were built, 26 by 1904, although the economies in construction cost cannot be discovered in the absence of surviving records. There was considerable flexibility on the arrangements beyond the hull design; for example ss *Tiberius* launched in June 1905, was described as having 'tween decks that were arranged *lofty* so that *cattle, troops or emigrants may be carried if necessary*. However, the problem of the shipyard size and design should be noted: although a vessel of 370' was seen as the Company's normal output the yard was designed to build up to 650'. It was *fully equipped for the building of large and speedy passenger steamers, floating docks, and any other type of floating craft which may be required*.

No other yard Tyne yard increased its output at the rate achieved at Howden; tonnage launched doubled in the first 6 years with 40,500t in 1904; seven years later it was

Standard 7,000 tonner ss Queen Christina

---

[10] The system was 3-phase 40 cycles at 5500 volts. A sub-station reduced the voltage to 420v and duplicate feeder cables to the generating station at Wallsend to prevent any stoppage of supplies. Their 36 motors were placed where required on ordinary concrete foundations, on wall brackets and in one case fixed to the roof.

[11] There was amble accommodation on bridge and water ballast in the cellular double bottom and an aft peak tank. Special attention was given to the loading & discharging gear with a complete set of steam winches and derricks.

66,400t. By 1908 the Company regarded itself as *somewhat restricted* because it was so hemmed in that the works could not be extended. *The Marine Engineer* rightly paid tribute to the management for maintaining employment in the depression; the annual average of 40,315t over the years 1908-10 was 86% of the good years 1905-7. Northumberland SB were fifth [in 1909] and sixth [in 1910] in the UK national table, exceeding every Tyne yard except Swan Hunter. Over the years 1911-3, output averaged 64,000t; only Armstrongs and Swan Hunter did better. At first many engines came from the nearby NEM. After 1902 most of the engines were supplied by the Scotia Works, part of Richardson Westgarth, which was also a Furness company. NEM continued to supply about two engines a year. Only 10 ships exceeded 6,000t, the first being ss *Filippo Artelli* [6,522t], launched in 1904. She was the largest cargo vessel owned in Austria and more than 11k was *easily obtained* on her trials. The largest ship built before 1914 was ss *Kangean* [7,070t] in 1911. A notable vessel was the twin screw passenger and emigrant ss *Patris* [4,650t]. The engines by Clark exceeded 5,000 ihp on trials and reached a speed of 13.8k. In output terms this yard had a remarkable first 15 years. In 1906, *The Shipbuilder* believed that the yard achieved *the largest number of steamers ever built off one model*- 46 ships. This use of the same ship's lines by Northumberland SB gave a lead that none were prepared to follow.

On the Tees and at Hartlepool.

On the Tees and at Hartlepool output in 1890 was above that of 1889 and the high level of output continued into 1891. [see diag 10.04] The combined output of the Tees & Hartlepool exceeded that of the Wear in 1893 and 1894, as it did in the three years 1898-1900. In 1895 this combination was greater than the Tyne as well the Wear; Gray took the Blue Riband for output and Ropner reached the position of third in the U K. Craggs ceased to build in 1909 and a year later Smiths Dock was building on the Tees so the number of yards stayed the same. At Hartlepool during this period the Withy and Irvine yards were consolidated into a Furness company. Over the years, 1889-1913, the Tees newcomer Ropner built 800,000t. Raylton Dixon was not far behind with 743,000t, then Richardson Duck at 634,000t and Craig Taylor at 402,000t. In their shorter period Craggs built 275,000t and at a much lower level Harkess not quite 75,000t. Gray's almost one and a half million tons was of course much greater and was equal to 60% of the output at Hartlepool. About two and a half million tons were built on the Tees compared with almost three million at Hartlepool between 1889 and 1914. Dixon headed the output on the Tees from 1886 to 1892 and in 1894. Ropner gained first place in 1893 and usually had the highest output on the Tees. An exceptions was in 1910 when Craig Taylor headed the river, when all four Tees yards were between 23,000t and 27,000t. Seven of the ten largest vessels built on the Tees were by Raylton Dixon, nearly all Dixon's ships were built on the *cantilever frame* principle. Furness Withy built the largest ships at Hartlepool. These were smaller than the largest ships on the Tyne, with only one Tees ship exceeding 8,000t and four at Hartlepool.

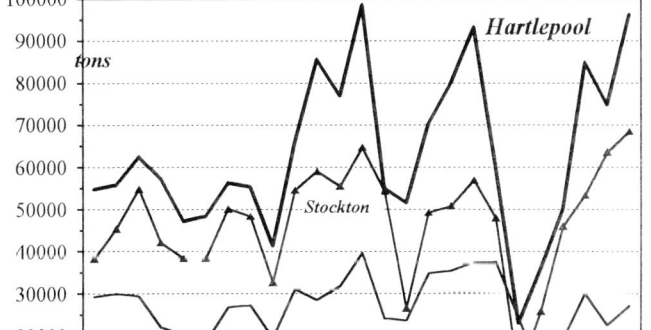

Diag 10.04

Only four firms in the whole of the UK exceeded the 40,687t launched by Raylton Dixon in 1889. Robert Ropner entered shipbuilding with a great flurry of success - the twelve vessels totalling 29,441t, which was a higher output than Laing achieved on the Wear and was almost 7,000t more than Pearse launched from the same premises in the peak year of 1883. Almost two-thirds was sold to Hartlepool owners, no doubt a tribute to this man's business acumen and the contacts he had built up by working in the area from the late 1850s. From his South Stockton yard, Richardson Duck launched 21,585t, almost half with iron hulls. Output at Craig Taylor's advanced steadily from the mere 1,300t in 1886 to 10,460t in 1889 and output increased by almost 50% in the following year [15,398t]. The smaller yard of Craggs launched five vessels, a total of 5,561t, which was 16% above the 1883 peak. These were of course relatively small vessels, the average of 1,112t being not much above half the average for the Tees. The three vessels launched by Harkess at 900t were even smaller. A comparison of the three largest yards is shown in diag 10.05. Over the years 1894-1900, Dixon's tonnage never fell below 30,000t with the high point of 36,111t in 1896. The other two yards plunged deeply in 1897, both to about half of two years earlier. In 1893 Richardson Duck increased output by nearly 20% an example of success against the trend. Between 1894 and 1895 output increased on both the Tees and at Hartlepool, in contrast to the Tyne and Wear. Together 208,000t were launched; Ropner increased output by 16,400t and Gray by 13,300t. Dixon built the largest vessel in 1896 ss *Albertville* [3,812t]. A year later this yard launched the first Tees ship of more than 5,000t ss *Montrose* [5,431t]; in 1898 they built the ss *Manchester City* [7,696t] and ten years later the largest vessel built on Tees, ss *Vasari* [10,117t]. This ship was the only one from the Tees in Kludas's *Great Passenger Ships of the World* [1858-1912] and was sold to the Soviet Union in 1935 and only left the register in 1960![12] Richardson Duck had their best period ever in 1898-1901; output never fell below 33,000t. There was a similar achievement during 1911-4 with an average of 32,200t. Raylton Dixon secured important orders in both Belgium and Portugal connected with trade with Africa, including in 1899 the twin screwed ss *Phillippeville* [4,060t] powered by engines which provided about 1 hp/ton. The yard was building *first-class passenger vessels of expensive type*. Ropner's vessels had a relatively low horsepower per gross ton on average about 0.4 hp/ton and sometimes less.

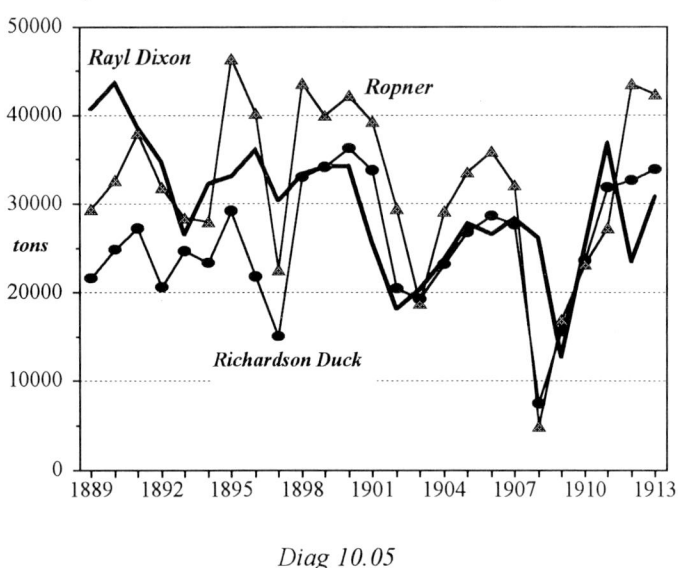

Raylton Dixon - Richardson Duck - Ropner 1889-1913

Diag 10.05

Despite a relatively good year in 1894, both Craig Taylor and Craggs were on a downward trend from 1890 to 1895-6. Both had the occasional vessel with an iron hull. More than half the output of Craig Taylor in 1892 was an iron hulled oil tanker [3,328t]. A year later they built a steel tanker ss *St Helens* [4,007t]. Craggs built a spar deck oil carrier for Odessa. There was sharp rise in the output of both Craig Taylor and Craggs from the mid-1890s as well as the considerable fluctuations. From an average of 5,500t in 1895-6, Craig Taylor exceeded 20,000t in 1900 and averaged more than 25,000t over the years 1899-1902. Over the years 1893-5, Craggs averaged less than 2,500t and reached 24,000t in 1900. Output at Harkess shrunk from 5,600t in 1890 to a mere two pontoons of 250t in 1892. It then increased to 3 vessels [2,460t]. Most of the 6,009t built by Harkess, in 1901, were for Cardiff owners and of the double-raised deck type introduced by the yard. The combined output of the three years, 1902-4, was only two-thirds of 1901. Repair work probably enabled this small yard to survive.

---

[12] *Vasari* was temporarily registered at 8,401t as shelter decker and carried 250 1st class, 130 2nd class and 200 3rd class. The *Vasari* began in Lamport & Holt's New York- La Plata service and was briefly on charter to Cunard sailing Liverpool-New York [1919-21]. Back with Lamport Holt for seven years, she was sold in 1928 and renamed *Arctic Queen*, with the passenger accommodation removed then 10,078t. In 1935 renamed *Pishchevaya Industriya*.

Hartlepool.

There were only three shipyards at West Hartlepool by 1890, and Gray on many occasions headed national output figures, then usually also the figures for leading shipbuilders in the world. The other two yards, Withy and Irvine, were before long to become part of the industrial interests of Christopher Furness; from 1898 there were effectively two shipbuilding businesses at Hartlepool. Over the years 1888-95, Grays output only once fell just below 50,000t and in 1890 exceeded 64,000t, which was the second highest in the country. The average annually was 57,000t. In 1889 Grays formed a private limited liability company.[13] There were then 9 building berths, three for ships up to 500', only 5 vessels [475'] built exceeded 450'. Not far short of 1,500,000t were constructed by Gray's yards up to the war, though as diag 10.06, shows with rough times along the way. Many orders were secured in South Wales; F C Strick, the yard's best customer, purchased 27 ships over the 18 years 1896-1913; three ships every two years would bring pleasure to any shipbuilder's heart. Pyman and Morel were each supplied with a vessel a year; Pyman 15 ships during 1889-1904 and Morel 13 ships during 1893-1909. Three other customers each purchased about 50,000t between 1890 and 1913 - London & Northern SS [16 ships], J & C Harrison [11] and Samuel [10]. Ten ships were supplied to a Falmouth shipowner R Chellew, the seventh largest customer, and nine to Cockerline at Hull.

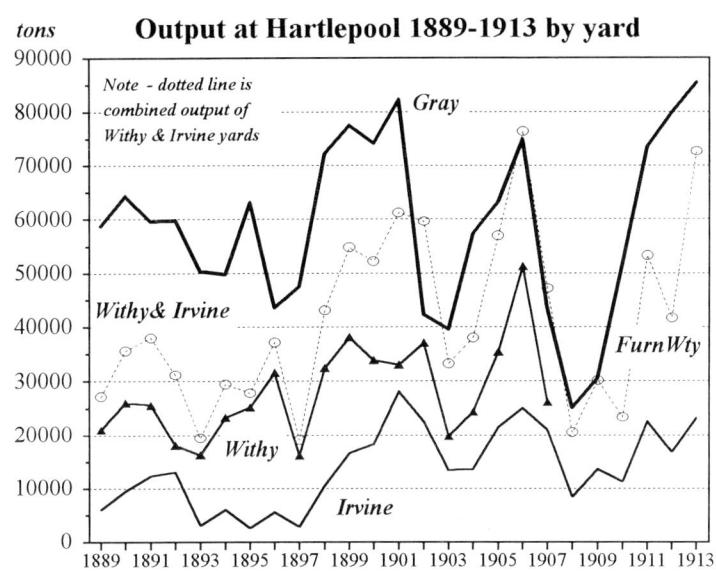

Diag 10.06

Gray usually launched 20 ships or more a year were during 1889-1899. The 27 vessels in 1890 was an average of three per berth! In 1898-9, while 150,000t were launched, alterations and extensions were underway. Completed in 1900, the addition repair facilities at the Central Dock were improved and the building of two berths, up to 500 feet, increased capacity to 11 berths. Grays launched 82,262t [27 ships] in 1901 and 75,000t [26 ships] in 1906; the annual average for 1911-3 was just under 80,000t. In between output was much less and the yard was producing below a comfortable capacity of 100,000t. Ships did get larger, with an average of about 4,000t in 1911-3 compared with about 2400t during 1890-2 [see diag 11.07]. The Scottish shipping magnate Burrell purchased four *Strath* ships from Gray and together they were almost one third of the yard's output of 49,733t in 1894. A year later Gray headed world output with 63,086t and again in 1898, second place followed in 1899 and then in 1900 for the last time Gray headed UK output. Two sister ships, built in 1890 were the first Hartlepool vessels over 4,000t, ss *Rangitira* [4,045t] carried lamb from New Zealand.[14] Five years later, the powerfully engined ss *Cambrian* [4,000ihp and 14k] was built, at 5,626t the largest by Gray to that time. There were stalls for 700 cattle on the shelter deck and *tasteful* accommodation for passengers; she traded between London and Boston. Gray's first ship above 6,000t was the twin screw ss *Toronto* [456' long] for the Wilson Line of Hull. Provision was made for the carriage of cattle as well as a grain capacity 450,000 cubic feet. When sailing light she carried 2,630t of ballast in two deep tanks, fore and aft peak tanks in addition to the double bottom. Her engines delivered 5,300 ihp, working at 200 psi under forced draught; the bunker capacity was 873t. Overall, Gray

---

[13] The other directors were: Gray's sons Matthew [died 1896], William Cresswell, the son in law G H Baines [1844-1913], George Jones [shipyard manager], T Mudd and R W Brydon became the company secretary.

[14] The second ss *Tekoa*, ordered by Furness and was sold on the stocks to the New Zealand Shipping Co. Dimensions were 376.5' x 47' x 29.3', about 6,250 dwt and triple expansion engines 1,600 ihp boilers at 160psi.

built smaller ships than Furness; only five Gray ships out of 476 exceeded 430'. A double blow was suffered by the Company in 1898, when both Sir William Gray and Thomas Mudd, their engineering chief, died. Gray's surviving son, William Cresswell [1867-1924][15] became chairman, George Jones[16] managing director, Archibald McGlashan [1855-1945] shipyard manager and Clydesider T B Borrowman took charge of the engine works. [Gray's yard layouts shown opposite]

Christopher Furness increased his investment in the Edward Withy's firm and in 1891 amalgamated the two businesses as Furness Withy & Co Ltd [nominal capital £700,000]. Withy continued as managing director of the yard, with R W Vick in charge of finance. Sister ships for the Greek company Fosgolo Mango spanned the changeover: ss *Zanni Stefanovich* [2,333t] was the last in the old company and ss *Marietta Ralli* [yard #188] the first in the new. Two ships ordered by Furness and launched in 1891, were immediately sold on and never entered his fleet. Robin Craig described this entrepreneur's tactics in the 1880s and 1890s:

> Furness ... could make most British shipbuilders jump, was not averse to using Gray's quoted prices in negotiations with Alexander Stephen ... to beat the latter down; and with the acquisition of Withy's shipbuilding yard he had an even more powerful weapon in his armoury. Furness placed many orders with both Stephen and Gray, but often contracted for tonnage only to dispose of ships to other parties before or soon after completion, generally at a profit, which cannot have endeared him to the shipbuilding community.

Three of the 6 ships launched in 1893 were for the American cattle and cargo trade; ss *Appomattox* was equipped to distil water for the cattle and had telescopic masts for use in the Manchester Ship Canal. She could travel at 12k. Output increased steadily to 31,600t in 1896, a year of important changes in the shipyard. The slipways were extended to 450', 550' and 700' and their own triple expansion engine generated electric power for 35 motors. The yard used very large shell plates, 32' long in 1893 and later up to 70' x 64" wide.

Output at Irvine's yard increased steadily until 1892, when 5 ships were launched totalling just over 13,000t [one was for Irvine's own shipping company] and then followed a sharp decline to a single vessel, ss *Sidra*, in 1893. A sequence of ten yard numbers [#80-89] were not used and over the five years 1893-7 their total output was just over 20,000t, including four small barges. Ship #100 was ss *Jacob Bright* [2848t] and after its launch the yard was closed during alterations. Furness became the principal shareholder and so from 1898 there were effectively two shipbuilding businesses at Hartlepool.[17] Robert, son of the yard's founder David Irvine, became managing director and A S Purdon, of Glasgow, was brought in as his assistant. The re-opened yard had three berths to build vessels up to 10,000 dwt and a graving dock increased in length from 315' to 380'. Henry Withy [1852-1922] retired in 1908. Ships launched at the Middleton Yard [Furness Withy] from 1909 were constructed by Irvines and the ship number sequence was shared between the two Furness yards.[18] This take over clearly opened up new market opportunities, given Furness's substantial shipping interests. The largest customers for the Irvine yard were the West Hartlepool S N Co, which Furness also took over, and other Furness companies. There were other related takeovers. Wilson, Pease & Co reopened Teesside & Iron Works [closed in 1883] but when it ran into financial difficulties Furness headed a syndicate to purchase the business. W B Peat, the

---

[15] Gray formed the South Durham Steel and Iron Co Ltd, from two Stockton iron works purchased in 1898, the Malleable Iron Co and Moor Steel Works with the West Hartlepool Steel Co. He acquired estates in Shropshire and Devon. He was made a baronet in 1917 and endowed a museum to the town to commemorate the safe return of his son from the Great War; open in Nov 1920 it was in the former home of George Pyman and later his brother's widow.

[16] Jones served his time at Richardson Duck, where he later became chief draughtsman, before becoming shipyard manager at Gray; he was for many years President of the Shipbuilders' Federation.

[17] The other directors of *Irivine's Shipbuilding & Dry Docks Co Ltd* were: Vick, Withy and S W Furness

[18] The Middleton-Furness sequence runs to #313, with 309-313 built by Irvines; the sequence at the Harbour Dock yard of Irvines ran to #172 and from #486 the numbers are divided between the two yards.

liquidator, announced on 11 July 1896 that three companies would be formed by Furness: *Westgarth English Tees Furnace Co. Ltd*; *Teesside Bridge & Engineering Co* and *Furness Westgarth*, with Tom Westgarth as managing director, which built marine engines. Four years later, in June 1900, Thomas Richardsons, the Middlesbrough engineering facility was acquired and an amalgamation with Allan's Sunderland Scotia works formed Richardson, Westgarth & Co [see chap 14]. Furness acquired shares in Palmers in 1898 and for a time in Stephenson's shipbuilding firm. Other acquisitions in 1898 were South Durham Steel & Iron Co , 1899, Weardale Steel, Coal & Coke Co Ltd and in 1900, Cargo Fleet Iron Co.

Combinations of various functions in the same ship which would now seem surprising were not unusual in the Victorian period. Two sister ships built by Furness Withy in 1897, carried in addition to 120 first class passengers, cattle and horses in the upper 'tween decks. Two sister ships in 1898 for the Furness Wilson Line, were the first to exceed 6,000t at Hartlepool: ss *Chicago* [6,438t] was designed to carry 850 head of cattle and on her trials reached 16.75k! Also 485.5' long was ss *Rapidian* [7,557t] built for Furness Withy. No vessel built at the yard exceeded 476' and only 10, were more than 430'. The Houlder[19] companies ordered ships from both the Furness yards and Gray. Houlder's ss *Everton Grange* [7,274t] could carry 130,000 cattle carcasses. This Line ordered the largest vessels built at the Middleton yard: two sister ships each 8,508t launched in 1912 [ss *Duquesa* #555 at 8,663t was not launched until 1918]. Five vessels were built for the German Company Hapag, including the ss *Frankwald* [4,060t], which carried 50 first class passengers, 44 second 50 third and 4,775 tons of cargo. Launched in 1908, she was the last ship built under the Furness-Withy label. The Middleton and Harbour Dock yards built nearly a million tons over the years 1889-1913.

Output 1901-13 on Tees & Hartlepool.
Overall after four years [1898-1901] of high output, both the Tees and Hartlepool suffered very serious falls in tonnage launched between 1901 and 1902. In the rest of the country there was a rise between those two years before a sharp fall in 1903. Output at Grays almost halved between 1901 and 1902. At Ropners the fall was almost a quarter and in 1903, Ropners went down to less than half the 1901 level. The proportionate reduction of new shipping was greater than on the Tyne and the Wear. The combined fall in output on the Tees and at Hartlepool made up just over one-third of the reduction in the whole country, which was twice what might have been expected. On both the Tees and at Hartlepool over the three years 1905-7, the average annual output was of 140,000t and 122,000t respectively; this was approximately equal to the earlier good years. At Hartlepool, Gray fell short of this by about 15% and did not exceed the output of 1901 until 1913. The combined output of the two Furness Withy yards exceeded that of Grays, which they had not previously done. Both Ropner and Richardson Duck were in a similar position to Gray; Ropner only reached the level of 1900, twelve years later and Richardson Duck never reached it. Craggs was the yard that showed an improvement, with an annual average of 27,700t over 1905-7, compared with 19,100t in the previous good years and in 1907 increased to more than 30,900t.

New developments on Teesside and the arrival of Smiths Dock Co Ltd.
There was such concern in Hartlepool that all Gray's shipbuilding would move to the new site when in 1913 Grays acquired a site at Greatham Creek on the Tees [later known as Graythorpe] to construct a new yard with a capacity of ships up to 20,000 dwt. Clearly their existing site, which required ships to pass through the dock locks, with a maximum width of 70', would cause serious problems with 20,000 dwt ships.[20] Gray's original lease at Hartlepool with the North Eastern Railway Co was due to expire in 1925; however, that the Company negotiated an extension of their lease there to 1950. The Tees site required

---

[19] E S Houlder [1828-1901] with his brothers became leading shippers in the Australian meat trade. In 1899, ten single ship companies merged in the Houlder Line Ltd, which regularly ordered ships in the north east. Greenhill wrote the company *clung to clippers well into the 1880s ...such caution should not be confused with entrepreneurial failure.*

[20] In 1960 the *Joya Mccance*, at 16,830dwt, just over 69' wide, passed through the dock!

substantial land reclamation and the Great War shelved the whole project for almost a decade [see chap 21]. A new yard was however established on the Tees. The steady demand for trawlers inspired Smith's Dock to seek an expansion of their building facilities and there was little if any scope for this on the Tyne. James Edwards, in 1905, inspected the sites on the Tees which were being offered by the Conservancy Commission at low costs. An option was taken on 16 acres at South Bank, largely mud flats with much of it only visible at low tide. Within the year it was purchased and Smith's Dock agreed to build to dry docks. Excavation began in April 1907 and six months later the coping stone of the dock was laid. Smiths last sea-going vessel launched on the Tyne was a coaster ss *Mountcharles*. On 10 December 1909 the first keel was laid at their new South Bank yard for the grab hopper barge ss *Priestman*, which was launched on 28 February 1910 and delivered on 12 April. Key personnel, including draughtsmen, moved to Teesside from the Tyne yard. Before long the first whale catcher was launched, vessels which became a Smith's Dock speciality. A total of 33 vessels [5,037t] were launched during 1910, mainly trawlers, and in the next year almost 12,000t, including 51 fishing craft and 3 tugs. The first engine from their own works was fitted in the trawler *Lord Percy*, with purchased boilers. This level of output was sustained over the next two years, in which three minesweepers were built for the Russian Navy. An interesting experiment was undertaken in 1913, when Smiths built the *Tynemouth*, powered by a combination of a diesel engine and electrical drive. This yard was an invaluable addition to the Teesside economy and sustained shipbuilding there until its final demise in 1987.

The Wear.

Engineering wrote on the Wear in 1901: *It is scarcely necessary to refer in any detail to the vessels built, because they belong to a well-known type that does not lend itself to any flights of imagination.* Cargo ships were main type of vessel built on the Wear. Although they form the bedrock of international trade, too often the cargo vessel is looked down upon. The durability of these ships is a tribute to the skills of the yards that built them. *Engineering* described the Wear output of 1889 as *unprecedentedly great*; just over a quarter of the 217,000t launched were for north east owners. More than five and half million tons were built on the Wear over the period 1889-1913. Doxford built the highest aggregate tonnage, followed by J L Thompson. From 1887 to 1899, Thompsons topped output on the Wear, with the exception of 1896, when Doxford took first place, a position the Pallion yard went on to occupy from 1902 to 1914. Only in 1900 & 1901 did Laing head the river, but less than 100t separated Laing from Doxford in 1901. Frequently the annual outputs were so close that distinguishing second and third place was not meaningful, for example in 1894, Shorts launched 25,615t and Doxfords 25,595t. Short Bros in total built slightly more than Laings. Five yards, Bartram, Blumer, Sunderland SB, Priestman and Robert Thompson, each produced between 320,000t and 340,000t over this 25 year period. Austin built 180,000t and like Crown/ Strand Slipway [82,000t] had substantial repair work. [see diag 10.07]

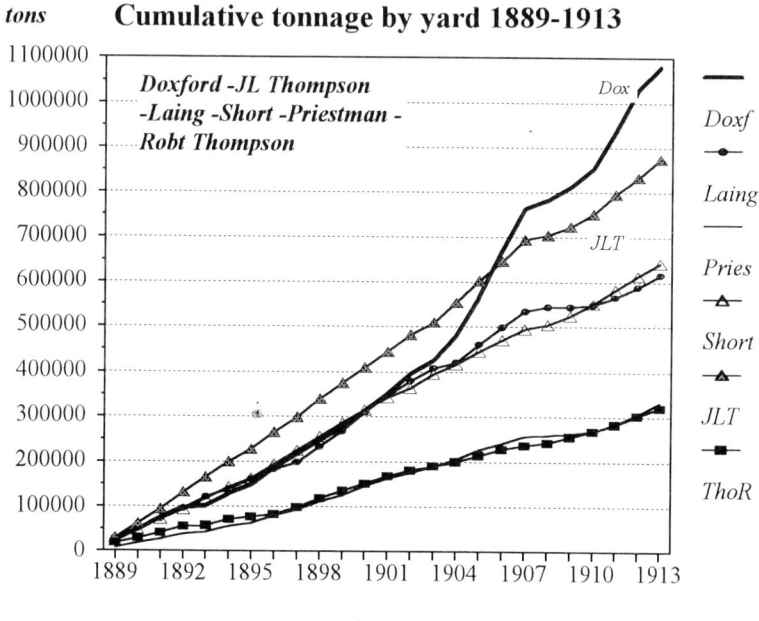

Diag 10.07

Scottish owners continued to buy vessels from the Wear and in 1889 four Sunderland ships [10,918t] were sold there, including the largest vessel ss *Mombasa* [4,662t] for British

India Steam Navigation Co, and a Glen liner of 3,100t. Six other vessels were over 3,000 tons. Sixty-three ships exceeded 2,000t in 1889 compared with 39 a earlier year. There was a noticeable increase in the locally owned tonnage in the Wear's output of 1890, 47% compared with less than 26% in 1889. All 11 vessels built by Shorts were owned at either Newcastle or Sunderland; over a five year period they had completed 14 steamers for the Prince Line owned by James Knott [1855-1934]. Doxfords built the three Wear ships which exceeded 4,000t. Changes in the tonnage launched in 1889 and 1890, when overall output fell by 11.5%, clearly showed the year on year variations between different yards,. Four yards increased their output, Pickersgill by almost 54% and Priestman by more than 30%, while the tonnage launched by Osbourne Graham fell 43% Sunderland SB fell by a third and Laings by 22%. Output on the Wear in 1891 and 1892 was almost the same as in 1890. However, in 1892, output at Sunderland SB was less than 6,000t, barely a quarter of that of 1889, and in contrast Osbourne Graham had almost doubled the output of 1890, to reach a peak not exceeded until 1907. This was a prelude to a collapse to no new tonnage in 1893! Doxfords launched the first Wear ship of more than 6,000t, ss *Samoa* [6,812t][21] for the Liverpool owners Crow Rudolf. In the bad year of 1893, Wear shipbuilders said it was *scarcely possible to make contracts pay* even with the *greatest economy*. Output fell by more than a third to 122,535t, once again with a sharp contrast between yards. Four yards increased their output, including Laings [by 11%], Shorts [9%] and Austins [14%]. A 30% increase was achieved by Sunderland SB but even that was less than half its capacity and more than half the tonnage launched was due to one ship: ss *Warrigal* [4,387t]. She was the largest ship launched on the Wear in 1893 and was for the London Australia trade, with accommodation for 16 passengers and could be used as a troopship. The ss *Warrigal* was powered by 3,500 ihp quadruple expansion engines. Doxfords had a very poor return, only two ships [4,370t], and Robert Thompson only launched only one ship ss *Arested* [1,817t] compared with 7 ships in 1892. Output on the Wear increased by 43,584t from 1893 to 1894 only to fall back again almost to the low level of 1893. The increase was mainly due to Doxford [+21,225t] Robert Thompson [+12,120t] and Priestman [+8,300t]. These three yards together added 41,645t. Laing's output fell by almost 30% [-7491t]. Blumer's output collapsed from almost 13,600t in 1892, through 8,065t to a single ship [1,645t] in 1894. Even the head of the river for ten years, J L Thompson, suffered a fall of more than 8,000t [24%] in 1895. Similar rates of fall occurred at Doxfords and Shorts and output was halved at Robert Thompsons and Priestmans. A total of 215,615t [83 ships] were launched on the Wear in 1896 to almost equal 1889. Three yards exceeded 30,000t and Doxfords built the first Wear vessel to exceed 7,500t, ss *Algoa* in 1896. Next in line of size was the 5,078t ss *Narrung* by Sunderland SB. A year earlier this yard launched only a single ship of 639t. Less than 50 days were required by Short Brothers from laying keel to launch of the ss *Truma* [1,570t]. In all they launched 12 vessels [32,321t] from their four berths, a very clear indication of their speed of construction!

The five years 1898 to 1902 must have seemed glorious years for Wear shipbuilders; the annual average was nearly 260,000t. New launchings in 1901 were more than 50,000t higher than the previous peaks. Laings and Priestman both launched ships exceeding 7,000t in 1899 and 1900 respectively. A frozen meat trade vessel of 7,332t by Laing was the largest on the river and Laings completed their 17th ship for Neptune Steam Navigation Co. Priestman's *Pontos* [7,586] was the last of 3 large boats designed specially for the Argentine cattle trade, for A C de Freitas & Co of Hamburg. These had electrically driven fans, together with special sanitary arrangements. Priestman received a telegram of congratulations from the Minister of Agriculture. An almost feverish burst of activity at Sunderland SB, in 1899, saw output leap up from just over 15,000t to more than 26,000t, including ss *Norfolk* and ss *Suffolk* each of 6,756t This activity was not sustained. In 1900 the tonnage launched was 16,388t and although in a few years this yard approached 20,000t it did not exceed it again until the 24,078t of 1912. Laings, in 1900, achieved the highest output on the Wear with 40,307t: their 8 ships averaged more than 5,000t, compared with 3,814t for the whole river. Pickersgill and Priestman each launched 20,000t for the first time; all Priestman's output was for overseas, including ss *Seville* [6,175t] for a German owner. The largest vessel built on the

---

[21] In 1894 a sister ship, ss *Maroa* made 10.5 k with 2,800 hp [0.41 hp/ton], 465' x 52' x 34.7', 9,550 dwt .

Wear to date, a 500' long beautiful passenger ship, ss *Yamuna* [10,606t] was launched by Laing for the British India Co. After her maiden voyage she sailed as *Slavonia* for Cunard. Colonel J T North, who managed ships in the nitrate trade, ordered probably the first steamers in this trade [as distinct from sailing ships]. In June 1895, Shorts launched ss *Avery Hill* [3,142t] and many more such ships followed in the *Anglo*s series.

A *very large number* were out of work in 1903 and vessels built *on spec* remained on the stocks. The Wear came back quickly from that low point. About half of the 40 berths were occupied in January 1904, with work in hand at 155,158t, but the year's output almost equalled that of 1902. Output exceeded a million tons during 1905-7, with more than 320,000t launched in 1905, and 99 ships in 1906, a total of 36,5951t. A low 85,000t was launched in 1908 and the combined output of 1909-10 just exceeded that of 1907. An annual average of 300,000t was launched during 1911-3. Bartrams were particularly successful in those years, with an annual average of 24,800t, 20% above any previous year. Laings though were progressing to better times with 27,000t in 1913. Only Laing [40,796t] and Doxford [62,928t] increased output in 1914.

J L Thompson at North Sands.

J L Thompson's first vessels exceeding 4,000t - *Port Chalmers* [4,154t] and *Yarrawonga* [4,010t] were launched in 1891. Maintaining its leading position, the North Sands yard headed the Wear's output in 1892, with 37,649t [13 ships], including ss *Gisela* [4,369t]. A year later the family yard became a limited liability company. Thompsons headed the river's output for the 10th time in 1895, with 27,262t, and in 1899 for the last time with 36,013t. Output averaged 46,000t over the years 1904-7, representing a high point not again achieved until World War II. James Marr [1854-1932][22] and Peter Phorson were appointed to the new Board. Marr became one of the leaders of the Wear shipbuilders and played an active role nationally in the Shipbuilders' Federation. At the age of 14 he started at Oswald's yard and when the yard closed he moved to Thompsons, where he quickly rose to be general manager. [The size of ships built see diag 10.09] Among the 9 ships in 1899 was ss *Isel Holme* [4,092t] the yard's 17th vessel for the Hine Brothers. All 7 ships built in 1900 were shelter deckers for the Atlantic trade. In 1888 the *Shipping World* reporting that the North Sands yard was to install *additional machinery of an improved type ... as is well known, in this respect they have for years compared more than favourably with their competitors.* The *Mechanical Engineers* visited the North Sands Yard and the Manor Quay Repair Works in 1902 and their *Journal* described the works as *being among the best kept and most up-to-date on ... the North-east Coast*:

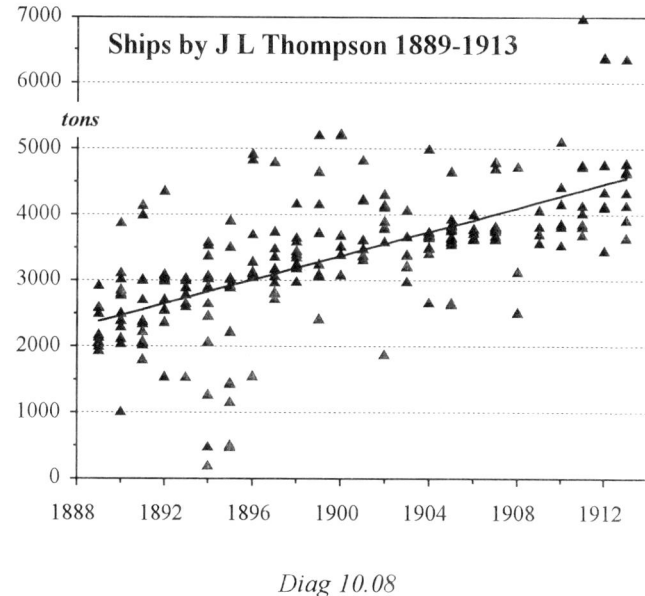

Diag 10.08

> The five building berths each had 12 powerful overhead hydraulic jib-cranes for hoisting plates, &c, the lifting capacity was 35 cwts and a radius of action of 28', with a lift of 52'. There were five hydraulic tower stacking cranes, lift up to 5 tons and radius of action 34'; these stacked plates on their edges in a

---

[22] He was born in Newcastle. His mother's father, Archibald Bell, was the manager of the Ford Paper Mill. He married Mary Abigail Ann [1855-1943] daughter of John Lynn, a paper maker, in 1876; they had two sons and a daughter. The elder son, John Lynn, died before his father. The son of his second son William Bell [b.1881] became chairman of Laings. Marr was awarded a CBE in 1918, made a baronet in 1919 and left £189,730 [gross].

circular fashion round the crane. Practically the whole of the hauling and lifting in the yard is done by mechanical power [only steel ropes were used]. All the frame and beam hoisting, &c., in connection with the framing stage was either done by hydraulic or electric winches. In the shell plating department there were four punching machines placed in close proximity to the planing, scarphing and countersinking machines the large rolls and Doxford joggling machine. Hydraulic cranes were provided so that plates were moved with a minimum amount of labour.

There was only one steam boiler in the yard, which was used for the gas furnaces and the ballast [for testing the ship's ballast tanks]. Numerous gas engines provided the power for hydraulic, electrical and compressed air equipment. The regenerative gas was made by a special plant on the premises. All the water required was obtained from an artesian well, 177' deep with a 6"bore pipe.

At the Manor Quay the latest wood-working machinery, powered by electric motors, was installed. A steam crane traversed the 690' of the quay frontage and there was a stationary masting crane with a lift of 66' and 15 tons. Sunderland Forge & Engineering Co had supplied all the electrical equipment for both works.

As this shows this progressive shipyard did not receive an outside electrical supply until after 1902.

Blyth.

Often overlooked are the shipbuilding activities at Blyth;[23] partly because the output was often included with larger neighbouring ports for statistical purposes. Output by the Blyth SB matched that of more well known yards and it carried out substantial repair activity; about 230,000t were launched at Blyth between 1880 and 1913. The formation of the Blyth Harbour Commission in 1882 was a turning point and, in October 1883, the *Shipping World* wrote that Blyth *is gradually becoming an important shipping and shipbuilding centre on the north east coast*. There were extensive improvements to the harbour. Coal shipments began an upward trend from 394,600t in 1884 and more than a million tons left the port in 1888. This was doubled by 1891 and rose to more 3,000,000 tons in 1898. Four million tons were shipped in 1908 and 4,732,000 tons in 1913. An equally rapid change could not take place in shipbuilding. The newly formed Blyth SB made *rapid progress*, the number of men was increasing *daily*. This company had taken over the shipyard of Hodgson & Soulsby[24], which was started in the early 1860s. A *large and influential meeting* of shipowners and *influential* gentlemen met in July to consider the *advisability* of forming a company to set up an iron shipyard. During the next year Hodgson & Soulsby began to build in iron and completed 4 ships and two steam hopper barges for Russia. Ships greater than 2,000t were built in 1881 and 1882. The yard number sequence was continued by the Blyth SB Co, and ss *General Napier* [1,731t] was in frame when they took over the yard. She was launched on 4 August 1883 for Cardiff owners and ss *Swansea* followed a month later. More than 10,000t over the first two years was a sound start but then the yard felt the impact of the mid-1880s depression. Output reached almost 11,000t in 1889. Like other shipbuilders the yard was subject to fluctuations [diag 10.09] and only exceeded the peak of 1889 on three occasions: 1905, 1912 and in 1913, with 14,879t. The first ship over

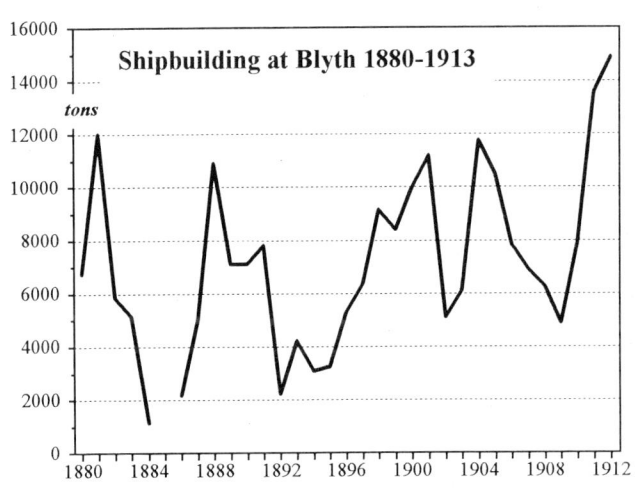

Diag 10.09

---

[23] Blyth does not even appear in the index of Duggan's *History of North East Shipbuilding*.

[24] Robert Soulsby's photograph appeared in the Journal of the Amal. Society of Shipwrights in 1903, when he was 80 years old. After his apprenticeship at Bowman & Drummond, he went to sea in 1844 and on his return became foreman shipwright in the same yard for ten years. From 1851 he had a share in the local floating dock.

3,000t was launched in 1896 and four vessels of about 4,000t in 1911-3; smaller colliers were the more usual output. There were many barges for both the Harbour Commission and the railway company, whose staithes maintained the port's coal trade. The chance fame of building *HMS Ark Royal,* the first British aircraft carrier, will be related in chap 20. There was also at Blyth the tiny Union Co-operative yard, which continued building small craft in wood for more than 30 years. After 1884 their vessels were steam powered, the last of which were launched in 1901- *Ethelbald* and *Ethelbert*, both of 85t.

Whitby.

The Crimea War brought some revival in shipbuilding at Whitby. In August 1853 two Barrick yards were operating. Henry Barrick was building a 230t vessel and repairing a collier and at the Henry & George yard a 360t vessel was under way for speculative sale. There was much more activity at Hobkirk's where two vessels were under construction for Smales. For his Lloyds visitors Hobkirk *appeared to be a Man who took an active part in his Business, he was very civil and obliging and on the whole his work appeared to be very creditable*. Although he continued until 1880, Hobkirk registered only 16 sailing vessels over 30 years, a total of 4,498t. A Lloyds visiting committee was pleased to find that Turnbull *had absolutely adopted* the late increase in the thickness of the Topside Planking, although he *did not ... so readily concur in the increased size of the Topside Timbers*. The 350t vessel nearing completion at Turnbull's yard was found to be *very* satisfactory. The future of Whitby's shipbuilding rested with the Turnbulls. An annual average barely above 1,000t during the 1850s & 1860s only too clearly confirmed the decline of shipbuilding at Whitby in the final phase of wooden hulls. A mere nine ships were 400t or more and the average was just above 250t. Bankruptcy overcame Thomas Hobkirk, whose last ship the *Merrie England* [444t] was launched in October 1862 and sold to Smales Bros. Smales Bros built the last *wooden* vessel in 1871, the composite *Monkshaven* [371t].[25] They had held a quarter share in the H & G Barrick yard from 1862.[26] In 1865 H & G Barrick built their final vessel the *Victory* [399t]. At the oldest shipyard, Henry Barrick launched his last vessel the *Revenge* [354t] in 1866. Both of these ships were sold to London owners. Four yards were operating at Whitby in 1862 but without Turnbull all shipbuilding would probably have been ended by 1871! No ocean going vessels were launched in 1869. Only Thomas Turnbull made the changeover to iron building. The first steamer built at Whitby was in 1871. The railways consumed the wood yards, and the new companies acquired most of the sites.[27]

The Turnbulls at Whitby.
In the early 1820s the clockmaker Thomas Turnbull [died 1867] began investing in small coastal vessels and became a major shipowner. When in 1840 he leased a small wood shipyard at Larpool Wood, the foundation was laid for the continuance of shipbuilding at Whitby into the 20th century. The first vessel, a 242t brig, was typical of the 24 vessels built in the 30 years until iron was adopted. His son Thomas [1819-1892][28] showed a keen interest in ship design on leaving school at 16 and was apprenticed to Henry Barrick. A new and larger yard at Whitehill was purchased by Turnbull in 1850 and Thomas jnr developed

---

[25] Laden with 657 tons of coal from Swansea to Valparaiso in Sept. 1876, the vessel caught fire. [Weatherill 191]

[26] After Smales built the *Monkshaven* the residual part of the yard was acquired by the Whitby & Robin Hood's Bay Shipbuilding and Graving Dock Co. Ltd and this Company built many fishing smacks. Later the Urban District Council built an Electric Power Station on the site [Weatherill 29]

[27] In 1845 the York & N Midland Railway purchased the former shipyard of Robert Barry [closed in 1830] and later acquired part of the yard of Henry Barrick and when he stopped building the site was completely taken over by the N E R Co. The dry dock was filled in and *entirely obliterated all signs of the shipyard*. In 1836, the Fishburn-Broderick premises became the offices of the horse drawn Whitby & Pickering Railway and the York & Midland Railway in 1845 completely cleared away the shipyard but leased the dry-dock to Turnbull [filled in 1902]. N E R acquired Hobkirk's yard and filled in the dock.

[28] see biography by Stephanie Jones in DBB v.5 pp 562-4.

the yard successfully as the wood era ended at Whitby. Output was overwhelmingly for the shipping companies of the Turnbull family: Turnbull & Co, Turnbull Bros of Cardiff and Turnbull, Scott & Co of London. These took more than 63% of the steam tonnage. In addition, Pyman bought nine ships and J Gray eight. The *Whitby Gazette* related the excitement as 5 p m on 20 June 1871 approached for the launch of the port's first iron steamer ss *Whitehall* [1,100t]: *The shores of the opposite side of the river were literally covered with spectators ... there was also an immense number of boats plying about in the vicinity.* Two tugs took her to Stockton, where Blair fitted her engines. Blair supplied the engines for almost all Turnbull's ships, 103 of the 114. It was no small achievement to build the first iron vessel in six months. The second vessel *Isaac Pennock* [1,200t] was launched on 7 December. Thomas III attended the Royal School of Naval Architecture for 4 years and worked at the Chatham Dockyard, a sound preparation for partnership with his father in 1870. The yard's annual output [1860-1902] is shown in diag 10.10; a large number of Turnbull built ships had the same overall dimensions.[29] Although the family provided a regular market this did not mitigate the usual trade fluctuations, indeed these were clearly related to the conditions of the freight market. Eight ships were launched in 1882 and 1883 but none in 1885. After the launch of ss *Mandalay* in February 1886, apart from a hopper it was 14 months before another vessel was launched. The first steel vessel ss *Dora* was constructed in 1887. Between 700 and 800 workers were employed at the high point of 1888, when almost 20,000t were launched. The next peak of just over 15,000t was in 1891 and in 1896 ss *Alton* was the first ship over 5,000t. A moment of final achievement was supplying ss *Theodore Wille* [5,700t] to Germany in 1901 but then only one more vessel was built, #145 ss *Broomfield*, launched on 10 April 1902. This completed 31 years of shipbuilding with metal hulls and ended Whitby's major contribution to the British merchant marine. There was a hope at Whitby, according to *The Glasgow Herald*, that Armstrong-Whitworth would take over Turnbull's yard. This was surely wishful thinking and the yard was dismantled in 1903.[30]

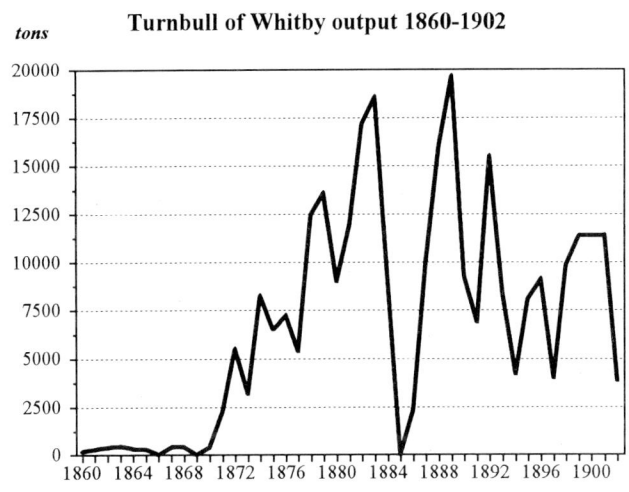

Diag 10.10

Doxfords and the Turret Ship.[31]

During 1889-1892, Doxford's maintained a relatively steady output, the lowest was 21,646t and highest 27,134t but a mere two ships [4,370t] followed in 1893. However, the yard was immediately back on track in 1894, with 25,600t. Refrigerated vessels were significant in Doxford's output. In 1889 ss *Mamari* [3,600t], for Shaw Savill Line could carry 40,000 carcasses from New Zealand and although the ss *Maori King* was larger at 3,800t, its refrigerated capacity was for only 18,000 carcasses. The three Wear ships in 1890 over 4,000t were built by Doxfords, two for Glasgow. The ss *Mary Beyts* [3,764t] was the pioneer ship of a Line for the Indian trade by Beyts, Craig & Co. The topmast could be lowered in case it used the Manchester Ship Canal. The Pallion yard had two achievements in 1892, the launch of the largest cargo

---

[29] Thirteen ships 240' x 34'; eleven of each 288' x 38' and 225' x 30' and eight 258' x 37'.

[30] Wartime conditions brought a brief hope of revival and in 1917 the yard was sold to the Albion Trust and although two concrete craft were built nothing further happened. See below re Whitby SB Co.

[31] This does not refer to the warships described as *turret ships* see D J Brown pp 41-3 and INA vols 4, 7, 9 and 10. A V Haver, who was chief draughtsman at Doxford's, sued the Company claiming that the was the actual inventor of their turret ship. Doxfords argued that a salary increase to £500 a year, a gratuity of £500 and shares valued at £500 was *ample reward*. The Board minutes make no reference to this matter, Havers was awarded £1,250 by the court. He later became a consultant and read two papers to NECIES on *Monotoria* see below

ship afloat ss *Samoa* [6,812t] and the completion of their first *turret* vessel. The two half sections show the relative sizes of the first *turret* ship and ss *Queda* of 1905. As these views show the hull swept round and then upwards to a turret like shape, without a deck in the usual way. This new design of ship remarkably transformed Doxford's fortunes with a sharp increase in their output [as diag 11.07 above showed]. For many years the turret design was very popular. In addition to 10 turret vessels, Doxfords launched in 1896 ss *Algoa* of 7,574t, the largest ship built on the Wear. In 1906 the yard launched 25 ships, in all more 106,000t.

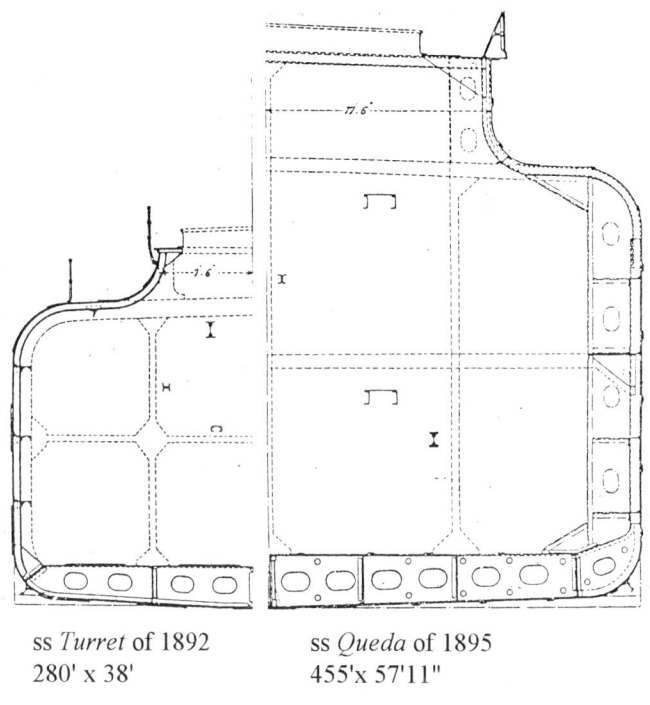

ss *Turret* of 1892
280' x 38'

ss *Queda* of 1895
455'x 57'11"

Driel, the author of a major study of tonnage, pointed out that north east shipbuilders successfully combined self-trimming vessels with *the advantage of doing away with useless corners* of the vessel and so gained in tonnage. He specifically identified the turret-deck, by Doxford, Ropner's trunk-deck and the Harroway-Dixon cantilever system. An American design, *the whale back,* was the inspiration for the Doxford's *turret deck* ship; a model and plans of such a vessel were considered by the Board on 15 December 1891. Both the freeboard and scantlings caused problems with both Lloyds and the Board of Trade. Charles Doxford reported in February 1892 his failure to get any *satisfactory settlement* during two visits to London. In December he travelled to Rotterdam, Bremen and Hamburg in his efforts to gain support for the new vessel. A Veritas Surveyor, Otto Schlick[32] was not only *favourable to the new type* but introduced Doxford to six German shipowners. Back in London Doxford found a San Francisco shipowner who also expressed an interest in *turrets*. Nonetheless back in Sunderland he reported that Lloyds' Mr Martell *objects without giving any distinct reason* but had pointed out that *plenty of types can be built under existing rules without introducing new types* and that by the time he got to Sir Digby Murray, at the Board of Trade, *Mr Martell's views on the question of Freeboard* had got there before him. W T Doxford discussed with the Scottish shipbuilder Archibald Denny, the possibility of the British Corporation classing the *turrets* and full plans of a 4,700t ship were sent to them. Even after many *turrets* were built, the argument on freeboard continued. Two representatives from each of the Board of Trade, British Corporation, Lloyds and Bureau Veritas, the assigning bodies, met on 17 July 1894. The Doxford minutes recorded the outcome:

> A scheme was drawn up & passed which was considered very unsatisfactory by British Corporation and ourselves as it meant a considerable addition to the freeboards already passed & which had proved entirely satisfactory in every case. The working out of the details for the *Turret Bell* were only finally settled three weeks ago & resulted in that vessel having a greater freeboard than her sister ship by $4^{3}/_{4}$ inches. [We] understand that the main argument used by Lloyds ... was that it would be unfair to the older types of vessels to allow the Turrets to load to such a degree as to enable them to carry a greater deadweight cargo than other vessels of corresponding size, this irrespective of strength or seagoing qualities! That this argument was used has been practically confirmed by what has passed since at interviews between your Directors and Mr Martell who still does not think it beneath the dignity of his position as the head of the scientific department of Lloyds to use his influence to prevent improvements if there should be any danger of such improvement being detrimental to the interests of owners of vessels of older and inferior types.

---

[32] Otto Schlick read many papers to the INA, was awarded their Gold Medal in 1894. His invention of a gyroscope to reduce ship rolling was patented and Swan Hunter acquired British and American rights. See below.

The Board of Trade agreed that the matter could be raised again in two years. To propagate their intentions, Doxfords passed information to Goodall, of Trinity House, for his paper on *Whaleback Steamers* given to the INA meeting in April 1892. Meanwhile, Charles secured a preliminary agreement with Runciman for a 4,700t *turret deck* vessel but his brother after discussions with more than half a dozen companies in London failed to secure any definite results. Petersen, Tate of Newcastle agreed to purchase a 3,200t turret steamer for £22,500 to be classed by Bureau Veritas and the British Corporation. Perhaps strangely, on 29 December 1892 Doxfords agreed to build an American Whaleback steamer to McDougall's design for £24,000 cash!

On 28 January 1893 ss *Turret* sailed from Sunderland, to be loaded with a full cargo of patent fuel and railway plant at Cardiff. Capt. Petersen commanded the vessel to the Azores and was satisfied with *the thoroughly good sea qualities of the vessel*.[33] The Board minutes noted that *all connected with the* [Turret] *vessel having satisfied themselves that this type of vessel is superior to any other type afloat for almost all cargo trades*. Petersen featured prominently in the early days of the turret ship and during visits to Pallion in March 1893 it was agreed to pay him a commission on orders secured of 1s per net ton. Orders for *turrets*, at £25,500 and £24,250, were reported in October and in January 1894 Angier Bros ordered four *turrets* at £33,250 each, to carry 5,000 tons. The Turret SS Co Ltd was formed to stimulate orders.[34] Many visitors came to Pallion to see the new ships under construction. For example, in January 1893, two from Dundee and various shipbuilders were interested in licences to build *turrets*. Furness was offered building rights on a royalty of 5s/dwt with a rebate of 50% on first vessel and 33.33% thereafter. Swan Hunter was allowed a rebate of 20% and on joint account with Doxfords they built *turret* #13, *Forest Brook*, launched in August 1895.[35] Two other *turrets* were built at Wallsend: ss *Mayo*, with a Doxford engine and ss *Mountain Ash*, later *Norham*, which was finally sold for £12,500 cash, plus ss *Ovingham* valued at £8,500. After inspecting ss *Turret Crown* in March 1895, Ernst H Craggs expressed an interest in the same terms as Swan Hunter. Vickers of Barrow had a licence to build *turrets* on a royalty of 7.5s/gt but Clan vessels were exempt from this.[36] The only *turrets* built at Barrow were for the Clan Line. Hawthorn Leslie launched a *turret* vessel, ss *Heathdene*, [renamed *Forest Dale*] in 1898. After seeing the *Turret Bell*, Henry Swan expressed the opinion that turrets were suitable for the bulk oil trade. Doxfords agreed to *assist him in preparing plans for a small vessel for the Caspian oil trade* and Swan was to seek orders. A royalty of 5s per ton dwt and bunkers was proposed and Doxfords agreed to send any inquiries or orders from the Caspian area to Armstrong Mitchell. To introduce the *turret* vessel to the coal trades Doxfords offered to build for the Broomhill Coal Co a vessel to carry 1,070t at net cost price - £10,000. Many of these inquiries never came to fruition. A notable international licensee was Krupp, the great German firm, and turret ship #126 ss *Narvik* was built under this agreement of February 1904. A special expensively bound book was produced for the first 100 turret ships, a feature of advertising at that time.

Doxfords supplied four more *turret* vessels to the Clan Line in 1899, the *turret* ship almost became a symbol of the Clan Line, Pallion delivered 30 of these ships. Speed of unloading was a matter for regular attention, especially for ore carriers and ss *Skandia* [7,500dwt] was therefore fitted with 10 masts and 18 derricks. Launched in 1903 the ore carrier *Grangesburg* [turret #84] carried 10,300t, with gear to discharge the cargo in 30 hours, 14 derrick poles, 24 derricks, 12 double ended winches and 12 hatches to the 24 holds. In June 1904, *Whateley Hall*, the 100th turret, was the first from the new section of their

---

[33] In April 1893 models and ship's lines were discussed with Frank Caws presumably as a result of tests in his tank

[34] In April Doxfords *contemplated* increasing the capital to £250,000. A syndicate was formed to take debentures of the Turret SS Co at 6½%, Lambton agreed to lend the syndicate about £31,000 at 5% for 3 years and 4½% for six years, this sum to be reduced by £4,000/ year. This helped to reduce the problems *of the financing ... the Turret SS Coy. paper* [bills of exchange].

[35] The agreed cost for the hull was £16,250, with £1,000 builder's margin and a royalty £1,000 plus the cost of machinery. The ship was sold for £26,000.

[36] Sir Charles Cayzer was elected Conservative MP for Barrow in 1892 and ordered 6 Clan vessels there.

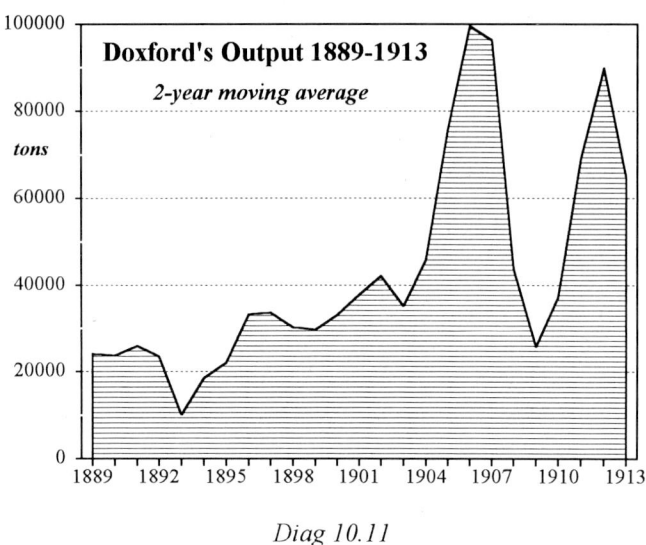

Diag 10.11

yard. Effectively; Doxford had doubled production capacity [see diag 10.11]. Headlines such as *The Rush for Turrets* appeared. Twenty *turret* vessels [86,632t] from Pallion, in 1905, placed Doxfords at the top of the Britain's output; five were for Sweden. The largest single deck ships then afloat, *Queda* [7,650t], *Querimba* and *Quiloa* for British India SS were also built in 1905. More than 100,000t was launched in 1906. As Doxford came out of the 1908-10 depression their *turrets* faced grave difficulties. Two vessels had capsized and a Board of Trade Inquiry followed. New loading instructions were issued and only one of the 10 ships built in 1910 was a *turret*. The Glasgow Herald commented that this *shows that there is little necessity for retaining any longer designs for which the need has passed away*. Only four years earlier it had written that Doxford's output proved that the *turret* steamer had *taken a very definite place in the shipping trade of the world*. Despite this setback Doxfords continued to head the output by Wear shipbuilders up to the Great War.

Depression - 1908-1910.

Nationally the tonnage under construction began falling in the summer of 1906 and new starts were reduced by more than half between the first quarter of 1907 and that of 1908. In January 1907, *Engineering* wrote of *a closing of shipowners' order-books*, when shipbuilders were quoting lower prices, *willing to keep their works going by dispensing with half the establishment charges and all profit*, despite an increase in costs of up to 10%. From June 1907 in shipbuilding, unemployment began to move steeply upwards; the industry was once again on the road to a grave depression [see diag 10.12 below]. New tonnage in 1908 was not much more than half that of two years earlier and this severe depression continued for a further two years. In the UK the tonnage of merchant ships and foreign warships averaged 644,000 net over the period 1908-10, compared with 1,160,000 net in 1906. The collapse in the north east was more severe than on the Clyde. Output in 1907 fell by a sixth in the region as a whole and in 1908 tonnage launched was less than 38% of 1906, while two years later output was still only 56% of the peak. On the Wear for every 4 tons launched in 1906 only one was launched in 1908. From February 1908 to March 1910, unemployment in shipbuilding on the Tyne was never below 19% and exceeded 30% in six monthly returns; over that same period on the Wear it was below 30% in only three months and exceeded 50% over a four month period. Unemployment on the Tees fell roughly between that on the Wear and the Tyne; for two months more than half the craftsmen were out of work. Laings faced extinction and

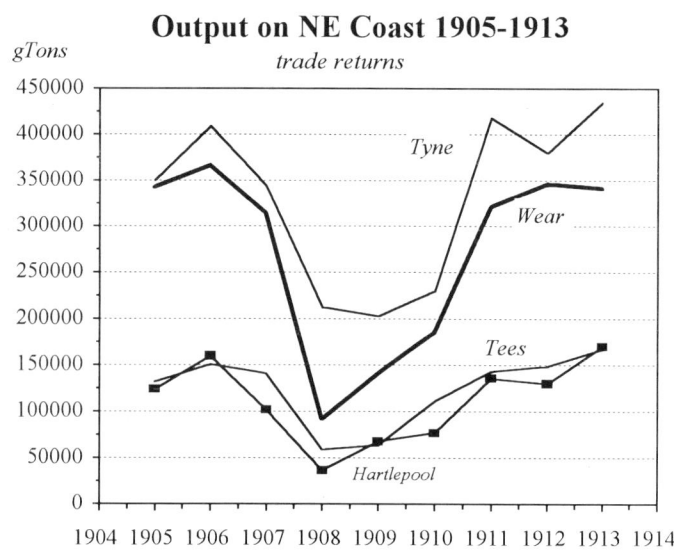

Diag 10.12

Craggs ceased to function. New shipbuilding at Stephenson's Hebburn yard was ended, after launching less than 6,000t in 1908 and a single vessel in 1909. Palmers took over the site.

Over the years, 1908-10, Tyne output averaged 215,000t, compared with 368,000t over the period 1905-7. The proportion of output for individual yards in the three depressed years compared with 1905-7 was -
        Dobson 47%; Armstrong 50%; Palmer 54%; Readhead 55%; Wood & Skinner 60%;
        Hawthorn Leslie and Tyne Iron SB 66%; Swan Hunter 74% and Northumberland SB 86%.
Swan Hunter [29%] and Armstrongs [24%] together accounted for more than half the Tyne's output in 1908. Oil tankers formed the backbone of the Tyne's work in that year and exceeded 71,000t; Armstrongs built 6 tankers, Swan Hunter - 3, Tyne Iron - 2 and Palmers one, the largest, *Hesperus* [6,389t]. Five of these tankers were under 5,000t. Well established customer connections helped Swan Hunter; the modest 2,300t *Merganser* was the 20th ship for the Cork SS Co, and ss *Fangtrum* the 27th by Neptune for the Hansa Co of Bremen. Over the previous 13 years these two Companies together ordered about 3 ships a year. Three South American warships accounted for 42% of Armstrong's output [engines by Vickers of Barrow]. Destroyers and torpedo boats were built at Palmers and Hawthorn Leslie. Remarkably, Dobsons, following a very sharp drop from 24,811t in 1906 to just over 10,000t in 1907, increased their tonnage to 17,000t in 1908. An almost total collapse followed in 1909, with a single vessel of 1,387t. As many as 59 vessels built on the Tyne were under 500t; the average of Wood & Skinner's 8 ships was only 604t. Smith's Dock, with 6,151t, reached place 45 of the 144 shipyards listed nationally; their 31 vessels were mainly trawlers.

While output in the region increased modestly in 1909, it fell marginally on the Tyne.[37] Serious falls in launches at Armstrongs and Palmers were the main cause of this; other yards improved. Although the Elswick yard remained reasonably active, the Low Walker yard was very slack and less than 16,000t was launched. Launches at Jarrow sank to the almost unbelievably low point of 1,630dpt, and Palmers fell to 79th place in national rank order. More significant than the new launch figure was the construction work on the battleship *HMS Hercules* [20,000t]. Swan Hunter advanced significantly and almost reached the 1907 output with 23 ships. Swans were second behind Workman Clark in national output; their largest ship was ss *Tortuna* [8,157t], an Atlantic passenger and emigrant steamer. Northumberland SB with 48,025t, almost equalled their output of 1907 and at fifth reached their highest place in the national table! At the beginning of 1910 all the berths were occupied. A fifty percent increase by Readheads only took the yard to half the level of 1906. Two of their four ships were for their reliable customer Hain. Armstrong's output improved slightly in 1910 with 5 merchant vessel from the Walker yard, but a total under 22,000t was only a small fraction of the available capacity. In the 1910 trade returns for shipbuilding the North East held the 2nd [Swan-Hunter], 4th [Gray], 6th [Northumberland SB] and 7th [Doxford] places among British yards behind the leaders Harland & Wolff. An American company the Great Lakes Engineering Works, with 58,908t held the place above Northumberland SB.

Probably no district has suffered more than the Wear *from the prevailing depression* wrote *The Shipbuilder*. Over the three depressed years the Wear launched only just over 2 tons for every 5 in the good years. Clearly Laing's problems, with no ships in 1908, seriously affected total output on the Wear. In 1907 with 91,254t Doxfords were top of the UK national output table. *Engineering* pointed to Doxfords as *the most striking case of diminished work on hand*, citing, after 22 ships launched in 1907,they had only three ships on the stocks in January 1908. Quarterly wages paid at Doxfords fell from from more than £13,000 in 1907 to not much more than £3,000 in 1908. The total output at Pallion for 1908-10 was less than 1907. J L Thompson only launched three ships in 1908, a mere 10,521t, which was the lowest for 24 years. Robert Thompson and Crown maintained the highest proportion relative to their good years, respectively 83% and 91%. For the other yards the ratios were: Short 72%; Sunderland SB 68%; Osbourne

---

[37] The rate of unemployment among trade unionists in shipbuilding began a downward trend in the autumn of 1909 but a year later stopped falling at about 15% on the Wear, 12% on the Tyne and 8% on the Tees! See chap 13.

Graham 59%; Austin 54%; Bartram 47%; Blumer 36%; Priestman 24%.

Given the disastrous level of 1908 it was hardly surprising that ten of the twelve yards increased output in 1909. Doxford headed the output with just above 28,000t and Shorts and J L Thompson were either side of 20,000t. Not a single vessel above 5,000t was launched into the Wear, evidence of the smaller craft ordered in a depression. The Wear's average at 2,485t was only slightly larger than 20 years earlier. In 1910, almost a quarter of the output was due to Doxford's; the 41,575t launched was less than half the yard's capacity but 46% above the previous year. The other yards experienced mixed fortunes. Output fell in five cases and an equal number improved. Doubling output at Priestman's still left it under 6,000t and a similar increase at Pickersgill only took the yard just over 10,000t. Shorts at 25,820t was approaching a usual level of output but J L Thompson with 27,251t was hardly at two-thirds of normal capacity.

Output on the Tees was effected by the closure of Craggs, and over the depressed years tonnage launched was just over half that of the good years. Cragg's yard was in financial difficulties in 1907, when it was necessary for Summers Hunter, of NEM, to enter discussions to avoid the issuing of a writ for outstanding debt. Despite these very considerable financial difficulties Craggs pursued an innovative policy and were constructing the first vessel based upon Isherwood's longitudinal *bracketless* construction, a tanker ss *Paul Paix* [see below]. She was launched in 1908 and there followed the cargo vessel *Gascony* [4,200t]: alas, for Craggs that was the end. Despite being owned by a ship owning family Ropners only built 44% of the level of the good years, in 1908 only ss *Leeds City* [4,298t] apart from barges. Although Richardson Duck had two ships in that year, over the years 1908-10 it was only at 56% of the previous three years. Craig Taylor had poor years in 1908-9 but was back to capacity in 1910 and so managed over the three years to reach two-thirds of 1905-7. Only 1909 was a bad year for Raylton Dixon, and even then they launched 12,661t. Two sister ships of 6,250t, ss *Berwindmoor* and ss *Berwindvale*, built in 1910 were believed to be the two biggest colliers ever built. Overall Dixon's output was 77% of the period 1905-7. Only the small yard of Harkess sustained its output through the depressed years. At Hartlepool Gray managed better than the Furness yards, with launches in 1908-10 at about 59% of 1905-7. Unlike most yards, however, Gray's output in 1905-7 was significantly below the yard's best performances. The average of 1905-7 was 60,501t, whereas 82,262t were launched in 1901 and for 3 years the tonnage was never below 72,000t. The combined output of the Furness yards was less than 62,000t during 1908-10, whereas in 1901 alone these yards launched 63,000t.

The voluntary liquidation of Laings.

Sunderland celebrated the centenary of Laings shipbuilders in 1893, and James Laing's 70th birthday. He had also completed 50 years in charge of the shipyard.[38] More than 500 ships and half a million tons had been constructed by this great firm. Officials and foremen travelled by special train to Etal Manor, Cornhill on Tweed for a day of celebration on 7 August. Six weeks later at the Victoria Hall a portrait and an illuminated address were presented to Laing. A Drinking Fountain, with a woman representing *Temperance - In memory of Philip Laing - Shipbuilder - 1793-1843 - by his son, on the Centenary of his Firm Deptford Yard* was given to the town. Five years later on 3 October 1898 a Limited Co [£300,000 capital] was established and Laing sold the shipyard and foundry to the new company for £127,429. All the directors were Laings: Sir James, Arthur, Hugh and Bryan. Many fine vessels were built by the Deptford yard in those hundred years, including passenger ships, such as ss *Ville De Havre* [3,100t] of 1889, as well as so many cargo ships. The yard's first ship over 5,000t, ss *Obra* [5,456 t] was launched in 1895, five years later ss *Tomoana* was 7,332t.

---

[38] On 1 Nov 1883, in the *Shipping World,* James Laing questioned the claim that Scott of Greenock was the oldest shipbuilding firm in the UK. He asked for the founding date and wrote *I think I can tell you a "senior".* Walker gives the starting date for Scott as 1711.

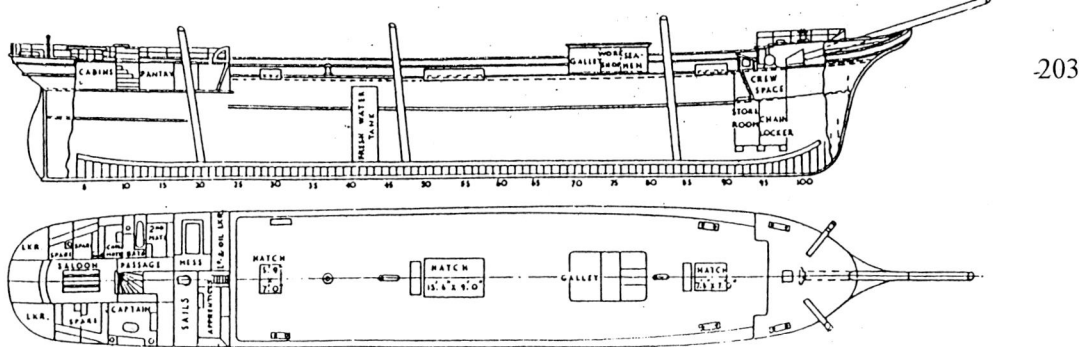

Bartram's sailing ship Castle Holm of 1875.

Grim years followed the death of Sir James Laing in 1901; output fell by almost 7,000t between 1901 and 1902 and by almost another 5,000t in the next year.[39] Only three ships were launched in 1904, which did not even reach 14,000t, at a yard whose output had been 40,000t in 1900. One of these was ss *Bermudian* [5,817t], an Australian liner, described as *one of the finest examples of naval architecture yet produced on the Wear.* She reached 18.25k on her 4 hour trial. From Laings there was a very mixed output in 1905, a large repair ship for the Admiralty, six barges for Buenos Ayres, a steamer for each of the Argentine, Melbourne and Rotterdam, the remaining three for British owners. An annual average of almost 38,000t, in 1905-7, was as good as the yard had ever achieved in a three year period, but it was not profitable business. There was a nett loss of about £40,000 on the conversion in 1905 of *Indrabarha* into the Navy Workshop, *HMS Cyclops* [14,660t], and serious financial problems in regard to three Italian emigrant ships. Lloyd Sabaudo Co signed a contract for three emigrant ships on the basis of one-third cash and two-thirds after satisfactory trials, partly cash and partly in shares on delivery to Genoa. The invoice worked out as £360,000 with extras, but the outstanding amount was not paid as the Italian owners claimed more in damages for alleged non-fulfilment of contract.[40] Trials in Italian Courts were subject to many delays. Hugh Laing went to America with papers for the arrest of one ship, which was carried out when it berthed on the Canadian side of the river; the owners had to pay for release. Laings suffered a loss of over £100,000. Barclays Bank secured the withdrawal of a claim for £410,250 by the Federal Government of Australia for non-fulfilment of contract, this would surely have been an insurmountable blow. The claim related to a contract by Laings, in July 1906, to carry mails between Australia and the UK. However, a syndicate formed to raise the capital to build the vessels was unsuccessful. Financial losses of about £60,000 by the Laing SS Co added to the shipyard's difficulties. The depression caused losses in the value of shares held by Hugh and Bryan Laing, who handed over their private property to Barclay's Bank as securities to secure advances to the Company.

Trading by Laing ceased on the voluntary liquidation of the main Limited Company in 1908. In addition to disputed claims, £273,726 was owed to unsecured creditors. H S Squance, as liquidator, dispensed with the services of H Trevisa Clarke, Bryan Laing and John H Clarke, while Hugh Laing acted as manager to complete the two oil tankers in hand, and the Brass Foundry stayed open to fulfil contracts. A re-organisation and re-opening was agreed with shareholders on 29 April 1909. The creditors were given 10s in £ in ordinary shares in a reformed Sir James Laing & Sons Ltd, and the new directors were J H H Clark of George Clark [left Board 1913]; James Marr [chairman Dec 1913] of Sunderland Forge and Hugh Laing. After court delays, the yard restarted in February 1910 on ss *Umona* a passenger and cargo steamer for Bullard & King. As steel plates and sections went down the road to the yard, the workmen cheered; they were only too eager to work after nearly two years of idleness. Their efforts resulted in *remarkably low labour costs on this ship.* No one thought it an ill omen when the first attempt to launch failed and after the

---

[39] A decision in 1903, by the Laing SS Co to trade with East African ports, was from a shipbuilding point of view unwise; it *offended the British India Co.*

[40] Laings argued that coal consumption guarantees were not met because of poor Italian coal; the owners contended the cost of an extra 0.5 lbs/ihphr amounted to £100,000 over 20 years. There was also the loss of emigrant beds. Laings contended that the Italian Emigration authorities regulations for doubled staircases to both tween decks reduced the space for 60 beds; loss for this was put at £90,000, with other items the total was over £240,000.

ways were altered all went *well. The Shipbuilder* welcomed back the re-constructed Sir James Laing & Sons as *again well to the fore, measuring their activities not so much by tonnage produced as by the high class of the single vessels launched.* From happier times, Laings may offer an introduction to a brief review of yard improvements.

Yard Improvements.

Many yards carried out substantial improvements to their production facilities in the 1890s and the early years of the 20th century. When after two years at NEM, Hugh Laing returned in 1894 to the Deptford yard he began putting improvements in hand; old machines were scrapped due to the increased size of ship plate and the use of electric power was considered.[41] The amount of loft work was increased and hydraulic rivetting extended. The adjacent old Bottle Works had already been acquired[42] and on 6 October 1896 the first keel was laid on one of the two 500' berths in the *East Yard*. Further improvements included -

> A new *Platers Shed* equipped with bending rolls to take plates 32' long and the *very small Plumbers Shop* was replaced. Steam driven *travelling* cranes were introduced and the necessary wide gauge rails, sleepers and turn tables were fitted throughout the yard; this enabled the transport of the heavier items from machine shed to the hydraulic rivetting machines, and then on to the building berths. Narrow gauge *tram lines*, with steel bogies replaced the older wood bogies, with large flat iron wheels, which were pulled through mud. On the building berths Loco Cranes were employed and *Electric Winches* for 3 ton lifts replaced older steam winches and donkey boiler. Again because of the increased weight of plates, new *steel derricks* and jibs, with 4 or 6 to a berth were set up. These were strongly held in position by heavy wire ropes with necessary concrete stays in the ground. *Fitting Out Quay* with a travelling elecectric crane 7.5 ton with a 40' radius.

Many changes were also made between 1895 and 1900 in the *Middle Yard* [or Low Yard], where the demolition of the old fitting out quay enabled a single berth [up to 420'] to replace the two unsatisfactory berths.[43] Access to the public ferry, through Ferry Road, created problems to modifying the *High Yard*, where the two berths launched down river, and in order to launch larger ships it was decided rearrange the ground to launch in the up river direction. Suitable arrangements were made in regard to the ferry; old buildings were cleared and in the early years of this century the new arrangements carried out. The expenditure involved over a ten year period was over £70,000 on new buildings and £19,000 on yard and foundry Plant.

As the building of *turrets* got underway Doxfords pioneered an important advance in construction technique, joggle plating, in which the plate at the edges was shaped to overlap adjacent plates and so enable rivetting without packing pieces.[44] A machine to shape plates in this way, first patented by Bell & Rockcliffe, enabled the wider use of this technique. This new system eliminated packing pieces between the frames and outside plating and rivets could be shorter. The weight saving could amount to 37.85 tons on a 2,700t ship and there was also some saving in the cement required. *An entirely new yard is being prepared* for Doxfords, wrote the *Glasgow Herald* in early 1902. Major re-organisation was taking place, including management responsibilities. In July 1901 tenders for work on the yard, totalling £43,665, were accepted. Most of the Wear yards were re-arranged and often extended. About 1896 both Austins and Bartrams carried out such changes, usually with additions to plant. Similar changes took place on the Tees.

---

[41] In a letter of 29 Apl 1896, Doxford commented on Laings - *I can hardly fancy him following our lead - but perhaps Arthur and Clarke together are getting more of their own way 510'* [length of ship] *will be a caution for them to build and launch.*

[42] Laing's son-in-law Featherstone was a director of Kirk & Co, who owned the site.

[43] These were at slight angles towards Cornhill Dock, so that the limited launching space restricted the size of ship very considerably. The new berth could launch up river towards the east end of Robert Thompson's yard. The old Boiler Houses were demolished when electric power was introduced. Shaw's Hill, adjoining Ayres Road, was excavated to provide a new Blacksmiths Shop. In the space of the old shop a Mould Loft of *ample dimensions at that time* was built, and beneath this was the angle-iron smiths fires, beam bending, and angle punching machines.

[44] These plates eliminated liner pieces, which also meant shorter rivets and saved some weight.

Taking advantage of the lull in trade in 1903, Ropner was reported as *making further improvements and developments* in order to build the largest cargo steamers *likely to be required in the future*. However, they underestimated how big vessels would become; his slipways were 450' long. In 1902 the *Glasgow Herald* noted that as a result of the extensions in the previous two years Palmers, Hawthorn-Leslie, Armstrong and Wigham Richardson had 600' berths. In the 1880s Wigham Richardson had purchased an Otto gas-engine to drive their heavy machine tools and it had given *every satisfaction*; it indicated 40hp. The management were surprised that the cost was *substantially* less than the cost of *coal, water and attendance* for *a high-pressure factory engine*. Many shipyards, such as J L Thompsons preferred gas engines to steam engines for driving machinery in the yard, and as others used them in their engineering works. In 1896 this Company ordered two additional gas engines with total of 250bhp.

For more than 30 years the sky line of Jarrow was dominated by the overhead cableway at Palmer's shipyard. A paper on methods of handling materials in American shipyards to the INA in 1902 was the inspiration for the building of a cableway, as the shipyard manager J L Twaddell[45] unhesitatingly admitted. The system was first installed over a battleship berth and then added to other berths. He rejected the argument of some shipbuilders, perhaps most, that a sufficient number of derricks *meet the requirements of construction very well*. Palmers decided to have a series of wire cables 100' above the ground, between supports 500' apart, and a load of 3 tons was to move transversely in addition to the weight of the trolley. Five firms were invited to submit detailed designs and estimates in the autumn of 1904; three firms condemned the idea as impracticable and two of these saw Twaddell and argued for a permanent steel structure with cranes.

Overhead cableways at Palmers at Jarrow

The contract was given to J M Henderson of Aberdeen. The cableway erected in 1906 covered a rectangle 700' x 150', which was two berths with 4 cableways. It was an impressive site as the longitudinal travel was designed for up to 600 feet per minute [normally 400 feet was used], transverse travel was 25 feet per minute and while a 1 ton load was hoisted at 150 feet per minute, those of 3 tons were at 100 feet per minute. A small but interesting point, the estimated cost of painting the structure annually was about £45 [approximately a labourer's pay for a year]. Electrical power enabled the Jarrow system to work.

Electricity in works and shipyard.

As with the rest of the community electricity was first employed by shipyards and engine works to provide light. *The Shields Gazette* on 23 January 1879 reported: *Last night the electric light was in operation for the first time in South Shields, at ... Edwards' High Dock ... A bright light was thrown over the whole ground and a pin might be discerned on the ground with the same ease as if it had been daylight*. Swan Hunters used electric light from 1883; there were four 2,000 candlepower arc lamps in the machine shed and two in the open on poles 60' high. By then many shipyards were using such lighting. Tyneside was one

---

[45] James Lindsay Twaddell [1857-1932] served his time in the Glasgow. He reached the post of chief draughtsman on the Clyde before going to Palmers as assistant works manager [1890-3]. After a further period in Scotland, he returned as works manager at Jarrow and became general shipyard manager in 1899.

of the greatest pioneering areas in electrical engineering and power supply. DISCo was a company in which Charles Parsons had a major interest. The NESCo network of Merz[46], was described by one historian of the industry, as *the biggest integrated power system in Europe* in about 1911, and that contemporaries *referred to it in awed tones as the harbinger of future development*. From a local lighting company serving an area of 16 square miles in 1900 it expanded by 1914, with its associate companies, to cover 1,400 square miles with a system of 3-phase 45 Hz AC supply. By then electrical power was widely used in shipyards. NESCo built two new power stations, at Neptune Bank, 2,100 kW, opened in June 1901, and then at Carville *a land mark in the evolution of power station design* in 1904. In opening the Neptune plant, Lord Kelvin said: *We have seen at work what many have not seen before - a system realised in which a central system ... delivers electricity to consumers at great distances ... This is of interest to the whole civilised world.*

A claim that Swan Hunter *installed electrical power for driving machines* in 1893, by Pollard, certainly should not be understood to mean that this applied to all their plant or even extensively throughout the yard. A description of Swan Hunter's works in October 1900 stated: *A large number of machines in various parts of the yards are driven by electrical power, the current being generated in a power house situated in a central position. The works are also exceptionally well lighted by arc and incandescent lamps.* For many years those who wished to use electrical power needed to generate their own supply. However, NESCo and DISCo offered a remedy to that situation. The North East Coast Institution [NECIES] included many electrical engineers who were pioneers of the new technology. This enabled local shipbuilders and marine engine manufacturers to be conversant with the new opportunities offered. In October 1894 their President Richardson had urged the use of electrical power, pointing particularly to the loss from condensation in *long range of steam pipes* usually found in shipyards. Thompson said that his firm were *just contemplating a step* in that direction. Someone would have been expected to mention an extensive use of electrical power at Swan Hunter; 16 people contributed to the discussion over two evenings. An electrical engineer, Selby Bigge, made the very bold claim that the whole of the power plant could be replaced within a works and *the cost would be paid for by the saving of fuel, water, and other expenses in under four years*. Bigge assured a doubting Price of Jarrow that this included the *cost of fitting motors to the machines ... in position*. Newitt, an electrical engineer from Elswick, noted the limitations, particularly in the necessary speed reducing gear. If a machine was more than 100 yards from its steam engine *the motor* had advantages. Experience with drilling in a shipyard illustrated some of the early problems. The motor was *continuously moved*; two men were required to lift it about and the delay made the work *equal to that of two good drillers*. It was not *a great success*. There was also the need for supervision if failures were to be avoided.[47]

In October 1900 Withy claimed that the Middleton shipyard was the first in the world to be *wholly worked by electricity*. The plant had been running for over 5 years, and in 1896-7 the cost of power production, attendance and repairs was 6.4d per £ of wages paid. [about 1% of turnover; cost per BoT unit 0.9d]. Electric driving was *a large factor* in enabling the doubling of the wage bill and the number of machines but with the cost of superintendence *not relatively increased*. At one time the works used 5 boilers, 3 steam engines, 5 winches and 2 gas engines, instead 2 main boilers and 2 main triple expansion engines were coupled directly or connected by belts to dynamos. A comparison of the cost of producing power with wages paid for consecutive 5-year periods showed a saving of 47% due to electric driving. A lively

---

[46] Charles H Merz [1874-1940] was born at Gateshead the son of J H Merz [1840-1922] and Alice Mary [nee Richardson], sister of the shipbuilder. He left the Newcastle College of Science before completing his course and became an apprentice at the Pandon Dene Power station. Further details of his considerable engineering achievements are given in Hannah DBB. He with two of his children and some of his servants was killed by a direct hit in a London air raid.

[47] Later in that session of the NECIES in January 1895, W C Mountain read a paper on *The Design and Efficiency of Plant for the Transmission of Power by Electricity*. v.11 pp 113-

discussion took place at the NECIES in February 1905 following a paper by Snell of the Sunderland Electric Co on the *Application of Electricity to Industrial Purposes*. Local works took 5.7 million units a year and load factors of 34.5% for engine builders, where night shifts were common, and 19.6% in shipyards. Another contributor claimed that the combined load factor for shipyards and marine engine works was 22%. There were disputes about the level of tariffs and initial construction costs and one contributor contended that once electricity could be purchased for 1d a unit or less there was no point in generating within a firm. Presumably for some time old plant must have remained at least in some works. Hugo McColl recalled that in one firm when the quarterly electricity bill arrived the foreman was instructed to cut off the current and start up his boiler fires. Gas engines could still be more economical according to McColl. One of the pioneers, R P Sloan, NESCo managing director, recalled that while the shipyards and engine works on the Tyne gave *the first impetus* to the use of electric motive power on a large scale, it was *no simple task to persuade* them *to adopt a new system to drive their works, and to obtain their power requirements from an outside source*. Sometimes the power company had to install trial installations on *sale or return* terms. Resistance to an outside power source may have been seen as a loss of control, since any interruption of supply could be damaging to tight delivery dates. British manufactures were not building polyphase motors and most motors were foreign imports largely from America. In 1906 the NESCo installed electrical capacity included:

Armstrong Whitworth Elswick	1807 kW	Armstrong Whitworth Walker	780 kW
Hawthorn-Leslie St Peters	707 kW	Swan Hunter & W Richardson	972 kW
North Eastern Marine	1590 kW	Northumberland SB	682 kW
Wallsend Slipway & Engineering	850 kW		

Charles Merz claimed in 1908 that *there is now, apart from the Power Company, practically speaking no coal burned on the Tyne for power purposes except in chemical factories. The Tyne shipyards and engineering works may be said to have adopted electricity to the exclusion of all other forms of motive power*. Later he modified this to say that all shipbuilders or engineers on *the north bank* of the Tyne *inside the Power Company's area* take 95% of their power from NESCo and the remainder from small gas-engines or from *boilers fired with scrap wood*. The contribution of Merz to both advocating and establishing a central system of electrical supply was outstanding. However, it seems unlikely the adoption of electrical power was as extensive at that time as he claimed.[48]

Ship Structures.

In addition to Doxford's turret reviewed above, some notable developments in ship design should be noted, at least briefly. Ropner patented their version of a *turret* type, in which the side above the water was like Doxford's rounded inwards but the upper part of the side was vertical instead of rounded. *Engineering* wrote *the idea is to secure the advantages of the well deck and partial awning deck steamers as well as those built as spar-deckers, with one deck only laid*. The first of these was ss *Trunkby* built in 1896 and 44 were launched by 1909. Very soon after the first use of his patent Side Tank design in ss *Mancunia*, McGlashan provided details to the NECIES in 1898 in a paper *Water Ballasting of Steamers*. He focussed attention on the widely agreed fact that *steamers were not sufficiently ballasted when proceeding light ship*, indeed their propellers could be seen coming out of the water.[49] At Raylton Dixons, Harroway[50] designed the cantilevered frame type of ship with topside water tank [see illustration] to offer another solution to the ballasting problem. It was first used in 1904 on the *Hedwig Heidman*, and over the next five years 22 ships of this type were built. Driel wrote of the Harroway-Dixon cantilever system: *in addition*

---

[48] In 1916 Stoney and Richardson echoed Merz: *Electricity has been adopted in practically every shipyard and engineering works to the exclusion of other forms of motive power* but that was nearly ten years later.

[49] Double sides were fitted for water ballast, extending from the double bottom to the underside of the upper / main deck and longitudinally from ½ to ¾ of the length of the ship. Extra strength and safety was also claimed.

[50] George Mitchell Harroway died in 1944, aged about 76. He served his time at Wigham Richardson and then went abroad for a time and returned to Neptune as chief of the designing & estimating department. He moved to Raylton Dixon, where he became general manager and in 1912 a director. He donated funds for a NECIES scholarship.

to securing excellent self trimming operation, also made the ship easier to navigate when in ballast, came to be widely adopted ... trouble at first to satisfy the Board of Trade that these topside tanks might only be used for water ballast.

Longitudinal framing of iron ships was advocated by the great naval architect Scott Russell in 1862. It was a man from Hartlepool however, J W Isherwood, who successfully introduced the technique to regular commercial use when Craggs had the courage to use it. The contemporary naval architect David Pollock unequivocally gave credit to Isherwood for introducing *a system of shipbuilding which has obvious structural, economical and commercial advantages*. Joseph William Isherwood was born in 1870 and his parents ran a grocers & beer retailers. At 15 years of age he was appreciated to Edward Withy and he continued to work there as a draughtsman until 1896. He became Lloyds surveyor at Hartlepool and later moved to the London office. He took out his patent in 1906 and a year later he resigned from Lloyds and became a director of Craggs. When the firm collapsed he established a consultancy firm. His innovative work continued and at the time of his death in 1937 more than twenty million deadweight tons of shipping, about 2,500 ships, were based upon his system. While Craggs were constructing the tanker ss *Paul Paix* [4,695t] in 1908, both Isherwood and E Hall Craggs presented papers on this longitudinal technique. Craggs recalled in his paper *The Framing of Ships*, that when he started in business *it was ... a matter of serious consideration to leave the tier of beams out of a vessel 24 feet in depth*. Isherwood reminded his audience, at the INA, that in 1895 Furness Withy *... in the face of great opposition* built a single deck steamer without hold beams and *beyond the mystic depth of 24 feet*. According to Craggs, The *real cause* of Scott Russell's failure to introduce longitudinal framing generally was his rejection of the use of the shell plating in connection with the transverse strength.[51] This Teesside builder for many years fitted some longitudinal framing underneath the midship portion of the uppermost deck in all vessels to overcome the collapse of decks, and in every ship of *extreme proportions*, he used longitudinal girders on *all decks to ensure increased longitudinal strength*. An American naval architect, Frear, said the *Paul Paix*'s construction *alleviated the inherent leakage at bulkheads of transversely framed tankers and strengthened the deck, especially in compression*. Many recognised that the new structure would be suitable *especially for petroleum tank steamers*, it reduced structural weight and simplified construction. Osbourne Graham launched an unusual ship in 1909, ss *Monitoria*, had corrugated sides form. Her designer Haver argued this saved 14-16% on coal consumption while carrying 3% more cargo. Some further *monitor* ships were built.

Sailing ships.
A short term upsurge during 1888-1892 in sailing ships had a limited impact on the north east coast. Many fine sailing vessels were built on the Clyde. *Engineering* pointed out that the north east *never attempted to compete with the Clyde in the construction of those magnificent sailing ships which are attaining great proportions,* such as the 5-masted *France*. Nationally steam tonnage fell from 717,582t in 1889 to 514,476t in 1892, while sail more than doubled, increasing from 137,147t to 287,072t! The Clyde contributed massively to this increase, sail tonnage increased threefold from 1888 to 1892, from 51,330t to 159,886t. The north east was hardly involved at all, with the exception the contribution of the Wear, where 40,000t of sail in 1891 constituted just over 20% of annual output. Doxfords built five large sailing ships, some 4-masted. On the Clyde, however, the ratio of sail was 32%. Less than 10% of the Wear output was sail in 1892 when on the Clyde it was not far below 48%. Pickersgill built five of the 11 sailing vessels, - the two largest being 3,440t and 2,873t. A small iron barquentine was launched sideways by Robert Thompson - *Regent* [3,86t]. They also built a barque the *Linden* [1,114t]. Pickersgills built the only two sailing vessels [2,223t] in 1893, including *Margarita*, the last sailing ship from the Wear. Swan Hunter built a 3-masted sailing vessel - *Flottbek* [1,988t] in 1891, the first such vessel built on Tyne for many years, and a year later, a 4-masted barque 327' long, the *Milton Stuart* [3,178t]. Palmers also made

---

[51] Russell's use of bulkheads for the transverse strength resulted in great weight and a very poor cargo ship and so *generally speaking, longitudinal framing disappeared from practice for many years.*

its contribution to the late expansion of sailing vessels, as noted above. Two were launched in 1884, followed by two more in 1885 and finally in 1893 the *Lydgate*. The *Lydgate* was described as a *most unusual occurrence* and similar words *an unusual sight* were used for the two sailing ships for Nova Scotia by Richardson Duck in 1891. Many sailing vessels built on the Tees had iron rather than steel hulls.

Colliers, Trawlers & Tugs.
Ships for transporting coal continued to be an important part of the work of many north east yards, such as Austins and Osbourne Graham; all yards however built some colliers. Their characteristics varied with the market supplied, for example a London distributor might want a limited quantity of coal whereas a large gas company often required larger supplies delivered to their works. Likewise a vessel with bunkers designed for the coastal trade would be too small for longer voyages. Price regularly influenced both the level of equipment on board colliers and the quality of the design. For example, ss *Holmwood* had *the absolute minimum of equipment ... probably little or no profit for the* builders when built in 1902 for £15,000. When Osbourne Graham supplied France Fenwick with *Needwood* [1985t], ballast capacity was reduced to only 487t to save costs. In bad weather that series of self-trimmers proved difficult to handle and in ballast were *easily blown off course*. The *Glasgow Herald*, in 1905, described several north east coast vessels as approaching *very near the type of large grain and ore carriers of the American Lakes*. In 1910 Osbourne Graham's ss *Ladywood* [2,314t] proved to be structurally weak and the propeller shafting was continually going out of alignment. Orders were then placed with Robert Thompson, who applied their ideas to produce *very well* built vessels with more power and better ballast arrangements, such as ss *Wedgewood* [1,674t]. The *Portwood* [2,248t - £32,000] was the first of three delivered by Austin starting in 1913. These north east colliers, supplied to a variety of coal carriers, played a vital part in the supply of the nation's energy.

A variety of small craft played an essential part of the marine activity of the world and were of particular importance for some north east yards. In 1893, for example, a third of the vessels built on the Tees were under 500t, including many trawlers. Edwards Bros [later Smith's Dock] specialised in building trawlers: 27 in 1896 and in the next year 30 fishing craft. Fishing craft and tugs were important for both Elthringham and Rennoldson; Clelands also built fishing vessels. These vessels were also more costly per ton than the usual general cargo ship.[52] Trawlers used relatively small triple expansion engines, such as the 12", 20", 33" / 23" stroke built by Shields Engineering for *Annie Melling* [125' x 21.4' x 12.3'], in 1904. The fishing industry was very important for north east ports such as North Shields. The wooden tug finally, departed. While the changeover to steel hulls was getting under way in 1885, nine of the last ten wood tugs were built on the Tyne. Rennoldson built three of these, including the *Australia*, the design of which showed little change over the previous 20 years. Four others were built at South Shields and at North Shields the family of Wouldhave with Johnston built the *Pera*. Elthringham built the last wooden tug on the Tyne, *Tyne Dock No.4*, for the North Eastern Railway Co at Grimsby in 1889. Renamed *Enable* she returned to work on the Tyne in 1911. One north east tug sails of the east coast of USA and another is firmly set as an exhibit in the National Maritime Museum. These small craft should never be forgotten as we admire the majestic giants of the sea.

---

[52] These small craft could mislead in regard to the average tonnage per ship at a port or individual yard. In 1901, for the Tyne, 43 of the 121 vessels built were such craft, then over the whole 121 ships the average is 2,529t. However, if the 43 ships are excluded the average becomes 3,846t [fully 52%] and directly comparable to the average for the Wear.

Floating Docks &c.[53]

When required some shipyards built metal structures such as cassions, dock gates and, particularly at Swan Hunters, floating docks. In 1896, Armstrongs built two caissons and a floating dock, Stephensons two dock gates for Glasgow and a caisson for the port of Barry. Iron gates for locks on the Manchester Canal were constructed by Eltringham. Stephenson built a pontoon for the Spanish government and a floating dock with a 12,000 ton lift capacity as well as 2 dock gates for the North Eastern Railway Dock extension at Middlesbrough. In 1900 Crown built the cassion that was used for the roundhead of Roker pier. The structural parts, pontoons, girders &c of the two landing stages for the Shields ferry were erected and fitted by Craggs in 1904-5.

Floating Dock

Civil engineers played a central role in the design of floating docks and the leading specialists were Clark & Stansfield who provided the designs for construction by Swan Hunter. In 1894, the Wallsend yard built the *Taylor* type dock for the Tyne Pontoon & Dry Dock Co; it was 300' long with 56' between the walls. Two years later an off-shore *L* shaped dock was built for Smith's Dock, with a length of 430', this dock could lift a 6,000 dwt vessel in 30 minutes. A similar dock [359' lift 3,600 tons] was supplied to Austin in 1903. Floating docks were supplied to the British Admiralty, the Spanish, Japanese and Natal governments as well as a number of commercial companies. In 1896, a dock to lift 10,000t and take warships to 500' long was required by the Spanish government for Havana and to be delivered in 11 months. Wallsend supplied their first *self-docking principle* floating dock and it reached Havana with three days to spare after a voyage of 58 days. A 510' long dock for Stetin left the Tyne 7 months after the first plate was laid. When the Admiralty wanted a dock for Bermuda which would not only take battleships of 16,500dpt but also liners such as ss *Campania*, Clark & Stansfield designed a dock which was 545' long with a clear docking width of 99' within the overall width of 126'. Extensive tests were carried out by the Admiralty and the Bermuda dock was considered the finest of its kind in the world. Its machinery pumped 34000t of water in 4 hours. Two *box* type docks were built, in 1902-3, by Swan Hunter for the Japanese Navy and shipped out in pieces for final assembly. The first plate of a *box* type dock for the Suez Canal Co was laid on 7 May and was launched on 11 August 1904; Wallsend Slipway fitted the machinery, the two centrifugal pumps in bottom of dock driven by electric motors. Clarke Chapman supplied all the electrical equipment. It reached Port Said on 4 October! Only one further example can be noted here. A dock to lift 2,700 tons was delivered on the Forcados River for an Elder, Dempster subsidiary, the Nigerian Dry Dock & Engineering Co, in not much more than five months, after a voyage of 57 days. Swan Hunters built more than 20 first class floating docks before 1913.

Progress with tankers.[54]

There can be no doubting the dominant role of the north east coast in building tankers; almost a million tons were built before 1914. Shipbuilders on the Tyne played the leading role, with 70% of that output. Lloyd's list of bulk oil carriers in 1913 shows that 60% of the world tonnage came from the north east, 161 of the 273 tankers over 500t. The Tyne built about two-thirds of British built tonnage. The dominance of

---

[53] The reasons for using a floating dock cannot be pursued here - see references

[54] A summary to 1906 gave north east built tankers, as follows: 147 on Tyne, 32 on the Tees and 21 on the Wear.

Armstrong before 1914 is clear in diag 10.13 as is the importance of Swan Hunter. In sharp contrast tankers were only a small part of the work of Hawthorn Leslie, an early starter in the field and later a major builder of tanker. Laing was even more dominant in the Wear tanker production than Armstrongs on the Tyne. Hugh Laing devoted particular attention to tankers. At Hartlepool, although Gray played a very important part in advancing tanker construction through the yard's association with Samuel, overall tankers were a small part of their output. Tanker sizes varied considerably and some in 1913-4 reached 10,000t vessels [see diag 10.14]. By 1892, north east yards had built 100,000t of tankers and the 19 tankers built in 1893 totalled than 58,000t. Many of these were 4,000t, including Gray's ss *Bullmouth*: she could carry 5,000t of oil and was intended to carry general cargo on return trips. Palmer built the

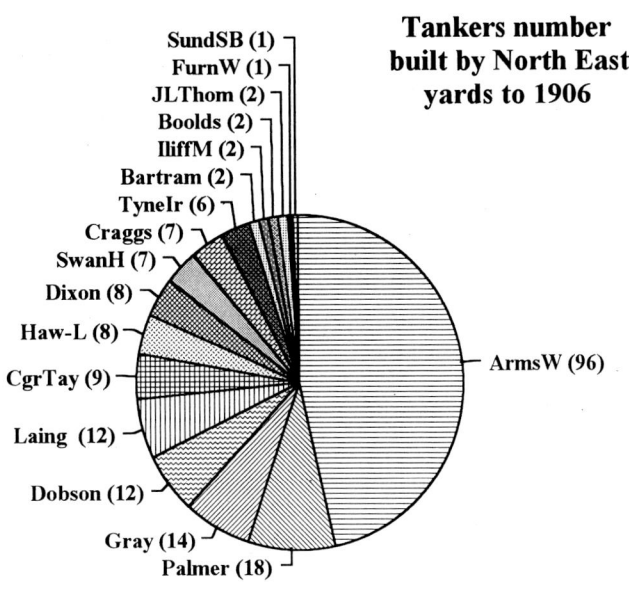

Diag 10.13

Crenella [5,500t] in 1897 and a year later Laings built the first tanker with a carrying capacity of 8,000t, ss *Tuscarona* [420' x 53' - 6,117t]. Armstrong's sixth tanker for Shell ss *Strombus*, carried of 8,500 tons of oil, once again it was to carry general cargo on the outward voyage; her oil burning boilers were installed by Wallsend Slipway. Gray continued to supply Samuel, including the *Pectan* [7,387t] and *Spondilus* in 1902: they were described as the two *largest bulk oil carriers afloat*. Although less tanker work was done in Scotland ss *Narranansett*, the first tanker of over 10,000t dwt, was built by Scotts in 1903 for Anglo-American Oil Co; she was 512' long. When on her second voyage the deck cracked, she was dry docked at Stephensons in 1905. More than half a million tons of tankers were built by the end of 1908 in the north east. Like other cargo ships, output was low in 1909-10. There was, however, a sharp increase in both the size of tankers and the volume of production during 1912-4. Nearly 95,000t of tankers were launched in 1912 and a year later this reached 170,000t. Swan Hunter built the largest part of this in both years 46,000t in 1912 and then 76,440t in 1913. Laing built the first *Standard Isherwood* oil tanker, the 10,250 dwt *San Joacquin* [6,975t] in 1913 for Wilhelmsen of Tonsberg.[55] Massive orders were placed by the Eagle Oil company and 14 of the *SAN* series were built. Both Armstrongs and Palmers built their first tankers of over 10,000t in 1913 and three Swan Hunter's tankers were 9,600t [see drawing of *San Isidoro*]. A were a late starter in building tankers, Doxfords began in an outstanding way, two of their four tankers in 1913-4 were 540' long, ss *San Jeronimo* and ss *San Nazario* both carried 15,000t of oil.

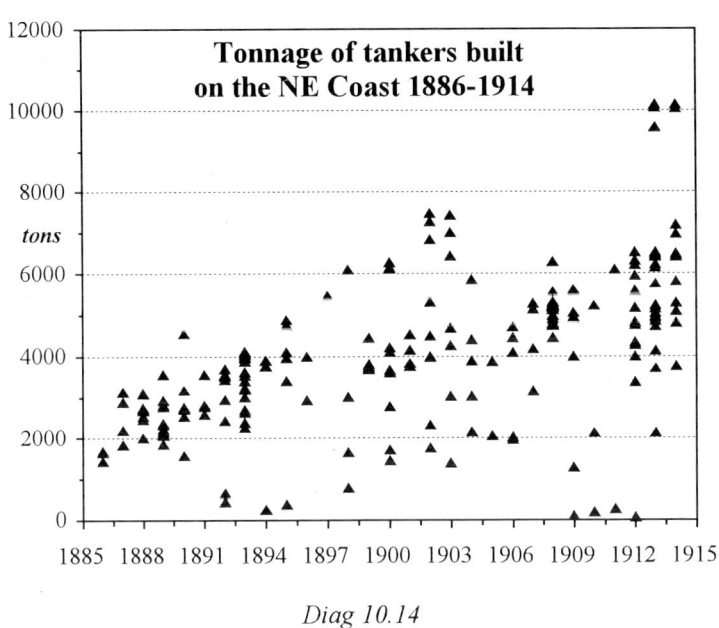

Diag 10.14

---

[55] W Wilhelmsen's daughter was educated by Laing's brother-in-law Dr Carter; five further tankers were ordered.

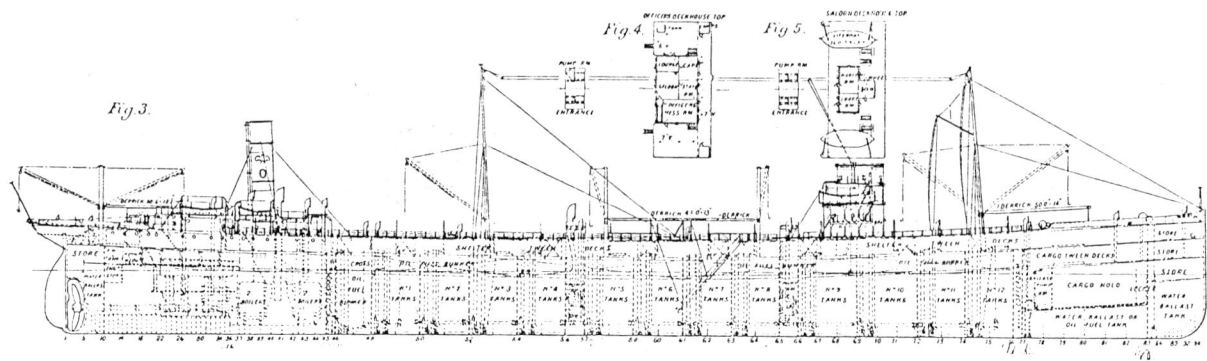

San Isodoro oil tanker

These ships remained for many years the largest vessels built on the Wear. A very able young Tyneside naval architect, Harry Bocler, in 1905 commented on tanker size: *Whether these large oil carriers will prove sufficiently remunerative to justify a further increase in size, remains to be seen.* Four *large steamers* each carrying 9,000t of oil had just been built locally for Samuel. Swan Hunters had completed ss *Goldmouth* [7,446t], at Wallsend, and Armstrongs ss *Silverlip* [7,492t] at Walker. Following experiments in the use of liquid fuel, the Admiralty placed the order for their first oil carrier at Swan Hunter. The *Petroleum* [4,686t] could carry a cargo of about 6,100 tons of oil in plus her own 500 tons of fuel oil, and she could pass her oil to another vessel while in tow.

Swan Hunter and Wigham Richardson.

C S Swan & Hunter formed a private limited company in 1895. The yard then employed some 2,000 men and boys. Just before this they completed the important development of two glass roofed berths in their East Yard. Many of the Tyne's largest merchant ships came from Swan's Wallsend yard, such as ss *Westmeath* [425' long] in 1893 the first over 6,000t. When in 1897, the 470' long ss *Milwaukee* [7,371t] was launched, work was already underway on ss *Ultonia* [8,056t], their first ship to enter the service of Cunard. She was ordered by Furness and purchased by Cunard on the stocks.[56] Orders for intermediate liners followed; ss *Invernia* [13,800t] was completed in 1900; her quadruple expansion engines by Wallsend Slipway reached 12,000 ihp.[57] In that year Swan Hunter began building in the newly erected covered berths. Over the three years 1900-2, the Wigham Richardson's Neptune yard averaged almost 37,000t and Swan's Wallsend yard 52,000t. This ratio corresponds with the allocation of ordinary shares when the two yards merged in 1903.

Amalgamation of Swan Hunter and J Wigham Richardson.[58]

By the spring of 1903 matters for amalgamating these two successful shipbuilding companies had reached the point of arranging the details of a new joint company and a series of letters were exchanged between George Hunter and Wigham Richardson, one of which summarised the key proposals[59] as in inset:

---

[56] She began in cargo and cattle trade, when Cunard got a ten year emigrant contract from the Hungarian Government it was switched to that work [Fiume-Gibralter-New York]. She was torpedoed in 1917.

[57] She carried 164 1st, 200 2nd and 1,600 3rd class passengers and 14,000 tons of cargo. The funnel was 106' from boat deck to rim cowl. Like *Ultania* was sunk in 1917 carrying 2,800 troops; 87 troops and 36 crew lost.

[58] Dr Ian Buxton regards the securing of the *Mauretania* order as the decisive factor in this merger. He wrote *On the strength of this expression of intent, an Extraordinary General Meeting of the Swan & Hunter shareholders was called on 26 May... they agreed to merge with Wigham Richardson.*

[59] Other points related to Wallsend Slipway, setting aside shares for the acquisition of the Tyne Pontoons Co and Wigham Richardson's London office. By May, Hunter saw no gain from speaking further to Renwick about Tyne Pontoons, but suggested that Richardson as a large shareholder in the Pontoons Co might induce Renwick *to recommend to the Shareholders the amalgamation ... on terms which we should be willing to accept.*

> *A summary of key proposals on the merger of Swan-Hunter & Wigham Richardson.*
>
> We will convene our shareholders ... obtain consent to an amalgamation with your Firm and to securing control of the Wallsend Slipway Co and also providing for the inclusion of the Tyne Pontoons Coy if that should subsequently be considered desirable, provided that your Company will now enter into an agreement with my Company upon the basis of the following essential particulars.
>   1. nominal capital £1500000 - 800000 Ord 700000 - 5% Pref; power to issue Deb up to 1/3 capital
>   2. sell all shares of both companies sold to the new Company
>   3. work in progress to be reduced by £325000 and goodwill correspondingly increased for ... prospectus
>   4. total consideration both companies £929000 - J Wigham Richardson £364250 Ord and £161700 Pref and Swan Hunter £564750 Ord and £ 232000 Pref
>   5. A board of not more than 15 members - first twelve: George B Hunter chairman; John Wigham Richardson vice-chairman; J Tweedy, W Denton Sir W White T H Bainbridge Charles J D Christie P Wig Ric J Denham Christie C S Swan G B Richardson G Ernest Hunter , which left three vacancies for Pontoon Co or others.
>   6. Directorships for five years from 1 Jan 1903; no competing interests - patents come over to new Company. *I understand that some members of your Board do not wish to be bound ... my Board prefer to have a fixed agreement.*
>   7. Salaries chair as Chair £1000 - GBH, WD, THB, CSS, GEH aggregate £4900 + 7% of profits. Nett profits ... after charging all Directors salaries, depreciation and amortization and all other usual charges. Interest on Debenture stock will form a prior charge to Directors' commissions but will not be deducted from nett profits and other points. WigR JDC JT PWR JSC GBR aggregate £4600 + 6.5%; White £1000 + 1.5%
>   Total paid for management and direction [excluding any new directors] £11500 / yr + 15% of profit.
>   8. Basis of capital for working extensions - may be 4.25% - 4.5% Deb or placing balance of Ord and/or Pref [either public or private issue or both] or issue both Debs & shares together.
>   15 New Company pay such registration costs *as it may legally pay* and others costs - 61% SH 39% WR.

The agreements of sale of 17 June 449,215 Preference & 345,082 Ordinary shares were allocated as follows: to C S Swan Hunter Ltd 225,900 Pref. & 338,850 Ord; Wighan Richardson Ltd 158,025 Pref. 206,225; Wallsend Slipway 31,820; Eliza Highat Mitchell 27,670; others 7,800. It was recognised that various customers would wish to continue to have their vessels built at their usual yard and normally the work was placed accordingly. Hudson [60] of Swan Hunter was to be appointed secretary, with Winstanley as assistant secretary. In May, Hunter wrote to Wigham Richardson that the stockbrokers consulted said that Preference shares *would not readily be taken up by the public,* so it was proposed only to offer 4.25% Debentures. The merger was successfully accomplished.

Some ships built at Wallsend & Neptune Yards.
The following are some examples of the ships built at the two yards. Neptune built the largest cable ship

---

[60] Robert Hudson [1835-1905] was a farmer's son and nephew of George Hudson the Railway King. He abandoned an intention to enter the church for a commercial career. After working for a railway company, in 1858 became traffic manager of the Sunderland Dock Co; he joined Swan Hunter as commercial manager in 1881and became secretary of the limited company in 1895. He was *an active supporter* of the Wallsend Shipyard Ambulance Corps. A *moderate Conservative* and prominent Freemason and was for 21 Provincial Grand Secretary [Durham]. He never married.

afloat, *Colonia* [7,976t][61] in 1902, and continued this Tyne tradition with ss *Cambria* for the Telegraph Construction & Maintenance Co in 1904. This twin screw vessel carried 2,800 dwt, with three cable tanks, and had an elliptical stern and overhanging bow, both fitted with cable sheaves. *RMS Carpathia*,[62] built at Wallsend, crossed the Atlantic in May 1904 with an average speed outwards of 14.9k and 15.1k on the return trip. [see illustration] Three ships for the Elders & Fyffe banana service were built at Wallsend. The ss *Matina* launched in January 1904 was the first vessel with all the internal space [excluding machinery] insulated for the carriage of fruit. Her sister ship ss *Manistee*[63] followed in March.

The Wallsend yard built a floating coal depot for the Admiralty in 1902-3; with a storage capacity of 12,000 tons. A train ferry *Drottning Victoria* was delivered to the Swedish government in 1908; on her trials the mean speed was 17.5k. *The Shipbuilder* described Swan's output in 1910 as *very varied* as indeed it was. The sixteen ships [70,012t] included: *Franconia* [18,146t] for Cunard, *Indrabarah* [7,395t], *Kioto* [6,182t], *Carthage* [5,036t] a French mail and passengers ship, *Harmattan* [4,791t]. Those for Canada included ss *Cartier* for hydrographic service, ss *Prince George* [3,372t] a fast passenger ship for Grand Trunk Pacific Co, ss *Keystorm* [1,673t] a Lake cargo ship. *HMS Hope* torpedo boat destroyer and a floating dock caisson were built for the Admiralty. There was also the *Toiler* with a Diesel engine. The passenger liner *Reina Victoria Eugenia* launched in 1912 was powered by the *combination* system [steam from reciprocating engines to low pressure turbine]. In 1906 the *Mauretania* showed that Swans could produce ships the equal of any in the world.

MAURETANIA - a Queen of the Atlantic.[64]

Great excitement spread along the banks of the Tyne on Thursday 20 September 1906, as the moment of the launch of Swan Hunter's ship #735 ts *Mauretania* arrived. This fine ship, the north-east's most famous passenger vessel, evoked amongst Geordies a sense of pride unequalled by any other vessel. The minutes of the Board for 7 May 1904 recorded the beginnings:

> Cunard S S proposed contract.
> The conditions of Contract & the outline of specification of the fast Turbine Steamer proposed to be constructed by this company for the Cunard S S Co Ltd, were submitted to the Board by the Chairman, and the Board unanimously approved of the same subject to the Engine Builders, (the Wallsend Slipway & Engineering Co Ltd) confirming. The penalties to be shared equally between this Company & their Company.

George Hunter reported in August that *No 735 is being proceeded with*. At that time there was no *formally*

---

[61] When she left the Thames to lay the Vancouver-Fanning Island section of a new Pacific cable, loaded with 3,540 knots of cable weighing 7,684 tons; the 3,455 knots laid *without a hitch of any kind*, was then *the longest length of cable ever laid*, and *the work is credible to the vessel and her builders*. *Glas Her* 1902.

[62] The vessels description included saloon accommodation for 400 passengers [1st class] and third class cabins 2, 4 and 6 berth for over 2,000 passengers. If required for the conveyance of troops she could carry 3,000 officers and men and if cavalry about 1,000 officers and men, with sufficient coal for 11,000k-12,000k at about 15k/hour.

[63] With her holds completely filled with a light cargo, fruit, she only drew 19.5' of water. She had the last Wallsend Swan ship number- #296. The last Richardson Neptune was #411. A new number sequence began with #709.

[64] Dr Ian Buxton has reviewed Cunard's approach to the building of their two fast Atlantic vessels in *Mariner's Mirror* Jan 1996. This includes a most useful chronology. Costs were also considered this is reviewed in chap 19.

Mauretania with Turbinia alongside

drawn contract, however, the printed outline specification and conditions, which have been initialled, with the correspondence constitute a contract. This story had begun three years earlier.

At the end of May 1901, the Board of Cunard discussed *new fast steamers* and on 2 August plans for a 23-24k vessel by their General Superintendent were considered. Before the end of the year Parsons proposed turbine machinery and early in February submitted turbine plans for a 725' ship with 48,000ihp. Four shipbuilders were invited to submit proposals, two Clyde yards, Vickers and Swan Hunter. There was one notable omission, Harland & Wolff, probably the most suitable shipyard to build such a vessel but excluded by a complex of financial interests and political concerns.[65] Fairfield and Vickers withdrew and so John Brown built one and Swans the other. On 30 September 1902, the government's financial support was announced; the historian Ensor wrote *after the Germans had, with three successive ships[66], won and held the 'blue riband' of the Atlantic, it was decided that national prestige warranted state aid to recover it.* Cunard was to construct two steamships,[67] capable of maintaining a minimum average speed of 24k to 25k in moderate weather. There was a capital loan, up to £2,600,000, at 2.75% interest and an annual subsidy of £150,000. The Cunard vessels surpassed the requirements in every way.[68] Brown's *Lusitania* secured the blue riband on her second voyage [23.99k westward and 23.61k eastward], she had a mean speed of 26.45k on her trials.

In the words of one of those who helped build her, A G Hood, *some of the greatest living experts in the world of naval architecture* were occupied for about two years before the *Mauretania*'s keel was laid; her dimensions were 790' long [760' bp], 88' broad, with a moulded depth of 60.5', and was not far short of 32,000t. Such a large ship[69] presented a vast range of design problems, including the materials to be used

---

[65] A syndicate, the International Mercantile Marine inspired by the American financier J Pierpont Morgan, involving the shipyard, the White Star Line and two German lines was being formed. They vainly hoped that Cunard might be enticed to join. Moss & Hume wrote: *When the scheme became public there was a storm of protest. There were fears that the interests of the British mercantile marine were being subordinated to those of America and on international finance; and there was a deeper anxiety that British control of the sea was being eroded by the machinations of Jewish financiers and of Imperial Germany. Lord Inverclyde, the Cunard chairman, was able to exploit the public reaction to force the Government to help finance the construction of Cunard ships.* [pp 106-9]. In March 1903, the German shipbuilders Vulcan of Stetin inquired if they might be considered.

[66] *Kaiser Wilhelm Der Gross*, won the riband in 1897 and the *Kronpriz Wilhelm* in 1901. The *Kaiser Wilhelm II* [1902], like the other vessels had Atlantic speeds above 23k, she was 706.5' long - 20,000t - 38,000 ihp. There were then 17 large fast transatlantic liners, including *Campania* of 1893 [22k]

[67] The *Lustitania* was completed before the *Mauretania*, launched on 7 June 1906. The Clyde vessel never quite equalled her sister and was sunk by a submarine in on 7 May 1915; 1,198 passengers and crew were lost. A paper on constructing this ship was given to the INA on 21 Mar 1907.

[68] The ships were required to meet the Admiralty standards for auxiliary cruisers and could be used in time of war.

[69] *The Glasgow Herald* commented that the move from the *Invernia* and *Carpathia* to the *Mauretania* was *a much larger step in naval architecture* than that on Clyde to *Lusitania*. [1906 p.30]

and the stresses to which they would be subject; a significant part of the upper plating was of high tensile and silicon steel. When the calculations were done and designs prepared, experiments were carried out in the Admiralty testing tank at Haslar and later with a much larger model [47.5' long] in the Northumberland Dock on the Tyne. A critical decision was the choice of engines. Initially it was intended to have quadruple expansion engines; and in October 1902 the Cunard Board stated they would not adopt turbines. Inevitably, given Parsons' pioneering record, he was not so easily dissuaded, and sought to overcome Cunard's reluctance. A very distinguished committee[70] was set up and spent many months considering this question. It was finally agreed to use turbines on 24 March 1904; this decision was a key factor in the speed achieved. *Engineering* commented: *To his [Parsons] genius the success of the vessels is largely due, and the engineering world no less than the firms concerned, render him full credit for this great advance in marine engineering.* This comment should not take away the vital contribution of Andrew Laing, and his assistant Tom MacPherson, in the design work and in particular to the successful construction of the steam turbines. Without such construction skills, the best designs will fail. *Mauretania*'s turbines could develop 70,000 shp. A description of the building of this great ship cannot be given here [the illustration shows a section outline in the building shed], however, some points may be briefly noted related to rivetting to illustrate the scale of the work. About 4 million rivets were used; these weighed 700 tons and were heated in specially designed oil furnaces, which could heat 3,000 rivets 3" long $^7/_8$"diameter. Many rivets were much larger; a *considerable proportion* were hydraulically rivetted. Special measures were taken to ensure that the holes were properly countersunk and that all rivet heads were free of burrs. Three thicknesses of plating [1"- 1.25"] made up the keel, these plates were clamped together and portable electric drills used to provide *perfectly fair* holes, avoiding the *deterioration* due to punching thick plates. All holes in the high tensile steel plates were also drilled. New railway sidings, directly connected to the NE Railway, were added to enable the materials to be brought directly to the building berths.

Mauretania in shipbuilding shed.

Cunard had agreed to provide 15% upon cost for establishment charges and 5% for profit. However,

---

[70] The committee was: Sir William White; C A Parsons; Rear Admiral H J Oram ; J T Milton [Lloyds]; James Bain [general superintendent Cunard]; Andrew Laing [Wallsend Slipway]; Thomas Bell [John Brown]; William Brock [Denny] and as secretary Eng-Lt W H Wood. George Hunter was prevented by his work from actively participating.

Wallsend Slipway wanted 17.5% for charges, which according to Hunter would have left about 12.5% for the hull.[71] Financial disputes with the engine builders followed. More serious cost problems were evident at the shipyard in the late autumn of 1906 and an exchange of letters with Cunard began on 12 December. It seemed the shipowner was withholding payments and that work could be stopped. Hunter told his Board, on 22 May 1907 *Mauretania will, for various reasons, be a more costly vessel than was estimated.* Cunard had protested and wanted details of the original estimate and in the meanwhile would make no further payments. Swan Hunter made less profits than they expected [see chap 19]. Their Board agreed that the ship must be finished, whether or not there were any further immediate payments. In November 1907 Hunter and Cunard chairman, Watson, agreed a further £45,000, in cash, and £100,000 in acceptances would be despatched. By the time the latter was received on 11 November, the *Mauretania* was within five days of her maiden voyage. The engine costs were 10% to 15% above estimate and the hull *very much more*.[72]

Mauretania's maiden voyage to America took 5 days 5 hours 10 minutes; her return journey was quicker. After fitting a new type of propeller, in June 1909 she reached America in 4 days 17 hours 21 minutes at an average speed of 25.88k. When 22 years old, in 1929, she sailed at an average of 27.48k for 24 hours, and four years later maintained 32k, her highest speed ever, for a distance of 112 miles. She held the *blue riband* for twenty years. In all this beautiful ship made 350 voyages across the Atlantic, which meant she covered more than 2,500,000 miles, equivalent to a hundred times round the equator. As she ended her life the *Queen Mary* was launched on the Clyde. Just how affectionately this ship was regarded is shown in these the words of one man's boyhood recollection of this noble ship's journey to be broken up in 1935:

> [as the] *Mauretania* ... passed the mouth of the Tyne, they brought her in as close as they could to the shore, in order that she and the people who built her might pay their last respects, one to the other. I have a clear memory of standing, surrounded by crowds of people, on St Mary's Island, and watching her as she moved slowly north ... during all this time, or most of it, my father and dozens of other fully grown men around me, wept openly ... I had never seen a grown-up man cry before, and I cannot remember ever seeing my father cry again, ... that day, he was surrounded by dozens of men whose faces were as wet with tears as his.[73]

Gyroscope

Perhaps hopes of much more passenger work inspired an interest in acquiring control of gyroscope patents. From 1895 Wigham Richardson developed the methods of Schlick to reduce vibration and in 1906 Swan Hunter actively pursued another innovation by this German engineer. The great Brunel produced a rather bizarre design of an inner structure that could swivel to overcome the problem of rolling in a passenger ship. A more practical solution was offered by E O Schlick, who patented his gyroscope in 1903 and a year later presented his ideas to the INA. Swan Hunter began negotiations in the autumn of 1906 in regard to this patent and received an offer from Schlick of *all interests in his patents in the United Kingdom, France and the United States* for £3,000 in cash and 40% of the net profits of working the patents. After attending the trials of the *Seebar*, fitted with a gyroscope, with Max Wurl, Sir William White formed a very

---

[71] In fact given an approximate ratio of 5:4 for hull: machinery costs, 17.7% for machinery would have left 13% for hull. As Swan Hunter refused to accept a 17%-13% split, R Saxton White as arbitrator, on 1 Aug 1905 decided 16.7% for Wallsend Slipway and 13.3% for shipbuilder, if this did not equal 15% the difference [excess or deficit] was shared equally. In February 1907 Hunter was still discontented and said that Wallsend Slipway had mislead the arbitrator by claiming that all their 1906 engine work would be on #735 when in fact they also completed a number of other sets of machinery. The 15% percentage yielded £68,000 in 1906 *more than sufficient to cover all their establishment charge*.

[72] It seemed that Wallsend Slipway agreed to contribute one half on any allowance Swans made to Cunard. By November 1908 the differences between Cunard and the builders was £70,000 to £60,000, which was finally split, however at the beginning of January there was in addition a matter of £10,978 for *doubtful debits*.

[73] Letter from Hylton Charlton of Seaton Delaval, dated 12 mar 1988: he was 8 years old at the time.

favourable opinion of the apparatus but thought its use would be limited in practice. The complex negotiations cannot be pursued here. White took steps to secure publicity with a paper at the INA and arranging for the *Seebar* to be in the Thames at the time of the meeting. Meanwhile, Wurl on holiday in Germany conferred with Schlick and secured *full particulars* of the apparatus for ss *Sylvana* for the Hamburg America Line. For some time every Board meeting agenda carried an item on the gyroscope. By early 1908 a little over £4,500 had been spent and the first one was being made; after workshop trials the Neptune device was fitted in ss *Lochiel*, the first British vessel with a gyroscope. The expected results were achieved:

> *In a rough sea rolls of 15 or 16 each side have been at once reduced to 2 or 3 and the efficiency of the gyroscope as a means of steadying ships against rolling in ordinary work at sea has been proved in an entirely satisfactory manner.* Christie, perhaps sadly noted - *from a technical point of view ... very gratifying but it cannot be said with any certainty that the financial success ... is at all secured.* It was realized that the *size, weight and power required* meant a *more costly piece of apparatus* than shipowners were *likely to readily adopt without a good deal of persuasion*.[74]

Swan Hunter Expands.

A spate of expansion measures were taken by Swan Hunter about 1912[75] and there were early endeavours related to North America. George Hunter showed a considerable interest in opportunities in the whole of North America and made a number of visits to explore the possibilities. There was a proposal for the Company to provide the whole or part of the capital for a floating dock at Sydney, Cape Breton. It was believed the Canadian Government would provide a subsidy of 3% for 20 years and that the city would contribute towards the 350,000$ of capital for a shipbuilding facility; without such public financial support shipbuilding would not be profitable, particularly as Halifax was more suitable for shipbuilding but already had a graving dock. Later land was purchased at Halifax, in association with B F Pearson. Bainbridge, in May 1905, raised the question of the £3,000 invested in Canadian land and six months later it was reported the business was in a dormant condition. Contacts were made with Canadian Ministers visiting Britain in 1909 in the hope of interesting them in Swan's land at Halifax for a projected shipyard at Montreal to build warships. An attempt by Hunter to act jointly in the matter with Armstrong-Whitworth through Sir Andrew Noble also failed. When Hunter reviewed the Canadian situation for his Board in November 1909, it emerged that in June Swan Hunter had proposed the formation of million dollar Company to provide a dock for the St Lawrence with a lift of 18,000t, half the capital from either the Canadian government or the Montreal Harbour Commissioners and the other half by shipowners and Swan Hunter, a nominal rent and certain other conditions.[76] The Board agreed to subscribe up to £10,000 to secure an order for a floating dock and continued to review the position at almost every Board meeting, but were not willing to take a large interest in any shipbuilding venture. Finally, in April 1910, they decided that there was no point in any amended offer.[77] In April 1911 a joint proposal by Armstrong-Whitworth, Swan Hunter and Wallsend Slipway to establish shipyard and engine works in Canada and to tender for Canadian war vessels was approved. However Armstrongs, very quickly, decided to act independently. They had also asked Wallsend Slipway to quote for the engines and the Board decided to tender for building 4 cruisers and six destroyers jointly with Wallsend Slipway in Canada. Swan Hunter continued to seek joint action

---

[74] The 60" dia solid steel disc weighed about 5.5 tons, enclosed in an iron casing, rotated at 1,500 rpm driven by an electric motor. A model was made to help persuade shipowners. George Hunter reported his meeting with Elmer A Sperry, of New York, whose name became almost synonymous with gyroscope. Following a German invention Sperry invented his widely used gyroscopic compass and his stabilizer for ships was introduced in 1913.

[75] Swan Hunter had direct investments in shipping. The minutes of 4 Dec 1911 recorded a number of sales: ss *Arconia* - for £17,000; ss *Ancroft* £26,250; ss *Dunbeth* £32,000; ss *Folgate* -£27,500; ss *Ayton* -£28,625 [prices were less commission]. Hunter stated that *broadly speaking this Company's investments in shipping have not been profitable.*

[76] Later discussions revealed that a subsidy of 4% for 40 years was being sought or a loan for 30 years at 3%

[77] Various other people expressed interests in developments in Canada, as George Hunter reported to his Board, for example Vickers Maxim, Sir Robert Perks, the Canadian Pacific Railway Co, Allan Line and Harland & Wolff.

with Armstrongs but in August George Hunter reported that such co-operation *could not be relied upon.* An attempt to increase the tender by £50,000 was rebuffed with the message that if the tender was accepted and not proceeded with the £20,000 deposit would be forfeited.[78] Finally none of the tenders were accepted and after December 1911, Canada was not on the agenda again for two years. In the summer of 1914 Hunter again went to Canada and New York and reported that there was not sufficient local capital support for a shipyard enterprise in Canada.

In New York, Hunter had discussions with the Donald SS Co and the Atlantic Fruit Co. Donald was still owing Swan Hunter £67,000 for 6 ships built on credit terms [the estimated value of their fleet was £121,038]. Three of the Donald steamers were employed by Atlantic Fruit. Hunter, described Di Giorgio of Atlantic Fruit as *a capable man and ... highly spoken of* and that prospects *appear to be very good ... and the business... likely to develop very considerably.* While the Donald SS would manage the steamers, Di Giorgio would control the business. The Board decided to invest 50,000$. Early in 1913, Hunter again went to North America, to look into the ongoing saga of the Atlantic Fruit Co., which was not going according to Hunter's hopes. At the end of 1913, a further bond was issued to provide funds *for discharging indebtedness* and Moorgate Investments [Hunter had a financial interest] underwrote 1,300,000$ of the two million dollar issue of 6% bonds at 80%. In a reorganisation of Atlantic Fruit, Di Giorgio *voluntarily* retired from the Presidency. N A McLeod, chairman of the Moorgate Investment took over.[79]

Swan Hunter and repair facilities on Tees.

Swan Hunter came close to establishing a works on the Tees. Early in 1911 they considered with Furness Withy acquiring the failed Craggs shipyard. Figures, not recorded, of book values were given and the yard price was £50,000; the Board approved *in principle subject to the valuation ... being favourable.* One of the factors in Hunter's mind was a returned floating dock as the minutes of 10 April 1911 show:

> the receiver of ... Craggs... arranged a conditional sale at £45,000, but the acceptance is opposed by the Liquidator... The Chairman attached importance to the association with Furness, Withy ... and had informed Mr Stephen Furness that he is willing to recommend our Board to follow him, but he advocated caution as to values, and the present being an inopportune time to get together a staff and workmen ... this negotiation [may] be an opportunity for finding employment for the Elder, Dempster pontoon dock.

Before the end of the month these negotiations had fallen through but throughout the summer enquiries were made *as to what facilities there are on the Tees for establishing a dock.* Explorations for a site for the stock pontoon and a repair works continued and by December offer prices were under consideration on both banks of the Tees. Although by February repair facilities were under consideration at Methil, in Scotland, and on the Mersey, Furness Withy still wanted a joint company with Swan Hunter for a graving dock on Cargo Fleet land on the south bank of the Tees and the Board agreed to continue these negotiations. Two months later the Swans were waiting to hear from Furness and the Board heard a report on the costs at Methil. By mid May the Tees proposal was *practically dropped.* Costs at Methil would have required at least a capital of £75,000 and Swan Hunter were not prepared to venture this alone and although learning in May that shipowner George Renwick would not join the project, it continued to be considered until the end of 1912.

Swan Hunter on the River Wear.

During April 1912 negotiations to acquire an interest in a Sunderland shipyard fell through because of unacceptable terms. The Board agreed on 21 May 1912 to establish a yard for building dock & cassion at

---

[78] The Canadian government took no chances and cashed the cheque, they agreed to pay interest after this action.

[79] During one of these trips Hunter held discussions with the Munson Steamship Line, at the time chartering ships at about £100,000 a month. Munson sought a shipbuilder who would offer them credit terms for *superior cargo boats of good speed* at about £50,000 and the Vice President of Canadian Pacific Railway spoke of requiring ten ore steamers. When Munson finally placed an order it was on the Clyde at *a much lower price* than Swan Hunter.

Southwick.[80] By July the terms of the lease were agreed and by the third week in October work commenced on a cassion for the Admiralty. By December it was stated *that very little now remains to be done in the way of equipping the yard so far as we wish it to be at present.* Although rivetting work had started, difficulties with the riveters continued for some time. By mid February 65 men were employed and it was reported to the Board that: *hand rivetting is now proceeding very satisfactorily, they are making progress with pneumatic rivetting but the compressed air plant is old and somewhat unsatisfactory.* A comment which makes the early remarks on equipment seem strange. On 21 July 1913, the first cassion was launched and was found to be *thoroughly efficient* sliding in its groove at the Portsmouth naval yard. The second cassion was launched 11 months later and this was followed by a large floating dock 500' long. In September the yard was asked *to retard the completion of this dock, if possible, to suit the convenience of the purchase.*

The Scottish Connection - Barclay Curle.
Shipping magnate and financier, Sir John Ellerman, suggested that Swan Hunter acquire a Scottish shipyard and on 18 June 1912 the Board discussed some such working arrangements under the heading Barclay, Curle & Co. A month later Hunter introduced the matter substantively as *the proposal made by Sir John Ellerman.* This was to take over the Scottish company on a valuation basis similar to the merger of Swan Hunter & Wigham Richardson and payment by an issue of ordinary & preference shares and debenture stock. Directors from each Company would serve on the Board of the other and the Board of Barclay Curle would continue to manage the business under its own name.[81] General approval was given by the Swan Hunter Board to the proposed deal and T E Thirlaway, an accountant, was *to go into the question of the figures.* It was later agreed that the Diesel engine works should be a separate development but the extensions for building ships were to be put in hand. Hunter told his Board met in December 1912, that he *would not attempt to influence* [them] *one way or the other.* After discussing the valuation, including the proposed new shipyard [£50,000-£60,000], Eldersie dry dock &c; it was unanimously agreed to purchase at £520,000.[82] Hunter, Denton and Thirlaway were nominated for the Barclay Curle Board and from Barclay Curle, W R Ferguson, James Gilchrist and N E Peck joined the Board of Swan Hunter. A temporary loan of £50,000 was made Swan Hunter to Barclay Curle in August for the Elderslie extensions and by December £100,000 was advanced.

The proposed engine department was realised in the form of the *North British Diesel Co Ltd.* As understood on 22 October 1912 the new company would be *promoted by others, represented by Mr F Lane,* who would purchase a site, erect a works and acquire certain patent rights. The first intention was only to provide *a small part* of the capital but three months later the tone had changed and Hunter spoke of being *closely interested in it and manage it.* When the first Board met on 4 February 1913 the directors were: F Lane, G B Hunter, W R Ferguson, G F Tweedy, C S Gulbenkian and H J Lane [capital £1,000,000 split equally between ordinary and preference £1 shares]. North British Diesel secured exclusive rights to use certain Krupp patents in Great Britain, the British Empire and Egypt for ten years. Krupp was paid £25,500 in cash for marine patents and was due to get another £21,250 over the following ten years, while Ehrardt & Sehmer of Saarbrucken for land engine patents, £4,500 cash and £3,750 over ten years. Perhaps, hardly surprisingly, *Contrary to assurances given by Mr F Lane to Dr Hunter the Diesel Works Ltd have not received a guarantee that the patents and designs will be successful, so we*

---

[80] A site of 9.5 level acres with a further 1.5-2 acres which required to be levelled. The lease offered was 21 years with a rental of £300 [5% of the purchase price of £6,000], and there was on offer two electric cranes, with their rails and wooden foundations, from the Craggs yard [£1,135 each + £600]. A probable outlay of £5,000 was envisaged for machinery, *small offices* &c but some doubts on whether the Bridge over the Wear was a problem.

[81] Barclay Curle estimated that £210,000 might be needed for extensions, £120,000 for an engine works to build Diesel engines and £90,000 for new shipyards, this *shall be reduced.*

[82] Swan Hunter paid with £115,000 - 4.25% Deb, £184,000 - 5% Pref and £220,800 £ ordinary shares all fully paid.

are in the dark as to their value. When war came in August 1914, the German workers erecting the shops were all arrested, part of the machinery was half paid for and other debts were outstanding. By November the Company was working making shell cases. In the spring of 1912 Swan Hunter were invited by the promoters to invest £5,000 in a new company, Burmeister & Wain [Diesel System] Oil Engine Co Ltd, who intended to set up a works on the Clyde and G F Tweedy would join the Board. This venture failed due to a lack of the public investment. When a new proposal emerged requiring both Burmeister & Wain and Swan Hunter each to subscribe one half [£125,000] with the works on Swan Hunter land, the Board decided not to pursue the negotiations. This was a missed opportunity in the field of diesel engine building

A Shipyard at Londonderry.
George Hunter saw another opportunity to gain assistance from public finance. In May 1912, he proposed renting a small shipyard at Londonderry, which had not been used for some time. The yard [valued at £10,000] occupied 6.75 acres and had three berths, with a graving dock and a 60 ton crane. The Harbour Commission were willing to rent it at a nominal £5 per annum and spend £2,000 on roof and other repairs. With the possibility of withdrawing at any time, the Board approved renting and agreed to expenditure up to £5,000-£6,000 and for the formation of a separate company. The North of Ireland Shipbuilding Co Ltd was formed [nominal capital of £50,000] and Trevisa Clarke became managing director. By October the yard was in working order but having difficulties in securing supplies of materials. In December 300 were employed including six squads of riveters. Hunter stated that there were *good prospects* of a profitable investment but it would mean *a larger capital expenditure than was expected*.[83]

Neptune Works.
Decisions related to the Neptune Works offer an insight into the prolonged and tortuous process of renewing shipbuilding facilities and plant. As early as 1898 a re-arrangement of the berths at Neptune was projected. So clearly changes were needed when the amalgamation took place and *contemplated improvements* were discussed in November 1903, when the view was expressed that as there was *only a small amount of work in hand* it was a suitable time to act. Matters were rarely that straightforward and although three months later an expenditure of £30,000-£40,000 was to be submitted, the outline plans with estimates were not considered by the Board until November 1905. John Tweedy argued against spending £11,000 on necessary repairs, since much of this would be wasted when remodelling of the yard took place and the Board concurred. The window of opportunity had passed and Hunter pointed out [1] it was then *inconvenient to finance* [2] *The work would be more costly ... than in slack times* [3] *The disorganisation due to alterations would cause greater inconvenience ... than in slack times*. A clear example of the argument repeated over and over again within the industry, together with the point that in slack times it could not be afforded. However, the Board voted £15,000 for *special improvements & alterations* and a Committee was set up to review the matter.[84] More than two years later, in May 1908, J Denham Christie *explained the necessity for re-building ... the quay and extending it and the desirability of having additional piling east and west of it to form a quay berth 550 feet long*. The estimated cost, including alterations to sheer legs was £6,000. Amongst other items identified was *say £200* to build latrines as required by the Factory Act ! A considerable list of contemplated changes was presented to the Board, including the re-arrangement of Nos 1,2,3 & 4 berths. £1,000 was provided for new wall planing machine

---

[83] An invitation from a German entrepreneur, in 1910, to set up a yard in Sweden was not considered. In 1912 a new company was set up to take over the salvage business of Lindsay, Caverhill & Co with a view to expansion to the West Indies. Swan and Thirlaway became directors of Lindsay Swan Hunter Ltd. By Feb 1914 *very little salvage work* so their workshops began making *a new type of small engine*. The West Indian station was established.

[84] Tweedy pointed out to Hunter that before the new bay could be added to the Engine Department, the berths would have to be re-arranged and so it was decided to spend £11,000 instead on fitting overhead appliances over the three berths in the North Yard. About £2,500 would be spent on small machine tools to be put in existing buildings.

in September 1909 *in place of one worn out*, and further sums were approved at later Board meetings, for example £9,000 in November 1909 for improved Engine Works and Boiler Shop and in December £2,400 for a new office block and office extension. In June 1911 because *the present Neptune siding which is now in an unsafe condition*, £2,200 was noted for additional N E Railway sidings at dry dock department and a connection made to them from *our railway lines* for the Neptune Works traffic; this was to include a new locomotive. The £1,200 voted in October was to cover a punching & shearing machine, an electrical winch and a centrifugal pump to *supply of river water for testing tanks* and also to be *available as a fire pump*. An expenditure of £27,000[85] was approved in May 1912 following a report for extensions to the Neptune engine works for the building of Diesel oil engines *economically* and using the existing shops for shipyard purposes. The impression from surviving records suggests that a considerable level of independent action continued at Neptune and Wallsend and probably for many years personal loyalties were associated with each man's own works rather than the amalgamated company.

The Mid-Tyne Link.

A Magazine conducted by the Staffs of Swan, Hunter, & Wigham Richardson, Wallsend Slipway and North Eastern Marine first appeared in July 1904 under the editorship of A G Hood. Priced at 6d, it had 52 pages, which were filled with illustrations and many insights into the activities not only of the companies named but over a much wider field. The second issue carried a new sub-title devoted to *the Shipbuilding and Engineering Industries of Wallsend and District* and it cited the many approving remarks on the first issue. Comments came not only from the trade journals; *The Syren and Shipping* welcomed *the organ of a great industrial centre*, but also many newspaper including the Liverpool Journal of Commerce, which referred to an excellent example of literary ability and the printer's art. The Workmen's Committee of the Wallsend Shipyard offered congratulations for *an interesting and useful magazine*, which they trusted the workmen *will appreciate it as a medium for the exchange of ideas on shipbuilding and engineering*. It was too successful to remain within its original function. Issue no.8, Spring 1906, began *A Departure*, the local *Mid-Tyne Link* was to become a national magazine *The Shipbuilder*. Subscribers throughout the United Kingdom had perhaps made this changeover inevitable as the Tyne initiative was closing a serious gap in the journals available to cover the whole country; the annual subscription was 3s for four issues.

Some summary comments.

In most respects the years 1906-13 represented the pinnacle for north east shipbuilding. Over the 13 years 1901-13, Swan Hunter, with Wigham Richardsons achieved an annual average output of 93,000t, a feat unequalled by any other firm in the world [see diag 10.15]. Harland Wolff were 10,000t less and the Scottish yard of Russell was at 65,000t.[86] The next five north east yards were Gray [62,000t], Doxford [59,000t], Irvine [53,000t], Armstrong [50,000t] and Northumberland SB [45,000t]. It should of course be noted that Barclay Curle averaged 34,000t, which enhanced still further Swan Hunter's position. Ropner [31,000t] on the Tees was next amongst north east firms, followed by Palmer [30,000t], J L Thompson [28,500t], Hawthorn Leslie [25,500t] and then three at 25,200t - Short, Readhead and Raylton Dixon. The annual average for the north east yards was about 63% of the best year's output. Total output in the boom year of 1889 was 718,000t compared with an average of 1,050,000t in 1911-3. If output in the best year indicated capacity then it was 1,250,000t. Isherwood regarded the North East Coast as *in the fore in all developments that have taken place in ship construction* during this period - well decker, part awning deck steamer, Doxford's turret ship, Dixon's *admirable type of steamer*, Ropner's *well known trunk steamer*, McGlashan's *side tank steamer* and Armstrong's oil tanker; he should have added his longitudinal frames. The rate of adoption of electricity on the north east coast was remarkable and offered a lead to the rest of the country. There were other yard improvements, though probably not enough, and a particular

---

[85] estimate: Buildings £12,000; new machines £4,500; removing existing machinery £2,500; cranes £3,575; railways £500; contingencies £500 - say £25,000. Also testing machine £1,000; to adapt present Engine Works for Plumbers Shop, Rivet Store and Smiths' Shop £1,000.

[86] Figures from the returns published in *Engineering* and the qualifications of tonnage alone has been emphasised.

slowness to adopt adequate cranage and handling equipment. The lack of systematic research, no test tank, and far too few young men entering higher technical education were serious weaknesses pursued elsewhere, yet there was the outstanding innovation of the marine steam turbine. Any comparison of the performance of the shipbuilding industry, with its violent fluctuations, over these years compared with the rest of the world cannot sustain the all too frequent denigration of the British industrial and technological achievement at this time.

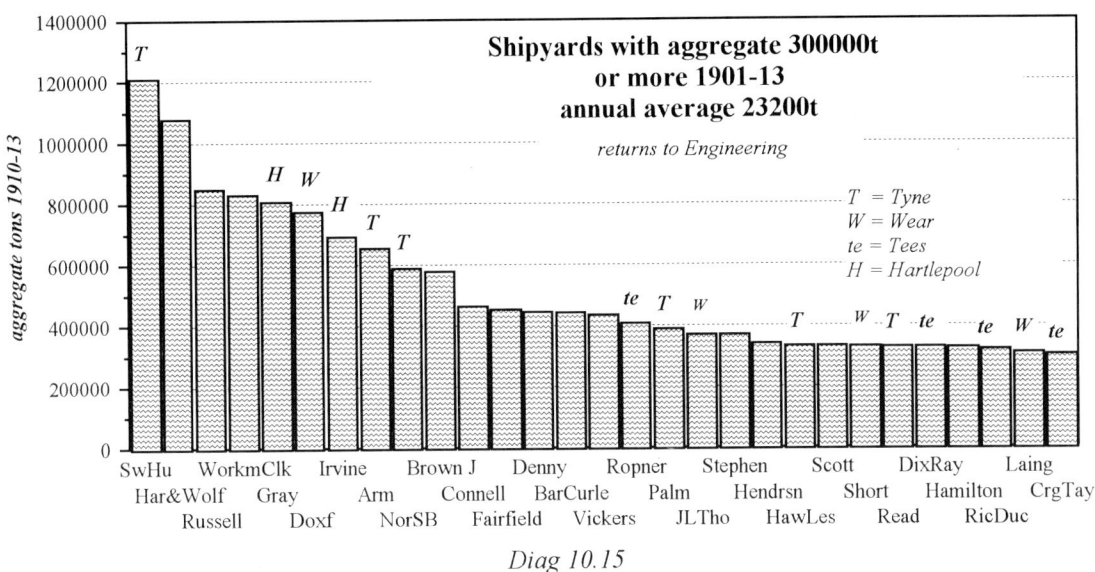

Diag 10.15

Doxford's *Nullus Secundus*

Chapter 11

Warship Building and Supplying Overseas Markets to 1914.

A significant part of the shipbuilding industry's output of merchant vessels and warships went to foreign customers up to 1914. Nationally one ton of every five built went overseas between 1888 and 1913. Undoubtedly, a well established major arms manufacturer such as Armstrong at Elswick, was a major asset for warship building on the Tyne; a successful supplier of the huge guns could propose to his customers the advantages of local shipbuilding. In the second half of the nineteenth century, Tyneside became a major world warship building centre. Almost 800,000dpt, nearly 300 warships, were built on the north east coast between 1850 and 1913. Navy contracts were substantially more valuable than those for merchant ships and invariably took more time to complete. Higher quality materials were normally used and subject to careful inspection, likewise the workmanship was required to be of the highest standard. *The Shipping World* regarded Armstrong-Mitchell as *the greatest warship builder, perhaps, in the world,* in 1890. Twenty years later the *Glasgow Herald* described Palmers as looking more like *a naval base than a private shipyard.*[1] While the *wooden walls* persisted, the south of England retained a very strong control over naval work but the arrival of iron warships dramatically changed the situation. The north with its iron and steel making facilities as well as iron shipbuilding skills enabled new yards to secure Admiralty contracts. In addition, substantial contracts were secured from many overseas countries, from the Argentine to Japan. Extensive sales initiatives were undertaken by Armstrongs as the financial rewards were high. A loss on the first naval order, the price of learning, was accepted by yards entering warship work but thereafter it was expected to be more profitable than merchant construction, and it usually was. North east firms provided many of the marine engines for locally built warships and were important suppliers to the Royal Dockyards. When the navies of the world adopted Parson's steam turbine, there was clearly a local advantage in making this machinery. This also contributed to the special expertise which the Tyne acquired in constructing torpedo boat destroyers, their machinery being more costly than the hull. Naval contracts were especially important for certain marine engine builders. Overwhelmingly the warship work was concentrated in a small number of yards on the Tyne and even in of periods of war had a limited impact on the shipbuilding in the rest of the region, with the exception of Doxfords. Warship building carried grievous risk of the consequences of a drastically curtailed naval building [see chap 22]. This chapter reviews both the warship work and merchant building for foreign customers. The first part examines events to the 1880s, following a broad overview of the period c1885-1913, a consideration of the destroyer, the contributions of Hawthorn-Leslie and Swan Hunter and then the creation of the new Naval Yard at Walker.

The Crimea War

During the Crimea War T & W Smith built seven gunboats in 1856, and two more in 1860, *HMS Britomat* and *HMS Cockatrice*. The latter were part of a class of *wooden gunboat designed as an improvement on the Crimean gun boats...rigged as a three mast schooner, with some additional square sails on the foremast*. The *Hesperus* [1,220 dpt], a troopship launched in 1854, was the first war vessel built by Mitchell, the start of a very important development for the Walker yard. Briggs on the Wear also built some gunboats for the Crimea. Palmers first warship building was the floating battery *HMS Terror*, launched on 23 March 1856. Under the threat of a severe financial

HMS Defence 1861

---
[1] Fourteen war vessels, either new or undergoing repairs, were being dealt with at the time.

penalty it was built and armour plated in about three months. The armour plates were rolled at Jarrow instead of being forged, which enabled this delivery date to be achieved.

Palmers early warships.

Five years later, in 1861, the armour plated frigate *HMS Defence* was launched, and the yard's third warship, a troop carrier, in 1866. The contract for *HMS Jumna* was £187,650 [£30.2/dpt] and, typical of the longevity of many Palmer vessels, she was still in use as a coal hulk 80 years after her launch. *The germ of the modern battleship*, in the words of naval historian David Brown, was launched at Jarrow on 2 December 1868: *HMS Cerebus* [3,340t] was the first of breastwork monitors designed by Reed.[2] This vessel was as *a complete break from established tradition* according to Parkes, while Archibald wrote that *her novel design clearly foreshadowed the Devastation and the class battleship layout that eventually emerged*. The absence of sails allowed a low freeboard vessel, which meant that less armour plating was required. It was surely indicative of confidence in Palmer's yard that they secured this order. Work on the slipway lasted for 15 months, a much longer time than that required for a merchantmen. Completion took even longer and , she was not ready until September 1870. She cost £117,556 and her engines came from the London firm of Maudslay. Until north east yards received Admiralty recognition a number of warships had London built engines. *HMS Cerberus* was finally scuttled as a breakwater outside Melbourne, where she may still probably be seen. A sister ship, *HMS Magdala,* built on the Thames, cost £132,400, an indication of a price advantage for the northern yards. Palmer built *HMS Gorgon* at the lowest cost [£141,254] of the 4 vessels in the *Cyclops* class of coastal defence vessels [the others were £143,310-£194,334]; she was launched on 14 October 1871. Once again the machinery came from an established Admiralty engine builder, Ravenhill. While building the *Cerberus*, Palmers were also working on two battleships, *Swiftsure* and *Triumph*,[3] each contract exceeding £250,000; both with Maudslay machinery. Copper sheathing was added by introducing a double layer of 3" planking to 3' above the water level; this was then covered with a tarred felt before being coppered.[4] Work began in August 1868 and they were launched in June and September 1870 respectively. A dozen flat bottomed gunboats[5] for river use were built by Palmers in 1876-7; this was very welcome work during a trough of merchant orders. Palmers were then also building *torpedo mining boats* [104dpt]; they built 22 of these small war vessels during 1876-81. By the mid-1880s, not only were two despatch vessels, *HMS Surprise* and *HMS Alacrity* under construction, but also two cruisers. Their high speed machinery for the despatch vessels was much admired. *HMS Orlando*, launched in August 1886, gave her name to the class of 7 first class belted cruisers and her sister ship, *HMS Undaunted* [5,600 dpt], was launched 16 weeks later. The hull of the *Orlando* cost £206,700 and her sister £195,900.These two were the only north east vessels among 13 Royal Navy fighting ships, over 700 dpt, launched in 1886; Scottish yards dominated with 6 ships, there was one each from Hull and Barrow and three by the Royal Dockyards. Palmers launched 31 ships for the Admiralty before 1887.

Armstrong-Mitchell.

Mitchell built 9 warships before 1866. In that year the yard built the *Prince Pojarski* [4,137t] for Russia, their largest armourclad for 20 years,. About 1867, Armstrong decided to embark upon the building of war vessels, and arrangements were made with Mitchell to build such vessels; details of these arrangements are not known. Mitchell built an armourclad *Ne Tron Menya* [3,031t] in 1864. It is not clear if warships of 1866 came through Armstrongs nor if later ships were sub-contracts from that firm. Some writers state that

---

[2] Armstrong-Mitchell were anxious to maintain good relations with Reed, White wrote to Noble [13 Feb 1884] *I quite agree with the view of Sir William and yourself, that we should do nothing to make him ill-disposed towards our Company , but should rather encourage any disposition he may have to put work in our way.* [Manning 127]

[3] These vessels were the end of a line- the last capital ships of under 8,000t, no guns above 9" and a propeller hoist.

[4] This was to reduce fouling of the hull because there were no British docking facilities in the Pacific until 1886.

[5] They were 110' x 34' x 10' 8" deep, about 255 tons. Eight were engined by Hawthorns, each had 2 boilers at 60psi.

Walker yard warships were built by Armstrong for example Hovgaard so described *HMS Staunch*. The importance of warship work at Walker should not be exaggerated, between 1866 and 1881, it amounted to about 7% of the tonnage built. If 1866 is excluded the proportion drops considerably and warships were only launched in 7 of 15 years. The Navy used coastal gunboats of the *Ant* class during 1867-1881; Mitchell built the first of these, the *Staunch* [160t], which was designed by G W Rendel of Armstrongs.[6] The rather larger, *HMS Mastiff* and *Bloodhound* [290t] were supplied in 1870. The *Alpha, Beta, Gamma* and *Delta* in 1876-7 were the first of 12 gunboats built for China. When Armstrongs decided to build naval vessels at Elswick, George Rendel expressed his doubts. He wrote, in March 1881, to his brother *I dread commencing shipbuilding*.[7] This involved the amalgamation of Mitchell's firm was with Armstrong's vast armaments works. The shipyard was valued at £250,000 and Mitchell became a director of the new enlarged company. Contracts for the purchase of the Walker yard were settled in November 1882. A manager with substantial naval expertise was required and efforts were made to recruit Nathaniel Barnaby, which filled Rendel with apprehension. A future Director of Naval Construction [DNC] William White [1845-1913] was advancing his career at the Admiralty. He was *top student by a large margin* of the first graduates from the new School of Naval Architecture, which was followed by 24 years *of brilliant and dedicated service to the Admiralty*. In September 1882, soundings were then taken to see if he had any interest in the post and after a number of discussion with Swan, White signed a five year agreement on 5 January 1883, with a substantial gain in his personal income.[8] Before the end of January, Mitchell presented plans for the Elswick yard.[9] The combined industrial knowledge and capacities of Armstrongs and Mitchells were complemented by close connections between personnel of the Tyneside company and key men at the Admiralty. A *series of appointments*, in McCord's words *cemented* links with the Admiralty.[10] Philip Watts first visited Elswick in 1870, as an overseer at the Pembroke Dockyard preparing a report for Reed on shipbuilding capacity on the Tyne. In his own words he *had remained in touch with the firm in various capacities* from then onwards.

As these matters were proceeding, Armstrong challenged naval design policy. When President of the Civil Engineers in 1882, he called for *small fast, heavily armed cruisers, protected by an armoured and a cellular layer ... almost to exclusion of the armour clads*. The Chilean cruiser *Esmeralda* [3,000t] launched 1884, was the first constructed on these lines. Rendel[11] was responsible for the design, and Watts, who was appointed his assistant by the DNC Sir Nathaniel Barnaby, said a Japanese delegation showed *much interest* in the ship. Warship historian Hovgaard, described these Armstrong-Mitchell vessels as

---

[6] G W Rendel [1833-1902] was the son of a civil engineer J M Rendel [1799-1856]. He worked for his father and in 1858 became a partner in Armstrongs and worked on the hydraulics on heavy guns. An extra professional civil lord of the Admiralty in 1882-5. Settled in Naples as director in Armstrong's Pozzuoli Co.

[7] George Rendel wrote to his brother Stuart in March 1881 *I am not satisfied to create a fine business for Mitchell for nothing, and I doubt if the present plan of contracting for ships to be sub-let can long be maintained, especially for important vessels like ironclads or large cruisers.* [Quoted from Warren]

[8] His Admiralty salary was £600 a year plus £51 for lecturing at Greenwich. His earnings from outside work, included £1,631 [1% of cost of production] for his design of the cruiser *Almirante Brown* for the Argentine Government. His earnings for the post of Armstrong's Warship Designer & Manager of the Warship Building Department were a salary of £2,000 a year plus 2s/ton for warships and 1s/ton for merchant ships built at Elswick.

[9] In April tenders for £9,075 were accepted and in September 1884 it was estimated that about £10,000 was required for an ironclad berth; Swan and Mitchell were to continue to direct construction of yard. £11,000 was allocated in March 1885 for a second berth - the tender for piling was £9,940, if Armstrong supplied the timber.

[10] The following Directors of Naval Construction [period of office in brackets] worked at some time at Elswick: William White [1885-1901], Philip Watts [1902-11] and Eustace H W Tennyson D'Eyncourt [1912-23].

[11] Rendel's outline design was developed by Mitchell, Swan and W Dobson and David Black. W H Whiting, who almost became a DNC, commented that *Rendel rendered to the shipbuilding industry of this country services which [he] supposed were never equalled, save those of Brunel*. NECIES v. XXX p 403.

characterized by the total absence of sail power, by high speed, good manoeuvring qualities, exceptional power of attack, and relatively good protection for ships of that class. These qualities were attained on a small displacement; but ... the freeboard was low, which was more particularly felt forward, where wetness restricted the use of the bow gun. On the whole ... the *Esmeralda* was a success, and its influence can be traced in the design of cruisers during the following years.

The Controller of the Navy attended the trials of the *Esmeralda*, and his aide Assistant Constructor, W E Smith[12] was *much struck with the very special features of her design*. He recalled that it was *for a time a very moot point* whether *on the whole* the new design was preferable to that of four similar vessels the Admiralty were building. Finally the *Esmeralda* type *won most favour*. During White's two years in Newcastle designs were produced for *Naniwa*[13] and *Takachiho* [Japan], *Panther* and *Leopard* [Austria], *Dogali* [Italy], *Chih-Yuan* and *Ching-Yuen* [China] as well as two small cruisers for Spain. The *Panther* was the first vessel laid down at Elswick The keel was laid late in October 1884 and launched on 13 June 1885. Just over six weeks later, White became Director of Naval Construction. Philip Watts replaced him at Elswick and in 1902 Watts returned to the Admiralty as DNC. Watt's successor Tennyson D'Eyncourt[14] was preparing to start his apprenticeship at Elswick as White was leaving Newcastle.

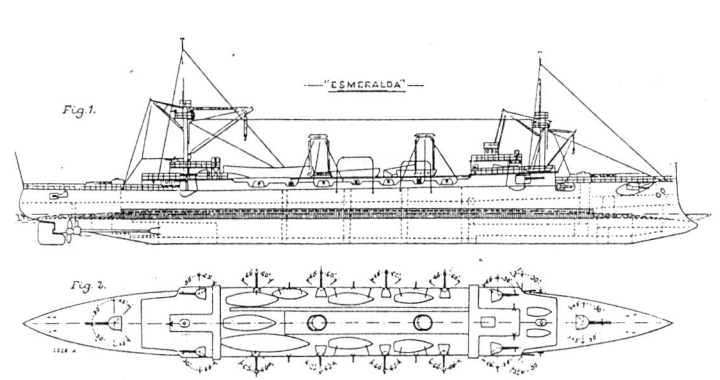

HMS Esmeralda

Five British gunboats were built at the Walker yard in 1884 and in the next year three cruisers, one for Italy and two for Japan. At Elswick the *Panther* was followed by her sister ship in 1886, together with two gunboats for the British Navy. In 1887 came the *Dogali* and the two cruisers for China and Spain. *HMS Victoria* was the first British battleship built at Elswick and at 10,000 dpt represented a major challenge. She was double the size of any ship previously built by Mitchell and work began in the summer of 1885. With supporting overseeing staff, Smith was appointed to see *Victoria*[15] was *properly built in accordance with specifications, and handed over satisfactorily.* He recalled her first voyage down river,

> Philip Watts on the navigating platform looking out with characteristic Napoleonic attitude as the bridges were approached. In those days it was considered a great feat to get the vessel safely through the bridges,

---

[12] Smith was appointed Superintendent of Contract Work in 1905. In 1912, he was due to become Director of Naval Construction when Watts left to join Armstrongs but Churchill became First Lord of the Admiralty. Smith was *rather careless in regard to his personal appearance*. Browne described a visit by Churchill to Portsmouth : *When Churchill fired a question, Smith was some distance away, talking to some workmen. Unimpressed by this ill-informed, ill-dressed man, Churchill demanded that the Secretary, Graham Greene, sack Smith forthwith. Smith, whose work in building the fleet of the First World War was unequalled, resigned that night...* pp 104-5.

[13] After the battle of Yalu in 1894, Admiral Ito wrote to White: *Not only are they indispensable as scouts, but they have also proved themselves to possess in an eminent degree the qualities of powerful battleships.* [Brown p 70]

[14] [Sir] Eustace H W Tennyson D'Eyncourt FRS [1868-1951] was a second cousin of Alfred Tennyson and educated at the Naval College Greenwich. He stayed at Elswick for 7 years after his apprenticeship. To gain experience of merchant work he went to Fairfields as naval architect; he got the job, *because of being personally known to* Francis Elgar [consulting naval architect]. Perret brought him back to Elswick in 1902. He headed the Admiralty Committee, which produced the first tank [*a land ship*]. He became managing director of the shipbuilding section of Armstrong-Whitworth [1924-8] and then joined the Board of Parsons Marine [1928-48].

[15] *HMS Victoria*, as the flag ship of Vice Admiral Sir George Tryon [1832-93], met a tragic end when rammed by *HMS Camperdown* during manoeuvres in the Mediterranean in June 1893. Tryon with 358 officers and men were drowned. She carried two of the heaviest guns in the Navy, each 111 tons of 16.25"calibre.

and although the Tyne people were then very proud of their tugs he could not help regarding it as almost impossible that she could be satisfactorily navigated with such small tugs ... after some difficulty and slight delay, the vessel was safely got to sea. [a site below the bridges would have been best]

That Syndicate [Armstrong, Barnaby & White].

When on 31 March, *The Daily News* reprinted a story from the *Nautical Gazette, a somewhat peppery little weekly* New York paper, that a syndicate [Armstrong, Barnaby & White] was designing American Warships, it caused *quite a sensation. The Shipping World* discussed this *attack upon some of the most prominent names connected with Naval Architecture and Construction* and argued that the charge of *pushing trade* in designing warships for foreign governments required *no refutation where the gentlemen* [were] *known. The Shipping Gazette* suggested White still had interests in Elswick. Despite denials, including from the Secretary of the United States Navy, *The Daily News* returned to the charge on 5 April. Given the *large foreign connection* of Armstrongs, *The Shipping World* commented: *No sensible person will question the right of the firm to build ships and guns for foreign governments, or to furnish such governments or other customers with plans, drawings, and specifications of warships, guns and machinery of every class and character whatsoever, in times of peace.* Barnaby's right after retirement to earn a living as a naval architect was defended. Armstrong told his shareholders how matters stood as White returned the Admiralty,:

> the Company should be entitled to his advice in a consultative capacity during the remainder of the term for which he was engaged. Much of the work which Mr White has inaugurated renders his temporary intervention absolutely necessary, and considering the sacrifice we made in liberating him, it is also perfectly fair that we should have the benefit of his opinion whenever we require to consult him ... provided that by so doing we do not encroach upon the time required for the discharge of his duties at the Admiralty.

In the House of Commons, Lord George Hamilton [ex-First Lord of the Admiralty] stated the one stipulation of Armstrongs, to which assent was given: *Several of Mr White's designs were not completed, and others were not commenced. Under these circumstances they asked they might, if necessary, consult with Mr White upon questions connected with these designs.* A slightly more limited approval than Armstrong's statement, which indicated right to consult in more general terms. According to Hovgaard: *The preliminary plans for the new cruisers were bought in England and prepared by Sir William White.* In 1885 the first of these the *Charleston* was authorised: it was *essentially a duplicate of the Armstrong cruiser Naniwa.*[16]

The overview 1885-1913.

About 31,000 dpt [32 warships] were built by Mitchell before the merger with Armstrongs and in the six years 1884-9, Armstrong-Mitchell turned out 53,361 dpt. This combined output of about 84,000 dpt compared with Palmers output of 54,000 dpt up to 1889. Up to that time Doxford [3,485 dpt] and Raylton Dixon [3,970 dpt] had built four and three craft respectively. A *large and hitherto unparalleled increase in naval strength* was authorized by the Naval Defence Act of 1889 and four years later a programme to match the advances of France and Russia was agreed. Over the 24 years, 1890-1913, the 162 warship built on the north east coast exceeded 623,000 dpt. Armstrong's dominance continued with 432,794 dpt, followed by

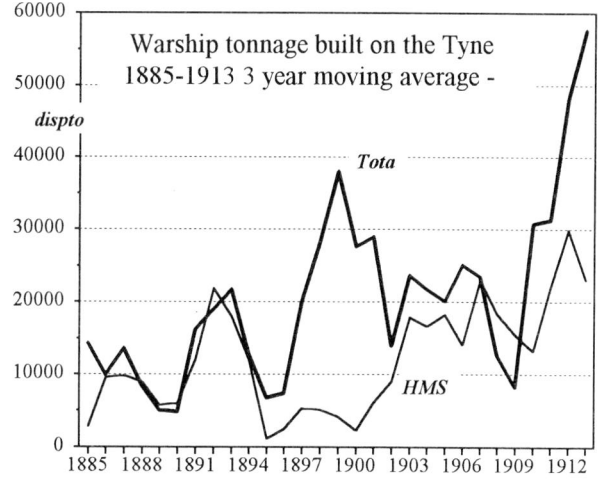

Diag 11.01

---

[16] The continued relative backwardness of American development, was reflected in a competition for the design of the *Texas* [6,300t], which was built in 1892 to a design by John of Barrow, the best of 13 designs submitted.

Palmer with more than 142,000 dpt and from Hebburn, 32 destroyers and torpedo boats added up to 19,540 dpt. Swan Hunter came into naval work later than other Tyne yards and built 8 vessels [11,500 dpt] during 1910-3. Doxford built six craft over the years 1895-1901, in all 2,040 dpt and both Raylton Dixon and Laing built repair ships for the Navy. Warship output by the Tyne yards is summarised in diag 11.01.

A comparison of the tonnage in the Royal Dockyards, the Clyde and the North East Coast is shown in diag 11.02 based on a 3-year moving average; this shows that for many years the Clyde secured a much higher proportion of British Navy work than the north east. From high points in the early 1890s, the north east remained substantially below the Clyde until the era of the turbine. From about 1900 the north east moved upward but only for a few years directly compared with the Clyde. The value of British Navy work over the period 1895-1914 was placed at £62,220,000 for the Clyde and £46,420,000 for the north east. At Elswick overseas orders were very important, with 13 foreign countries supplied apart from the Indian and Australian governments. Just about one-third of the tonnage from Armstrongs was for the British Navy. Japan took almost 19% of the output, and more than a quarter went to South America. In addition to many warships for Chile and Brazil, three cruisers and three gunboats were supplied to the Argentine. The customer for some Elswick vessels offers more than a little confusion. Reed designed the battleship *Constitution* for Chile, and Armstrongs proceeded to build her but she was commissioned as *HMS Swiftsure* in 1903. Ten years later the intended customer for the dreadnought *Almirante Latorre* was Chile. In fact she became *HMS Canada*, and was afterwards sold to Chile in 1920.[17] Another dreadnought, *Rio De Janeiro* was intended for Brazil but sold to Turkey. Just as she was due to depart, armed troops marched on to the Tyne quayside and surrounded *Sultan Osman I* to prevent her delivery in August 1914. She was then commissioned as *HMS Agincourt. The Mid-Tyne Link* commented on the Russo-Japanese War [1904-5] -Tyneside as a shipbuilding centre was *well represented in both the belligerent fleets*. Elswick built 13 of the 50 Japanese armoured and cruising ships and Armstrongs supplied all the guns on the Japanese vessels that defeated the Russian Fleet in the Tsushima Straits. As that battle continued Armstrongs were completing their largest vessel for Japan the battleship *Kashima* [16,400 dpt][18].Like all the Japanese warships after 1885 her engines were by Humphrey Tennant.

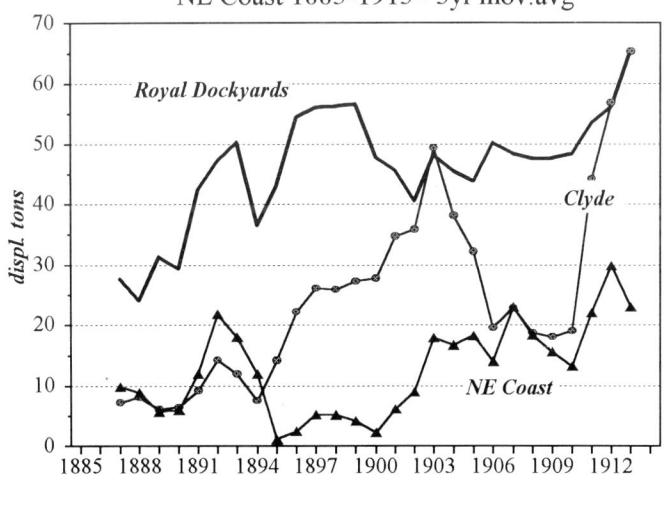

Diag 11.02

Palmers, in 1889-93, were very successful in securing Admiralty contracts; a total of £1,400,000 almost equalled John Brown and amounted to more than a quarter of all private yard work. In 1890-1, three *Apollo* class wood sheathed cruisers were built at the Howdon Yard - *HMS Pique, Rainbow* and *Retribution*. The battleships *HMS Resolution* and *HMS Revenge* were launched in 1892; they were of the *Royal Sovereign*

---

[17] Two cruisers *Almirante Barroso* [1897] and *Amazonas* [1898] were built for Brazil and soon afterwards were both purchased by the USA and served as *USS Albany* and *USS New Orleans*.

[18] Other vessels were gunboat *Tsukushi* [1880], five cruisers *Izumi* [1883], *Naniwa Kan* [1885], *Takachiho* [1885], *Yoshino* [1892], *Takasayo* [1897], four armoured Cruisers *Tokiwa* [1898], *Asama* [1898], *Idzumo* [1899], *Iwate* [1900]. torpedo gunboat *Tatsuta* two battleships *Yashima* [1896], *Hatsuse* [1899]

class.[19] *HMS Russell* a first class battleship was launched in 1901 and sailed in February 1903 [speed 15k]. British naval contracts at Jarrow from 1889 to 1905 exceeded £3,000,000. *HMS Lord Nelson* was launched in 1906, powered by Palmer built triple expansion engines; she had a speed of 18k and cost £1,540,000, and the larger dreadnought *Hercules* followed four years later. The largest warship built at Jarrow, a 700' long dreadnought cruiser *HMS Queen Mary* [26,350t], was launched on 20 March 1912.[20] Her turbines came from John Brown on the Clyde and Palmers built 14 of the 42 boilers. A total of 44 warships, battleships, cruisers and torpedo boat destroyers were built at Jarrow between 1887 and 1914. Palmers provided designs for foreign governments, including three cruisers for Spain, which were built at Bilbao: the *Maria Theresa*, *Viscaya* and *Almirante Oquendo*. A destroyer the *Planet* was built for Austro-Hungarian fleet in 1889.

Before 1914, Hawthorn-Leslie's shipyard built mainly destroyers, but their first naval contract was for the cruiser *Bellona* launched in August 1890. Their chairman Browne argued that the substantial loss of £16,119 on the £45,000 price for the hull was a cost to be borne *for getting our experience as War Vessel Builders*. He hoped it would not have exceeded £2,000! Marshall was not happy when the Company once again put in tenders for warship work; indeed he thought they had abandoned that field. His mind was perhaps set at rest when five torpedo boats built in 1894-8, yielded a profit of 18.6% on turnover. It was the company's engine works which was deeply engaged in supplying warships engines; it was the principal supplier to Armstrongs. After 1886 there was rarely a time when a naval marine engine was not passing through the St Peter's Works, and although losses were made on some it was overwhelmingly profitable. The turbine work here and at Wallsend Slipway is considered in chap 14. The tonnage of different types of warship built over the ten years 1895-1914 in each region and the Royal dockyards is shown in diag 11.03 [above].

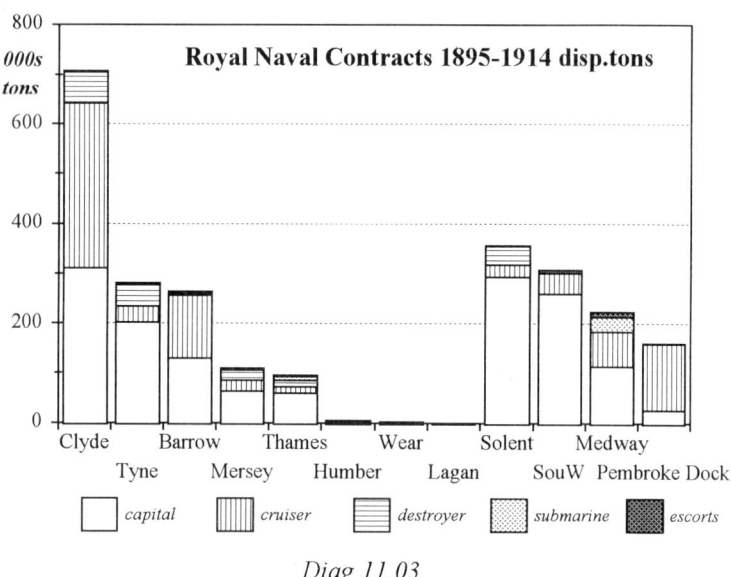
Diag 11.03

The torpedo boat destroyer.[21]

The torpedo boat destroyer became a specialty of Tyne shipbuilders; they built at least 79 during 1892-1913. Both Armstrongs and Palmers occasionally laid down stock destroyers. *HMS Copra* was laid down for stock by Armstrongs and one built at Jarrow was purchased in 1900 and sailed as *HMS Kangaroo*. Almost as soon as White took up his appointment as DNC he had to face the threat posed by the Whitehead

---

[19] Only *HMS Revenge* of this class to survive in the Royal Navy to 1914. She served as monitor and was renamed *Redoubtable* in 1915. The designer, White gave the cost breakdown of his class: hull & fittings £320,000; armour £260,000; propelling & other machinery £97,000; gun mountings &c £76,000; torpedo tubes £6,000. This was a sub-total of £759,000 and there was then ammunition & reserves £219,000, which gave a grand total of £978,000.

[20] She was first in action on 28 August 1914 in Heligoland Bight and was sunk at the Battle of Jutland with the loss of 1,265 lives. This ship with two others were sunk before they *had received heavy punishment and the deduction is that flame reached the turret magazines causing them to explode* - from official report in Brown.

[21] See Edgar J March's historical survey of the first 60 years of the destroyer ; this section draws on that study. Twenty seven firms built more than 900 destroyers up to 1953. In destroyers built before 1919, approximately 35% of the displacement was due to machinery and 41.5% to the hull.

torpedo.[22] After some initial unsatisfactory attempts at a solution, according to Brown, *The idea of* [destroyer] *seems to have crystallized in a discussion between Sir Alfred Yarrow and Sir John Fisher the Controller in 1892.* White passed an early Admiralty sketch to Yarrow and Thorneycroft and so from the outset these two shipbuilders played a leading role in designing and building the torpedo boat destroyer. Opposition by White to building the new craft in the Royal Dockyards opened an important opportunity for the private yards. He stated:

> To secure remarkably high speeds in small vessels it is absolutely necessary to devote the most careful attention to every detail of hull and machinery. The responsible designer must scrutinise and control every portion of the work. In fact design and construction are practically inseparable in this class of work.

Understandably, the first orders, the 1892-3 programme, were placed with Yarrow and Thorneycroft. Fourteen yards built the 35 vessels of the 1893-4 programme. Palmers launched *HMS Janus* on 12 March 1895,[23] Hawthorn-Leslie's first launch was on 23 May and Armstrongs on 7 June. On the 3-hour speed trials the Palmer vessels were faster than the others, 27.8k- 27.94k against Hawthorn's best 27.58k and Armstrongs 27.46k; it is debatable whether these differences were significant. In this programme for 27 knotters, Doxford and Armstrongs each built two destroyers, while there were three each from Palmers and Hawthorn-Leslie; it was not until 1910 that Swan Hunter launched their first destroyer.

Commanding Officers gave their assessment of various TBDs to the Committee on Torpedo Boat Destroyers in July 1903. Brown summarised as follows: they *claimed to recognise significant differences in seaworthiness between builders and the accounts are mutually consistent. Palmer's boats are almost always seen as the best, rivalled by Hawthorn Leslie as sea boats while Laird's are described as weak. Thorneycroft boats were the worst due to slamming under their wide, concave stern and inadequate freeboard and flare forward.*[24] Among individual assessments were the following :

> *Destroyers built by Hawthorn-Leslie were more roomy and somewhat better accommodation ... All the Palmer- built TBDs with Reed boilers were good steamers, able to maintain speed in seaway.* Vice-Admiral Sir J A Fisher *Everyone speaks highly of the Palmer boats ... all the engineer officers without exception mention them as superior to all others.* Cdr Mark Kerr *Cheerful* and *Mermaid* by Hawthorn-Leslie *the best without doubt and Thorneycrofts the worst.* C in C Portsmouth Adm. Hotham praised Palmer boats *by far the best in the division ... Myrmidon, is particularly good. Their boats are good at sea, engines satisfactory, good accommodation.*

Serious breakdowns in machinery occurred during 1904 manoeuvres in heavy weather; there were 16 reported defects, from hot bearings to cracked cylinders and breakdowns in condensers. The boilers burned out on Doxford's *Violet* and she was towed 130 miles. Capt Charlton reported that the *Racehorse* class, by Hawthorn Leslie gave the least trouble, but the *Bittern* class by Vickers, *the most they were also coal eaters*. A possible explanation was poor stoking due to a *complete lack of training for stokers*!

TURBINIA - and destroyers.

William White was kept fully informed of the progress Parsons was making on the *Turbinia*[25] and when he inspected her in February 1897 he suggested that the stern could have been improved if built up square. On its final trials, the Navy's Engineer in Chief was on board and both Parsons and his works manager Barnard managed the controls. In 40 seconds 30 knots was reached and the vessel stopped in 36 seconds. *The almost complete absence of vibration and noise,* Marsh wrote, *amazed the naval men used to the reciprocating engine.* A new revolutionary engine, particularly suited for naval vessels, had arrived.

---

[22] Robert Whitehead [1823-1905], manager of a marine engine works at Fiume, made a locomotive torpedo in 1867. In 1870 he demonstrated his torpedo to the Admiralty and within three years Yarrow supplied vessels armed with torpedoes. By 1890 there was a much improved torpedo. In 1906 Armstrong-Whitworth acquired £200000 of shares in the Whitehead Torpedo Co.

[23] Davidson wrongly claimed that Palmer's order was the pioneering one, *watched by warship builders throughout the country with very great interest.* Undoubtedly Jarrow was a very successful builder of destroyers.

[24] Concern was expressed upon the multiplicity of designs by 11 builders and its impact on spares !

[25] *Turbinia*, with both *HMS Viper, HMS Copra* and *HMS Velox* are further reviewed in chap 15.

Although it first established its merits propelling destroyers it is appropriate to quote how naval engineers first enjoyed the steam turbine in a capital ship. Admiral Bacon wrote :

> When steaming at full speed in a man-of-war fitted with reciprocating engines, the engine room was always a glorified snipe marsh; water lay on the floor plates and was splashed about everywhere; the officers often clad in oilskins to avoid being wetted to the skin. The water was necessary to keep the bearings cool. Further, the noise was deafening; so much so that telephones were useless and even voice-pipes of doubtful value. In the *Dreadnought*, when steaming at full speed, it was only possible to tell that the engines were working, and not stopped, by looking at certain gauges. The whole engine-room was as clean and dry as if the ship was lying at anchor, and not the faintest hum could be heard.

Undoubtedly, Parsons' prestige, determination and application were very significant factors in securing the success of the turbine. The Admiralty placed contracts with his Marine Turbine Co, who then sub-contracted the hull. Parsons was the main contractor for- the *Viper* and *Velox*, hulls by Hawthorn-Leslie, the *Badger* and *Beaver* [hulls - Denny] and the *Garland* [hull Cammell-Laird], the *Leonidas* and *Lucifer* [hulls - Palmer]. Each of these represented critical phases of development, the beginning, semi-geared turbines and finally geared turbines. Parson's standing alone would never have secured such a speedy adoption without a receptiveness among some senior naval constructors and the Engineer in Chief's department. [see chap 15]

Hawthorn's *HMS Eden* was the only one of the *River or E Class* destroyers [1901-4] with Parsons turbines. At £87,400 the contract was significantly higher than the others: Palmers built for £67,779 and Yarrow for £77,000. Hawthorn's *HMS Derwent*, with triple expansion engines cost less than Yarrow. *HMS Eden* was launched on 3 March 1903 and on trial reached the highest speed 26.23k compared with 26.07k by Yarrow's *Usk*, the best of the others. Coal consumption by the *Eden* at 7.66t / hour was below the 7.8t required in contract. On the repeat *Acorn* programme, 1910-11, Parsons secured a contract for two vessels, the *semi-geared HMS Badger* and *HMS Beaver*; the hulls were built by Parsons' friend and supporter Denny. Tenders submitted to the Admiralty showed wide variations. For the *Tribal class*, tenders from £95,000 by Yarrow to £137,500 by Palmers were rejected, all the designs being unacceptable. These two builders were not invited to re-submit when Lairds, Armstrong and Hawthorn-Leslie were asked for new tenders. Prices quoted for the Flotilla leader *Swift* were described as *breath-taking*: Armstrong's tender at £284,000 was the highest and John Brown's the lowest at £191,717. For the *Beagle class*, the Doxford, Palmer and Thorneycroft tenders were *prohibitive*. Palmers offered a destroyer built *on spec* to the Admiralty in September 1903, *practically identical* to the *Erne class* at £72,000, it was accepted in 1904 and named *HMS Rother*.

HMS Talisman one of four torpedo boat destroyers designed for Turkey and taken over by Admiralty

Swan Hunter.

Some concern was expressed, in 1907, on the Swan Hunter Board at the absence of Admiralty enquiries in recent years. White advised writing to the secretary of the Admiralty and Lord Tweedmouth, drawing attention to the Company's close association with Wallsend Slipway, whose machinery was highly regarded. White had already left the Board before more active consideration was given to warship building. Comments by George Hunter, in April 1909, were hardly optimistic: he understood *that the Contracts for warships recently built were not remunerative and that the prospect of our securing remunerative Contracts for such work is not good*. Early in 1911 the Board considered a proposal to construct 6 destroyers for Chile, at about £60,000, and authorised the provision of a Drawing Office for additional Admiralty work at an estimated cost of £3,000. It was agreed in August to establish a separate department for sheet iron work if an order for a cruiser or battleship was received. The facilities for warship production, including submarines, were reviewed in March 1913 and the Board considered appointing an officer from the Royal Corps of Naval Constructors. E L Peacock, of the Lake Torpedo Boat Co, applied to be manager and designer of a department for submarines and he was interviewed by Hunter during a visit to New York. Peacock was appointed and within months two draughtsmen were working with him. The Wallsend yard was placed on the Admiralty list and not long afterwards they were invited to tender for submarines. Before mid-December the tenders were submitted and a submarine was being designed for Russia. Designs to met the requirements for the U S Navy were prepared and negotiations began with an American Company to construct to these designs under a Royalty payment. It was *practically decided* by mid April 1914 that if no order was received Swan Hunter would build a submarine on their own account. A possible means of lowering prices was considered; it was to build Diesel engines for *the coastal type of submarines* at the Neptune Works. No immediate action was taken to build *on spec*. In August design work was underway for *submarines of different types* and not long after war began tenders for Greece were suspended. However, it was not until November 1914 that approval was given for the expenditure for a new shed, with cranes, for building submarines and plant for charging their accumulators: it was not to exceed £6,500. Meanwhile not far away a new naval yard was completed.

Cartoon in *Jarrow Guardian* 31 March 1911

Armstrong's Naval Yard.

Capital ships were steadily increasing in size. Two of the Elswick warships for Chile were 92' wide, compared with 82' for *HMS Dreadnought*. Armstrong-Whitworth[26] faced the necessity of building a new yard because of the problem of vessels from Elswick reaching the sea. So the new yard was constructed at Walker in what was probably the biggest single investment in shipbuilding on the Tyne. The Naval Yard was opened in the summer of 1914, four years after the first decisions were taken by the Board. A report to the Directors in September 1912 by the shipyard manager G J Carter [1860-1922][27] shows that the original intention was to set *up the new yard with an output at least equal to that in Elswick Shipyard*. However, as the size of vessels that *may be built will be very much increased*, buildings were to be

---

[26] In 1897- Armstrong incorporated Whitworth's business into his company forming Armstrong-Whitworth Ltd [Warren - the *sweeping gains* expected *were not realised*]. Vickers bought the Naval Construction Co at Barrow.

[27] G J Carter who left Elswick in 1912 to become managing director of Cammell Laird at Birkenhead. He came to Tyneside in 1886 and joined Elswick in 1894. His departure seems surprising, Warren commented: *Some evidence that Armstrongs undervalued the skills of managers and innovators...* [p 96]

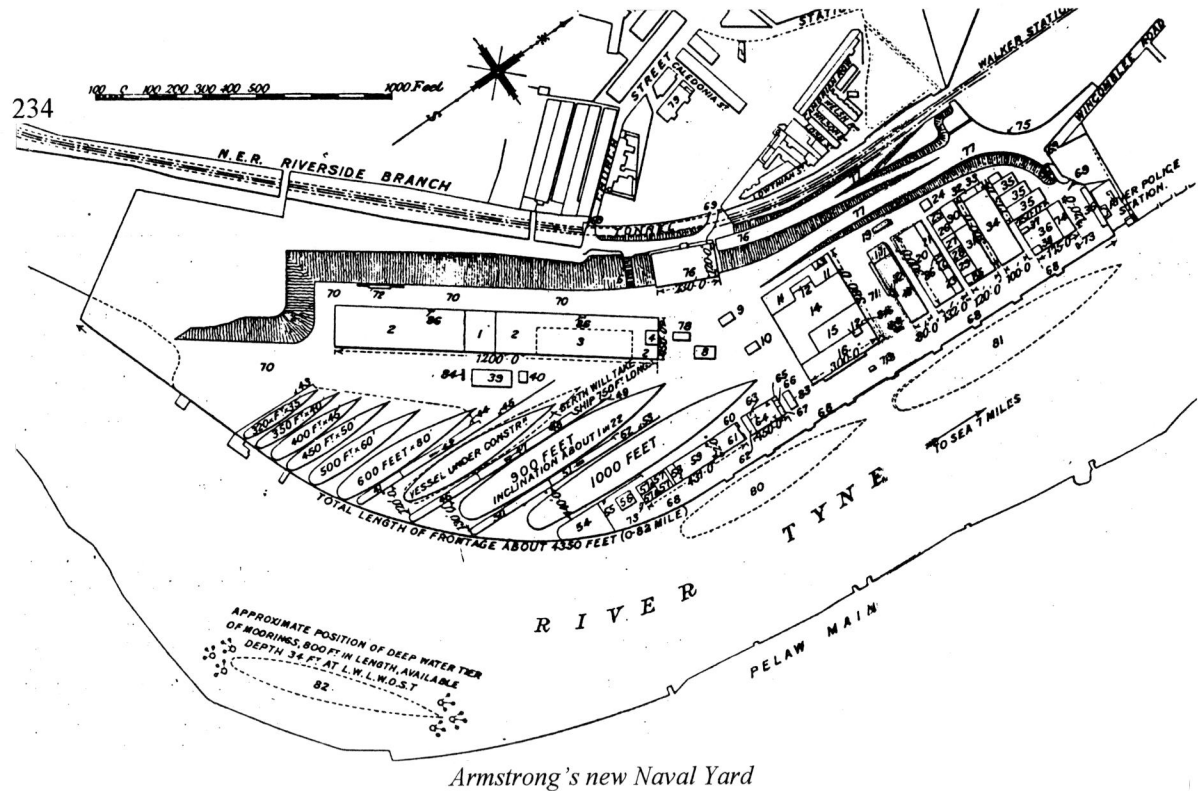

Armstrong's new Naval Yard

arranged ... to allow extensions. J R Perrett,[28] as general manager had overall responsibility for the new yard. Reports on the *New Walker Yard* from the Company secretary's office survive up to September 1912. Instructions were received on the 4th of August 1910 to obtain *certain properties to allow the extension of the Naval Equipment Yard, to meet the requirements of a constructing yard.* Acquiring the land required involved the purchase of many business premises and there were complications with the length of leases that could be secured. Within a month various options had been secured.[29] Deals were finally worked out with the Gas Company to include 900' river frontage. The ongoing relationship with existing work influenced progress on the new yard. Estimates were first obtained on the basis of the excavation work being completed in 12 months [quotations varied from 15.5d to 27d/ cubic yard]. Due to the work at Elswick, 18 months was then allowed for excavation and a lower price was secured, which saved £13,000. The cost was still going to exceed £200,000. By the beginning of October preparations were underway for the excavation. Work was about to be started on a Brazilian battleship, which would not be launched for eighteen months, and *cannot reach a state when she can be removed from Elswick certainly under two years*. This not only affected the removal of any plant but also made it desirable to secure an order to build another ship on the berth then occupied by the *Monarch*.

More dredging was required than was first anticipated. Subsistence and a problem of shifting sand meant that the old jetty needed to be *very much strengthened* and the new part to be of a *much more substantial nature* than was *originally contemplated*. Tenders were sought for ferro concrete piling. Early in September plans for the new jetty were submitted to the Tyne Commissioners and before the end of 1911

---

[28] Perrett [1848-1918] trained at the Devonport Naval Yard and the Royal School of Naval Architecture; he then worked under Froude for many years. After two years as Assistant Constructor joined Armstrongs, as assistant to Watts and later general manager of the Elswick yard and then the Naval yard.

[29] They could buy the *Hope & Anchor* for £2000 if spirit license transferred to *Refreshment Arms* on Walker Shipyard property, otherwise £3500; the magistrates granted the licence. Central Government would only sanction 99 year leases where there was *some monetary advantage* to the local authority. *Several interviews* were held with representatives of the various committees to acquire City Council land; 21 acres were offered on a 75 year lease at £750 per annum with £250 reversion charge and all the buildings *to be removed at our discretion...as far as the* [Corporation] *have power, to close all roads on the land in question*. Both committees *unanimously* recommended approval to the full Council.

work was about to begin on the first buildings. A remarkably late decision was recorded in the Report of 7 December 1911:

> Seeing subsidence which has taken place at the Pallion Yard of Doxfords owing to the working of coal mines under that yard, and knowing that under certain portions of the new Walker yard coal was worked many years ago enquiries of Dr J B Simpson [Simpson's costs were not to exceed £100].

Despite two months of much bad weather and rough seas *good progress* was noted at the beginning of 1912. Work was further delayed by a London dockers' strike, which was followed by a national transport strike. The 80 acre site was levelled to suit the needs of the new shipyard. More than four million cubic yards excavated from ground in places as high as 130' above quay level. Some half a million tons of material was dredged from the river to provide a depth of 30' for 100' alongside the quay at low water. Keel launch ways for these vast ships required very strong foundations; this was secured by driving 4,500 pitch-pine piles, each 14" square into the ground to an average depth of 18'. No less than ten miles of railway track were laid on the site. NESCo provided the electrical power at 6,000 volts 40 Hz, which was transformed down to 440v for the various shops and to 110v for lighting. The river frontage of the yard was 4,376' and 50 acres of the site were occupied by the yard. Battleship berths were laid almost parallel to the river by utilising the bend. Nine completed berths ranged from 320' to 1,000'. The fitting-out wharf was 2,133' long and traversed by a 30 ton electric crane and it was intended to use a floating crane for heavier loads. This vast investment was, in many ways, too late. When the war was over in 1918 an entirely new situation existed. Armstrongs had for some time actively considered acquiring a marine engine works. A sub-committee was examining the position and there were discussions with Benjamin Browne and J M Allan, managing director at St Peters. Finally it was agreed there was ground available on which, should it be so desired, to construct a marine engine works in connection with this yard. This did not come into to operation until after 1919.

It should not be assumed that British yards had the overseas markets all to themselves; they did not. The French built foreign warships from an early stage and after 1880 the Germans were also very active in this field; they were building two Chinese warships [*Ting Yuen & Chen Yuen*] at the same time as Elswick. When in 1910 it looked as though the Germans would secure the order for a Brazilian battleship Tennyson d'Eyncourt hurried to Rio de Janeiro and with great skill managed to secure the order for £1,821,400; this was the vessel that finally became *HMS Agincourt*! The man from Elswick was smarting from a rebuff in Buenos Aires, where the Americans had secured an order for two dreadnoughts at a loss leader price. For many years the Argentine ordered from Italy. Prompt delivery may be noted - in 1902, the *Glasgow Herald* pointed out while all 52 US warships under construction were 12 months behind time, British builders were *rarely behind with naval work*.

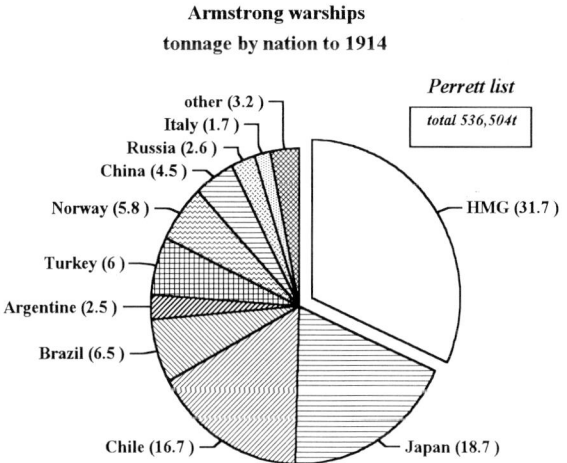

Merchant Tonnage Built for Overseas Customers.

On Sunday 22 June 1862 a clergyman in the Danish village of Allinge must have been very surprised when a young Tynesider tried to talk to him in Latin. Wigham Richardson was the young man, on his way to personally deliver a ship to Warsaw. This paddle steamer *Isabell* was only 134' long and the whole episode illustrated the initiatives which shipbuilders took to secure orders and satisfy customers.[30] The substantial foreign sales by the Neptune yard are presented below. Export opportunities were greatly improved after the introduction of iron hulls and steam power. Despite its role as a leading builder of wooden ships, the

---

[30] For the whole excitement of this episode, which began on the streets of Newcastle, see his *Autobiography*.

Wear sold few ships abroad in the 1850s and 1860s. Overseas customers were more important for the yards on the Tyne than in the rest of the region.

Overseas customers in 1850s & 1860s

Less than 1% of the Wear tonnage went overseas in the 1850s, only 17 ships, totalling 5,643t, including the Channel Islands and British colonies. Three ships were built for German owners; in 1852 Naisby supplied the *Washington* [486t] and the other two were in 1855 and 1858. Not until 1871 did any more ships go to Germany. One ship to each of Norway and Greece completed sales to Europe except for a 343t ship to Malta. A craft of a mere 47t was sent to Cape Town and the *Mary* [109t] to St Helena. Exports in 1860s increased substantially but only reached 2.64% of the tonnage built, made up of 25 wood ships [8,590t], two composites [1,392t] and 12 iron vessels [6,909t]. Spain headed the list with 7,100t, almost equally divided between wood and iron hulls. France followed with 5,400t; the average size of their five iron vessels, at 634t, was double that of the wood ships. Three ships were delivered to Greece in 1866, two to Italy and a single vessel to each of Sweden, Russia and Manilla. Twenty two different yards sold abroad, Doxfords in three different years and Laing in four. Laings were the biggest single exporter; two ships went to St Nazaire in 1862, the iron ss *Francoli* [1,000t] to Barcelona in 1865 followed by composite *Sumatra* [733t] and ss *Oran* [758t] for Marseilles. Pile only exported a single vessel, the *Charente* [842t] which went to France in 1862. In the 1860s Leslie's Hebburn yard alone exported a greater tonnage than all the Wear shipyards.

Not many vessels were exported from the Tees. Richardson Duck built ss *Palikara* for Stephanos Xenos of *the Greek and Oriental Steam Navigation Co* in 1860. This yard also supplied a steamer to Spain in 1861 and Russia in 1865. Pearse built a small number of vessels for Germany, Spain and France in the 1860s and early 1870s. At least three steamers were built by Backhouse for Spain and one for Germany. In all twenty vessels were built for overseas. There were regular overseas sales from Hartlepool. In 1857, the Richardson Brothers built the iron sailer *Armenian*, for the Indian trade. She was later modified for steam power, and was a relatively large vessel at that time at 999t. Two iron paddle steamers were built for Sweden before the Richardsons abandoned shipbuilding. Pile completed their final vessel *Wave Queen*, which was then sold to Xenos as *Admiral Miaulis*. This Greek shipowner was an important customer for Pile. He purchased six more vessels in 1858-1860; Xenos also bought ships from Leslie. A St Petersburg shipowner Elisekeff purchased the 729t ship, launched as *Screw Queen*, and renamed *Alexander II* in 1860. Four years later the ss *Kalioub* [1,150t] was supplied to the Turkish government and ss *Asie* [1,164t] was sold to a French owner. Flensberg Navigation Co, of Germany, regularly placed orders with Denton Gray, six over the years 1869-74. Six ships were supplied to other German owners up to 1875. Withy also supplied ships to Germany, four to the Kosmos Nav Co, three of these at 1,530t were the largest of those exported. His yard's first vessel, in 1869, was a small sailing ship, 158t, for Spain followed by a second of 282t in the same year. A Spanish owner bought the iron barque *Francsisca* [231t] from Irvine & Currie's yard in 1866 and their ship #8 ss *Fuh Le* was for the Shanghai Tug & Lighter Co. Twelve years passed before another ship was sent abroad ss *Normand* [1,238t] to France. Denton-Gray's first steamer was ss *Dessouk* [1,389t] for the Egyptian government. Up to 1879, Hartlepool supplied 30,700t to foreign owners and almost three fifths of the tonnage went to Germany. The Denton-Gray yard built nearly half this tonnage.

Perhaps the more diverse trade passing through the Tyne offered more opportunities for securing overseas orders. From Leslie's Hebburn yard over the years 1855-7, one ton was sold abroad for every ton on the home market and 20,000t went overseas in the 1860s. There were only seven over the 25 years 1855-1879 without an overseas sale. Russia proved a good market for the Hebburn yard, more than 18,000t before 1880. Although the first batch of vessels were small sailing craft of only 200t, in 1857 ss *Mougoutschi* was 1,000t powered by 80 nhp engines. Ten years later ss *Azoff* [1,414t] was the first of many for Russian Steam Navigation Co. More than half the output of 1869 was for overseas customers, three small craft for

France and almost 8,000t for Russia; ss *Cesarevitch* and ss *Korniloff* were each 2,030t and ss *Tcherkask* [1572t]. Maudslay & Field provided 170 nhp engines for the larger ships. The yard's largest ship to date was built for Italy in 1873, ss *Maddaloni* [380' long] was 2,700t. Overseas work was particularly important for Wigham Richardson's yard [see diag 12.07 below]: two barges for Cape Town were among the early vessels built at Neptune and in 1862 the small steamer *Elba* was built for Genoa. A Captain Whitakker was their contact for a number of ships for carrying coal to Australia and along the Australian coast. Lloyd's surveyor Thomas Luke introduced Richardson to Captain Durham, who acted for the Armenian house of Apcar at Calcutta, and this brought a number of orders, including the *Catherine Apcar*, although some of these ships had London owners. A recommendation by Armstrongs to the Prussian government resulted in an order for the paddle steamer *Ruhr*, which carried railway trains. This was the forerunner of a number of such ships from Neptune. In Richardson's words *the transactions* for several steamers for the Droutheim Co *were always pleasant, if not very profitable*. Many ships were purchased by overseas customers from Charles Mitchell.

ss Yat Sing 1904

Some exports in the 1870s on the Wear.
About 93000t were exported from the Wear in the 1870s, just over 10% of the output. No doubt the changeover to iron and steam played a part in this but 12 were wood ships. Three ships with wood hulls went to Spain, two each to France, Greece and Australia and one each to Denmark and Russia. More than half of exported tonnage was in 1872-3. Spain headed the list with 23,500t and Germany was not far behind with more than 22,000t. Italy took more than 13,000t and France almost 12,000t and the first ships went to Japan. Oswald blazed a final trail of glory, with 25,000t sent overseas during 1870-3, albeit some completed by his liquidators. Two others on their way to bankruptcy also contributed significantly: Watson almost 9,000t and Pile more than 6,600t. These three yards accounted for 43% of the overseas buyers. Some fine large vessels left from Oswald's yard, including four vessels of more than 2,500t, one for Bilbao and three for Stettin, including ss *Ernst Moritz Arndt* of almost 2,600t. In 1871 two sister ships, the *Humbolt* [1820t] and *Franklin*, were also built for Stettin and two for Bilbao, each exceeding 2,000t. Laing's Deptford yard sent nearly 11,000t overseas, the second highest on the Wear. Among three ships for German owners, ss *Buenos Aires* [2,401t] was the largest and was engined by Humphry Tennant. Doxford's 7,300t included the *Bermuda* [1,159t] for Canada. A number of ships were built for Australian owners, Blumer launched *E J Spence* [519t] in 1871 and two ships went to Adelaide, Laing's the *Flinders* [489t] in 1875 and Austin & Hunter's *Ridge Park* [969t] in 1878. In that year Osbourne Graham built the *Wollabra* [930t] for Sydney and the *Alexa* [441t] for New Zealand. However, Empire territories took less than 7% of the tonnage going overseas. Five Short vessels went to Germany including ss *Kron Prinz* [10,76t] in 1873, two more *Prinz* ships followed in 1878 [one of these later joined a Japanese fleet]. The Wear's later strong connections with Scandinavia hardly existed, less than 3,000t went there in the 1870s; in 1873 Bartram built ss *Nordtiernen* [1,262t] for Copenhagen. Twenty-three yards sold to overseas owners but for eight of them it was a single ship.

Japan as a customer.

Among its many other distinctions Robert Thompson's Southwick yard supplied the first Wear vessel to Japan. In 1874, ss *Min* [*Hyogo Maru*] and ss *Sumida Maru*, were built to the order of the Japanese government, probably through London agents.[31] They were near sister ships of about 1,250t and powered by 200 nhp engines. Six years later Thompson built the smaller ss *Yoretomo Maru* [986t]. Although the fourth vessel may have been intended for another customer [The name *Gratitude* was crossed through in yard list.], ss *Totoni Maru* was launched for Kyado Unyu Kaisha. This ship of 1840t although shorter than ss *Min*, was significantly broader and almost 10% greater in depth. Two much larger ships, almost 50% above the Wear average, were supplied later to the Nippon Yusen Kaisha [*NYK*]: ss *Miike Maru* [3,198t -320'] was built in 1888 and two years later ss *Hiroshima Maru* [3,170t]. These vessels were of the latest technology, steel hulls, and the ss *Miike Maru* [yard # 144] was a double first for Robert Thompson - the new material, steel and the triple expansion engine. This achievement by a Wear yard is almost if not entirely unknown, while the successes of larger yards are given prominence.

During the summer of 1883, Armstrong Mitchell secured the contracts for the first two steamers for the Great Japanese Trading Co. [32] Rear-Admiral Ito, *with a suite of scientific advisors*, spent several days in Newcastle arranging matters; ss *Yamashiro* was launched in 1884. *The Shipping World* wrote: *The Japanese are showing signs of commercial enterprise of no mean order. Dress peculiar to Christian nations is becoming common on the streets of Yokohama, and the people are embarking in International trade now chiefly carried on by Christian nations*. The Tyne Iron Co launched ss *Fushiki Maru* in 1885. Two years later Hawthorn-Leslie supplied ss *Kuishui Maru* [1856t]. On Teesside, Pearse supplied two, the first in 1881 and the *Yawata Maru* [3,981t] in 1886 and Craig Taylor supplied a ship in 1890.

In November 1886, *The Shipping World* reported on *Iron Shipbuilding in Japan* the launch of the first iron vessel on 18 August from the Onohama yard at Kobe, a branch yard of the Imperial Navy. Amongst those at the launch were Rear Adm. T Y Ito, and a distinguished French naval architect Charles Bertin, who had been appointed an advisor to the Navy. Work began on 29 September 1885 to designs prepared at Tokyo and it was carried out under the supervision of Chief Engineer Constructor Yamagata entirely by Japanese workers. Although 11 months was a longer period of construction for a vessel of 614 dpt than in a British yard, it was a considerable achievement. The *Maya-Kan* was 154' x 26' and her engines were horizontal compounds with surface condensers. She was the first of 10 gunboats made with material imported from England. At the Yokosuka yard they were constructing a torpedo boat from the sections supplied from Britain. Leading naval architects and engineers from Britain helped to staff the Japanese technical academies and skilled craftsmen and foremen went to their yards to help establish their new shipyards. Mitsubishi, then a shipping company, purchased the Nagaski shipyard from the government in 1887. North east builders were aware of the potential competition and those starting in other countries continued to come to Britain to learn.[33]

Thirty-one merchant ships, more than 80,000t, were directly exported to Japan between 1874 and 1911. Armstrongs, with six ships [17,412t], was the largest north east supplier of these ships, including the tanker *Joyo Maru* [5,135t] in 1908. J L Thompson built 4 ships for the *OSK* [Osaka Shosen Kaisha] shipping company, two sister ships of 1,566t in 1896 and a year later ss *Tainan Maru* [3192t]. This Company was

---

[31] Conte-Helm states the *Min* was *ordered directly by A R Brown* and sold by Brown to the Japanese government and renamed. The yard list distinguished the two only by port of registry London for *Min* and *Tokei* for *Sumida*..

[32] Four ships built by Mitchell between 1873 and 1876 were later acquired by Japanese owners: *Bankoko Maru* [*Monte Video*], *Takashiho Maru* [*Lotus*], *Katsuno Maru* [*Arratoon Apcar*] and *Kumanto Maru* [*Gadshill*].

[33] It is reported that Swan & Hunter helped establish Hitachi Shipbuilding in the 1880s. In October 1886 *The Shipping World* in an article on shipbuilding in Norway stated their materials came *from England*, which prevented them, despite their lower wages, from being able *to build more cheaply*. One yard was managed by Mr Cucheron, *who had previously held a responsible post* at Palmers..

extending its services to Korea and China and also acquired a 3,221t ship from Laing, as well as two vessels from Wigham Richardson and one from Blyth. Five merchant ships were supplied in 1911. These included the *Tenpaisan Maru* [6,985t] by the Thompsons, which was the largest vessel built by the yard up to the Great War and the largest sent to Japan. Raylton Dixon[34] provided one of the others and Armstrongs supplied two through Samuel's Japanese interests. *TKK* [Toyo Kisen Kaisha], founded in 1896, began its service to San Francisco with three north east ships; Swan Hunter built *American Maru* [5,870t] and Laing the other two. In 1898, Samuel said no one who saw these two passenger & mail steamers *could doubt that the North East could build as fine a vessel as could be built anywhere*. Japanese owners bought many second hand north east built ships. Up to 1912 *NYK* had used 51 such ships.

Exports from the 1880s.

The Clyde as the pioneer of steam was an attractive supplier for many years to overseas buyers, but by the early 1880s the position was changing. In May 1883, *The Shipping World* noted: *In former years our foreign customers have shown a preference for steamers of Scotch build; but this seems no longer the case*. In 1882 the north east's 50,000t for overseas customers exceeded the 47,000t by the Clyde: the rest of the country was a long way behind, only 18,181t in all.[35] The number of ships was almost the same on the north east coast [48] and the Clyde [47], with an average size of about 1000t. At the depth of the depression in 1886, when the whole country exported almost 80,000t, the Clyde and Tyne both contributed about 32,000t. Not many months later, *The Shipping World* wrote: *it must be remembered that the bounty and protection policy has spread over nearly all the shipowning countries in the world ... despite cheaper labour and a bounty upon building and sailing ships, our shipbuilders are able to book orders from protecionist countries*. Output for overseas customers over the period 1884-92 is shown in diag 12.05. Over those years the Clyde built 639,884t for overseas markets compared with 795,039t on the north east coast; after 1885 the north east surpassed the Clyde. Within the region the dominance of the Tyne in exports was very clear. With almost 470,000t it was nearly double the Wear's 236,500t; the combined Tees & Hartlepool output was about 85,000t.

Much of the Tyne's figure was naval work and so commercially more significant than tonnage figure alone suggests. Armstrong-Mitchell was responsible for almost 140,000t, followed by 79,000t from Wigham Richardson, then Swan Hunter [64,000t], Palmers [48,572t] and Hawthorn-Leslie [36,881t]. At South Shields, Readheads turned out 9,326t for foreign buyers in 1883 and although none was sold overseas in 1892, for the period the yard totalled more than 27,000t. Most of the new yards secured overseas work, with Wood & Skinner, sent 29,000t overseas in the six years 1887-92. Ten yards launched ships for overseas customers in 1884 and 1885 and although the number fell to eight in 1886 it rose to a dozen

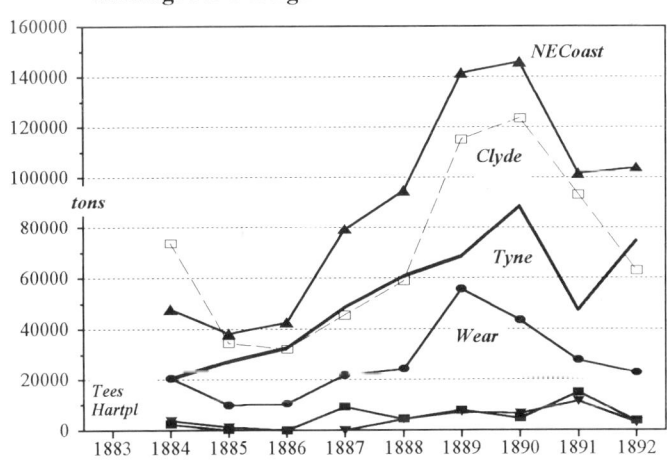

Diag 12.05

yards in 1888 and 1889. Amongst examples of these exports were the following. An early Tyne steel ship ss *Czar* was built by Armstrong-Mitchell for the Russian Steam Navigation Co. and launched in 1883. She had a clipper stern, topgallant forecastle, long poop, and hurricane-deck amidships and her decks were of teak, with excellent passenger accommodation. Massive engines were supplied by Wallsend Slipway; the

---

[34] Wayman Dixon in 1901 became Honorary Japanese Consul at Middlesbrough, NYK called bimonthly at the port.

[35] Pollard & Robertson wrote [p 38]: *Between 1870 and 1890 all modern fleets were in the habit of ordering their new tonnage from British yards, usually the Clyde...*

low pressure cylinder was 78" diameter with a 48" stroke. Later in 1883 Leslie launched the ss *Garcia De Vinuesa* for Spain. South American Companies received four paddle driven ships from Hebburn in 1884, including the *Para E Amazona*. In 1885 both Palmer and Swan Hunter sold vessels to Spain. Swan Hunter launched the ss *Gullivara* in May 1888 for the Anglo-Scandavian SS Co. its main function was to carry 4,000 tons of Swedish iron ore from the port of Lulea in the Gulf of Bothnia. Twelve first class passengers could also be accommodated, in this case in addition to the electric lighting there were also the *usual oil lamps*. Ore carriers continued to be an important export type.

The Russian Volunteer Fleet.[36]

The Russian Volunteer Fleet was the outcome of the actions of some wealthy Russians to assist their government by *providing vessels which would be used as transports and auxiliary cruisers, and be self supporting as liners in times of peace*. Committees raised funds and four Scottish built ships, owned by the North German Lloyd Co, were purchased. Three of the remaining four ships in the orginal fleet were built in Scotland and the fourth in France. Three new ships were later bought, which were not specifically designed for the Fleet; these were Tyne vessels from Hawthorn-Leslie [1888], Armstrong [1890] and Wigham Richardson [1900]. Specially designed vessels were in three categories: *low speed* [about 12k] and *high speed* [19k] for overseas service and special service in the East. Hawthorn-Leslie's yard played a very important part in the designed Fleet. There remained however a significant Scottish contribution. Denny built 4 of the 7 *low speed* craft [1893-6] and John Brown one *low speed* [1896] and one *high speed* [1898]. From the technical side, William White said, that Hawthorn-Leslie's work was of the *greatest value*.[37] At their suggestion *the Russian authorities made not a few experiments in both the construction of the vessels and the machinery*. In White's words *these new departures were of great value outside the Volunteer Fleet*. Water-tube boilers were adopted. Hawthorns built five of the fast speed ships, including the *Smolensk*[38] [7,270t] and the *Habarovsk* and two ice breaking tugs for the Far East service. When ss *Orel*[39] was ordered the intention was to have 10 *high speed* ships, the lack of potential profitability particularly as the Trans-Siberian Railway[40], resulted in a decision to have four as intermediates. The *Smolensk* could transport 1,650 troops, 3,000 tons of supplies 4,000k in nine days, without touching a port. These vessels made 9 round trips a year from Petersburg or Odessa to Vladivostock and the *Saratov* steamed 461,862 miles between December 1891 and 1 January 1904. *It is our business as technical men to fulfil conditions laid down by those for whom we build ships*, White stated; there was general agreement that from a technical point of view the Fleet was a success. The Hebburn yard also built 13 ships [16,000t] for the Russian Steam Navigation Co. In 1891, *The Marine Engineer* described ss *Grand Duke Alexis* and ss *Grand Duke Constantine* - *as quite unique specimens of modern shipbuilding work ... for beauty of design, stability of construction, or elaborateness of interior ornamentation, it is safe to say that it would be no easy task to find their equals*.

---

[36] There were discussions as to whether this Fleet should transfer into the Russian Steam Navigation Co and this was rejected. The organisation was transferred to the Ministry of Marine and its objects were *defined as being for the maintenance of a cargo, passenger, and postal service between Odessa and the East, and the general development of national commerce, all operations ... on a commercial basis*. See Rowell INA 1905 pp 63-79.

[37] Hawthorn's success raised opposition in Russia. Rowell recalled that a number of the leading journals immediately before the tenders were due published articles and letters pointing out that orders for the best vessels had invariably gone to Hebburn. It was asked if the R.V.F. was *run for the benefit of Hawthorn Leslie or of Russia or whom?* It was too much for the R.V.F Committee, and Colonel Linden told Rowell *privately* that they had decided to give the Clyde a turn.

[38] The armament was 8 -120mm and 8 - 75mm rapid-fire guns:

[39] The *Orel* was launched as a flush decked vessel of spar-deck class in 1889 and carried 1,380 troops [113 crew]; poop, bridge and forecastle were added in 1897. Converted at La Seyne into a hospital ship [including Rontgen Ray department] - attached to Adm Rodjestvensky's squadron. Hawthorn's *Kostroma* was also converted

[40] A French loan was raised for construction in the summer of 1891 and Port Arthur was reached in 1901.

On the Wear - 1888-1913.

From about 22% of the Wear's total output going overseas in 1888-9, there was a downward trend until the mid 1890s. Over ten years 1883-92, it was the newly formed Sunderland SB which headed the overseas table with 43,456t, including many for Hansa ships, with five in 1889. J L Thompson were next, exporting more than 40,000t; there followed Doxford [36,281t], Robert Thompson [26,357t], Blumer [20,455t] and then Laing at 18,000t. On average annually, over the whole period 1888-1913, exports on the Wear were about 21% of total tonnage. Almost 35,000t were sent overseas in 1890, more than any single Wear yard launched that year. The principal countries supplied were Spain 6,358t, France 6,287t Germany 5,952t Norway 4,580t and Spain 4,580t.[41] In the boom year of 1896 almost one-third of the tonnage went abroad - 69,792t. Germany took more than 20,000t, Norway 13,834t, the Dutch 8,314t and Russia 5,301t. Japan with 6,403t came third behind France and Germany in 1897. Only 27,000t was sent abroad in 1902, the poorest year between 1896 and the outbreak of war, less than one eight of the Wear's tonnage. Germany, with 7,294t, came just a head of the Scandinavians with 7,120t. During the great boom year of 1906 overseas work seems to have been squeezed out to less than 50,000t [15% of output]. A very different picture emerged over the next three years when on average more than 35% of the output went abroad. In 1907 as much as 112,000t was exported, a quarter of this to Italy, nearly as much to Scandinavia and 19,000t to the British Empire. One example of the securing of a satisfied customer was Ybarra of Seville, 15 of the 17 ships in their fleet of 1893 were built on the north east coast, ten of these by J L Thompson; the other two coming from Scotland. *The Shipping World* described passenger boat *Vega ... as one of the finest crafts ever turned out on the Wear, and is in every way a credit to the builders* [she] was *specially constructed to navigate the fjords of Norway*. This was seen as the replacement of the *maid of all work* by the *specialist* craft. Over the years 1910-13, just over 260,000t was sent overseas. The Wear's export tonnage at 22% of output over the years 1888-1913 matched the ratio of the UK as a whole.

Tees & Hartlepool.

Only about 5% of the Tees output was sold abroad at the end of the 1880s. After two years at about 12%, there followed a remarkable four year spell during which more than 150,000t was exported. During 1893-6 foreign customers bought more than one-third of total output. In 1895, of the 52,000t sent abroad; 43% went to Norway. Just over 19,000t was exported in the bad years of 1897-8 and this was followed by a relatively good five years, averaging about 33,000t sold to foreign customers. In the boom year 1907, the highest total ever 55,000t was exported. The next three years barely averaged 12,000t a year. Raylton Dixon's yard was one of the main seekers of overseas work; Richardson Duck and Ropner rarely built for foreign owners. Over the whole period 1888-1913 just over 20% of Tees output went abroad. A more complete picture of markets is available for Hartlepools, thanks to the work of Bert Spaldin [see diag 12.06]. In the ten years 1888-97, exports from Hartlepool were less than 87,000t compared with 214,000t on the Tees. Exports from Hartlepool were substantially larger in the next ten years [1898-1907] and were 77% of those on the Tees, compared with only 41% in the earlier

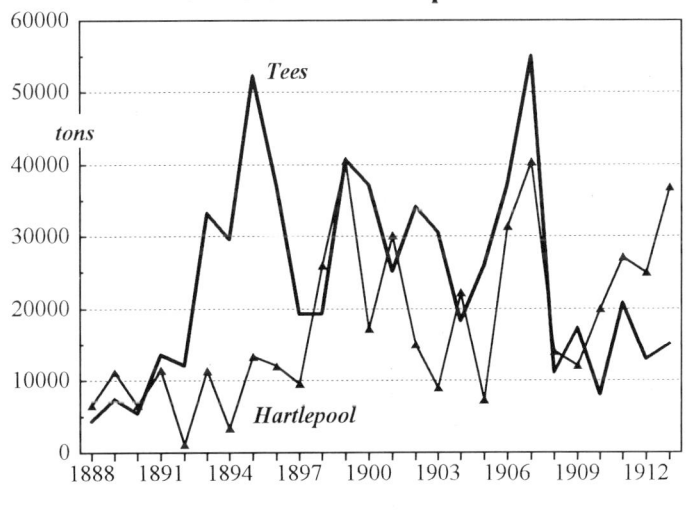

Diag 11.06

---

[41] Other places in 1890 were one each for Japan, Fiume, Singapore, Melbourne and Montreal.

period. In the years 1909-13, Hartlepool sold substantially more abroad than the Tees, 121,000t compared with 74,000t. However over the whole period, 1888-1913, only 17.4% of Hartlepool's output went abroad, the lowest of the three north east rivers. Until 1899 only Gray sold abroad, with hardly any such activity by Irvine and not much by Withy. Gray remained the highest exporter. Norway and Sweden together took just under 118,000t, followed by Holland 108,000t and Germany 101,000t. Denmark and Greece were next in importance and the British Empire accounted for 20,500t [4.4 %]. Only in two years 1899 and 1907 was more than 40,000t exported. After supplying the sailing barque *Apollo* [1,196t] to Germany in 1884, Gray did not supply that country again until 1889, when he despatched no less than six ships! Four for a J Lange were each of 1,600t and two for Anderson, 2,630t each. Andersen placed further orders in 1894 and 1899. Danish shipowner L Carl purchased his first two ships from Gray in 1896 in all buying 14 ships up to 1907; no overseas buyer had more vessels. The Norwegian Christensen got his first ship in 1888 and his final total of 9 ships almost reached 30,000t, including in 1911 ss *August* [5,254t]. A year later a similar ship was also supplied to Norway. Four vessels were built at the Central yard for the Netherlands SS Co in 1913-4, each about 6,450t. The Hamburg-America Line placed ordered five ships from Gray, ss *Nubia* [3,622t] and ss *Numidia* were delivered in 1900 and the others in 1901. The Holland America Line bought ships from Furness and Gray. Furness Withy supplied five, including the sister ships ss *Soestdijk* [6,440t] and ss *Amsteldijk* launched in 1901. The largest ships this firm sent overseas were ss *Oosterdijk* [8,250t] and ss *Westerdijk* [8,260t] in 1913. Gray launched ss *Noonderkyk* [7,156t] in the same year.

Exports from the Tyne.

There cannot be a substantive review of the ships for overseas customers for individual Tyne yards. Wigham Richardson's Neptune yard however is reviewed below and the following are some other examples. Swan Hunter supplied their most powerful ship to date, in 1890 to Genoa, ss *Citta De Venezia* [3,551t] with engines rated at 3,350 ihp. Nine ships were exported that year, in all 20,000t. Four were for Hamburg, and one each for Rotterdam, La Havre and Dantzig. This Wallsend yard built more vessels for the Empire and Colonies than other yards. Huddart & Parker of Australia received Swan's first steel ship in 1885, together with a sister ship. There were other ships in 1887, 1889 and in 1892 three fast steamers *Tasmania*, *Warrimoo* and *Miowera*. German shipowners purchased four large cargo vessels from Palmers in 1900, of which ss *Belgia* at 9,785t was the largest north east ship for the year and the other three were all over 7,600t. Jarrow also launched the largest cargo steamer owned by Austria, the ss *Ellenia* of 4,450t. A special design was used in 1905 by Armstrongs to satisfy their customer's desire to carry a very large number of passengers in relation to size, 130' x 23'7" x 9'3". *Bhosphorus 53* and *Bhosphorus 54* were built for the Turkish passenger service near Constantinople with the deck was extended beyond the ship's sides and supported on sponsons with cabin accomodation in deck houses. Small yards also sent vessels abroad; for example, a Rennoldson built tug *Nyore* went to Melbourne for heavy ocean going fire and salvage service, and for the P & O service in Bombay a twin screw tug *Dewan*, with a powerful fire pump.

The Neptune Yard and overseas customers.
For the twenty years 1884-1903, no north east merchant yard matched Wigham Richardson's success at securing overseas orders. He launched *a very handsomely- modelled* ss *Eeta* for Demerar & Berbice S S Co, for the carriage of mahogany in 1883. The usual hold beams were removed to provide for the stowage of the logs and replacement strength was provided by strong web frames. At this time the yard also

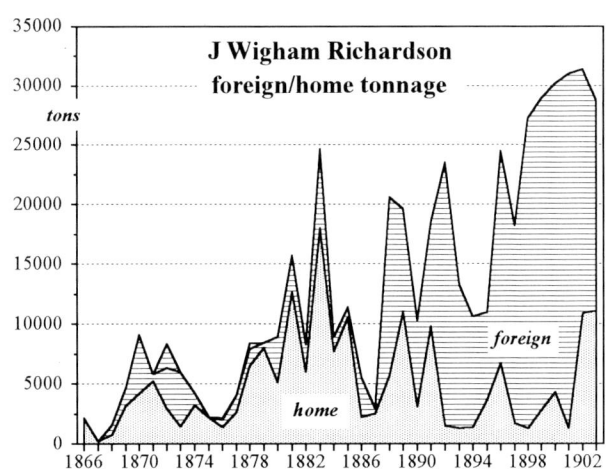

Diag 11.07

turned out two sister ship for Marseilles: ss *Isly* and ss *Emir*, built under the supervision of two French naval architects. Large cabin accommodation was provided and ss *Isly* was for carrying the mails from France to ports on the Algierian coast. The overall performance of the Neptune yard is shown in diag 11.07. The outstanding vessel ss *Alfonso XII* built for the Spanish mail service in 1887-8, was described above. Emigrants were carried from Genoa to the River Plate in a fleet of ships owned by the Lavarello Co. Neptune supplied their first ship to this Company in 1870, ss *Espresso*, followed by three sister ships in 1872-3. After a gap of 12 years six ships were supplied during 1886-9, including ss *Adelaide Lavarello* [1,907t] and ss *Aquila* [2,542t]. A total of 18,537t was supplied to the Italian Company. Almost 90,000t, a total of 20 ships, were built by Wigham Richardson for Deusche D G Hansa over the years 1882-1903; at an average of 4,500t these were large vessels. In 1899 ss *Drachenfels* [7,143t] was 456' long and powered by powerful quadruple expansion engines working like a number of these German vessels at 210psi. Nine of these vessels exceeded 5,000t, starting with the ss *Neidenfels* [5,327t] in 1896. Five ships were supplied to Deusche D G Kosmos, including ss *Sakkarah* [4,660t] in 1897. Nordeutscher Lloyd was supplied with ss *Hannover* [7585t] in 1899, she was the second largest ship [by tonnage] built at Neptune but at 431' shorter than ss *Drachenfels*. Seven ships [15,118t] were supplied to Indo-China Steam Navigation. These vessels mainly traded in Chinese waters carrying passengers and cargo. The first was ss *Fau Sang* [2,251t] and in 1905 ss *Kut Sang* [*Lucky Increase*][42] was built for trade between Hong Kong and Calcutta. In addition to a large cargo, passengers were carried by *suitably* separated: European passenger accomodation was on the bridge deck, first class Chinese passengers under the bridge deck and a number of second class Chinese passengers in the poop! Outstanding among these overseas orders were 19 ships supplied to the Royal Hungarian Steam Nav. Co over the eleven years 1892-1902. Few yards ever enjoyed such a sequence of work from one company. Only two of the top ship tonnages by Neptune were not for one or another of sixty overseas customers.

After the formation of Swan Hunter & Wigham Richardson Ltd substantial exports continued. The emigrant ship ss *Madonna* [5,551t] launched in 1905, carried 1,700 emigrants and 50 first class passengers. One of five ships for the Ungaro-Croata S N Co of Fiume, ss *Salona* reached 14.5k on her trials. The engines on the Yarrow, Schlick & Tweedy system provided the *freedom from vibration ... peculiarly suitable for passenger steamers*. She carried 65 first class and 23 second class passengers, with the accommodation *artistically decorated*. Walls of polished oak graced the first class saloon, where *fine panels of gesso work, depicting seascapes and land views* were executed by Ruston of the Art School in the Armstrong College. The following description provides a limited insight into the additional work required on a passenger vessel:

> The upholstery is in a scheme of old gold for the seats and sofas, with carpet-runners of rose du Barry on the polished parquet floor... a handsome entrance-house and smoke-room, where the walls are of polished mahogany with ash-bur panels and gesso plaques. The sofas are covered with deep moss-green frieze velvet, and the windows are draped by gold damask curtains. In the staterooms special care has been taken to provide comfortable accommodation, with good iron bedsteads and ample wash basins. The floors are covered with cork carpet and Axminster carper-runners. Curtains are provided for doors, windows and beds, and every cabin has a comfortable sofa, upholstered in Tashmere velvet. The scheme of the colour is a handsome blue, all woodwork being painted in white enamel.

With nine weeks of the launch, ss *Salona* went on her trials, a prompt completion. A further nine ships were built for D G Hansa during 1904-13. Among the many notable vessels sent overseas ss *Drottning*

---

[42] Others included in 1903-4 ss *Foo Shing* [*Wealth & Promotion*] and ss *Yat Shing* [*Daily Promotion*].

Train Ferry Drottning Victoria for Swedish State Railways 1908

Victoria a train ferry for the Swedish government [see illustration]. The *combination system* was used on the general cargo *Birma* [4,896t], built for Rotterdam Lloyd in 1912. In the same year splendid *Reina Victoria Eugenie* was launched at 9,726t, only five Cunarders were larger at Swans before 1914.

Ice-breakers and ore carriers.

A Russian merchant transformed his tug *Pilot* into the first recorded icebreaker, and the port of Hamburg built their own vessel in 1871.[43] A number of these vital craft, some ferries with ice breaking characteristics for northern ports and waters, were built at Armstrong's Walker yard. H F Swan discussed two of these, the *Sampo* supplied to Finland and the *Ermack* supplied to Russia at the INA in 1899. The *Sampo* was of 2,000dpt, with a propeller forward and aft; the engines developed 3,000 ihp. Swan described the *Ermack* as marking *an immense stride* in the construction of these craft, three times as powerful as any vessel previously constructed; it was 8,000 dpt and 10,000 ihp. She had three propellers aft and one forward. Both bronze and nickel steel was used on the propellers and although many times the engines were brought up *all standing* there had been no broken blades. The *Ermack* had travelled at 2.5k-3k through an icefield 40" thick and made about 10k through clear ice of 24"; she had remarkable manoeuvring qualities, with her helm only she could turn a circle of only twice her own length [305'].[44] Adm Makaroff, of the Imperial Russian Navy, was full of praise for those who produced the *Ermack*: *the problem was very difficult, but difficulty is not a thing before which English engineers stop. There is no ice so thick that the skill of the English engineer cannot overcome it.* Vessels were also designed to link railway terminals on either side of large stretches of water. One such was designed to operate on the Volga. This ferry could load and unload railway wagons at various heights and could operate in up to about 20" of ice without the assistance of ordinary ice-breakers. In 1899 another ferry ice-

Icebreaker Ermack in dry dock

---

[43] The *Pilot* was built for a Russian merchant in 1864 and *Eisbrecher I* in 1871. See INA Tuxen pp 105-115 vol 39 [1897] Swan H F pp 325 -332 vol 41[1899] Arpianen & Danska in *European Shipbuilding* [1984]

[44] The commercial value of this vessel was illustrated by Swan. On her arrival she went to Reval where 33 steamers were trapped and then went to Cronstadt and St Petersburg where about 40 steamers were able to proceed *several weeks* earlier than waiting for the *ordinary opening of the navigation*.

breaker was being built on the Tyne.[45] After erection to check all parts, it was disassembled and transported about 5,000 miles with a considerable part of the journey was by sledge. On the shores of Lake Baikal it was re-erected and entered service. Ships to carry Swedish ore, frequently from Narvik, provided orders for a number of north east shipbuilders and two of these ore carriers built by Hawthorn-Leslie received special attention, the 8,000t ss *Vollrath Tham* [1909] and the 10,800t ss *Sir Ernest Cassel* [1910]. These were described by Foster King of the British Corporation as *the most highly specialised cargo steamers which have yet been evolved*. They were designed to use the mechanical system [Johnson-Welin] for handling the ore, which had already been tried on an existing vessels in 1907. Electric cranes were fitted to eliminate all hands on deck apart from the crane drivers[46]; there were 10 cranes [lift 2.5 tons] on ss *Vollrath Tham* [1909] and 12 cranes [3.5 tons] on ss *Sir Ernest Cassel*. Both J L Thompson and Doxford supplied Wilhelmsen of Tonsberg with ore carriers [10,000t & 12,000t] for the Canadian ore trade and for the Pacific from Norway.

Ore carrier Sir Ernest Cassel

Shipyards & engine works on the Continent and designs for Overseas Builders.
Restrictive legislation on the use of national shipping, at least in part, inspired some Tyneside companies to established business connections on the Continent. Armstrongs and Hawthorn-Leslie were involved in Italy and Palmers in Spain. Armstrongs were for a time part owners of the Ansaldo shipyard and linked with Maudslay in regard to the marine engine plant. At Pozzuoli Armstrongs had a machine shop, a sawmill and wood working department when Rowell went there in 1888 to complete two gunboats built at Elswick. The firm considered erecting a shipyard there. George Rendell became resident director in Italy, where steel manufacture and armaments work became the principal activity. Two Japanese cruisers *Nisshin* and *Kasugo* were launched from Ansaldo in 1904. For some years Palmers operated a shipyard in Spain as well as providing designs and specifications for three armoured cruisers for the Spanish government. T R Guppy of Bristol set up a small nail factory in Naples in 1853 and this works later built marine engines. In 1888, Hawthorn-Guppy was established with the Tyneside firm holding 2,000 - £10 shares, the St Peter's works manager Nelson Foley was transferred there and Marshall became a director.[47]

---

[45] Her dimensions were 4,200 dpt - 290' x 57' x 28.5' to the rail deck. She had three sets of engines [4,000 ihp]; two sets aft drove twin-screw propellers and one set in the bow. The Lake at the point of travel was 40 miles wide.

[46] See INA vol 53 pt II 1911 paper by Johnson. 120 men working 40 hours to discharge a vessel equivalent to *Vollrath Tham* were replaced by 20 men in 36 hours.

[47] It was a financially successful venture for Hawthorn-Leslie for some years - see *Power on Land & Sea* p59.

Some comparisons with the Clyde.

In export terms the north east coast and the Clyde were even more significant than their their overall proportion of the nation's shipbuilding. In aggregate the *rest* of the UK fell short of the River Wear alone. Fluctuations in the tonnage for foreign owners were similar on the Clyde and the north east coast, with the exception of 1893-4, when the Tees boosted north east exports. From a level of 35.6% for overseas customers, the Clyde slumped to 12.5% in 1894; over that same period the Tyne also fell but only to 23.1% and both returned to the one-third level in 1895. Nationally the percentage fall was from 21.3% to 14.3%. Tyneside was the most important exporter in the north east. In round figures however the Tees's 33,000t in 1893 came close to the Tyne's 39,000t, and two years later 52,000t on the Tees compared with 60,000t on the Tyne. The two ports never again came so close to each other. Both regions recovered sharply in 1895 and entered a very good period for exports, the Clyde hardly ever slipped below 100,000t in any year, averaging about 115,000t over the years 1895-1902. Only in 1896 and 1898 did the Tyne exceed the Clyde. The next lean time began in 1901 on the Tyne, a year earlier than on the Clyde and lasted for about four years [Clyde average about 80,000t and the Tyne about 70,000t]. From the low point of 1903-4 there was a a climb to 1906-7 and the fall that so severely hit the whole industry followed. When the Clyde moved up from 1910 it reached more than 170,000t for overseas buyers by 1913, fully 70,000t more than the Tyne. [see diag 11.08] Over the three years 1911-13 the north east exported more than 230,000t annually.

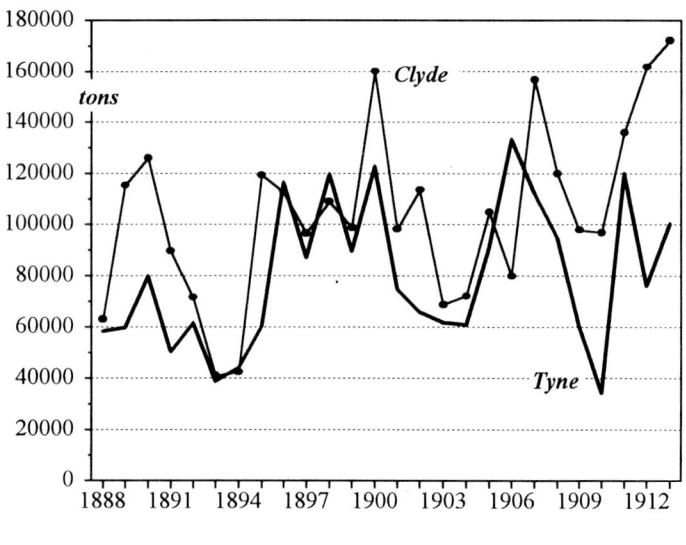

Diag 11.08

Despite protective laws and subsidised rail freight, *The Glasgow Herald* pointed out in 1905 that German builders required from 10s to £1 per ton more for cargo steamers than British builders. Some subsidised German steel was used in Britain. Germany did take special materials from Britain and large quantities of shipbuilding materials were exported from the North East to Italy. A year later the *Glasgow Herald* wrote that British builders were *quite well aware ... they retain their hold on Continental shipbuilding by reason principally of their ability to execute orders quickly. It is becoming to be less a question of prices and of workmanship and more a question of time.* A Hartlepool yard had recently secured a Dutch contract over Dutch builders on *early delivery*. From the late 1880s there certainly was an internationally competitive market and many commentators underestimated the extent to which other countries had developed the potential for shipbuilding. It should be stressed that over the 1890-1911, the colonies and dominions accounted for only about one eighth of the British built tonnage for overseas registration and the proportion was less for the north east. For the UK as a whole Germany and Sweden & Norway [taken together] both took a greater tonnage than the British overseas territories. The export of almost 4 million tons of shipping from the north east over twenty-five years was a great achievement.

Chapter 12

The Workforce - to about 1870 and the formation of Employers' Organisations.

It is a very great mistake to suppose that the relation between the working classes and their employers has reference only to labour and its remuneration. Responsibility does not terminate with the payment...there are duties beyond and above the contract which cannot be neglected without the worst consequences for the community. The *Newcastle Courant* 1854.

Shipbuilding depended upon a workforce that was both manually dexterous and physically strong. This situation continued well into the 20th century. While the wooden hull continued, the shipwrights were very much independent minded craftsmen, each with his own bag of tools; money was allocated from earnings to cover tool replacement and the trade union paid compensation for the loss of tools. As already seen, the iron hull brought dramatic changes at all levels in the industry, not least for workers. Up to the mid-nineteenth century there was a marked contrast in trade union activity on the Tyne and the rest of the north east. Craftsmen on the Tyne certainly had trade unions from 1795 and shipwrights' associations continued on an individual port basis until the 1880s. From the 1870s persistent efforts were made to form stable organisations amongst the *semi-skilled* workers, such as the *plater's helpers*. This chapter will examine the position of the workers, their trade unions up to about 1871 and the formation of employers' organisations.

Early Shipwrights' Associations.

The Articles of the Shipwright's Association in South Shields, established in 1795, are the earliest surviving Rules. Such opening words as: *agreed...in the thirty-fifth year of the Reign of our Sovereign Lord George the Third, by Grace of God, of Great Britain, France, Ireland, King, Defender of the Faith...* were hardly the terms of a very radical political body. The objects were stated as: *to make some provisions for ourselves and families, in case of sickness, affliction, misfortune, old age, or death...and also for the relief of our widows and children.*[1] Membership was limited to those who had served *a regular apprenticeship to a Shipwright* and were less than 45 years of age and of *healthful and of good character.* A committee of 15 was to manage *the affairs and funds* and two of these men were required to sign all applications for admission. Meetings were held weekly for those *at home*, a recognition that many men went to sea. No member was to return to sea until his dues were paid under a penalty of 6s. Subscriptions, 10d for every 20s earned [just over 4%], were paid at the weekly meeting except for those at sea, then either monthly or at the end of the voyage. Seven shillings a week were paid for loss of work due to *sickness, accidental misfortune, or old age* [after a year's membership] *become unable to follow his ... employment.* Widows were to receive an annuity of £10 a year and those without family or next of kin could nominate someone else to *his legacy*, which was set at £15. There was provision for expulsion for those who seriously broke the Rules and a 5s fine for striking another member and for being *notoriously immoral or irregular, so as they shall be hurtful to the said association*; no benefit was paid to those with venereal disease. Proper conduct at meetings was required; the fine for entering the society room *disguised in liquor* was 1s and 6d for swearing or talking obscenely at any meeting, or not remaining seated and silent *when demanded*. Those members, *at home*, who did not attend the funeral of a dead brother were fined 1s. The box was held, under a bond, at their meeting place, George Wilson's inn. Almost no details have survived of the activities of this association.

---

[1] Professor McCord pointed out that registering with J Ps for legal protection as friendly societies may have influenced the language used.

A recruiting drive flysheet in 1819 was entitled *First established Shipwrights' Association in this town*, South Shields. Meetings were at Mrs Sarah Weatherburn's *Sign of the Ship* and the fund worth £2,330 was *in an improving state*. Men under 25 years were to be admitted free, and between 25 and 30 would be entitled to benefits in six months. There were probably other societies, as indicated by the words *first established*. The lack of strength of separate societies probably resulted in an increasing recognition that only by acting together could the shipwrights hope to maintain their wage rates. Joseph Welsh, whose father and father-in-law had both been in societies, told the Select Committee on the Combination Acts in 1825: *we found that no society would be any good without we had one society of shipwrights in each town ...we never want any more wages than what is fair and right*. On 23 June 1823 shipwrights' trade unions were formed independently at Newcastle and South Shields; unions were also formed at Howdon Panns [*Houghton Pans* in report] and North Shields, as well as Blyth. Spokesmen for both stressed their independence; William Temple [Newcastle] said *they are all separate; the payments are different* and George Ribbon [South Shields] stated that full responsibilities were *[the whole might] upon ourselves*.[2] Although continuity cannot be proved from this point, it is most likely that from that time the Tyne shipwrights always had trade unions, albeit with only occasional formal contact between the separate societies. A very informative introduction preceded the rules of at least two Union Societies of Shipwrights[3]:

> Passive obedience and non resistance are doctrines which do not accord with the feelings of an independent mind; therefore in acknowledging our "pastors and masters", we certainly should not always tamely submit to everything which they please to propose, the result of which is to benefit themselves alone. Seeing, therefore, the necessity of establishing a just and lawful equilibrium of right between the employer and the employed, it becomes the latter as reasonable men to stand or pause at every measure likely to be adopted, which bears not a like advantages to master and servant: to effect such a laudable purpose, and remove some of these grievances which have long existed among us, which have been the bane and ruin of our trade.

In 1834 the South Shields Shipwrights' Union Society met monthly at Mrs Sarah Dobby's. These new unions met with very determined opposition by both the shipbuilding employers and the shipowners; these were of course roles held jointly by many of them.

Rules of the Shipwrights' Associations.

The Rules of the South Shields Association [1824] began:

> We, the Shipwrights of South Shields ... taking it into our serious consideration that man is formed a social being, and that the Sovereign Ruler of the World has been pleased to place us in life dependent upon each other, and in continual need of mutual assistance and support, Do severally agree to form ourselves into a Friendly and Benefit Association for our mutual relief.

There was a sharper message here than in the earlier society. The Rules stated that *any member using disrespectful language against His Majesty or his Government shall be immediately excluded*, effectively preventing political discussion. On this point, the *General Laws* of the Wear Shipwrights were unequivocal: *to prevent all party contention, members of the Society will not interfere in matters of religion or politics or allow any such subjects to be introduced into any of their meetings*.[4] Members were required to have served a 7- year apprenticeship or to *have been regularly employed as journeymen shipwrights*. Well aware of how quickly funds could be exhausted, new applicants were required to be healthy and free from *any defect which may prevent him earning a competent livelihood for himself and his family*. Those entering immediately at the end of their apprenticeship were made *free members* [entitled to all benefits] on the payment of 5s, about a week's pay. Admissions were approved by a majority vote. Failure to pay the 1s subscription at each monthly meeting resulted in a fine of 3d; those who lived more than two miles

---

[2] By the 1850s there was a much closer collaboration between these numerous port unions - see below.

[3] The Union Society meeting at Mr Booth's House Sun Inn West Holborn South Shields [est 23 June 1823] and the Union Society at Nag's Head South Blyth [3 October 1823] printed 1827.

[4] Shipwrights' and other rules: South Tyneside Reference Library, text in the *Bulletin of the North East Group for the Study of Labour History* no.1 pp 21-40, Rules were given to Sel Ctte on Combination Acts App. No 5.

from the meeting place might pay the contribution every six months. Those impressed into His Majesty's service or taken prisoner by an enemy were exempt their dues until their return, and £1 was allowed to help shipwrights who had lost their tools. When a member could no longer follow his trade, *whether by old age, infirmity, or sickness*, he was entitled to 2s a week from the funds and *a voluntary subscription* taken at the next meeting after notice was given to the committee. The death *benefit* was £5: a member was paid once for the decease of his mother or wife, and when a member died his widow, or next of kin, was given the same amount.[5] Each member contributed 6d to the box to replace such death benefits. With her consent, a further sum was raised for the widow by selling the dead member's tools at the club house. At their annual general meeting, a committee of 11 was elected, including a chairman / president, secretary, two stewards and a treasurer and members dined together at 2s/head.[6] Fifty pounds was always to remain in the box and a general meeting could decide on the management of the *overplus* funds, either by investing in *government funds, or real securities at interest, or in the purchase of property, or otherwise*. The society could only be dissolved by the consent of five-sixths of the existing members together with all those entitled to any benefit or relief. Many of the Bye-Laws reflected the rules of earlier societies, for example 6d fine for cursing or being drunk and 2s 6d for calling a man a liar or otherwise reflecting on his character, and a fight cost 5s. Any attempt to defraud the society was subject to a fine of 10s 6d. William Booth, the innkeeper of the *Sun Inn*, was required to enter into a bond of £1,000, *with sufficient securities*, for the safe keeping of the box and its contents. No superannuation was paid until 1829, and the weekly sickness allowances were to begin only when the fund was £800.[7] If an accident was notified to the stewards in three days, a weekly allowance of 6s would be paid on the *eight day after such misfortune*; all members contributed 2d to raise this money. Subscriptions at Newcastle at 1s every six weeks were lower than those of the 1795 Society but it was increased in April 1825 to the level as South Shields. Temple emphatically told the Select Committee they did not give relief to *men who refused to accept wages that are offered ... by their masters - None, never, not yet, never*. Regularly trade unions coped with special cash needs by one or another form of levy on those members in work; their financial stability was firmly dependent upon the overwhelming bulk of their members having regular work.

Early industrial disputes.

Few accounts of industrial disputes from the early 19th century survive. However, Home Office documents dealt with a strike by the shipwrights in December 1801 at South Shields. Shipwrights assembled *in large bodies, preventing any of their own fraternity working, and even attempting to decoy the foreman*. Richard Bulmer, the largest shipbuilder at South Shields, was described as *acting spiritedly* and the admission of the errors of their ways by six of the men was reproduced as a handbill:

> We have committed a great abuse in clandestinely entering the dockyard of Messers Bulmer...and endeavouring to prevail upon the foremen to quit their work; and declare, in this public manner, our thanks to Messers Bulmer for withdrawing the prosecution commenced against us, on the late Act of Parliament for preventing unlawful combinations of workmen: and promise that we will not invade the peace of the town or neighbourhood by a repetition of these acts.

The strike continued and a threatening letter was sent, *You Bulmer, if you do not give the carpenters a guinea a week as sure as Hell is hot O before winter is done you must be shot O . . .* A reward of 100 guineas was offered for information leading to a conviction.[8]

---

[5] On the Wear [1860] the death sum was £10 also, £3 for *wife, mother or nominee* and then £7 for member

[6] The quorum was five. The committee was to meet as business required [2s 9d allowed for expenses]. A 2s 6d fine could be imposed for refusing to act. The first committee was: William Copley, *President*; John Carr, John Henderson, William Gunn, James Heddle, Robert Jewitt, John Downey, John Copley, Edward Rutter, Joseph Welsh, William Smith - *Stewards*: Edward Young and George Ribbon - *Secretary*: John Harper - *Treasurer*: John Lawson.

[7] If 400 members @ 1s = £20/meeting - thus 40 meetings to accumulate £800 but there were outgoings.

[8] quoted from Aspinall A *The Early English Trade Unions. Documents from the Home Office Papers...* [1949]

Disputes in the 1820s.
James Laing, of South Shields, had trouble with the newly formed union in October 1823. During repairs on the *Lavinia* the foreman considered the men caulking were not working hard enough and when there was no improvement he dismissed them: Laing said when *other men were desired to go into their births [sic], not one of them would, the whole took up their tools and left us*. For ten days no work was done on the ship and finally apprentices finished it in another dock. Early in 1824 the shipbuilders of South Shields *resolved to break up this union if possible, for it was intolerable*. During a dispute at Sunderland, the South Shields shipwrights' union steward Ribbon took a collection from the Tyne men over to the Wear and then Laing discharged his men. At Forsyths the men took strong exception to a perceived threat to recruit 3-year apprentices. Straker informed his men through Welsh's brother-in-law, that because of a bond between the shipbuilders he would have to lay them off unless the disputes were ended. They were all discharged.[9] At Newcastle, T & W Smith was the first to suspend men. All but five or six Newcastle shipowners decided not to employ any ship's carpenters who were members of the union. Insurance cover was normally only available to vessels with a ship's carpenter; the underwriters however sent out *a written notice, that ships might without impeachment of the insurance sail without a carpenter, and many did so*. It was a substantial risk to take to break the union. In May, Laing and other employers[10] asked each man to sign an oath:

> That I am not now, nor do I intend to become, a member of any association at Newcastle-upon-Tyne, or elsewhere, not having the purpose of charity and benevolence for its sole object ... That I will not object to work with any builder on account of his engaging apprentices for a term of a less term than seven years; nor will I object to work with any journeyman who is not a member of the same society as myself; and that I will not attempt to dictate to my employer or employers in any manner whatever in the conducting or management of his or their business.

A few men did sign but not many. Ribbon set out his response: *I thought it was quite inconsistent; I thought I was an Englishman, and it was infringing my rights as an Englishman, because I considered that I and my forefathers had always gone to work without signing any paper.*

Although the employers presented the 7-year apprenticeship as the heart of the problem it is difficult to accept this, since they gained substantial benefits from the cheap labour of these lads. In 1850 the Tyne shipwrights' rules required that final year apprentices were not paid more than 10s a week! Even though temporarily many employers may have wanted to employ youths for shorter periods, few if any who were technically knowledgeable believed that a boy was going to acquire the all round skills they required of their journeymen in three years. Shipwrights' Association did not attempt to limit the intake of apprentices, although undoubtedly at times they said there were too many, but did try to insist on the 7-year term. In January 1825, Laing had 49 apprentices and at other times he employed 100, 120 or even 150, according to shipwright Ribbon and *sometimes none at all*; thus the ratio to craftsmen was very variable! While facing hostile questioning at the Commons, Ribbon calmly explained where he stood: *I do not conceive we have a right to dictate to them in that matter* [years of apprenticeship], *but however we thought it was an injury to us, and ... it was our right to do the best for ourselves that we could*. Shipowner and shipbuilder Richmond said of the employers' failure: our resolution *was in vain, because the men are consistent and united in their purpose, even to the extent of starvation to themselves; and I am afraid masters never can or will successfully combine against their workmen ... I believe they did bear great privations last year*. The men were in *a state of starvation*, reported Laing, *we ourselves began to feel the effects of our contracts not being finished ... an arrangement was entered into...men to work without any conditions*. Shipwright Temple noted that when the shipbuilders could no longer do without the men, the shipwrights were recalled and they returned on their old terms. The apprentices continued working during the dispute. Within weeks of the return to work, wages were increasing and the men at St Peters wrote to T & W Smith:

---

[9] Welsh - explained in a more qualified way *all they could discharge*; Temple, at Newcastle 120-130 laid off.

[10] One shipbuilder Jonathan Brown offered to strike off the oath if men would accept 21s wages instead of 24s

In consequence of the wages having rose in several places from 4s to 4s 6d per day, we expect you will advance the same. If you have any objections, will you please to state the same, as we consider striking of work to be injurious to both masters and men. We remain, with due deference and respect, your obedient servants,   *The Shipwrights in your employ.*

Smith replied *we have no objections whatever; but it is not our intention at present to carry on the new work. We perfectly agree with you, that it is much better to come to an understanding than to strike work. Your obedient servants, W.S. & Co.* Letters were also sent to builders at South Shields and Metcalfe, Ribbon's employer immediately gave the advance and indicated he had been expecting the request.

The working of the Shipwrights' Unions.

In 1825 there were 239 members of the separate Newcastle union, and according to Ribbon *no man in South Shields but that is in the society* - 600. Three Tyneside shipwrights presented evidence in a clear and forthright manner to the *Select Committee on the Combination Acts* and rebutted questions suggesting secret rules. Ribbon was convinced it was much better than before they had the Society; he believed the employers met twice or three times a week and he, Ribbon, had met Laing twice and a ten-man deputation followed. Previously *Very often it was done very suddenly, because at one yard they were knocked off, and then they mustered, and it went through the whole river in a day; and we felt that it was very inconvenient, and it did not answer a good end.* Wage disputes occurred from time to time and wages were once as low as 2s 9d a day [16.5s/week]. Shipwrights worked *all by day*, rejected *job work* [piecework] which was considered *an evil.*[11] Piecework was successfully resisted even when it became the principal mode of payment in iron shipbuilding. *The Tyne shipwrights*, wrote the *Sunderland Herald*, in February 1851, were *pretty well known as close unionists*. Probably on Tyneside few craftsmen felt they could become masters; however, on the Wear, the possibility of having their own yard continued to inspire shipwrights. There were occasional endeavours by Shipwrights' Unions to set up their own yards. When the employment of shipwrights at South Shields fell from *upwards of 700* to no more than 100 in the depression of the 1830s, according to MacKenzie & Ross, *the funds of their benefit society were dissipated by speculations in shipbuilding on their own account* and in other attempts *to struggle against the circumstances of the time.*[12]

Shipwrights used three methods to try to protect their employment: the 7-year apprenticeship,[13] the refusal of piecework and an unwillingness to work with non-society men. If all craftsmen were Society men then the possibilities of enforcing their policies were much greater. The separate Tyneside societies met in September 1850 and revised the *Working Rules... of the Shipwrights of the Port of Tyne* and they specified:
>   3. we shall not work with anyone that is not a member of the Society, except ... carpenter of the ship, and if the ship be in dock such carpenter to work by himself and not come amongst the men.
>   4. if any member or members belonging to this Society take piecework, or solicit for any other master in this river, he or they shall be suspended during the Society's pleasure.

Such regulations almost mirror the early masters' organisation, the Shipwrights' Company. These new Rules contained many detailed statements in regard to work to be done, for example a day's work for caulking new decks was 80 feet and on old decks 90 feet. Sunday was to count as a double day and no overtime was to be worked if *any men off work belonging to this society, except at the finishing of a vessel*

---

[11] Schloss in *Methods of Industrial Remuneration* [1892] wrote that workers regarded piecework as *incompatible with really first-class quality of execution,* [it] *is detested by workmen who take a pride in their work.* p.70. Scattered evidence suggests that there was some contract / piecework by both shipwrights and joiners [see chap.13]

[12] Taylor Potts stated the Wear carpenters' union began shipbuilding in Tiffin's former yard and the managers appointed later separated and each built on his own account. Sunderland shipowner Joshua Wilson said in 1848: *These Men who built this Ship of ours had been I think Committee-men in a Strike in the Year 1823. The Masters would not employ these Men, and they began building on their own Account.*

[13] Unions accepted a legal indenture *or a few lines to specify ... served seven years as a regular shipwright*, The legal indenture was rare except for premium apprentices. Membership was for those proficient at the trade.

and then one quarter day if required.[14] Although the overtime rule remained in the rule book, it was certainly interpreted so as to cause few difficulties. Palmer's General Manager said in 1894 that the shipwrights would always help an employer in difficulties. A distinguished British economist Alfred Marshall, as a member of the Commission on Labour, described this regulation as *an excellent rule*. Limitations were placed upon the work other trades might do. Sailors were not to be allowed to black [tarring] vessels on the shore alongside shipwrights; no blockmaker should cut hawseholes nor millwrights put in hawse pipes where shipwrights were working. Much more was identified in regard to the joiners, a portent of the demarcation disputes to come:

> Rule 33... no joiner be allowed to make iron knee moulds, build chain trunks, lay half-deck or forecastle floors, and bulwark round the bows, or build sterns up in any new or old ship, or build bulk heads in any old ship when any member or members are working.

Such prohibitions imply that these tasks were sometimes carried out by joiners. A Wear bye-law suggested that unskilled workers may also have impinged on *their* work. Rule 9 stated *no labourer be allowed to carry any prepared material, make stages, lay or assist to lay ways or any other shipwright's work. Any member or foreman allowing this* to be fined 2s 6d. Wear shipwrights also tried to retain *boring* for their members. Around 1800 Laing employed borers at little more than labourers' rates of pay. At Thompsons in 1847-9 a borer worked on 26 of 90 weeks, this man might have been a former shipwright but he was paid 18s compared with 24s - 27s for craftsmen. Working hours were 6 to 6, except in the winter quarter: the first 4 weeks were 6.30 am - 5.30 pm, followed by 8 weeks from mid-November through to January, 7 am - 5 pm and then 3-4 weeks 6.30 am - 5.30 pm. Mealtimes were breakfast $\frac{1}{2}$ hour and dinner $\frac{3}{4}$ hour. Allowances were to be given to men caulking the deck top of new ships and these Rules expected *all masters to provide an allowance house for the men*. This rarely occurred, an exception being the large room with a deal table, forms and a kitchen fire, oven and cooking utensils at Smith's St. Peters yard. Such luxury caused the Sunderland men to point to it, in 1856, as an example of what was desirable when they were seeking a shelter from the north wind. Many foremen, often assisted by their wives, set up a beer house in their shipyard.

Shipwrights on the River Wear.

Perhaps on the Wear, if only because of its dominant position, shipbuilding was truly more *a way of life* than merely an occupation or business. Many Wear employers had worked side by side with the craftsmen, some for many years, as in the case of the Thompsons, and had a good understanding of the lives of their men. Towards the end of 1847, Robert Thompson sr was taking a wage of 33s/week and leading his shipwrights building ship #10; his son Joseph Lowes on 27s was in charge of #8 and Robert jnr on 30s looked after the building of #9; the shipwright's rate was then 27s. Early in 1849, another son John was on 27s and the others remained unchanged when the craftsman's rate dropped to 24s. Almost all Wear master shipwrights had served genuine yard apprenticeships and so, for seven years, worked under the same hours and conditions as the men, and many yards began as a partnership of a group of shipwrights. Jacky Crown was *never afraid to doff his jacket* and help his workers in the yard and William Pile personally knew all his men. These workmen met their employers in the streets of Sunderland. During one dispute, the employers complained of being exposed to abusive language from the men; there was not yet a great social barrier between the employer, the manager and his workers. There was a concern for the men. In times of depression Pile *saw to it that good workers and men with large families were kept on*. In practice some employers accepted the union regulations which provided work for infirm or aged shipwrights. Shipbuilder Haswell acknowledged that sufficient disabled shipwrights were always available to supply the need for borers, but the employers resisted trade union efforts to impose any such conditions. The father of the man who built the *Mauretania*, George Hunter, was so exhausted by his work as a shipyard apprentice, in the 1820's, that he was found *more than once, fast asleep in a field by the wayside due to exhaustion*.

---

[14] Shipwrights tried to restrict movement between jobs - Rule 32: *no member be allowed to come from a new ship to an old one, nor to go from one old ship to another while there are any men off work, except their work is finished.*

Techniques had changed little, if at all, by the 1850's when the boy George was apprenticed in Pile's yard. He later wrote: *The old Sunderland wood shipwrights were among the most capable and hard working in the world.* Very often, these skilled men were unable to stay in the full vigour of their trade all their working lives.

Shipwrights were not infrequently educated to at least a reasonable degree of literacy. Interest in literature was sometimes high, as was shown by a group of Wear shipwrights who met regularly for four years, in the blacksmiths' shop, to read and discuss such works as - De Lolme, *On the Constitution*, Paley's *Natural Theology*, and the *New Testament*, as well as their own compositions. Their activities resulted in the establishment of a library at Monkwearmouth in 1851 [note events a century later[15]]. A Sunderland shipwright, John Hopper, won a literary prize, in 1851. This letter, signed by *An Operative Shipwright* in the *Sunderland Herald* of 15 Sept.1851, reflected a literary style typical of the period:

> In a nation where the light of reason is but as the dimmest dawn of a cloudy morning, where the millions are purely physical men, and mind lacks cultivation, where science and machinery are unknown, where intelligent and skilful workmen are like a few grains of sand scattered amongst a huge pyramid of stones, competition and monopoly may be the means of calling forth the energy and inventive powers of such a nation... but in a nation where science reigns in glory, where machinery and capital reign in omnipotence over manual labour, where skilled workmen are counted by millions, and there is only sufficient work for thousands, in such a nation science and machinery in the hands of competition and monopoly, will reduce the working classes to the lowest ebb, and perhaps be the means of ruining our nation.

For many years, the independent attitudes of these craftsmen increased the problem of elected representatives negotiating with the employers. The men were very reluctant to give full powers to their delegates and always wished to retain a final sanction, after talks were held. This remained a continuing problem even after stronger national unions were established. A keen pride and interest in their craft characterised these men. *They took the same pride and pleasure in their day's work as many shipyard workers of the present day do in football and racing,* and when iron arrived in the shipyard *Great were the discussions among them as to whether such ships would float*[16], wrote Hunter & De Russett in 1909. On Sunday mornings, small groups of shipwrights walked along the banks of the Wear, critically surveying and commenting on the ships under construction. Much of their work was carried out by rule of thumb and there was little advanced planning. Even in the mid-1860s, at Pile's yard, there were only one draughtsman and two apprentices in the drawing office, even though four or five ships might be under construction. As the shipyards were open to the view of all, the shipwright had a good insight into his employer's order book and, indeed, could reasonably estimate the employment opportunities in the port in a way that engineering or other workers rarely, if ever, could. This knowledge could inspire or restrain action on the wages front. The shipwrights, like the other trades of joiner, mast and blockmakers, riggers, sailmakers and painters, had their own tools, and they regarded themselves as equal to their masters as men and had little or no sense of subservience.

Undoubtedly there were shipwrights' societies formed on the Wear at various times before the 1840s;[17]

---

[15] The Rev C H G Hopkins recalled that in the early 1950s in Doxfords engine works a group of men *generally ate their mid-day bait together, meeting round four machines ... nick named the red square - because the debates were fast and furious. The arguments ranged from politics to economic and religious and social problems."* When foreman Harry Oxley noticed *that they were deeply concerned,* he asked the Vicar for the use of a room on the Saturday night *a lot of men turned up ... I asked them into the house because the old iron room. . . was a pretty grim example of a Victorian parish room. From that day to this, the Forum has met once a month.* pp 52-3

[16] The issue was not the specific gravity of iron, many metal utensils were seen to float, but watertightness of hull.

[17] There is no reason to doubt Tyneside business man Thomas Brown's view, that there was *no combination of the carpenters* on the Wear in 1833. Shipbuilder Thomas Young's claim of *shipwrights taking them by the piece, and we can get nothing of the kind done with us,* may refer to a squad of shipwrights undertaking to build a hull for an agreed price. He said wage rates were 4s a day and 6d allowance [about the same as 1825], shipowner Anderson thought Shields wages *about 6d a day higher than Sunderland.*

probably separately based at Sunderland, Monkwearmouth, Bishopwearmouth and Hylton. It is also likely that, craftsmen occasionally took strike action, even without a formal society. The very sharp reduction of wages at Laings in 1801 from 5s to 4s resulted in no shipwrights going to work for a week but it seems likely if the men were in a union a longer struggle would have lasted longer. Members of Shipwrights' Unions from other ports came to the Wear, if only as ship's carpenters, which would be a stimulus to organisation. The provision of welfare benefits were as necessary at Sunderland as elsewhere and in 1846, the Wear shipwrights established an enduring association. Whit Monday was the shipwrights' annual day of celebration and demonstration. In 1850, some 900 men went from the Wear to South Shields where they were joined by 800 more and they all proceeded on eight steam boats, with bands and banners, to Newcastle. At this city, three hundred more swelled the ranks so that about 2,000 marched through the main streets to the Music Hall. It was not surprising that the local press described it as a *formidable force*. Two years later, a similar number marched and, in 1853, the *Newcastle Courant* described how some thousands of carpenters marched and 500 dined at the Lyceum. Models of the vessels under construction were carried with great pride on these annual holidays. The deep regard men felt for their wooden ships was reflected in a booklet, published in 1858 at Sunderland, which as well as defending trade union activities argued the case for the wood ship against the iron vessel. The new material was seen as offering *unskilled labour's opportunity in shipbuilding*. There were 1,389 members in the Wear Society in 1850 and in June 1851 a local press report gave the membership as 1,186. The 1851 census return of 1,372 shipwrights [over 20 years] in Sunderland suggests that membership covered almost all journeymen, allowing for those retired or in final year of apprenticeship. A total of £436 in benefits and paid out in 1849-50 and £303 in 1850-1. The number of shipwrights under 20 years was 653. In 1860 there were eight branches of the Wear Union, two at both Sunderland and Monkwearmouth, the others were at Bishopwearmouth, Ballast Hills, Deptford and Southwick and a separate society at Hylton. Every member was required to carry his contribution card and *will not be allowed to start work if he be found to be 4 meetings in arrears*. Such inspections were probably rare, since in a closely knit small community the standing of the men were known to each other and their employers. Such limited evidence as there is, usually at the time of disputes, suggests a good attendance at trade union monthly meetings; an unemployed man was required to attend to have his card franked so that he might pay his contribution later [Wear Rule #11]. One delegate was elected per 100 members. Meetings were held on every Tuesday, at Sunderland, and every Wednesday, at Monkwearmouth, such regular contact provided a wide knowledge of the labour in the port. The yard steward was available as a final check on the *interloper*.

1850s - new rules & strikes.

Within weeks of the Tyne shipwrights revising their rules, the employers declared they would restore the old rules from 1st February 1851. Despite the three months available for discussion, no agreement was reached in time to prevent a strike by about 1,100 shipwrights. Even though at South Shields the employers were firm in their opposition to the men, work was available on other parts of the river. On 22 February, delegates of the strikers and representatives of the shipwrights at Sunderland, Stockton, Hartlepool and Blyth met at South Shields. The 7-year apprenticeship was the critical issue, the employers insisting on their right to more limited periods if they so wished. These craftsmen resisted this claim with great vigour; they regarded the trade as theirs and retained a keen professional pride. The young lads were trained by the craftsmen, as Robert Knight, the Boilermakers' Secretary, pointed out in 1870; the employers played no part in this training. These men had a strong sense of their right to some control over their work situation and desired no reduction in the period of training. Once a man was acknowledged as a shipwright, he enjoyed the status of a craftsman of high standing and this position was not to be lightly gained. This attitude was reinforced by the desire to protect their wages and jobs by some limit on entry to the trade; if the labour market was the prime consideration the shipwrights would seek to restrict the number of apprentices, Towards the end of February, the Sunderland men sent £50 to aid the Tyne strikers and, by 7th March, a settlement was arranged without a modification of the apprenticeship rule.

A significant labour dispute at Hylton.
Many famous shipbuilders began at the village of Hylton, despite the absence of the finishing trades. There was *but one resident class of artizan (with the exception of blacksmith and joiner, who are indispensable) shipwrights ... the sailmaker, mast and blockmaker, rigger, painter and many others ....who are required for the finishing of a vessel, are not to be found in Hylton*. These shipwrights worked shorter hours than the Sunderland men and normally received refreshment at their work. Such variations, the *custom of the port* as it was called, persisted in the north east well into the 20th century. When the Hylton employers posted a notice, on 25 October 1851, that as and from 1st November *the restrictions and limitations shall be such as generally acknowledged in Sunderland*, their shipwrights came out on strike. Two weeks later, the sawyers joined the strike and the local press, describing the cause of the dispute as a *trivial matter*, proposed arbitration. No immediate solution was found. After a fruitless meeting in late November, the Town Council urged the Mayor to overcome his scruples as a large scale employer and intervene. Just before Christmas the Mayor, after consulting the men, arranged a conference under his chairmanship. Each of the 11 yards involved elected a delegate and the men were to accept the decisions of the conference; therein was a stumbling block. The conference met for three and a half hours on Monday 29 December, but failed to settle the strike. The shipwrights refused to confer full powers on their delegates, merely allowing them *to mention certain rights*. In welcoming the Mayor's intervention, a shipwrights' delegate, J. Walker, expressed a view which was often to be repeated by labour leaders in the north east: *The time had arrived when both the masters and men would see their interests were reciprocal and ... for the future act in unison*. Such an attitude, on a widespread basis, was a necessary starting point for effective conciliation or even acceptable arbitration.

Discussion at the conference clarified the points at issue, which were:
    (a) the *allowances*;
    (b) whether or not when caulking a worker could leave the yard before finishing time,
        if he had completed the acknowledged stint;
    (c) fines;
    (d) finishing time on Saturday;
    (e) the employment of labourers on boring.

No complaints as to the quantity of work done were made by the employers, although this was subject to regulation in all the yards. Comparisons were made with the Tyne rules, and figures quoted from the Sunderland yards of Laing, Austin and Pile showed that there were variations in the different yards but, in each, a clearly understood day's work was apparently acceptable. On the issue of *fines*, the shipbuilder, Bartram, complained that he had once paid a fine of 22s to the union. Delegate R Young explained that if a shipwright left a yard or was suspended and the Society thought his action was justified they paid him 2s and they expected the shipbuilder to contribute half this sum; if he did not, his yard was declared *black*. It appears unlikely, from these discussions, that the fines were always paid. A shipwright, R Hume, stated that the fines system at Sunderland was never brought into use because *the intelligent and respectable shipbuilders of that district never came into collision with their men*. Even allowing for some exaggeration in this statement, it suggested that the rules and regulations of the shipwrights enjoyed an acceptance on the Wear. The original notice by the Hylton shipbuilders stated that certain matters were *generally acknowledged* at Sunderland [these were not detailed it was assumed the men would be familiar with the regulations]. Some measure of agreement on the first four points was reached at the conference but there was no progress on the use of labourers for boring. There was division among the employers on this issue; shipbuilder Haswell said it was not an important issue and only two yards used labourers for boring. Shipwright J Pratt said there was only one non-union labourer in the two yards he represented. The men remained adamant that boring must be restricted *to provide the old and disabled shipwrights with employment*; although these men were lame, they could do a *sufficient day's work on boring*. These jobs reduced money paid from benefit funds. A delegate stated that they were advocating the rights of about 10,000 men throughout the country. Consultation with the men reinforced the delegates' stance, and the decision was firm; only men who had been *legally apprenticed* would be allowed to bore. Hume, the

chairman of the strikers, blamed the dispute on the masters:
> it was their intention to deprive us of certain privileges or regulations which we have been in quiet possession of for a number of years, regulation which time and custom had legalised, and the tacit agreement of the masters had ratified.

The hours of work were settled long before some of those *so-called masters* knew anything about Hylton or shipbuilding. Unless the allowance was made at the conventional time, the men argued, once the top of the vessel was caulked and so protected against the weather, shipbuilders often discharged the bulk of the men, later finishing the vessels at leisure or when a buyer arrived. It was claimed that the drink of itself was of little consequence and Hume's statement ended by declaring that all the men wanted was *the right to live by our labour*. In March 1848, Thompson paid £4-17s *for Tea & allowances in Coffee for Tee Total men*.

The Wear Shipbuilders' Protection Society was formed to match with equal determination the resolve of the men and on 20 January 1852, the builders decided to continue to insist on the right to use whom they chose as borers. Some shipwrights found jobs at South Shields and others went to sea; plans for a cooperative shipbuilding venture did not go beyond discussion. Sunderland shipwrights sent £100 to support the 130 men out in the sixteenth week of this Hylton strike. A casual street contact between a Lloyd's agent and a shipwright was reported in the press as an attempt to secure a settlement. However, the Lloyd's agent was said to have agreed that the standard of boring by the labourers, Irish and others, was inadequate. Fresh negotiations followed an initiative by the Sunderland shipwrights. On March 15th, G Gamsby, with two other Sunderland shipwrights, met with the employers and presented credentials showing they had full powers to negotiate. They explained the practices at Sunderland but failed to resolve the boring issue. The employers rejected arguments based on custom and stated that this regulation restricted their freedom and so was unreasonable, and, in any event, it was not the general rule of the port. This last point was the fundamental weakness in the stand of the Hylton men and it was unlikely that these men could maintain special privileges, if the employers were determined to end them. After further consultation, Gamsby offered, on behalf of the Hylton shipwrights, to do all boring at 3s a day, instead of the usual 4s, thus reducing the cost to something only slightly higher than a labourer's wage. When this was rejected, the men returned defeated after a strike lasting 21 weeks. There was to be no limitation on the number of labourers employed in the yards, though a preference would be given to old hands for boring work.[18] The Hylton yards were not at peace for long. The hiring of two non-union sawyers at Hodgson's yard caused another strike. The foremen and apprentices continued to build 12 ships on the stocks. The men began to drift away to jobs elsewhere as output was increasing and the dispute was finally settled in mid-June with the adoption of the general rules for the Wear.

An early conciliation board 1853-4.

Those prolonged disputes of 1852 and the formation of a shipbuilders' association stimulated a very important development. The minute book of the Wear Employers began with the following entries:
> 25 Jan. evening Bridge Hotel Sunderland: to take into consideration several regulations respecting the hours of labour, wages & other matters - motion moved by Geo Booth, sec Jno Smith: the time has arrived, when for the mutual benefit of Shipbuilders of the Port of Sunderland and their men a proper understanding, and a feeling of good will should exist between them.
>
> 26 Jan. each shipbuilder request the workmen to nominate a workman to meet with the Shipbuilders.

That Saturday evening meeting in January 1853, at the Lyceum, Bishopwearmouth, *to consider whether a better understanding between the masters and men could not be established*, resulted in one of the earliest joint industrial boards in Britain. James Laing was chairman and his recollection 40 years later was the basis of a number of inaccurate accounts of these events.[19] Masters and men agreed to form a

---

[18] It is unlikely that this led to a widespread use of labourers. It was claimed that John Blumer employed *all skilled workmen* over many years, he started at the end of the 1850s. A newcomer was unlikely to increase his labour costs.

[19] His account in 1892 became a source: L Jones dated the Board as 1850, lasting two years [p 162]. Sharpe also gave 1850 and followed Laing on the break-up and he errorneously stated *it was re-established in 1883-4*. [p 52]

committee of shipbuilders and shipwrights and they resolved: to refer to this committee *any question of dispute, either between an individual master and his men or the whole body of builders and shipwrights ... with a view to their amicable settlement.* They also declared their recognition of *the principle that the interests of the employer and employed are combined and cannot be separated without disadvantage to both parties.*

Separate meetings of the masters and men followed and the local press welcomed the moves but also pointed to the difficulties involved. On Saturday evening 5 February, the delegates and employers reassembled to establish the formal machinery. There were 45 shipwrights present, one from each yard, representing about 1,500 men. Gamsby explained how the men showed *great reluctance* about handing over decision making and so it was agreed that the proceedings of the Arbitration Court should be open to all members of the trade on the river. By this decision it was hoped to allay the fears of the men in regard to any underhand negotiations or agreements. This was a clear illustration of the independent attitude of these craftsmen, each one feeling that he had a right to know how matters proceeded and to participate in decision making. This aspect was also reflected in the insistence of the men, against the opposition of some employers, that the press should be present; this was finally decided by majority vote. According to the agreement *The Court* was to be composed of nine members from each side. Each shipyard was to elect a delegate, then a meeting of these forty-five delegates elected 14 representatives of whom nine sat in *The Court*, the remaining five being available as deputies. When the joint board failed to agree, the matter was to be referred to the independent chairman. A vice-chairman, with technical knowledge, attended with the chairman and a disputed decision could be delegated by the chairman to this technical assessor. It was agreed in the 4th clause that:

> all disputes, alleged grievances, partial or general and all projected changes or alterations affecting the builder and the workmen, shall be referred to this Court with a view to amicable adjustment, without the intervention of strikes or the interruption of business and the decision of this court to be final and binding on all parties.

What had been established was a Board of Conciliation rather than a simple court of arbitration. Henry Crompton, in 1876, stressed the important difference between the two - arbitration occurred *after the fact*:

> Arbitration... and implies a cause of difference and dispute have arisen...conciliation aims at something higher - at doing before the fact ... It seeks to prevent and remove the causes of a dispute before they arise ... Arbitration is limited to the larger and more general questions of industry, those of wages or prices...

Such wider aims were recognised to some degree by both sides on the Wear in the words - *all projected alterations, amicable adjustment* and no strikes. However, it should be noted that the references to the Court do refer to arbitrators and the names of the Masters and Shipwrights were entered under the heading *Committee of Arbitration.*[20] All seemed set for industrial peace; trade was improving, masters and men met regularly around the same table. The shipwrights drew attention to the Councils de Prud'homme and their success in preventing strikes at Lyons. The *Sunderland Herald* subsequently printed a long article on the work of these French Councils. A former Mayor, Dr. W. Mordey, was the first chairman of the Court and William Knott, foreman blacksmith of the River Wear Commissioners, as a working man vice-chairman. Shipbuilder John Candlish had known Knott for several years as *a good high-minded and intelligent man* and he *would have no hesitation in submitting any matter in dispute to him*. Knott wrote to the local press describing the setting up of the Board as *the best evidence that we are, in truth, in a civilised and intelligent community*. Editorially, the paper commented that the masters and men were *wiser in this port than other places*. A belief in the peaceful settlement of industrial differences was held by many labour leaders in the north east, from shipwright Gamsby [in 1850's] through John Kane, the iron worker [in

---

[20] The Wear Shipbuilders Association's first minute book contains material related to the Board, the Committee members were: *Masters*- James Laing, S P Austin, John T Alcock, Jno Pile. Peter Gibson, Geo Booth, Robt Thompson jnr., John Candlish, John Watson, Jno Pile secretary; *Shipwrights* - Stephenson Rowntree, Geo Gamsby, James Dobson, Jas Emmerson, Elisha Taylor, William Robson, John Lamb, John Foster, David Davies, Thomas Harris secretary.

1860's], John Burnett, the engineer, [in late 1860's & 1870's] to Arthur Henderson, the foundry man.[21]

The shipwrights' request for uniform caulking conditions on the river was the first case examined by the Wear Court. Mordey delivered his verdict on 26 February 1853; the *scale of work* for caulking then decided remained in the 1860 edition of the Wear shipwrights' Rule Book.[22] Further decisions in that Rule Book were those given by Mordey and Knott, on *A Scale of Time*, in October 1853 and in April 1854, on the *Regulation of Tide Work*. Press reports gave the impression of the employers going to the meetings with little if any prior consultation, for example when one shipbuilder raised the issue of runaway apprentices, a fellow employer declared it to be a purely masters' question. The shipwrights' delegates volunteered their cooperation and did help to secure the return of the runaways involved. Despite the wideness of the original terms of reference, the wages issue was strangely excluded by employers from the Board. The first evidence of this was the increase of April 1853, when the press stated it was mentioned in *a short jocular chat* and that the Court *decided such matters* were *never contemplated*. The events preceding this increase in pay began in February when the shipwrights, then earning 4*s* a day asked for 5*s* a day, apparently anticipated an offer by the employers and 4*s* 6*d* a day was readily agreed. On 24 March, three ships were launched on the Wear [together about 2,000t]. The opportunities for profit-making were such that Briggs offered 5*s* a day plus two pints of beer. When the shipwrights circulated the employers that they were unwilling to accept less than 5*s* a day, after 9 April, all the employers could only reply was *it was unreservedly stated ... that the increase having already been granted by one or two masters, there was little doubt they would have to follow.*[23]

Excluding such a critical issue as wages was a serious weakness in the Board's work and was the basic immediate cause of the break up of the Board in November 1854. James Laing, Sunderland's foremost shipbuilder, in 1892, told the Royal Commission on Labour that following a number of decisions adverse to the men, the Board broke up. He stated - *The original idea of a Council of Conciliation was in 1850* and lasted *about two years I think*. Laing was speaking from memory and said that the records were mislaid. The local press reported matters rather differently. A leading article on *Strikes* in the *Sunderland Herald*, on 7 January 1854, failed to mention the Board, which suggested perhaps at least temporary inactivity.[24] During the Crimea War, the wages of the shipwrights increased, it was claimed up to 12s and even £1 in some places. Wages on the Wear reached 6s a day in February 1854 and the trade was so busy that, in September, the *Newcastle Courant* wrote: *There is not a shore on the Tyne and Wear, from the sea five or six miles up, but it is employed in shipbuilding.* It was with some surprise that the Wear shipwrights read the employers' notice that from 13 October 1854 wages would be 5s a day; the men requested arbitration but the employers rejected this. The *Newcastle Courant* wrote [3 Nov 1854]: *The men...[are] willing to allow this course but the masters would not allow that wages could be a subject of arbitration* by the *Court*. Eight hundred men struck work, perhaps half the labour force, while 6 yards continued on a partial basis with individual shipbuilders paying 6s whenever they particularly wanted a

---

[21] John Kane [1819-76] born in Alnwick; worked at Hawkes of Gateshead; gen. secretary Ironworkers Assoc. In 1869 with Quaker David Dale set up a board for the North of England Iron & Steel Trade. Arthur Henderson [1862-1935] district organiser the Ironfounders, 1892-1902; MP, with breaks - 1903-35, was Home Secretary and Foreign Secretary.

[22] The Caulking scales set out the length of caulking per day, e.g.- decks - 130 ft; over the side $2^{1}/_{2}$" - 65 ft and 4" - 50ft.; this award of 26 Feb 1853 was signed by J Pile for the shipbuilders and T Harris for the shipwrights.

[23] At this time, the blockmakers advanced to 27*s* a week, while the riggers gained 30*s*, after a one day strike. The pieceworking sawyers fought a longer struggle to secure their advance. Tyne shipwrights were on strike for two weeks in May 1853 for 5s / day and offered to forgo an increase of 6d, if they were allowed a half hour break for tea. G Marshall immediately conceded the increase revealing a division among the employers. Elsewhere only the apprentices were working. About 200 Tyne shipwrights found jobs at Sunderland. Gradually the employers weakened and some 300 men resumed their usual jobs, before 5s /day was generally agreed.

[24] The last award given on 15 Apl. 1854 was for the Regulation of Tide Work [13 clauses].

vessel finished. Work was offered to 100 men by a shipbuilder in the South. Knott had contacted the employers on using the Court, to which they replied that a meeting with the shipwrights was acceptable *but not in the Court of Arbitration*. In a letter to the *Sunderland Herald* [3 Nov 1854], a shipwright stated that the two chairmen supported the view that the Board could decide wage issues; this should not have been doubted given clause 4. He rejected the opinion that the Board could not arbitrate because wages were subject to *the laws of supply and demand*, and argued that all questions between masters and men, e.g. hours, were likewise affected by *supply and demand*. A week later, some masters were paying 6s 6d a day. When the shipwrights went to meet the employers on 13 November, both chairmen Mordey and Knott were at the meeting place; the shipbuilders asked them to leave. Their minute book referred to their objection to the *interference* of the Chairman of the Court of Arbitration. Hutchinson and Laing spoke to the men but without resolving anything. On the next day, Knott wrote:

> the Arbitration Court may be considered at an end, from the discourtesy we met with last night. . .I cannot however, omit the opportunity of thanking and complimenting that portion of the workmen who represented that body in the Arbitration Court, for their uniform, intelligent and courteous demeanour.

Laing's recollections were inaccurate and Knott placed responsibility for the break up on the employers. The irony of the situation was that Knott, as an arbitrator, would probably have reduced wages, judging by an open letter of 24 November. He wrote: *You* [the shipwrights] *seem to imagine that a powerful combination can reverse this axiom (supply & demand) of political economy ... you will be mistaken*. Gamsby reported the failure of the meeting of 13 November and cheers greeted his statement that if a fair inquiry had decided on a reduction they would have accepted it *like sensible men*. With no such inquiry, the strike continued.

Further struggles on the Wear.

When Laing and Hutchinson discovered that 6s was the general wage on the Tyne and Tees, they attempted to secure a reduction along the whole north east coast. A visit by Hutchinson to Tyneside secured the posting of reduction notices, except at Howdon. Reduction notices were also posted at Hartlepool but Pile, one of the principal builders, soon withdrew his. While nearly 1,900 men were out when the Tyne yards stopped, 9 yards were working on the Wear, including Thompson's, despite assurances given by the Wear secretary that they would not pay the disputed rate. Accounts of the discussions between the shipwrights' leaders and the Wear shipbuilders reveal a high degree of frankness. An impression emerges of a discussion between equals, in which indiscreet words sometimes slipped out, for example when Hutchinson's contacts with the Tyne employers were revealed, it was probably never intended the men should discover this. Laing condemned the men's combination although the absence of some organisation would have prevented effective consultation and conciliation. A shipwright retorted that without the union there was *lump work* and ships were *clagged together*. The benefit of the union was good work and well trained apprentices.[25] The debate was frank and vigorous. By 6 December, the employers' urgent need for men was such that Byers and Smith had resumed full work at 6s a day, in addition to Briggs at Michael Clarke's yard. Four others were about to offer 6s also. Seven masters said they should give due notice to Shields before yielding. It was too late; even Laing said *it was little use holding out any longer*, pay the 6s. *A great deal of dissent* was recorded in the Employers' minutes and they adjourned *indefinitely, with the understanding that the above resolution or proposition would generally be adopted*. The Employers' Association did not meet again for more than 13 months. Work generally resumed on 9 December. On the Tyne, Smiths and three others reopened. By mid-December, the strike was over. After 10 weeks, the men had won and the notices were withdrawn. The trade was *brisk and the men pretty well employed*. This stoppage cost the men about £2,000 a week in lost wages. Even with the strike 67,000t were launched in 1854 on the Wear, only just below the level of 1853. The lost time may partially explain a 10% fall in output in 1855, when industrial peace reigned.

---

[25] Mayhew 8 August 1850: *In almost all trades there are broadly distinguished classes of workmen, known as society and non-society man... These society men constitute what may be termed the aristocracy of the trade. They are not only for the most part the more intelligent and respectable of the craft but by far the more skilled workmen.*

Early in 1856, the wages of the 300 or so men employed on the Wear constructing gunboats increased; the shipwrights advanced to 8s 6d a day and the sawyers were paid 5s / 100 feet compared with 4s 3d in other yards. A claim for 7s a day by the shipwrights was unanimously rejected by the employers on the morning the notice expired. The shipwrights reviewed the situation and decided to continue working at 6s, despite the opposition of the Hylton men. Although the Hylton men turned out on Saturday, during the weekend, more reasonable counsels prevailed and they were at work on Monday. About 2,000 men were dismissed from the Woolwich Dockyard when the Crimea War ended. Output on the Wear remained high, and in November three shipbuilders spoke against posting a notice of a 1s reduction. A general meeting of the shipwrights resolved by a large majority to resist the reduction on the grounds that there were not similar reductions in other ports. By Christmas 1856, 1,400 men were out of work and 7 yards continued working at 6s a day. The *Newcastle Courant* reported on 22 December that the employers were *not to be unanimous*. This division among the employers gave the shipwrights confidence that the dispute would not outlast the holidays. On 2 January 1857, the *Sunderland Herald* wrote that it would be no surprise if the men won. Later that day the employers met and after considerable discussion agreed to withdraw the reduction notices. It was however only a postponement; inevitably once output fell on the Wear wages would be reduced. By the late spring about 1,000 men were unemployed. On 14 May 1857 representatives from neighbouring ports met with the Wear Shipbuilders' Association; Forsyth, McLeod and Young came from South Shields, Laing from North Shields and Denton and Blumer from Hartlepool. At first Forsyth and Denton proposed 1s reduction and then agreed jointly with the other employers to serve notices of a reduction from 6s to 4s 6d a day on the shipwrights, the wages of other trades and sawyers' piecework rates were also to be reduced. Wear shipbuilders avoided a stoppage by accepting the shipwrights' offer of a 1s reduction to 5s a day, on 3 June. Nearly 3,000 men went on strike on the Tyne and at Blyth and finally a similar settlement was agreed.[26] A proposed reduction to 4s a day caused a general stoppage of work by the shipwrights on Saturday 12 December. Again division among the employers was such that they agreed, with no dissent, on 8 January 1858 that each builder should act as he chose. It was another short term respite for the men, before the end of April 4s was the ruling rate.

Exodus of Shipwrights From Sunderland, was the headline of a Newcastle paper's report of the departure of 600 men from the Wear to the government dockyards. On 2 May 1859 a telegraphic message from the Secretary of the Navy asked for more men. Single men were give 15s by their trade union and married men 20s to assist in the journey; the leaders appeared unaware that this was only short term relief to local unemployment. Almost 200 men left Hylton, where empty houses reflected their departures. By mid May there was a local scarcity of skilled men and a strike was called for an extra 1s a day on Wear and Tyne. Shipbuilders on the Wear were in no mood to concede any advance and on 10 June decided to send Barker and Taylor to Scotland to recruit workers [20 for Laing, 10 each for Alcock, Taylor and Austin]. As on other occasions, there were difficulties with the ship repairers; Hutchinson was asked on 17 June to lay off his men. Soon afterwards efforts were agreed to bring the repairers into line. Another factor changed the whole picture; at the naval yards the men were paid off and were coming home. Before long such men as had jobs were back at work without any increase. A South Shields builder offered £50 for the names of those who had attacked non-union men from Aberdeen, one of the few allegations of the use of violence. When the *Sheffield outrages* were being investigated, Charles Mark Palmer commented *whatever might have been the misunderstandings, the North had witnessed no trade outrages*. Thus ended a decade of considerable strife in shipbuilding on the Wear, which also had the very positive feature of that early Arbitration Court. This Court was a worthwhile attempt to eliminate strikes. The serious fluctuations in shipbuilding would have strained any agreements but, if the employers had established a more consistent unity among themselves, the attempt might have survived longer. The shipwrights, as a body, were capable of disciplined decisions and sufficient of their leaders favoured peaceful settlements to have maintained the Court, if they had enjoyed the employers' support. Conciliation is always a two-way process and a modest beginning was *made. The process of discussion*, Asa Briggs pointed out, *was often more important*

---

[26] No details survive of *a lengthened discussion* by Wear shipbuilders on Union or non-union men on 8 November.

than the decisions arrived at; in this respect, conciliation was a more satisfactory pointer to the future than arbitration.

National connections of shipwrights' unions.

Shipwrights continued to organise on a port basis until the 1880s. These port based trade unions[27] corresponded with each other and came together annually from about 1850. Such annual meetings were held at South Shields in 1851, Newcastle 1855, when the question of national amalgamation was discussed, and at Sunderland in 1860.[28] Wear shipwrights maintained a separate association from 1846 until 1907, even after a national trade union was formed in 1883, with its headquarters in Newcastle. In their own locality, these unions were strong by virtue of embracing within their ranks the bulk of the skilled men, but their power extended beyond this. The *Sunderland Herald* stated in 1851 that the *corresponding machinery reaching to other place ... rendered* [the local society] *more powerful.* In 1856, strikers at Whitby confidently declared that no north east port would handle their work.

Trade unions for shipbuilding and marine engineering.

The first north east branch of the Society of Friendly Boilermakers was founded in 1843 at Newcastle and thereafter John Parker[29] of Stephenson's works played a major role in building up the membership. The importance of the area to this national Society was reflected in the decision in 1845 to send the General Secretary to Newcastle to recruit new members, with the entrance fee reduced to 2s 6d to assist his efforts. This society was founded in 1834 and its early emblem shows a marine boiler; it became the dominant trade union in shipbuilding once the iron hull arrived and indeed the Union's title became in 1852 the *United Society of Boiler Makers and Iron Shipbuilders.*[30] The last two words were added before Lloyds had established formal rules for building iron ships! Four years later the first branch was opened at Sunderland, by which time there were three branches on the Tyne as well as at Stockton and Middlesbrough. Many of these early members were in engineering. However, on the Wear members were in shipbuilding and Thomas Vickers, secretary of Sunderland #1 branch, played a prominent part in the Society's delegate conference of 1862. A Thomas Vickers was foreman riveter at Doxfords in 1863. This union was always willing to help to provide workers by advertisement in union journal and fares, as secretary, John Allen, made clear to a Royal Commission in 1868. The union paid fares to unemployed men so that they could reach an employer or foreman who wanted them. More than £10,000 was paid for members to travel in search of work by the Society in 1867, almost £16,000 in the six years to the end of 1867.

---

[27] Among other locally based trade unions were the sailmakers, who formed an association at South Shields in 1825, and at North Shields in 1845. These unions in 1899 had 31 members at South Shields, 24 at North Shields, at Sunderland about 40. Blacksmiths formed the Co-operative Smiths of Newcastle in 1849.

[28] The meeting places were: 1853 Newcastle; 1854 London; 1855 Liverpool; 1856 London; 1857 Dublin; 1858 Glasgow; 1859 South Shields; 1860 Sunderland; 1861 Swansea; 1862 London; 1863 Greenock; 1864 not known; 1865 Belfast; 1866 North Shields; 1867 Bristol; 1868 Liverpool; 1869 Glasgow; 1870 London; 1871 Hartlepool; 1872 Cardiff; 1873 Belfast; 1874 Monkwearmouth; 1875 Liverpool; 1876 Glasgow; 1877 Swansea; 1878 Liverpool; 1879 Southampton; 1880 Belfast; 1881 South Shields; 1882 London; 1883 Cardiff; 1884 Portsmouth; 1885 Hull; 1886 Belfast; 1887 Liverpool; 1888 Southampton; 1889 Bristol; 1890 London; 1891 Liverpool.

[29] Parker died in 1871 from injuries sustained when the casing of a marine boiler fell on him; he had served the Company for 33 years and the works was closed on the day of his funeral. He was branch secretary for 25 years.

[30] Religious language was present in the earliest Society books; there was a prayer at both the start and end of Lodge meetings. Early subscriptions were 1s 9d per four weeks, of which 3d was spent on liquors. Sick benefit was 10s/week for six months, 5s for the second half year and then 3s 6d. Superannuation was 3s 6d - payable at 60 after 20 years memberships. A penny a mile was allowed to members travelling to find work. Death benefit was £8 for member, £7 for wife; a widow could by contributing 1s / quarter secure a funeral benefit of £4.

A very important national trade union came into being at mid-century. Engineering workers were organised in various societies throughout the country; chief amongst these were the *Steam Engine Makers' Society* [begun in Liverpool in 1824] and the Friendly Society known as the *Old Mechanics*, started two years later. A steamship on the membership emblem of the latter showed a perceived marine connection. Early in 1850 steps were taken to amalgamate as many as possible of these societies. By no means all joined, the *Steam Engine Makers* and a significant part of the *Old Mechanics* staying out. Nonetheless there were 5,000 members in the *Amalgamated Society of Engineers, Machinists, Smiths, Millwrights and Patternmakers* [*ASE*] when it began on 6 January 1851. The four branches on the North East Coast totalled only 145 members. The subsequent growth of the *ASE* in the region is compared with Leeds in diag 12.01. Following the national lockout, [largely centred on London and Manchester], in 1852, membership fell sharply in the Tyneside *ASE* branches. The drop was a loss of almost 37%, from 122 to 77 compared with a national loss of less than 18%. Although a new branch was formed at Middlesbrough, there were only 128 *ASE* members in the whole area, while there were more than 2,000 Engine & Machine Makers, over 20 years, in Northumberland and Durham. Perhaps part of the explanation was that north east workers preferred to avoid national entanglements and the 1s subscription, equivalent to two hours pay if you were able to earn 30s a week, was also probably a deterrent to joining the *ASE*. New branches were established at Hartlepool [1854] and at Jarrow [1855], this latter no doubt related to Palmer's

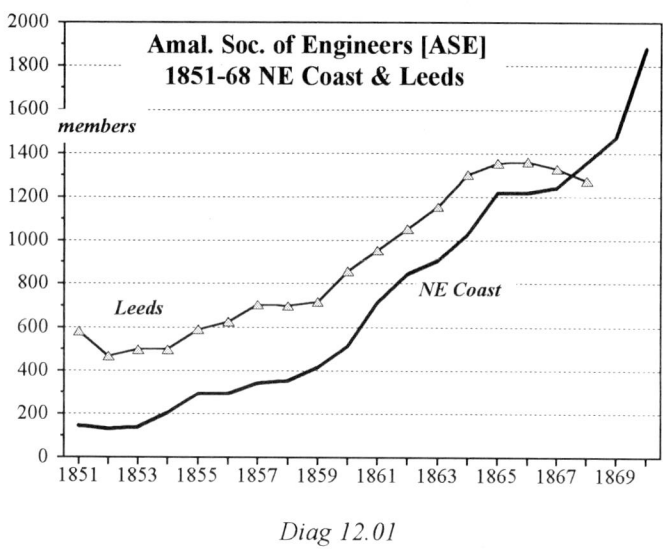

Diag 12.01

and Leslie's shipyards. Apart from the shipwrights, there was a low level of trade union organisation, the complex reasons for this are not pursued here. Men joined a trade union to advance their working conditions, including wages, and also, in particular, as a protection against the ups and downs of industrial life, and the latter was uppermost in the intentions and actions of the craft unions.[31] This provident theme was prominent in the preface to the *ASE* rules.

> Members of a trade ... who are cognisant of much of the misery which is necessarily attendant on a precarious employment, would be inhuman indeed, if they did not make some arrangement for relieving the distress of their fellow workmen, whom sickness or a want of employment should befall them... It is not necessary to overcharge the picture. We are willing to admit that, whilst in constant employment, our members may be able to obtain all the necessaries and perhaps some of the luxuries of life...there is a fear always... that it may not continue ... and [so]... mutual assistance in time of need, a regulation of the condition of labour that its benefits may be mutually enjoyed and a well regulated organisation to prevent a surplus of labour in our trade.

Up to the early 1870s the union organisation of engineering workers in the north east was very limited.

Boilermakers resented any attempt by shipwrights, *our wooden enemies*, to master the working of iron;

---

[31] D.C.Cummings [1861-1942]- joined the Labour Dept. of the Board of Trade in 1908], secretary of the Boilermakers [1899-1908], wrote: *In its very infancy the objects of the Friendly Boilermakers were ... mutual relief in cases of sickness, old age and infirmities, and for the burial of the dead.* In the six years to 1868, the Society spent on Sickness benefit £18,145, Funerals, £4,213, Surgeon, £5,052; Travelling to work: £15,966, Aged members & superannuation £ 2,502. Of the £5805 spent on disputes in the five years to 1867, £3,667 was for one dispute in London and on the Clyde.

however there were few if any industrial stoppages on this issue.[32] The iron workers mocked the shipwrights' efforts and attempted through a more comprehensive organisation of their trade to deny the shipbuilder who employed shipwrights, the help of caulkers. Normally in engineering, boilermakers embraced all branches of the trade and there was not a separate trade of caulker, but as already noted iron shipbuilders subdivided the work of boilermakers. Members of the Boilermakers' Society on the Tyne and Wear, who had accepted the change, urged their executive council to recognise this new situation. When, in 1865, the Executive rejected a proposal to admit caulkers, the branches of Stockton, Hartlepool and Middlesbrough issued a circular explaining the case for change. They argued that the caulkers enabled the shipwrights to build iron vessels; without the assistance of two caulkers *our wooden enemies*, at Piles[33] and Smiths would see all their ships sink. Caulkers were paid the same rates as fitters. They argued that in the iron shipbuilding areas caulkers formed *a very marked and distinct branch* of the trade and continued:

> we know that caulking is part of our trade, and if the employers separate it and form it into a distinct branch both for speed and economy - and as we all know this is an age of improvement and advancement - why should we as a society refuse to keep pace with the age.

This was the voice of men confident of the growth of their trade and the premium their scarce skills could bring, who were prepared to co-operate in technical change. Unmoved, the National Executive's reply reflected the cautious friendly society attitude as to the possible cost to the funds. They wrote:

> Now the evil of admitting men who can only caulk or cut holes in iron must be very plain to anyone who has visited the inland towns or shipbuilding districts. The holder-up is a man who can caulk or hold up in either the boilershop or the shipyard ... and thus in depression of trade, stands two chances to one of getting employment and relieving the funds from travelling money which would be received by him who could not hold-up or do anything but caulk or cut holes ... we think that the Caulkers, as a class, having a claim upon the funds of our Society would be most detrimental to us in slackness of trade.

Later their general secretary Cummings described this as *foolish opposition*. Ultimately caulkers were admitted but not the hole cutters or the drillers, who organised their own separate society, at Sunderland, in 1875, and later elsewhere.

Labour in the 1860s.

During the 1860s industrial disputes were less frequent on the Wear. As shipbuilding output increased from the low point of 1859, the shipwrights' wages stayed constant, until the height of the boom. Hence it was not surprising that, in January 1863, the *Newcastle Courant* described the relations between the masters and men as *more satisfactory to both parties than they have been for a very long time*. Just over a year later, in February 1864, some shipwrights on the Wear gained 6s/day and it was confidently predicted that this would be general. In March, the other shipyard trades of joiner, sawyer and blacksmith attempted by strike action to obtain the same advance. The employers resisted and attempted to restore the earlier shipwrights' rate of 5s a day. Many of the joiners moved into the building trade at 24s a week. The shipwrights responded to the employers' pressure by offering to work at 5s 6d, which was accepted. The blacksmiths and sawyers stayed out but after a while the shipwrights were sawing their own timber, so undermining the resistance of the sawyers. This action again demonstrated the rift between the various groups of workers which could only too readily be widened. In later years, black squad craftsmen on occasion carried out the work of other workers with whom they were in dispute. One of the earliest examples of a strike by the boys in a shipyard was at Hartlepool in 1864, when the magistrates' court was used to discipline and punish strikers, a response frequently used at this time. A policeman was employed at the shipyard of Denton, Gray & Co., and the lads decided to refuse to work until the policeman was removed. Thirteen lads were taken into custody and, when they appeared in court, the supposed leader was sentenced to 14 days imprisonment. The other lads detained agreed to return to work and pay the costs of

---

[32] Mortimer [1973] states there was a strike at Middlesbrough (?1864-5) against shipwrights doing *iron-work*. The words *Wooden Enemies* were used in a circular from Stockton, Hartlepool & Middlesbrough 1866.

[33] When Pile's yard closed, the Boilermakers warned against employing these shipwrights through the Union Journal- *All our Yard and shop delegates to keep a watchful eye on all strangers coming amongst them.*

the action. At Jarrow, Palmers took out summonses on a fairly wide scale, in 1864, when their iron workers took industrial action against a wage reduction. Eight men were tried under the *Combination Acts* [sic]; a labourer John Cooper was sentenced to three months imprisonment and the others to one month each. A week later, with the dispute ended, the other cases were withdrawn. The sound selection of foremen was an essential element in successful management. A failure in this regard in 1865 resulted in Tyne shipwrights demonstrating their organised strength. Following the serious illness of the yard foreman, the Tyne Ironshipbuilding Co. replaced him with a Mr Blackwood. In the words of the *Newcastle Courant* Mr Blackwood was *in bad odour amongst the men* and the shipwrights asked for his removal. When the foreman was not removed, the men struck and a deputation went to London to see the directors of the company, who simply said the works was open and those who wished could leave. Before the end of June the management gave way and the news of Blackwood's resignation[34] was received *with acclamation* by the men, who returned to work and completed a 650t vessel in less than three months.[35]

At Jarrow Palmer made the iron for his ships and marine engines. Charles Palmer's hostility to the union organisation at his iron plant may have influenced his attitude to all trade unions, despite the fact that John Kane, the leader of the ironmen, was a conciliator.[36] As a prior condition to allowing his Tyneside iron plant men to return to work after a dispute, Palmer insisted they pledged not to send any support to those still on strike in the Midlands, although many had relations there.[37] At the opening of the Jarrow Mechanics' Institute in 1864, Palmer denounced unions as *a hindrance to free intercourse*, claiming they enabled the *idle and lazy to get the same as the hardworking and intelligent*. He was addressing men, who had just marched under the banners bearing the words - *Let Jarrow Flourish*. Again, three years later, he spoke of the evil of the *fever of trade unionism*. He told a Royal Commission that his Company did not allow unions to come between them and the workers and they had *a free conference with them*; they always refused to meet trade union delegates. Palmer looked upon trade unions *as simply efficient in times of prosperous trade*; in the iron manufacturing trade unions had raised wages sooner than they would otherwise have risen. He could not conceive masters acting *unfairly* to unorganised men. Despite these denunciations, he added: *We have never had any special trouble ... from the unions at our works excepting ... the rolling mills department.*

The Nine Hours Day - the first attempts 1865-6.

Action by the London building trades to secure a 9-hour day, in 1859-60, probably inspired workers elsewhere to seek this reduction from ten hours. George Potter, leader of the London workers, spoke on this issue in Newcastle in April 1861. Hours were reduced at Stephensons in 1864: work finished on Saturdays at 12 noon instead of 4 p.m. On Teesside, many carpenters gained a 9-hour day and Pile at Hartlepool, conceded the 9-hour day in 1865. The 9-hours movement became an issue on Tyneside and Teesside, including Jarrow. *Newcastle Courant* reported that for some time it was *eagerly discussed on the banks of the Tyne*. The time for achieving this seemed favourable. In January 1866, the *Chronicle* described the engine building trade as *so brisk during the past year* that there was considerable difficulty in getting both suitable material and good men. Piecework, introduced in some places to overcome these

---

[34] In February 1866 Blackwood became manager of Irvine's shipyard at Hartlepool.

[35] A similar but more violent struggle occurred at Bolckow & Vaughan in Middlesbrough. *Riotous proceedings* was the *Newcastle Courant*'s headline when the workers struck after the overseer, George Bushell locked the factory gates preventing the men from leaving, as was customary, after a young man was killed. Many arrests were made and the 8th Hussars arrived. By the end of the week, Bushell had resigned and with *general rejoicing* the men returned to work.

[36] Kane pioneered from the labour side The Iron Industry Arbitration Board, described as *the most famous and successful of the nineteenth century boards* by Clegg, Thompson & Fox.

[37] The iron trades employers were organised and when a major strike in North Staffordshire continued through 1864-5, lockouts were arranged in the north east. In 1866 there was a strike of some 12,000 to resist a wage reduction.

difficulties, was continuing. Not long afterwards, an organised movement developed. While events on the Tyne, Tees and Hartlepool were related, in particular the joint organisation of the employers, certain phases of the struggle are best examined separately. The 9-hour day *was one of more importance than that relating to a mere advance of wages, as it affected their social and intellectual condition*, Rea, of the North Eastern Railway Works told a meeting at Newcastle on 19 February 1866. Speakers pointed to the 8-hour day, in the USA, and *considerable enthusiasm* was displayed. With *acclamation* a motion was carried by that:

> in the opinion of this meeting, the time has arrived when the employers ought, as a tribute to the intelligence of their workmen, concede, without struggle, the reduction of the hours of labour from ten to nine per day.

The intellectual and social benefits to be derived from the reduction were stressed throughout the discussion. Holyoake, Fawcett and Mill[38] were quoted by the trade unionist Keir and he referred to the daily reading of newspapers in the workshops. He was against strike action because of the effects upon those earning less than £1 a week, some only 15s, and said *they had deliberated calmly ... in order to avoid the strike stigma ...* [they] *had given the employers ample opportunity to consider the matter*. If the employers refused, they should bear the blame for subsequent actions. The meeting also resolved that workmen should share the gains from the use of improved machinery. John Hill, probably a boilermaker, reported on the developments on Teesside. Only a Mr Green, while *regretting that so few of those* present were union members, urged that the way to success was through trade unions: *they should make it a trade union question*. The chairman intervened to prevent a speech along these lines continuing, a clear confirmation of the elementary condition of trade unionism on Tyneside. Less than 600 men belonged to the 6 *ASE* branches on Tyneside in 1865.

Following this meeting, the workmen of Jarrow sent a letter to their employers.

> Gentlemen,
>
> We ... beg to acquaint you that an association has been formed on Tyneside, for the reduction of the hours of labour from ten to nine per day; and also to inform you that we have identified ourselves with this movement, believing that the period has arrived when such reductions may reasonably be expected. We submit the following reasons as grounds for our request: -
>
> By the introduction of improved machinery into the various departments of labour, the profits of the employers have been considerably increased, while no corresponding benefits have accrued to the working classes, though in most instances such improvements in machinery are mainly attributable to the increased intelligence and application of the artisans themselves. No suggestion is required to prove that machinery, however complicated or simple, is safer in the charge of intelligent and moral workmen, than men without education and moral rectitude; and as the shortening of the hours of labour will afford opportunities for mental and moral training, thereby a mutual advantage could not but be realised by both employer and employed. We could advance other reasons equally powerful for the reduction of the hours of labour but we trust those already given will be sufficient.
>
> We submit this memorial for your careful consideration and respectfully request your answer on or before March 1st 1866.

Any suggestion that the *memorial* meant the men would strike on 1 March was repudiated by Henry Savage, of the marine engine works. Palmer acted promptly and called a meeting for the evening of Thursday 22 February in the new engine erecting shops. About 2,000 workers greeted with loud cheers the arrival of Palmer, accompanied by H D Pochin, of Manchester, a member of the board of directors. Earlier in the afternoon of that day, Palmer, with employers from a large area, had met and resolved on a common policy; with his hand that much stronger, Palmer might have taken a tougher line. He proceeded with *tact and cleverness*, to use the words of John Burnett, who later praised *the conciliatory tone adopted by that gentleman, who met his workmen and discussed the matter with them calmly and fairly*. The vastness of

---

[38] *George Jacob Holyoake* [1817-1906] - tinsmith & white smith at Birmingham, reformer, Chartist and advocate of co-operation - gaoled for his rationalist views. *Henry Fawcett* [1833-84] Professor of Political Economy at Cambridge- *Manual of Political Economy* [1863]; a Liberal MP, who favoured proportional representation. *John Stuart Mill* [1806-73] philosopher who wrote *Political Economy and Representative Government* [1861].

the meeting gave Palmer the opportunity to exercise his considerable personality to the full, in a manner which might not have been so effective in a smaller negotiating situation. A published pamphlet was entitled *Conference between C.M.Palmer and the Workmen of Jarrow* [it truly was a company town!]. It could hardly be called a conference, except on the very widest use of that term; it was a works meeting addressed by two directors. Beginning by complimenting the men, Palmer probably secured their confidence and said

> where differences arise ... for the best interests of both parties concerned, they should meet together and have the question in dispute thoroughly discussed. [Their letter was] a respectful and intelligent document and surely ... I appeal to enlightened men, and I will ask you whether by the introduction of machinery, the intelligent labourer, the steady industrious man has not been raised up to the condition of the mechanic.

He sympathised with the aim and should *be thankful* if something could be done throughout the country and the continent but meanwhile his labour costs were higher than the Clyde, the Mersey and the Thames [he quoted figures for the Clyde; it was not true of the other two rivers]. There was also the threat of foreign competition. Palmer referred to *a most influential meeting* with representatives of nearly all the large firms in the North of England. The employers had resolved *to resist the demand* and that

> the respective trades engaged in the manufacturing industry of this district should separately combine for their own protection, and that a general committee, consisting of representatives from each trade, be appointed to consider the best means of resisting the nine hours movement.

Then came the hint of a threat. While he, Palmer, repudiated a lockout as a means of settling the dispute, the Teesside employers intended to offer to open their yards on the basis of a 59-hour week and, if this was not accepted, a general lockout on the Tees would follow.

In this very large meeting and faced with the knowledge of united opposition from a combination of employers, it was not surprising that there was a pause before any worker spoke. A fitter, Bannerman, stated briefly that, since they had the views of the management, they might now be patient. No one else seemed to wish to speak and Pochin gave his advice: *The only legitimate means of raising wages was this; that there should be two masters competing for one man's work; then the man could fairly demand a wage increase*. Subsequently, when a shipyard worker explained how much higher his earnings had been on the Thames than on the Tyne, Palmer taunted him as to why he had left there. Palmer was anxious that all remained at work so, while urging then not to be *a cat's paw* for other districts, he made it clear that if any section came out, all would suffer: *yet if one class of workmen chose to combine to the injury of their masters and their fellow working men, the evil effects of that combination must fall on all alike*, a statement hardly consistent with his earlier rejection of a lockout. It was agreed that each section of the works appoint delegates to meet the employers. Palmer had quelled the movement in his own works.

Further talks continued at Jarrow and a strike was only just avoided. The ship's joiners, at Jarrow and at Willington Quay [Palmers other yard], decided not to strike, pending the discussions. At Willington Quay the manager, W M Cleland, met the joiners. Bannerman explained the proposals of F C Marshall, the manager of the engine department, to the men. These were: [a] to work 59 hours per week, the same as the Newcastle men, a reduction of $3/4$ hour, [b] to abolish the $1/4$ day worked on Friday night. The men made a counter proposal and *pledged*:

> to refrain from enforcing the nine hours movement until it shall become a general demand throughout the country, on condition that the Company concede us the Saturday half holiday entire. The pay to take place on the Friday evening, and to allow seven o clock mornings, in the winter months, to remain as at present.

This resolution was given to Marshall, on Tuesday morning, but, late on Wednesday, Palmer refused to meet the engineers separately from the rest of the workers. A large meeting at South Shields, on Saturday 3 March, heard a report from a Newcastle delegation on developments there. The *Newcastle Chronicle* reported *a generally expressed aversion of strikes which were denounced as being alike detrimental to the men as well as the employers*. By then, the joiners were on strike in a number of yards. At Wallsend, they decided to levy 5s on single men and 3s on married men who were working to provide support for those striking. The connection of these craftsmen with the building trades probably increased their determination to stay out.

Strikes on Tees & at Hartlepool.

On 7 February 1866, after giving a fortnight's notice, workers in the iron shipbuilding yards on the Tees and at Hartlepool struck work.[39] In response to the demand for a 56-hour week, the employers [except Pile, Spence] offered a half holiday on Saturday [work to stop at 1pm] thus reducing the normal hours to 59. A lockout began on 14th February; while persistently urging the need for free access to the men as individuals, the employers wanted the workers to oblige any minority that was holding out to return to work. A strong union capable of exerting leadership and discipline might have gone far towards meeting the employers' desire but this was seen as an unpalatable solution. Such a solution required bargaining with a more equal force than unorganised men, however militant they might be individually. Later, the Boilermakers' Society played such a role, but as yet it was only gaining the necessary strength of organisation and clarity of policy. Workers at Middlesbrough held a number of meetings on 8 February and established links with the men at Stockton. At the shipyard of Fox & Candlish, a deputation met the management without any success. By 11 February, committees existed in both towns to organise the strike. A stoppage was avoided at Pile & Spence's yard, when Pile privately assured a deputation that the *nine-hours* system, which they had worked for five months, would continue until an arrangement was made for the whole river. This yard employed between 2,000 and 3,000 men. A small yard, Riddell & Brays, of Middlesbrough, conceded the men's demand.

The Teesside men continued to meet regularly and there were occasional meetings with individual employers, for example the joiners with Pearse, Lockwood & Co. The employers, organised on an area basis at least temporarily, were determined to maintain their resistance. On 24 February, they took steps to strengthen their organisation; using the Iron Manufacturers' Association as a model they sought

> to draw up codes of rules, based upon the principle of subsidising manufacturers whose men strike for any concession which shall not receive the sanction of the association. ... that this committee pledges themselves to afford material support to those employers whose men remain on strike.

The ability of this smaller group of larger employers on Tees and at Hartlepool to stand firmly together contrasted with the less successful efforts of the more numerous and smaller shipbuilders on the Wear. The Teesside employers met about 100 workers in the drafting loft of Pearse & Lockwood on Monday 26 February. Like Palmer, the employers headed by George Lockwood were confident of their new persuasive powers and confronted the men with the resolutions and pointed out that they represented the full support of the Northern employers. He asked if the men were prepared to sacrifice their wives and children in a futile struggle; *a desultory conversation* followed. The next day, the men meeting at Middlesbrough decided to stay out. Differences were appearing; some men were willing to return at $9^{1}/_{2}$ hours a day and the financial difficulties of non-society men were increasing. Then the employers used the Courts to try to break the strike. Pearce & Lockwood issued 26 summonses and 25 cases were heard on 3 March. W.P.Roberts[40], the Chartist lawyer, represented the men on a charge of breach of contract. The first cases heard were against the frame turners, Charles Steel and Thomas Potter, hired on 3 July 1865. Counsel for the employers stated that the hours reduction was given to the carpenters [shipwrights] because *they were few in number and found their own tools*. It was contended that the terms of the verbal contracts were: *To serve in the capacity of frame turners for an indefinite period determinable nevertheless on the completion of the frame turning of a certain vessel.* The firm held back 10% of the men's earnings until

---

[39] A meeting of various trades, at Low Walker, in mid-February, decided to take no action and await the outcome of the Teesside struggle. About 360 ships joiners were on strike; some found work in the building trade and at other ports. On 10 March, when only 120 were out of work, they decided *we stand out for the nine hours... but... are open to confer with the masters directly at any time.*

[40] William Prowting Roberts [1806-71], son of a clergyman and trained as a solicitor, an enthusiastic Chartist and from 1843 associated with most trade union actions. Known as the *Miners' Attorney General*. See R Challinor *A Radical Lawyer in Victorian England: W P Roberts and the struggle for workers' rights.*

they finished. The men had given 7 days notice before leaving work but the court rejected Roberts' argument that the lock-out notices terminated the contract. Steel and Potter were sentenced to one month in gaol. Roberts told the others that all the cases would go the same way and they decided to return to work but expressed doubts that any labourers would be available. On the basis of this undertaking, the sentences were suspended.[41]

Reports in the *Newcastle Chronicle* suggested that the men would return on the next Monday. Pile & Spence were sufficiently confident that the strike was defeated to serve notice that, from March 15th, the hours at their yard would be 59 hours per week, under a threat of closure. The court cases however stimulated the national leadership of the Boilermakers to take action. On Teesside, a telegram from Manchester on Sunday was read as meaning that all those on strike would receive 10s a week strike pay. When William Swan from the Boilermakers Executive arrived he made clear that there was no intention of paying 10s to all on strike [presumably it was the home donation for Society members]. As predicted, when the craftsmen, who were sentenced, arrived for work on Monday morning, there were no labourers, whose militancy was high despite a low income. Summonses issued by Backhouse & Dixon were adjourned while negotiations continued. Swan addressed a mass meeting on Tuesday in Stockton, and said he was *there as a stranger, and desired to obtain truthful information.* He made it quite clear that the local workers who initiated the movement acted against the advice of his executive. When one of those who had been in Court, Sparrow, explained why he had agreed to return to work, an Irish voice interrupted him with the message *you'll get no labourers*. Swan tried to secure a settlement. After a meeting at Pearce & Lockwood, he suggested a conference, to bring *the unhappy dispute ... to an amicable termination.* Swan's limited powers became clear when in accepting Lockwood's proposal to meet on Thursday, he explained the representatives would be chosen at public meetings in Middlesbrough, Stockton and Hartlepool. Although Swan added that these representatives would have full powers to act on behalf of the men and their decisions would bind the whole district, this was not the reality of the situation. The Boilermakers' Society only represented a minority of the men; about 300 of Pile's 2,000 workers were trade unionists. The union was many years away from establishing a good standing with the employers on Teesside and even when the Society did represent the men, difficulties continued in securing acceptance by the rank and file of agreements made by their leaders.

While these events proceeded at Stockton, the men at Middlesbrough received a boost by the unanimous decision of the local *ASE* branch to provide *substantial support weekly* while the strike lasted. These strikers were determined to gain the *nine hours* and elected delegates only on the basis of 9-hours or nothing. They wished this conveyed as their unanimous verdict to the employers. There was anxiety as to whether or not the attitude of the Middlesbrough men would prevent the meeting taking place, but George Lockwood gave a written assurance that the employers would meet Swan, with delegates from Hartlepool and Stockton. After a vigorous debate at Stockton, hands were counted three times and each result was disputed. A secret ballot showed how close the division was: 168 for a compromise and 154 for 9-hour day. The workers' delegates were clearly disappointed that the employers made no fresh offer when the conference met. Like Palmer, they spoke of competition at home and abroad and Gray claimed that it was an advantage to the employers to have the men out at the moment. Swan made the offer that the *contractors* [the skilled craftsmen] would not ask for higher prices until August if the nine hours was agreed. Lockwood made clear that the offer of 59 hours could not be improved without consulting the Tyne employers. After consulting the delegates, Swan offered 56 hours or the continuation of the strike and so the dispute continued. It is difficult to know if there was any intention of real negotiations, since the gates were already open on the 59-hour basis, unless the employers thought that Swan would modify the attitude of the men. The employers' quick response to Swan's approach suggests that despite Gray's comment, they desired a settlement. On the very evening of the conference, which began at 5 pm, further summonses were issued

---

[41] It is not clear if any men went to gaol [other cases see below]. Mortimer [1973] wrote, the men *were sentenced* [p.66] and, on p.73 *were sent to prison* [also p.219]. Cummings failed to state that the sentences were suspended.

against men from Pearce & Lockwood.

Voices for the 56 hour week became stronger. It was supported by workers at Middleton shipyard, Hartlepool, who dissociated themselves from their then fellow employees of Richardsons, at Stockton.[42] When at Pile's the 9-hour day ended from 15 March, the men offered to continue working on a 56-hour basis; this yard was facing a financial crisis and was in no position to offer any concessions. When Pile's men came out, there were an estimated 3,000 strikers in Hartlepool.[43] A final pressure that failed to deter the men was the public announcement by the grocers of the town that they would close their books on the men. They refused their wives credit. Strike leader G Hill travelled to the main industrial centres of Lancashire to raise financial support and was unwise enough at one meeting to raise the hope of 15s a week strike pay. A collection was made at a meeting of more than 500 at the Darlington Railway Works. Finally, an appeal was issued to *the workingmen of the United Kingdom*. Regular meetings of the men continued. John Allen[44], secretary of the Boilermakers, was present to support Swan at a meeting in Stockton and there were hopes of increased financial assistance from the travelling delegates. Pressure through the Courts continued. Under the threat of prison, two apprentices acted as labourers to frame turners at Backhouse & Dixon. Stockton magistrates refused an adjournment so that the work's rules might be produced and then passed sentences of one month with hard labour. On the motion of counsel, however, for a *case stated* [at a higher court], the men were allowed bail on two sureties one of £25 and one of £50. When two men said they would return to work, their cases were adjourned. A few days later, witnesses gave evidence in a case against a plater that workers had been discharged on 7 days notice, before vessels were completed and with contracts unfinished. It was argued, that if the employer could act in this way, why could not the worker who had given 7 days notice before leaving work? This did not affect the magistrates, who passed a one month sentence on the plater, who was bailed to await another *case stated*. Five caulkers, at Middlesbrough, were sentenced to 14 days for not returning to work.

An unexpected conference followed the front page advertisement in the *Newcastle Chronicle* on 22 March:

> Nine Hours Movement Jarrow.
> Fellow Workmen, - As there is to be a meeting of the Masters of the Tyne and Tees on Saturday First, the 24th, in Newcastle, Mr Palmer, Chairman of the Masters' Committee, has invited us to send Delegates to settle or arbitrate the question. We hereby request the workmen to send Delegates from all the yards on both Rivers, to meet on Saturday at 10 am at the Willington Hotel...Newcastle. By order of the Committee.

Forty delegates from all but two of the yards on the Tyne and Tees met in Newcastle. The *Newcastle Courant* reported later that *the masters seemed to be taken by surprise by this unlooked for* proposal of a meeting with the men. They did however agree to meet the men but they would not give Swan any voice in such a meeting. Palmer presided over the employers, including Leslie, Lockwood, Fox, Richardson, Dixon, Swan, Schlesinger, Davis, Hepple and two of Palmer's managers. The discussion was vigorous but ineffective; the men reiterated their arguments and reaffirmed their intention to resist but made no offers. Palmer declared with pride that his men of Jarrow remained faithful to their word and did not strike. He later blamed Marshall for the confusion which brought the men to the meeting. All was not yet over at Jarrow. Bannerman reported on the situation to a meeting of Palmers' men on the evening of 30 March. Andrew Gourley moved a resolution that, on 2 April, notice be given that if 9-hour day was not conceded

---

[42] This dispute took place during the short lived company of Richardsons, Denton Duck & Co Ltd see chap 8.

[43] Reports in the *Newcastle Chronicle* suggested that the bait of 10s a head had brought out Pile's men, but this alleged offer was publicly repudiated. It was more likely that the men who were working reduced hours would not give up their gains without a struggle, especially when so many other workers were out on strikes for just this.

[44] John Allen [1804- 88] was born in Cork, Ireland; he migrated to Bristol and then after he learned boilermaking in the U S A, he was employed for a time by the Steam Navigation Co. of Bristol. Joined Society in 1836 -General secretary 1857-71. Favourite authors - Jeremy Bentham and the two Mills. Retired on £1/week pension.

by 2 May, all would turn out. This was rejected after much discussion and amended to seven days notice only. *Tremendous cheering* greeted this amendment. Realising that such a decision would almost certainly close every yard on the Tyne, some of the men's leaders attempted to prevent precipitous action. A *cooling off* device was secured by Young's motion that sectional meetings should be held in the workshops to consider the question and report to a general meeting in the following week. Bannerman, Aitken, Gourley and others supported this.

The *Newcastle Chronicle* intervened with an editorial on 5 April 1866. The *Chronicle* was widely read and looked to as a progressive and Radical paper, as indeed it was under the ownership of Joseph Cowen Jr. [1831-1900] Its attitude may well have influenced significantly the final decision on the Tyne, as it certainly did five years later when the *nine-hour* question re-emerged. Under the title *The Labour Movement*, the editor wrote:

> Several weeks have now been consumed in fruitless efforts to procure a settlement to the nine hours question. Meetings, negotiations, conferences have all ended in failure. The prospect is decidedly not encouraging ... For this hostile movement, the masters are already prepared. Their organisation is at this moment sufficiently complete. In event of a strike ... they have arranged to assist and subsidise each other. Furnished with ample funds, backed by a powerful combination of capitalists, the menaced employers of Tyneside occupy a commanding position. It was an economical question ... The masters will not give way; the state of the trade will not justify them in giving way ... Is it not now, therefore, the interest and the duty of the men to abandon the scheme? It is impossible to disguise the fact that further agitation on the question promises no success whatever ... A strike for the object the men now claim could in no case be beneficial.

When Palmer's men reassembled on 10 April, those for strike had lost the debate. Although the voting was incomplete, only about a quarter of the votes were for strike action. Bannerman declared that the sectional meetings were against strike action. They agreed to seek the 57 hours as recently agreed on the Clyde. The *Newcastle Courant* reported *tremendous cheering*, when a delegate proposed asking for the weekly payment of wages, which he said would be worth an increase of 2s a week. A proposal to accept 59 hours was rejected. This became the basis of the final settlement which took place some seven weeks after the meeting which Palmer claimed had *stopped the movement*. Two of the deputation which met Palmer, blacksmith John Burnett and fitter Andrew Gourley were later leaders of strikes which won the 9-hour day [see below].[45] The joiners[46] remained a source of difficulty for many employers. By the end of March they had been out for six weeks. Wigham Richardson sent joiner work to Scotland, Hepple recruited cabinet makers and Mitchells despatched unfinished ships to other ports. On Tyneside joiners returned at the time of the Jarrow settlement. The *Newcastle Chronicle* wrote of *the present prudent policy* of the Jarrow men and sent out a message: *The joiners who left the locality during the struggle will doubtless be glad to learn that their usual workshops are again in harmonious operation.* Joiners were still out at Middlesbrough and Hartlepool.

In the continuing dispute on Teesside, the labourers continued to be vocal at meetings and their spokesman argued that any concession by the *black squad* would be seen as a betrayal and the labourers would never again trust these craftsmen. Court cases continued, with 30 convictions at Stockton and 5 at Middlesbrough. At the end of March 1866, some Manchester trade unionists pledged support of 6d / man /week and a distribution of 12s to Society members and 10s to non-society men and labourers was made. Teesside strike leader Hill rejected Richardson's claim that the bulk of the men were back, at Stockton, on the basis of 59 hour week and weekly pay for time workers; he said that only 27 out of 300 men were working. Men were recruited in Scotland to replace strikers. Irvine's men were reported back at work on 7 April. A new keel was laid at Richardson's Middleton yard. On 10 April, the *Newcastle Chronicle* days reported: *Virtually the nine-hours movement agitation is now at an end in Stockton, at least [in] iron*

---

[45] In the midst of all this, another relationship between managers and men at Jarrow was shown when the workers' spokesman, Aitken, seconded the motion moved by the manager, F.C.Marshall at a Reform meeting on 6 April.

[46] The Kenwood Index of residential building: 37.8 in 1864, 50.9, in 1865, and 50.3 in 1866.

shipbuilding. The police, who stood ready for trouble at the shipyard gates, were not needed. Richardson had all the men he required and large numbers were going in at Pearse & Lockwood. At Middlesbrough, activities by the strikers continued, but, even there, *a few men now and again* returned to different yards. At West Hartlepool, the non-society men were returning and two delegates went from the town up to the Boilermakers' headquarters at Manchester to seek approval for the return of the Society men. The workers were back in Pile's yard on 13 April. Workers at Backhouse & Dixon still hoped to persuade the management to concede 57 hours and there was only a small return to work at Middlesbrough, *a mere handful* compared with what the employers required, about 70. When towards the end of April, it was reported that labourers in some yards were learning plating the craftsmen faced a grievous threat. After 12 weeks of strike a general return began at Middlesbrough on 2 May. The loss of earnings was probably of the order of £12,000, no small sacrifice for those involved. The final settlement was a 59-hour week and weekly pay. The weekly payment of wages was an important achievement; it greatly reduced dependence on credit to bridge fortnightly pay periods. There is no evidence of trade union organisation among these unskilled men, who unusually had acted side by side with the craftsmen in this particular struggle, albeit with tension at times. A downward phase of the trade cycle as these strikes took place undoubtedly weakened the men's position.[47]

Between the strikes of 1866 and 1871 there was a public speaking contest on *Strikes and how to prevent them, showing their disadvantages to nations and individuals*. On two evenings in January 1867, the Newcastle Town Hall was crowded, while more than 30 workers spoke on their remedies for strikes. Joseph Cowen jr. chaired the event under the Mayor's patronage and with prizes provided by a local firm. Admission charges were 1d or 6d, with reserved seats at 2s 6d. Speakers repeatedly proclaimed the need for Courts of Arbitration and others advocated the usefulness of workmen having a direct interest in the firm, *Workingmen as Co-capitalists*.[48] In *an excellent address*, John Burnett *forcibly* pointed out the evils of strikes and proposed a system of cooperation. This meeting illustrated the discussions that went on in many workshops concerning industrial disputes. Strikes in 1871 demonstrated the power of joint workers' action to gain a most important advance when economic conditions were favourable, without significant union support.

1871 - Engineers' strikes on the Wear and Tyne.[49]

The centre piece of a commemorative plate shows John Burnett under the words *the King of the 9 Hours Movement Commenced Whit Monday 1871*, which shows how highly this blacksmith was regarded, although it does less than justice to the campaign on the Wear in which Andrew Gourley played such a key part. Although both men were active *ASE* members this was not a union led movement. Overwhelmingly, those who participated were not members of a trade union. This struggle embraced engineering as a whole and on Tyneside this meant that Armstrong's, not a marine engine works, was the key player. All the marine engine works were involved, in one way or another, and the outcome therefore affected the shipyards as well.

---

[47] Depressions had very serious effects on union funds. Years of *long and painful stagnation* were the words of the Boilermakers' Society report in October 1868, and, at the end of the year, the balance of their funds was a mere £873. In 1867, the Boilermakers spent £10,546 [28s 5s per member] helping members travelling in search of work. The *ASE* funds were reduced from 83s / member in 1865, to 45s, in 1869. The funds of the Steam Engine Makers Society [about 2,830 members], were almost halved between December 1867 and December 1870 [from £9,286 to £4,794]. A shilling a week was the normal subscription for the Ironfounders but they found it necessary to raise a special levy of 5s per member, in 1868; nonetheless, the cash in hand per member fell from 50s 2d, in 1866, to a mere 1s 5d three years later. In such critical situations, as Robert Knight pointed out, there was a trade union spirit which preserved the organisation even if the funds ran out.

[48] Some attempts were made in this direction after the 1871 strike, e.g. at Hawthorns and Bell Goodman, but there is little evidence these efforts got seriously started.

[49] More detail is available in E Allen & al *The North-east Engineers' Strikes of 1871* [1971]; and Clarke [1966]

Fortnightly pay, with its associated evils of *subbing* and credit purchases by housewives, began a sequence of actions by engineering workers on Tyneside. Deputations of workers approached their own employers in August 1870 for weekly pay; although received *with courtesy and consideration*, only one firm granted the request. Delegates reported to a meeting on 10 September and a committee was set up to campaign for weekly pay, with representatives from six Newcastle firms.[50] Early in 1871 more firms were promising to begin such payments. When Hawthorns failed to begin in February as promised, a deputation met the management. No reply was given until 7 March, when the workers were told there would be no weekly payments until further notice. After a dinner time mass meeting, the management tried to prevent a stoppage by suggesting payments might begin in 4 to 6 weeks. The men had been there before and agreed to stop work at 3.30 p.m. except in the foundry where the men remained to finish metal work in progress. Twelve hundred men came out. After a meeting in the Cattle Market a deputation went to the management, who firmly promised weekly payments in ten days. Triumphantly the men returned to work on Thursday morning. This successful action moved Armstrongs to announce a few days later that they would begin weekly payments from 15 April.

Emblem of the ASE

Nine-hours movement on Wearside in 1871.

By then matters were afoot at Sunderland, where engineering was mainly related to shipbuilding requirements. Andrew Gourley,[51] working at Dickinsons, became president of a Wear committee organising a movement for a shorter day. Boilermaker Cain, at a meeting on 22 March 1871, spoke of his contacts with Tyne delegates, who represented 900 union and 8,000 non-society men. This meeting decided to reject any wage increase as an alternative to the reduction of hours. There was a clear recognition that wages went up and down but reduced hours were more difficult to increase. The primary aim was shorter working time. Circulars were sent out and it was estimated that 800 attended the next meeting in the Theatre Royal. The chairman *trusted that in the conduct of this agitation they would behave themselves as Englishmen and honourable citizens* [he] *denied that this was a Society movement ... the masters were greater trade unionists than the men.* The employers' rejection was posted on the gates on 31 March but was handled differently at various works. At Dickinsons a printed notice was circulated; at NEM the manager with the cashier handed the notice to the deputation and at Clarks there was a brief discussion. Oswald discussed the matter with a boilermaker and an engineer. Pile was *rather offended*, his manager explained, since his men already worked only $55\frac{1}{2}$ hours and the delegates agreed that was a special case; there were, however, a thousand workers in other firms. Two companies agreed to reduce the hours when Newcastle firms did. Wearside engineering works[52] were deserted by adult workers on Monday 3 April when 2,000 attended an open-air meeting. By the end of the week Newcastle and other employers pledged support for the Wearside

---

[50] Three of these Hawthorns, Thompson Boyd and Black-Hawthorn were established marine engine builders; Stephensons were not included they stayed aloof from employers combinations and Palmers was a special case.

[51] Burnett wrote: *The chances are that had Gourley been allowed to remain at Jarrow, he might very possibly have got a house through the medium of the Factory Building Society; the possession of the house would have kept him quiet at Jarrow (the possession of a house having that effect upon a man, a fact which Mr Palmer has not failed to note) he would never have originated the Sunderland strike, and the Nine Hour Movement would still have been left in the limbo of unfulfilled aspirations.* [*The Nine Hours Movement*] Frankly a doubtful opinion.

[52] Reported that a single machine operator was working at NEM, two labourers & three chargehands at Clarks, half a dozen at Oswalds and 18 at Piles. None were fitters or turners.

firms, and said that they would prevent the men securing jobs. As earlier on Teesside, the Courts were brought into play, George Clark and Oswald issued summons under the Master & Servant Act and their Counsel frankly declared that he *did not bring the men there to take money from their pockets but to get them to return to work.* Unlike the magistrates at Stockton, fines and costs were usually imposed; when 70 men appeared in court in April, the cases were adjourned pending a settlement. When Oswald's men came for their pay on 9 April he spoke to them but refused to pay their *lying-in money.* Former MP, W S Lindsay, issued a statement to the *intelligent engineers of Sunderland* and the iron workers' leader John Kane urged arbitration. *ASE* leaders in London were furious at the strike action, two officials were despatched to the District Committee in Newcastle and they condemned *the hasty action of a few members of the Sunderland branch which participated the strike.* These officials tried to secure a settlement with the Sunderland employers and arranged for a return to work with the 9-hours from 1 June. Local leaders of this overwhelming non-union action resented this intervention and the strikers rejected June 1st and returned with the *9-hour* day on 5 May 1871. [There were 407 *ASE* members on the Wear] Good relations existed between the employers and the men during this dispute; a Sunderland man spoke of the *good feeling* between both sides in Newcastle on 22 April. *Success to the Sunderland Employers Who Granted the Nine Hours Movement* were the words on the banner the Wearsiders later carried in support of the Tyneside workers.[53]

Activity on Tyneside.

The workingmen *in the engine building trades of Newcastle and Gateshead* discussed the reduction of hours from ten to nine per day on 22 April. The local press reported cheers when the chairman Johnson said they had *one object in view throughout, to try to carry their point without injury to their employers, and above all to do it without having what they got at Sunderland - a strike.* They agreed arbitration would be far better than a strike. A week later it was agreed to form The Nine Hours League[54], and on 2 May an elected committee considered six drafts of a letter to the employers. A letter was sent on 5 May; it began -
> Coming events so often cast their shadow before ... the events ... in Sunderland, within the last few weeks, must have prepared you for the request, which we, as the appointed representatives of your workers now respectfully prefer, viz: - That you kindly consent to the reduction of the hours of labour from ten to nine per day - or more properly speaking from 59 hours to 54 ...

A reply was asked for by the 12th and it was hoped it would be *in a similar spirit of goodwill.* Armstrong was determined to defeat this campaign for reduced hours. The Manufacturing Engineers met together and sent a unanimous rejection as from the Associated Employers through a firm of solicitors. On this failure to reply directly Burnett later commented: the third party was *in the most objectionable form of a firm of solicitors - to the Radical workingmen of Newcastle the most obnoxious firm ...that could be chosen the solicitors of the Conservative Association.* To avoid a strike the men's leaders suggested a meeting of six representatives from both sides. Events took a dramatic turn at the Gateshead works of Clarke, Watson Guerney on Tuesday 16 May. At breakfast time a deputation meet with the management. Despite Clarke's plea for patience, a dinner time meeting decided to stop work and about 300 men left the works.[55] This was

---

[53] Most general histories give little or no attention to this pioneering action on the Wear and can also be misleading [perhaps due to brevity] by seeming to merge the action with the Tyne strike: *In 1871 a rank and file movement for a nine-hour day on Tyneside began with a strike in Sunderland, and in due course the local employers' association let the unions know they would welcome a conference... the convenience of a central settlement carried the day ... and the nine-hour day agreed.* p. 11- Clegg, Fox & Thompson

[54] The Webbs wrote this as *in fact though not in name, a temporary Trade Union.* Burnett claimed that it became *to all intents and purposes a trade society.* Both views appear nearer to reflecting their attitude to the importance of trade unionism rather than a recognition of the loose character of the organisation and its limited role.

[55] This company used the Master & Servants Act to compel some workers to continue. Their foreman in evidence stated that he agreed a price of 45s per windlass on 9 February [three months before the strike began] and the men must continue on that contract till he decided they should stop, and so they worked throughout the strike.

used to justify refusing any meeting. Again the solicitors sent a message and stated that their earlier statement was final. On Saturday 20 May, 60 to 70 works delegates decided that the time for *energetic action has arrived* recommending that after working their legal notice men should stop at nine works. Almost 7,500 men[56] given notices to their foremen on Monday morning. Armstrong decided to close his works. The prospect of this massive loss of wages caused great anxiety amongst shopkeepers and the Chamber of Commerce urged the Mayor to act as mediator. On Thursday morning seven workers met the Mayor. When about 30 representatives of the employers came in the afternoon, they made clear they would not talk to the men and would only receive a written communication. In the principal workshops, the strike began on 27 May and regular working did not start again for five months. It is certain that the employers never contemplated such a sustained dispute, indeed they appeared confident of an early victory as they were certainly losing business. From the very first day of the strike men were moving elsewhere to jobs, with employers seeking them from all over the country. There were only 3,092 men on the books when the first strike benefit [3s per man & 6d per child] was distributed in the third week of the strike. This suggests that some 4,000 men had found work elsewhere. By 19 September less than 2,000 were paid benefit [1s each for 2534 children and 8s per man, later increased to 11s and then 12s]. Armstrong acknowledged in a letter that most of *the best old hands ... have gone away and found work elsewhere*. Work continued at three important firms. At Jarrow the men honoured their settlement of 1866; this was not a national claim for a *9-hour* day. At the Gateshead railway workshops the men donated £50 per week to support the action. More than 600 men at Stephensons balloted in support of the 9 hours but there was no strike. This firm stayed aloof from employers' combination and the management met a deputation from the various departments. G R Stephenson was away but sent a long letter setting out his position. General Manager Douglas offered a 57-hour week, but the men decided to wait for the 9 hours.

John Burnett

Not until 22 July did the *ASE* union leadership take any action.[57] Little wonder that such a staunch supporter of official union policy as Cummings wrote *The gaining of a nine-hour day may be said in every sense of the word* [to be] *a victory of the rank and file against the apathy of many of their leaders*. Although Jarrow was working normally, Charles Palmer entered the scene in mid-July as an intermediary and met a deputation of eight workers on 19 July. He believed the employers had agreed to attend a meeting on the following evening but they failed to arrive. This was only the first of a series of confusions. When both sides were finally brought together with the Mayor, the employers wanted to insist on how the men should decide on any proposal. This meeting ended without the issue of the dispute ever being discussed[58]. Still hoping for discussions, the men's leaders proposed to a meeting on Saturday 22 July that the mode of voting should be decided by the Mayor after the employers' offer was made. Swiftly the employers replied that it was *useless to attempt further negotiations*. By the end of July only 170 trade unionists had not found jobs elsewhere. At the end of the first week in August the employers opened their gates, with notices of *working hours inside 57 hours*. No workers appeared at nine factories and about a score at three others. During the following week imported workers arrived first from Norway and later from Germany

---

[56] Armstrongs 2,700; Hawthorn 1,200; Abbott 1,000; Thompson & Boyd 700; Hawkes & Crawshay 500; Black & Hawthorn 500; Clarke, Watson & Guerney 500; T Clark 300; Joicey 100; Wylie 90; Pattison & Atkinson 40.

[57] In a circular they stated: *This silence is not to be construed as indifference*. They desired *to stimulate all branches to greater activity in raising timely and substantial support for our friends in the North*.

[58] The *Pall Mall Gazette* wrote: the only conference the employers proposed to the men was accompanied by a condition the concession of which would have been equivalent to an abandonment of all trade union organisation.

and other places; the intention was to bring in 2,000 men. Armstrong's school at Elswick was closed to house such workers.[59] At Dundee about 200 with a bounty of 5s were recruited but only 100 turned up to travel; some of these later said they were told the strike was settled. Even *The Times* was *inclined to consider the conduct of the employers throughout this dispute as imprudent and impolitic*. *Masters who reply cavalierly by lawyers' letters to the demands of the men, refuse personal discussion*, wrote the *Spectator*, *act as nearly as they can like despotic governments against revolutionary bodies can hardly expect their moral claim on the sympathy of the public to be conceded*. Such comments stung Armstrong into a lengthy reply in the *Times*. Many public figures tried to bring the employers into negotiations, including two MPs, the iron master Bernhard Samuelson[60] and A J Mundella.[61] After meeting Mundella, the strike leaders were willing to accept a wage cut to bridge the gap between the 54 hours and the offer of 57 [only 300 voted against this proposal]. This too was rejected; instead Armstrong offered a 5% increase for all skilled trades. It is difficult to see any rationale behind the employers' stance unless they feared all overtime would be stopped, in their interpretation of the slogan *Nine Hours Pure and Simple*. Joseph Cowen and the Town Clerk, R P Philipson, may have sensed this overtime issue and proposed that if 54 hours were conceded the men would agree to work overtime when and to the extent required by the employers, with the *9-hour* day to begin from 1 January 1872. When Philipson secured Armstrong's agreement and Cowen that of the workers' delegates, a team of six men were to work out the precise details. Overtime would only be paid after all 54 hours were worked. An attempt by the employers to secure individual applications to return was successfully resisted. It was agreed that those who had worked during the strike could continue and those still out would be taken back as work was available. There were difficulties in persuading the men to accept the overtime regulations; nonetheless the final details were settled on 9 October for the firms involved in the strike. At the end there were only 1858 non-society men on the League's books, further evidence of jobs found.[62]

Rapidly the new hours were applied. Stephensons started on 9-hours on 1 November, two months ahead of the settlement date; the N E Railway Co. and Palmers both accepted the new arrangements. Before the end of October the engineering works of Teesside adopted 54 hours and by the spring of 1872 it might reasonably be claimed that it applied in all the principal engineering centres. *The Shipping World* later wrote: *It is to the Tyneside engineers that the skilled workers of the United Kingdom are indebted for establishing the day's work at nine hours*. The leaders of the Tyneside strike displayed considerable organisational talents; its first secretary James Parkinson was struck down by smallpox early in the dispute and we only know his successor as Mr Short; others included Matthew Pletts and R Gillander. At a celebration rally Gillander expressed views held by many of these men: *There was a duty to be discharged by the workingmen ... to exert themselves more actively during the hours of labour, that there might be little or no loss to the employers from the concession ... to be diligent and show the masters that we were right*. He urged them to use the spare time to improve their minds and not waste it *at public houses, upon dog fighting or horse racing*. For Burnett there was little hope of avoiding strikes unless *men have a perfect right to treat with their employers on terms of perfect equality* and there was an *absolute need* to establish courts of arbitration. Such thoughts were far from Armstrong's mind; he was endeavouring to establish a powerful employers' organisation, which was later usually seen as *predominantly a union-fighting and strike break organisation*.

---

[59] Browne in 1904: *It is absurd to suppose that we could import a thousand high class engineers ... during a strike*.

[60] Sir Bernhard Samuelson FRS [1820-1905 - baronet 1884] owned various engineering works but was principally an iron master, established Britannia Iron Works at Middlesbrough; Liberal MP for Banbury 1859 & 1865-85 and North Oxfordshire 1885-95. A promoter of technical education, he chaired Royal Comm. on Technical Instruction.

[61] A J Mundella [1825-1897] was a partner in hosiery firm at Nottingham, where he formed a conciliation board. He served as MP for Sheffield 1868-85 and 1885-97 for Brightside; a key figure in passing 1874 Factory Act and the 1870 Education Act, introduced Compulsory Education Act 1881 and set up the Labour Department in 1886.

[62] These included at Armstrongs 583; Hawthorn 345; Abbott 287; Thompson & Boyd 178; Hawkes & Crawshay 116; Black & Hawthorn 101; Clarke, Watson & Guerney 79; T Clark 82; Joicey 35; Wylie 27.

Wages.

Nominal wages were always only a part of the story. For the worker and his family it was what that money might buy that was the most important thing and in addition whether or not a full week's work was available. Craftsmen sought to maintain traditional parities; if shipwrights were used to a 1s a week more than joiners then they expected to retain that differential. Labourers tended to get about two-thirds of the craftsman's rate of pay. More than a little imagination is required to grasp the significance of wages and earnings in past times, because much was very different from recent times. Firstly, even within the same trade there was frequently a range of wage rates even if one rate dominated; likewise it was accepted by both the worker and his employer that wages would rise and fall with the movement of trade. Secondly, before the 1850s there is very little reliable information on how much unemployment there was or how much short-time working.

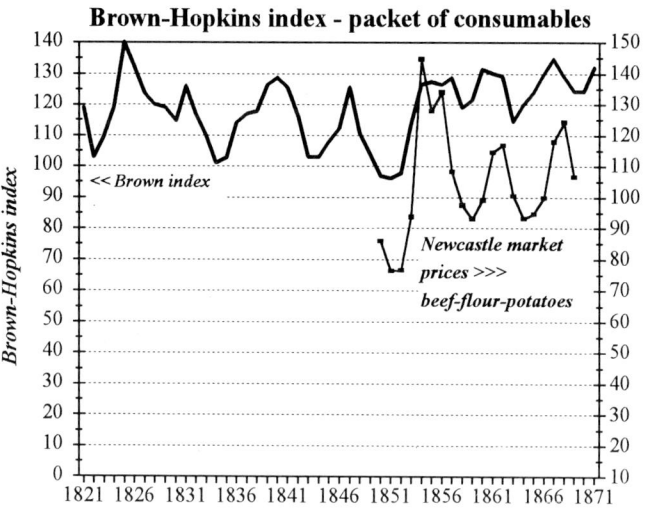

Diag 12.02

Patterns of household expenditure were very different and changed significantly in the latter part of the century, before the dramatic changes which took place in the second half of the twentieth century. Just as wages had a spread so did prices, for example the wholesale price of beef in the Newcastle wholesale market was quoted in January 1850 as varying from 4s6d to 5s9d per stone [28% difference]. The Brown-Hopkins index and some wholesale prices in Newcastle, as can be seen in diag 12.02 [above] show there were substantial fluctuations. No attempt will therefore be made here for this period to present a *real wage*, the data being too unreliable for this to be very meaningful. An awareness of fluctuations is however important and some comparison on the prices of budget items may be more useful than an overall index. A further factor in regard to the north east was that a significant amount of home baking [or sometimes collective baking] took place. This may well have reduced at least for one product the adulteration that plagued large cities such as London. As the budget below shows, less than 9% of income was spent on rent, and coal and water took only 2%; in contrast flour took more than 36% and food overall made up more than 77% of the budget. For poor families at least 4s out of every five was probably spent on food. It may also be noted that tea was very much more expensive than coffee, 4 ozs of tea cost 12d but a pound of coffee only 16d!

Often the budgets printed in contemporary journals were examples by the writer rather than what the worker's family may actually have spent. One of the shipwrights' leaders, during a strike, G.Gamsby, presented the following budget, for himself, his wife and four children, to justify the current level of wages. This offers a rough base line for any comparisons the reader might wish to make. This was the budget of a well paid craftsman describing expenditure relating to a full week's pay of 30*s* [6 days at 5*s*/day]. Gamsby was a teetotaller; a majority of workers would have spent money on beer and also on tobacco, the latter might have been included within sundries. Food accounted for just over 77% of this budget and flour for 46.5% of the food

Shipwright's Family Budget - 1854

House rent............................	2s 6d
Coals and Water......................	7d
3½ stone of Flour at 3/- a stone.	10s 6d
8lbs meat at 7d per lb................	4s 8d
2½ stone Potatoes @ 9d a stone	1s 10½d
3½ lbs sugar........................	1s 2d
¼ lb tea............................	1s 0d
1 lb coffee..........................	1s 4d
1½ lbs Soap........................	1s 0d
1½ lb candles.....................	1s 0d
Milk and Butter......................	2s 0d
Sundry..............................	1s 0d
Tools...............................	6d
TOTAL	29s 1½d

expenditure. Many north east housewives baked their own bread. Wage rate changes for various trades are shown below in diag 12.05 for 1850-79. Worker's earnings in a wood yard [Thompsons 1847-9], an iron yard [Leslie's at Hebburn 1855-6] and at Doxford's provide specific examples. Such individual information is certainly more helpful for understanding from a human standpoint than the nominal daily wage rate.

Hours worked.
Usually wage data is on the basis of full regular weekly hours; some records however provide evidence of the time actually worked. With winter variations, in shipbuilding there was nominally a 60-hour week; however, from about 1850 a full six day week was probably the exception rather than the rule for the workforce as a whole. Overwhelmingly the blacksmiths, at Thompson, usually worked a full six days; indeed almost a fifth of them were paid for $6\frac{1}{2}$ days or more[63] and the apprentices usually worked a full week. Although many shipwrights were paid for a full week the average was often nearer to five days per week [see diag 12.04]. Among the labourers work was far more irregular with perhaps a third on five days or more. At Leslie's ironyard wages were paid fortnightly and men did not always start on a Monday, so for example a labourer starting on a Wednesday and leaving on the following Tuesday, if he worked for all 60 hours would appear as only 50% over the pay period so making estimates of time worked more complicated. Labourers, who were at the yard for at least 20 weeks, averaged rather less than 50 hours/week. Shipwrights normally worked a full week, allowing for occasional lateness, at Hebburn. A calculation of average hours per week for men, who were at the yard for at least 300 hours or five weeks in 1855-6, shows as usual the rivet boys worked longer hours than the men, an average of 52, compared with the riveters 48 hours [range 58-43] and holderups averaged $46\frac{1}{2}$ [range 50.3-41.7]. In January 1863, at Doxford's 14 shipwrights worked a full six days, 10 lost a quarter day, 5 a half day and three quarters of a day was lost by two men; four other men worked $4\frac{3}{4}$ days, 3 days, $1\frac{3}{4}$ days and 1 day respectively. Excluding the last three the average was 5.7 days in a week, the same as the 5 borers employed.

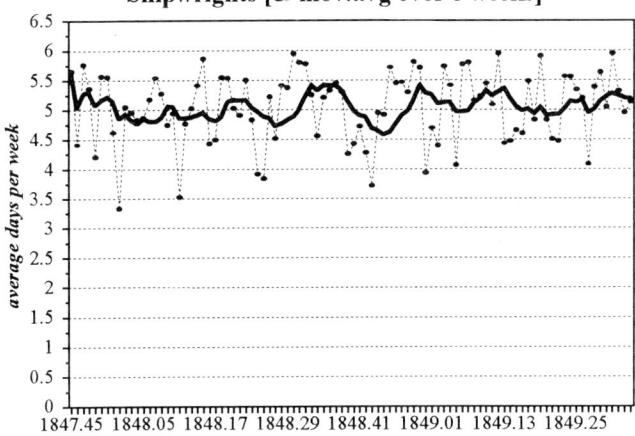

Diag 12.04

Earnings at Thompsons [1847-49].
A paybook from Thompson's yard on the Wear provides exact information on the actual pay men got from late 1847 to mid-1849. The shipwright's rate was 27s for a full week in 1847 and it was 24s in 1849. In pay week 9 February 1849 at Thompsons, 38 shipwrights working a full six days got 24s and the foreman 27s. The remaining ten worked 5 days or less; there is no means of knowing if these men had been employed elsewhere for the time missed; they averaged about 20s. One apprentice had the very abnormal payment of 24s! Only one of the labourers was paid for a full six days, for which he was paid 18s. Three shipwrights, who were regularly employed, illustrate what was probably typical earnings: Topless averaged almost 23s a week, Binney earned 20.71s, almost 10% lower and Nipper averaged less than 20s. The daily rate was usually 4s early in 1847 and 4.5s by the end of the year and then returned to 4s, in the manner characteristic of shipbuilding. Sawyers, who worked in pairs on piecework, could have very variable rates; three teams were employed by Thompsons during almost the entire period 1847-9; they also used at least 11 other teams one of them for 40 weeks. Welsh's team averaged 25.53s despite one very bad week and the Forest pair 23.35s. Two other teams exceeded 25s whereas Bell's team over 14 weeks were down to

---

[63] Days paid may not be a direct measure of days worked. 2 days overtime were entered as *3* for wages purposes.

20.41s. These averages are half the amount paid to the team, but the *top man* would have got more than the man in the pit. Clearly the sawyers through their piecework were earning more, if not a lot more, than the shipwrights. The two sawyers named at Doxfords in January 1863 were almost certainly the senior of the paired sawyers; their earnings were 48s 9d and 74s respectively.[64] Labourers, at Thompsons, were on day rates between 2.5s and 3.5s but usually 18s a week, the borers normally 15s a week. Sixteen years later labourers' wage rates were similar at Doxfords, although Hair ,probably a chargeman, was paid 21s.

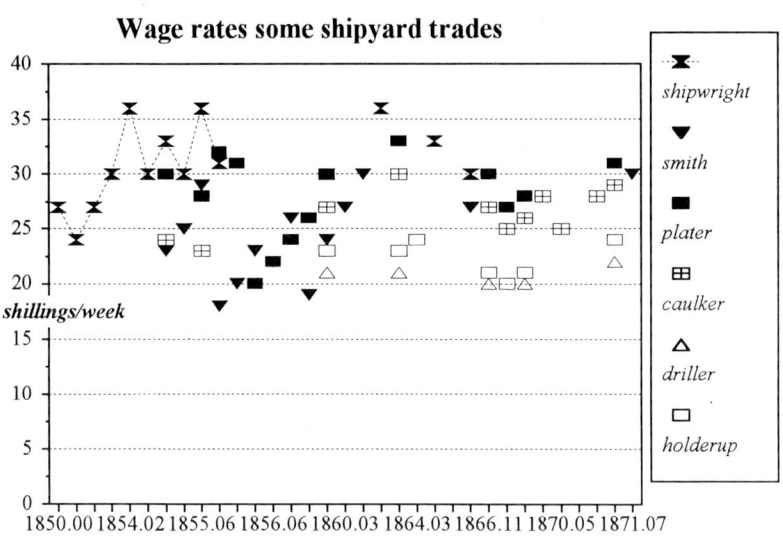

Diag 12.05

The borers were better paid, two at 18s, two others at 21s and one at 20s. The costs given in Gamsby's budget show that life could not have been easy for these lower paid workers.[65] At Thompsons, joiners, painters and blockmakers were paid by contract; for example *George Baxter joiner & men 55s 6d* and in another pay Baxter was paid 11s 3d for $2^1/_2$ days which was 4s 6d/day. A typical rate for joiners was 24s/week. The maker of treenails was paid 10s, sometimes 12s; it is not clear if this was a full week. George Salter *at the Boiler* was paid 12s, and James Dixon who was with him 9s. Mrs Sarah Moore regularly supplied punches and was paid for the number supplied, for example 13s 4d [16,000], 7s 6d [9,000], 3s 4d [4,000]. For some time Doxford's joinery work was on a contract: £17 - 5s was paid to *Joiner*. Later in 1863 apparently they were directly employed; six joiners were named and paid at a daily rate of 5s, the same as shipwrights. An average of $4^1/_4$ days was worked by five joiners.

Earnings at Doxfords 1863-4.

Doxford's shipwrights were paid 5s/day. Foreman, William Johnson, was on 40s a week and two other Johnsons, Jonathan & Ralph, were on 33s & 30s, possibly the same family. As foreman of the wood building Low Yard, George Shevill was paid 42s in 1864. One Stothard was paid 21s 7d for treenails and a week later 16s 3d in 1863; both sums were related to a price for number and size, so either he was on piecework or a subcontractor. At this time pay books do not always clearly distinguish payments to an outsider: there was an item *land of coals- 9s* which probably labourers did. Blockmaking was contracted outside the yard until in October 1863 and then Doxford employed a blockmaker at 33s. A foreman Blacksmith Patton was paid 5s a day and headed a list of 15 workers in pay-week 4 of 1863. The others were not identified as smith or striker but the pay shows: a senior man at 4s 6d, four at 4s and one at 3s 6d; men at 3s 6d, 3s and two at 2s6d; one at 1s4d and two at 1s2d plus two lads at 6d and 7d / day. A lad called Patton was perhaps the foreman's son. Four *platers & riveters* were paid 5s, 4s8d and 4s6d [2] per day, while two *drillers & caulkers* were paid 3s and 2s6d. A third was paid 19s7d for drilling 280 holes [at 7s/100]. Labourers were paid at *3s* and *3s4d*. In mid April the three yard labourers earned *18s*, and two men with short weeks *14s5d* and *7s6d*. In August 1863, Iron foreman, R Hall, was paid 50s and the Rivet foreman Vickers 36s. The fitters were listed with the blacksmiths. James Whyte, foreman blacksmith, was paid 6s/day and W Robson 33s. Of the 19 others, three were on 5s, three were on 4s6d, one on 4s, two on

---

[64] Details were :-1,501 Eng Oak 3s3d *48s 9d* = [15 hundred ft x 3s3d] and 720 Eng Oak *23s5d* plus 1,200 Teak [?] @ 3s6d *43s9d* plus 185 Elm @ 3s9d *6s11d*. This totals a penny more than 74s paid.

[65] *Round About a Pound a Week*, by Maud Pember Reeves, a New Zealander who came to London in 1896, provides useful insights, although her work is not based on the North East. See Lady Bell- *At the Works* [1907].

3s8d, one on 3s6d. Three were paid 2s and one each at 1s8d, 1s5d, 1s4d and 1s2d; finally two boys at 7d and 8d / day. At the sawmill[66] two men were paid weekly - 36s and 30s. Two other men were on 4s / day and one on 3s and presumably two youths at 1s2d. In August 1863 the fireman was paid 21s 8d.

This Pallion wage book also provides some insights into changing jobs held by two men; similar examples occur in later depressions. Mitchell, a boatbuilder, was paid at the shipwright's rate of 5s and his lad at 6d a day; later he became the store & timekeeper at 27s a week. Wm Toward was the highest paid man at 45s; it seems likely he had some managerial functions. *Draft &c*, was written above his name for 6 February 1863 pay-week; three months later he was *Manager, Iron Yard*, but not for long, for he reverted to *draughts*[man] but at the higher salary of 55s. A payment of only 9s on 18 July 1864, indicated his departure. James Parkinson, on 33s/week, was one of two *Assist Drf* in August, and George Parkinson on 6s: which suggested a drawing office staff of three when Toward left Doxfords. This account book, from 29 August 1863, separated the pay of those not covered by *Wages per time book*. The list included W.Wilson, Manager, at 60s, the office staff, foremen and Blackwell as gatekeeper at 20*s* and finally Alf Doxford. Young Alfred was born in 1842 and was paid 6s/week in January 1863. This increased to 8s in May. His pay was 30s in March 1864, and rose to 40s in May 1865 and just over a year later to 50s. These sums appear to be included in summary as foreman costs but no specific function was indicated. At the beginning of 1868 he was paid 60s, which was the same as manager Hornby; at the end of that year neither of these salaries appeared in this record. The office in summary combined manager and draughtsmen/lads. After draughtsman James Parkinson left, another lad joined George in the office, so it must be assumed that either the manager or one of the Doxfords provided the required designs. In 1869 a draughtsman, John Parkinson, was recruited from Pile & Spence at 30s/week but he did not stay long. Until April 1871 there was no reference to a qualified draughtsman, but there were two lads in the drawing office at 15s and 12s. There is an entry of £26 for J D Skinner, draughtsman, before he was on the regular staff; by July he was paid £3 a week. This was the salary Boyd offered to E F Wailes when he joined Wallsend Slipway in 1875 as a draughtsman.

Earnings at Leslie's yard at Hebburn 1855-6 and at Palmers 1871.
The shipwrights were on the highest weekly *time* rate at Leslies Hebburn shipyard in 1855-6, four of them earning 36s/week, while 25 were paid 33s and three others 30s. Platers varied from 28s to 32s and the typical rate for riveters and caulkers was 24s; one caulker was a shilling higher and the lowest was paid 20s. Drillers, at 15s-18s, were not much better paid than the labourers, half of whom were on 15s/week but some were paid 18s. Blacksmiths earned from 18s to 26s and one man was on 31s, mainly they were in the 23s-25s range. Exceptional craftsmen such as the blockmakers were on 31s, as were sparmakers who got 31s and 33s.

Variation of pay even within the same trade continued into the 1870s, with only the shipwrights usually managing to secure a minimum rate. In the iron shipyards, wages fell from 1866; at Jarrow, platers' wages fell from 6s a day to 5s 6d and, finally 5s. Rivetting piecework for 100 rivets was reduced from 9s 6d to 9s and then to 8s 4d. Evidence from Palmers of Jarrow offers a useful summary of the position in 1871. John Price did not provide data on labourers' earnings in the shipyard but in the engine works their average rate was just under 18s, [17s 8d] and in the boiler shop 17s 5ds. Neither did he give figures for holders-up, however, in the boilershop they got 22s or 76% of the riveters' rate which was a usual ratio between these two crafts. The craftsmen's time rates and average earned on piecework are shown below. Shipwrights were on 29s and the platers head the list with 31s, while the rates for others were, riveters 30s, caulkers 28s, drillers 20s and riggers 27s. Joiners were on the same rate as the shipwrights and the painters a shilling a week less, 28s. Piecework earnings were substantially higher; platers at 54s 8d were 76% above time rate,

---
[66] All this sawmill output may not have been for Doxford shipbuilding. Doxfords also sold timber.

angle iron smiths 47.6%[67] [45s 9d], caulkers 37.5% [38s 6d], drillers 77.9% [35s 7d], riveters 14.7% [34s 5d]. What is surprising here is the apparent position of the riveters; in the absence of any rate for holder-up it may be a squad average. Riveters' earnings certainly moved ahead of both the caulkers and the drillers, who within ten years had fallen back at Jarrow. It is clear that best platers and AI smiths could make 10s a day and the others about 7s. The time rates are similar to those on the Wear [diag 12.05].

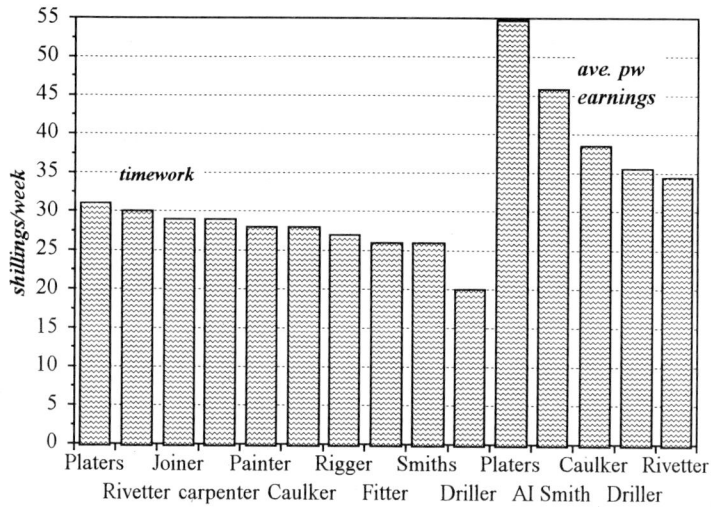

Diag 12.06

In the Jarrow Engine Works boilermakers were normally on time rates which meant there were not the high earnings of the same trades on piecework in the shipyard. The skills developed by the flangers had secured them the high rate of 34s, which was above the plater at 30s 6d, sixpence less than in the shipyard. The drillers at 22s 6d were above the shipyard time rate but the actual earnings would have been substantially less in 1871. Blacksmith's strikers, in the Boiler Shop, were paid 20s 7d, just over two-thirds of the craftsman's 29s; however in the Engine Dept. they only got 17.8s, a labourer's rate, but in that shop the smiths were on 26s $5\frac{1}{2}$d so maintaining the $\frac{2}{3}$rds ratio. Coppersmiths, of whom there were probably about ten, headed the Engine Works rates at 38s and most craftsmen were on about 27s/week. At this time both were at a relatively higher rate than they would later have, the planers at 25s [in Boilershop] and machinemen 26s 9d [Engine Shop]. Machine drillers, in the Engine Shop, at 19s, were lower than either the shipyard rate and or the 22s 6d in the Boiler Shop. Marine engine shops on the Clyde paid platers 32s, riveters & caulkers 28s 2d, erectors 26s 5d, turners 29s 3d, smiths 28s 2d and patternmakers 27s in 1872s: the Tyne and Clyde were on similar rates.

Apprentices & Boys.

Usually boys would go to work at 13 or 14 years of age; they were frequently the sons of men already in the yard or engine works, Their apprenticeship would begin at 16. Very young workers[68] were rare in shipyards and there were few in engine works; the physical demands of the work severely limited their usefulness. There were exceptions, as the Children's Employment Commission[69] showed:

> *Sidney Smith foreman of Pearse's shipyard*: each set of riveters have two boys to heat the rivets for them. The boys are paid by the men when they are on piece-work. At 14 years of age these boys are, most of them, apprenticed to the trade. I believe nearly all these boys can read and write; they have all to write on the time-board the particulars of their day's work. We keep another account to check them. They nearly all write for themselves; the boys often write for the men.
>
> *James Little, heater for riveter* - I am going 11. I have worked here going two years. I went to school before I came here. I can read. I read the Bible and little books. I come at 6 and leave at 6. I never work after 6. I go home for dinner. I get my breakfast here. I blowed when I first came. I get 4s6d a week on time, and 6s on piece. I like working on piece better than on time, because I get more wages. It is not hard work. I give my money to my mother. I have four sisters [two worked at the pottery].
>
> *William Anderson, boltsmith and rivet-maker*: I employ a lad as striker. We never have boys to blow the

---

[67] This 47.6% is calculated on platers time rate. Price lists *smiths* at 26s, this must refer to blacksmiths; if it was the rate for angle iron smiths the gain from piecework was 76%.

[68] W. Allen, of the *ASE*, stated in 1868 that there were *in an engine factory very few boys in comparison with men...*

[69] Evidence was given for three Thames shipyards with boys : Langleys of Deptford, Hepworth's Milwall Wigrams at Blackwall and at Vernon of Liverpool there were 20 under 13 years and 193 aged 13 <18 years and 758 adults.

forge fire ... The man must mind his work ... He must have one boy and work quick.

Tom Atkinson started work at Smith's Dock in 1888 at the age of ten as a catcher; he became foreman driller in 1919. An eleven-year old boy was entered in the 1861 Hebburn census as a labourer in an iron shipyard; ten years later there were two of 12 years and three of 13 years with this job description. A twelve-year old was also described as an apprentice in a shipyard in 1861. In 1871 two rivet boys were 11 and 13, and the rivet heaters 12 and 13 years. Boys usually came in at 13 or 14 and apprenticeship as a shipwright began at 14, in other trades at 16 years [riveters at 18]. There was no more uniformity in the pay of apprentices than there was for the adults; the rates paid by Edwards on the Tyne began at 3s6d in 1811 and was at the same rate in 1845. The amounts in the following years were: 4s, 4s6d, 5s, 5s6d, 6s and 8s in the seventh year. By the 1840s there were 1s increments after the 4s and so the final year was 9s, less than 38% of a journeyman at 4s/day. Laing and Thompson paid some lads as little as 2s6d when they started. Shipwright apprentices were normally provided with personal tools as they proceeded through their training. A notebook from Edward's yard recorded this practice in the 1830s and it certainly continued through the 1860s as shown by a list from Thompsons of May 1868. Mainly augers were listed but also six adzes. It is likely that later the lads may have contributed to the cost of these tools. In 1863, wages for 13 shipwright apprentices at Doxfords varied from 5d a day to the highest at 3s a day. Apprentice riveters were paid at daily rates of 2s [7 lads], 1s 8d [2] and one each at 1s 2d and 1s, which is from 6s to 12s a week. The lowest paid to a boy at Hebburn was 4s and some apprentices on piecework earned £1 a week. In many wood shipyards there was one apprentice to every two craftsmen, including foremen. The high proportion of apprentices of the wood yards was probably not possible in the iron yards and it was certainly never reached in normal times.

Trade unions certainly desired to have some control of apprenticeship, as the rules of the shipwrights' societies clearly showed. *It is our duty to exercise the same care and watchfulness over that in which we have a vested interest as the physician who holds a diploma or the author who is protected by a copyright-* declared the rules of the *ASE*. Adults could, however, qualify for skilled work, as John Price explained, and, in practice, the trade unions accepted as members the worker at the trade who could earn the union rate for the job. William Allan explained the meaning of the expression *legal to the trade* to the Erle Commission: *We suppose that a man who has been five years at the trade, whether apprentice or not, is capable of earning his livelihood at it.* Apprenticeship issues were a primary cause of the longest strike on the north east coast in 1883-5 [see chap 13]. The old system of bound apprentices had largely broken down by the 1870's. In 1871, the Sunderland boilersmith, Willis, decried the *great number of unbound* [apprentices]. In the iron shipyards, according to Heslop, the Tyne delegate of the joiners, it had *scarcely ever been the custom to bind them*. Robert Knight told a Royal Commission in 1886: *unfortunately*, the lads were not apprenticed in the shipbuilding business and he added the employers *discharge them the same way as they discharge ordinary workers*. Six years later, the Wear Shipbuilders' Association informed the Royal Commission on Labour, that they had no apprentices by indenture. Apprentices usually worked piecework[70] in the shipyards; this was not a normal practice in engineering with the exception of Armstrongs. Formal agreements were on apprenticeship were negotiated in the 1890s with the organisation of employers on a national scale.

Employers organise.

Shipbuilders on the Wear.

A form of alliance began among Wear shipbuilders as a result of the Hylton strike of 1850, but once the immediate issue had passed the builders always had difficulties in sustaining collective action. Nonetheless they did form a continuous organisation earlier than employers on the Tyne or Tees. Despite lapses in activity it may be argued that the *Wear Shipbuilders' Association* existed from 1853. On 8 November 1853, James Laing chaired the meeting at the *Crown & Sceptre Inn*, when 45 men agreed that:

---

[70] The Scottish shipbuilder, Inglis, claimed that *In iron shipbuilding, the apprentices can afford to go idle nearly as well as the journeymen because their pay is so high.*

as Shipbuilding is the chief branch of trade carried on in this town it is desirable that a feeling of mutual protection should exist amongst the various parties connected with trade, as far as regards all subjects affecting its interests; to effect which object it is proposed to form a Society ... it shall consist of a President, Vice-President, Treasurer, Secretary and a Committee together with the Shipbuilders of the River Wear. The subscription was to be £2, paid in four quarterly instalments paid in advance. The committee would meet monthly and general meetings would be held quarterly. Any member having a complaint to make or any business to bring forward, connected with the trade, shall give notice in writing to the Secretary, who shall be empowered to call a Special meeting. ... no Shipbuilder shall take an apprentice from any yard on the river, without a certificate from his late master, stating the length of time he has served, the rate of wages paid him, and the said master has no further claim on his Services.

No Shipbuilder shall employ any man or men that are on strike until the dispute in question be decided by the Court of Arbitration or otherwise; and that the Master with whom the dispute arises shall immediately give notice to the Secretary together with a list of the men's names, who shall give immediate notice thereof to each member of the Association.

To abide by the Rules and use our best endeavours to further the Interests of the Association.

Those involved by location of yard were as follows:

Deptford	*Monkwearmouth*	*Southwick*	*Pallion*
James Laing	M Byers & co	John Crown	R Wilkinson
John Robinson	W Harkess	T Stonehouse	Newby Stothard
Low Street	G Booth	J & R Mills	G Short
T Alcock	*North Sand*	W Crown	J Watson
R H Potts Bros	W Pile jr	Jas Hardie	Edw Bailey
Ayres Quay	Jas Pile	S Austin & Mills	Arrow Leithead
Peter Gibson	Havelock & Robson	Geo Worthy	Robt Watson
Wilson Chilton	R Thompson & sons	Dennis Douglas	*Hylton*
Panns Slipway	*Wreath Quay*	J & R Candlish	Forrest & Jackson
W H Pearson	Geo Barker	Pickersgill & Co	Wm Petrie
Panns	John Barkes	*Southwick pat.slipway*	Hume & Easson
S P Austin	T & B Tiffin	Robt Thompson jr	John Smith
J Hutchinson			
North Dock	*Bridge Dock*	*Wear Slipway*	
Ratcliffe & Spence	G W & W J Hall	Wm Mills	
Hartlepool - John Pile			

A deputation visited those who had not joined, such as James Briggs and Pickersgill & Co. The topics discussed at their December meeting included modifications to Lloyds Rules. This issue, together with labour relations were topics which usually brought them together. For just over a year they met regularly to consider wage changes, until the meeting of 6 December 1854 [as related above]. Builders who employed apprentices before their time was completed were discussed and James Briggs was particularly condemned for *this unfair proceeding*. More than a year passed without a meeting, before a claim for 7s brought the shipbuilders back together in January 1856. At the end of this meeting 1s each was collected *to defray the expenses of the room &c*; clearly any funds held earlier had gone. In an attempt to establish a more viable association, George Barker proposed that the Association was reorganised, contacts established with the Tyne shipbuilders and that there should be a bond with a penalty. When they met on 1 February, chaired by Alcock, the sanction of a £200 bond by the Hylton builders was noted. The Hylton builders were invited to join the reorganised association; they were to be admitted free on handing over their funds. Presumably the Hylton organisation had continued after the other Wear builders' group had lapsed. Details were worked out on 29 February, including a bond and a £2 annual subscription [paid half yearly]. A noticeable absentee when the 27 builders paid their first £1 was James Laing. Press reports stated that the association intended to fix the hours of labour and wages by themselves alone and stated their determination to prosecute anyone who attempted to limit the number of apprentices or intimidate any man regarding the *disposal* of his labour. This does not appear in the minute book. They next met on 11 April and Laing was back at the helm as Chairman on 9 December. There was a lengthy discussion on Lloyds Rules in May 1857 and they wanted ships launched in November and December, which had not sailed, to be classed from the following

1 January. Unfortunately *a lengthened discussion* on Union or non-union men minuted on 8 November was not even summarised. Too few were present at the next two meetings, 19 November and 15 December, so they were adjourned. Before the end of the year proposals on Timber Duties resulted in a flurry of activity, including public meetings.

Once again more than a year passed before an Association met in July 1859 and then it was a claim from the sawyers which brought them together on 14 September 1860. When on 20th September only six employers came the meeting was adjourned. After settling a sawyers' wage claim no further meeting was called until 12 July 1861, when again a small attendance required them to adjourn and this occurred twice more. On 30 July, a meeting with the men ended with *no arrangement or conclusion.* Following a gap of 18 months, Alcock asked for a meeting and then failed to attend on 21 January 1863. Two days later Alcock provided the list agreed by the shiprepairers for the sawyers. Wage claims in February 1864 led Blumer to propose meetings with the iron shipbuilders on the Tyne, Tees and at Hartlepool. A joint meeting was held on 10 March to consider pay demands and the relative prices of various trades. Those present were *Wear*: Laing, Percival; R. Thompson; Oswald; Robinson; G. Barker. *Tyne*: Palmer; Rogerson; Richardson; Metcalfe; Henderson; Crosswaite. It emerged that the Tyne wood yards were paying same rates as on the Wear.[71] In September 1866, E G Haswell replaced Pearson as secretary. Twenty shipbuilders attended a dinner in December at 7s 6d per head, which included a pint of claret or sherry! From May 1867 to January 1870 there were long periods between meetings. From then on meetings were held on a regular and routine basis. This task was made easier by steady reduction in the number of shipbuilders.

Organisation amongst Tyne Employers & the first attempt at a national organisation.
Palmer was no doubt capable of bringing together the shipbuilders on the Tyne should the need arise, as in 1866. It may be that a Tyne association continued for a short time but as Palmer said in 1868 they seldom needed to use the Shipbuilders' Association. Within four years, however, Tyne shipbuilders were meeting regularly in a formal organisation. Before 1871, Tyneside engineering employers showed little if any inclination to form an employers' association. These men built up their own loyalties, although, no doubt, meeting and talking informally. The *9-hour* demand in 1871 enabled Armstrong successfully to bring these employers together, as seen above. Before that strike was over, Armstrong and Westmacott were taking steps to establish a national Iron Trades Employers' Association. On 8 August 1871 Armstrong chaired a meeting of employers from the North East Coast, Hull, Leeds, Liverpool and Glasgow; a committee was set up on *the best mode of establishing an association of employers in the engineering and shipbuilding trades throughout the United Kingdom.* Westmacott and Ure of Elders, the Clyde shipbuilders, were to sound out other districts.[72] When the Iron Trades Employers' Association [ITEA] came into existence on 4 April 1872 in London, *somewhere along the road the firms of the Tyne and Clyde ... had pulled out.* The new organisation was mainly supported from Manchester, Liverpool, Leeds and London. When the 9-hours strike was over the *bond that held them* [local employers] *together was relaxed* [Boyd]. A view confirmed by the sluggish response to a letter [22 April 1872] from Armstrongs to firms

---

[71] Tyne iron shipbuilders paid joiners 26s-28s; blacksmiths 23s-29s; shipwrights 32s. Thompson said *Wear sawyers having an advantage of about $^2/_3$rds over Tyne*; it was accepted that any shipbuilder was allowed to employ Shields sawyers by the day but might not do so on the Wear, where piecework ruled.

[72] They reported on 28 Dec.1871 at Stafford, that with a few individual exceptions- *it was universally admitted that the combination and perfect organisation of trade unions, aided by powerful agitation to enforce unwarrantable demands upon employers chiefly by intimidation, is damaging to the interests of the several trades, being contrary to the natural law of supply and demand, and opposed to the freedom of labour and freedom of contract, and that it now behoves employers in self defence to secure unity of action and mutually to aid, counsel and support each other by forming and organising a General or National Association of Masters.* Remarkably extravagant language! Boyd was at Stafford and wrote that Tyne & Wear *definitely decided* not to join in April 1872.

offering to put £2,000[73] at the disposal of an employers' association provided it was formed within a year of the offer. Employers of iron shipbuilding & engineering labour met in Newcastle on 22 March 1873 to establish an employers' association. Names in the first membership list were *Engineering* - Armstrongs; Abbott; Clarke, Watson & Guerney; T Clark; Dunston Engine Works; Thompson & Boyd; Keeney & Marshall and Nicholson & Wilson[74]. *Shipbuilding*: Cole Bros.; Coulson Cook; Leslie; Mitchell; Readhead-Softley; Schlesinger & Davis; Wallsend Slipway; Wigham Richardson, Palmer and Cleland Ltd. The following was minuted:

> 1. It is proposed to form an Association of Shipbuilders and Engineers on the River Tyne on a basis so simple that no employer need have any hesitation in joining it.
>
> 2. It is believed that the existence of such an association would not only afford ready means of consultation between the members on Legislature and other general matters affecting the interests of the Trades in question but also would be [to any member who required it] a voice of information and advice on questions of difficulty which might from time to time arise between himself and his workmen, and further be a basis for any other concerted action which circumstances might at any time render necessary.
>
> 3. Experience shows that the chief weakness of an employer in resisting an unreasonable demand on the part of any section of his workmen is the knowledge that when work is plentiful such workmen if on strike against him are readily employed elsewhere.
>
> 4. To remedy such a state of things it is proposed that one simple rule of such an association be *That each member shall pledge himself not to employ any workman who may be one strike against any other member*. It is believed that a general adherence to such a pledge would so strengthen the hands of an employer as to materially assist him in resisting undue demands from his workmen.

Early in April the formalities were completed under the chairmanship of Charles Mitchell; the subscription was to be £10 per year [£5 if less than 500 *hands*]. Benjamin Plummer was elected secretary at £160 a year [This included the use of an office].[75] Noble, Mitchell, W Thompson, John Palmer and Leslie were elected to the committee. Two Armstrong men agreed to attend the London meeting of the ITEA, which aimed to frustrate efforts *by Trade Unionists and others to induce Parliament to modify in favour of workmen, the Masters & Servants Act and other measures bearing on the relations between Capital and labour*.

In December 1873 the committee informed the secretary of the Iron Trades, Ephraim Hutchings, that the Tyne Association was formed and that they *would be glad to be of service to the London Master Engineers should a strike arise*. If, Noble, Palmer and Mitchell thought such support would be forthcoming, there was little evidence to support that opinion, indeed the Tynesiders stayed out of the national body for another ten years. William Boyd wrote *the class of work turned out in the Tyne district was very different from that done in Lancashire and Yorkshire*. On 31 January 1874, shipbuilding members[76] considering a 6d claim by the shipwrights revealed the various attitudes usually present when joint action was sought. Leslie, true to his usual stance, was for resisting, Swan suggested that arbitration offered *a medium course* and Coulson explained that as a *young firm would object* to a stand which would lead to a strike. He was for asking the *heads of Unions* to sign 6-month agreements to enable contracts to be worked off. Mitchell's comments that he *had found some of the delegates very useful in settling and avoiding disputes and as the men's unions were formed it was advisable to make use of them*, confirming views expressed by Browne, Doxford and others. Later that year the Boilermakers' delegate Jones made clear they had no objections to three or six months notice. Tyneside shipbuilders[77] worked under the same

---

[73] It transpired ten years later that this was *money that the firm was entitled to receive out of the Funds subscribed to aid the Tyne Engineers in the 9 hours strike* - minutes 30 Nov. 1883

[74] These last two do not appear in list of those paying subscription. Also present were representatives from Hawks, Crawshay and Black-Hawthorn, they referred back to their companies.

[75] Plummer was secretary to the Newcastle Chamber of Commerce and the Exchange. James Robinson became acting secretary in 1890 and on Plummer's death in May 1902 he became sole secretary; after various office moves the employers' associations, in 1909, joined the NECIES in Bolbec Hall.

[76] Mitchell, Coote, H F Swan, Sclesinger, Davis, C S Swan [Coulson], Leslie, R E Cole, J Couslon and Readhead.

[77] A slip of the pen? - *A meeting of Shipwrights was held on April 8th 1874*; it was, of course, the shipbuilders.

umbrella organisation as the engineering employers at least until the spring of 1874; there is no doubt the shipbuilders continued to meet regularly and act together. It seems likely that any formal organisation of the engineering employers lapsed.

The Response of the Tyne Employers to the Wear Engineers' Strike of 1883.
The Employers of Engineering Labour on Tyneside met on 25 June 1883 to organise support for the Sunderland employers, with Cruddas, of Armstrongs, as chairman. This organisation became the Tyneside branch of the Iron Trades Employers' Association [ITEA] in 1884.[78] Although engineering employers on the Wear came together to resist the demand for a 9-hours day, they then reverted to acting individually. In response to the Sunderland *ASE* strike of 1883 they formed the Wear Engine Builders Association. A year later this organisation like the Tyne also became a branch of the Iron Trades. This Wear association was composed of four firms who between them employed 2,500 workers; a fifth marine engine firm did not join the organisation. The historian of the Employers' Association, Wigham, wrote of the ITEA:
> It was not a negotiating body like a modern employers' organisation. In fact it had no direct contacts with trade unions. Its main activity was to help employers in disputes by financial assistance and providing non-unionists to take the place of strikers.

The Tyneside branch told a Royal Commission in 1894 that its objectives were the settlement of disputes, mutual support to each other against attacks by trade unions and to negotiate with workmen.

Employers on the Tees and at Hartlepool.
Col. Dyer of Armstrongs was a very active advocate and organiser of employers' associations. At a meeting of Tees and Hartlepool engineering employers on 20 July 1893, he argued that the workmen's societies were *consolidating and strengthening themselves, and were becoming every day more powerful and aggressive*, hence the necessity for employers to federate. If the Tees joined the Wear & Tyne Association *so great would be the power of a North East Coast Association that strikes and disputes would become very rare*. Eight days later it was resolved to form an Association and in August the Tees & Hartlepool Engineering Employers' Association was formed dominated by the marine engine builders. In 1894, following strikes by patternmakers and foundry workers, they acted jointly with the Tyne and Wear employers *on all general questions*. The *ASE* unsuccessfully attempts to ignore this joint committee.

Employers' National Associations.
Nationally the Employers' Federation of Engineering Associations was formed in June 1896 and those employers in the North East already organised collectively were immediately involved. Col. Dyer was the first President and he was succeeded by Sir Andrew Noble, who held the office until 1915, clear evidence of the status of the Armstrong management in this field. The consequences of this new link to a national policy caused considerable trouble in 1897 [see chap. 13]. A National Federation of Shipbuilders [including marine engineers] was formed in 1889 and re-formed ten years later. In 1894, there was a national Shiprepairers' Association, five years later a North East Coast Shiprepairers' Association. The large size of engineering and shipbuilding firms led them fairly readily to combination once the stage of personal owner manager was passing. It is probable that a national policy by the employers increased rather than decreased local labour problems by reducing if not eliminating flexibility. However, in shipbuilding, local customs were respected much longer than in engineering. North east industrialists played an active part in the national organisations of employers. Armstrongs provided the first presidents of both Engineering Federation and Shipbuilders & Repairers Federation, respectively, Col. Henry Dyer [1896-8] and Philip Watts. Dyer was followed by Andrew Noble [1898-1915], Hawthorn Leslie provided Sir Archibald Ross [1926-30] and Philip Johnson [1946-9] as Presidents of the Engineers. Three men from Hawthorn Leslie became Presidents of the Shipbuilders, Herbert Rowell [1912-4], his son Robin [1941-2] and J T Batey

---

[78] Hawkes Crawshay and Eltringham declined to join. At first there were doubts about NEM & Wigham Richardson. Boyd described the record of June 1883 as the first Minute Book *now discoverable*. Earlier minutes had survived.

held the office in 1927-8. Among 16 other north east Presidents were: George Jones [1906-8]; W H Dugdale [1919-20], L Ropner [1922-3], J H Edwards, Sir Tristram Edwards, Sir Charles S Swan, F C Pyman [1937-8], J R Gebbie [1944-5], Sir John Hunter [1956-7] and G R Towers [1959-60]. Wigham, as historian of the Engineering Employers' Federation was puzzled by the *inability of shipbuilding and engineering employers to settle down in the same organisation*, particularly as many of the big firms built both ships and marine engines. As late as 1964 the Shipbuilders successfully resisted a merger bid from the Engineers. He noted such important differences as more extreme fluctuations in shipbuilding and a *quite different* system of payment by results. In the 1890s, the dominant union in shipbuilding, the Boilermakers, were still following the *tradition of the craft societies*, with which the employers had *learned to live, if not always very happily*, and Knight was *an exceptionally able and thoughtful secretary*. In contrast the *ASE* was regarded as *tainted* with socialism and behaved with *an arrogance, as it seemed to the employers, which threatened the industry's future. The shipbuilders would want to avoid being involved with that.*

Housing.

Providing living accommodation for their workers was undertaken by employers in both shipbuilding and marine engineering, sometimes from necessity. Housing conditions were far from satisfactory in the north east.[79] *The available space for human habitation is as precious as the ground in a grave yard-* was an observation made of a part of Newcastle in 1850. Housing available for mechanics was *not much better than those of the poor*, a writer complained, adding that the rents were *enormous* for the poorer dwellings. He continued: mechanics were charged £5 per annum for single rooms, *little better than those described (for the poor, e.g. broken window panes, size 9ft x 11ft)*. Most mechanics could only afford to pay for one room, two rooms could not be rented for under £9, with water extra, and few of the houses were *furnished with conveniences*. Gateshead's Town Clerk told a Parliamentary inquiry in 1853 that half the town's population *are lodged in places which rarely if at all are fit for human habitation*. Our population, he continued, *consists mainly of skilled artisans, many of them of a very intelligent character; and it is a painful reflection to think that persons of that character should be so badly housed*. During the 1860's, Newcastle had more persons per house than any other large town in England. A special sanitary report to the Town Council, in 1867, stated that nearly half of the population lived under conditions of 2.4 persons per room. There were 9,639 families in single room accommodation and 6,191 families in two-room households. No fewer than 13,747 persons lived in 4,171 rooms, or at a density of 3.3 persons per room. One in eight of the inhabitants were without water supply, good ventilation or drainage. It was hardly surprising that the death rate was 36.7 per 1000, substantially higher than Liverpool at 33.1 per 1000. Deaths in Sunderland in 1869 clearly shows how the deaths of children dominated the numbers dying at this time [see diag 12.07].

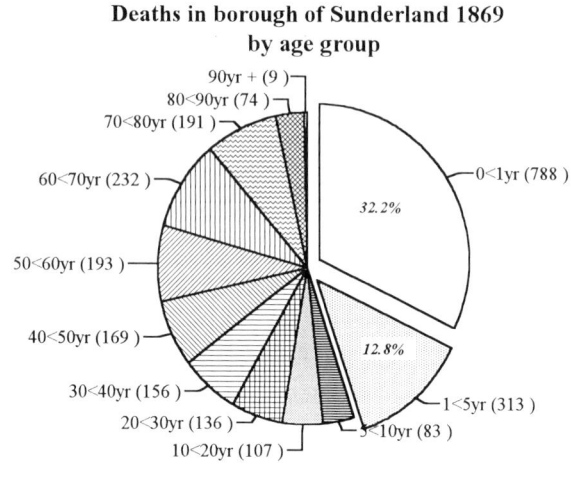

Diag 12.07

By the mid-1870s, the housing conditions of the workers in the north east, showed little, if any, improvement. The Medical Officers of Health reported the low standards, for example at Newcastle,
> [in 1874] Yet the small amount of vacant house room - very little beyond that of a box, 6 feet x 7 feet x 7 feet - is scarcely to be found by the poor, even though of bad quality and exorbitant rent ... The chief difficulties in the way of sanitary progress ... have been the want of fit habitation for the poor and means of isolation. [in 1875] the rent of tenement property in Newcastle is high, some dark and damp cellar

---
[79] See also Clarke [1967]; *Working Class Housing on Tyneside 1850-1939* [Lancaster] and Wilkinson pp 73-7.

kitchens (recently closed) bring 2/6 and 3/6 a week ... with the present scarcity of dwellings, the shutting up of rooms, even under conditions such as the above, is to a great degree, impracticable, a bad room being better than none.

Water was only supplied once a week in some parts of Walker and Wallsend, in 1874. At South Shields there was a similar position and in 1876 the Medical Officer described the *Newcastle Flat*, which became the typical dwelling for many workers:

> A large proportion of the property which is now built is of this description: The houses are in flats; each tenement consists of two rooms, front and back; there is no passage, at least on the ground floor; the two rooms forming the tenement communicating directly by a doorway in the partition wall. Now in several houses...this door of communication between the two rooms was nailed up and each room, front and back, let off to a separate tenant. [That] *practice* [was threatening] to become quite general in certain locations.

Some improvement in the distribution of property types [with a valuation of under £15] was noted by Dr Campbell Munro in the *Borough* of South Shields. Of every 1000 such dwellings in 1871, there were 541 with a valuation under £5 [1 roomed] and there 408 [2 roomed] in £5<£10 valuation group. Only 5% were in the 3 roomed category [£10<£15]. Sixteen years later, in 1887, the proportion of 3-roomed had doubled to 10.9% and the 1 roomed group had fallen from 54.1% to 28%. In the older area of the *Township*, however, there was virtually no change in the 3 room group at just over 4% and the lowest category had only fallen from 82.1% to 72.2%. Sunderland was seriously overcrowded. In 1850, the local paper described *the greater part of the parish* [as] *occupied by the labouring classes, living in tenemented houses*. There were 11.6 persons per house in East Sunderland and 9.7 persons per house in West Sunderland in 1851.

In 1864, Charles Palmer acknowledged the problem when speaking to the men's wives; after suggesting that some of them lacked a good education in housewifely duties and others had sickly children, he continued

> too many of you are ill-provided with houses, or rooms, suitable for healthy family arrangements ... I believe they (the Local Board) fully recognise that the improvement of the workingman's dwelling is indispensable to the success of every attempt to ameliorate his condition and render him sober and thoughtful.

Lodging house conditions were not good; in January 1853, the lodging houses of South Shields housed 803 Irish, 375 Scots and 499 English persons. Old colliery houses, such as existed in Elswick, often constituted the only available accommodation for newcomers. Verbal tradition, if not the written record, suggests that successions of shift workers occupied the same beds and that food was prepared in wash houses, at the rear of the buildings in a communal manner. The persistent desire of the workers to be as near as possible to their place of work increased the pressure on housing. The secretary of a society for building industrial dwellings in Newcastle, defended the lack of gardens and other amenities - *the majority of the workingmen regard the convenience of residing near their work as superior to all other advantages or attractions*. Walking was the usual way to work to arrive not later than 6 am. In 1864, some 300 workmen petitioned for a public road from North Shields to Howdon, to facilitate their journey. Arriving late lost a quarter day's pay and very often this meant a long and chilly wait at the factory gate. An explosion at the Morrison works, at 5.30 am, in July 1858, gave direct evidence of this: two men were killed and many injured, waiting to go into work.

One of the earliest employers to provide workmen's cottages was the Willington Slipway Co., founded in 1835. Hawks & Crawshay was described as *leading the way in erecting comfortable cottages for their workmen*, in 1850. In the mid-fifties, the *Northern Examiner* urged Armstrong to build cottages:

> His workmen are either scattered throughout the town ... they come in swarms along the road in the darkness of the wintry morning or they are forced to inhabit the pestilential cribs of such places as Greenhow Terrace - a place from its nastiness and filth, fatal to many a man and woman ... Mr Armstrong's example would tell on the whole district and tend to promote that kindness and co-operation which is so necessary for the peace and comfort of employer and employed...surely the very man to realise our notions of a model cottage.

The paper's hopes were not realised. Armstrong did not develop homes for his workers. There was some accommodation in Newcastle, but Jarrow's remoteness from a large town and lack of dwellings may have reinforced Palmer's paternalism. He built both dwellings and established a building society for his workers. Many extolled his virtues in this direction. Lawson, in his *Tyneside Celebrities* [1873], wrote of *the erection of model dwellings for his workpeople*. Richardson, as historian of Wallsend, wrote:

> Palmer's ... connection with Wallsend had one good permanent result. They secured a considerable parcel of land and drew up an excellent *hire purchase* scheme for small self-contained houses for workmen. [These] were in advance of almost any of their class and, after the rent had been paid for a certain period, the houses became the property of the tenants... sixty workingmen became owners of their own houses.

According to Davidson: *whole streets were built by the more thrifty and enterprising of the men*. The ownership of their homes by workers extended furthest at Jarrow. In 1886, John Price thought that about half the town belonged to the workers. Serious overcrowding continued, in 1901, more than 16,000 people lived in St. Paul's Parish at a density of 8.1 persons per house, and there was an average of 10 per house in the parish of St. Peters. Nearly 40% of the tenements in Jarrow were one or two-roomed dwellings.

When in 1860, Wigham Richardson began shipbuilding at Wallsend, he too erected dwellings. His motives partly arose from his Quaker background, which inspired a desire to look after the well-being of his workers but there was also the necessity of housing them. Low Walker, the nearest village, was very isolated. Only a rough road to Newcastle joined Byker, which consisted of only a few cottages. In Wallsend *practically the only accommodation* available was old colliery houses with *the floor of the living room covered with stone slabs, and in most cases below the level of the street*. The dwellings built by Richardson gradually improved in quality; he resisted strong pressure to build one room dwellings for each family and, in those first erected, there was one *fair sized room* and one *small room*. There were three stories in each building with a common staircase to six tenements and a common backyard. So they were very much akin to the occupation of rooms in a large house. Later, a row of dwellings was added back to back with those just described. In the second block, a separate entrance was provided for those on the bottom floor and a common stair for two tenements. Later, allotments were secured for some workers and a house purchase scheme similar to the one at Jarrow. By the 1890s, to accommodate his foremen, new dwellings were built - *a self-contained house with a parlour, a kitchen, a wash house, three bedrooms and a bathroom with hot and cold water, a small garden in the front and a backyard*. The rents of these were such that they were only likely to be occupied by *a well-paid artisan or foreman*. Richardson built in all 200 houses. The Carville estate cost £30,000 and realised, in 14 years, £60,000, so it was not an unprofitable venture, apart from the gains in goodwill and a reliable labour force which also flowed from it. When Schlesinger & Davis started their Wallsend shipyard, in 1864, they bought 44 tenements for their workers. The Wallsend Co-operative Society purchased land, in 1868, and erected *workingmen's houses, so superior to the average available that they were extended rapidly*; some years later other north east co-operative societies also built housing. In the early 1870s, Wallsend was *a dreary looking place* and for the workmen residence near their work was almost *an impossibility. Almost all* came from Newcastle or places between Wallsend and Newcastle, with no riverside railway or tramcar; all communication was carried by water or on foot. In the late 1860s, NEM faced similar problems to Wigham Richardson at Wallsend, and their general manager, William Allan organised new housing. There were houses for the foremen, at Northumberland Villas, *pretty villas, each with a large garden attached*, for the mechanics, at North Terrace and at South Terrace for the *lower paid employees*; in all more than 100 houses. Under existing housing conditions, it is hardly surprising that there was *a continual rush* for these houses, described at the time as *of the very best construction and arrangement, and their popularity is easily seen by the long list of applicants who wish to occupy them*.

Andrew Leslie's first two houses at Hebburn were for foremen, and for a time were known as *Gaffers Row*, until a local used the derogatory term *Oatmeal Terrace*. By 1861, there was accommodation for 43 households of his shipyard workers. Twenty-five of the heads of households were born in Scotland, seven in Ireland; amongst the others was James Skinner, his draughtsman and future shipyard owner. Many of these occupants took in lodgers, so that in all 101 workers slept in Leslie houses. One of the earliest

Ellison Street Hebburn 1871 Census — examples of households

John Grant boilersmith
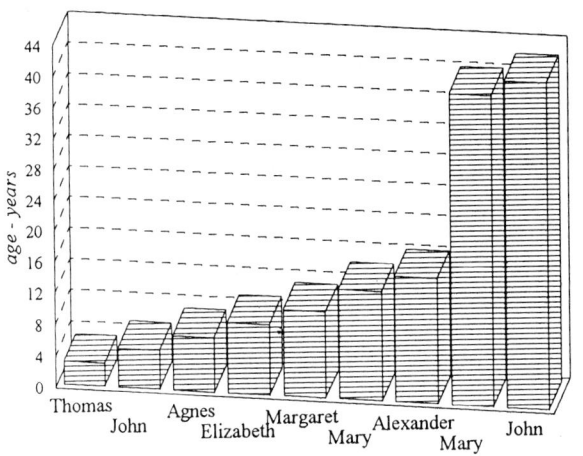

Wm McLoughlin rivetter household at 18 Ellison St
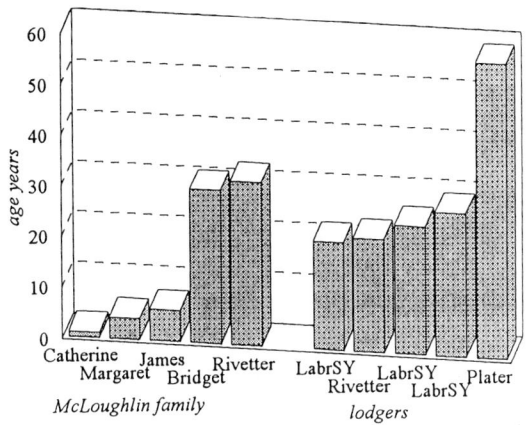

Household of midwife Ann Cox in 18 Ellison St
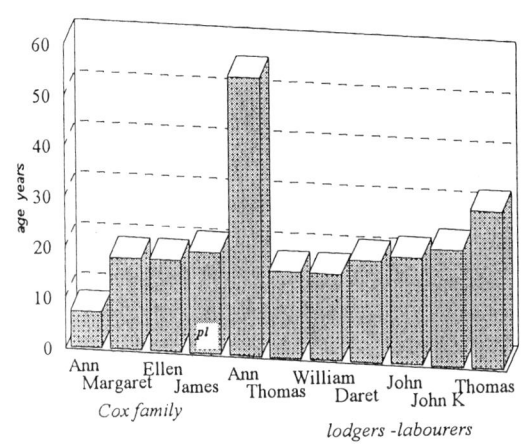

Ellison St. Hebburn 1871 number living in each house
993 persons lived in 80 houses
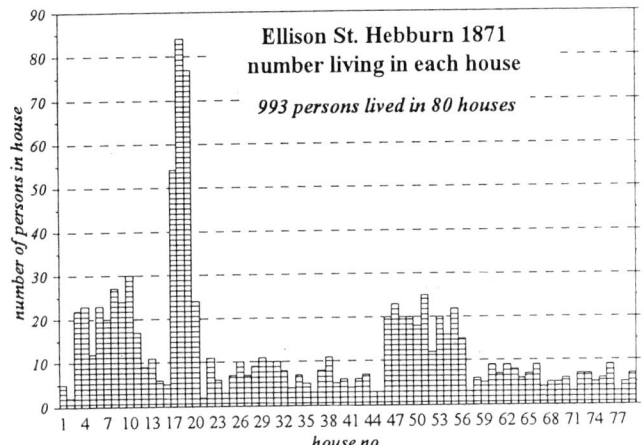

map shows location of Ellison Street and the Shipyard
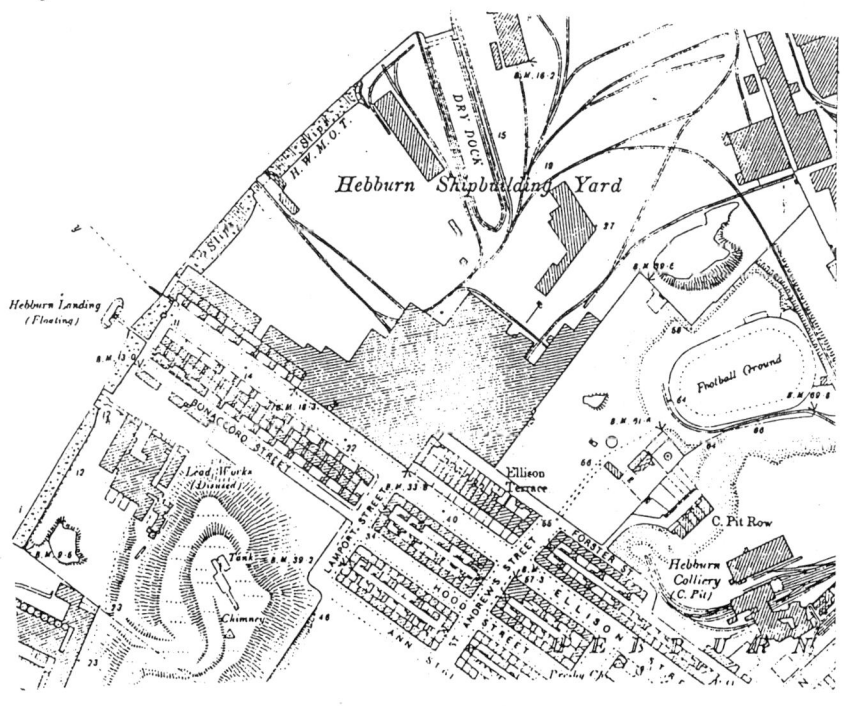

Ellison Street Hebburn 1871 Census - Andrew Leslie's houses
Paid workers [that is not including wives, who certainly worked very hard]

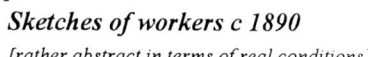

Sketches of workers c 1890
[rather abstract in terms of real conditions]

Trade	no. of workers	average age		no. of workers	average age
joiner	91	26.6	Presbyterian		
Labourer ISY	86	28.4	Minister	1	37.0
Carp ship	53	26.5	Police constable	1	50.0
Riveter	32	28.1	L Chem	2	42.0
Boilermaker	26	30.0	Coalminer	1	21.0
Blacksmith	18	34.9	Tailor	1	42.0
Painter	13	26.0	Butcher	1	31.0
Fitter	11	33.4	app Butcher	1	17.0
Joiner ship	11	25.5	Grocer	1	30.0
Plater	11	30.6	Grocers asst	1	17.0
carpenter	8	34.4	Shoemaker	1	27.0
Caulker	8	26.5	Ferryman	1	39.0
Boilersmith	7	35.0			
Boat builder	5	23.4	Rivet boy	2	15.0
Boilerbuilder	5	34.4	Rivet heater	1	12.0
Foreman	5	34.0	app Riveter	1	17.0
Driller	4	27.0	app Boat Bld	1	16.0
Cabinet maker	4	25.5	app Boilsm	1	15.0
Engineman	2	39.5	app Brassfin	1	13.0
Holderup	2	29.5	app Joiner	3	14.7
Stone Mason	2	26.0	app Plater	3	19.7
Timekeeper	2	27.0	app fitter	1	15.0
Upholsterer	2	36.0	app Blacksmi	4	14.7
Bolt Fitter	1	37.0	Messenger	1	13.0
Brass finish	1	49.0	Errand Boy	1	12.0
Engineer	1	23.0	Stoker	1	12.0
File Grinder	1	28.0			
Foreman L	1	34.0	*ISY=Iron Shipyard*		
Forgeman	1	30.0	paid female workers		
Gatekeeper	1	43.0			
Iron finisher	1	26.0			
Iron Sb firm	1	25.0			
Mason	1	38.0	paid female workers		
L Mason	1	61.0		no.	av.age
Labourer	1	22.0	Servant	16	15.8
Manager ISY	1	35.0	Charwoman	4	38.5
accountant	1	36.0	Charmaid	1	13
Shipwright	1	52.0	Housekeeper	1	28
Weighman	1	42.0	Midwife	1	55
Patternmaker	1	22.0	Nurse	2	14
Planer	1	39.0	Milliner	1	21
Plumber	1	27.0	Dressmaker	1	18
Rigger	1	39.0			
Sawyer	1	22.0			

a caulker at work - sealing edge of plate

angle iron in furnace prior to shaping
bending slabs can be seen
below shaping heated angles for frames

arrivals, *iron shipbuilder* Alexander Cowan, lived with his wife, age 42, and his 16-year old son a shipyard worker together with five lodgers aged 16 to 45. Ten years later when his son was a plater they still had five lodgers, two platers, two joiners and a plumber, all from Scotland, aged 23-27 years. In 1861 Cowan's immediate neighbours each had three lodgers, Agnes Smith a blacksmith's widow had a son at the yard and two daughters, 15 & 10 years, in addition to the lodgers. William Thom, a labourer and another early arrival from Scotland, was married with four children [12, 10, 8 & 4 years], so there were nine in all in his flat. By the census of 1871, Leslie had built many more houses and the streets were named. Ellison Street was the western boundary of the shipyard and contained almost the whole range of social classes amongst its 993 residents in 164 households lived in 78 numbered dwellings. Leslie himself never lived in Hebburn, but his manager's house was in Ellison Street with his foremen, as well as the Presbyterian minister. The occupations of the residents are shown opposite. Just how crowded these dwellings[80] were is illustrated by three households in no.18 Ellison St. There were eight households at that address, in all 84 persons. Boilersmith John Grant had no lodgers but there were seven children. The widowed midwife Ann Cox in addition to her own four children had six lodgers and riveter William McLoughlin, in addition to his wife and three children, housed five lodgers. It is not difficult to accept that there was rotation in the use of beds and cooking in the wash house. The average for the whole street was almost 13 persons per dwelling. This was of course much reduced by the smaller households where there was only a single family in the dwelling. In Bon Accord St. the average was more than 21 persons per dwelling; the four households in no.11 were headed by a riveter, a joiner, a driller and a labourer, in all 31 people living there. Amongst the ten lodgers was a family of an Irish labourer, his wife and two children aged one and two years.

Housing and benefits to the employer.
Like those of Wigham Richardson, the Hebburn houses were a profitable investment. About 400 were built and 319 were part of the shipyard property, and these were described as *a steady source of income, and of considerable indirect value in attracting a good class of Workman to the Yard* when the Hawthorn Leslie Ltd was formed in 1886. Over the period 1886-1898, rents collected amounted to £37,485, a substantial income for very little current expenditure. Over these years a number of dwellings were reconstructed. A block of single roomed cottages was changed into four 3-roomed cottages [at a cost of £235] in 1889; two further blocks were also modified in this way. Similar alterations took place in 1899 and 1905. In 1893 there were *grave sanitary defects connected with most of the ashpits ...The evil applies to the whole of the property* [say 200 tenants]. £100 was voted by the Hawthorn-Leslie Board to deal with this problem. Such housing helped to establish, or reinforce, a bond of attachment between the employer and at least a part of his workmen. The house was a prize to be won and John Burnett claimed it might well restrain the more militantly minded; the influence of occupying an employer's house need not be doubted. When the Blyth & Tyne Railway Co. were building workmen's dwellings, the *Newcastle Chronicle* commented: *They would be the better able to retain good servants in their employ and would not incur any expense because the houses would be let at a fair rent.* Wigham Richardson's literary executor wrote: *The ownership in fee simple of his dwellings, the profit of his allotments and the attractions of his garden, have, it is believed, contributed much to make the workman of Walker what he so often is today - the ideal of a self-respecting citizen.* There seems little doubt that the workers sought these dwellings since they combined the attractions of nearness to the workplace and were newly erected. While this was not perhaps a major factor in labour relations, it was of some significance. The able man who would rise to be a trade union leader was the kind of man who sought satisfactory housing, if he could. Despite these efforts, only a small part of the labour force was housed in this way.

---

[80] A Company report of 1904 stated *although the rooms are larger than in the average modern houses, they were ... built on the principle of getting as many houses as possible on the land ... as soon as they were occupied the Yard policeman was sent round to ask the tenants of one and two-roomed houses how many lodgers they were prepared to take ... The houses were originally built without any downcomers to the spouts in the front, and the water was carried from the front to the back by means of a lead pipe through the roof ... many leaks and dampness.* Earlier reference was made to the *disadvantage of ... one passage and stairs common to two houses upstairs.*

Wife & Mother - the essential support.

A much neglected aspect of life at that time is the exacting almost unending work carried out by women, on which the following is only a brief comment. In the words of the compiler of the 1861 census: *These women are sometimes described as of no occupation. But the occupation of wife and mother and housewife is the most important in the country, as will be apparent if it be assumed for one moment to be suppressed.* Consider for one such moment the work carried out by those women coping with the overcrowding and housing conditions just related. Their men were at work at 6 a.m. and usually returned for their dinner midday; evening meals were subject to the variations caused by overtime. During the evening there were the worn and frequently torn clothes to be mended, not forgetting the care of the children. Washing by hand was all the more demanding in a situation where alternative sets of clothing were rare and the work made clothes very dirty. Any thought that this, or indeed other industries, could have prospered without this mountain of unpaid work is badly mistaken. Likewise these women faced the recurring task of providing food when there was a reduced pay packet, due to bad weather or other causes, no pay because of unemployment or only the earnings of an apprentice son. The early experiences of the first women to arrive from Scotland was described in the *Hebburn Monthly* in 1874. On her first night Mrs Cowie tried to find water, finally succeeding in a stagnant pond by the ballast hill, the next morning

> the female portion of the new settlers sallied forth on a voyage of discovery, and found water in small quantities at a time was to be obtained at the Cock Row. Thither they sojourned with their water utensils, and grudging much the distance they had to carry, and still more the time required to wait upon it, were yet thankful that after all they should be able to obtain a drink of pure water. As they trudged home with their liquid burden they had to pass the workmen engaged in making the yard and before they were aware the thirsty navvies and masons had consumed every drop ... early rising became the only escape ... A canny housewife would slip out early with the prudent resolve that she would be first at the well ... a race ensued and the nearer they came to the well the more numerous the competitors ... almost every house sent forth its water nymph ...[a local gardener saw his opportunity and] began to bring regular supplies by cart as he returned from the market. At first ... once a week, but as settlers increased he extended his operations, and twice, thrice and sometimes oftener was his liquid freight required. It is needless to say that scenes occurred on the arrival of the water cart. The rule was to lay down the pails from a given point in the order of arrival, but you might as well expect to have street honour and discipline in a number of drunken men scrambling for beer, as with women panting for water to make the tea ... our colonists having found themselves so destitute of the common domestic requirements, and so isolated from the rest of the world, required strong nerves to continue in a land where they were evidently unwelcome, and where the comforts promised to be few. They had not yet, however, got the full measure of the trials that awaited them, for the hostility of the Tynesiders had not yet been fully evoked.

This cannot be pursued here but it is important to realise that starting a shipyard on what we now call a greenfield site could have many problems if your workers were coming from another part of Britain.

Unmarried men.

Single men, who were not living at home, were usually accommodated as lodgers but there were in the early 20th century efforts to provide directly for these workers. A proposal to build a Rowton house[81] for Wallsend, was debated at the Board of Swan Hunter in May 1906; it then appeared this scheme might be extended to other parts of Tyneside and Sunderland. In August Swan Hunter agreed to offer £2,500 in capital support. Following an exchange of correspondence, Northern Rowton decided they wanted more experience at Newcastle before proceeding.[82] A Dr Simpson was successful in establishing lodging houses and after an inspection of his Tower House, Workmen's Hotel in Newcastle Swan Hunter decided, in December 1912, to acquire a site in Buddle St. for £726 which would be suitable for a *Simpson's Hotel*. Building costs were estimated at about £9,000 to accommodate 350 persons and it was intended to sell it to a Company set up by Dr Simpson, on a mortgage at 6.75% of the unpaid price. This new Company

---

[81] M W L Corry [1838-1903], created Baron Rowton in 1880. He became trustee of the Guiness Trust [Industrial Dwellings] Fund in 1889 and resolved to provide a poor man's hotel; built *Rowton House* at Vauxhall in 1892.

[82] In October 1911, estimated cost of a 264 bed Rowton House at Station Road £8,500, regarded as *a high figure*.

would spend about £2,000 furnishing &c and take the entire management. Revised estimates of perhaps as much as £12,000 for 320 bed accommodation for the Carville House Workmen's Hotel were approved in May 1912. A year later, again the need for additional workmen's houses at Wallsend was discussed and a subcommittee set up to make a detailed report. Before the end of the year, Swan Hunter agreed to commit £15,000 - £20,000. Tyneside Tenants Ltd [Workmen's Houses] was formed and by February 1914 there was a scheme for houses near Fisher St. and building was under way by April.[83]

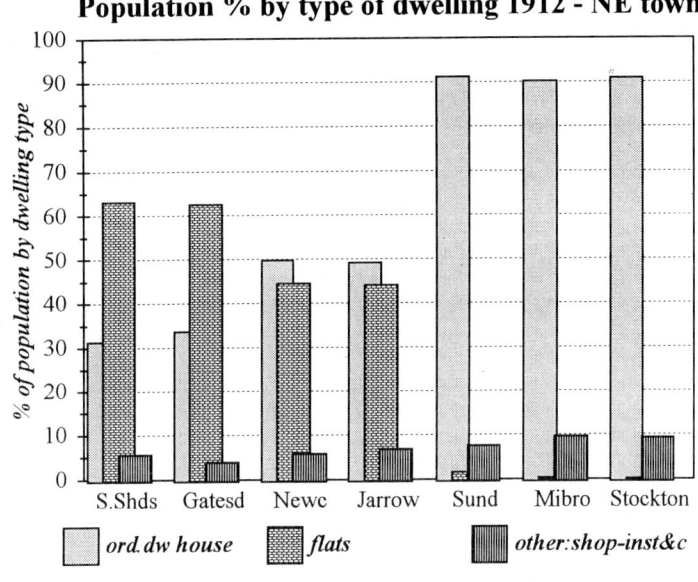

Diag 12.08

Severe overcrowding on both the Tyne and Wear[84] persisted into the 20th century, with three out of every ten people overall living two or more persons per room. Even greater crowding would have afflicted those on lower incomes. Approximately 63% of the people lived in flats in South Shields and Gateshead and 45% in Newcastle and Jarrow. Nowhere else in England had such a concentration of flat dwellers. At Sunderland it was only 1.5% and it was negligible on the Tees. Although the Tees and Hartlepool occupancy was higher than the national average, at about one person in ten [2/room] this part of the region was dramatically less crowded than its northern neighbours. These figures illustrate how little progress was made towards adequate housing. It is very surprising, with the relatively high earnings among many north east coast workers in this latter period, that better housing was not provided. The explanation does not appear to be an unwillingness to pay adequate rent, since, wherever housing was available, there was considerable competition for it. Types of dwelling are shown for 1912 in diag 12.08.

Rents.

This scarcity of housing was reflected in relatively high rents. A letter in the *Newcastle Chronicle,* in 1878, set the rent for flats at £14 to £16 per annum, plus £3 rates; that was about 7s weekly. A further letter from Sunderland gave the rent of a flat as 5s but this was one mile from the town centre. In 1890, the Newcastle Medical Officer reported a house in Bath Lane

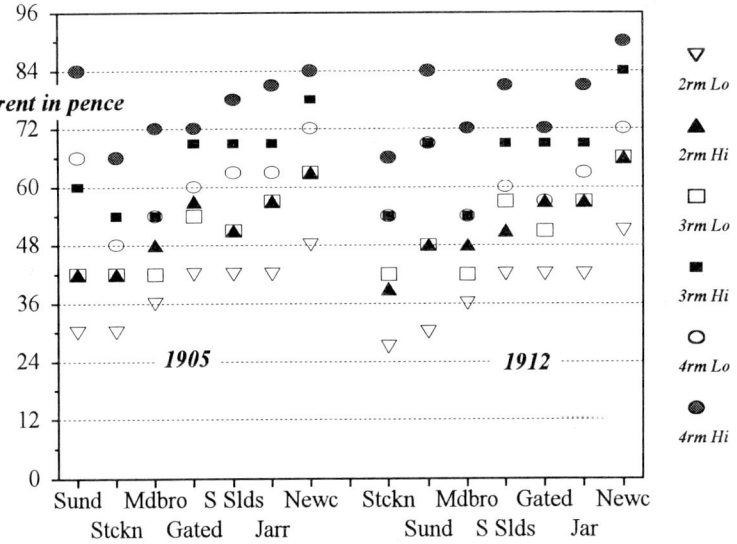

Diag 12.09

---

[83] A summary of commitments Aug. 1914 was as follows: Houses at Fisher Hill £7,500; Land at Wallsend £7,400; Contract price tenement Wallsend £15,332 - Heating[£1,045], fees[£766] extra roads[£247] £2,058; this made a total of £32,290. A proposal to build houses at Wallsend at cost of £37,000 was also considered.

[84] Indeed, Sunderland was one of the towns selected by the economic historian Prof. J H Clapham to illustrate a failure to make any improvement during the 20 years 1891-1911.

with 10 sub-tenancies yielding 61s 6d and gave instances of single rooms let at 5s to 8s, and pairs 6s to 8s. A distribution of rent paid by members of the *ASE* in 1892, showed that almost two-thirds of those outside London paid between 5s and 6s 6d in rent. For those trade unionists the average rent at Hartlepool, Darlington and Newcastle was 5s and, at Middlesbrough and Stockton, 5s 6d. The Manchester average was 5s 6d, Liverpool 7s 6d and London 9s. North East rents for engineering workers were on a par with Manchester. The *ASE* figures seem low compared with local figures. It might also be suggested that the available accommodation in the North East was less satisfactory than in many other parts of England. Twenty years later a Board of Trade survey gave a rent index, in which London [Middle Zone] was taken as a 100, Newcastle upon Tyne was next at 84, Jarrow was 73 [a point behind Birkenhead], Gateshead was 67 and Sunderland 66 [both higher than Manchester at 64] Middlesborough 61 [the same as Birmingham] and Stockton on Tees 55. A summary of the predominant weekly rents is shown in diag 12.09 [above], this clearly indicates the wide range depending on type of dwelling and location. At Gateshead the Co-operative Society offered flats at rents of 4s 6d and 7s 6d per week, it was said these were *above the level of the district*. The rents were 5*s* to 8*s* per week for Society dwellings at Sunderland, where the Co-op built some for sale at Roker. In the official *cost of living index* of 1914, rent & rates was allocated 16%, compared with food 60%.

Some summary comments.
These working men also wanted political advance and many of them participated in the parliamentary reform movements. A Great Reform Demonstration marched through Newcastle in 1867, estimated to be about 25,000 strong, accompanied by the large number of their bands[85]. The workers demonstrated their emerging new organisations in the era of iron steam ships and mechanical engineering and their dedication to their trades:

    Iron Shipbuilders & Boilermakers: *Industry the Wealth of Nations*
                          England's greatness - the working men.
    Amal. Society of Engineers: *May honest integrity ever be fairly rewarded.*
    Jarrow & Howdon Ironfounders & Shipbuilders :   *Success to Iron Shipbuilders*
                                          Let Trade in Jarrow Flourish
    Jarrow Ship Painters - Ironfounders & Smiths - Co-operative Smiths Society -
    North of England Chainmakers Assoc. - Brassfounders & Finishers
    Tyne Operative Plumbers Newcastle & Gateshead - Amal. Society of Joiners & Carpenters
    Jarrow Joiners - *models in wood ... Crystal Palace and a spiral staircase.*
    Workmen of the North-eastern Railway Workshops -
    Stephenson Workmen -   *Coal and iron the sources of national wealth -*
                                  By hammer and hand, All arts do stand
    Hawthorn's Workmen - Joicey's Workmen - Elswick Ordnance & Engine Works -John Abbott Ironworks
    Ouseburn Engine Works - banner included *a fine steam ship and a locomotive.*

There were of course many others, including miners under 15 colliery banners and chemical workers. These men even in their politics associated with their workplace, which was an integral part of their lives! Scottish and Irish workers and men from East Anglia had joined the expanding shipbuilding industry; many maintained their own cultural heritage and so enriched the social life of the north east. By the early 1870s there was a firm base of trade unionism, even though it was still weak in engineering. The *black squad* in the iron shipyards earned good money on piecework. Skilled leaders regularly emerged amongst the workers and some such as Burnett went on to become national trade union leaders. Winning the nine-hours day was a national advance won on the north east coast but no organisation of workers could stop the ravages of unemployment, the inevitable companion of the fluctuations of shipbuilding.

---

[85] These included: Hawthorn's Band, Howdon Drum & Fife Band, Elswick Ordnance & Engine Works; North-Eastern railway Workshops; Elswick Glee Club; Boiler-builders Band; Hawkes, Crawshay & co Band

Chapter 13

The Workers - Labour Relations in the Later 19th Century

So many contemporary readers have been subject to a sustained media and political campaign against workers' organisation that is perhaps important to start by recognising that there is the need to consider that our attitudes are conditioned by various fundamental considerations. If we view workers, by *hand or head*, as industrial units who should behave like machines then any of their *negative* or disagreeable responses are condemned. However, if workers are free human beings operating in a democratic society then they and their actions will be seen in a different light. Overwhelmingly most consumers were firstly workers and their role as workers is the source of the income they spend. Perhaps the words spoken in 1898 by Benjamin Browne, the head of Hawthorn-Leslie and a Conservative in politics, may illustrate these points:

> I must speak of our workmen, of their legitimate hopes and aspirations of matters which are liable to cause friction between them and their employers, and the hopes of improvement ... One of the greatest problem, if not the greatest problem in the life of a shipbuilder of today is the labour question ... When we consider the enormous number of men that are employed, each man has his own interests, his own difficulties, and the possibilities of misunderstanding, we see how very easy it is for friction to arise, and I sometimes question whether any transaction between man and man are, on the whole, carried on more smoothly than between employer and workmen, even our great strikes, enormous as they are, bear a very small proportion to the large numbers of men in the country who are working peaceably and quietly; and when you think often people quarrel with their neighbours and sometimes with their customers.[1]

Workers on the north east coast became famous for their trade union strength. It was not always so, but union membership advanced considerably after 1870. Some employers at the time had a more hopeful view of dealing with sound leaders of well-organised workers than facing the chaos of the diverse groups of the multitude of trades which formed a shipyard's workforce. This diversity resulted in more inter-worker differences than in many other industries and the employers indirectly used unions such as the Boilermakers to help *manage* their workforce. Workers, in the 1890s, achieved a further one hour reduction, the 12 o'clock Saturday, and for a few the 8-hour day. Earnings increased and for many pieceworkers substantial pay packages, but the fluctuations of the industry always made a comfortable life hazardous. A small proportion of women were in paid employment in the north east and hardly any of those were in shipbuilding although they were a significant part of the workforce in rope making.[2] Industrial disputes are almost akin to illnesses for a person. They were not the day by day relationship between worker and employer but rather the culmination of a breakdown in the normal conditions, sometimes leading to a stoppage of work. From the end of the 1870s, almost all the problems, which later so troubled the industry were present: demarcation, overtime, conflicts within the workforce, the ability or not of officials to persuade the men to accept advice, securing the regular operation of agreements and the haunting fear of

---

[1] Browne continued ... the idea that there would be no labour difficulties if there were no trade unions is wrong,... what grounds have we for thinking if there were no unions all men would be... self reliant workman, who thinks out every question for himself ... all our knowledge and all our experience goes to show that, at all times ... among men and women of all classes, the natural tendency of most people is to take the conventional view... Conventional customs, conventional wages and hours exist where there are no unions ... in cases of dissatisfaction, ... men, hitherto disunited, are liable at any time to hold a mass meeting, guided by impulse, elect the most plausible or violent men as their leaders and make demands of the most extreme order, such as the leaders of an experienced union would never adopt; and, worst of all, if an employer comes to a compromise with these ephemeral authorities, there is no safeguard that the men will not throw these leaders over and adhere to their old terms or demand something worse ...we are safer dealing with wise and experienced union leaders. See fn 32 re Palmer.

[2] In 1881 census: *Rope twine&c*: Sunderland 145m 65f, Gateshead 51m 91f and Newcastle 75m 23f. Rowe gave the economic activity rate in 1911 for females as almost 20% in South Shields and 25% at Sunderland. Males were nearly 83% of the occupied population in Durham, 78% in Northumberland and 70% for England & Wales.

no work. This brief account by a great character of shiprepair George Scorer is a way into our story. When he joined T & W Smiths in 1883, he found:

> all the shipbuilding tradesmen were members of a new union ... they called themselves Iron Shipwrights, but really they were wood shipwrights who worked at either trade as it suited them. I had a year or two of real misery and trouble. They were not organised, there was no one to appeal to in time of trouble, and men were allowed to call themselves rivetters, who would shovel in a few hundred rivets, get the Trade Union rate of pay and clear out - leaving us to cut out and replace their rivets as we found the leaks out when testing.

Robert Knight, general secretary of the Boilermakers,[3] visited Scorer, while he was off work with a sprained foot, and after Scorer related his difficulties, the Boilermakers agreed to take *our good men as full members*. Meetings were held and the men joined the regular black squad trade union.

The Boilermakers' Society.

Knight was a union leader who combined great qualities of leadership, substantial technical knowledge and the constant desire to lead a disciplined workforce. He always wanted members to abide by the negotiated agreements. He matched the qualities set out in the Union journal during an election for a full-time official: The applicant should be:

> A first class mechanic, and know ... the value of work, as he is ofttimes appealed to by both foremen and members.
> He should be a thorough honest man, one on whose word the employers and members can depend.
> ... a peacemaker ... remove all little causes of irritation as they arise, and not add fuel to the fire.
> He should be a man of unimpeachable character.

It was not only such leaders who were against strikes and hasty action. In 1873 *after mature consideration*, the Executive Council wanted a ballot taken upon any important questions, but *especially in cases of dispute that were likely to end in strikes, lockouts, or members losing their situations*. Two years later, the Teesside District Committee was hoping to avoid *that fearful curse, a strike* and described the winning of all non-members to the union as *the greatest guarantee against strikes*. Petty disputes were regularly condemned as well as the *unprincipled men* who block jobs without authority. They cautioned members against holding shop or street meetings *as such are illegal, unconstitutional and contrary to our rules*. As 1883 began, the Tyne & Wear District Committee hoped the year would be *exceptionally free from disputes*, and that members would *co-operate with us, in every way they can, to secure this result*. As much as possible petty disputes were to be avoided in the best interests of the Society. The Committee promised to do their best *to still further cement the good feeling which for a long time has existed in this district between ourselves and the employers*. A remarkable level of mutual trust was achieved by men such as the delegate James O'Neill[4], who related to a Royal Commission the normal procedure that every shipbuilder in Sunderland *sends me a book, made up by the draughtsmen, showing the sizes of the plates with the shells, decks, stringers and tanks throughout the ship, and I weigh those plates up and send them to the yard* if there are any differences O'Neill arranged matters and so the men had no cause for dispute. On occasions a vessel went to sea before prices were fixed for plating, such was the high standing built up by this man. The Wear membership supported O'Neill's attitudes as was reflected in the illuminated address given to him in 1891:

---

[3] Knight's son was a draughtsman in Smith's Pontoon Dept. and later manager at South Bank of the Docks Dept.

[4] O'Neill [1838-1913] was born in Manchester and started work at 14. He became foreman and joined the Boilermakers at Birkenhead in 1862. He was a Justice of the Peace at Sunderland. He refused nomination as a Parliamentary candidate and rejected various offers to become a technical delegate for the employers. In 1882, the Wear Platers made a presentation of a gold watch & chain and a purse of gold. Nine years later accompanying an illuminated address, the Wear members gave him 100 guineas, a silver-mounted walking stick, a gold appendage, a dressing gown and Mrs O'Neill a silver tea and coffee service and for Miss O'Neill a secretaire. He retired on the same pension as any other member of the Society; the severe depression when he retired meant that the usual collection for retiring officials was not made. The Wear Shipbuilders' Assoc. presented him with a cheque for £100 and a silver salver as *a token of respect and esteem* in 1907.

> You came among us a stranger, but your ability, straightforwardness, and honesty in all your dealings, soon endeared you to all ... We have also to thank you for bringing us safely through the many troubles and trials in which we have been placed from time to time, and also for the many disputes averted by your integrity and kindly counsel - not peace at any price, but peace with honour.

The District Delegate for Teesside, Richard Rothwell stated: *I have free entry to all the yards; in fact, the employers send for me as often as the workmen themselves, by these means we keep down disputes as ever we possibly can. I look upon a dispute in my district as being a sort of reflection on my character.*

The opening of the Boilermakers' Headquarters.

The key of the door of Boilermakers' new headquarters, Lifton House, was held by Sir Benjamin Browne, who was a major asset for north east industrial relations. Tom Mann, the famous trade union leader and socialist, related an encounter with Browne in Newcastle in 1887:

> we arranged to attend the cathedral church of St Nicholas in an orderly way, but in large numbers ... On the Sunday morning I was addressing a large meeting of the unemployed prior to marching to church, when I saw the chief superintendent of the police and the mayor [Benjamin Browne] come along and stand listening. Ignoring their presence I proceeded to arrange the procession for starting, when the mayor approached, saying, *Are you going to church?* I replied, *Yes, Mr Mayor*, and he inquired, *May I come with you? - With pleasure, Mr* Mayor. The mayor walked by my side into church and sat throughout the service with the unemployed. No disorder took place, and the same week at the town council meeting the mayor heartily supported some of the proposals we had made for the council's consideration. One of these, which was adopted, was the planting of trees around the Town Moor to give work some and to beautify the town.

Three years later, there was a different march. September 22nd 1890 was a great day for the 7,000 members of the Boilermakers' Society assembled for the opening of Lifton House in Jesmond; The local press reported:

> by noon the huge space from the foot of Grainger Street to the Cattle Market, and extending some distance along Westmoreland and Scotswood Roads was a dense sea of moving people... From a distance nothing could be observed but the constant wheeling of banners and other emblems carried high above people's heads ... At the order to move forward a dozen bands equally distributed over the whole line commenced to play, and the flying banners, the martial strains of the music, and the tramping of thousands of feet made an imposing and inspiring scene. Not only were the banners carried but there were some splendid models of ships, bridges, engines, boilers, furnaces, hammers, and other implements of work, all eloquently demonstrative of hardy toil.

Thomas Bell, Mayor of Newcastle, the Sheriff, the ex-Sheriff and others were present with Browne. Sir Benjamin was heartily cheered and he congratulated them all

> on the work they had accomplished. It was ... a great epoch in the Labour history of the country. [and] would be remembered with pride and satisfaction by all those who took a real interest in the well being of the working classes or in the industrial future of this country ... He was one of the employers ...who had always with his whole heart believed in and upheld Trade Unionism ... it was of very great benefit to employers of labour like himself - *nay, more, he said frankly that he very much doubted if it would be possible for the enormous enterprises of this country to go on as they did now if the workers were not organised so as to act with unanimity and system all through the country great.* [5] [emphasis-JC]

The Mayor, a substantial shipowner, described the Society of the Boilermakers as one of the *most powerful* in the country. He described shipbuilding as Britain's *chief industry of this great country - for without ships, and without the boilers and the engines which were fitted to navigate these ships, the future prosperity of this country would be in very considerable doubt.* Frank Fox[6] called the new buildings *a*

---

[5] These were not just sweet words for the occasion, as his speeches and writings after the *9-Hours* strike show. He also commented: *If every two or three men here and there were to rise up and attempt to carry out the fetish of competition and the law of supply and demand to an unlimited extent, and all the rest of it, he did not believe large industries would go on at all. It was better for everybody that there should be a steady organisation.*

[6] Fox was born at Sunderland in 1854 and joined Sunderland #2 in 1874. He became branch secretary 1879 and served on Executive Committee before going to South Wales. He headed the ballot for post of General Secretary in 1899 but then decided to take up post of Technical Delegate to Bristol Channel Ship Repairers' Association.

monument to the men who held aloft the banners ... when the night was the darkest and the storm raged the fiercest. He was followed by Durham born James Conley[7], who said:

> Very often the finger of scorn had been pointed at Trade Unionism... if their Society worked in the future as it had done in the past, hand in hand with the employers, it would be acknowledged and dealt with justly. They wanted a better share of the profits of their labour than hitherto. Employers like Sir Benjamin Browne they could always deal with, and he was very glad to say that other employers[8] were coming round to view Trade Unionism in the same light.

Location of Boilermakers' National Headquarters

Until 1897 the Executive Council of the Society was elected from the membership of the district in which the union's Headquarters was located. The growing importance of shipbuilding in the north east was no doubt an important factor in the Union's decision by ballot vote in the summer of 1879 to move the general office from Liverpool to Newcastle. This move was very important for industrial relations in the north east, as national officers were always at hand if required. In 1880 Knight entered his new office in 28 Archbold Terrace, where in the evenings the working boilermakers and shipyard workers of the Executive Council met with him to make decisions on the union's business. In evidence that was markedly hostile to trade unionism, M C James, Chairman of the North East Shiprepairers, said: *I have had frequent cases where I have had to telegraph to the head office, in Newcastle, to the General Secretary, and the Executive Council sits there every day, and then we get some sort of satisfaction.* Members of the last Executive Council elected from Tyne and Wear branches were C Laws, J Corbett, W Pye, J Matthews, G T Redhead and M Charlton.[9] Joseph Matthews joined the Boilermakers at Jarrow in 1880, became a shop steward and served on the local Trades Council. He was elected a member of the full-time Executive in 1897 and three years later became the Tyne delegate. He left this post in 1903 to take up *a responsible position of trust in a repairing establishment.* This was not seen as a betrayal as the *handsome testimonial* given to him and his wife by the Tyne members showed. Tynesider Readhead joined in 1878 and was Treasurer, Matthew Charlton joined at Sunderland in 1882, and was probably the youngest man to hold the Chairmanship of the Executive Council. These men, like many others, devoted much of their spare time to enabling their union to function and in helping to resolve the problems of its members. Full-time executive members were elected from 7 electoral district and R W Lindsay was one of those elected. He was born in Hartlepool, where he served his time and joined the union in 1882. He became secretary of #4 branch at Sunderland and in 1895 tried to secure a Boilermakers' Hall in the town. William Ryan succeeded Mathews on the full-time Executive in 1901 and although born in the North, he served his time as a plater at Oswalds in Southampton. After many jobs, returned to Howdon and became chairman of the Tyne District Committee. R Dunn was elected Tyne District delegate in 1892 and

Robert Knight

---

[7] James Conley was born in Tow Law on 29 May 1850. He worked at Readheads for 15 years and joined Boilermakers' Society in Feb. 1872and became branch secretary within a year. He was secretary of committee *instrumental in locating* General Office in Newcastle and unsuccessful in a bid to be Asst. Gen. Sect. in 1881. In 1887 became the Clyde District delegate. He was on the Boilermakers' panel of parliamentary candidates, as a Liberal *but unpledged to party measures*; in 1903 adopted as Labour candidate for Wednesbury [later withdrew]. In 1906 he polled 3,157 against Conservatives 3,749 in Kirkdale. Member of Partick Council and a J P.

[8] Shipbuilder Doxford: *very strongly in favour of strong unions, both ... of the men and the employers. I believe the stronger the unions are, the less likely there will be strikes.* Tees shipbuilder, Henry Withy, *the better relations ... are amply demonstrated* by the meetings of the employers and unions, *as a rule, we have little difficulty in dealing with the Unions which are old enough to have found out for themselves the value of organisations.*

[9] Cuthbert Laws joined in Newcastle in 1872, J Corbett also from the Tyne joined in 1880. W Pye joined when he was 20 at Howdon in 1877 and after moving to Sunderland was one of first elected to the Wear District Committee.

resigned in 1900; he later became the technical delegate of Tyne Shiprepairers Association.

Labour discipline - timekeeping & absenteeism.
The Society and its District Delegates played a part in the establishment of labour discipline within the shipyard. The following were amongst the most serious problems in the shipyard, aggravated when business was booming: [a] absenteeism and drunkenness, [b] the unfinished contract, including the failure to pay helpers, [c] pressure for higher payments when work was urgently needed. High earnings by the skilled shipyard workers sometimes meant that men would take days off, after pay day, either for leisure or drink. They were also inclined to extend the layoff period at unpaid holiday times. In 1901, shipbuilder Henry Withy said: *A very serious matter, especially in connection with shipyards, is the large amount of time lost by the workmen. The large amount of cheap excursions almost every week no doubt aggravates this evil, which has assumed startling proportions.* Two years later, *Palmer's Record* wrote: *as usual, on each occasion the holiday was extended by a full day*, the scale of the absenteeism was rarely given. The Boilermakers' monthly and annual reports regularly reported these problems. In May 1877, the Tees District Committee condemned drinkers in response to complaints from the employers. A year later the Tyne & Wear Committee reported that employers were *making great complaints against those losing time through drinking* and condemned such behaviour. At J L Thompsons in 1882, some were *behaving in a most unjust manner towards their employers, by remaining away from their work drinking.* The Council gave their only warning that *unless better time is kept* [they] *will be compelled to make an example of the defaulters.* Price of Palmers told a Royal Commission, in 1886, that during the previous ten years :

> we have seen a very marked improvement in the habits of the men and their general conduct ... more attentive to their duty ... more amenable to law and order, both amongst themselves and in all their relations to us; they are more thrifty and a great deal more sober; and in every respect in which we can be affected by their personal conduct ... we have found an immense improvement. I was anxious ... to state that, in connexion with what has been said about their wages, I believe we get more and better work from our men than we ever did.

In January 1884, *The Shipping World* wrote that with *this remarkable prosperity* [the 1883 boom], holidays had increased and they had *the authority of a large and accomplished builder for saying that, whilst the workmen are anxious for additional time for amusement and leisure, there is a manifest reduction in the excessive use of strong drink*, and that to be *drunk* was now looked upon *as a positive disgrace among the various craftsmen engaged in the shipyards*. At the annual meeting of the Hartlepool branch, Coulson, of Irvine's, spoke favourably of the sobriety and steadiness of the members of the Boilermakers' Society.

A determined campaign was waged by the Union against absenteeism. The Teesside secretary regretted *very much* having to call attention to men absenting themselves for two and three days after pay every fortnight. In 1878, foremen *could only muster 18 sets out of 32 at 9 a.m. Wednesday.* This was *very bad behaviour to employers, and the utmost folly to themselves.*[10] Tyne & Wear District officers wrote:

> Now is the time, in the height of the prosperity, to prove to our employers that, under all circumstances, we have never lost sight of the fact that their interests and our own are identical; ... the most substantial proof we can offer is regular attendance at work. Hoping the complaints...will grow less [and] cease entirely.

A year later, *by far the most important* problem was the irregular attendance of some of members at their work. Some were *disgracing our Society* by only working three days a week. Pieceworkers earning £1 a day may have placed leisure high on their scale of preferences. In 1889, there were complaints every week on the Tyne and *a great deal of trouble* due to *losing time*. Absenteeism at a Tees shipyard was *a disgraceful record*: in February one squad lost seven working days and six days were not worked by frame turners and two platers. Members were reminded of the fine [10s to £5] for misconduct injuring any employer. The Executive Council resolved that members losing more than one day each week *when he*

---

[10] Missing a quarter day was not confined to the Boilermakers. In the 1890s the marine engineering employers complained about bad timekeeping particularly on Monday morning, without giving any precise figures.

might be at work, shall be fined 5s for each day's absence; branch and district committees were charged to see this resolution was *rigidly enforced*. In 1889 at a special conference with north east employers Knight voiced his concern for the *serious effect on the character and life of the men* of such absenteeism and asked for the evidence *to enable the Society to convict* those guilty of this behaviour. This problem was never entirely mastered in the 19th century and an important local football match resulted in absenteeism well into the 20th century.

Paying helpers.
As part of their general philosophy of co-operation and joint interest, the Boilermakers' officials made great efforts to secure that their members honourably fulfilled all contracts with both employers and helpers. The *Monthly Reports* regularly named men who were in debt to their helpers and the Society expelled persistent offenders, for example the five members who refused to pay what they owed at Dixon's in 1883. Where members had defaulted, the Society paid direct compensation to individual firms. Early in 1884, Palmers accepted £7.72 in settlement of a claim for £11-6s. Knight explained to the Royal Commission, in 1892, that firms were paid for unfinished work and the members fined; this procedure he believed was *unique*. He made it clear *Our Council always compels our men to complete their* undertakings even if they were unable to make day rates of pay.[11] In 1882, two men were expelled at Sunderland *for bringing the Society into bad repute while working at the Mushroom yard, on the Tyne. They also left their helpers unpaid.* On Teesside, the District delegate said he was *dunned at every street corner by gangs of helpers who have thus been robbed* [with] *language a great deal more forcible than pleasant*. When finally the employers, took responsibility for the direct payment of wages[12] to the helpers and these men joined regular trade unions [from 1889] this problem became a minor matter. It was not raised as an important issue, when Labourers' Union leader Owen Wade gave evidence to the Royal Commission on Labour. [see below]

The growth of the Boilermakers' Society in the North East is shown in diag 13.01. Membership moved forward in leaps, usually in periods of prosperity and then levelled off. At a local level such set backs often meant members moving away rather than a man leaving the union. An unemployed man was required to travel in search of work and was issued with a travelling card. Membership dropped on Wearside during 1875 by 200. However, in the first three months, 53 new members were recruited, 51 members left [failure to pay dues &c] and 29 members were given travelling card to seek work; thus what appears as a loss of membership of 27 was a net gain of two members for the Society. Only in December, when only two joined and five left, did the number of new members fail to exceed the run-outs. The strength of the Society steadily increased, not only numerically but also in the quality of leadership. Bad conditions of trade always seriously affected trade union finances. In the badly depressed year of 1879, the Boilermakers were forced to raise subscriptions and the General Secretary's salary was reduced by 8% and the District delegates by 7½%. Three District posts were temporarily suspended including that at Teesside.

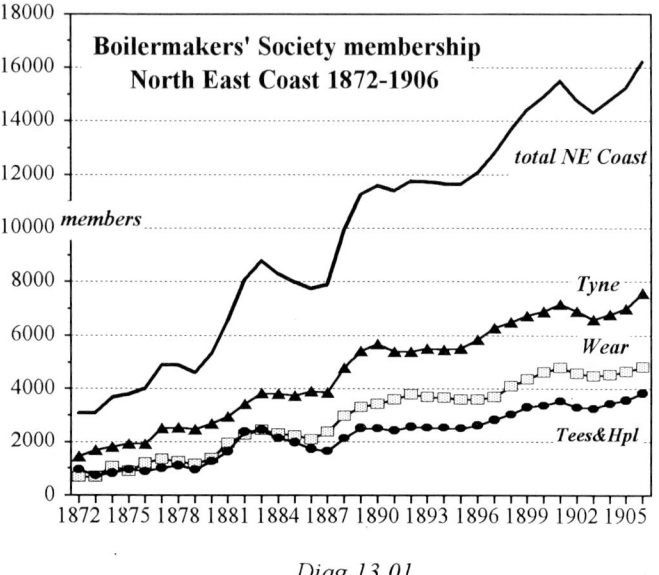

Diag 13.01

---

[11] At the Royal Commission of 1904, Inglis, of the Shipbuilding Employers', agreed that the Boilermakers insisted on no breach of contract and *paid damages for breach of contract by their members...on being asked.*

[12] Deductions continued, however, to be made from the craftsman's payment for his helpers.

Other important trade unions.

The shipwrights.

More shipwrights, on the north east coast, were trade union members in 1870, than iron shipbuilders [i.e. Boilermakers]. By 1883, the societies of shipwrights had only 2,971 members compared with the 8,768 in the Boilermakers' branches. Never registered as a trade union, the Wearside Shipwrights' Association[13] continued as a separate association until 1907. The membership was about 1,200 over the years 1892-5 and then rose sharply to 1,700 in 1897 before falling back to about 1,500, which remained the level of membership until what the Webbs called *a belated amalgamation* brought them into the national union. A very small Wear Shipbuilders' Association formed in 1872 joined the national Association in 1898. Those Wear shipwrights, who worked in iron, formed their own Society in 1882, and continued independently, until it joined the Wear Shipwrights' in 1899. This persistence of local societies was remarkable once a national trade union of shipwrights was formed, especially since the new society's headquarters was in Newcastle.

Blacksmiths & Drillers.

Trade unions for smiths and drillers began on Wearside in the 1870s. The Sunderland Smiths' Association had 212 members in 1876. When this union' wanted to join the Boilermakers', in 1882, Knight wrote: *their amalgamation will considerably strengthen our hands at Sunderland.* Frank Fox[14] led the opposition and the membership voted against. Eleven years later these smiths joined the *ASE*. In 1874, the drillers and hole-cutters formed a union and recruited just over 200 men; the 1870s slump reduced it to 96 members. These lower paid workers had even less chance than the skilled men of supporting a trade union, when unemployment was widespread. During the more prolonged slump of the mid-1880s membership fell to 68. During the upsurge of trade union activity in the boom of 1889-90, the Wear Drillers and Hole-Cutters Society was joined by the Sunderland and District Drillers and Hole-Cutters; these two societies amalgamated in 1904. Trade unionism among drillers on the Tyne and Tees began also in that late 1880s boom: no fewer than seven separate societies were formed on the Tyne. A Newcastle Drillers & Holecutters Society was formed in 1888, soon followed by others at Jarrow and South Shields. It seems likely that these societies or their members joined the National Drillers and Holecutters Union, when it began in 1892. The Rose of Tyne Society certainly did so, with 100 members, in 1893. Three years later the Byker Society with 63 members dissolved. When the National Drillers' association merged, in 1899, with the Associated Shipwrights, it had 2,327 members. Four associations of drillers were formed on the Tees: the Amalgamated Drillers of Stockton-on-Tees, the Onward Drillers & Holecutters of Stockton, Drillers and Holecutters of Hartlepool and the Cleveland Drillers & Holecutters. These amalgamated, in 1896, to form the Amalgamated Drillers and Holecutters, with some 300 members; the Onward Drillers remained independent, for another three years. Thus slowly did these small local societies merge into larger district groups and finally national unions.

Unions for the semi-skilled and labourers.

Probably the first independent strike action by the helpers occurred in May 1871, at three Wearside yards, and a short lived trade union was formed. Quite unworthily the *Sunderland Times* described them as *the very lowest form of unskilled labour*. A striker denied this stating they were not *unskilled* men, many had *been 13 years at the business* and *frequently* instructed an apprentice or *unskilled 'wright*. Without organised support they lost and were replaced. At the first annual dinner of the Amalgamated League of Shipyard Workers & Labourers, the shipwright Boldon spoke of the *two great antagonists, the employers and the Boilermakers societies*. Both the Trades Councils of Newcastle and Sunderland offered moral

---

[13] In 1898, the Hylton shipwrights after a half century of independence joined the Wear Shipwrights Society.

[14] Fox later acknowledged this was an error of judgment. In 1899 when a small society of iron shipwright wanted to join the Boilermakers' Society, the Sunderland members through a local employer stopped these men working. They finally found jobs elsewhere.

support to the helpers and raised their case, without success at the TUC in both 1877 and 1878. James Lynch, the leader of the helpers' union, in 1885[15]described the position as he saw it:

> the ship-platers and their assistants, commonly known as *helpers*. The system of work and payments ... involves a most unfair division of wages earned, and subjects the helper to many grievous injustices besides the mere disparity of remuneration ... a mixed system of piecework for the platers and time-work for the helpers, both being engaged conjointly on the same work. The plater being paid by result at high-pressure speed, and the helpers, although paid by the day or hour, must of necessity keep pace with them. It will be easily understood how the helper who has no special incentive to exertion is made to keep up with the plater ... I need hardly say that the means by which this is accomplished are demoralising to both the plater and helper. They are nominally fellow work-workmen, but *they are actually taskmaster and serf.* [emphasis -JC] Those ... acquainted with shipyard work will know these terms...are not misplaced. To show the unfairness of the division of piece wages ...In the recent busy period the helpers' time wage on the Wear was 4s. per day, and the platers' time wage was 6s. per day. The price for shell-plates requiring six men to work them was at that time not less than 10s. per plate ... in a fairly well-regulated and well-appointed yard ... the receipts of helpers and platers ... were scandalously disproportionate. Three platers working in company completed 18 plates per day ... for ... £9... they paid 3s to a boy, the remainder ... between themselves and the helpers ... two squads of six men each ... each helper received 5s ... each plater received £1 19s.
>
> On other classes of work the disproportion is not so great, but there is no instance in which the plater does not receive at least three times as much as the helper, while in strict justice he is entitled to no more than three-fifths to the helper's two-fifths, [the] proportion usually found to exist between the time rates of each class... in the shipbuilding industry the injustice and inequality are immensely aggravated, owing to the precariousness of employment. Stoppages from various causes are of constant occurrence... in brisk times only four days a week can be worked ... while in slack times ... two days per week ... speaking of stoppages over which the men have no control ... [in addition] The platers frequently lie off work for purposes of pleasure or dissipation, and sometimes two or three days together are lost in this way,[16] the plater can make up for the loss when he returns ... by driving still harder the helpers... The platers will not start work of a morning if there is a sign of bad weather to be observed, or they cannot see the prospect of being able to make what they term *a good day's work*. Both summer and winter they absent themselves from work during the first quarter ... very frequently - as often as three or four mornings a week. All the abstentions are a loss to the helpers, for the platers invariably refuse to pay them for lost time. When the plater stops off *first thing*, the helpers who are on the ground at six o'clock...have to wait till breakfast time, and then start for a three-quarter day, or perhaps only a half or quarter day ... I will not say that there is not now and then to be found a liberal-minded plater, who is willing to pay his men for at least a portion of the time lost through his fault, but such are rare exceptions, and if they do pay their men they must do it secretly, to avoid the displeasure of the others. Not to be unjust ... I ... admit that the helpers are sometimes absent when the platers are present, but this need never be a cause of loss to the platers, as there are always plenty of the helper class on the ground to supply the places of absent men, while the places of temporarily absent platers are seldom or never filled up.
>
> The shipbuilders will not move in favour of the helpers, and the platers will not voluntarily relinquish their unjust privileges. There is not the smallest chance, at least in this generation, of the helpers being able to conquer justice for themselves. They have tried it more than once, but have always failed, and the recollection of these failures will prove an effectual preventive (for many years to come at all events) to their making any further efforts. The chief cause of their failures ... the little difficulty met with in filling their places by the importation of men from other districts... I know of no way to remedy the helpers grievances except legislation.

At first Lynch seemed to make progress in contacts with the Wear Shipbuilders' Association in 1879 but this did not continue very long. A sustainable trade union came with the newly formed unions of the 1880s.

---

[15] This extended extract shows how Lynch presented his case and should be viewed in the light of points made throughout this history of shipbuilding. [at *Industrial Remuneration Conference*, pp 114-8 in reprint of 1968].

[16] The Wear shipbuilders wrote to Knight on 5 June 1883 complaining *they feel bound ... to repeat their dissatisfaction with the very irregular attendance of a large proportion of your members which is now become so frequent an occurrence*. Even allowing for exaggeration, it does confirm in boom times this was a problem.

The National Labour Federation[17] was founded on Tyneside in 1886 with the help of *ASE* members to recruit unorganised workers. In March 1888, this general union established a dispute fund. Drillers at Hartlepool and helpers in Stockton were recruited in 1891, besides women in South Shields glassworks and trimmers at Sunderland. Early in 1889, there began a much more important development which led to the extensive and permanent organisation of the helpers in the shipyards and the unskilled in the engineering works. A labourer [Elswick Works] wrote to the *Newcastle Chronicle* pointing out their lack of organisation and calling for assistance. The leaders of the Newcastle & Gateshead Trades Council immediately responded and called a meeting, which was chaired by Councillor J C Laird, the man who had raised the helpers' problems at the TUC. Thomas Burt was the principal speaker at a very well attended public meeting on 16 February, where William Stanley moved that *it could be to the advantage of the Labourers on Tyneside that they at once join this association, which has for its object to better their condition, and for the social elevation of the labouring classes generally*. The Tyneside Labourers' Association[18] was formed on 23 February 1889 and grew rapidly. On 2 March, the *Newcastle Chronicle* reported that six Lodges already existed in Newcastle, one in Walker and one in Jarrow. The committee was in touch with other bodies of labourers and *some meetings were so crowded that many intending members could not come forward to register their names*. This union included the unskilled in chemical works, dockyards, cement works, masons, labourers and those in shipyards and engineering workshops. On 21 May, the Executive of the Engineering Employers' met a delegation from the Tyneside Labourers' Association, with Stanley as secretary. A few weeks later, the Wallsend branch was in contact with Swan & Hunter. Armstrong's manager Black sent for both Knight and Stanley to help resolve a stoppage by angle-iron smiths' strikers. In November, Price contacted the Labourers' Union when union members tried to oblige twenty others to join the union. At the annual meeting on 4 August 1890, Stanley reported:

> The employers resented for a time what they preferred to believe an unwarrantable intrusion but now, instead of being ordered off the premises as interlopers, your delegates are eagerly sought after by employers, whenever a hitch in their works occurred.

This recognition probably owed something to the approach of these union leaders, not their *pliability* but that they, like many of their craft brothers, eschewed strikes as far as possible. Stanley said: *Arbitration - the watchword of well regulated labour combinations - became an everyday factor in the carrying on of society*. Owen Wade, delegate of the Tyneside & National Labour Union [later the National Amalgamated Union of Labour], also rejected strikes and declared himself for voluntary boards of conciliation and arbitration. Before the end of 1889, Mitchell of the Labourers' Association was negotiating for a wide range of *labourers*, such as the sailor gangs, iron shifters, scrap gatherers, screwers down at planing machines, as well as the labourers to the painters, joiners, shipwrights and furnace men.[19]

Owen Wade[20] together with a plater's helper Andrew Hare, then the Hartlepool branch secretary, in their evidence to the Royal Commission on Labour in May 1892, repeated many of Lynch's comments. When

---

[17] E R Pease [1857-1955], of the Fabian Society chaired the first meeting. Rev Moore Ede was a trustee.

[18] Clegg, Thompson & Fox suggested that the *initial motive behind the formation ... had been to provide protection for the platers' helpers and other assistants employed by the skilled craftsmen of the Boilermakers' Society*. Current press reports offer little to support this view, nor the evidence of Owen Wade, to the Roy Comm, in 1892: *I can scarcely go over them all* [the workers covered] in early April they were organising the tramway workers.

[19] In May 1892, Wade referred to Stanley as *the late general secretary*. The new secretary was Londoner A P Dipper who worked from 169 Westgate Road Newcastle. Twelve men served on the Executive Council, their President John Raffery worked in Palmers Boiler Shop. There were 24,000 financial members with a further 16,000 above 8 weeks in arrears with subscriptions; most were in the north east and *a fair share in* Lincolnshire.

[20] Wade claimed that half his Union members working in the shipyard were *competent to ... do the same work as the platers are doing*. If platers caught a helper *making any signs of to do a bit of a job for himself he is very soon told about it not to do it. In regard to lining a plate off, or anything like that, for his mates, he is told to put the chalk line down ... and to mind his own business*. Wade acknowledged to former Tyneside apprentice and Belfast shipbuilder Eric Harland that the plater had learned his skill through an apprenticeship, an opportunity the helper had not had but tried to maintain his point for some cases.

informed that the Labourers' Union's complaints were *principally against* his Society, Knight indignantly retorted -*Indeed*. He continued *I could occupy your time for about two hours in giving you an idea of the tyranny of the labourers and the helpers... We do not want to pay the helper*. For him, the divergence of interests between the two unions would go *if we could only get the labourers to keep their places; that is the difficult point of the dispute. I mean the plater is the mechanic, and as a matter of course the helper ought to be subservient and do as the mechanic tells him*. Wade pointed out that although the foremen hired the helpers the plater dismissed men without notice; however, he acknowledged that with the foreman's help they did secure the return of men. Only in some yards did the office deduct the helpers' pay from the amount due to the plater, elsewhere the plater put his hand in his pocket and said *That is yours*. On the Tyne, only the small yards paid through the plater. Wade rejected the suggestion that some men in a squad were paid more than others and claimed that payments were no longer made in pubs and concluded that how the helpers were paid made *very little difference* to their condition. Only three north east yards then were paying helpers piece work, according to Hare. O'Neill of the Boilermakers could not recollect *any friction* in relations with the helpers for the previous ten years and set out the agreement on the Wear between the platers and their helpers:

> [1] where the plater is absent from work and his men have to lose their quarter, they will be paid for the same by the plater. [2] If in during the same pay [week], any individual helper lose a first quarter, he forfeits his claim under the first clause. [3] plater only responsible for paying helpers actually in the yard and ready to work within ten minutes of the regular starting time in the morning. In another yard, the actual times were set out and that *Any dispute between the platers and helpers, the local secretaries of the workmen to be informed, for the purpose of arranging any question in dispute; in the meantime, no stoppage of work to take place*.

The growth of Trade Unionism in Engineering.

Some engineering union leaders evoked more hostility and difficulties than their fellows in shipbuilding. In the north east there was no equivalent in shipbuilding to Armstrong's dominant position in engineering and the attitude of this giant to unions was very important. Technological change, in the form of advances in machine tool design[21], more quickly threatened the status of the craftsman in engineering than was possible in the shipyard, where such advances were due to 20th century technology. However, given the *tailor-made* nature of much of marine engineering, these technical changes had a lesser impact in marine work than in others fields of engineering. None the less, in the Jarrow works a potential road to higher skills was available for many years. *Any labourer can make a driller,* Price said in 1886, and *a drilling machine man is occasionally moved up to a slotting machine or a planing machine, and a planing machine man ultimately in some cases, but not frequently, becomes a lathe man.* Eight years later, Thomas Richardson was saying the *unfortunate doctrine ... as to our superior craftsman is by no means as true as formerly. The chief cause of this levelling up* was the *extended and universal adoption of machinery;* the opportunities for this in

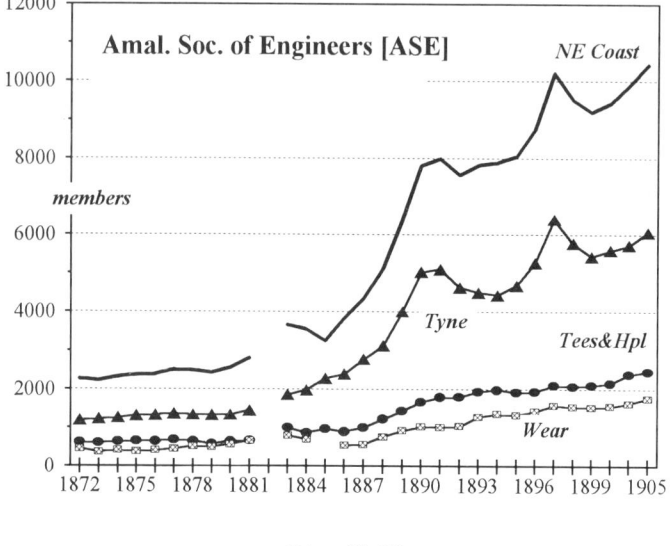

Diag 13.02

---

[21] The *chief difficulty of the ASE,* Clapham wrote, was the *ease, the growing ease, with which engineering could be picked up by the smart lad or labourer, who started perhaps as a minder of some straight forward machine* [or] *as a general utility hand in a little agricultural shop.* This was an oversimplification; some firms were instaling semi-automatic machines, which enhanced the opportunities for *machinists* as distinction from all round craftsmen.

engineering was *practically unlimited*. Less than 2,000 workers in the north east were *ASE* members in 1871; membership grew sharply after 1881 and before the end of the century more than 10,000 were in the union [see diag 13.02]. An important part of the rise was due to the expansion of engineering. The region made up just over 5% of the total *ASE* in 1871 and about 11% in 1891-1901; it was 9% in 1911.[22] An estimate of 90% union membership, in 1892, by the local *ASE* secretary Glennie was optimistic, even for skilled workers. A *very large number* of non-Society men were *employed on Tyneside, especially at Elswick*, when the 1897 engineering dispute began, according to the *Newcastle Chronicle*. Craftsmen formed and lead the *ASE* but its policy of recruiting only skilled workers was a drawback to the advance of trade unionism in engineering for many years.

Other New Trade Unions & Trades Councils.
Until *the turbulent period* following the *9-hours* strike, many patternmakers[23] joined one or other of the existing engineering unions, then the United Patternmakers' Association was born on Tyneside. General secretary W Mosses believed his trade was then *highly probable ... the worst organised* in engineering; apathy among the men made it difficult to form a union. A few enthusiasts, who circulated rules written on sandpaper and then contacted those who showed interest, finally achieved their objective. At Sunderland 27 men were enrolled in March 1872, and 15 attended the first Tyneside meeting at Gateshead. Members were also recruited in Stockton and South Shields. Simply starting a branch was never enough and an attempt was made to disband the Newcastle branch before its first anniversary. At Middlesbrough a branch was re-established twice in the first ten years, in other words three starts before a stable branch succeeded. Such were the difficulties of establishing a new trade union. At this time, Mosses thought the union was *too insignificant and sectional to attract the attention of the employers*. In 1882 in the Pattern Shop of the main Stockton firm, the 29 workers were in three unions: 11 - United Patternmakers; 10 - *ASE*; 2 - Carpenters and Joiners [6 older men were outside the union because of entry age &c]. *War to the knife* was the attitude of the *ASE* to the Patternmakers, in 1885, according to their historian. Such could be the intensity of inter-union rivalry. In 1892 their were 466 members in the 8 branches of the Patternmakers .

At the *Nine Hours Inn* in mid-February 1872 a meeting of delegates of machine-men, from many firms, considered establishing a trade society. A week later, the branch formed became part of the Combined Metal Planers, Shapers & Slotters Society, a union centred on Manchester. During the 1880s, the United Machine Workers were recruiting on the north east coast and, by 1891, had branches in Newcastle, Sunderland, Hartlepool [160 members] and Stockton [74]. Excluded from the ranks of the *ASE*, the semi-skilled workers formed their own unions. The National Trade Society of Engineers had members from Hartlepool to Jarrow. To this multitude were added unions for plumbers, coppersmiths, brass workers, iron founders and workers in wood. The mere number of these societies is a small indication of just how complicated problems of labour relations could be in both shipyard and marine engine works. Two years after the first attempt, a Newcastle Trades Council was established in January 1873, at *a very enthusiastic* meeting under the leadership of a patternmaker, a printer, a baker and a blacksmith. A Trades Council was set up South Shields in 1872 and two years later the Sunderland United Trades Council was formed. Not until 1890, were trades councils formed at Hartlepool and Stockton & Thornaby. These trades councils provided a forum where trade unionists exchanged ideas, formulated policies of common interest and could organise mutual support. The South Shields Trades Council organised a 3,000 strong joint procession on the Criminal Amendment Act, in 1873. Trades councils helped to organise the unskilled.

---

[22] *ASE* membership increased nationally from 98,666 [1905] to 110,084 [1907] a rise of 12%; it fell back in two depressed years and reached 121,469 in 1911 and exceeded 200,000 by 1915. Trade unions became *approved societies*, under the 1911 National Insurance Act and this probably helped increase membership.

[23] These highly skilled craftsmen made the wooden patterns for the moulds required for iron castings. In 1870s at Palmer's engine there were about 20 men, 10% of the number of fitters & turners. The 1901 census - 523 patternmakers [6,588 fitters &c] in Northumberland and 1,049 patternmakers [10,361 fitters &c] in Durham.

The Foreman.

It would be difficult to exaggerate the importance of the foreman, and his role increased in significance as growth in size of businesses reduced the ability of the master-employer to keep contact directly with his men; then in Spence's words only foremen could *know most of the men intimately.* An engineer, J W Haldane, wrote in 1887 of the foreman's *considerable responsibility,* standing between the masters and the men, and their object was *to please the former by getting as much good work out of the latter as possible, and at the same time, to be kind, just and not overbearing to them.* Those *very disagreeable and exacting* foremen could not keep their *hands,* if they could get a job elsewhere, the men *dislike such overseers far more than bad masters, because they are always among them ... it was not considered etiquette for masters or managers to interfere with or give directions to men or boys except through their chiefs in the workshops.* There was also another essential function of the foreman, that of *an inspector* to see that the work was performed satisfactorily. *One of the most important matters,* said the Teesside engineering employer Tom Westgarth, was the selection of works managers and foremen; there were *few more difficult positions than that of works manager, because there must be a sufficient firmness to secure obedience and respect, yet there must be a feeling on the part of the men that the manager is their friend.* He added pointedly that many works managers *consider too much the former question.* Works managers were *head foremen* for much of the nineteenth century. Westgarth was one of those who clearly grasped that this two-way character of the job lay at the core of labour relations problems - mutual interest. In the 1890s, W G Spence of Wigham Richardson's emphasised that it was *more than ever important* to have foremen of such a character that they were *not afraid* to present the workers' case to the manager, and added that firms were more depended upon good foremen *than they ever got credit for.* Summers Hunter recognised that *friendly feeling ... really commenced with the foreman.* Glennie, in 1892, spoke of the tyranny of the foreman and the secretary of the Steam Engineers Society claimed that the men were *worked much harder and kept under closer surveillance* than 20 years earlier. Drawings were often inadequate and, sometimes, nonexistent; the order of operations as well as the requisition of materials were often decided on the shop floor by foreman and craftsman. Over the years 1860-1880, *almost every yard had its own practice, very much according to the vagaries of the foreman plater,* according to R H Muir: such technical influence by foreman continued long after 1880. The inventor of many hydraulic machines, R H Tweddell, regarded *the foreman* classes a source of *valuable information* for the NECIES. Foremen were paid much less than their responsibilities merited; 431 foremen on the north east coast in 1906 averaged only 51s/week in shipbuilding, those in engineering a little more at 52s 2d. Those men working *a full week* averaged 54s in the yards with a quarter of them on 60s or more; the median rate was 50s and the lowest quarter was on 45s or less. On average there were 83 workers per foreman but many were responsible for a much larger number of workers. As early as 1853, the London Association of Foremen Engineers & Draughtsmen was formed and a similar body began in Manchester, three years later; these organisations were primarily devoted to technical matters. A similar body began in Newcastle in 1871, and local employers spoke at its meetings and dinner functions.

William Mould of T & W Smith a typical foreman

Hiring & the Foreman.

Men were hired and fired by the foreman. As Alex Wilkie, of the Shipwrights, said, the foreman when taking on workers *had to judge as to whether the men suit him or not.* They also engaged the semi-skilled and unskilled. There were some occasions on which the higher management intervened, for example in June 1876, the office stopped the employment of boilermakers engaged by Dixon's foreman. Until trade union minimum rates were negotiated, a man's wage rate was usually left to the foreman, even at a firm as large as Armstrongs. Before the mid-1880s there was considerable variation in the rates paid for the same job in one firm, apart from different companies. By and large, the shipwrights had achieved a minimum rate before their fellow wood workers. It was not until 1884 that the joiners managed to secure a uniform 35s a week when accepting a wage reduction. Previously, Tyne delegate W Patterson explained, the men were *paid anything they could get. The foreman used to fix the price*. Some joiners, on as little as 27s, received an increase when with this reduction a uniform rate was introduced. As the hirer of labour, the foreman had considerable arbitrary power, especially among unorganised workers, and the abuse of this authority caused much distress. The foreman was certainly in a position to aid or hinder trade union development. He might either directly employ trade unionists, or indirectly help by showing a tolerant attitude to the shop steward or trade unionist who attempted to recruit members in the works or shipyard. To build a trade union in the face of the serious hostility of the foreman, when he had such power as he had, would have been difficult. Wear Boilermakers frankly stated, in 1877, they were *very likely to get full possession* of Thompson's shipyard since a member was now foreman. He had *already done good service by discharging several of the blacks and employing our members in their stead*. If as the Webbs claimed no plater or riveter outside the union could get a job on the north east coast, this must have meant that foremen would refuse them employment. Jeffreys, the historian of the *ASE*, wrote *A further obstacle to finding jobs was the growing insistence that foremen should not be Society members*. He probably over estimated the success of the employers' attempt to get foremen to leave their society. The unions played a role in placing workers in jobs.[24] Employers came to regard the services of the Boilermakers as useful, no doubt largely because, as suggested above, the trade societies usually contained the best craftsmen. When a dispute at Leslie's yard was settled, in 1878, the management made it a condition that members of the Boilermakers' Society would apply for work there as elsewhere on the river. Almost any issue of the Boilermakers' Monthly Reports provided ample evidence of this. Details of the requirements of North East firms often appeared in the Monthly Report, for example No 115: *Leslie's seek 200 men* and No 126: *shell platers & riveters wanted J L Thompson, (Sunderland)*. Following his successful efforts to regain entry of Society members to the important marine engine works of Blair's[25], Knight received an acknowledgement of the value of his men. *The result has proved as you said it would, that we could not do better than employ your Society men*, Blair wrote on 5 January 1882, *long may you live to assist in giving reasonable counsels, and thus making your Society men not objectionable but desirable to all employers who need their services*. Most likely the foreman generally played a neutral role. Westgarth did *not think that foremen as a rule knowingly allow the influence of their trade societies to have weight with them*, but added *it is contrary to nature that they should be able to act entirely independently of the Society of which they have been a member for many years*. From the 1880's employers insisted *the character note* was issued when a man left any firm; this was a source of continuous concern to workers. The note *would pursue the workman who dared to make a complaint*, according to Glennie and even Sir Andrew Noble acknowledged that *no doubt if a foreman has a grudge, it might affect the character as entered in the book, but we cannot help that ... You must take the character the foreman gives*.

Undoubtedly there was a persistent pressure on foremen to minimise costs and this was particularly strong in periods of depression. Henry Withy told his fellow employers of *a little plan*. The *total time* was made up to Tuesday night and on Thursday each foreman was informed of the amount due to every man, which enabled *the foreman to see where the money was going, and induced him to keep his list down as small as possible*. Such cost cutting efforts caused difficulties for the Boilermakers' Society directly but also in regard to the position of the foreman; in general the union had no sympathy with those members who tried to take unfair advantage of the foreman. Indeed their Reports were frequently urging members to do their

---

[24] In 1883, a shiprepair foreman Clouston saw the Society secretary to arrange to get 20 men *as early as possible will wire him to night* [send a telegram].

[25] Mortimer wrote that the Union recruited 80% for the trade at Blairs during 1872-3, *despite the hostility of the firm*, but after a locked out in 1874 jobs were found elsewhere. He did not relate the events of 1882.

duty by their foremen, in 1882 members were told to be *true to our Society, and honest to their foremen.* In the mid-1870s depression the Teesside Boilermakers complained that some foremen were *trying to reduce prices still further*. At Leslie's of Hebburn, the men claimed they faced dismissal if they did not accept the foreman's reductions. In 1885, a few foremen [union members] were acting *in a very arbitrary and unprincipled manner ... to reduce wages to the lowest ebb* on the Tyne and Wear. Even sharper comment came from Teesside: *some foremen are worse than the employers for cutting down prices*, while pressure from the employers was recognised it was hoped *these remarks will be taken home and the results prove beneficial*. Later a Tyne foreman was accused of seeking estimates in Scotland and that foremen members in some yards on the Tyne and Wear were *not slow to take every advantage of their men*. In more comfortable times the Union supported its foremen. When a foreman faced a claim for an extra 2s, at Hartlepool, he telegraphed Knight who replied that the men should be given the money to avoid delay and an account of the extra cost sent to him. He despatched a cheque to the firm to cover the cost and later recovered it from the men.

The foreman might have been a thorn in the worker's side but he may also have been a significant ally. At the first Sunderland rally for the 9-Hours Day, a cry from the audience against the foremen was rebuffed by the platform with the remark *Leave the foremen alone*. It is very likely that many foremen, and in some trades almost all, were trade unionists. Undoubtedly in the early years of shipbuilding and in the small engineering works, the foreman was *a superior workman, himself, executing, or assisting in the execution of some, usually the more difficult, portions of the work*. However, as a superior craftsman, they were likely to have been trade unionists and there is much direct evidence of this.[26] Manager W G Spence, well understood the position, and pointed out that generally when a foreman was appointed he had *sunk a good deal of money in some trade society ... unions were, so far as he knew, the only friendly societies which paid out of work benefit*. A foreman at Clarke's, of Gateshead, sued the *ASE* over his expulsion, following the *9-Hours* Strike, after being a member for ten years. The Boilermakers' Reports contain many references to foremen members; and in a ballot vote 4,605 members voted for and 5,784 against foremen being allowed to sit on the Executive Council.[27] W J Watson, gave up his post as Howdon branch secretary to become head foreman plater at Stephensons at Hebburn in 1897, then returned with the tools at Hawthorns before being elected a Tyne District delegate 1901.The Tees District delegate was a foreman for 14 years and the following is a sample of others in Boilermakers' Society:

J Young, platers and caulkers - Swan & Hunters.   W Smith, - Oswalds
R S Webster, plater - Scotswood yard.   D Patrick, plater - Armstrong-Mitchell.
S Brooks, plater left Leslie's for Hartlepool   J Robertson riveter - Doxford
B Black, under manager Newcastle   P Muir plater - Schlesinger, Davis & Co
J Cameron, head foreman Richardson & Duck.   John Hall, Sunderland.
J Bell, riveter - R. Thompson.

The rules of the Wear Shipwrights provided penalties for foremen who did not follow the union rules. Many foremen were amongst leading members of local Co-operatives including:

Thomas Cockburn - shipwright, Armstrong's Walker yard. 17 years Treasurer of the Shipwrights' Society.
William Graham [died 1894] - foreman Armstrong, 37 years secretary of the ASE
R Casson [died 1909] - engineer in a shipyard, played a leading part in trade union and socialist circles.
Thomas Brandon [died 1894] - sawyer at Wigham Richardson [not stated to be a trade unionist].

Before the 1890's, there is little if any evidence of pressure on foremen to leave their union. After the engineers' dispute of 1897, the Engineering Employers' Federation attempted to secure a much more active policy of exclusion from union membership. Dyer of Armstrongs was the leader of these employers and

---

[26] At the Erle Commission, W Allan of the *ASE* denied that trade unionism prevented men becoming masters and said: *it has the contrary effect ... because the bulk of the superintendents of railway works and large managers have at one time been members of the society*. His questioner, W Matthews, agreed. W Knighton, chief foreman of the Stavely Coal & Iron Co foundry said: *I paid to the union till two or three years ago.*

[27]The north east coast voting by branch was : *For*:- Sunderland, Howdon, Wallsend, Byker, E Hartlepool. *Against*:- Newcastle no2, Gateshead, Hebburn, Jarrow, North Shields, Middlesbrough, Stockton.

the Federation's view was reflected in the north east. The following were some opinions expressed:
> Westgarth: *foremen on being appointed should certainly cease to be members of trade societies*
> Boyd: it was certainly *inconsistent and objectionable* that foremen *should at the same time be allowed to remain members of trade unions* and
> Henry Fownes: *foremen and managers were doubtless better clear of any connection which did not enable them to exercise their function absolutely impartially.*

It was recognised that other means than trade unions must be found for foremen to insure provision for old age and sickness; that of course left out unemployment. Foremen's Benefit Societies were formed but their success was hardly encouraging for the employers. Foremen at Elswick opposed a superannuation scheme which seemed *to contemplate that all foremen give up their connection with the several unions to which they belong.* At the Wallsend Slipway, the Foremen's Benefit Society was formed in January 1899 and Boyd wrote: *Several difficulties prevented the foremen from joining the new Society for many years, and it was not until May 1907 that they joined in any numbers.* There were 15 members in October 1911. Trade unions remained the chief benefit societies for foremen for many years after 1900.

Workers continued to be prepared to attempt to secure the removal of undesirable foremen, if need be, by strike action. Workers of a Sunderland shipyard turned out, in November 1872, when a recently appointed manager discharged the old foreman. Considerable discussion preceded the stoppage with meetings at both the breakfast and dinnertime breaks. Those against strike action secured the support of a branch meeting in the evening and the men resumed work; a deputation discussed the matter with their employer when he returned from London. Early in 1874, Hawthorns appointed a young man *unknown to the department* as under-foreman and the *greatly respected* head foreman of 27 years service was paid off. Fifty craftsmen took strong exception to this and gave in their notice: these men admitted the firm's right to appoint whom they wished but they would not work under him. When in 1876, iron shipbuilders at Gray's yard struck against a foreman, *who was obnoxious to them*, it was *amicably arranged* after the foreman gave a month's notice. Such disputes did not often occur for the Boilermakers after this.[28] Over 400 shiprepair workers, in 1900 at Wallsend, were out for 8 days in an attempted to remove an offending official. A dispute involving 38 drillers, at Sunderland, was resolved after 6 days, when an objectionable foreman was replaced by his assistant. In 1901 at Walker, 425 Boilermakers refused to work under a draughtsman appointed foreman; they stopped work for 4 days and made a further 450 men idle: they resumed when it was agreed that this man would have no dealings with the workmen, although he would supervise the shipyard. Later, at Hebburn, 96 ships' smiths and their strikers were out for three days in sympathy with a foreman they believed wrongly dismissed. At West Hartlepool, the trade union leadership intervened to secure the return to work of 225 striking riveters and their assistants, who had objected to the foreman's action in changing the mode of work.

Industrial Disputes & labour issues 1870s & 1880s.

There were a number of significant disputes in the 1870s. Managers at Palmers's mishandled the outcome of the *9-hours* strike. New overtime regulations resulted in 700 Engine Shop workers stopping work on Thursday 7 January 1872. A delegation elected at a mass meeting secured sufficient satisfaction to return on Monday. [29] A notice posted on Saturday 20 January that the shipbuilding department hours from the following Monday would be 6.30 a.m. to 5.30 p.m. [5 p.m. was part of *9-hour* agreement] caused nearly 2,000 men to turn out on Monday; a deputation of 16 men was elected to meet manager McIntyre, who agreed to 5 p.m. After hearing the deputation's report the men decided that a committee should continue to look after their interests, a further example of the *ad hoc* arrangements when so many were outside any

---

[28] A major dispute at Armstrongs in 1885 over the manager McDonnell is not related here [see Clarke 1967 - pp 382-395]. In 1891, blacksmiths and their strikers were out for a month at Hebburn to secure the removal of a new foreman because of *unacceptable conduct* and at Hartlepool platers stopped work until the union took up the matter with the management.

[29] More than 200 shipyard *labourers* struck for an extra 6d, which was quickly conceded to give them 4s 6d a day.

trade union.[30] This meeting also thanked McIntyre and the chairman urged the men *to use their spare time in raising themselves in the moral and social scale*. Further conditions were posted on Wednesday 14 February, with new rules for hourly pay from the next day. A deputation saw the general manager J P Palmer and despite his threat of the *gate* [dismissal] the men decided to work under protest until Saturday. They prepared a written statement

> We...request that we be employed on the day and quarter day system ... that a code of rules be drawn up for the whole year...That fines be entirely struck off the said rules; and should ... those rules to be adopted be altered, a week's notice be given before the said rules take effect.

Palmer insisted on hourly pay, which he said was *the distinct understanding* for the 54 hours,[31] and issued the hours for the whole year. A legal threat followed, it was for the workers to decide if they wanted cases of misconduct dealt with according to the law rather than *an agreed system of fines*. He agreed to a week's notice and suggested the men's decision should be made by ballot. Only five votes at a packed meeting supported the motion to give the hourly system a trial and rejected any offer of a compromise. Many men simply asked for their money, handed in their tools the next day and left. When Charles Palmer returned from London, he again blamed his subordinates and appeared to achieve *another triumph of tact and conciliation*. A large placard on the gate announced a meeting with the men in the Drill Shed at 3 p.m. and the men elected their delegation at the old Pit Heap. Palmer said that many of the rules were foolish and were withdrawn, it was all a misunderstanding but the *inside men* must accept hourly pay. The men did so, gave three rousing cheers for Palmer[32] and expressed a cordial attitude towards the foremen. Following a strike by platers in April over a non-unionist, who was moved elsewhere, the helpers, who had lost their wages, refused to start unless they were guaranteed a $5^3/_4$ day week. In response the platers offered the guarantee [with the exception of sickness, wet weather and holidays] provided it also applied to the helpers. Effectively that meant if a helper was missing, he paid the plater and the other helpers; no helper could make such payments and this offer was rejected. Both the manager and under-manager met the platers and the platers agreed to secure 25s $10^1/_2$d weekly for the helpers - an example of their role as sub-employers. Mismanagement, at Palmers, again caused a brief stoppage. When *winter hours* did not begin on 21 November as expected, 1,200 left work but within the day the matter was resolved but the *inside* men failed to secure the same change

Local strikes in support of wage demands occurred in 1873 and joiners at two South Shields yards gained 2s to make their pay 32s. In a remarkable case the Newcastle sailmakers refused to take up an increase they had won, *with a view to placing our masters on an equal footing with others*, when the men at North Shields and Sunderland had resumed work on the old terms [30s/week]. Newcastle engineering workers, early in 1874, agreed to simultaneously ask for an advance of 1d/hour and the employers readily offered the advance to good time keeping steady workmen. Offering to go to an *impartial* Board of Arbitration, the men replied:

> There is no desire on our part to do anything that will cause you serious loss; but after discussing the question in all its bearings, the meeting could not resist the conclusion that the working engineers of Tyneside are fairly entitled to a liberal advance of wages.

An offer of 5% in February, a further 5% in May and the last 5% in January 1875,[33] came close to the men's demand [a penny = 16.6% on 6d/hour]. A mass meeting approved the first two dates but hoped the

---

[30] The Jarrow branch of the Boilermakers had about 300 members, that of the *ASE* less than 140.

[31] The settlement related to engineering. At Palmers both *inside* and *outside* men were involved. The final arrangements allowed the *outside* men to continue under shipyard conditions, while the others went on hourly pay.

[32] Palmer signed the Minority Report of 1886 Roy Comm, in part it read: *many employers fully recognise the advantage they obtain in being able to deal with large bodies of men through their appoint officers (who are generally selected from the most intelligent members of the society), rather than directly with numbers, who, though in default of organisation may be weaker, are also less likely to know in which direction their true interests lie* - not his practice.

[33] As in 1871 Stephensons made their own separate settlement.

third could be brought forward to August. There was no stoppage of work and the men's committee remained in place, a continuing reflection of the relative weakness of trade unionism in engineering. Depressed trade intervened before the final 5% was due and except for Armstrong's workers, none benefited from the third instalment. Tyne shipwrights claimed an increase of 3s/week early in 1874; the only stoppage was at Cole Brothers. The arbitration of Thomas Hughes, the author of *Tom Brown's School Days*, was an advance of 1s 6d on 23 February and a further 1s 6d on 1st June. Given that Hughes's *Honeymoon with Labour* was already over[34], added to the significance of his comments that after many years experience:

> I have rarely seen an instance of so much fairness and courtesy on both sides. It is an example which is much need at the present time, and if followed, would take away all the bitterness from trade disputes, and go far to establish healthier and more friendly relations between employers and their workmen.

Shipwrights, joiners, blacksmiths and painters on the Wear wanted to finish at 12 o'clock Saturday to achieve the 54 hour week and left work. The Shipwrights' union secretary was asked to send 150 men to Hull, and 50 each to Blyth and Hartlepool. An offer of 1 o'clock with arbitration on the other hour was rejected with the words *believing the hour to be infinitely more vital importance to the health of the workman than the commercial value to the employers*. The 54 hours was conceded on 30 April 1874.

Following proposed wage reductions of 10% on day rates and 15% on piece rates by the shipbuilders on Tyne, Wear and Tees, their workers held meetings in December 1874. The joiners moved towards strike action but the shipwrights were more cautious. Early in January the recently formed Sunderland Trades Council called meetings on the broad question of wage reductions. Unity amongst the employers broke down and there was a very late withdrawal of the notice first on the Wear and then on the Tees. When the strikes began on 1 February 1875 there was such a stillness over the Tyne that the *Shields Gazette* wrote *such a sight had not been witnessed on Tyneside since the inauguration of shipbuilding on the river*. There was no stoppage at Smiths, Readheads and Eltringhams. Although 800 Boilermakers were out, the union did not expect the dispute to last long. James Conley, as secretary of the South Shields branch, wrote to the local paper *we ignore the word strike altogether. We consider that as we are asking for nothing it is not a strike, but a lockout*. The *Shields Gazette* estimated that 15,000 men were involved. Joiners went into house building, reportedly earning 35s 5d for a 50-hour week, and the Boilermakers paid the fares of 40 men to go to Hull to work. After four days employers offered to withdraw the notices for the forgemen, blacksmiths and general labourers. When the blacksmiths returned at Leslies, they were sent away because the firm was not ready for them. A celebration broke out when Clelands opened their yard on the old terms, a band playing at the yard gates. Hugh Taylor, coal merchant and President of the Newcastle Chamber of Commerce succeeded in arranging a conference in the fourth week of the strike and after further discussions the yards were reopened on the existing wages. A few months later, when reductions were proposed a Tyneside Shipbuilders' Conciliation Board was formed, on 15 November 1875. This Board arranged immediate reductions for all except the Boilermakers, who declined to join the Board. The Rules specified that each representative was *deemed fully authorised to act for the body of men who elected him* and this representative was to confer with the employer over any complaint and *use his best endeavours to get the complaint adjusted*. This Board [35] at least partially recognised the advantages of collective bargaining but it did not last long. In March 1876 painters at Cole Bros struck before the Board considered a wage claim and they were excluded. Not long afterwards joiners rejected arbitration on a claim for a 15% advance. Leslie withdrew and so effectively the Board ended. No doubt benefits were gained from the discussions to work out the rules but the establishment of successful Boards on the Tyne was some years away.

---

[34] His biographers, Mark & Armitage, called 1870-4 *Divorce from Labour*. He told iron workers *You ought to be ashamed of yourself [behaving] like children ... Particularly disastrous were his continuing attacks on labour*.

[35] The 25 clauses included: The Board shall at all times be a substitute for strikes, or lockouts, and shall adjust by conciliatory means, or ... arbitration, all questions of dispute [9] A Departmental Board for each class of workmen, a delegate from each yard ... and an employer [25] Awards remain in force for at least three months.

Workers, their delegate and the national leadership - the Wear 1876.
Events in 1876 were unhappy ones for both the national leadership of the Boilermakers' Society and the workers on the Wear. *Equalisation* was what the employers were calling what the riveters saw as *new lists of reductions*. A list, sent to the union on 8 April, was discussed with the shipbuilders on 29 April. After waiting four weeks for a reply, the employers informed the full-time official Richard Dimberline[36] that from 29 June the list would operate. Dimberline's immediate reply suggested that he was having difficulties in obtaining full details of rates within particular yards. Wage rates for the angle-iron smiths were prepared and again the membership rejected the new lists. On 23 June, Dimberline sent *a correct average of the prices for the two branches* [of the trade] and added that our members *state that if the said lists cannot be accepted* [they] *prefer to work time work*, lower piecework prices were not acceptable. The employers offered to put the differences to the arbitration of Thomas Burt M P[37] or some other gentleman to avoid a strike and stated that if any prices proved less remunerative consideration would be given *to build them up to standard*. Following a prolonged discussion, a very large meeting unanimously rejected these proposals. Recalling two previous 5% reductions, Dimberline wrote to the employers pointing out that much of the *allow* was taken off and that no other district had *suffered general reductions*. They objected to *a uniform rate if not an average one*. Riveters and angle iron smiths stopped work. Dimberline and four workers met the employers on 13 July and a proposal by Cain, a leader in the *9-hours* strike for a resumption of work at the old prices for not more than a month, while a joint committee of fully empowered representatives resolved prices differences was accepted. This move failed: neither the persuasive powers of the official nor the delegates could change the attitude of the men. The employers did not reply to a letter of 14 July. After another meeting of the men, Dimberline threatened on 25 July to call out all their members by the end of the month if their proposals were not accepted. Such short notice was a breach of a recent agreement of one month's notice and the shipbuilders wrote to Knight at Liverpool. Haswell's letter suggested that if he Knight or a member of his executive inquire into the matter *we believe an impartial consideration of [the points in dispute] by you would result in a settlement*. Once it was known this letter was sent, the strike notice was withdrawn. Dimberline protested:

> it was never our desire to break faith with our employers... seeing a number of our members were paid off without a moment's notice, at the same time plenty of work in hand that was not affected by the dispute, we had no alternative than to allow all hands to cease work. as some ... were informed that the yard would be closed the next day, therefore our members felt justified in the action they took.

Matthew Smith[38] was sent by the Boilermakers' Executive and he, together with the earlier delegation met the employers on 1 and 2 August. Average prices, calculated from each firm's books, were offered except for keel rivets, iron decks, beam knees, tank shoes and large hatchways, which should either be at their prices or submitted to arbitration. Again the men rejected this. When Smith reported to the Executive Council, of Merseyside members, it unanimously ordered the men back to work for a month on the old rates while a fully empowered negotiating committee sorted matters out or submitted prices not agreed to arbitration.[39] Knight wrote to the employers, who accepted the proposals, before informing Dimberline or the Wear branches. A regrettable action and many Wearside men were furious. Dimberline wrote to Knight:

> [our members] feel sorry to think that our Executive Council ... have so far forgot themselves as to send any resolution to our employers, without first consulting the members of Sunderland. If the Council had first reasoned with us and then submitted any resolution that might have been agreed upon, that would have been respectful towards our members, but they cannot allow any such prerogative even to our Council ... they cannot accept the Council's resolution ...we have not a uniform system of working, neither arbitrator or committee would be able to give satisfaction to each yard.

---

[36] Dimberline from Hull was elected after the death of Peter Jones; he loaned his branch £100 during a strike.

[37] Thomas Burt [1837-1922], one of the first two working men members of parliament, began in the pits aged 11 years, general secretary Northumberland Miners Assoc. 1865-1913, Liberal M P for Morpeth 1874-1918.

[38] Smith [born 1840] at 14 was a rivet heater at Bradford and joined the union aged 20. He became secretary of the Birkenhead branch and was elected a district delegate in 1874. He became the longest serving full-time official.

[39] In hoping the employers would agree Knight wrote *as no one can be more opposed to conflicts than I am*.

Haswell protested to Knight that they believed the Council had *full powers*; Knight replied he was *exceedingly sorry*, but all the Council could do was to withhold any support from the Society's funds and as officials have always had to say the Council *cannot force them to work*. A delegation from Sunderland on 11 August failed to change the Executive's decision. Finally the attitude of the national leadership prevailed. On 23 August the men decided to return at Austin & Hunters, *in order to keep the yard from the blacks*, and there was no general stoppage. In his annoyance Knight claimed Blumers was lost to the carpenters *after spending hundreds of pounds of Society's money*,[40] *which has also been utterly wasted*. Within two months it was claimed that Blumer's yard was regained.

One of the most unpleasant chapters of the Society's history was Cummings' shorthand for this episode. He wrote that Dimberline *had not worked smoothly with the General Office, and strong words were used which ended in the members voting by a large majority in favour of* [his] *removal ... the full details ... are neither good nor beneficial*. Mortimer, the Boilermakers' historian, saw the issue as a struggle for more central control: *The significance of this bitter controversy was that, irrespective of the merits of the particular strike, the authority of the Executive Council had in the ultimate been upheld*. Neither account enables the reader to judge the case. Understandably, the Sunderland men wanted to defend their actions and issued a circular stating their case, this circular was rejected in a national ballot by 5,642 votes to 4,771. Mortimer described this as *somewhat to the discomfiture of the EC, the view of the EC was upheld by only a narrow majority*. Controversy continued and a second circular was issued. Patience was running out at the Liverpool union headquarters and the Executive resolved that Dimberline should leave his post by 28 February 1877 or they would resign. A national ballot supported the Executive by 5,532 votes to 2,266; North Shields was the only north east branch to vote. Anxious to ensure that justice was seen to be done, the Executive asked Lloyd Jones[41] and two former members to review the case. Their report on 24 April 1877 supported the Executive and Dimberline retired. The only positive outcome of those turbulent months was James O'Neill's arrival to take up the post. Dimberline[42] asserted his right to stand and secured almost 3,000 votes but he was overwhelmed by the 20,256 votes for O'Neill in the national ballot.

Strikes by the helpers.
Their new union gave helpers a confidence to advance their claim to the corner system, a form of piecework. At Hartlepool a helper claimed it had operated in his yard from 1876 and certainly some worked this system on the Wear. Early in 1877, the Tyne Boilermakers stated the labourers *have caused us a great amount of trouble this last month by demanding an advance in some yards and the extension of the corner system in others*. There were partial strikes at Doxfords in February 1877. Craftsmen tolerated workers brought in by the employers from outside the region, if the helpers were in dispute.[43] There were further disputes with helpers including at the Austin & Hunter yard and such disputes continued into 1880 with a month long unsuccessful strike by helpers to the frame turners in an attempt to establish piecework payments. During the summer of 1880, the Wear shipbuilders discussed the supply of helpers and in September they decided that *no labourer be set to work* until it was established he was free of his previous employer. The employers' secretary spoke to O'Neill on the possibilities of *men employed from a distance* as helpers. A delegation, of Lynch and five others had a long discussion with the Wear builders in February 1881. The prices discussed were minuted as equivalent to an advance of 1d per corner. A month later

---

[40] *Journal* #52 Oct. 1876 reported that the Sunderland branches had spent more than £1,393, nearly £1,000 above their income. It should be noted that Jan-Jun over the Tyne & Wear all their income £2,437 was spent.

[41] Lloyd Jones [1811-86] an advocate of co-operation: joint author *Progress of Working Classses* [1867]

[42] Knight commented spitefully *If there are any member or members who feel disposed to vote for him we shall be prepared to record the votes...*, amongst his votes were 546 from Jarrow, 225 -Sunderland #2, 280 -S.Shields, 180 -Howdon, 130 -Wallsend, 110 -Middlesbrough #2 and at Hebburn 200 for Dimberline & 130 for O'Neill.

[43] In 1875 platers helped each other to break a strike by their helpers, who wanted an extra 6d/day at Pearse's yard. The *Journal* wrote *all honour to them*. Unemployed platers and riveters worked as helpers for 8 weeks in a dispute at Cole Bros.

Lynch wrote about the pay of helpers to the frame turners and adjusters; at that time in five Wear yards these helpers were paid piecework but at the seven others it was time work. In May the union stated that platers' helpers would only work plates of 6 cwts with 4 helpers from 21 July and a scale[44] was offered before that date. Almost immediately afterwards the employers threatened to lay off all helpers if the strikes at Sunderland SB and Bartrams did not end. In a letter, O'Neill suggested that piecework was the *direct cause of all the trouble* and asked the employers to help *terminate* the strike. The platers refused to resume unless the *corner system* was ended and the dispute continued into August and September. Both Robert Thompson and Shorts continued to operate the *corner system*.[45] Helpers' strikes on the Tees in June and July 1881, failed to secure the *corner system*. In the summer of 1883, O'Neill's house was *beset with Platers' Helpers claiming their pay* as some craftsmen moved on without paying them. As disputes ranged on, in March 1884 shipbuilder Robson argued that it was a *mistake* to interfere between platers and their helpers. Helpers at Stockton claimed the same rates as at Hartlepool in May 1888 and the platers conceded 1s a week. On the Tyne, 8 firms locked out 2,000 helpers when asked for an advance of 3s; the men accepted 1s from 25 June and a further 6d in August. Early in February 1889, T Simpson & G Mitchell wrote on behalf of the helpers to the Wear Shipbuilders seeking an increase, which was refused. Platers' helpers went on strike on 20th and although there were discussions, the men did not return until 4th March. About 2,000 men were out and they returned with an advance of 6d, making their wages 29s [outside] and 30s 6d [block & board] and the attention of the employers was to be drawn to any losses of ½ days. These union men on the Wear were active before the union led by Stanley existed. However, it is likely that Mitchell became secretary to the helpers' on Wear as part of the new union; in July, during discussions Laing objected to the name Tyneside & District Labourers' Association.

Wages and disputes.
Sometimes there were fruitless local strikes, as when 67 *ASE* members walked out at Palmers in 1877 for a 3s advance and they simply ended up 8 weeks later without jobs. A Teesside strike by the Boilermakers for a 10% increase in March 1877 was averted on the brink by an agreement to return to 1875 prices. The Union noted this as a success in that the District delegate *now is accepted ... by all employers in the District*. The Executive refused financial support to the men striking at Leslie's yard for weekly pay in 1878; the manager offered a three months trial for those who wanted it. Notices of reductions on the Tyne resulted in a strike, when negotiations failed to bridge the gap between the employers $7\frac{1}{2}$% and the union's offer of 5%. Joiners and blacksmiths were on strike. Not all yards were affected; neither Readhead nor Eltringham had sought any reduction and at Schlesinger & Davis, dispute free for four years, the men accepted the need for a reduction. For seven hours, the Boilermakers debated before finally calling the strike. Once it began the employers began to seek solutions; arrangements were made with the drillers on the fourth day and on the first Saturday Palmer met a delegation of the Boilermakers; a settlement was reached on the Monday for a return on Tuesday. Tyne Iron SB settled at this time and others settled over the following ten days. The joiners were the last to settle on 15 March; once again the employers were far from having a united approach.

Both weekly wages and piecework earnings fell in the slump to 1879 but once production began rising, demands were made to regain lost ground. Piecework increases were negotiated on 8 April 1880 for the platers on the Wear; those for angle iron smiths and caulkers began later. From the end of August there was a general 5% advance on the Tyne, and, three months later, a further $2\frac{1}{2}$% was conceded. So rapid was the increase in production that it was *almost impossible* to find men to fully supply the demand on the Tyne and Wear, according to the May 1880 Boilermakers' Monthly Report. Matters did not proceed so easily on the Tees, where 1880 began with a dispute at Withy's yard. As a result the Boilermakers stated:

---

[44] 4 helpers up to *7cwt*; 5 helpers *7-8.5 cwt*; 6 helpers *8.5 - 10 cwts* and 7 over *10 cwt*.

[45] Lynch said one yard on the Wear paid 6d. per plate for each helper and 1s. per plate for each plater. *This was not strictly just ...but it was sufficiently near approach to justice to satisfy the helper perfectly*. They did more work, on average twenty plates per day, and got 10s/ day and the plater a £1.

Sunderland carpenters and Sunderland blacklegs have succeeded in getting possession of two of our best shipyards. The union was hopeful that their members would get back, if the company failed to recruit riveters. By the end of June, Withys were discharging their substitute labour and re-engaging members of the Boilermakers' Society. As usual, the Monthly Report announced where work was available: G R Smith of North Shields *are badly in want of 2 or 3 good steady platers* - Edwards & Craig and Dobsons *now require all the assistance we can render in the supply of men, so as to keep pace with their increasing wants*. In addition to its general policy of helping to supply labour, the Union was very much aware that the lack or absence of certain workers deprived others of employment. On the Tees a lack of good holders-up meant riveters were out of work and the *utmost diligence* was called for to try to supply foremen with *this class of member*. Wage rates advanced on the Tyne and Wear in 1881. In March 1882, at Sunderland, an increase of 2s was granted just ahead of a similar increase at Newcastle, Hartlepool and Shields. The division into separate craft unions effected the effectiveness of wage claims in engineering; for example settlements were reached on different dates. Not until 1882 was the fitters' rate restored to the level of 1878, although no doubt in some firms this position was gained sooner. Following a general advance in 1880, the United Patternmakers with only 16 unemployed members in January 1881 made new pay demands on the North East Coast. An offer by the Sunderland employers was rejected and then after two days of strike it was accepted; 2s extra for those earning less than 30s and 1s for those earning 30s or above. In Newcastle, advances of 5%, $7^1/_2$% and even 15% were given.

Shipwrights & joiners.

Both the local leaders of the shipwrights and joiners welcomed negotiating with employers' associations. Joseph Heslop, Tyne & Tees delegate of the Associated Shipwrights, said in 1892, that relations with employers were *very cordial*, based on his experience over the previous 13 years of negotiating for the Tyne men. Since 1879 there has been no dispute on the wages question. Conferences had arranged all the changes and he preferred dealing with employers' associations than individual shipbuilders; the associations were, *as a rule, better and more permanent arrangements*. William Patterson, Tyne delegate of the Amalgamated Society of Carpenters and Joiners, also regarded 1880 as the turning point. Before that year, all the yards settled their own affairs and so there were frequent disputes. Then, a district committee was established *to look after the interest of the trade in the district, to meet the employers, and to use their best endeavours to arrange questions in dispute in a conciliatory manner*. The men then had a united body to face the united employers. Wage advances were arranged, in November 1880 and April 1881, and finally, in 1882, this trade union secured the abolition of both piecework and subcontracting [within the shipyard] for their members. Until then, any one of three systems might operate: [1] all the work on the vessel would be given to a group of men for a set price, [2] the various sections of the work was given out in parts and [3] the work was given to two or three men who then hired those who worked under them[46]; this was regarded as *practically ... a sweating system*. Joiners raised their wages again, in 1882, but it was only two years later in the negotiations for a reduction that they achieved a uniform minimum rate of pay. Unfortunately demarcation disputes between the shipwrights and joiners, caused as much distress as the wage disputes previously did and resulted in a great deal of ill feeling between the workers themselves.

Shipbuilding avoided serious disputes in the early 1880s, until depression brought a sequence of wage cuts [chap 9 above]. Recurrent short strikes irritated both the employers and trade union officials, revisions of wages caused difficulties and so disputes. The 1883 annual wage agreement negotiated between the Wear Boilermakers and the shipbuilders was a big step forward. Knight, a staunch believer in stable wage rates, recommended this practice to all his union: *We should be pleased if all our members would follow this good example. We should have peace and ... would profit much ... in the end.* John Price [of Palmers] *read with much interest* a speech by Knight in 1882, and then wrote to him:

---

[46] For a time this system occasionally caused difficulties among the Boilermakers. In Report No.139 [1884], it was noted with regret that some members on the Tyne were *in the habit of contracting for work on a large scale on old jobs and employing their fellow members under them*. Such members were warned that it must stop.

> I ... feel that I ought personally to thank you for the frank and outspoken manner in which you placed your views ... I allude more particularly to what you said in reference to the law of supply and demand, and as to the relations which should subsist between employers and employed at all times; and moreover as to the wages that are received by workmen, and the feeling of contentment that ought to pervade. I feel quite sure that the temperate but firm enunciation of such views will add materially to the good understanding now subsisting between the masters and men, and tend to promote the interests of both... I feel your efforts towards pacification were entitled such support as I could give them in this way.[47]

Engineers strike at Sunderland -1883-5.

No one realised in May 1883 that a strike by craftsmen at Clark's Engine Works was the forerunner of one of the longest strikes in history. They wanted an increase from 28s to 30s and objected to the employment of a 24 year old apprentice. After a few days Clark's men returned and the local *ASE* adopted both issues as general problems of Wearside. A notice was sent to the marine engineering employers, which included:

> owing to other trades restricting the apprentices, our trade is being resorted to by a proportion of apprentices which far exceeds the proportion in any other trade. We have... decided ..: No apprentice to start at the trade after the age of 16 years [and] No apprenticeship to terminate before the age of 21 years. The proportion of apprentices be not more than one to two bona fide mechanics. In order that the proportion be not more than one to two in slack times it would be necessary to limit them to two to five in brisk times; and we have to ask that no apprentices be engaged until the proportion is two apprentices to five men.

The Wear Engine Builders' Association was formed and refused to concede any limitation of apprentices. The Tyne engineering employers' organisation promised help and *considerable pecuniary assistance.*

These workers had not chosen the best time for raising such a critical issue as apprenticeship. A month earlier, the Boilermakers' Report noted *conflicting reports* on the employment prospects and considered the threat of a depression. With only one *ASE* member out of work, such thoughts did not deter the Sunderland men. On 21 June, about 1,400 men left work, including many non-society men. Most shipbuilding firms and smaller engineering works conceded the demand, Doxfords however would not guarantee the required conditions, although with only 31 apprentices to 75 men they fulfilled it, so they too were affected by the strike. Haswell, the employers' secretary, stated their objections to the limitation of apprentices:

> [a] the general standard of wages would be forced up, in the first place, without any corresponding benefit to ourselves [b] an invasion of their just right to conduct their works in such a way as they thought fit, [c] would tend to reduce the amount of lawful employment for the rising generation ... there was always on the books of the Sunderland employers a large number of boys ... waiting their turn to be taken on.

These points confirmed the workers' fears; firstly, that boy labour kept wages lower than they might be, and secondly that their job security was threatened as machines became available which boys could work. The apprentice ratios in Sunderland are shown in diag 13.03 [below]. If Doxfords is excluded the ratio was four craftsmen to three apprentices. The strikers were confident that the *figures will speak for themselves as to whether we have a grievance or not*. It would seem that although even Haswell was prepared to agree that the ratio, *considered simply as a proportion, is large* but there was *still a surplus of boys available*.[48]

The strike began with the usual open air meetings and an organising committee mobilising funds and support. An estimated 200 men left for jobs in other places in the first fortnight. Obviously anxious to

---

[47] The Society of Boilermakers was acceptable to some employers. R S Hooper, General Manager of the Pearse's yard, attended the annual dinner of the Stockton branch in 1883. At Hartlepool, William Gray and his manager Mitchell attended a similar event. Knight quoted Raylton Dixon and W J Bone of the Tyne Iron Shipbuilding Co. Ltd, in rebutting criticisms in the *Glasgow Herald*.

[48] In two other works: 25 journeymen to 37 apprentices and 25 journeymen to 54 apprentices. [Jeffreys] In the 1891 census in England & Wales - the ratio of those <20 to those over 20 for fitters & turners was 3.78 and 3.71 for engine & machine makers; if $1/5$ of 20yrs < 25yrs was added to <20s the ratio changes to 3.08 and 3.14.

prevent this the Sunderland Engine Builders circulated a letter [21 July 1883] to fellow employers, marked *Private*.

> I am instructed to inform you that the workmen in the engineering establishments of Sunderland are on strike in consequence of the refusal of their employers to comply with the demand of the Sunderland District Branch of the Amalgamated Society of Engineers to restrict the number of apprentices at the trade. The strike has already lasted a month and still continues. The employers of Sunderland feel assured that you will agree with them that such a movement as this cannot but be detrimental to the general interests of the trade, and I am requested to ask your kind co-operation with them by your declining to employ any more hands in the engineering departments of your works until the present dispute is settled.

A letter from Ray, of the Patternmakers, to Burnett, quickly involved the *ASE* at national level. Early in July, Burnett unsuccessfully attempted to gain a hearing at an area meeting of the employers. The strikers received monies from the *ASE* and from other workers and began by distributing 6s per man plus 6d per child to the non-society men. This payment varied but gradually increased, until by August, the child's allowance was 1s and, by the end of the month, there was 9s per man. A long struggle was by then generally accepted and in early October, there was 14s per man. The weekly outlay by the strike committee was about £350 [the *ASE* fund provided £150]. All the apprentices were still on the job and with their foremen were turning out work. There were two unsuccessful efforts to resolve the dispute in September. The Mayor's suggestion of arbitration was rejected by an overwhelming majority. The *Sunderland Echo* commented on the local M P Col. Gourley's efforts that there was *no difficulty in the way of a conference* so far as the men were concerned ...*Unfortunately... the employers do not seem to reciprocate this feeling*. Their mood was reflected in their decision to bring in men *from other centres of industry*.

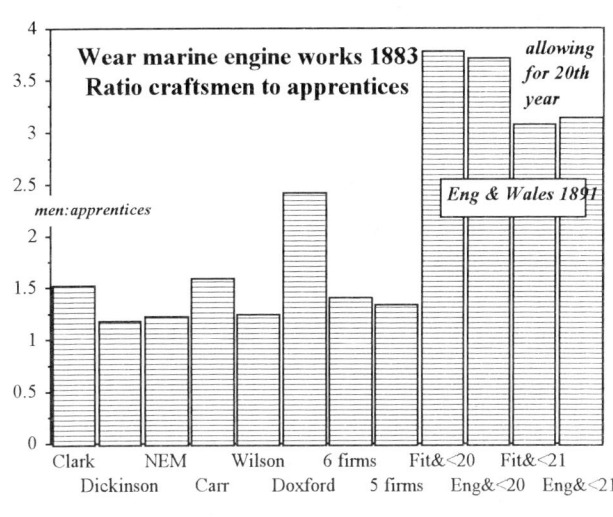

Diag 13.03

Men started arriving from Scotland and the South of England, and over *a hundred strangers* were reported on the Wear by the end of September: 35 men went to NEM and 21 to Dickinsons. None the less, the strikers remained *practically unanimous* and placarded the town with notices asking the *strangers* not to take the work. A great demonstration was organised, with the banners of 1871, including a pictorial representation of *The Great Charter May 2nd 1871*. The struggle had sharpened and the strikers alleged that the employers *have discharged every foreman in their employ who would not sacrifice his principles and his membership of the Society to which he belonged at their bidding*. The arrival of the *strangers* brought an unexpected event - the apprentices stopped work. Apprentices at Dickinsons lead the way and about 300 lads were out. More than 200 met at the *Royal William* and at a regularly conducted meeting resolved:

> We, the apprentices in the engineering trade ... pledge ourselves not to resume work until the strange workmen now employed in our shops are removed, as we do not consider them qualified to teach us our trade.

Within a week, the courts had forced the lads to return. *Rightly or wrongly*, their counsel explained *they took the step on their own judgement*. A view accepted by the *Sunderland Echo* which wrote:

> Their plea that the strangers are incompetent to teach them about their business is, we dare say, a specious cover for the real reason for their strike: namely objection - not unnatural - to work with what they term blacklegs ... we are bound in fairness to accept ... the emphatic declaration of the Strike Committee that they had done nothing to encourage the lads in the course they had taken.

Many of these lads, almost certainly most, were the sons and nephews of men on strike and could have been brought out earlier. Indeed, the readiness with which trade unionists accepted the neutrality of apprentices might be considered a surprising feature, unless due allowance is made for the reluctance of men to see their sons imprisoned or their apprenticeships ended. All working class parents wanted their sons *to have a trade*. The newcomers led to a few cases of assault and sentences of six weeks to two months with hard labour were passed in such cases, under a Bench headed by the shipbuilder, James Laing.

On 30 October, the men offered the employers: [a] to accept an advance of 2s [i.e. 37s a week[49]], [b] the abolition of the character note and [c] mutual concessions regarding the regulation of apprentices. The first two points were rejected outright and the employers declined the third because of vagueness and said that *any special regulations which are not applied to or acknowledged by the trade generally throughout the country* were not acceptable. The men's next circular began *from the tone of the employers' reply, we can see no course but to fight the question out to the bitter end*. Almost as many non-society as society men were on strike. In November, 237 men received 17s, another 396 took smaller amounts and allowances were paid for 271 children. Picketing was stepped up and a police witness claimed [surely an exaggeration] that 2,000 people obstructed the entry to Clark's. Summonses were issued on a wide scale, with 266 issued in one week in December. Much distress was caused as *old hands* faced Christmas in jail. Summonses were withdrawn at the Court hearing, when the Chairman and Secretary of the strikers signed a formal undertaking that there would be no further interference with any works. The local press regarded this withdrawal by the employers as a gesture in the *spirit of conciliation*; it was unlikely that the strikers took so sanguine a view. The strike committee distributed £577 in Christmas week, about £100 above previous weeks.

A bleak future faced the strikers as 1884 began. By then the *Sunderland Echo inclined to think the aim of the employers is nothing less than a determined effort to free themselves from the trammels of trade unionism among the men*. Such a view most surely was dawning on the men and Burnett told a mass meeting that the *avowed object* of the employers was to make Sunderland *a non-Society town*. This was almost entirely an *ASE* dispute. The Boilermakers' Society members continued to work during the dispute, except where the strike meant there was no work available and this Society was a considerable force in the boilermaking shops. However, 24 of 33 members of the Patternmakers' Society joined the strike. A new Sunderland Trades Council gave moral support to the men and publicity to the discharging of workers in other towns, as a result of the employers' letters concerning the employment of strikers. In October 1884, there were still 520 men receiving financial assistance[50] from the Strike Committee. Six months later, when nearly all the shops were full, the strikers again vainly tried to achieve a settlement by offering to withdraw their original circular. Now the employers felt able to change the local *9-hours* agreement. At Sunderland, overtime counted on a daily basis, i.e. after 5 p m, not as on the Tyne only after the whole 54 hours were worked. Negotiations dragged on and for some time the economic depression had meant any effective struggle was over. After 93 weeks, with 450 men still on strike benefit, the *ASE* Executive[51] told the men to find work where and when they could. On 28 May 1885 the strike ended officially.

From a trade union standpoint, the strike was seen as disastrous. It is *scarcely an exaggeration to say that we are still feeling the effects ... at the present day*, wrote the Patternmakers' leader Mosses in 1922; the membership of his Sunderland branch dropped from 33 to 13. The *net result was the virtual annihilation of the Sunderland [ASE] branches*, wrote Jeffreys the *AEU* historian, *and the abandonment of large scale attempts to limit apprentices*. Any claim of *virtual annihilation* is a gross exaggeration, as the diag 13.04

---

[49] Bowley & Wood believed this was conceded: *they received 37/- which was not only higher than they ever had before but higher than they have ever had since*. p.594 J Roy.Stat Soc. 1905.

[50] Financial support was regularly received from engineering workers for much of the strike; Newcastle men sent about £25 weekly and Stockton £16 per week; such contributions came from as far away as Malta.

[51] This strike was a costly one; the Report on Strikes & Lockouts of 1888 gave the cost to the trade union as £43,000 and the local press a similar figure. Jeffreys's estimate of nearly £100,000 seems too high.

shows, not only did the *ASE* survive in the town but its secretary was public spirited enough to submit evidence to the *Royal Commission on the Depression*, in 1886. Coming out of the 1889-90 boom 1,000 engineering workers were members of the *ASE* in Sunderland and about double this number in eight branches by 1914. Jeffreys, continued his assessment: *A sound policy and plenty of courage was not enough of itself; the engineers of Sunderland were defeated by lack of leadership in choosing the time to strike and the tactics to be pursued, as much as by the superior strength of the employers.* This suggested strategic planning by the local leaders, which was hardly the case and it omitted a recognition of the uncontrollable factors of the state of the trade. The timing was clearly bad, as the *Shipping World* wrote, at the end of the strike, it is folly to strike in a falling market. It was not so obvious, in May 1883, that such bad times were at hand. There were serious strategical problems not grasped by those leading the strike. It may be asked, how were the strikers to win against the consistent opposition of employers to apprentice limitation, especially when there were so many apprentices in the workshops? These lads, with their foremen, provided a significant labour force. In addition, there were so very many unorganised engineering workers in the country generally, including the North East, and wages in Sunderland were good. Another factor was the Boilermakers; with their aid victory might have been won, but without it success was most unlikely. In the marine engine shops, the Boilermakers were very important. The census group *Machine & Implements* for Sunderland, in 1881, contained 633 Boilermakers compared with 1,431 machine makers, turners and fitters. In 1891, the ratio for the same two groups was 1,048 and 1,505. While such a highly skilled group stayed on the job, the engineers' position was weak. There was a marked difference, in Sunderland, between the attitudes of the engineering employers to trade unionism and that of the shipbuilders. Compared with centuries of shipbuilding on the Wear, marine engineering had existed for a short space of time and the employers remembered the success of the striking engineering workers in 1871. They did not want a repeat performance. Engineering firms on the Wear were determined to avoid being placed in a disadvantageous position compared with other employers. Some employers saw the *ASE* as having interests beyond shipbuilding, whereas for other unions this industry was their central concern.

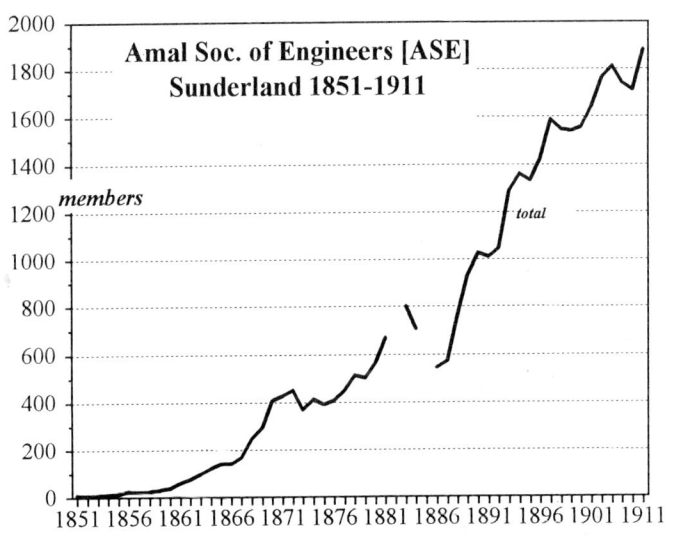

Diag 13.04

Demarcation - who does a particular job?

Job insecurity lay at the heart of the ever present problem of demarcation, the desire of one trade to restrict particular areas of work exclusively for its craftsmen. Such practices by the shipwrights and other guilds went back to the very early days of wood shipbuilding. Iron ships, with their machinery and far more elaborate outfitting required a vast array of trades which added new dimensions to the problem. Busy times, up to the 1870s, often created precedents for later disputes; when everyone was working probably the fitter may not have been very concerned about a plumber doing certain jobs [the shipwrights always were],[52] however once jobs were scarce then the task must be protected. *It is difficult to imagine the intensity of the men's feelings or the fierceness of their passions*, wrote Wigham Richardson, *Image what your*

---

[52] At Hartlepool, in 1881, patternmakers took no action when joiners were first brought into pattern shops. When a third joiner was hired in one firm and the Patternmakers' union threatened a strike no further joiners were hired.

feelings would be, if you believed (as if it were Gospel) that you had a prescriptive right to certain work of which you were being unjustly deprived. He characterised the delegates of two trades facing each other across a conference table as seeming *to glare at each other like wild animals*, no doubt more than a touch of exaggeration. *Exceedingly difficult* was Doxford's description of the differences between the shipwrights and the joiners but the Wear employers showed that their Conciliation Board could help resolve this problem. The complexity of the problem was illustrated by the 300 headings in the shipwrights' claim for work vis-a-vis the joiners. After many meetings, at the Conciliation Board, the points of difference reduced to 11. Matters were *amicably arranged*, when the last three points were submitted to the employers for decision, the agreed allocation was signed in January 1891. The leaders of the Carpenters commented favourably on this to the Royal Commission adding there was *no disturbance of any kind since*.

On the Tyne, the intractable problem of demarcation caused many difficulties. Noble acknowledged in 1892, that serious difficulties were *a recent development*. The deep and protracted Depression of the 1880's aggravated the craftsman's normal protective attitude to his job. Reinforcing evidence was provided by the fact that the transition from wood to metal was free of disputes; indeed, Price of Jarrow said it was *entirely without disputes*. The fear of no work and the limitations which increasing specialisation placed on men were also sources of anxiety. In addition increased trade union organisation allowed the fears to be expressed; the shipwrights had this strength before 1850. A comprehensive survey of the demarcation issue was given to the Royal Commission on Labour by Price. The starting point was *whenever two trades work the same material*, after that, the character of the work was a factor, a *line* was *generally though not invariably drawn between the rougher and finer jobs, or those in which the heavier as against the lighter masses of material are used and for which different tools are required.* He listed the disputes which had affected Jarrow:

1. fitter-plumber
2. shipwright-joiners
3. fitters-drillers
4. fitters-caulkers & hole-cutters
5. fitters-blacksmiths
6. plumbers-tin & iron platers workers
7. tin & iron plate workers - platers
8. angle iron smiths - blacksmiths
9. iron shipwrights-caulkers
10. platers-caulkers
11. caulkers-drillers
12. painters-red leaders.[53]

This list gives some idea of the diversity of the problem between trades, while the absence of an all-embracing industrial union did not help the solution of such questions. Jeffreys claimed too much for the *ASE*, when he wrote: *The unifying influence of the ASE and the relatively small changes of methods and machines in the engineering industry proper, kept (demarcation) disputes in this section to a minimum.* Technical change was important and no industry was subject to so many changes as shipbuilding, nor to such violent short-term fluctuations. Different practices in the various works and shipyards and in different districts complicated the issue still further. In some yards, practices had changed over the years. At times, unions sought uniformity but, on other occasions, to maintain a yard tradition, they stood out against a district pattern. Price and Noble stated the employers' attitudes. Price wanted demarcation ended to allow work to be done in *[a] the best, [b] the cheapest* and *[c] the quickest manner.* To end such *ruinous disputes*, the employer should decide, *not being bound by precedent and current practice in his neighbourhood, but guided by his judgement alone ... until ... finally fixed by some properly constituted body.* Noble was unlikely to have accepted this last point; for him the employer paid the wages and *should have full liberty to say what class of workmen shall work the machines.* Understandably, all employers deeply resented these disputes, as did many of the workers indirectly affected. It cost both the loss of so many working days.

Woodworkers were frequently involved, in particular the shipwrights and joiners. The joiners were convinced that the shipwrights were seeking joiners' work because they had lost much to the Boilermakers.

---

[53] Wade [Labourers' Union] said that his members did paint. Early in 1893 the Tyne employers refused to set demarcation lines and that they alone would decide who would do any work. In July 1893 at Wallsend, 26 painters struck for 18 days because *red leaders / labourers* were painting the second coat on ships' bottoms.

At the Elswick shipyard, joiners struck, on 1 September 1887, because the making of the magazine on *HMS Victoria on contract* was given to the shipwrights and did not return until 7 October. The joiners claimed that all such work on war vessels was done by them; in the Crimea War period, they built the magazine on *HMS Terror*. However, it was the shipwrights who had caulked that magazine, an example of how their work met and mingled. *In fact*, said the secretary of the Carpenters, *their work comes so close that they meet, and the difficulty is to determine where one class of work ceases and the other begins*. At the end of the dispute, Armstrongs agreed that

4
SHIPWRIGHTS' WORK.

Boats' Beams, to make, fit, and secure.
Boats' Skids to make, fit, and secure.
Boats' Chocks, to make, fit, and secure, with all fittings.
Boiler, packing with wood.
Bow Chocks, to make, fit, and secure, with all fittings.
Bowsprit Bits, to make, fit, and secure.
Bobee Hatches, to fit and secure.
Breakwaters, wood to make, fit, and secure.
Brass Caps, covering pipes or pumps (thro' deck), to fit and secure when wood deck.
Breadrooms, to build, above 2 ins. thick, when out of cabin.
Belting on Steamships and Barges, to make, fit, and fasten.
Beds, water-cask, spar, and anchor, to make and fit.
Bilge Blocks, to build up.
Battens, wherever bolted on frames.
Bulkheads, wood dividing cargo spaces.
Bulkheads, wood dividing forecastle from 'tween decks, or cargo spaces above 2 ins. thick.
Bulkheads, all requiring to be caulked.
Bulwarks, Topgallant, solid fit and fasten, when bolted to main rail.

5
JOINERS' WORK.

Bucket Racks, to make and fit.
Bull's-eye lights to put in and finish in wood deck houses.
Berths, making and fitting up of all mates, engineers, electricians, boatswains, carpenters, cattle, and men's berths.
Breadrooms, to build out of cabin, 2 ins. and under.
Boiler Cleading, make and fit.
Binnacle Poles, to make.
Beds, water casks, to dress.
Binnacle stands, to make and fix, when not bolted through decks.
Bridges, to prepare, clead, and finish all pilot or flying bridges.
Bridges and fore and aft Gangways, to make, if framed.
Bulkheads, to prepare and fix in cabin and forecastle, and all linings and bulkheads for officers, crews, or passenger accommodation, irrespective of thickness.
Bulkheads, wood dividing cabin from hold.
Bulkhead, dividing forecastle from cargo space, 2 ins. and under.
Bulwarks, to prepare, fix, and finish, if of wood; excepting bow bulwarks.

Pages from agreed division of work 1890 at Hartlepool

in future the joiners would get this work, but the joiners would not accept contract work. After a nine day strike at Wallsend, the shipwrights put the rails on iron stanchions and rail ends; however it was agreed that, in future, this was joiner's work. Joint trade union action resulted in Thomas Burt MP acting as umpire on a list of 168 jobs in 1890. After five and a half months of consideration, he allocated 96 jobs to the joiners and 72 to the shipwrights.[54] Much to the annoyance of many local trade unionists, the joiners struck work against this award on 1 August 1890 and this strike had a very critical side effect. In early October, about 950 joiners stopped work in 13 shipyards on the Tyne and it was early November before they were back at work. The cost to the trade union in funds was £6,400 but the loss of goodwill was probably more serious. Employers began to bring in men from outside the area and such *imported hands* were not acceptable to many trade unionists still at work in the yards. On 3 October, 1,000 men struck at the Elswick yard and this action spread to Stephensons, Hawthorn-Leslies and Palmers. With little hesitation, the leaders of the Boilermakers ordered their members back to work. Only after a conciliation board was formed with the Mayor of Newcastle as Chairman and a representative nominated by both sides, was the joiners' dispute ended. One of the joiners' objections to the Burt award was that he did not have expert knowledge of the trade, hence the two technical assessors to work with the Mayor; 32 jobs were submitted to this Board.

Engineers v Plumbers.

In late October 1890, at Hebburn, 76 engineers struck for a month in a demarcation dispute with the plumbers and finally returned, pending a conference. The United Operative Plumbers' Association's secretary accused the engineers of desiring to get rid of the plumbers at the Royal Commission on Labour, reflecting the bitterness of these disputes. He said that many plumbers came to ship work from house plumbing. Palmer's manager stated that a government contract might increase their need of plumbers two or threefold. The immediate problem related to a cover of iron pipes used to protect lead pipes from rats. Plumbers who learned their trade in the shipyard could work these iron pipes. *ASE* men claimed the right to work on certain $2\frac{1}{4}$" diameter pipes because they were made of iron, but the plumbers objected it was pipe work used for sanitary purposes and so was their work. The fact that, on earlier occasions, the fitters had refused to do this work clearly weakened their case but the *ASE* claimed the reason the employers wanted the plumbers to do the work was that they would do it cheaper. The plumbers claimed that the rates of pay refuted this argument but the *ASE* declared that the foreman's estimates were different and it was

---

[54] A dispute followed the application of the award at Blyth; a committee of the shipyard *kindred trades* raised the matter and when the joiners rejected the outcome, the employers decided the Burt award did not apply to Blyth.

this that was relevant, not hourly rate of pay. The employers, a little naively, rejected this aspect of the affair entirely and said it made no difference to them. Finally in January 1891 an agreement was reached to apply to the Tyne district.

The settlement did not last long. On 27 April, engineers were again in dispute with plumbers at Jarrow, which continued until 18-22 June. Two factors contributed to this stoppage, definitions in the agreement were not clear and there was no provision for third party interpretation. At Jarrow there were 329 strikers in the Engine Dept. and 230 in the Shipbuilding Dept. Their action laid off 1320 skilled, 569 unskilled men and 12 apprentices. At the end of May, with the *ASE* still on strike, the employers announced that unless there was a settlement, they would discharge all *ASE* members in the district, in groups of 25% of the workers.[55] The first 25%, about 2,000 men were discharged, and the next 25% were under notice when the dispute ended. A conference was arranged by the ex-Mayor of Newcastle between the employers, the engineers and the plumbers. It was resolved on 18 June to set up a joint conference of the two parties with the employers to collect evidence from all the Tyne shipyards and then decide an allocation of work. Difficulties, fortunately quickly resolved, began at the first meeting on 22 July, when the *ASE* objected to Arthur Coote's election by the conference as chairman. Coote, who was accompanied by George Hunter, Philip Watts, Doxford and Arthur Laing, proposed that in order not to waste time they met from 11.30 a.m. to 4.30 p.m., with a half hour break at the convenience of the conference. Clearly with two employers present from the Wear, it was raised whether or not the outcome would apply to the Wear. At the next meeting the specific firms to be covered were identified.[56] On 30 & 31 July evidence was collected from the Elswick shipyard and over another seven days further evidence was taken including that from the marine engine works on the Wear. Both sides were asked, on 20 August, to present summaries of their evidence and the employers suggested that the *ASE* and the Plumbers should meet to settle as many points as possible mutually. On 7 September, the employers hoped to present a provisional list on the 21st, at the end of September the *ASE* asked for more time. Two weeks later complications threatened when the engineers said the blacksmiths were claiming the right to iron pipe bending. Just when some areas appeared to be settled, a newspaper reported on 13 October that *disagreement* was *probable*. Acrimonious accusations followed as to who had inspired the story. Everyone denied doing so. Later that day the *ASE* objected to the division of wrought iron pipes at 3"diameter between the two trades and withdrew.[57] After 17 meetings, the work was completed and a list was circulated to all yards. Within months, the decisions were opposed by a strike, the main disruption in shipbuilding in 1892.

At Jarrow, the engineers stopped work on 7 January 1892 against the award of October. After discussing the strike the employers served notice on 25% of the engineers that they would be discharged seven days after 23 January, and a further 25% would go each week until all were locked out. On 30 January, all *ASE* members on the Tyne and Wear stopped work and other engineering workers as well. Twenty one firms controlling 31 establishments were involved. The official report stated that 7,122 men were involved in 22 establishments whilst the indirect numbers involved made the total 10,785. In all, as many as 15,000[58] may have been involved. The shipyards were more or less idle, there was a lack of engines and since few orders were pressing, the shipyards closed. After 13 weeks of lockout, the engineers returned. On April 22nd, the *ASE* agreed to accept the arbitration of Mr Chitty QC, who after two hearings confirmed the award of the previous October. Jeffreys' account was too slight, if not actually misleading, *after three months*

---

[55] Surviving Employers' Assoc minutes begin on 7 Feb 1891, noted likelihood of trouble at Hawthorn-Leslie due to *imported hands*. The next meeting is 8 July; so some other meeting not in those minutes made the lockout decision.

[56] These were: Armstrongs, both yards, Wigham Richardson, Palmers, Hawthorn-Leslie, Swan Hunter, Readheads, Doxfords, J L Thompson, Robert Thompson, Shorts and Laings.

[57] The *ASE* made clear they had *no complaints* on how Coote had conducted the conference, as chairman.

[58] The estimate of the *Shipping World*. The 5000 in Glennie's evidence to the Royal Commission and in the official history of the *AEU* presumably referred to members of the *ASE* alone.

resistance, the engineers had to return on the employers' terms and the plumbers kept the jobs ... the *ASE* had *not only tended to suffer more at the hands of the employers but received the lion's share of public condemnation.* The Labour Department Report commented *perhaps* [it was] *the most unfortunate and ill-advised conflict of the year.* Many would have omitted the *perhaps*. Mosses of the Patternmakers wrote they were affected *as victims but there is no doubt that this squabble accelerated the depression in trade which was rapidly developing, at the beginning of that year.* Demarcation disputes were a cause of grave harm within the trade union movement and antagonised employers so as to threaten to jeopardise normal relations with the unions.

Caulkers and Drillers.

A demarcation dispute between the caulkers and drillers at Jarrow involved over 1,000 men at the end of July 1896; work resumed after a week. A month later the same trades were in dispute at Armstrong's Walker yard when 400 boilermakers stopped work. Union efforts got the men back after two days and the matter was referred to arbitration. The decision[59] was given on 13 November and stressed that the allocation of work only applied to the yards at Walker and Jarrow and must not be *used as an argument by either party to secure work in any other yard or shop.* Again local yard custom was respected and general principles were avoided. Dissatisfaction continued and 147 caulkers stopped work at Walker on Christmas Eve. Haswell, for the shipbuilders, said that matters were *on the verge of a great crisis on the North East Coast.* The employers decided on 29 December, that if the caulkers were not at work by 5 January, a week's notice would be given to all members of the Boilermakers' Society. It seemed they were determined to test Knight's ability to maintain discipline within his union. Knight castigated the strikers and told them: *they know full well we could not grant support.* Overwhelmingly north east members voted that the caulkers should return to work [6,296 to 935] but four branches supported staying out. The caulkers returned on 13 January, only just in time to prevent dismissals. A month of extreme trade union pressure was needed to secure their return a clear illustration that even a disciplined and well led union had moments of great difficulty.

Painters & labourers.

Continued disputes between the painters and labourers over painting finally resulted in the laying down of guide lines at the Hebburn shipyard in September 1899. Ten points were defined including:

> *Labourers* would do - [1] all scraping inside and outside; [2] first coat red or any other colour; [3] second and succeeding coats if red; [5] all anti-fouling composition so far as it extends; [10] all first coating with oil on iron or steel and cement & lime wash, tar and bituminous substances
>
> *Labourers may* do [8] deck machinery, timberheads, fair leads, waterways and hatch coamings and hatch covers; [9] all tanks other than those in accommodation or on deck, double bottoms and peaks below 'tween decks, funnels, stokehold, ventilator cowls and fidleys
>
> *Painters would do* - [3] second and succeeding coats other than red; [6] all cork dusting and painting; [7] all painting wood work, except sparring, pipe castings in holds and 'tween decks which are finished by *Labourers*, also deck planks which are to be painted before laying on steel deck, in which cases they also may be done by *Labourers*.

This left limited areas in the hands of the painters, probably only those that required craft skills.[60]

---

[59] 1. Cutting off the squares used for screwing in tap bolts and dressing up or caulking such heads on government vessels was drillers' work. 2. When bolts with cant heads are used instead of rivets in bars, and such bars have to be watertight, whose work is it to put the grummet round the bolts and run the bolts in? When such bars have to lifted and clean and felt is to be put under and made watertight ... to be caulkers' work. However, when bars are rivetted and occasional tap bolts are screwed in ... drillers' work. 3. Use of a certain machine for cutting out side lights or other holes of a similar nature. Drillers' work on all vessels built in that yard. Decisions only applied to the yards mentioned.

[60] In 1902 at Jarrow, a strike by 141 painters failed to stop labourers painting; they were charged with breach of contract.

Conciliation & Arbitration - Joint Standing Committees for the Demarcation of Work.
The hopes of a permanent demarcation board raised in 1892, were realised on 20 October 1893, when a joint committee of the employers, shipwrights and joiners was established.[61] This did not abolish demarcation problems, but provided a basis for a more orderly settlement of a particular issue. The shipwrights, boilermakers and blacksmiths formed a joint committee with the employers in 1898 to deal with any demarcation disputes in the shipyards on the Tyne and Blyth. It was agreed that work on any disputed job was suspended while efforts were made to settle at yard level, but all other work must proceed. A failure to agree was notified by the firm, and within eight days of the original dispute, the Employers' secretary convened a joint committee to consider the matter. A board of referees from a list of local employers constituted a final court of appeal. The original six months agreement was superseded by a more substantial and detailed agreement a year later. This new agreement was between the Tyne Shipbuilders' Association and all trade unions affiliated to the trade union Shipbuilding & Engineering Federation, the *ASE* and the National Association of Drillers. A disputed job might continue in an emergency:

> Temporary Decision. If the disputed work is urgent, the management shall have the right to give a temporary decision to allow the work on the disputed job or jobs to proceed, but such a decision shall be without prejudice to the final settlement. [clause 2]

The section on Custom made it clear that only if a job was not previously done, or not done more than once in the Tyne & Blyth District was *outside evidence ... relating to the practice in any other district* to be considered. The Tyne Joint Committee of Shipwrights and Joiners did not prevent disputes in 1894 but it helped to reduce their length. Thirty joiners struck over work on accommodation gangways, which was given to the shipwrights and stoppages at Howdon [6 days] and Walker [10 days] were referred to the Joint Committee. After labourers were given the job of removing the staging after a launching, a one day stoppage by shipwrights re-established their right to that work. The Shipwrights' Society urged restraint: on demarcation questions all members were *seriously* urged not to take *any precipitate action in connection with this matter. Let us always have an opportunity of having the differences investigated.* In 1895, the Joint Tyne Board considered 14 cases, 3 of which went to the shipwrights, 6 to the joiners and 4 were divided between them. One case was settled on the basis of individual yard practices. Shipwrights went on strike twice at Hebburn, in June when a subcontractor gave shipwrights' work to joiners and in September, 175 men were out for 7 days in a dispute with the joiners. In 1897 there were 6 stoppages by shipwrights or joiners before their demarcation disputes were referred to the Joint Board. A prosperous period in 1898 reduced the stoppages due to demarcation, nonetheless 17 cases were considered by the Tyne Board.

On Teesside, a demarcation Board for shipwrights and joiners was formed in 1895; four years later a similar Board began at Middlesbrough and not long afterwards the two boards were united into one. As in the Tyne agreement, the employer could settle the matter in cases of emergency and the custom of the port was respected. The employers agreed that three members of the Tees & Hartlepool Shipbuilders' Association would

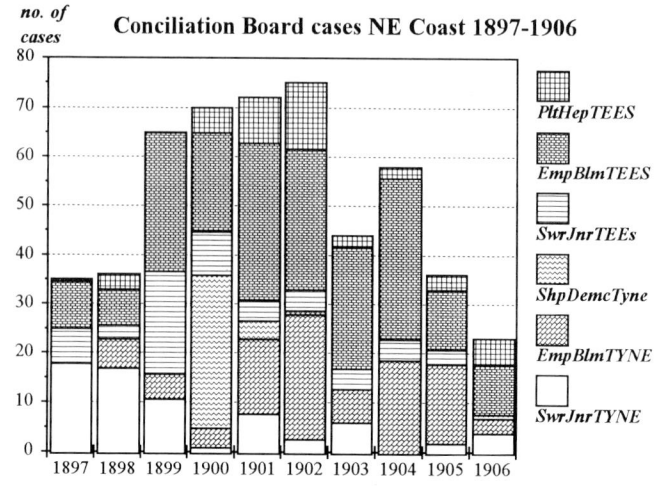

Diag 13.05

---
[61] Before the Board was formed for three weeks at Wallsend, shipwrights were in dispute with the joiners, when it was claimed the employers had not operated an agreement. Work allocation also involved labourers at Walker where they were employed to lift a portable ceiling in the oil tank of a vessel; 139 shipwrights stopped work for a week and 300 others were idle. It was agreed that the labourers would only carry the ceilings to and fro and the shipwrights would fit them.

decide disputes arising from the interpretation of a scale of help agreement affecting the helpers. A comprehensive agreement on demarcation disputes was also negotiated for Teesside; eight unions were involved - the Boilermakers, the *ASE*, two drillers' unions, the plumbers, the mill sawyers, wood cutting machinists, carpenters & joiners and the shipwrights. Any disputes arising between the latter two trades went to their own Board but the general Board considered disputes with any other member trade. The procedure had the usual three tier form - firstly, the shop steward, district delegate and the firm, then the joint committee, three from each trade with an employer as chairman, and finally the board of three arbitrators drawn from a list of local employers. When this Board was formed, it was the eleventh in the region. Sharp wrote in his study of industrial conciliation :*The North East Coast was the only region where conciliation and arbitration machinery was developed to any extent*. The prospects of conciliation improved when the Conciliation Act was passed in 1896; this gave the Board of Trade powers of intervention in disputes. A summary of the scale of the north east Boards is presented in diag 13.05. Almost 560 cases, were reviewed by these boards over the years 1897-1906, only ten of which began as strikes. During that period there were 87 strikes in engineering & shipbuilding in the north east recorded in official reports, less than 12% of the total.

The division of labour.

A small strike but with a wider significance occurred at a Sunderland marine engineering works in 1893. A wood turner, described in the official report as a cabinet maker, was employed to do all lathe work in connection with patternmaking and no patternmaker was allowed to turn his own work. Although only 16 men were involved, the craftsmen regarded the principle as very important. The wider issue was the division of labour and the separation of a part of a craftsman's work away from him altogether and the union also saw it as a threat to wages and job opportunities. An 1890 agreement, approved by the Wear Engine Builders stated in clause 1: *That all parts of the engine and machine work where castings are required is patternmaking.* No other shop on the North East Coast had introduced a man as a wood turner. Nonetheless, employers argued a wider principle - *that it was advantageous to keep one man continuously at the lathe, and as this man was proficient, they were justified in so employing him, or indeed any other man they wished.* Despite staying out from April to July, the men failed to secure the replacement of the man but only agreement that, in future, the work would be done by patternmakers.

Employment of non-unionists

At Hartlepool in 1893, 80 moulders struck against the employment of a non-unionist and secured his dismissal and, at Blyth, the helpers, in a two day strike, forced the management to ask four men to join the union or leave.[62] Those distinguished historians, Clegg, Thompson & Fox, seem to have accepted at its face value the union claim in 1901, that *in Palmer's shipyard, every man who is not a member of our union and refuses to do so will be sacked.* It is unlikely that any such rigid policy would have been company's policy. Owen Wade of the NAUL explained that when a man came into a shipyard, their shop steward discovers whether he is a member of any organisation and if not he is given a week to join the union. If he did not they want him to go and the union got *a man a card to go there*. There is no reason to suppose that this worked in every case. Two hundred helpers, at West Hartlepool, were on strike in 1894 for 8 working days in an unsuccessful effort to persuade one man to leave one union and join another; this dispute made hundreds more idle. Two other attempts by helpers to assert control over the trade union membership were unsuccessfully in 1895. At Palmers, helpers refused to work with a member of another union; these men were replaced but the union continued the strike for over three months. At Thornaby, 150 helpers failed to remove a run-out member [i.e. out of benefit] of the Boilermakers' Society working as a helper despite a 12 day strike.

---

[62] At Walker, more than 300 smith's strikers stopped work from 21 August until 1 September because a man in arrears in one labourers' union joined another and the matter was referred to a joint committee and the man finally left the job.

Major disputes - 1894- 1897- 1908
Conflict in the Foundry - the strikes of 1894 - new Conciliation Boards.

Industrial production is a complex relationship, in which a wide range of activities form a vital network with a critical time sequence; a breakdown in one part can have the most profound consequences throughout the system. Two parallel major dispute by the iron founders and the patternmakers in 1894, only too well illustrated the point. Finally the combined number on strike reached about 2000. It was estimated, by the Board of Trade, that this dispute *ultimately kept out of work seven times that number*. Little inconvenience was felt for some weeks as existing castings were used up, but idleness soon began to spread. The patternmakers appear to have been particularly effective in preventing work from the north east being produced elsewhere.[63] Unemployment among engineering craftsmen in the district rose from 14% in March to 23% in July; at the July count, 43% of the Boilermakers were unemployed. The work of the two trades on strike was at an early stage in the manufacture of many engineering products; the wooden pattern was the first step to making a casting. These castings machined by engineering workers became the components of engines and other products. Without patterns the ironfounders could not work. The engineers were at a standstill, once all the castings were machined, and so, later, were the assembling trades and finally the shipbuilders.

Few would have believed that the Newcastle Ironfounders attempt to regain the ground they lost in wage cuts a year earlier was the beginning such a large dispute.[64] When the employers rejected the claim for an advance of 3s 6d, a strike was called for 21 March. There were militant elements in the local leadership but not the union's district delegate Arthur Henderson.[65] A *tough negotiator*, according to the union's historians, who *believed profoundly in conciliation*. His opposition to *the idea of a general confederation of unions* may have partly explain the lack of joint activity with the patternmakers, who were also soon on strike. The official report noted that although the strikes took place *simultaneously*, they were *carried on separately by the two sections of the workers*. About 1,000 members of the Iron Founders struck work and were joined by hundreds of non-union men[66], 1549 workers were involved. Overall the men were *very firm*, but a small number continued to work. A reduced claim to 2s was rejected. The employers were determined on no increase.

It was hardly a surprise when the employers refused a claim by the patternmakers. Following a ballot vote of 290 to 20, strike notices were served, expiring between 4 April and 9 April in different places. The *Labour Gazette* reported that 400 stopped work on Tyne & Wear; 50 at Hartlepool; 45 at Stockton and 13 men at Middlesbrough, making 508 in all. Union secretary Mosses stated that of 354 on strike, 308 were members of the Patternmakers, 31 *ASE* and 15 non-Society men. He estimated that 60 patternmakers went into work on the Tyne, including 40 *ASE* members. The *ASE* national leadership was prepared to help the patternmakers but their local men refused to sanction such support. In retrospect, the men wrongly read the economic barometer. The Rev. Moore Ede, of Gateshead, made the first peace moves in May and secured a meeting but the employers would offer nothing in regard to wages, instead proposing a Conciliation Board. Overwhelmingly the men rejected this; a mere ten votes were cast in favour and more than 1,300 against by the foundry men. The very serious impact on local employment intensified efforts

---

[63] Patternmakers struck at Bradford and Leeds rather than do *black work*, Mosses, secretary of the Patternmakers, wrote that *black work* was traced and generally stopped, except in Huddersfield and Halifax. The Iron Founders also stopped jobs from Tyneside being placed outside the district and castings coming in.

[64] At Hartlepool and Stockton, these workers had successfully recovered wage reductions early in 1894.

[65] Browne wrote to Ridley [5 May 1896]: *To be the chief delegate in a first class strike or lockout (whether successful or not) secures to the delegate notoriety and that to men like Glenny [sic], Henderson and Radcliffe is of incalculable value and goes a long way to secure them a permanent position - besides Public Honours of sorts.*

[66] Trade union branch reports confirm this e.g. on strike 121 with 81 in the union, 209 [174], 312 [238] for those 3 branches only two out of three were trade unionists; in other branches nearly all the strikers were in the union.

to find a solution. Knight wrote: the men *have been out for four months and the result is that trade in all the shipyards and engineering establishments on the North East Coast is completely paralysed. Some of them are closed altogether, and others are discharging most of their hands*. He pointed out that the tens of thousands who were idle[67] had no voice in the dispute and argued those in the wrong should *at once end the unfortunate dispute and not stand on their dignity*. Efforts to secure a settlement by both the Bishop and the Mayor of Newcastle failed. A delegate meeting of iron founders prepared the way for discussions with the employers on 8 August. A fortnight later terms of reference for arbitration were seriously examined and the employers wanted the question to be: *Does the state of trade justify an advance or reduction of wages, and if so, how much?* The men objected to the word *reduction*. The question finally agreed was: *Shall we form a permanent Conciliation Board, whose first business will be to consider the wages of the moulders in this district?* If a majority was *yes* the men would return to work immediately, which they did after voting 709 to 452 for acceptance. After a strike of 138 working days, the iron founders returned on 1 September at their old wages together with a conciliation board which became an important factor in maintaining industrial peace.

According to Mosses, the Patternmakers *were rather pleased to see them* [the iron founders] *out of the way, believing that our chance of success would be much more favourable*. Members certainly reflected this spirit by voting 256 to 58 in October against submitting their claim to a conciliation board. Just as the general state of trade was wrongly estimated earlier, so too now the strikers overlooked the fact that there were patternmakers at work. *ASE* and non-Society men continued to work, so there were patterns awaiting casting. On 19 November, a last attempt by the union leaders made to gain some advance failed. Then the men voted by 235 to 86 to end the strike. Some branches remained closely divided, e.g. at Newcastle, the vote was 45:34 and at Stockton 17:17. Boyd said it was *a complete victory for the employers*.[68] The patternmakers were out for 33 weeks and their journal described it as *probably the most protracted and most stubbornly contested struggle in the engineering trade*. The *primary reason for our failure was that we did not make a clean sweep of the shops* and continued that the patternmakers of the Tyne, *who remained at their work ... can plume themselves upon the decisive victory they achieved over their fellow workmen*. It was recognised that the demand for *our labour was not indicative of a genuine revival in trade*. The employers were united and the men were not. Two years later recognising that the Moulders' Conciliation Board was working well, the patternmakers voted 146-55 to form such a Board. This new board first met on 2 November 1896, with its *primary object ... to regulate general advances and reductions*, although other questions, exclusively the concern of the patternmakers could be considered. About 600 workers received a backdated advance of 1s to when the discussions began to form the Board. It was later decided that Board awards would also apply to the patternmakers in shipyards.

1896 Engineering wage advance & strike.
A long spell of industrial peace was broken in 1896, when in opposition of the national leadership of the *ASE* claims for wage increases were made on the north east coast. When Tees district asked for an advance of 2s and 10% from mid-March, the North East Associated Employers replied that any advance must apply also to the Tyne, Wear and Hartlepool. On 16 March the *ASE* refused an offer of 1s and 5% immediately and 6d in July. However, a week later the other engineering unions accepted an agreement for increases in April and September. Those over 30s/week got two 1s increases and 5% on piecework; those between 25s and 30s, only got a second increase of 6d and those under 25s only two 6d increases. On 31 March, the *ASE* reached

---

[67] Boilermakers paid out £48,000 in unemployment money that year.

[68] The settlement included: the men will be reinstated on Tuesday morning 27th as far as work can be found for them at the old rate of wages. For two months, the old hands are to be taken on in preference to strangers; No interference with men who worked during the dispute; Strangers actually engaged to start on a definite day without reference to the end of the strike to be allowed to start; No distinction is to be made between the men of different societies. The employers will make *every effort* to secure work, and give employment to as many hands as possible.

an agreement:

> [1] No general alteration until six months elapsed from the last alteration and only after the customary month's notice and [2] an increase 1s and 5% in April and 1s in September, which settled wages up March 1897.

Trouble soon followed. On 22 April, the employers complained that they had just discovered that the *ASE* had members other than fitters, turners and patternmakers, and some of these were earning less than 30s a week. The employers said that the lower paid men must accept the graduated scale agreed with the other unions. This was reneging on the agreement in the eyes of the *ASE*; negotiators could fairly have supposed that the employers were familiar with the changes made at their delegate conference in 1892.[69] It was a very small part of the labour force of 12,000 who were the subject of the employers' complaint. The *Labour Gazette* estimated that less than 5% of the workers were on less than 30s /week. A quarter of these workers were non-unionists, about 900 were in unions other than the *ASE*, which had about 8,200 members.

On Teesside *ASE* members gave notice that they would stop work on 5 May.[70] Unfortunately the employers waited until 4 May before offering to go to arbitration which was too late to stop the strike. Eight firms and about 1,000 men were involved. Notice of a lockout was given on 9 May; the Associated Employers would discharge 325 *ASE* members in a fortnight and the remainder were to be locked out during the three weeks after the notice expired. *ASE* men at Hartlepool stopped work and the Sunderland Co-operative Engineers decided to ban overtime during the lockout. After meetings on 18th and 19th May the employers retreated:

> The employers have been advised that the construction of the agreement ... should rest upon the literal interpretation of the written terms, irrespective of any verbal explanations given at the time of signature. They have ... decided to give operation to the agreement ... and to give a general advance of 1s in September next. It is distinctly understood that an amnesty is to be declared on both sides, the men on strike to return to work as soon as work can be found for them ... Overtime is to be resumed.

On 21 May, the men returned and the other unions were informed that the new terms also applied to them. Ironfoundry workers refused terms of the engineers' settlement. When their Conciliation Board failed to resolve the matter; Judge Greenwell as the umpire, advanced the date of the second increase to July.

Blacksmiths at Blyth and the three unions with blacksmiths [*ASE*, the Co-operative Smiths and Associated Blacksmiths] on Teesside submitted a pay claim for 3s towards the end of 1896. Only the *ASE* rejected an offer of 1s and 5% on piecework. *ASE* smiths on Teesside wanted the same wage rate as on Tyneside and 18 smiths stopped work at Stockton and 54 at Hartlepool. The region's shipbuilders posted notices on 13 February that all *ASE* blacksmiths [260 smiths &their strikers] would be discharged in a week if the strike was not ended. Before this notice was effected, 78 smiths were out at Elswick in support of a claim for 2s and 7%. The locked-out blacksmiths were joined by 476 other *ASE* members in the shipyards. The dispute was resolved, on 12 March, when the employers conceded an equalising advance of 1s to the Teesside men and a general advance on the three rivers of 1s 6d and 5% on piecework. Normal working was delayed until 25 March as the *ASE* unsuccessfully attempted to secure the dismissal of those who worked during the strike.[71]

---

[69] The *ASE* added *and other machine men* to the rules. This was a belated recognition of the increased use of special machines and the need to embrace within the union all skilled men in engineering. In 1894, the Metal Planers' Society, with about 130 men in the north east, joined the *ASE*, some of these earned less than 30s/week.

[70] from Browne letter [5 May]: Clarke's resolution is quite premature. I told Dyer that he is simply playing into the hands of Radcliffe and the Tees men. (the war party) As you say it is not pleasant to be one against the whole meeting, but I think more men are of our way of thinking than dare say so. I have always insisted that a lockout required unanimity. I don't quite know how far I could carry my opposition. If we left the association I fear we should have a very bad time with the men, and also incur the intense hostility of the masters (Elswick for one).

[71] 5% on piecework was offered to the labourers and on time 1s for men on wages of more than 25s and 6d if less than 25s. The offer was rejected as it was not clear that the hammermen / smiths' strikers would get 1s. When it was made clear that all the would get an advance of 1/- the offer was accepted by a small majority in a ballot vote.

Machine manning & the 1897 Lockout.

The year 1897 *opened stormily*, wrote the normally sedate *Report on Strikes and Lockouts*. The whole character of trade union relations with the employers in the engineering industry was tested in the prolonged lockout of that year. Although primarily national in character, this dispute needs consideration not only because of its general consequences but also as certain aspects of its origin were located in the north east. A *small dispute at Sunderland Forge* achieved an unexpected national significance. Twenty six engineers came out on strike, on 13 February 26, against a machine man working a horizontal boring machine, which they claimed should be worked by a skilled man. Item no.1 on the list sent by the Engineering Employers to the *ASE* on 26 February 1897 was the Pallion dispute. This letter was the opening shot in a dispute which lasted almost twelve months. *The increasing militancy of the Society, the rapid growth of its membership and the mobilisation of the employers for hostilities could not but produce a conflict,*[72] wrote Jeffreys. Under Col. Dyer's leadership, the engineering employers were willing to seriously challenge the *ASE*. A Clydesider W C Borrowman, who came to the Tyne in 1898, said a year later *in the old days*:

> the apprentices used to be taught a definite craft and his trained hand was of the highest value in the work, demanding the use of the hammer, the chisel and file ... he was trained in all details of his trade...Now, he learns only a portion of his trade [and] is trained amongst men who are only capable of doing little more than one thing ... the introduction of exact machinery has almost banished handicraft altogether and cheap and rapid production by minute sub-division of labour renders it impossible for a workman, unless he be of exceptional character, to so exercise his hand and his mind as to develop deeper insight, broader view and capacity and brighter intelligence, and so, if he be only skilful with his hands, he becomes no better than the unskilled labourer the moment his work can be performed by means of a new machine.

This was an exaggerated picture of the situation in marine engine works. Fear of being *no better than an unskilled labourer* was very real for many. Those Sunderland men feared unemployment, due to easier replacement, and the lower earnings that would follow a reduction in their skills and status. The *ASE* refused to order these men back to work unless these boring machines were stopped until the matter was settled, when the employers refused to do this the situation worsened.

The employers resolved to post notices on 20 March of a progressive lockout in all member firms at the rate of 25% per week. On 22nd, the *ASE* Executive instructed all members to stop overtime and gave notice of a strike from 27 March, the first day of the lockout. Other items in the letter of 26 February were: a partial strike at Barrow; working of automatic grinding machines at the Elswick Ordnance Works and lodging allowances, trial trip wages & allowances and overtime problems at Sunderland, Hartlepool, Barrow, Belfast and on the Clyde. It is difficult to believe that the employers considered that these separate issues were inspired by central direction but they were clearly challenging the *ASE* to exercise the kind of control they experienced from Knight and the Boilermakers. On Tyneside, comment was made on the difference between dealing with the more remote central *ASE* office and with the Boilermakers in Newcastle.[73] The employers wanted lower labour costs for machines that could be worked with semi-skilled or unskilled labour. If this principle required a major struggle with the *ASE*, then this was accepted. Knight and the Federation of Engineering & Shipbuilding Trades paved the way for a conference between the employers and the *ASE* by arranging for the temporary withdrawal of the disputed worker, a member of an affiliated union. Both parties accepted this and the Sunderland men returned on 29 March, with both notices suspended. The engineering employers refused to discuss disputed machine questions. They were not prepared to have anyone interfere with what they regarded as a function of management. Shipbuilding

---

[72] Others agree on the increased militancy Pelling: *the union's militancy continued to grow*; Clegg, Fox & Thompson wrote of the growing strength of the *militants* and the dismissal of the general secretary Anderson, who was of a more *pacific* tendency, by the Executive in August 1896. His successor was G N Barnes [1859-1940].

[73] The *Shipping World* took this view in 1888 -The iron hands who manage their affairs locally gained the advance without any cessation of work. The joiners, directed from Manchester, had to undergo two or three weeks of strikes, while the engineers, acting under the guidance of the Head Committee in London, were out of work for four weeks.

employers, in contrast to this, readily accepted full participation in demarcation disputes, which were no less an interference with the allocation of work, the same basic management function. This different attitude probably reflected both differences in trade union strength and the attitudes of the employers to the unions involved. Meetings were held in London between the 1st and 15th April. After various proposals were discussed, the Union agreed to make certain recommendations to their members in regard to trial trips etc.[74] At Sunderland, the boring machine was working again on 27 May. There were *no definite conclusions as to the main point in dispute, nor were the provisional agreements ratified by the men*. Another development widened the dispute.

The *ASE* Executive called for a special levy of 9d per member for the *Assistance of Our Own Trade* but denied any wish to *widen the breach between ourselves and the employers*. A joint trade union committee in London began a movement for an *8-hour* day. Within six weeks, 95 employers agreed to an *8-hour* day. This London issue was the immediate cause of the closing of engineering works throughout the country and, to a considerable extent, in the north east. On 5 June the Engineering Federation firmly rejected an *8-hour* day. The militants were confident of their ability to win: Tom Mann wrote, in the *ASE Monthly Journal*:
> The employers have sought the quarrel... let them have it. Everything favours the men; the state of trade, the prospects for the next year, the unions' finances and the opinion of the members.

ASE members were refusing to work overtime and the London men stated they would stop work on 3 July unless their demand was met. The employers promised a lockout if there was a strike *in any workshop* of the Federated Employers. Immediately, the Boilermakers informed the employers that their members were under instructions to take no part in the strike and withdrew from the London *8-hour* day Committee. Lockout notices were posted on 6 July.[75]

A full account of this strike is outside the scope of this book. The opinion of the Labour Correspondent [the Board of Trade] was that *though the immediate cause* was the 8-hour day issue *the real questions* became of *a much more far-reaching kind, and ... involved the questions of workshop control and the limits of trade union interference*. This was a better interpretation than Jeffreys - the issue *was the demand... for the eight-hour day*. Pressure was increased on non-Federated firms to join the organisation and lock out their workers;[76] the number of firms locking out increased from under 200 to more than 700 finally, almost 45,000 workers were directly involved in the stoppage. On Tyneside, the stoppage affected about half the engineers and about one third at Sunderland. Unemployment increased because of the dispute; it varied on Tyneside from 47.9% to 55.5%, and at Sunderland from 28.8% to 34.2% and on Teesside, there were about 950 out, about 27%. Many non-Federated firms reaped benefits during the lockout. On the Wear such firms were *busy* in July and in August *brisk and overtime* and later *full of work*. The *Newcastle Chronicle* showed little sympathy for the *ASE*, and on 5 July commented: *The employers are not the aggressors. But the other side will not so easily be acquitted of a grave responsibility*. Workers in the North East were surprised that a remote London issue should affected them. At Hartlepool, the *ASE* unanimously resolved:
> That this meeting of engineers strongly protest against the arbitrary and tyrannical action of our employers in depriving us of our employment at a time when we are working harmoniously and without dispute of any kind ... we are entirely free from all responsibility in this dispute. They referred to activities in *a distant part of the country* and that the result would be to *engender perpetual strife and bitterness*.

They had never discussed the 8-hour question nor had it been discussed in the area.

Leaders of the *ASE* on Tyneside instructed their members not to act until given precise instructions.

---

[74] Although the engineering employers said they would recommend dispensing with overtime where possible, they offered working 248 hours / month for guidance, which was 18 hours more than the existing Tyneside agreement.

[75] Members of the ASE, Steam Engine Makers, United Soc. of Smiths & Hammermen, London & Prov. Soc. of Coppersmiths, London United Soc. of Drillers, United Machine Workers Assoc., London Soc. of Brassfinishers, London & Soc. of Hammermen, Amal. Soc. of Tool Makers, Scientific Instrument Makers *will be dispensed with*.

[76] F W Hirst, an economist: *the organisers of the Federation have exercised pressure of the most extraordinary kind upon employers who did not wish to join them, and had no complaints against their workpeople*.

Col. Dyer wrote in the *Times*, 7 September 1897, that the employers *were obliged to resist the attempt made to deny British employers the same freedom in managing their works which is enjoyed by every manufacturer with whom they have to compete.* There had been little or no interference in machine manning at Elswick. Some years later, Sir Andrew Noble stated:

> we had introduced [milling machines] *very early ... hundreds* [were] *at work at Elswick, and at not one of these machines was there a turner or a high class machine man employed, as it was not at all necessary. We were never interfered with in that matter.*

Browne was one of the first to declare that there was no intention to break the unions and Haswell, for the Wear employers, quickly followed him with a similar statement. In all probability considerable differences existed amongst employers as to the kind of strength that was to be left to the trade unions. In November, *Engineering* claimed that the chairman of one of the largest engineering firms on the Tyne had told Mr Livesey[77] that *the degrading doctrines of the new unionism have so poisoned the ASE as to make them a class fully 20% less valuable than they ought to be.* Benjamin Browne accepted that the new unionism *advocated extreme demands, and some actually taught in many cases that the employers and workmen were natural enemies* but added *Happily, I believe this wicked nonsense had never taken a deep hold of the working classes.* He described his workers, in 1897, as *a thousand high class engineers*; this would hardly have been a fitting description of men working at 80% efficiency. Palmer, in 1902, at a company dinner, said: *The workingmen of Tyneside formed a class equal to any which could be found in this country, America and Germany.* Some might suggested that this was after dinner rhetoric but it more nearly reflected the view normally expressed than the views of an anonymous Chairman, quoted at second hand. Engineering workers in the Federated firms in the north east were locked out until the dispute ended. A lack of marine engines finally caused layoffs in the shipyards. By September, two Tyne yards were *practically closed.* By the end of 1897, unemployment on Tyneside, apart from the strikers was approaching 15% and was 20% on the Wear. Just before Christmas, in the Newcastle district, the benefits paid were 15s to adult trade unionists, 8s to the non-unionist, 5s to labourers and 6d per child. Benefits were given to 3,800 men, there were 3,080 wives and 9,140 children. When the strike began, the Trades Council appealed for 100,000 sixpences to help the strikers and local trade unionists were helped with regular contributions. The Board of Trade after much effort secured a conference of the parties on 17 November. Only 752 out of almost 70,000[78] were prepared to accept the employers' terms in the first of a series of ballot. Less than 43,000 voted in the final ballot - 28,588: 13,727. It was a humiliating defeat.

The final agreement was signed on 28 January 1898; some of its main features were:
> *General Principles of Freedom to Employers in the Management of Their Works.*
> The Federated Employers, while disavowing any intentions of interfering with the proper functions of Trade Unions, will admit no interference with the management of their business, and reserve to themselves the right to introduce into any federated workshop ... any condition of labour under which any members of the Trade Unions here represented were working at the commencement of the dispute in any of the workshops of the Federated Employers...
> 1. *Freedom of Employment.* Every workman shall be free to belong to a Trade Union or not as he may think fit. Every employer shall be free to employ any man, whether he belong or not to a trade union. [a note -The Federation ... advise the members not to object to Union workmen.]
> 2. *Piecework.* The right to work piecework at present exercised by any members of the Federated Employers shall be extended to all members of the Federation and to all their Union workmen.
> 3. *Overtime.* When overtime is necessary, the Federated Employers recommend the following as a basic guide; - no man shall be required to work more than 40 hours overtime in any 4 weeks after full shop hours have been worked, allowance being made for time lost through sickness or absence with leave. In certain cases, such as breakdowns *urgency and emergency*, no restrictions applied. All other existing restrictions as regards overtime are to be removed. Unless mutually satisfactory to the Local Employers and the workmen concerned.

---

[77] Sir George Thomas Livesey [1834-1908] promoter of labour co-partnership, joined Metropolitan Gas Co. 1848, this Company operated a partnership scheme from 1889, director 1898; knighted 1902.

[78] The votes were [1] 752: 68,966 [2]1,041: 54,933; 51 hour compromise - 8,515: 42,065; [3] 28,588: 13,727.

4. *Rating of Workmen*. Employers shall be free to employ workmen at rates of wages mutually satisfactory. They do not object to the Unions or any other body of workmen in their collective capacity arranging amongst themselves rates of wages at which they will accept work, but while admitting the position they decline to enforce a rule of any Society. ... The Unions will not interfere ... with the wages of workmen outside their own Unions. General alterations in the rates of wages in any district...will be negotiated between the Employers' Local Association and the local representatives of the Trade Unions or other bodies of workmen concerned.

5. *Apprentices*. There shall be no limitation of the number of apprentices.

6. *Selection, Training and Employment of Operatives*. Employers are responsible for the work turned out by their machine tools and shall have full discretion to appoint the men they consider suitable to work them, and to determine the conditions under which such machine tools shall be worked.

Provisions for Avoiding Disputes[79]

With a view to avoid disputes in future, deputations of workmen[80] will be received by their employers, by appointment, for mutual discussion of questions, in the settlement of which both parties are directly concerned. In case of disagreement local associations of employers will negotiate with trade union officials. Failing settlement by the Local Association...the matter shall be forthwith referred to the Executive Board of the Federation and the central authority of the Trade Union; ... there shall be no stoppage of work either partial or of general character, but work shall proceed under the current conditions.

For more than 50 years this agreement, with amendments, governed procedure in engineering. Marsh wrote in 1965: *The basic notions of procedure ... have remained remarkably constant to the present day* [*Industrial Relations in Engineering*]. Many trade unionists in the north east greatly resented the loss of local autonomy, especially when, after the first central conference, local delegates could only attend such conferences in a consultative capacity. Radcliffe, the north east organiser of the *ASE* was in open revolt against the agreement but later apologised. At the next round of *ASE* elections, the sitting north east member on the Executive was defeated; it was the first time a sitting member had been defeated. The occasional attempts to enforce the use of skilled men on particular machines, such as a 7 day strike by 190 men at Middlesbrough, in 1901, failed.

1908 strike.

Once again two major north east coast strikes were conducted in parallel over comparable time periods and disputed issues [wage reductions]. On 6 November 1907, the employers gave two months notice to the engineering workers that piecework prices would be cut by 5% and time rates by 2s/week. The *ASE* leadership, true to its policy of avoiding stoppages, went through all the procedures, together with the Steam Engine Makers and the United Machine Workers Association. It reached a Central Conference decision on 31 January 1908. The north east employers were prepared to modify the reductions to 2.5% of piecework, and on time rates 1s for those on 26s or more, and 6d for those on 22s -26s, likewise men between 20s-22s, if they had been advanced in 1906, and no reductions for those under 20s. Union leaders, unable to recommend acceptance, balloted their members, who rejected the reductions. A strike by these three unions began on 20 February. More than twenty other unions accepted the reductions. Some 8,000 workers were out with perhaps as many as a further 3,000 indirectly affected; the strike lasted 179 days and caused the loss of an estimated 1,700,000 working days. Precise voting figures do not appear to be available but the Shields press reported a ballot vote in early March, in which the *ASE* voted 296 to 88 against the employers' terms and the Steam Engine Makers were for acceptance by 80:44. Lloyd George[81]

---

[79] Patternmakers, at Sunderland and Middlesbrough, resisted an attempt to apply the *Provisions for Avoiding Disputes* to them, their union pointed out they were not a party to the January 1898 agreement.

[80] This was the policy of the Armstrongs as Sir Andrew Noble told a Royal Commission in 1904, his company wanted no direct contact with trade unions. Clegg, Fox & Thompson wrote *These requirements represented a major setback to the authority and pretensions of the unions of craftsmen involved*.

[81] David Lloyd George [1865-1945] a solicitor, first elected a Liberal MP in 1890; President of the Board of Trade [1905-Apl.1908] then Chancellor of the Exchequer - Prime Minister 7 Dec 1916-1922 - made an earl in 1945

quickly intervened, to the annoyance of some employers and secured agreement that work could be resumed at the old rate while the matter was submitted to a referee. Despite the recommendation of the national leadership to accept this proposal, 5,834 votes were cast against and only 2,699 in favour. Still hopeful of ending the dispute Lloyd George secured a second ballot in which it would be made clear that a list of impartial persons would be prepared by the Board of Trade and the person selected with the concurrence of both *ASE* leader Barnes[82] and Andrew Noble. The gap narrowed substantially [4,356 to 3,693], whereas less than 32% were for arbitration on first vote it was almost 46% on the second. The men on the Wear, Tees & Hartlepool were in favour, the Tyneside branches against. Proposals from another Conference, at national level on 15 June, were also rejected. An *ASE* ballot, with a 60% turnout, on 14 August divided as follows [any outcomes to be put to a ballot vote]:

    1,115 for the NE Coast Committee to get best terms possible;

    3,523 for the Executive Committees of the three unions to get best terms possible;

    2,021 were against both these proposals.

Four days later the Employers' Federation dramatically decided that if the north east workers did not return to work there would be a general lockout of all members of the three unions on 26 September.

A new principle was raised by these striking engineering workers, that of a minimum wage[83] below which they were not prepared to fall. It was this that reluctantly brought the employers' decision to treat a local wages dispute as a national issue. A Federation circular stated:

> If the men succeed in establishing in so large a district as the North-east coast the principle they now contend for, their success cannot fail to have an effect on all other federated districts where a similar stand may be taken and the possibility of securing a reduction in wages seriously affected. The action of the men in discarding the advice of their leaders will tend to greatly weaken all arrangements that have been made with the unions for the amicable settlement of labour questions.

On 9 September, at the Board of Trade offices, a provisional agreement was worked out: *in view of the continued depression in the Engineering and Shipbuilding Trades ...the best terms possible ...To return to work at the reduction. No further alteration of wages to take place for 6 months* and in a future conference between both sides were to seek the means of avoiding stoppages over wages. Even under this national threat and the severity of their condition after such a long dispute the north east workers were only barely willing to give in, the majority for the settlement was only 870 votes in a ballot of 8,348, almost 45% were for continuing the struggle [in *ASE* only 52.5% for agreement]. Work resumed on 24 September 1908. Labour historian Croucher regard this strike as *the high point in the campaign for 'local autonomy'*.

Meanwhile, work in the shipyards was also disrupted. All trades faced reductions and the Boilermakers voted to accept the proposals [6,085 to 2,168] as did the helpers' unions. Other shipyard trades held three conferences in Newcastle during

Wallsend Shipwrights & Drillers Branches Committee 1906

---

[82] The vote was all too much for George Barnes who felt he had to resign as general secretary; he regarded the north east men as undermining collective bargaining. Jeffreys wrote: *the sum total of his action was to weaken the men on strike and deprive the Society of one of the most efficient and able secretaries since William Allen.*

[83] *NewcWJrl* [6 Jun 1908] reported that employers saw minimum wage as socialist agitation and *the transformation of commercial problems into class problems.*

December 1907 but the employers refused both a postponement of the wage cut and arbitration. Only after the New Year's Eve meeting, did the employers allow a week's suspension of the notices so that a ballot might be held. With a stoppage imminent on 14 January the shipbuilders offered the same terms that the engineering employers produced at the end of the month, except they wanted a further 6d reduction in March. Current wages continued for a week while the branches decided. Union leaders recommended this offer and the smaller unions were willing to accept. The key trades, shipwrights, joiners and other woodworkers, rejected the reductions, *by a most decisive majority*. About 3,000 men stopped work on 22 January. An embarrassing position faced the Wear shipbuilders, who had delayed their notice and so the Conciliation Board rules applied. They decided *to keep employment to a minimum*, no yard to have more than on 22 January. Their conduct during this time hardly reflected any honour on them. Directly the notice was completed, at the end of April they posted notices to discharge their shipwrights and others, virtually immediately *terminate Saturday first*. They were soon reminded of their obligations of a months notice under the working rules of July 1887. At other north east yards notices were posted on 3 February that without a resumption of work the yards would close on 15 February. The severe gravity of such a closure brought many efforts to bring the parties together. Samuel Storey[84] secured a meeting on 14 February and the notices were postponed for a week. A further meeting was planned with trade unions but this did not take place because the branches would not allow any representatives to agree to any reduction. As with the engineers, Lloyd George intervened and held discussions with Noble and Benjamin Browne. Notices were withdrawn from those not on strike but the employers wanted parity with Clyde wages. Lloyd George saw Wilkie of the shipwrights and local leaders of the joiners and drillers. The Boilermakers' Society was extremely annoyed at the loss of work by their members and refused to complete an agreement with the employers until the strike ended. On 25 March at Edinburgh, all the unions, including those who accepted the reductions, meet with the employers, who withdrew the unachievable attempt to bring pay down to the Clyde level and stated that they would have Federation backing for the original reductions. In a new ballot on 3 April, 5,284 votes were cast against accepting the proposed cuts, a mere 304 for accepting and only 914 for negotiations for the best possible terms. Notice was given of a lockout of the striking trades from 25 April and that in future all wages were to be set nationally. This dispute involved 13,000 directly and many more indirectly. A national ballot of the unions was for arbitration rather than forcing the north east men to concede The Federation responded with lockout notices for the whole country. Winston Churchill, now President of the Board of Trade, took a hand in the dispute. He outlined a scheme for an arbitration board when he finally brought both sides together. Another national ballot was held, with a vote of 24,125 to 22,100 for acceptance; it was likely the north east voted heavily against. With perhaps not a little bitterness the men returned on 31 May. In all 3,400,000 days were lost between these two 1908 disputes. There remained the Wearsiders. They rightly resisted in negotiation the full reduction since they had already accepted 1s reduction through the Conciliation Board. To avoid a second lockout the national Federation suggested the employers settled locally, and the union leaders obligingly modified their original offer of a 6d reduction to that of 1s. In accepting the offer, the Wear employers gave notice they would raise the issue of inequality with the Tyne and Tees.

Phelps Brown, a major contributor to the understanding of labour relations, commented on both strikes [and another in cotton] that the employers would not have held out as they did *if it meant losing much profitable business*. The men knew that the industry was depressed and that more than ten years work would be required to recover the pay lost even if they stopped the cut. Brown gave two reasons staying out so long:

> the younger men especially wanted wages determined by human needs and common decency as a first charge on their industry ... To cut the existing wage was the more indefensible when a rising subjective standard of living made it appear scandalously low already [and secondly] there was an aversion of either side to give way to force even when what was conceded was not unreasonable in itself.

---

[84] Samuel Storey [1841-1925] one of the founders of *Sunderland Echo*, had links with Andrew Carnegie in building up ½d evening newspaper chain, Liberal MP 1881-95.

Probably the workers inadequately appreciated just how far the employers had moved towards national organisation and national policies, although it is doubtful if such a realisation would have modified their actions. Cummings and Wilkie, as leaders of the two main shipbuilding unions, showed where they stood in their unsuccessful resolutions at both the TUC meetings of 1908 and 1909 that either side should be able to ask the Board of Trade to inquire into a dispute and *Pending such ...report no strike or lockout shall take place*; both wanted to avoid stoppages and even more so lockouts.

One outcome of this dispute was the agreement of 9 March 1909 between the Shipbuilding Employers' Federation and the Unions.[85] Seventeen unions signed, notable exceptions were the *ASE* and the Plumbers. The settlement had features of Knight's 1894 North East Coast agreement [see p], six months intervals for changes and these were subject to a maximum alteration. There were nine principal headings including,

General Fluctuations in Wages, were *Changes due to the general conditions of the Shipbuilding Industry-* there was to be no change for six calender months after previous change and the movements limited to 5% on piecework and 1s/week or $^1/_4$d per hour.

Questions Other Than General Fluctuation in Wages These were similar to the arrangements of 1898 agreement provisions for avoiding disputes, proceeding through a Local Conference to a Central Conference. Finally a Grand Conference, *attended by Federation and all Unions parties to this agreement, this may be called if the central Conference has not resolved matters prior to any stoppage of work.*

Piecework Questions - Settlement of - Local arrangements may continue or be established with the following further provisions ... until any dispute resolved ... two or three employers not connected with the yard will set a price at which the job will be worked, without prejudice to ultimate settlement.

Demarcation, existing local arrangements to continue.

General Provisions At all Meetings ... the representatives of both sides shall have full powers to settle, but it shall be in their discretion whether or not they conclude a settlement ... Until the whole procedure of this Agreement ... has been carried through there shall be no stoppage or interruption of work either of a partial or of a general character. The agreement was to last three years and then subject to three months notice.

A major dispute in 1910 challenged this agreement and a *supplementary and subsidiary agreement* had to be added. Disputes at Armstrong's Walker shipyard and at Henderson's in Scotland were held by the employers to be in breach of the new procedures. Notices were posted that members of the Boilermakers would be locked out from 3 September and there was to be no resumption until satisfactory assurances were received on the observation of the 1909 Agreement. Efforts by the Boilermakers' Executive to secure the authority to give these assurances failed badly. In a ballot members voted two to one against leaving it to the Executive [10,193: 5,087]. Following a representative conference on 21 September at Newcastle, there was a three day meeting of the Executive of the Federation with representatives of the Boilermakers. A small subcommittee carried these discussions forward and a provisional agreement was worked out in a Conference at York on 11 October. On 14th the directors of Swan Hunter believed it was *likely to be settled, but questions of yard discipline, wages, &c have not been dealt with. Meanwhile the loss in establishment charges is heavy in consequence of the reduced turnover.* The new proposals substantially increased the number in favour, with a slight increase in the vote against [10,212: 9,054]. After certain clauses were clarified by the Employers the vote swung more heavily against 15,563: 5,650. The Board

---

[85] Boilermakers; Shipwrights; Co-operative Smiths; Assoc. Blacksmiths' Society; Combined Smiths of Gt.Brit & Ire; Sheet Iron Workers..; Gen Union of Braziers & Sheet Metal Workers; Drillers & Hole Cutters; Amal. Soc. of Carpenters & Joiners; Ass of Carpenters & Joiners Soc.; Gen. Union of Carpenters & Joiners; Amal. Union of Cabinetmakers; Nat. Amal Furnishing Trades Assoc.;Amal. Soc. of Wood Cutting Machinists; Nat. Amal. Soc. of Operative House & Ship Painters - it was these last two which had separate Scottish unions.

of Trade continued to observe developments. G R Askwith[86] informally met the Boilermakers' Executive and the Emergency Committee of the Shipbuilders met the President of the Board of Trade, with Sir H Llewellyn Smith and Askwith. On 24, 25 & 26th November, Askwith chaired a conference attended by the Boilermakers' Executive, the district delegates and representatives from the affected districts. After two days a small committee began drafting propositions, which were forwarded to the Shipbuilding Employers. With the principal ground work done on 7 & 8 December a Conference was held at Edinburgh, when all participants in the Board of Trade discussions, representatives of the other union signatories to the 1909 agreement met with the Employers. An agreement was signed and the Boilermakers present *unanimously agree that the foregoing is a fair and equitable settlement, and we unanimously pledge ourselves, individually and collectively, to recommend it* to our members. Work resumed on 15 December after a ballot vote with a large majority in favour. Some 15,000 were locked out for 87 working days and 20,000 were indirectly affected. The new accord set out a procedure to decide who was in breach of the agreement; a committee of six with three from both sides would consider the question; if they disagreed the matter was to be referred to a referee already agreed. Whoever was found to be in breach must be dealt with according to the rules of the organisation involved followed by proof of enforcement. Certain procedures were to be speeded up. While a question was under discussion, the price paid should be settled *in the Yard wherever possible* [taking] *into account the practice of the district and the average wages earned by the workman or workmen...on the same class of work on previous similar vessels in the Yard*. Step by step efforts were made to try to minimise stoppages of work, but the ultimate limitation remained. Men cannot be forced to work.

Some disputes and other changes 1890-1905.
This section notes some of the disputes not discussed elsewhere. Again in 1890 Teesside shipbuilding was the scene of numerous small disputes. At a Middlesbrough shipyard, helpers gained 1s 4d in a two day strike, and a hundred ships' joiners, only half of whom were trade unionists, gained 1s advance after a two-day strike. After fines were imposed by the employer on 550 platers and riveters who extended their holiday, action by the Boilermakers' Society prevented the subsequent walkout on 3 June continuing. A proposal for an extra hour's work in winter was defeated by a 3 day strike by 1,200 shipyard workers at Middlesbrough in October. In December, 30 *unskilled* workers gained an advance after a strike of four day at West Hartlepool. At the end of January 1890, nearly 900 engineering labourers stopped work for six days at Jarrow and in Newcastle, claiming 2s advance, a further 750 men and boys were idle; they gained an advance of 1s for *suitable men*. During that year of 1891, shipyards on the Tyne and Wear were free of stoppages directly arising out of actions of the Boilermakers' Society, although members did feel the impact of the various demarcation disputes involving the engineers. Boilermakers were on strike twice on the Tees: 240 platers were out for 4 days and 80 men for 5 days. On Wear in January 1892, an 11 day strike by 1200 helpers failed to stop a reduction in wages. Similarly in their first strike for 17 years, 300 ships' smiths on the Tyne were unsuccessful after a prolonged stoppage [26 Jan-4 Apr]. After Knight had negotiated a 5% reduction in December 1892, the *Shipping World* wrote: *The way in which the Shipbuilders and the Boilermakers' Society manage their negotiations with the employers cannot be too highly commended. If their enlightened and dignified policy had more followers, disastrous and recriminating strikes would be less frequent than they are.* Most workers accepted the wage reductions in 1892 without stoppages. Some 1,200 helpers, against union advice, struck at ten Wear shipyards 21 January 1892 against their reduction: they returned on 3 February having only postponed the reduction. It was accepted on the Tyne without a stoppage. At Hartlepool, 32 riveters gained an advance for shell plating after 20 day stoppage. In the employer's words disputes with the ships joiners in his Hartlepool yard were a *rare* occurrence, but this *respectable and reasonable body of men* successfully resisted the

---

[86] Lloyd George recruited George R Askwith [1861-1942], a barrister, to the Board of Trade by and took charge of the Labour Dept in 1909 - Chief Industrial Commissioner 1911-19, knighted in 1911, a baron in 1919. H Llewellyn Smith [1864-1945] permanent secretary to the Board of Trade 1907-19, planned the unemployment insurance scheme.

withdrawal of a 6d repair allowance. During the *very depressed* 1893, the *Labour Gazette* recorded 27 strikes in North East shipbuilding, compared with 8 in 1892. Wage reductions continued, mainly negotiated without major stoppages; the Boilermakers accepted a 5% reduction, in April, and the engineering workers were reduced by a shilling in both May and July. *Thanks to their better organisation*, the *Shipping World* wrote, *The workmen have been able ... to stave off the reductions to the last possible moment.*

When in June 1893, the employers wanted a reduction of 1s for the joiners, these tradesmen argued that they had plenty of work, and by the laws of supply and demand why should they accept a wage cut. The shipbuilders contended that all shipyard workers must accept a reduction. Unable to be attend an Employers' meeting on 5 June, Arthur Coote in a letter urged that the reduction notices for the joiners should be withdrawn pointing out that in some places joiners were asking for increases. Opinion among the employers was divided: five of those at the 5 June meeting wanted to insist on the reduction and four were for trying to keep the men at work. More than 600 joiners stopped work on 7 June at 13 Tyneside yards.[87] Employment opportunities in house building weakened the employers' case. Some shipyard labourers were going into house building. With a display of his usual militancy, Col. Dyer said *we might try & check-mate the Joiners by establishing a Joiners Shop at Flushing or some other suitable place on the continent, & thus teach these men that their action was resulting in a loss of work to themselves.*[88] When the Wear Conciliation Board endorsed a reduction, the employers tried to use the decision against the Tyne men, but their leaders countered by pointing out that hours were less on the Wear, by 104 hours per year due to a shorter week and *winter hours*. In return the employers said they paid extra 6d for the hour; this did not cover the winter hours. The employers considered hourly pay but Dobson pointed out that this would only mean a cut of $3\frac{1}{2}$d a week. Dyer in arguing the case for the reduction said they were losing passenger ship orders due to cost and claimed an engine contract was lost over £1-14s 7d! While the workers wanted *winter hours* for all their members, the builders only wanted them for the outside men, some employers did not want to change the hours. By July 17 the employers recognised they had lost: *it was not an undignified course*, said Price, *to say they had made a mistake* and in Tweedy's words *it was no use trying to cover up our position*. To the end Dyer opposed withdrawing the reduction but agreed to follow majority. After five weeks the reduction was withdrawn and work resumed on 19 July. The minutes ended as follows *after some words of advice to the Joiners by Col. Swan & Mr Price the meeting terminated*. It can only be wondered what those words were.

Wage cuts for craftsmen often caused disputes with their helpers when they tried to pass them on. Helpers, at Howdon, prevented platers cutting their wages by a strike lasting two weeks in March 1893, and these workers also resisted a cut at Thornaby. To avoid the consequences of the piecework reductions, at Wallsend platers tried to use only two teams of helpers, instead of three; the helpers left work and after 11 days secured the usual three teams. The number of helpers for the larger *steel* plates that were replacing *iron* plates caused many disputes [see 1895 agreement below]. At Walker, in July 1893, the helpers secured an extra man when working certain plates but at Stockton they failed to gain all they wished and the firm expedited the return of the men by offering to pay half the cost of an extra helper. Four disputes in 1894, at Blyth, Wallsend, Thornaby and Sunderland raised the same basic point: the number of helpers to be used with the large plates. With an increase of teams of five men to six, the helpers won their point. An attempt at Thornaby to replace helpers with apprentices extended the strike. A single strike of helpers on the Wear in 1894, compared with 16 strikes on the Tyne and 6 on the Tees, demonstrated the success of the Wear Conciliation Board.

---

[87] The employers listed the joiners in 11 yards : Palmer [234], Elswick [86], Wigham Richardson [82], Swan-Hunter [47], Readhead [34, Dobson [20], Hawthorn-Leslie [12], Tyne Iron [12], Blyth [9] and Wood-Skinner [2].

[88] Armstrongs and Wigham Richardson bought in furniture work and this caused minor problems in the autumn.

336

Half of the 14 stoppages in 1898 involved helpers. One of these disputes in a Teesside shipyard showed one of the many complications that could emerge. In January 1898 the yard was on short time of $32\frac{1}{2}$ hours per week but on 21 January there was a changeover from the *48 winter hours* per week to 51 hours. As a result the helpers who were getting 3s 11d a day on 20th [the correct fraction of 48 hours] but on the changeover to 51 hours there was a reduction of 3d a day [6.4%] for working the same hours each day. Five hundred helpers stopped work and another 600 workers were laid off. Ten working days were lost before the employer agreed to pay 3s 11d until full working was resumed.[89] There was that rare event, a strike of boilermakers for an advance on a piecework price; the men were out for nearly a month before gaining their demand. The *ASE* ordered 166 members, striking over alleged victimisation, back to work at Hartlepool; officials said the man was not victimised. Other stoppages by helpers related to alleged loss of earnings due to the absence of platers and lying-in money.[90] Four strikes in Sunderland shipbuilding, in 1899, was an unusually large number compared with a total of seven in the previous five years. Two of these strikes concerned helpers and the skilled men - the smiths' strikers gained an increase in 3 days and the platers' helpers extra help on steel plates after 9 days. The Conciliation Board reduced to a day a stoppage of shipwrights who refused to take labourers as mates on some jobs. In 1900, only a strike by 20 labourers for a week soiled an unblemished record in engineering. Chippers and Painters at Shields were out for 36 working days and gained a 1s advance. An old problem surfaced at Sunderland, nearly 100 helpers struck because of alleged loss of earnings due to the absence of platers. The most significant dispute was at Hartlepool, where 470 Boilermakers and others were out for 23 days to compel some members to pay fines for breach of apprenticeship rules. At Howdon, 37 platers stopped work for two days before allowing the demarcation board to examine their dispute with the ships' smiths. The Wear continued to be the most strike free port with no stoppages in 1901. There were three short strikes by black squads at Hartlepool and a one-day strike by 50 helpers.

Michael Narey's novel timeboard at Tyne Iron SB horizontal stroke a full day - vertical stroke an extra quarter day

Although in October 1902 more than 28,000 shipyard workers suffered wage reductions, only the plumbers and joiners offered resistance by strike action. This dispute lost an estimated 180,000 working days. Opportunities[91] in the building trade probably accounted for the rejections of the proposed cuts of 1s6d for joiners and 1s for plumbers. On the three rivers 270 plumbers stopped work and 125 joiners were on strike on the Tyne and Tees; the Wear joiners continued to work as members of the Conciliation Board. Within two days the employers offered to postpone the reductions until December or alternately reductions of 1s and the remaining 6d, referred to arbitration and then rejected a counter offer of a 6d reduction. The leaders of the unions who had accepted the reductions failed to secure a return to work. Not until 24 February 1903, were the plumbers persuaded to returned at their old rates, while the reduction was submitted to arbitration. The joiners stayed out for another month, before returning on a 6d reduction and a second 6d reduction three months later. At the end of November 1904, some 500 ship smiths and their

---

[89] A futile attempt by the shipwrights, drillers and others [283 men] to stop only working $\frac{3}{4}$ time began at Middlesbrough on 3 December 1902 and last three months; a further 336 workers were indirectly affected.

[90] The amount held by the employer as wages were made up some days before pay day.

[91] The Kenwood index of north east building work was *94.2* in 1901 and rose to *119.2* [1902] and *126.1* in 1903.

strikers decided to resist a wage cut across the whole region, they were out 169 days, before having to accept the reduction.

Hours of Work.[92]

The 12 o'clock Saturday.
On 11 October 1889, the Sunderland Committee of the *ASE* were setting the scene for the major issue of 1890. No wage claims were possible until January 1890 and so it was decided to ask for a reduction of the hours of labour, *by establishing a twelve o' clock Saturday*. They claimed this would create jobs for some of the 6,500 members unemployed. Business was booming but the employers were anxious to resist this demand for a reduction of one hour in the normal week. The *Shipping World* expressed their anger:
> It were difficult to conceive a more ill-considered step, a more useless strike than that at present prevailing among the engineers ... It is to the Tyneside engineers ... that the skilled workers are indebted for establishing the day's work at nine hours; and it is not easy to understand how the same class of men, if not the same individuals, came to inaugurate this wretched strike for a diminution of work by one hour per week ... This squabble lacks all the elements of a reforming movement.

Work stopped at 32 engineering establishments on the North East Coast on the 17th March; the most widespread dispute yet of engineering workers in the area.[93] The trade unions estimated that 20,000 were involved and the employers 25,000. Some firms conceded in a day or two, conditional on following the general settlement, and the men rejected an offer of a 1s increase[94] to retain the 54-hour week. The Mayor of Newcastle presided over a conference, on 24 March, which prepared the way for the agreement of the 53-hour week from 10 May and the strike ended on 26th March. Once again, the North East had led the way, and by the end of 1891 engineering workers in fifty two important centres enjoyed a longer Saturday afternoon. Engineering employers, on the Wear, failed to form a conciliation board because *the men could not come to any agreement among themselves*. Perhaps the bitter memories of the long strike of 1883-1885 remained too strong. Overtime hours were the next question waiting in the wings.

Overtime.
Night shifts were regularly worked in the marine engineering shops in the mid 1880s with no objections from union members. Payment was usually time & a quarter [a shift from 5 p.m. to 6 a.m. with mealtimes 9.15 to 10.15 p.m. and 2 -2.30 a.m was counted as 15 hours]. This was the normal enhanced payment for overtime, except that in some cases if it continued after 10 p.m. when it was time and a half. A long strike, more than two months, in 1888, by fitters in the shipbuilding department at Hebburn failed to change amounts of overtime worked; the strikers were replaced. There seems little doubt that systematic overtime was normal. Employers acknowledged, in 1892, the widespread use of overtime. Price of Jarrow said that regular overtime *has been continued up to recent times* and Noble said that to abolish overtime would be *exceedingly inconvenient and detrimental to all concerned*. Armstrongs would avoid a night shift if 5 or 6 hours would do the work. The *ASE*, in 1890, asked the Iron Trades Employers Association to agree to an ending of overtime and proposed a total time limit of 10% additional overtime in any one firm in any one week. As negotiations dragged on, workers began to refuse to work overtime and the union claimed that men were discharged for refusing overtime. Help was sought from the factory inspector and the union was

---

[92] Closer control of time-keeping [mechanical clocking in] irritated many workers. There was a 3 day strike in Jan. 1895 at Palmers yard, against new time boards and the system was slightly modified. In 1899 at South Shields, after a two day strike 200 engineers were allowed to clocking-in in the employer's time. One senior manager, Alf Harrison did not see how the time clock *will help towards a better feeling*. Mechanical clocking at Palmers engineering departments in 1904 resulted in a 92 day strike [nearly 26,000 days lost] before an *amicable arrangement* was reached. In 1910, 1,450 shipyard workers stopped over time-keeping methods.

[93] The *Shipping World* claimed the votes on Wearside, including labourers, decided on the strike issue.

[94] William Boyd told his fellow employers on 7 March *he had reliable information that 6 meetings had been held on the previous night in the Mid-Tyne district* and gave voting figures [first for 53hrs- second 1s advance] Byker 14; 74; Wallsend 107:15; Hebburn 27:17; Willington 24:79; Walker 27:21; Jarrow 79:105. totals 280 : 329.

assured that overtime would stop for youths under 18 years. Workers at the NEM [Wallsend] alleged that an apprentice was compelled to work overtime and went on strike to stop it. The Employers' Association responded vigorously and stated that unless the men returned they would discharge the engineers in all affiliated works in groups of 25%. When the first 25% were due for dismissal, the engineers stopped work. About 5,700 men were out in 18 firms on Tyne and Wear and a further 8,000 were indirectly affected. The serious implications of the strike for the local economy and other workers brought immediate efforts to settle it. Both Robert Knight and the Mayor of Newcastle took steps to bring the parties to an arrangement. On a ballot vote, the men accepted terms which basically limited overtime to 18 hours per month. There were the exceptions to the limitation: steam trials or breakdowns during trials, repairs to employers' plant and all *old work* [repairs on ships or machinery]. Glennie attributed the settlement as principally due to the Mayor of Newcastle. Officially the dispute was recorded as lasting from 21 October to 9 November; in fact, the general stoppage only lasted a week. The *Shipping World* 's view that *systematic and excessive overtime has been abolished on the Tyne, Wear and Tees* must be considered too sanguine.

The final vote, 3,511 to 2,920, on accepting 18 hours at least casts some doubt on the view of the Patternmakers' leader Mosses that *there was no enthusiasm amongst the rank and file to abolish overtime. Most of them were too anxious to get it.* He claimed that the other trades abandoned the restrictions straight away. Just over a year later, Price said *we now find we can do without it* [systematic overtime] and Noble declared that the new arrangements were not causing inconvenience. Glennie was not convinced that the employers were honouring the agreement and even claimed that men were discharged at the end of the 18 hours of overtime; Noble rejected both suggestions. There is little doubt that overtime continued although it was probably reduced. *Systematic overtime* was worked in areas where more than 70% of the *ASE* members worked in 1892, and less than 16% were in areas of *little or no overtime*. The national settlement in 1898 as for 40 hours, reduced to 32 in 1907. Part of a leaflet, issued in September 1912 illustrates how the problem was persisting and there were *ASE* men who were regularly working overtime.

Overtime and an ASE rule change.
Overtime was always held to be wrong by active trade unionists when other members were out of work. Despite the opposition of their national leaders, in October 1904, the *ASE* members voted for a very strict change to their rules: *In no district shall overtime be worked on new work whilst there are members of the same trade signing the vacant books and receiving the benefits of the Society.* Action by north east district committees caused serious problems. At Hartlepool overtime was stopped at the CMEW in March 1905 and later at Richardson Westgarth. On Tyneside many works were affected including both Parsons works. In vain did the national leaders explain that this was all contrary to specific agreements with the employers and they finally obliged the local leadership to refer the matter to a Conference. Even as the Central Conference assembled in London in August overtime was still being refused, and it was agreed to leave the matter in abeyance. Much acrimony against the Newcastle leaders flowed over into the *ASE Journal*, to the pleasure of employers who reproduced extracts that

Amalgamated Society of Engineers.
TYNE DISTRICT COMMITTEE.

Instructions *re* Working of Overtime.

SEPTEMBER, 1912.

MEMBERS are hereby instructed that they must not work overtime in excess of the limit, viz., 32 hours in any four weeks, as, by doing so, they render themselves liable to be fined the sum of **Three Pounds.**

Also members are instructed that they must not work **systematic** overtime, i.e., while they may not work 32 hours in any four weeks, they work a regular amount of overtime every week or every alternate week, thus systematically working a certain amount of overtime. Members accustomed to so work must report same to their Branch Secretary, as by not reporting they also render themselves liable to be dealt with. Further, members must not exceed the 32 hours' limit in any four weeks under the plea of **Emergency** without first obtaining the consent of **District Committee.**

Committee's instruction *re* not working more than 32 hours in any four weeks means that members when required to work overtime must date back three weeks, and the amount of overtime worked in those three weeks, less than 32 hours, is the amount of overtime that may be worked in the current week.

EXAMPLE:—A member works during the 1st week 10 hours,
                                 "   "   "   2nd   "   8   "
                                 "   "   "   3rd   "   6   "
or 24 hours in the three weeks; thus he can only work 8 hours in the fourth or current week.

displayed the divisions.[95] A total ban was an unworkable policy and not necessarily a means of protecting jobs; there were times when overtime by patternmakers and moulders provided work for the other trades. While that rule continued the national leaders were in an impossible position and it was changed at a special meeting.

The Eight Hours Day. [96]
Hardly now remembered was the glory Sunderland should have gained as a pioneer of the 8-hour day in 1892. At Short Brothers' Shipyard and the Scotia Engine Works of William Allan, hours were reduced from 52 to 48 per week. Neither of these two employers were members of the employers' associations. Initially, the reduction of hours was linked to a 5% reduction in wages, but by August, this reduction was restored when it was clear that output was not affected by the reduced hours. As the Board of Trade correspondent pointed out -*Under the old system, there was a considerable loss of time in the early morning*. At the Scotia Works, the day began at 7.30 a.m. [instead of 6 a.m.] and so the workmen could breakfast at home; the midday break was from 12 noon to 12.48 p.m. and the day finished at 5 p.m., Saturday was a half day. The *Shipping World* regarded the action as *creditable alike to employers and employed* and pointed to the following lessons:

    1. where the employers act in a spirit of generosity, the men are not slow to do the same,
    2. the more intelligent of the working classes have grasped or are grasping, the economic principle, that beyond a certain point, shorter hours must necessarily mean less weekly pay...,
    3. where the men's unions are strong enough (as in this case referred to they undoubtedly are) the men are perfectly able to negotiate an eight hour day without the intervention of the State.

When the *Shipping World* reported a presentation from his 400 workers to William Allan, it called for *a few more experiments*. Allan in both private correspondence,[97] evidence to committees and speeches advocated the gains of the 8-hour day but few followed his example.

Three very important agreements.
North East Boilermakers & Wages.
A most important agreement was negotiated by the Boilermakers' Society on the timing and amount of wage changes. Upsurges in conflicts caused by attempts to increase and to cut wages with trade fluctuations were undesirable events that Knight passionately wanted to reduce. At the Royal Commission on Labour, he proposed a 5-year wages agreement, restricting changes in wage rates to a limited amount - 5% or 10% - and alterations only at intervals of 6 or 9 months. This suggestion was almost treated with scorn. James Laing doubted if his fellow shipbuilders would stick by such an agreement once they had full order books. Knight worked patiently and on 4 July 1894, signed such an agreement for the North East Coast.

There should be no misunderstanding that a majority vote of the *whole Society* imposed this agreement on the rank and file Boilermakers of the North East Coast. Nationally 15,954 voted for the agreement and 11,840 against [excluding the north east the vote was *13,788 to 4,493*]. More than 77% of the members in the north east voted against. In many branches all the votes were against, including West Hartlepool [800], Hartlepool [577], Middlesbrough [741], Wallsend [571], Walker [405], Hebburn [413], North Shields [161], Blyth [136] and Newcastle #1. Sunderland was massively against by 1,485 votes to 330, at Stockton more than 3 to 1 against and the vote at Thornaby was 230 for and 260 against. The votes at

---

[95] The employers regularly monitored trade union journals and circulated financial and other details, including in 1904 the candidates and the votes cast for the General Secretary of the *ASE*.

[96] In 1842 shipwrights of Charleston Massachusetts secured an 8 hour day. [Roediger & p.81]. There was quite unnecessary concern amongst employers in the mid-1880s over an 8- hours movement. [Wear Assoc 1 Dec 1886]

[97] Companies who made inquiries included: Ransomes & Rapier of Ipswich, the Montrose Foundry, T Bushell & Sons of Coventry, MacConnall and Peter Shore of Liverpool, G F Chance of Birmingham. When Lancashire engineer Sir William Mather [1838-1920] ran a year long experiment on an 8 hour day - he concluded it could be economical.

Byker [220 *for* - 226] and Howdon [187-189] and South Shields [292-318] were nearly equally divided. Majorities *for* the deal were recorded at Jarrow [324: 260], Gateshead only 10 of 251 against and Newcastle #2 [297] unanimously *for*. Such a large hostile vote in the region affected obliged Knight to defend this agreement and he wrote:

> a careful perusal...will, we hope, convince those who voted against it that it will not only secure to us the blessings of peace, but all the other conditions of fair dealing. It is not a leap in the dark with us, as the agreement contains the principle on which the Society has been conducted for many years past... we have proved...that disputes can be settled without stoppages of work.

The Provisions of the July 1894 Agreement included

1. *Alterations in Wages.* No general alteration to be made until six calendar months have elapsed from the last alteration, and no single change to be more than 5%. Four weeks notice of any proposed alteration.
2. *Sectional or Individual Disputes.* any such disputes ... shall, in the first instance, be referred to the Society's officials and the employer, or his representatives. If any dispute takes place respecting the price of work, the job shall proceed as on piece, and, whenever the price may be settled, the same shall be paid from the commencement of the job, and, in the meantime, if a pay-day comes before a settlement ... the men can draw customary ... or the disputed job can be done at day rates, if so agreed upon between the firm's officials and the district delegate. Failing a settlement of a dispute by ordinary means, the terms ... shall be adjusted by a committee representing the employers and the Boilermakers' and Iron Shipbuilders' Society within 14 days.
3. *Appliances.* Shipbuilders are to be entitled to revision of rates on account of labour saving appliances, now existing and not already sufficiently allowed for or hereafter to be introduced; for improved arrangements in yards; for rates in vessels of new types where work is easier, and other special cases... these revisions to be adjusted by a committee of employers and the Boilermakers ... The men may also ask for revisions
4. *Work pending the Settlement of Disputes.* Work shall in all cases be proceeded with without interruption, pending settlement of any dispute, whether to prices or otherwise.
5. *Standing Committee.* A standing committee of three on each side (exclusive of delegates on each side) shall -be appointed for each river to consider local disputes. [if] more than one river ... a joint committee.
6. *Duration of Scheme.* five years, and to be afterwards terminated by six months notice on either side.

There seems little doubt that this agreement was a major contribution to industrial peace because it eliminated those disruptive but effective pressures which could be exerted by the men in very busy times. The men objected to losing this means of gaining a temporary advantage when circumstances were favourable to them. No other area in the country followed the example of the north east. There was much in this agreement to appeal to the employers, its essential elements being the basis of the national agreement of 1909. In particular, it required the continuation of work in times of dispute or disagreements and gave them a reliable guide to labour costs for a reasonable period ahead. It is unlikely that the Boilermakers suffered in terms of general wage movements; their organisation was too strong to allow the employers to prevent them sharing in any general upward movement. An exact comparisons between 1894 and 1906 for the north east with the rest of the country is not possible but in 1906, the north east was better paid than the national average. However, groups of workers might have found it possible, in the years of very low unemployment, 1898-1901, to have gained local advances on a temporary basis. There must, however, be set against that the maintenance of rates in times of falling trade when employers might equally quickly have depressed wages. For Knight this agreement was a major success; he was rightly convinced that his men were the best and could justify their high earnings. He wanted to reduce the drain on trade union funds which disputes brought and the shipyards were most prone to strike than the engineering workshops. A Joint Committee of the Boilermakers and the employers was quickly established on the Tyne and Wear, and there were no disputes for the Tyne committee to consider in 1894. Arrangements took longer on Teesside and the joint committee was not finally established until nearly the end of 1895. No formal agreement can of itself eliminate the need for employers and men to agree locally and there were strikes.

Repairs on Oil Tankers.

Oil tankers created new conditions of work and hazards not previously experienced. The Boilermakers signed an agreement in 1894 with the Shiprepairers of the United Kingdom on pay and the following requirements:

> The employers undertake that, before men are put to work ...an expert's certificate shall be obtained daily to the effect that the tanks are absolutely safe... Ordinary repair rates only are to apply with regard to oil vessels that have been cleansed, and have carried perishable goods as the last cargo. It is agreed by the Boiler Makers' Society that ... piece-work speed must be worked.

The daily rates were: platers 15s, riveters 12s 6d, caulkers 12s 6d and holders-up 10s. The ASE had no such agreement and there were two strikes by fitters for extra payments, both unsuccessful; their employers contended that the vessels were cleaned and apprentices carried out the work.[98]

A *Scale of Help for use in Tyne and Blyth Shipyards.*

By the summer of 1891 the helpers felt strong enough to attempt to remedy the recurring problem of the use of varying numbers of helpers for apparently the same tasks at different yards. When Stanley[99] asked for a uniform scale for the Tyne, the shipbuilders said it would be *impossible* to agree such a scale *for the whole river*. He pressed out for a guide, which could be adjusted to different conditions. Employers continued to reject a common scale and their technical delegate Cameron favoured a scale for each yard; persistent difficulties finally changed attitudes. Actions by the Labourers' Union had *disorganised* one yard for 50 days in the 16 months to August 1893, according to the employers. When a dispute began in April 1894 at Swan-Hunter, George Hunter proposed taking steps to set up scales for the whole river. With the dispute continuing into July, Hunter again pressed for a general solution and a subcommittee was formed to explore the question on 24 August. Some employers disagreed with a suggestion to consult Robert Knight. When on 11 September Hunter, Charles Reynolds [Armstrongs] and W H Dugdale [then of Palmers] met to start work on the question, Knight was invited. Once assured that the interview was *quite private and unofficial* and was not a matter of wages, Knight happily discussed the issue and offered to provide any helpful information available to the Society. The Boilermakers' leader suggested visits to yards on the Clyde, at Belfast and Barrow for two men from the helpers' union, accompanied by employers' representatives. This proposal was carried out by the employers, who paid the expenses of the union men. The subcommittee invited Dipper, the helpers' secretary to arrange for not fewer than five delegates to meet with them.

Three days later Dipper, together with Hughes [mid-Tyne], Wade [Shields] Kelly [Newcastle] and Mitchell [Sunderland] began discussions with Hunter, Reynolds, Dugdale and Bone [Tyne Iron SB] Agreed scales were needed, Dipper argued, to avoid disputes but he did anticipate difficulties with their members. He was opposed to going outside the Tyne for information, pointing to the previous reluctance of the employers to

---

[98] The Wear Conciliation Board, towards the end of 1894, settled the rates for repairs on oil vessels for shipwrights, joiners, drillers and painters. Time and a half for particular named jobs and all other jobs to be paid at time and a quarter.

[99] Hughes of the Labourers' Union had a difficulty mastering negotiation procedures. In August 1892, trying to resolve a dispute at Wigham Richardson's, Cameron invited to his office Knight, Hughes; and two others. He later reported: Hughes *grossly insulted these gentlemen & behaved in a most dogmatic and high-handed fashion, so much so, that no one else could speak except himself ... broke up in disorder, no one being able to do anything with Hughes.*

do so. Hughes wanted the weight of plates to be a criteria and Mitchell pointed out that the facilities at Belfast were not available locally and *better... not to legislate for non-existing circumstances*. The employers overcame any objections to going to other ports and a report on the visits was made on 31 October. It was then agreed that those in the visiting party should carry out the negotiations and propose suitable scales. This remarkable development meant that the employers' secretary, Robinson, with technical delegate Cameron worked out proposals with the working helpers Chapman and Gaffney and the first draft was before the employers on 15 January 1895. The employers insisted there on no separate *tackle* men. Given the slow progress, it was agreed that the employers' representatives could consult privately with Knight and such members of his Executive, who could be trusted to keep it private. On 20 March, the employers met with the helpers and tried to press matters through so that they could start immediately after the Easter holidays. Various allocations were gradually sorted out and when finally settled on 15 July there were *mutual congratulations*.

A *Scales of Help for use in Tyne and Blyth Shipyards* agreement was signed between the Tyne Shipbuilders' Association and the National Amalgamated Union of Labour on 25 July 1895; it covered shells, decks, stringers, tank-tops, centre keelsons and tank sides, for all vessels built by members of the Association, and arrangements for the helpers on blocks and boards. For all other inside work the custom which has hitherto prevailed in the respective yards was to be continued. This phrase showed the persistence of variations and indeed in a more limited way so did the body of the agreement. Plates were categorised by weight and number of men, for each of four scales and for each of these the men for the Punching Squad and Hanging-up Squad.

> *Scale no.1 Where no facilities are available for working plates for both squads;*
> *Scale no.2* Hanging-up Squad *Where no cranes are available for lifting plates, but where winches are set for hoisting plates on to deck or tank top.*
> *Scale no.3* for the Punching Squad *Where cranes are available for taking plates from rack or pile and placing them on bogies for men, but where no facilities are available for working plates punching squads* Hanging-up Squad *Where there are fairly good roads to vessel, steam winches for heaving plates into position on shell, and gib derricks for hoisting plates on to deck and tank top.*
> *Scale no.4* Punching Squad *Where cranes are available for taking plates from rack or pile and placing them on bogies convenient to shed, and where cranes are available for placing plates on to vertical and plane, scarphing machine and mangle, and, where necessary, for turning plates over at rolls.*
> Hanging-up Squad *Where tram lines, or cement, or paved, or planked roads are laid to the vessel, and when steam or hydraulic winches and gib derricks for hoisting plates on deck.*

These arrangements did not apply to protective decks and armour plates for warships, which remained yard custom. It did apply to all beams and angles &c worked under similar conditions; however when *so turned or bent or otherwise so unwieldy that bogies or other appliances cannot be used* such work was on scale of 1 cwt [50.35 kg] per man. The shop steward arranged with the firm the number of men according to scale; in case of weight dispute the firm was to allow the men's representative access to the books. No plates were to be worked with fewer men than the scales allowed. Work was to go on in the event of any dispute, which should be referred to official delegates on both sides and when new labour-saving appliances were introduced revisions could be made and the men could also raise any jobs that may require revision. Three months notice was required for any changes. Yards were allocated to the various scales[100] as follows:

> *Scale 2*: Tyne Iron and Wood & Skinner
> *Scale 3*: Hawthorn-Leslie; Swan Hunter West yard; Readhead; Blyth SB and Palmers for *Hanging Squad*
> *Scale 4*: Armstrong yards Elswick & Walker; Swan Hunter East yard and Palmers for *Punching Squad*.

Not unusually with a radical departure from previous practice, the new scales had initially problems of interpretation, firstly at Wallsend, where 24 helpers were out for seven days. Two months later at this yard

---

[100] On scales 1 & 2 men were allocated up to 15 cwt with provisions for calculations for greater weights; on scale 3 up to 18 cwt and scale 4 was up to 25 cwt and above. On the Wear in 1901, squads at Bartrams were made up as followed: on the *hanging up* squad the plater had 8 helpers and an assistant at the tackle; plater *at the punch* had 7 helpers, while the plater *templating* had 7 helpers and 2 marker boys. This squad could complete 13 plates a day amidship; the machines were not adapted for *larger plates*, so these were turned on the bogey.

there was the interesting appointment of a local driller, Councillor Hanlon, as arbitrator. This was a far more prolonged dispute, 119 helpers were involved and 33 working days lost. At Walker, 800 men put out of work when forty helpers would not work *scale 4* and stopped work on 28 October. This strike ended on 11 December when the scales were varied and a special hanging tackle was provided; the official estimate was more than 32,000 days lost. Nonetheless this agreement was almost certainly the means of reducing conflict in one of the most fragile areas of the industrial relations that between craftsmen and their helpers. Ten years later conditions continued to vary in individual yards and the scales of help and prices were in dispute. After a survey of facilities by the Chairman prices were adjusted for different yards in 5% stages.

Moves to national decisions and control.

From 1902 moves were underway towards reducing, if not eliminating local arrangements with the trade unions. A subcommittee of the Shipbuilders Federation was working a draft on Conditions of Labour, Yard Management and Discipline. Doxford moved and Hunter seconded a resolution to *organise simultaneously a movement to take Foremen out of trade unions* and enrol them in the Foremen's Mutual Benefit Society. By the beginning of 1904 serious discussion was taking place on a draft letter to the trade unions, beginning

> For some considerable time the Employers have had constant and increasing difficulty in securing orders owing to the advance made in the Shipbuilding Industry abroad. This advance has been so great that the Shipbuilding Industry in this Country has already lost a considerable part of its international prestige ... re-organisation is necessary if this National Industry is to be preserved.

The shipbuilders agreed to meet with the engineering employers to co-ordinate their approaches to the matter. By the end of October 1906 it was noted that the Tyne employers had served notice to end the 1894 agreement and that it was desirable that the Wear Conciliation Board was ended.

The end of the Wear Shipbuilding Conciliation Board.

After years of resistance, those Wear shipbuilders arguing for a closer co-ordination with the national Federation won the day. A general meeting decided to inform the affiliated trade unions that unless they accepted the hours on the Tyne, the employers would serve notice of withdrawal from the Conciliation Board. On 19 August 1907 a special meeting[101] decided unanimously against taking up the hours question with the Board trades, because it was not clear *whether it was within the scope and objects of the Shipbuilding Employers' Federation to support* them on that matter. They wanted guarantees of *effective assistance* from the Federation in any dispute or strike on the Wear with Trade Societies of purely local organisation, including assistance in cancelling district agreements. It was resolved *subject to satisfactory assurance* from the Federation, that three months' notice would be given in November of withdrawal from the Wear Board of Conciliation. Haswell's letter noted that Federation members had commented on the *incongruity of a Board within the Federation with provision in its rules for the settlement of disputes by arbitration* but went on:

> *many* of the Wear Shipbuilders *have always held strongly that the Wear Board* established in 1885, long before the existing Federation was formed - has served *a most useful function* locally and should not be given up ... unless and until the results which would follow thereupon are mutually recognised as between this Association and the Federation. But there is a growing desire in Sunderland to fall into working line as completely as possible with other Federated Associations within the Federation [emphasis -JC].

At their next meeting the Wear shipbuilders wrote to the Federation asking for moves for a reduction in *Boiler Makers' wages*. There was a delay and November passed. In January, however, the Tees & Tyne Association asked them to serve notice to withdraw and promised that disputes on the Wear *shall be joint Association questions*.[102] So ended one of the most successful endeavours in industrial relations in shipbuilding after more than twenty years of peacefully resolving many disputes.

---

[101] R A Bartram [chairman]. Those present were W T Doxford, W Blumer, W H Dugdale Bryan Laing and J Marr. It is difficult to understand how Haswell could describe this as *largely attended* in his letter to the Federation.

[102] In November 1906 the Tees & Tyne shipbuilders were not willing to give that guarantee

Young Workers.

Rivet heaters and shipyard lads.

Apprentices were barred from industrial action but on occasion before they started their *time* they did stop work. One of the earliest strikes by rivet heaters occurred in 1871, when 40 lads earning 8s a week struck for an extra 1s; the threat of prosecution sent them back to work. A year later the lads stopped work at Palmers, Leslies and Schlesinger & Davis for higher rates; rises of 1s and 2s were gained at Jarrow and after a three day stoppage at Hebburn, Leslie personally secured a settlement at 8s and 9s, with 14s on piecework. Trouble returned with the next boom and in July 1883 Austin was appealing to his fellow Wear shipbuilders as to what he should do with his heater boys *who were continually striking*; they were out three times in seven weeks - he was told to sack them. When they struck at Laings in September *firm treatment was used ... the only remedy for evils of this sort*. Rivet heaters stopped work twice in 1893 because of apprenticeship priority and once because of an alleged unjust discharge. More than 30 boys were out at Howdon for three days in support of the advance of one lad: 100 men were idle and after two boys were sacked, the others resumed work. A half day stoppage at Blyth secured the removal of a lad the heaters said was made an apprentice ahead of them. At Walker, 50 youths struck and secured the re-employment of a dismissed lad, after he apologised. In March 1894, after striking for two weeks against a wage reduction 18 lads returned under the threat of summons. Fourteen of them signed the following declaration:

> We ... having left our work on strike improperly, are now willing to return to work, and on your withdrawing the summons now in force against us we agree to pay the costs thereof. We sincerely regret the trouble and annoyance you have been put to in this matter.

Directly this strike was over, the apprentices were out at Wallsend against a reduction; after nearly three weeks, they returned on a uniform weekly rate but with a reduction. At Blyth, in May, rivet heaters secured an increase when working on repair work. When 272 apprentices resisted an agreement between the Boilermakers and the Tyne shipbuilders to reduce their rates, their strike lasted from the 5th to the 24th of September. The lads returned on the reduced rates after the largest dispute of this kind. These young men and boys were not in a union, and despite a militant mood, they had little hope of success unless their case was endorsed by the mens' unions. That support was not available when attempting to overthrow an agreement made by the union to which most of their fathers belonged. At Low Walker, in August 1895, the rivet heaters successfully asserted their claim that apprentices should only be chosen from their ranks; 70 lads were out for five days and 210 men were made idle. Court actions continued to be taken against young strikers.

Apprentices.

Apprentices continued to play a vital role in both shipbuilding and marine engineering. Too often overlooked was the fact that many of them went on to be key technicians in the engine room with some becoming chief engineers. The ratio of craftsmen to apprentices varied with the level of trade activity; on Tyneside during 1909-14 it varied from 2.1 to 3.4. [see diag 13.06] From the lowest point the number of journeymen increased by 93% but the number of apprentices by only 37%. [The employers did not separate the *improvers*, those who finished their apprenticeship but not on full rate.] The proportion of apprentices varied between firms. On the Wear, in July 1905, three out of every ten shipwrights were apprentices. At Crown, Laing and Shorts more than 40% were apprentices, while at Doxfords, J L

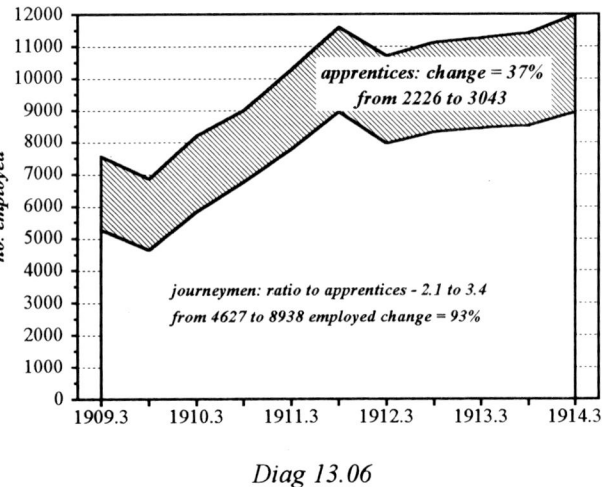

Diag 13.06

Thompson and Austins only 21% were serving their time.[see diag 13.07] In December 1893, an agreement between the Iron Trades Employers' and the Boilermakers covered Boiler & Bridge Yards. Boys about 14 years of age were taken on as Probationers and worked as *Rivet boys* or similar work. Apprenticeship would begin at 16, with the lads selected from the *most capable and best conducted* Probationers. They would serve five years [if no apprenticeship vacancy existed their time could begin up to 18 years]. Apprentices were barred from union membership and they must not be *interfered with in any way by any Trade Society*. A minimum rate of pay began at 6s/week and increased by a shilling up to 10s, with piecework arranged locally. Employers recognised that *the sons of men working...[at] the trade have a claim to be taken on as Probationers*, and although not so bound they would *endeavour to give these lads the preference*. This agreement specifically excluded restrictions on numbers, *which has been admitted in Ship yards*, did not apply. When eight years later the Boilermakers negotiated their agreement with the Shipbuilding Federation, the wording was

> Employers are opposed to any limitation in the number of apprentices to be employed; but it is not their intention to overstock yards with Apprentices, and if the Boilermakers' Society finds it necessary to prefer a complaint [on] the number of Apprentices, this must be done through the Secretaries of the ... Federation.

Apprenticeship could begin up to 19 years of age. Riveters usually started at 18 and did not finish until they were 23 years old. Time lost had to be made up at the end of the normal time served period. Pay rates began at 6s [except for riveters] and in the last two years were 10s and 12s; riveters started at 7s and finished on 14s. Starting at less than one fifth of the journeyman's rate, apprentices finished their time at less than one third of the rate. Piecework meant that some lads in shipyards earned much more than those on a time rate. About 1900, with the sole exception of patternmakers, north east engineering firms had a higher ratio of apprentices to journeymen than other districts of their Federation. Nearly four out of every ten fitters were apprentices and in the case of the boilermakers it was a third. For both the blacksmith's trades in engineering and boilermaking the ratio was less, just over one in five; lads were still learning this trade in villages and it was not so easy to give a learner work to do that he might not spoil beyond correction. In 1936, the North East Shiprepairers wanted in *no circumstances* apprenticeship to be less than five years and argued that

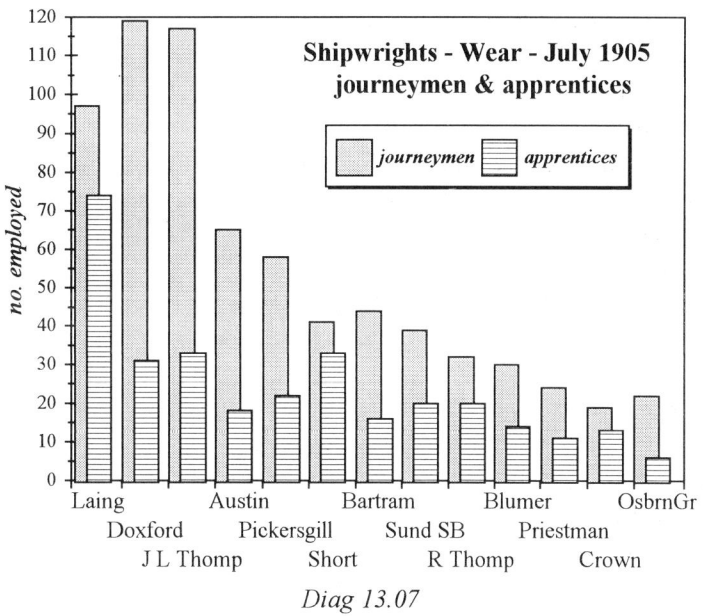

Diag 13.07

the *greatest usefulness* of the apprentice to his employer was in the fourth and fifth year. Many young men as they finished their time in a marine engine shop went to sea as engine room staff if only for a few years although many then made it their career.[103] Of 296 fitting shop apprentices, from the Scotia Works, 103 were chief engineers at sea, 34 second engineers and 2 junior engineers; in other words almost half had a career at sea.

Improvers.

Some employers not infrequently called for reductions in the period of apprenticeship but they all showed

---

[103] The handbook of the engineering unions of the Tyne District listed *Superintendent Engineers to whom Sea-Going Members may apply for situations* [39 in edition of 1915, such handbooks began about 1900].

a reluctance to pay the young man of 21 years the full rate. Henry Watson asked the Engineering Employers' Association to set an agreed rate for these men; he proposed 26s as *standard*, for the apprentice who had performed in a *satisfactory manner*, 24s for those of *moderate ability* and only 22s-23s for the *inferior*. Any agreed rate was regarded by the Association as *very undesirable*; as their policy was opposed to *any standard or minimum rate for any class of workmen*. *Improvers* were paid this *loosing rate* for from six months up to two years before getting the journeyman's pay. In 1912 the most frequent time period was two years, but in 7 firms it was up to three years. At a few firms the journeyman rate was reached in 6 to 12 months and in some increases changed according to ability. An increase of a shilling every four or six months was not unusual. Some *improvers* started at 20s/week, more usually at 24s-25s and a dozen firms started at 27s or more and one on the Wear at 31s.

National Insurance & an apprentice strike.
When an issue was seen to be serious enough, union membership was not necessary to see workers old or young striking. A major social reform by the Liberal government of 1906 reduced the pay packet of apprentices. The National Insurance Act provided a contributory scheme for health benefit and old age pensions. These National Insurance contributions for lads 16 to 18 were deducted at 5d per week and in August 1912 this brought a widespread stoppage of apprentices in north east marine engine works as well as in other parts of Britain. At NEM on the Tyne 365 apprentices from ten different trades stopped work on 20 August and claimed 1s/week increase to cover cost. Three days later they were joined by 69 from Parsons Marine and a day later by 116 from the Neptune Works. During the following week 85 stopped at NEM on the Wear and 60 at Doxford's engine works. Many other works were affected at Sunderland; almost 160 came out at Clarks, 34 at John Wigham, nearly 100 at Richardson Westgarths and although 19 struck at Lynns 60 continued to work. Names of the strikers were circulated by the employers' association, although it is difficult to understand why, as the lads wanted more money to pay the insurance, which presumably no employer was going to give them. These lads began returning at Parsons on 9 September, however, and some stayed out at Clarks until 11 November. More than 1,000 apprentices were involved, the largest single group being fitters. In order to gain a better control over the apprentices, the employers adopted an entirely new attitude on indentures; at Neptune they signed up most of these lads and other firms sought simplified documents. A new concern emerged from Tees, when it was realised that many of the lads would become members of the union benefit societies [under the Act unions could and did become approved societies]. However small 5d/week may have seemed, for a boy of 16 on 6s a week it was almost half a day's pay. This was another example of extensive action by a non-unionised group of workers. There does not appear to have been any action in the shipyards on this issue, perhaps because about half the apprentices were on piecework.

Work and the lack of it - the ever present spectre of unemployment.
Scanning the early morning sky was a regular activity by the shipyard worker and his employer: shipbuilder Bartram regularly began his diary by noting the weather.[104] This was one of many factors which normally affected whether the men had work or not and contributed to seasonal variations in employment.[105] Cyclical fluctuations in shipbuilding were however the most serious cause of unemployment. Short time was the other factor; work might be slowed down if the shipowner wanted the delivery delayed. When order books were depressed, the employers collectively discussed working three-quarter time; joint action was not usually decided but individual employers did restrict the working week in this way. Other factors, such as lack of materials or co-workers, could lead to the loss of quarter days. Extended unpaid holidays were regularly used in depressed periods; the yards would close on the Saturday before Christmas and not re-open until after the New Year. For many workers there were only 48 to 50 working weeks in the year. A combination of these things caused Knight to wish that his members could average a 48-hour week. Marine

---

[104] Time lost *through stresses of weather* or *want of materials* did not count against apprentice.

[105] Unemployment was usually higher in the winter months.

engineering was similarly affected given its direct relationship with shipbuilding. For some workers there was employment on maintenance and repairs through the holiday periods. Precise figures for unemployment are not available before the 1890s, although there is little doubt that the output of new tonnage is a very good indicator of the level of work available. Craft trade unions, who paid unemployment benefit, provided a guide as to unemployment levels but it is important to realise that unemployment was probably higher amongst non-union craftsmen, as well as certainly being so for the less skilled and labourers.

Between May 1893 and April 1894 unemployment among trade unionists in engineering on the Wear was lower than on Tyneside; over the first three months of 1894 the rate was 9%, when on Tyneside it was 20%. Labour disputes affected the returns; non striking workers did at times lose their jobs and this may have affected the figures in April 1894. At that time London had 7.7% unemployed while it exceeded 25% on the Tyne. At Middlesbrough it was 13.7% and at Sunderland 10.6%. Both the Stockton and Hartlepool *ASE* branches, however, had less than 5% out of work. Ten years later the comparisons were similar. Over the years 1894 to 1901, each month the *Labour Gazette* printed unemployment figures combined for Engineering and Shipbuilding on the Tyne and Wear. [see diag 13.08][106] Unemployment in shipbuilding was usually greater than in engineering. More than one fifth of these workers in the north east were without pay packets at Christmas 1894. This unemployment continued into 1895, and not until June did the unemployment rate fall below 10% on the Tyne, while it remained at twice that level on the Wear. The annual mean monthly level on the Tyne was 14.3% and on the Wear it was 21.5%. By June 1897 the level was down to about 2% until the shock impact of the engineers' dispute. There were 10-12% unemployed at the start of 1898, but this fell to about 2% on the Tyne and there were hardly any men out of work on the Wear where for five months it was under 1%. Good times were experienced until November 1901, when unemployment increased and in the summer of 1902 was at about 6%.

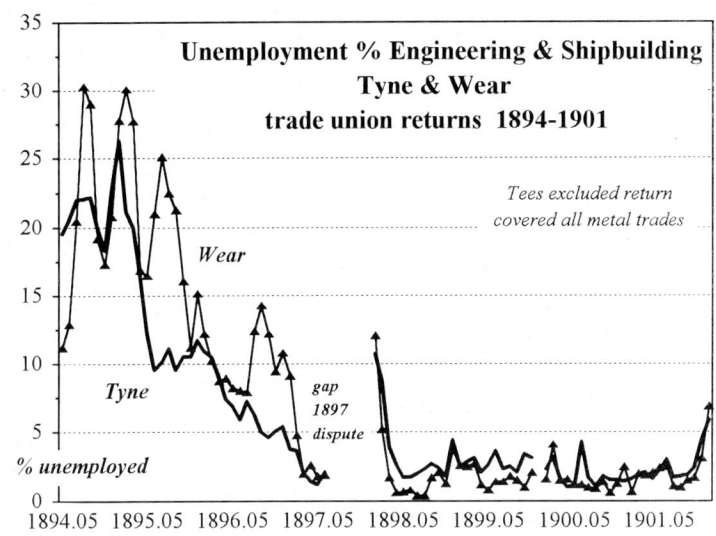

Diag 13.08

Unemployment 1902-13.

From 1902 a new statistical series separated unemployment in engineering and shipbuilding. The reports did not separate north east engineering data for the three rivers. Clearly engineering included much more than marine engineering activities but these were certainly a very important part of the region's work. Before 1913, except for the 1906 boom, rarely did unemployment in engineering fall below 4%. It was 6% in June 1907 and then swept upwards to at its worst a year later, with about three in every ten engineering workers were unemployed for a period of six months [Apl-Sept 1908]. For about a year unemployment fluctuated around 20%. In the spring and summer of 1910 it was at 8%-9% but the winter months saw a return to 14%. The average for 1911 was 3.2% and was at about 2% from the autumn of 1912. A comparison is made between the rate of unemployment in shipbuilding nationally and on the Wear in diag 13.09, which vividly demonstrates the appalling impact of the 1908-10 depression at Sunderland. A yearly

---

[106] The gap in the graph is to exclude the distortion due to the 1897 engineering dispute; unemployment for July to Dec.1897 was given as 50% or more for the Tyne and from 29 to 34% on Wear.

moving average[107] of unemployment in shipbuilding shows that the Tyne normally did better than the other ports in the region, probably due to the naval work which builders on that river secured. Overall the other parts of the region did not differ much, though the Wear suffered more in 1908-10 through a lack of work than the Tees but did better in the previous few years. During 1912-3 all were in a very similar position. The pattern of fluctuations on the Tees & Hartlepools and the Tyne were similar to those on the Wearside. Unemployment on the Tees was never below 10% from June 1902 until November 1905, and in many months exceed 20%; on average about one man in six was without work. Within a year 10% was again exceeded and the 1908-10 depression soon followed. Three months after the Tees the Tyne moved over the 10% mark.

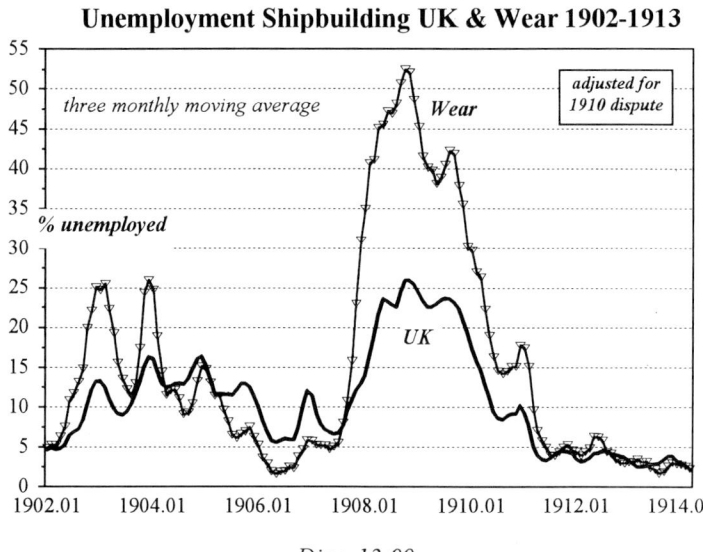

Diag 13.09

Employers' records for the river Wear of the employment available for the principal trades for 1902-1910 show that unemployment between the trades varied [see diag 13.10]. A workforce of 12,672 in September 1906 was reduced to a mere 4,068 two years later. The five groups with detailed information made up 35% of the workforce in normal times. This dropped to about 30% in 1907-9. If 1906 is regarded as full employment, then for the Boilermakers, between 1904-5 they were at 85%. As the depression deepened they fell from 47% in 1907 to less than 22% at the beginning of 1908, just over 31% in the next year and were still under 50% during 1910. Shipwrights faired slightly better, almost 95% in January 1905, although they were at 88% in March 1902. In August of that year they were at less than 72%. These craftsmen began 1907 at 54% of the 1906 level and fell to 35% a year later, then progressed through 46% to 64% in January 1910. Overall the joiners, a fitting out trade, did better; indeed in September 1903 and January 1905 joiners were substantially above the 1906 norm, at 113% and 125% respectively. The type of vessel built influenced how many were required. The Joiners' low point in 1908 was just under 29%. At that time the drillers were at 23% and they were at only 46% at the beginning of 1910. Blacksmiths did better throughout, their worst point reaching 42%, almost twice the proportion of jobs available to the Boilermakers, and exceed 52% in 1909. Such a better position was small mercy; in 1910 one blacksmith in three had no job available on the Wear. Many Wearsiders were probably without work for perhaps as much as two years and it is difficult to see how given the general figures it could have been otherwise. From these unemployment figures it may reasonably be concluded that there was rather more famine

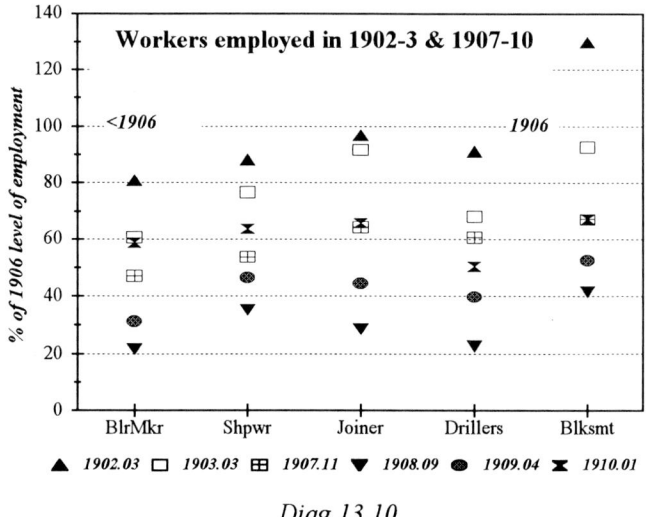

Diag 13.10

---

[107] The dispute of Sep-Nov 1910 - resulted in unemployment returns for the Tyne of 32-53%, the Wear 39-49% and the Tees 42-81%; these values were replaced with 12.6, 15.1 and 7.6 [the August levels] to avoid gross distortion.

than feast in merchant shipbuilding. Over a period of 147 months, the average monthly unemployment rates nationally exceeded 10%, while for the Tyne it was almost 12% and both the Wear [14.75%] and Tees were more than 14%. For four months out of every ten on the north east coast at least one worker in eight was seeking a job. On the Wear and Tees it was as high as one man in five for one quarter of the time. Engineering nationally averaged 5.2% and the north east at 8.2% was more than 50% higher. For nearly a quarter of these months one engineering worker in ten was seeking a job and for almost 10% of the time one in five were unemployed in the north east.

Engineer Robert Allan finds work.
One engineer's efforts to secure work was shown by Robert Allan's diary;[108] he was obliged to change his job thirty times between 1905 and 1912. There is a gap between completing his apprenticeship and going to sea. At Shields Engineering, in 1905, he was in charge of steam drifters and trawlers and stayed there until suspended on 28 March 1908. On 10 April he secured a start at Middle Docks but was paid off on 24th. After illness he was back at Shields Engineering on 11 June but after ten months he was again laid off there. The next day he started at G T Greys, where the job lasted four months. After a week without a job he secured work at J P Rennoldsons for six weeks, then went to sea again. On his return, it took six weeks to get his next job at Greys, but it only lasted from 14 February to 3 March. Four days later he started at Shields but only for six weeks, then back to Greys 23 May to 4 June. Then the first of a few days work at Clousens at the Albert Edward Dock and he had four days at Smiths at the Bull Ring. In summary Allan worked six times at Middle Dock and Shields Engineering, four times at Rennoldson before the continuous period that began on 16 September 1912 and continued until he moved to Palmers in April 1918. This trade unionist showed a tenacity to secure work typical of the north east craftsman.

Co-operatives & profit sharing.
There were a few examples of co-operative ventures and profit sharing on the north east coast. At Blyth the wood shipwrights set up a yard and registered it as the Union Co-operative Shipbuilding Society in 1869; the founding members were Richard Lough and a Mr Heron. It was intended to both build and repair wooden vessels. Twenty members in 1871 had a share capital of £1,200 and that year's trade amounted to £9,039. A profit of £849 was made in the next year and £524 in 1874, when with one member less the share capital had increased to £3,032. Three years later only seven members remained with a share capital of £450 and loans of £1,300; the business carried on as a co-operative certainly until 1888. In that year the Registrar had been informed by the secretary that *Owing to wooden vessels dying out, and consequent lack of employment, the society has a very feeble existence; and as we cannot take stock owing to vessels lying in dock remaining unsold, it is impossible to make a return.* Work continued at the yard until about 1902, although whether as a co-operative is uncertain.

A radical clergyman and pioneer of technical education, the Rev. Dr. Rutherford opened a co-operative marine engine works in an engine works which had remained closed for almost six years in the midst of the Newcastle 9-hours strike. This venture the *Ouseburn Co-operative Engine Works Co* is discussed in chap 14. A 54-hour week was part of the articles of association or *such other terms* as mutually agreed. It adopted the usual engineering practices: wages were to be determined between the workman and his foreman. Each workman was required to become a shareholder, and if he did not have the necessary £5, deductions were made from his regular pay packet. The workforce increased from 130 to a maximum of 800. This co-operative works failed after four years. Following the 9-hours strike, in December 1871, Hawthorns proposed *to establish more direct and mutual interest between the Firm and their Workmen; to prevent the occurrence of disputes.* Every person was to have a *direct pecuniary interest* in the business

---

[108] Allen began serving his time in December 1898 at the Northern Press & Engineering, but completed his apprenticeship at Shields Engineering in April 1904. In January 1905 he signed on ss *Lugigen* and was paid off on 17 March [*Came home bad with gastric Catarrh*], still under the doctor he returned to work at Shields Eng. Allan returned to sea in October 1909, on ss *Skerne*; two months later he had to leave through ill health.

and after financial costs and a fixed rate of return on capital were met, the remainder would be divided equally between the capitalist and all employees. This does not appear to have made much if any progress. Christopher Furness[109] in 1908 took steps to establish a scheme both for his shipyard and coal mines; again this did not work out, only surviving at the shipyard for about a year. In 1910, George Hunter suggested profit sharing to his Board, with the idea of a certain percentage of profit for the shareholders, then to divide the surplus by three, with equal parts to the shareholders, the workmen, and reserves. This was seen as a move *towards an increase in efficiency, and a decrease in costs*; the matter appeared regularly on Board agendas but there was no decision by the end of the year. A year later, £5,000 was set aside *for some purpose ... for the benefit of the Company's employee's* and the Board favoured a proposal to help the lower paid labourers. A similar £5,000 was set aside in 1912 accounts and in May £1,000 was taken for investment in preference shares, the income to be used for the benefit of old workmen and widows. A scheme was developed to receive deposits from employees, but there was very limited take up. Each of these proposals were well intended but not adequately prepared in terms of the times in which they were launched. Most workers saw too little of significance to themselves in these various proposals

Wages and Earnings.

Accurate information on precisely what individual workers were paid, as distinct from nominal rates is not easily established. With great regularity shipbuilders cited high earnings by Boilermakers on piecework but rarely the distribution between jobs and men. Trade unions never regarded their negotiated rate as anything other than a minimum and the employers always insisted they did not operate fixed rates. This variation of payment to those in the same occupation is of no small importance in trying to understand levels of income. Generally wages rose and fell with the movement of trade, although individual unions did influence how swiftly a cut might fall or an advance was gained.[110] Retail price variations and whether the bread winner, a valid term at the time, retained his job, were decisive in determining the impact on family life. An official survey of 1906

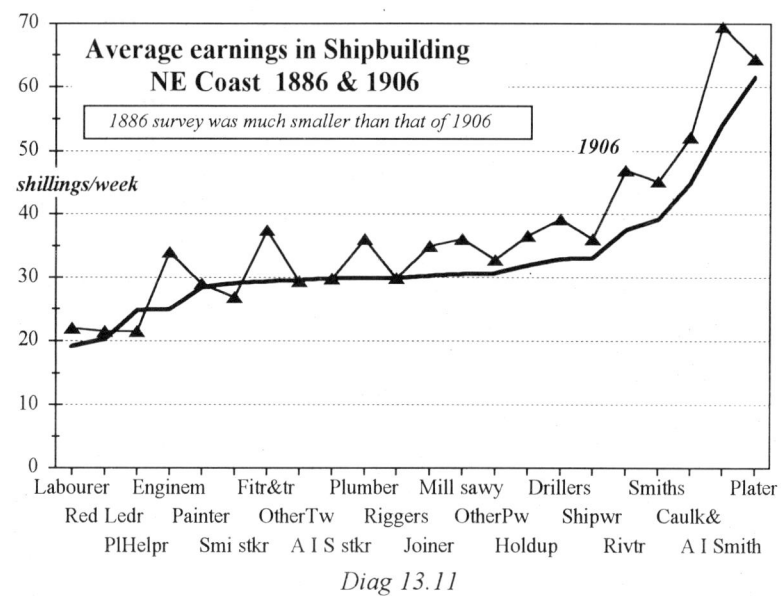

Diag 13.11

provides a basis for comparisons between trades and offers a bench mark, an earlier survey in 1886 was on a much smaller scale, for a summary of the average earnings see diag 13.11.

---

[109] Furness wrote *Industrial Peace and Efficiency* in 1908 and a year later *Co-operation in Coalmining*. His maiden speech in the House of Lords called for a commission on wider use of co-partnership.

[110] *Glasgow Herald* wrote: It was late in the season before the depression now general on the North East Coast took affect on the yards ... Wages have come down - naturally - and the operatives, to their credit be it said, have in most cases accepted the reductions with a good grace, recognising that this is their share of a falling market. 1902

Piecework earnings.
A division of the workers in 1906 between trades and piece and time payment is shown in diag 13.13. Just under half [47%] the shipyard workers were on piecework and they received 57% of the wages. The time rate was much less significant for the piecework trades and their earnings did not necessarily move proportionately to changes in time rates; when piecework was not available they were on lieu rates. In all cases it is very important to recognise the spread of earnings amongst the workforce, even amongst the best paid trades. Weekly earnings at the Jarrow shipyard, in September & November 1871, 1882 and 1885 are shown in diag 13.12.[111] Clearly the platers were capable to earning 60s/week and reached

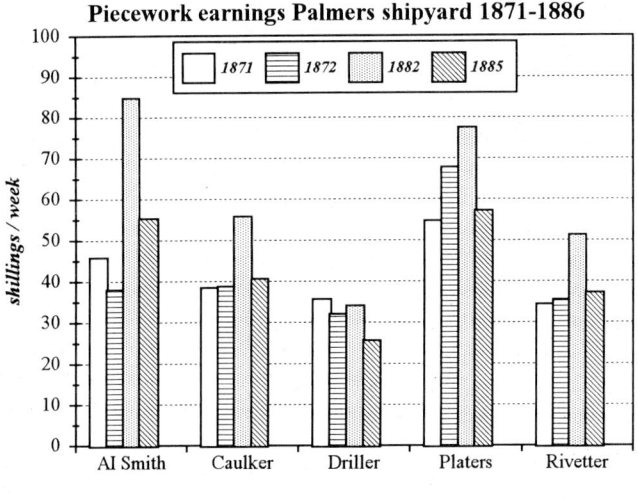

Diag 13.12

77.5s in 1882. The substantial fall back between 1882 and 1885 was from a boom year to a depressed year and the wage reductions already discussed. Angle iron smiths and frame benders almost reached 85s in 1882. Their average over the four pays was 45.7s compared with 64.25s for the platers. Rather surprisingly the caulkers [average 43.4s] were earning more than the riveters [39.6s]. The platers at an average 61.5s and AI smiths at 54.08s in the 1886 survey, were very close to Jarrow figures but caulkers at 49s and riveters 40.67s earned more. Likewise 41 drillers averaged 34.83s, which was substantially more than 25.68s earned at Jarrow in 1885! Holders-up earned 35s and the platers helpers 24.68s. The average for the shipwrights was just over 33s and the joiners 30.25s. General labourers were paid 19.08s. However, the hours worked for the 1886 earnings were not given. Helpers were paid 30s on the Tyne & Wear in the early 1890s but only 28.5s on the Tees, where it was suggested they averaged about four and half days a week. The *Engineer* in 1887 cited as average earnings in *some Representative* Tyne and Wear shipyards AI smiths 75s, platers 67.5s, riveters 52.67s and caulkers 52s. Gray reported the earnings per day on two vessels: 12.16s for each of the frame benders, platers both *inside* and *outside* [this seems a remarkable coincidence], riveters 9.75s, caulkers 8s [some earned 12.67s, 16.5s and 19.25s]; if these figures were over five days then the weekly amounts were 60s

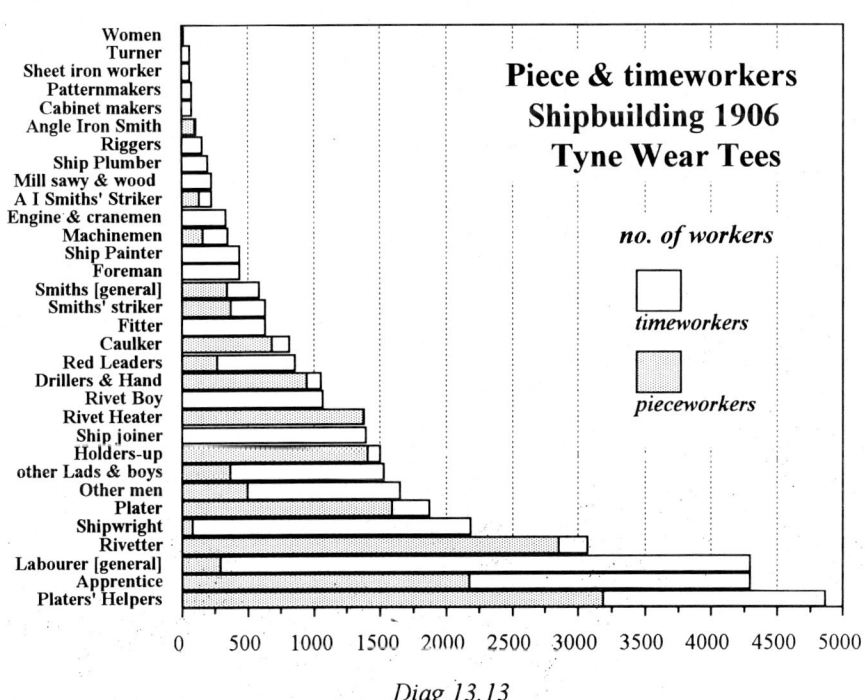

Diag 13.13

---

[111] John Price said there was an *Average increase* of 21.8%; this statement might be considered misleading; it was not referring to the weekly income but to average hourly earnings calculated on the basis of 60, 57 and 54 hours. Not of itself invalid but was not pointed out at the time, an illustration of how wage data was presented.

10ds, 58s 6d and 48s. The overall average at Grays was 6s 8d/day or 33s 4d/week, which was higher than an average of 32s $4^{1}/_{2}$d for the best month in 1906 on the north east coast.

Occasionally data appeared in the employers' records but unfortunately few of the detailed returns have survived. A return, in January 1886, gave the average daily earnings of platers as 11.32s, over 16,554 days, AI smiths 12s [3,982 days], riveters 8.77s [11,786 days], caulkers 8.67s [12,935days]. In 1888 slightly lower figures were returned for the Tyne - AI smiths 11s and platers 10.52s and drillers earned 5.62s and the holder-up 6.37s. Palmers reported in 1889 a range for the platers of 9.33s to 11.16s/day [apparently on an individual ship basis]. The figure of 11.16s was also given by Swan Hunter. AI smiths at Jarrow ranged from 10.13s to 11.69s and at Swans 13.33s. Ten years later there were similar figures and according to the employers squads of riveters with steel rivets were making 10s a day. A working week of five days, allowing for lost time, was probably the norm. It would be rash to suppose that because a plater could make 60s or £3/week that he earned more than £150 a year, even though the Inland Revenue wanted details of men earning more than £150 a year. The nature of the tasks in many shipyard trades did allow for substantial piecework earnings, with increased dexterity, better organisation or simply everything sometimes going just right. Ready accessibility to equipment and materials or tools also played their part and different parts of the vessel, although on same rate, could be worked more readily. So much was done completely manually that it allowed wide variations as a result of successful team work, exacting physical effort and intelligence, as well as chance. There were 24 changes in piecework rates for platers over the years 1879-1906, the accumulated effect of which was a reduction of 13%; other trades also had a similar number of changes.

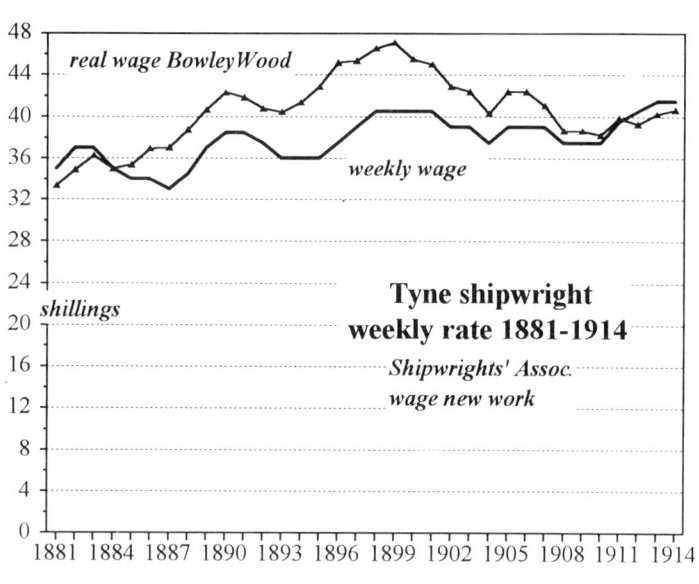

Diag 13.14

Over the years 1881-1914, the union rate for the Tyne shipwrights frequently changed. Beginning at 35s and rising to 37s before the fall back to the low point of 33s in 1887, then the path upwards in the next boom and 41s was reached in 1898, which held for three years then down again before the upward climb to 42s in 1912. These changes with an index of retail prices are plotted in diag 13.14. As already suggested precise links to *real* wages are rarely possible. The index however, can indicate broad trends and in a paradoxical way as wages fell in the mid-1880s, for those who continued to work their shillings could buy more. Apart from that the two lines follow similar trends; there was an upward trend to the end of the century but after that it was downwards, until it steadied at the time of the 1908-10 depression.

Shiprepair work, *old work*, was normally at a higher minimum rate than new building. The position for the Tyne & Blyth before the reductions of October 1902 showed a range of pay for both occupation and between firms. Shipwrights on repair were paid 43.5s compared with 40.5s on new building. Piecework rates for platers were given as 10s-18s, for riveters & caulkers 10s to 15s, with the holder-up at the usual $^{3}/_{4}$ of riveter. Many joiners were paid the same amount as the shipwrights 43.5s [new work 39.5s] but at both Palmers and Blyth it was a shilling less and only 39.5s at Wallsend Slipway. Blacksmiths were usually paid 41s; again it was less at Palmers [38.5s] and the Slipway [38s], but more at Clelands [42.5s].

Their strikers ranged from 24s to 26s. For the fitters there were different rates for *inside* work 38.5s and *on vessel* 41.5s; again the Slipway was 2.5s less on both. Fitters' labourers were paid 22s-23s *inside* and 24.5s-25.5s *on vessel*. Drillers were usually on piecework, but the day rates were at Blyth 6s, Clelands 6.25s and three other repairers at 6.5s; at Wallsend Slipway the driller's rate was 10d/hr per hour [7.5s for 9 hours]. General labourers were at 21s-25.5s, compared with shipyards at 21.5s and plater's helpers at 33s, chippers and painters at 28s. Plumbers working *inside* were on 36s or 36.5s but on board ship 3s more.

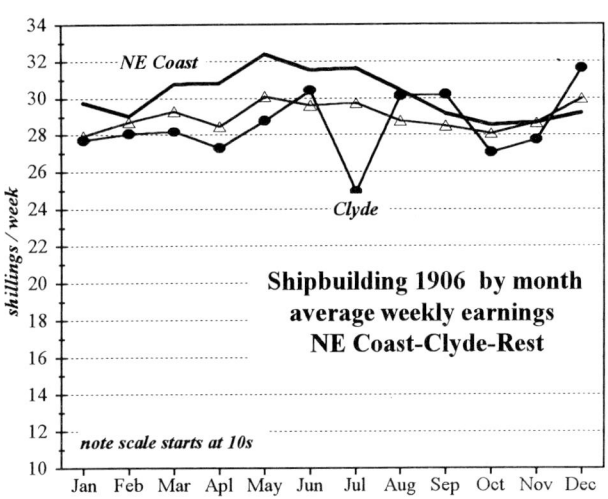

Diag 13.15

1906 Wages Survey.

The 1906 wages survey presented data combined for the Tyne, Wear and Tees, which prevents any comparisons between the rivers. This is a most comprehensive set of information, albeit in a boom year. For each month of 1906, the total of *amount of wages* and *number of workpeople* in shipbuilding in six regions is given. In the north east shipyards the number of workers varied between 38,319 in December to 43,706 in July. Average earnings show that for most months the North East was above the Clyde and the rest of UK [see diag 13.15]. There is a detailed account of wages for the last pay week of October, covering 36,036 workers by trade. The numbers working *full-time* were given but there is no indication of whether the remainder were on overtime or short time. Earnings of those not full-time suggest that many pieceworkers probably lost time and that time workers worked overtime. About 6,000 pieceworkers [36%] earned more than 40s /week but less than 1,000 timeworkers [5%] earned that much. There were 18858 on time and 16,747 on piecework. About 3,000 piece workers exceeded 50s but hardly any timeworkers. The normal week was 53 hours for 57% of the workers; the remainder were on a 54-hour week, which was the norm on the Clyde and in the *South*

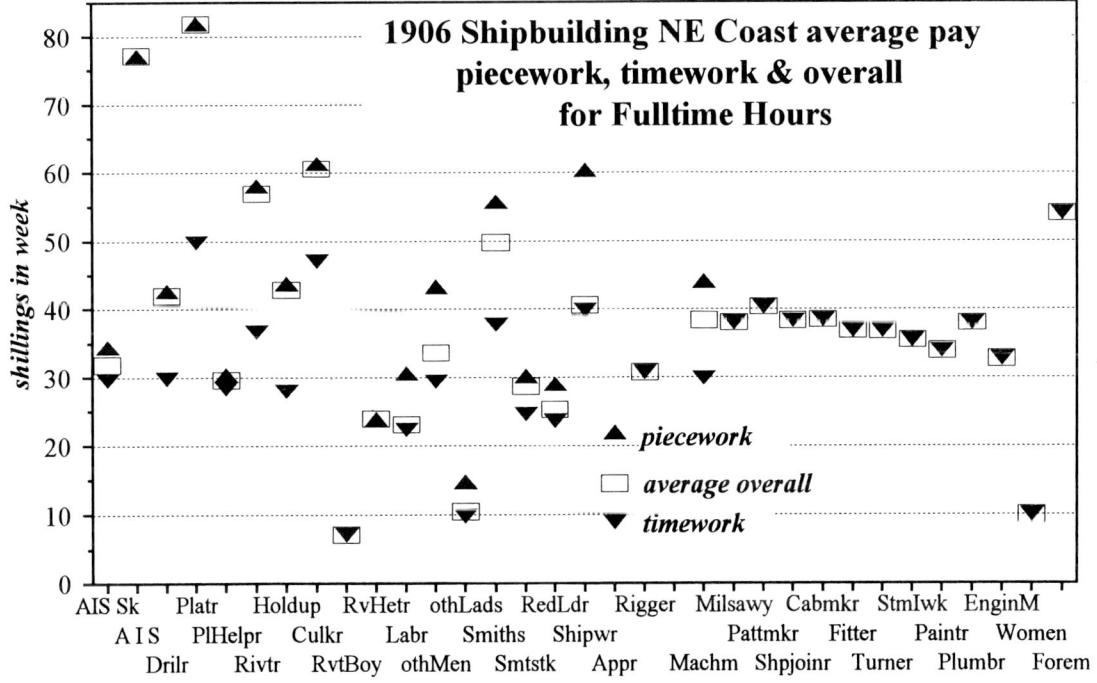

Diag 13.16

of England 82% had a 48-hour week. The *usual number of holidays per annum* was given as 11 to 19 in the north east, 10-21 on the Clyde, 6-17 on the Mersey & Barrow with the *South* on 4 to 9. These were, of course, unpaid days when the yards were closed! The recognised holidays for enhanced payments were: Christmas Day, Good Friday, Easter Monday, Whit Monday and on the Tyne Race Week Wednesday and Thursday. An overall picture of the earnings for a full-time week by trade is shown in diag 13.16. A box shows the overall average by trade; timework is an inverted triangle and piecework a triangle. Where the inverted black triangle, timework is enclosed in the square, no piecework was worked, for example the patternmakers. Likewise if triangle is enclosed only piecework, the AI smiths and the platers. Where both were worked by the same trade then the position of the square shows roughly the balance between the two types of payment. Apprentices were almost equally divided between time and piecework; on time lads earned 8.91s and the pieceworkers 22s, [average 14.5s]. Only 22 out of 639 of shipwrights worked piecework, [the piece men earned 60s] the overall average at 40.6s was only just above the timeworkers earnings of 39.9s.

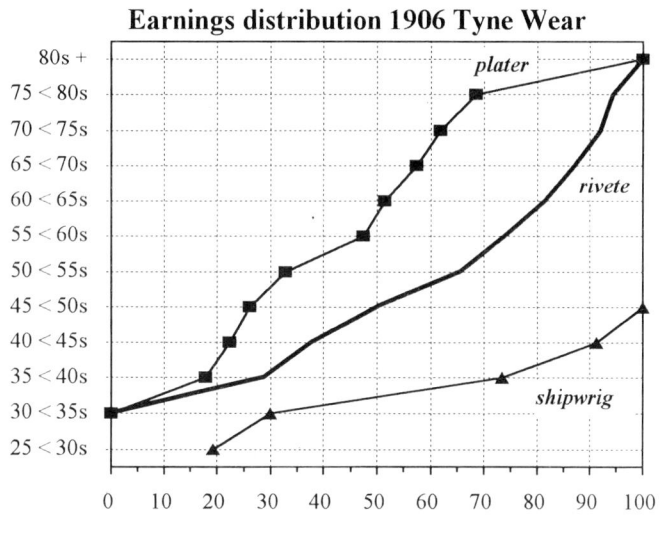

Diag 13.17

In 1906 north east platers had higher weekly earnings than other regions. An average of 82s was by the *fulltime* platers [63% were not *fulltime*] compared with 71.25s for the UK as a whole and 63.08s on the Clyde. Once all the platers are included, it fell to 70.08s [UK- 64.58s and Clyde 59s]. On the Clyde almost 40% of all platers earned less than 50s, compared with about 26% in the north east; similarly more than 30% exceeded 80s compared with less than 19% on the Clyde. There is no regional breakdown for the 249 platers who earned 100s or more [just over 7% of the total]. Although north east riveters earned more than elsewhere the difference was small, 48.75s compared with 47.91s on the Clyde and 47.83s for the UK.[112] The 1,373 rivet heaters averaged 14.42s, but the 176 who worked a full week got 24s, a quarter of them 25.5s or more. Rivet boys on time averaged 5.75s and on a full week earned 7.16s. Caulker's fulltime earnings at 61.33s were 9% above the riveters. Platers Helpers working *fulltime* [572] earned 30.42s on piecework, however the 2,611 who did not work a normal hours only got 20.16s. There was a much smaller difference between, time and piece for these workers; overall the time men averaged 20.5s and those on a full week got 28.42s, only 6% below the piece workers. Four women were employed at 9s. Every occupation group cannot be examined here but the average is plotted in diag 13.18. Most shipwrights earned between 35s and 40s, although about 1 in 4 earned more, platers roughly earned twice as much as shipwrights [see diag 13.17].

Pay in Marine Engine Works.
Most engineering workers in marine engine plants were on time rates. Average pay per employee at the Wallsend Slipway from 1876 to 1914 is shown in diag 13.18; there is no information of the hours worked. The weekly pay varies from as little as 26s to as much as 35s. After each boom wages fell. From the low point of 1893 there was a steady increase up to nearly 34s in 1900. Another fall back followed by a rise to 34.5s in 1907, then the fall in the 1908-10 slump. Workers in this leading world marine engineering plant

---

[112] Those working full-time on the Mersey at 61.75s were higher than the north east 58.08s; as were the holder-up.

earned 28s weekly over the years 1908-10, thereafter it rose to 35s in 1914. At the Jarrow engine works, fitters averaged 26.77s in 1871 and 32.43s in 1882 and labourers advanced from 17.65s to 20.52s; this was an increase of more than 20%. The overall average at St Peters was just over 27s in 1888, with fitters at 32s and labourers at 20s, however, nearly 20% of the fitters were under 30s and the top 20% were over 34s. A quarter of the labourers were on 18s or less and one in six were over 22s. In 1905, the fitter's rate was 35s in the north east, the Clyde and Barrow. The Mersey was 1s higher and London 4s.

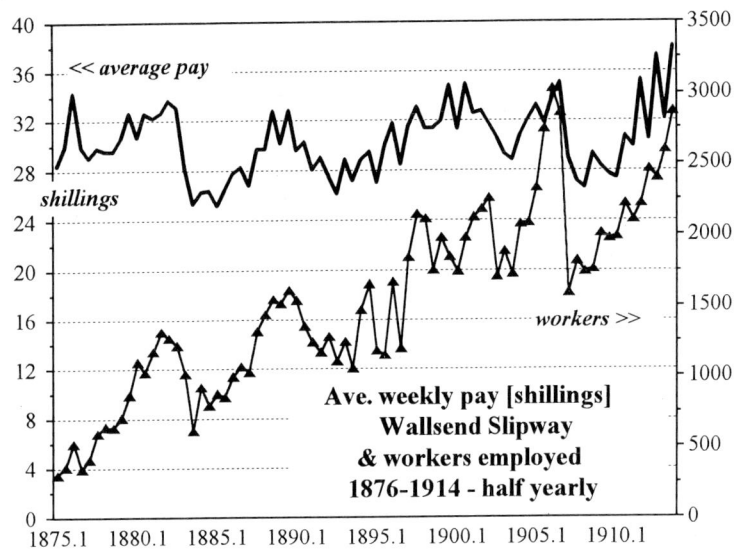

Diag 13.18

Standard of Living.

In personal human terms there is no means of balancing the success of the many by the deprivation of a minority and unfortunately too often that minority in terms of not having a job was frequently very large. This proviso is pertinent to all that follows. Undoubtedly for those in work life was much better at the end of the period 1871-1913 than it was at the beginning; indeed something would have been very wrong given the advance in technological knowledge and skill, if there had not been a substantial improvement. The meagre budget of a skilled craftsman such as Gamsby of 1850s had greatly expanded. An illustration of this was the prices for provisions given by a German coal miner in his report on how Englishmen live for a Social Democratic newspaper in the mid-1890s: *pence per pound* [see inset table]

The Engineer of 1887 in a wages survey stated that in Newcastle rents could vary from 3s per week for a single room to 5s/ week. In the blocks of industrial dwellings a single room flat cost 2s 6d/week and two rooms 3s3d. Board & lodgings males 12s 2d to 16s 2d and for females 9s 2d to 12s 2d. Some north east prices for 1905 and 1912 are given at the end of the chapter and the official return noted a price range; these show the kind of purchases made and also may provide a guide to spending power. Throughout this period about two-thirds of a family budget was spent on food.[113] Almost certainly with lower income and unemployment, wives and mothers switched their purchases from higher up to lower down the price scale or buying the remainders no longer suitable for normal sale such as burnt loaves, bacon off-cuts and offal. At this time official surveys were beginning, from which a retail price index was later constructed. The

Prices per lb weight in pence by German miner living on Tyne	
Wheat-flour [per stone]	10 - 18
beef	3½ - 8
mutton	4 - 6
corned beef	6
American salt pork	3½ - 6
Fine sugar	1 - 1½
loaf sugar	2
currants	1½ - 2½
raisins	2½ - 3½
rice	1½ - 2½
tea	12 - 18
beans & green peas	1½ - 2½
butter	12 - 16
margarine	5 - 11
American lard	5
salt in the block	¼
Dutch cheese	5¼

---

[113] *The Engineer* in 1887 gave for Hartlepool ironworker an *Example of Cost of Living for a family of Six:* Butter, fish & meat 124d [32.2%]; flour & potatoes 49d [13.8%]; groceries & milk 32d [8.3%]; rent & fuel 57d [14.8%]; lighting 19d [4.9%], clothing 102d [26.5%]: total 385d from income of 438d. This was similar to the ratios in Lady Bell's book: food at only 54.3%, more than a quarter spent on clothing was much higher than found elsewhere.

proportion of different purchases by urban families in 1904 on an average income of 32s [a skilled craftsman] is shown in diag 13.19. The continuing dominant role of bread and potatoes is clear.[114] Meat and bacon consumption increase substantially with increased income, butter and fresh milk even more so. Suggestions of precision in deciding *real* wages are misguided and no attempt is made here to quantify these advances. Side by side with the general advances there were certainly periods of devastating poverty for skilled as well as labouring men and women. Great ingenuity by mothers, often at their own sacrifice, achieved much in those bad periods. A critical indicator of

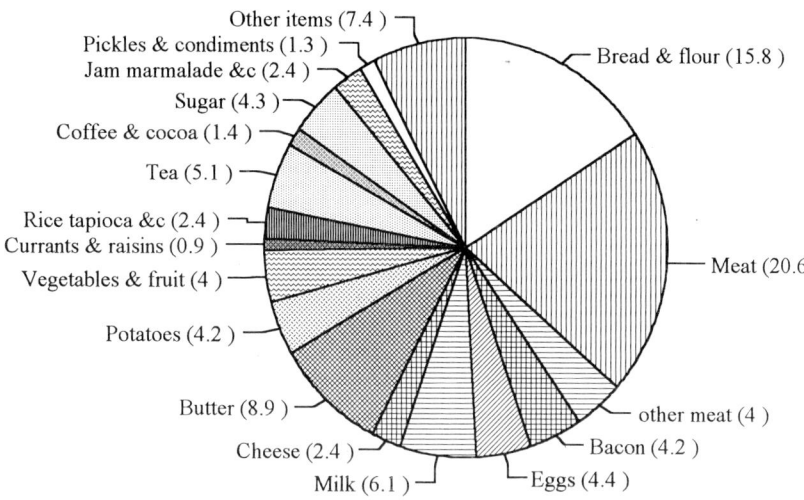

Diag 13.19

social progress, infant mortality, remained tragically high; it was 123 deaths under a year per 1000 births in South Shields[115] in 1911-3 and still over 100 ten years later. Men stayed in employment as long as they physically could, if they reached their late 60s taking more lowly tasks to continue to have some income. Those craftsmen, who had contributed for 25 years or more to their trade union received superannuation. Up to 1897, this ranged from 4s to 7s [a shilling increment for each five years of contributions up to 40] and it was then increased to 6s to 11s. In the case of the Shipwrights in 1907 the amount was 5.5s. This only affected a part of the workforce. From 1909 there was a means tested old age pension of 5s/week from the age of 70 [7s 6d for a married couple]. Any Boilermaker on 11s was excluded, since an income of 10s/week disqualified person from state pension. Unless men as trade unionists had sickness benefit there was no income during illness. One fifth of the members of the Shipwrights' Union received sickness benefits payments during 1907, with an average payment per sick man of 64s 3d, nearly two weeks pay. Among adults there was a significant increase in life span. The median age of death was 38 years in 1878 for north east Boilermakers' Society members. Thirteen years later it was 45 and by 1906 had reached 51 years. A year later the members of the Shipwrights' Union were living on average about three years longer. Wives of Boilermakers also advanced from 28 years through 36 years to 44 years in 1906; this only, of course, effects those who died before their husbands; women had a longer life expectancy than men. However, in the Boilermakers' Rules of 1852, there was a £7 death benefit for the death of a first wife and a similar amount for a second wife. At that time the premature death of many young wives was recognised. No doubt this sample has its limitations. These were craftsmen, but the size of the sample was increasing and it does indicate a clear improvement. Injury and death stalked the shipyard [see chapter 23 in Part II].

The central role of shipbuilding in north east communities is summarised from the 1911 census. More than one man in five at Sunderland was directly employed in shipbuilding, as the diag 13.20 shows. At Hartlepool it was more than one in six, at South Shields one in every nine, at Tynemouth almost one in ten

---

[114] *Round About A Pound A Week* by Mrs Pember Reeves, first published in 1913, although largely based upon London budgets, is a most useful insight into the problems of the low paid.

[115] Clapham supported the view that infant mortality was *the most sensitive index of social welfare and sanitary administration.* [v III, p 460]. The following were comparative figures for other parts of Tyneside: Hebburn - 134; Jarrow - 131; Newcastle - 120; Wallsend - 116; Gosforth - 93 and Whitley Bay - 54.

and so on. Less than 1% of the male working population of England & Wales was in the industry. This industrial concentration profoundly affected the whole community, not only because of the numbers employed but also because a significant part of the industry were well paid men. When they were without work and pay packets, the effect quickly spread through the shop keeper and beyond. That was why not merely unemployment but industrial disputes became the concern of all. The North East was a great industrial centre, with more than one third of the shipbuilding workers in the kingdom working there and about one seventh of the workers in engineering. Industrial peace was the normal situation. Trade union divisions, and even rivalries, did not help the workers'

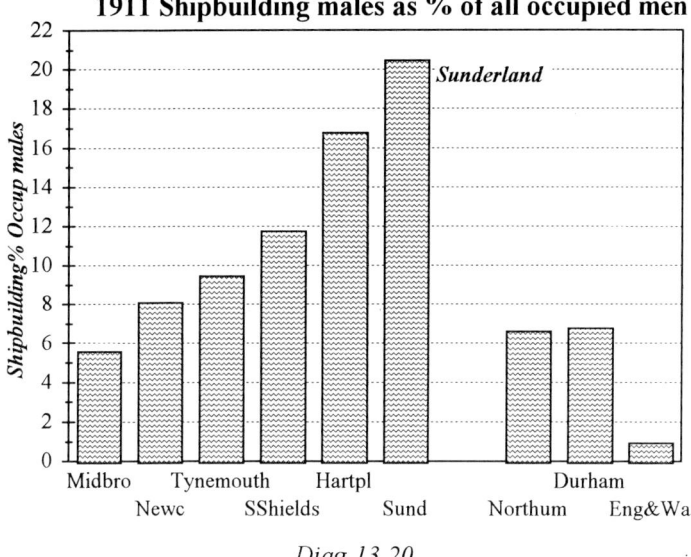

Diag 13.20

cause nor that of the industry. An industrial union embracing all the shipbuilding trades would probably have helped both the worker and the employer. However, 1907 saw the ending by the employers of the 1894 north east wage agreement with the Boilermakers' for far less satisfactory national arrangements. The Wear Conciliation Board, a fine child of much travail, was sacrificed on the same altar. Yet a spirit survived the many buffetings and disputes of 1907-13 so that when in 1917, Lloyd George sent forth Commissioners *to inquire into ... the causes of industrial unrest.* They reported:

> that past experience of the advantages of Trade Unions in adjusting labour difficulties and bringing about good relations between employers and employed on the North East Coast convinces us that nothing ought to be done to interfere with the usefulness of the Unions. If the North East were wholly independent of the other fields of industry it might well be left to employers and employed to settle by themselves any differences that might arise.

This ability of employers and employed to work together was the product of decades of experience in struggle, organisation and talk. Craftsmen struggled to maintain the status of their craft and their pay differentials and indeed to do all they could to improve their standard of living. For them their welfare benefits were always important and their leaders tried to avoid putting these in jeopardy by prolonged strike action and unnecessary disputes. The more extensive their trade union membership the more successfully they achieved their objectives. Labourers and semi-skilled workers by creating their own trade unions secured some voice in negotiations with both the employers and the craftsmen they frequently worked under. Amongst the employers there were those who sought to find a resolution of differences by negotiation and an agreed framework which minimised conflict. As among trade union leaders there were also some who sought to secure their position by strength and if need be by lock-out. Overall industrial relations on the north east coast were better than in most other regions of shipbuilding. Most workers felt an attachment to their company and even if they were unemployed, locked out or on strike they expected to return to that yard or workshop: that was how they lived.

From official survey pence per lb weight	South Shields 1905 Price	1905 HighPr	Newcastle 1905 Price	1905 HighPr	Sunderland 1905 Price	1905 HighPr	South Shields 1912 Price	1912 HighPr
Bacon sides	6.00	7.50			7.00	8.00	9.00	11.00
Bacon collar	6.50				7.00			
Bacon roll Amer	6.00	7.00	6.00	8.00	6.50	8.00	8.50	10.00
Bacon streaky	6.00	7.50			7.00	8.00		
Beef flat or top rib	8.50	9.50	7.00	9.00	8.50	9.00	8.00	10.00
Beef shin & bone	3.00	4.00			4.00		4.00	5.00
Beef shin no bone	8.00		8.00		7.00		8.00	10.00
Beef silverside	9.00		9.00		8.00	9.00	10.00	10.50
Beef thin flank	6.00		6.00	7.00	5.50	6.50	6.50	7.00
Bread	6.00		6.00		5.50	6.00	6.00	7.00
Butter fresh	14.00	15.00			12.00	15.00		
Butter salt colonial	12.00		12.00		12.00		13.00	14.00
Butter salt Danish	14.00		14.00		14.00		15.00	16.00
Butter salt Irish							13.00	14.00
Cheese North America	7.00		7.00	8.00	7.00		8.00	9.00
Cheese Cheshire							9.00	10.00
Eggs [foreign]	0.75	1.00	0.86	1.00	0.75		0.75	1.00
Flour	8.00		8.50	9.00	8.50	9.00	9.50	10.00
Milk	4.00		3.50		4.00		4.00	
Mutton breast	5.00	6.00	5.00		4.50	5.00	6.00	7.00
Mutton Chops [trim]	10.00		10.00		8.00	10.00	10.00	12.00
Mutton leg	9.00		9.00	10.00	8.00	9.50	9.50	11.00
Mutton Nech scrag	6.00		6.00		6.00		6.00	8.00
Mutton Neck best	9.00		9.00		8.00	9.50	9.00	10.00
Mutton shoulder	9.00		7.50	9.00	7.50	9.00	7.50	9.00
Pork belly	7.00	7.50	7.00		7.00	8.00	9.00	
Pork chops	8.00	9.00	8.00	10.00	9.00		10.00	
Pork fore loin	8.00	9.00	9.00		8.00	10.00	9.00	11.00
Pork leg	7.50	8.50	9.00		8.00	10.00	10.00	12.00
Potatoes	2.25		3.00		2.25		3.00	4.50
Steak beef	7.00	9.00	9.00	10.00	9.00	9.00		
Steak rump	10.00		10.00	11.00	9.00	10.00	10.00	12.00
Steak shoulder					8.00	9.00	10.00	11.00
Sugar lump	2.50		2.50		2.50		2.25	2.50
Sugar white gran	2.00		1.75	2.25	2.00		1.75	2.00
Sugar white moist	1.75		2.00	2.25	1.50			
Tea	16.00	18.00	20.00	24.00	18.00		16.00	18.00
Rent 2 rooms	42	51	48	63	30	84	42	51
Rent 3 rooms	51	69	63	78	42	9	57	69
Rent 4 rooms	63	78	72	84	66	10	60	81

NOTES

The Custom House Registers and Lloyd's Register are sources throughout and are not cited for chapters. From 1874-5 Lloyd's Register contains substantial detail. Norman McCord's *North East England ... 1760-1960* provides a general background. *The Dictionary of Busiiness Biography* has entries for Bartram, J T Batey, Boyd, Benjamin Browne, G Clark Raylton Dixon, Doxford, Gray, Geo Hunter, Laing, Leslie, Marr, F C Marshall, palmer, Parsons, J Wigham Richardson, Ropner, Rowell, Short and R Thompson.

This work is based upon the considerable archive collections of the following companies in TWAS 1811 records of Crown, Doxford, Laing, J L Thompson and George Clarke [there are other holdings for these companies], Armstrong Whitworth, [held at TWAS], Bartram & Sons [TWAS 990 & 1708], Readheads [TWAS 1061, 1202 & 1926], Short Bros [TWAS 714 - 1391], Hawthorn-Leslie [TWAS 962 &c], Swan Hunter & Wigham Richardson [under many TWAS nos.] Robert Thompson [TWAS 1508 & 1081], Wallsend Slipway, NEM [TWAS 1993]. Smaller collection, for example on Austin [TWAS1658] and Palmers were also used. The records of Edwards & Smith's Dock now at TWAS, previously in Cleveland Archives were also a major source. Extensive use was made of the records of employers associations - Tyne, Wear & Tees Shipbuilders [TWAS 708 & 895] Wear Shipbuilders [TWAS 708], NE Coast Ship Repairers [978], Tees & Hartlepool Shipbuilders [TWAS 895] and the Engineering Employers [EM/EN/4] and holdings at the National Maritime Museum. These records are only identified by company name in following notes.

Chapter 1
Bourne H *History of Newcastle upon Tyne* [1736]
Davis, Ralph *Seamen's Sixpences: An Index of Commercial Activity, 1697-1828* [*Economica*]
Dietz B The North-East Coal Trade 1550-1750. [*NorHist*]
Ellis Joyce *A Bold Adventurer: The Business Fortunes of William Cotesworth, c1668-1726* [*NorHist*]
Gardner R *England's Grievances Discovered in relation to the Coal Trade* [1655]
Hughes E *North Country Life in the Eighteenth Century*
Mackenzie E *An Impartial History of ... Newcastle* [1801]
Moir D R *The Birth and History of Trinity House, Newcastle upon Tyne*
Nef J U *The Rise of the British Coal Industry*
Willan T S *The English Coasting Trade*

Chapter 2
TWAS GU/SH/1-4 [Shipwrights' Conpany]
NRO 650; NRO ZCE 10; NRO 92 - 2/DE12/2/1-4 & 2/DE43/6/1-19.
Anon Delaval Papers
Abell Sir Wm *The Shipwright's Trade*
Bourne H *History of Newcastle upon Tyne* [1736]
Brand J *History of Newcastle upon Tyne* [1789]
Charlton L *The History of Whitby and Whitby Abbey* [1779]
Davis Ralph *The Rise of the English Shipping Industry*

Defoe Daniel *Tour through England and Wales* [1727]
Dendy F W *Records of Company of Hostmen*
Flagg, Amy C *Notes on ... Shipbuilding in South Shields*
Fraser C M & Emsley K *Tyneside*
Chorographia Or A Survey of Newcastle Upon Tyne [1649]
Hedley W Percy *Northumberland Families* v 1
Hinderwell Thomas *The History... of Scarborough* [1798]
Hughes E *North Country Life in the Eighteenth Century*
J C *The Compleat Collier* [1708]
Jackson Gordon *Hull in the Eighteenth Century*
Lane F C *Venetian Ships & Shipbuilders*
Lavery Brian *Nelson's Navy*
Lipson E *The Economic History of England* v II
Manders F *History of Gateshead*
Parry J H *Trade and Dominion*
Rowe D J *The Records of the Company of Shipwrights*
Rowntree Arthur [edit] *The History of Scarborough*
Sowler *The Town and Borough of Stockton-on-Tees*
Summers *History of Sunderland* [1858]
Thompson E P & Yeo Eileen *The Unknown Mayhew*
Unger R W *Dutch Shipbuilding before 1800*

Chapter 3
PRO ADM 49/102 PRO CUS 36/5
Laing archive
Parliamentary Papers 1805 *Ships of War...*
Parliamentary Papers 1806 *Ships and Vessels built in Great Britain 1790-1806.*
Sel Ctte on Navigation Laws [1848] *Return of ... Men of war ... built Merchant yards ...1793-1815*
Newcastle Directory 1778
Papers by *The Society of Shipowners of Great Britain 1807*
Smith's Dock Monthly 1920
Archibald E H H *The Fighting Ship in the Royal Navy*
Aspinall A *The Early Trade Unions ...*
Clay M, Milburn & Miller *An Eye Ma p of Sunderland and Bishopwearmouth 1785-1790* by John Rain
Colledge J J *Ships of the Royal Navy : an historical index*
Flagg, Amy C *Notes ... Shipbuilding in South Shields*
Goldenberg J A *An analysis of shipbuilding sites in Lloyd's Register of 1776 MarMirr*
W. J. Hausman *Size and Profitability of English Colliers in the Eighteenth Century - BusHistRev v.LI*
Morris Roger *The Royal Dockyards during the Revolutionary and Napoleonic Wars*
Richardson Wm *History of the Parish of Wallsend*
Surtees R *The History and Antiquities ... of Durham* [1820]
Wallace John *The History of Blyth* [1869]

Chapter 4
A Return ... of Steam Ships Registered in United Kingdom ... 1861 Accounts & Papers 1861 LVIII [371]
Sel Cttes on Shipwrecks 1836 1839 1843
Select Ctte on Manufactures... 1833
Bartram's Journal a photocopy in Tyne & Wear Archives
Corder MSS
TWAS 1081 Thompson Robt
TWAS 1811/1- [Laing] 1811/ 77 - [Doxford] 1811/ 214 - [Thompson J L]

Doxford *TWAS* 2276
Edwards papers
Lloyd's *Visitation Books* 1851-
Lloyd's *Reports of Surveyors &c No.1* 1844-
Shipwrights' Work NRO *312*
Sunderland Rate Books TWAS 209/84
White J TWAS 730
The Shipping World
Cleveland Industrial Archaeologist no.15
Bocler *Shipbuilder v. III pp 73*
Gilchrist A *Early examples of iron shipbuilding* 1865
NECIES v.4 Sivewright; v 54 Baker
Moorsom, G *On the new tonnage law* INA 1860
Abell, Sir Wm *The Shipwright's Trade*
An Operative Shipwright *Causes of Distress Amongst the Shipwrights* [1858]
anon *Where the Wall Ends*
anon *Annals of Lloyd's Register*
Blake G *Lloyd's Register of Shipping 1760-1960*
Campell, R *The London Tradesman* [1747]
Charnock J *A History of Marine Architecture* [1800]
Clarke J F *The Changeover from Wood to Iron Shipbuilding*
Deane's Doctrine of Naval Architecture [1670]
Dodds & Moore *Building the Wooden Fighting Ship*
Driel, A van *Ship Tonnage Measurement*
Estep E Cole *How Wooden Ships Are Built* [1918] repr 1983
Farr G - *Shipbuilding in North Devon*
Farr G *Shipbuilding in the Port of Bristol*
Fincham J *A History of Naval Architecture* [1851]
Flagg Amy C *Notes ... Shipbuilding in South Shields*
Garbutt G *History of Monkwearmouth...* [1819]
Gilchrist *A Early examples of iron shipbuilding* [1865]
Grantham J *Iron Shipbuilding* [1858]
Grantham J *Iron as a material for Shipbuilding* [1842]
Hardy A C *From Slip to Sea*
Harris D G *F H Chapman, the First Naval Architect and his work [1721-1808]*
Holms C *Practical Shipbuilding* [1916]
Horsley John E *Tools of the Maritime Trades*
Hume J *Shipbuilding Machine Tools*
Keys R E *The Sailing Ships of Aln & Coquet*
Mitchell J *Shipbuilding*
Nell T *Shipbuilding in Sunderland 1834 AntqSund* v.XXV
Newman Brian *Plate and Section Working Machinery in British Shipbuilding 1850-1945*
Paasch H *Illustrated Marine Encyclopedia* [1st 1890]
Ponsford, C N *Shipbuilding on The Exe*
Rees *Naval Architecture* [1814]
Richardson J Wigham *Memoirs* [1911]
Salaman R A *Tools of the Shipwright 1650 Folklife v 5*
Salisbury W *Early Tonnage Measurement in England - MarMirr* [1966 1967 1968]
Sinclair N T *Industry to 1914 in Milburn & Miller* [1988]
Singer Charles & al [edit] *A History of Technology*
  v III Naish; v IV Naish; v V Robb.
Thompson *Memoir of John Thompson*
Unger R W *Dutch Shipbuilding before 1800*
White *Manual of Naval Architecture*

Chapter 5
Corder Family records
Corder MSS
Sel Ctte *Navigation Laws* 1848
Sel Ctte on *Manufacturing, Commerce and Shipping* [1833]
Sel Ctte on *Ship Wrecks* 1836 -1839
Shipbuilding in Liverpool evidence before a committee of the Town Council [1850]
Lloyd's Visiting Committee Reports
Sunderland Herald
Pigot's *Directory* 1834
Appleby Miller *The First Tug-boat Smith's Dk Jrl* 1929
Armstrong W G and others *The Industrial Resources of Tyne, Wear and Tees*
Barton Peter *The Port of Stockton-on-Tees and its Creeks...*
Barton Peter *A decade of iron shipbuilding*
Flagg, Amy C *Notes ...Shipbuilding in South Shields*
Hedderick P *A Treatise on Marine Architecture* [1830].
Jackson G *Hull in the Eighteenth Century*
Jones, S *A Maritime History of the Port of Whitby ...*
Martin & McCord *The Steamship Bedlington 1841-54 Maritime History*
McLaren-Kerr D *John Winspear*
Proud J H *Seahorses of the Tees*
Proud J H *150 years of the Maltese Cross*
Rutherford W *The Man who built the Mauretania*
Thomas P N *British Steam Tugs*
Williamson James *Clyde Passenger Steamers 1812-1901*

Chapter 6
Corder MSS
Doxford -Laing - Thompson JL -Thompson Robt archives
Lloyd's *Visitation Books* 1851-
Lloyd's *Reports of Surveyors &c No.1* 1844-
Thompson J *Memoir of Mr John Thompson*
Wear Shipbuilders Association TWAS 708/1-
Webster & Co account books
SundHer annual output tables
An Operative Shipwright *Causes of Distress Amongst the Shipwrights*
Armstrong W G and others *The Industrial Resources of Tyne, Wear and Tees*
Bain G W *Antiquities of Sunderland* [1904]
Banbury P *Shipbuilders of the Thames & the Medway*
Bell R C ed. *Diaries from the Days of Sail*
Clarke J F *Shipbuilding 1780-1914*
Clarke J F *Shipbuilding on the River Wear 1780-1870*
Graham, G *The Ascendancy of the Sailing Ship 1850-85* [1956 EcHistR 9 74-88]
Lubbock, Basil *The Blackwall Frigates*
MacGregor D R *The Tea Clippers 1833-1875*
McCord N *North East England The region's development*
Newspaper clippings Southampton Library on Oswald.
Phillips M *A History of Banks, Bankers and Banking in Northumberland, Durham and North Yorkshire*
Potts T *Sunderland, a History of Town, Port, Trade and Commerce*
Rance *Victorian Shipbuilding at Southampton*

Chapter 7
NRO 693 [Tyne Iron SB]
Achives Readhead - Wigham Richardson- Swan Hunter - Hawthorn Leslie
Palmer TWAS 1357/1-
Lloyd's *Visitation Books* 1851-
Shields Gazette
The Engineer
Mid-Tyne Link
Palmer's Record 1902-6
Practical Mechanic's Journal
Smith's Dock Jrl
The Works of Palmers Shipbuilding and Iron Co Ltd [1912]
RINA v 18 Martell; v29 Messent 1906 Twaddell
John Readhead & Sons *A Hundred Years of Shipbuilding at South Shields* [1965]
Armstrong W G and others *The Industrial Resources of Tyne, Wear and Tees*
Clarke J F *Power on Land & Sea*
Duckworth C L D & Langmuir G E *Railway... Steamers*
Flagg, Amy C *Notes... Shipbuilding in South Shields*
Guthrie J *The River Tyne: its history and resources*
Johnson, R W *The making of the Tyne*
MacGregor David R *The Chinabird*
Richardson J Wigham *Memoirs* [1911]
Richardson Wm *History of the Parish of Wallsend*
Richardson Wigham *Official Local Guide- Industrial Section* [1889]
Robinson N J *Stag Line and Joseph Robinson and Sons*
Runciman, Sir Walter *Collier Brigs and their Sailors*
Rutherford Wilfred *The man Who Built the Mauretania*
Wilkinson Ellen *The Town that was Murdered*
Swan Hunter *Launching Ways*

Chapter 8
Barton P *A decade of iron shipbuilding* in *Sea Breezes*
Barton P *The Port of Stockton-on-Tees and its Creeks ...*
Brewster J *The Parochial History ... of Stockton*
Craig R *William Gray and Company... 1864-1913*
Fallows W *Fragments of the Early History of the Tees*
Heaviside H *The Annals of Stockton-on-Tees*
Hogg P *RICHES*
Hogg P *Central Marine Engine Works*
Hogg P *The history ... of the ports of Hartlepools NECIES*
Lilley W *The History of Middlesbrough*
Martin R *Historical Notes on West Hartlepool and its founder.*
McLaren-Kerr D *John Winspear*
Richmond T *Local Records of Stockton ... [1868]*
Sharp C *A History of Hartlepool* [1851]
Sowler T *The Town and Borough of Stockton-on-Tees* 1972
Spaldin B *Shipbuilders of the Hartlepools*
Wood R *West Hartlepool*
visits to Tees & Hartlepool by IMechEng 1893 August; Iron & Steel Inst 1908

Chapter 9
Papers at the INA
v7 Rochussen [Application of Steel to the Building of Ships].
v8 [Treatment of Steel Plates in the Shipbuilder's Yard]
v9.p.11 - 275. The Treatment of Steel Plates. Henry Sharp 10-18 INA v16 p.141 INA v.22 p.13 INA v19 p.185 v19 p1-Martell, p 27 Reed; v23 pp167-8v29 p80.INA v.29 p.88. INA v. 22 Parker INA v.17 pp135-6. Siemens.
INA v.21, v.12
I.Civil v.84 v.80 p.19
I.Mech 1881
Iron & Steel Institute 1878 1879 1880 1884 1889 1896
NECIES v14 p88;
The Engineer
Engineering 1867
Shipping World 1883, 1892, 1895
Cleveland Institute of Engineers 1881-2
Denny List v1-4
Report of the Naval Board on Mild Steel Washington 1886.
Annals of Lloyd's Register
Bell I Lowthian *Iron Trade of the United Kingdom* [1886]
Bessemer H *Autobiography*
Boyd Cable *One Hundred Years of the P & O*
Brown D K *A Century of Naval Construction [1983] p 48;*
Clapham Sir John *An Economic History of Modern Britain ... 1850-1886.*
Clarke J F & Storr F *The Intro' of the Use of Mild Steel*
Duckworth C L D & Langmuir G E *Railway ... Steamers*
Faupel J H *Engineering Design [1964]*
Haws D *Merchant Fleets in Profile [1979 - to vol.10].*
Jeans J S *Steel: its History, Manufacture ... and Uses.*
Knight R *The Practical Boilermaker, Iron-shipbuilder and Mast Maker* [1880]
McCloskey D N *Economic Maturity and Entrepreneurial Decline British Iron &Steel*
On Waste in Combustion [1869]; NECIES v.9 p.194
Pole W *Iron As A Material of Construction* [1872]
Pollard & Robertson *The British Shipbuilding Industry*
Turner T *The Metallurgy of Iron* [1908 - 3rd edit.]
White W *A Manual of Naval Architecture* [1877] p 396;
Wilson R A *A Treatise on Steam Boilers* [1879 - 5th edit.]
Frear H P *History of Tankers* 1943 Hist Trans SNAME

Chapter 10
TWAS 1361/659
Archives Wallsend Slipway - Clarke Chapman - Short Bros - NEM - Hawthorn-Leslie - Readhead - Swan-Hunter - Laing - Thompson J L - Doxford &c in TWAS 1811
Scotia Works Archives [in private hands]
S.World 1889 p.165
Hannah L *Electricity before Nationalisation* [1979]
Bowers Brian *A History of Electric Light & Power* [1982]
Hughes Thomas P *Networks of Power* [1983]
Middlemass N L *The Gathering of the Clans*
INA v.49 pp 157-
NECIES v. 11 p.14; ENNG 1895 p. 25? NorSB-ENNG 1900 p.30
Browne H B *Chapters of Whitby History* [1946]
Ensor R C K *England 1870-1914* [1936]
Weatherill pp 437-445
Buxton I *MarMirr* 1996
Vale V *The government and the Cunard contracts 1903* Jrl of Transport History NS v.5 [1979] pp 36-45.

Chapter 11

Archives Armstrong - Swan Hunter - Hawthorn-Leslie - Doxford
NECIES v XXX
ICivE 1882 Armstrong vol lxviii
RINA 1897 [pp105-115], 1899 [325-332], v 47 Rowell, v 1911 pt II [Johnson] - 1914
The Glasgow Herald
Mid-Tyne Link vII
Palmer's Record 1902-
Shipping World 1884 1887 1890 1894
Smith's Dock Monthly
Archibald E H H *The Fighting Ship ... Royal Navy*
Bacon *Lord Fisher* vI p263
Baxter J P *The Introduction of the Ironclad Warship* [1933]
Brown D K *A Century of Naval Construction*
Brown D K *Sustained Speed at Sea in the Royal Navy* in NECIES *Centenary Conference* [1984]
Buxton Ian *The Big Gun Monitor*
Colledge J J *Ships of the Royal Navy : an historical index*
Conte-Helm M *Japan and the North East of England* [1989]
Davidson J F *From Collier to Battleships*
Hough Richard *The Big Battleship or the curious career of HMS Agincourt* [1966]
Hovgaard W *Modern History of Warships* 53-4, 74, 173-8
Manning W *The Life of Sir William White*
Marsh E J *British Destroyers*
McCord [1979] pp 133-8
Parkes O *British Battleships* 156-8 167 213
Pollard S & Robertson P *The British Shipbuilding Industry*
Tennyson D'Eyncourt Sir E H W *A Shipbuilder's Yarn* 1948
Warren Keith *Armstrongs of Elswick*

Chapter 12

Working Class Rents & Prices [1912]
Articles of the Shipwrights' Association South Shields 1795
Conference between Palmer and Workmen of Jarrow [1866]
Archives Doxford - Hawthorn-Leslie - Swan Hunter - Thompson JL - Edwards
Employers Association Records
Wear Shipbuilders Association
Hawthorn-Leslie Report on Housing Properties 1904
Leslie Paybooks 1855-6
Thompson Paybooks 1847
Census of Population 1851 - 1861 - 1871
Cholera Inquiry Commission [1854]
Commission on the Employment of Children
Reports of the Medical Officer of Health for Newcastle
Reports of the Medical Officer of Health for South Shields
Roy Comm on Labour 1892-5
Roy Comm on Depression [1886]
Roy Comm on Trade Unions 1867-8
Sel Ctte on Combination Acts Appendix 5
Newcastle Courant
Newcastle Chronicle
Sunderland Herald
Shields Gazette
Hebburn Monthly 1874
Bulletin of the North East Group for the Study of Labour History #1

Bell Lady *At the Works*
Brown E H Phelps *The Growth of British Industrial Relations [1959]*
Burnett J *A History of the Engineers' Strike in Newcastle & Gateshead [1872 Newcastle]*
Campell Munro *A Twenty Years in the life history of a North Country Doctor*
Chapman D *The New Shipwright Building Co of Dundee [1940 EcHistR v X]*
Clapham J *An Economic History of Modern Britain v 3*
Clegg H A, Fox Alan & Thompson A F *A History of British Trade Unions since 1889 v I [1964 Oxford]*
Cummings D C *History of the United Society of Boilermakers & Iron & Steel Shipbuilders [1905]*
Davidson J F *From Collier to Battleship: Palmers of Jarrow 1852-1933*
Jeffreys J B & M *The Wages, Hours and Trade Customs of the Skilled Engineer in 1861 [1947 EconHistR]*
Jeffreys J B *The Story of the Engineers*
Lancaster Bill *Working Class Housing on Tyneside*
Lawson W D *Tyneside Celebrities* [1873]
Mortimer J E *History of the Boilermakers' Society v 1* [1834-1906]
Potts T *Sunderland, a History of Town, Port, Trade and Commerce*
Reeves Maud P *Round About a Pound a Week*
Report of the Industrial Remuneration Conference [1885]
Rutherford Wilfred *The man Who Built the Mauretania ...*
Schloss *Methods of Industrial Remuneration* [1892]
The Northern Examiner: Sketches of Public Men of the North [1855]
Webb S & B *The History of Trade Unionism*
Wigham Eric *Power to Manage*
Wilkinson E *The Town that was Murdered*

Chapter 13

Archives Doxford - Hawthorn-Leslie - Laing - Swan Hunter - Thompson JL
Employers Association Records
Hawthorn-Leslie Report on Housing Properties 1904
Wear Shipbuilders Association TWAS 708/1-
Scotia Works archive - Allan correspondence
Census of Population 1881 - 1891 - 1901 - 1911
Roy Comm on Labour 1892-5
Roy Comm on Labour 1904-5
Roy Comm on Depression [1886]
Labour Gazette [monthly] *1893-1951*
Reports on Strikes & Lockouts 1888-1913 [Board of Trade]
Wages Survey 1906
Amal Society of Engineers... [1851-1920] Monthly Reports
Associated Shipwrights' Society [1885-] Monthly Reports
Society of Boilermakers & Iron & Steel Shipbuilders *Monthly Reports* [1870-]
Reports of the TUC Annual Conference
Smith's Dock Jrl
Shipping World
Newcastle Chronicle
Newcastle Weekly Jrl
Sunderland Herald

Sunderland Times
Shields Gazette
BulNELab
NECIES v 9; Thompson; v 15 Browne - Westgarth; v 18;
Brown E H Phelps *The Growth of British Industrial Relations*
Clapham J *An Economic History of Modern Britain* v 3
Clarke J F *Labour relations in Engineering & Shipbuilding c1850 -1906*
Clarke J F *The Foreman NELabB9*
Clegg H A, Fox Alan & Thompson A F *A History of British Trade Unions since 1889* v1 & v2
Croucher R *The North East Engineers Strike of 1908 NELabB9*
Cummings D C *History of the ... Boilermakers* [1905]
Davidson J F *From Collier to Battleship: Palmers of Jarrow 1852-1933*
Fryth & Collins *The Foundry Workers*
Hopkins C H G *The Moving Staircase ... 1939-1972*
Jeffreys J B *The Story of the Engineers*
Mortimer J E *A history of the Association of Engineering and Shipbuilding Draughtsmen*
Mortimer J E *History of the Boilermakers' Society* v 1 & 2
Reeves Maud P *Round About a Pound a Week*
Report of the Industrial Remuneration Conference [1885]
Rutherford *The man Who Built the Mauretania...George B Hunter*
Schloss *Methods of Industrial Remuneration* [1892]
Webb S & B *The History of Trade Unionism*
Wigham Eric *Power to Manage*
Wilkinson E *The Town that was Murdered*

Early emblem of the Boilermakers' Society

Selected Bibliography.

Parliamentary & other official reports
[This is only a selection see the list given by Pollard & Robertson pp 287-9.]
A Return ... of Steam Ships Registered in United Kingdom ... 1861 Accounts & Papers 1861 LVIII [371]
Census of Population Reports 1801-1911
Labour Gazette [monthly] 1893-1915
Official Publications
Reports on Strikes & Lockouts 1888-1913 [Board of Trade]
Return of Wages 1830-66 [Board of Trade]
Roy Comm on Trade Unions 1867-8
Roy Comm on Labour 1892-5
Roy Comm on Depression [1886]
Sel Ctte on Combination Acts Appendix 5
Statistical Abstract of the United Kingdom
Working Class Rents & Prices [1912] [Board of Trade]

Archives
L A Ritchie's *The Shipbuilding Industry* [1992] is an invaluable guide to British shipbuilding archives and is organised under the name of the shipbuilder. Tthe two volumes produced by R J B Knight as a *Guide to the Manuscripts in the National Maritime Museum* showed the scale of the source material held at Greenwich. Much of this is relevant to the north east both in regard to information collected nationally by the employers but also the collections such as the ships' plans from north east shipyards. Some Armstrong-Whitworth records are held at Greenwich. The many records held in the *Public Record Office* at Kew, provide statistical and other material collected by government departments and are particularly important in regard to naval work.

Ship plans are held at *National Maritime Museum* from: Hawthorn-Leslie [ships #1 and #259-#500], J L Thompson, Armstrong-Whitworth, Austin & Pickersgill, Bartram, Palmers [12], Richardson Duck [about 500 constructional drawings] and Smith's Dock.

Custom House Registers
Custom House Registers are held at *Tyne & Wear Archives Service* for Newcastle [EX/NC/1- 1786-], for South Shields [EX/SS/1- 1859-] for North Shields [EX/NS/1-1850-] and for Sunderland [EX/SU/1- 1786-]. At *Cleveland County Archives* the registers are held for Middlesbrough, Stockton and Hartlepool.

Tyne & Wear Archives Service
The collection of archival held by the Tyne & Wear Archive Service merits a major survey and the following can only be some brief comments. A major collection related to the shipbuilders on the River Wear are listed under TWAS 1811. This collection includes material from Laings, Doxfords, Thompsons J L, Crown,[for each of these there are separate holdings also] and Sunderland Shipbuilders [1971-81]. Inevitably the series are not always continuous, so that some records cover only a short period of time.
The *Laing* collection includes particulars books from 1794[1811/33/1-6], some ships contracts & specifications [1811/35/-

and 1811/44/1-] and a considerable number of business ledgers [e.g 1811/10/1-5 and 1811/13/1-] covering costs as well as the Company's trading activities; see also TWAS 1338. *Doxford*'s series begins 1811/77/1- and in addition to ledgers and other account books from 1834, there are correspondence files and a number of personal notebooks. There are very detailed particulars books, with sketches, ship costs [e.g 1811/ 121/1-494], and diesel engine costs [e.g. 1811/122/- & 1811/123/-]; a number of detailed wage records also form part of this collection. Six other collections related to Doxfords, including TWAS 898, which includes insurance material and drawing office pay for 1894-1911 and TWAS 1687 - Keller. Similar records to Laing are available *J L Thompsons* [1811/214/1-] but the accounts are post 1874 and there further holdings TWAS 1045/1-2 covers a list of ships and the dates of stages of construction by berth for ships #214-#373 and TWAS 1202, 1338 and 2234 also relate to this yard, there is also material .Records of *J Crown*, after the formation of the limited company are held in TWAS1811/202 - 1811/208, there is also holdings TWAS 1658 and 2209.

A major collection of *Hawthorn-Leslie* records is held under TWAS 962, 1248 ,1836 and 1850. These include material from the original Hawthorns, minute books, a wide range of ledgers and cost books cover both ships and engines [mainly 1884-1950s]. Material related to *Palmers* are held in TWAS 770, 1211, 1357, 1479, 1810 and 1969; these are records covering short time periods [further records are held at the Bede Gallery Jarrow, Greenwich and Cambridge]. A very comprehensive collection relates to Readheads, the business records start in the 1870s and there are cost books for 1909-68, the main collection is TWAS 1061 with further material in TWAS 1202 & 1926. Two collections, TWAS 714 & 1391, contain a very wide collection of records from Short Bros, these include cost books which cover more than 150 ships, wage data, specifications, private notebooks and a valuable record of quotations for both engine and ships [1900-28]. *Smith's Dock* .... Eight collections contain the very extensive *Swan Hunter* records, the business records mainly relate to the period after 1903 TWAS 964, 1266 1304, 1826 [includes detail wage bills at Neptune], 1836, 1989, 2029 and 2263. *Wigham Richardson*' early ship payments are in , Ship contracts of *Austins* are held in TWAS 1658, some of this yard's records are in *Austin & Pickersgill* TWAS 2296 also covered by TWAS 1708. Two collections relate to Bartram's TWAS 990 & 1714, journals for 1865-78 and most of the remainder is twentieth century and this includes a years individual workers pay sheets. *Clelands* TWAS 1615, slipway and particulars register and some general arrangement plans. The Armstrong Whitworth Collections cover all the Company's activity: there are many items in TWAS 130 related to shipbuilding including minute books and TWAS 450 is for ships built 1898-1908. Shipyard cost [1897-1909] and report books [1883-1913] are held at Cambridge University Library. *Robert Thompson's* ships [1855-1933] are listed in TWAS 1081, with dimensions and a facsimile of his will [TWAS 1508]. William *Dobson*, TWAS 1571, a small collection includes almost 300 photographs. Collections relate to ship outfitting include TWAS 238 [Farrow of Sunderland] TWAS 694 [Linkleter N Shields] TWAS. 713 [Parker Sunderland]

Shiprepairers
Brigham & Cowan there are 20th century business records and a foreman shipwright's journal for 1919-39. Three collections TWAS 538, 1338 and 1632 are for *T W Greenwell*: these are business accounts [1902-73] and some correspondence, TWAS 538 relates to *Wear Arc Welding Co* [1920-60]. *Tyne Dock Engineering* [1882-1977] a major collection of business records TWAS 1224, includes accident books 1948-77.

Engine builders
George Clark an item in 1811/284 and 1361 there is an index of contracts but particularly valuable are the engine trial and performance reports. in TWAS 1993. The minutes of *NEM* [1865-1924] and other records are held in TWAS 1993 together with some engine plans, *Parsons Marine Turbine*, three collections relate to this works 927, 1321 and 1802: these include plans of Turbinia and design records 1906-63 [further material held at the Science Museum London]. Extensive records covering both the building of engines and repair work by Wallsend Slipway are held in TWAS 1551

Employers Assocuations.
Among employers' association records are *Wear Shipbuilders Association* TWAS 708 - *Tyne Shipbuilders' Association* TWAS 895. *North East Coast Shiprepairers Association* TWAS 978 [1903-1977] .This includes many of the circulars issued, their handbooks of repair charges and important statistics on accidents. Records of the *Engineering Employers Association* TWAS EM/EN [1873-1970] concern through the marine engine builder s very important links with shipbuilding.

Shipping Companies & Organisations.
Many records are held of north east shipping companies, for example Tyne Tees SS Co, Stag Line, Common Bros, Souter, Turret SS Co and Pyman Bell and these can provide information related to shipbuilding.

Tyne & Wear Museum Service
Many ship plans and photographs are held by the Museum Service e.g general arrangements of Mitchell, Armstrong-Mitchell and Armstrong-Whitworth ships, Crown, Priestman. *Shipbuilding History Project* Department of Marine Technology University of Newcastle upon Tyne. Amongst the holdings are records of William Allan's Engineering Company [1888-1929]

Durham County Records Office
Amongst the ship plans held are Pickersgill [ships 76-111], Priestman, Short Bros [1876-89] Plans of 7 engines built by Dickinson for Short Brothers [1879-92]

Cleveland County Archives
The records held include Office pay book 1897-1923 for Raylton Dixon U/S/39U/S/39, the very useful harrison papers and trade union journals

Northumberland Record Office
A labour cost book for ships [1898-1924] of William Gray and records of Tyne Iron SB [1876-1928] are held in NRO 693.

Stockton Museum Service
Records include Furness SB Yard detail books, general arrangement drawings and photographs.

Hartlepool Museum Service
Amongst the holdings here are - Furness SB some specifications and photographs W Gray a substantial collection of both ship and engine plans [general arrangements], particulars books, launch and trial notebooks. One of the few holdings of cinematic film.

Hartlepool Central Library [Local Section]
Yard books of William Gray and for Ropner SB. Business records of Luke & George Blumer [1850-65], including detailed repair costs are held here.

Whitby Museum
Letters [1870-96] and plans [1840-96] of Thomas Turnbull

Local Libraries
Sunderland Library holds the very valuable Corder MSS material on shipbuilding and local families. Most of the local libraries hold some photographic and other material on the shipbuilding industry and the local press is a valuable source. Unfortunately unknown and unrecorded are the various items held by individuals such as the Thompson Pay books 1847 and *Bartram's Journal* [known in these two cases].

Trade Union Records
The *Monthly Reports* and *Annual Reports* of the trade unions are invaluable sources of information, including cash receipts & payments but also the sick benefits paid and the cause of death.
   Amalgamated Society of Engineers... [1851-1920]
   Amalgamated Engineering Union [1920-
   Associated Shipwrights' Society [1885-
   United Society of Boilermakers [1870-
Reports of the TUC Annual Conference

Museums
A valuable insight into the history of shipbuilding and marine engineering is available in many museums, not all items held are on display. This material includes both full scale exhibits and models, may to which were created by the craftsmen in the industry and many paintings and drawings.

Newcastle Discovery
This is the successor to the Museum of Science & Engineering. The *Turbinia* gallery, contains the restored original vessel. Weighton's experimental engine is also held by this museum [but not on display] and the triple expansion marine engine used at the South Shields Marine College.
At the *South Shields Museum* there is a display of shipwright's tools and models. Other exhibits are shown at the Sunderland Museum & Art Gallery and at the *Hartlepool Maritime Centre*

Science Museum London
Many models related to north east shipbuilding are held in the *Science Museum* London: these include the tugs *Monarch* [Wait of North Shields 1838], *Albatross* [Hepple 1878], Oswald's *Durham* [1866], Smurtwaite's *Stonehouse* [1866] designed by Gilbert Row [Topsham], Short's RFA Celerol [1917], Swan Hunter's mv *Dominion Monarch* [1939] , midship section of *Paul Paix*, a Hawthorn boiler of 1868, a model of *Auris* turbine and *Turbinia's* radial turbine

National Maritime Museum Greenwich
The complete paddle tug *Reliant* built on the Tyne is housed at Greenwich. Models include Palmer's *HMS Queen Mary*, Doxford's turret ship *Nonsuch* and mv *Silver Elm* [1924].

Trade papers & journals and house journals.
Engineer
Engineering
Heaton Works Journal
Marine Engineer
The Motorship
Steamship
The Shipping World [SWrld] [1882-
Shipbuilder
Shipbuilding & Shipbuilding Record
The Glasgow Herald
Smith's Dock Monthly
Shipyard
Mid-Tyne Link
Palmer's Record

Technical and Professional Institutions
The papers to these Institutions and the discussions which followed are an invaluable source for understanding both the history of industry and technology. Their visits to various towns were accompanied by very useful descriptions of local industry and their obituaries are a neglected source of information of their members and so of industry.

Institute of Marine Engineers [*IMarE*] {1889-
Institution of Civil Engineers [*ICivE*] {1818-
Institute of Mechanical Engineers [*IMechE*] {1847-
[Royal] Institution of Naval Architects [*RINA*] (1860-
Iron & Steel Institute [*I&SInst*]
North East Coast Institution of Engineers & Shipbuilders [NECIES] [1884-1993]
Institution of Engineers & Shipbuilders in Scotland [*IESSc*] (Institution of Engineers in Scotland founded in 1857; Scottish Shipbuilders' Association in 1860; they merged in 1865 as Institution of Engineers in Scotland with which is incorporated Scottish Shipbuilders' Association. In 1875 adopted title given)
Mariner's Mirror *MarMirr*
North East Group for the Study of Labour History Bulletin : from no 24 *North East Labour History NELabB*

Statistical & other tables, together with lists of ships - see p iv. These will be available in computer format.

Books

Abell Sir Wm *The Shipwright's Trade* [1948]
Aldcroft D H *The mercantile marine* in *The Development of British Industry and Foreign Competition 1875-1914* [1968]
Allan W *The Shipowners' and Engineers' Guide to the Marine Engine* [Sunderland 1882]
Allen E, Clarke J F, McCord N & Rowe D *The North-east Engineers' Strike of 1871* [1971 Newcastle]
Allen G C *British Industries and Their Organisation* [1970]
An operative shipwright *Causes of Distress Amongst the Shipwrights* [1858 Sunderland]
anon *A General Directory for Newcastle* [1824 Durham]
anon *A Hundred Years of Howden Engineering* [1954]
anon *A Shipbuilding History 1750-1932* [Alex Stephen] [1932 Glasgow]
anon *Annals of Lloyd's Register* editions from 1884 [1934]
anon *Annals of Lloyd's Register* [1884]
anon *Austin and Pickersgill: 150 years of history* [1976]
anon *Bartram & Sons, Centenary Souvenir of the Company's History* [1938]
anon *Delaval Papers*
anon *John Readhead & Sons A Hundred Years of Shipbuilding at South Shields* [1965]
anon *Mowbray Quay to Pallion Yard 1850-1950* [1950]
anon *Swan Hunter and Wigham Richardson* [1906]
anon *Thomas Royden & Sons Shipbuilders 1818-93* [1953]
anon *Two Centuries of Shipbuilding by Scotts* [1920]
anon *William Doxford & Co* [1921]
Appleyard, H S *Turnbull Scott & Co Fleet List* [1978]
Appleyard, Rollo *Charles Parsons...* [1933]
Archibald E H H *The Fighting Ship in the Royal Navy* [1987]
Armstrong W G and others *The Industrial Resources of Tyne, Wear and Tees* [1864]
Aspinall A *The Early Trade Unions ...* [1949]
Ayre W *A Shipbuilder's Yesterday* [1968]

Baldwin C A *The History of the Port of Blyth* [1929 Newcastle]
Banbury P *Shipbuilders of the Thames & the Medway* [1971]
Barnaby K C *The Institution of Naval Architects 1860-1960* [1960]
Barnaby N *Naval Development in the Nineteenth Century* [1902]
Barrow A *The North East Coast Whale Fishery 1750-1850* PhD University of Northumbria 1989
Barry P *Dockyard and Naval Power* [1863]
Barry P *The Dockyards and Private Shipyards of the U K* [1863]
Baxter J P *The Introduction of the Ironclad Warship* [1933]
Bell Lady *At the Works* [rpt 1985 - 1st edit 1907]
Bell R C ed. *Diaries from the Days of Sail* [1974]
Bentham M S *The Life of Brigadier-General Sir Samuel Bentham K S G* [1862]
Blake, George *Lloyd's Register of Shipping 1760-1960* [c 1960]
Bourne H *History of Newcastle upon Tyne* [1736 Newcastle]
Bourne J *A treatise on Steam Engine* [1848]
Boyd W *Story of Wallsend Slipway & Engineering Co. Ltd 1897-1911* [1911 Wallsend]

Brand J *History and Antiquities ... of Newcastle* [1789]
Brewster J *The Parochial History ... of Stockton* [1796]
British Association Reports of Annual Meetings
Brockie W *Sunderland Noteables* [Sunderland 1894]
Brown D K *A Century of Naval Construction...* [1983]
Brown E H Phelps *The Growth of British Industrial Relations* [1959]
Burnett J *A History of the Engineers' Strike in Newcastle & Gateshead* [1872 Newcastle]
Butt J & Ward A ed. *Scottish Themes* [1976 Edinburgh]
Buxton I L *Big Gun Monitors* [1978 Tynemouth]
Buxton I L ed. *Index to the Publications of the NECIES*

Campell Munro A *Twenty Years in the life history of a North Country Doctor* [1894]
Campell, R *The London Tradesman* 1747 [repr 1968]
Carozzi J L [ed] *British Shipbuilding* [1919]
Carter R O *Index to the Publications of the North East Coast Institution of Engineers and Shipbuilders* [Newcastle 1993]
Carvel J L *Stephen of Linthouse 1750-1950* [1950 Glasgow]
Charlton, Lionel *The History of Whitby...* [1779 York]
Charnock, J *A History of Marine Architecture* [1800]
Chorographia Or A Survey of Newcastle Upon Tyne [1649]
Clapham J *An Economic History of Modern Britain* 3 vols [1930 -1932-1951]
Clarke J F *The changeover from wood to iron shipbuilding - with particular reference to the North East* [1986]
Clarke J F *Labour relations in Engineering & Shipbuilding c1850-1906* [1967 MA Newc]
Clarke J F & Storr F *The strength of marine boilers & the design of the furnace* [1983 Newcastle]
Clarke J F *A century of service to Engineering & Shipbuilding* [1984 Newcastle]
Clarke J F *An Almost Forgotten Great Man - Charles Parsons ...* [1984]
Clarke J F *Power on Land & Sea* [Hawthorn-Leslie] [1977]
Clarke J F & MacDermott T P *Newcastle & District Trades Council 1873-1973* [1973 Newcastle]
Clarke J F & Storr F *The Introduction of the Use of Mild Steel into the Shipbuilding ...* [1983 Newcastle]
Clay M, Milburn & Miller *An Eye Map of Sunderland and Bishopwearmouth 1785-1790* [1984]
Clegg H A, Fox Alan & Thompson A F *A History of British Trade Unions since 1889* v I [1964 Oxford]
Clegg H A *A History of British Trade Unions since 1889* vII [1985 Oxford]
Cocker M P *Royal Navy Submarines 1901-1982* [1982]
Colledge J J *Ships of the Royal Navy : an...index* [1990]
Collinge, J M *Navy Board Officials 1660-1832* [1978]
Conference between C.M.Palmer and the Workmen [1866]
Conte-Helm M *Japan and the North East of England* [1989]
Cormack W S *An Economic History of Shipbuilding & Marine Engineering* [1930 Glasgow Univ PhD]
Cummings D C *History of the United Society of Boilermakers & Iron & Steel Shipbuilders* [1905]

D'Eyncourt Sir E H W T *A Shipbuilder's Yarn* [1928]
Darvill P *A Contribution of Co-operative Societies... North East Coast Area* [Durham M Litt 1953]

Davidson J F *From Collier to Battleship: Palmers of Jarrow 1852-1933* [1946]
Davis, R *The Rise of the English Shipping Industry in the 17th and 18th Centuries* [1962]
Deane's *Doctrine of Naval Architecture* [1670]
Defoe Daniel *Tour through England and Wales* [1727]
Dendy F W *Records of the Hostmen of Newcastle ...* [1901]
Denny List [edit D Lyons] v1-4 [1976 Greenwich]
Devon J R ed. *Where the Wall Ends - recollections of a Tyneside town* [1977 Wallsend]
Dickinson H W *A Short History of the Steam Engine* [1963]
Dillon M *Palmer's Shipbuilding and Iron Co Ltd* [1904]
Dobson, C R *Masters & Journeymen* [1980]
Dodds J & Moore J *Building the Wooden Fighting Ship* [1984]
Dougan D *The Shipwrights* [1975]
Dougan D *The History of North-East Shipbuilding* [1968]
Driel, A van *Ship Tonnage Measurement* [1925 Hague]
Duckworth C L D & Langmuir G E *Railway and Other Steamers* [1968 Prescot]
Estep E Cole *How Wooden Ships Are Built* [1918 repr 1983]

Fairburn W A *Handling Materials over Shipbuilding Berths in American Shipyards* [1902]
Fallows W *Fragments of the Early History of the Tees* [1878]
Farr G *Shipbuilding in North Devon* [1976]
Farr G *Shipbuilding in the Port of Bristol* [1977]
Fassett F G jr *Shipbuilding Business in the U S A* [1948]
Finch R *Coals from Newcastle* [1973 Sussex]
Fincham J *A History of Naval Architecture* [1851]
Finden E *Ports Harbours ... of Great Britain* [1838]
Fisher S [ed] *British Shipping & Seamen 1630-1960* [1984]
Flagg, Amy C *Notes on the History of Shipbuilding in South Shields 1746-1946* [1979 South Tyneside]
Fordyce T *Local Records ... 1833-1867*
Fordyce W *Chart of the River Tyne* 1846
Fraser C M & Emsley K *Tyneside* [1973 Newton Abbot]

Garbutt G *History of Monkwearmouth...* [1819]
Gardner R *England's Grievances Discovered in relation to the Coal Trade* [1655]
Garnham Ann *Education for Industry: the Newcastle Experience, 1889-1902* [Sussex MPhil 1978]
Gaskin, R T *The Old Seaport of Whitby* [1909 Whitby]
Gilbert K R *The Portsmouth Blockmaking Machinery* [1965]
Grantham J *Iron Shipbuilding* [1858]
Grantham J *Iron as a material for Shipbuilding* [1842]
Griffith J W *The Shipbuilder's Manual* [1856 New York]
Guthrie J *The River Tyne: its history and resources* [1880]

Haldane J W C *Engineering Popularly and Socially Considered* [1887]
Hamer F E [ed] *Personal Papers of Lord Rendel* [1931]
Hannan Bill *Fifty Years of Naval Tugs* [Cornwall]
Hardy A C *A History of Motor Shipping* [1955]
Hardy A C *From Ship to Sea* [1926]
Harris D G *F H Chapman, the First Naval Architect and his work...* [1989]
Heaviside Henry *The Annals of Stockton-on-Tees* [1865]
Hedderick Peter *A Treatise on Marine Architecture* [1830]

Hedley W Percy *Northumberland Families* v 1 [1968]
Hepplewhite P *'Wor Lass' Sources for Women's History in the North East* [1988 Newcastle]
Hill R I *Power from Steam* [1989 Cambridge]
Hinderwell T *The History ... of Scarborough* [1798]
Hodgson G B *Borough of South Shields* [1903 Newcastle]
Hoffman W *British Industry 1700-1950* [1955]
Hogg P *Central Marine Engine Works* [1995 Hartlepool]
Hogg P *RICHES* [1994 Hartlepool]
Holland A J *Buckler's Hard* [1985]
Holland A J *Ships of British Oak* [1971]
Hollet D *From Cumberland to Cape Horn* [1984]
Holms A C *Practical Shipbuilding* [1916]
Hopkins C H G *Pallion 1874 to 1954: Church and people in a shipyard parish* [1954 Sunderland]
Horner J G *Encyclopaedia of Practical Engineering* [c1905]
Hough R *The Big Battleship ... HMS Agincourt* [1966]
Hovgaard W *Modern History of Warships* [1920 rept 1978]
Hughes, E *North Country Life in the Eighteenth Century The North East 1700-1750* [1952]
Hume J R & Moss M *Shipbuilders to the World* - Harland & Wolff [1986 Belfast]
Hume J *Shipbuilding Machine Tools* in *Scottish Themes* edit Butt J & Ward J T [1976 Glasgow]
Hutchins J G B *American Maritime Industries & Public Policy 1789-1914* [1941- Camb Mass]
Hutchinson W *A Treatise on Naval Architecture ...* [1794]
Hutchinson W *History of the County of Cumberland* [1794]

J C *The Complete Collier...* [1708 - rept 1968]
Jackson G *Hull in the Eighteenth Century*
James W *Naval History of Great Britain 1793-1837* 1847
Jeans J S *Notes on Northern Industries* [1879]
Jeffreys J B *The Story of the Engineers* [c 1946]
Jeremy D J ed. *Dictionary of Business Biography* [1983-6]
Johnson I *Beardmore Built* [1993 Glasgow]
Johnson, R W *The making of the Tyne* [1895]
Jones John A Rupert *Chronological Order... Steam ... Royal Navy - Notes & Queries* 1927
Jones S *A Maritime History of the Port of Whitby 1700-1914* 1982 London Univ PhD
Jung Invar *The Marine Turbine* I-III [1986 Greenwich]

Kenwood A G *Capital Investment in North Eastern England, 1800-1913* [1962 Ph D London]
Keys, R E *The Sailing Ships of Aln & Coquet* [1993]
Keys, R E *A Dictionary of the Sailing Ships of the Tyne* [forth coming 1997-8]
Kludas A *Great Passenger Ships of the World v.1* [1975]
Knight R J B *The Royal Dockyards of England at the time of the American War of Independence* 1972
Knight R J B *Guide to the Manuscripts in the National Maritime Museum* - 2 vols [1978 & 1980]
Kruger R & Symes G *Launching Ways* [Swan Hunter] 1953
Lancaster Bill *Working Class Housing on Tyneside 1850-1939* [1994]
Lane F C *Venetian Ships & Shipbuilders* [1934 reprint 1975]
Lavery, B *Nelson's Navy* [1990]
Lavery, B *Ships of the Line* [1983]
Lawson W D *Tyneside Celebrities* [1873]

Le Guillou M *A History of the River Tees* [1978]
Lee C H *British Regional Employment Statistics 1841-1971*
Lindsay W S *History of Merchant Shipping...* [1874-6 - 3v]
Lingwood J & Appleyard H *Chapman of Newcastle - the story of a Tyneside Tramp Shipping Co.* [1985]
Lipson E *The Economic History of England* [1956]
Long, A & Russell *A Shippimg Venture: Turnbull, Scott & Co 1872-1972* [1974]
Lorenz E & Wilkinson F *The shipbuilding industry 1880-1965* in Elbaum
Lorenz E H *Two Patterns of Development: Labour Process in British & French Shipbuilding Industries 1880-1930* [1984]
Lubbock B *The China Clippers* [1914 Glasgow]
Lubbock B *The Blackwall Frigates* [Glasgow]
Lubbock B *The Arctic Whalers* [1937 Glasgow]
Lubbock B *The Coolies Ships and Oil Sailers* [1955 Glasgow]
Lubbock B *The Nitrate Clippers* [Glasgow]

MacGregor D R *Merchant Sailing Ships 1775-1815* [1980]
MacGregor D R *Fast Sailing Ships 1775-1875* [1973]
MacGregor D R *The Tea Clippers 1833-1875* [1983]
MacGregor D R *Merchant Sailing Ships 1815-1850* [1984]
MacGregor D R *The China Bird*
MacGregor D R *Merchant Sailing Ships 1850-1875* [1984]
Mackenzie E & Ross E *View of the County of Durham* [1834]
Mackenzie E *An Impartial History ... of Newcastle upon Tyne and its Vicinity* [1801 Newcastle]
MacKenzie & Dent *Directory for Newcastle ...* [1811]
Manders F W D *A History of Gateshead* [1973]
Manning F *The Life of Sir William White* [1923]
Marsh A *Industrial Relations in Engineering* [1965]
Marsh E J *British Destroyers 1892-1953* [1966]
Martin R *Historical Notes on West Hartlepool ...* [1924]
Mathias P & Pearsall A W H *Shipping: A survey of historical records* [1971]
Mc Closkey D N [edit] *Essays on a Mature economy : Britain after 1840* [1971]
McCord N *North East England The region's development 1760-1960* [1979]
McCord N [edit] *Essays in Tyneside Labour History* [1977 Newcastle]
McLaren-Kerr D *John Winspear* [1982 Hartlepool]
Middlemiss N L *British Tankers* [1989 Newcastle]
Middlemiss N L *Pride of the Princes* [1988 Newcastle]
Middlemiss N L *British Shipbuilding Yards, v1: North East Coast* [1993 Newcastle]
Middlemiss N L *Gathering of the Clans* [1988 Newcastle]
Middlemiss N L *Travels of the Tramps* [1989 Newcastle]
Middlemiss N L *The Anglo-Saxon/Shell Tankers* [
Milburn G E & Miller S T *Sunderland River, Town and People* [1988].
Mitchell, B R & Deane Phyllis *Abstract of British Historical Statistics* [1962 Cambridge]
Mitchell J *Directory of Newcastle* 1801
Mitchell J *Shipbuilding & Shipbuilding industry* [1926]
Mitchell W H & Sawyer L A *Sailing Ship to Supertanker* [1987]
Moir D R *The Birth and History of Trinity House, Newcastle upon Tyne* [1959 Glasgow]

Morris R *The Royal Dockyards during the Revolutionary and Napoleonic Wars* [1983 Leicester]
Morsom, G *On the new tonnage law ...* [1860]
Mortimer J E *History of the Boilermakers' Society* [1834-1906] 1973 and [1907-39] 1981
Mortimer J E *A history of the Association of Engineering and Shipbuilding Draughtsmen* [1960]
Murray A *Shipbuilding in Wood & Iron* [1863 - 2nd ed]

Nef J U *The Rise of the British Coal Industry* [2v 1932]
Newman B *The development of sites and facilities in the ship & marine engine building industries of Britain 1850-1945* [MPhil Newcastle 1994]
Newman B *Materials Handling in British Shipbuilding 1850-1945* [1996 Glasgow]
Newman B *Plate and Section Working Machinery in British Shipbuilding 1850-1945* [1993 Glasgow]
Oliver, T *A General Directory for Newcastle ...* [1833]
Oppenheim M M *The Maritime History of Devon* [1968]
Osler A G *Mr Greathead's Lifeboats* [Newcastle 1990]
Osler A G & Grieve G R *Turbinia Report* Nos 1-9 [1980]
Osler A G & Barrow A *Tall Ships Two Rivers*

Paasch H *From Keel to Truck* [1901]
Parkes O *British Battleships 1860-1950* [1957]
Parry J H *Trade and Dominion* [1971]
Pering R *A Brief Inquiry into the Causes of the Premature Decay in our Wooden Bulwarks* [1812]
Phillips M *A History of Banks, Bankers and Banking in Northumberland ...* [1894]
Pollard S & Robertson P *The British Shipbuilding Industry 1870-1914* [1979]
Pollock D Modern *Shipbuilding and the Men ...* [1884]
Pollock D *The Shipbuilding Industry, Its History...* [1905]
Ponsford, C N *Shipbuilding on The Exe* [1988 Exeter]
Potts A & Jones E R *Northern Labour History - a bibliography* [1981]
Potts A ed. *Shipbuilders and Engineers: Essays on Labour ... of the North East* [1987]
Potts T *Sunderland, a History of Town, Port, Trade and Commerce* [1892]
Prothero, Iorwerth *Artisans & Politics in Early Nineteenth Century London* [1979]
Proud J H *Seahorses of the Tees* [1985]
Proud J H *150 years of the Maltese Cross* [1993?]

Rea V *Palmers Yard and the Town of Jarrow* [1975 Jarrow]
Rees *Naval Architecture* [1814]
Reeves M P *Round About a Pound a Week* [rpt 1979 - 1913]
Reid A *Division of Labour in the Shipbuilding Industry 1880-1920 : Clydeside* [1980 Glasgow PhD]
Report- Medical Officer of Health for South Shields 1875
Report of the Industrial Remuneration Conference [1885]
Richardson, G B & Tomlinson W W *Official Handbook to Newcastle & District.* [1916 British Assoc]
Richardson J Wigham *Memoirs* [1911]
Richardson, M A *A General Directory for Newcastle* [1838]
Richardson W *History of the Parish of Wallsend* [1923]
Richardson, Wigham *Official Local Guide- Industrial Section.* [1889 British Assoc]

Richmond T *Local Records of Stockton* ... [1868]
Ritchie L A [edit] *The Shipbuilding Industry - a guide to historical records* [Manchester 1992]
Robinson N J *Stag Line and Joseph Robinson* ... [1984]
Rowe D J ed. *Records of the Company of Shipwrights of Newcastle upon Tyne 1622-1967* [1971 Gateshead
Rowe D J ed. *Northern Business Histories - a bibliography* [1979]
Rowntree A [edit] *The History of Scarborough* [1931]
Runciman, Sir Walter *Collier Brigs and their Sailors* [1926]
Rutherford W *The man Who Built the Mauretania...George B Hunter* [1934]

Schloss D F *Methods of Industrial Remuneration* [1892]
Scott E Kilburn *Matthew Murray Pioneer Engineer* [1928]
Scott J D *Vickers A History* [1962]
Sennet R & Oram H J *The Marine Engine* [1882-1911]
Sharp Cuthbert *A History of Hartlepool* [1851]
Singer Charles & al [edit] *A History of Technology* v III Naish; v IV Naish; v V Robb.[1954-1957-1958]
Slaven A ed. *Business, Banking & Urban History* [1982]
Slaven A ed. *Dictionary of Scottish Business Biography* v1 [1986 Aberdeen]
Smith E C *A Short History of Naval and Marine Engineering* [1953 Cambridge]
Smith J W & Holden T S *Where Ships are Born* [1953]
Sowler T *The Town and Borough of Stockton-on-Tees* [ ]
Spaldin Bert *Shipbuilders of the Hartlepools* [1986]
Storr F *The Development of the Marine Compound Steam Engine* [1982 PhD CNAA]
Sturgess R W [edit] *The Great Age of Industry in the North East* [1981 Durham]
Sullivan, W R *Blyth in the eighteenth Century* [1971]
Summers J W *History ... of Sunderland* [1858]
Surtees R *The History... of Durham* v 2 [1820]
Sutherland H *The Blockmills in H M Portsmouth Dockyards* [1968]
Sutton, J *Lords of the East - The East India Co...*[1981]

Thomas P N *British Steam Tugs* [1983]
Thompson F M L ed. *The Cambridge Social History of Britain 1750-1950* [1990 Cambridge]
Thompson J *Memoir of Mr John Thompson* [1893]
Tuckett A *Blacksmiths History* [1974]
Unger R W *Dutch Shipbuilding before 1800* [1978]
Ville S P *English Shipowning during the Industrial Revolution* [1987 Manchester]

Walker F M & Slaven A [ed] *European Shipbuilding One Hundred Years of Change* [1984]
Walker James & Richardson M A *The Armorial Arms of the several ... companies of Newcastle* [1824]
Wallace, J *History of Blyth* [1862]
Warren K *Armstrongs of Elswick* [1989]
Weatherill, R *The Ancient Port of Whitby...* [1908 Whitby]
Wedderburn K W *The Worker and the Law* [1971]
Welford R *Men of Mark 'twixt Tyne and Tweed* [1893]
White, W H *A Manual of Naval Architecture* [1875]
Whitehead, W *Account of Newcastle upon Tyne* [1787]
Whitehead, W *Newcastle Directory...* 1778

Wigham E *The Power to Manage A History of the Engineering Employers' Federation* [1973]
Wilkinson E *The Town that was Murdered* [1939]
Willan T S *The English Coasting Trade* [1938 Manchester]
Williamson J *Clyde Passenger Steamers 1812-1901* [rpt 1987 - 1st edit 1904]
Wood R *West Hartlepool* [1967 West Hartlepool]
Young, Rev George *A History of Whitby* ... [1817 Whitby]

Articles

Appleby Miller R N *The First Tug-boat Smith's Dock Jrl* 1929
Bain G W *Antiquities of Sunderland* 1904
Baker R *John Wilkinson & the early iron barges* J. of Wilkinson Society 1987
Barton P *A decade of iron shipbuilding* in *Sea Breezes*
Barton P *The First Blockade Runner and 'AnotherAlabama'* [1995 MarMirr]
Barton P *The Port of Stockton-on-Tees and its Creeks, 1825-61...*
Bowley A L & Wood G H *Wages in Engineering & Shipbuilding* [1905-6 J Roy Statistical Soc]
Brown D K *The Structural improvements to wooden ships instigated by Robt Seppings* 1979 Naval Architect

Chapman D *The New Shipwright Building Co of Dundee* [1940 EcHistR v X]
Clarke J F *Engineering Workers on Tyneside* [in McCord 1977]
Clarke J F *Labour in Wearside Shipbuilding* [in Potts 1987]
Clarke J F *Labour at the N E Coast Institution of Engineers & Shipbuilders* [in Potts 1987]
Clarke J F *Shipbuilding 1780-1914* in Milburn & Miller 1988
Clarke J F *Shipbuilding on the River Wear 1780-1870* in Sturgess 1981
Clarke J F *The Foreman* NELabB9
Clarke J F *Workers in Tyneside Shipyards* in *Essays in Tyneside Labour History* [in N McCord] 1977
Craig J *Some Effects of War on Merchant Shipbuilding* [1918 IE&S 61]
Croucher R *The North East Engineers Strike of 1908* BulNELab 9

Davis, R *Seamen's Sixpences: An Index of Commercial Activity, 1697-1828* Economica 328-343 Nov 1956
Fairburn W A *Handling Materials over Shipbuilding Berths in American Shipyards* RINA 1902
Frear H P *History of Tankers* Hist Trans SNAME 1943
Gilchrist A *Early examples of iron shipbuilding* IE&S 1865
Goldenberg J A *An analysis of shipbuilding sites in Lloyd's Register of 1776* MarMirr v 59 1973
Graham, G *The Ascendancy of the Sailing Ship 1850-85* EcHistR 9 74-88 1956
Haas J *Methods of Wage Payment in t Royal Dockyards* Maritime History V 99 1977
Haas J *The introduction of Taskwork into the Royal Dockyards 1775* J British Studies 8 44 1969

Harley C K *Persistence of Old Techniques : the Case of North American Wooden Shipbuilding* JEconHist 33 1973

Harley C K *Shift from Sailing Ships to Steamships 1850-1890* in McCloskey 215-234

Harley C K *Skilled Labour and the Choice of Technique in Edwardian Industry* Expl in Econ Hist 11 1973

Harris J R *Copper and Shipping* EcHistR 1966

Hausman, W J *Size and Profitability of English Colliers in the Eighteenth Century* BusHistR LI 4 1977

Hebburn Monthly 1874 [extract copied by John Gascoigne]

Jones John A Rupert *Chronological Order... Steam ... Royal Navy* - Notes & Queries 1927

Jones, S *The Builders of Captain Cook's Ships* MarMirr 1984

Martin S B & McCord N *The Steamship "Bedlington" 1841-54* Maritime History 1971

Maxton, J *Register tonnage and their Relation to Fiscal Charges* RINA 1903

Morsom, G *On the new tonnage law ...* RINA 1860

North D C *Sources of Productivity Change in Ocean Shipping 1660-1850* Jnl of Pol Econ 76 - 953-70 1968

Pering R *A Brief Inquiry into the Causes of the Premature Decay in our Wooden Bulwarks* 1812 Quarterly Review

Price S F *Rivetters' Earnings in Clyde Shipbuilding 1889-1913* Scot Econ & Soc Hist-1 42-65 1981

Ramage, A G *Minimum Net Register, and Its Effects on Design* RINA 1898

Rees, Gareth *Copper Sheathing ... Technological Diffusion in the English Merchant Fleet* JTrans Hist 85-94

Rowe D J *Occupations in Northumberland and ... Durham 1851-1911* NorHist v VIII 1973

Rowe D J *The economy of the North-East in the Nineteenth Century* NorHist v VI 1971

Salisbury, William *Early Tonnage Measurement* MarMirr 1966 1967 1968 1963

Todd D *Regional variations in Naval Construction : British Experience 1895-1966* Regional Studies 1981

Unger R W *Technology & Industrial Organisation: Dutch Shipbuilding before 1800* BusHist 17 1975

Ville, S P *Patterns of Shipping Investment in ... Newcastle, 1750-1850* v XXV NorHist 1989

Ville, S P in IntJMarHist v I no1 p65-, v II no2 p183- [Clarke] p195- [Ville], v III no 2 p109 [Craig]

Ville, S P *The Problem of Tonnage Measurement in the English Shipping Industry 1780-1830* IntJMarHist v I no2

Walker F M *Early iron shipbuilding - Vulcan* IE&SS 1990

Wall, A T *The tonnage of Modern Steamships* RINA 1919

Cleveland Industrial Archaeologist no.15

Many useful books are published by the World Ship Society which are not listed here. These frequently cover individual shipping lines with accounts of the individual vessels

Part of Laing's Wage book 1800-1

Part of Thompson's Wage book 1847

INDEX

Personal and Company Names

A

Abbay 99, 101
Abbott 62, 68-9, 274-5, 284
Abell, Westmacott 7
Adamson 35, 56, 68, 82, 100,164-5
Adamson & Ronaldson 129
Airey 28-9
Aitken 50, 56, 270 [worker]
Alcock 98, 102, 257, 260, 282
Alexander 148
Alison 56
Allan 98, 134, 219, 235, 281, 288, 306, 339, 349
Allen 261 [John], 269, 271 [E], 280, 331
Almory 14, 27, 31
Anderson 84, 242, 253, 280 [Wm], 327 [ASE]
Anderson Mrgt brewer 12
Anderson & Laverick 184
Andrew, Mary 12
Apcar 129, 144
Appleby 146, 148, 150
Archibald 29
Arkley 87, 90
Armstrong 44, 768
Armstrong [A-Mitchell8, A-Whitworth] 124-5, 127, 131, 156, 158, 170, 177, 179, 183-5, 187, 197, 199, 201, 205, 207, 210-28, 218, 222, 224-229, 231-5, 237-89, 242, 244-5, 271-2, 274-5, 281, 283-5, 287, 301, 305-87, 319, 330, 335, 337, 341-22
Arvin 85
Ashby [see Head] 138
Askwith 334
Aspinall 249
Atkinson 84, 281 [Tom]
Attley, Swan 45
Austin 82, 84, 95, 98, 101-2, 107, 135, 155, 159-160, 193, 202, 204, 209- 210, 237, 255, 257, 282, 345
Austin & Hunter 108, 311

B

Backhouse [& Dixon] 142, 236, 268-9, 271
Bacon Adl 232
Bailey 282
Bain James 216
Bainbridge 75, 213, 218
Baines 189
Baird 14
Baker 29, 96, 232 [Adml]
Banbury 96-7
Banks 115, 118
Banks, Liddle 32
Bannerman [fitter] 266, 270
Barclay Curle 220, 222
Barker 85, 260, 282-3
Barkes 103, 282
Barnaby 168, 226-8
Barnard 232
Barnes 119, 327, 331

Barrass 75
Barrick 36, 38, 86, 196-7
Barry 36, 38, 80, 86, 196
Barton 139, 158
Bartram 45, 48-9, 52, 55, 84, 107-8, 131, 155, 159, 192, 194, 8202, 204, 238, 255, 312, 342-3, 345-6
Barwick 178, 185
Bates 36, 184 [Lindon W]
Batey 129, 285
Baxter 156, 278 [Geo]
Bayley 51-2, 54, 56, 101
Beardmore's 156
Beckwith 13-4, 120
Beer 80
Bell 84, 89, 96, 158, 172, 194, 204, 216 [Thomas], 277 [sawyer] 295, 306
Bell, Cookson, Carr & Airey 73
Bell Goodman 271
Bell John E 99
Bell & Miller 116
Bell & Rockcliffe 204
Bentham 269
Berrier-Fountaine 164
Bertin 238
Bessemer 163-8
Bider 89-90
Bigge 124, 206 [Selby]
Bilbe & Perry 67
Biles 172
Binney 277
Black 226 [David], 301 [manager Armstrongs]
Black Ball Line 140
Black-Hawthorn 148, 153, 272, 274-5, 284, 292, 307, 365
Blackburn 45
Blackwood 264
Blair 134, 139,141, 148, 153, 185, 197, 305
Blankley 46
Blenkinsop 34, 75
Blumer 85, 88, 106, 110, 143, [Hartlepool] 155, 160, 170, 192-3, 202, 237, 241, 256, 260 [Hpl], 282, 311, 343
Blunt 16
Bocler 212
Bolbec Hall 284
Bolchow & Vaughan 141, 144, 153
Boldon [shipwright] 299
Bone 130-1, 135, 314, 341, 388
Boolds 156
Booth 34, 75, 99, 248-9 [Wm], 256-7 [Geo], 282
Borrowman 190, 327
Boult 16, 30
Boulton 119
Bourne Henry 2, 5, 8-9
Boutland 79, 85
Bowes 120-133,
Bowley & Wood 316
Bowlt 75, 89
Bowman & Drummond 36, 134, 195
Bowstead 129, 133, 156
Boyd [see also Thompson Boyd] 279, 283-4, 307, 325, 337
Boyd Cable 169
Bradley & Potts 98

Brand 7-8
Branfoot 50
Brassey 167
Brewhouses 7, 9
Briggs 84, 97-8 [Wm also a James], 111, 224, 258-9, 260 [Asa], 282
Brock 216
Brockie 21
Broderick [Brodrick] 18, 27, 30-1, 36, 39, 85, 197
Broderick Ann 30-1
Brown 19 [John 1792], 35, 45, 56 [Thomas], 68 [Wm], 80, 82, 84, 238 [A R], 250 [Jonathan], 253 [T],
Brown David 168, 197, 225, 227, 230-1
Brown Edw 828
Brown John [Clyde] 215-6, 230, 232, 240
Brown Thomas & Robert 33
Brown & Shaw 49
Brown-Hopkins index 276
Browne Benjamin 160, 227, 230, 235, 275, 284, 293, 295, 324, 326, 329, 332
Browne T 10
Bruce 16, 120
Brunel 129, 218, 226
Brunton 52, 54-5, 102
Brydon 189
Bucknall 179
Bulmer 30, 32-3, 39, 45, 74, 249
Burden 14, 129
Burmeister & Wain 221
Burn [s] 21, 35, 50, 88
Burnett 258, 265, 270-5, 289, 292, 315-7
Burn Mrs 35
Burrell 189
Burt 159, 301, 310, 319
Bushell 85, 264 [Geo], 339 [Coventry]
Bushnell 59
Buxton 212, 214
Byers 69, 82, 99, 259, 282

C

Cain 272, 310
Caird 169
Cairds 129, 166
Calla 88
Cameron 306, 341-2
Cammell 166, 232, 233
Campell, Mackintosh & Bowstead 133
Campbell Munro 287
Campion 15, 36
Candlish 56, 106, 257, 282
Candlish-Fox 141, 267
Carr 9 [Robt], 49, 82-3, 249 [John]
Carr Jane 9
Carrier 11-2 [widow]
Carse 27-8, 41, 74
Carter 211, 233
Casey 176
Cato 37-8
Caws 199
Cay 11
Cayzer 199

Chaloner 45
Chambers 10
Chapman 36, 38, 86, 178, 342 [helper]
Chapplelow 39
Charles I 7
Charles II 5
Charlton 19, 27, 36-7, 49, 68, 110, 218, 231, 296 [Matthew]
Chellew 189
Chilton 10, 84, 100, 282
Chitty 320 [Q C]
Christie 41, 129-130, 213, 218, 221
Church 66 [Roy]
Churchill Winston 227, 332
Clapham 165, 291, 302, 356
Clark Chas & Taylor Henry 36 [Blyth]
Clark T 274-5, 284
Clark & Stansfield 210
Clarke [Michael] 98, 100, 259
Clarke H Trevisa 203-4, 2218
Clarke Watson Guerney [see Clarke Chapman]
Clarke Chapman 178, 210, 273-5, 284, 3068
Clark Geo 103-4, 107, 123, 129, 148, 153, 187, 203, 2738, 314-6, 346
Clay 86
Clegg, Thompson & Fox 264, 301, 323, 327
Cleland 121, 133, 209, 266, 284, 309, 352-38
Cleugh 131
Clover 45
CMEW [Central Marine Engine Wks - Gray's] 148, 153, 338
Coates 19, 36, 139, 142
Cockerill 20
Cockerline 189
Coke 6
Cole [Bros] 130-1, 284, 309, 311
Collier [Colier] [Colyer8] 9, 14, 17, 19 [anon]
Common, 131
Conley 296, 309
Conrad 110
Cook 6, 19, 127, 284
Cooke 127, 136
Cooper 89, 168, 264 [John]
Coote 128, 136, 284, 335
Copley 249 [John]
Corbett J 296
Corder 82, 97, 105, 108, 109
Cornforth 82
Cory 149, 151, 185
Corry [see Rowton]
Cotesworth 2
Coulson 127, 284, 297
Coutts 62, 81, 86, 119, 124-5, 128, 142
Cowen 159, 270-1, 275
Craggs 139, 141-3, 178, 199-202, 208, 210, 219-220
Craig-Taylor 141, 200-3, 238
Craig [Robin] 147-8, 190, 200-2
Craister [Craster] 30-1 [80-1 Dock]
Cram 26-7
Crawshay see Hawks Crawshay
Creuze 44, 54, 86, 101-2

Crompton 257
Crosbie 8
Cross 45, 167,
Crosswaite 283
Crown[e], 35, 55, 77, 82, 84, 101, 105, 108, 155, 192, 202, 210, 252, 282, 344
Cruddas 285
Cucheron 238
Cudworth 87
Cummings 161, 262-3, 268, 274, 333
Cunard 188, 194, 212, 214-7, 244
Cunningham 85, 118
Currey [Curry8] 11, 268
Currie 151

D
Darling 102
Davidson 36, 231, 288
Davies David 257
Davis [see Schlesinger & Davis] 3, 6,[Ralph] 127, 129, 284, 307
De Russett 147, 253
De Lolme 253
Deane's 46
Debord & Morrison 36
Defoe 6
Delaval 9, 18, 218
Dendy 12
Dennison & Pearson 100
Denny 111, 128-9, 180-2, 198, 232, 240
Denton [see Denton-Gray] 52, 63, 87-8, 102, 143-4, 260, 2698
Denton W [Swan-Hunter] 213, 220, Denton-Gray 67, 146-7, 149, 151, 236-7, 263
Devitt & Moore 95, 104, 110
Di Giorgio 219
Dickinson 107, 272, 3158
Diesel 60, 214, 220-1, 233
Dimberline 310-2
Dipper A P 301, 341
Ditchburn 43
Dixon 67, 84 [T S], 119, 129, 140-2, 155, 157, 170, 184, 187-8, 202, 207-8, 222, 229, 239, 298, 304, 314
Dixon James [at Doxfords] 278
Dobbinson 82, 84
Dobby, Mrs Sarah [inn] 248
Dobson 19, 133, 136, 170, 179, 185, 201, 226, 257 [James],313, 335
Doeg [Doag] 278, 30, 56, 74
Donald 219
Donkin 75
Douglas 101, 274, 282
Dowey 89
Downey 249 [John]
Doxford 44, 49, 60, 65, 82, 84, 97, 103, 105-6, 109, 111-2, 155, 159, 160, 169, 181, 183, 192-5, 197-202, 204, 207-88, 211, 222, 224, 228-9, 231-2, 235-7, 241, 245, 253, 261, 278, 281, 284, 296, 306, 311, 314, 343-4, 346
Dredge 163
Driel 198, 207
Dring 144, 149
Duckworth & Langmuir 125

Dugdale 286, 341-3
Dunbar Duncan 96
Dunn 296
Durham 7, 9, 16, 237 [Capt]
Dyer 88 [c1811], 285, 306, 326, 329, 335

E
Earle 2
Easson 282
Ede 301, 324
Edwards 49, 56, 77, 86, 89-91, 129, 170, 183-5, 192, 209, 281, 286, 313 [E & Craig]
Elder 148, 194
Elder, Dempster 210, 219
Elders 167-8, 214, 283
Elgar J [c 1825] 61, 227
Elizabeth I 2, 12
Ellerman 219
Elliott 50
Ellis 95, 160
Eltringham 90, 133, 210, 285, 309, 312
Emmerson Jas 257
Erle [Royal Comm] 281, 306
Eskdale 37-8
Evans 32, 39, 43, 45, 75-6

F
Fairbairn 66, 67
Fairfield 215
Fairles 32, 39
Fairs 75
Falkingbridge 86
Farmer 14
Farr 43, 58
Farringdon 75, 77
Farrington 74, 75
Farrow 16
Faupel 164
Fawcett 150, 265
Fawdon 11, 15
Feater 84
Ferguson 220
Fielding & Platt 186
Fincham 60-1
Fishburn [e] 19, 30, 36, 38, 86, 197
Fisher 11, 14-5, 231
Fitch 88
Flagg 17, 32, 74, 79, 129
Flannery 177-8
Fletcher 13, 21, 96, 173
Foley 245
Forest [shipwright] 277
Forrest 282
Forster 11, 13, 17, 30, 39 [Mrs]
Forster Catherine 30
Forsyth 27, 33, 39, 45, 74, 85, 250, 260
Foster 108, 156, 257 [John]
Fownes 307
Fox 96, 295 [Frank], 299
Fox & Candlish see Candlish
Fox Smith 96
France Fenwick 209
Frater 82, 84
Frear 208
French Ron, 119
Froude 233
Fulton 88

Furness [Furness Withy] 144, 146-8, 150-1, 162, 166, 184, 188-191, 204, 208, 212, 219, 242, 350

G
Gaddy & Lamb 85
Gaffney [helper] 342
Gainer 158
Gale[s] 36, 53, 56, 75-7, 91-3, 99
Gamsby 98, 256-7, 259, 276, 326, 355
Gardner 10, 99, 111
Gebbie 286
George 273,
George, Lloyd 330-2, 334, 357
George II 20
George III 247
Gibbon 100
Gibson 11, 62, 80, 257 [Peter], 282
Gilchrist 173, 220
Gilkes & Wilson 153
Gill 100
Gillander R 275
Glennie [ASE], 303-5, 320, 338
Goddard 15
Goldenberg 25
Goodall 199
Goodchild 35-6
Gordon 11
Gothard [Gothart] 14-5, 27
Gourley [Andrew] 269-272
Gourley M P 315
Graham [see Osbourne Graham]
Grantham 60, 61, 65, 67, 166
Gravell 178
Gray 5 [1649], 63, 67, 79, 88, 137-8, 8143-4, 146-151, 153, 155, 162, 178, 183, 197 [J], 200-205, 211, 222, 236, 237, 242, 264, 268-9, 314, 351-2
Gray Mrs baker 49
Grey 349
Green 78, 95-6, 100, 265 [trade unionist]
Greene , 9, 227
Greenwell 129, 326 [Q C]
Griffith 48, 61
Grimshaw 36, 45, 68
Gross 164 [Sheffield steel maker]
Gulbenkian 220
Gulston 111
Gunn 249 [Wm]
Guthrie 113

H
Hackworth & Fossick 139, 153
Haggie [see Hood]
Hain 132, 201
Haldane 304
Hall 18, 35, 110, 278 [R], 282, 297, 306
Hall Jane 12
Halliday 20
Hamilton 36, 228
Hanlon 343
Hannay 36
Harbord & Twyman 164
Hardcastle 10
Hardy 100, 324
Hare Andrew 301-2
Harkess 67, 141, 158, 200-2, 282

Harland 166, 301
Harland & Wolff 147, 183, 201, 215, 218, 222
Harle 31
Harper 249
Harris Thomas 257-8 [sect. Shipwrights]
Harrison 20, 35, 49, 189, 337
Harroway 207-8
Harroway-Dixon 198, 208
Haswell 96, 107-8, 131, 159, 252, 255, 283, 311, 314, 321, 329, 343
Havelock 35, 282
Haver 197, 208
Haws 39
Hawks / Hawkes see Hawks-Crawshay
Hawks-Crawshay 30, 862, 68, 79, 88, 258, 274-5, 284-5, 287, 3158
Hawthorn R & W [see also Hawthorn-Leslie] 70, 88, 105, 129, 139, 153
Hawthorn-Leslie 155, 172-3, 178, 183-5, 199, 201, 205, 207, 211, 222, 230-2, 238, 240, 245, 271-2, 274-5, 285, 289, 293, 306-7, 319, 335, 342
Hay [s] 95, 104
Head [& Ashby] 79, 98, 138, 153, 297, 307-8
Head Wrightson 151
Headlam 14, 17, 20, 27, 30, 39
Hearn 13, 27-30
Heaviside 39, 138-140, 142
Hedderick 56
Heddle [James] 249
Hedley 8, 18, 51, 80, 96, 107
Helmsley 84
Henderson 15 [Wm], 66 [Capt Andrew H-], 68 [Thomas Hood H-], 84, 88, 205, 249 [John], 258 [Arthur], 283, 324
Henry 127
Henry VIII 2
Henzell 32, 82
Hepple 90, 133, 170, 270
Heron 33, 134, 349
Heslop 281, 313
Heward 34, 75
Higgins 144
Hill, 194, 204, 265 [John], 269-270 [G]
Hinderwell 20
Hindmarsh 14
Hine 194
Hodge 186
Hodgson [& Soulsby] 41, 77, 134, 195
Holmes 87, 129, 141
Holt [& Lamport] 37, 86, 129, 188
Holyoake 265
Hood 75-7, 222
Hooper R S 314
Hopkins Rev C H G 253
Hopper 56, 75, 81, 85, 253 [John]
Horn see Nicholson Horn
Hornby 279
Horsley 44-5, 150
Hotham 231

Houlder 191
Howard 35
Hubert 10
Huddart [& Parker] 127, 150, 243
Hudson 11, 20, 213
Hughes 2 [Edw], 309, 341-2 [helper]
Hume 255-6, 282
Humphrey Michael [c1750] 208
Humphrey Tennant 229
Hunter 3, 95, 108, 116, 135, 147, 158, 252, 253, 286,
Hunter J 75
Hunter Mary 95
Hunter Summers 8202, 3048
Huntley 75, 79
Hurry 27-9, 32, 40
Hustler 37
Hutchings 284
Hutchinson 3 [Wm. author 1794], 35, 54-6, 84, 259, 260, 282

I

Iliff & Mounsey 103, 108-9, 111, 156
Inglis 281, 298
Irvine 151, 155, 187, 189-191, 222, 237, 242, 264, 270
Isherwood 208, 211, 222
Ito Rear-Adl 227, 238

J

Jackson 129, 139, 144, 158, 151, 282
James M C 130, 296, 368
James I 2
Jeans 164, 165
Jeffreys 305, 314, 316-8, 320, 327-8, 331
Jewitt [Robt] 249
Jobling 105
Joblings [widow] 12
John 167, 172-3
Johnston 209
Joicey 274-5
Jones 67, 166, 189, 190, 197, 256 [Leslie], 284, 286, 311
Jones, Quiggin 166
Jordan 66-7, 128
Joy 153

K

Kane 257-8, 264, 273
Keeney & Marshall 283
Keir 265
Kell 32, 74, 81
Kellock 141
Kelso 104
Kelvin 206
Keeney & Marshall 2848
Kerr 88, 231
Keys 57 [Richard], 111 [John]
Kimber [see Rake Kimber] 80
King 203, 245 [Foster]
Kirby 184
Kirk 163, 204
Kirkbride 84
Kish 156
Knight 158, 160-1, 173, 181, 254, 271, 281, 286, 294, 296,
298-302, 305, 311-2, 313, 321, 325, 327, 333, 338-341, 346
Knott 141, 178, 193, 257-9 [Wm]
Krupp 199, 220
Kyd 28

L

Laing 34-7, 45, 50, 53, 55-6, 59-60, 62, 68, 79, 82, 95-6, 108, 110-4, 129, 135, 153, 155, 171-3, 184-6, 187, 192-4, 202-4, 211, 229, 236-78 239, 241, 250-2, 255-260, 281-3, 313, 316, 339, 343-4
Laing 87 [Middlesbrough]
Laing Andrew 216
Laird 61, 165, 232-3, 301 [J C]
Lamb 129, 257 [John]
Lamport [Lamport & Holt] 75, 127, 188
Lane 87, 220
Langborne 37, 37
Langdale 87
Langdale's site 138
Lashley 26
Laslie 27, 31, 32
Lattany 9, 20
Laverello 130
Laverick [see also Anderson & L-] 28
Lawrence 101-2
St Lawrence 5, 218 [river]
Laws 84, 85, 296 [Cuthbert], 364
Lawson [John] 84, 249, 288
Leach & Coates 139, 142
Leithhead 82, 84, 84
Lennard 142, 178
Leslie 119, 128-9, 133, 155, 262, 277, 279, 284, 288-9
Letany 20
Liddell 56, 102
Lidgett 87
Lidster 20
Lightfoot Mary 48
Lightfoot 84, 99
Lindsay 50, 60, 119, 128, 144, 205, 273, 296 [R W]
Lindsay, Caverill [Lindsay Swan Hunter] 221
Linklaters 69
Lipson 5, 12
Lister 55, 84
Little James rivet heater 280
Livesey 329
Livingstone 166
Lockwood [see Pearse & Lockwood] 139, 151, 267-271
Londonderry [Marquis of] 150
Lough 134, 349
Love 85
Lowson 14
Lubbock 96, 98, 104, 110, 141
Luke [Thomas] 237
Lumsden 698, 84, 100
Lumsdens
Lynch, James 300-1, 312
Lynn 194, 346

M

MacGregor 66-7, 85, 96-7, 118
MacKenzie [& Ross] 28, 62, 77, 89, 251
Mackie 56, 84
Mackintosh 129, 133, 156
MacPherson 216
Manders 68
Mann 295, 328
Manner & Bates 36
Mannesmann 167
Markham 39, 139
Marley 120
Marr 194, 203, 343
Marsh 230, 330
Marshall 62, 97, 103, 112, 118, 131-3, 230, 245, 252 [Alfred], 258 [G], 266 [F C], 269-70
Martell 54, 102, 134-6, 153, 166-8, 171, 177-8, 198
Martin 53-4, 68 [Francis], 180-2
Martindale 129
Masterton 30
Matheson 128
Matthews J 296
Maudslay 124, 225, 237
Maughlin 9, 11
Maughline 9
Mavor 178
Mayhew 7, 43-4, 63, 259
McAllister 175
McCloskey 172
McColl 207
McCord 62, 73, 226, 247
McCulloch 43
McGlashan 190, 207
McGovern 177
McIntyre 121, 307-8
McKinnon 145
McLaine 75
McLeod 79, 129, 129, 219, 260
Mellanby 39, 87
Merz 206-7
Messent 78, 116
Metcalfe 45, 49, 56, 77, 80-1, 85, 100-1, 120, 251, 283
Middle Dock [& Co] 18, 32, 39, 106, 129, 147, 349
Middlemas 27
Milburn 69, 67, 125,
Miles 102
Mill J Stuart 265, 269
Miller 88, 108, 119
Mills 56, 82, 84, 97-8, 282
Milton 216
Mitchell[s] [see also Armstrong-M] 119, 124, 128, 130, 132, 136, 166, 176, 213 [Mrs Mitchell], 270
Mitchell 279 [boatbuilder], 284, 301 Labourers' Union], 341-2
Mitclam 83
Money Wigram 49
Monson 59
Moor 5-
Moore 12 [Philip], 18, 100, 278 [Mrs Sarah]
Moore [Moor] widow 12
Moorsom 60
Mordaunt 109
More 20
Mordey 257-9
Morel 189
Morris 41
Morrison 110, 287 [explosion]
Mortimer 263, 268, 305, 312
Mosley 28, 29

Moss & Hume 215
Mosses [Patternmakers] 303, 316, 321, 324, 325, 338
Mould Wm 304
Mounsey see Illiff & Mounsey
Mudd 188-90
Muir 304, 306
Mumford 102
Mundella 275
Munroe 36
Muntz 85
Murray [Sir Digby8] 198

N

Naisby 84, 100, 236
Napier 134
Nef 2-3, 7
Nell 59
Nelly 42
Nelson 74,
NEM 187, 202, 204, 272, 285, 288, 315, 338, 346
Newitt 206
Nichol 146
Nicholson 21, 35, 69 [Wm], 111, 131
Nicholson & Horn 30, 39, 45, 748
Nicholson & Watt 178
Nicholson & Wilson 283
Nipper [shipwright] 277
Nixon 15
Nobel 174, 176, 178
Noble 84, 129, 218, 225, 284-5, 305, 318, 329-332, 337
Northumberland SB 185-7
North of England SB 157
North of Ireland SB 221
Nourse 95, 104

O

O'Neill 294, 302, 311-28
Oram 216
Ords 87
Osbourne [see Osbourne Graham]
Osbourne Graham 111, 159,193, 202, 208-9, 227, 237, 306
Oswald 113-5, 118-123, 148, 237, 273, 282-3
Oswald Partis 75
Oxley Harry 253

P

Palmer 60, 67, 69, 103, 113, 116, 119-125, 127, 133-4, 136-7, 147, 160, 165, 169, 170, 175, 177, 183-5, 191, 201, 205, 208, 211, 222, 224, 225, 228-232, 239, 240, 243, 245, 252, 260, 264-270, 272, 280, 283-4, 287, 297-8, 308, 313, 319, 322-3, 329, 335, 337, 342, 344, 349, 351-2
Parker 165, 174, 261 [John]
Parkes 225
Parkin 87
Parkinson 119, 275, 279
Parry 6
Parsons 155, 169, 185, 206, 215-6, 227, 232, 338, 346
Partis 75

Patterson 58, 305, 313
Pattison [partner of Dring] 144
Pattison & Atkinson 274
Patton 279
Paley 253
Peacock 233
Pearce 99, 160, 238
Pearse['s] 138-140, 151-82, 166, 171, 188, 236, 280, 314
Pearse-Lockwood 267-71
Pearson 100, 102, 218, 282-3
Pearson Mary 78
Pease 80, 184, 191, 301 [E R]
Peat 191
Peck 220
Penney 108
Percival 283
Perret 227, 234
Perring 68
Petersen 199
Petrie 282
Petries 55
Peverall 110
Phelps Brown 332
Philipson 275
Phillips 73
Phorson 194
Pickersgill 101, 108, 156, 170, 193-4, 202, 208, 282
Pile 55-6, 62, 95-7, 99, 101-5, 108, 111-2, 119-123, 143-147, 151-2, 236-7, 252-3, 255, 257-9 263 [Hartlepool], 272 [Wear], 282, 341
Pile & Spence 267-8, 279
Pletts 275
Plummer 284
Pochin H D 121, 265-6
Pole 163
Pollard 164, 206, 240
Pollitt & Wigzell 141
Pollock 54, 166, 208
Poppelwell 85
Potter 17, 264 [Geo], 267-268 [Thomas]
Potts 9, 35, 50 [P & Burn], 56, 75, 82-4, 98, 251 [Taylor], 282
Potts & Burn 50
Pratt 255
Preston 9, 12 [Isabele], 14
Price John [Gateshead] 88
Price John 121, 123-4, 159, 169, 173, 206, 279, 281, 288, 297, 302, 313, 318, 351
Priestman 156, 192-3, 202
Proud J H 88
Purdon 191
Pye 39, 296
Pyle 82, 84
Pyman 144, 146, 148, 150, 189, 190, 197, 286

R

Radcliffe 35, 324 [ASE], 326, 330
Raffery John 301
Raincock 130
Rake Kimber 50, 80, 87, 139-140, 142
Rance 109
Rankine 66-7
Ratcliffe [ASE] 282

Ravenhill 119, 225
Ravensworth 120, 159
Ray 315
Rea 265
Readhead 10, 90, 131-3, 136, 155, 185, 201, 222, 284, 296 [G T], 312, 335, 342
Reay 35-6, 56, 81, 82, 84, 100, 105, 119
Reed 14, 16, 20, 41, 97, 98, 135, 166-7, 177, 225, 226, 229, 231
Rees 50
Reinhard 168
Rendel 226, 227
Rennison 27
Rennoldson 27, 90, 118, 133, 183, 209, 243, 349
Renwick 30, 213, 219
Reynolds 341
Ribbon Geo 248-251
Richardson 28-9, 100-1 [Wm]
Richardson Duck 68, 138-141, 143, 149, 155, 171, 187-8, 190-1, 202, 209, 236, 241, 269-270, 306
Richardson J Wigham 89, 113, 115, 118-9, 129, 130, 152, 155, 181, 183-4, 205, 207, 212-3, 217, 222, 235, 237, 239, 240-2, 244, 8270, 283-5, 288-9, 304, 306, 317, 320, 335, 341
Richardson Thomas [R - Bros] 87, 141-6, 148-151, 153, 166, 182, 191, 206-7, 302
Richardson Westgarth 187, 1918, 338, 346
Richmond 250
Rickaby 95
Riddell & Brays 267
Riddle 67, 141
Ridley 12 [Ann], 108, 324
Riedemann 176, 177
Riley 167-8, 172
Ritchie 54
Roberts 79, 267-8 [W P]
Robertson 121, 164, 240, 306
Robinson 17, 19, 100, 131, 134, 282-4, 341-2
Robson 45, 52, 79, 84, 88-9, 129, 257 [Wm], 278, 282, 312
Rochussen 166
Rogerson 125, 156, 169, 174, 283
Ropner 138, 146, 148, 150, 171, 187-8, 191-2, 198, 202, 205, 207, 222, 242, 286
Rose 127
Ross 285
Rothwell 162, 295
Row [e] , 11, 16, 30, 40, 878, 120, 293
Rowell 158, 240, 245, 285
Rowntree 39, 77, 84, 257 [Stephenson]
Rowton 290
Royden 45
Rumsey 88
Runciman 133-4, 199
Russell 112 [W Clark R-], 143 [Clyde], 166, 208 [Scott R-], 222
Ruston 244
Rutherford 349
Rutter [Edw] 249

Ryan W 296

S

Salter 278
Samuda 166-8
Samuel, 178, 189, 211-2, 239
Samuelson 275
Sanderson 87, 124
Sauver 163
Savage 265
Saxton White 176, 217
Schlesinger [see Schlesinger & Davis]
Schlesinger & Davis 127, 130, 133, 155, 170, 183, 269, 284, 288, 306, 312, 344
Schlick 198, 218
Schloss 251
Scorer 294
Scott 11, 35, 56, 75, 166, 197, 202,
Scott Russell see Russell
Scrafton & Smith 138
Scurfield 56
Seaton Sluice 18-9, 31
Seaton Delaval 218
Selby 17
Shafto 7, 14
Sharer 41, 156
Sharp 41, 202-4, 323
Sharpe 256
Shaw 7 [Richard], 9, 16, 41,
Shaw Saville 105, 140, 197
Shevill 278
Short 107, 129, 136, 170, 187-9, 193, 202, 8204, 206, 208, 222, 237, 258, 260, 269, 282, 311-2, 320, 339
Short 275 sect 9 hours League
Siemens-Martin [steel] 124, 150, 8165, 167-170
Simey 100, 102
Simpson 6 [Robt], 11, 12 [his daughter], 37, 124, 235, 312
Simpson [Dr] 290
Sivewright 150-2
Skinner James [see Wood & Skinner] 288, 279 [J D],
Slaven 66
Sloan 207
Smales 37-8, 86, 196
Smart 96
Smith 9, 30 Wm, 75-8, 91, 107-8, 227-8 [W E], 249 [Wm], 289 [Agnes], 307, 310 [Matthew], 313, 334 [Llewellyn]
Smith John [c1850] 98-9, 256, 282
Smith George 18
Smith Sidney [foreman] 280
Smith T & W 56, 67, 75, 81, 85, 96, 115-6, 129, 155-6, 183, 192, 209-10, 224, 250-2, 259, 263, 281, 304
Smith Wasteney 69
Snell 207
Softley 131-3, 284
Sollitt 20
Soulsby see Hodgson & Soulsby
South
Spaldin 63, 148, 152, 241
Sparrow 268

Spence 80, 86-7, 102, 135, 143-158, 279, 282, 304, 306
Spencer 129
Squance 203
Stanhope [Lord] 88
Stanley 301, 312, 341
Steel [Thomas], 151 [Steel & Young] 267-268 [Charles]
Steele 7
Stephenson 75, 116, 121, 129-131, 156, 184-5, 191, 196-8, 210-1, 264, 272, 274-5, 306, 308, 319
Stewart 179
Stockton Iron Shipbuilding Co 139
Stoker 36
Stokoe 179
Stonehouse 102, 282
Stoney 207
Storey 15-6, 56, 77, 84, 332
Storr 163
Stothard 278, 282
Stoveld 36, 80
Straker 75, 77, 81, 85, 250
Stromeyer 164
Strother Mrs 12
Stuart 141, 178
Summers 17, 19, 27, 30
Sunderland SB 193, 201, 312
Surtees 34-5
Sutherland 59, 84
Swainston 112, 144
Swan 108, 124-5, 127, 176-7, 8178, 226, 284, 286
Swan Wm 268-9 Boilermakers Soc
Swan Hunter 3, 116, 124-8, 130, 148, 155-6, 170-1, 173, 176 181, 183-6, 198-201, 205-7, 210-223, 224, 229, 231-3, 238-240, 242-4, 290-1, 301, 306, 320, 333-5, 341-3, 350, 352
Sykes 77, 87
Symington 88

T

Tanner 39, 79
Taylor [see also Craig Taylor] 36, 39, 84, 134, 257, 260, 309
Temple 18, 27, 30-3, 39-40, 248, 250 [Wm -shipwright c1820s]
Tennyson, Alfred 226
Tennyson D'Eyncourt, E H W 226, 235
Thackray 99-100
Thirlaway 220
Tholander 164
Thomas P N 88, 90
Thompson 36 [James], 884 [Wm], 97, 100-1 [Richard]
Thompson J L 155, 157, 170, 172 [Robt], 178, 192-5, 201-2, 205, 222, 241, 245, 297, 305, 345
Thompson 9 [Robt] see also J L, 46, 57, 66, 77, 95, 102, 106-7, 252, 277-8, 281-4
Thompson Robt jnr 106, 110, 159, 170, 192-3, 201, 208-9, 238, 241, 257, 282, 312, 345
Thompson & Boyd 121, 141, 153, 274-5, 284

Thorneycroft 231-2
Thowburn 11
Tiffin 51, 99, 251, 282
Tindall 20, 38, 49
Todd 40, 84
Topsham 19
Topless [shipwright] 277
Totherick 12
Toward 62, 133, 279
Towers 286
Trenchmann 165
Trewent 173
Trewhitt [Trewitt] [Trawitt] 7, 11, 14, 17, 32
Trotman 77
Trotter 85
Trumble 11
Tryon Vice-Adl 227
Tully 131
Turnbull 62, 94-7, 138, 196, 197
Turner 165
Twaddell 205
Tweddell 304
Tweedmouth 233
Tweedy 129, 213, 221
Tyne Iron SB 185, 201, 238, 312
Tyne Ironshipbuilding Co 264
Tyser 95
Tyzack 69, 99
Unger 66
Ure 113, 283 [of Elders]

V

Vaughan [see Bolchow & Vaughan] 134
Vaux 21
Vernon 120, 280
Vick 190-1
Vickers 199, 201, 215, 219, 231, 233, 261 [Thomas], 278

W

Wade, Owen 298, 301-2, 318, 323, 341
Wailes 179, 279 [E F]
Wait 90
Wake 35
Walker 95, 104, 255 [J]
Wall 11, 77
Wallace 110
Wallas 11, 13, 17
Wallis 9, 17, 39, 51, 62, 74-5, 81, 85
Walmsley 27
Wallsend Slipway 124, 148, 157, 179, 207, 214, 217-8, 230, 279, 284, 302, 307, 352-48
Wang 95, 102
Watkins John 90
Watson [see also Clarke Chapman], 28, 36, 66, 82, 95, 97, 102, 111-2, 158, 175, 217, 237, 257 [John], 282, 306, 346
Watt 17, 88, 119 [Boulton & Watt]
Watts 36, 67 [Watts & Milburn], 148, 168, 174, 184, 226-8, 233, 285, 320
Waymouth 53, 98, 136
Weatherburn Mrs Sarah 248 *Sign of the Ship*
Webbs 273, 299, 305

Webster 68, 306
Welsh 101, 232, 249-250 [Joseph shipwright c 1820s], 277 sawyer
West 167-8
Westgarth [see also Richardson Westgarth] 127, 142, 153, 191, 304-7
Westmacott 283
Wetherley 56
White 14, 16-7, 44, 56, 59-60, 134, 168, 176, 213, 214-8, 225-8, 230-3, 240, 388
Whitehead 96, 231
Whyte foreman blacksmith 278
Wigham 285 [Eric], 346 [John]
Wigram 49, 78
Wilhelmsen 211, 260
Wilkie 305, 333
Wilkinson, 10-11, 17, 55, 61, 77, 94, 121, 282
William & Mary [charter 1695] 3
Williamson [Hedworth8] 106
Willington Slipway Co 287 [houses]
Willis 75, 95, 281
Wilson 11, 50, 85, 100, 118, 130, 163 [Robt], 166, 189, 247 [Geo], 251 [Joshua], 279 [W]
Wilson, Pease & Co 190
Winlo8 1188
Winlow 56, 858
Winship 17
Winspear 88, 143
Winstanley 213
Withy 135, 147-152, 155, 169, 187, 189-191, 206, 236, 242, 296, 305, 312-3
Wood 87, 89, 216 [Eng Lt W H]
Wood William see Wood & Skinner
Wood & Skinner 128, 130, 133, 155 170, 184-5, 201, 239, 335, 342
Woodcroft, Bennett 678
Woodhouse 62, 89
Woodroffe 56
Workman Clark 201
Worthy 101, 103, 112, 282
Wouldhave 209
Wrangham 7, 9
Wrangham Mary 11
Wright 19, 27, 31, 36, 45, 75-6
Wurl 217-8
Wylie 274-5
Xenos 145, 236

Y

Yamagata [Chief Engineer Constructor] 238
Yarrow 231
Ybarra 241
Yeoman F 152
Young 20 [Wm], 44 [G F London], 74-5, 79-80, 85-6, 118, 178, 249 [Edw], 253 [T], 255 [R], 260, 264, 270, 306 [J]

SHIPS

A

Aaron Manby 61
Achillens 129
Achilles HMS 185

Acorn 74 [1807]
Acute HMS 40
Adam Lodge 81
Adelaide Lavarello 243
Admiral Aspin 32
Admiral Gambier 33
Admiral Kanaris 104
Admiral Miaulis 236
Advance [1854] 63, 139,
Affiance 34, 34
Afghanistan 141
African 96 [tug]
Agenoria 5, 77
Agincourt 229, 235
Agricola 82
Aid 318
Alacrity 40 [HMS 1806], 105 [1856], 225 [HMS 1885]
Albany 229
Albertville 188
Albion 29, 34
Aldworth 153
Alexa 237
Alexander II 236
Alexandra 106
Alfonso XII 117, 130, 170, 181, 243
Algoa 193, 198
Alliance 88
Alma 98
Almirante Barroso 229
Almirante Brown 168, 226
Almirante Latorre 229
Almirante Oquendo 230
Alpha 226
Alton 197
Amaryllis 130
Amazonas 229
Amelia Mary 82
American Maru 239
Amity 60, 62, 103
Amphitrite 74
Amsteldijk 242
Amy 146
Ancroft 218
Andromeda 176
Anglo series 194
Ann Brass 99
Anne 50
Annie Melling 209
Ant HMS class 241
Antwerpen 171
Apollo 229 [HMS class]242 [sail]
Appomattox 190
Aquila 243
Arab Steed 104
Arawa 185
Arconia 218
Arctic Queen [later Pishchev Industriya] 188
Ardmore 107
Arested 193
Argo 29
Ariadne 105
Ark Royal HMS 196
Armais 87
Armeniak 175
Armenian 236
Arno 95
Arracan 141
Asama 229
Ashton 150

Asia 74, 104
Asiatic 118
Asie 236
Assam 66
Astrae 34
Atlantic 174
Attila 142
August, 93, 242
Aurora 39
Auspicious 29
Australia 209,
Australian 46, 127,145
Avalon 171
Avery Hill 194
Avon 145
Ayton 218
Azoff 236

B

Babthorp 118
Bacchus 81
Badger 232
Bahama 139
Bakuin 148, 177-8, 180
Bankoko Maru 238
Banshee 166
Banter HMS 40
Barambio 108
Barbara 82 [1832], 99,
Baronsmore 108
Beagle HMS 232
Beaufort 108
Beaver HMS 232
Bedlington 62
Belgia 242
Belgravia 106
Bellona 230
Beltane 110
Benholm 141
Bermuda 139, 237
Bermudian 203
Bertha 150
Bertha Marion 110
Berwindmoor 202
Berwindvale 202
Beta 226
Betsey & Jane 82
Bhosphorus [#53 & #54] 242
Bilboa 33
Birma 244
Biscayan 133
Bittern [HMS class] 231
Black Sea 107
Blenheim 140
Blessing 131
Bloodhound HMS 226
Blowden 156
Blyth 104
Bolivar 140
Border Chief 132
Borneo 146
Bouncer HMS 40
Bride 98
Brighton
Brisbane 67
Britannia 79, 105
Britannias 116
British Queen 79
Britomart 98, 118, 224
Brodrick 31
Broomfield 197
Brunswick 29

Bucephalus HMS 40
Buenos Aires 237
Buenos Ayrean 169
Bullmouth 211
Burrumbeet 170
Buteshire 183

C

Cadiz 105
Calabar 55
Calais-Douvres 129
Caledonia 33
Cambria 214
Cambrian 189
Cambridgeshire 130
Campania 210, 215
Camperdown 228
Canada 60, 229 [HMS]
Canadian 106, 184
Carlo Alberta 116
Carmargo 108
Carolina 120
Carn Tual 108
Carnation 79
Carpathia 214-5
Carrie 141
Carthage 214
Cartier 214
Castle Eden 87
Catherine 32
Catherine Apcar 237
Celandie 105
Celsus 107
Cerebus HMS 225
Cesarevitch 237
Challenge 67
Champion 112
Champion of the Seas 107
Charente 236
Charles 174
Charleston 228
Charlotte Dundas 88
Charlton 26, 37, 49, 110
Chase 105
Chasseur 118, 123
Chaudiere 106
Chaumin 178
Cheerful HMS 231
Chen Yuen 235
Cherwell 142
Chicago 191
Chieftain 89
Chigwell 178
Chih-Yuan 227
Chilean 140
Chih-Yuan 227
Ching-Yuen 227
Choles 108
Christobal Colon 145
Chusan 119
Cicero 74
Circassian Prince 127, 178
Citta De Venezia 242
City of Adelaide 107, 110
City of Agra 144
City of Sidney 140
Clarendon 128
Claudia 101
Clermont 88
Clytemnestra 166
Cockatrice HMS 224
Colonia 214

Colonist 99
Colorado 104
Colpitts 30
Columbian 145
Commerce 79
Concord 138
Connaught 123
Conqueror 67, 145
Constantia 99
Constitution 229
Content 30
Copernicus 128
Coppename 108
Copra HMS 230-1
Cornelia 40 [HMS], 98
Coundon 87
Courier 127
Coverdale 36
Crenella 211
Crest of the Wave 96
Crewe 184
Cricket 101
Crocodile HMS 40
Crostafels 237
Crowley 7
Crown 29[1794]
Crusader 81
Cuba 50, 56
Cullandsgrove 36
Cumberland 19
Cyanus 150
Cyclops HMS [was Indrabarha] 203, 225 [HMS class]
Czar 170, 239

D

Dalhousie 63, 146
Danube 118
De Brus 63, 79, 139
Defence 51-53, 224-5 HMS
Delta 226
Demetrius 144
Denmark 50, 140,
Dependent 105
Derwent 232
Dessouk 146, 236
Devastation HMS 225
Devonshire 134
Dewan 242
Dhu Hearth 129
Dogali 227
Dolmenbaktchi 146
Dolphin 142
Domitilla 166
Don 81
Dora 197
Dovenby Hall 123, 209
Drachenfels 243
Dreadnought 232-3
Drottning Victoria 214, 243-4
Duke of Northumberland 78, 105
Duke of Roxburgh 78
Duke of Sutherland 128
Duke William 21
Dunbeth 218
Duncan Dunbar 97
Duquesa 191
Durham City 147

E

E J Spence 237
Eagle 88

Earl Percy 29
Early Morn 144
Eden HMS 232
Eeta 242
Eisbrecher 244
Elba 237
Elbruz 177
Eleanor 33
Electric 129
Elizabeth 20, 49,
Elizabeth I 2, 12, 19
Elizabeth Graham 141
Elizabeth Watts 174
Ellenia 242
Ellens 75
Emir 243
Emperor 90, 139
Empress Eugenie 98
Emulous HMS 40
Enable 209 [see Tyne Dock no 4]
Endeavour 19
Energia 131
Enfield 148
English Rose 87, 153
Enrique Maynes 132
Era 177
Erin 122
Ermack 184, 244
Erne [class HMS] 232
Ernst Moritz Arndt 237
Esmeralda 226-7
Espresso 130, 243
Essequivo 139
Essex 112
Ethel 125, 170
Ethelbald 196
Ethelbert 196
Euphrosyne 139
Europa 123, 130
Europe 181
Euxine 147
Everton Grange 191
Excelsior 66
Expedit 141
Expedition 18, 29
Experiment 17 [1752], 39

F

Faith 105-6
Fame 34, 99
Fangtrum 201
Faraday 125, 130, 136
Fau Sang 243
Favourite 99
Fenton 108
Ferdinand Corvilain 108
Fergusons 178
Fergusson 142
Fiery Cross 133
Fifeshire 127
Filippo Artelli 187
Fiume 119
Fi-wan 110
Flash 62
Flinders 237
Flora 81
Flor de Maria 111
Flottbek 208
Flying Dragon 96
Flying Dutchman 89
Folgate 218
Foo Shing 243

Forest Brook 199
Forfarshire 110
Formby 166
Fort Augustus 79
Fortitude 87
Forward HMS 40
Four Winds 123, 209
France 208
Francoli 236
Franconia 214
Francsisca 236
Francunion II [see Hooper] 175
Franklin 237
Frankwald 191
Frau Jung 106
Free Briton 20
Friends' Adventure 88
Fuh Le 236
Fushiki Maru 238

G

G.F.D. 119
Galatea 105
Gamma 226
Ganges 104
Garcia De Vinuesa 240
Garland 232
Garry Owen 61
Gascony 202
Gem 98
Gemini 34
General Napier 195
George Elliott 21
George Green 78
George Marshall 118
George Pyman 144
Georgia 123
Germany 140
Gertrude 118
Gipsey Queen 145
Gisela 194
Gladiator 139
Glance 112
Glenaros 104
Gluckauf 125, 176-7
Golden Horn 146
Golden Sunset 106
Goldmouth 212
Gorgon HMS 225
Gosforth 118
Grand Duke Alexis 240
Grand Duke Constantine 240
Grangesburg 199
Gratitude 238
Great Eastern 129, 134
Great Northern 147
Great Western
Greece 123
Gresham 110
Gulf of Venice 147

H

Habarovsk 240
Hafis 178
Halia 101
Hannover 243
Happy Jannet 21
Happy Returns 29
Harmattan 214
Harriet Pinkney 141
Harriot 30
Hatsuse 229

Havilah 124
Hawk Packet 30
Hawkhope 118
Heathdene 199
Hector 104
Hedwig Heidman 207
Helena Mona 106
Henry, 257
Her Majesty 99
Herculean 32
Hercules 104, 201 [HMS], 230
Hesperia 44, 106
Hesperus 125, 201, 224
Heversham 51, 118
Hew Singers 74
Hibernia 123
Highland Lass 39
Highlands 141
Hilton 33
Himalaya 105, 145
Hindoo 130
Hindostan 129
Hiroshima Maru 238
Hokkaido Maru 140
Holland 50, 123,
Holly Bough 98
Holmsdale 98
Holmwood 209
Honour 99 [858], 312
Hooper [Silvertown in 1916 - Francunian II in 1924] 125, 130, 175
Hope, 41, 88, 166, 214 [HMS]
Hopper 56, 75
Horta 34
Hotspur 118
Hound 33
Hudson 123, 140,
Hugh Streatfield 107
Humbleton 100
Humbolt 237

I
Idzumo 229
Incertus 82
Indrabarah 214
Indrabarha 203
Indus 32, 139,
Ingram 150
Intrepid 32
Invarine 106
Invernia 212, 215
Iquique8 119
Ireland 144
Ireshope 106
Iris 32, 74, 168
Iron Age 139
Iron Ore 60
Isaac Pennock 197
Isabel Craggs 142-3
Isabell 235
Isabella 77
Isabella & Dorothy 18
Isel Holme 194
Island Queen 151
Isly 243
Istanboul 144
Itsukushina Maru 127
Iwate 229
Izumi 229

J
Jackdaw 40
Jacob Bright 190
James 312, 316
James Shepherd 98
Jane 89
Jane Kelsall 133
Janus 231
Japan 125
Jarrow 121
Jessica 65
John 818
John & Thomas 17
John & Mary 143, 146
John Allan 98
John Bowes 120-1, 134
John Dixon 130
John Line 82
John Mcintyre 121, 123
John Myers 98
Jonas 33
Jones Brothers 141
Jumna 104, 225
Jung Frau 106
Juno 74, 81
Justitia 141

K
Kaiser Wilhelm 215
Kaiser Wilhelm Der Gross 215
Kalioub 236
Kangaroo 230
Kangean 187
Kara 171
Kashima 185, 229
Kasugo 245
Kate Fawcett 150
Katsuno Maru 238
Kelso 104
Kent 112
Keystorm 214
Kielder Castle 130
King Arthur 63, 144
King of Italy 63, 144
King Richard 96
Kioto 214
Knight Templar 108
Knutsford 171
Kong Sverre 142
Korniloff 237
Kostroma 240
Kron Prinz 237
Kron Prinz Wilhelm 215
Kuishui Maru 238
Kumanto Maru 238
Kut Sang 243

L
La Hogue 55, 96
Lady Eleanor 111
Lady Zealand 110
Ladywood 209
Lamport 75, 127
Lasborough 108
Latona 98, 123
Launceton 98
Laurestina 131
Lavinia 250
Leander 41
Leeds City 202
Leinster 123
Leipzig 145
Leonidas 232
Leopard 227
Lewis M Lamb 118
Liberty
Linden 208
Little Lucy 140, 166
Lizzie English 152
Lizzie Leslie 132
Lizzie Scott 99
Llandaff 130
Lloyds 145 [see Sea Queen]
Lochiel 218
Loftus 103
Looch 178
Lord Collingwood 33
Lord Duncan 35
Lord Eldon 32
Lord Nelson HMS 185, 230
Lord Percy 192
Lord Seaham 82
Lord Sidmouth 74
Lord Warden 104
Lucifer 232
Lucknow 99
Lugigen 349
Lumen 177
Lusitania 215
Lux 179
Luxor 147
Lydgate 123, 209
Lydie 150

M
Ma Roberts 166
Maddaloni 237
Madona 29
Madonna 243
Madrid 170
Magdala HMS 225
Magnet 108
Magpie HMS 40
Maize 105
Majestic 88
Mally & Jenny 49
Mamari 197
Manchester City 188
Mancunia 207
Mandalay 197
Maori King 197
Margaret 41
Margaret & Winifred 17
Margarita 208
Maria Theresa 230
Marietta Ralli 190
Marion Macintyre 66
Marlborough [see Scotsman] 150
Marmion 104
Maroa 193
Marquis Scicluna 178
Mars 98
Martin
Mary 17, 75, 236
Mary Beyts 197
Mary Rogerson 174
Mary Shepherd 98
Mary Sophia 82
Massis 175
Mastiff 226
Matina 214
Mauretania 185, 212, 214-7, 252
Maynards 105

Mayo 199
Mediator 39, 274
Medusa 98
Mei Shih 181
Memora 119
Mercury 168
Merganser 201
Merlin 115, 118
Mermaid 231
Merrie England 196
Merrington 118
Miaza 98
Middlesbrough 87
Middleton 88, 271
Midnatsol 147
Miike Maru 238
Milburn Tower 130
Milton Stuart 208-9
Milwaukee 212
Min 106, 238
Miowera 242
Mirage 144
Miss Preston 112
Missouri 148
Modern Greece 141
Mombasa 192
Monarch 89, 90, 184, 234
Monkseaton 127
Monkshaven 196
Montauk Point 185
Monte Moro 127
Montrose 188
Mougoutschi 236
Mount Kembla 171
Mountain Ash 199
Mozart 157
Murex 178
Muskoka 141
Myrtle 107

N
Nairnshire 171
Naniwa 227
Naniwa Kan 229
Nanuphar 107
Narranansett 211
Narrung 193
Narvik 199
Nautilus 88, 111
Navarra 185
Ne Tron Menya 225
Nederland 175
Needwood 209
Neidenfels 243
Nereus 40
Nerva 34
Nevada 123
New Orleans 229
Newcastle 119
Niger 108
Nile 108
Nisshin 245
Noonderkyk 242
Nord America 130
Nordtiernen 237
Norfolk 193
Norham 199
Normand 236
Normania 181
North Sands 34
Northenden 127
Northumberland 17 [1758], 120

Northumbrian 30, 99 [1855]
Norval 113
Nubia 242
Nullus Secundus 223
Numidia 242
Nyore 242

O

Obra 202
Ocean Flower 87
Ocean Mail 106
Octavia 118
Oka 177
Old Trafford 90
Olive Branch 49
Oosterdijk 242
Oran 235
Orel 240
Oriental Queen 110
Orlando HMS 225
Ortinashell 141
Oscar 75
Oscar II 153
Osprey 139
Otnaburgh 87
Otterspool 123, 209
Ouse 147
Ovingham 199
Oweenee 141

P

Palambam 79
Palikara 236
Palikari 140
Pandour 40
Panther HMS 227
Para 150
Para E Amazona 240
Parramatta 104
Patras 141
Patris 187
Paul Paix 202, 208
Peace 107
Pectan 211
Per Ardua 106
Pera 109, 209
Perseverance 88
Persia 145
Persian Prince 141
Perthshire 183
Peteroff 145
Petrel 87
Petriana 178-9
Petrolea 141, 179 [Swedish]
Petroleum 212
Phantom 98
Phillippeville 188
Pishchevaya Industriya 188
Phosphorus 177
Pilot 244
Pique 229
Planet 230
Plantagenet 33
Pleiades 77
Polly 34
Pontos 193
Porcia 77
Port Chalmers 194
Port Denison 171
Port Fairy 130
Port Jackson 144
Portwood 209

Poseidon 175
Pouyer Quertier 125
President 132
Priam 99
Priestman 192
Prince Albert 62, 119
Prince George 214
Prince of Wales 32, 99
Prince Pojarski 225
Prince Regent 29
Priscilla 100
Providence 21

Q

Q.E.D. 62-3, 119
Queda 198, 200
Queen Christina 186
Queen Mab HMS 40
Queen Mary 217, 230 [HMS]
Queen of the Age 104
Queen of the North 98
Querimba 200
Quiloa 200

R

Racehorse HMS 231
Rainbow HMS 229
Raleigh HMS 29, 40
Ramsey 174
Rangitira 189
Rapidian 191
Ravenna 169
Ravenshoe 185
Rebecca Stout 110
Red Riding Hood 75
Redoubtable 230
Regent 208
Reina Victoria Eugenie 214, 244
Reliant 90
Remembrance 139
Renovation 118
Resolution 124, 229
Restitution 130
Retribution 229
Revenge 124, 196, 229-230
Reward 105
Richmond Lass 87
Ridge Park 237
Rio De Janeiro 229
Robert & Hannah 18
Rosamund 40
Rother HMS 232
Rotomahana 169
Rouen 70, 135
Rover 40
Roxburgh Castle 96
Royal Family 99
Royal Sovereign 229
Royal Victoria 140
Ruhr 129, 237
Russell 17 [1751], 184 [HMS], 230

S

Safety 89
Sagunto 132
Saint Lawrence 118
Sakkarah 243
Saldanha 40
Sally 118
Salona 243
Sam Mendel 144

Samoa 193, 198
Sampo 184, 244
Samuel Laing 135
San Isodoro 180, 211-2
San Jeronimo 211
San Joacquin 211
San Nazario 211
Sanspareil 68
Santiago 142, 171
Sappho 34
Sarah & Jane 21
Sarah & Mary 101
Sarah Jane 50
Sarah Scaling 34
Saratov 240
Saratovskaia Ledokol 184
Saratovskaia Pereprava 1848
Scotia 184
Scotsman 10, 123, 150 [later Marlborough], 209
Screw Queen 236
Sea Queen 145
Seebar 217
Sepia 146
Seville 193
Sexta 147, 153
Shagbrook 148
Shannon 35, 61
Shearwater HMS 40
Sheldrake 145
Sidra 190
Sir Colin Campbell 144
Sir Ernest Cassel 245
Skandia 199
Skylark HMS 40
Slavonia 194
Smiling Morn 134
Smolensk 240
Smyrna 128
Snowdrop 99
Sobraon 110
Soestdijk 242
Solebay 28
Solway 106
South Milton 101
Southern 139
Southwick 106
Spartan 145
Spec 120
Spirit of the Age 96
Spirit of the North 96
Spondilus 211
Spray of the Ocean 96
Springhall 131
St Clears 171
St Helens 188
St Leonards 105
St Magnus 125
St Osyth 125
St Vincent 110
Star 62
Starling HMS 40
Stelvio 127
Stentor 35
Strenuous HMS 40
Staunch HMS 226
Strombus 211
Stuart 108, 265
Sud America 130
Suffolk 193
Sullamut 130
Sultan Osman [see Agincourt] 229

Sumatra 110, 236
Sumida 106, 238
Sunbeam 87
Sunda 142
Sunniside 81
Surprise HMS 225
Surrey 118
Swansea 195
Swift 88, 232 HMS
Swiftsure HMS 225
Switzerland 175
Sylvana 218
Syren 29
Syria 104

T

Taeping 169
Tainan Maru 238
Takachiho 227, 229
Takasayo 229
Takashiho Maru 238
Talisman HMS 232
Talpore 139
Tasmania 242
Tatsuta 229
Taunton 67, 146
Tcherkask 237
Tekoa 189
Temesa 106
Tenpaisan Maru 239
Termagant 116
Terror 122, 224, 319
Teucer 185
Texas 228
Themis 35
Theodore Wille 197
Thisbe 50
Thomas Wood 87
Thorwald 112
Tiberius 186
Tide 113
Tigris 29
Ting Yuen 235
Toiler 214
Tokei 238
Tokiwa 229
Toronto 189
Torrens 104, 110
Tortuna 201
Totoni Maru 238
Tottenham 39
Tourmaline 142
Transit 120
Traveller 75
Trent 145
Trevelyan 105
Trewidden 132
Triad 29
Trial 61
Triple [class HMS] 232
Triumph 225 HMS
Truma 193
Trunkby 207
Tsukushi 229
Tubal Cain 66
Turbinia 184, 215, 231
Turret 198
Turret Bell 198-9
Turret Crown 199
Tuscarona 211
Two Friends 74
Tyne 89, 118-9

Tyne Dock No4 209
Tynemouth 67, 192

U

Ulidia 141
Ultonia 212
Umona 203
Undaunted 33, 225 HMS
Unione 132
United Services 68
Unus 132
Urbino 130
Usk 232

V

Vaderland 175-6
Valentine Fierro 120
Van Tempest 150
Vanguard 96
Vasari 188
Vega 241
Velox HMS 231-2
Venezuelan 145
Vesta 81
Vibilia 105
Victor 139
Victoria 68, 181 HMS, 227
Victory 196, 274, 318
Vigilant 99
Viking 185
Villa Selgas 120
Ville De Havre 202
Violet HMS 231
Viper HMS 231-2
Virginia 123
Viscaya 230
Viscount Melbourne 81
Vistula 79
Vollrath Tham 245
Vulcan 61-2

W

W H Harkess 67
W S Lindsay 60, 119, 273
Wallace 112
Wanderer HMS 142
Wandle 150
Warkworth 18
Warrigal 193
Warrimoo 242
Warrington 127
Warrior HMS 608
Warrior Queen 98
Washington 112, 132, 236
Washington City 150
Wastwater 150
Water Witch 89
Waterlily 50
Waterloo 129
Wave Queen 145, 236
Waverley 125
Wedgewood 209
Wellington 87
West Point 185
Westerdijk 242
Westmeath 212
Westminster 138
Westmoreland 18 [1765]
Whately Hall 199
Whisper 145
White Sea 107
Whitehall 197
Whitley 127

Wild Flower 178-9
William & Catherine 82
William & Jane 19
William C Steed 108
William Wallis 81
Winchester 112
Windsor Castle 166
Wisbech 104
Wollabra 237
Woodham 146
Woodlark 40
Wye 111

Y

Yamashiro 238
Yamuna 194
Yang 176
Yariso 30
Yarrawonga 194
Yashima 229
Yat Shing 243
Yoretomo Maru 238
Yoshino 229
Young Regulus 81

Z

Zaire 139
Zanni Stefanovich 190
Zanibar 147
Zeus 107
Zingari 118
Zanzibar 147
Zoe 106
Zoroaster 174
Zulu 118

General

8-hour 265, 328, 339
9-hour 264-275, 283-4, 307-8, 310, 316, 337, 349

A

Aberdeen 62, 110, 119, 124, 128, 205, 260
accident 96, 108, 134, 179, 249
Admiralty 6, 26, 30, 36, 40, 60, 68-9, 96, 98, 111, 113, 118, 125, 164-5, 168, 174, 203, 210, 212, 214-6, 220, 224-232
AEU 316, 349
Africa 51-2, 618 [colonies], 186, 188
8African8 oak 458, 57-61,
AI Smiths [see angle iron smiths]
All Saint's Church 9
allowances 13, 80 [ale],149, 249, 252, 255-6, 317, 327
America [American] 83, 22, 25, 41, 45, 48, 50, 51, 53, 55, 57-9, 61, 79, 84-85, 88, 93, 99-100, 103, 113, 115, 8130, 139-140, 163-4, 171, 175-6, 182, 190, 198-9, 201, 203, 205, 207-9, 211, 8215, 217-9, 227, 229, 232, 235, 239-40, 242, 326, 329
anchor[s] 27, 30, 49, 68-9, 80, 77, 79, 81, 848, 96, 100, 133-6, 218, 233
angle iron smiths 160, 161, 279, 311, 313, 319, 323, 325, 351
Ansaldo 245

Appledore 30
apprentice [see also boys] 5-12, 14-8, 20, 26-36, 38, 40-1, 49, 74-8, 85, 98, 119, 128-130, 133, 144, 153, 157-8, 166, 178, 206, 247-8, 250-68, 258-9, 269, 277, 280-2, 299, 301, 314-7, 320, 327, 330, 335-6, 338, 341, 344-6, 349, 354
arbitration - see board and conciliation
Argentine 168, 193, 203, 224, 229, 235
ASE 157, 262, 265, 268, 271-4, 280-1, 285-6, 292, 299, 301-3, 305-6, 308, 312, 314-31, 333, 336-9
Australia [Australasia] 55, 93, 112, 119, 193, 203, 227, 237
Ayres Quay 77, 99, 108, 282

B

ballast [see also water ballast] 57, 68, 81, 115, 122, 175, 190-2, 195, 254, 290 [b-hill]
Baltic 50, 52, 79, 80-1, 85, 100, 103, 135, 175
banking 73, 142
bankruptcy 19, 29, 30, 32, 73-4, 84, 998 , 109, 110, 112, 196, 237
barge 61, 142, 145, 192
bark 32, 50, 56, 58
barque 19, 55, 57, 63, 96, 99, 108, 131-2, 141, 145, 208, 235, 242
Barrow 167, 181, 199, 225, 230, 233, 325, 326, 327, 341,
beech 45-6, 50-1
Belfast 108, 167, 302, 327, 341
Berwick 1, 38, 40, 134
Bessemer steel 163-8, 173
Bilbao 108, 111, 229, 237
Bill Quay 75, 133, 155
birch 46, 50
Birkenhead 134, 165, 233, 294, 311
Bishop Auckland 16, 156
Bishopwearmouth 21, 35, 73, 82-3, 254, 256
black squad 63, 159, 161-2, 263, 270, 292, 294
blacksmith 6, 40-1, 49, 61-2, 65, 88, 128, 253, 255, 257, 261, 263, 270-1, 277-80, 283, 299, 303, 307, 309, 312, 318, 320, 322, 326, 333, 345, 348, 352
Blackwall Frigates 96-7, 119
blockmaker 252-3, 255, 258, 278-9
Blyth 1, 18, 26-7, 31, 36, 42, 83, 107, 113, 115, 134, 146, 181, 195-6, 239, 248, 254, 260, 289, 309, 329, 322-3, 326, 335, 339, 341-2, 344, 349, 352-38
Board of Arbitration see conciliation
Board of Trade 153, 162, 179, 198-9, 208, 262, 315, 324, 328-32, 334, 339
boiler 62, 63, 66, 68-9, 79, 88, 122-3, 128, 131-2, 151, 163-5, 181, 173-4, 177-8, 190, 192, 195, 204, 206, 207, 211, 222,225, 229,231, 241, 261, 278-280
Boilermakers [incl Boilermakers' Society] 62-3, 128, 170-6, 179, 180, 254, 261-3, 265, 267-9, 271-2, 280, 284, 286, 292-9, 301-2, 304-14, 316-9, 321-5, 327-8, 331-6, 339-41, 343-5, 348, 350, 356-78
borers [boring] 14, 40-1, 252, 255-6, 277-8
boys 5-6, 11, 814-5, 20, 26, 30, 36, 42, 63, 68, 76-7, 83, 85, 88, 156, 157, 212, 250, 253-4, 263, 272, 277-9, 280-1, 302, 304, 314-5, 317, 334, 342, 344-6, 354
Brazil 229
brig 7, 17, 20, 32, 39, 46, 57-8, 66, 78, 73, 131-2, 174, 197
brigantine 57-8, 134
Bristol 25, 99, 112, 245, 261, 269, 324
Britain see Great Britain
budget [domestic] 276, 278, 326-78
builders measure 59, 116
Bureau Veritas 198-9
Byker 288, 299, 306, 337, 340

C

cabinet maker 270, 323
Calcutta 78, 141, 237, 243
Canada [Canadian] 50, 68, 112, 145, 172, 184, 203, 214, 218-9, 229, 260, 237
Cape Town 78, 99, 235, 2378
Carville House Workmen's Hotel 291
Cardiff 145, 186, 189, 196-7, 199, 261
carpenters [see also shipwrights] 1, 6, , 10, 13-4, 19, 37, 50, 85, 96, 101, 118, 158-9, 249- 251, 253-4, 264, 267, 311, 313-4,
Carpenters & Joiners trade union 303, 314. 318-9, 323, 333
Castle Eden 87, 153
Castletown 109, 112
casualties 30, 44, 74, 1778
catcher 65, 192, 280
caulkers [caulking] 845, 48, 56, 63, 65, 66, 96, 134, 173-5, 250-2, 255, 258, 263, 269, 278-280, 306, 312, 318-9, 321, 341, 351-2
cedar 50, 53
census 46, 83, 85, 254, 281, 289-90, 293, 303, 314, 317, 356
chain 49, 68-9, 879-80, 85, 135-6, 252, 332
chaldrons 1-3, 12, 19, 21, 29, 36, 58
Chamber of Commerce 274, 284, 310
Chatham 43, 197
Chester-le-Street 101, 108
Chile 170, 229, 248
China [Chinese] 67, 96, 127, 170, 174, 226, 227, 235, 239, 243

379

380

civil engineers 69, 134, 210, 226
clipper 67, 78, 96, 104, 110, 119, 240
Clyde 61, 73, 88, 113, 121, 138, 143, 157, 164, 166, 172, 181-2, 200, 205, 208, 215, 217, 219, 221, 229, 239-241, 245-6, 262, 266, 270, 280, 283, 296, 327, 332, 341, 353-5
coal 1-3, 5-8, 10, 12, 17, 20-3, 28, 33, 37-9, 51, 58-9, 61-2, 69, 79, 78, 73, 85, 87-8, 103-4, 113, 115, 120, 134-5, 141, 144-5, 147-8, 150-1, 153, 179, 182, 186, 190-1, 195-6, 199, 203, 205, 207-9, 214, 225, 218, 235, 237, 276, 309, 350
coasters 3, 135, 1928
collier [s] 2, 6-7, 18-22, 32, 46, 54, 58, 59, 62, 78, 80, 115, 118, 120-122, 129, 132, 134, 139, 145, 148, 177, 181, 196, 202, 209
colonies 25, 50-1, 61, 235, 227, 246
Company of Shipwrights 3, 6-17, 21, 27, 31, 75-8, 251
composite ship 66-7, 98, 100, 103-4, 106, 110-1, 142, 146, 165, 176, 196, 236
conciliation 4, 155, 158-160, 255-261, 275, 301, 308-9, 318-9, 312, 322-6, 332, 332, 335-337, 341, 343
copper 32, 30, 36, 48-9, 52-3, 66, 68-9, 74, 80-1, 85, 94, 122, 225
copper bottom [coppering] 48-9, 80, 1168
coppersmiths 68, 280, 304, 328
cordage 20, 68, 81
costs - related to ships 4, 14, 19, 29, 35, 39, 41, 48, 49, 50, 52, 62, 69, 79-81, 84-6, 90, 106, 131-2, 134-85, 165, 169, 171-2, 178, 186, 199-200, 203, 217, 225-6, 232-48
court of law 147, 159-160, 198, 203, 263, 2678-273, 315-68, 322, 344
Coxgreen 21, 105
Co-operative [s] 196,219, 261,265, 287-8, 306, 349-50
crane[s] 43, 84, 116, 125, 150, 186, 195, 204-5, 220-2, 232, 235, 245, 342
Crimea 61, 93, 95-6, 99, 115, 118, 124-5, 196, 224, 258, 260, 320

D

Dantzic 46, 51, 52
Darlington 269, 292
deadwood 48, 51, 53
demarcation 50, 252, 263, 313, 317-23, 327, 332, 334-5
Denmark [Danish] 850, 140, 235, 237, 242, 388
Deptford 35, 43, 88, 100, 104, 202, 204, 237, 254, 280, 282
derricks 62, 80, 185-6, 199, 204, 205, 341
destroyers 201, 214, 219, 224, 229-

displacement 58, 60, 123, 184, 227, 231
dock 13, 16, 17, 19, 22, 29-34, 36, 39, 41, 43, 45, 51, 55, 69, 74-5, 77-818, 83-4, 87-88, 102, 116, 118-9, 123, 8131-4, 141, 144-5, 147-8, 150-1, 156, 183-4, 186-87, 189, 191-2, 196-7, 201, 204-5, 209-10, 213-4, 216, 218-222, 249-51, 281-2, 294, 349
double bottom 63, 105, 134-5, 151, 175, 177-8, 186, 190, 207, 3218
draughtsman 111, 119-20, 124, 128-130, 1586, 159, 179, 190, 192, 198, 205, 208, 232, 8253, 279, 288, 294, 3048, 307
drillers [drilling] 44, 63, 65,140, 160, 206, 263, 278-281, 289, 299, 301-2, 307, 312, 318, 321-3, 331-3, 341, 343, 348
Dumbarton 61, 88, 111, 122, 128, 118, 169
Dundee 275
Dunston Engine Wks 284
Durham 3, 49 [gaol], 93, 128, 139, 147, 190-1, 237, 262, 293, 296, 303
Dutch 7, 241, 246, 326
dyer 158

E

earnings [see wages]
East Anglia 25
education 4, 124, 118, 147, 223, 265, 275, 287, 349
electricity 186, 190, 205-7
Ellison Street 289
elm 46, 57-62, 79, 80, 85, 278
Elswick 44, 125, 156, 201, 206-7, 224, 226-9, 232-5, 245, 275, 287, 292, 301, 303, 307, 319-20, 326, 327, 329, 335, 342
employers- employer' organisations 1, 4, 65, 68, 76, 98, 118, 133, 145, 158-163, 180, 190, 195, 247, 250-276, 281, 283-7, 289, 293-299, 301, 303-46, 348, 350, 352, 357
engine [engine works - engineering] 4, 43, 59, 60- 62, 66, 68, 73, 79-81, 88-90, 105-6, 109, 111, 115, 118, 122, 125, 127, 130, 133-4, 139, 141-151, 153, 155, 158, 163, 164, 166, 178, 179, 181-2, 184, 187, 190, 192-3, 220-2, 224-5, 230-2, 235, 238, 243, 245, 253, 258, 261-263, 265, 272-5, 281, 283, 286, 295, 301-9, 314-32, 341, 343-7, 349, 354-5, 357
The Engineer 103, 109, 112-3, 123, 139, 140, 163, 170, 195, 201, 203-205, 205-210, 215-68 231, 351,
engineer - in engines [engineering]
Engineering 81, 216
engine room 90, 344-5
England & Wales 1, 3, 58, 12-3,

26, 37, 42, 48, 50-1, 69, 73, 85, 87, 93, 118, 120, 123, 128, 147, 157-8, 181, 186, 196, 224, 227, 238-9, 258, 266-7, 286, 291, 315-6, 322, 324, 328
Esk river 19, 368

F

factory 43, 68, 84, 124, 125, 205, 222, 245, 264, 272, 280, 287, 338
Factory Act 222, 275
Felling 30, 45
ferry 35, 111, 118, 156, 170, 184, 204, 210, 214, 243, 245
Fifeshire 34, 1118
fir 48, 57-60, 79, 80, 103
fishing 19, 184, 192, 196, 209
fitters 29, 68, 66, 266, 270, 273, 278, 303, 313-4, 317-9, 326, 337, 341, 345-6, 353. 355
fitting out 4, 49, 81, 85, 109, 132, 136, 140, 204, 348
Fleetwood 108
floating dock 134, 184, 196, 209, 210, 214, 218-220
food [including prices] 9,157, 276, 287, 290, 315, 326
foreign 1, 5, 19, 21, 25, 50, 51, 53, 60, 85, 135, 139, 156, 167, 177, 201, 207, 224, 227-229, 235-237, 239, 240, 242, 246, 258, 266
foreman 40, 846, 54, 55, 62, 68, 75, 87-8, 95, 106, 108, 118, 8120, 128, 132, 151-2, 159, 174, 181, 8196, 202, 8207, 249-250, 252-3, 2587, 261, 264, 273, 277-81, 8288, 294, 297, 302, 304-7, 313, 315, 317, 3438, 349
forge 43, 195, 203, 280, 327
fouling 68, 66, 67, 225, 321 [anti-fouling]
foundry 68, 8113, 202-4, 258, 272, 286, 306, 324, 326, 339
France [French] 51, 61, 88, 125, 158, 165, 168, 173-4,214, 235-6, 257
freeboard 153, 198, 199, 225, 227, 231
friendly society 20, 262, 263
frigate [s] 29, 32, 39-40, 78, 106-7, 116, 166, 225
futtocks 48, 51, 53-4

G

Gateshead 10, 14-7, 30, 62, 68-9, 79, 88-9, 118, 129, 258, 273-4, 286, 291-3, 301, 303, 306, 324, 340
Germany 50, 68, 95, 107, 112, 127, 147, 150, 176, 182, 197, 215, 218, 235-8, 241-2, 246, 275, 329
Glasgow 61, 116, 134, 142, 195-9, 191, 204-5, 209-210, 216, 224, 235, 246, 261, 283
Glasgow Herald 182-3, 172, 197, 199, 204-5, 209, 216, 224, 235, 246, 314, 350
Gosforth 327
government 7- , 20, 39, 40, 59,

68, 74, 110, 116, 119, 123, 125, 130, 132, 139, 145-6, 156, 161,181, 169, 184, 186, 203, 210, 212, 214-5, 218-9, 226, 233, 235-8, 240, 243, 245, 248-9, 260, 320, 3288, 350
graving dock see dry dock
Great Britain 19, 25-6, 29, 37, 39, 48, 61, 66, 83, 88, 93, 99, 173, 178, 218, 221, 238, 239, 246-7, 256, 290, 3288
Great Yarmouth 29
greenheart 46, 50, 52, 54-5
Greenock 26, 36, 61, 129, 202, 261
Greenwich 3, 79, 88, 226-7
Grimsby 51, 184, 209
guild 2, , 43
gunboats [guns]29, 36, 39, 40, 98, 116, 118, 125, 130, 139, 170, 224-9, 238, 245, 260

H

Hamburg 18, 85, 129, 125, 193, 198, 242, 245
hardwood 51, 55
Hartlepool 52, 55, 62, 67, 69, 83, 95-98, 107, 118, 124, 133, 137, 138, 140, 142-155, 157, 162-3, 165, 171, 178, 181, 200-5, 208, 211, 235, 237, 240, 242, 246, 254, 259-265, 267-271, 283, 285, 291-2, 296-7, 299, 301, 303, 306-7, 309, 311-4, 317, 319, 322-8, 8331, 334, 336, 338, 347-8, 355-6
Hartley 18
Hebburn 113, 128-9, 131, 136, 156, 171-2, 179, 184, 201, 229, 235, 237, 240-1, 277, 279, 281, 288-9, 306-7, 311, 319, 321-2, 327, 337, 339, 344, 3568
Hebburn Monthly 290
helpers 4, 63, 65, 158-9, 163, 173, 247, 297-302, 308, 311-2, 323, 331, 334-6, 341, 343, 351, 353-4
hemlock 50
Herefordshire 55
hewer 40
hickory 50
Hillgate 17, 30, 79
holder-up 63, 65, 263, 279, 323, 325
hole-cutters 65, 300, 319
Holland 43, 50, 68, 242
holy days 8-9
Holy Island 2
Horseley Iron Works 61
Hostmen 12-3, 28
hours 79-80, 109, 139, 145, 158, 160-1, 178, 199, 203, 210, 214, 217, 231, 245, 247, 252, 255-6, 258-9, 262, 264-275, 277, 282-5, 292, 293, 295, 300, 302-3, 306-310, 312, 316, 328-9, 333-9, 343, 346, 349, 351, 353-4
house 7, 9, 14-16, 17, 27, 29,32, 16, 50, 68-9, 80-1, 73, 75, 84, 96, 113, 115, 120, 120, 118, 128, 130, 135, 140, 145, 199, 204, 206, 237, 243, 249, 252,

260, 272, 275-6, 277, 286-289, 291, 312
house building 309, 355
Howdon 18, 29, 115, 118, 123, 156, 162, 229, 248, 259, 287, 292, 296, 306, 311, 322, 335-6, 340, 344
Hull 5, 19, 25-6, 76, 79, 108, 123, 130, 141, 189, 225, 283, 309-10
Humber 20, 129
Hylton 21, 35, 84, 95, 98-9, 102, 108, 111, 254-6, 260, 281-2, 299

I

improvers 345, 328
INA [RINA] 67, 111, 125, 134, 142, 166-9, 173, 177, 197-9, 205, 208, 215, 217-8, 240, 244-5
India [Indian] 29, 39, 43, 46, 56-9, 66, 68-9, 78-9, 98, 103,119, 123, 125, 130, 139, 144, 146, 166, 193-4, 199, 203, 221, 229, 2358
inside men 309
insurance 32, 59, 94, 131, 146, 153, 250
Ipswich 2, 5, 13, 339
Ireland [Irish] 61, 221, 247, 256, 268-9, 288, 292
iron 4-5, 30, 36, 48-51, 53-7, 63-5, 67-71, 73-80, 81, 890, 893-6, 99, 108-110, 113-120, 122-6, 127-131, 132-5, 138-151, 155, 158, 160-1, 176-188, 196-9, 201-4, 196, 208-210, 218, 224, 232, 235-8, 240, 243, 247, 251-4, 258, 261, 263-4, 267, 271, 273, 275, 277-285, 288,
Iron Trades Employers' Assoc [ITEA] 264 [iron], 283, 285, 338, 345
Italy [Italian] 60, 178, 203, 227, 235, 237, 241, 245, 246

J

Japan [Japanese] 896, 106, 123, 1258,140, 172, 210, 224, 227-9, 237-9, 241, 245
Jarrow 30, 32, 81, 83, 89, 113, 120-5, 135, 137, 156, 162, 169, 170, 173, 196-8, 201, 205-6, 225, 229, 231-2, 243, 262, 264-6, 269-70, 272, 274, 279-80, 288, 291-2, 296, 299, 301-3, 306, 308, 311, 318, 320-1, 334, 337, 340, 344, 351, 355-6
joiners 9, 41, 49, 50, 66, 131, 159-60, 251-3, 255, 263, 266-7, 270, 276, 278-9, 281, 283, 289, 301, 303, 305, 308-9, 312, 317-9, 322-3, 332-336, 341, 348, 351-2

K

keel 7, 13, 19, 32, 36, 43, 46, 48, 58-60, 58, 59, 68, 63, 65, 66, 79, 73, 88, 94, 101, 125, 131, 146, 166, 176, 192, 193, 204, 216, 217, 227, 235, 271, 311
keelmen 7, 15, 88
keels 6, 7, 13, 17-9, 39, 58-9, 88, 94, 161
knees 46, 54-59, 56, 136, 311

L

Labour Gazette 324, 326, 335, 347
labourers 6, 9, 13, 22, 42, 44, 50, 63, 65, 84, 128, 140, 153, 155, 252, 255-6, 264, 266, 268-272, 276-81, 289, 8298-9, 301-2, 309, 311-2, 318, 321-3, 326-7, 3298, 334-7, 341, 347, 350-1, 353, 355, 357
lads [see boys]
larch 50
Leeds 262, 283, 324
lengthened [ships] 21, 32, 33, 102, 104, 145, 260, 282
Lifton House 295
Liverpool 4, 25-6, 45, 56, 61, 66, 69, 76, 88, 99, 90, 94-5, 98, 103, 106, 108-9, 122-4, 129, 135, 136, 141, 144-6, 152-3, 164, 166-7, 179, 184, 188, 193, 222, 261-2, 281, 283, 286, 296, 310-1, 339
Lloyd's 3, 18-20, 25, 37, 50, 52-6 5, 69, 79-80, 88, 90, 94-8, 101-2, 109, 115, 119, 129, 132, 134-7, 143-5, 151-3, 164-6, 172, 174, 177-8, 196, 198-9, 208, 210, 261, 282
London 2, 4, 5, 7, 19-22, 25-6, 37, 43-4, 54, 57-8, 67, 69-71, 78, 85, 87, 90, 93, 95-6, 98-9, 113-5, 106, 118-123, 125, 130, 134, 141, 144-8, 150, 153, 169, 174, 178, 189-190, 193, 196-9, 206, 208, 209, 213, 225, 235, 237-8, 261-2, 264, 273, 276, 278, 283-4, 292, 301, 304, 307-8, 327-8, 338, 347, 355-6
Low Lights 29, 77
Low Walker 69, 89, 119, 125, 133, 162, 179, 201, 267, 288, 344

M

Madras 78, 166
mahogany 46, 51, 80, 227, 243
Malta 235, 317
Manchester 85, 122, 150, 167, 190, 198, 210, 266, 268, 271, 283, 294, 303-4, 327
Manilla 235
marine engineering 4, 88, 143, 153, 153, 216, 261, 286, 297, 302, 314, 317, 323, 337, 344, 347
mariners 2, 5, , 11,815,18, 328, 86
Marseilles 120, 235, 227
masons 9, 290, 302
mast [incl mastmaker] 4, 13, 17-8, 20, 25, 27, 33, 38, 43, 849, 51, 56-9, 79-80, 86, 104-5, 107, 141, 150, 152, 172-5, 178, 190, 1998, 224, 253, 255
Melbourne 96, 203, 225, 241, 227
Memel 46, 50, 51, 53, 80
Mersey 88, 113, 166, 220, 266, 325, 326
Middle Dock 19, 32, 39, 106, 118, 129, 129, 147, 349
Middlesbrough 63, 67, 80, 87, 139-142, 155, 162-3, 181, 191, 210, 239, 261-4, 267-271, 275, 292, 303, 306, 311, 322, 324, 330, 334, 336, 339, 347
Mid-Tyne Link 127, 222, 229
mild steel 150, 163-172
millwright 13, 61, 132, 181, 252
Monkwearmouth 35, 68, 77, 83, 85, 253-4, 261, 282
moulders 323, 325, 339
Mushroom 26, 118, 298

N

National Insurance Scheme 303, 334, 346
naval architecture 7, 54-5, 60-1, 77, 112, 167, 197, 203, 216, 226-7, 233
navy 2, 19, 21, 29, 142, 166, 167, 169, 192, 203, 210, 224-229, 232, 238, 245, 260
NECIES [North East Coast Institution of Engineers & Shipbuilders] 111, 124, 131, 148, 152, 159, 172, 179, 198, 206-7, 227, 284, 305
New Zealand 99, 104, 150, 169, 190, 198, 237
Newcastle 1-3, 6-9, 10-1, 13, 15, 18-23, 25-29, 30, 32, 34, 36, 42, 43, 45, 50, 51, 54, 56-7, 61, 67, 69, 73, 75, 76, 78, 80-1, 85, 88, 95, 101-2, 113, 125, 127, 129-123, 134-5, 139, 142, 145-6, 156-7, 173, 175, 178, 193-4, 199, 206, 227, 235, 238, 247-251, 254, 260-1, 263-6, 268-73, 276, 284, 286-93, 295-6, 299, 303-4, 306, 308-9, 313, 316, 319-20, 324-5, 8327-9, 331, 333-4, 337-41, 349, 355-6, 358
Newcastle College of Science 206
Newcastle Chronicle 139, 156, 264, 266, 268-270, 289, 291, 301, 303, 329
Newcastle Courant 85, 122, 247, 254, 258-260, 263-265, 269, 270
nine hours [see 9-hours]
Noah's Ark , 23-4
North Dock 84, 102, 106, 108, 282
North Sands 34, 77, 107, 110, 156-7, 170, 194
North Shields 10, 13, 17-18, 29-30, 39, 69, 85, 89, 95, 104, 108, 116-8, 130, 184, 209, 248, 260-1, 287, 306, 308, 311, 313, 339
North Shore 15, 26, 32, 81, 96
Northern Examiner 2878
Northumberland 3, 18, 85, 93,118, 120, 128, 207, 216, 262, 288, 293, 304, 310
Northumberland SB 183, 185-7, 201, 222-38
Norway 57-9, 147, 184, 235, 239, 241, 242, 245-6, 275

O

oak 5-6, 19, 45-6, 48, 51, 538 57-63, 79-80, 85, 103, 118, 243, 278
oakum 42, 45, 48-9
OM [old measure] 58-60, 103, 140
on spec see speculation
Otto Gas engine 205
Ouseburn Works 107, 315, 349
outfit 49, 80, 85, 86, 100, 103, 106
outfitting 39, 66, 318
outfitting trades 66
Overseers 11, 13

P

Pacific 214, 219, 225, 245, 327
paddle steamer 89, 118-9, 123, 125, 133, 139, 140, 145-6, 169, 170, 184, 235, 237, 240
painters [painting] 49, 50, 66, 80, 99, 135, 160, 177, 205, 8253, 2558 278-9, 302, 309, 318, 321, 333, 336, 341, 3538
Pallion 98, 102, 106, 112, 156, 193, 198-200, 201, 235, 279, 282, 327
Palmer's Record 297
patternmakers 262, 280, 285, 303, 313, 315-8, 321, 323-6, 330, 338- 9, 345, 348, 354
Pembroke 43, 226
Petersburg 127, 178, 235, 241, 245
piecework [ers] 4, 65, 140, 153, 158, 160, 173-6, 173, 179, 251, 258, 264, 265, 277-281, 283, 293, 297, 300, 310-3, 325-6, 329-30, 333, 335-6, 344-6, 350-4
pine 46, 57-60, 79, 80, 235
pitch 30, 45, 46, 48, 53, 56-8, 250
platers 63, 65, 66, 141, 173-175, 204,247 269, 278-280, 288, 294, 296-7, 300, 302, 304-8, 311-3, 318, 334, 336, 341-2, 351-4
plumbers 12, 49, 66, 204, 222, 288, 303, 317-321, 323, 333, 336, 353
Plymouth 43, 68, 110
Poland 50
Portrack 39, 87
Portsmouth 40, 43, 44, 61, 69, 220, 227, 231, 261
Prussia[n] 50,51, 130, 166, 237

Q

Quebec 50, 52-3

R

Raff yard 43
railway 83, 93, 111, 120, 125, 127, 131, 144, 145, 150, 163, 169, 184, 192, 196-7, 199, 209, 210, 213, 217, 219, 222, 235, 237, 241, 2438, 245, 265, 274-5, 288-9, 306
rate of pay see wages
red leaders 319
register [see also Lloyds] 26-30,

36, 37, 57, 73, 78, 81, 90, 94 [Liverpool], 118, 123 [Liverpool],
rent 13, 20, 45, 73, 84, 86, 120, 169, 219, 221, 276, 286, 288-98, 291-2, 355, 358
repair work 2, 3-4, 7, , 14-15, 18-20, 21, 29-34, 37, 44, 63, 73-5, 79, 80-2, 87-8, 96, 99, 103, 108, 115, 118, 133,130, 139, 142, 144, 145, 151, 158, 160, 161, 177, 183, 189, 193, 195, 203, 219, 220, 229, 294-7, 305, 307, 335, 338, 341, 344-5, 347, 349, 352-3
rigger 253, 255, 258
Riga 50-51
RINA [see INA]
rivet heaters 65, 178, 281, 310, 344, 3548
riveters 63, 65-6, 68, 141, 158, 161,173, 220-1, 261, 277-281, 289, 294, 305-7, 310-311, 313, 321, 334, 341, 344-5, 352, 354
rope [ropery] 4, 27, 29, 36, 45, 48-9, 68, 80, 74, 77-8, 95, 145, 195, 204, 293
Rowton House 290
Royal Commission 152, 155, 157, 159, 160, 162, 252, 258, 262, 264, 281, 285, 294, 297-299, 302, 318-349, 330, 339
Royal Navy 19, 21, 29, 142, 169, 225, 229
Russia [Russian] 50, 51, 127, 128, 170, 187, 177, 184, 192, 196, 225, 229, 232, 235, 237, 241, 245
Russian Volunteer Fleet 240

S
Sandwich 2
safety 4, 21, 88, 153, 167, 179, 207
sailcloth 20, 49
sailing ships 4, 18, 57, 63, 879, 83, 86, 88, 104-8, 111, 130-2, 134, 139-142, 144-7, 149, 151, 172, 181, 208-9, 235, 240
sailmakers 19, 27, 49, 68, 253, 255, 261, 309
sailors 252
salted [salting] 53, 103
sawyers 27, 40-46, 255, 256, 258, 260, 263, 277, 278 [piece rates], 282, 283, 307, 323
Scandinavia [n] 50, 53, 238, 241
Scarborough 1-2, 20, 25, 26, 37, 39, 49, 76, 86, 91, 108, 139
schooner 36, 57, 58, 80, 88, 178, 224
Scotch fir 53
Scotia 184, 187, 191, 209, 339, 328
Scotland 1, 10, 26, 61, 90, 95, 100, 101, 111, 120, 128, 133, 172, 174, 181, 205, 211, 220, 240, 241, 260, 270, 271, 288-289, 290, 306, 316, 332
Scots [Scotsmen] 10, 65, 88, 90, 96, 104, 111, 119, 164, 169, 287
seamen 2-3, 13, 21, 74, 81, 86, 179
Seaton Sluice 18-9

Seine 70, 88
Shannon river 61
Sheerness 43, 166
Shields 2, 13, 25, 41, 84, 86, 88
Shields Gazette 129, 205, 309
shipbuilder [under names]
shipbuilding - throughout
ship - construction - see chap 4, 174-9 [tankers], 197-8 [turret], 207-8.
shipowner 21, 22, 27, 29, 32, 35-7, 39, 48-9, 51-2, 54, 56-7, 59, 60, 69, 73, 876, 78, 80, 85-6, 88, 94-8, 99, 100,8102, 105-7,120, 125,8127, 129, 130-1, 133-4, 142, 144, 146, 150-3, 156, 164-5, 167, 169, 170-1, 177-9, 181-2, 186, 189, 196-7, 199, 217-9, 220, 227, 235, 242, 248, 250-1, 253, 295, 346
Shipping World 69, 123, 124, 130, 131, 144, 148, 157-8, 165, 169,173-175, 177, 193-195, 202, 224, 227, 238-241, 275, 297, 318, 349, 328, 335, 337-9
shiprepair see repair
shipwrights 1, 3-19, 20-3, 26-38, 40-6, 48-51, 49, 50, 54, 56, 59, 618, 63, 65, 66, 78, 80, 82-6, 88, 95, 98-9, 103-4, 106, 118, 138, 140, 149, 151-82, 171-3, 166, 196, 247-67, 294, 301, 304, 306, 309, 313, 317-19, 322-3, 331-3, 336, 339, 341, 344, 377, 348-9, 352, 354, 356
Shipwrights' Association 247, 261 [annual national meetings]
Shipwrights' Company see Company of Shipwrights
ship's carpenter 129, 250
Siemens-Martin steel 165-169
Simpson's hotel 290
slipway 5, 29, 36, 74, 75, 79, 86, 99, 102, 106 [Candlish patent], 108-9, 116, 119, 127, 129, 130, 133, 134, 140, 143, 179, 184, 190, 193, 205, 222, 225, 229, 232, 240, 282, 283, 307, 323-5
sloops 19, 39, 40, 57-88, 788
smith [s] see blacksmith and angle iron smith
Smith's Dock see Smith T & W
snows 37, 53, 57-58, 1448
South Dock 102, 108, 156
South Shields 5, 9-12, 17-8, 26, 30-33, 39, 43, 45, 51, 56, 67, 74-5, 77-8, 80-1, 83, 85-6, 89, 118, 120, 131-3, 139, 157, 162, 183-4, 205, 209, 235, 239, 247-252, 254, 256, 260-1, 266, 287, 291, 293, 299, 301, 303, 308-9, 327, 337, 340, 356-8
South Shore 16, 17, 27, 30, 79, 116
Southwick 34, 82-93, 96, 100, 106, 156, 220, 238, 254, 282, 282
Spain 107, 108, 120, 149, 227, 227, 229, 235, 237, 240, 241, 245
speculation 4, 36-7, 39, 74, 94, 107, 108, 128, 146, 184, 194,

196, 232
St Lawrence 5, 118, 218 [river]
St Petersburg 20, 127, 178, 235, 245
St Peter's 29, 40, 78, 116, 118, 127, 175, 184, 207, 8229, 235, 245, 250, 3268
standard of living 332, 326, 328
steam boat 79, 88-9, 96-8, 113, 118
Steam Engine Makers' Society [Old Mechanics] 262, 271
steel 1, 4, 57, 124-125, 127, 130, 139, 141, 147, 150, 151, 155, 156, 161, 163-174, 188, 190, 195, 197, 202-205, 209, 216-232, 224, 238, 240, 245-246
Stettin 48, 52, 80, 237
Stockton 2, 20, 26, 39, 76, 83, 86, 87, 138-142, 144-5, 147, 152-3, 155, 158, 162-3, 166, 188, 190, 197, 254, 261, 263, 267-271, 273, 299, 301, 303, 306, 312, 314, 316, 324-6, 335, 339, 347
strikes 45, 84, 89, 8159-160, 162, 171-176, 249-251, 254-2788, 281, 283-58, 293-4, 296, 301, 308-9, 311-4, 316, 323-84, 327, 330, 332, 334-6, 341, 344
Sunderland 2-3, 19-23, 25-6, 33-5, 39, 42, 44-5, 48, 57-59, 54, 63-66, 68-9, 82-85, 87, 89-95, 99, 103-105, 108-113, 119-121, 135, 144-5, 153, 156-175, 186, 191, 193-195, 199, 202,-203, 207, 213, 220, 241, 250-261, 263, 272, 273, 282, 284, 286, 287, 290 293-6, 301, 303, 305-17, 323, 326-8, 332, 335-7, 339, 341, 343, 346-7, 356, 358
Sunderland SB 201
Sunderland Echo 315, 316, 332
Sunderland Forge 195, 203, 327
Sunderland Herald 83, 93, 108-110, 103, 251, 253, 257-261
Sunderland Technical College 156
Sunderland Times 300
Swansea 30, 147, 168, 196, 261
Sweden 51, 52, 144, 175, 200, 221, 235, 242, 246

T
tankers 4, 60, 125, 127, 141-2, 155, 161, 187-194, 201-3, 208, 210-2, 222, 239, 341
teak 46, 57-62, 103, 240, 278
technical education 4, 223, 275, 349
Tees [Teesside] 20, 39, 63, 67, 69, 80, 86, 98-100, 138-143, 147, 150-5, 157-8, 160, 162-3, 166,171, 178, 181-3, 187-8, 191-2, 201-2, 204, 208-10, 220, 222, 233, 235, 238, 240, 242, 246, 259, 264-271, 273, 275, 281-2, 285, 291, 294-9, 304, 306, 309, 312-3, 322-3, 325-6, 328, 331-2, 334-6, 338-9, 3418, 343, 346,

348, 349, 351, 353
Thames 2, 7, 18, 25, 26, 29, 40, 42, 52, 59, 61, 69, 78, 88, 99, 96, 108, 113, 120, 139, 166, 214, 218, 225, 266, 280
The Engineer [see *Engineer*]
Thornaby 304, 323, 335, 339
timber [see wood] 88-82
timber merchant [yard] 18, 39, 82, 87, 99, 100, 118
timework [ers] 160, 324-5
Tokyo 238
tonnage - measurement of 58-60
torpedo boat [torpedo]201, 214, 224-5, 229-232, 238
trade union 4, 41, 157, 160, 161, 173, 247, 252, 254, 260-2, 264-5, 267, 271-3, 275, 289, 293-6, 298-300, 302-9, 313, 315-9, 321-4, 327-30, 332-4, 337-40, 343, 347, 350, 357
trade unionism - see trade union
trades council 159, 296, 299, 301, 303, 309, 316, 329
trawlers 30, 171, 181, 184, 192, 201, 209, 349
treenails 41, 48, 57-9, 55, 278
Trinity House 2, 29, 118, 199
TUC 300-1, 332
tug 61, 88-90, 96, 113, 120, 127 132, 138-9, 145, 192, 209, 237, 227, 245
turbines 4, 155, 164, 169, 172, 215-216, 223, 224, 229- 229, 232
Turkey 229, 232
turners 65, 165, 2867-9, 273, 280, 298, 304, 312, 315, 318, 323, 326, 329
turret ship 197-200, 222
Tyne [Tyneside] 1-3, 5-8, 13, 15, 22, 25-30, 32-3, 35-6, 40, 42-3, 45, 54, 56, 58, 61-2, 67-9, 73-880, 83-6, 88-91, 93, 95, 98, 103, 106, 108, 110, *chap 7* pp 113-137, 153, 155-8, 159-163, 166, 169-170, 174, 176, 181-8, 191-2, 200-1, 205-7, 209-12, 214, 216-7, 222, 224, 226-7, 229, 231, 233-238, 240, 242, 245-7, 250-1, 253-5, 258-266, 268-273, 275, 280-7, 289, 290-1, 294, 296-9, 301-3, 305-6, 308-9, 311-4, 316, 318-320, 322, 324-9, 331-2, 334-8, 341-9, 351-6
Tynemouth 2, 28, 68, 83, 96, 119, 128, 134, 328, 356

U
unemployment 77, 84, 157, 161-2, 173, 200-1, 254, 260-1, 276, 290, 292, 295, 298-9, 307, 311, 313, 324-5, 327-9, 334, 337, 340, 346-8, 349, 355, 357
United Machine Workers 303, 328, 330
United States of America USA 25, 43, 61, 88, 99, 168, 174, 177, 209, 229, 265

383

W

wage[s] & earnings 4, 6, 11, 13, 15, 840-2, 49-50, 65, 85, 106, 121, 128, 140, 158, 160, 162-3, 172-4, 201, 206-7, 226, 232, 239, 247-8, 8232-254, 256-260, 262-6, 271, 276-281, 290-1, 293, 297-8, 300, 306, 308-9, 312-4, 317-8, 323-7, 330-6, 339-341

Wales [see England & Wales] 101, 109, 189, 295

Walker [see Low Walker] 81, 119, 123-5, 133, 135, 170, 175-6, 212, 224, 226-7, 233-4, 244, 287, 289, 301, 306-7, 321-3, 335, 337, 339, 342-3

Wallsend [see also Wallsend Slipway] 10, 127-8, 130, 180, 186, 199, 207, 210-5, 217, 222, 227, 229, 240, 248, 267, 279, 283, 286-8, 290-1, 301, 306-7, 311, 318-9, 320, 322, 331, 335, 337-9, 342, 344, 352-4, 356

war [s] - wartime 1, 3, 7, 25, 30-1, 37, 40, 42-3, 50, 57, 61, 69, 73-4, 86, 93, 95-6, 99-100, 103, 113, 115, 118, 120-1, 125, 139, 145, 169, 181, 183, 189, 190, 192, 194, 196, 198, 200-1, 224-5, 227, 229-230, 232-3, 235, 239, 241, 258, 260, 319

Warsaw 235

warships 1, 6, 14, 33, 40, 115, 123, 127, 130, 156, 168, 176, 172, 184, 198, 201, 210, 232, 224-235, 340

water ballast [see also ballast] 62-3, 115, 120-1, 134-5, 150, 176, 178, 186, 207-8

Wear [Wearside] 81, 3, 7, 9, 20-3, 33-4, 39-42, 51-2, 54, 56-7 61-2, 67, 69, 73, 75-8, 81-5, 89-91, chap 6 pp 93-1128, 115, 118-123, 131, 135, 137-8, 144-5, 155-163, 170, 181-3, 187-88 192-4, 197-204, 208-211, 219-220, 223, 236-9, 241, 246, 248-261, 263, 267, 271-3, 277-9, 281-285, 291, 294, 297-302, 305-7, 309-316, 318-9, 323-5, 328-9, 331-8, 341 343-9, 351

Wear Commissioners 21, 257

well-deck 152-3

Whitby 1-2, 6, 19, 22, 25-6, 33, 36-8, 42, 57, 76, 80, 83, 86, 88, 91, 98, 121, 131, 144, 181, 196-7, 261

Whitehaven 76

wife [wives & widows] 9-12, 15, 21, 29, 128, 130, 139, 247, 252, 261, 267, 269, 276, 287-290, 296, 329, 354-6

Willington Quay 118, 123, 129, 131, 266

winch[es] - windlass 4, 77, 80, 150, 178, 186, 195, 200, 204, 206, 222, 274, 341

women [see also wife] 830, 41-2, 68, 249, 280, 293, 301

wood [including *wood yard*] 3-5, 7-11, 13, 15, 20-2, 28-30, 38-9, 43-6, 48-57, 60-1, 66-7, 77-80, 85-6, 95, 99-100, 103-123, 127, 130, 132-5, 138-144, 146, 149, 155, 170-1, 178, 184-5, 195-197, 201, 204, 207, 209, 226, 229-8230, 235, 237, 240, 245, 253-4, 263, 276, 278, 281-2, 293, 304-5, 315, 317-9, 323, 332, 335, 342, 3498-350,

Woolwich 43, 116, 125, 134, 260

Y

Yarmouth 2, 5, 19, 28

yeoman 9, 15, 16, 34

LAUNCH OF THE "BLENHEIM," EAST INDIAMAN, 1600 TONS BURTHEN, AT NEWCASTLE-UPON-TYNE.